Capital Budgeting and Long-Term Financing Decisions

Third Edition

Neil Seitz
St. Louis University

Mitch Ellison
Quincy University

CAPITAL BUDGETING AND LONG-TERM FINANCING DECISIONS

Third Edition

Neil Seitz
St. Louis University

Mitch Ellison
Quincy University

Harcourt Brace College Publishers

Fort Worth   Philadelphia   San Diego   New York   Orlando   Austin   San Antonio
Toronto   Montreal   London   Sydney   Tokyo

Publisher	George Provol
Acquisitions Editor	Mike Reynolds
Market Strategist	Charles Watson
Developmental Editor	Laura Hayes
Project Editors	Claudia Gravier, Elaine Richards
Art Director	Burl Sloan
Production Manager	Lois West

ISBN: 0-03-023789-0
Library of Congress Catalog Card Number: 98–85989

Address for Domestic Orders
The Dryden Press, 6277 Sea Harbor Drive, Orlando, FL 32887-6777
800-782-4479

Address for International Orders
International Customer Service
The Dryden Press, 6277 Sea Harbor Drive, Orlando, FL 32887-6777
407-345-3800
(fax) 407-345-4060
(e-mail) hbintl@harcourtbrace.com

Address for Editorial Correspondence
The Dryden Press, 301 Commerce Street, Suite 3700, Fort Worth, TX 76102

Web Site Address
http://www.hbcollege.com

Printed in the United States of America

9 0 1 2 3 4 5 6 7 039 9 8 7 6 5 4 3

Harcourt Brace College Publishers

THE DRYDEN PRESS SERIES IN FINANCE |

Amling and Droms
Investment Fundamentals

Berry and Young
Managing Investments: A Case Approach

Boone, Kurtz, and Hearth
Planning Your Financial Future

Brigham
Brigham's Interactive Guide to Finance
CD-ROM

Brigham and Houston
Fundamentals of Financial Management
Eighth Edition

Brigham, Aberwald, and Gapenski
Finance with Lotus 1-2-3
Second Edition

Brigham, Gapenski, and Klein
*1998 Cases in Financial Management:
Dryden Request*

Brigham and Gapenski
Financial Management: Theory and Practice
Eighth Edition

Brigham and Gapenski
Intermediate Financial Management
Fifth Edition

Brigham and Houston
*Fundamentals of Financial Management: The
Concise Edition*

Chance
An Introduction to Derivatives
Fourth Edition

Clark, Gerlach, and Olson
Restructuring Corporate America

Cooley
*Advances in Business Financial Management: A
Collection of Readings*
Second Edition

Dickerson, Campsey, and Brigham
Introduction to Financial Management
Fourth Edition

Eaker, Fabozzi, and Grant
International Corporate Finance

Fama and Miller
The Theory of Finance

Gardner and Mills
*Managing Financial Institutions:
An Asset/Liability Approach*
Third Edition

Gitman and Joehnk
Personal Financial Planning
Seventh Edition

Greenbaum and Thakor
Contemporary Financial Intermediation

Harrington and Eades
Case Studies in Financial Decision Making
Third Edition

Hayes and Meerschwam
*Financial Institutions: Contemporary Cases in
the Financial Services Industry*

Hearth and Zaima
Contemporary Investments
Second Edition

Hearth and Zaima
*Contemporary Investments: Security and
Portfolio Analysis*

Johnson
Issues and Readings in Managerial Finance
Fourth Edition

Kidwell, Peterson, and Blackwell
Financial Institutions, Markets, and Money
Sixth Edition

Koch
Bank Management
Third Edition

Columnists and other pundits of the business press decry the short-run focus of managers. Managers, on the other hand, profess to have a consuming interest in the long term, hampered only by the short-term focus of investors, analysts, and pundits of the business press. There seems to be general agreement on the importance of focusing on long-term investment and financing decisions. The only disagreement is on who is guilty of limiting that emphasis.

Fortunately, the crime of short-term focus may be less prevalent than suspected. Most executives depend on the long-term health of their company to give value to their stock options and retirement plans. A number of the corporate restructurings and takeovers that made headlines throughout the 1990s changed the asset structures to enhance the potential for long-term survival and profitability. Many of us are heartened to find classrooms populated by students who actually want to manage a business for the long term rather than seeking quick profits in investment banking. This book is for those who want to practice long-term financial management in businesses and nonprofit organizations.

Academics and practitioners have become increasingly sensitive in recent years to the necessity of integrated decision making. Capital investment decisions must, for example, be made in the context of the organization's strategy, and must be made within the organization's resource constraints, particularly within the organization's financial resources. This book is for those who want to take an integrated approach to capital investment decisions so that capital investments do, in fact, contribute to the organization's goals.

Intended Use

This book was written primarily as a textbook in capital budgeting and long-term financing decisions and is appropriate for any of these settings:

1. A business school course dealing with long-term financial decisions, including both capital investments and long-term financing.
2. A business school course focusing on capital investment decisions.
3. An engineering school course focusing on capital investment decisions.
4. Desk reference for a manager involved in long-term financial decisions.

Business school students will typically have introductory courses in accounting, finance, and management before the course using this book. The course using this book may focus on capital budgeting, with both working capital management and long-term financing decisions covered in other courses; this would typically involve a three-course sequence in financial management. Alternately, the course using this book may cover capital investments and long-term financing, with working capital covered in the other course of a two-course sequence. Either sequence may appear at either the M.B.A. or the undergraduate level.

Industrial engineering schools have traditionally taught a capital investment course, often carrying the title "Engineering Economy." Like business schools, engineering schools have become increasingly sensitive to the necessity to integrate the various functions of the business; they have come to appreciate the importance of integrating capital investment choices with strategic planning and financing decisions. The students taking this course often will not have had a prior finance course. The first four chapters, which will serve primarily as a needed review for business students, will serve engineering students as the introduction to finance, strategy, and valuation principles that provide the foundation for optimal capital budgeting.

Organization of the Book

The book follows a natural progression from the development of basic principles to the application of those principles in increasingly complex circumstances. We start by recognizing that wealth maximization is the common goal of capital budgeting. We first address the strategy and the competitive conditions that must exist if there is to be a potential for wealth creation. We then cover the basic rules of time value analysis and apply those rules to develop general principles of valuation. Next, we apply those rules and principles to the selection of capital investments given (1) a single goal of wealth maximization, (2) known costs and benefits, (3) efficient financial markets, and (4) independence between capital investments. We then expand the basic model to deal with competing investments, risk, relationships between investment and financing decisions, and goals other than wealth maximization. The book is divided into six sections:

I. Introduction
   Wealth-creation objective of capital budgeting, strategic basis for wealth creation, basic principles of time value, general principles of valuation.

II. Capital Investment Choice
   Evaluation of the basic net present value (NPV) rule, comparison of NPV to alternate capital budgeting methods, ranking attractive projects.

III. Estimating Cash Flows
   Taxation principles and current tax laws that affect capital investments, marginal cash flows concepts, and the impact of inflation and foreign exchange rate movements on capital investment analysis.

IV. Risk and Investment Choices
   Single-investment risk analysis, risk analysis from the perspective of top management, risk analysis from the perspective of a fully diversified shareholder, option pricing and arbitrage pricing.

V. Financing Decisions and Required Return
   Cost of capital, capital structure choice, dividend policy, interactions between investment and financing decisions, leasing, and capital rationing.

VI. Special Topics
   Decisions in nonprofit organizations, multicriteria capital budgeting and linear programming, and mergers.

Features of the Book

The goal in writing this book was to bring as much of our current understanding as possible to bear on practical capital budgeting and long-term financing decisions. Development efforts were focused on making the book *comprehensive, applicable, understandable,* and *flexible.*

It was necessary to bring a comprehensive set of decision-making tools to bear on a comprehensive set of problems. The book contains, for example, problems of nonprofit organizations, service businesses, and financial institutions along with the traditional problems of manufacturers. A range of profitability measures and a variety of tools for dealing with risk are introduced because a number of techniques are used in practice.

The applicability standard resulted in numerous examples that provide models for applying various techniques. Reference to surveys of corporate usage are also included. Surveys are supplemented by frequent references to the experiences of specific corporations. There are approximately 20 application problems at the end of each chapter and a case at the end of almost every chapter. The applicability goal leads to some sharp contrasts between some other books and this book in the treatment of topics like portfolio models, capital asset pricing models, option pricing models, and arbitrage pricing theory. The emphasis is not on the theory as an interesting side trip, but on its applications for capital budgeting and long-term financing decisions.

Understandability has been pursued in various ways. A direct writing style was pursued with, for example, enthusiastic avoidance of acronyms and jargon. Proofs are relegated to footnotes in the great majority of cases so that the students can continue with the main line of thought and review the proofs as they desire. Numerous examples provide models to follow in the application of the various techniques. Feed-back from the first edition and second edition as well as class testing at St. Louis University and Quincy University was used to weed out sources of confusion.

Several flexibility objectives were pursued. The book was designed to fit the needs of a course focusing only on capital budgeting or a course dealing with both capital budgeting and long-term financing decisions. Furthermore, the book was designed to allow use by students at several different levels of preparation. Certain chapters are identified in the suggested course outlines as candidates for inclusion or deletion, depending on the students' level of preparation. The movement of most proofs and all calculus into the footnotes allows the instructor to skip over those issues or draw the students' attention to them. Extensive sets of questions, problems, and cases at varying levels of complexity give the instructor considerable flexibility in choosing pedagogical techniques. Flexibility in use of computers is also designed into the book, as discussed in the ancillary materials section of this preface.

We also emphasize integrated decision making. The relationship between strategy and value is treated early in the book because capital budgeting must support, and be supported by, the organization's strategy if wealth is to be created. Likewise, financial choices are not treated as a separate topic, but as a set of decisions inseparable from the capital budgeting decision of the firm.

Features of the Third Edition

The treatment of cash flow estimation was expanded and reorganized in this edition. Surveys of corporations and discussions with students lead to the conclusion that forecasting future cash flows is the most challenging part of capital investment analysis. Chapter 8 begins with a discussion of what makes a cash flow relevant to a decision. We then illustrate, by example, the individual steps necessary to convert a proforma income statement and balance sheet (which are constructed using accrual accounting) into a cash flow statement that can be used to judge the investments desirability. Taxes have been moved to Chapter 9 following the discussion on how to estimate cash flow so that a greater emphasis could be placed on the significant role that taxes have on the amount and timing of a projects cash flow. The particular problems associated with estimating cash flows for an international investment are also discussed in this chapter. The inflation chapter has been expanded to discuss the role that differing international inflation rates have on exchange rates and consequently cash flows from foreign investments.

International business considerations have been integrated into the book instead of being treated as a separate chapter. For example, recognition of the global marketplace as a strategic issue is treated in chapter two while tax and foreign exchange rate impacts on cash flows to the parent company are treated in chapters nine and ten. This change was made to reflect the reality of business, in which most activities are now carried out in a global marketplace.

Material for the instructor has been expanded. PowerPoint® presentations have been prepared to aid the instructor. Additional test questions and reading quizzes have been added to the instructor's manual. The instructors disk now has exam question files in a Microsoft Word format to ease test preparation.

Other chapters of the book were revised to respond to changes in the environment, such as new tax laws and to comments received from numerous reviewers and students. We believe that those hundreds of small changes will combine to make a much stronger book.

Pedagogical Features

We wanted to present a strong pedagogical structure to the book to support our objectives of comprehensiveness, applicability, understandability, and flexibility. Every chapter begins with a set of specific learning objectives. It has been our experience that students can more easily plan their learning if the expectations for learning are established up front.

Within each chapter are extended examples that illustrate, step-by-step, the analysis associated with each calculation. These examples prepare students for the end-of-chapter problems. Many of the examples include suggestions for using Lotus or Excel to solve the problems. These spreadsheet examples show the student how to use the advantages of spreadsheets to perform the analysis.

We include a comprehensive set of review questions that reinforce students' understanding. As a part of these questions, in many chapters we have added "Ethical Consideration" questions to get students thinking about the social and ethical ramifications that their decisions may have.

Every chapter ends with numerous problems to reinforce students' understanding of the key decision-making concepts, applications, and calculations.

Within these problems are several problems that utilize the spreadsheet template disk offered for professors to use with the textbook.

Many chapters end with a case study that draws together all the ideas of the chapter and applies them to a real-life capital budgeting situation. Most parts end with a case study that draws on concepts throughout the part for application to an actual decision making process.

Possible Course Outlines

This book is designed to serve a broad range of needs in terms of prior preparation of students and emphasis preferred by the instructor. A chapter outline for a capital budgeting course follows. Chapters that can be omitted for students who have less preparation are identified, as well as chapters that are recommended only for advanced students.

Chapters 1–4	Foundations for Capital Budgeting (Various portions will be review, depending on the backgrounds of the students.)
Chapter 5–7	Capital investment evaluation tools
Chapters 8–9	Marginal cash flow identification and taxes
Chapter 10	Inflation, foreign exchange movements, and capital investment analysis (Instructors not wishing to emphasize these issues can omit Chapter 10 without loss of continuity.)
Chapters 11–14	Risk analysis (Use of Chapters 11 and 12 alone is possible if the instructor wishes to focus on single-investment risk analysis. Chapters 13 and 14 can be used alone if students have a good background in basic probability and the instructor wishes to focus on nondiversifiable risk.)
Chapter 15	Applications of option pricing models and arbitrage pricing theory to capital budgeting (Include for an advanced class.)
Chapter 16	Cost of Capital
Chapter 20	Interactions between investment and financing decisions (Include for an advanced class.)
Chapter 21	Lease analysis (If the instructor does not wish to deal with leasing, this chapter could be omitted without loss of continuity.)
Chapter 22	Capital rationing (Include for an advanced class.)

Choice among these last four topics—on profits, multicriteria capital budgeting, and mergers— depends on remaining time and the preferences of the instructor. The following outline is appropriate for a course dealing with both capital budgeting and long-term financing decisions.

Chapters 1–4	Foundations for Capital Budgeting (Various portions will be review, depending on the backgrounds of the students.)
Chapter 5–7	Capital investment evaluation tools
Chapters 8–9	Marginal cash flow identification and taxes
Chapter 10	Inflation, foreign exchange movements, and capital investment analysis (Optional)
Chapters 11–14	Risk analysis
Chapter 15	Applications of option pricing models and arbitrage pricing theory to capital budgeting (Include for an advanced class.)
Chapter 16	Cost of Capital
Chapters 15–19	Capital structure and dividend policy
Chapter 20	Interactions between investment and financing decisions (Include for an advanced class.)
Chapter 21	Lease analysis
Chapter 22	Capital rationing (Include for an advanced class)

If chapters 1 through 22 are treated in detail, with use of cases and problems, there will probably be little time left for special topics. Any of the special topics in chapters 23 through 25 can be used if time permits.

Supplementary Materials

The text is accompanied by an instructors manual containing:
—Suggestions for use of the book
—Answers to end-of-chapter questions
—Answers to end-of-chapter problems
—Suggested solutions to cases
—Answers to selected problems and cases in a form suitable for reproduction as overhead transparencies
—Sample examinations
—Additional cases that can be used for examinations or further discussion
—PowerPoint presentations
—Chapter reading quizzes

Certain problems are designated with an ▦ to indicate that they are appropriate for use with a spreadsheet program such as *Lotus 1-2-3* or Excel. A diskette, with data and templates for the analysis of selected problems and cases, is available to adopters of this book. Template solutions for those problems are included on a second disk that is shrink-wrapped with the instructors manual. This second diskette is appropriate for distribution to students.

Acknowledgments

We have run up an extraordinary number of debts. We have benefited from input provided by James Ang (Florida State University), Stanley Atkinson (University of Central Florida), Richard H. Bernhard (North Carolina State University), Lyle Bowlin (University of Northern Iowa), Edward C. Boyer (Temple University), Sris Chatterjee (Rutgers University), Dale Cloninger (University of Houston–Clear Lake), John Cotner (Loyola University of Maryland), Gary Fay (Cooper Tire & Rubber), William E. Gardella (Montclair State University), David Goldenberg (University of Maryland), Nicholas Gressis (Wright State University), Janice Jadlow (Oklahoma State University), Dana Johnson (Virginia Tech), Sayeed Kayvan (Towson University), Carol Kiefer (Eastern Illinois University), Penny Kleen (Quincy University), Howard Lanser (University of Notre Dame), Dennis Logue (Dartmouth College), Dick Magliari (Quincy University), Roger Miller (Northern Illinois University), Norman Moore (University of Texas–Arlington), Roger Morin (Georgia State University), Chris Muscarella (Southern Methodist University), Aliriza Nasseh (Saint Louis University), Don Panton (University of New Mexico), Ralph Pope (Illinois State University), Ricardo J. Rodriguez (University of Miami), Emmanuel Santiago (Kansas State University), John Thatcher (University of Wisconsin—Whitewater), Raj Varma (Pennsylvania State University), J. D. Williams (University of Akron), and Thomas Wright (Webster University).

Cases have been contributed by Fred Yeager and Ellen Harshman (Saint Louis University) as well as Anil Mital and R. Vinayagamoorthy (University of Cincinnati). Kay Drey provided information for the Callaway case that was available virtually no place else. Adam Gehr (DePaul University) helped me to think about arbitrage pricing theory and capital budgeting. Our colleagues at St. Louis University and Quincy University have given us intellectual support and encouragement. Judy Janes has performed countless hours of proofreading.

It is impossible to be too extravagant in praise for the fine work done at Dryden Press. The third edition confirmed the warm memories of the first two editions. Mike Reynolds, Laura Hayes, and Claudia Gravier were effective managers and cheerleaders, who kept the project moving.

Bente, Laura, and Kirsten Seitz continue to tolerate and even support eccentric work habits here in St. Louis while Janet, Myles, Mason, and Merrill Ellison do the same in Quincy. Their tolerance and support is appreciated. Bente also logged immeasurable hours on research. The Callaway case, for example, resulted primarily from her digging. Janet's editorial hand can be seen frequently. Our parents, Walt and Peggy Ellison and Everett and Anna Mae Seitz have encouraged us for more years than we deserve. Freckles who was a continual supporter during the first edition, is still helping out. She still admires every word, as long as an occasional dog biscuit or walk is provided. Like the others whose support we appreciate so much, Freckles is innocent of any remaining flaws.

BRIEF TABLE OF CONTENTS

DETAILED TABLE OF CONTENTS |

PART 1

STRATEGY AND VALUE

The financial decisions of the firm begin with the choice of a business strategy designed to create value. The strategy is then implemented by making investments, by committing resources to particular courses of action. The investment decisions are the primary source of risk, and risk must be considered in the investment selection process. Investments require money, so they also result in financing needs. Financing costs and, therefore, the return that must be earned on an investment depend on the types of investments, including the riskiness of those investments. The figure below summarizes those relationships. Part I of this book, Chapters 1 through 4, focuses on the first box: strategy and goals, with particular emphasis on how value is created and measured, as well as how value is related to strategy. Chapter 1 provides a general overview of the financial decisions faced by the firm, as well as the linkage between value, strategy, and financial decisions. Chapter 2 deals with strategy in more detail because strategy is the basis for value. Chapter 3 introduces time value of money, the basis for understanding value. Chapter 4 applies time value principles to the valuation of companies and specific assets. These four chapters lay the foundation for capital investment choice, risk analysis, and financial structure choice.

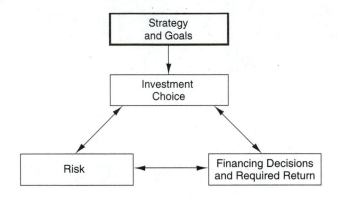

CHAPTER 1

LONG-TERM FINANCIAL DECISIONS

After completing this chapter you should be able to:

1. Describe why capital budgeting and appropriate financing is important to the firm, society, and to you personally in your career or private life.
2. Discuss the merits of wealth maximization versus the other goals of the firm.
3. Identify the different parties that benefit from optimal capital budgeting and financing decisions.
4. Explain current business events in relation to the parties that benefit and the parties that may have lost in a particular event.
5. Recognize and discuss the sources of competitive advantage.
6. List and describe the importance of the steps involved in the capital investment process.
7. Describe the variables important in planning the long-term financing of the firm.

Imagine yourself as John McDonnell, CEO of McDonnell-Douglas Corporation. Military contracts, which make up the bulk of your $18.5 billion annual revenue, are shrinking rapidly as peace threatens around the world. You can find something else to produce, or just say good-bye to most of your 100,000 employees. Commercial airliners would be the logical product for you, but the challenges are nearly overwhelming. McDonnell-Douglas is only a minor player in the commercial airliner business. You would be going up against Boeing, which dominates, and the European consortium, Airbus, which is gaining market share with the help of government subsidies. To add to your difficulties, airlines currently have excess capacity and are canceling more orders than they are placing. The only strong segment of the market is in the jumbo jets that airlines use mostly for international flights.

Development of a new jumbo jet would cost $5 billion. This would be a heroic commitment because you can only guess about demand and price years from now, when the first airplane will roll onto the runway. But heroism is not enough. You also need investors who are willing to wait most of a decade with no assurance that they will ever earn a profit. Possible financing arrangements include a joint production and ownership deal with the government of Taiwan, which would require congressional approval.[1]

John McDonnell's problem may have been more dramatic than most, but it represents the types of decisions faced by all leaders. Every leader must (1) establish a vision, (2) accumulate resources to realize that vision, and (3) deploy resources to realize that vision. The vision is a general description of how the company will position itself to offer to customers something with value in excess of cost. Business leaders establish and seek realization of a vision because they believe that it will allow their company to compete effectively for customers and resources, both surviving and prospering in the long run. They believe that jumping from one seemingly attractive opportunity to the next without a clear vision as a compass is a formula for eventual failure. They seek a vision not as an alternative to profitability, but because they believe it is the surest route to profitability in the long run.

Finance is not a side show to the activities of leaders; it is an integral part of the action in the center ring. The vision itself must be justified in financial terms: Do the expected benefits exceed the cost of resources used? The fundamental resource that must be accumulated is money, because you can buy other resources if you are able to attract money from investors. Every use of resources must be thought of as an investment. To be judged attractive, an investment must typically meet two tests: (1) Does it contribute to the vision? and (2) Will it provide enough benefits to satisfy the investors who furnished the money? The two primary functions of financial management, *arranging funding* and helping to *select investments* of those funds, are clearly central to the responsibilities of business leaders.

Financial management is not limited to the CEO or a few wizards in the back room. Whether you are an engineer, an advertising manager, or a human resource specialist, you will allocate resources, and thus make investment decisions, every day. Most managers participate at least occasionally in decisions about investments that require years to pay off fully. Many managers will someday participate in that watershed strategic investment decision that determines the success or failure of their company. To make those investments, the company must design financing that fits the investments and that meets the objectives of investors. As with McDonnell-Douglas, the investment, financing, and sale of resulting products increasingly occur in world markets. This book is about how to make those investment and financing decisions.

---

[1]The rest of the story: McDonnell-Douglas decided not to make the investment. After losing out on a competition to build the next generation of fighter jets, the company was sold. Boeing made the capital investment decision to acquire McDonnell-Douglas over the alternative of building additional factories to meet demand for commercial airliners.

CENTRAL ROLE OF WEALTH MAXIMIZATION |

The purpose of this book is to help current and prospective managers make better investment and financing decisions. If a choice is better, it must be better by some standard. Otherwise, one alternative is as good as the next. That standard is *wealth maximization.*

An action increases wealth if the benefits gained exceed the benefits given up. We will measure benefits primarily as money gained and given up. Money is a uniquely convenient benefit because it can be exchanged for virtually any other product. To supplement the general focus on money, we will take a few side trips to deal with benefits that cannot be measured entirely in dollar values, such as healthy babies.

The wealth criterion is so general that it fits a vast range of decisions. In single-period business decisions, wealth is created if cash inflow exceeds cash outflow by more than we would have earned by investing our money somewhere else during that period. In Economics 101, this wealth creation was called *economic profit.* In multi-period decisions, the *present value* of an expected future cash flow is the amount that must be invested elsewhere, at the same risk, to generate the same expected cash flow. The *net present value* of an investment or course of action is the present value of all cash inflows, minus the present value of all cash outflows. Thus, net present value is the economic profit or wealth created by a multi-period investment. Companies develop strategies, goals, and visions so they will be in a position to create economic profit and wealth.

Some considerations that immediately seem to create conflicts with the wealth maximization goal are actually ways to implement the wealth maximization goal. Business leaders develop and work toward visions as the most likely method of achieving long-term wealth creation, not as an alternative to wealth creation. When we discuss competitive advantage and strategy, these are again methods of creating wealth. Financing alternatives are also analyzed in the context of wealth creation.

Risk is inherent in most business decisions, and consideration of risk is part of the process of making wealth-maximizing choices. We are, after all, making decisions about future costs and benefits. We are seldom certain about future events. Investors require higher expected returns as compensation for taking on additional risk. If $60 invested in a bank account would grow to $100 in ten years, the present value of a *certain* $100 ten years from today would be $60. Suppose, on the other hand, there is a highly uncertain payoff in ten years, which could be $0 or $200 with equal probability. The present value in this case might be as low as $30, or even less, depending on investor attitudes toward risk at that particular time. Risk is such an important consideration that it is given five chapters of explicit coverage in this book: Chapters 11 through 15.

The wealth standard applies equally well to the financing decisions of the firm. Financing arrangements that decrease tax liabilities or minimize transaction costs of financing can increase wealth by leaving more money available after providing investors their required return. A financing arrangement that minimizes risk for the investors can decrease the return they require, and can therefore create wealth by leaving more money available after providing them with their required return.

WHO BENEFITS FROM WEALTH MAXIMIZATION? |

Stakeholders are parties who share in the results of business or nonprofit organization activity. The corporation serves as a framework for bringing together the money or labor of numerous stakeholders to create products that meet the needs of other stakeholders who, in turn, provide revenue that is used to pay the stakeholders providing money and labor. The interests of these various stakeholders are discussed in relation to the wealth maximization objective.

OWNERS

Shareholder (owner) wealth maximization is the most common answer when we ask whose wealth is to be maximized. In fact, finance textbook authors routinely assume that shareholder wealth maximization is the dominant goal of the firm, if not the only goal. As an example of the importance of shareholders, the cover of Shering-Plough's 1986 annual report contained the company's name and three other words: "Maximizing Shareholder Wealth."

Reasons cited for use of the shareholder wealth maximization goal include both the ethical standards and self-interests of managers. It is frequently argued that maximization of shareholder wealth is the professional responsibility of managers because they are legally the agents of the shareholders. Lawyers, real estate brokers, and stockbrokers are but a few of the professionals who are required by both law and standards of their profession to act on behalf of their principals, subject to other ethical constraints such as the requirement that they behave honestly and legally when dealing with others. Thus, a belief that you as a manager have ethical obligations toward the stockholders would not seem far-fetched.

The net present value of an investment is the amount by which the investment increases the current wealth of the shareholders. We would expect an increase in the value of the company's stock equal to the net present value when an unanticipated capital investment is announced, unless investors expect managers to use part of the investment's future cash flows for something that is not in the best interests of the shareholders. If competing projects are being considered, the combination that increases total net present value the most will maximize the wealth of the owners. If the present value of the benefits from an investment does not exceed the present value of the outlays, the owners would be better off to pass up the opportunity and invest their money outside the firm.[2]

---

[2] For a detailed discussion of the relationship between value maximization and the welfare of shareholders, see Ezra Solomon, *The Theory of Financial Management* (New York: Columbia University Press, 1963).

MANAGERS

Some observers base their analysis on the assumption that *management welfare maximization* is the dominant business goal. Belief in this goal follows from the assumption that managers, like everyone else, are interested in their own welfare. In perfect competition, managers must maximize wealth just to survive. But in the absence of perfect competition, managers have some leeway and may decide to act in their own self-interest. Stockholders are not privy to every decision made by managers, and attempts to closely monitor managers involve costs in terms of both time and money.

Managers have several interests that may conflict with those of shareholders. Managers are frequently accused of preferring size over profitability, partly because compensation is related to size, and therefore making some investments that cannot be justified in terms of shareholder wealth maximization. Managers may also be tempted to consume excessive perquisites, such as luxury offices and golden parachutes.[3] Finally, managers may have different attitudes toward risk.

Different attitudes toward risk are particularly difficult to deal with because they are often difficult to observe and can often be observed only well after irreversible results. One problem occurs when the personal wealth of a manager consists primarily of human capital and company stock, both of which are affected by the company's performance. Because many managers have all their eggs in one basket, they may be more risk-averse than shareholders. Another problem occurs when the wealth of managers is primarily in the form of options, so that they will gain large amounts if the company succeeds but will not share in the losses if the company fails. A contributing factor to massive losses in the savings-and-loan industry was a structure that allowed managers to share generously in the gains while transferring the losses to the taxpayers.

The conflicts between the goals of managers and stockholders create *agency* problems. An agency problem exists whenever one person (the agent) is employed to act on behalf of another person (the principal). The principal always faces the risk that the agent will be less than faithful. The principals in this case are the stockholders, and the agents are the managers. When Ralston-Purina invested heavily in the St. Louis Blues hockey team, for example, questions were raised about whether this was a decision to maximize shareholder wealth or a decision based more on the interests of executives. When top management changed a few years later, the hockey connection was severed as part of a general restructuring. When the risks of problems like this exist, the principal either faces the cost of closely monitoring the agent or accepts less than would be expected if the agent were completely faithful. These agency problems may be resolved by managers accepting shareholder wealth maximization as an ethical obligation. Alternately, these agency problems may be resolved through close monitoring or compensation plans.

---

[3]A *golden parachute* is an employment contract guaranteeing top executives large payments, often in the millions of dollars, if they are forced from their positions through a takeover by another company.

Monitoring of top executives is difficult and expensive, but compensation plans have proved to be a powerful tool for limiting these agency problems. Incentive pay systems, including bonuses and stock option plans, serve to tie the managers' wealth to the value of the common stock at over 90 percent of the large corporations in the United States. Even though the top executives of major corporations typically own only a small percentage of the corporation they lead, their interest in the corporation represents the great bulk of their personal wealth. They are motivated to protect and increase that wealth. In addition, managers who do not concentrate on the interests of the shareholders may risk being sued, fired, or pushed aside through hostile takeovers or as a result of a proxy fight. Thus, even managers who do not recognize a professional responsibility to the shareholders may spend most of their time trying to increase the wealth of the shareholders.

Conflicts between managers and shareholders do occasionally arise with regard to nonmonetary objectives and use of wealth created by wealth-maximizing decisions. These conflicts are the stuff of newspaper headlines or courtroom drama and are probably the reason why many corporations are more interested in prescribing a code of ethics or conduct for their employees today than they were in the past.[4] The fact that a conflict or choice may exist should not obscure the dominance of common interests. Both groups favor capital investments that maximize wealth, and both groups generally prefer less risk to more risk, even if they do not have identical views about risk. Thus, the objectives of increasing wealth and avoiding risk dominate investment and financing decisions whether the goal is shareholder wealth maximization or management welfare maximization.[5]

CREDITORS

In general, the creditors' protection increases when wealth increases. There are, however, exceptions. An investment that increases risk may decrease the value of the creditors' claims, even if it increases the value of the firm. In these cases, which are discussed in more detail in Chapter 15, the wealth maximization criterion must be extended to consider not only total wealth but also the wealth of shareholders and creditors separately.

CUSTOMERS, EMPLOYEES, AND SUPPLIERS

The shareholder wealth maximization standard does not leave customers and employees high and dry. You must attract customers and sell your products above cost if you are to increase wealth. Thus, the desire to maximize wealth motivates

---

[4]It is important for the student to realize that the alternatives confronted in reality are not black and white. To facilitate understanding, we have added at least one ethics question or problem at the end of each chapter.

[5]For a discussion of the relationship between management and shareholder interests, see Michael C. Jensen and William A. Meckling, "Theory of the Firm: Managerial Behavior, Agency Costs, and the Ownership Structure," *Journal of Financial Economics* 3 (October 1976): 305–360.

companies to strive for better products and more efficient production. The same desire drives companies to design compensation packages that will attract and motivate the employees who can contribute to quality and efficiency.

Competition is critical in aligning the interests of shareholders, customers, and employees. Competition keeps companies from overpricing products and underpaying employees and suppliers. Competition for high-quality employees pressures the company not only to pay wages but also to provide stable employment and a desirable work environment. Strong relationships with suppliers are increasingly seen as a source of competitive advantage by assuring a stable source of high-quality inputs, such as parts. Suppliers want more than just the price of their goods. They want clear product quality expectations and stable demand, which will allow them to invest in their own futures. This, in turn, assures the company a stable source of high-quality inputs. Other producers of products and other employers force companies seeking wealth maximization to jointly pursue product quality, efficiency, strong supplier relationships, and the attraction and retention of employees.

Problems sometimes arise when it is time to divvy up the wealth. Should it all go to the shareholders, or should it be divided among workers, suppliers, managers, and shareholders, for example? Before foreign competition reshaped the automobile industry, General Motors created a substantial pool of wealth. The wealth was shared by stockholders, managers, and workers, all of whom earned more than they could have earned by taking their respective time and money elsewhere. The problem of dividing up wealth will not be solved in this book, but it will not arise unless some wealth is created in the first place. A plan for sharing wealth gains is often a key part of management's plan to encourage wealth-maximizing behavior.

SOCIETY

Society wealth maximization is sometimes cited as the ultimate goal of business activity. Fortunately, the benefits of an attractive capital investment often extend to broad segments of society. Consider, for example, an investment to improve the efficiency of a factory. Customers benefit when reduced production costs lead to increased price competition. Workers benefit because increases in wages over the years have followed from increases in productivity.[6] Overall economic growth is enhanced because increased productivity frees up resources to be used in other areas of the economy. Finally, the tax revenues to support government services are enhanced by increased profitability.

Conflicts between business and society in terms of wealth maximization arise in two areas. First, there are problems with nonpriced costs such as pollution and nonpriced benefits such as community stability. If commercial fishing in Lake Michigan is destroyed by mercury waste, for example, the cost is

---

[6]The benefit is not necessarily limited to the industry in which the improved efficiency occurred. Average wages in an economy tend to move with changes in the marginal productivity of labor in that economy.

widespread, but the polluting companies may not be charged for the damage. Second, there are questions about how wealth is to be allocated among members of society. For example, a company may choose an investment solely to reduce its taxes, the collection of which is one of society's tools for allocating wealth. In these cases, the investments that maximize the owners' wealth may not maximize society's wealth. These problems often arise from poorly thought-out government policies that inadvertently encourage companies to behave in ways not really desired by the public. If government policies in areas such as taxation and pollution are properly designed, the investments that maximize shareholder wealth will generally contribute to the wealth of society as well.[7]

A statement by John M. Henske, chairman of Olin Corporation, reflects one executive's recognition of a responsibility to consider the role of the business firm in society:

> I believe that every corporation must serve several constituencies. Shareholders are certainly an important one. So are employees, so are customers. We have a responsibility to the communities in which we work, to the public who use and are exposed to our products, and to our suppliers, who have committed resources to supply us reliably. To my mind, the chief executive officer has the responsibility of serving all of these. [Olin Corporation 1986 Annual Report]

COMPANY GOALS AND NONMONETARY CONSIDERATIONS

Nonmonetary considerations are sometimes important, regardless of whether managers are focusing on the interests of owners or themselves. Some nonmonetary goals that appear to be used instead of wealth maximization are actually policy guidelines designed to implement the vision of the corporation. Requiring that investments support the company's vision is a tool for seeking wealth creation, not an alternative to wealth creation. As an example, consider the capital budgeting process at Xerox Corporation. Executives there have identified leadership in information management as their route to the creation of products with value in excess of cost. If Xerox managers want to be sure they have identified the investments that will maximize wealth, they must evaluate the fast-food business, the rubber tree plantation business, the movie production business, and so on prior to every capital budgeting decision. The search would take forever, cost unlimited amounts, and distract attention from the vision. Because the attempt to identify and evaluate every possible capital investment on and off the earth would paralyze the company, top executives must provide guidance as to where to search for attractive investment opportunities. Generally, top executives will direct the search to areas in which the company can enjoy an advantage in

---

[7]There may be situations in which monitoring costs are so high that the societal wealth decreases caused by certain activities are less than the monitoring costs needed to modify companies' behavior. In these cases, there is a genuine conflict between corporate and societal wealth maximization.

relation to competitors, because those are the areas in which attractive investments are most likely to be found. A goal of capturing 30 percent of the office typewriter market, for example, would tell managers to focus on finding attractive investments in the office typewriter businesses, in which Xerox is already a strong competitor.

As another example, goals stated in terms of accounting income may arise because management compensation is tied to accounting income and accounting income is reported to investors. A chief executive who hears on the evening news that the price of a competitor's stock fell following unfavorable earnings news may be hesitant to select investments that will temporarily hurt income, even if those investments have positive net present values. Trade-offs between accounting income and net present value of cash flows may sometimes be necessary, but these conflicts can be minimized. Income is important because investors use it to predict future cash flows. A history of honest communication with investors helps managers to decrease reliance on accounting income as a communication tool.

Some nonmonetary goals represent conflicts between interests of owners and managers. You may, for example, want to be chief executive of the largest company in the industry even if that does not mean maximizing wealth, as long as you can earn a "satisfactory" return for the owners. You may also be less willing to take risks than the diversified shareholders, even if wealth could be increased by adopting a more risky position. When other, nonmonetary goals are also important, capital budgeting involves trade-offs between nonmonetary goals and wealth maximization. It is the responsibility of management to be aware of the nonmonetary goals of the stakeholders and to decide which of those goals result in a management obligation.

NONPROFIT ORGANIZATIONS

Nonprofit organizations such as hospitals and churches are also involved in capital investment decisions. Many so-called nonprofit organizations seek to maximize wealth just as if they were profit-seeking businesses. For example, many hospitals face such vigorous competition that wealth-maximizing decisions are necessary just to survive. In other cases, such as deciding whether to make a church building more energy efficient, the decision process is not significantly different from that in a profit-seeking company; the decision that creates the greatest wealth gives the organization the most resources to allocate to the pursuit of its mission.

When a nonprofit organization faces alternate ways of achieving its mission, the basic wealth maximization model also works. If either of two capital investments will achieve the mission, the one with the smallest present value of costs is desirable, leaving the maximum amount available for other purposes.

When competing investments lead to the achievement of different missions, the wealth maximization principle is more difficult to apply. One approach is to use resources to maximize the wealth of the organization's constituency. This may be a useful guideline for an association of doctors, lawyers, or accountants, but charities have more difficulty identifying and measuring benefits. To use the wealth maximization criterion for a charity, you must be willing to assign relative values to various missions. However, decision makers are often unwilling to assign relative values to saving a starving child in the sub-Sahara and educating a minority student in the United States. If you are not willing to assign relative values to missions, minimization of the present value of outlays may help you find the most efficient way to achieve each mission and the amount of one mission that must be given up for a unit of another mission. The topic of capital budgeting in a nonprofit setting is discussed in greater detail in Chapter 23.

COMPETITIVE ADVANTAGE AND WEALTH CREATION |

We know from Economics 101 that perfect competition has the following characteristics:

- There are no restrictions keeping producers from entering or exiting the market.
- No one producer or buyer is large enough to affect price through any action.
- All producers manufacture identical products.
- All producers have identical costs.
- Everyone is perfectly informed about what everyone else is doing.

We also know from Economics 101 that nobody can expect continued economic profit in these conditions because a price that allows an economic profit will attract new producers until the extra supply causes the price to fall. Where there are no opportunities to increase a firm's economic profit, there are no opportunities for wealth creation. It was noted earlier that competition helps solve conflicts between the goals of owners, managers, customers, and so on. Perfect competition solves these problems perfectly, but does so by assuring that the company will create no wealth. Most managers would prefer to create wealth and struggle with the agency problems that follow.

A company sets the stage for wealth creation by creating *competitive advantage,* which is the elimination of some of the conditions for perfect competition so that an economic profit is possible. When executives talk about vision and strategy, they are talking about the process of positioning themselves to achieve competitive advantage, therefore economic profit, and positive net present values. *Strategy* includes decisions as to what businesses we are in and how we intend to position our organization in relation to others in those businesses to gain competitive advantage. The investment decisions of successful companies create wealth by implementing their strategies.

Competitive advantage is typically achieved by product advantage or cost advantage. A *product advantage* exists if your product is differentiated from those of your competitors so that you are selling your product without matching their prices. A *cost advantage* exists when you can produce your product at a lower cost than your competitors so that you can earn an economic profit while matching their prices. Investments that create wealth are then aimed at giving the company lower costs or a superior product.

Financing decisions of the most successful companies are also coordinated with their strategy. Financing arrangements that minimize the annual cash flows required by investors may, for example, increase the company's ability to withstand competitors' attempts to increase market share by reducing price. The company's ability to withstand such an attack may be sufficient to discourage the attack in the first place. Financing choices may also give the company a cost advantage by reducing the return that investors require.

OVERVIEW OF THE CAPITAL INVESTMENT PROCESS |

A *capital investment* is defined as an outlay that is expected to result in benefits in the future. *Capital budgeting* is the process of selecting capital investments.

Capital investments can be classified as physical, financial, or intangible. *Physical assets* such as factories and machinery are familiar capital investments, but computers, airplanes, and highways are also physical assets that qualify as capital investments. A *financial asset* is a claim against some other party for monetary payment; examples include savings accounts, bonds, and stock. Financial assets generally have value because money was used to acquire some other asset that will provide cash flows. *Intangible investments* are not physical in nature and do not serve as claims for payment by some other party but are expected to result in future benefits. Examples of intangible assets include a training program for marketing representatives, a membership drive for a symphony orchestra, and a franchise. For McDonnell's jumbo jet development, investments would have included both special tools and the wages of engineers who would work on the project. The tools are tangible assets, while the wages are an intangible investment because they are expected to result in future benefits, even though they do not result directly in an identifiable asset.

The decision process is similar for all capital investments regardless of how those investments are classified. Because capital investments are so important to the success of the organization, most companies have formal policies guiding the decision process. Figure 1.1 illustrates the typical capital investment process, and a discussion of each step in that process follows.

Establish Goals

Wealth creation is generally the overall goal, but wealth creation is abstract. It is difficult to know if shareholder wealth was maximized, for example, because we do not know what share price would have been if we had taken other courses of action. Therefore, chief executives often translate the wealth goal into more concrete goals against which performance can be measured. When John F. McDonnell took over McDonnell-Douglas, for example, he identified four standards by which progress would be measured: rate of return, size of government contracts, response by financial markets, and ranking among *Fortune*'s most admired

| **FIGURE 1.1** | **FLOW CHART OF THE CAPITAL INVESTMENT PROCESS**

This flow chart represents the sequence of steps followed in a typical, well-organized capital investment process.

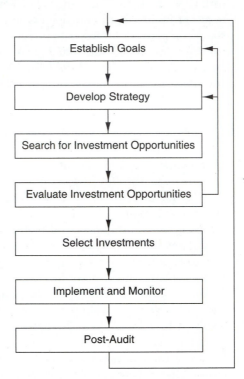

corporations.[8] Ideally, these are the *attainable* goals that managers believe will increase wealth the most. There may also be nonmonetary goals such as reduction of injuries, improved reading ability, or cleaner water. Monetary goals are dominant for businesses, while governmental and nonprofit organizations often focus on nonmonetary goals.

Develop Strategy

Strategy sets the general direction of the organization and provides the framework within which capital investment opportunities are sought. The goals and strategy of the corporation are typically combined in the vision. According to General Electric chairman Jack Welch, the job of the boss is to "develop a vision" and then oversee a change in the set of shared values and beliefs that make

[8]*St. Louis Post-Dispatch* (May 8, 1988): E,1.

up the organization's culture in order to accomplish it.[9] As discussed at the beginning of this chapter, the job of the boss is also to accumulate and allocate resources in support of that vision. Goals and strategy therefore set the framework for leading people, accumulating resources, and allocating resources.

The major focus of strategy is the generation of wealth through creation and use of competitive advantage. Strategic assessment often begins with an analysis of *opportunities* and *threats* in the environment, followed by an analysis of the company's *strengths* and *weaknesses*. From this analysis, general directions for development are chosen.

Strategy is the foundation of a successful capital budgeting system. Strategy is the framework in which resources are marshaled in pursuit of goals. Strategy also tells members of the organization where to search for profitable capital investments. Successful capital budgeting and wealth maximization are therefore dependent on sound strategy. Likewise, sound strategic planning will not lead to wealth creation unless strategy is implemented with the goal of maximizing wealth. Thus, sound strategic planning, sound capital budgeting, and sound financing plans are essential.

An example was Southwestern Bell Telephone's decision to focus on its core business after deregulation and to convert its trunk system to fiber-optic technology. This strategy, which required capital investments measured in the billions of dollars, gave Southwestern Bell a clearer signal and better ability to handle the rapidly growing data transmission business. The adoption of this strategy provided guidance to the capital budgeting process for years. It proved to be more successful than strategies followed by some other telephone companies, such as expansion into business unrelated to telecommunications.

A less successful strategy was Sony's decision to severely limit licensing of its Beta video-recorder format and keep most of the manufacturing investment opportunity to itself. Managers knew the beta format was technically better than the competing VHS format and therefore assumed that beta would win out in the marketplace. By refusing to license the beta format to other manufacturers, Sony would have competitive advantage and control over price; it would create the opportunity for large, highly profitable capital investments. Unfortunately, the strategy failed. VHS became the dominant format because it was freely licensed. After a long, expensive struggle, Sony was eventually forced to switch to VHS format production itself. Apple computer followed a similar strategy in protecting its operating system, and like Sony, lost the industry standard position to Microsoft, which did not sell computers and therefore was not tempted to restrict the use of its operating systems to one manufacturer.

Each strategic decision is in itself a general capital budgeting decision, in that it is based on estimates of wealth creation and other contributions to company goals that can be expected from later capital investments in pursuit of a particular strategy. Goal setting and strategy choice are interactive processes, as

[9]"Jack Welch: How Good a Manager?" *Business Week* (December 14, 1977): 92–94.

shown in Figure 1.1, because goals are often readjusted in response to information about feasibility gained in the strategic assessment process.

Search for Investment Opportunities

The identification of potential capital investments is a critical stage in the capital budgeting process. The remainder of the process can only assure that the best of the proposed investments are selected. Fortunately, companies that want to be successful in identifying capital investment opportunities can organize themselves for success. The first part of that organization is development of realistic goals, sound strategy, and appropriate rewards for successful managers. Then, specific attention must be devoted to the search process.

The search for investment opportunities must be supported by a corporate culture that encourages creativity; otherwise, there will be no good proposals to evaluate. 3M Corporation has been widely recognized for encouraging creative thinking about new business opportunities. Results include such home-run new product investments as Scotchgard and Post-it. For comparison, consider the (mercifully) anonymous quote from a manager of another company: "The trick to getting ahead here is to never make a mistake. Nobody would submit a capital request if there was any doubt that it would test out." This company languishes with an outmoded product line in a stagnant market.

A successful search process generally requires the commitment of resources. Research, product development, and consumer attitude surveys are all ways to identify investment opportunities. If the strategy involves acquisition of other companies, an acquisition group may be responsible for searching out and evaluating opportunities. These various approaches have in common the willingness to spend money on people to search for attractive capital investments.

Training in support of strategy is another example of organization for a successful search. Executives are increasingly realizing that training of employees is not a sideline activity for good years but an important part of strategy implementation. Managers at all levels must be aware of company goals and strategy if they are to search out the right types of capital investment opportunities. In addition, managers at all levels must have some skill in capital budgeting so that they can perform at least preliminary analysis of potential investments.

A successful search for investment opportunities will be carried out at all levels of the organization. Major capital investments that involve a *change in strategy* will probably be identified at a top management level. General Motors' decision to build the Saturn plant, for example, involved a new strategy as well as a capital investment of $5 billion.[10] This project was developed at the highest levels of the company. *Major investments in support of existing strategy* will typically be developed at a high level, such as the senior executive in charge of marketing or production. Examples include the introduction of a new cereal by

---

[10]During the implementation stage, General Motors backed away from the strategy (a new strategic decision, in effect), scaling down the size of the investment and relying on less radical production methods.

General Mills and Chrysler's addition of a new factory to increase production of its minivan. *Smaller investments* are identified and given preliminary screening by the person in a position to perceive a need. Examples include thousands of decisions by industrial engineers to replace or modernize specific pieces of equipment, by supervisors to send employees to training programs, by marketing managers to run advertisements, and so on. Although these investments are smaller in scale, they are vitally important due to their cumulative effect. Because people are involved at all levels, efforts to encourage the search for attractive investments must reach people at all levels of the organization.

Evaluate Investment Opportunities

The ideal corporate culture will result in numerous capital investment proposals, each of which must be evaluated. The fundamental question is whether the present value of the cash benefits or savings to be generated by an investment exceed the present value of the outlays. Identifying these outlays and benefits is by no means a trivial exercise. In fact, survey respondents have identified project definition and cash flow estimation as the most difficult stage of the evaluation process,[11] and there is evidence that estimates are systematically biased.[12] Cash flow estimation requires sales forecasts, cost forecasts, engineering analyses, inflation estimates, tax estimates, and so on. Deciding which cash flows will be affected by a particular investment is a major challenge. Chapters 8 through 10 are devoted to the identification of cash flows. Chapters 11 through 15 deal with uncertainty surrounding cash flows.

Strategic considerations are often on an equal footing with cash flow analysis because investments that are not consistent with the corporation's strategy are not likely to create wealth. Chrysler Corporation's decision to shortcut testing and rush its Aspen automobile to market may have made sense in terms of cash flow related to that car. But repair problems damaged Chrysler's competitive position for years.

Risk analysis is a standard part of the evaluation of most capital investments. We are estimating future events, and those estimates are almost always fraught with uncertainty. Total project risk is often analyzed by looking at the sources of uncertainty, then estimating the wealth effects of changes in those values. If sales levels are a key variable, for example, analysts may compute net present values using several different sales forecasts. Risk that cannot be diversified away is of particular importance and receives special attention. Results of changes in overall economic conditions are hard to diversify away, while factors related to a particular project, such as technological life or shifting customer tastes, can be diversified away when the company or its shareholders spread their money among a number of different projects. Managers must ultimately use this information

[11]David F. Scott, Jr., and J. William Petty II, "Capital Budgeting Practices in Large American Firms," *The Financial Review* 19 (March 1984): 111–123.

[12]David I. Levine, "Do Corporate Executives Have Rational Expectations?" *Journal of Business* 66 (April 1993): 271–293.

to decide if the potential benefits are worth the risk. Chapters 11 through 15 are devoted to risk analysis and decision making.

Other considerations come into play as well. Companies often lack sufficient resources to acquire all attractive investments and must make choices. An investment might have good cash flow characteristics but seriously reduce reported income for several years. Conflicts between accounting income and wealth creation would not occur in a world of perfect information, but these conflicts are sometimes important to managers. An investment may look good in isolation but have disastrous public relations consequences. Because of these and other considerations, the evaluation process commonly includes review by finance, production, engineering, marketing, legal, and public relations departments.

The information gained from the evaluation of scores of investment proposals feeds back into strategy development. If an area of emphasis identified in strategic planning cannot provide attractive investments, it may be necessary to revise the strategy.

Select Investments

The selection of investments is typically a multilevel process. A plant manager may, for example, have authority to approve individual capital investments of up to $100,000 in cost, *provided* that the investments meet the company's criteria and the sum of those investments is within the total budget limit. Capital investments endorsed by the plant manager, but beyond the plant manager's authority, may then go to a division vice president who can approve capital investments up to, say, $500,000, provided that they meet company standards and fall within an overall budget. Decisions on the largest investments are then made at the top management level.

Committees are commonly involved in the decision process. A capital budgeting committee may prioritize investment opportunities at the factory or division level. The largest investments may ultimately be chosen by a corporate capital budgeting committee, the executive committee, or the board of directors. The decision makers on these committees bring a wide range of interests, expertise, and communication skills to the table. Some are highly trained in the use and explanation of financial analysis tools, while others may have expertise in the areas of engineering, law, human resource management, marketing, and so on. Some will focus primarily on the forecasted financial numbers, for example, while others are more interested in strategic issues or employee implications. The discussion can therefore be far-reaching, and the analysis required to support this discussion can be extensive. Higher-level executives will be very comfortable with the search for consensus among people with varied interests and different levels of understanding, while junior members of the corporation may be new to this type of decision process.

Not every company follows the process just outlined. The president of one multibillion-dollar, multidivision company insisted on personally signing off on *every* capital investment proposal. His average analysis time was under five minutes per proposal, and his approval rate approached 100 percent on all but the largest projects. Obtaining his signature was obviously a formality, with the real decisions on most proposals being made informally at other levels.

Unfortunately, capital budgeting is sometimes viewed as little more than an exercise in saying no. This view is understandable on the part of a manager who submitted proposals and received no feedback other than "request denied." Viewed in broader context, though, capital budgeting begins with encouraging people to search for investment opportunities and culminates with the selection of the investments that make the greatest contribution to company goals. Clear guidelines and reasonable feedback on how and why choices were made, along with some positive reinforcement for people whose proposals were not chosen, should contribute to a positive view of capital budgeting.

Implement and Monitor

The implementation and monitoring process begins once a capital investment has been approved. Capital investments are monitored during the actual period of acquisition or construction because deviations, either good or bad, should be recognized, taken into consideration, and dealt with. Cost overruns are the most common deviations during construction or acquisition and are dealt with by changing control procedures or taking another look at the attractiveness of the investment. Likewise, the capital investment should be monitored as it goes into operation to spot deviations and take corrective action.

Post-Audit

The post-audit is primarily a learning tool because it is carried out at the end of a capital investment's life or after the investment has matured to a stable level of activity and profitability. The post-audit includes an assessment of the actual performance of the investment and a comparison with forecasted performance. Reasons for deviation from anticipated performance are sought. Post-audits will allow you to identify the strengths and weakness of your capital budgeting systems. Some companies construct business case histories from post-audits and use those cases in their management education programs.

Monitoring and post-audit encourage managers to be accurate in the estimates used in their capital investment proposals and help counter the tendency to adjust the numbers to make proposed investments look better. Managers receiving proposals frequently express concern that the numbers have been adjusted to make the projects look good, and managers submitting proposals sometimes brag (privately) about adjusting the numbers to get the result they know they will need to sell the project. As an example, a regional telephone company sent back the year's capital budgeting requests with a note that a post-audit process was being introduced. Managers were given an opportunity to revise their proposals in light of a future post-audit. Hundreds of proposals were withdrawn and benefit estimates were scaled back for scores of others.

When conducting a post-audit, the distinction between a good *decision* and a good *outcome* must be kept in mind. An oil company may, for example, drill hundreds of exploratory wells knowing that only one out of ten will hit oil. Penalizing an engineer who chose one of the sites that turned out to be dry is counterproductive if the site met the required conditions for exploratory drilling at the time the well was drilled. Likewise, the treasurer who sinks all of the company's cash into the state lottery is not vindicated just because he chooses a winning number. The company may decide to change the decision process if the number of successful outcomes is smaller than expected, but in a world of uncertainty, some good decisions will result in bad outcomes, and vice versa.

The information garnered from a series of post-audits can result in a new look at goals and strategies. Consequently, the capital investment process is dynamic, with the entire process being continually reviewed and modified as new information becomes available. The fundamental objective of this dynamic process is the identification and selection of the capital investments that will make the greatest possible contribution to the firm's value and other goals.

OVERVIEW OF LONG-TERM FINANCING DECISIONS |

A finance theory called the separation principle holds that investment and financing decisions of the firm can be dealt with separately. The principle is correct under perfect market conditions, in which wealth is unaffected by the ways in which the firm finances its activities. In the imperfection-loaded world of normal activity, financing choices matter, and the use of financing appropriate for your company's investments can increase wealth. Capital investments that meet customer needs cost-effectively can make you a big winner in the wealth creation race. Likewise, you can raise funds on favorable terms, and therefore increase wealth, if you meet the needs of investors. The importance of satisfying investors is why David Weslink, chief financial officer at Household International, described his group as "the other marketing department." It is their job to meet the needs of investors so that the company will have a continual supply of funds with which to take advantage of attractive investment opportunities.

The plan for long-term financing begins with the amount of money needed for attractive investment opportunities, both now and in the foreseeable future. The decisions about how much is needed, what it is needed for, and how to raise that money are interactive. The wealth impact of a capital investment is affected by the rate of return that must be paid to investors. The rate of return that must be paid depends on how much money is needed, risk, and how that money will be raised. The lower the rate of return that must be paid to investors, the greater the number of attractive investment opportunities the company will have. Because investment and financing decisions are interrelated, you need at least some familiarity with financing considerations even if your personal responsibility is only related to investment decisions.

FINANCING CHOICES

Financing sources are divided primarily between stock (equity) holders, who share in ownership of the residual after other claims have been paid, and creditors, who are promised a fixed return for the use of their money. The first choice, then, is the *debt-equity mix*.

The financing job is, however, much more complex than simply choosing a mix of debt and equity. *Maturity* of debt is one key issue. For companies, like individuals, the ability to carry debt is not determined by the absolute amount of debt but by the payments. From academics like Gordon Donaldson[13] to practitioners like conglomerate builder Meshulah Ricklis, the role of cash payments in the measurement of debt capacity has long been stressed. When considering maturity, the company must consider not only the minimum payment it must make but the maximum payment it is allowed to make. In other words, the company is concerned about its right to repay the loan early if it no longer needs that funding.

The *priority of each claim* is another important consideration. Some debt may be senior to other debt, meaning that the senior debt holders have a higher priority in the event of bankruptcy. Creditors may also be given liens against specific assets. We may, for example, give one creditor first claim against the office building and another creditor first claim against the inventory in the event of bankruptcy. Even when raising additional equity capital, the company faces a choice between selling common stock, which is the final residual claim, and preferred stock, which is typically assured dividends before anything is given to the common stockholders.

Source of financing is also given careful consideration. The company may sell debt in the public markets, typically through investment bankers, or it may prefer private borrowing, from banks, insurance companies, or pension funds, for example. Sale of additional stock involves similar choices. The company may seek a private placement in which stock is sold to one or a few investors. Alternately, the company may seek to sell the stock exclusively to employees or to distribute it as widely as possible to the public.

The range of financing choices becomes even broader when we realize that for every two alternatives, there is a hybrid choice in between. The distance between debt and common stock, for example, can be bridged by issuing convertible debt, which the lender can later exchange for common stock, or by issuing preferred stock. Likewise, the company may issue warrants, which allow investors to acquire stock later, at a price fixed today.

CONSIDERATIONS IN FINANCING

Cost is, of course, a principal consideration in financing choice. The lower the rate of return required by investors, the greater will be the net present value and wealth contribution of each capital investment. Cost is affected by a number of

---

[13]Gordon Donaldson, "New Framework for Corporate Debt Capacity," *Harvard Business Review* 40 (March–April 1962): 117–131.

considerations. Because interest expense reduces taxes while stockholders must be paid from after-tax income, we would expect debt to be a cheaper source of funds. However, the tax advantage of debt is offset by several other costs. Large amounts of debt, for example, may increase the risk of bankruptcy or other problems that arise when companies cannot pay their creditors on time. Furthermore, the larger the amount of debt, the smaller is the probability that the company will have enough income before tax to take full advantage of the interest deduction from debt.

Agency costs are a particularly difficult and important category of costs that must be considered when choosing financing. Recall that agency problems occur whenever one person (the agent) is employed to act on behalf of another person (the principal). The principal either incurs the cost of monitoring the agent or accepts less than would be expected if the agent were completely faithful. An all-equity capital structure leaves the stockholders with the risk that managers will not always act in their interest. Because there is no requirement to repay stockholders, investors are concerned about the risk that managers will continually reinvest in projects that do not create wealth. Debt reduces this concern because debt must be repaid, forcing managers to return to the investors to justify new investment plans. Debt has its own agency costs, though. Managers might take more risks than the creditors anticipated, for example. The higher the level of debt, the greater is this risk. Specific asset pledges and repayment schedules help to decrease this risk, but these arrangements also have costs.

A good deal of the effort in designing a financing mix is aimed at minimizing these agency costs. A mix of senior debt, with first priority in bankruptcy, and junior debt that gets paid only after the senior debt is one example of a solution. The senior creditors are substantially relieved of monitoring cost, and the monitoring problem is concentrated in the hands of the junior creditors. The company might, for example, sell the senior debt to a broad group of investors while selling the junior debt to one or a few investors who are in a good position to monitor the company. Asset type obviously affects the monitoring problem as well. The use and maintenance of a hotel can be easily observed, for example, while the use of a research laboratory is much more difficult to monitor. Not surprisingly, investors will generally lend a high percentage of the cost of a hotel compared to what they will lend for a research program.

Beyond cost, the company is concerned about *availability* and *flexibility*. The financial markets as well as the company are subject to a wide variety of influences, and the company does not want to be in a position where it has excellent investment opportunities but cannot raise money. The company also wants to be able to change its financing by, for example, repaying debt before maturity. Keeping a lower debt-to-equity ratio than creditors would accept is one way of assuring access to either the equity or credit markets at all times. Maintenance of numerous credit arrangements as well as international listing of the firm's stock keeps the company from being dependent on one market. Banking problems decreased the supply of bank loans in the early 1990s, for example, and companies that had relied exclusively on bank credit complained bitterly that they could no longer raise funds. Companies have sold stock to the public when they did not really need the money, just so they could establish a market for their stock in case of later need.

Strategy plays a role in financing choice. The strategy that is designed to create competitive advantage and guide the capital investment process also guides financing plans. If your strategy calls for gaining market share from strong competitors, for example, you may expect a period of low profitability that will be more than compensated by higher profitability later. You cannot commit yourself to large cash payments to investors in the low-profitability period. You can avoid this problem by using more equity and using long-term rather than short-term debt. You may also use convertible debt so that creditors will see an opportunity to participate in the success if you win. As another example, secrecy may be an element of your strategy, and you would then need to seek private financing to avoid publishing the intended use of the money. Thus, financing decisions support investment decisions not just by providing money but by supporting the strategy behind those decisions.

Obvious from this discussion of financing considerations is the point that it is impossible to completely divorce investment and financing decisions. Low-cost financing always makes investments more attractive. Stability of cash flows from the investment allows more fixed payments to creditors than would be possible with unstable cash flows. Some assets are more easily monitored than others, and creditors may be more willing to advance large amounts of money for those assets. Finally, some sources of financing, such as industrial revenue bonds and leases, are available only for a particular capital investment. For these reasons, capital investments and long-term financing decisions are both treated in this book. Financing decisions and their relationship to capital investment choice are covered in detail in Chapters 16 through 22.

THE CAPITAL INVESTMENT "CRISIS"

Capital investments are important to the economy for two reasons. In the short run, the business cycle is affected by the amount of demand for new capital investments. Current discussion of a capital investment "crisis," though, focuses on the long-run problem. Troubles are seen with regard to both the amount and type of capital investment that is being carried out.

The *amount* problem is seen by observing in Figure 1.2 that reported capital investment as a percent of gross domestic product is lower in the United States than in leading competitor countries, particularly Japan. There is fear that the United States will fall behind as a competitor in the world markets if it does not make adequate investments. Possible causes of lower investment rate include government deficits, tax policy, cultural attitudes toward saving, and accounting differences that distort the statistics.

The discussion about problems with *types of capital investments* being made was brought into focus with a study led by Michael E. Porter at Harvard University. He concludes that "the U.S. system of allocating investment capital both

| **FIGURE 1.2** **CAPITAL INVESTMENTS BY COUNTRY**

This figure shows gross fixed capital formation as a percent of gross domestic for the United States and a set of competitor countries.[*]

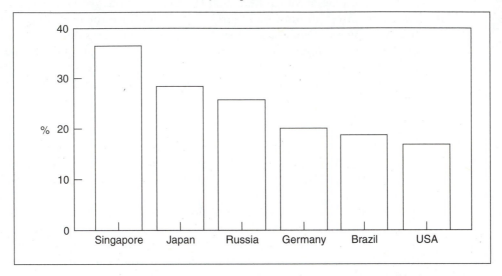

[*]*International Financial Statistics*, Volume 51 (January 1998), International Monetary Fund.

within and across companies is failing."[14] Porter summarizes a research project involving 18 separate studies, so it is not surprising that he finds multitudinous problems. Chief among these is an emphasis on actions that produce short-term results. Reduced investment in promising research and development is an example of how a company might increase short-term income, because R&D is treated as an expense in the accounting records, at the expense of long-term success. He blames this short-term focus on stockholders who rapidly churn diversified portfolios and focus on short-term income because they are unwilling to learn about the company or wait for long-term results. He also blames CEOs who reward managers primarily for short-term financial performance and who assemble diversified corporations with no understanding of what really goes on in the various divisions. He suggests numerous cures by both government and business, including changes in accounting rules, reduced restrictions on disclosure of "insider" information to significant long-term owners, changes in tax rules to encourage long-term investment in stock, and a management goal of maximizing long-term shareholder value rather than current stock price. He does not directly object to the wealth maximization criterion, but rather suggests that much current practice does not result in capital investment decisions that result in long-run wealth maximization.

[14]Michael E. Porter, "Capital Disadvantage: America's Failing Capital Investment System," *Harvard Business Review* (September–October 1992): 65–82.

Porter's view has considerable support, including the 18 studies he summarizes. The general business press has been reporting on perceived national problems in the capital investment arena for years. As early as 1987, a Conference Board survey confirmed the existence of a general concern about excessive focus on short-term thinking that may reduce the international competitiveness of U.S. businesses in the years ahead. A favorite refrain of managers is that investors force them into a short-term focus.

Others have been quick to argue that managers are on thin ice when they blame investors for their myopia. Woolridge, for example, observed that only a small fraction of the value of the typical stock can be accounted for through anticipated dividends over the next few years,[15] and dividends are the only thing the company gives the shareholders in most cases. While an individual stockholder may sell shares to another investor, the only thing the stockholder is selling is a stream of future dividends. As a typical example of Woolridge's point, Dow Chemical's stock sold for $94.37 a share on February 2, 1998, and annual dividends were $3.48 per share. Barring a major change in dividend policy, the dividends over the next five years accounted for less than 25 percent of the value of the stock. Therefore, investors were buying the stock primarily for cash flows expected to be paid out over the long term.

Stock prices do, of course, respond to news about company plans and profits, even though the news is not directly about cash flow. An increase in profits, a new patent, or new factory at Dow Chemical would likely lead to an expectation of increased future cash flows, and therefore to a change in the stock price. The primary job of a security analyst is to interpret the news about a company in terms of its impact on future cash flows and therefore value. The principles of stock value are developed in detail in Chapter 4, but in the meantime we should not misread changes in expected long-term cash flows based on current news as a short-term focus. Executives who believe there is excess reaction to transitory events may be seeing evidence that they have not done an adequate job of educating investors and security analysts about their strategy.

Woolridge is one of a number of researchers who have provided evidence that investors not only respond positively to capital expenditure announcements but also to research and development expenditure announcements, even though the R&D expenditures often push income down in the short term.[16] Announcements of large short-term earnings declines as a result of a change in accounting for retiree benefits did not lead to corresponding drops in stock prices, which would be expected if investors cannot see beyond current income. Porter himself observes that the U.S. capital budgeting system is more effective than that of Germany or Japan when it comes to providing funding for emerging high-tech industries that are expected to be the basis for future economic growth, even though current income is typically low or nonexistent.

[15]J. Randall Woolridge, "Competitive Decline and Corporate Restructuring: Is a Myopic Stock Market to Blame?" *Journal of Applied Corporate Finance* (Spring 1988): 26–36.

[16]Ibid.

The debate over the quality of current capital budgeting policies will go on for years, and we cannot afford to wait. Fortunately, we have more agreement about how to do it right than we have about whether people are doing it right. The capital budgeting "crisis" will be addressed in this book by focusing on capital budgeting methods that increase the likelihood of selecting wealth-maximizing investments in both the short and long run, and on management policies that support those methods.

THE GLOBALIZATION OF INVESTMENTS AND FINANCING |

International business was once defined primarily in terms of imports and exports, but managers increasingly view the entire planet as the bazaar in which to search for the best places to:

1. Acquire raw materials.
2. Acquire production equipment.
3. Acquire labor.
4. Acquire financing.
5. Sell the product.
6. Invest the profits.

It would be surprising if the same country turned out to be the best choice for all six activities. Reasons for choosing different countries for each activity include comparative advantages of a particular country such as lower labor costs or proximity to raw materials, diversification, differences in capital accumulation rates, differences in tax treatment, and differences in regulation. These considerations will be discussed more fully in Chapter 2 because they are central to the strategic decisions of the firm.

Globalization of business leads to some special considerations for capital investment and financing decisions. Cash flow and reported income are both affected by exchange rates between the various currencies. Financing decisions are affected by tax laws, regulatory rules, and supply-demand relationships in each country. Additional risks experienced in global operations include unanticipated exchange rate risk movements, economic instability, and government instability. Because of the broad range of issues encountered in global business, we will return to global considerations in most chapters of this book.

A NOTE TO ENGINEERS |

Many readers of this book are or have been engineering students rather than business students. The topics covered in this book are broader than those typically covered in an engineering economics textbook. This is necessary because your responsibilities are likely to be broader than those of the prior generation. Integrated decision making is a major focus of leading companies. You will be concerned about more than how to generate the desired production or even the cheapest way to achieve the desired production. You must also consider how manufacturing decisions affect company strategy, risk, ability to raise money from investors, and so forth. You will be promoted farther and faster if you are able to deal with all of the implications of your capital budgeting proposals.

SUMMARY

This book is about the investment and financing decisions of the firm. The goal pursued in these decisions is *wealth maximization*. An increase in wealth increases the amount that can be divided among the owners, managers, employees, suppliers, creditors, and society. For a single-period decision, wealth is created if cash inflow exceeds cash outflow by more than we would have earned if we had invested our money elsewhere. The amount of wealth creation is called *economic profit*. The *present value* of an expected future cash flow is the amount that must be invested elsewhere, at the same risk, to generate the same expected cash flow. For a multiperiod decision, wealth creation is the *net present value*, which is the present value of cash inflows minus the present value of the outflows.

Shareholder wealth maximization is generally considered to be the goal of investment and financing. The interests of managers are similar to the interests of shareholders in most cases, and the interests of customers, employees, and society are also served in most cases by shareholder wealth maximization. In general, shareholder wealth maximization is achieved by choosing investments for which the present value of benefits exceeds the present value of outlays. This same selection procedure also works for nonprofit organizations when they are considering investments with monetary benefits.

Economic profit is not possible in perfect competition. Therefore, all wealth creation comes from competitive advantage, typically in the form of product advantage or cost advantage over competitors. Thus, the investment and financing actions of the firm have as their goal the generation of wealth by creating or exploiting competitive advantage.

Capital investments are key components of the plan for achieving wealth. A *capital investment* is an outlay that is expected to result in benefits in the future. *Capital budgeting* is the process of selecting capital investments. Capital investments include physical assets such as factories and airliners, but also include monetary assets such as securities and intangible investments such as advertising campaigns.

The capital investment process consists of seven steps: establishment of goals, development of strategy, search for investment opportunities, evaluation of investment opportunities, selection of investments, implementation and monitoring, and post-audit. Careful management of each stage of this process leads to capital investments that make the maximum attainable contribution to shareholder wealth.

Financing choices begin with the amount of money needed and a decision about the proportions of debt and equity. Then managers look at specific characteristics of financing, such as maturity, priority of claims, and which particular investors will be approached. The company seeks the lowest possible cost of funds. This requires meeting investor needs, consideration of taxes, and dealing with agency costs as effectively as possible. Beyond cost, managers are concerned about availability, flexibility, and consistency with strategy.

For both the individual organization and the corporation as a whole, selection and financing of capital investments are key components of success. Much has been written about actual and potential problems caused by inappropriate methods. The objective of this book is to help people make capital investment and financing decisions that will maximize wealth.

Questions |

1–1. Why is wealth maximization used as the guiding goal for financial decisions?

1–2. How is wealth generation measured for (a) a single-period decision, (b) a multiperiod decision?

1–3. How can the wealth maximization criterion help a nonprofit organization in making capital investment decisions?

1–4. Define the terms *present value* and *net present value*.

1–5. Define the terms *capital investment* and *capital budgeting*.

1–6. List the seven steps in the capital budgeting process.

1–7. What are the main factors considered in deciding if a proposed capital investment is attractive to the company?

1–8. Who in the corporation is involved in the capital budgeting process?

1–9. Who makes the final decision on whether a proposed capital investment is to be made?

1–10. List the main categories of financing choices.

1–11. What is the primary consideration in choosing a financing method?

1–12. There is probably an abandoned retail store in your town. It was pointed out in the chapter that coming up with investment opportunities is often the most difficult, most critical, and most profitable element in creating wealth. You are now going to be given the chance to test your abilities in this area. Develop at least three different capital budgeting ideas (projects or businesses) that you believe might use this abandoned property and have a positive net present value.

1–13. For the above projects, what information or studies would you want to collect or perform before you approach the loan officer or investing public with your idea?

1–14. Recently Monsanto decided to split into two companies, one specializing in biotechnology and the other specializing in chemicals. They issued two different shares of stock to formalize the split. List the benefits of this action in terms of the financing variables discussed in the chapter. What are the disadvantages?

1–15. USX, the company formed in the early 1980s by the purchase of Marathon Oil by United States Steel, split back into two separate companies and issued stock in the steel company and stock in the oil company. The stock prices of the two separate companies reflected more total value than the stock of the combined company. Why?

1–16. The tax rates on capital gains from increases in asset values have recently been reduced. In respect to the parties that benefit from capital investment or wealth creation, explain why investment would decrease or increase as a result of the change in tax rates.

1–17. (Ethical considerations) How would the following actions redistribute the size of the claims of parties discussed in the chapter (shareholders, creditors, employees, managers, suppliers, customers, government, and society)? Is this redistribution ethical in your opinion?

a. GM decides to move production from a plant in Michigan to a plant in Texas.

b. Northwest Airlines negotiates with the unions to take pay and benefit concessions to encourage the creditor to delay possible bankruptcy proceedings.

c. IBM reports a record loss due in part to the high cost of severance packages paid to terminated workers.

d. An astute company president terminates an overfunded pension plan and takes the excess to the company coffers.

e. A group of executives of a particular company line up an investment banker to float a debt issue to take the company private for a 20 percent equity stake for themselves. They suspect that the company is undervalued in the marketplace and they will reap tremendous benefits after this leveraged buyout.

CASE PROBLEM

Night Baseball[17]

After the Chicago Cubs baseball team had sustained several years of operating losses in the early 1960s, William Schlensky, a minority stockholder, brought suit to force the Cubs management to equip Wrigley Field, where the home games were held, with lights so that games could be held at night. Baseball was first played at night in 1935, and Wrigley Field remained the only major league ballpark without lighting for night games.

[17]Contributed by Ellen Harshman, St. Louis University.

Schlensky concluded that the Cubs' losses were directly attributed to inadequate attendance at home games and that if the directors maintained their refusal to equip Wrigley Field with lights, the Cubs would continue to sustain losses and the corporation's financial condition would continue to deteriorate. Schlensky argued that funds for the financing could be obtained readily through financing and that the cost of the installation would be recaptured quickly by increased revenues from growth in attendance.

Philip K. Wrigley was president and owner of approximately 80 percent of the stock of Chicago National League Ball Club, Inc., which operated Wrigley Field, concession sales during home games, and television and radio broadcasts of Cubs' home games, as well as leased the field for football games and other events. He opposed the installation of lights. He expressed his personal opinion that baseball is a daytime sport. Wrigley also noted his concern that the lighting and night traffic would cause deterioration of the residential neighborhood around the ballpark.

Schlensky alleged that the other corporate directors simply acquiesced in the policy set out by Wrigley and that they permitted him to dominate the board of directors even though they knew he was not motivated by the best interests of the corporation, but solely by his personal views.

The court observed that Schlensky did not show that increased revenue from night attendance would be sufficient to cure the corporate deficit; nor did he address possible increases in operating costs associated with night games.

Case Questions

1. What facts and arguments could Schlensky have provided to strengthen his case?
2. Do you see any tensions between a corporation's commitments to its community and to its shareholders?
3. Was Wrigley's insistence on playing baseball according to his personal perception of the game responsive to the interests of the corporation?
4. What, if any, are the responsibilities of the other directors if they disagree with Wrigley?

Selected References

Agrawal, Anup, and Ralph A. Walking. "Executive Careers and Compensation Surrounding Takeover Bids." *The Journal of Finance* 49 (July 1994): 985–1014.

Anstaett, Kurt W., Dennis P. McCrary, and Stephen T. Monahan, Jr. "Practical Debt Policy Considerations for Growth Companies: A Case Study Approach." *Journal of Applied Corporate Finance* 1 (Summer 1988): 71–78.

Baldwin, Carliss Y., and Kim B. Clark. "Capabilities and Capital Investment: New Perspective on Capital Budgeting." *Journal of Applied Corporate Finance* 5 (Summer 1992): 67–82.

Bernstein, Peter L. "Are Financial Markets the Problem or the Solution? A Reply to Michael Porter." *Journal of Applied Corporate Finance* 5 (Summer 1992): 17–22.

Bierman, Harold, Jr., and Seymour Smidt. *The Capital Budgeting Decision,* 8th ed. New York: Macmillan, 1993.

"Capital Budgeting." *Financial Management* 18 (Spring 1989): 10–17.

Chan, Su, John Kensinger, and John Martin. "The Market Rewards Promising R&D, and Punishes the Rest." *Journal of Applied Corporate Finance* 5 (Summer 1992): 59–66.

Comment, Robert, and Gregg A. Jarrell. "Corporate Focus and Stock Returns." *Journal of Financial Economics* 37 (January 1995): 67–87.

Dean Joel. *Capital Budgeting.* New York: Columbia University Press, 1951.

Denis, David J., and Diane K. Denis. "Performance Changes Following Top Management Dismissals." *The Journal of Finance* 50 (September 1995): 1029–1057.

Donaldson, Gordon. "Voluntary Restructuring: The Case of General Mills." *Journal of Applied Corporate Finance* 4 (Fall 1991): 6–19.

Emerick, Dennis, and William White. "The Case for Private Placements: How Sophisticated Investors Add Value to Corporate Debt Issues." *Journal of Applied Corporate Finance* 5 (Fall 1992): 83–91.

Fama, Eugene F. "Agency Problems and the Theory of the Firm." *Journal of Political Economy* (April 1980): 288–307.

Froot, Kenneth, Andre Perold, and Jeremy Stein. "Shareholder Trading Practices and Corporate Investment Horizons." *Journal of Applied Corporate Finance* 5 (Summer 1992): 42–58.

Jensen, Michael C., and William A. Meckling. "Theory of the Firm: Managerial Behavior, Agency Costs, and the Ownership Structure." *Journal of Financial Economics* 3 (October 1976): 305–360.

Kester, W. Carl. "Governance, Contracting, and Investment Horizons: A Look at Japan and Germany." *Journal of Applied Corporate Finance* 5 (Summer 1992): 83–98.

Lessard, Donald R. "Global Competition and Corporate Finance in the 1990s." *Journal of Applied Corporate Finance* 3 (Winter 1991): 59–72.

Levine, David I. "Do Corporate Executives Have Rational Expectations?" *Journal of Business* 66 (April 1993): 271–293.

Lippert, Robert L., and William T. Moore. "Monitoring Versus Bonding: Shareholder Rights and Management Compensation." *Financial Management* 54 (Autumn 1995): 54–62.

May, Don O. "Do Managerial Motives Influence Firm Risk Reduction Strategies?" *The Journal of Finance* 50 (September 1996): 1291–1308.

Mehran, Hamid. "Executive Compensation Structure, Ownership, and Firm Performance." *Journal of Financial Economics* 38 (June 1995): 163–184.

Narayanan, M. P. "Form of Compensation and Managerial Decision Horizon." *Journal of Financial and Quantitative Analysis* 31 (December 1996): 467–491.

Park, Sangsoo, and Moon H. Song. "Employee Stock Ownership Plans, Firm Performance, and Monitoring by Outside Blockholders." *Financial Management* 24 (Winter 1995): 52–65.

Porter, Michael E. "Capital Choices: Changing the Way America Invests in Industry." *Journal of Applied Corporate Finance* 5 (Summer 1992): 4–16.

———."Capital Disadvantage: America's Failing Capital Investment System." *Harvard Business Review* (September–October 1992): 65–82.

Prueitt, George C., and Chan S. Park. "Monitoring Project Performance with Post-Audit Information: Cash Flow Control Charts." *The Engineering Economist* 36 (Summer 1991): 307–335.

Shapiro, Alan C. "International Capital Budgeting." *Midland Corporate Finance Journal* 1 (Spring 1983): 26–45.

Shleifer, Andrei, and Robert W. Vishny. "A Survey of Corporate Governance." *The Journal of Finance* 52 (June 1997): 737–783.

Smith, Michael P. "Shareholder Activism by Institutional Investors: Evidence from CalPERS." *The Journal of Finance* 51 (March 1996): 227–252.

Sridharan, Uma V. "CEO Influence and Executive Compensation." *The Financial Review* 31 (February 1996): 51–66.

Stewart, G. Bennett III. "Market Myths." *Journal of Applied Corporate Finance* 2, no. 3 (Fall 1989): 6–23.

Sullivan, G. William. "A New Paradigm for Engineering Economy." *The Engineering Economist* 36 (Spring 1991): 187–200.

Szewczyk, Samual H., George P. Tsetsekos, and Zaher Zantout. "The Valuation of Corporate R&D Expenditures: Evidence from Investment Opportunities and Free Cash Flow." *Financial Management* 25 (Spring 1996): 105–110.

Woolridge, J. Randall. "Competitive Decline and Corporate Restructuring: Is a Myopic Stock Market to Blame?" *Journal of Applied Corporate Finance* (Spring 1988): 26–36.

Zantout, Zaher, and George P. Tsetsekos. "The Wealth Effects of Announcements of R&D Expenditure Increases." *The Journal of Financial Research* 17 (Summer 1994): 205–216.

CHAPTER 2 |

MARKET IMPERFECTIONS AND VALUE: STRATEGY MATTERS

After completing this chapter you should be able to:

1. List the conditions necessary for a perfectly competitive product market and resource market.
2. Explain how competitive advantage results from the successful identification of existing and potential opportunities, the formulation of a coherent strategy, and the implementation of plans that exploit these opportunities.
3. Identify and discuss the different industry characteristics that allow competitive advantage.
4. Discuss the different product and cost characteristics that allow a specific company to enjoy a competitive advantage.
5. Describe what is meant by *comparative advantage*.
6. Develop a strategy.
7. Describe the wealth-enhancing process when capital budgeting supports the long-term strategy, and be aware of the pitfalls that beset those who forget this relationship.
8. Explain the supporting role that financing plays in implementing strategy and how your financing errors can be used by your competitors to limit your ability to profit from competitive opportunities.

When James Stover took charge of Eaton Corporation in 1986, the three major businesses of the company were defense electronics, controls, and drivetrains (primarily heavy truck). Within a year, Stover made a major strategic decision. He began to change the focus of the company by selling off the defense electronics business and concentrating on the profitability of the two remaining lines. Some of the considerations leading to this change of direction were (1) relative profitability in the three lines, (2) prospects for future growth and profitability, (3) Eaton's position in each market, and (4) the internal strengths and weaknesses of Eaton. These strategic decisions were affected by past financial decisions—both capital investment and financial structure choices—and will guide future financial decisions. It is important, therefore, to understand the interactions between strategy and financial decisions.

PERFECT MARKETS |

Perfection is not always good. In fact, a perfectly competitive market is a bleak prospect to a business manager. Few, if any, markets are perfectly competitive, but it is important to understand perfectly competitive markets because wealth can be created only if perfection can be eliminated. You will recall from Chapter 1 that economists define a perfectly competitive market for a product or service as having the following characteristics:

- There are no restrictions keeping producers from entering or exiting the market.
- No one producer or buyer is large enough to affect price through any action.
- All producers manufacture identical products.
- All producers have identical costs.
- Everyone is completely informed about what everyone else is doing.

In perfect competition, each of your competitors produces identical products at identical costs, to be sold to a public that knows what everyone else is charging. No producer can charge more than any other producer of that product and hope to sell anything. If the prices being paid in the marketplace were providing an economic profit, new producers would be attracted to the industry, and they would drive prices down as they attempted to sell their output. The long-term result is that in perfect competition all producers must charge identical prices and produce at the lowest possible cost just to survive.

If all producers have identical costs, they must all be paying the same prices for inputs. One of those inputs is the money needed to invest in the business. All producers will have the same cost of funds if financial markets are perfect. A perfect financial market satisfies the following conditions:

- There are no taxes, transaction costs, or other restrictions keeping buyers of funds and sellers of funds from entering or exiting the market.
- No one buyer of funds or seller of funds is large enough to affect price (interest rate) through any action.
- Identical information is costlessly available to everyone, resulting in identical beliefs.
- All participants are rational wealth maximizers.

With all this perfection, the business can just barely satisfy investors and earn an economic profit of zero. Few people enter business with the goal of just barely surviving. Fortunately, businesses can go beyond survival to create wealth if they can avoid significant aspects of market perfection. The rest of this chapter is about competitive advantage, the art and science of getting out of perfect competition, and about the strategic basis for capital budgeting and long-term financing decisions.

COMPETITIVE ADVANTAGE

Competitive advantage is a departure from perfect competition that makes it possible to earn an economic profit. The key considerations are industry characteristics, product differentiations, and cost advantages.[1]

INDUSTRY CHARACTERISTICS NECESSARY FOR COMPETITIVE ADVANTAGE

A wheat farmer is severely handicapped in the search for competitive advantage. Farmer Smith's wheat is completely interchangeable with that of Farmer Jones in the marketplace, so Smith cannot possibly charge a higher price. Furthermore, Smith and Jones have the same production technology available, so Smith cannot achieve a lower cost. If some fortuitous event should temporarily drive the price of wheat above the cost of production, new entrants would soon drive the price back down to cost, or the prices of inputs would be bid up to eliminate economic profit.

Fortunately, most of us are not wheat farmers, and most of us will never sell in perfectly competitive markets. A market will be perfectly competitive only if *all* of the conditions for perfect competition exist. Each of the following market characteristics decreases the likelihood of perfect competition, and therefore increases the potential for competitive advantage.

- *Barriers to entry exist.* Barriers to entry include regulatory restrictions on new entrants as well as patents, copyrights, and economies of scale that discourage new entrants. Television stations have been protected from competition by limits on the number of licenses in a particular area. The value of this barrier to entry is clearly illustrated by the multimillion-dollar prices bid for TV stations in large metropolitan markets. The "big three" automakers of the United States enjoyed limited competition for decades because economies of scale were sufficient to fend off new entrants until the Japanese breached the wall.

---

[1]For a more extensive coverage of competitive advantage see Michael Porter's groundbreaking works: *Competitive Advantage: Creating and Sustaining Superior Performance* (New York: The Free Press, 1985) and *Competitive Strategy: Techniques of Analyzing Industries and Competitors* (New York: The Free Press, 1980).

- *Customers are not price sensitive.* We observe, for example, that people are much less sensitive to interest rates on credit cards than to interest rates on home mortgages. It is not surprising, then, that credit card issuers are often more profitable than mortgage lenders. One reason for lack of price sensitivity is that the *purchase is small relative to the buyer's wealth.* The monthly interest charge on the typical credit card balance is only a fraction of that on a typical home mortgage, even though the interest rate on the credit card is substantially higher. *Difficulty of comparing prices* is another factor that can make customers less sensitive to price. We can easily shop for gasoline because stations post their prices out front, but shopping for medical services is difficult. Doctors do not advertise their prices, and the patient receives a complex set of services that cannot be defined in advance.

- *Customers care about product features.* A well-trod path away from perfect competition leads to a product that is different from everyone else's, but this is possible only if the customers of that industry care enough about product features to pay the costs of providing those features. TWA announced that they were increasing leg room in coach class by taking out seats. Although customers liked the extra leg room, they were not willing to pay much for it. TWA eventually dropped the experiment.

- *Customers are not fully informed.* This may seem contradictory to a manager who is lamenting consumers' unwillingness to recognize the superiority of her company's product. But do we want our customers to know about the new producer, who is offering more features at a lower price? Reputation is one way for a customer who is not fully informed to decide on product quality without investing in extensive research. Reputation is therefore a valuable asset for many existing companies and a barrier to entry for potential new players.

- *Demand is stable.* Stability of demand creates the opportunity for economies of scale and makes life difficult for new entrants, who must wrench customers from existing players. One of the problems with the mortgage market is that the combination of highly cyclical demand and low barriers to entry assures us there will be a flock of new competitors every time demand for loans picks up.

- *Competitors are limited.* The most desirable type of competitor is none, but monopolies are rare. Our second choice is a few competitors because vigorous price competition is less likely when there are only a few players. We also prefer competitors who are weaker than we are.

Wealth-seeking managers can either find markets that have the potential for creating competitive advantage or change the markets in which they operate. The franchise idea, for example, converted hamburger sales from an industry made up of thousands of struggling individual restaurants to one in which a few large chains, dominated by McDonald's, enjoy competitive advantage and economic profit.

PRODUCT DIFFERENTIATION

If conditions in the industry give us the potential for creating a competitive advantage, then product differentiation is a common method of gaining that competitive advantage. Many successful capital investments are aimed at the creation of product differentiation. Product advantages come in several varieties:

- *Features.* If customers in the industry care about product features, and are willing to pay for the costs of such features, then competitive advantage can be gained by selecting a set of features that will differentiate your product from those of the competition. Direct price comparison becomes impossible, and the opportunity for economic profit is created. Both you and your competitor may be able to earn an economic profit once your products are differentiated, because neither of you is forced to compete on a pure price basis. Differentiation of products through features is the norm, as witnessed by the scarcity of advertisements saying, "Our product is just like theirs." A critically important feature of Microsoft Windows' operating system is that it gives the user the greatest ability to exchange files with other users and use software provided by a host of vendors. Few of us would choose an alternate operating system, even one with superior features, if it did not offer this broad compatibility advantage.

- *Quality.* Quality advantage is surprisingly hard to copy. The source of quality often lies in the set of shared values and beliefs that comprise the company's culture, and culture is not changed easily. Even if a competitor finally matches your quality, its reputation is likely to lag well behind that reality. When Toyota gained a quality advantage over General Motors, the time required to close that gap and recover lost reputation was measured in decades, not months or years. It is, of course, critical that the customer be willing to pay for the cost of quality.

- *Image.* Many producers have succeeded in creating valuable images for their products. We see, for example, a beer advertisement that promises you can be a "Mountain Man" if you just drink that brand. The taste of the beer is never mentioned. Likewise, makers of athletic shoes have converted them from utilitarian products to fashion statements. Like a reputation for quality, image can survive and provide competitive advantage decade after decade.

- *Service.* In its heyday, IBM knew that the top executives of its customer corporations did not want megahertz and megabytes; they wanted paychecks delivered reliably on Friday afternoon. A high level of service gave IBM a competitive advantage by assuring a high-quality result. Quick response in the case of failure was one part of service for IBM, but not the primary point. Service was designed to provide the support to prevent failures in the first place. Service included close attention to meeting the outcome expectations of the customer both before and after the sale. The reputation for service quality lasted for decades.

- *Distribution.* People cannot buy what they cannot find. Anheuser-Busch has succeeded for years in earning an economic profit, increasing market share, and increasing sales in a declining beer market. A cornerstone of their strategy was an early capital investment to build the dominant beer distribution system in the country. A person may spend hours searching for a favorite vintage cognac, but beer is a convenience good. A strong distribution system means that Anheuser-Busch's advertising cost per customer who can actually find the product at the local convenience store is lower than the costs for competitors.

COST ADVANTAGE

While product quality basks in the limelight, cost advantage is often the unsung hero of the profitability quest. Honda did not invent the idea of good alignment between the doors and fenders on an automobile. Rolls-Royce and Lamborghini have been lining up body parts almost since the invention of sheet metal, but not at a price the average driver could afford. Honda and its contemporaries achieved quality results at costs that made their products widely affordable. Southwest Airlines has grown and earned steady profits while the airline industry has been floundering in a flood of red ink. Southwest ranks near the top in quality measures such as on-time performance and baggage handling, while staying near the bottom in cost. Several techniques are available to create a cost advantage:

- *Economies of scale*. A local automobile dealer cannot compete against General Motors or Honda by building automobiles in the back room. Lower costs per unit are achieved by spreading fixed costs over a large number of units. Economies of scale can give cost advantages that keep out new entrants for half a century, as was the case in the U.S. automobile industry. Because long-lived advantages are especially good, economies of scale are especially beneficial.
- *Technology*. Several banks have invested large amounts in modern technology in order to develop processing centers with low costs per credit card transaction. Those who have made the technology investment have a cost advantage when they set out to attract new business. Although the number of credit card issuers seems to be continually growing, processing is being concentrated into the hands of a few highly efficient operations. Other issuers simply contract with these efficient and profitable operators. A limitation of technology as a cost advantage is that it may be copied, but technology developed in-house and patented or kept secret may protect your cost advantage from competitors.
- *Corporate culture*. A critical basis for cost advantage is a commitment to efficient operations. The shared values and beliefs that make up the culture of the organization must include an understanding that efficiency is important and will be rewarded. Part of the planning process at 3M, for example, requires that each manager develop a plan to get a 3 percent productivity gain each year. Cooper Tire has a stated goal of reducing the cost per tire by 5 percent a year. Where does Southwest Airlines achieve lower costs than its competitors? Everywhere. As an example, the short-flight focus and lack of seat

assignments minimize food and passenger loading times, allowing the airplanes and their pilots to spend less time at gates and more time in the air, earning revenue.

■ *Control supply of inputs.* Companies develop delayed compensation plans aimed at discouraging voluntary movement of employees to competitors. Thus, they gain a cost advantage by controlling the supply of skilled and talented people all the way from assembly-line workers to senior executives. Other companies buy suppliers to create monopoly control over raw materials. These actions can create cost advantages.

SURVIVAL OF COMPETITIVE ADVANTAGE

Few competitive advantages last forever, but remember the comforting words of John Maynard Keynes: "In the long run, we are all dead." We do not worry about forever, but when we invest resources to gain competitive advantage, the life of that particular competitive advantage is a critical concern. Some product features, such as an ice maker for a refrigerator, are easily copied, so that the competitive advantage may last for no more than a few weeks or a few months. Other advantages, such as a quality reputation or economy of scale, may last for decades. Microsoft's advantage as the industry standard operating system is in the second decade of its life, with no sign of weakening. General Motors benefited for decades from the economies of scale that limited the automobile industry to a few competitors until Japanese companies entered the market. The Japanese automobile manufacturers, in turn, developed a reputation for superior quality that lasted for more than a decade.

GLOBALIZATION AND COMPETITIVE ADVANTAGE

Caterpillar, Inc., provides an excellent example of globalization of business as a competitive advantage. Caterpillar and International Harvester were companies in traditional Rust Belt manufacturing industries. It was widely predicted that companies such as these would not be able to compete in the world markets or even in the United States because their costs would be above those of competitors in other countries, such as Japan's leading heavy-equipment manufacturer, Kumatzu. International Harvester proved the gloomy forecasts right and went out of business. Caterpillar, on the other hand, developed a world view, selling, manufacturing, and acquiring inputs around the globe. While International Harvester disappeared, Caterpillar thrived.

Comparative Advantage

The theory of *comparative advantage* is one explanation of the success of Caterpillar. The theory of comparative advantage is an extension of the principle that specialization increases total productivity; wealth is increased when each country does what it does best. Take, for example, a fully developed and a less developed country, each of which produces only for its own consumption. Use of labor in producing shirts and computers in the two countries is as follows.

	NUMBER PRODUCED		LABOR PER UNIT		Total Labor Used
	Computers	Shirts	Computers	Shirts	
Fully developed country	1,000	50,000	50	1	100,000
Less developed country	500	10,000	200	2	120,000

The fully developed country requires less labor for either shirts or computers, but the advantage is greater for computers. Suppose the less developed country offers to exchange 30,000 shirts for 500 computers. To maintain identical consumption in each country, production is changed as follows:

	Computers	Shirts	Total Labor
Fully developed country	1,500	20,000	95,000
Less developed country	0	40,000	80,000

Each country is able to maintain its consumption of computers and shirts while using less total labor. Labor is freed up for other production, and the wealth of both countries increases. As a shirt manufacturer from the developed country, you could establish a factory in the less developed country to increase the wealth of your shareholders while also increasing the wealth of the citizens of both countries.

Natural resources often contribute to comparative advantage. Israel's weather gives it an advantage over Finland in the production of oranges, and a country with extensive iron-ore deposits has an advantage in the manufacture of products using large amounts of iron. *People* are a particularly important natural resource. People vary in health, education, and cultural attitudes toward cooperation and work. A country that has invested in education has a comparative advantage in high-tech industries, for example.

Economies of scale also come into play. Denmark does not have a domestic automobile industry, for example. Economies of scale make it cheaper to import cars than to build them for a population of five million people. A larger automobile industry, based on export, could be developed, but a highly educated population does not provide a comparative advantage in industrial production of that type.

Technological advantage is also important. A country that invests heavily in one area of technology can often develop an advantage in that area. Many countries find it cheaper to pay the United States to put their communications satellites in orbit than to develop their own rockets. Denmark is a leading producer of high-quality insulin and uses the revenues to import automobiles. The information superhighway is an attempt to gain a technological advantage.

Because of the factors leading to comparative advantage, there will be many situations in which market forces do not quickly eliminate the benefits of comparative advantage. Companies can create substantial wealth by taking advantage of comparative advantage. The truly global companies, such as Caterpillar and Citicorp, go wherever they find comparative advantage and also leverage their investments by applying their knowledge around the globe. This globalization is a cornerstone of their competitive strategy.

COMPETITIVE ADVANTAGE AND WEALTH CREATION

In perfect competition, there are generally no positive net present value projects, and therefore no opportunities to create wealth. The only positive net present value project in perfect competition would be an investment that brought an inefficient producer with negative economic profit back down to the same cost as the rest of the industry and back to an economic profit of $0. Competitive advantage allows us to charge more than cost, including the rate of return investors could earn elsewhere as one of the costs, and therefore earn an economic profit. Since net present value is economic profit for multiyear investments, competitive advantage creates the opportunity for positive net present value projects. Thus, competitive advantage is the only route, not just a route, to wealth creation.

Whose wealth is affected by competitive advantage, and when? Competitive advantage creates wealth for the shareholders when investors first learn about that competitive advantage. They adjust their estimates of future cash flows and adjust the price they are willing to pay for the stock. Investors who buy after that price adjustment will earn only the opportunity cost of their funds, even though the company continues to earn the expected economic profit, because the price they paid included the present value of that anticipated future economic profit. The investors who buy the stock after competitive advantage is known will earn superior returns only if the competitive advantage turns out to be more valuable or longer lasting than originally anticipated. For example, when do you think the stock price will move for the pharmaceutical company that discovers the cure for AIDS? The reverse of this is observed in the market also. Monsanto was in the unfortunate position of having two highly profitable products go off-patent, Treflan and NutraSweet. With no certain replacement in sight, the market had already discounted the reduced cash flows into the stock price, even before the patents expired.

Do gamblers create wealth? Numerous managers have resorted to gambles when they were in trouble, and a few have even won. Some savings and loans were in such deep trouble that they could not be rescued through prudent lending, and they gambled by making highly speculative loans. The average returns on these speculative loans turned out to be negative, but a few of these gamblers won and saved their institutions, while the taxpayers got the bill for the losers. To avoid these problems, it is important to distinguish between gambles and competitive advantage. The $20 million winner of the Illinois lottery may view that as a lot of wealth creation for a dollar investment. But the payoff for a gamble is a random redistribution of wealth, not a creation of wealth. A crucial issue in executive compensation is designing the package to encourage creation of wealth and not to encourage or reward gambling.

Does no risky decision create wealth? Many excellent business decisions involve risk. When Eli Lilly spends money on drug research, the probability of failure is always high. These research investments make sense only if there is more than enough profit to compensate investors for taking risk when the successes and failures are averaged together. In the case of the lottery, the amount returned is *less than* the amount invested when the winning and losing tickets are averaged together.

Many companies and professional organizations have attempted to formalize the exclusion of these actions on the part of management and their members by drawing up codes of ethics. The success of any code of ethics rests with the individual because no code can detail all courses of actions, and the definition of an ethical risk-return trade-off is particularly difficult.

STRATEGIC PLANNING |

The competitive advantage concepts discussed in the previous section are applied through strategic planning, because the primary focus of strategy is the positioning of the company so that competitive pressures will not eliminate economic profit and positive net present values. Strategy coordinates the diverse actions of myriad decision makers throughout the organization in achieving the organization's goals. The major financial decisions of the organization—both investment and financing decisions—must be coordinated with and in support of the organization's strategy.

Figure 2.1 provides an overview of the strategic management process. We begin by assembling the information necessary for a strategy decision. This includes the first three steps: establishment of goals, identification of threats and opportunities in the environment, and analysis of the organization's strengths and weaknesses. Then a strategy is developed. The *strategy* defines the business that the company is in and how it intends to position itself within that business. Leaders sometimes refer to the strategy as their *vision* for the organization. The strategy must then be translated into policies for functional areas such as marketing, production, personnel, and finance. These functional area policies are sometimes called operating strategies. Those policies are implemented through plans, budgets, and so on. Performance is monitored and the whole process is continually evaluated so that the organization learns from its experiences and responds quickly to change.

We begin with an overview of the steps leading to a strategy decision. Next, conceptual models for strategic decision making are developed. Then, operating policies are discussed. The final topic for the chapter is long-term financing strategy in imperfect markets.

STEPS TO A STRATEGY

The development of a strategy requires: (1) a statement of goals, (2) an analysis of the environment, and (3) an analysis of the organization itself.

Goals

Most U.S. businesses cite shareholder wealth maximization as a major goal, but building business strategy on the goal of shareholder wealth maximization is like building a military strategy on the goal of stamping out evil. Progress is more likely

| **F I G U R E   2 . 1**   **THE STRATEGIC MANAGEMENT PROCESS**

This figure summarizes the strategic management process, from development of goals through implementation and monitoring.

when goals are not only measurable but also achievable and based on variables that managers can control. Thus, top executives often translate their wealth maximization objective into specific goals that can be pursued by lower-level managers. Mead Corporation, for example, translated an overall goal of financial performance among the top quarter of its industry into four specific, measurable goals:

1. 12 percent return on net assets.
2. Maintenance of a debt/equity ratio of .50.
3. 17 percent return on equity.
4. 10 percent growth rate.[2]

A fair question is "Do they know that pursuing these goals will maximize shareholder wealth?" The answer is almost surely "No!" Commenting on the overhaul of Cummings Diesel, CEO Henry Schacht observed that "We'll never know whether we could have made higher net present value returns" by simply distributing cash to investors instead of using it to rebuild.[3] But they act on the hope that there is a strong relationship between their chosen goals and actual wealth creation.

Nonprofit organizations also need clear goals. An army general must know whether the objective is to distract the enemy, conquer ground, or destroy opposing forces in order to develop an effective strategy. In the Vietnam War, for example, the generals were hampered in strategy development by the lack of a clear statement of national goals. Nonprofit organizations often use the term *mission* to describe their overall goal. The strategic decisions of a hospital manager will vary, for example, depending on whether the primary mission of the hospital is to make a profit, aid the sick, or spread the sponsor's religion.

Environmental Assessment

Environmental assessment focuses on the threats and opportunities facing the organization from outside. Environmental assessment usually begins with a broad view. The state of the overall economy and the state of international relations are considered along with demographic and cultural changes. Important trends in recent years include changing trade barriers, increasing life expectancy, increasing participation of women in the workforce, decreasing birthrates, a shift of population from the Northeast to the Sun Belt, and increasing interest in diet and in health.

The attitudes of government are also of considerable importance. An increased belief in competition instead of regulation characterized government attitudes toward business in the 1970s and the 1980s, while there is some indication of a reversal of this trend in the 1990s. The aerospace, medical research, and defense industries depend on government spending and are always subject to the direction of the fickle breezes blowing across the Potomac. An expectation of decreased demand for defense electronics was an important part of the environmental assessment at Eaton, as was the possibility of an investment tax credit that would encourage purchase of more heavy trucks. Companies maintain offices in Washington not just to influence legislation but also to help managers predict changes in government policy. Developments in state legislatures are often equally important.

[2]Warren L. Batts, "Planning and the Corporation: What the Future Holds," a speech at *Business Week* Strategic Planning Conference, New York, October 4, 1978.

[3]"A Long-Term Bet Pays off at Last," *Fortune* (August 23, 1993): 79+.

The international political and business climate deserves special attention. Opportunities and threats often go hand-in-hand. The end of the cold war has opened up both new markets and new sources of competition. Trade barriers have been declining in recent years, again increasing both competition and opportunities. Rising incomes in many Asian countries mean new markets along with new competition. The North American Free Trade Agreement (NAFTA), for example, puts increased cost pressures on some manufacturers while giving others a new way to compete in world markets. At the same time, NAFTA opens up new markets for goods produced in the United States.

Narrowing the focus a bit, you must look at the industry in which you operate. The industry analysis usually begins with an examination of how the industry will be affected by broader trends in the economy, demographics and so on that were previously identified. An aging population, a decreasing birthrate, and the rise of two-income families have combined with inflation and unstable interest rates to restructure the housing market. Condominiums, requiring less maintenance and often providing less space, increased their market share, while the lower end of the single-family house market was particularly hard hit by unaffordable interest rates. Companies that took advantage of these trends increased their profits, and those who continued with business as usual lost out.

After looking at factors affecting the industry from outside, managers turn their attention to things happening within the industry. Changes in customer preferences are important, as are changes in technology. The airline industry, trucking industry, telephone industry, and financial services industry have all undergone radical restructuring as a result of deregulation. Some companies anticipated the changes and prospered; others are no longer a part of the American business scene. In the financial services industry, for example, savings and loans failed by the score when they failed to plan for unstable interest rates and were unable to compete in new lending markets, while more nimble mortgage bankers and credit card specialists prospered. The entire airline industry suffered from excess capacity following deregulation. Just as the hyenas eliminate the weakened wildebeests, competition eliminated airlines that did not anticipate this new environment with improved efficiency and a clear market strategy. At the same time, upstart airlines thrived in well-selected niche markets.

A major focus of industry analysis is on the characteristics that create the potential for competitive advantage. Are opportunities for product differentiation increasing or decreasing? Are barriers to entry increasing or decreasing? How are the competitors changing? As an example of the extent of this analysis, one of the authors' acquaintances works full-time to follow and predict the actions of *one* competitor.

Internal Strengths and Weaknesses

Following environment assessment, some introspection is in order. Managers must identify the organization's strengths and weaknesses, then develop strategy accordingly. The focus of internal analysis is also on sources of competitive advantage, either product advantage or cost advantage. Do our factories make us a high- or low-quality producer, a high- or low-cost producer? A company with products at the leading edge of its industry and with a reputation for quality, service, and reliability will develop one strategy. A company that was forced to withdraw a product from the marketplace because of bad publicity over quality will develop quite another strategy.

The most difficult part of the internal analysis process may be an analysis of the top managers and the culture they have created. Top executives who spent their careers in regulated industries are often unprepared to respond quickly and aggressively in a deregulated environment. The bureaucracy that served them so well for decades simply does not work when fast action and risk-taking are required. Culture conflicts between drivetrain people and defense electronics people contributed to the lack of success in Eaton's defense business.

The combination of environmental and internal analysis is often referred to as SWOT analysis, for Strengths, Weaknesses, Opportunities, and Threats. Once the SWOT analysis is completed, managers can begin the development of a strategy. Managers often apply various conceptual models for this purpose.

CONCEPTUAL MODELS FOR STRATEGIC DECISION MAKING

Conceptual models are designed to capture the meaning of large amounts of information quickly. Decision makers are often crippled by the existence of too much information. Critical information may be overlooked or the organization may be paralyzed because nobody can decide which information to focus on. Consulting organizations have attempted to overcome these problems by developing conceptual models such as the strength/attractiveness grids and product life cycle models that are discussed in the following sections.

Strength/Attractiveness Grids

As suggested by the discussion of competitive advantage, we cannot look at the company or the marketplace in isolation. Strength/attractiveness grids provide a way to look at each of a company's products or businesses in terms of both the attractiveness of the industry and the position of the company in the industry. A number of these models exist, including the Boston Consulting Group Model and the Hofer Product/Market Evolution Matrix. They all consist of a grid such as that in Figure 2.2, in which the desirability of the industry is placed on one axis and the competitive strength of the company is placed on the other axis. The fundamental point of all such grids is that we want to be in a strong position in a desirable industry.

The drivetrain business of Eaton would be placed in the upper part of the grid, for example. The industry is attractive to Eaton because barriers to entry are high, quality is more important than price, and so on, so there are opportunities for competitive advantage and economic profit. There is no dominant player other than Eaton. The drivetrain business would be placed on the left side of the grid because Eaton is the dominant player. The upper-left position of the

| F I G U R E 2 . 2 STRENGTH/ATTRACTIVENESS GRID

This grid is used to view the strength of the company in the context of the attractiveness of the industry.

Competitive Position

	High	Low
High	Continue to build and maintain competitive strength	Improve competitive position or get out
Low	Milk for cash	Get out or milk for cash

Industry Attractiveness

drivetrain business caused Eaton to focus on that area. In contrast, the defense business was in the lower part of the quadrant because of falling demand, and Eaton was on the right side with no advantages in that market. It is not surprising that Eaton pulled out. Controls, on the other hand, were seen as being in the upper part of the grid, and Eaton set out to move its position well to the left by gaining a strong position.

The models differ with regard to the specifics of how you measure industry desirability. Some models focus on narrow definitions of desirability, such as growth rate, and narrow definitions of strength, such as market share, but we know from the study of competitive advantage that these limited measures are insufficient. Ultimately, we must consider all the factors that make a market attractive and create the foundation for competitive advantage. Weighing all of those factors and placing a product or business in the matrix necessarily requires a major dose of seasoned judgment.

Eaton, for example, concluded that the demand for the type of military electronics it produced would not be growing, and there would be few new government contracts available. Price competition would probably be severe because all producers would be stuck with excess capacity. This made the military electronics industry relatively unattractive. Furthermore, Eaton's competitive position was weak. The culture that worked well for the drivetrain business did not work well for the aerospace business. Eaton's major defense product—a radar jamming device—was not working well and new product development had been neglected. The military electronics business was clearly in the lower right quadrant of the grid, so the possibility of economic profit was remote. Eaton decided to get out.

The heavy truck drivetrain industry was mature and had only modest growth. Nevertheless, several factors made the industry attractive to Eaton. There were only a few main players and there were substantial barriers to entry. Product quality was more important to the customers than price because the cost of time lost due to a breakdown was high. Furthermore, customers determined product quality by reputation, to a large extent. Eaton had an excellent reputation for quality. In addition, Eaton had made heavy investments in efficiency for its drive-train business, so it had a cost advantage as well. The drivetrain business was in the upper left quadrant, and Eaton set out to capitalize on that position.

The controls business had more potential for growth, and Eaton was an industry leader in many aspects of controls. Their strategy was to invest in expansion in areas related to their existing controls markets, so that they would have the advantage of dominance. Prior to selling its military electronics business, Eaton generated 73 percent of its sales in markets in which it had the largest or second-largest share. Chief Executive Stover pursued a policy of acquisitions and sell-offs aimed at further increasing the proportion of sales that were in markets in which Eaton was dominant.

Product Life Cycle Model

Most products pass through a life cycle, and optimal strategy varies by phase of the life cycle. Figure 2.3 illustrates a typical product life cycle curve. In the development phase, the product does not yet have wide market recognition. Using video recorders (VCRs) as an example, the units first came on the market priced in the $2,000 range, with few movies available to rent. Several different formats were being offered by competing companies, which further limited the supply of rental movies. Sales were, needless to say, limited. As less costly production methods were developed and rental movies became available, VCRs entered the growth stage of their life cycle. While sales grew rapidly, the VHS format won

| **FIGURE 2.3** **PRODUCT LIFE CYCLE CURVE**

This figure illustrates the phases during the life of a typical product, from introduction and growth through maturity and decline.

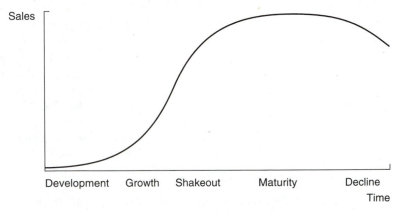

dominance, driving other players from the marketplace. Within a few years, 60 percent of the U.S. households owned VCRs and the product began the transition into the maturity phase. At this writing, it appears that the video recorder market may remain in the maturity phase for some years, as have the automobile and refrigerator markets. However, new technology such as compact video disks may make existing units obsolete, leading to a new round of growth. Future developments in communications technology may start the decline phase by making driving to the video rental shop an obsolete method of gaining access to a movie.

Identification of the position in the life cycle is helpful in identifying industry attractiveness and developing a strategy. In the development phase, for example, companies try to position themselves so that they can become the industry leader when the growth phase begins and to differentiate themselves so that they will not have to rely on pure price competition to develop market share. Their focus is not on current income but on positioning themselves for future profits. This is why several companies were trying to gain dominance for their format during the development stage of the VCR life cycle.

During the growth phase the inability of the industry to keep up with ballooning demand sometimes makes profits easy to come by. Some business advisors have become so enamored as to suggest that the major focus of business strategy should be to stay positioned in the high-growth part of the life cycle. Growth of sales does not, however, produce profitability unless there are restrictions on the rate of supply growth. Thousands of neighborhood video rental stores failed during the rapid growth part of the cycle because there were no barriers to entry and larger entrants such as Blockbuster Video were preferred by customers. If growth temporarily removes competitive pressures on price, it creates a window of opportunity to establish the competitive advantage that will give you the lead position and continued profitability in the maturity phase. Even a company with no competitive advantage may profit temporarily in this phase before pulling out at maturity. If there are no barriers to entry, supply will catch up with demand immediately, and competitive advantage must be gained immediately if you are to continue to create wealth.

If supply cannot keep up with demand during rapid growth, that situation will change as we approach maturity and growth slows. Those who were complacent because of the large profits during the growth stage will fail in this transition period. Successful companies will continue to follow the strategies developed earlier and will not be buffeted or panicked by temporarily low profitability caused by the death throes of competitors. They will often consolidate their power by acquiring failed competitors.

In the maturity or saturation phase, growth stops or is limited by the overall growth of the population and economy. It is not necessarily a bad place to be. Eaton's 30 percent return in the drivetrain business is one example of the many companies that have carved out very profitable businesses in the maturity phase of the life cycle. The secret of profitability at this stage is to have planned earlier for competitive advantage. The small neighborhood video rental stores failed to do this, while Eaton's investments in drivetrain design and efficient drivetrain production give Eaton the competitive advantage.

Proper strategy can maximize profitability in the decline phase, as witnessed by the success of Anheuser-Busch in a declining beer market. Efficiency and cost controls are often critical at this stage. The decline stage may last for decades and provide satisfactory profitability to the industry leaders during that stage. Finally, the most profitable abandonment time must be chosen. Finding the right abandonment time is not always easy. Ford decided to abandon the Mustang, for example, but an unexpected surge in demand kept the car alive for another generation.

The conclusion from studies of numerous companies over the product life cycle is that there is no one right place to be. With competitive advantage, you can create wealth at any stage. Without competitive advantage, you can lose money at any stage. Nevertheless, it is important to recognize the stage you are in so that you can plan accordingly.

IMPLEMENTING THE STRATEGY ACROSS THE ORGANIZATION

A change in strategy generally requires changes throughout the organization. Changes include organizational structures, marketing and distribution methods, production methods, and human resource policies. Financial policy, control methods, and reward structures must also be brought in line with the strategy. When Ralston Purina restructured itself from an agricultural feed company to a diversified packaged consumer goods company, a restructuring of the organization to allow rapid decision making was also required. Scott Lawn Seed's decision to achieve a dominant market position through saturation depended very heavily on a marketing and distribution plan that would allow their products to dominate retail store space. The service quality we find acceptable at a Days Inn is different from the level we find acceptable at a Hilton resort, for example. Like an orchestra conductor, the CEO must bring all the parts together in harmony to support the company's strategy.

ALIGNING CAPITAL BUDGETING WITH CORPORATE STRATEGY

Strategy should guide decisions about where to look for capital investment opportunities and which types of investments are most likely to have positive net present values.[4] A decision to expand in a particular direction will not be

---

[4]For additional studies of factors affecting profitability, see Ivan E. Brick and Daniel G. Weaver, "A Comparison of Capital Budgeting Techniques in Identifying Profitable Investments," *Financial Management* 13 (Winter 1984): 29–39; Ronald W. Melicher, David F. Rush, and Daryl N. Winn, "Industry Concentration, Financial Structure and Profitability," *Financial Management* 5 (Autumn 1976): 48–53; Allen Michel and Israel Shaked, "Does Business Diversification Affect Performance?" *Financial Management* 13 (Winter 1984): 18–28; and Thomas J. Peters and Robert H. Waterman, Jr., *In Search of Excellence* (New York: Harper and Row, 1982).

implemented unless capital investment proposals are generated. Expertise and manpower are required to generate capital investment proposals. Thus, the strategic decision must often be backed up with research-and-development staffs, an acquisition unit, and so on. These units will increase the probability of a flow of proposals from areas expected to generate competitive advantage.

Capital budgeting policies are often biased against strategically important capital investments. The bias is typically unintentional, which makes it that much more difficult to correct. Recognizing some of the forms of this bias is helpful in designing appropriate capital investment policies to support corporate strategy.

One common type of bias is a policy favoring replacement decisions, which often lead to continuation of "business as usual." These investments are viewed as low risk by managers who often approve them with less rigorous justification than is required for investments involving departures from the past. While adjusting required returns for risk makes sense, the required returns for investments involving new ways of doing business are often set artificially high. These policies may leave managers continually frustrated in their attempts to implement corporate strategy.

An undue focus on short-term results also inhibits implementation of strategy. Companies sometimes set a limit such as three years on the payback period, the time it takes a project to return the amount invested. The justification is often that they do not want to take too much risk. A high discount rate and a short payback-period requirement favor assets with short lives, while investments of major strategic importance may take years to begin paying off. Thus, a policy designed to assure profitability may inadvertently assure that an economic profit is never achieved.

A narrow or shortsighted view is another culprit hindering implementation of strategy. Strategic investments must be evaluated in the context of their impacts on other investments now and in the future. As Myers points out, capital investment analysis will lead to the wrong decision if it does not include the value of future investment opportunities that may be created by the investment currently under consideration.[5] A test-market investment may, for example, include such high costs that it loses money in even the most favorable scenario. But the purpose of the test market is not to make money. If the test market confirms an adequate customer demand, nationwide investment opportunities are thereby created. A potential source of conflict between the strategists and the capital investment analysts often arises in the recognition of potential future investment opportunities created by the current investment. Consistent with Myers's suggestion, option theory is used in Chapter 15 to analyze investments that create future investment opportunities.

Investing in growth for growth's sake is another impediment to strategy implementation. Growth is often desirable because it takes advantage of economies of scale, creates barriers to entry, and so on. But companies that want to grow

[5]Steward C. Myers, "Finance Theory and Financial Strategy," *Midland Corporate Finance Journal* 5 (Spring 1987): 6–13.

simply to be bigger may find funds diverted from the activities that create economic profits. The business press is full of examples of declining stock prices in the face of rapid growth because investors do not believe the company's growth will lead to economic profits.

Failure to give up is another barrier to strategy implementation. When a business can no longer generate an economic profit, it should be sold or abandoned. This principle shows up in the various conceptual models and in Shapiro's analysis of capital budgeting and strategy.[6] But giving up is often seen as failure. Furthermore, managers and employees in the unprofitable area will develop one scheme after another for returning the business to profitability. The decision that a viable scheme is unlikely is a painful one and is often avoided for years while capital and attention are diverted from strategically important capital investments.

Allocating capital among divisions according to past profitability is another potential detriment. First, accounting profitability is the wrong measure. A division with a functional factory that is fully depreciated for accounting purposes will have an extremely high accounting return on investment, while a division with a new factory will have a lower return on capital. Even more fundamentally, historical performance is the wrong measure. A division that requires a capital investment to become profitable is forever doomed while capital is allocated to divisions with historical profitability and no opportunities for profitable new investment.

Capital investment analysis that ignores market dynamics is another blow to implementation of strategy. One of the more common errors is forgetting that competitors will change too. Eastman Kodak dominated the 35 millimeter film market in the United States for decades. But foreign competitors have made huge strides in recent years, and Kodak's competitive advantage has declined. Furthermore, digital technology may mean that computer diskettes will be the main competitors in the near future. A proposal for a "business as usual" capital investment in the film division will overstate profitability if it ignores declining competitive advantage. As a result, the "business as usual" investment may beat out a capital investment that would help the company improve its competitive advantage and generate economic profits.

Finally, the management reward system should be consistent with the profitability goals of the company. Many companies give lip service to profitable capital investments but base the management reward system entirely on this year's sales or accounting income. This focuses attention on short-term results rather than on the capital investments that create wealth. A compensation system based on longer-term profitability helps.

Eaton again provides a good illustration of strategically focused capital budgeting. Eaton was dominant in the drivetrain business. Dominance in terms of quality was maintained through heavy investment in research and development. Dominance in cost was maintained by heavy investment in efficiency. Dominance

---

[6]Alan C. Shapiro, "Corporate Strategy and Capital Budgeting," *Financial Management Collection* 1 (Winter 1986): 1–2+.

in size resulted from quality and price. As a result, Eaton earned substantial profits and cash flows in the mature, staid drivetrain business, while companies in faster growing and more glamorous businesses were scraping by. Eaton's reorganization aimed at focusing its investment in areas where it could achieve similar dominance and profitability while selling off or closing down businesses without that potential.

FINANCING IN IMPERFECT FINANCIAL MARKETS |

Just as imperfect product markets are the norm, imperfect financial markets are the norm also. Taxes and transaction costs are ubiquitous and information sets available to managers and outsiders almost always differ. Thus, financing decisions can affect cost of funds, strategy, and shareholder wealth.

Taxes and transaction costs are simply part of the reality that must be dealt with. In Chapters 17 and 18 we will discuss how a mix of debt and equity funding can contribute to value because of these considerations. Likewise, we will discuss how the debt-equity mix can be used to help overcome conflicts between management and shareholder interests in the absence of complete information. In this section, we focus on how the financing mix can support the corporation's strategy.

Power in the marketplace is one aspect of corporate strategy that is clearly affected by capital structure. Companies attempt to differentiate their products and use competitive advantage to generate profitability. But profitability attracts new entrants. The decisions of new entrants depend on their perceived strengths and those of the entrenched companies. Likewise, the decisions of entrenched companies depend on the perceived strength of the new competitors. An entrenched company may avoid battles for market share if competitors realize that it is financially strong, and can outlast them in a battle. Likewise, an entrenched company may decide not to respond vigorously to a new entrant if it is clear that the new entrant has the financial strength to persevere.

People's Express entered the airline market with a low-price, no-frills service strategy. Unfortunately, People's Express also entered the market with a large debt burden. The debt burden made People's vulnerable, and People's was eventually forced out of business when major airlines responded with lower fares of their own. A capital structure that did not place excessive demand on cash flows for principal and interest payments may have saved People's Express from competitive reaction in the first place.

Flexibility is another key issue. Flexibility is achieved by maintaining a capital structure that makes it possible to raise or retire various types of capital under widely varying financial market conditions. Long-term debt with restrictive covenants and no call provision is the classic example of financing that eliminates flexibility. Likewise, a financing mix consisting of as much debt as anyone will provide means that you may be shut off from the financial markets in future periods if your stock price is depressed. A depressed stock price is impossible with perfect information, but undervalued stock is possible if investors are not fully informed. Failure to provide flexibility may force you to abandon a strategy in midstream. Pan Am's strategy of dominating the Caribbean market by serving every location was abandoned in midstream, providing an example of how hundreds of millions of dollars can be lost when a company starts a strategy it cannot carry through. Pan Am, once the star of international air travel, went out of business.

Takeover issues are important in designing a financing mix, whether your strategy includes acquisition of other companies or the desire to avoid being acquired. Companies with very little debt in their capital structure have found themselves vulnerable to takeover, for example, because the acquirer could borrow money against their assets. Companies attempting takeovers, on the other hand, have found that unused debt capacity may allow them to buy another company more cheaply because they could close the deal while a competing bidder was still looking for financing.

Information asymmetry between managers and investors is a chief reason that financing affects strategy and value. This information inequality generally works to the detriment of the corporation, because investors are likely to assume (often correctly) that the news they did not get is bad. Excessive investor focus on this quarter's accounting income, for example, typically arises from investors' suspicions that they do not know the rest of the story. Consequently, a strong, credible investor relations program can be an invaluable contribution to corporate strategy by assuring that money is available on favorable terms to fund attractive investments. In the long run, the only credible investor relations program is based on a pattern of honest, candid communication.

SUMMARY

In a perfectly competitive market, large numbers of producers with identical cost structures compete to sell identical products to customers who are aware of all the other producers and know that all the products are identical. No economic profit is possible is this market, and producers must operate at peak efficiency just to survive. Thus, companies seeking to create wealth are of necessity seeking to break out of perfect competition.

The likelihood of success in breaking out of perfect competition depends on the nature of the industry in which the company operates. Desirable industry characteristics include:

- Barriers to entry exist.
- Customers are not price sensitive.
- Customers care about product features.
- Customers are not fully informed.
- Demand is stable.
- Competitors are of the right type (intelligent wealth maximizers, for example).

If industry conditions are right, the company seeks to establish competitive advantage by product differentiation or cost advantage. Product advantage is achieved by differentiating the product from those of competitors through different features, higher quality, better distribution, a distinct image, and so on. Cost advantage can be achieved through technology, economies of scale, capture of a supply source, and corporate culture. Lower-cost financing is one type of cost advantage, and it can be achieved with a strong investor relations program that establishes the credibility of the corporation.

Globalization is often important in creating and maintaining competitive advantage. Globalization can take advantage of comparative advantage, conducting each part of the business in a country that has an advantage in that part of the business. Globalization also allows companies to leverage knowledge investments in additional markets.

The ultimate goals of strategic planning are competitive advantage and economic profit. Strategy is the grand design of the organization, involving the decision as to what business we are in and how we intend to position our organization in relation to others in that business. The major financial decisions of the organization—both investment and financing decisions—follow from and support the organization's strategy.

The strategy of the company defines the business that the company is in and how it intends to position itself within that business. The development of a strategy is based on three major sets of information: (1) a statement of goals, (2) an analysis of the environment, and (3) an analysis of the organization itself.

The objective of most strategic analysis is economic profit: a rate of profit above that just necessary to cover the opportunity cost of capital. To achieve economic profit, the company must avoid operating in perfect competition. Profitability is achieved by creating, enhancing, protecting, and using competitive advantages, either product advantage or cost advantage. Product advantages can include features, quality, image, service, and distribution. Cost advantages can come from economies of scale, technology, corporate culture, or control of the supply of inputs.

A number of conceptual models are used in the process of strategic analysis. These include the product life cycle curve and the strength/attractiveness grid. The conceptual models are used in the process of developing a strategy or grand design. The grand design is then implemented through a number of strategies applied to operation of the business. These include organizational strategies, marketing and distribution strategies, production and processing strategies, personnel strategies, financial strategies, and control strategies.

Financial decisions in support of strategy include both capital investment policy and capital structure policy. Capital investment policy must be designed to assure that the investments chosen are those that will contribute to the corporation's strategy. This requires the design of a capital investment policy and a management reward policy to avoid traps that deflect capital to other uses and encourage the flow of capital to the uses that will generate the greatest value.

Financial structure analysis must go beyond simply minimizing the cost of capital to consider ways in which capital structure can increase the value of the firm by contributing to strategy. Market power, flexibility, and the ability to continue to finance corporate strategy are all affected by capital structure decisions.

A properly developed strategy coordinates decision making from all areas of the organization. Optimal decisions are made in the framework of the corporation's overall objectives, not just in isolation. The result is achievement of overall goals in general and maximization of wealth in particular.

QUESTIONS |

2–1. Define the term *strategy*, as used in business decision making.

2–2. What are the characteristics of perfect competition, and what are the implications for economic profit?

2–3. List the industry characteristics that create the potential for competitive advantage, and give an example of each.

2–4. List the types of comparative advantage that might lead to international business activities.

2–5. What are some of the factors considered in an environmental assessment?

2–6. What are some factors considered in analyzing internal strengths and weaknesses?

2–7. What types of investments are likely to contribute to the earning of an economic profit?

2–8. Does net present value analysis have a role in strategic planning? Explain.

2–9. List and describe the various types of operating strategies.

2–10. Discuss some ways in which capital budgeting policy can inadvertently thwart corporate strategy and thereby limit profitability.

2–11. Discuss ways in which the financing decisions can support the corporation's strategy.

2–12. Pick either Coke, Nike, Disney, McDonald's Corporation, or Southwest Airlines and answer the following:

    a. What do you consider to be the largest potential threat of maintaining this company's competitive advantage?

    b. What do you suggest the company do in a strategic, and more specifically, in a capital budgeting or financing sense to lessen the potential threat identified above?

2–13. Clearly Canadian, the bottled water company, has made millions of dollars in recent years selling bottled water to the consumer. If anything should be a commodity that faces a perfectly competitive market, you would think it would be water.

    a. If you were the president of this company, how would you explain your competitive advantage to a group of potential investors.

    b. Do you personally (as an outsider) believe that this competitive advantage is sustainable in the future? What are the potential threats?

    c. What projects would you recommend to protect this advantage in the future?

2–14. Answer question 13 with regard to Orville Redenbacher popcorn.

2–15. Assume that the following demographic or social changes are taking place: the population is getting older, crime is increasing, and wealth is becoming more concentrated.

    a. Take one of these changes and identify an opportunity that might develop for an industry or company.

    b. Develop this opportunity into a wealth-generating project for the firm, as if you were presenting this project to an executive committee for the organization. (Ignore specific numbers.)

2–16. Consider the changes identified in question 15 and the following technology changes:

- Computer processing capabilities are getting faster and capable of handling more data.
- Engineered materials continue to get stronger and cheaper.
- Genetic engineering continues to produce more durable produce.
- Pharmaceuticals promise (and are delivering) breakthroughs in health care.
- Another technological change (you supply) is occurring.

Identify the benefits and the disadvantages these changes will have on the following businesses:

    a. Exxon Corporation

    b. Kinko's Copies

    c. Ford Motor Company

    d. Federal Express

2–17. Caterpillar Corporation recently threatened to hire replacement workers rather than guarantee job security. One of the reasons cited for this position was that strong foreign competition could necessitate labor force reductions and work rule changes.

    a. From the perspective of a union leader, how would you persuade your membership into dropping the job guarantee requirement in terms of strategy, competition, and wealth presented in this chapter?

    b. What are the ethical considerations associated with this situation?

PROBLEMS

2–1. Labor use per unit for two products is shown below for countries A and B, along with units of each product being produced. Can the two countries benefit from trade? Who has the competitive advantage with regard to which product?

	COUNTRY A		**COUNTRY B**	
	Unit Labor	**Units Produced**	**Unit Labor**	**Units Produced**
Shoes	100	1,000	50	2,000
Computers	500	10	200	10

2–2. Perform an environmental assessment from the perspective of one of the smaller manufacturers of general-use personal computers.

2–3. You will probably be marketing your services in the near future. Perform an environmental assessment with regard to the market for your services.

2–4. Identify the goal of your school (it is probably stated in the front of the catalog) and perform an environmental assessment. List both threats and opportunities.

2–5. Identify the internal strengths and weaknesses of your school.

2–6. Develop a strategy for your school.

2–7. A new line of business for Hartford Corporation will require a $1 million cash outlay to enter and will generate perpetual cash inflows of $100,000 a year. Investors could earn 12 percent elsewhere by taking the same risk. Will this investment generate an economic profit?

2–8. New Haven Corporation is considering a new capital investment that will cost $1 million and will generate perpetual cash flows of $200,000 a year. Investors could expect to earn 10 percent elsewhere while taking the same risk. Will this investment generate an economic profit?

2–9. Identify a currently available product in each of the stages of the product life cycle.

2–10. You are a leading manufacturer of an electronic home entertainment product. You are positioned at the high-quality end of the market. Your business is still growing rapidly, but you anticipate that growth will slow sharply in the next year or two as the market reaches maturity. Sales will be dependent on replacement needs and population growth once maturity is reached. What are the strategy implications of this position?

2–11. Select three of your school's major fields of study, and locate each of these on a Strength/Attractiveness Grid. What strategies would you recommend to the administration with regard to each major field?

2–12. Place General Motors' top luxury car in a Strength/Attractiveness Grid based on your own perceptions. Place the two major competitors on the same matrix. What are the strategy implications for General Motors?

2–13. We can acquire another company by purchasing its stock for $1 million. The company is earning $150,000 a year, which is available for dividends, and that level of income is expected to continue whether the company remains independent or we acquire it. If we acquire the company, though, we can use its patents to increase our income by $50,000 a year indefinitely. The acquisition candidate has about the same risk as our company, and our investors require an 18 percent return. Is the investment attractive?

CASE PROBLEM |

Micromaster

Patricia Jennings was a computer science major in the early 1980s, when microcomputers were just entering the growth stage. Jennings wrote several term papers on microcomputer applications. In addition, she bought an IBM PC within a few weeks of its introduction and began to spend most of her time studying the machine's potential.

Jennings's brother, Jim, was a certified public accountant who had set up his own practice, concentrating on small business customers. The bookkeeping for these customers was still being done by hand, and the typical business had an in-house bookkeeper who manually recorded transactions. Jim designed the bookkeeping systems, conducted the audits, and handled tax forms. In talking with her brother, Jennings quickly concluded that there was a large market for small-business accounting software for microcomputers. With her brother's guidance on accounting principles, Jennings wrote a simple small-business accounting program as an independent study project. Jim tested the program and put it to use, persuading a number of his clients to buy microcomputers for use in maintaining their accounting records.

Jim offered to put up several thousand dollars to advertise the system for sale through microcomputer magazines. They marketed the system under the name Micromaster Accountant. Micromaster was one of the first small-business accounting programs on the market, and sales started out well. Unfortunately, though, Jennings quickly learned the importance of market power. Major software houses brought out small-business accounting packages backed by 20 times the advertising budget. The advertising budgets gave the major software houses access to retail shelf space in computer stores. In addition, the software houses provided free seminars nationwide on how to use their products. Despite rapid growth in sales of microcomputer-based accounting systems, sales of the Micromaster system fell to the point where marketing efforts were abandoned.

Jennings had been in and out of the computer software business prior to the start of her senior year. The venture had left the entrepreneurs with a small profit of $60,000, and she was fascinated by the prospect of reentering the software market. She thought about making another attempt at capturing a national market, but realized that at least a million dollars in promotional expenditures would be needed, with only a small probability of success. Arrangement of funding seemed unlikely.

Jennings decided to identify market segments that had special needs and custom-design programs to meet those needs. She chose church record keeping as her target. The potential customers could be reached through specialty advertisements that would be much less expensive than national advertising for general products such as word processing. Direct-mail selling would be used, so she would not need to fight for space on the retailers' shelves. Furthermore, she would be working in a market in which competition was limited and demand would therefore be less sensitive to pricing.

During her senior year, Jennings developed a church management program she named Churchmaster. She again used the advise of her brother, who audited several churches as part of his practice. In addition, she interviewed pastors of a dozen churches of various sizes and denominations about their needs. The system consisted of five independently priced modules: a basic church accounting package, accounts payable, personnel records, membership records, and contribution records. She priced the modules separately so that a church could buy only what it needed and could add on later if desired. A small church, for example, could operate with only a basic accounting package. A large church would benefit from using all of the packages. A church with a limited budget might start with basic accounting and then add other packages as funds became available. Jennings decided to sell the basic unit for $995 and price each of the other modules at $495. She estimated that a tenth of the nation's 340,000 churches would be large enough to benefit from the program.

Jennings devoted her full time to the Churchmaster, dividing her time between marketing, enhancing the program, and adding modules. Initial expenses were covered by $60,000 of profits retained from the earlier venture, plus additional funding from her brother, who became part owner of the business. She budgeted $10,000 a month for promotions, which included free seminars in large cities, church magazine advertisements, and direct mail. To free up her time and avoid fixed costs, Jennings contracted out the actual production of disks and manuals as well as shipment. The charge was $30 for each unit shipped, whether a basic accounting package or a module. Sales of basic accounting modules by month for the first three years appear in Table 2.1.

TABLE 2.1	UNIT SALES PER MONTH FOR THE CHURCHMASTER BASIC UNIT				
Month	Units	Month	Units	Month	Units
1	12	13	16	25	127
2	12	14	19	26	141
3	12	15	23	27	154
4	13	16	27	28	156
5	13	17	33	29	156
6	13	18	39	30	153
7	14	19	46	31	149
8	14	20	55	32	140
9	14	21	65	33	131
10	14	22	78	34	123
11	15	23	93	35	118
12	15	24	110	36	115

By the end of three years, sales had begun to decline. Jennings attributed this to two factors: market saturation and competition. Several companies introduced church software packages, and Jennings was forced to reduce her prices, to $695 for the basic package and $295 for additional modules. Additional price decreases would probably be required. In addition, handling questions for existing church customers and enhancing the program to stay competitive were steadily adding to fixed costs and reducing profitability. Jennings guessed that she had as many systems in use as any competitor, but nobody published their sales records.

Jennings had no intention of abandoning the church computer software. After all, it had given her income of over $900,000 in three years and was still generating profitable sales. Nevertheless, she realized that this source of income would probably continue to decline and began to focus her attention on new products. She had been thinking about new areas of development for some time and began to concentrate on two alternatives: a database for churches and marketing of the small-business accounting package.

ALTERNATIVE I

Church database. Like other organizations, churches needed to monitor their progress and manage their finances. Businesses often compared their progress to that of other companies using industry average ratios. A similar approach could be used by churches, but data sources were extremely limited; nobody published an extensive set of statistics on church performance. One reason for lack of statistics was that churches had not kept their records in a consistent manner. With almost 3,000 churches using her information system, there was now a reasonable base of churches using a consistent reporting form.

Jennings envisioned a new module that would be distributed free to churches. When run, this module would lift information from the church's database and transfer it to a diskette that would be mailed to Jennings. Jennings would write another program that would compile information from the various churches into an annual statistical report on trends in contributions, expenditures, membership, attendance, and so on. The service would not be labor intensive because data would be entered and compiled automatically.

Jennings estimated a fee of $100 per year per member church. She estimated that the system could be maintained by one person who would run each church's disk through a program to transfer data to a master file, check the data for reasonableness, and do the follow-up inquiries when data seemed unreasonable. That person would also have time to handle promotional efforts during slack periods. Wage, space, and supply costs would be approximately $30,000 a year. Printing and mailing out reports would be handled by the same firm that reproduced and mailed the programs. Two mailings would be needed each year: one mailing with the disk and reminder letter, and a second mailing with the report. Printing and mailing would cost approximately $4.50 per church per year. Promotion would be inexpensive as she would focus on churches that were already customers.

Jennings would not have time to write the programs and estimated that it would cost her $25,000 to hire the work done under her supervision. She would have to start the programming project before promoting the service, so she would have to spend approximately $15,000 on programming before receiving any orders. Initial promotion would consist of a brochure mailing to all existing customers, at a cost of $4,350. If response was favorable at this level, a general mailing could be used for 30,000 churches on her "target" mailing list. That mailing would promote Churchmaster plus the added benefit of a complete comparative statistics service. Less material would be included in this mailing, and the recipients would be invited to ask for additional information. The cost would be $0.75 per church. In addition, advertising in church publications would be intensified.

ALTERNATIVE 2

Revised small-business accounting system. After three years of neglect, the original small-business accounting system was still being used by some customers. This vote of confidence encouraged Jennings to think of ways to capitalize on this product. Two alternatives were possible. She could market the system at a greatly discounted price, such as $99 for the entire package, and hope for volume sales through a small advertising campaign costing $50,000 a year. Production and shipment would cost $30 for each package. With over 10 million small businesses operating in the country, the potential sales volume was substantial.

A second alternative was to spend $300,000 on a one-year development effort, then invest $1 million in an advertising program to sell the system to retail stores for $350, with a suggested retail price of $499. Again, production and shipment costs would be $30 per unit. Stores would be able to demand very favorable credit terms and return policies, so store inventory would effectively be carried by Micromaster. Potential sales were in the hundreds of thousands of units, but actual sales would depend on reviews by software reviewers, satisfaction of early customers, and the success of the advertising campaign.

Jennings could fund the church database package alternative and/or the marketing of the existing accounting package from her existing profits. However, outside funds would be required to develop and market a revised small-business accounting package. With $300,000 of equity and $90,000 of marketable securities on hand, Jennings doubted if she would be able to borrow the $1.3 million she would need to launch this promotion. She did not know if she would be able to sell equity and was hesitant to try. Jennings and her brother were the only stockholders, and she did not want to give up control of her business.

CASE QUESTIONS

1. What would be your primary goal(s) if you were in Patricia's position?
2. For each of the alternatives, discuss possible threats and opportunities in the environment.
3. For each of the alternatives, discuss competitive strengths and weaknesses of Micromaster Corporation.
4. For each of the alternatives, discuss the potential for Micromaster to gain a competitive advantage.
5. Recommend a course of action for Patricia.

SELECTED REFERENCES |

Aggerwal, Raj. "The Strategic Challenge of the Evolving Global Economy." *Business Horizons* (July–August 1987): 38–44.

Arzac, E. R. "Do Your Business Units Create Shareholder Value?" *Harvard Business Review* (January–February 1986): 121–126.

Balachandran, Bala V., Nandu J. Nagarajan, and Alfred Rappaport. "Threshold Margins for Creating Economic Value." *Financial Management* 15 (Spring 1986): 68–77.

Baldwin, Carliss Y., and Kim B. Clark. "Capabilities and Capital Investment: New Perspective on Capital Budgeting." *Journal of Applied Corporate Finance* 5 (Summer 1992): 67–82.

Berkovitch, Elazar, and M. P. Narayanan. "Timing of Investment and Financing Decisions in Imperfectly Competitive Financial Markets." *Journal of Business* 66 (April 1993): 219–248.

Bhide, Amar. "Reversing Corporate Diversification." *Journal of Applied Corporate Finance* 3 (Summer 1990): 70–81.

Bruns, William J., Jr., and Kenneth A. Merchant. "The Dangerous Morality of Managing Earnings." *Management Accounting* (August 1990): 22–25.

Castle, Douglas E. "Financing Options for the Corporate Strategist." *Journal of Business Strategy* 9 (January–February 1988): 12–16.

Dobson, John, and Robert Dorsey. "Reputation, Information, and Project Termination in Capital Budgeting." *The Engineering Economist* 38 (Winter 1993): 143–152.

Donaldson, Gordon. "Voluntary Restructuring: The Case of General Mills." *Journal of Applied Corporate Finance* 4 (Fall 1991): 6–19.

Giammarino, Ronald, and Robert L. Hienkel. "A Model of Dynamic Takeover Behavior." *Journal of Finance* 41 (June 1986): 465–480.

Hamel, Gary, and C. K. Prahalad. "Do You Really Have a Global Strategy?" *Harvard Business Review* 63 (July–August 1985): 139–148.

Hofer, C. W., and M. J. Davoust. *Successful Strategic Management*. Northbrook, Ill. A.T. Kearney, Inc., 1977.

Jose, Manuel L., Len M. Nichols, and Jerry L Stevens. "Contributions of Diversification, Promotion, and R & D to the Value of Multiproduct Firms: A Tobin's q Approach." *Financial Management* 15 (Winter 1986): 33–42.

Kensinger, John W. "Adding the Value of Active Management into the Capital Budgeting Equation." *Midland Corporate Finance Journal* 5 (Spring 1987): 31–43.

Liberatore, Matthew J., Thomas F. Monahan, and David E. Stout. "A Framework for Integrating Capital Budgeting Analysis with Strategy." *The Engineering Economist* 38 (Fall 1992): 1–18.

Melicher, Ronald W., David F. Rush, and Daryl N. Winn. "Industry Concentration, Financial Structure and Profitability." *Financial Management* 5 (Autumn 1976): 48–53.

Michel, Allen, and Israel Shaked. "Does Business Diversification Affect Performance?" *Financial Management* 13 (Winter 1984): 18–28.

Myers, Stewart C. "Financial Theory and Financial Strategy." *Midland Corporate Finance Journal* 5 (Spring 1987): 6–13.

———. "Notes on an Expert System for Capital Budgeting." *Financial Management* 17 (Autumn 1988): 23–31.

Opler, Tim C., and Sheridan Titman. "Financial Distress and Corporate Performance." *The Journal of Finance* 49 (July 1994): 1015–1040.

Porcano, Thomas M. "Factors Affecting the Foreign Direct Investment Decision of Firms from and into Major Industrialized Countries." *Multinational Business Review* 1 (Fall 1993): 26–36.

Porter, Michael E. *Competitive Advantage: Creating and Sustaining Superior Performance.* New York: The Free Press, 1985.

———. *Competitive Strategy: Techniques of Analyzing Industries and Competitors.* New York: The Free Press, 1980.

Rappaport, Alfred. "Linking Competitive Strategy and Shareholder Value Analysis." *Journal of Business Strategy* 7 (Spring 1987): 58–67.

Reimann, Bernard C. "Stock Price and Business Success: What Is the Relationship?" *Journal of Business Strategy* 8 (Summer 1987): 38–49.

Shapiro, Alan C. "Corporate Strategy and Capital Budgeting." *Financial Management Collection* 1 (Winter 1986): 1–2+.

Thakor, Anjan V. "Game Theory in Finance." *Financial Management* 20, no. 2 (Spring 1991): 71–94.

Walls, Michael R. "Integrating Business Strategy and Capital Allocation: An Application of Multi-Objective Decision Making." *The Engineering Economist* 40 (Spring 1995): 247–266.

CHAPTER 3 |

MEASURING WEALTH: TIME VALUE OF MONEY

After completing this chapter you should be able to:

1. Explain to somebody why you have to put future dollars on a common basis before you can add them. For example, can you add a dollar expected in year one and a dollar expected in year two to get a meaningful answer?
2. Calculate the present dollar equivalent (present value) of a future amount.
3. Compute the future dollar equivalent (future value) of a present amount.
4. Define an *annuity* and find the present value or future value of an annuity.
5. Recognize the numerous instances in which you come in contact with the pricing of future cash flows.
6. Price future cash flows so that you know a bargain when you see it.
7. Adjust for instances in which the interest is compounded more than once a year.
8. Value cash flows that are received at various points in the year.
9. Value perpetual cash flows.

For-profit education is now estimated to be in the billions of dollars worldwide. Sylvan Learning Systems, founded in 1979, now has over 700 franchised learning centers and a market capitalization of over $2 billion. To open one of these centers an entrepreneur must invest $34,000 to $42,000 for the franchise and another $76,000 to $137,000 in start-up costs. For this investment, the owner receives training and an exclusive right to use the Sylvan name and Sylvan programs designed to help grade school and high school students with reading, math, and study skills. In addition, several professional continuing education programs and testing services are being offered at these centers. Fees for these programs average $30 to $40 per hour or $1,000 to $3,000 per course. Instructors' wages for these educational services average 40 percent of the revenue charged for the service. The remainder of the revenue must cover the fixed costs with enough profit left to allow the entrepreneur an adequate return on his or her average $140,000 investment. With investors demanding returns in the neighborhood of 12 percent, these entrepreneurs must determine if there is enough demand to justify the investment. The time value concepts developed in this chapter will help you to make these decisions.

These same time value concepts are invaluable for a myriad of planning purposes. Valuation of a potential acquisition is primarily an exercise in determining the present value of future cash flows. Amounts required for sinking fund and pension fund contributions depend on the rate at which money will grow over time if invested. Choice of financing methods also involves trade-offs between money now and money later. In the personal realm, retirement planning, house financing, and savings programs all involve trade-offs between money now and money later. The principles covered in this chapter are the key to making optimal choices in these and hundreds of other situations, as well as optimal capital budgeting decisions.

SINGLE AMOUNT PROBLEMS |

The basis for all time value analysis is that a dollar invested today will grow to a greater amount in the future. The mathematical formula describing that growth is for finance what the laws of motion are for astronomy; it is the foundation for much of our understanding of how the financial world operates.

Every day individuals, businesses, and governments give up dollars with hopes of receiving more dollars in the future. How much more is determined by the forces of supply and demand in the market for particular funds. At the very least, one would expect to be compensated for forgoing present consumption and for any risk involved. This compensation is referred to as the cost of money or the cost of capital. For debt securities, this cost is referred to as interest, and for equity securities this cost is a required rate of return. How the market operates to determine the interest rate or required rate of return will be discussed in the next chapter. For now we know there is a cost of money, and this dollar cost is determined by the size of the cash flow, the present value (PV) or future value (FV), the amount of time the money is invested (n), and the cost of the money in percentage terms (k). In this section we will illustrate how to solve all four types of single amount problems using formulas, tables, and computer spreadsheet packages. We begin with a discussion of future value of single amount problems, then discuss rate of return problems, and conclude this section with present value of single amounts.

FUTURE VALUE OF A SINGLE AMOUNT

A simple savings account can be used to develop the future value principle. Suppose a savings account at Montgomery National Bank pays 10 percent interest, compounded annually. This means that at the end of each year, if there were no deposits or withdrawals during the year, the bank adds to the account 10 percent of the balance at the beginning of the year. Letting FV_n be the amount in

the account at the end of n years, the growth of the account over a 2-year period can be summarized as follows:

$$FV_1 = \$100 + .10 \times \$100 = \$100(1 + .10) = \$110$$

$$FV_2 = \$110 + .10 \times \$110 = \$110(1 + .10) = \$100(1 + .10)^2 = \underline{\$121}$$

This growth pattern can be generalized for any present value, any interest
rate, and any number of periods:

$$FV_n = PV(1 + k)^n \tag{3-1}$$

where

PV = the present value

n = the number of periods, and

k = the interest rate or rate of return per period

The mechanical problem of solving for $(1 + k)^n$ when n is large can be resolved by use of a financial calculator, a computer spreadsheet program such
as Excel, or Table A.1 at the back of this book. Table A.1 contains values of
$(1 + k)^n$ for numerous values of k and n.

Table Example. One hundred dollars will be invested in the previously discussed
savings account at Montgomery National Bank, and the deposit will be left to
grow for 20 years at 10 percent annual interest. The problem can be stated as
follows:

$$FV_{20} = \$100(1 + .10)^{20}$$

By turning to Table A.1, going to the 20 period row, and then going across
to the 10 percent column, $(1 + .10)^{20}$ is found to equal 6.7275. In 20 years, the
$100 deposit will grow to:[1]

$$FV_{20} = \$100 \times 6.7275 = \underline{\$672.75}$$

[1]If you need a factor from one of the time value tables (A.1 through A.5) for an interest rate not
shown in the table, you can find the approximate amount using the following linear interpolation
formula:

$$F(k) = F(k_b) + [F(k_a) - F(k_b)][(k - k_b)/(k_a - k_b)]$$

where k is the interest rate for which a factor is desired, k_a is the interest rate immediately above
k in the table, and k_b is the interest rate immediately below k in the table. $F(k_a)$ and $F(k_b)$ are the
factors from the table for interest rates k_a and k_b, respectively.

Suppose, for example, you want to find $(1 + .094)^{20}$ using Table A.1. Using interpolation, the
value is approximately:

$$5.6044 + [6.7275 - 5.6044][(.094 - .09)/(.10 - .09)] = \underline{6.0536}$$

In other words, at 9.4 percent interest, $100 would grow to approximately $100 \times 6.0536 = \underline{\$605.36}$.

Spreadsheet Examples. To solve the above problem using Lotus or Excel, you need to set up one of the following spreadsheets:

In Lotus:

	A	B	C	D	....	U
1	100	+A1*1.1	+B1*1.1	+C1*1.1	....	+T1*1.1
2	Or 100 * ((1+.1)^20					

In Excel:

	A	B	C	D	....	U
1	100	=A1*1.1	=B1*1.1	=C1*1.1	....	=T1*1.1
2	Or = 100 * ((1+.1)^20					

After entering the $100 dollar amount in cell A1 and the formula in cell B1, the formula in cell B1 should be copied across to cell U1. The result in cell U1 is the future value of $100 after growing at 10 percent for 20 years, or $672.7499. Any slight difference from the table answer is caused by rounding the table at four decimal places. Later in the book when we estimate growing cash flows this spreadsheet command will come in handy. A shortcut command is shown is cell A2. Note the only difference between Lotus and Excel in this example is that Lotus uses a + sign where Excel uses an = sign.

RATE OF RETURN ON A SINGLE AMOUNT

Table Example. The rate of return earned on an investment can also be found using Equation 3-1. An investment of $1,000 today in a mutual fund offered by Troy Securities is expected to grow to $4,661 in 20 years. To find the rate of return, we need to solve for k in the equation:

$$\$4,661 = \$1,000(1 + k)^{20}$$

Dividing both sides of the equation by $1,000 yields:

$$4.661 = (1 + k)^{20}$$

The value of k can be found by using a calculator to take the 20th root of both sides of the equation or by going to the 20-year row in Table A.1 and looking for the number 4.661. This number is found at the 8 percent column, so the rate of return earned on the investment is 8 percent.

Spreadsheet Examples. An investment of $1,000 today in a mutual fund offered by Troy Securities is expected to grow to $4,661 in 20 years. Lotus and Excel have built-in rate functions that calculate the rate of return. To use these functions you enter the given information in the following order in any empty cell in the spreadsheet:

Lotus's rate function:

$$@RATE(\text{future value, present value, term})$$

Excel's rate function:

$$= RATE(\text{number of periods, payment, present value, future value, type, guess})$$

You would enter @RATE(4661,1000,20) or = Rate(20,0,−1000,4661,1,.1). When you press ENTER the computer will return with an answer .08000, or 8 percent. Note that in Excel, the present value must be entered as a negative number. The type field is a 1 if the cash flow is at the beginning of the period and a 0 if it occurs at the end of the period. The guess is needed as a starting point for the computer, and 10 percent is usually adequate.

Equation 3-1 is written in terms of rates of return, but it applies to any situation in which growth occurs at a rate of k each period. At a 5 percent inflation rate, for example, the price of a building lot selling for $20,000 today will increase in 10 years to:

$$FV_{10} = \$20,000 \ (1 + .05)^{10} = \$20,000 \times 1.6289 = \qquad \underline{\$32,578}$$

PRESENT VALUE OF A SINGLE AMOUNT

The amount we would be willing to pay now in exchange for a dollar at some future date would not exceed the amount we would need to invest today to have a dollar by that future date. The present value of a future amount can be found by rearranging the terms in Equation 3-1:

$$PV = FV_n/(1 + k)^n = FV_n[1/(1 + k)^n] \tag{3-2}$$

In this context, k is the interest rate or rate of return that can be earned elsewhere. Table A.1 at the end of this book contains values of $(1 + k)^n$ for numerous combinations of k and n, while Table A.2 contains values of $1/(1 + k)^n$. Again, a financial calculator or a spreadsheet program such as Lotus 1-2-3 or Excel can also be used.

Example. Shares in a timber stand near Tuscaloosa cost $10,000 today, and will be worth an estimated $20,000 in 5 years. Other investments provide returns of 10 percent. The present value of the $20,000 future amount is therefore:

$$PV_5 = \$20,000[1/(1 + .10)^5] = \$20,000 \times .6209 = \underline{\$12,418}$$

In other words, \$12,418 invested elsewhere at 10 percent would result in \$20,000 in 5 years, so the present value of the timber stand is \$12,418. The shares are therefore a bargain at \$10,000.

Spreadsheet Example. Using the same information, shares in a timber stand near Tuscaloosa cost \$10,000 today and will be worth an estimated \$20,000 in 5 years. Other investments provide returns of 10 percent. The present value of the \$20,000 future amount can be calculated with Lotus by using the formula +20000/((1 + .10)^5) or in Excel with =20000/((1+.10)^5). An alternative solution is the following spreadsheet:

	A	B	C	D	E
1	0	0	0	0	20,000
2	In Lotus: @NPV(.1,A1..E1)		In Excel: =NPV(.1,A1..E1)		

The formula in cell A2 is @NPV(*the discount rate, range*) for Lotus and = NPV(*the discount rate, range*) for Excel. When you press ENTER the answer \$12,418.42 will be returned. This is a very powerful function and it will be used again in the following chapter to calculate net present values. In this case zeros are entered in the first four columns to tell the computer that the \$20,000 is received at the end of the fifth year.

The relationships between rate of return, time, and present value are illustrated in Figure 3.1. The same relationship can be seen by scanning across rows and down columns in Table A.2. The longer the time between present and future amounts, and the higher the required return, the smaller will be the present value of the future amount, and vice versa.

ANNUITY PROBLEMS

Annuity problems come in two types. Ordinary annuities have cash flows that occur at the end of the period and annuities due have cash flows that occur at the end of the period. Unless otherwise stated, please assume that we are talking about ordinary annuities. In this section we will discuss future value of annuity problems and then present value of annuity problems.

FUTURE VALUE OF AN ANNUITY

As part of its capital investment planning, Normal Corporation wants to put away money each year to replace a major asset when it wears out. This is but one of hundreds of situations in which managers need to know the amount to which an *annuity*—a payment each period—will grow. These questions could be an-

| FIGURE 3.1 RELATIONSHIP BETWEEN PRESENT VALUE, RATE OF RETURN, AND TIME

These figures show the relationship between present value, future value, and rate of return. The two curves in each figure show the difference between the impacts of 5 percent and 10 percent rates of return.

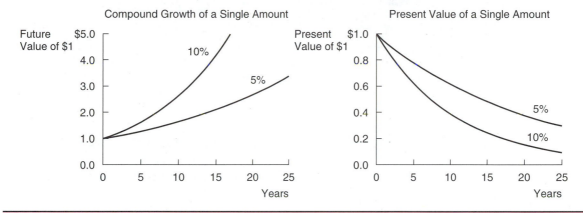

swered using Equation 3-1, but the process would be tedious. Future value of annuity formulas and tables are created to eliminate the tedium. A good financial calculator or a spreadsheet program like Excel or Lotus 1-2-3 can also be used to solve these problems quickly.

To develop the process for finding the future value of an annuity, consider what will happen if you deposit $1,000 in an account at Florence National Bank at the end of each year for 3 years, with the account paying 10 percent annual interest. Since payments are made at the end of the year, the first annual payment will have had 2 years to earn interest, the second annual payment will have had 1 year to earn interest, and the third payment will have earned no interest. The growth of each payment can be determined using Equation 3-1, and the individual future values can be summed to find the future value of the annuity, as illustrated in Table 3.1. Figure 3.2 illustrates the analysis from Table 3.1 in the form of a time line. The future value of this annuity can be rewritten as:

| TABLE 3.1 FUTURE VALUE OF AN ANNUITY

This table illustrates the growth of $1,000 invested at the end of each year for 3 years at a 10 percent annual interest rate.

Payment #	Years to Grow	Compound Value
1	2	$1,000(1 + .10)^2 = $1,210
2	1	$1,000(1 + .10)^1 = $1,100
3	0	$1,000(1 + .10)^0 = \underline{$1,000}
TOTAL FUTURE VALUE		$3,310

| FIGURE 3.2 TIME LINE ILLUSTRATION OF THE FUTURE VALUE OF AN ANNUITY

This figure illustrates the future value of an annuity of $1,000 a year for 3 years, at a 10 percent rate of return.

Year	0	1	2	3
		$1,000	$1,000	$1,000
				1,100
				1,210
				$3,310

$$FVA_3 = \$1,000(1 + .10)^2 + \$1,000(1 + .10)^1 + \$1,000(1 + .10)^0 = \underline{\$3,310}$$

Extending this concept, the general formula for the future value of an annuity is:

$$FVA_n = \sum_{t=1}^{n} PMT_t(1 + k)^{n-t} \tag{3-3}$$

where PMT_t is the payment at the end of period t. As previously defined, k and n are the rate of return and the number of periods. When the payment is the same each period, Equation 3-3 can be simplified with a little rearrangement of terms to:[2]

$$FVA_n = PMT \times [(1 + k)^n - 1]/k \tag{3-3a}$$

$$FVA_n = PMT \times FVA1_{n,k} \tag{3-3b}$$

where $FVA1_{n,k} = [(1 + k)^n - 1]/k$, the future value of an annuity of $1 at the end of each period for n periods, at a rate of return of k per period.

The annuity just described is a *level* or *uniform* annuity because the payment is the same each period. The term *annuity* without a qualifier is generally used to refer to a level annuity.

As with the other time value formulas, Equation 3-3 can be readily solved using a calculator, a computer program, or Table A.3 at the back of this book. To find the future value of an annuity, it is only necessary to find the future value of an annuity of $1 for the appropriate values of n and k in Table A.3, then multiply that factor by the amount of cash flow per year (PMT).

[2]First, substitute PMT for PMT_t in Equation 3-3. Then multiply both sides of Equation 3-3 by $(1 + k)$ and rearrange terms to give:

$$FVA_n(1 + k) = PMT \times \sum_{t=1}^{n} (1 + k)^t$$

Subtracting Equation 3-3 from this new equation gives $FVA_n \cdot k = PMT[(1 + k)^n - 1]$. Dividing both sides of this equation by k gives Equation 3-3a.

Table Example. You decide to deposit $1,000 in an Individual Retirement Account at the end of each year for the remaining 40 years of your working life. The money can be invested at an interest rate of 10 percent a year. The $1,000 per year will then grow to:

$$FVA_{40} = \$1,000FVAI_{n,k}$$

$$= \$1,000 \times 442.59 = \underline{\underline{\$442,590}}$$

The value 442.59 is found at the intersection of the 10 percent column and 40-year row in Table A.3.

Spreadsheet Example. Using the same data, you decide to deposit $1,000 in an Individual Retirement Account at the end of each year for the remaining 40 years of your working life. The money can be invested at an interest rate of 10 percent a year. The future value of this equal stream can be calculated by using the =FV function in Excel or the @FVAL function in Lotus. To use this function you find an empty cell in the spreadsheet and enter =FV(rate, number of periods, payment, present value, type) in Excel or @FVAL(payment, interest, term, type, present value) in Lotus. In this example your entry would look like this:

In Excel: =FV(.1,40,−1000,0,0)

In Lotus: @FVAL(1000,.1,40,0,0)

After entering this, press ENTER and the answer $442,592.5 will appear in the cell. In Excel, please remember that you must use a negative sign in front of the $1,000 amount to signify an outflow of cash so that the answer returned by the computer is positive. The "type" field in both programs uses a 1 to signify an annuity due (where the cash flows occur at the beginning of the period) and a 0 to signify an ordinary annuity (where the cash flows occur at the end of the period).

FUTURE VALUE OF AN ANNUITY – PAYMENT PROBLEMS

Table Example. Birmingham Corporation needs to replace a piece of equipment in 5 years, at an estimated cost of $1 million. The company wants to make equal payments into an investment account at the end of each year for 5 years to accumulate the $1 million. The invested funds will earn 10 percent interest annually. The annual payment can be found as follows:

$$FVA_5 = PMT \times FVAI_{5yrs,10\%}$$

Using the 10 percent, 5-year factor from Table A.3 and substituting $1,000,000 for FVA_5 gives the annual payment needed (PMT):

$$\$1,000,000 = PMT \times 6.1051$$

$$PMT = \$1,000,000/6.1051 = \underline{\underline{\$163,797.48}}$$

Spreadsheet Example. Using the Birmingham Corporation information in the prior example, both Excel and Lotus have payment functions that can be used to solve for the payment in a future value of an annuity problem. In Excel you enter =PMT(interest rate, number of periods, present value, future value, type). In Lotus you enter @PAYMT(principal, interest rate, term, type, future value). Using the Birmingham example, you would go to an empty cell in the spreadsheet and enter:

In Excel: =PMT(.1,5,0,0,1000000)

In Lotus: @PAYMT(0,.1,5,0,1000000)

When you hit return the answer would be ($163,797.50) in Excel, indicating an outflow of cash is needed each year. In Lotus the answer would be $163,797.50. If you enter the $1,000,000 requirement as a negative number in Lotus the answer will match the Excel answer. It is important for the user to determine the sign of the answer based on whether the cash flow is an inflow (positive) or an outflow (negative).

FUTURE VALUE OF AN ANNUITY – RATE OF RETURN PROBLEMS

Table Example. You invested $1,000 in mutual fund shares at the end of each year for the last 10 years. Your shares are now worth $19,337. To find the effective rate of return, it is first necessary to solve Equation 3-3b for $FVA1_{10yrs,k}$:

$$\$19,337 = \$1,000 \ FVA1_{10yrs,k}$$

$$FVA1_{10yrs,k} = \$19,337/\$1,000 = 19.337$$

In the 10-year row of Table A.3, the factor 19.337 is found at the 14 percent column, so the effective rate of return was 14 percent.

Spreadsheet Example. Using the same data from above, you can solve this problem using the @IRR function in Lotus or the =IRR function in Excel. The spreadsheet would look like this:

	A	B	C	D	....	J
1	−1,000	−1,000	−1,000	−1,000	....	+18,337
2	@IRR(.1,A1..J1)		=IRR(A1..J1,.1)			

The .1 in the @IRR or =IRR functions is a guess that begins the process for the computer. If an "ERR" message is returned, you should guess a higher or lower number. The $18,337 is the $19,337 value less the $1,000 put into the account at the end of the tenth year. After entering the formula in cell A2 press ENTER and the answer of .139996, or 14%, will be displayed.

ANNUITIES DUE VERSUS ORDINARY ANNUITIES

The annuities previously examined are called *ordinary annuities* or *annuities in arrears* because payment occurs at the end of each period. An *annuity due* or *annuity in advance* has payments at the beginning of each period. Payments for a $1,000, 3-year ordinary annuity and annuity due are as follows:

Year	0	1	2	3
Ordinary annuity		$1,000	$1,000	$1,000
Annuity due	$1,000	$1,000	$1,000	

Equation 3-3a and Table A.3 are used to find the future value at the end of year n when payments are made at the end of each year. If payments are to be made at the beginning of each year for n years, the future value of an annuity factor from Table A.3 must be multiplied by $(1 + k)$, or the right-hand sides of Equations 3-3a and 3-3b must be multiplied by $(1 + k)$ to recognize the extra interest earned by having the funds invested for one more year.[3] When using either Excel or Lotus functions, you specify ordinary annuity or annuity due by entering a "0" for an ordinary annuity and a "1" for an annuity due.

Table Example. Athens Life Insurance Company will sell you a 20-year term policy for $500 at the beginning of each year. If you are still alive at the end of 20 years, you get nothing back. A whole life policy, on the other hand, requires a payment of $1,500 at the beginning of each year for 20 years. If you are still alive at the end of 20 years, you can cash in the policy for $40,000. To make a decision, you consider the amount you would have if you bought the term insurance and invested the other $1,000 at the beginning of each year in an alternate investment earning an 8 percent annual return. The amount you would have at the end of 20 years is:

$$\$1,000 \times 45.762 \times 1.08 = \underline{\$49,423}$$

You would end up with more money if you bought the term policy and invested the extra money somewhere else.

[3]*Proof:* If payment is at the beginning of the period,

$$FVA_n = PMT_1(1 + k)^n + PMT_2(1 + k)^{n-1} + \ldots + PMT_n(1 + k)^1$$

$$= \sum_{t=1}^{n} PMT_t(1 + k)^{n-t+1} = (1 + k)\left[\sum_{t=1}^{n} PMT_t(1 + k)^{n-t}\right]$$

The bracketed portion is the right-hand side of Equation 3-3, which is $FVA1_{n,k}$ if $PMT_t = \$1$ for all t.

Spreadsheet Example. Using the Athens Life Insurance Company example you would enter one of the following functions in either Excel or Lotus:

In Excel: = FV(rate, number of periods, payment, present value, type) or
= FV(.08,20,−1000,0,1)

In Lotus: @FVAL(payments, interest rate, term, type, present value) or
@FVAL(1000,.08,20,1,0)

After hitting ENTER the answer will come back $49,423. The computer adjusts for the annuity due payment when you specify a "1" in the type field.

PRESENT VALUE OF AN ANNUITY

Trade-offs between costs now and streams of benefits in the future are typical of capital budgeting. The purchase of a business or a share of stock also involves payment now in exchange for a series of cash benefits in the future. Present value of annuity concepts provide a convenient method of deciding if the stream of future cash benefits is worth the present cost.

To develop the present value of an annuity, consider an investment that will pay you $1,000 at the end of each year for 3 years. You could earn 10 percent a year if you invested your money elsewhere. The present value of each individual cash inflow can be found using Equation 3-2 and Table A.2, and the individual present values can then be added to find the value of the investment:

Year	Cash Flow	Present Value at 10 percent
1	$1,000	$1,000[1/(1+.10)^1] = $1,000 \times .9091 = $ 909.10
2	$1,000	$1,000[1/(1+.10)^2] = $1,000 \times .8264 = 826.40
3	$1,000	$1,000[1/(1+.10)^3] = $1,000 \times .7513 = 751.30
TOTAL PRESENT VALUE		$2,486.80

If the market price of the investment is less than $2,486.80, it is attractive. This present value can also be illustrated in the form of a time line:

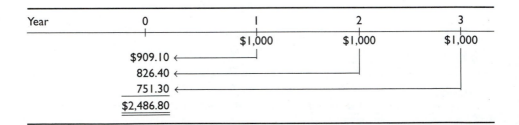

This procedure could be used even if the investment was expected to generate cash flows over a period of 50 years, but the calculations would become tedious. The present value of annuity formulas and tables make calculations faster and easier. The present value of an annuity formula can be developed using the investment example just analyzed. The computation procedure for this problem can be rewritten:

$$PVA_3 = \$1,000/(1 + .10) + \$1,000/(1 + .10)^2 + \$1,000/(1 + .10)^3$$

This procedure can be generalized as the present value of an annuity (PVA_n):

$$PVA_n = \sum_{t=1}^{n} PMT_t/(1+k)^t \tag{3-4}$$

where PMT_t is the payment at the end of period t, k is the required return, and n is the number of periods. When the payment is the same each period, Equation 3-4 can be simplified with a little rearrangement of terms to:[4]

$$PVA_n = PMT \times [1 - 1/(1+k)^n]/k \tag{3-4a}$$

$$PVA_n = PMT \times PVA1_{n,k} \tag{3-4b}$$

where $PVA1_{n,k} = [1-1/(1+k)^n]/k$, the present value of an annuity of \$1 at the end of each period for n periods at an interest rate of k per period.

As with other time value formulas, Equation 3-4 can be readily solved using a calculator, a computer program such as Lotus 1-2-3 or Excel, or a table. Table A.4 at the back of this book contains present values of annuities of \$1 at the end of each period for various rates of return and numbers of periods. To find the present value of any annuity with equal payments, it is only necessary to find the present value of an annuity of \$1 for the appropriate values of n and k in Table A.4 and multiply that factor by the amount of cash flow per period (PMT).

Example. A winner of the Super Lottery will receive \$20 million, but the lucky winner should not expect a \$20 million check. The winner receives an immediate payment of \$1 million, then \$1 million at the end of each year for 19 years. At a 10 percent discount rate, the present value of the payment is:

$$Present\ value = \$1,000,000 + \$1,000,000 PVA1_{19yrs,10\%}$$

$$= \$1,000,000 + \$1,000,000 \times 8.3649 = \$9,364,900$$

---

[4]First, recognize that $PVA_n = FVA_n/(1 + k)^n$. This equality can be verified by dividing the right-hand side of Equation 3-3 by $(1 + k)^n$ and rearranging terms to yield Equation 3-4. Substituting from Equation 3-3b for FVA_n gives:

$$PVA_n = \{PMT[(1 + k)^n - 1]/k\}/(1 + k)^n$$

Rearranging terms yields Equation 3-4a.

Spreadsheet Example. The present value of these winnings can be determined by using the Lotus functions @PVAL or @NPV or the Excel functions =PV or =NPV. The @PVAL or =PV functions can only be used when there is a constant equal payment, while the @NPV or =NPV functions can be used with equal or un-equal cash flows over time. The spreadsheet would look like this:

	A	B	C	D	....	T
1	1,000,000	1,000,000	1,000,000	1,000,000	....	1,000,000
2	@PVAL(1000000,.10,20,1,0)			=PV(.1,20,1000000,0,1)		
3	@NPV(.1,B1..T1,1)			=NPV(.1,A1..T1)+A1		

If you use the @PV or =PV functions, you do not need to enter the $1,000,000 amounts in cell B1 through T1 but only the function illustrated in cell A2 or D2 to get the answer $9,364,920. The @NPV or =NPV functions illustrated in cells A3 and D3 are more commonly used because they work for both equal payments and the more common unequal cash flow problems. In this case we are dealing with an annuity due, so the @NPV function uses a "1" in the type field. In both cases the answer is $9,364,920. The extra accuracy is due to the fact that the tables are rounded at the fourth decimal place. Of course, the winner will pay about 40 percent of all winnings in taxes, so the present value of what she will get to keep is $5,618,940.

Equation 3-4 and Table A.4 are for payment at the end of each period. If payments are at the beginning of each year (annuity due), it is only necessary to multiply the present value of the annuity or the right-hand side of Equation 3-4 by $(1 + k)$.

Example. The lottery winner in the previous example received $1 million immediately, plus $1 million a year for 19 years. This is equivalent to $1 million at the *beginning* of each year for 20 years.

$$\text{Present value} = \$1{,}000{,}000 PVA|^{20\text{yrs},10\%} \times 1.10$$

$$= \$1{,}000{,}000 \times 8.5136 \times 1.10 = \$9{,}364{,}960$$

The small difference from the prior solution is simply a result of rounding in the time value tables.

PRESENT VALUE OF AN ANNUITY—PAYMENT PROBLEMS

Table Example. A senator once used the purchase of a letter opener for $475,000 as an example of government waste. The letter opener, produced by AES Systems of Elk Grove, Illinois, was designed to save substantial amounts of labor for public utilities, insurance companies, and other organizations that receive large numbers of payment envelopes. Assuming a 10 percent required return, a

10-year life, and year-end cash flows, the annual expense reduction needed to justify this letter opener is found as follows. (We ignore taxes for simplicity.)

$$\$475,000 = PMT \times PVAI^{10yrs,10\%}$$

$$\$475,000 = PMT \times 6.1446$$

$$PMT = \$475,000/6.1446 = \underline{\$77,303.65}$$

Spreadsheet Example. Using the letter opener example from above, this problem can be solved with Lotus by using the @PMT function or with Excel using the =PMT function. To use these functions you enter the following in any cell in the spreadsheet:

In Lotus: @PMT(principal, interest, term) or @PMT(475000,.1,10)

In Excel: =PMT(rate, number of periods, present value, future value, type) or =PMT(.1,10,−475000,0,0)

After you press ENTER the computer will return with the answer $77,304.06. The computer answer is not rounded like the table solution.

The investment would be profitable if it did the work of half a dozen people opening letters manually at an annual labor cost of greater than $12,884 each.

PRESENT VALUE OF AN ANNUITY— RATE OF RETURN PROBLEMS

Table Example. Equation 3-4b and Table A.4 can also be used to find the effective rate of return on an investment. If Jacksonville Repair Service buys a new microcomputer for $3,790.80, bookkeeping expense will be reduced by $1,000 a year for an estimated 5 years. The problem can be written as:

$$\$3,790.80 = \$1,000 \times PVAI^{5yrs,k}$$

$$PVAI^{5yrs,k} = \$3,790.80/\$1,000 = 3.7908$$

The present value of an annuity of $1 a year for 5 years is 3.7908. Going across the 5-year row of Table A.4, 3.7908 is found at the 10 percent column, so the effective rate of return is 10 percent. If Jacksonville Repair's cost of funds is less than 10 percent, the investment is attractive.

In more general terms, the effective rate of return is the discount rate that leads to a present value of benefits equal to the present value of costs. When the stream of cash flows is complex, it is often necessary to use trial and error to find the rate of return. Fortunately, some calculators and computer programs like Lotus 1-2-3 or Excel have built-in financial functions for solving these otherwise tedious problems. In this case you would use the @IRR or =IRR functions that were illustrated under the "Future Value of an Annuity—Rate of Return Problems" heading earlier in the chapter.

COMPLEX CASH FLOW PROBLEMS |

The problems addressed thus far have been solved by using one equation and one table. Frequently, the equations and tables are used in combination to solve more complex cash flow problems. A complex cash flow is one where the cash flow amounts are not equal and consistent but instead either miss periods or change in amount.

Example. Oakland Chips, which has a 10 percent required return, is considering a new extractor. Because of anticipated start-up delays, cash flow will be $1,000 at the end of each year for years 4 through 20. We could find the present values of the 17 cash flows separately, then add them up. This would, however, be tedious. We can speed the analysis with the following calculation procedure:

$$
\begin{array}{l}
\text{PV of \$1,000 a year for years 1 through 20} = \$1,000 \times 8.5136 = \$8,513.60 \\
\underline{- \text{ PV of \$1,000 a year for years 1 through } 3 = \$1,000 \times 2.4869 = 2,486.90} \\
= \text{ PV of \$1,000 a year for years 4 through 20} \underline{\$6,026.70}
\end{array}
$$

This same solution procedure can then be written as:

$$
\text{PV} = \$1,000(8.5136 - 2.4869) = \underline{\$6,026.70}
$$

Spreadsheet Example. When there are unequal amounts like the Oakland Chips problem, the benefits of using the computer really become evident. To solve this problem with the computer, you would set up the following spreadsheet:

	A	B	C	D	....	T
1	0	0	0	1,000	....	1,000
2	@NPV(.1,A1..T1)		=NPV(.1,A1..T1)			

Note that zeros need to be entered in the first three columns to tell the computer that the cash flow will not start until the end of the fourth year. After you press ENTER the computer will return the answer of $6,026.71.

Example. Fairbanks Partners are considering the purchase of a small retail outlet. The outlet will cost $100,000, and $50,000 will be spent in the next year to make the outlet serviceable. After that, cash inflows will be $25,000 a year, and the outlet can be sold in 10 years for an estimated $80,000. The cash flows are summarized as follows:

Year	0	1	2 through 10	10
Cash flow	−$100,000	−$50,000	$25,000 a year	$80,000

The firm can evaluate this investment by subtracting the present values of the outflows from the present values of the benefits to provide a *net present value*. At a 10 percent required return, the net present value is:

Year	Cash Flow	Present Value of $1 Factor (10%)	Present Value
0 (now)	−$100,000	1.0000	−$100,000
1	− 50,000	.9091	− 45,455
2−10	25,000	(6.1446−.9091)	130,888
10	80,000	0.3855	30,840
		Net Present Value	$16,273

Since the net present value is positive in this case, the present value of the benefits is greater than the present value of the costs and the initial outlay. Thus, the investment is attractive.

Example. As another example dealing with a complex pattern of cash flows, assume a rental property in Stockton can be purchased for $40,000. The property will generate cash flows of $8,000 at the end of each year for 7 years, before equipment replacement. A new $6,000 furnace will be needed at the end of 5 years, and the building will be worth an estimated $50,000 at the end of 7 years. If you can invest elsewhere at 10 percent, the present value of the cash flows is as follows:

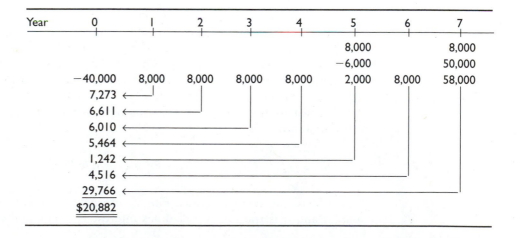

An alternate solution form is as follows:

Year	Cash Flow	Present Value Factor	Present Value
0	−40,000	1.0000	−40,000
1–7	8,000	4.8684	38,947
5	−6,000	0.6209	−3,725
7	50,000	0.5132	25,660
			$20,882

COMPOUNDING MORE THAN ONCE PER PERIOD |

This chapter was introduced with an example in which a year's interest was added to a savings account at the end of each year. However, your bank probably adds interest earned on a monthly or even daily basis. Most bonds pay interest twice a year instead of once a year, and interest on the typical loan to an individual, whether a credit card loan or a mortgage loan, is charged on a monthly basis. Many capital investments provide benefits on a daily or weekly basis rather than in annual lump sums. This section covers the extensions needed to get accurate answers in these situations.

If a savings account pays 10 percent interest, with interest compounded annually, a $100 deposit will grow to $110 by the end of one year. If semiannual compounding is used, the account will pay 5 percent interest in each six-month period. The amount in the account after one year will be:

$$\$100 \times (1.05)^2 = \underline{\$110.25}$$

The account effectively grows at a rate of 10.25 percent a year rather than at 10 percent a year because of the semiannual compounding. The annual rate before considering the effect of compounding more than once per period (10 percent in this case) is called the *nominal* interest rate; in lending circles it is called the *annual percentage rate* (APR). The effective annual growth rate with compounding more than once per period considered (10.25 percent in this case) is called the *effective* interest rate.

The situation with compounding more than once per period can be generalized as follows:

$$FV_n = PV \times (1 + k'/q)^{nq} \tag{3-5}$$

where k' is the nominal annual rate of return (10 percent in the previous example) and q is the number of times interest is compounded during the year.

The effective annual interest rate (k) with interest compounded q times a year is[5]:

$$k = (1 + k'/q)^q - 1 \qquad \text{(3-6)}$$

Example. Anchorage Service Workers Credit Union pays interest of 10 percent a year, compounded semiannually. A $100 deposit will grow in 3 years to:

$$FV_3 = \$100(1 + .10/2)^{3 \times 2} = \underline{\$134}$$

The effective interest rate is:[6]

$$k = (1 + .10/2)^2 - 1 = \underline{10.25\%}$$

To find the present value or future value of a single amount with compounding more than once a period, Equation 3-1 or 3-2 can be used, with k being the effective interest rate. Alternately, these equations can be used with k'/q as the rate of return and qn as the number of periods.

Spreadsheet Example. To adjust for multiple compounding of interest within a year in the spreadsheet, you simply fill the cells with the semiannual, quarterly, or monthly cash flow and adjust the interest rate within the function to a semiannual, quarterly, or monthly interest rate. For example, the balance outstanding on an 8 percent mortgage requiring a $460 monthly payment for the next 20 years can be calculated by using the @PVAL function and entering @PVAL(460,.08/12,20*12). The computer will return with an answer of $54,994.97. The .08/12 in the function is the annual interest rate divided by 12 months in the year. This works the same way for Excel functions.

Example. The present value of $10,000 to be received in 10 years at a nominal required return of 16 percent a year, compounded quarterly, is:

$$PV = \$10,000[1/(1 + .16/4)^{10 \times 4}] = \$10,000 \times .2083 = \$2,083$$

Alternately, Equation 3-6 can be used to find the effective interest rate of $k = (1 + .16/4)^4 - 1 = 16.986\%$ and the value of k can then be used:

$$PV = \$10,000[1/(1 + .16986)^{10}] = \underline{\$2,083}$$

[5]For a discussion of the importance of recognizing the correct required return in these cases, see Philip A. Horvath, "A Pedagogic Note on Intra-Period Compounding and Discounting," *Financial Review* 20 (February 1985): 116–118.

[6]The bank that advertises the 10.25 percent effective interest rate will not make the same adjustment for loans. A 10 percent mortgage loan with monthly payments and monthly compounding of interest—the standard procedure for mortgage loans—has an effective interest rate of $(1 + .10/12)^{12} - 1 = 10.47$ percent, but a 10 percent rate will be advertised. In other words, financial institutions typically advertise k for their deposit accounts and k' for their loan accounts, calling k the effective interest rate and k' the annual percentage rate (APR).

ALTERNATE PAYMENT PATTERNS |

Payments often occur at some time during the year other than at year-end. It is easy to handle a payment received during the year because the future value of a single payment is found in the same way whether n is a whole number or a fraction. To see that this is true, consider a $100 deposit in a savings account that has semiannual compounding and pays 5 percent each 6-month period. If the money is left on deposit for $3\frac{1}{2}$ years, this is equivalent to a 7-year period at 5 percent a year. The amount in the account at the end of $3\frac{1}{2}$ years is:

$$FV_{3.5} = \$100(1 + .05)^7 = \underline{\$140.71}$$

Note that the effective interest rate for this savings account is $k = (1 + .05)^2 - 1 = 10.25\%$, and that:

$$FV_{3.5} = \$100(1 + .1025)^{3.5} = \underline{\$140.71}$$

Thus, the future value of this single payment could be found with Equation 3-1 even though n was not an integer.

To generalize this concept, we assume that money received any time during the year can be immediately invested as profitably as if it were received at the end of the year. This is probably a reasonable assumption in most cases, because there is nothing magical about year-end that causes superior investment opportunities to become available. Capital investments, for example, are made throughout the year. Stated formally, we *assume that the rate earned during any fraction (1/q) of a year is compounded q times a year*. Given this assumption, the future value of a single payment can be found with Equation 3-1 whether or not n is an integer.[7] It also follows from the justification for Equation 3-2 that the present value of a single payment can also be found with that equation whether or not n is an integer.

Example. The present value of $1,000 to be received in $3\frac{3}{4}$ years, at an effective annual required return of 10 percent, is:

$$PV = \$1,000/(1 + .10)^{3.75} = \underline{\$699.48}$$

For an annuity with payments 1/q of a year before year-end, the present value or future value is found using Equation 3-3a or 3-4a, and then multiplying by $(1 + k)^{1/q}$. At a 10 percent effective required return, for example, the present value of $100 received at the end of each year for 10 years is:

$$PVA_{10} = \$100PVA|_{10yrs,10\%} = \$100 \times 6.1446 = \underline{\$614.46}$$

---

[7] *Proof:* The effective interest rate per fraction (1/q) of a year is $k_q = (1 + k)^{1/q} - 1$. Assume money is left to grow for y + 1/q years at an interest rate of k_q per 1/q of a year. Then, $FV_{y+1/q} = PV(1 + k_q)^{yq+1} = PV(1 + k)^{y+1/q}$. Substituting n for y + 1/q gives us Equation 3-1, with n being an integer or noninteger number.

If payment is received at the end of the third quarter rather than at the end of each year, the present value is $614.46 \times (1 + .10)^{1/4} = \$629.28$.

PAYMENTS SPREAD EVENLY ACROSS THE YEAR

Many payment series are spread over the year, with a payment received at the end of each period of 1/q of a year. The effective interest rate per payment period is:[8]

$$k_q = (1 + k)^{1/q} - 1$$

Present and future value of an annuity procedures can then be carried out as previously explained, recognizing that there are n × q (n times q). payment periods, a required return of k_q per payment period, and a payment each payment period 1/q times the total annual payment. If we receive $1,000 a year for 10 years, divided into equal daily payments, with an effective annual interest rate of 10 percent, Equation 3-4b can be used as follows to find the present value:

$$k_{365} = (1 + .10)^{1/365} - 1 = .000261158$$

$$PVA_{3650} \text{ days} = (\$1,000/365)PVA\,|_{3650\text{days},.0261158\%} = \$6,446.07$$

Example. A management contract for Resorts International had the potential to pay $30 million a year for 10 years. We want to find the present value for year-end payments, midyear payments, and daily payments with a 10 percent required return. The patterns are illustrated graphically as follows. (Numbers in the figure are in $ thousands.)

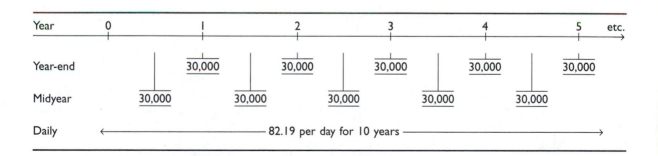

[8]The effective interest rate per period of 1/q of a year is defined as the rate that, when compounded q times a year, gives the same growth rate of money as investing at a rate of k with compounding once a year:

$$(1 + k_q)^q = (1 + k)$$

Rearranging terms gives $k_q = (1 + k)^{1/q} - 1$.

If the payments are received at year-end, the present value is:

$$PVA_{10} = \$30,000,000 PVA|_{10yrs,10\%} = \$30,000,000 \times 6.1446 = \underline{\$184,338,000}$$

If payments are received at midyear, the present value is:

$$PVA_{10} = \$30,000,000 PVA|_{10yrs,10\%}(1 + .10)^{1/2}$$
$$= \$30,000,000(6.1446)(1 + .10)^{1/2} = \underline{\$193,335,325}$$

If payments are spread evenly over the year on a daily basis, the interest rate per day is:

$$k_q = (1 + .10)^{1/365} - 1 = .0261158\%$$

The present value is:

$$PV = (\$30,000,000/365)PVA|_{3650days,.0261158\%} = \underline{\$193,382,189}$$

Note that treating daily cash flows as if they arrived at the end of the year would lead to an error of 4.68 percent in this example, but treating daily cash flows as if they were a midyear lump sum resulted in an error of only 0.02 percent. The similarity of the present value with daily cash flows and midyear lump-sum cash flows follows from the assumption that cash flows arriving anytime during the year can be immediately invested as profitably as if they were received at the end of the year. *To simplify calculations, many companies treat cash flows spread evenly across the year as if they arrive in a lump sum at midyear*[9]. Many of the problems in later chapters use the midyear assumption to approximate the daily cash flows that most businesses experience. It is important to remember that the cash flows are not received at midyear but are instead received daily. We use this shortcut only to approximate the value of daily cash flows without all the columns of work.

Example. Boeing Corporation spent a total of $100 million on its 7J7 jet design over a 3-year period before backing off. Assuming one-third of the $100 million is paid each year, payments are at midyear, and the investment opportunity rate is 10 percent, the compound cost of Boeing's investment at the end of 3 years was:

$$(\$100,000,000/3)(3.310)(1 + .10)^{1/2} = \underline{\$115,718,576}$$

In other words, Boeing would have had $115,718,576 by the end of 3 years if it had invested the money elsewhere at a 10 percent rate of return.

[9] For additional discussion of intraperiod cash flows, see G. A. Fleisher, "Discounting an Intraperiod Cash Flow," *The Engineering Economist* 32 (Fall 1986): 56–58.

PRESENT VALUE OF A NO-GROWTH PERPETUITY |

A perpetuity pays cash each period forever. A bank account is the simplest example: $1,000 left in a 10 percent bank account will earn $100 a year forever if the interest is withdrawn each year rather than reinvested. We can state the annual return on this bank account as an equation:

$$PMT = PV \times k \qquad \text{(3-7)}$$

where PV is the amount deposited in the account and k is the interest rate paid by the bank. To find the present value of a perpetual stream of constant cash flows, then, it is only necessary to rearrange terms:

$$PV = PMT/k \qquad \text{(3-7a)}$$

At a 10 percent required return, the value of $100 at the end of each year forever is:

$$PV = \$100/.10 = \$1,000$$

This makes sense; if $1,000 deposited in a savings account will earn interest of $100 a year forever, there is no reason to pay more than $1,000 for an investment that provides $100 a year forever.

Example. Preferred stock of Duke Power pays an annual dividend of $7.80, or 7.8 percent of the $100 par value. Interest rates in general had fallen by 1998, so investors could earn only 7.46 percent elsewhere in similar investments. Using Equation 3-7a, the present value was then:

$$PV = \$7.80/.0746 = \qquad \underline{\$104.56}$$

If holders of Duke Power's preferred stock wanted to sell their shares in 1998, they could expect to find buyers at a $104.56 price, more than the $100 par value.

PRESENT VALUE OF A CONSTANT-GROWTH PERPETUITY |

A special type of perpetual investment is the investment that provides a constantly growing stream of cash flows. If cash flows will grow at the percentage rate g and PMT_1 represents the cash flow expected at the end of the first period, the value of this perpetual investment is:[10]

$$PV = PMT_1/(k - g) \qquad\qquad (3\text{-}8)$$

Equation 3-8 is called the *constant growth model*. Sometimes it is referred to as the Gordon Model, after the person who popularized it. To avoid misuse of this equation, several points should be stressed. First, note that PMT_1, not PMT_0, is used in the formula. PMT_1 is the payment at the end of the first period. If a payment is due immediately, that payment must be added to the present value found using Equation 3-8. Second, growth of payments must be *perpetual* at the rate of g for the formula to apply. Finally, the constant growth model is derived under the assumption that the growth rate, g, is less than the discount rate, k.

Example. Auburn Corporation's common stock is expected to pay dividends of $4 a share at the end of the first year. Thereafter, dividends are expected to grow at a rate of 5 percent a year forever. The required return is 10 percent. The present value of the dividends is:

$$PV = \$4/(.10 - .05) = \underline{\underline{\$80}}$$

If no future growth in dividends were anticipated, the present value would be:

$$\text{Present Value} = \$4/.10 = \underline{\underline{\$40}}$$

The formulas for finding present values of perpetuities are, of course, not limited to securities. A capital investment that allows the company to move into a new market, for example, may be perceived as having perpetual benefits, either constant or growing.[11] The present value of the perpetual stream of benefits should be compared to the present value of the cash outlays to decide if the venture is attractive.

---

[10]The present value of a constantly growing annuity with a life of n periods is:

$$PV = PMT_1/(1 + k)^1 + PMT_1(1 + g)/(1 + k)^2 + PMT_1(1 + g)^2/(1 + k)^3 + \ldots + PMT_1(1 + g)^{n-1}/(1 + k)^n$$

$$(A)$$

Multiplying both sides of Equation A by $(1 + k)/(1 + g)$ and subtracting Equation A from this new equation yields:

$$PV[(1 + k)/(1 + g) - 1] = PMT_1/(1 + g) - [PMT_1(1 + g)^{n-1}/(1 + k)^n]$$

As the life, n, goes to infinity, the last bracketed expression goes to zero (as long as $k > g$). Rearranging the remaining terms gives Equation 3-8.

[11]In some of these cases, growth may be negative as the product declines in profitability. Suppose, for example, a product will generate cash flows of $100,000 the first year, with cash flows declining 5 percent a year thereafter. The present value at a 10 percent required return will be $V = \$100,000/[.10 - (-.05)] = \$666,667$.

SUMMARY |

Time value of money concepts are the basic tools for evaluating capital invest-ments. These concepts are also useful for dealing with a wide variety of business and personal financial decisions. The basis for all time value analysis is the con-cept of compound growth, which is captured in the future value of a single pay-ment formula:

$$FV_n = PV(1 + k)^n \tag{3-1}$$

where FV_n is the amount to which the present amount PV will grow if invested for n periods at a rate of k per period. The extensions of this formula to various patterns of payments are summarized in Table 3.2.

When interest is compounded more than once a year, the *effective* annual interest rate is:

$$k = (1 + k'/q)^q - 1$$

where k' is the *nominal* annual interest rate (the rate without compounding more than once a period) and q is the number of compounding periods per year.

| **TABLE 3.2** **TIME VALUE FORMULAS**

These formulas serve as convenient tools for applying the basic compound value principles to a broad variety of problems.

Description of Payments	Value Formula	Equation Number
Future value (compound value) of a single payment	$FV_n = PV(1 + k)^n$	(3–1)
Present value of a single payment	$PV = FV_n[1/(1 + k)^n]$	(3–2)
Future value of an annuity[a]	$FVA_n = PMT \times FVAI_{n,k}$	(3–3b)
Present value of annuity[b]	$PVA_n = PMT \times PVAI_{n,k}$	(3–4b)
Present value of a perpetuity	$PV = PMT/k$	(3–7a)
Present value of an amount PMT_1 in period 1, thereafter growing at a rate of g per period	$PV = PMT_1/(k-g)$	(3–8)

$$^aFVAI_{n,k} = \sum_{t=1}^{n}(1+k)^{n-t} = [(1+k)^n - 1]/k$$

$$^bPVAI_{n,k} = \sum_{t=1}^{n}1/(1 + k)^t = [1 - 1/(1 + k)^n]/k$$

QUESTIONS |

3–1. List several personal decision problems for which you or other individuals might use the concepts in this chapter to help you make a decision.

3–2. Why is a dollar received in the future worth less than a dollar received today?

3–3. Define the terms (a) *annuity*, (b) *level annuity*, (c) *annuity due*, (d) *annuity in arrears*, (e) *ordinary annuity*, (f) *annuity in advance*.

3–4. Give an example of a business application for each of the formulas in Table 3.2.

3–5. Give an example of a situation in which you would know the cash flows involved and would want to find the effective rate of return.

3–6. A capital investment requires payment in anticipation of future returns. What are the conditions necessary for a capital investment to be attractive?

3–7. List several examples of investments that would be perpetuities.

3–8. Differentiate between the terms *nominal* interest rate and *effective* interest rate.

PROBLEMS |

(*Note*: You may notice that taxes will affect the net benefits received in some of the following problems. Assume no taxes in working these problems. Taxes will be incorporated in later chapters.)

3–1. The Phoenix Growth Opportunity mutual fund claims to have provided an effective average annual return of 16 percent in recent years. If the fund continues to earn this rate of return, a $10,000 investment will grow to how much in 20 years?

3–2. If the inflation rate continues at 4 percent a year over the next 10 years, a college education that presently costs $14,000 will be expected to cost how much then?

3–3. You purchased a piece of land in Alberta 10 years ago for $20,000 and sold the land today for $74,144. What effective annual rate of return did you earn?

3–4. If you sold the piece of land described in problem 3 for $39,343, what effective annual rate of return would you have earned?

3–5. To replace a piece of machinery, Tuscon Cement will need $100,000 in 10 years. If funds can be invested at an effective return of 12 percent a year, how much must Tuscon Cement invest today to have $100,000 in 10 years?

3–6. A zero-coupon bond pays no interest and simply pays the principal amount at maturity. A 20-year, $1,000 principal amount, zero-coupon bond is currently priced at $258.40. What is the effective annual interest rate?

3–7. An investment will generate the following cash inflows.

Year	0	1	2	3
Cash Inflow	—	$20,000	$40,000	$60,000

At an effective annual required return of 10 percent, what is the present value of these cash flows?

3–8. You decide to invest $2,000 in an Individual Retirement Account at the end of each year for the next 40 years. You will have how much at the end of 40 years if you earn an effective annual return of 10 percent? 12 percent?

3–9. Suppose you decide to invest $2,000 in an Individual Retirement Account at the *beginning* of each year for 40 years. If a 12 percent return is earned, you will have how much at the end of 40 years?

3–10. Flagstaff Fabricating Company will need $100,000 for machinery replacement in 10 years. The treasurer wants to make equal payments at the end of each year into a fund for the purpose of accumulating this amount. If the fund can earn an effective annual return of 10 percent, how much must the company invest each year?

3–11. A $100,000 loan from First State Bank of Poplar Bluff carries an annual percentage rate of 12 percent. It will be paid off through equal year-end installments, including both principal and interest, over a 20-year period. What is the annual payment required?

3–12. What would be the monthly payment if the loan in problem 11 were paid off in monthly installments, with an annual percentage rate of 12 percent and interest compounded monthly?

3–13. Second National Bank of Jonesboro pays a nominal interest rate of 12 percent on deposits. What is the effective interest rate if interest is compounded quarterly? monthly?

3–14. Batesville Manufacturing is considering a capital investment that will provide cash flows of $1,000 a year for 20 years. The payments are spread across the year in daily payments rather than being made at year-end. The effective annual required return is 12 percent. What is the present value of these benefits? What would be the present value of benefits if all cash flows occurred at midyear?

3–15. United Airlines plans to buy 34 airplanes for $120,000,000. Flight operations and ground costs are expected to be $7,000,000 per year and $4,000,000 per year respectively. United expects to sell 300,000 tickets and variable costs are expected to be 20 percent of revenue. With a 14 percent required rate of return, what annual revenue is needed to justify the purchase of the airplanes? (Assume a 20-year life and no salvage value for the airplane at the end of 20 years.)

3–16. You intend to place 10 percent of your salary in a mutual fund at the end of each year for 20 years. Your salary will be $40,000 the first year, and you anticipate average raises of 7 percent a year. If the fund earns an effective annual return of 12 percent, how much will you have at the end of 20 years?

3–17. You are considering the purchase of a rental property for $100,000, with a $20,000 down payment. Cash flows after loan payments will be as follows.

Year	1	2	3	4	5	6	7–10
Cash flow	$2,000	$2,120	$2,240	$2,360	$2,480	$2,600	$2,720

The loan balance will be $70,000 at the end of 10 years. For what price must you sell the property at the end of 10 years to provide an effective annual return of 15 percent on your equity investment? (Assume year-end cash flows.)

3–18. Several salary surveys indicate that accountants who hold the Certified Public Accountant designation earn on the average $7,500 more than their noncertified counterparts. If this certification raises your average salary by $7,500 over your 40-year working life and money costs you 8 percent, how much is this certification worth today? (Assume year-end cash flows.)

3–19. You plan to retire in 40 years and can invest to earn 8 percent. You estimate that you will need $38,000 at the end of each year for an estimated 25 years after retirement, and you expect to earn 8 percent during those retirement years. How much do you need to set aside at the end of each year to accumulate the money necessary for your retirement? (Assume year-end cash flows.)

3–20. You have two options for the purchase of a new car. You can either receive a $2,000 discount off of the $20,000 price, or you can receive 3 percent financing for 5 years. Assume annual, year-end payments and a 12 percent cost of funds. Should you take the 3 percent financing or the $2,000 discount?

3–21. Under the Taxpayers' Relief Act of 1997 individuals are allowed to place $500 per year into an "educational IRA" to be used for college tuition. How much will the average student have accumulated when she enters college after saving in one of these plans for 18 years and earning 12 percent on her investment?

3–22. Currently only 14 percent of the population smokes cigarettes. If smoking cost $10 per week or $520 per year, and this amount were saved and invested at the end of each year for 40 years at 8 percent, how much would the individual have accumulated at the end of 40 years?

3–23. In 1998 the national debt of the United States stood at approximately $5.2 trillion. If this debt is allowed to grow at a rate of 3 percent annually for 30 years, how much will be owed in 2028?

3–24. If a college education cost $80,000 and money can be invested to earn 12 percent, how much does the annual salary for a college graduate have to exceed that of a high school graduate for the college education to be financially feasible? (Assume a 40-year working life.)

3–25. (Application) It was reported in *The Wall Street Journal* that 307 companies out of 366 surveyed by Goldman Sachs & Company were using a discount rate of 8 percent or more to calculate their pension obligations. They were assuming that the funds in their plans would earn 8 percent or better even though the market rate at this time on long-term high-grade corporate bonds was roughly 7 percent. Several *Fortune* 100 companies were using a 9 percent rate. Assume for simplicity that you have $600,000,000 in your pension plan and have estimated your pension obligation to be $40,000,000 per year for the first 10 years and to be $60,000,000 per year for the next 40 years. Is your pension fund over- or underfunded at a 7 percent interest rate? an 8 percent interest rate? a 9 percent interest rate? (Assume year-end cash flows.)

3–26. (Ethical considerations) Please reread problem 3-25. Assume that you are the president of one of these companies, and you are using a 9 percent rate. As a result, you have a pension surplus and are contributing income to the income statement each year. In reality you have not "locked in" this 9 percent rate and will more likely "roll" into a 7 percent rate as current securities mature. This will cause your company to move into a position where an unfunded pension liability will exist, and income will be reduced to accrue pension expense each year. What is the ethical dilemma? Do you think that in the absence of the Securities and Exchange Commission's recommendation, companies would move to the lower rate? What would you do?

A p p e n d i x   3 - A

CONTINUOUS COMPOUNDING |

For many capital investments, the cash flows come in continuously over the year rather than in a lump sum. While it is often assumed, for simplicity, that the cash flows occur once a year, a more precise approach is to actually recognize the continuous nature of the flows. Also, the values of cash flows that occur at frequent intervals, such as daily, can be closely approximated using continuous compounding.

Future Value of a Single Payment |

Continuous compounding is the extreme special case of compounding more than once a period. Recall from Equation 3-5 that the compound growth formula with compounding more than once a period is:

$$FV_n = PV \times (1 + k'/q)^{nq} \qquad \text{(3-5)}$$

where FV_n is the amount to which a present amount PV will grow in n periods if invested at a nominal interest rate of k' per period, with interest compounded q times per period. If compounding was on a daily basis, q would be 365. If compounding was on a continual basis, q would be infinity. You can confirm with any elementary calculus text that:

$$\lim_{q \to \infty} (1 + k'/q)^{nq} = e^{k'n} \qquad \text{(3-A-1)}$$

where e is the base of the system of natural or Napierian logarithms: 2.7183. . . . .. The future value of a single payment with continuous compounding is therefore:

$$FV_n = PV \times e^{k'n} \qquad \text{(3-A-2)}$$

Values of $e^{k'n}$ appear in Table A.5. With continuous compounding, the effective interest rate is:

$$k = e^{k'} - 1 \qquad \text{(3-A-3)}$$

and

$$k' = \ln(1 + k) \qquad \text{(3-A-3a)}$$

where $\ln(\cdot)$ refers to the natural logarithm.

As an example, a 10 percent nominal interest rate with continuous compounding is an effective interest rate of $e^{.10} - 1 = 10.52$ percent. An investment of \$1,000 at a 10 percent nominal interest rate with continuous compounding will grow in 5 years to:

$$FV_5 = \$1,000 \; e^{.10 \times 5} = \$1,000 \times 1.6487 = \underline{\$1,648.70}$$

Table A.5 was used to find $e^{.10 \times 5}$. These problems can also be solved with a pocket calculator that has a built-in function for finding e raised to any power. Computer programs like Lotus 1-2-3 also have built-in functions for this purpose.

To see the closeness of daily compounding to continuous compounding, note the amount to which \$1,000 will grow with various compounding schemes if invested at 10 percent a year for 5 years:

	Amount	Difference from Continuous Compounding
Continuous compounding	$1,648.70	NA
Daily compounding	$1,648.60	$ .10
Annual compounding	$1,610.50	38.20

Because of the similarity between daily and continuous compounding, continuous compounding often serves as a convenient approximation. Continuous compounding is also used in the development of theoretical models because the resulting integrals are easier to manipulate than the sums that result with discrete compounding.

PRESENT VALUE OF A SINGLE PAYMENT

The present value of a future payment with continuous compounding is found by rearranging terms in Equation 3-A-2:

$$PV = FV_n/e^{k'n} \tag{3-A-4}$$

Example. Your deferred compensation plan will pay you $1,000 in 5 years. The required return is a nominal 10 percent a year, with daily compounding. Continuous compounding is used as a convenient approximation:

$$PV = \$1,000/e^{.10 \times 5} = \$1,000/1.6487 = \underline{\$606.54}$$

The value 1.6487 was found in Table A.5, at the 5-year row and 10 percent column; it could have been computed directly with a calculator.

FUTURE VALUE OF AN ANNUITY

The future value of a series of continuous payments, continuously compounded, can be stated as an extension of Equation 3-A-2 in the form of the integral:

$$FVA_n = \int_{t=0}^{n} a_t e^{k9t} \, dt \tag{3-A-5}$$

where a_t is the amount received instantaneously at time t. This integral is analogous to the future value of a discrete payment annuity in Equation 3-3. The future value of continuous flows can also be found by rewriting Equation 3-3a for the continuous case. The future value of an annuity of PMT/q at the end of each 1/q of a period for n periods can be written by substituting PMT/q for PMT, k'/q for k, and nq for n in Equation 3-3a:

$$FVA_n = (PMT/q)[(1 + k'/q)^{nq} - 1]/(k'/q)$$

Substituting into this equation for the value of $(1 + k'/q)^{nq}$ as q approaches infinity—see Equation 3-A-1—and rearranging terms yields:

$$FVA_n = PMT[e^{k'n} - 1]/k' \qquad \text{(3-A-6)}$$

Example. You decide to invest $10,000 a year for 20 years in a bond mutual fund, with payments spread continuously over the year. The money is expected to earn an effective annual interest rate of 10.517 percent. With continuous compounding, k' is therefore $\ln(1 + .10517) = 10$ percent. The future value of the annuity is:

$$FVA_{20} = \$10,000[e^{.10 \times 20} - 1]/.10$$

$$= \$10,000[7.3891 - 1]/.10 = \$638,910$$

The value 7.3891 is the 20-year, 10 percent value from Table A.5.

PRESENT VALUE OF AN ANNUITY |

The present value of a continuous stream, with interest continuously compounded, is commonly stated as an extension of Equation 3-A-4 in the form of the integral:

$$PVA_n = \int_{t=0}^{n} a_t/e^{k9t}\, dt \qquad \text{(3-A-7)}$$

where a_t is the amount received instantaneously at time t. The present value of a continuous stream of payments can also be found by rewriting Equation 3-4a for the continuous case, substituting PMT/q for PMT, k'/q for k, and nq for n:

$$PVA_n = (PMT/q)[1 - 1/(1 + k'/q)^{nq}]/(k'/q)$$

Substituting into this equation for the value of $(1 + k'/q)^{nq}$ as q approaches infinity—see Equation 3-A-1—and rearranging terms yields:

$$PVA_n = PMT[1 - 1/e^{k'n}]/k' \qquad \text{(3-A-8)}$$

This formula can be applied with a calculator that has a function for raising e to a power, or by looking up $e^{k'n}$ in Table A.5 and then using the formula.

Example. Searcy Hat Company is considering a building expansion that will provide cash flows of $100,000 a year, arriving continuously over the year, for 20 years. At the end of the 20-year period, the investment can be sold for $200,000. The effective required return is 10.517 percent a year, and k′ is therefore ln(1 + .10517) = 10 percent. Using Table A.5, the present value of the benefits is:

$$PV = \$100,000[1 - 1/e^{.10 \times 20}]/.10 + \$200,000/e^{.10 \times 20}$$

$$= \$100,000[1 - 1/7.3891]/.10 + \$200,000/7.3891 = \$891,732$$

The value 7.3891 is from the intersection of the 20-year row and 10 percent column of Table A.5.

Continuous compounding is frequently used for theoretical analysis because it is easy to use for mathematical derivations. In practical application, continuous compounding is a convenient tool when cash flows occur continuously over the year or when very frequent compounding periods, such as daily compounding, are used.

PROBLEMS |

3–A–1. A $1,000 investment will earn a return of 16 percent a year. How much will the investment grow to in 10 years if interest is compounded annually? quarterly? continuously?

3–A–2. Talladega National Bank is advertising that its savings accounts have continuous compounding for an effective annual interest rate of 12.75 percent. What is the nominal interest rate?

3–A–3. A payment of $1,000 is to be received in 20 years. What is the present value at a 12 percent return compounded annually? quarterly? continuously?

3–A–4. A sum of $10,000 is to be invested at the end of each year into an investment account that earns a return of 10 percent a year, compounded continuously. What is the *effective* interest rate? What will be the amount in the account at the end of 20 years?

3–A–5. Tempe Electric is considering a capital investment that will provide cash benefits of $20,000 a year for 10 years, with cash flows being continuous over the year. The required return is 14 percent, compounded continuously. What is the *effective* required return? What is the present value of the cash flows?

3–A–6. A capital investment will provide cash benefits of $100,000 a year for 20 years. The effective required return is 12 percent (k = 12 percent).
   a. What is the present value if the cash flows are received at the end of each year?
   b. What is the present value if the annual cash flows are divided into four equal payments, one at the end of each quarter?
   c. What is the present value if the cash flows arrive continuously over the year?

SELECTED REFERENCES |

Fleisher, G. A. "Discounting an Intraperiod Cash Flow." *The Engineering Economist* 32 (Fall 1986): 56–58.

Glasco, P. W., W. J. Landes, and A. F. Thompson. "Bank Discount, Coupon Equivalent, and Compound Yields." *Financial Management* 11 (Autumn 1982): 80–84.

Horvath, Philip A. "A Pedagogic Note on Intra-Period Compounding and Discounting." *Financial Review* 20 (February 1985): 116–118.

Linke, Charles M., and J. Kenton Zumwalt. "The Irrelevance of Compounding Frequency in Determining a Utility's Cost of Equity." *Financial Management* 16 (Autumn 1987): 65–69.

CHAPTER 4 |

VALUE-DRIVEN MANAGEMENT

After completing this chapter you should be able to:

1. Explain how arbitrage works to ensure that the prices of financial claims are equal to the present value of the expected future cash flows.
2. Differentiate between value and price.
3. Value bonds.
4. Know the different yield terminology.
5. Value stock using a constant growth model.
6. Describe the variables important to the market when valuing stock.
7. Discuss the shortcomings of assuming constant growth and some of the ways used in practice to overcome these shortcomings.
8. Define what factors the market values and what ones it does not value.
9. Explain the relationship between the intrinsic value of the stock and the market price.
10. Explain how purchasing power parity and interest rate parity explain currency values.

When Michael Eisner earned over $250 million in his first six years as CEO of Disney, there were cries of outrage and numerous claims that something had gone wrong in the world of finance. Before reaching your own judgment, you might want to think for a moment about how he earned the money. The company was in trouble when he was hired as CEO in 1984, and his compensation agreement was mostly in the form of stock options. He would do well only if the price of Disney stock improved. During the six-year term of his initial contract, the price of Disney stock increased from $14 to $102 a share. The shareholders gained $12 billion, so Eisner's compensation was 2 percent of the shareholders' wealth gain.[1] Furthermore, he set the stage for additional growth, which resulted in the share price rising to $125 in 1998, *after* a stock split which gave shareholders four shares for each share previously held. Eisner apparently earned his money by doing what he was supposed to do, create wealth.

---

[1]For a more detailed discussion, see Stephen O'Byrne, "What Pay for Performance Looks Like: The Case of Michael Eisner," *Journal of Applied Corporate Finance* 5 (Summer 1992): 135–136.

Knowing the source of Eisner's fortune, you might also want to know why a stock purchase of $14 in 1984 grew to $500 by 1998. In this chapter, we will focus on the determinants of asset value and wealth creation, taking a look at Disney stock in particular. The general principle of asset value and wealth creation is that we create wealth by acquiring assets that have values in excess of their costs. The general answer as to how we can acquire such assets is *competitive advantage*. This chapter uses the arbitrage pricing principle to tie together the concepts of competitive advantage and time value, thereby providing an understanding of how value is created in general, and how capital investments or capital investment opportunities, in particular, contribute to wealth. This chapter completes the foundation for an analysis of specific capital investments, which begins in Chapter 5.

ARBITRAGE VALUATION |

In Chapter 3, we found the present values of numerous patterns of cash flows. The present value is essentially an application of the arbitrage pricing principle. *Arbitrage* is the process of increasing benefits without increasing cost or risk by taking advantage of market imperfections. The *arbitrage pricing principle* states that identical streams of cash flows will have identical prices. The basic argument for the arbitrage pricing principle is that buying and selling pressures from people trying to take advantage of arbitrage opportunities will immediately eliminate any differences in the prices of identical streams of cash flows.

To see how the arbitrage pricing principle works, we look at asset types A and B, each of which provide identical streams of future benefits. If asset type A is for sale at a price of $1,000, there is no incentive to pay more than $1,000 for asset B. Thus, holders of B cannot sell unless they reduce their price to equal that of A. If B is offered at a price below $1,000, all holders of A will attempt to sell so that they can buy B. Of course, no rational person will buy A, so the prices of the two assets will be forced back to equality.

We can extend the arbitrage principle to the case in which B and C together provide future benefits equal to what A provides alone. The arbitrage pricing principle requires that the sum of the prices of B and C equals the price of A. Otherwise, the previously described arbitrage attempts will drive the prices back into equilibrium. This extension of the arbitrage pricing principle is simply another way of saying that the sum of the parts equals the whole. The conclusion that identical sets of benefits sell for identical prices is sometimes called the *law of conservation of value*.

Example. Investments X, Y, and Z have the following year-end cash flows:

	Year 1	Year 2
X	$100.00	$200.00
Y	$100.00	0
Z	0	$200.00

A savings account pays an effective annual interest rate of 10 percent. Therefore, the amount that must be deposited in the savings account now in order to withdraw $100 in 1 year is:

$$PV = \$100/(1 + .10) = \$90.91$$

The arbitrage pricing principle will lead to a price of $90.91 for asset Y. The amount that must be deposited in order to withdraw $200 in 2 years is:

$$PV = \$200/(1 + .10)^2 = \$165.29$$

Therefore, the arbitrage pricing principle will lead to a price of $165.29 for asset Z. Since X provides cash flows equal to those of Y and Z combined, the arbitrage pricing principle requires that its price be $90.91 + $165.29 = $256.20. If the price of one of the three assets changes while the other two remain constant, an arbitrage opportunity exists, and attempts to take advantage of that opportunity will quickly drive the prices back into equilibrium.

To generalize, the fundamental valuation principle that follows from the previous discussion is that the value of any asset is the present value of future cash flows to and from the owner of that asset:

$$Value = \sum_{t=0} CF_t/(1 + k)^t \qquad (4-1)$$

where CF_t is cash flow in period t, and k is the rate of return that could be expected from opportunities of equal risk. Throughout the book, we will apply this formula to the valuation of bonds, stocks, companies, and capital investment opportunities.

For arbitrage pricing pressures to be completely effective, it is necessary that financial markets meet specific standards of perfection. As discussed in Chapter 2, a financial market is defined as perfect if

- there are no taxes, transaction costs, or other restrictions keeping buyers and sellers from entering or exiting the market;
- no one buyer or seller is large enough to affect price through any action;
- identical information is costlessly available to everyone, resulting in identical beliefs; and
- all participants are rational wealth maximizers.

If the financial markets are perfect, they will also be *informationally efficient*, which means that prices reflect all available information. It may be possible for the markets to be informationally efficient without being perfect, though.

Perfection is, of course, an unattainable ideal. Transaction costs exist in even the most sophisticated financial markets, and the cost of a *Wall Street Journal* means that information is not free. Distortions are, however, relatively small compared to those in other markets, such as those for real estate, used cars, and

Persian rugs. Thus, we can reasonably expect actual prices to be quite close to those predicted from arbitrage pricing principles.

The fundamental arbitrage pricing principle is that identical sets of benefits have identical values. How can we reconcile this principle with the goal of wealth creation? The answer is that we want to acquire assets for which value exceeds cost. Competitive advantage allows us to acquire assets for which value exceeds cost. The cost of a new airplane is the same for a profitable and an unprofitable airline, but the stream of benefits has a higher value for the profitable airline, which is exploiting its competitive advantage.

Valuation based on arbitrage principles and returns available from alternate investments will be used extensively in this book to evaluate capital investments and to estimate required returns. Many capital investments are not traded independently in the markets, so we cannot always observe price. We can, though, use *arbitrage valuation*, which is the application of arbitrage pricing principles, to estimate the price of a set of benefits, as if that set were for sale. The concept can also be applied to the valuation of securities and perpetuities, as illustrated in this chapter.

VALUE AND PRICE

Much of the confusion and debate in the area of valuation, as in so many other endeavors, comes from failure to agree on definitions. We hear one person talking about value, a second person talking about intrinsic value, and a third person talking about fair value. We may also hear someone talking about price, bid price, or fair price. What does all this mean?

Price refers to an amount of money per unit, pound, liter, or some other form of measure at which someone buys, or is willing to buy or sell. In a perfect market, there is a single price at which one can buy or sell. In an imperfect market, there may be both bid and ask prices. *Bid price* is the price at which someone offers to buy, and *ask price* is the price at which someone offers to sell. The highest bid and lowest ask prices are frequently posted in securities markets, along with the price paid in the most recent transaction.

Price without a qualifier often means the price agreed to in the last transaction. Alternately, price without a qualifier may also mean either the single price in a perfect market or an estimate of what the single price would be if the market were perfect. However, we are frequently forced to rely on context to discern the exact meaning. When the shoe store advertises a price of $49.95, for example, we know that it is actually publishing its ask price. If the shoes are not sold, the store will eventually reduce its ask price until buyers are found.

Value is used to mean the price at which an item would be bought and sold in a market that is perfect (or perfect except for taxes), based on the information set currently available to investors. The value of a company to the stockholders is the value of a single share of stock, multiplied by the number of shares. Real estate appraisers attempt to estimate the "price to which a willing buyer and willing seller would agree." Analysts tracking the values of stock may use prices from actual transactions, bid prices, or an average of bid and ask prices as their estimate of value. Value is an important concept in capital budgeting because the present value of a future cash flow is our estimate of the price at which the claim to that cash future flow would sell if it were being bought and sold in perfect financial markets, or at least informationally efficient markets.

Because value depends on some information set, we sometimes want to estimate the impact of additional information. *Intrinsic value* is the value that would exist if all potential investors had the same information that was available to the person determining the intrinsic value. We can estimate intrinsic value, but we can never observe it. The net present value of a capital investment is the amount by which it would increase the value of the company if investors shared management's information set. If shareholders do not have or do not believe management's information, stock price may not increase to that intrinsic value immediately in response to a positive net present value capital investment. We would expect though, that stock price would converge with intrinsic value as time passes and investors become convinced of the benefits of the new capital investments.

Although the terms *fair price* and *fair value* are frequently bandied about, their meaning is unclear. These terms seem to follow from a belief that moral principles, rather than supply and demand, should be used to set prices. Unfortunately, we lack general principles to use in determining a price that is fair to buyer and seller, and we lack market mechanisms that would assure adequate, but not excess, supplies to meet demand at the so-called fair price. Attempts to determine a *fair price* often occur when it is believed that markets are not working well, and the *fair price* is usually an estimate of what the price would be in a competitive market. The main problem with the determination of a fair price is that fair depends on the perspective of the decision maker. Food is a good example. Many farmers argue that the price is unfairly low, so that they cannot give their families a decent living, while advocates for the poor may argue that prices are too high, so that people cannot afford to eat.

VALUE OF BONDS

A bond is simply an IOU issued by a business, a nonprofit organization, or a government. Bonds are typically in $1,000 denominations, so they break the debt of the organization into small pieces. This allows the organization to attract a wide variety of investors. The bond provides a promise to pay a fixed interest payment on the $1,000 face value, and a promise to repay the face value at the maturity date specified in the bond contract.

Because there are markets in which bonds can be bought and sold, bondholders do not necessarily have to wait until the bonds mature to get their money back. The price received by an investor wanting to sell a bond may not be $1,000, though. The price the investor can get will be the *present value* of the interest payments and the principal payment. The price may be above or below $1,000, depending on whether interest rates on alternative investments of similar risk and maturity are above or below the interest rate on the bond.

Example. IBM bonds maturing in 2013 pay annual interest of 7.5 percent of face value. Like most bonds, IBM's bonds pay half the annual interest each 6 months, so the interest payment is $37.50 (.075 × $1,000/2) each 6 months until 2013. In 1998, you could earn 3.287 percent on your money each 6 months by buying other bonds of equal risk. The price you could expect to receive for an IBM bond would be the present value of $37.50 each 6 months for 15 years, plus the $1,000 face value in 15 years:

$$PV = \$37.50PVA|_{30periods, 3.287\%} + \$1,000/1.03287^{30}$$

$$= (\$37.50 \times 18.89321) + (\$1,000 \times .37901) = \underline{\$1,087.50}$$

Lotus/Excel Example. Using Lotus to solve the IBM problem, you would set up the following spreadsheet:

	A	B	C	D	....	T
1	37.50	37.50	37.50	37.50	....	1037.50
2	@NPV(.03287,A1..AD1)					

Using Excel, the formula in cell A2 is = NPV(.03287,A1:AD1). After typing the formula in cell A2, press ENTER, and the computer will return the answer $1,087.50.

The *yield to maturity* is the interest rate that would be earned by a bond-holder who bought the bond at the current price and held it until maturity. The yield to maturity is the discount rate that causes the present value of the future payments to equal the price. At a price of $1,087.50 in 1998, the yield to maturity of the IBM bonds would have been 3.287 percent each 6 months.

Suppose the IBM bonds were selling at $1,000 or $1,147. The yield to maturity would have been 3.75 percent or 3.00 percent semiannually, respectively:

$$PV = \$37.50PVA|_{30periods, 3.75\%} + \$1,000/1.0375^{30} = \$1,000$$

$$PV = \$37.50PVA|_{30periods, 3.00\%} + \$1,000/1.03^{30} = \$1,147$$

Suppose the IBM bonds were selling at $1,000, so that they provided a yield to maturity of 3.75 percent each 6 months, when the yield to maturity for other bonds of similar risk was 3.287 percent. Bond investors would want to buy IBM bonds so that they could earn 3.75 percent instead of the 3.287 percent they were earning with other investments, but nobody would want to sell when alternative investments pay less. The only price at which both buyers and sellers could be found is the price that gives the buyer a yield to maturity equal to the

interest rates available on other investments. Thus, the arbitrage pricing principle leads to a bond value of $1,087.50.[2]

A similar price adjustment situation would occur if IBM bonds were selling
at $1,130. All holders of IBM bonds would want to sell them at $1,130, because
they could invest the money to earn 3.287 percent somewhere else, but nobody
would want to buy. Again, the equilibrium price would be $1,087.50.

INSTITUTIONAL DETAILS OF BONDS VALUATION

If you were to check the IBM bond in the newspaper, you would see a price of
108 3/4 and a yield to maturity of 6.57 percent. Neither number looks consistent with our discussion of IBM. The discrepancies are not real, but simply arise
from the customary methods of reporting bond prices and yields. The price is
quoted as a percent of the face value, so 108 3/4 percent of $1,000 is $1,087.50.

We know from our study of alternative compounding periods in Chapter 3
that 3.287 percent each 6 months is an effective annual interest rate of:

$$\text{Effective annual interest rate} = (1 + .03287)^2 - 1 = 6.682\%$$

However, it is customary to state bond yield to maturity by simply doubling the
6-month yield. Furthermore, the yield is rounded to the nearest hundredth of a
percent, so 3.287 percent is doubled and rounded, to become 6.57 percent. The
quotation method does not change the facts, though. Banks advertise both an
annual interest rate and an effective annual interest rate on savings accounts. If
bond yields were published the same way, this bond would have a yield to maturity of 6.574 percent and an effective yield to maturity of 6.682 percent.

Bond prices also are affected by the time until the next interest payment.
The calculations shown here assume it is 6 months until the next payment. The
general principles of time value analysis would cause a bond to be worth more
if the next interest payment were closer. If the next interest payment for the IBM
bond is only 4 months away, all payments are moved closer by a third of a
6-month period, so the value increases to $1,087.5(1.03287)^{1/3} = $1,099.29.[3]

SOME ALTERNATIVE YIELD DEFINITIONS

As long as we are looking at customs, we should note also that several different
interest rates are sometimes quoted, and it is important to be sure you know
which is which:

[2]The price of $1,087.50 depends on IBM bonds being an extremely small proportion of total
bonds outstanding. The equilibrium adjustment process would include attempts to buy IBM bonds
and sell other bonds. Increased supply and decreased demand for other bonds would drive their
prices down and consequently their yields up, so that the eventual equilibrium would result, with
all bonds reaching the same equilibrium yield, somewhere between 3.50 percent and 3.75 percent.
IBM bonds are, of course, an extremely small percentage of all debt, so the only *measurable* adjustment would probably be in the IBM bond price.

[3]The price quoted in the newspaper will be lower because the buyer pays that price *plus* accrued
interest. For a more detailed discussion, see Marcia Stigum, *Money Market Calculations: Yields,
Break-Evens, and Arbitrage.* (Homewood IL: Dow Jones-Irwin) 1981.

Yield to maturity: interest rate that would be earned by a bondholder who bought the bond at the current price and held it until maturity; discount rate that causes the present value of the future payments to equal the current price.

Coupon rate: annual interest payment divided by face value ($75.00/$1,000 = 7.50 percent for IBM).

Current yield: annual interest payment divided by current price ($75.00/$1,087.50 = 6.897 percent for IBM).

Yield to call: interest rate that would be earned by a bondholder who bought the bond at the current price and held it until it was called. Many companies issuing bonds retain for themselves an option to call the bonds (buy them back from the investors) prior to maturity, typically by paying a predetermined call price that is in excess of the $1,000 face value. The yield to call is computed the same as the yield to maturity, except the time is changed to be the time until the bond can be called, and the $1,000 face value is replaced with the call price. The IBM bond is not callable.

In perfect markets, the value of the bond equals the price and also equals the present value of future payments. Intrinsic value could be different, though. If the manager has inside information that IBM will go bankrupt tomorrow morning and pay nothing to the bondholders, the manager knows that the intrinsic value of a bond is $0. The market value will equal the intrinsic value as soon as everyone else learns of the bankruptcy.[4]

If you follow bond prices, you will see that they fluctuate from day to day. Consequently, people who buy bonds and then sell them a few months later may experience large gains or losses. These fluctuations are a confirmation, not a violation, of our value principles. General interest rates change on a daily basis, so rates of return on alternative investments change continually. Arbitrage valuation principles require that the values of bonds change so that they provide yields to maturity that are the same as the returns available on similar investments. Speculators make or lose large amounts of money by guessing correctly or incorrectly the direction of general interest rate movements.

VALUE OF STOCK

While bond values are straightforward enough, stock values are often viewed as almost mystical. Experts, either self-designated or recognized for their *recent* track records, are referred to as *seers, magicians, gnomes,* and *elves.* They seem to imply that they have dimensions of insight that cannot be transcended by mere mortals. They need to convey this impression in order to earn a living, but fortunately, it is not true.

---

[4]If the bankruptcy were not so immediate there would be an ethical dilemma for the manager. He/she could collect his/her salary as long as the truth is withheld from the market but, at the same time, may be violating his/her fiduciary duty to the shareholders by withholding the truth.

The principles of stock valuation are the same as those for bonds; both have value because they provide future cash flows. The main complication is that future cash flows from stocks are often more difficult to predict than those for bonds. For bonds, the cash flows are principal and interest payments. For stocks, the cash flows are dividends. Unless the company is acquired or liquidated, we do not expect it to distribute anything besides dividends and glossy annual reports to its shareholders. Thus the typical stock purchaser is buying the expectation of a future stream of dividend payments. The practical difficulty is that future dividends are difficult to predict, but the general principles are easy enough to grasp. The general value formula for a share of stock is an application of Equation 4-1:

$$\text{Stock value} = \sum_{t=1} D_t/(1 + k)^t \qquad \text{(4-2)}$$

where D_t is the dividend in period t, and k is the return that could be expected from alternative opportunities of equal risk.

If dividends will remain constant in all future periods, the value of common stock is determined as is the present value of any perpetuity:

$$\text{Stock value} = D/K \qquad \text{(4-3)}$$

where D is the annual dividend.

We sometimes assume, as a convenient approximation, that dividends will grow forever at a constant rate. In those cases, the formula for constantly growing cash flows (developed in Chapter 3) can be used:

$$\text{Stock value} = D_1/(k - g) \qquad \text{(4-4)}$$

where D_1 is the expected dividend at the end of period 1, and g is the expected growth rate of dividends thereafter.

Preferred stock provides the simplest illustration of stock valuation. Most preferred stock pays a specified annual dividend to the shareholders and has no maturity. It is, therefore, a promise to pay the dividend forever. If the preferred stock of Allied Power pays an annual dividend of $1.70, and investments of similar risk pay an expected return of 6.77 percent, the value of the preferred stock is:

$$\text{Value of Allied Power preferred stock} = \text{Dividend}/k = \$1.70/.0677 = \$25.11$$

Valuation of common stock is more complicated than valuation of preferred, only because it is more difficult to forecast dividends. Stockholders do not receive a specific promise of dividends, but receive dividends that depend on the success of the company.

Returning to the stock of Disney, the price was $125 a share in 1998. Dividends were forecast to be $0.70 a share in 1999. Assuming that investors could expect 15 percent elsewhere in opportunities of equal risk, we will discuss how that opportunity rate estimate was made in Chapter 16. They are certainly not buying this stock with the expectation of receiving $0.70 a year forever, which is less than 1 percent of share price. They are expecting future growth of dividends. With 15 percent required return, 14.44 percent growth is required to justify a $125 price:[5]

$$\text{Value} = D_1/(k - g)$$

$$\$125 = \$0.70/(.15 - .1444)$$

What about investors who expect to sell their stock for capital gains? Valuation is no different for an investor who expects to sell stock for a capital gain than for an investor expecting to hold it forever and receive dividends. The present value of Disney's anticipated dividends over the next 5 years was only about $3.00, so $122 of the $125 price was for dividends more than 5 years in the future. At a 15 percent compound rate of return, money slightly more than doubles in 5 years, so the stock price in 5 years must be slightly more than double the $122, or $245, if investors are to earn a 15 percent rate of return. How could the price go to $245? Assuming a 14.44 percent growth in dividends, the dividend will grow from $0.70 at the end of year 1 to $1.37 at the end of year 6:

$$D_6 = D_1(1 + g)^5 = \$.70(1 + .1444)^5 = \$1.37$$

The price of the stock at the end of year 5 will then be:

$$P_5 = \$1.37/(.15 - .1444) = \$245$$

Is the 14.44 percent growth rate believable? Bear in mind that the constant growth model is a handy approximation, but no company maintains the same growth rate forever. Most companies move through a life cycle in which they start out reinvesting most of their earnings, as Disney is doing, and then pay substantial dividends as they reach maturity. Security analysts at that time were forecasting dividends from Disney to grow at annual rates substantially *higher* than 14.44 percent in the near term.

Note that the investor who bought at $125, received 5 years of dividends, and sold at $245, only earned the 15 percent rate that could have been expected elsewhere, because the $125 is the present value of 5 years of dividends, plus $245 in 5 years.[6] Superior returns would occur if the price rose to more than $245 in 5 years, either because dividend forecasts had been revised upward or

---

[5]If you are enthusiastic about details, you might note that the formulation implicitly assumes all dividends are paid out at year-end. You know from your mastery of time value of money that dividends spread over the year would cause the same stock value, with a slightly lower dividend growth rate.

[6]$125 = $0.70/1.15 + ($0.70 × 1.1444)/1.15^2 + ($0.70 × 1.1444^2)/1.15^3 + ($0.70 × 1.1444^3)/1.15^4 + ($0.70 × 1.1444^4)/1.15^5 + $245/1.15^5

the rate that could be earned elsewhere had declined. All you need to do to earn superior returns is forecast more accurately than other investors, so that you can buy stocks that will pay higher future dividends than other investors expect. This means that your predictions of future competitive advantage and resulting cash flows must be more accurate than those of other investors. The minor difficulty is that we cannot all be better, on average, than each other. Even the professional stock analysts have not, as a group, established consistent records of superior performance.

What about companies that do not pay dividends? One problem with the dividend valuation model is that there are hundreds of examples of companies that do not pay any dividends. Reference to Equation 4-2 provides a ready answer to that question. The value of a share of stock is the present value of all future dividends. The fact that dividends are expected to be zero in some years does not change the basic valuation principle. Stockholders are still buying the expectation of future dividends, but the dividends are just farther in the future. Note that the value of a share of Disney stock would have been only $1 less if the company were expected to pay no dividends during the first 5 years, then start with $1.37 in year 6, with a 14.44 percent growth rate thereafter.

Why do stock prices fluctuate from day to day? As summarized in Figure 4.1, a change in stock price must be a result of a change in the present value of future dividends. The present value of future dividends can change either because the expected dividends themselves change or because the required return changes. Expected dividends can change because news about the specific company or the economy in general changes investors' expectations about that company. Discouraging news about Eurodisney attendance, for example, caused investors to lower their forecasts of future dividends. The required return can change either because general interest rates change or because the riskiness of the company changes. Additional news about companies and the economy reaches investors every day.

We are left with several questions. Why would a company pay no dividends at first, then large dividends later? What would cause Disney's dividends to grow? How is an investment analyst to estimate that growth to determine value? The answers to all these questions, and to wealth creation, lie in a company's investment opportunities; that is the next topic.

| **FIGURE 4.1**   **SOURCES OF CHANGE IN STOCK PRICE**

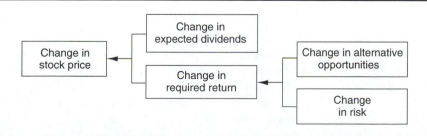

VALUE OF INVESTMENT OPPORTUNITIES

We can look at a company as a set of investments and a set of investment opportunities. The current set of investments provides cash flow, which a wealth-maximizing company will pay out as dividends if it cannot invest at a return at least as high as stockholders could expect from other opportunities of equal risk. In the absence of other investments, the value of the company is the present value of the dividends. If the company has additional investment opportunities, and plans to exploit those opportunities, its value is increased by the present value of those investment opportunities. The value of the company and a share of stock is independent of whether the equity needed for those opportunities will come from retention of earnings or the sale of additional stock.

Example. Suppose, just to make things simple, Delta Corporation has no attractive expansion opportunities, but that it is profitable enough to justify replacement of worn-out assets to maintain its current level of production. Further suppose that the accountants have done a good job in estimating depreciation, so that income is actually the amount left after setting aside enough money to replace assets as they wear out. Then, dividends will equal income. Delta has 100,000 shares of common stock outstanding and does not expect income to change from its current level of $100,000 a year. Dividends will, therefore, be $1.00 a share. If investors could earn 10 percent elsewhere in opportunities of equal risk, the value of a share of stock is:

$$\text{Value} = \$1.00/.10 = \$10.00$$

Let's introduce some good news. Delta suddenly discovers a new opportunity that will give it a competitive advantage. The opportunity will require an additional $50,000 of equity at the end of the year, to earn additional income (available to distribute as dividends) of $10,000 a year thereafter.

The present value of a future opportunity is the present value, today, of the net present value on the future date when the investment will be made. The net present value a year from now will be:

$$\text{NPV} = \$10,000/.10 - \$50,000 = \$50,000$$

The value (today) of the future investment opportunity is then:

$$\text{Present value} = \$50,000/1.10 = \$45,455$$

With 100,000 shares outstanding, this is $0.45 per share, so the investment opportunity increases the value of a share to $10.45.

To confirm the $10.45 value, suppose Delta gets the needed equity by reducing dividends the first year. The dividends and the value of a share of stock are then as follows:

Year	1	2−	Total
Income	$100,000	$110,000	
Dividend per share	$0.50	$1.10	
Present value factor	.9091	9.0909*	
Present value	$0.45	$10.00	$10.45

$$*9.0909 = \frac{(1/.10)}{1.10}$$

The future investment opportunity, therefore, causes the value of a share of stock to increase from $10 a share to $10.45 a share. An increase in the price of the stock despite the fact that dividends will be cut the first year is consistent with the principle that the value of a share of stock is the present value of the expected dividends. The short-term reduction of dividends is more than offset by higher dividends later.

To see that this value gain is independent of how equity is obtained, assume Delta wants to maintain its dividend and sell additional shares at the end of the first year, immediately after the dividend payment, to get the equity needed for the new investment. We must determine the number of new shares to be sold at the end of the year (S_n) to raise $50,000. To find the number of shares, we need the price per share at the end of the year (P_1). To find the price per share, we need to know the dividends per share in year two and beyond (D_{2+}). Assuming investors are informed about the investment opportunity, so that price equals value, we can find these values by solving three simultaneous equations:

$$S_n = \$50,000/P_1$$

$$P_1 = D_{2+} /.10$$

$$D_{2+} = \$110,000/(100,000 + S_n)$$

Saving you the boredom of reading through the algebra for solving three simultaneous equations for three unknowns, the solution is:

$$S_n = 4,762$$

$$D_{2+} = \$1.05$$

$$P_1 = \$10.50$$

The value of a share today is the present value of the $1.00 dividend at the end of year 1, plus the expected $10.50 price at the end of year 1:

$$\text{Value} = (\$10.50 + \$1.00)/1.10 = \$10.45$$

The main point from this illustration is that *the value of a share of stock is the present value of dividends that can be paid from current operations, plus the present value of investment opportunities expected to be taken in the future.* The value is the same whether the equity needed for the new investment comes from curtailing dividends or from selling additional shares, and this sameness of value is completely consistent with the principle that the value of a share of stock is the present value of future dividends.

ECONOMIC PROFIT AND WEALTH

What is the relationship between economic profit and wealth? Wealth creation is the present value of future investment opportunities, and also the present value of economic profit created by investment opportunities. As an illustration, the investment of $50,000 of new equity at the end of the first year in the previous example generated cash flow of $10,000 a year for the equity holders forever. At a 10 percent required return, the annual economic profit in year 2 and beyond is:

Annual cash flow	$10,000
Normal profit (.10 × $50,000)	5,000
Economic profit	$5,000

The previously computed $50,000 NPV at the end of year 1, when the new investment is being made, also equals the present value of the economic profit:

$$NPV = \$5,000 \times .10 = \$50,000$$

The wealth creation at the beginning of year 1 is the present value of that future NPV and also the present value of the future economic profit:

$$\$50,000/1.10 = \$5,000\left(\frac{1}{.10} - PVA_{1yr,10\%}\right) = \$45,455$$

The total value of the company increases $45,455, and the price of a share increases $0.45 to $10.45 based on the present value of future economic profit, which also equals the present value of the future NPV of the investment.

One point driven home by the focus on economic profit is the importance of competitive advantage in wealth creation. Recall that a positive economic profit is impossible in perfect competition; therefore, a positive NPV is impossible in perfect competition. *Investments that create wealth do so by creating or exploiting competitive advantage.*

WHAT IF INVESTORS DO NOT KNOW?

Before we are declared incompetent, we should note that the $10.45 share value that is supposed to occur today, based on the announcement of an investment opportunity a year from now, depends on the information being immediately absorbed by investors. Thus, $10.45 is the intrinsic value, and will be the actual value only if complete information is immediately and believably available to investors. If investors are not well informed, cutting dividends might even be translated as bad news about future growth, causing divergence between intrinsic value and the price at which shares are currently being bought and sold.

Suppose it is the end of year 1 and we have just paid out dividends at Delta Corporation. If we do not make any new investments, the stock will have earnings and dividends of $100,000 a year forever, or $1 a share. At a 10 percent required return, the intrinsic value is $10 per share. We announce our plans to invest an additional $50,000 of equity, telling investors that we expect it to provide $10,000 a year, and telling them we intend to sell additional shares of common stock to pay for it. The intrinsic value at the end of year 1 increases to $10.50.

Unfortunately, investors do not know what a great company this is, and the stock is actually selling for $4.00 a share. What should we do now? If we drop the plan, we will have earnings and dividends of $1 a year forever, giving our stock an intrinsic value of $10. If we go ahead and invest, things get worse. The number of new shares and dividends in year 2 and beyond are:

$$S_n = \$50,000/4 = 12,500$$

$$D_{2+} = \$110,000/(100,000 + 12,500) = \$0.98$$

The intrinsic value of a share at the end of year 1 then declines to $0.98/.10 = $9.80.

Because investors are misinformed, the intrinsic value of existing shares at the end of year 1 will actually decline as a result of the new investment. Even if the investors become fully informed later, the price of a share will only recover to its $9.80 intrinsic value, which is below the $10 intrinsic value prior to the investment announcement. Wealth-maximizing managers will be forced to forgo this opportunity because the investors are not informed.

We will extend the analysis in later chapters to deal with market imperfections. For the moment, though, be cautioned against excess emphasis on imperfections. Investors have strong incentives to keep informed, and numerous professionals devote their careers to collecting and disseminating information about companies. Furthermore, it is the job of senior management to keep shareholders well informed so that price reflects intrinsic value. A reputation for honesty in past communication is an important asset for a manager wanting to keep investors well informed. One CEO describes his view of the degree of imperfection by suggesting that his goal is to reduce his cost of funds by a 10th of 1 percent by overcoming imperfections. Imperfections of this magnitude are not going to switch many projects between the wealth creation and wealth destruction categories.

WEALTH AND VALUE

Shareholder wealth, share price, and value generally move in the same direction, but not always. Suppose Delta Corporation had retained $50,000 of income at the end of year 1 for an investment that would provide $3,000 a year forever, instead of $10,000. This is not an attractive investment:

$$NPV = \$3,000/.10 - \$50,000 = -\$20,000$$

Dividends and future price are as follows:

$$D_1 = \$.50$$

$$D_{2+} = \$1.03$$

$$P_1 = \$10.30$$

The stock price would have been $10.00 a share right after the year-1 dividend if the company had paid dividends of $1.00 a share, so the dividend cut for reinvestment purposes leads to a $0.30 increase in stock price. Unfortunately, the $0.30 increase in price comes at the expense of a $0.50 reduction in the dividend, so year-end wealth is decreased by $0.20 per share. If Delta announces this intention today, the price of a share will be expected to fall from $10.00 to:

$$P_0 = (\$10.30 + \$.50)/1.10 = \$9.82$$

Suppose the CEO brags at the next annual meeting that the initial stock price decline following the announcement of an intention to invest was proved incorrect and he cites as proof the $10.30 year-end price, while his nongrowth competitor's shares stayed flat at $10.00. He will probably be surprised by the enthusiastic chorus of boos. In fact, the price will probably decline further as investors factor incompetent leadership into their forecasts of future dividends.

Smoke and Mirrors

The prior example drives home again the fundamental point that *wealth is created by attractive investment opportunities*, which in turn are created by competitive advantage. We have seen that choice between retained earnings and sale of new shares does not change the amount of wealth that is created by an investment. We will take a look at a couple other nonevents.

Stock splits are a common part of the investment news. The basic idea is that we give the shareholders two shares, or some other multiple, in exchange for each share held previously. It sounds like the perfect Christmas present, but it is an illusion that fools few people. Delta Corporation, without the investment opportunities, could pay dividends of $1.00 a year on its 100,000 shares. With a 10 percent required return, the price of a share was $10.00. A two-for-one split would create 200,000 shares. If the company had the same $100,000 available to distribute as dividends, the annual dividend would be reduced to $0.50 a share and the price of a share would fall to $5.00. You would have twice as many shares, worth half as much per share.

When Disney split its stock four-for-one in April of 1992, the price fell from $150 a share to $39 over the weekend of the split. Were Disney managers surprised by this price drop? Almost certainly not. In the absence of other news, we would have expected the stock to fall to $37.50 a share, one fourth of the prior price. The $1.50 increase can be attributed to investors becoming more optimistic about Disney in particular or stocks in general.

Stock dividends are close cousins of stock splits. We announce that things are going so well at Consolidated Sludge that we are sure that you would rather have more shares than more cash, so we are giving you a stock dividend. For each ten shares of stock you now own, we will be giving you one additional share at no cost. As with the stock split, this action simply divides ownership into more pieces, and does not change the total value of the pieces. If you owned 1 percent of the company and its cash flows before, you own 1 percent after. An increase in the number of pieces of paper representing your cash flows does not affect the value of those cash flows, any more than five $1 bills can buy more than a $5 bill.

Why do companies engage in stock splits and dividends if they achieve nothing? One argument is that they want to attract a broad group of investors. Stocks are normally sold in 100-share multiples. Commissions are higher for smaller quantities. A split or stock dividend that reduces the price from $60 to $30 reduces the amount required to purchase 100 shares, from $6,000 to $3,000; this may make the stock available to more investors. Another argument is that the splits and stock dividends provide a signal that management expects the company to increase its competitive advantage in the future. If past stock splits for a particular company have always been followed by earnings or dividend increases, for example, then another stock split announcement would create similar expectations.

A final explanation for stock splits and dividends is that some people are fooled into believing they received something of value, even though educated investors know better. Splits or stock dividends for this purpose raise serious ethical questions and damage the reputations of managers, making later communication with stockholders even more difficult.

What is the conclusion? Forget smoke and mirrors. Do what is both ethical and wise. Concentrate on finding attractive investments and communicating honestly with the shareholders.

WHAT ABOUT EARNINGS?

CEOs and academic researchers can provide anecdotal and scientific evidence that stock prices respond positively to announcements of income that was more than expected, and vice versa. But earnings are an accounting concept, not cash flow and certainly not dividends. Why would investors be willing to pay more for Disney stock just because the company reported more income? Accountants may not have created perfect measures, but income is generally useful for predicting future cash flows. Thus, shareholders would be using the reported income to change their forecasts of future dividends. We will see in the next section that announcements of actions that will decrease income in the short run will cause stock price to increase if investors expect those actions to result in increased cash flows in the future.

Stock Price Responses to Firm Investment Announcements

Can we be sure that investors will respond when we make investments that create or exploit competitive advantage, and thereby increase intrinsic value? If you require certainty, find another profession. If you just want some assurance, you are in luck. A common fear of managers is that investors are myopic, uninterested in long-term decisions and care only about next quarter's earnings. Massive amounts of evidence suggest that investors do indeed respond favorably to good investment decisions, even if the short-run result is a decrease in accounting income.

McConnell and Muscarella studied capital budget announcements extensively. They found that for industrial companies, announcements of increased capital investment lead to an increase in stock price, while announcements of decreased capital investment lead to a decrease in stock price. In contrast, announcements of increased or decreased capital investment by utilities did not lead to a significant stock price change. They interpreted these results as consistent with investor belief that managers are making positive net present value investments. Industrial companies have a choice, and presumably invest because they expect to make a positive net present value. Public utilities, on the other hand, can expect regulated returns which are neither above nor below the rates required by investors.[7] Blose and Sheih found that the stock market's reactions were related to past corporate success.[8]

Studies of R&D announcements provide us a more detailed understanding of investor response. Chan, Kensinger, and Martin studied announcements of R&D expenditures exhaustively. Because accountants treat R&D as an expense, the immediate effect of an R&D expenditure is a decrease in earnings, and the benefits of R&D are many years in the future. If investors care only about short-term income, stock price would fall when companies announce increased R&D. Stock price would rise, on the other hand, if investors thought R&D was a positive net present value investment. What happens? In general, stock price rises when increased R&D is announced. The response is uneven, though. Investors are much more positive about R&D investments in growing high-tech industries than in old, stable industries[9] and are more positive when the company has been successful in the past.[10] Doukas and Switzer found that R&D announcements had positive price effects in concentrated industries (industries in which only a few companies compete) and negative results in low-concentration industries.[11] Since high concentration is one way of getting out of perfect competition and gaining competitive advantage, these results also are consistent

[7]John J. McConnell and Chris J. Muscarella, "Corporate Capital Expenditure Decisions and the Market Value of the Firm," *Journal of Financial Economics* 14 (1985): 399–422.

[8]Laurence E. Blose and Joseph C.P. Shieh, "Tobin's q-Ratio and Market Reaction to Capital Investment Announcements," *The Financial Review* 32 (August 1997).

[9]Su H. Chan, John Kensinger, and John D. Martin, "The Market Rewards Promising R&D—and Punishes the Rest," *Journal of Applied Corporate Finance* 5 (Summer 1992): 59–66.

[10]Samual H. Szewczyk, George P. Tsetsekos, and Zaher Zantout, "The Valuation of Corporate R&D Expenditures: Evidence from Investment Opportunities and Free Cash Flow," *Financial Management* 25 (Spring 1996): 105–110.

[11]John Doukas and Lorne Switzer, "The Stock Market's Valuation of R&D Spending and Market Concentration." *Journal of Economics and Business* 44 (May 1992): 95–114.

with the theory that investors respond positively to what they perceive as attractive investments.

The cited studies and numerous others, some of which are referenced at the end of this chapter, lead to the conclusion that investors respond positively to investments they believe to have positive net present values, even if the short-term impact on income is negative. The evidence supports the idea that wealth is maximized by seeking positive net present value investments, which have competitive advantage as their foundation, and communicating honestly with investors about those investments.

VALUE OF A COMPANY

The value of a company is the value of the benefits that can be paid out by that company. We generally interpret that to mean the total value of the owners' claim: the value of a share of common stock multiplied by the number of shares. A broader interpretation, which is sometimes used, is the total value of all claims: the total value of common stock, plus the value of all preferred stock and debt.

Other measures of company value are occasionally discussed, although they are not generally useful for financial management purposes. Book value of common equity is the total equity shown on the balance sheet. Likewise, book value of assets is the amount of assets shown on the balance sheet. Book value of total claims also might be considered, but it equals total assets by definition. The problem with these accounting measures is that they are based on amounts raised from investors and paid for assets in the past. They are adjusted for depreciation, which may *not* be a good estimate of actual value loss. They do not necessarily reflect what the assets, debt, or equity could be sold for. Likewise, they say nothing about the ability of any of those items to generate future cash flows. At the end of 1999, the total market value of Disney's equity was over $80 billion (over 675 million shares at $125 a share), while the book value of equity was only $18 billion. This difference reflects investors' expectations that the existing assets plus future investments will generate dividends with a present value substantially in excess of the book value of assets.

Occasionally, we see companies valued in terms of the sale price or the replacement cost of their assets. Sale price of assets sets a floor on the value of a company, because we can always get that amount by liquidating the firm. Similarly, replacement cost creates a ceiling on the value of a company in certain circumstances. If you are buying another company solely to use its assets in your business, the *maximum* price you would be willing to pay is the replacement cost of the assets.

The organizational expertise, reputation, and other sources of competitive advantage in a successful business create a value substantially in excess of replacement cost of assets. Thus, it is cash flow of the business and not the sum of its individual assets that determines value. These components of company value are summarized in Figure 4.2.

| **FIGURE 4.2** **COMPANY VALUE**

Competitive advantage is a key determinant of future investment opportunities as well as return on existing capital. Dividends arise from current investments and future investment opportunities. Value is the present value of the dividend stream.

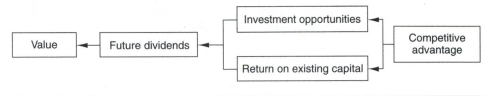

VALUE OF CURRENCY |

The value of currency provides another important example of arbitrage pricing principles at work. Two important factors affecting the exchange rates between currencies (the number of units of one currency that must be exchanged for a unit of the other currency) are *purchasing power parity* and *interest rate parity*.

PURCHASING POWER PARITY THEORY

Purchasing power parity theory states that equilibrium exchange rates between two countries will result in identical goods selling at identical prices. If a Big Mac sells for 1.1 pounds in London and $1.54 in Detroit, the purchasing power parity price of the pound is $1.40 so that 1.1 pounds can be exchanged for $1.54. If the inflation rate over the course of a year is 20 percent in Great Britain and 10 percent in the United States, prices of Big Macs will increase to 1.32 pounds and $1.694 respectively. For purchasing power parity to hold, the value of a pound will decline to $1.694/1.32 = $1.2833.

If purchasing power parity theory holds, the movements of exchange rates can be reduced to a simple formula:

$$ER_t' = ER_{t-1}(1 + INF_D)/(1 + INF_F) \qquad \text{(4-5)}$$

where ER_t is the exchange rate at the end of period t, expressed as the price of one unit of the foreign currency, INF_D is the domestic inflation rate for the period, and INF_F is the inflation rate in the foreign country for the period. We can confirm this formula by finding the end-of-period value of the pound for the previous example:

$$ER_t = 1.40(1 + .1)/(1 + .2) = 1.2833$$

Purchasing power parity theory does not always hold in practice, though. Differences in interest rates and perceived safety between countries can increase demand for one currency and decrease demand for the other. Market forces are not strong enough to assure rapid movement to equilibrium. Londoners will not rush to Detroit for lunch to take advantage of the price disparity in Big Macs, for example. Nevertheless, movements in exchange rates over the long run are strongly influenced by differences in inflation rates.[12]

INTEREST RATE PARITY THEORY

Interest rate parity theory, which predicts a specific relationship between spot exchange rates (exchange rates for immediate delivery), forward exchange rates (exchange rates for delivery at a specified future date), and interest rates, follows from the no-arbitrage-profit principle that is central to so much finance theory. Investors will always search for opportunities to make a risk-free investment at a superior rate of return. Suppose interest rates on risk-free government securities are higher in Great Britain than in the United States. You can convert dollars into pounds, and buy the pound-denominated securities. You can make this a risk-free investment by also entering into a futures contract to repurchase dollars at the maturity date for the pound-denominated security. The futures contract makes this a risk-free investment. If the investment provides a return above the domestic risk-free rate, numerous investors will join you in seeking to take advantage of the opportunity and will drive the return back into equilibrium. For the foreign investment to provide the same return as the domestic investment, the relationship between interest rates and exchange rates must be as follows:

$$R_{Foreign} = (ER_{Spot}/ER_{Forward})(1 + R_{Domestic}) - 1 \qquad \text{(4-6)}$$

where $R_{Foreign}$ and $R_{Domestic}$ are the foreign and domestic nominal risk-free interest rates, respectively. ER_{Spot} and $ER_{Forward}$ are the spot and forward exchange rates, respectively. The exchange rate is expressed as the price of the foreign currency, in terms of the domestic currency.

To illustrate the use of Equation 4-6, we return to the pound which was suffering an inflation rate of 20 percent while the dollar inflation rate was 10 percent. Assume the spot exchange rate is $1.40 per pound, and the 1-year forward contract rate is $1.2833 per pound. The risk-free interest rate in dollar-denominated securities is 12.2 percent. The equilibrium interest rate in pound-denominated securities is therefore:

$$R_{Foreign} = (1.40/1.2833)(1 + .122) - 1 = 22.4\%.$$

There are powerful forces at work to enforce interest rate parity. You can make deposits in a London bank in any one of a number of currencies, with all

---

[12]For additional reading, see Richard Roll, "Violations of the 'Law of One Price' and Their Implications for Differentially Denominated Assets," in *International Finance and Trade*, ed. M. Sarnat and G. Szego (Cambridge, Ma.: Ballinger Press, 1979); and Rita Maldonado and Anthony Saunders, "Foreign Exchange Futures and the Law of One Price," *Financial Management* 12 (Spring 1983): 19–23.

of these deposits being virtually risk-free with regard to interest and principal payments. At the same bank, you can exchange one currency for another and enter into a futures contract. As a result, it is easy to take advantage of any violation of interest rate parity theory, and investors will respond quickly to these money-making opportunities, bidding rates back into equilibrium.[13]

Interest rate parity theory can be used to understand how a government can temporarily drive exchange rates out of purchasing power equilibrium. Suppose the exchange and interest rates between Great Britain and the United States are in equilibrium as previously defined. The spot and 1-year forward exchange rates are $1.40 and $1.2833 respectively. The interest rate is 22.4 percent in Great Britain, and the United States federal reserve bank decreases the money supply, driving interest rates up to 14 percent. The British government, on the other hand, commits itself to a monetary policy that will maintain the 22.4 percent interest rate. Investors view these disturbances as temporary, so the future contract exchange rate does not change. For interest rate parity to hold, it is necessary for the spot rate to change as follows:

$$224 \; 5 \; (ERSpot/1.2833)(1 \; 1 \; .14) \; 21; \; ERSpot \; 5 \; 1.378$$

The increase in interest rates in the United States drives the relative value of the pound down, and the relative value of the dollar up. This change violates purchasing power parity, but it can be maintained at least temporarily through a high interest rate policy.

In summary, we know from observations that inflation rates are the primary determinants of exchange rate changes over the long run, but there are numerous disturbances to the purchasing power parity relationships. For example, the Polish labor uprising of 1981 caused concern about European stability, and there was a rush to the U.S. dollar as a safe-haven currency, temporarily driving up the value of the dollar. We also know that exchange rates are sensitive to monetary policy, because monetary policy affects interest rates.

SUMMARY |

Arbitrage is the fundamental concept underlying the valuation of stock, bonds, companies, and investment opportunities. The basic *arbitrage pricing principle* is that identical streams of cash flows will have identical prices. Thus, the

---

[13]For additional discussion, see T. Agmon and S. Bronfield, "The International Mobility of Short-Term Covered Arbitrage Capital," *Journal of Business Finance and Accounting* 2 (Summer 1975): 269–278; J. A Frenkel and R. M. Levich, "Covered Interest Arbitrage: Unexploited Profits?" *Journal of Political Economy* 83 (April 1975): 325–338; F. X. Browne, "Departures from Interest Rate Parity: Further Evidence," *Journal of Banking and Finance* 7 (June 1983): 253–272; and Ian H. Giddy, "An Integrated Theory of Exchange Rate Equilibrium," *Journal of Financial and Quantitative Analysis* 11 (December 1976): 883–892.

present value of any set of expected future cash flows is the amount that must be invested elsewhere today at equal risk to generate the same expected set of future cash flows.

Price refers to an amount of money per unit of measure at which someone buys, or is willing to buy or sell. *Value* is used to mean the price that would exist in a market that is perfect (or perfect except for taxes), based on the information set currently available to investors. *Intrinsic value* is the value that would exist if investors had the same information that was available to the person determining the intrinsic value.

When the arbitrage pricing principle is applied to bonds, the value of a bond equals the present value of the interest payments and the repayment of principal. The value of a share of stock is the present value of the dividend stream from that share, and the equity value of a company is the value of a single share multiplied by the number of shares outstanding. The value of a company can also be stated as the present value of all dividends that can be paid from existing investments, plus the present value of investment opportunities. The present value of a future investment opportunity is the present value of the net present value at the time the investment will be made. The value impact of an investment opportunity is the same whether the equity required is obtained by selling new shares or retaining earnings.

Competitive advantage is a key determinant of investment opportunities as well as return on existing capital. Wealth is created by earning more than the investors' required return from existing assets, or by creating positive net present value investment opportunities. Wealth creation thus depends on earning more than the investors' required return—on earning an economic profit. It is helpful to understand the relationship between economic profit, value, and wealth creation because that relationship focuses our attention on the importance of competitive advantage in determining wealth and value.

The statements about value are based on the assumption that shareholders know about the company's existing assets and its future investment opportunities. If investors are not well informed, it may be necessary to forgo otherwise attractive investments. If investors understand cash flows at all, superficial changes such as stock splits and stock dividends do not affect value. Earnings affect value only to the extent that they give investors information about future cash flows. Investments such as research and development, which reduce income as measured by accountants in the short term, result in price increases if investors believe the company has made good investment decisions.

The value of a company is the value of the benefits that can be paid out by the company. Other measures, such as book value, liquidation value, and replacement value, are of limited significance. Liquidation value would, for example, determine a minimum value because it is the amount that can be realized if the company is liquidated because the value of future dividends is not sufficient to justify continued operation.

Currency prices provide yet another example of arbitrage pricing principles at work. Purchasing power parity has a major impact on the exchange rates between currencies in the long run, pushing exchange rates toward that which causes goods to cost the same in each country. Interest rate parity theory causes short-term equilibrium between spot exchange rates, forward exchange rates, and interest rates.

Questions |

4–1. What is the basic arbitrage principle of valuation, as identified in this chapter?

4–2. Define the terms *price*, *bid price*, and *ask price*.

4–3. Define the terms *value* and *intrinsic value*.

4–4. Define the terms *yield to maturity*, *coupon rate*, *current yield*, and *yield to call*.

4–5. If bond and stock prices are determined by logical principles, why do they fluctuate from day to day?

4–6. If the value of a share of stock is the present value of future dividends, how is it possible that value could actually increase with a reduction of dividends to invest in new assets?

4–7. Explain the role of economic profit in determining wealth increases.

4–8. If cash flow in the form of dividends is what matters, why does stock price react to unexpected changes in accounting income?

4–9. Do investor responses to firm investment announcements support the valuation principles presented in this chapter? Explain.

4–10. Define the terms *spot exchange rate* and *forward exchange rate*.

4–11. Describe each of the following theories. Indicate the extent to which each theory holds in practice.
　a. Purchasing power parity theory
　b. Interest rate parity theory

4–12. (Applications) Recently, The Gap started to experience much slower growth in earnings than the 30 percent to 40 percent rate it had experienced in the past. At the same time, the stock price fell from the $50 range to under $30. In your own words, why did the value of The Gap stock change?

4–13. (Applications) In the past, Wal-Mart's earnings have grown at an average annual rate of approximately 30 percent. Assume that Wal-Mart's expected dividend is $0.11 for next year, and is expected to grow at 30 percent a year thereafter. Applying Equation 4-4, the value of a share should be $0.11/(.10 − .30) = −$0.55. Obviously, the stock cannot have a negative price. Explain why Equation 4-4 does not work for Wal-Mart.

4–14. (Ethical considerations) As chief executive officer, you are chosen by the board of directors, which is, in turn, chosen by the stockholders. You know that an investment that has been proposed will generate an economic profit. Investors are, however, not convinced. Your investor relations experts tell you that the stock will most likely decline in price if you announce the new investment, although it will eventually increase in price in future years as the results of the investment become known. In the meantime, though, you could face a hostile takeover or a proxy battle if the stock price declines. What should you do?

PROBLEMS |

(Note: You may notice that taxes will affect the net benefits received in some of the following problems. Assume no taxes in working these problems. Taxes will be incorporated in later chapters.)

4–1. Asset A will pay $1,000 in 1 year, and asset B will pay $500 in 2 years. Asset C will pay $1,000 in 1 year and $500 in 2 years. The value of asset A is $900, and the value of asset B is $400. What is the value of asset C? What would happen if asset C could be bought for less than its value?

4–2. Some real estate in Montreaux is expected to be worth $10 million in 10 years. Annual rent will just cover operating costs. Alternate investment opportunities pay annual interest of 10 percent. What is the value of this real estate? If the real estate can be acquired for $2 million, what is the impact on wealth?

4–3. Suppose the real estate discussed in problem 2 also generates annual rent of $100,000 in excess of operating costs. What is the value of the real estate?

4–4. If Fayetteville Copy Center joins a national franchise, annual year-end cash flow is expected to increase by $10,000. At a 12 percent effective required return, what is the value of the franchise affiliation?

4–5. Suppose the franchise discussed in problem 4 would generate cash flows of $1,000 at the end of the first year, and cash flows are expected to grow at 5 percent a year thereafter. At a 12 percent effective required return, what is the present value of the franchise affiliation?

4–6. Zero coupon bonds pay no interest, and investors receive the face value, normally $1,000, at maturity. If other investments of equal risk earn an effective return of 12 percent, what is the value of a $1,000 face value, 20-year zero coupon bond?

4–7. A 20-year, $1,000 zero coupon bond is presently selling for $61.10. What is the effective annual interest rate? (Zero coupon bonds are defined in problem 6.)

4–8. Monticello Employees Pension Fund can buy a mortgage that provides payments of $1,000 at the end of each year for the next 20 years. At a 10 percent effective required return, what is the value of this mortgage?

4–9. A $1,000 bond matures in 10 years. The bond pays interest of 10 percent a year, with half of the annual interest paid at midyear and the other half paid at year-end. The bond is selling below $1,000, so that the yield to maturity earned by an investor is actually 6 percent each 6-month period. What is the price of the bond?

4–10. You purchased new 20-year 6 percent bonds of Amalgamated Corporation for $1,000 each when they were issued a year ago. Interest rates on investments of this type have fallen to 5 percent since then. What is the value of one of these bonds today, and what rate of return did you earn on your investment over the 1-year period? (Assume year-end interest payments for simplicity.)

4–11. For the bonds in problem 10, what rate of return would you have earned on your investment if interest rates on investments of this type had risen to 7 percent over the 1-year period?

4–12. Helburn Corporation issued $1,000, 20-year bonds 5 years ago. The bonds pay interest of $100 at the end of each year. The bonds are currently selling at a price of $1,100 because interest rates have fallen. The bonds can be called when they are 7 years old, at a call price of $1,050. Compute the yield to maturity, coupon rate, current yield, and yield to call. Assume year-end interest payments for simplicity.

4–13. Heidleburg Corporation has annual income of $2 million and has 1 million shares of stock outstanding. The company has no expansion opportunities, and depreciation equals the replacement cost necessary to maintain the current level of output, so income is available to distribute as dividends and is expected to continue indefinitely. Dividends are paid annually and the last dividend was just paid. Similar investments pay a rate of return of 16 percent. What is the value of Heidleburg Corporation and a share of Heidleburg Corporation stock?

4–14. A new opportunity arises for Heidleburg Corporation (problem 13). The investment will require $1 million of equity a year from now, and will earn income (available for dividends) of $200,000 a year indefinitely. What is the value today of that future investment opportunity?

4–15. Show how today's stock price for Heidleburg Corporation (problem 14) is affected if investors become aware of the new investment opportunity and know the equity requirement will be funded with retained earnings.

4–16. Show how today's stock price for Heidleburg Corporation (problem 14) is affected if investors in a fully informed market become aware of the new investment opportunity and know the equity requirement will be funded with the sale of new shares.

4–17. For Heidleburg Corporation (problem 14) compute the annual economic profit from the new investment. Use the economic profit to compute the value today of the future investment opportunity.

4–18. For Heidleburg Corporation (problem 14) suppose investors are not well informed, and the stock is selling at $8.00 a share. What would happen to the intrinsic value of a share of stock if the company decides to fund the equity needed for the future investment opportunity by selling new shares? Would the investment be attractive if the company used retained earnings instead?

4–19. Frankfurt Corporation has annual income of $4 million and has 1 million shares of stock outstanding. The company has no expansion opportunities, and depreciation equals the replacement cost necessary to maintain the current level of output, so income is available to distribute as dividends and is expected to continue indefinitely. Dividends are paid annually, and the last dividend was just paid. Similar investments pay a rate of return of 16 percent. An investment opportunity available 1 year from now would require equity of $4 million, and would provide income of $600,000 a year thereafter, available to distribute as dividends. The company would retain earnings to generate the equity for this investment. Assuming investors are fully informed, what will be the price of the stock 1 year from now, and what rate of return will stockholders earn over the year, with and without the new investment? Will investors be happy because of this new investment?

4–20. Hamburg Corporation has $5 million of income and 1 million shares of stock outstanding. The stock is currently selling for $40 a share. The company decides to issue a 10 percent stock dividend since things are going so well. What is the expected price of a share of stock after the stock dividend, and what is the wealth effect for an investor who owned 1,000 shares before the announcement?

4–21. Mt. Hamilton Corporation is considering the purchase of a division from another company. The division is what is often referred to as a "cash cow." Sales are declining, but cash flows are excellent. Cash flows are expected to be $10 million at the end of the first year and are expected to decline at the rate of 8 percent a year indefinitely. At a 10 percent required return, what is the value of that division?

4–22. The Israeli Shekel is currently priced at $0.6224. Suppose an apartment that would rent for $400 a month in New York is renting for $800 in Tel Aviv. Does this relationship violate purchasing power parity theory? Are there any market forces that would bring the prices in line?

4–23. The Swiss franc is currently priced at $.6645. A coat that would sell for $120 in Chicago is in a store in Zurich. What price for the coat would be consistent with purchasing power parity theory?

4–24. The value of country X's currency is $.50 on January 1 and $.60 on January 1 of the following year. Inflation over the period was 10 percent in the United States and 30 percent in country X. Is the change in currency value consistent with purchasing power parity theory?

4–25. The spot rate and 6-month forward rate for the Japanese yen are 143.81 yen per dollar and 142.10 yen per dollar respectively. The interest rate per 6-month period is 3 percent in the United States and 2.5 percent in Japan. Are these relationships consistent with interest rate parity theory?

4–26. The 1-year forward exchange rate for British pounds is $1.56 dollars per pound. If the interest rates are 12 percent in the United States and 10 percent in Britain, what spot rate is consistent with interest rate parity theory?

4–27. The spot and 6-month forward exchange rates for the German mark are $.5496 and $.5544 respectively. If the interest rate in the United States is 3 percent for the 6-month period, what interest rate in Germany is consistent with interest rate parity theory?

CASE PROBLEM |

Martin Quality Systems[14]

Martin Quality Systems was a privately held firm that manufactured specialty instruments, used primarily to monitor quality on assembly lines. Sales had increased nearly 50 percent from 1988 to 1992, aided by the introduction of new products and by strong customer relations based on satisfaction with products produced in the past.

The firm's founder and controlling stockholder, Jim Martin, was approaching retirement and had decided in early 1993 to sell the firm. The senior management team was considering a buyout plan, and had approached an investment banker for help in determining a price and arranging financing. Since Martin's stock had never been publicly traded, there was no direct market test. However, investors seemed to require a return of about 15 percent on stock of similar risk to that of Martin's. Of course, required returns were only estimates, and it was possible that the required return was closer to 16 percent.

Five years of financial history for Martin appear in Table 4.1. Return on equity was well in excess of the 15 percent required return in all years except 1990. The problem in 1990 was a combination of an unexpected fall in revenues and Martin's long-term policy of avoiding layoffs. It was estimated that the decision to avoid layoffs took almost $1 million from the bottom line in 1990.

If sales at Martin were to just remain stable, depreciation would approximately equal replacement cost, so income would be available to distribute as dividends. If the business were to continue growing, on the other hand, it would be necessary to either retain earnings or sell additional shares of stock so that equity would grow at the same rate as sales. If equity did not grow at the same

| TABLE 4.1 | FINANCIAL STATEMENTS OF MARTIN QUALITY SYSTEMS FINANCIAL RESULTS (IN THOUSANDS)

Year	1988	1989	1990	1991	1992
Sales	20,051	26,852	24,502	27,694	30,140
Net income	996	1,264	(237)	1,345	1,436
Current assets	7,058	9,673	8,404	9,789	10,645
Fixed assets	2,193	2,769	2,783	3,030	3,058
Total	9,251	12,442	11,187	12,819	13,703
Current liabilities	3,665	5,023	4,982	5,052	5,442
Long-term debt	637	803	803	885	891
Equity	4,949	6,616	5,402	6,882	7,370
Total	9,251	12,442	11,187	12,819	13,703

[14]Contributed by Fred Yeager, St. Louis University.

rate as sales, the company would have great trouble raising the debt capital it would need.

Based on orders on hand, Martin was certain that revenues and income would increase 10 percent in 1993. He believed that revenue and income growth could be maintained at that level for the indefinite future as long as the new management continued the standards he had maintained.

CASE QUESTIONS

(For simplicity in answering these questions, assume that all cash flows occur at midyear, and that you are valuing the business as of the start of 1993.)

1. Assuming that revenue and income does not grow, what is the value of the equity of the business?
2. Assume that revenue and income remain unchanged in 1993, grow 10 percent in 1994, and remain constant after 1994. The $737,000 of equity needed to fund the 1994 growth will come from retained earnings at the end of 1993. What is the value of the business's equity at the start of 1993?
3. Assume the same revenue growth, income growth, and equity need as in question 2. Assume, however, that the $737,000 is obtained by selling new equity. If potential investors are fully informed, what is the value of the equity of the business at the start of 1993?
4. Rework the answers to questions 1 and 3 so that you can compare the value implications of 15 percent and 16 percent required returns.
5. What is a reasonable price for the remaining managers to pay to Martin for ownership of the firm?

SELECTED REFERENCES

Bansal, Ravi, David A. Hseih, and S. Viswanathan. "A New Approach to International Arbitrage Pricing." *The Journal of Finance* 48 (December 1993): 1719–1747.

Blose, Laurence E., and Joseph C. P. Shieh. "Tobin's q-Ratio and Market Reaction to Capital Investment Announcements." *The Financial Review* 32 (August 1997): 449–476.

Branch, Ben. "Corporate Objectives and Market Performance." *Financial Management* 2 (Summer 1973): 24–29.

Browne, F. X. "Departures from Interest Rate Parity: Further Evidence." *Journal of Banking and Finance* 7 (June 1983): 253–272.

Chan, Su H., George W. Gau, and Ko Wang. "Stock-Market Reaction to Capital Investment Decisions: Evidence from Business Relocations." California State University, Fullerton, Working Paper (August 1993).

Chan, Su Han, George W. Gau, and Ko Wang. "Stock Market Reaction to Capital Investment Decisions: Evidence from Business Relocations." *Journal of Financial and Quantitative Analysis* 30 (March 1995): 81–100.

Chan, Su H., John Kensinger, and John D. Martin. "The Market Rewards Promising R&D— and Punishes the Rest." *Journal of Applied Corporate Finance* 5 (Summer 1992): 59–66.

Cornell, Bradford. "Spot Rates, Forward Rates and Exchange Market Efficiency." *Journal of Financial Economics* 5 (1977): 55–65.

Doukas, John, and Lorne Switzer. "The Stock Market's Valuation of R&D Spending and Market Concentration." *Journal of Economics and Business* 44 (May 1992): 95–114.

Findlay, M. Chapman, III, and G. A. Whitmore. "Beyond Shareholder Wealth Maximization." *Financial Management* 3 (Winter 1974): 25–35.

Froot, Kenneth, Andre Perold, and Jeremy Stein. "Shareholder Trading Practices and Corporate Investment Horizons." *Journal of Applied Corporate Finance* 5 (Summer 1992): 42–58.

Gombola, Michael J., and George P. Tsetsekos. "The Information Content of Plant Closing Announcements: Evidence from Financial Profiles and Stock Price Reaction." *Financial Management* 21 (Summer 1992): 31–40.

Grossman, S. J., and J. E. Stiglitz. "On Value Maximization and Alternative Objectives of the Firm." *Journal of Finance* 32 (May 1977): 389–402.

Ikenberry, David L., Graeme Rankine, and Earl K. Stice. "What Do Stock Splits Really Signal?" *Journal of Financial and Quantitative Analysis* 31 (September 1996): 357–375.

Keane, Simon M. "Can a Successful Company Expect to Increase Its Share Price? A Clarification of a Common Misconception." *Journal of Applied Corporate Finance* 3 (Fall 1990).

Khaksari, Shahriar, and Neil Seitz. "A Real Return Test of International Capital Market Efficiency." In *The Changing Environment of International Financial Markets: Issues and Analysis.* Dilip K. Ghosh and Edgar Ortiz, ed. (New York: St. Martin's Press, 1994), 189–200.

McConnell, John J., and Chris J. Muscarella. "Corporate Capital Expenditure Decisions and the Market Value of the Firm." *Journal of Financial Economics* 14 (1985): 399–422.

Rappaport, Alfred. "Don't Sell Stock Market Horizons Short." *The Wall Street Journal* (June 27, 1983): 22.

———. "Linking Competitive Strategy and Shareholder Value Analysis." *Journal of Business Strategy* 7 (Spring 1987): 58–67.

Reimann, Bernard C. "Stock Price and Business Success: What Is the Relationship?" *Journal of Business Strategy* 8 (Summer 1987): 38–49.

Roll, Richard. "Violations of the 'Law of One Price' and Their Implications for Differentially Denominated Assets." In *International Finance and Trade*, ed. M. Sarnat and G. Szego (Cambridge, Ma.: Ballinger Press, 1979).

Solomon, Ezra. *The Theory of Financial Management.* New York: Columbia University Press, 1963.

Statman, Meir, and James F. Sepe. "Project Termination Announcements and the Market Value of the Firm." *Financial Management* 18 (Winter 1989): 74–81.

Stewart, G. Bennett, III. *The Quest for Value.* New York: Harper Business, 1991.

Szewczyk, Samual H., George P. Tsetsekos, and Zaher Zantout. "The Valuation of Corporate R&D Expenditures: Evidence from Investment Opportunities and Free Cash Flow." *Financial Management* 25 (Spring 1996): 105–110.

Woods, John C., and Maury R. Randall. "The Net Present Value of Future Investment Opportunities: Its Impact on Shareholder Wealth and Implications for Capital Budgeting Theory." *Financial Management* 18 (Summer 1989): 85–92.

Woolridge, J. Randall. "Competitive Decline and Corporate Restructuring: Is a Myopic Stock Market to Blame?" *Journal of Applied Corporate Finance* 1 (Spring 1988): 26–36.

Zantout, Zaher, and George P. Tsetsekos. "The Wealth Effects of Announcements of R&D Expenditure Increases." *The Journal of Financial Research* 17 (Summer 1994): 205–216.

INTEGRATIVE CASE FOR PART I: |

Rolm

In 1984, International Business Machines (IBM) was considering its first acquisition in almost 20 years. Giant IBM, with a 70-year history, a strong record of profitability, and total assets of $23 billion, was considering the acquisition of corporate teenager Rolm, which had assets of half a billion dollars and a spotty earnings record over its 15-year history. Rolm and IBM were also a study in contrasting management styles. Rolm was a casual, open-collar Silicon Valley technology company while IBM's pin-striped formality was legendary.

The condition that brought such unlikely partners together for merger discussions was the evolution of both the computer and telecommunications market. Rolm had gained a strong position in the market for private branch telephone exchanges (PBXs), such as those used in large organizations. Telephone systems might seem to be outside IBM's normal area of interest, other than fitting into the general definition of office information handling systems, but information was transferred between computers using telephone lines, and the telephone systems of the country were converting to digital technology so that they could handle data more efficiently. IBM wanted to be able to offer a complete information processing package, and set the standards for communications between computers.

Management at IBM identified four key components of its strategy: "Central to IBM's strategy are four key business goals—growth, product leadership, efficiency and profitability" (1983 annual report). Management had confidence in the continued growth of the information processing industry, and it intended to grow by maintaining or increasing its share of that market. Product leadership was sought through refinement of traditional lines, such as mainframe computers, microcomputers, and typewriters. In addition, IBM explored new areas such as industrial automation, graphics systems, and telecommunications. It might surprise some who view IBM as differentiating itself with product and service quality, but IBM also sought to be the low-price producer in its industry. In its 1983 annual report, the company reported on important steps to reduce costs in both manufacturing and distribution of its products. Management believed that pursuit of these goals was the primary route to profitability, and it believed that a special emphasis on quality was necessary while pursuing these goals in a highly competitive market.

An important part of product leadership was fully integrated information processing, both voice and data, for the automated office. IBM had a full line of computers, copiers, and typewriters. It had introduced new products, such as voice mail. Nevertheless, IBM had not been successful in its own attempts to enter the telecommunications market. Entry through joint ventures seemed to be an ideal strategy, and IBM responded favorably to an overture from Rolm.

Rolm was incorporated in California in 1969. By its 1976 fiscal year (ending June 30, 1976) gross revenue reached $17.5 million. From there, it grew at an average annual rate of 57 percent through 1984, as shown in Table I.1. The company gained strong positions in two fields. Its Mil-spec division produced rugged computers for harsh environments, primarily military use. While the market for these Mil-spec computers was not huge, Rolm had an 8 percent market share. Rolm was also a formidable competitor in the PBX market; its sales of PBXs accounted for 19 percent of the total market. Eighty-six percent of Rolm's sales were PBXs and related items, while Mil-spec accounted for the remaining 14 percent. Like IBM, Rolm had a reputation for product dependability and service quality.

Unfortunately, profitability growth at Rolm did not keep up with sales growth, as shown in Tables I.1 and I.2. Return on equity had declined for several years, and earnings per share declined in 1984. This decline in profitability was attributed to cut-throat competition in the PBX market. Industry analysts suggested that Mil-spec accounted for up to half of Rolm's profit, and most of the rest came from interest on marketable security reserves created by purchase of its newly issued shares by IBM.

IBM gained a 15 percent interest in Rolm in 1983, by acquiring newly issued Rolm stock of $228 million, or $59 a share. IBM then increased its share to 23 percent over a period of a few months. The two companies then attempted to work together on joint ventures, with their sales people making joint sales calls to offer a complete system to customers. Unfortunately, these efforts were not successful, because it had proved difficult to mesh the efforts of highly motivated sales people interested in selling their particular piece of equipment. IBM had acquired controlling interest in a long-distance carrier, Satellite Business Systems, although a merger had not been proposed, and was working on joint ventures with that company. The acquisition of Rolm might allow better coordination of efforts and would position IBM to challenge AT&T for control of the information market in the decade ahead.

The merger was not without its potential problems. IBM had failed in attempts to enter the market in the past. Furthermore, the joint ventures IBM had attempted with Rolm had not proved successful in the past. In addition, the PBX

| **TABLE** **I.1** **PERFORMANCE HISTORY OF ROLM** |

(Items other than share-related numbers are in $ millions.)

	1976	1977	1978	1979	1980	1981	1982	1983	1984
Sales	17.5	30.0	50.3	114.4	200.7	294.6	380.6	502.6	659.7
Net income	1.1	1.9	3.6	11.3	17.3	23.8	29.8	35.5	37.7
EPS	.11	.15	.26	.75	1.09	1.39	1.70	1.80	1.49
Div. per share	0	0	0	0	0	0	0	0	0
P-E Ratio	NA	11.0	37.5	23.1	31.0	27.2	31.9	33.4	32.2

| TABLE 1.2 ROLM FINANCIAL STATEMENTS | | | | | |

(in $ thousands)	FISCAL YEAR[a]				
	1980	1981	1982	1983	1984[b]
Sales	$200,729	$294,576	$380,577	$502,642	$659,700
Cost of sales	95,306	141,210	185,754	249,848	
Marketing, etc.	58,016	89,313	118,272	163,424	
Product development	13,379	20,056	24,410	35,326	
Net operating income	34,028	43,997	52,141	54,044	26,388
Interest expense	458	−1,772	−2,904	−6,908	
Earnings before tax	33,570	45,769	55,045	60,952	
Income tax	16,230	21,992	25,218	25,409	
Net income	$ 17,340	$ 23,777	$ 29,827	$ 35,543	$ 37,700
Cash		$ 36,163	$ 28,927	$213,211	
Accounts receivable		35,597	64,580	103,163	
Inventories		48,748	60,273	73,705	
Prepayments, etc.		2,154	2,470	3,945	
Current assets		122,662	156,250	394,024	
Net property, etc.		72,665	99,449	120,710	
Other assets		11,587	11,425	5,181	
Total assets		$206,914	$267,124	$519,915	
Accounts, etc. payable		$ 38,489	$ 58,683	$ 85,002	
Income taxes		11,456	13,484	21,437	
Current liabilities		49,945	72,167	106,439	
Long-term debt		35,135	35,122	23,559	3,528
Deferred income tax		0	0	8,198	19,522
Common stock		59,732	67,906	254,247	
Retained earnings		62,102	91,929	127,472	
Net worth		121,834	159,835	381,719	541,336
Total liability & net worth		$206,914	$267,124	$519,915	
Net working capital	31,700	72,717	84,083	287,585	386,600
Total capitalization		156,969	194,957	413,476	564,386

[a]Ending the end of June.

[b]Complete detail on 1984 was lacking because Rolm was acquired by another company.

market was suffering from cut-throat competition and declining profit margins. In this environment, Rolm was having trouble matching the research and development budgets of larger competitors; Northern Telecom was spending twice as much, for example. IBM would have to pump substantial increases into R&D in order to remain competitive. Last, but not least, IBM competed directly with Mil-spec, and the Justice Department might force divestiture of the profitable Mil-spec division as a condition of approving the merger.

The merger had disadvantages for Rolm as well. Many employees were concerned about being forced to adapt to the IBM management style, and sales people were not excited about spending their time on joint sales calls. In addition, there was concern that IBM would lose interest in funding the needed R&D if competitive pressures continued. This was a serious concern as a bitter struggle for the information-processing market was expected and major R&D investments were needed. IBM might simply decide to abandon the PBX market if satisfactory profit margins did not develop.

On the positive side, Rolm needed three things that IBM had: funding, access to large customers, and access to foreign markets, particularly Europe. Furthermore, management at Rolm was concerned about being left on the outside as industry leaders such as AT&T developed integrated information-processing systems for their customers.

The merger promised opportunities and threatened problems for both sides. It was necessary for both sides to weigh the merger in terms of strategic importance, risk, and value. Managers at IBM and Rolm needed to answer two questions: (1) was a merger desirable? and (2) what price should IBM pay for Rolm stock?

The stock of Rolm had declined from an all-time high of $80 a share in 1983 to the $30 range in early 1984, before rebounding to $44 a share. Rolm had 23,333,000 shares outstanding, and IBM owned 23 percent of those shares. Financial institutions held another 47 percent of Rolm's shares. IBM's stock was priced at $125 a share, very near its all-time high (adjusted for stock splits) of $134.25.

CASE QUESTIONS

1. From the information available, identify the threats and opportunities faced (1) by IBM, and (2) by Rolm.
2. From the information available, identify the strengths and weaknesses (1) of IBM, and (2) of Rolm.
3. Identify the strengths and weaknesses of a combined IBM and Rolm.
4. Discuss the potential for competitive advantage in office computing for:
   a. IBM alone
   b. Rolm alone
   c. A combined IBM and Rolm
5. Would you recommend to IBM that it seek to merge with Rolm? Would you recommend to Rolm that it seek to merge with IBM?
6. Assume an 18 percent required return on equity, no further growth, and continuation of the present profitability level. If all income is available to distribute as dividends, what is the value of Rolm as an independent company? (Assume mid-year cash flows for simplicity.)

PART II

CAPITAL INVESTMENT CHOICE

The strategy and value goals of the corporation are implemented by making investments, by committing resources to particular courses of action. These investments in turn determine the risk and financing needs of the corporation. The financing choices and risk in turn determine the required return, and help to determine which investments are desirable.

A successful strategy creates numerous investment opportunities. The company must find ways to identify those investments that will contribute to its wealth-creation goals. This part of the book develops the techniques used to evaluate capital investments and measure their contribution to the value of the firm. Chapter 5 focuses on net present value, the most widely recommended method of capital investment analysis. Chapter 6 compares net present value to some alternative evaluation methods. Chapter 7 moves beyond the question of whether or not an investment is attractive to the ranking of competing, attractive investments.

CHAPTER 5

MEASURING INVESTMENT VALUE: YOU CAN TRUST NPV

After completing this chapter you should be able to:

1. Calculate the net present value of a project with even or uneven cash flows.
2. Value a perpetual no-growth project and value a perpetual project with growing cash flows.
3. Measure the wealth created for the shareholders using net present value.
4. Describe the relationship among market imperfections, economic profit, and net present value.
5. Demonstrate that NPV measures the wealth created whether or not the company includes debt in its capital structure, and in the presence of corporate income taxes.
6. Appreciate the role of management in practicing due diligence in estimating the cash flows and NPVs and in keeping the shareholders informed, so that the market price of the firm's stock will approximate the intrinsic value over time.
7. Describe the difficulties faced by management when investors are not fully informed, so that the market price is substantially different from the intrinsic value.

Bill Gates of Microsoft fame and Craig McCaw, who sold his company McCaw Cellular to AT&T for billions of dollars, are now partners in a new company called Teledesic. The objective of Teledesic is to blanket the earth with 288 low-level satellites that would form an information superhighway in the sky. Unlike with traditional phone lines, the user could transmit data or voice information from a moving car, the beach, or anywhere else in the world with the use of a small parabolic disk that sends the information to the nearest satellite to be relayed across the network of satellites until it reaches its intended destination. The cost of placing the satellites into orbit and building the initial system is estimated to be at least $9 billion. Gates and McCaw believe that this system will be so superior to existing line and cellular systems that they will attract a significant portion of the $140 billion that is spent on telecommunications services annually. The success of this venture depends on the ultimate ability of this system to attract enough customers to pay for the initial $9 billion investment. The focus of this chapter is on the frequently faced question of whether future benefits are worth the investment required.

Since Chapter 1, net present value (NPV) has been described as the present value of benefits, minus the present value of costs. It has also been claimed that NPV measures a project's contribution to wealth and is, therefore, *the* criterion for project desirability. In this chapter, we will define net present value more rigorously and explore more fully its role as the investment selection criterion that leads to wealth maximization.

The focus of this chapter is on *absolute desirability:* considering this investment in isolation, are the benefits worth the outlay? If a proposed investment does not conflict with any other investments, the decision can be based on absolute desirability. There are, however, many types of conflicts between desirable investments, such as two investments that are different ways of doing the same thing, or desirable investments that exceed the amount of money available to invest. In these cases, investments must be chosen according to *relative* desirability. The techniques developed in this chapter are extended in Chapter 6 to measure relative desirability.

Except where indicated otherwise, the analysis in this chapter is based on the assumption that all costs and benefits are monetary and have been adjusted for tax implications. Taxes are introduced in Chapter 8, nonmonetary considerations are discussed in Chapter 24, and risk is dealt with in Chapters 11 through 15.

DEFINITION AND ILLUSTRATIONS OF NPV

An investment's *net present value* (NPV) is the sum of the present values of its expected benefits, minus the present values of all expected cash outlays. Benefits are generally in the forms of cash flows. Let k be the rate of return that can be earned elsewhere if the money is not used for this investment. Letting I_o be the initial outlay and CF_t be the cash flow at the end of period t, the net present value is:[1]

---

[1]In the case in which the required return changes from period to period, the net present value formula is:

$$NPV = \sum_{t=1}^{n} CF_t / \prod_{i=1}^{t}(1 + k_i) - I_o$$

where

$$\prod_{i=1}^{t}(1 + k_i) = (1 + k_1)(1 + k_2)\cdots(1 + k_t)$$

Required return could vary by period because of anticipated changes in general interest rates or in the company's debt-equity mix over time.

$$\text{NPV} = \frac{CF_1}{(1 + k)^1} + \frac{CF_2}{(1 + k)^2} + \cdots + \frac{CF_n}{(1 + k)^n} - I_o$$

$$= \sum_{t=1}^{n} \frac{CF_t}{(1 + k)^t} - I_o \tag{5-1}$$

Recall that $CF_n/(1 + k)^n$ is the *present value* of amount CF_n; it is the amount that could be invested elsewhere today at rate of return k in order to have amount CF_n at the end of period n. The arbitrage pricing principle then requires that the value of an investment is the sum of the present values of all future cash flows. The difference between the value of future cash flows and the initial outlay needed to achieve those cash flows is the increase (or decrease) in wealth for the investor acquiring that investment. A company investing on behalf of the stockholders would create shareholder wealth increases equal to the NPV.

Example. If you invest $1,500 today, you will receive $1,000 at the end of each year for two years. If you could invest elsewhere to earn a 10 percent return, the net present value is:

$$\text{NPV} = (\$1,000 PVAI_{2yrs,10\%}) - \$1,500$$

$$= \$1,735.50 - \$1,500$$

$$= \underline{\$235.50}$$

You would be required to invest $1,735.50 elsewhere to receive $1,000 at the end of each year for two years. Thus, the future cash inflows have a *value* of $1,735.50. When you buy a stream of payments for less than its value, you create wealth. In this case, you create wealth of $235.50 by spending $1,500 to generate cash flows with a value of $1,735.50. Looking at the investment in a slightly different way, an entrepreneur who had identified this opportunity, but who had no capital, could raise $1,735.50 based on a promise to provide the investors with the future cash flows from the project and could pocket the $235.50 excess as her wealth increase.

COMPLEX CASH FLOWS

Cash flows are typically not even over the life of a capital investment, and there may be outlays in more than one period. Equation 5-1 makes it clear that even cash flows are not required. Likewise, there is no requirement that all future cash flows be positive. Suppose an investment has the expected cash flows shown in Table 5.1. As shown in Table 5.1, this project can still be evaluated using Equation 5-1 because no restrictions are placed on the signs of the cash flows in that equation.

The wealth effect of the NPV may not be as obvious when there are additional outlays in future years, but it is still there. Suppose, for example, we wanted to put away enough money today to fund both present and future outflows for

TABLE 5.1	ILLUSTRATION OF NPV FOR UNEVEN AND MIXED CASH FLOWS

This table demonstrates that NPV still measures wealth impact when cash flows are uneven and when cash outflows are mixed between inflows.

Time	Cash Flow		Present Value
Now	−1,000		$−1,000.00
End of year 1	+1,000	$+1,000 \div 1.10^1 =$	909.09
End of year 2	−2,000	$−2,000 \div 1.10^2 =$	−1,652.89
End of year 3	+3,000	$+3,000 \div 1.10^3 =$	2,253.94
Net Present Value			$ 510.14

this investment in Table 5.1. An amount of $1,652.89 temporarily invested at 10 percent would provide $2,000 to cover the outlay at the end of year 2. Thus, the total investment that must be made today is:

$$\text{Total investment: } \$1,000 + \$2,000/1.10^2 = \$2,652.89$$

For that investment, we receive $1,000 at the end of year one and $3,000 at the end of year three. The amount that must be invested elsewhere to acquire those same benefits is:

$$\text{Value of future inflows: } \$1,000/1.10 + \$3,000/1.10^3 = \$3,163.03$$

Thus, this investment allows us to buy the set of benefits for $510.14 less than it would cost to buy those same benefits elsewhere. The net present value still measures the wealth impact in the case of complex cash flows.

PERPETUITIES

Some investments are essentially perpetuities. Expansion into a new market area and acquisition of another company are examples of investments with no natural ends to their lives. When UPS spent $30 million on TV advertisements to publicize its new overnight letter service, for example, managers certainly expected to gain a permanent position in that market.

The net present value of a perpetuity with a constant annual cash flow is an application of Equation 3-8:

$$\text{NPV} = \text{CF}_1/(k − g) − I_o \qquad (5\text{-}2)$$

where CF_1 is the expected cash flow at the end of the first year, and cash flows are expected to grow at a constant rate of g per year.[2]

___

[2]Recall from Chapter 3 that g must be less than k, and it is reasonable to expect g to be less than k.

Example. When Eastman Kodak paid $5.1 billion for Sterling Drug, perpetual cash flows were anticipated. Suppose the required return is 15 percent and Sterling will generate $700 million at the end of each year. The net present value, in millions, is then:

$$NPV = \$700/(.15 - 0) - \$5,100 = \underline{-\$433}$$

The investment is not attractive because it decreases wealth. If, however, cash flows are expected to grow at 4 percent a year, after beginning at $700 million at the end of the first year, the net present value, in millions, is positive, so the investment is attractive:

$$NPV = \$700/(0.15 - 0.04) - \$5,100 = \underline{\$1,264}$$

NET PRESENT VALUE AND WEALTH CREATION: PERFECT FINANCIAL MARKETS |

We have talked about the NPV as the gain to an investor making a decision about the use of his or her money. If we are acting on behalf of that investor, the same decision rules hold. The impact of an investment on the investor's wealth depends on the characteristics of the choice, not the identity of the person making the decisions. We will see, though, that imperfect financial markets can change the optimal investment choice, particularly when we are making decisions on behalf of other investors. Because imperfect markets increase choices, difficult decisions arise with regard to both wealth-maximizing choices for the shareholders and implied ethical obligations to other stakeholders.

We will first examine the position of a stockholder in a firm that operates in perfect financial markets. Recall that in perfect financial markets there are no taxes, transaction costs, or other restrictions keeping buyers and sellers from entering or exiting the market; no one buyer or seller is large enough to affect price through any action; identical information is costlessly available to everyone, resulting in identical beliefs; and all participants are rational wealth maximizers.

We will begin with a firm financed entirely with equity. Then we will consider a firm funded with both debt and equity. Then we will introduce financial market imperfections in the form of taxes and incomplete information. We will see that the net present value directly measures wealth in perfect markets and is robust with regard to the handling of imperfections.

ALL-EQUITY FINANCING

In these perfect market conditions, there is no difference between making the decision for ourselves and making it for our shareholders. In the case of all-equity financing, cash flow from an investment is also cash available to distribute to the shareholders or reinvest on their behalf. This is the simplest case, and we showed in the prior chapter that the wealth of the shareholders is increased by the net present value of the investment. We demonstrated in the prior chapter that the value of an investment opportunity was the same in perfect markets, whether the equity portion of its funding came from retention of earnings or the sale of new stock.

Example. Berner Corporation is financed entirely with equity, and Berner's stockholders could earn a 12 percent return elsewhere. Berner is considering an investment that requires an initial outlay of $1,500 and generates the year-end cash inflows in Table 5.2.

  If 12 percent is the rate shareholders could earn elsewhere, then they would be required to invest $1,709.18 elsewhere to buy the same benefits generated by this asset, so the benefits have a value of $1,709.18. The value of the benefit exceeds the required investment by $209.18, the amount by which the wealth of the shareholders is increased.

DEBT-EQUITY MIX AND NPV

When companies finance their investment with a combination of debt and equity, we refer to the average opportunity cost—the average rate of return investors could earn elsewhere—as the weighted average cost of capital. The weighted average cost of capital (WACC) is:

$$\text{WACC} = W_d K_d + (1 - W_d) K_e \tag{5-3}$$

where

W_d = debt as a percent of the present value of remaining future benefits from the investment

K_d = the rate of return creditors could expect elsewhere by taking the same risk they are taking when they lend to this company

K_e = the rate of return stockholders could expect elsewhere by taking the same risk they are taking when they invest in the stock of this company

| TABLE 5.2 ANALYSIS OF BERNER CORPORATION CAPITAL INVESTMENT

This table illustrates the computation and meaning of NPV when a company is financed entirely with equity.

Year	0	1	2
Cash flow	(1,500.00)	1,200.00	800.00
Present value (12%)	(1,500.00)	1,071.43	637.75
Total present value	1,709.18		
Net present value	209.18		

Suppose Berner Corporation were to buy the prior asset but maintain debt equal to 50 percent of value. Further, suppose that stockholders could earn 14 percent elsewhere with the same risk they are taking by investing in this company, and bondholders could earn 10 percent elsewhere. For this company, the weighted average cost of capital is then:

$$\text{WACC} = .5 \times .10 + (1 - .5).14 = 12\%$$

Since Berner's cost of capital is still 12 percent in this example, the net present value is still $209.18, but are the shareholders still better off by $209.18? The key to answering the question is to analyze the cash flows to and from the shareholders, as is done in Table 5.3. Remember that we assumed debt would remain at 50 percent of the *present value of future benefits,* with the WACC used as the discount rate to compute that present value. At time 0, the present value is $1,709.18, so the amount of debt is half of that amount, or $854.59, and the initial equity required is only $645.41 ($1,500 − $854.59). In later periods, debt must be reduced to half of the present value of remaining benefits, so part of the cash flow from the investment is used to repay debt as well as to make interest payments.

The cash flows to the shareholders are discounted at the return shareholders could have earned elsewhere by taking the same risk: 14 percent. The share-

| TABLE 5.3 | NPV TO STOCKHOLDERS WITH DEBT |

This table demonstrates that NPV also measures wealth creation for shareholders when debt is included in the financing and maintained at a constant percentage of the present value of future cash flows.

Year	0	1	2
Cash flow from investment	(1,500.00)	1,200.00	800.00
P.V. of remaining cash flows (12%)	1,709.18	714.29	0.00
Debt (50% of P.V. of remaining cash flows)	854.59	357.14	0.00
Borrow (repay)	854.59	(497.45)	(357.14)
Cash flow from investment	(1,500.00)	1,200.00	800.00
Interest expense*		85.46	35.71
Borrow (repay)	854.59	(497.45)	(357.14)
Cash flow to (from) equity	(645.41)	617.09	407.15
PV (14%)	(645.41)	541.30	313.29
PV	854.59		
NPV	209.18		

*Debt outstanding at time zero is not repaid until the end of year 1, so first-year interest is .10 × $854.59 = $85.46, and second year interest is .10 × 357.14 = $35.71.

holders would have to invest $854.59 elsewhere to get the same expected cash flows, but they can buy these cash flows for $645.41 by joining the creditors in funding this investment. The wealth of the shareholders is increased by the difference of $209.18.

What can we conclude? The net present value computed using the weighted average cost of capital as the discount rate is the amount by which the wealth of the shareholders is increased if the company acquires the investment. This conclusion rests on the assumption that debt remains a constant percentage of the present value of future benefits. The net present value would still measure shareholder wealth creation if the debt ratio were determined in some other way, but the opportunity cost of debt and equity would probably change from period to period. It was also assumed that the financial markets were perfect. We will see that the net present value computed using the weighted average cost of capital still holds if taxes are introduced as a market imperfection.

INCOME TAXES, NPV, AND WEALTH CREATION |

While taxation of business income causes a variety of annoying problems, including reductions in the *amount* of net present value, they do not change the *meaning* of the net present value. With or without taxes, and with or without debt, the net present value is the amount by which an investment increases the wealth of the shareholders.

We will avoid a lengthy discussion of taxes at this time, but there are two important tax considerations that must be recognized. Tax law does not allow a company to deduct the cost of acquiring an asset from its taxable income. Instead, tax law generally allows the company to recognize the wearing out of an asset as depreciation expense each year over the asset's life, so taxable income after the asset acquisition year is typically less than cash benefits. Tax laws specify the amount of depreciation expense that can be used each year to reduce taxable income. Second, interest expense is treated in the tax laws as an expense that reduces taxable income, while payments to stockholders and repayment of debt do not reduce taxable income.

To illustrate the unchanged meaning of net present value when taxes are introduced, assume that Berner now pays tax equal to 40 percent of income. The initial $1,500 purchase price of the asset does not reduce taxable income, but tax laws allow depreciation expense of $900 in year 1 and $600 in year 2. There are no tax consequences from the asset purchase at time zero, but later income taxes, in the absence of interest expense, are as follows:

$$\text{Year I tax: } (\$1,200 - \$900) \times .40 = \$120$$

$$\text{Year 2 tax: } (\$800 - \$600) \times .40 = \$80$$

After-tax cash flows near the top of Table 5.4 reflect these tax implications.

| **TABLE 5.4** **NPV TO STOCKHOLDERS WITH DEBT AND TAXES**

This table demonstrates that the NPV also measures wealth creation for shareholders when debt is included in the financing and the company must pay income tax.

Year	0	1	2
Cash flow from investment	($1,500.00)	$1,200.00	$ 800.00
−Tax		120.00	80.00
After-tax cash flow from investment			
without interest expense	(1,500.00)	1,080.00	720.00
P.V. of remaining cash			
flows at WACC of 10%	1,576.86	654.55	0.00
Debt	788.43	327.28	0.00
Borrow (repay)	788.43	(461.15)	(327.28)
After-tax cash flow from			
investment	(1,500.00)	1,080.00	720.00
Interest expense		(78.84)	(32.73)
Interest tax savings		31.54	13.09
Borrow (repay)	788.43	(461.15)	(327.28)
Cash flow to (from) equity	(711.57)	571.55	373.08
Present value (14%)	(711.57)	501.36	287.07
PV	788.43		
NPV	$ 76.86		

The company still uses debt equal to 50 percent of the present value of remaining cash flows. The equity holders could still earn 14 percent (after corporate tax but before personal tax) by investing elsewhere at equal risk. Bondholders could earn 10 percent before personal tax by investing somewhere else at equal risk. A dollar of interest expense reduces taxes by $0.40, so the after-tax cost of debt is:

$$K_d = .10(1 - .40) = 6\%$$

The weighted average cost of capital is then:

$$WACC = .50 \times .06 + (1 - .50) \times .14 = 10\%$$

We continue in Table 5.4 to identify the cash flows to and from the shareholders. The first step is to compute the present value of future benefits using the 10 percent cost of capital as the discount rate. The next step is to determine the amount of debt each period, in order to maintain debt equal to 50 percent of the present value of future benefits. Cash flows to shareholders are then determined by subtracting debt repayment and interest expense from cash flows.

The computation of cash flows to shareholders is the same as in Table 5.3, except that each dollar of income is taxed, and each dollar of interest expense reduces taxable income by one dollar.

The analysis of cash flows to and from shareholders yields a NPV of $76.86, so we know that the wealth of the shareholders is being increased by $76.86. This is lower than the NPV in the absence of taxes, because part of the benefits of the project was shared with the government.

As was true in the absence of taxes, we can also find the same NPV by computing the present values of after-tax cash flows as they would be in the absence of interest expense, discounted at the weighted average cost of capital:

$$NPV = \$1,080/1.10^1 + \$720/1.10^2 - \$1,500 = \$76.86$$

This example again illustrates the following relationship.

Net present value of after-tax cash flows from the investment, before considering the impact of financing choice, discounted at the weighted average cost of capital	=	Wealth gain to the shareholders, based on an analysis of the cash flows to and from the shareholders, considering the shareholders' opportunity cost

We will avoid delving further into taxes until later, and avoid delving into the details of weighted average cost of capital until later as well. For the time being, though, we can be comfortable knowing that if we are given some cash flows and a weighted average cost of capital, the net present value of those cash flows, using the weighted average cost of capital, is the amount by which the investment will increase the wealth of the shareholders.

ECONOMIC PROFIT AND NPV

Economic profit and net present value are closely linked strategically in that competitive advantage is needed for economic profit, and net present value can be thought of as economic profit for a multiyear decision. Therefore, positive net present values have competitive advantage as their foundation. It was mentioned in Chapter 4, and demonstrated for a perpetuity, that *net present value is the present value of economic profit*. The same relationship holds for other capital investments. To demonstrate this point, assume that the tax people were right in determining the depreciation of $900 the first year and $600 the second year that was used to determine taxable income for Table 5.4; the asset actually loses value at that rate. If we define profit as actual cash flow plus or minus any change in the value of the asset, then profit, as shown in Table 5.5, is $180 in year 1 and $120 in year 2. The normal profit is the 10 percent weighted average cost

| **TABLE 5.5** **ECONOMIC PROFIT AND NPV**

This table demonstrates that net present value is the present value of economic profit when the asset's life is limited.

Year	1	2
After-tax cash flow in the absence of interest expense	$1,080	$720
Depreciation	900	600
Profit (Cash flow − Loss of value)	180	120
Normal profit (10% of beginning value)	150	60
Economic profit	30	60
Present value (10% WACC)	27.27	49.59

NPV = $27.27 + $49.59 = $76.86

of capital applied to the value of the asset: $1,500 at the beginning of the first year and $1,500 − $900 = $600 at the beginning of the second year.[3] The present value of the economic profit exactly equals the NPV that was previously computed using both cash flows without interest expense and cash flows to and from stockholders.

The important point from Table 5.5 is the linkage between net present value and economic profit. We can say two things about economic profit:

NPV = Present value of benefits − Present value of cash outlays

NPV = Present value of economic profit

The relationship between economic profit and net present value is important because it highlights the role of competitive advantage in creating wealth. It will also prove important in the final chapter of this book, when we deal with management policy in support of wealth-creating financial decisions.

[3]For the purpose of concluding that NPV is the present value of economic profit, we need not be overly concerned about whether the tax collector was right in determining depreciation amounts. Letting D_1 be the amount of actual loss in value in year one, the calculations in Table 5.5 can be written as the following formula:

$$NPV = (1,080 - D_1 - .10 \times 1,500)/1.10 + [720 - (1,500 - D_1) - .10(1,500 - D_1)]/1.10^2$$

Rearranging terms,

$$NPV = (1,080 - .10 \times 1,500)/1.10 + (720 - 1,500 - .10 \times 1,500)/1.10^2 - D_1/1.10 + 1.10 \, D_1/1.10^2$$

D_1 cancels out of the formula. Therefore, the NPV does not depend on the amount of actual loss of value each year, as long as the total loss is $1,500; otherwise residual value would be part of the cash flow. A change in the amount the tax collector allows each year would matter, on the other hand, because it would change the timing of the tax reduction from depreciation.

UNCERTAINTY AND **NPV**

Our conclusions about the meaning of the net present value also hold in the face of risk. We assume here that all investments being considered are equally risky. (Differences in risk will be dealt with in Part III of this book.) To deal with risk, we define k_o a bit more precisely as the return available elsewhere on opportunities of equal risk to those of our company. This is, of course, not a radical redefinition. After all, k_o is the average return we must pay to investors, and investors generally require compensation if they are to take risks. Therefore, other companies with similar risks must provide investors with similar expected returns. We substitute expected cash flow at time t, $E(CF_t)$, for known cash flow at time t. By saying that other investments of equal risk have an expected return of k_o, we mean that the price of an alternate investment that provides a single expected amount $E(CF_t)$ at time t has a price of:

$$\text{Price of alternate investment} = E(CF_t)/(1 + k_o)^t$$

The net present value of an investment that provides expected cash flows in a number of future periods is then:

$$NPV = \sum_{t=1}^{n} \frac{E(CF_t)}{(1 + k_o)^t} - I_o \tag{5-4}$$

Net present value has the same general meaning in risk and certainty. The present value of an expected cash flow is the amount that could be invested elsewhere to generate the same expected cash flow.

UNINFORMED INVESTORS AND **NPV**

If investors are not well informed about future profitability of the company's existing assets and investment opportunities, the market value of the stock may be different from its *intrinsic value,* which is the value that would exist if all potential investors had the same information that was available to the person determining the intrinsic value. This problem was first discussed in Chapter 4, when valuation principles were being established. Difference between current market price and intrinsic value can cause otherwise attractive investments to actually decrease shareholder wealth and can, therefore, lead to the rejection of otherwise attractive investments. Poorly informed investors are a serious problem, which management must work to correct. Nevertheless, the net present value criterion can still be applied, with a modification.

A key point about the problem of investors being misinformed about the current value of the company is that the investors' mistaken view is temporary. Investors become informed over time as cash flows come in. Eventually, they will most likely be properly informed and share price will equal intrinsic value per share. Even if the share price is never properly adjusted, the bulk of the value will be in the benefit stream over a long time horizon, and all of the value will be in the benefit stream over an infinite time horizon. A reasonable approach is to measure the impact of a new investment on intrinsic value. For this purpose, we define the intrinsic net present value of a proposed capital investment:

$$NPV_I = IE_n(S_o/S_n) - IE_o \qquad (5\text{-}7)$$

where

IE_n = intrinsic value of the equity with the proposed capital investment

IE_o = intrinsic value of the equity without the proposed capital investment

S_n = number of shares of stock if the new investment is made

S_o = number of shares of stock already outstanding

Example. Albers Corporation generates cash flow of $1 million a year for the shareholders, after reinvesting a sufficient portion of income to assure continuation at the current level of profitability. The company has 100,000 shares of stock outstanding. Cash flow per share is therefore $10. Stockholders could earn 10 percent elsewhere taking the same risk. The stockholders are misinformed, so they expect cash flow of only $8 a share.

	Per Share	Total Equity
Intrinsic value	$10/.10 = $100	$100 × 100,000 = $10,000,000
Actual price	$ 8/.10 = $ 80	$ 80 × 100,000 = $ 8,000,000

The company has an opportunity to make a new investment that would require $2 million of additional equity. The present value of the cash inflows to equity would be $2.4 million, so the project is attractive. If investors were properly informed, the project would have a net present value of $400,000. Because investors are not informed, the total number of shares that will exist if the new investment is made is:

$$S_n = 100,000 + 2,000,000/80 = 125,000$$

Thus, the intrinsic net present value is:

$$NPV_I = \$12,400,000(100,000/125,000) - \$10,000,000 = -\$80,000$$

The investment is unattractive because investors are not well informed, despite the fact that the investment would have created wealth of $400,000 for existing shareholders if investors were properly informed.

What about using retained earnings to fund the project and avoid the problem of selling stock below its intrinsic value? Bear in mind that a stockholder who receives dividends can use those dividends to buy more stock at the lower price, and a stockholder who wants cash will be forced to sell some stock at the lower price if dividends are not paid. Thus, the retention of earnings to fund new investments does not mitigate the problem of a stock price below the intrinsic value. What about funding the new project with debt to avoid using undervalued equity? This is sometimes done, but changes in the debt-equity mix involve a complex set of trade-offs that will be discussed later in this book.

What is the best solution to the problem of misinformed investors? Work hard to ensure that your estimates of future benefits are correct. Then communicate honestly with the investors. Honesty might be viewed as its own reward, but in this case ethical behavior has more direct benefits in that it helps you establish a reputation for honesty. A reputation for honesty is an extremely useful tool for keeping investors informed so that the price does not diverge from the intrinsic value.

SUMMARY

Wealth creation is generally considered to be the goal of the firm. Net present value measures the amount by which a proposed investment will increase the wealth of the shareholders, assuming the cash flows from the investment are used for the benefit of the shareholders. Net present value is defined as:

$$= \sum_{t=1}^{n} \frac{CF_t}{(1 + k)^t} - I_o$$

where CF_t is cash flow at time t, I_o is the initial investment, and k is the rate of return investors could earn elsewhere by taking the same risk. The net present value measures both the wealth creation of the shareholders and the ability of the shareholders to increase consumption today while holding consumption constant in all future periods. It can also be thought of as the economic profit for a project with a life longer than one period.

The net present value is a robust measure of investment desirability. Three different forms of computation result in precisely the same net present value as long as a constant ratio of debt to value is maintained:

NPV = present value of cash benefits, minus the present value of cash costs other than financing costs, discounted at the average cost of debt and equity funds.

NPV = present value of cash flows to stockholders, minus present value of cash flows from stockholders, discounted at the stockholders' opportunity cost.

NPV = present value of economic profits, discounted at the stockholders' opportunity cost

The validity of the net present value as the measure of wealth creation is easily demonstrated in the case of perfect financial markets. Fortunately, the net present value also measures wealth creation when there are taxes and when results are uncertain. A modification called the intrinsic net present value can even measure wealth creation from the shareholders' perspective when investors have biased expectations.

If our goal is to create wealth, and net present value measures the amount by which a capital investment creates wealth, it then follows that net present value is the key guideline for capital investment decisions. We will be applying net present value throughout the remainder of this book.

QUESTIONS |

5–1. Explain in your own words the meaning of net present value.

5–2. How is the meaning of net present value changed when cash flows are uncertain?

5–3. How is the meaning of net present value changed when investors are not fully informed?

5–4. What conditions define a perfect financial market?

5–5. Explain the relationship between economic profit and net present value. Why is that relationship important?

5–6. Why is it in management's best interest to keep shareholders informed of the size and the nature of the capital projects accepted in a given year?

5–7. Why is it in management's best interest to have the market price equal the intrinsic price?

5–8. What may happen if the market price is greater than the intrinsic value?

5–9. It can be said that net present value measures three things. What are they?

5–10. Given the market's propensity to extrapolate the growth in the past into the future, is it better to excel in a slow-growth industry or to be middle-of-the-road in a rapid-growth industry? What dangers are involved with each situation?

5–11. Many firms have encouraged their employees to own stock in the company they work for. Using this chapter and what you have learned so far about wealth creation, how would you explain to the employee the importance of his job in increasing the stock price? Assume that this employee is an operations person meeting the customer.

5–12. (Application) Pfizer Corporation announced a new capital investment program, and its stock price increased. Western Digital (a disk-drive maker) Corporation announced a new capital investment program, and its stock price decreased. How do you explain these opposing responses? What should a company that is considering a new capital investment conclude from this evidence?

5–13. (Ethical considerations) There are several ways you might earn an economic profit, and therefore a positive net present value. For each of the methods discussed below, indicate whether it is ethical to earn a positive net present value in that way.

a. Take advantage of economies of scale.

b. Force competitors out of business by temporarily cutting your price until they go bankrupt.

c. Charge more than cost for a lifesaving drug that you invented and patented.

d. Develop a superior product.

e. Develop a unique image through advertising.

f. Acquire all of your competitors to create a monopoly.

g. Meet with your competitors to agree on a common price.

PROBLEMS |

(Assume no taxes unless taxes are specifically mentioned in the problem.)

5–1. Sealand Corporation is considering acquiring a newer, more modern machine. The machine, which requires an initial outlay of $3 million, will generate cash flows of $1 million at the end of each year for five years. Investors could earn 10 percent elsewhere in opportunities of equal risk. Compute the net present value and explain what it means to investors.

5–2. Compute the net present value for the asset in problem 1 if cash inflows are received at midyear.

5–3. Claremont Corporation is considering starting a new division. The required investment is $1 million. Cash inflows are expected to be $50,000 at the end of the first year and are expected to grow at 6 percent a year thereafter. At a required return of 10 percent, compute the net present value.

5–4. Conway Auto is considering a new business development program. Anticipated benefits are $100,000 in the first year, $200,000 in the second year, and $400,000 in the third year. Benefits will decline 10 percent a year after the third year, and will end after the tenth year. Assume these benefits are received at year-end. The effective required return is 10 percent. What is the present value of these benefits? If the development program requires an initial outlay of $500,000, what is the net present value?

5–5. Alborg Corporation is considering the introduction of a new product. The required investment is $1 million, and anticipated year-end cash flows are as follows:

Year	1	2	3	4
Cash flow	$300,000	$400,000	$500,000	$200,000

Compute the net present value using a 10 percent required return.

5–6. Find the net present value for the investment in problem 5 if cash inflows arrive at the end of the third quarter each year rather than at the end of the year.

5–7. A machine can be purchased today for $1 million. It will generate cash flows of $200,000 at the end of each year for ten years. However, a $300,000 overhaul will be required at the end of year 5. At a 10 percent opportunity cost of money, compute the net present value of this investment.

5–8. A new factory at Arcata requires an initial outlay of $1 million. Of this $1 million, $400,000 must be paid immediately and $200,000 will be paid at the end of each year for the next three years. At the end of the three-year construction period, the factory will go into service and will last for ten years, after which it can be sold for a salvage value of $200,000. Sales will be $1 million during the first year of operation and will grow at a rate of 10 percent a year after that. Variable costs will be 50 percent of sales and fixed costs will be $300,000 a year. All costs are in cash. Assume cash flows occur at year-end. At a 10 percent required return, is the factory an attractive investment? If there are 1,000 shares outstanding, how much wealth per share has been created?

5–9. Alpha Corporation is considering a new $3 million capital investment that will generate cash flows of $1 million at the end of each year for four years. The company, which pays no taxes, finances its investments with debt equal to 40 percent of the present value of future cash flows. Lenders charge 6 percent and stockholders require a 16 percent return.

   a. Compute the net present value of the capital investment using a weighted average cost of capital.

   b. Compute the net present value of the cash flows to and from shareholders using the shareholders' required return.

5–10. Beta Corporation pays a 40 percent tax rate. A new $3 million investment will generate after-tax cash flows of $1 million a year for four years if the company uses no debt. The company will, however, use debt equal to 60 percent of the present value of future cash flows. Pretax interest on debt is 10 percent, and stockholders require a 16 percent return on their investment.

   a. Compute the net present value of the capital investment using a weighted average cost of capital.

   b. Compute the net present value of the cash flows to and from shareholders using the shareholders' required return.

5–11. A $1 million capital investment will generate cash flows of $700,000 at the end of each year for two years, after which it will be worthless.

   a. Compute the net present value using a 10 percent required return.

   b. Assume depreciation of $600,000 the first year and $400,000 the second year, compute the economic profit for each year, and compute the present value of the economic profit.

5–12. Kerlagen Corporation's existing assets will provide cash flows for the stockholders of $1 million a year indefinitely, and stockholders require a 10 percent return. The company has 500,000 shares of stock outstanding, dividends are $2 per share per year, and the stock is currently selling for $20 a share. A new $100,000 capital investment will provide cash flows of $30,000 a year for five years, which will be paid out as additional dividends.

    a. Compute the net present value. Is the investment attractive?

    b. By how much will the investment increase the intrinsic net present value of the project?

5–13. For Kerlagen Corporation (problem 12), is the investment attractive if investors are not informed and the stock is selling for $12 a share? $18 a share?

5–14. An asset needed by La Jolla Corporation can be purchased for $100,000. Maintenance and other ownership expenses will be $20,000 at the end of each year for the asset's ten-year life. Alternately, the company can avoid the purchase price and ownership costs by leasing the asset for $45,000 at the end of each year for ten years. If the required return is 10 percent, which alternative should the company use?

5–15. Nancy Geer is considering an MBA degree. She estimates that she will forgo after-tax income of $9,600 a year (she will have a part-time job), during the two years it will take her to complete the degree, but her expenses will be $3,600 a year less than if she were working. Tuition will be $10,000 at the beginning of each year. She estimates that her income will be $4,800 a year higher, after tax, for her 40-year working life if she receives the MBA. She can borrow the money needed at an interest cost of 8 percent, after tax. Would you recommend that she pursue the MBA degree?

5–16. Suppose Geer (problem 15) will have income that is $4,000 higher the first year, and the difference will grow at 4 percent a year thereafter. What does this do to the attractiveness of the MBA degree?

5–17. If Texarkana Retread Tire Company purchases an automatic blender, material waste will be reduced by $10,000 in the first year. Because of inflation, the savings will increase 8 percent a year over the blender's ten-year life, after which the blender can then be sold as scrap for $20,000. Assume savings occur at year-end. At a 10 percent effective required return, what is the maximum price the company can afford to pay for the blender?

5–18. An investment being considered by Siloam Spring Water Distributing requires an initial outlay of $1 million and an additional outlay of $500,000 at the end of five years. The investment will provide returns of $200,000 a year for the first five years and $300,000 a year for the second five years. These cash inflows will be received at midyear. At the end of 10 years, the investment will be sold for a salvage value of $250,000. At a 10 percent effective required return, is this an attractive investment?

CASE PROBLEM |

Midcity Center, Inc. (A)

The board of trustees meeting of Midcity Center, Inc., was called to order at 7:30 P.M. There was considerable interest in several proposals before the board, and the discussion promised to be lively.

Midcity Center, Inc., was located in a run-down part of an old industrial city. The center was a nonprofit corporation formed by a coalition of churches to serve the needs of inner-city poor. Services provided by the center included temporary quarters for the homeless, hot meals once a day for the indigent, and the General Store. The General Store carried free used clothing and free nonperishable foods for the poor. In addition, the center housed a store called the "Center Boutique," which sold donated items to help cover the center's costs.

Midcity Center was funded by annual pledges from the coalition churches. The center also had an endowment fund as a result of several substantial bequests. The endowment fund was controlled by the center's board of trustees, who had complete discretion with regard to investment policy. The board also had the authority to spend the entire endowment fund, but they had always maintained a strict policy of preserving the principal and spending only the income.

The endowment fund had a balance of $1.2 million, invested entirely in corporate bonds. The average interest rate on the bonds was 7 percent, but many of the bonds were selling at a discount due to rising interest rates since their purchase. Yields to maturity for bonds of this type were currently 10 percent.

The proposals before the board that evening involved the use of endowment principal. The center had been plagued by rising energy costs, with heating bills for the past year totaling $14,230. T. Haley, the board member who chaired the building committee, had brought in a consultant to conduct an energy survey. Two proposals arose from that survey.

One proposal involved 68 storm windows at a cost of $230 each. This would decrease heat usage by 20 percent. Another proposal called for the acquisition of a new high-efficiency furnace for $27,630. This furnace would reduce the amount of fuel used for each unit of heat by 40 percent. Haley analyzed both proposals assuming a ten-year building life, and recommended both. Since the building budget included only $12,000 a year for improvements, this would mean dipping into the endowment. Several members objected strongly to spending the endowment principal, suggesting that this would start a trend leading to bankruptcy. One member suggested that borrowing money would be preferable and indicated that a local bank would charge 12 percent with the endowment assets as security. Another member said that the endowment should serve the poor, not the building, and took the opportunity to argue again for an allocation of $100,000 of endowment principal to develop a center for abused children.

After a long discussion, the president broke in. "I believe all positions have been clarified. May we have a motion so that we can vote?"

CASE QUESTIONS

1. Using a 10 percent discount rate, compute the net present value of the storm window investment without a new furnace.
2. Using a 10 percent discount rate, compute the net present value of the furnace investment without new storm windows.
3. Using a 10 percent discount rate, compute the combined net present value from investing in both furnace and storm window investment.
4. Is an investment in energy reduction more risky than an investment in corporate bonds?
5. What discount rate should be used to evaluate the energy savings project?
6. Which investments, if any, should the board accept?
7. If you recommended accepting one or both investments, how should these investments be financed?
8. Would you characterize the board's approach to capital investment decisions as guided by strategy or as reaction as proposals arise?
9. Comment on the capital investment policy of Midcity Center. How could that capital investment policy be improved?

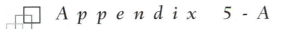

Appendix 5-A

ENTREPRENEURS, WEALTH, AND CONSUMPTION

In the chapter we have addressed the net present value from the point of the wealth of equity investors who gain from attractive investments. Suppose, instead, that the investment opportunity has been discovered by an entrepreneur who has no personal capital. Inspection of Table 5.2, 5.3, or 5.4 should make it clear that the present value of the future cash flows from an investment, discounted at the weighted average cost of capital, is the amount that could be raised from a combination of external equity investors and lenders by promising them all the future cash flows from the investment. If that present value exceeds the required outlay for the investment, the resulting net present value is the entrepreneur's wealth increase. In Table 5.4, for example, the entrepreneur could raise $1,576.86, half from stockholders and half from creditors, in exchange for the future cash flows from the investment. Since only $1,500 is actually required, the entrepreneur can pocket the remaining $76.86 as her wealth increase.

The entrepreneur provides a convenient launching point for the observation that the net present value also measures the change in current consumption made possible by an investment, *for any given pattern of future consumption.* To show this to be true, start with a person who has some wealth and a capital investment opportunity, hereafter called the *wealth holder*. This wealth holder wants to increase present consumption without decreasing planned future consumption. The wealth holder has decided to spend amount C_t on consumption at time t and is considering an investment that will provide CF_t at time t.

The present value of a series of future cash flows is the amount of money that can be raised from a combination of creditors and equity investors, based on the promise to give them the future stream of cash flows. Thus, the amount of capital that can be raised *today* based on a promise to pay $CF_t - C_t$ at time t is:

$$\text{Capital raised today} = \frac{(CF_t - C_t)}{(1 + k_o)^t}$$

where k_o is the weighted average cost of capital: $W_d k_d + (1 - W_d)k_e$. If the capital investment will provide cash flow over n future periods, and the wealth holder wants to consume in each of those periods, the amount the wealth holder can consume at present (C_o) is:

$$C_o = \sum_{t=1}^{n} \frac{CF_t - C_t}{(1 + k_o)^t} + (W_o - I_o) \qquad \text{(5-5)}$$

where W_o is the wealth holder's beginning wealth and I_o the cost of the proposed capital investment. Rearranging terms gives Equation 5-6:

$$C_o = \left[\sum_{t=1}^{n} \frac{CF_t}{(1 + k_o)^t} - I_o \right] + \left[W_o - \sum_{t=1}^{n} \frac{C_t}{(1 + k_o)^t} \right] \qquad \text{(5-6)}$$

The first bracketed expression in Equation 5-5 is the net present value of the proposed investment. The second bracketed expression includes wealth and consumption that were not changed as a result of the investment. Thus, the net present value is the change in ability to consume now as a result of the investment. Instead of present consumption, the wealth holder may wish to maximize consumption in some future period t, while holding consumption constant in the present period and all other future periods. The change in the amount that can be consumed in that one future period increases by:

$$\text{Change in period t consumption} = NPV(1 + k_o)^t$$

Example. Assume the Berner Corporation investment opportunity in Table 5.4 was discovered by an entrepreneur whose personal wealth of $500 was invested in a combination of corporate stocks and bonds, providing an average return of 10 percent. The entrepreneur could use part of her own money for this investment, but to keep it simple we will assume she does not. She will consume $100 now and leave the remaining $400 invested at 10 percent so she can consume $240 at the end of the first year and $220 at the end of the second year, which will exhaust her wealth.[4] The entrepreneur raises $1,576.86, half in debt and half in equity. She uses $1,500 to acquire the project, and the entire future proceeds will be required to pay off the creditors and stockholders. The $76.86 difference between the amount raised based on a promise of all future benefits and the amount needed for the investment can be used by the entrepreneur to increase immediate consumption, while holding future consumption constant. Using Equation 5-4, the same conclusion is drawn:

$$C_0 = \frac{(\$1,080 - \$240)}{1.10^1} + \frac{(\$720 - \$220)}{1.10^2} + (\$500 - \$1,500) = \$176.86$$

Recall that the entrepreneur was going to consume $100 immediately, without the capital investment. Immediate consumption is increased by the amount of the NPV, with no change in future consumption. Alternately, the extra $76.86 could be invested at 10 percent to increase consumption in some future period by more than $76.86.

It is not surprising that the net present value, which measures the impact of an investment on shareholder wealth, also measures the impact of an investment on the ability of the shareholder who owns the company's investment opportunities to consume goods and services. This is simply another confirmation of the usefulness of net present value as a decision tool.

PROBLEMS |

5-A-1. John Smith has $1 million invested at 10 percent return. Smith can either invest or borrow at the 10 percent rate. A new $200,000 investment opportunity has come up. The investment will provide cash flows of $60,000 a year for five years.

    a. Compute the NPV of the new investment.

    b. Smith intends to consume $100,000 at the end of each year forever. How much more can Smith consume today with the new investment?

5-A-2. Suppose Smith does not want to increase present consumption. Instead, Smith would like to increase consumption at the end of each year from $100,000 to some higher amount. By how much can Smith increase consumption at the end of each future year as a result of this investment?

---

[4]The $400 grows 10 percent to $440 in one year, and $240 is then consumed, leaving $200. The $200 grows 10 percent to $220 at the end of the second year.

SELECTED REFERENCES |

Aucamp, Donald C., and Walter L. Eckardt, Jr. "A Sufficient Condition for a Unique Nonnegative Internal Rate of Return—Comment." *Journal of Financial and Quantitative Analysis* 11 (June 1976): 329–332.

Bailey, M. J. "Formal Criteria for Investment Decisions." *Journal of Political Economy* (October 1959).

Beaves, Robert G. "The Case for a Generalized Net Present Value Formula." *Engineering Economist* 38 (Winter 1993): 119–133.

Brigham, Eugene F., and Richard H. Pettway. "Capital Budgeting by Utilities." *Financial Management* 2 (Autumn 1973): 11–22.

Dearden, J. "The Case against ROI Control." *Harvard Business Review* (May–June 1969): 124–135.

Dorfman, Robert. "The Meaning of Internal Rates of Return." *Journal of Finance* 36 (December 1981): 1011–1021.

Durand, David. "Comprehensiveness in Capital Budgeting." *Financial Management* 10 (Winter 1981): 7–13.

Fama, Eugene F. "Organizational Forms and Investment Decisions." *Journal of Financial Economics* 14 (March 1985): 101–119.

Fisher, Irving. *The Theory of Interest.* New York: Macmillan, 1930.

Fogler, H. Russell. "Overkill in Capital Budgeting Technique?" *Financial Management* 1 (Spring 1972): 92–96.

Gitman, Lawrence J., and John R. Forrester, Jr. "A Survey of Capital Budgeting Techniques Used by Major U. S. Firms." *Financial Management* 6 (Fall 1977): 66–71.

Gurnami, G. "Capital Budgeting Theory and Practice." *Engineering Economist* 30 (Fall 1984).

Hastie, K. Larry. "One Businessman's View of Capital Budgeting." *Financial Management* 3 (Winter 1974): 36–44.

Hayes, R., and W. Abernathy. "Managing Our Way to Economic Decline." *Harvard Business Review* (July–August 1980): 67–77.

Hirshleifer, Jack. "On the Theory of Optimal Investment Decision." *Journal of Political Economy* (August 1958): 329–352.

Khan, Aman. "Capital Budgeting Practices in Large U. S. Cities." *Engineering Economist* 33 (Fall 1987): 1–12.

Klammer, Thomas P., and Michael C. Walker. "Capital Budgeting Questionnaires: A New Perspective." *Quarterly Journal of Business and Economics* 26 (Summer 1987): 87–95.

———. "The Continued Increase in the Use of Sophisticated Capital Budgeting Techniques." *California Management Review* 27 (Fall 1984): 137–148.

Lewellen, Wilbur G., Howard P. Lanswe, and John J. McConnell. "Payback Substitutes for Discounted Cash Flow." *Financial Management* 2 (Summer 1973): 17–23.

Martin, John D., Samuel H. Cox, and Richard D. MacMinn. *The Theory of Finance: Evidence and Applications.* Hinsdale, Ill.: Dryden Press, 1988.

McConnell, John, and C. Muscarella. "Corporate Capital Expenditure Decisions and the Market Value of the Firm." *Journal of Financial Economics* 14 (September 1985): 399–422.

Middlaugh, J. Kendall, II, and Scott S. Cowen. "Five Flaws in Evaluating Capital Expenditures." *Business Horizons* 30 (March–April 1987): 59–67.

Mukherjee, Tarun K., and David F. Scott, Jr. "The Capital Budgeting Process in Large Firms: An Analysis of Capital Budgeting Manuals." Paper presented at the Eastern Finance Association meeting, April 1987.

Narayanan, M. P. "Observability and the Payback Criterion." *Journal of Business* 58 (July 1985): 309–323.

Reimann, Bernard C. "Stock Price and Business Success: What Is the Relationship?" *Journal of Business Strategy* 8 (Summer 1987): 38–49.

Ross, Marc. "Capital Budgeting Practices of Twelve Large Manufacturers." *Financial Management* 15 (Winter 1986): 15–22.

Samuelson, Paul A. "Some Aspects of the Pure Theory of Capital." *Quarterly Journal of Economics* (May 1937): 469–96.

Schall, Lawrence D., Gary L. Sundem, and William R. Geijsbeek. "Survey and Analysis of Capital Budgeting Methods." *Journal of Finance* 33 (March 1978): 281–287.

Scott, David F., Jr., and J. William Petty III. "Capital Budgeting Practices in Large American Firms: A Retrospective Analysis and Synthesis." *Financial Review* 19 (March 1984): 111–125.

Sundem, Gary L. "Evaluating Capital Budgeting Models in Simulated Environments." *Journal of Finance* 30 (September 1975): 977–992.

Woods, John C., and Maury R. Randall. "The Net Present Value of Future Investment Opportunities: Its Impact on Shareholder Wealth and Implications for Capital Budgeting Theory." *Financial Management* 18 (Summer 1989): 85–92.

CHAPTER 6

ALTERNATE MEASURES OF CAPITAL INVESTMENT DESIRABILITY

After completing this chapter you should be able to:

1. Calculate and explain the meaning of:
   a. Profitability index
   b. Modified profitability index
   c. Internal rate of return
   d. Modified internal rate of return
   e. Payback period
   f. Present value payback
   g. Accounting rate of return
2. Explain the reinvestment rate assumption underlying the internal rate of return method and explain when this can be a problem.
3. Recognize the causes and remedies for multiple internal rates of return.
4. Describe why companies use multiple measures of capital investment desirability.

When Southwestern Bell Telephone Company designed a new computerized capital investment analysis system called Finplan, capital budgeting managers knew that net present value was the best measure of capital investment desirability. Naturally, they designed the computerized analysis system to compute the net present value. They also designed the system to compute profitability index, internal rate of return, payback period, even accounting rate of return. Why would they use all of these other measures when they knew net present value was right?

They knew that capital budgeting decisions would be made by committees of finance people, engineers, marketing managers, and so on. In addition to different areas of primary responsibility, the participants would have different training and backgrounds. The capital budgeting managers knew that people might be persuaded to focus on net present value, but would still want to look at measures with which they might be more familiar. The capital budgeting managers also knew that each measure conveyed some information about the investment being considered.

Like the managers at Southwestern Bell, you need to be familiar with all of these measures if you want to argue credibly for the capital investments that will maximize wealth. The objective of this chapter is to give you that familiarity. The definition and meaning of each of these measures is discussed in this chapter.

PROFITABILITY INDEX |

The profitability index (PI) is the value increase per dollar invested. If an initial investment I_o will generate cash flows in future years, with cash flow in year t designated CF_t, the profitability index is:

$$PI = \left[\sum_{t=1}^{n} \frac{CF_t}{(1 + k)^t} \right] / I_o \qquad (6\text{-}1)$$

This equation can also be written as:

$$PI = 1 + NPV/I_o \qquad (6\text{-}1a)$$

As an example, a computer store requires an initial outlay of $500,000 and is expected to generate cash flows of $100,000 at the end of each year for ten years. At a 10 percent required return and using Equation 6-1, the profitability index is:

$$PI = (\$100,000 \times 6.1446)/\$500,000 = 1.23$$

In other words, this investment will generate $1.23 of present value for every dollar invested, and it will increase net present value by $0.23 for every dollar invested.

If the net present value is positive, the profitability index will be greater than 1.00, and vice versa.[1] A profitability index greater than 1.00 means the investment is attractive.

There is a definition problem with the profitability index when investments are spread over several years rather than being made as a lump sum. The following investment, for example, requires a cash outlay now and again in two

---

[1]Suppose cash flows for a capital investment are divided between *investment flows* and *other flows*. The present values of the two types of flows are PV_i and PV_o respectively. Net present value and profitability index are defined as follows:

$$NPV = PV_i - PV_o$$

$$PI = PV_i \div PV_o$$

It can be seen by inspection that whether the net present value is positive and whether the profitability index is greater than 1.0 both depend on whether PV_i is greater than PV_o.

years. Is the investment amount just the first $1,000, is it $3,000, or is it some other number?

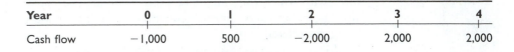

Year	0	1	2	3	4
Cash flow	−1,000	500	−2,000	2,000	2,000

The question of whether to subtract the present value of a future outlay from the numerator, or add it to the denominator does not matter as long as we are only concerned about whether the profitability index is greater than 1.0. If you want to compare projects using the profitability index, though, it is necessary to establish a standard rule for dealing with later cash outflows. The modified profitability index provides one such rule.

Modified Profitability Index

The modified profitability index[2] is based on the assumption that the initial commitment to a project should be in the denominator. The *initial commitment* to a project is the initial investment plus any amount that we would need to set aside today to provide funds for future outflows. The modified profitability index is then:

$$\text{Modified profitability index} = 1 + \frac{\text{Net present value}}{\text{Initial outlay} + \text{PV of future commitments}} \qquad \text{(6-2)}$$

The initial commitment for the prior investment, assuming a 10 percent required return, is determined as follows:

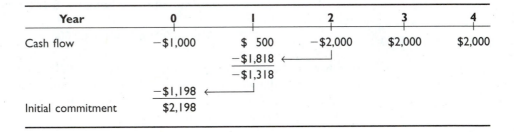

Year	0	1	2	3	4
Cash flow	−$1,000	$ 500	−$2,000	$2,000	$2,000
		−$1,818 ←			
		−$1,318			
	−$1,198 ←				
Initial commitment	$2,198				

An amount of $1,818 must be invested at the 10 percent required return rate at the end of year 1 to provide the $2,000 needed at the end of year 2. A cash flow of $500 coming in at the end of year 1 can be used as part of the $1,818, so $1,318 must come from $1,198 invested at 10 percent now. Consequently, the total initial commitment is $2,198.

The net present value is:

$$NPV = -1,000 + 500/1.10 - 2,000/1.10^2 + 2,000/1.10^3 + 2,000/1.10^4 = \$670$$

---

[2]The modified profitability index was suggested at Bellcore.

If your only question is whether the benefits exceed the cost, the two profitability indexes give the same signal. Both will be greater than 1.0 when the net present value is positive, and vice versa. If you want to use the profitability index to discuss the degree of attractiveness, though, the two measures are substantially different. The profitability index and modified profitability index are:

$$\text{Profitability index} = 1 + \$670/\$1,000 = 1.67$$

$$\text{Modified profitability index} = 1 + \$670/\$2,198 = 1.30$$

Net present value of $0.67 is generated for each dollar initially invested in the project, but only $0.30 is generated for each dollar of initial commitment to the project. Because the two measures give substantially different results, it is obviously necessary to apply consistent rules for handling later cash outflows if you are going to compare investments using the profitability index.[3]

Although companies sometimes use the profitability index to measure relative attractiveness of investments, it is a poor tool for this purpose. Even if you use consistent rules for handling later cash outflows, the rules are arbitrary so there is no clear relationship between the profitability index and wealth creation. Second, the profitability index ignores project size and, therefore, ignores the amount of net present value generated. A $1.00 investment with a profitability index of 1.31 looks more attractive than a $1 million investment with a profitability index of 1.30, despite the fact that the "superior" project creates wealth of 31 cents while the "inferior" project creates wealth of $300,000.

While the profitability index is limited as a tool for measuring relative desirability, it is sometimes used as a measure of the margin for error and, therefore, as an indicator of risk. A profitability index of 1.3, for example, suggests that benefits are 30 percent greater than what is required to generate a net present value of $0 and just break even on the project. Thus, the profitability index gives an indication of how much benefits can fall below expectations before the project begins to destroy wealth.

INTERNAL RATE OF RETURN |

The internal rate of return is the rate of return earned on money committed to a capital investment[4] and is analogous to interest rates generally quoted in the financial marketplace. The effective annual interest rate that a bank promises on its savings accounts is the internal rate of return, and the annual percentage rate

---

[3]An additional method for calculating the profitability index where there are additional investments in later years is to divide the present value of net yearly cash inflows by the absolute value of the present value of net yearly cash outflows. Using this method would result in a profitability index of:

$$(500/1.10 + 2,000/1.10^3 + 2,000/1.10^4) \div (1,000 + 2,000/1.10^2) = 1.25$$

[4]The term *internal* differentiates the return earned on funds tied up *in* an investment from required returns or returns that could be earned elsewhere.

on a loan (APR) is similar to the internal rate of return.[5] The internal rate of return, then, states the profitability of an investment in terms that are generally familiar to managers, whether or not the managers have strong financial backgrounds.

The internal rate of return is formally defined as the discount rate that results in a net present value of zero. In other words, it is the level of k that would result in a net present value of zero in Equation 5-1. A *conventional capital investment* requires cash outlays before any cash inflows are received and has cumulative cash flows that change from negative to positive only once. A higher discount rate results in a smaller net present value for a conventional investment. This relationship is illustrated in the net present value profile in Figure 6.1. The internal rate of return is the discount rate at the point where the net present value profile line crosses the horizontal axis—the point at which the net present value is zero.

To find the internal rate of return for a *conventional* capital investment, it is only necessary to apply the present value equations from Chapter 3 or look up a factor in Table A.2 or A.4. Take, for example, the $300 million George Steinbrenner's Tampa-based American Ship Building was planning to spend on two cruise ships for the Hawaiian market. Suppose the ships generate cash flow of $35,237,700 at the end of each year over a 20-year life. Setting this up as a present value of an annuity problem, using Equation 3-4b, gives:

$$\text{Present value} = \text{PMT} \times \text{PVAI}_{n,k} \tag{3-4b}$$

| FIGURE 6.1 NET PRESENT VALUE PROFILE

This figure shows the relationship between the net present value and the discount rate for a conventional capital investment. The internal rate of return is the discount rate, the value of k, that results in a net present value of $0.

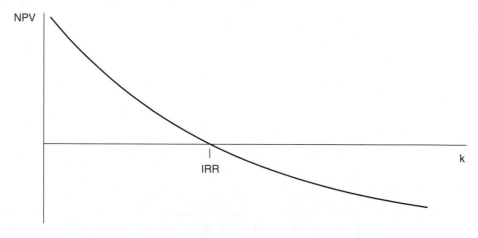

Substituting in the known values gives:

$$\$300,000,000 = \$35,237,700 \times PVAI_{20yrs,k}$$

$$PVAI_{20yrs,k} = \$300,000,000/\$35,237,700 = 8.5136$$

Going to the 20-year row of Table A.4 and searching across that row, 8.5136 is found at the 10 percent column; the internal rate of return on this investment is 10 percent. A discount rate of 10 percent will cause the present value of benefits to equal the initial outlay and the net present value, therefore, to equal zero.

This problem can be solved with Lotus 1-2-3 or with the Excel spreadsheet software. First set up the following spreadsheet and then use the @IRR function in Lotus or the =IRR function in Excel. The spreadsheet would look like this:

	A	B	C	$\longrightarrow$	U
1	−300,000,000	35,237,000	35,237,000		35,237,000
2	@IRR(.1,A1..U1)		=IRR(A1..U1,.1)		

The entry in cell A2 is a Lotus command telling the computer to calculate the internal rate of return in range A1 to U1 using .1, or 10 percent, as the starting point. The entry in cell C2 is the equivalent Excel command. Please note the range is entered first in the Excel command. After entering the formula in cell A2 or C2, press RETURN, and the computer will return 0.099996, or 10 percent for the answer. If the computer returns "ERR," then the 10 percent starting guess is too low or too high and another guess should be entered. Remember, you should not enter the commas in the numbers, or the computer will not accept the entry as a value.

UNEVEN CASH FLOWS

Finding the internal rate of return is tedious if cash flows are uneven over the asset's life. The objective is still to find the point in Figure 6.1 where the net present value equals zero, but that point is generally found by trial and error. For a conventional capital investment, the net present value is first computed with an arbitrarily chosen discount rate. If the net present value is positive, the process is repeated with a higher required return, and vice versa, until the discount rate that results in a net present value of zero is found.

Example. Berkeley Development Partnership is considering the purchase of two lots for $264,050. The first lot will be sold for $100,000 at the end of the first year and the second lot will be sold for $200,000 at the end of the second year. Arbitrarily selecting a discount rate of 10 percent, the net present value (NPV) is found using the present value factors from Table A.2:

$$NPV = \$100,000 \times [1/1.10] + \$200,000 \times [1/1.10^2] - \$264,050$$

$$NPV = \$100,000 \times 0.9091 + \$200,000 \times 0.8264 - \$264,050 = -\$7,860$$

Since the net present value is negative, a lower discount rate must be tried. A discount rate of 8 percent is chosen, again arbitrarily:

$$NPV = \$100,000 \times [1/1.08] + \$200,000 \times [1/1.08^2] - \$264,050$$

$$NPV = \$100,000 \times 0.9259 + \$200,000 \times 0.8573 - \$264,050 = \$0$$

The net present value is zero, so the internal rate of return is 8 percent. Using Lotus or Excel the spreadsheet would look as follows:

	A	B	C
1	−264,050	100,000	200,000
2	@IRR(.1,A1..C1)	=IRR(A1..C1,.1)	

The computer should return with the answer 0.080026, or 8 percent.

INTERPOLATION AND OTHER SOLUTION METHODS

The internal rate of return in each of these examples was conveniently equal to a whole percentage that could be found in the tables. If the internal rate of return is between two of the interest rates in the tables, it can be found exactly by iterative use of Equations 3-2 and 3-4b to find the value of k that leads to a net present value of zero, or the internal rate of return can be estimated by linear interpolation.[6] Manual searches for the internal rate of return, with or without interpolation, are being replaced by use of computers and financial calculators. The reader is encouraged to read the owner's manual to the financial calculator. Specific instructions differ depending on the make and model of the calculator.

USE OF THE INTERNAL RATE OF RETURN

As a decision criterion for conventional capital investments, the internal rate of return gives the same accept-reject signals as the net present value and profitability index. If the internal rate of return is above the required return, the net present value will be positive, and the profitability index will be greater than 1.0.

---

[6]The interpolation formula for the internal rate of return is:

$$IRR = k_b + (k_a - k_b)[NPV_b/(NPV_b - NPV_a)]$$

where b is the discount rate below the IRR and a is the discount rate above the IRR in the tables. NPV_a and NPV_b are the net present values at discount rates k_a and k_b respectively. By definition NPV_a will be negative and NPV_b will be positive.

If the internal rate of return is below the required return, the net present value will be negative and the profitability index will be less than 1.0.

The internal rate of return does provide additional information. First, because the internal rate of return is stated in terms of a rate of return or interest rate, it is often easier to explain to people who lack formal training in finance. They are familiar with similar measures, such as the interest rates on their mortgages and bank accounts. Second, because a higher internal rate of return is more desirable, other things being equal,[7] the internal rate of return can be used as a ranking method when choosing between competing investments. Third, the internal rate of return may give an indication of risk; the farther it is above the required return, the greater is the margin for error.

Unfortunately, there are also problems associated with the internal rate of return. Like the profitability index, it ignores the size of the project and therefore does not give an indication of the amount of wealth created. It also ignores project life. As discussed in the following sections, projects may have more than one internal rate of return, and managers may make implicit reinvestment rate assumptions that are unrealistic. These problems can lead to conflicts between net present value and internal rate of return selection.

REINVESTMENT RATE ASSUMPTIONS

Some observers fear that managers will mistakenly believe that the entire investment is earning the internal rate of return over its entire life when, in fact, only the *unrecovered* investment is earning that rate.[8]

Example. Two $10,000 investments generate the following cash flows:

Investment	Initial Investment	CASH BENEFITS	
		Year 1	Year 2
A	$10,000	$ 0	$14,400
B	$10,000	10,000	2,400

Each investment has a 20 percent internal rate of return and a two-year life. If the company has a required return of less than 20 percent, both investments are equally attractive using the internal-rate-of-return criterion. But most of the capital from investment B is received back at the end of the first year, so only a small amount is left invested at 20 percent in the second year.

[7] Although the internal rate of return is often used as a ranking method, "other things being equal" is a strong requirement. Projects must have equal costs, equal lives, equal risk, and similar cash flow patterns, such as level annual cash flows, to satisfy this requirement.

[8] John J. Clark, Thomas J. Hindelang, and Robert E. Pritchard, *Capital Budgeting: Planning and Control of Capital Expenditures*, 2nd ed. (Englewood Cliffs, NJ: Prentice-Hall, 1984), 62–64.

Suppose this company's required return is 10 percent, and any cash inflows will be reinvested at the 10 percent rate. If investment B is chosen, the total value at the end of the second year will be:

$$\$10,000(1 + .10) + \$2,400 = \underline{\$13,400}$$

compared to $14,400 with investment A. Thus, A gives more terminal value. The preference of A is also confirmed with the net present value:

$$NPV_A = \$14,400/(1 + .10)^2 - \$10,000 = \underline{\$1,901}$$

$$NPV_B = \$10,000/(1 + .10) + \$2,400/(1 + .10)^2 - \$10,000 = \underline{\$1,074}$$

As this example illustrates, the internal rate of return and net present value can give different measures of relative desirability. Since we have shown that the net present value measures the increase in wealth, a rule that leads to the choice of projects that does not maximize net present value is not desirable.

The internal rate of return incorrectly led to the conclusion that A and B were equally attractive because of an implied assumption about the reinvestment rate. When the internal rate of return is used, the implied assumption is that cash flows generated by the investment can be reinvested at the internal rate of return. When the net present value is used, the implied assumption is that funds can be reinvested at the company's required return. Since the required return is determined by investment opportunities available elsewhere, the net present value relies on a more reasonable implied assumption.

MULTIPLE INTERNAL RATES OF RETURN

Despite the superiority of net present value, the internal rate of return is used by many companies. It is, therefore, important to understand the problem of multiple internal rates of return and implications for investment choice.

An investment requires outlays in anticipation of future benefits. Financing, on the other hand, provides benefits in exchange for future outlays. Some projects have characteristics of an investment over part of their lives and characteristics of a financing arrangement during other parts. These projects are unconventional investments, having *cumulative* cash flows that change between negative and positive more than once. These projects may have more than one internal rate of return, and they may have negative net present values even though they have internal rates of return above the required return. Consequently, special care is needed when the internal rate of return method is used to analyze mixed cash flow projects. The reasons for and implications of multiple internal rates of return are discussed in the following paragraphs. A simple method of checking for the possible existence of multiple internal rates of return is explained in Appendix 6-A.

As an example of multiple internal rates of return, consider projects F and G, which have the following cash flows.

| **FIGURE 6.2** | **NET PRESENT VALUES FOR A PROJECT WITH MIXED CUMULATIVE CASH FLOWS** |

Net present value at various discount rates for an investment requiring an initial outlay of $100, providing a cash inflow of $275 at the end of the first year and then requiring an outflow of $180 at the end of the second year.

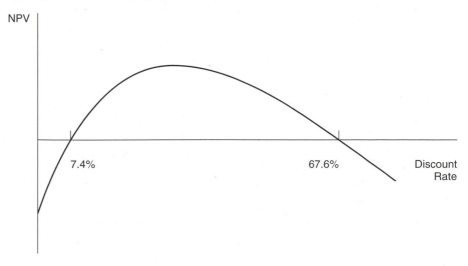

Year	0	1	2
Cash Flow F	−100	275	−180
Cash Flow G	100	−275	180

To calculate the internal rate of return for investment F, set the net present value equal to $0 and solve for k:

$$NPV = -100 + 275/(1 + k) - 180/(1 + k)^2 = 0$$

Using the quadratic equation formula, k equals 7.4 percent and 67.6 percent;[9] either value of k will result in a net present value of zero.

The net present values for various interest rates are shown in Figure 6.2. For project G, which simply has all the cash flows reversed, the graph would be inverted and the internal rates of return would be the same.

[9]First, let NPV = 0 and let R = 1/(1 + k). Then, rearranging terms:

$$-180R^2 + 275R - 100 = 0$$

Using the quadratic equation formula:

$$R = \frac{-275 + \sqrt{275^2 - 4(-180)(-100)}}{2(-180)}, \text{ so } R = .9311 \text{ and } R = .5966$$

Therefore, k equals .074 and .676.

Assume our required return is 15 percent; we can raise money by paying a return of 15 percent and can invest excess funds at 15 percent. The net present values for the two projects are:

$$NPV_F = -100 + 275/1.15 - 180/1.15^2 = +\$3$$

$$NPV_G = +100 - 275/1.15 + 180/1.15^2 = -\$3$$

Based on the net present value, F is attractive while G is not. The internal rate of return, on the other hand, gives ambiguous signals because each project has internal rates of return above and below the required return.

The correctness of the net present value rule in the face of multiple internal rates of return can be demonstrated with investments F and G. Suppose an investor with a 15 percent opportunity cost of funds is considering these two assets and wants to consume as much as possible now for a given pattern of consumption in future periods. Current consumption with the two investments is as follows:

Investment F: $\quad C_0 = W_0 - 100 + (275 - C_1)/1.15 - (180 - C_2)/1.15^2$

$\qquad\qquad\qquad = W_0 + 3 - C_1/1.15 - C_2/1.15^2$

Investment G: $\quad C_0 = W_0 + 100 - (275 - C_1)/1.15 + (180 - C_2)/1.15^2$

$\qquad\qquad\qquad = W_0 - 3 - C_1/1.15 - C_2/1.15^2$

Neither Investment: $C_0 = W_0 - C_1/1.15 - C_2/1.15^2$

where C_t = consumption at time t and W_0 = beginning wealth.

For any combination of C_1 and C_2, investment F increases present consumption by \$3 and investment G decreases present consumption by \$3. Therefore, anyone who preferred more wealth and consumption to less wealth and consumption would invest in F and reject G. As long as money can be raised or invested at the company's required return, the investment that maximizes net present value also allows the owners to maximize consumption.

MULTIPLE INTERNAL RATES OF RETURN AND CAPITAL RATIONING

Capital rationing is treated in Chapter 22. However, it is appropriate to comment briefly at this point on multiple internal rates of return and capital rationing. When a company is facing capital rationing, defined as having a fixed amount of money to invest and attractive investments in excess of the amount of money available, *the highest internal rate of return is the rate at which a capital base will grow if all cash flows from the project are invested in projects with the same internal rate of return.*[10] Thus, there is a potentially useful interpreta-

[10]Robert Dorfman, "The Meaning of Internal Rates of Return," *Journal of Finance* 36 (December 1981): 1011–1021.

tion of the internal rate of return in the case of capital rationing, even if the investment has more than one internal rate of return.

MODIFIED INTERNAL RATE OF RETURN

Managers wanting to use the internal rate of return sometimes use a *modified internal rate of return* to develop a single internal-rate-of-return measure when a project has multiple internal rates of return. This involves two steps:

1. Compute the terminal value of all cash flows except the initial outlay.
2. Calculate by interpolation or other means the modified internal rate of return that sets the terminal value equal to the initial outlay (or present value of the outlays if there are more than one).

Example. San Jose Development is considering the purchase of three lots for $264,050. The first lot will be sold for $100,000 at the end of the first year, the second lot will be sold for $100,000 at the end of the second year, and the third will be sold for $100,000 at the end of the third year.

The terminal cash flow is calculated by discounting to the end of the project all intermediate cash flows using the cost of capital as the discount rate. Stated differently, it is finding the future value of the cash inflows at the end or termination of the project life.

$$\text{Terminal value} = \$100,000 \times [1.10^2] + \$100,000 \times [1.10] + \$100,000$$

$$\text{Terminal value} = \$121,000 + \$110,000 + \$100,000 = \$331,000$$

$$\text{Initial outlay} \times (1 + \text{MIRR})^3 = \$331,000$$

$$\text{By interpolation the MIRR} = 7.8\%$$

This problem can be solved with Lotus or Excel by setting up the following spreadsheet:

	A	B	C	D
1		100,000	+B1*1.1	+C1*1.1
2			100,000	+C2*1.1
3				100,000
4	−264,050	0	0	+D1+D2+D3
5	@IRR(.1,A4..D4)		=IRR(A4..D4,.1)	

After the formulas are entered the spreadsheet will return with the following results:

	A	B	C	D
1		100,000	110,000	121,000
2			100,000	110,000
3				100,000
4	−264,050			331,000
5	.078236		.078236	

One of the purposes of calculating a modified internal rate of return is to give the analysts an unambiguous accept-reject signal when multiple internal rates of return are possible. Another advantage of the modified internal rate of return procedure is that it gives the user the most conservative estimate of the internal rate of return by using the company's cost of capital as the assumed reinvestment rate and financing rate. The last project for any firm that cannot generate projects that have returns greater than the firm's cost of capital is the returning of funds to the suppliers of capital. By definition, when a firm returns money to the debtors and shareholders (in the same proportions as were used to calculate the weighted average cost of capital), the firm earns the cost of capital. In other words, the modified internal rate of return calculates the internal rate of return on a project as if the cash flow coming off the project were returned to the suppliers of capital. This is a most conservative situation, but this measure does provide some information content in light of the fact that over 1,200 share repurchases were announced in 1997 alone.

Analysts using this method to compare projects will compute a terminal value as of the end of the life of the longest life project. When the modified internal rate of return is greater than the required return, the investment is attractive. However, the earlier cited problems with the internal rate of return as a ranking tool still exist. Most importantly, there is still no adjustment for project size and, therefore, amount of value contribution. Furthermore, the method does not work well for investments that have no initial outlay or for investments with the outlay spread over several years.

ON THE DOMINANCE OF DISCOUNTED CASH FLOW

The capital investment evaluation methods discussed thus far are based on the use of discount rates to compare cash flows occurring at different times. These discounted cash flow methods, as they are commonly called, are recognized as the best methods for evaluating a capital investment because they base the investment decision on whether or not the investment will increase the owners' wealth. As long as the objective of the firm is the maximization of owners' wealth, investments that are not in competition with each other and will not change the company's risk should be accepted if they meet the acceptability criteria of the discounted cash flow evaluation methods. (The decision rules are extended to competing investments and risk differences in later chapters.) These discounted cash flow methods are also the dominant capital budgeting methods in practice, and they continue to grow in acceptability.

The two remaining measures of capital investment desirability to be discussed in this chapter are the payback period and the accounting rate of return. These measures are sometimes referred to as primitive methods because they were developed before discounted cash flow concepts were widely understood and they do not recognize the timing of benefits. Today, these measures are more accurately viewed as supplementary information because many firms use them to supplement the information provided by discounted cash flow analysis. These measures are still used as the primary decision criteria for some firms, though.

PAYBACK PERIOD |

The payback period is the number of years it takes to recover the initial investment. Stated more precisely, the *payback period* is the number of years until the cumulative cash benefit equals the money invested. For an investment that requires an initial outlay of $100,000 and provides cash benefits of $20,000 a year, the payback period is:

$$\text{Payback} = 100,000/20,000 = 5 \text{ years}$$

As another example, consider an investment that requires an initial outlay of $100,000 and provides the following cash benefits.

Year	Cash Flow	Cumulative Cash Flow
1	$40,000	$ 40,000
2	30,000	70,000
3	25,000	95,000
4	20,000	115,000

As the cumulative flow column shows, all of the cash flows through the third year and part of the cash flows from the fourth year are required to recover the $100,000. Specifically, $5,000 of the cash flows from the fourth year are needed to reach $100,000. Since total cash flows for the fourth year are $20,000, one-fourth of these flows are needed. The payback period is therefore:[11]

$$\text{Payback} = 3 + (5,000/20,000) = 3\tfrac{1}{4} \text{ years}$$

Payback was the principal capital budgeting criterion in practice for a number of years. Simplicity was one reason for its popularity. You can establish a

[11]To be precise, we should note that the investment is recovered in $3\frac{1}{4}$ years only if cash flows are spread evenly over the year.

minimum acceptable payback period, such as three or five years, and easily explain the rule to employees with no background in finance. This approach works fairly well if all investments have identical lives and are characterized by one initial outlay followed by level cash benefits over their lives. For a given project life and constant annual inflows, any payback standard corresponds with some discount rate. For example, a five-year payback period, standard for investments with ten-year lives, is equivalent to a 15 percent required return.[12]

The payback period is also used as a risk measure. Managers often believe that the longer it takes to recover the original investment, the more chances there are for something to go wrong. When Hewlett-Packard committed itself to a compatible technology called Spectrum in 1982, one of the questions was certainly how long the technology would last before becoming obsolete. The payback period gives an indication of how long the technology must survive for the company to recover its costs. A high level of cash flow from a project is also important for *liquidity* purposes; a short payback indicates that the project makes a greater contribution per year, on average, toward cash flow needed for debt repayment and other purposes. Liquidity is often of particular importance for new companies.

Narayanan cites managers' concerns for their own reputations as another reason for using payback. Given two projects with identical net present values, managers would prefer a shorter payback because the public would become aware of their ability to find superior investments sooner, and the value of their human capital would increase.[13] The same argument applies to a manager who needs to establish credibility with investors so that additional funds can be raised.

The payback period has two important weaknesses. First, it ignores the timing of cash flows and the fact that a dollar received now is worth more than a dollar received later. With the payback measure, $10,000 in the first year and $50,000 in the second year is just as good as $50,000 in the first year and $10,000 in the second year. Furthermore, the payback measure ignores all cash flows after the payback period. A $100,000 project that provides cash flows of $20,000 a year will have the same payback whether it has a life of 5 years or 50 years. For these reasons, the payback is not recommended as a primary evaluation method, and its use for that purpose is declining.

The payback period is used today primarily as supplementary information. Some managers who relied on payback in earlier years will still want to look at the payback even if they rely primarily on net present value. Many capital investment decisions are made by committee, and members of the committee who are not familiar with discounted cash flow techniques may rely primarily on pay-

---

[12]A five-year payback period is equivalent to saying annual cash flow must be at least $20 per $100 of initial outlay. The internal rate of return, or implied discount rate, is found as follows.

$$\$100 = \$20 \times PVAI_{10yrs,k}$$

Using the internal rate of return solution procedure, k = 15.1 percent.

[13]M. P. Narayanan, "Observability and the Payback Criterion," *Journal of Business* 58 (July 1985): 309–323.

back, while other members are focusing on net present value or internal rate of return.

PRESENT VALUE PAYBACK (DISCOUNTED PAYBACK)

The present value payback is the number of years it takes for the cumulative present value of cash flows to equal zero. For an investment that requires an initial outlay of $2,000 and generates cash benefits of $1,000 at the end of each year, the present value payback with a 10 percent required return is found by first computing the cumulative present value:

Year	Cash Benefit	PV Factor	Present Value	Cumulative Present Value
1	$1,000	.9091	$909.10	$ 909.10
2	1,000	.8264	826.40	1,735.50
3	1,000	.7513	751.30	2,486.80

From this information, the cumulative present value will match the $2,000 outlay somewhere in the third year. Specifically, the amount of additional present value still needed at the end of year 2 is $2,000 − $1,735.50 = $264.50. The proportion of year 3's present value this represents is $264.50/$751.30 = .35, so the present value payback period is said to be 2.35 years. If risk increases with the passage of time, this investment would be less risky than an investment with a present value payback period of three years.

ACCOUNTING RATE OF RETURN |

The accounting rate of return, also called the average rate of return or return on investment (ROI), differs from the evaluation techniques discussed thus far in that it focuses on accounting income rather than cash flow. The *accounting rate of return* is defined as the ratio of average accounting income to average investment. The average accounting income for this purpose may be simply income after tax, income before interest and tax (EBIT), or the after-tax income that would be generated by the project if it did not result in more interest expense: EBIT × (1 − tax rate).

The after-tax measure is generally preferred because income after tax is the income that provides benefits to the owners. After-tax income that would be generated in the absence of debt is often used because it allows the capital investment analyst to focus on the project without being sidetracked by a study of the company's debt policy. Thus, a widely used computation formula for the accounting rate of return is:

$$\text{Accounting Rate of Return} = \frac{\text{EBIT} \times (1 - \text{tax rate})}{(\text{Beginning value} + \text{Ending value})/2} \qquad \text{(6-3)}$$

Example. The development of a new safety valve requires an investment of $1 million by San Diego Engineering. The product has an estimated technological life of ten years and is expected to generate profits of $184,545 a year before interest and tax. The company's tax rate is 36 percent. The company estimates a value of $0 in ten years, so the ending value of the fixed assets will be $0. The accounting rate of return is therefore:

$$\text{Accounting Rate of Return} = \frac{\$184{,}545(1 - .36)}{(\$1{,}000{,}000 + \$0)/2} = 23.6\%$$

To make an investment decision, the accounting rate of return is compared to a standard, such as the existing average accounting return on the company's assets, or to the company's target accounting return on investment. The investment proposal is accepted if the accounting rate of return is higher than the established standard.

There are a number of variations on the accounting-rate-of-return formula. Beginning assets are sometimes used instead of average assets, and average assets are sometimes found by averaging assets for each year or even each day rather than by using just beginning and ending assets. In some cases, total income over the investment's life, less the initial investment, is divided by the number of years to arrive at the average income. As previously mentioned, income may be measured before or after tax.

John F. McDonnell provides an example of the wide use of the accounting rate of return by managers. When he became chief executive officer of McDonnell-Douglas in 1988, he noted that the company was the leader in defense contract awards, but Lockheed, Rockwell, and General Dynamics earned higher rates of return.[14] Although he did not spell out a specific measure, he was apparently focusing on accounting numbers such as EBIT ÷ Total Assets, Net Income ÷ Total Assets, or Net Income ÷ Equity. A statement such as McDonnell's may send a message to managers, telling them that they should focus their attention on projects that will improve the company's income in relation to assets used. Managers would then use the accounting rate of return on assets as their capital investment decision guideline.

The accounting rate of return has three advantages that result in continued use despite some weaknesses. One advantage of the method is simplicity; the accounting rate of return is easy to calculate without worrying about things like present value formulas. If an investment is a perpetuity with constant annual income, depreciation is just sufficient to cover replacement, and there are no changes in working capital, then the accounting rate of return will often be approximately the same as the internal rate of return. The accounting rate of return is often used for the evaluation of new products and services by financial institutions, since the main assets of these institutions are generally financial instruments, and there is very little depreciation or working capital requirement.

[14]*St. Louis Post-Dispatch* (May 8, 1988): E1.

If development costs for the products are insignificant, these institutions can get the same accept/reject decision as the net present value, profitability index, or internal rate of return with less effort.

A second advantage of the accounting rate of return is that it is consistent with the numerous management reward systems that focus on accounting return on investment. If you are going to be evaluated according to the income of your division in relation to assets used, you will prefer to select capital investments using the same criterion. Advanced methods of simultaneously considering net present value and accounting profitability are explained in Chapter 24, but using the accounting rate of return is the simplest way to consider accounting income. A better alternative, of course, is to change the way success is measured, so that wealth creation is recognized and rewarded.

A third advantage of the accounting rate of return is that it reflects the importance of accounting income for managers who are concerned about the income they report to their shareholders. Once again, managers can reduce reliance on accounting income by establishing credibility with investors.

The accounting rate of return suffers from three weaknesses. First, like the payback period, it does not recognize the importance of timing. Income in the tenth year counts the same as income in the first year. Second, the method also ignores asset life. A $100,000 investment that generates income of $20,000 a year will have the same accounting rate of return whether it has a life of 2 years or 20 years. Finally, the accounting rate of return method focuses on accounting income rather than on cash flow. The measures that use cash flow focus on the benefits actually received, while the accounting rate of return focuses on accounting reports given to shareholders and others.

While the accounting rate of return has declined in popularity as a principal criterion, it continues to be used as supplementary information. It also continues to be used as the primary criterion in some cases because of its ease of use, its consistency with many management reward systems, and its consistency with accounting information given to shareholders.

SUMMARY EXAMPLE

Clutter Corporation of Pasadena is considering the purchase of microcomputers at a cost of $3,600 each. The computers will reduce labor expense, thereby saving the company $1,000 a year per computer. It is estimated that the computers will have a five-year technological life and will have no value at the end of five years. Clutter Corporation has a 10 percent required return and is not subject to income tax. The net present value and profitability index are:

$$\text{Net Present Value} = \$1,000 \times \text{PVAI}_{5yrs,10\%} - \$3,600$$

$$= \$1,000 \times 3.7908 - \$3,600 = \underline{\$190.80}$$

$$\text{Profitability Index} = \$3,790.80/\$3,600 = \underline{\$1.05}$$

To find the internal rate of return, we solve for the discount rate, k, such that:

$$\$1,000 \times PVAI_{5yrs,k} = \$3,600 = 0$$

$$PVAI_{5yrs,k} = \$3,600/\$1,000 = 3.60$$

Going to the five-year row of Table A.4, the value of 3.6048 is found at the 12 percent column, so the internal rate of return is approximately 12 percent (12.05 percent using a calculator or interpolating, if you want to be more accurate).

The payback period is $\$3,600 \div \$1,000 = \underline{3.6 \text{ years}}$.

The present value payback is found as follows:[15]

Year	Cash Flow	Present Value	Cumulative Present Value
1	$1,000	$909.10	$ 909.10
2	1,000	826.40	1,735.50
3	1,000	751.30	2,486.80
4	1,000	683.00	3,169.80
5	1,000	620.90	3,790.70

The present value payback period is therefore:

$$\text{Present value payback} = 4 + \frac{\$3,600 - \$3,169.80}{\$620.90} = \underline{4.7 \text{ years}}$$

Assume that the purchase will increase earnings before interest and taxes by $500 a year and the company has a 36 percent income tax rate. The accounting rate of return is:

$$\text{Accounting rate of return} = \frac{\$500(1 - .36)}{(\$3,600 + 0)/2} = \underline{\underline{17.8\%}}$$

The three discounted cash flow techniques—net present value, profitability index, and internal rate of return—all give the same accept-reject signal. The net present value is $190.80, meaning the purchase of one of these computers will increase shareholder wealth by $190.80. The profitability index of 1.05 means that $1.05 of present value is created for each dollar invested, which may be interpreted as a fairly narrow margin for error. The internal rate of return is 12 percent, which is above the required return, so the investment is again con-

---

[15]The $.10 difference between cumulative present value and the present value computed using the present value of an annuity formula is a result of rounding in Tables A.2 and A.4.

firmed to be attractive. Managers can compare 12 percent to the required return in gauging the profitability of this investment, and can use the difference between 12 percent and the 10 percent required return as another indicator of the margin for error.

The payback period of 3.6 means the first three years' cash flows and 60 percent of the fourth year's cash flows are needed just to recover the money invested. The present value payback of 4.7 means that the first four years' cash benefits and 70 percent of the present value of the fifth year's cash benefits are required to provide a 10 percent return. Once again, the difference between the 5-year life and the 4.7-year present value payback is a measure of the margin for error, and the margin for error is not extremely large.

The accounting rate of return gives an indication of the impact of the decision on accounting profitability. Managers can compare the 17.8 percent accounting rate of return to the company's existing return on assets to determine if this investment will improve or hurt return on assets. Suppose EBIT for existing assets is 28.3 percent, and the company's marginal tax rate is 36 percent, so after-tax return is $.283(1 - .36) = 18.1\%$. This investment will decrease return on assets as reported by the accountants.

With this information assembled, managers still have a decision to make. The net present value, profitability index, and internal rate of return tell them that the investment is attractive. However, the profitability index and present value payback tell them that the margin for error is narrow. (Risk analysis will be covered in detail later in this book.) The accounting rate of return tells them that the investment will decrease return on assets, as reported to the shareholders. If investors are fully informed and managers want to maximize shareholder wealth, the investment will be accepted. In practical decision making, managers may also consider their own risk and impacts on accounting profitability. Thus, managers may factor other considerations into the decision-making process. This is one reason major capital investment decisions are often made by a committee of executives rather than by following automatically from a decision rule, such as net present value.

CAPITAL BUDGETING PRACTICE

Surveys of corporate capital budgeting practices have been conducted extensively since 1959. Payback and accounting rate of return were the favored decision tools in the earlier surveys. Fewer than 30 percent of the companies surveyed in the earlier studies used discounted cash flow techniques at all. By 1977, 66 percent of the survey respondents in a study by Gitman and Forrester[16] indicated that the *primary* capital budgeting technique was a discounted cash flow method. By the time of Ferreira and Brooks's 1988 survey, over 75 percent of companies

---

[16]Lawrence J. Gitman and John R. Forrester, Jr., "A Survey of Capital Budgeting Techniques Used by Major U. S. Firms," *Financial Management* 6 (Fall 1977): 66–71.

were relying on discounted cash flow methods.[17] Surveys conducted into the 1990s confirm a continued trend toward using discounted cash flow techniques of net present value, profitability index, and internal rate of return.[18] These same surveys make it clear, though, that companies compute a number of different measures of desirability. Other measures, such as payback and accounting rate of return, are more likely to be used as supplementary information than as the primary decision tool.

Internal rate of return continued to be at least as popular as net present value, despite its well-known limitations. Ease of explanation and provision of a simple ranking system are apparently powerful advantages to practitioners.

SUMMARY |

The capital investment desirability measures in this chapter are best viewed as supplementary information to net present value because none directly measures the wealth created by an investment. Each does, however, provide some information. It is not unusual to compute each of these measures in addition to the net present value.

The profitability index is the ratio of the present value of benefits to investment amount. A profitability index of greater than 1.0 means the present value of net cash benefits exceeds the present value of investment, and the investment is desirable. It gives some indication of the margin for error. Unfortunately, it ignores project size and, therefore, total wealth creation. It also requires arbitrary rules for treatment of later cash outflows.

The internal rate of return is the rate of return earned on money committed to an investment. It is analogous to interest rates generally quoted in the financial marketplace. The internal rate of return is formally defined as the discount rate that results in a net present value of zero. For a conventional investment, an internal rate of return above the required return means the investment is desirable, and vice versa. The internal rate of return is limited as a rule of relative desirability in that it ignores both project size and project life: $1 invested at a particular internal rate of return for one year looks as good as $1 million invested for ten years.

[17]Eurico J. Ferreira and LeRoy Brooks, "Capital Budgeting: A Key Management Challenge," *Business* 38 (October–December 1988): 22–29.

[18]See, for example, Ravindra Kamath and Eugene Oberst, "Capital Budgeting Practices of Large Hospitals," *Engineering Economist* 37 (Spring 1992): 203–232; Thomas P. Klammer and Michael C. Walker, "The Continued Increase in the Use of Sophisticated Capital Budgeting Techniques," *California Management Review* 27 (Fall 1984): 137–148; Marc Ross, "Capital Budgeting Practices of Twelve Large Manufacturers," *Financial Management* 15 (Winter 1986): 15–22; Ferreira and Brooks, "Capital Budgeting"; A. Charlene Sullivan and Keith Smith, "Capital Budgeting Practices for U.S. Factory Automation Projects," Purdue University Working Paper #90-11-1 (November 1990); and R. H. Pike, "A Longitudinal Study of Capital Budgeting Practices," *Journal of Business, Finance and Accounting* 23 (1996): 79–92.

The payback period is simply the number of years it takes to recover the money originally invested. Payback ignores timing of cash flows and cash flows beyond the payback period, but it is simple to use and it also provides some information about liquidity and risk. The *present value payback* measures the number of years for cumulative present values of benefits to surpass outlays or, in other words, the number of years it takes for the cumulative net present value to surpass $0. The present value payback also gives some indication of risk in that it tells us how long the investment must perform as expected in order to earn our required return.

The accounting rate of return, also called the average rate of return or return on investment, is defined as the ratio of average income generated by the investment to the average book value of the investment. The accounting rate of return fails to consider cash flows or timing. It is used because it is consistent with the accounting data used for public reporting and incentive reward systems, and because it is easy to use.

QUESTIONS

6-1. Which capital investment analysis methods apply the discounted cash flow concepts discussed in Chapter 3?

6-2. What are the advantages of using discounted cash flow methods of capital investment evaluation?

6-3. If an investment has a positive net present value, it will also have a profitability index greater than 1.0 and an internal rate of return in excess of the required return. Likewise, an investment with a negative net present value will also have a profitability index less than 1.0 and an internal rate of return less than the required return. Since all three measures give the same accept-reject signal, why do companies bother to compute all three of these measures?

6-4. Explain in your own words the meaning of the profitability index, modified profitability index, and internal rate of return.

6-5. Explain in your own words the meaning of the payback period and accounting rate of return.

6-6. The internal rate of return is the most widely used measure of investment desirability in practice. Why might this measure be preferred by practitioners?

6-7. What supplementary information does the payback period provide if an investment has already been evaluated using one of the discounted cash flow methods?

6-8. What supplementary information does the accounting rate of return provide if an investment has already been evaluated using one of the discounted cash flow methods?

6-9. According to survey results, which methods of capital investment evaluation are increasing in popularity, and which are decreasing? Why?

6–10. What conditions can cause an investment to have more than one internal rate of return?

6–11. (**Applications**) Anheuser-Busch, like many other companies, uses the internal rate of return to evaluate proposed capital investments. The company has very substantial cash flows available for investment because its core beer business is profitable, but beer sales in the United States are not growing. Managers there are highly educated with regard to capital budgeting methods, so their choice of internal rate of return is a conscious one. Why might it be possible that Anheuser-Busch finds that internal rate of return provides satisfactory results?

6–12. (**Ethical considerations**) You are working as the capital investment analyst, reporting to the manager of a division of a company that uses internal rate of return to justify capital investments. You have computed net present values for projects as well, because you know it is the correct tool. The boss must recommend one of two competing projects. You know that the project that maximizes internal rate of return has a substantially lower net present value because it is substantially smaller. You explain this to your boss, and he decides to recommend the project that maximizes IRR anyway. The stated goal of the company is shareholder wealth maximization. What are your alternatives in this situation? Recommend and justify one of these alternatives.

PROBLEMS |

6–1. A quality-improvement investment at Los Angeles Leather requires an initial outlay of $100,000 and generates cash flows of $20,000 at the end of each year for ten years. The required return is 10 percent. Find the net present value and profitability index. Is the investment desirable? Why?

6–2. Find the internal rate of return for the investment in problem 1. Is the investment desirable according to this criterion? Why?

6–3. Find the payback and present value payback for the investment described in problem 1. What do the payback calculations tell you?

6–4. For the investment in problem 1, assume that EBIT(1 − tax rate) is the same as cash flow and the investment is depreciated to $0 over its ten-year life. Compute the accounting rate of return. What does the accounting rate of return tell you?

6–5. A capital investment at San Francisco Marine Electric requires an initial outlay of $1 million, and will generate cash flows of $300,000 at the end of each year for five years. The required return is 10 percent. Find the net present value. Is the investment attractive?

6–6. For the investment in problem 5, EBIT(1 − tax rate) is the same as cash flow. If the asset will be worth $0 at the end of five years, what is the accounting rate of return?

6–7. The shop foreman at Santa Barbara Rig Service proposed a portable service unit requiring an initial outlay of $100,000 and providing the following year-end cash flows:

Year	1	2	3	4	5
Cash Flows	$30,000	−$50,000	$70,000	$60,000	$50,000

At a 10 percent required return, find the net present value. Is the investment desirable? Explain why this is desirable or undesirable assuming your audience is not trained in finance.

6–8. Compute the profitability index and modified profitability index for the investment in problem 7. Interpret these measures for a manager who is not trained in finance.

6–9. Find the internal rate of return and modified internal rate of return for the investment in problem 7. Interpret these measures for a manager who is not trained in finance.

6–10. Find the payback period and present value payback period for the investment in problem 7. Interpret these measures for a manager who is not trained in finance.

6–11. Assume that EBIT(1 − tax rate) is the same as cash flow for the investment in problem 7. The asset is being depreciated to zero over its five-year life. Compute the accounting rate of return. Interpret this measure for a manager who is not trained in finance.

6–12. Find the profitability index for the investment in problem 7 if cash inflows arrive at midyear rather than at the end of the year.

6–13. San Jose Industries is considering a capital investment that requires an initial outlay of $100,000 and generates the year-end cash flows shown below. The required return is 12 percent. Compute the modified profitability index. Is the investment attractive?

Year	Cash Flow	Year	Cash Flow	Year	Cash Flow
1	−$20,000	6	−$50,000	11	$35,000
2	−10,000	7	50,000	12	30,000
3	0	8	50,000	13	25,000
4	10,000	9	40,000	14	20,000
5	30,000	10	50,000	15	20,000

6–14. Davis Corporation is considering an investment that requires an initial outlay of $400,000 and will provide cash benefits of $100,000 at the end of each year over its five-year life. In addition, the asset will have a salvage value of $200,000 at the end of its five-year life. At a 10 percent required return, compute the net present value and profitability index.

6–15. Compute the internal rate of return for the investment in problem 14.

6–16. Claremont Corporation is considering starting a new division. The required investment is $1,000,000. Cash benefits are expected to be $50,000 at the end of the first year and are expected to grow at 6 percent a year thereafter. At a required return of 10 percent, compute the net present value and profitability index.

6–17. Compute the internal rate of return for the investment described in problem 16.

6–18. Chico Manufacturing must choose between two methods of producing a new product. The outlays and year-end benefits are as follows:

Year	Method A	Method B
0	−$1,000,000	−$2,000,000
1	200,000	800,000
2	250,000	600,000
3	300,000	500,000
4	350,000	400,000
5	400,000	400,000

Assuming the required return is 10 percent, compute the net present value and internal rate of return for each production method. Which production method should be used? Why?

6–19. Compute the modified internal rates of return for the two production methods described in problem 18. Does the modified internal rate of return help you to make a choice?

6–20. You are considering the purchase of a rental property for $100,000, with a $20,000 down payment. Cash flows after loan payments will be as follows.

Year	1	2	3	4	5	6	7–10
Cash flow	$2,000	$2,120	$2,240	$2,360	$2,480	$2,600	$2,720

The loan balance will be $70,000 at the end of ten years. For what price must you sell the property at the end of ten years to provide an effective annual return of 15 percent? (Assume year-end cash flows.)

CASE PROBLEM |

Dash Buildings, Inc.

Ann Smith is the president of Dash Buildings, Inc. (DBI), a subsidiary of Dash, Inc., one of the new long-distance telephone companies that sprang up as a result of deregulation of long-distance telephone service in the United States. DBI is responsible for purchasing and managing real estate used by the various units of Dash. DBI acts like a private real estate investment firm—acquiring properties, managing those properties, and providing space to the other divisions of Dash. DBI occasionally rents space to other tenants when it acquires a building that has more space than is needed by Dash. DBI does not, however, purchase buildings for the express purpose of renting to non-Dash tenants.

DBI is a corporation rather than a department only for reasons of legal convenience. DBI acts like any other department within Dash. DBI does not raise its own funds but receives them from the corporate treasury.

When Smith first joined Dash as a property manager, internal rate of return was the primary tool for project analysis. This often forced DBI to acquire smaller, older, less efficient buildings. Her role on a task force leading the conversion to net present value was the source of recognition that lead to her eventual promotion to president of DBI. Net present value analysis had allowed DBI to acquire newer, larger, and more modern buildings. This had led to a dramatic decrease in complaints about buildings and greater overall employee satisfaction.

Oversight of capital budgeting at Dash was the responsibility of the treasurer. The prior treasurer had allowed each operating unit to use its own capital investment analysis methods, with some choosing net present value, some choosing internal rate of return, and some even choosing accounting rate of return. The new treasurer, who comes from a background in investment banking, wants to standardize analysis so proposals can be compared from one unit to the other. While the treasurer has not issued a formal policy, it is clear that he is leaning toward internal rate of return.

DBI has been formally evaluated as a profit center, being credited with revenue equal to the estimated cost of renting space of the same type in the local market. Smith and her employees receive bonuses based on the profit of DBI. Bonuses at DBI had been quite small in the early years, but rising rents along with some well-timed purchases at the bottom of a real estate depression made the division profitable enough to bring it up to the maximum allowable bonus. She is, therefore, able to concentrate on maximizing satisfaction, which she believes to be the source of any further career advancement. Smith is concerned that internal rate of return will force her to return to acquiring less desirable office space. Dissatisfaction and complaints about building quality could derail her career.

DBI is currently working on additional office space for Sun City. The alternatives in Sun City are typical of those in most other locations. An older building could be acquired for $7 million. Imputed rent savings from ownership would be $1.5 million the first year, and would then grow 3 percent a year. After deduction of operating cost and taxes from imputed rent savings, net cash flow would be $1 million the first year and would grow 3 percent a year thereafter. It is estimated that the after-tax sale price at the end of the ten-year planning horizon required by Dash would be $5 million.

Alternately, DBI could construct a new building of the same size at a cost of $10.1 million. Because the space would be more luxurious, imputed rent savings would be $1.8 million and would be expected to grow 5 percent a year because of the excellent location of the building. After deduction of operating cost and taxes from imputed rent savings, net cash flow would be $1.1 million the first year and would grow 5 percent a year thereafter. It was estimated that the building would be worth $12 million after tax at the end of the ten-year planning horizon.

The after-tax cash flow return available on other investments similar to the risk of the DBI division (real estate) is estimated to be 12 percent. The after-tax cash flow return available on investments with risk similar to the other divisions of Dash (telecommunications) is 15 percent. Dash is not earning its opportunity cost of capital, and its stock price is low, so management is under pressure to improve profitability. Most units are not earning bonuses at all because of low profitability.

QUESTIONS

1. Compute the net present value, internal rate of return, profitability index, and payback period for each of the alternatives. For present value calculations, assume midyear cash flows except for initial outlay and terminal value.
2. Recommend the alternative that should be chosen.
3. Prepare a presentation to the treasurer explaining how the company would benefit from using net present value instead of internal rate of return.
4. Comment on the company's methods for evaluating and rewarding success. Does the reward structure encourage optimal capital investments in DBI and the rest of the company?
5. Would you recommend that the reward structure be changed in any way?

A p p e n d i x   6 - A

TESTING FOR MULTIPLE INTERNAL RATES OF RETURN |

When using internal rate of return, it is important to determine if the investment being considered has more than one internal rate of return. One way to achieve this is to prepare a graph similar to Figure 6.2 by computing the internal rate of return at discount rates from 0 percent to some fairly high rate such as 1,000 percent. This is, of course, tedious. Fortunately, this effort can be avoided in most cases with a few simple checks.

From Descartes's rule, we know that the number of internal rates of return cannot exceed the number of changes of signs in cash flows. If all cash flows are positive or all cash flows are negative, there can be no internal rate of return. For an initial outlay followed by a stream of cash inflows, there can be only one internal rate of return. Thus, cash flows must be mixed, with more than one sign change, for there to be multiple internal rates of return. Cash flows for project H appear below.

Year	0	1	2	3	4
Project H Cash Flows	−100	300	−800	1,800	−1,200

There are four changes of sign in the cash flows, so this sign test would suggest that as many as four internal rates of return are possible. Note that this simple counting of signs does not identify the actual number of internal rates of return; it only identifies an upper limit. Fortunately, that upper limit can frequently be reduced with an additional simple test.

The number of *positive, real* internal rates of return cannot exceed the number of changes in the signs of cumulative cash flows. Cumulative cash flows for investment H are as follows:

Year	0	1	2	3	4
Project H Cash Flows	−100	300	−800	1,800	−1,200
Cumulative Cash Flows	−100	200	−600	1,200	0

A move from either a positive or negative number to zero does not count as a sign change, so there are three sign changes in cumulative cash flows; there could be as many as three internal rates of return.

Fortunately, more powerful tests for multiple internal rates of return have been developed. One of the easier-to-use tests was developed by Pratt and Hammond as an extension of the simple cumulation test. This test will often improve on simple cumulations to confirm the existence of only one internal rate of return when simple sign changes or cumulative sign changes indicate the *possibility* of more than one rate. Pratt and Hammond's test consists of repeated cumulations, in which the cumulative cash flows from one stage are cumulated to provide the cumulation in the next stage.[19] This is illustrated in Table 6.1 for project H.

After each stage, the maximum possible number of real, positive internal rates of return is found by counting the number of sign changes going across the bottom row, around the corner, and up the right-hand side of the table of cumulative values. The sequence to be checked after stage two is −100, 100, −500, 700, 700, 0. This involves three sign changes, so the number of possible internal rates of return is still three. Going on to stage three, the sequence to be checked is −100, 0, −500, 200, 900, 700, 0. Remembering that movement

[19]John W. Pratt and John S. Hammond III, "Evaluating and Comparing Projects: Simple Detection of False Alarms," *Journal of Finance* 34 (December 1979): 1231–1242.

| TABLE 6A.1 REPEAT CUMULATION TEST FOR MULTIPLE INTERNAL RATES OF RETURN

Each stage of the cumulations is a cumulation of the numbers in the preceding row. The maximum possible number of real, positive internal rates of return is found by counting the number of sign changes going across the bottom row, around the corner, and up the right-hand side of the table of cumulative values.

Year	0	1	2	3	4
Project H Cash Flows	−100	300	−800	1,800	−1,200
Cumulations					
Stage 1	−100	200	−600	1,200	0
Stage 2	−100	100	−500	700	700
Stage 3	−100	0	−500	200	900

to zero and back to the same sign does not constitute a sign change, there is only one sign change at stage three: from −500 to +200. Therefore, this investment has only one internal rate of return.

This cumulation process can be continued for any number of stages, with the minimum number of sign changes achieved at any stage being the maximum possible number of positive, real internal rates of return. There are also various extensions of this process as well as other processes for further narrowing the number of possible internal rates of return.[20]

If the possibility of multiple internal rates of return cannot be eliminated through these various tests, then the net present values should be plotted as was done in Figure 6.2 in order to determine if there actually are multiple internal rates of return, to determine the internal rates of return, and to determine the net present values at various discount rates. This can be done without too much difficulty using software like Lotus 1-2-3. Of course, use of the net present value criterion avoids these problems entirely.

[20]See Donald C. Aucamp and Walter L. Eckardt, Jr., "A Sufficient Condition for a Unique Non-negative Internal Rate of Return—Comment," *Journal of Financial and Quantitative Analysis* 11 (June 1976): 329–332; Richard H. Bernard, "A More General Sufficient Condition for a Unique Non-negative Internal Rate of Return," *Journal of Financial and Quantitative Analysis* 14 (June 1979): 337–341; Richard H. Bernard and Carl J. Norstrom, "A Further Note on Unrecovered Investment, Uniqueness of the Internal Rate of Return, and the Question of Project Acceptability," *Journal of Financial and Quantitative Analysis* 15 (June 1980); R. Capettini, R. A. Grimlund, and H. R. Toole, "Comment: The Unique Real Internal Rate of Return," *Journal of Financial and Quantitative Analysis* 14 (December 1979); Clovis De Faro, "A Sufficient Condition for a Unique Nonnegative Internal Rate of Return: Further Comments," *Journal of Financial and Quantitative Analysis* 13 (September 1978): 577–584; M. M. Hajdasinski, "A Complete Method for Separation of Internal Rates of Return," *Engineering Economist* 28 (Spring 1983); Anthony F. Herbst, "The Unique Real Internal Rate of Return: Caveat Emptor!," *Journal of Financial and Quantitative Analysis* 13 (June 1978); David Longbottom and Linda Wiper, "Necessary Conditions for the Existence of Multiple Rates in the Use of the Internal Rate of Return," *Journal of Business Finance and Accounting* (Winter 1978).

PROBLEMS

6-A-1. An investment being considered by Dover Corporation generates the following year-end cash flows. Is it possible that this investment has more than one internal rate of return?

Year	0	1	2	3	4	5
Cash Flow	−100	600	−1,000	1,000	−1,500	2,500

6-A-2. A capital investment at Newark Corporation has the following year-end cash flows. Given the Pratt and Hammond test, is it possible that this investment has more than one internal rate of return?

Year	0	1	2	3	4
Cash Flow	−1,000	3,000	−4,000	8,000	−6,000

6-A-3. Confirm your answer to problem A-2 by graphing the relationship between net present value and required return.

SELECTED REFERENCES

Aucamp, Donald C., and Walter L. Eckardt, Jr. "A Sufficient Condition for a Unique Non-negative Internal Rate of Return—Comment." *Journal of Financial and Quantitative Analysis* 11 (June 1976): 329–332.

Bailey, M. J. "Formal Criteria for Investment Decisions." *Journal of Political Economy* (October 1959): 476–488.

Bernard, Richard H. "Base Selection for Modified Rates of Return and Its Irrelevance for Optimal Project Choice." *Engineering Economist* 35 (Fall 1989): 55–65.

———. "Income, Wealth Base and Rate of Return Implications of Alternative Project Evaluation Criteria." *Engineering Economist* 38 (Spring 1993): 165–176.

———. "A More General Sufficient Condition for a Unique Nonnegative Internal Rate of Return." *Journal of Financial and Quantitative Analysis* 14 (June 1979): 337–341.

Bernard, Richard H., and Carl J. Norstrom. "A Further Note on Unrecovered Investment, Uniqueness of the Internal Rate of Return, and the Question of Project Acceptability." *Journal of Financial and Quantitative Analysis* 15 (June 1980): 421–423.

Bierman, Harold. "Beyond Cash Flow ROI." *Journal of Applied Corporate Finance* 5, no. 4 (Winter 1988): 36–39.

Brick, Ivan E., and Daniel G. Weaver. "A Comparison of Capital Budgeting Techniques in Identifying Profitable Investments." *Financial Management* 13 (Winter 1984): 29–39.

Brigham, Eugene F., and Richard H. Pettway. "Capital Budgeting by Utilities." *Financial Management* 2 (Autumn 1973): 11–22.

Calderon-Rossell, Jorge R. "Is the ROI a Good Indicator of the IRR?" *Engineering Economist* 37 (Summer 1992): 315–340.

Capettini, R., R. A. Grimlund, and H. R. Toole. "Comment: The Unique Real Internal Rate of Return." *Journal of Financial and Quantitative Analysis* 14 (December 1979): 1091–1094.

Cook, Thomas J., and Ronald J. Rizzuto. "Capital Budgeting Practices for R&D: A Survey and Analysis of Business Week's R&D Scoreboard." *Engineering Economist* 34 (Summer 1989): 291–304.

Dearden, J. "The Case against ROI Control." *Harvard Business Review* (May–June 1969): 124–135.

De Faro, Clovis. "A Sufficient Condition for a Unique Nonnegative Internal Rate of Return: Further Comments." *Journal of Financial and Quantitative Analysis* 13 (September 1978): 577–584.

Doenges, R. Conrad. "The 'Reinvestment Problem' in a Practical Perspective." *Financial Management* 1 (Spring 1977): 85–91.

Dorfman, Robert. "The Meaning of Internal Rates of Return." *Journal of Finance* 36 (December 1981): 1011–1021.

Durand, David. "Comprehensiveness in Capital Budgeting." *Financial Management* 10 (Winter 1981): 7–13.

Eschenbach, Ted G., and Alice Smith. "Sensitivity Analysis of EAC's Robustness." *Engineering Economist* 37 (Spring 1992): 263–276.

Fama, Eugene F. "Organizational Forms and Investment Decisions." *Journal of Financial Economics* 14 (March 1985): 101–119.

Ferreira, Eurico J., and LeRoy Brooks. "Capital Budgeting: A Key Management Challenge." *Business* 38 (October–December 1988): 22–29.

Fisher, Irving. *The Theory of Interest*. New York: Macmillan, 1930.

Fogler, H. Russell. "Overkill in Capital Budgeting Technique?" *Financial Management* 1 (Spring 1972): 92–96.

Gitman, Lawrence J., and John R. Forrester, Jr. "A Survey of Capital Budgeting Techniques Used by Major U. S. Firms." *Financial Management* 6 (Fall 1977): 66–71.

Gurnami, G. "Capital Budgeting Theory and Practice," *Engineering Economist* 30 (Fall 1984).

Hajdasinski, Miroslaw M. "A Complete Method for Separation of Internal Rates of Return." *Engineering Economist* 28 (Spring 1983): 207–250.

———. "On Bounding the Internal Rates of Return of a Project." *Engineering Economist* 33 (Spring 1988): 235–270.

———. "The Payback Period as a Measure of Profitability and Liquidity." *Engineering Economist* 38 (Spring 1993): 177–191.

Hastie, K. Larry. "One Businessman's View of Capital Budgeting." *Financial Management* 3 (Winter 1974): 36–44.

Hayes, R., and W. Abernathy. "Managing Our Way to Economic Decline." *Harvard Business Review* (July–August 1980): 67–77.

Herbst, Anthony F. "A FORTRAN VI Procedure for Determining Return on Invested Capital." *Management Science* (February 20, 1974): 1022.

———. "The Unique Real Internal Rate of Return: Caveat Emptor!" *Journal of Financial and Quantitative Analysis* 13 (June 1978): 363–370.

Hirshleifer, Jack "On the Theory of Optimal Investment Decision." *Journal of Political Economy* (August 1958): 329–352.

Kamath, Ravindra, and Eugene Oberst. "Capital Budgeting Practices of Large Hospitals." *Engineering Economist* 37 (Spring 1992): 203–232.

Khan, Aman. "Capital Budgeting Practices in Large U. S. Cities." *Engineering Economist* 33 (Fall 1987): 1–12.

Klammer, Thomas P., and Michael C. Walker. "Capital Budgeting Questionnaires: A New Perspective." *Quarterly Journal of Business and Economics* 26 (Summer 1987): 87–95.

———. "The Continued Increase in the Use of Sophisticated Capital Budgeting Techniques." *California Management Review* 27 (Fall 1984): 137–148.

Lewellen, Wilbur G., Howard P. Lanswe, and John J. McConnell. "Payback Substitutes for Discounted Cash Flow." *Financial Management* 2 (Summer 1973): 17–23.

Longmore, Dear R. "The Persistence of the Payback Method: A Time-Adjusted Decision Rule Perspective." *Engineering Economist* 34 (Spring 1989): 185–194.

Luxhoj, James T., and Marilyn S. Jones. "A Framework for Replacement Modeling Assumptions." *Engineering Economist* 32 (Fall 1986): 39–49.

Martin, John D., Samuel H. Cox, and Richard D. MacMinn. *The Theory of Finance: Evidence and Applications.* Hinsdale, Ill.: Dryden Press, 1988.

McConnell, John, and C. Muscarella. "Corporate Capital Expenditure Decisions and the Market Value of the Firm." *Journal of Financial Economics* 14 (September 1985): 399–422.

Meal, H. C. "Putting Production Decisions Where They Belong." *Harvard Business Review* (March–April 1984).

Middlaugh, J. Kendall, II, and Scott S. Cowen. "Five Flaws in Evaluating Capital Expenditures." *Business Horizons* 30 (March–April 1987): 59–67.

Mukherjee, Tarun K., and David F. Scott, Jr. "The Capital Budgeting Process in Large Firms: An Analysis of Capital Budgeting Manuals." Paper presented at the Eastern Finance Association meeting, April 1987.

Narayanan, M. P. "Observability and the Payback Criterion." *Journal of Business* 58 (July 1985): 309–323.

Pike, Richard H. "Do Sophisticated Capital Budgeting Approaches Improve Investment Decision-Making Effectiveness?" *Engineering Economist* 34 (Winter 1989): 149–161.

———. "An Empirical Study of the Adoption of Sophisticated Capital Budgeting Practices and Decision-Making Effectiveness." *Accounting and Business Research* (Autumn 1988): 341–351.

Porter, Michael. "Capital Choices: Changing the Way America Invests in Industry." *Journal of Applied Corporate Finance* (1992): 4–16.

Pratt, John W., and John S. Hammond III. "Evaluating and Comparing Projects: Simple Detection of False Alarms." *The Journal of Finance* 34 (December 1979): 1231–1242.

Proctor, Michael D., and John R. Canada. "Past and Present Methods of Manufacturing Investment Evaluation: A Review of the Empirical and Theoretical Literature." *Engineering Economist* 38 (Fall 1992): 45–58.

Ramis, Francisco J., Gerald J. Thuesen, and Tina J. Barr. "A Dynamic Targert-Wealth Criterion for Capital Investment Decisions." *Engineering Economist* 36 (Winter 1991): 107–126.

Reimann, Bernard C. "Stock Price and Business Success: What Is the Relationship?" *Journal of Business Strategy* 8 (Summer 1987): 38–49.

Robichek, Alexander A., and James C. Van Horne. "Abandonment Value and Capital Budgeting." *Journal of Finance* 22 (December 1967): 577–590.

Ross, Marc. "Capital Budgeting Practices of Twelve Large Manufacturers." *Financial Management* 15 (Winter 1986): 15–22.

Samuelson, Paul A. "Some Aspects of the Pure Theory of Capital." *Quarterly Journal of Economics* (May 1937): 469–496.

Schall, Lawrence D., Gary L. Sundem, and William R. Geijsbeek. "Survey and Analysis of Capital Budgeting Methods." *Journal of Finance* 33 (March 1978): 281–287.

Schull, David M. "Efficient Capital Project Selection through a Yield-Based Capital Budgeting Technique." *Engineering Economist* 38 (Fall 1992): 1–18.

Scott, David F., Jr., and J. William Petty III. "Capital Budgeting Practices in Large American Firms: A Retrospective Analysis and Synthesis." *Financial Review* 19 (March 1984): 111–125.

Stewart, G. Bennett, III. "Market Myths." *Journal of Applied Corporate Finance* 2, no. 3 (Fall 1989): 6–23.

Sullivan, A. Charlene, and Keith Smith. "Capital Budgeting Practices for U.S. Factory Automation Projects." Purdue University Working Paper #90-11-1 (November 1990).

Sundem, Gary L. "Evaluating Capital Budgeting Models in Simulated Environments." *Journal of Finance* 30 (September 1975): 977–992.

Wilner, Neil, Bruce Koch, and Thomas Klammer. "Justification of High Technology Capital Investment—An Empirical Study." *Engineering Economist* 37 (Summer 1992): 341–353.

CHAPTER 7

RANKING MUTUALLY EXCLUSIVE INVESTMENTS

After completing this chapter you should be able to:

1. Identify mutually exclusive projects and know how to choose the better project.
2. Demonstrate why net present value is superior to other methods in ranking mutually exclusive projects.
3. Compare projects with different life spans or durations.
4. Compute the equivalent annuity for different projects.
5. Explain when and why the equivalent annuity method is used to compare projects with unequal lives.
6. Determine the optimal abandonment time for a project.

After studying energy conservation decisions at numerous firms, Marc Ross developed the following composite profile:

> Bill Johnson is part of an energy-conservation team at a large plant of a basic-materials manufacturer. On the initiative of a vendor, he has identified an approach to cutting energy cost of a heater: advanced combustion controls, which would reduce excess air in the combustion zone.
>
> Bill looks into other approaches, such as total replacement of the heater or added heat exchangers (to capture heat from the stack gases to preheat the product.) However, the projects overlap; he can advocate at most one.[1]

Like Bill Johnson, managers are often forced to choose between attractive investments, and various discounted cash flow measures sometimes give

[1]Marc Ross, "Capital Budgeting Practices of Twelve Large Manufacturers," *Financial Management* 15 (Winter 1986): 15–22.

conflicting messages about which investment is best. What is Exxon to do, for example, if new supertankers have the highest net present values but smaller used tankers have higher internal rates of return? Acquiring both types of tankers is not the answer because the company can acquire enough of either type to carry all available oil. Some capital investments have more than one internal rate of return, and what should a company do about a capital investment that has internal rates of return of 2 percent and 200 percent? Choices between attractive investments must be made, and this chapter is devoted to capital investment choice when at least two alternatives are attractive.

Investments may compete because they are mutually exclusive or because the company faces capital rationing. Two investments are *mutually exclusive* if, like Exxon's tankers, there is a reason other than money that makes the selection of both infeasible. *Capital rationing* occurs when managers limit the total amount of money to be invested, so that they do not select all investments with positive net present values, even though the investments are not mutually exclusive. Mutually exclusive investments and investments with more than one internal rate of return are treated in this chapter, and capital rationing is treated in Chapter 22 as part of the section on financing decisions and capital investment analysis.

REASONS FOR MUTUALLY EXCLUSIVE INVESTMENTS |

Mutually exclusive capital investments are often alternative ways to achieve the same result or alternate uses of a scarce resource other than money. When an airline is comparing the purchase of new and used airplanes, it is looking at two different ways to carry the same passengers. When Boeing was considering production of the 7J7 airplane, managers knew that airlines needing additional capacity could buy a used airplane for $12 million or a new, fuel-efficient 7J7 for $30 million.[2] Boeing's managers thought that the airlines would rank used airplane investments higher than 7J7 investments and, therefore, decided not to build the 7J7.

Why do we get conflicting rankings? Addressing the question in mechanical terms, there are three conditions that can lead to ranking differences with the three discounted cash flow measures:[3]

1. Differences in the timing of cash flows for competing investments.

When Chrysler bought American Motors, it got a design (Jeep) it could sell immediately, while years would otherwise be spent developing a competing design. Chrysler also got older, less efficient factories with shorter lives and immediate production instead of new, efficient factories with longer lives.

[2]"Bright Smiles, Sweaty Palms," *Business Week* (February 1, 1986): 22–23.

[3]Reinvestment rate assumptions may also be an issue, if explicit assumptions of reinvestment rates different from the company's required return are used.

2. Differences in the sizes of competing investments.

Choices among investments of different sizes are illustrated by George Steinbrenner's decision to enter the Hawaiian cruise market by building $150 million, 1,200-passenger ships. Prior to this decision, $100 million, 800-passenger ships had been considered.

3. Differences in the use of scarce resources other than money.

The world is rich with examples of investments that are competing uses of scarce resources. Neiman-Marcus has more potential uses for floor space at its Union Square store than it has space available. Skilled personnel are another type of resource constraint, and airline manufacturers are often seen vying with each other for a supply of engineers that is fixed in the short run. Other companies are forced to limit growth because they cannot expand their management team fast enough to take advantage of all opportunities without losing control. When Bill Bidwell decided to move his Cardinal football team to Phoenix, he made a choice between competing uses of a scarce resource: an NFL football franchise.

Time is an essential element in many mutually exclusive investment situations. Suppose Neiman-Marcus wants to expand its Union Square store, but no adjacent space is available. Land must be found, a purchase must be negotiated, architectural plans must be drawn, permits must be obtained, construction must be carried out, and a buyer for the old store must be found. The marginal cost of the increased space may be so high that the project is abandoned. Even if the process is feasible, it may take years, and space must be rationed in the meantime.

These examples make it clear that mutually exclusive investments are not oddities but part of the daily life of anyone who deals with capital investment proposals.

REMINDER: NPV IS STILL BEST

Commerce Energy Service illustrates the problems faced in choosing among mutually exclusive investments and can be used to demonstrate the superiority of net present value as the tool for choosing among these investments. Commerce can provide electricity to an industrial park using coal, gas, or oil as fuel. The three competing investments are summarized in Table 7.1. Each investment has a four-year life in that it will produce electricity for four years, even though coal does not generate cash flows in all years. (The coal investment will just break even during the last two years, but the operation must be continued to meet contract obligations.) Given Commerce's 10 percent required return, each of the three investments is desirable according to net present value, profitability index, and internal-rate-of-return criteria. But each investment is best according to one of the measures and worst according to one of the others.

These reasons for differences in rankings are illustrated for Commerce Energy Service in Table 7.1. Coal is superior to gas in terms of internal rate of return, but

| **TABLE** **7.1** ILLUSTRATION OF INVESTMENT DESIRABILITY RANKING CONFLICTS

Initial outlays and year-end cash flows for the three fuel choices available to Commerce Energy are shown, along with net present value (NPV), profitability index (PI), and internal rate of return (IRR). The required return is 10 percent. Rankings depend on which of these three measures is used.

	CASH FLOWS							
Year	**0**	**1**	**2**	**3**	**4**	**NPV**	**PI**	**IRR**
Investment								
Coal	−1,000	750	500	0	0	95.04	1.095	18%
Gas	−1,000	350	350	350	350	109.45	1.109	15%
Oil	−500	180	180	180	180	70.58	1.141	16%

cash inflows from coal occur sooner, so the higher return is earned for a shorter time. Oil generates more cash flow per dollar invested than does gas, but the oil investment is smaller in size so its contribution to net present value is less.

In Chapter 5, we demonstrated that net present value measures the increase in wealth. We could just quit with that point, because we know that the choice that maximizes net present value maximizes wealth, so any other choice does not maximize wealth. Since you may come up against the use of alternate ranking schemes, though, it is worthwhile to explore the implications of these alternate rankings a bit more.

Reasons for conflicting rankings can be further illustrated by comparison of the net present value profiles for coal and gas, shown in Figure 7.1. This profile is constructed by calculating the net present value for each project at various required rates of return. As these profiles illustrate, the investment choice that provides the highest net present value depends on the required return. At very low discount rates the gas project is preferred to the coal project. The intersection of the two profiles, called Fisher's intersection due to exploration of its significance by Irving Fisher,[4] occurs at the discount rate of 11.45 percent. Coal is superior if the required return is above 11.45 percent, and gas is superior otherwise.[5] In this case, gas makes the greatest contribution to wealth because the required return is 10 percent.

Suppose we are faced with the three alternatives in Table 7.1. Suppose further that we are making the decisions on behalf of an investor who can invest elsewhere at 10 percent and has $1,000 to invest, after setting aside the present value of the amount she wants to consume over the next four years. If this investor likes more money better than less, her objective with the $1,000 will be to end up with as much money as possible at the end of four years. Coal or gas

---

[4]See Irving Fisher, *The Rate of Interest* (New York: Macmillan, 1907) and *The Theory of Interest* (New York: Macmillan, 1930).

[5]We can also note that when two investments are being considered, net present value and internal rate of return rankings agree if the required return is above Fisher's intersection, and disagree otherwise.

| FIGURE 7.1 NET PRESENT VALUE PROFILES FOR MUTUALLY EXCLUSIVE INVESTMENTS

This figure shows the net present values for coal and gas investments from Table 7.1, at various discount rates. The intersection of the two lines, called Fisher's intersection, is at the discount rate that results in the same net present value for both investments.

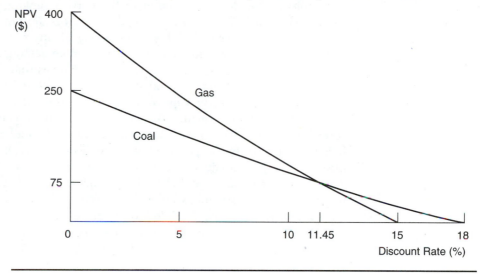

will take all of her money, while oil will leave her with $500 to invest elsewhere at 10 percent. All cash inflows from the investment will be reinvested until the end of the four-year period at 10 percent.

Her wealth at the end of the four years with each alternative is as follows:

Coal: $750(1.10)^3 + 500(1.10)^2 = \$1,603.25$

Gas: $350(1.10)^3 + 350(1.10)^2 + 350(1.10)^1 + 350 = \$1,624.35$

Oil: $500(1.10)^4 + 180(1.10)^3 + 180(1.10)^2 + 180(1.10)^1 + 180 = \$1,567.43$

Elsewhere (None): $1,000(1.10)^4 = \$1,464.10$

The project that maximized net present value also maximized terminal wealth. To be precise, the present value of the increase in terminal wealth, over the $1,464.10 from investing elsewhere, is the net present value:

	Terminal Wealth (TW)	Terminal Wealth Gain (TW − 1,464.10)	Present Value of Terminal Wealth Gain
Coal	1,603.25	139.15	95.04
Gas	1,624.35	160.25	109.45
Oil	1,567.43	103.33	70.58

We set aside this investor's consumption plans and concentrated on terminal wealth. Of course, the investment that maximizes terminal wealth also maximizes current consumption potential if the investor wants to borrow against future cash flows at 10 percent interest rate. Once again, we see that the net present value is the correct ranking tool when choosing among mutually exclusive projects. Net present value gives the correct ranking for maximization of current share price, maximization of the investors' terminal wealth, and maximization of the investors' ability to consume at any one time, while holding consumption at other times constant. The example demonstrates that use of the other ranking methods (IRR and PI) leads to choices that do not maximize current wealth, future wealth, or consumption by investors.

Having recognized the superiority of the net present value ranking, it is useful to compare the information content of the various discounted cash flow measures. The net present value measures an investment's *total* contribution to shareholder wealth while the profitability index measures wealth creation *per dollar invested*. The profitability index has some limited use as a ranking tool in certain capital rationing situations, but in the absence of capital rationing, money committed to one investment is not diverted from other uses that would generate positive net present values. Therefore, total net present value creation, and not net present value creation per dollar invested, is the appropriate standard for choosing among mutually exclusive investments so as to maximize shareholder wealth.

The internal rate of return measures the rate of return on *unrecovered* investment. It gives no indication of the dollar *amount of investment* earnings that are returned or the *length of time* that return is earned. Consequently, the internal rate of return does not measure the size of the value contribution of an investment, even though it continues to be the most widely used discounted cash flow method in practice.

It is clear that net present value is the right way to choose, but application of the net present value can be complicated. In the remainder of this chapter, we will look at ways to apply the net present value rule to mutually exclusive capital investments with unequal lives, to mutually exclusive capital investments with costs and no direct benefits, to repair/replace decisions, and to abandonment decisions.

USING NPV WITH UNEQUAL LIVES |

Unequal lives are a common problem in capital budgeting. The prospective choice of an airline between a Boeing 7J7 and a used airplane involved differences in life. A used airplane that cost $12 million might have a life of only 10 remaining years, while a new $30 million airplane might last 20 years. Thus, the 7J7 would provide both fuel economy and more years of usage. The question is whether the extra years of use and the fuel savings would be worth an extra $18 million of investment.

To deal with unequal lives, suppose that the coal investment in Table 7.1 has a life of only two years and that a new investment in electricity production can be made at that time. This is an important consideration. The goal is still to maximize net present value, but net present value must be measured over comparable periods. Assume that the industrial park will close after four years and none of the investments have salvage values if abandoned early. The oil and gas alternatives have equal lives, and we already know that the gas investment is preferred over the oil investment. The investments to consider are:

- Invest in coal, then invest in coal again at the end of two years.
- Invest in gas.

It would also be possible to consider sequences involving abandonment of an investment before the end of its life, but none of these capital investments happen to have positive net present values if abandoned early. Cash flows and net present values for the two sequences appear in Table 7.2.

In this example, the greatest net present value over the four-year life of the industrial park is achieved by starting with coal and then repeating coal after two years. The preferability of this sequence is dependent on the particular set of assumptions about future opportunities. A change in the life of the constraining resource (industrial park), a change in future investment opportunities, or an opportunity to sell one of the investments before the end of its life could change the sequence that has the highest net present value. Thus, the selection process is heavily dependent on assumptions about future opportunities. If the assumptions about future opportunities are correct, maximizing net present value over

| **TABLE 7.2 CASH FLOWS WITH ALTERNATE INVESTMENT SEQUENCES**

This table contains a cash flow and net present value analysis (at a 10 percent required return) for two possible investment sequences. The industrial park has a life of four years. The lives of investments end when cash flows stop, and none of the investments have salvage values if abandoned early.

Year	0	1	2	3	4
I. Start with coal and then repeat coal					
Invest in coal	−1,000	750	500		
Invest in coal			−1,000	750	500
Total	−1,000	750	−500	750	500
Net present value =	$173.59				
II. Invest only in gas					
Invest in gas	−1,000	350	350	350	350
Net present value =	$109.45				

the life of the constraining resource (the industrial park's life) will maximize wealth.

EQUIVALENT ANNUITY (EA)

Finding the investment sequence that maximizes net present value can be a difficult process when you can reuse a resource indefinitely. Suppose, for example, you were trying to choose between a new airplane that will last 21 years and a used airplane that will last 8 years, with an indefinite number of repetitions of either investment being feasible. A simple net-present-value ranking will not do because one investment provides service longer. You could evaluate the two alternatives by assuming that whichever investment was chosen initially would be repeated over the span of 168 years (8 × 21) that would be required to get a time horizon at which both assets would be reaching the ends of their lives simultaneously. This would, of course, be a bit tedious. The equivalent annuity, also referred to as the *annualized net present value,* is a useful tool for simplifying the analysis of problems of this type, as long as the projects being compared are of the same risk. The equivalent annuity is not an alternative to the net present value; it is a convenient way of selecting investments that will maximize net present value.

The *equivalent annuity* is the level annuity over the investment's life that has a present value equal to the investment's net present value. Expressed mathematically by rearranging terms in Equation 3-4b, the equivalent annuity (EA) is:

$$EA = NPV/PVAI_{n,k} \qquad (7\text{-}1)$$

The investment with the highest equivalent annuity will have the highest net present value of total cash flows if all competing investments are repeated to infinity or to a comparable time horizon at which the lives of all competing investments end.

Using the 10 percent required return, the equivalent annuities for coal and gas investments in Table 7.1, assuming coal can be repeated in two years, are:

$$EA_{coal} = \$95.04/PVAI_{2yrs,10\%} = \$95.04/1.7355 = \underline{\$54.76}$$

$$EA_{gas} = \$109.45/PVAI_{4yrs,10\%} = \$109.45/3.1699 = \underline{\$34.53}$$

The coal investment is superior to the gas investment using the equivalent annuity and will, therefore, be superior to the gas investment using net present value analysis with repeated investment out to any comparable time horizon.

To see the correspondence between the net present value and equivalent annuity ranking, note that the coal investment's equivalent annuity of $54.76, if continued for four years, is:

$$\$54.76 PVAI_{4yrs,10\%} = \underline{\$173.59}$$

This $173.59 is the same net present value found in Table 7.2 with the coal investment repeated after two years. If a capital investment is replaced with an identical investment at the end of its life forever, the net present value is:[6]

$$NPV_\infty = EA/k \tag{7-2}$$

The net present values for the coal and gas investments assuming repetition to infinity are:

$$NPV_{coal,\infty} = 54.76/.10 = \underline{\$547.60}$$

$$NPV_{gas,\infty} = 34.53/.10 = \underline{\$345.30}$$

Suppose the gas investment could be repeated indefinitely but the coal investment could not be repeated. If the coal investment were chosen, the company would have to switch to the gas investment after the end of the initial life of the coal investment. The value-maximizing choice would still be to start with the investment with the highest equivalent annuity and then switch to the investment with the second-highest equivalent annuity at the expiration of the first investment.[7]

The equivalent annuity leads to the choice between two mutually exclusive investments that maximizes net present value and shareholder wealth when the investment can be repeated to a comparable time horizon, or at least one of the two investments can be repeated indefinitely.

[6]Proof:

$$NPV_\infty = NPV + NPV/(1 + k)^n + NPV/(1 + k)^{2n} + \ldots$$
$$= [NPV(1 + k)^n]/(1 + k)^n + [NPV(1 + k)^n]/(1 + k)^{2n} + [NPV(1 + k)^n]/(1 + k)^{3n} + \ldots$$
$$= [(1 + k)^n NPV]/[(1 + k)^n - 1]$$

By definition, $NPV = EA[1 - 1/(1 + k)^n]/k$. Substituting for NPV gives:

$$NPV_\infty = (EA/k)(1 + k)^n[1 - 1/(1 + k)^n]/[(1 + k)^n - 1] = EA/k$$

[7]Proof: Let NPV_A be the net present value from perpetual reinvestment in project A, let NPV_B be similarly defined, and let NPV_{AB} be the net present value from initial investment in A and then perpetual reinvestment in B after the initial n year life of A. EA_A and EA_B are the equivalent annuities of A and B respectively.

$$NPV_A = EA_A/k \text{ and } NPV_B = EA_B/k$$

$$NPV_{AB} = EA_A PVAI_{n,k} + [EA_B/k]/(1 + k)^n]$$

Subtracting NPV_B from both sides and rearranging terms yields:

$$NPV_{AB} - NPV_B = [EA_A - EA_B] PVAI_{n,k}$$

Since both bracketed expressions on the right-hand side are positive if $EA_A > EA_B$, it follows that starting with investment A and then switching to investment B will create more value than starting and staying with investment B.

COST-ONLY ANALYSIS |

Some mutually exclusive investments do not generate cash flows directly. An example is Southwestern Bell's choice of an air-conditioning system for its San Antonio headquarters building. There was no need to spend time deciding if they should air condition the building. The question was simply which air-conditioning system has a series of costs with the lowest present value. If the lives of the two methods are equal, the one with the lower present value of costs should be chosen. If the lives are unequal and replacement will be needed to continue providing the service, each present value can be converted to an equivalent annuity, commonly referred to as the *equivalent annual charge* when used in this context.

Example. The Old Haven city government, with a 10 percent required return, is considering two alternative heating systems for city hall. Suppose the economy heating system will last five years and has costs with a present value of $100,000, while the deluxe heating system will last seven years and has costs with a present value of $120,000. The equivalent annual charges (using the five- and seven-year 10 percent present value factors from Table A.4) are:

Heating Method	Life	PV of Costs	Equivalent Annual Charge
Deluxe	5 years	$100,000	$100,000/3.7908 = $26,380
Economy	7 years	120,000	$120,000/4.8684 = $24,649

The deluxe system has a lower equivalent annual charge and is therefore more desirable, assuming either alternative can be repeated indefinitely. The same conclusion could have been reached with more tedious calculations by assuming a 35-year time horizon with the deluxe heating system replaced four times and the economy system replaced six times.

REPAIR/REPLACEMENT DECISIONS |

The choice between repairing and replacing a piece of equipment is effectively a choice between mutually exclusive investments. The city of St. Louis currently faces a choice between spending a few hundred million dollars to modernize its overburdened Lambert Field or build a new airport in Illinois for ten times the cost. The modernization of Lambert Field is generally viewed as a stopgap measure, with a more permanent solution still being required in the long run.

For the repair/replace decision, the cost of the old asset is the repair cost plus the forgone sale price or salvage value.[8] The equivalent annuity or equivalent annual charge can be used to account for uneven lives.

---

[8]We continue to ignore taxes or assume cash flows are on an after-tax basis throughout this chapter. Recognition of taxes in the estimation of cash flows is taken up in Chapter 8.

Example. You could sell your used automobile today for $6,000, or you could have it extensively repaired at a cost of $1,000 and use it for five more years, at which time it would be worth nothing. A new car could be purchased for $10,000 and would last for ten years, with no significant repairs and no salvage value. The cost of using the old car for five years is the forgone $6,000 receipt from the sale plus the repair cost, for a total of $7,000.

Using Equation 7-1 and a 10 percent required return, the equivalent annual charge over the five-year period is:

$$\text{Equivalent annual charge (old car)} = \$7,000/3.7908 = \underline{\underline{\$1,846.58}}$$

The equivalent annual charge for the ten-year life of the new car is:

$$\text{Equivalent annual charge (new car)} = \$10,000/6.1446 = \underline{\underline{\$1,627.45}}$$

Since the equivalent annual charge is based on costs, not benefits, the lower number is desired, and the new car is preferred.

The correctness of the equivalent annuity solution can be confirmed by comparing the two alternatives using marginal cash flows over a ten-year horizon. To do this, assume that if the old car is kept, another old car will be bought for $6,000 and repaired for $1,000 at the end of five years.[9] The immediate $3,000 marginal cash flow to buy a new car (the price of a new car minus the sale price of the old car, minus the avoided repair cost) allows us to avoid a $7,000 expenditure to buy and repair a used car in five years. To summarize, the marginal cash flows for the new car are as shown in Table 7.3.

At a 10 percent required return, the net present value of the marginal cash investment to buy a new car is positive:

$$\text{NPV} = -3,000 + (\$7,000/1.1^5) = \$1,346$$

This $1,346 net present value is also the present value of the difference between the two equivalent annual charges over ten years:

$$\text{NPV} = (1,846.58 - 1,627.45)6.1446 = \$1,346$$

This confirms the preferability of the new car, as determined using the equivalent annual charge.[10]

---

[9]Using the proof in footnote 7, it can also be shown that buying a new car now is cheaper than repairing the old car and replacing it with a new car in five years. This conclusion is based on the assumption that a car will be needed indefinitely and identical cars will be available at identical prices in the future.

[10]People will occasionally suggest that the cost of the new car is the purchase price minus the sale price of the old car, or $4,000, while the cost of keeping the old car is the $1,000 repair cost. This would give an answer consistent with net present value over a ten-year horizon if the old car would last for ten years with a $1,000 repair every five years. It is an appropriate solution, but for a different problem.

| **T A B L E   7 . 3   MARGINAL CASH FLOW ANALYSIS OF NEW CAR PURCHASE**

These calculations confirm that the equivalent annuity analysis of the cost-only car purchase decision leads to the same choice as net present value over time with repeat purchases.

Year	0	5
Purchase new car	−$10,000	
Sell old car	6,000	
Avoided repair cost	1,000	
Total Initial Outlay	−$3,000	
Avoid purchase of used car		$6,000
Avoid repair of used car		1,000
Net benefit in Year 5		$7,000
Present Value		$4,346
Net Present Value	$1,346	

COMPLEX INVESTMENTS |

The investments considered thus far were competing investments with only one constraining or scarce resource. A more complex situation would involve several scarce resources with each of a number of investments using different amounts of each scarce resource for different lengths of time. A factory, for example, may have limited assembly-line time, limited raw materials, and limited engineering time available, with each of a hundred competing products using these resources in different proportions. The objective in these cases is still to choose the feasible combination of investments that maximizes net present value, but finding that combination could require checking thousands or millions of combinations. Fortunately, tools like linear programming can be used to quickly find the optimal combination of investments in these situations. Linear programming applications are discussed in Chapter 24.

ABANDONMENT DECISIONS |

For many capital investments, the economic life is not fixed, and there are a number of different times at which the investment can be abandoned. Abandonment decisions are a form of mutually exclusive investment analysis because a choice between several streams of costs and benefits is required. Car rental companies such as Hertz and Avis have wrestled with this problem because a car could be kept in the rental fleet from a few days to a decade or more. Most rental car companies have opted to abandon (sell) their cars after a year or two, although some discount companies keep their cars longer.

If a project has no salvage value or other value that can be realized on abandonment, and it is not mutually exclusive with regard to other investments, it will generally be continued as long as it provides positive cash flows. If the investment has a value that can be realized on abandonment, you should abandon it at the point that maximizes net present value of all cash benefits, including abandonment value. Mathematically, the net present value with abandonment at the end of year d is:

$$\text{NPV} \sum_{t=1}^{d} CF_t/(1 + k)^t - I_o + S_d/(1 + k)^d \tag{7-3}$$

where S_d is the salvage value at the end of year d. The net present value is computed in this way for values of d from one to the maximum possible life of the investment. The project life (d) that gives the highest net present value is the economic life of the investment.

Example. Georgetown Corporation is considering a new hydraulic packer. The asset requires an initial outlay of $1,000 and then generates cash benefits at the end of each year for the next three years. The value that can be obtained on abandonment declines from $700 at the end of the first year to $50 at the end of the third year. Table 7.4 shows an abandonment analysis. The net present value is computed on the assumption the investment is abandoned at the end of the first year. The computation is then repeated on the assumption of abandonment at the end of the second year and again for the assumption of abandonment at the end of the third year. A 10 percent required return was used for the analysis. The net present value, in this case, is maximized by abandonment at the end of the second year.

| TABLE 7.4   ABANDONMENT ANALYSIS

Total net present value using a 10 percent required return is computed for each possible abandonment time. Net present value is maximized by abandonment at the end of year 2.

Year	0	1	2	3
Cash flow	−$1,000	$500	$450	$300
Salvage value at the end of year d: (S_d)		700	350	50

Abandon after	Net present value
1 year	$(500 + 700)/1.10 - 1{,}000 = 90.91$
2 years	$500/1.10 + (450 + 350)/1.10^2 - 1{,}000 = 115.70$
3 years	$500/1.10 + 450/1.10^2 + (300 + 50)/1.10^3 - 1{,}000 = 89.41$

It is sometimes suggested that a project should be abandoned when the present value of the future cash flows is less than the salvage value. The problem with this rule is that it ignores the future abandonment opportunities. This point can be illustrated with Table 7.4. At the end of the first year, the salvage value is $700 and the present value of the remaining cash flows is $450/1.10 + 300/1.10^2 = \$657$. This rule would lead to abandonment at the end of the first year, whereas the optimal abandonment time is at the end of the second year.

In the case of mutually exclusive investments with unequal lives, the use of the constraining resource after abandonment must be considered. If investment in an identical asset is assumed, the abandonment time that maximizes the equivalent annuity is optimal. For the three alternative abandonment times considered in Table 7.4, for example, the equivalent annuities are as follows:

Abandonment Year (d)	NPV ÷	PVAI$_{d,10\%}$ =	Equivalent Annuity
1	90.91 ÷	.9091 =	$100.00
2	115.70 ÷	1.7355 =	$ 66.67
3	89.41 ÷	2.4869 =	$ 35.95

Abandonment at the end of the first year gives the highest equivalent annuity. Therefore, abandonment at the end of the first year is optimal if abandonment frees up a constraining resource for reuse; net present value over time would be maximized by abandoning at the end of the first year and replacing the investment with an identical investment that is abandoned when it is one year old, etc. If the constraining resource is not freed up by abandonment, the net-present-value rule identifies the end of the second year as the optimal abandonment time.

Managers sometimes talk about the optimal replacement cycle rather than the optimal abandonment time. As an example, should San Jose Plastics replace injection pumps every two years or every three years? Reuse of a constraining resource is implied in these decisions, so a replacement cycle decision is really an abandonment time decision with a constraining resource.

In capital-rationing situations, other abandonment rules are sometimes appropriate, and these are discussed later, in Chapter 22. Abandonment opportunities can also be important in risk analysis, and the abandonment opportunity will be considered in that context in Chapter 11.

SUMMARY |

In Chapter 6, we noted that the three discounted cash flow techniques—net present value, profitability index, and internal rate of return—are preferable to the payback period and accounting rate of return because they recognize the importance of the time value of money. While the three discounted cash flow measures give identical accept/reject signals for noncompeting investments, they often give conflicting rankings for mutually exclusive investments. The net present value is the amount by which the investment increases wealth. Thus, if the firm is not subject to capital rationing, ranking by net present value will lead to the choice between mutually exclusive investments that maximizes wealth.

When mutually exclusive investments have unequal lives, the net-present-value ranking still leads to the choice that maximizes shareholder wealth, if the computation of net present value explicitly recognizes the difference in lives and possible later uses of the constraining resources. The equivalent annuity is not an alternative ranking method but simply a convenient way to develop the net-present-value ranking for mutually exclusive investments with unequal lives. The equivalent annuity formula is:

$$EA = NPV/PVAI_{n,k} \hspace{3cm} \text{(7-4)}$$

The net present value and equivalent annuity concepts were extended to abandonment, replacement, and repair/replace decisions. These applications illustrate the robustness of the net-present-value rule.

Although many of the companies that rely on the internal rate of return for project selection will choose the same investments that would be chosen using net present value, they will not know if conflicting signals exist unless both the net present value and internal rate of return are computed. When both measures are computed and there is a conflict, the net-present-value signal is the one that should be used if the goal is to maximize shareholder wealth.

QUESTIONS

7–1. List some examples of conditions that could result in investments being mutually exclusive.

7–2. What is meant by the term *capital rationing*?

7–3. Why is it possible for an investment to have a higher net present value than a competing investment but still have a lower internal rate of return and profitability index than that competitor?

7–4. Define, in your own words, the equivalent annuity.

7–5. Give several examples of mutually exclusive investments that are not expected to increase revenues.

7–6. What is the criterion for selecting the optimal abandonment time?

7–7. What are the conditions in which the equivalent annuity gives a ranking the same as that achieved with the net present value?

7–8. Explain why the net present value is generally considered the superior measure for choosing between mutually exclusive investments.

7–9. Why is it not necessarily correct to sell a project when the salvage value in greater than the present value of cash inflows from future operations?

7–10. List five examples of resources other than money that can be constrained, and can, therefore, lead to mutually exclusive capital investments.

7–11. (**Applications**) On pages 192 and 196 of this chapter, two airplane alternatives were discussed: a $12 million used airplane that would last 10 years and a Boeing 7J7 that might last 20 years. In addition to direct equivalent annuity analysis, what strategic considerations might come into play in the choice between airplane types?

7–12. (**Ethical considerations**) Eli Lilly took on the challenge of reducing cash outflow by $1 billion over three years. The purpose was to make the company more lean and competitive. The company had never had a layoff up to that time. Is it ethically acceptable to make capital investments that will improve productivity but will also lead to layoffs in a company that has never laid off workers in the past?

PROBLEMS |

(Continue to ignore taxes in analyzing these problems. The adjustment of cash flows for tax considerations will be taken up in Chapter 8.)

7–1. Initial costs, year-end cash flows, and desirability measures (net present value and internal rate of return) for mutually exclusive investments being considered by Stockton Corporation follow. The required return is 10 percent. Which investment should be chosen? Why?

Year	0	1	2	3	4	NPV	IRR
P	−1,500	50	400	800	1,000	160	13.60%
Q	−1,800	1,200	600	400	50	121	14.55%

7–2. Initial costs and year-end cash flows for two mutually exclusive investments being considered by Stanford Partners follow. The required return is 10 percent. Which investment should be chosen? Why?

Year	0	1	2	3
R	−4,000	1,000	1,000	5,000
S	−5,000	5,000	1,000	1,000

7–3. Prepare a net present value profile for investments R and S from problem 2. Identify and interpret Fisher's intersection.

7–4. Santa Clara Corporation is considering investments T and U. Initial costs and year-end cash flows follow. Investment T has a life of three years and investment U has a life of four years. The limiting resource that caused the two investments to be mutually exclusive cannot be reused. The required return is 10 percent. Which investment should be chosen? Why?

Year	0	1	2	3	4
T	−50,000	25,000	25,000	25,000	
U	−65,000	25,000	25,000	25,000	25,000

7–5. For the mutually exclusive investments described in problem 4, which investment should be chosen if the constraining resource can be reused at the end of either investment's life? Why?

7–6. For the investment described in problem 4, assume that the constraining resource can be reused, but an investment similar to investment T will not be available when T expires. The constraining resource must be used for an investment similar to U at the end of the life of either T or U. Which investment should be chosen in this case? Why?

7–7. An office in Fort Collins uses 1,000 photocopies per working day, and there are 200 working days a year. The brand A copying machine costs $3,000 and will produce a total of one million copies before it wears out. The brand B machine costs $5,000 and will produce two million copies in its life. Maintenance and material costs are $.03 a copy with either machine, and neither machine will have any salvage value. The required return is 10 percent a year. Which machine should the company acquire? Why? (Assume year-end cash flows for simplicity.)

7–8. Which of the two copying machines described in problem 7 should the company choose if it uses 5,000 copies a day?

7–9. The board of directors at Boulder Corporation is considering two alternate ways of dealing with a deteriorated, demoralizing, and difficult-to-maintain office building. The existing building could be refurbished at a cost of $4 million, or a new building could be built at a cost of $6 million. The old building, even if refurbished, would not be as efficient as the new one, and energy costs would therefore be $200,000 a year higher. Either the new or the refurbished building would be used for 20 years. The salvage value for the new building would then be $1 million, while the salvage value for the old building would be $500,000. If the new building is acquired, the old building can be sold now for $250,000 in its present deteriorated condition. The required return for Boulder is 12 percent. Which alternative should be chosen? (Assume year-end cash flows for simplicity.)

7–10. Assume the old building described in problem 9 would only last 15 years if refurbished. The salvage value in 15 years would be $500,000. In this case, which building should be chosen?

7–11. A fast-food chain headquartered in Denver prefers to run stores for a few years and then sell them to franchise operators. The franchise operators pay an average fee of $100,000 a year per store above the cost of services provided. The company earns an average of $350,000 a year by operating a store itself. Sales prices, which depend on the time of sale, follow. The operating life of a store is 20 years. The company's required return is

14 percent, and it costs $1.5 million to build a store. The sale of a store does not free up any resource other than capital (the company is not operating under capital rationing) because it takes as much supervision for a franchise store as for a company-owned store. What is the optimum sale time? (Assume year-end cash flows for simplicity.)

Year	5	10	15	20
Sale price	$1,250,000	$1,000,000	$800,000	$50,000

7-12. For the stores described in problem 11, what would be the optimal sale time if the sale of one store freed up management time so that another store could be put in operation?

7-13. A taxi driver acquaintance drives a taxi 50,000 miles a year. A new cab costs $12,000. He can drive the cab 200,000 miles with the original engine and transmission. (It lasts longer than an ordinary car because he changes oil every 3,000 miles and because a taxi engine never gets cold, he explains.) Repair costs will average $.04 a mile for the first 200,000 miles. After 200,000 miles, he can sell the car for $200 or spend $2,000 for a rebuilt engine and transmission. With a new engine and transmission, the cab will then last another 200,000 miles with additional repair costs averaging $.08 a mile. The salvage value after 400,000 miles is approximately zero. His required return is 10 percent. Should he get a new cab every 200,000 miles or every 400,000 miles? (Assume year-end cash flows for simplicity.)

7-14. An asset being considered by Greeley Corporation has a five-year life and a net present value of $100,000. At a 10 percent required return, what is the equivalent annuity?

7-15. Colorado Springs Technology must choose between two methods of producing a new product. The initial costs and year-end cash benefits are as follows:

Year	0	1	2	3	4	5
Method A	−$1,000,000	200,000	250,000	300,000	350,000	400,000
Method B	−$2,000,000	1,000,000	600,000	500,000	300,000	200,000

Assume all cash flows occur at year-end and the company's required return is 10 percent. Which production method should be used?

7-16. Storrs Corporation can sell an asset today for $1 million, or the asset can be kept for an additional five years and then scrapped for an estimated value of $200,000. If kept, the asset will generate cash flows of $200,000 at the end of each year for the next five years, exclusive of scrap value. The price will decline very rapidly, so the asset will not be sold until the fifth year if it is not sold immediately. At a 10 percent required return, should the asset be sold now or kept for another five years?

7-17. An asset costs $100,000 and will generate cash benefits of $30,000 at the end of each year for five years for Hartford Corporation. Salvage values are $50,000, $40,000, and $0 at the end of years 3, 4, and 5 respectively. The required return is 10 percent. When is the optimal time to abandon the investment? What is the net present value if the investment is abandoned at that time?

7-18. An electric utility spends $1 billion on a new generating plant. Half of this $1 billion will be paid immediately and half will be paid at the end of three years, when the plant begins operation. The plant will then operate for 30 years. Fuel costs will be $100 million a year and other operating costs will be $50 million a year, both spread evenly over the year. Salvage value will be negligible. The utility has a 10 percent required return. What must be the annual charge to customers to cover all costs, including the purchase price of the plant? (Assume the revenues occur at midyear.)

7-19. New Haven Corporation is considering a new factory. Shutdown costs are expected to be extremely high at the end of the factory's life because by-products of the manufacturing process are highly toxic and difficult to dispose of. It will cost $1 billion to construct the factory, and the factory is expected to generate cash flows of $200 million at the end of each year for its 20-year life. Shutdown costs at the end of its life are then estimated to be $4 billion. The company has a 10 percent required return. Draw a net present value profile. Is this investment attractive?

7-20. An investment being considered by Danbury Corporation generates the following cash flows. It has two internal rates of return: 7 percent and 39 percent. The company has a required return of 10 percent. Draw a net present value profile. Should the company invest in this asset?

Year	0	I through 19	20
Cash flow	−1,000	400 a year	−12,000

7-21. Fresno Corporation can sell an asset for $1 million or keep the asset for an additional ten years and then sell it as scrap for $200,000. If kept, the asset will generate cash flows of $200,000 at the end of each year for the next ten years, exclusive of scrap value. The sale price will decline very rapidly, so the asset will not be sold until the tenth year if it is not sold immediately. At a 14 percent required return, should the asset be sold now or kept for another ten years?

7–22. For the asset in problem 21, suppose cash flows decline 10 percent each year. Should the asset be sold now or kept for another 10 years?

CASE PROBLEM |

Zandts' Charter Sailboat

After spending over a decade of 12-hour workdays in successful management jobs, Barbara and Jim Zandt were in a comfortable financial position. But they had no time for themselves. Feeling a strong need to get away, the couple took a vacation on a charter sailboat out of St. Thomas in the Virgin Islands. By the end of the week, they decided this was where they wanted to spend their lives. For the next two years, they spent all of their vacation time in sailing courses and all of their spare time studying, both to enhance sailing skills and to understand the charter business.

The Zandts learned that most charter sailboats were owned by wealthy individuals who used the boats as tax-shelter investments, spending no more than two weeks a year on their boats. By joining several sailing clubs, advertising in a sailing magazine, and inquiring among their personal contacts, they found a physician who agreed to purchase a sailboat as an investment. The physician would bear all operating costs as the owner, while the Zandts would receive a percent of gross charter fees for their services as captain, crew, and manager.

The arrangement worked fine for five years, but the tax laws changed during that five-year period. Typically, boats were kept in charter for five years, until the advantages of rapid depreciation had been used up. The owner would then trade for a new boat or pull the old boat out of charter service for personal use. Unfortunately, the new tax law eliminated investment tax credits and decreased the rate of depreciation. The physician wanted to sell the five-year-old boat and did not want to replace it. Finding another investor seemed unlikely in the new tax environment. If they wanted to continue in this lifestyle, they would have to buy a boat themselves.

The Zandts faced several alternatives. They could buy the current boat from the physician for $50,000. It was due for refurbishing, which would cost $10,000. If they kept this boat for five years, it could be sold for approximately $25,000. If they kept this boat for ten years, it could be sold for $15,000, but an overhaul after five years would cost $20,000.

Another alternative was to buy a new boat for $100,000. At the end of five years, the alternatives with the new boat would be the same as those with the existing boat. It could be sold for $50,000 or refurbished and kept for either five or ten more years, with an overhaul when it was ten years old if it were kept for 15 years.

A newer boat would attract more charter business and bring higher weekly fees. Barbara and Jim estimated that revenue per year during the first five years of a boat's life would be $50,000, but revenue would decline to $45,000 a year in the second five years and $40,000 a year in the third five years. The opposite would happen with operating expenses. Annual operating expenses would be $20,000 during the first five years, $25,000 during the second five years, and $30,000 during the third five years.

A new boat would be nice. The Zandts would have to spend less time on maintenance, and would have more time for pleasure. Also, it was fun to buy a new boat. On the other hand, their net worth was $200,000, and they were hesitant to sink half of it into one investment. A boat dealer had suggested that they could avoid the use of their capital by making a 25 percent down payment and borrowing the rest at a 12 percent annual interest rate. This, though, did not seem wise when they were only earning 10 percent on their own investments, which they guessed to be of similar risk to a boat. The dealer pointed out that the interest payments would be tax deductible, but the Zandts were in an income category that made taxes a negligible consideration.

CASE QUESTIONS

1. List the alternatives to the Zandts.
2. Identify cash flows, net present value, and equivalent annuity for each alternative.
3. Discuss the risks that are inherent in each alternative.
4. Do the Zandts have a competitive advantage? Is there anything they can do to create or enhance a competitive advantage?
5. Which alternative would you recommend? Why?

SELECTED REFERENCES

Bacon, Peter W. "The Evaluation of Mutually Exclusive Investments." *Financial Management* 6 (Summer 1977): 55–58.

Brenner, Menachem, and Itzhak Venezia. "The Effects of Inflation and Taxes on Growth Investments and Replacement Policies." *Journal of Finance* 38 (December 1983): 1519–1528.

Brick, Ivan E., and Daniel G. Weaver. "A Comparison of Capital Budgeting Techniques in Identifying Profitable Investments." *Financial Management* 13 (Winter 1984): 29–39.

Capettini, Robert, and Howard Toole. "Designing Leveraged Leases: A Mixed Integer Linear Programming Approach." *Financial Management* 19 (Autumn 1981): 15–23.

Emery, Gary W. "Some Guidelines for Evaluating Capital Investment Alternatives with Unequal Lives." *Financial Management* 11 (Spring 1982): 14–19.

Fisher, Irving. *The Rate of Interest*. New York: Macmillan, 1907.

———. *The Theory of Interest*. New York: Macmillan, 1930.

Fogler, H. Russell. "Overkill in Capital Budgeting Technique?" *Financial Management* 1 (Spring 1972): 92–96.

Jones, Phillip C., James L. Zydiak, and Walace J. Hopp. "Generalized Imputed Salvage Values." *The Engineering Economist* 35 (Spring 1990): 214–229.

Luxhoj, James T., and Marilyn S. Jones. "A Framework for Replacement Modeling Assumptions." *The Engineering Economist* 32 (Fall 1986): 39–49.

Meal, H. C. "Putting Production Decisions Where They Belong." *Harvard Business Review* (March–April 1984): 102–110.

Reimann, Bernard C. "Stock Price and Business Success: What Is the Relationship?" *Journal of Business Strategy* 8 (Summer 1987): 38–49.

Robichek, Alexander A., and James C. Van Horne. "Abandonment Value and Capital Budgeting." *Journal of Finance* 22 (December 1967): 577–590.

Ross, Marc. "Capital Budgeting Practices of Twelve Large Manufacturers." *Financial Management* 15 (Winter 1986): 15–22.

Sachdeva, Kanwal S., and Lawrence J. Gitman, "Accounts Receivable Decisions in a Capital Budgeting Framework." *Financial Management* 10 (Winter 1981): 45–49.

Schrieves, Ronald E., and John M. Wachowicz, Jr. "Proper Risk Resolution in Replacement Chain Analysis." *The Engineering Economist* 34 (Winter 1989): 91–114.

Sundem, Gary L. "Evaluating Capital Budgeting Models in Simulated Environments." *Journal of Finance* 30 (September 1975): 977–992.

PART III

ESTIMATING CASH FLOWS

In the previous three chapters we have discussed investment choice first from a single project perspective and then concluded with a more realistic situation where multiple projects of unequal lines exist. In this section we take the book to a more realistic and practical level by introducing the reader to the difficult task of estimating the expected cash flows of a project. Chapter 8 focuses first on how to identify the relevant incremental cash flows from an investment, then expands the discussion with a detailed explanation of the construction of a projected cash flow statement for a typical project, and concludes with an introduction to some of the more common forecasting methods used in practice to estimate cash flows. Chapter 9 details the ramifications of taxes on cash flows. This chapter is important because of the significant and often increasing role that taxes (both domestic and international) play in influencing the size of the project's cash flow. In addition to the influence that taxes have on an international investment, Chapter 9 also introduces other unique concerns associated with estimating the cash flows for an international investment. Chapter 10 discusses the role of inflation in the estimation of cash flows for domestic investments. The chapter concludes with a discussion of the role that expected inflation in different countries has in the determination of future exchange rates and consequently the estimation of cash flows from a foreign investment to the parent company.

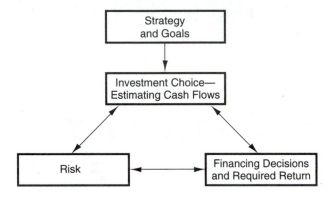

CHAPTER 8 |

ESTIMATING INCREMENTAL CASH FLOWS

After completing this chapter, you should be able to:

1. Differentiate between a relevant cash flow and an irrelevant cash flow.
2. Discuss several hard-to-quantify benefits and costs associated with a capital investment.
3. Understand the relevance or irrelevance of sunk cost, indirect cost, pure joint cost, and indirect benefits.
4. Describe the steps involved in estimating cash flow and in putting together a cash flow statement.
5. Construct a cash flow statement from an income statement by adjusting after-tax income for depreciation and adjusting for balance sheet working capital items such as cash balances, accounts receivable, inventory, accounts payable, and accrued expenses.
6. Estimate the incremental balance sheet impact resulting from a project in the form of land, buildings, and equipment and understand how these assets are depreciated, amortized, or depleted over time.
7. Calculate the net present value of a project by identifying all incremental cash flows, adjusting for depreciation and taxes, and discounting back to the present.

After an extensive investment in research, Gillette developed a new shaving system, the MACH3, that provided a closer and smoother shave at a slightly higher production cost than the existing Sensor system. Special manufacturing equipment to produce the razors and blades would cost close to $800 million. In principle, it was only necessary to identify and estimate the relevant cash flows and to make the investment if the net present value was positive.

Identifying and estimating all relevant cash flows is easier said than done, though. Managers needed to decide how to treat the research investment and alternate use of the factory into which the new equipment would be placed. In addition, it was necessary to forecast production costs, working capital needs, and taxes. It was necessary to forecast sales and recognize sales of existing razor lines that would be lost when the new shaving system was introduced. Perhaps the most difficult problem was forecasting the number of years until some new development made these razors technologically obsolete. Gillette's problem is typical of the problems faced by a company when it attempts to estimate relevant cash flows for a capital investment.

This chapter begins with a discussion of relevant and irrelevant cash flows. Next, models are developed for the identification of relevant cash costs and benefits over the life cycle of a simple stand-alone investment. A comprehensive example illustrates the complete process, and the chapter concludes with a discussion of common forecasting techniques.

RELEVANT CASH FLOWS |

A major part of capital budgeting is the separation of relevant from irrelevant cash flows. Considering a capital investment as a course of action, relevant and irrelevant cash flows can be defined as follows:

A relevant cash outflow is the incremental cash outflow that will be caused by the course of action—a cash inflow that will be eliminated or an investment in assets and the respective claims by suppliers of capital that will be created.

A relevant cash benefit is the incremental cash inflow that will be caused by the course of action—a cash outflow that will be avoided or a liquidation of assets and the claims by suppliers of capital that will be avoided.

An irrelevant cash flow is a cash flow that will occur regardless of whether the proposed course of action is taken.[1]

Incremental or additional actual cash inflows and outflows, as well as cash inflows and outflows that are eliminated by the selection of a capital investment, are readily accepted as relevant cash flows. There are, however, several types of outlays and benefits that deserve special attention. These are discussed in the following paragraphs.

---

[1]Capital is defined as long-term financing, to include long-term debt, preferred stock, and common stock. The present value of future payments on certain leases also is included. Deferred taxes are generally excluded, even though they appear in the long-term liability section of the balance sheet, because they are not a source of cash but a means of reconciling accounting income with the cash flows used for capital budgeting.

SUNK COSTS

Sunk costs, which are expenditures that occurred prior to the time when the decision is being made, are a common source of confusion. Suppose, for example, that Nestle has spent $1 million developing a new coffee flavor at its Maryville facility and must now decide whether to produce this flavor. Production of the new flavor will result in a net present value of $600,000 if the $1 million sunk cost is ignored. Recognizing the $1 million sunk cost leads to a net present value of negative $400,000. What should the company do? Consider that making the investment has the same value impact as selling the formula for $600,000; the company is $400,000 worse off than if it had never started the development, but $600,000 better off than if it simply forgot the whole thing. Managers may regret starting that particular development effort, but the sunk cost is not relevant for the decision about what to do with the results of that effort.

INDIRECT COSTS

Indirect costs are also called joint costs, common costs, allocated costs, or overhead costs. These costs are shared by more than one activity, and it is often difficult to determine how these costs will be affected by changes in one particular activity. When Chrysler Corporation considers an expansion of the Fenton plant, for example, what will be the impact on home-office overhead? We may not know where a particular computer operator or accountant is going to be added, but we do know that there is a relationship between home-office expense and the total size of all operations. Failure to recognize potential increases in home-office costs will lead to overestimation of profitability. The allocations of these costs by cost accountants are often based on a requirement that all such costs be allocated somewhere, not on an estimate of an operation's marginal impact on costs. Thus, accounting allocations may not be useful. Statistical tools like regression analysis can often be used to estimate the relationship between total size and total overhead expense for the purpose of estimating the actual impact of an additional investment.

PURE JOINT COSTS

Pure joint costs are the extreme case of indirect costs. Pure joint costs are costs shared by two or more activities in such a way that changing the level of one activity while holding the other constant will not affect the costs at all. United Airlines, for example, hauls both people and express freight on passenger flights from Los Angeles to Chicago. Some costs are associated specifically with only one type of hauling; cabin attendants are not needed for freight, for example. But most of the costs are indeed pure joint costs. Attempts to allocate the pilot's salary between passengers and freight are of no help in decision making.

You can make wealth-maximizing decisions in the face of pure joint costs through a two-step decision process:

1. Compute the net present value of each capital investment using the best estimate of its impact on indirect costs. Consider the capital investment in step 2 only if it has a positive net present value solution in this step.
2. Compute the net present values for sets of capital investments that share costs, with all joint costs considered. Select a set of capital investments only if the total net present value from all of the investments in the set is positive when all joint costs and benefits are considered. This approach leads to value-maximizing capital investment decisions and avoids the problem of how to assign joint costs.

Example. UPS is considering adding seats to its airplane and utilizing these planes on Saturdays and Sundays since these are lighter days given that next-day packages will be delivered on Monday and can be moved over a two-day weekend.

Step 1: Estimating the net present value (NPV) of the parts

■ NPV of the passenger service:
Identify and estimate all the incremental costs associated with the addition of the seats and the extra flights. This would include labor to install the seats, the pilot's salary for the extra flight (if it would not otherwise be flown), gas, food, gate fees, and other expenses associated directly with the addition of passenger service. Expenses that would not be included are, for example, the president's salary, general corporate overhead, taxes, and other expenses that would not change as a result of instituting this new passenger service. A NPV would be calculated using the incremental revenues and expenses, and let's say it comes to $100 million dollars.
■ NPV of the freight service:
Next, the freight service would estimate its incremental expenses the same way; assume that this solution is $250 million dollars.

Step 2: Estimating the NPV of the whole operation including joint cost

Calculate the NPV of the entire UPS operation. Let's assume that this number is $300 million. As long as the whole operation including joint cost has a positive NPV (passengers and packages), then UPS would offer both services. If, on the other hand, both projects had positive NPVs but when combined and joint costs are included, the NPV for the entire operation becomes negative, then the operation should seek higher NPV projects, lower its joint cost, or shut down. In looking for another project to combine with packages, should another proposed project (of equal risk) have a higher combined NPV of $320 million, then this alternative is superior to the passenger alternative.

INDIRECT BENEFITS

Indirect benefits are the reverse of indirect costs. When BankAmerica attracts additional customers by offering a new checking account, an indirect benefit is that some of the new customers will sign up for the bank's credit cards. Profitable capital investments are sometimes rejected because indirect benefits are ignored. A set of capital investments is attractive if that set produces a positive net present value, even if no individual investment has a positive net present value when considered as a stand-alone project. Of course, a particular capital investment is attractive only if it adds to the net present value of the set.

CHANGES IN CLAIMS BY SUPPLIERS OF CAPITAL

If the firm finances projects by retaining the current earnings of the business, it is changing the claims of the suppliers of capital. Recall that the required return used in present value analysis is the return necessary to satisfy suppliers of capital. A $1,000 asset acquired by signing a note rather than by making a cash payment increases the amount of capital supplied by $1,000, and a satisfactory return must be earned on the $1,000. Likewise, owners' profits that are retained in the business instead of being paid as dividends must earn a return at least equal to what the owners could earn elsewhere. Thus, increases in obligations to suppliers of capital have the same decreasing effect on value as an increase in direct cash outflows. This claim is not quantified in dollar terms and subtracted from estimated cash benefits. Instead, this claim is considered in the discount rate used to calculate the net present value.

INTEREST EXPENSE

Interest expense is another form of claim by suppliers of capital and, consequently, it is not included in the annual cash outlays of a capital investment. Interest expense is part of the cost of money that is used in determining the discount rate to use in computing net present value. A positive net present value means that the relevant cash benefits are more than enough to cover the relevant cash costs and pay the suppliers of capital their required returns. The actual cost of borrowed money, preferred equity, and common equity will be discussed and calculated in Chapter 16.

OPPORTUNITY COST

The opportunity cost of a particular course of action is the cost of the next best action not taken. For example, for years Dole, Inc., (formerly Castle & Cook) owned many thousands of acres of prime real estate in Hawaii. The chosen course of action for this land was to grow pineapples. The opportunity cost for this action was the income that could be earned by converting this land to residential home sites, resort hotels, or some other commercial real estate purpose. In the late 1980s, management realized the opportunity cost and began to expand the real estate operation and exit the pineapple-growing business. In 1991, they attempted to split the company and put the food-processing business up for sale. This plan was later abandoned due to market and creditor reaction, and Dole is now both a food processor and a major land developer. It is important for management to recognize that the opportunity cost can surpass the profits from the existing business, and they may want to alter their strategy to increase the net present value of the company for the shareholders. Opportunity costs are harder to quantify than out-of-pocket costs, but they should not be ignored.

ESTIMATING CASH FLOWS FROM A PROJECT |

Estimating the cash flows from a potential project is no small undertaking and it requires the help of engineers, cost analysts, marketing personnel, and others. We have broken down the process into the following steps:

Estimating the Income Statement:
1. Estimate the relevant revenues and/or expenses you expect to receive from the project.
2. Assemble these revenues and expenses into a preliminary income statement making an appropriate calculation of the after-tax income.

Estimating the Balance Sheet:
3. Determine all of the balance sheet accounts that are impacted by the project.
4. Estimate the initial size of the investment in these balance sheet accounts. In particular, estimate the incremental investment in fixed assets, such as buildings and equipment, and in working capital items, such as cash balances, accounts receivable, and inventory.
5. Determine size and growth of these accounts after the project is operational.

Roll the Income Statement and Balance Sheet into a Cash Flow Statement:
6. Calculate the depreciation charge flowing from the fixed assets on the balance sheet to the income statement.
7. Estimate the life of the project.
8. Determine the terminal values for fixed assets and the disposition values of working capital (net of taxes).
9. Roll all of this information together into a projected cash flow statement.

Making the Decision:
10. Calculate the net present value of the project using the appropriate discount rate.[2]
11. Make the appropriate accept or reject decision.

ESTIMATING THE INCOME STATEMENT |

DEFINITION OF CORPORATE INCOME

In simple terms, the income of a business is the revenue, minus the expenses. The main sources of revenue for most businesses are the sales of goods and services. Also included in revenue is investment income such as interest, rent, etc.

[2]Determination of the appropriate discount rate given the risk for the project is discussed in the risk section of this book, Chapters 11 to 15.

Companies may also receive revenue in the form of payments under licensing agreements or royalties for the use of their inventions or other creations. To arrive at ordinary income, expenses are subtracted from revenue. A typical income statement may look as follows:

+ Revenues
− Cost of goods sold
− Selling and administrative expenses
− Bad debt expense
− Wages, salaries, and employee benefits
− Repairs
− Rent expense
− Taxes paid (other than income tax to the taxing agency)
− Interest expense
− Depreciation expense (recognition of wearing out of fixed assets)
− Lease payment
= Taxable income
− Income tax
= After-tax income

Incremental revenues are recorded as positive numbers because they are assumed to be cash inflows, and expenses are recorded as negative numbers because they require cash payment and are therefore cash outflows.

ACCRUAL CONCEPTS OF INCOME

Most businesses and all publicly traded corporations keep their books on an accrual rather than a cash basis. A cash basis recognizes income and expenses during the period in which the payment is received or made. Under accrual accounting, revenue and expense are recognized in the period in which they constructively occur, whether or not payment occurs during that period. For example, an accrual-basis taxpayer will generally recognize revenue from a sale when title is passed, even if payment is not actually received for months.

With the accrual method, some expenditures are deemed costs in the period in which they occur, and other expenditures are deemed to be asset acquisitions. When goods are purchased or produced, the cost of purchase or production is considered to be an investment in inventory assets, not an expense. The cost of inventory is recognized as an expense when the inventory is sold. When an asset like a building or piece of machinery is acquired, the purchase itself is the acquisition of an asset, not an expense. The wearing out of the asset is recognized as a series of depreciation expenses over the life of the asset.

Example. To illustrate the determination of accrual income consider the activities of Georgetown Corporation summarized in Table 8.1. The company bought $100 worth of raw material in 1999, and paid for the material in 2000. The company also paid workers $200 in 1999 for work done in 1999, turning the raw

| TABLE 8.1 | COMPARISON OF ACCRUAL INCOME AND CASH FLOW USING ACCRUAL ACCOUNTING

This table illustrates the timing of accrual income recognition, and the difference between timing of cash flows and income, resulting from accrual accounting principles.

Year	1999	2000	2001	2002
Sell products on credit			$500	
Receive payments for credit sales				$500
Buy raw materials on credit	$100			
Pay for raw materials bought on credit		$100		
Recognize the material as an expense			−$100	
Use and pay for labor	$200			
Recognize the labor as an expense			−$200	
Taxable income—cash flow accounting	−$200	−$100	0	$500
Taxable income—accrual accounting	0	0	$200 [a]	0

[a]$500 sale price minus the $100 of raw material and $200 of production labor that were recorded as part of the value of the inventory.

materials into finished goods. The company sold these finished goods on credit for $500 in 2001 and received payment in 2002.

In addition to illustrating the difference between cash flow accounting and accrual accounting in measuring taxable income, the example in Table 8.1 also demonstrates the importance of adjusting the typical accrual-based income statement to a cash flow statement before making the capital budgeting decision. Timing of benefits is important, and there is often little relationship between the timing of income and the timing of cash flows. Had Georgetown Corporation acquired production equipment in 1999 and recognized depreciation expense on that equipment, the differences between timing of cash flow and timing of income would have been even more pronounced.

ESTIMATING THE BALANCE SHEET |

Most projects have an acquisition stage, an operating stage, and a disposition stage, and throughout these phases these projects affect both the balance sheet and the income statement. During the acquisition stage land is purchased, buildings are built, machines are installed, employees are trained, inventory is accumulated, and advertising is spent. The building, land, machines, and inventory are all first placed on the balance sheet as assets. As time passes, these assets are written off (except land) by recognizing yearly depreciation expense on the income statement. Training and advertising are recognized as expenses at the time these activities occur, resulting in a tax savings to the extent of the marginal tax rate of the organization.

In the first few days of operation, operating cash is needed to pay bills or transact business, credit is extended to customers, inventory is replaced, credit is granted by suppliers, and employees perform services for which they are not yet paid. The extension of credit to the customers is recorded on the balance sheet as an accounts receivable. The inventory purchased is placed into inventory on the balance sheet, while the inventory sold is recorded as a cost of goods sold expense on the income statement. The credit granted by the suppliers is recorded as an accounts payable on the balance sheet. The credit extended by the employees is recorded as an accrued expense on the balance sheet.

If all goes well in the first few years of operation, cash balances, inventory balances, and customers' accounts receivable balances will increase as sales increase and the firm grows. All of these increases will cause more cash to be tied up in working capital. As an offset, credit balances owed to suppliers (accounts payable) and employees (accrued expenses) will also increase and offset some of the working capital needs.

Table 8.2 summarizes the proper timing and treatment of many of the relevant balance sheet items for a typical project. As you can see, most assets begin on the balance sheet and then flow through to the income statement over the life of the project.

ROLLING THE INCOME STATEMENT AND BALANCE SHEET INTO A CASH FLOW STATEMENT

So far, we have introduced an accrual-based income statement and discussed the timing and treatment of the typical accounts on the balance sheet that result from a project. In this section, we will integrate the two by taking each account and illustrating the process by which it flows to the income statement and the adjustments that are necessary to construct a cash flow statement.

ACCOUNTS RECEIVABLE

Credit sales are an example of an item that is recognized as a revenue at the time of sale using the accrual basis of accounting but as a change in the accounts receivable balance on the cash flow statement. In the normal course of business, we extend credit to our customers for collection at some later date. As some customers pay, others are receiving credit. The net effect is that credit is extended at the beginning of the project's life (Year 0) and as sales grow, more credit is extended. These credit balances are not liquidated until the disposition stage of the project's life.

Since taxes are calculated based on the accrual accounting definition of revenue for most businesses, we typically include all incremental sales or revenues in the projected income statement and then adjust for the extension of credit as a line item in the cash flow statement.

The easiest way to measure the incremental extension of credit in a period is to look at the change in the accounts receivable balance for a given period. If the accounts receivable balances are increasing, then sales are being recognized in the income statement but cash is not being received. In reverse fashion, if accounts receivable balances are decreasing, then more cash is being received than is shown in the revenue numbers.

| TABLE 8.2 TREATMENT AND TIMING OF THE TYPICAL BALANCE SHEET AND INCOME STATEMENT ITEMS FOR A TYPICAL PROJECT

Item	Treatment	Timing
Buildings	A	Year 0 (and later if additional investment)
Equipment	A	Year 0 (and later if additional investment)
Land	C	Year 0 (and later if additional investment)
Initial training	B	Year 0 (additional expense recognized as cash expense)
Initial advertising	B	Year 0 (additional expense recognized as cash expense)
Cash balances	C	Year 0 (changes recognized yearly)
Accounts receivable	C	Year 0 (changes recognized yearly)
Inventory	C	Year 0 (changes recognized yearly)
Accounts payable	C	Year 0 (changes recognized yearly)
Revenues	D	Year 1, 2, 3, 4 until disposition
Cash expenses	D	Year 1, 2, 3, 4 until disposition

Types of Treatments

A—Begins as a balance sheet item and flows to income statement as a depreciation expense as the asset's economic or physical life expires (book depreciation) or due to the passage of time (tax depreciation). They are added directly to the cash flow statement as an investment in the time period in which the assets are paid for. Depreciation expense is deducted to calculate income tax but then added back to avoid double counting of the investment's impact on cash flows.

B—Starts as an investment of cash and is immediately expensed as a time 0 expense, thereby increasing the initial outlay. Since these expenses are tax deductible (and this tax saving will be assumed to be realized in time 0) the investment is not dollar for dollar but instead 60 cents on the dollar when the firm is in the 40 percent tax bracket.

C—Begins as a balance sheet item and continues as such over the life of the project. Any additional investment (or decrease in investment) is added (or subtracted) in the year of investment.

D—Flows straight to the income statement in the calculation of income. Any credit sale is handled as an account receivable and any credit purchase is handled as an account payable.

Example. Houston Corporation began operations on January 1, Year 1, and expects the following sales and cash expenses:

	Year 0	Year 1	Year 2	Year 3
Sales		$50,000	$100,000	$150,000
Cash expenses		$20,000	$ 40,000	$ 60,000

Present experience, in related lines of business, has shown that credit sales will probably average 73 days outstanding. In addition, Houston Corporation expects to lose $3,000 upon liquidation of the credit balances at the end of the project's life (Year 3).

The income statement for Houston would look like this:

	Year 0	Year 1	Year 2	Year 3
Sales		$50,000	$100,000	$150,000
Cash expenses		$20,000	$ 40,000	$ 60,000
Taxable income		$30,000	$ 60,000	$ 90,000
Taxes at 40%		$12,000	$ 24,000	$ 36,000
After-tax income		$18,000	$ 36,000	$ 54,000

The balance sheet would look like this:

	Year 0	Year 1	Year 2	Year 3
Accounts receivable	$10,000	$20,000	$30,000	$0

The accounts receivable balances are simply 73/365 times $50,000 for Year 0, 73/365 times $100,000 for Year 1, 73/365 times $150,000 for Year 2, and $0 to reflect the liquidation of these accounts at the end of Year 3. The $10,000 Year 0 balance is a Year 0 cash flow because the credit is extended to the first customer on day one of the project's life (in theory, no money will be received until the 73rd day if everybody takes the credit terms). Since this outlay is closer to Year 0 than to the end of the year, we place the cash flow as a Year 0 number. The $20,000 at the end of Year 1 assumes that sales begin to average $100,000 starting on day one of Year 2. This is a simplifying assumption made on the part of the authors.

The cash flow statement for Houston would look like this:

	Year 0	Year 1	Year 2	Year 3
Sales		$50,000	$100,000	$150,000
Cash expenses		($20,000)	($40,000)	($60,000)
Taxable income		$30,000	$60,000	$90,000
Taxes at 40%		($12,000)	($24,000)	($36,000)
After-tax income		$18,000	$36,000	$54,000
Change in working capital				
Accounts receivable	($10,000)	($10,000)	($10,000)	($0)
Disposition-stage cash flow				
Accounts receivable (net of tax)				$28,200
Net cash flow	($10,000)	$8,000	$26,000	$82,200

Although $36,000 in after-tax income is realized in Year 2, the amount must be adjusted for the $10,000 increase in accounts receivable. As a result, the cash flow for Year 2 is only $26,000. The disposition-stage cash flow for accounts receivable was calculated by taking the $30,000 balance and subtracting the $3,000 loss and then adding back the $1,200 tax savings from the loss (40% of $3,000).

INVENTORY

When Wal-Mart opens a new Super-Center, often the $10,000,000 worth of inventory inside the store is worth more than the land, building, and shelving combined. Add this to all the inventory at the supporting warehouses, and the cash invested in inventory accumulates to balances that are quite meaningful in a typical net present value analysis. Inventory comes in two forms: items that are sold to customers, and parts inventory necessary to support physical assets. Regardless of the form, as inventory is sold or used, it must be replaced, and as the businesses grow, the investment in inventory usually grows also.

As with accounts receivable balances, the inventory investment is usually made in advance of a store's opening or the placing of an asset into service. This investment is commonly recorded as a Year 0 (the first day of the project) investment. As the operation expands, additional inventory will be necessary to support the larger operation.

Over time, inventory can suffer holding losses due to obsolescence, theft, destruction, or many other reasons. These holding losses, if material, should be estimated and deducted from estimated benefits (revenues) of the project. Under current tax law, these losses are fully tax deductible.

Inventory Example. Dallas Corporation began operations on January 1, Year 1, and expects the following sales and cash expenses:

	Year 0	Year 1	Year 2	Year 3
Sales		$50,000	$100,000	$150,000
Cash expenses		$20,000	$ 40,000	$ 60,000

Present experience indicates that inventory levels will be maintained at 25 percent of sales. In addition, Dallas Corporation expects to lose $1,000 annually in shrinkage and $5,000 upon liquidation at the end of the project's life (Year 3). The income statement for Dallas would look like this:

	Year 0	Year 1	Year 2	Year 3
Sales		$50,000	$100,000	$150,000
Cash expenses		$20,000	$ 40,000	$ 60,000
Inventory shrinkage		$ 1,000	$ 1,000	$ 1,000
Taxable income		$29,000	$ 59,000	$ 89,000
Taxes at 40%		$11,600	$ 23,600	$ 35,600
After-tax income		$17,400	$ 35,400	$ 53,400

The $1,000 shrinkage is subtracted as a normal cost of doing business in the calculation of taxable income.

The balance sheet would look like this:

	Year 0	**Year 1**	**Year 2**	**Year 3**
Inventory	$12,500	$25,000	$37,500	$0

The inventory balance is simply 25% times: $50,000 for Year 0, $100,000 for year 1, $150,000 for Year 2, and $0 to reflect the liquidation of these accounts at the end of Year 3. The $12,500 is a Year 0 cash flow because inventory must be present on day one of the project's life. Since this is closer to Year 0 than to the end of the year, we place the cash flow as a Year 0 number. The $25,000 at the end of Year 1 is based on the same logic explained in the accounts receivable section earlier in the chapter.

The cash flow statement for Dallas would look like this:

	Year 0	**Year 1**	**Year 2**	**Year 3**
Sales		$50,000	$100,000	$150,000
Cash expenses		($20,000)	($40,000)	($60,000)
Inventory shrinkage		($1,000)	($1,000)	($1,000)
Taxable income		$29,000	$59,000	$89,000
Taxes at 40%		($11,600)	($23,600)	($35,600)
After-tax income		$17,400	$35,400	$53,400
Change in working capital				
Inventory	($12,500)	($12,500)	($12,500)	($0)
Disposition-stage cash flow				
Inventory (net of tax)				$34,500
Net cash flow	($12,500)	$4,900	$22,900	$87,900

The $1,000 in shrinkage is a negative cash flow because missing inventory has to be replaced to maintain inventory levels at 25% of sales. The original investment in inventory and additions in later years are recorded as negative cash flows. The cash proceeds realized from the final sale are recorded as positive cash flow at the end of the project's life.

In the disposition year of the project, the inventory will be liquidated. It is usually assumed that the original purchase price will not be realized and some liquidation loss will be experienced on the final sale. In this case the $34,500 was calculated by taking the $37,500 balance and subtracting the $5,000 loss and then adding back the $2,000 tax savings from the loss (40% of $5,000).

PREPAID EXPENSES

Prepaid expenses are expenses that are paid before the period of their use. Suppose, for example, an insurance premium covering the next 2 years is paid in advance on January 1, Year 1. Half of the payment is recognized as an expense in Year 1, and half is recognized as an expense in Year 2. On the Year 1 balance sheet, the amount applicable to Year 2 is an asset called prepaid expense. In the disposition year, prepaid expenses are usually projected to be fully recovered with no associated losses.

CASH BALANCES

Most, but not all, new projects will involve the need for some cash balance to transact business. For example, McDonald's adds a new outlet and on the first day that the doors open for business, the establishment must have enough cash in the register to make change for the level of purchases projected for the day. For simplicity's sake, we assume that the initial cash balance needed to operate through the first year is needed at the beginning of the project and would therefore be a Year 0 cash flow. As the business grows in outlets or as sales increase in dollars, cash balance increases must be estimated.

Example. Ted's Ice Cream Shoppe will open for business on January 1, Year 1, and will need $10,000 in operating cash to support $200,000 in sales. Sales are expected to increase to $350,000 in Year 2 and the cash balance is expected to grow to $17,500. In Year 2 sales are expected to stay at the $350,000 level and all cash is recovered in the disposition year.

Cash flows would be projected as follows:

	Year 0	Year 1	Year 2	Disposition Year
Cash investment needed	($10,000)	($7,500)	0	$17,500

The bracketed (or negative) cash flows signify the money is being invested or used by the project. In the disposition year the $17,500 is recovered and is consequently shown as a positive number. Even though sales probably grew gradually over Year 2, we assume that the $7,500 was needed at the beginning of that year and was projected as an end of Year 1 cash flow. When the mid-year convention is used to approximate daily cash flows, it is common to also use mid-year as the interval for the increased investment in cash.

ACCOUNTS PAYABLE AND ACCRUED EXPENSES

Accounts payable result when an asset is acquired on credit and payment for the assets follows. When inventory is purchased on credit, the inventory itself is treated as an asset, and the amount owed is treated as an account payable.

Wages and many other expenses are not paid on a daily basis. These expenses are often recognized for accrual income purposes in the period in which they are incurred, even if they are actually paid for with cash in a different period. When these expenses are recorded but not paid, an accrued expense is shown on the balance sheet until payment is made. As with accounts payable, this delaying of the payment is considered a source of cash or a positive number in calculating the estimated after-tax cash flow on the projected cash flow statement.

LAND

When a project requires the purchase of land, a building, and equipment as a package, then proper accounting requires that a portion of the purchase price be allocated to the land, a portion to the building, and a portion to the equipment based on appraised market values of each as if they were independently purchased. One reason for this is that land cannot be depreciated under IRS rules. Although it may seem unfair not to allow for the recovery of the investment in land over the life of the project, in the eyes of the tax code, land does not wear out and therefore it is not entitled to recovery.

The initial investment in land is recorded as a negative cash flow in Year 0 and the recovery of the purchase price in the disposition year is recorded as a positive cash flow. If the recovery price is less than the original purchase price, the resulting loss is fully tax deductible. Should the land be sold for more than its purchase price, the excess is taxable as a gain. For corporations, there are no special capital gain or loss treatments, and both gains and losses are taxed at ordinary rates.[3]

BUILDINGS

In the tax code, there are only two categories of investments in buildings—either residential buildings or nonresidential buildings. Residential buildings include houses that contain home offices as well as living quarters, apartment buildings, duplexes, and any place considered to be a private residence. Nonresidential buildings include office buildings, shopping centers, factories, and anything else not considered residential property.

The acquisition of either residential property or nonresidential property is recorded as negative cash flow at Year 0 (the year they are placed into service). The wearing out of the building is recognized through an annual depreciation expense which is fully tax deductible on the income statement each year.

The specific depreciation rates allowed by the IRS differ depending on whether the investment is residential property or nonresidential property. Under current tax law, residential property is depreciated over 27.5 years using a mid-month convention and commercial or noncommercial real estate is depreciated over 39 years also using a mid-month convention.

---

[3]Taxes and tax rates are discussed in Chapter 9.

Residential Property Example. An apartment building costing $1 million is placed into service on March 5, Year 1. It is sold on September 25, Year 8. What is the depreciation expense allowed for Year 1, Year 2, and the disposition year?

Depreciation expense for Year 1 is:

9.5/12 months times $1 million times 1/27.5 years

or
(9.5/12)(1,000,000)(1/27.5) = $28,788

Depreciation expense for Year 2 is:

12/12 months times $1 million times 1/27.5 years

or
(12/12)(1,000,000)(1/27.5) = $36,364

Depreciation expense for the disposition year or Year 8 is:

8.5/12 months times $1 million times 1/27.5 years

or
(8.5/12)(1,000,000)(1/27.5) = $25,758

The 9.5 months used in Year 1 are calculated by first going to the middle of the month, in this case March, counting March as one half of a month, and then counting the remaining months in the year (April, May, and so on). The 8.5 months used in the disposition year are computed by counting the months preceding the month of sale (January, February, and so on) and adding one half of a month for the month of disposition or September. Naturally, any full year between the acquisition year and the disposition year would be allowed a full 12 months of depreciation.

Commercial Property Example. An office complex costing $1 million is placed into service on March 31, Year 1. It is sold on September 1, Year 8. What is the depreciation expense allowed for Year 1, Year 2, and the disposition year?

Depreciation expense for Year 1 is:

9.5/12 months times $1 million times 1/39 years

or
(9.5/12)(1,000,000)(1/39) = $20,299

Depreciation expense for Year 2 is:

12/12 months times $1 million times 1/39 years

or
(12/12)(1,000,000)(1/39) = $25,641

Depreciation expense for the disposition year or Year 8 is:

8.5/12 months times $1 million times 1/39 years

or
(8.5/12)(1,000,000)(1/39) = $18,162

As before, the 9.5 months used in Year 1 are calculated by first going to the middle of the month, in this case March, counting March as one half of a month, and then counting the remaining months in the year (April, May, and so on). The 8.5 months used in the disposition year are computed by counting the months preceding the month of sale (January, February, and so on) and adding one half of a month for the month of disposition or September. Naturally, any full year between the acquisition year and the disposition year would be allowed a full 12 months of depreciation.

EQUIPMENT

Investment in a fixed asset such as a vehicle, equipment, and so on is recognized on the balance sheet at the purchase price plus any delivery fees, setup expenses, testing expenses, and other expenses associated with placing the asset into service. The wearing out of the asset is recognized through an annual depreciation expense.

The specific depreciation rates allowed by the IRS depend on the type of asset that is placed into service. Table 8.3 is a listing of the six classes of assets recognized by the IRS. The sampling of assets listed in the table is taken from the Internal Revenue Code. The actual listing in the Internal Revenue Code consists of page after page of assets for each category. As with all tax items, the

| **T A B L E   8 . 3   ASSET LIFE CATEGORIES UNDER THE ACCELERATED COST RECOVERY SYSTEM** |

This table lists the six asset life categories recognized under the Accelerated Cost Recovery System as modified by the Tax Reform Act of 1986, along with samples of assets assigned to each category.

Life Category	Sample Assets
3 year	Tractor units for over-the-road trucks, and special tools such as dies and jigs used in some specific types of manufacturing.
5 year	Automobiles, light trucks, busses, over-the-road trailers, computers and peripherals, typewriters, copiers, other data-handling equipment, general construction equipment, and telephone company computer-based central office switching equipment.
7 year	Office furniture, computer equipment, many types of production equipment (some specific types of production equipment are assigned 5, 10, and 15 year categories), airplanes used by commercial airlines, agricultural equipment, and assets that have not been assigned by law to other categories.
10 year	Vessels, barges, etc.
15 year	Oil and gas pipelines, and electric utility nuclear and combustion turbine power plants.
20 year	Telephone company distribution plant, and electric and gas utility transmission and distribution plant.

reader is referred to a good tax book, tax counsel, or the code to clarify situations not specifically dealt with in the table.

Once the asset has been located and the tax life determined, then Table 8.4 is used to determine the allowable depreciation rate. No adjustment for mid-year or mid-month is necessary because a mid-year convention is built into the rates in the table.

Year 1 in Table 8.4 is the year in which the asset was placed in service. An asset is considered to be placed in service when it is *available* for use, even if it has not actually been used full time.

Example. A laser copier costing $10,000 is placed into service on March 31, Year 1. It is sold on September 1, Year 6. What is the depreciation expense allowed for Year 1, Year 2, and the disposition year?

The first step is to determine the tax life of the copier. By referring to Table 8-3, copiers are found to have a 5-year tax life. Using the rates in Table 8.4 for 5-year property, the depreciation expense is calculated as follows:

| TABLE   8.4   DEPRECIATION RATES USING THE MODIFIED ACCELERATED COST RECOVERY SYSTEM

This table gives the depreciation rates as a percentage of original basis for assets in each life category eligible for declining balance depreciation. Year 1 is the year in which the asset is placed in service. The mid-year convention is assumed.

Year	3 year	5 year	7 year	10 year	15 year	20 year
1	33.33%	20.00%	14.29%	10.00%	5.00%	3.75%
2	44.44	32.00	24.49	18.00	9.50	7.22
3	14.82	19.20	17.49	14.40	8.56	6.68
4	7.41	11.52	12.49	11.52	7.71	6.18
5		11.52	8.93	9.22	6.94	5.72
6		5.76	8.93	7.37	6.24	5.29
7			8.93	6.55	5.90	4.89
8			4.45	6.55	5.90	4.52
9				6.55	5.90	4.46
10				6.55	5.90	4.46
11				3.29	5.90	4.46
12					5.90	4.46
13					5.90	4.46
14					5.90	4.46
15					5.90	4.46
16					2.95	4.46
17						4.46
18						4.46
19						4.46
20						4.46
21						2.23

Depreciation expense for Year 1 is:

$$.2000 \text{ times } \$10,000$$

or

$$(.2000)(10,000) = \$2,000$$

Depreciation expense for Year 2 is:

$$.3200 \text{ times } \$10,000$$

or

$$(.3200)(10,000) = \$3,200$$

Depreciation expense for the disposition year or Year 6 is:

$$.0576 \text{ times } \$10,000$$

or

$$(.0576)(10,000) = \$576$$

Careful inspection of Table 8-4 shows that the depreciation term exceeds the tax life by one year. For the copier, it is depreciated in Year 6 even though it has a 5-year tax life. The mid-year convention is what caused the term to exceed the tax life. In constructing the tables, the IRS reduces the first year's rate to assume that on average, assets will be placed into service throughout the year and will average one half of a full year's depreciation. Notice that in each case the second (or first full) year's depreciation exceeds the first (or half) year's depreciation rate.

ADJUSTING CASH FLOWS FOR DEPRECIATION

Depreciation is a common noncash expense included in the projected income statement. The accounting definition of depreciation is the systematic writing off or expensing of a physical asset over the shorter of its economic or useful life. The acquisition of the physical asset involves the use of cash but the expensing of the asset over its life is a noncash item.

Where you choose to adjust for depreciation in the cash flow statement is a personal choice. Table 8.5 illustrates the two typical treatments for depreciation in practice. The first and more common method is to deduct depreciation in arriving at taxable income, calculate taxable income, and then add the full depreciation amount back to get after-tax cash flow. A second method is to leave depreciation out of the income calculation and add back depreciation (net of taxes) to the after-tax income number to get after-tax cash flow. Either method is acceptable and both will yield the same after-tax cash flow. The first method is our preferred method and is the method used on the spreadsheet template that is included with the textbook.

TIMING OF CASH FLOWS

Up until now we have assumed that all land, buildings, and equipment have been placed into service on one day, and we have called that first day of the first year "Year 0." Many acquisition outlays do not typically occur all on one day. A major capital investment may be put together over a period of several years, and

| **Table** **8.5** | **Two Common Treatments of Depreciation Used to Project After-Tax Cash Flows** |

Method 1

+ Increases in sales revenue
− Increases in (+ decreases in) operating expenses before interest & depreciation
= Earnings before interest, depreciation, and taxes (EBDT)
− Depreciation
= Earnings before tax (EBT)
− Income tax (tax rate × Earnings before tax)
= Net income
+ Depreciation
= Net after-tax cash flow (outlay)

Method 2

+ Increases in sales revenue
− Increases in (+ decreases in) operating expenses excluding depreciation
= Earnings before depreciation and taxes (EBDT)
− Income tax (tax rate × EBDT)
= Net income before depreciation
+ Depreciation expense net of taxes [depreciation × (1 − marginal tax rate)]
= Net after-tax cash flow (outlay)

additional investment may be required after a capital investment is first placed in service. In addition, working capital may continue to increase through the growth of inventory and accounts receivable, particularly if sales grow. As a practical matter, capital investments for which almost all of the relevant initial cash outlays occur over a period of a few months are frequently treated as if all the initial costs occurred at one time. When the investment is spread over several years, the net present value can be accurately computed by discounting all future cash costs and benefits, including future investment, to the date when investment first occurs. Some managers prefer to compute the net present value as of the date an asset was placed in service. To do this, they compute the *future value* of outlays prior to the date the asset is placed in service.

Example. A capital investment being considered by Evanston Technology requires a $1,000 after-tax cash outlay at the end of each year for 3 years, with use to begin at the start of the 4th year. The asset will then generate after-tax cash inflows of $1,000 at the end of each year for 5 years, and the company has a 10 percent required return. The future value of the investment outlay as of the date the asset is placed in service would be:

$$\$1,000 \times 1.1^2 + \$1,000 \times 1.1 + \$1,000 = \$3,310$$

If $1,000 had been invested somewhere else at the end of each year for 3 years, it would have grown to $3,310.

The net present value, as of the date the asset is placed in service, is:

$$NPV = \$1,000 \times PVAI_{5\ yrs.,\ 10\%} - \$3,310$$
$$= \$1,000 \times 3.7908 - \$3,310 = \$480.80$$

The net present value as of the date the asset is placed in service gives the same accept/reject signal as the net present value as of the date the first outlay occurred.[4]

NET WORKING CAPITAL

For brevity in reporting, companies sometimes report a net working capital requirement as one line in the analysis. When this is done, net working capital is calculated by adding all of the individual current assets accounts (cash, accounts receivable, inventory, and prepaid expenses) requiring incremental or additional investment and then subtracting all of the current liability accounts (accounts payable, and accrued expenses) that typically supply funds.

DISPOSITION-STAGE CASH FLOWS

Cash flows at the time of termination are an important part of the analysis of a capital investment. To calculate the cash proceeds from the sale of fixed assets we must first find the remaining basis by subtracting the depreciation taken from the original purchase price. Taxable gain is calculated by subtracting the remaining basis from the selling price. If the remaining basis is higher than the selling price, a tax-deductible loss is incurred that will reduce taxes. This amount should be added to the selling price to get net proceeds from disposition. If the selling price is greater than the remaining basis, then a taxable gain will result. Taxes are calculated on this gain using ordinary income tax rates for corporations. Individuals, partnerships, and subchapter S corporations are allowed to use capital gains rates that are discussed in the next chapter. To get net proceeds from the sale, simply subtract the taxes due from the selling price. Table 8.6 illustrates the proper format for calculating the net proceeds from the sale of fixed assets or working capital.

INDIANA LEGAL EAGLES: A COMPREHENSIVE EXAMPLE |

A successful Indianapolis law firm, Indiana Legal Eagles, was considering the opening of a legal clinic in the Fort Wayne area. Approximately $10,000 had already been spent on a feasibility study. The firm was taxed as a corporation, with a marginal tax rate of 34 percent. Land for the building would be acquired on

---

[4]See, for example, Norbert L. Enrich, *Marketing and Sales Forecasting: A Quantitative Approach*, rev. ed. (Melbourne, Fla.: Krieger Publishing, 1979); Donald L. Hurwood, *Sales Forecasting* (New Work: The Conference Board, 1978), and *Sales Forecasting: Timesaving and Profit-Making Strategies That Work* (Glenview, Ill.: Scott Forseman, 1978).

| **Table 8.6** | **Spreadsheet for Calculating the Cash Flow from Disposition for Fixed Assets and for Working Capital**

Proceeds from the sale of fixed assets

Original purchase price
− Depreciation taken
= Remaining basis
Selling price
− Remaining basis
= Taxable gain or (loss)

Taxable gain or (loss)
× Tax rate
= Tax on gain or loss

Selling price
+ Tax on loss or − tax on gain
= Net proceeds from disposition

Proceeds from the sale of working capital

Liquidation value
− Accumulated value
= Taxable gain or (loss)

Taxable gain or (loss)
× Tax rate
= Tax on gain or loss

Liquidation value
+ Tax on loss or − Tax rate
= Net proceeds from disposition

January 1, 2000, at a cost of $200,000. A building would be built on the site at a cost of $500,000, including architects' fees and building permits. Of this building cost, $100,000 would be paid at the beginning of 2000, when construction started, and the remainder would be paid for on January 1, 2001, when construction was completed. Office equipment (word processors and so on) and office furniture would be acquired and paid for around the end of 2000, at a cost of $50,000 for each of the two categories. The building and other assets would be considered placed in service on January 1, 2001. Various forms and other supplies would result in a total inventory need of $4,000. Prepaid expenses—insurance and so on—would initially be $3,000 as of January 1, 2001. At the time operations began, accounts payable and accrued wages would total $1,000 each. Recruiting of new personnel to staff the business would cost an estimated $10,000. Personnel would be trained at the home office during the last couple of months of 2000 and would receive wages of $10,000 during that time. A promotion campaign to launch the clinic would cost an estimated $30,000. These promotional expenditures would occur in late 2000 and early 2001. The land and fixtures would be paid for from funds currently available, while the building would be financed with a 20-year, 9 percent term loan. Considering other expansion opportunities available, and the fact that both their equity capital and borrowing capacity was limited, the owners required a 10 percent after-tax return on all new investments. The cash flows associated with acquisition of the investment are summarized in Table 8.7.

The cash flows in Table 8.7 have been grouped into two time periods, in keeping with normal conventions, rather than being separated by exact day for payment of each item. If the net present value is to be computed as of the beginning of Year 2000, the present value of relevant acquisition outlays is $300,000 + ($538,000/1.10) = $789,091. If the net present value is to be computed as of the end of 2000 and beginning of 2001, the value of acquisition outlays is ($300,000 × 1.10) + $538,000 = $868,000.

| TABLE 8 . 7 | ACQUISITION CASH FLOWS FOR A LEGAL CLINIC |

Summary of cash flows to begin operation of a legal clinic, recognizing the approximate timing of cash flows.

	EXPENSES	
	Start of Year 2000	End of Year 2000 Start of 2001
Promotional costs		(30,000)
Recruiting and training		(20,000)
= Total expenses		(50,000)
Tax savings from expenses		17,000
Net expenses		(33,000)
WORKING CAPITAL		
Increase in supplies inventory		(4,000)
Increase in prepaid expenses		(3,000)
Increase in accounts payable		1,000
Increased accrued expenses		1,000
Net increase in working capital		(5,000)
CAPITAL OUTLAYS		
Land	($200,000)	
Building	(100,000)	$(400,000)
Equipment and furniture		
Purchase price		(100,000)
Delivery and installation		0
= Net Capital Outlays	$(300,000)	$(500,000)
RELEVANT CASH OUTLAYS	$(300,000)	$(538,000)

Note: Outflows or investments of cash are in parentheses, and inflows of cash are not.

Note, again, that financing methods and interest expenses do not affect the cash flow estimates. The requirement that the assets generate a rate of return sufficient to satisfy all suppliers of capital is captured in the required return or discount rate used in computing present values. The computation of that required rate, based on a study of the financing sources available, will be taken up in Chapter 16.

ESTIMATING CASH FLOWS FROM OPERATIONS

Having calculated the acquisition-stage cash flows, the next step is the construction of an income statement. Legal Eagles' new Fort Wayne legal clinic is expected to generate the following revenues and cash operating expenses over a 20-year planning horizon:

	Year 2001	**Thereafter**
Revenues	$300,000	$700,000
Wages	220,000	420,000
Other operating expenses	100,000	120,000
(excluding depreciation & interest)		

- Accounts receivable are expected to increase each period by 5 percent of the increase in sales.
- Supplies inventories are expected to be maintained at 3 percent of sales in addition to the initial $4,000 investment.
- Prepaid expenses are expected to be 2 percent of sales in addition to the $3,000 initial investment.
- Accounts payable are expected to be 4 percent of wages and other cash operating expenses for that period in addition to the initial $1,000 investment.
- Accrued expenses are expected to be 1 percent of wages and other cash operating expenses for that period in addition to the initial $1,000 investment.
- Equipment will be depreciated using the rates in Table 8.4.

Based on this information, the relevant cash flows through 2003 are shown in Table 8.8. The only changes in cash flows after 2003 result from the changing depreciation rates on the building and equipment.

For this law firm, the benefit is increased revenue but part of the increased revenue is offset by increased cash operating expenses. For other investments, the benefit could be decreased cash operating expenses, with no increase in revenue. As mentioned earlier, the differences between dates of recognition of revenue or expense and dates of payment or receipt are captured in the change in net working capital. Collections that lag behind sales mean, for example, that cash inflow from sales is less than sales, and the increase in net working capital is the measure of how much less. Remember also that interest expense was not deducted in arriving at net income because the cost of money is captured in the discount rate used for capital investment analysis.

In this law clinic example, each year is given a single column, as if each type of cash flow occurs at the same time or is spread across the year in the same pattern. This is a common-enough assumption in practice, but it is not an essential assumption. Suppose, for example, that sales are expected to be at the $300,000 per year rate immediately in 2001. The working capital commitment will occur very early in the year as January revenue will not be collected until mid-February, and so on. The other cash flows, on the other hand, would be spread through the year. These cash flow patterns can be handled more accurately by creating two or more columns for 2001—one for beginning relevant costs and benefits and another for cost and benefits spread continuously over the year—and additional columns for significant cash cost or benefits occurring at other times during the year. Alternatively, the working capital requirement occurring in the first month or two can be treated as part of the initial outlay.

An Alternative Format. Some analysts prefer a format for estimating cash flows that focuses more directly on cash impacts, rather than following a financial statement format. This format, and its application to 2002 for the previous law clinic example, is illustrated below.

ALTERNATIVE CASH FLOW STATEMENT	
	Year 2002
Revenue	$700,000
Wages	(420,000)
Other operating expenses, except depreciation	(120,000)
Earnings before depreciation and tax (EBDT)	160,000
Income tax (.34 × EBDT)	(54,400)
Operating cash benefit	105,600
Depreciation tax savings (.34 × depreciation)	13,962
Increase in accounts receivable	(20,000)
Increase in supplies inventory	(12,000)
Increase in prepaid expenses	(8,000)
Increase in accounts payable	8,800
Increase in accrued expenses	2,000
NET RELEVANT CASH FLOW	$ 90,362

    Note: This format is simply another way to organize the information, and it leads to the same estimate of net relevant cash flows.

ESTIMATING DISPOSITION-STAGE CASH FLOWS

Continuing with the legal clinic example, assume that this project has an estimated life of 20 years. After 20 years, the remaining basis for the land would still be the original cost of $200,000 because no depreciation can be taken on land. The remaining basis for the building would be the $500,000 original cost less depreciation taken of $275,876 to leave a remaining basis of $224,124.

| **TABLE** **8.8** **OPERATING CASH COSTS AND BENEFITS FOR THE LEGAL CLINIC**

Revenues, wages, and cash operating expenses were given. Balances in accounts receivable, supplies inventory, accounts payable, and accrued expenses are 5%, 3%, 2%, 4%, and 1% respectively. The building is depreciated over 39 years as is allowed by the IRS. Equipment is depreciated using the rates in Table 8.4.

INCOME STATEMENT

Year	2000	2001	2002	2003
Revenue	$300,000	$700,000	$700,000	
Wages	($220,000)	($420,000)	($420,000)	
Other Operating Expenses	($100,000)	($120,000)	($120,000)	
Depreciation Expense				
Depreciation, Building	($12,286)	($12,821)	($12,821)	
Depreciation, Office Equipment	($10,000)	($16,000)	($9,600)	
Depreciation, Office Furniture	($7,145)	($12,245)	($8,745)	
Total Depreciation	($29,431)	($41,066)	($31,166)	
Earnings before Taxes	($49,431)	$118,934	$128,834	
Income Taxes at 34%	$16,807	($40,438)	($43,804)	
Net Income	($32,624)	$78,496	$85,030	

BALANCE SHEET

Year	2000	2001	2002	2003
Accounts Receivable Balance	$0	$15,000	$35,000	$35,000
Supplies Inventory Balance	$4,000	$13,000	$25,000	$25,000
Prepaid Expenses Balance	$3,000	$9,000	$17,000	$17,000
Accounts Payable Balance	($1,000)	($13,800)	($22,600)	($22,600)
Accrued Expenses Balance	($1,000)	($4,200)	($6,400)	($6,400)
Net Working Capital Balance	$5,000	$19,000	$48,000	$48,000

Furniture and equipment would be fully depreciated and would therefore have a remaining basis of $0. Management estimates that the furniture and equipment would be worthless in 20 years while the building and land could be sold for $500,000 with $200,000 allocated to the land and $300,000 allocated to the building based on appraised values. The gain on the sale of the building is taxed at the 34 percent rate. Working capital accounts are projected to be $35,000 for accounts receivable, $25,000 in supplies inventory, $17,000 in prepaid expenses, $22,600 in accounts payable, and $6,400 in accrued expenses in 20 years. The receivables would be collected, but management estimates a loss of $4,000 on supplies inventory. The prepaid expenses would terminate in the last year and the accounts payable and accrued liabilities would be paid at face value. Disposition-stage cash flows are shown in Table 8.9.

Given the initial outlays in Table 8.7, the annual cash benefits in Table 8.8 (extended to cover the remaining years of operation), and the terminal cash flows

| TABLE 8-8   OPERATING CASH COSTS AND BENEFITS FOR THE LEGAL CLINIC (*CONT.*)

CASH FLOW STATEMENT

Year	2000	2001	2002	2003
Revenue	$300,000	$700,000	$700,000	
Wages	($220,000)	($420,000)	($420,000)	
Other Operating Expenses	($100,000)	($120,000)	($120,000)	
Depreciation Expense				
Depreciation, Building	($12,286)	($12,821)	($12,821)	
Depreciation, Office Equipment	($10,000)	($16,000)	($9,600)	
Depreciation, Office Furniture	($7,145)	($12,245)	($8,745)	
Total Depreciation	($29,431)	($41,066)	($31,166)	
Earnings before Taxes	($49,431)	$118,934	$128,834	
Income Taxes at 34%	$16,807	($40,438)	($43,804)	
Net Income	($32,624)	$78,496	$85,030	
Add Back Depreciation	$29,431	$41,066	$31,166	
Increase in Accounts Receivable	($15,000)	($20,000)	$0	
Increase in Supplies Inventory	($9,000)	($12,000)	$0	
Increase in Prepaid Expenses	($6,000)	($8,000)	$0	
Increase in Accounts Payable	$12,800	$8,800	$0	
Increase in Accrued Expenses	$3,200	$2,200	$0	
After-Tax Cash Flow	($17,193)	$90,562	$116,196	

Supporting Calculations

2001 depreciation on the building = (11.5 months / 12 months) times 1/39 times $500,000 = $12,286

2002 depreciation on the building = (12 months / 12 months) times 1/39 times $500,000 = $12,821

2001 increase in accounts receivable = 5 percent times $300,000 = $15,000

2002 increase in accounts receivable = 5 percent times $400,000 = $20,000

2001 increase in accounts payable = 4 percent times $320,000 = $12,800

2002 increase in accounts payable = 4 percent times $220,000 = $8,800

Note: Again, inflows of cash are denoted as positive (non-bracketed) numbers and outflows of cash are negative or bracketed numbers.

in Table 8.9, the only remaining task is to compute the net present value of these flows to determine if the investment is attractive.

Tables 8.7 through 8.9 are summaries that result from substantial volumes of analysis. For example, detailed construction cost estimates were probably used for the initial cost estimates, and detailed market forecasts were probably used to estimate revenue. Table 8.10 is a further summary of all relevant cash costs and benefits from Tables 8.7 through 8.9. As shown in the present value analysis, the investment is attractive when evaluated at the 10 percent required return. For the net present value computation, it was assumed that operating cash flows occurred at midyear.

| **TABLE 8.9** **DISPOSITION-STAGE CASH FLOWS FOR THE LAW CLINIC**

Land with a cost of $200,000 and a building with remaining basis of $224,124 are sold for $200,000 and $300,000, respectively. Current assets are $77,000, and a loss of $4,000 is experienced on the liquidation of supplies inventory. Current liabilities are $29,000. Sale of assets and liquidation occurs at year-end 2020.

LIQUIDATION OF FIXED ASSETS

	Building	Land	Equipment
Original purchase price	$500,000	$200,000	$100,000
Depreciation taken	$255,876	$0	$100,000
Remaining basis	$244,124	$200,000	$0
Selling price	$300,000	$200,000	$0
Less remaining basis	$244,124	$200,000	$0
Gain or (loss)	$ 55,876	$0	$0
Gain or (loss)	$ 55,876	$0	$0
Tax rate on gain or (loss)	34%		
Tax on (gain) or loss	($18, 998)	$0	$0
Selling price	$300,000	$200,000	$0
Tax on (gain) or loss	($18,998)	$0	$0
Cash proceeds	$281,002	$200,000	$0

LIQUIDATION OF WORKING CAPITAL ITEMS

	Receivables	Inventory	Prepaid	Payables	Accrued Expenses
Liquidation value	$35,000	$21,000	$17,000	$22,600	$6,400
Accumulated value	$35,000	$25,000	$17,000	$22,600	$6,400
Gain or (loss)	$0	($4,000)	$0	$0	$0
Gain or (loss)	$0	($4,000)	$0	$0	$0
Tax rate on gain or (loss)	34%	34%	34%	34%	34%
Tax on (gain) or loss	$0	$1,360	$0	$0	$0
Liquidation value	$35,000	$21,000	$17 000	$22,600	$6,400
Tax on (gain) or loss	$0	$1,360	$0	$0	$0
Cash proceeds	$35,000	$22,360	$17 000	($22,600)	($6,400)

FORECASTING SALES, OPERATING COST, AND WORKING CAPITAL NEEDS

The analysis thus far has been based on the assumption that revenue and expense streams have been determined, that collection patterns for accounts receivable have been estimated, etc., and that the job at hand is the conversion of this information into relevant cash flows. Developing the projections that provide the basis for cash flow identification is obviously a major part of the capital investment analysis problem. Engineers, market researchers, cost accountants, human resource specialists, economists, and regulatory environment analysts are

TABLE 8.10 CAPITAL INVESTMENT ANALYSIS OF THE LEGAL CLINIC

This table summarizes the cash flow analysis for the Indianapolis legal clinic. Present value analysis is based on a 10% required return and the assumption that operating cash flows occur at mid-year.

Year	Beg. 2000	End 2000 Beg. 2001	2001	2002	2003	2004	2005	2006	2007	2008	2009 to 2020	END 2020
Revenue			$300,000	$700,000	$700,000	$700,000	$700,000	$700,000	$700,000	$700,000	$700,000	$700,000
Expenses												
Cash Expenses in the Acquisition<None> Stage	($50,000)											
Cash Expenses												
Wages			($220,000)	($420,000)	($420,000)	($420,000)	($420,000)	($420,000)	($420,000)	($420,000)	($420,000)	
Other Operating Expenses			($100,000)	($120,000)	($120,000)	($120,000)	($120,000)	($120,000)	($120,000)	($120,000)	($120,000)	
Depreciation Expense												
Depreciation—Building			($12,286)	($12,821)	($12,821)	($12,821)	($12,821)	($12,821)	($12,821)	($12,821)	($12,821)	
Depreciation—Office Equipment			($10,000)	($16,000)	($9,600)	($5,760)	($5,760)	($2,880)	($0)	($0)	($0)	$0
Depreciation—Office Furniture			($7,145)	($12,245)	($8,745)	($6,245)	($4,465)	($4,465)	($4,465)	($4,225)	($0)	
Total Depreciation			($29,431)	($41,066)	($31,166)	($24,826)	($23,046)	($20,166)	($17,286)	($15,046)	($12,821)	
Earnings before Taxes		($50,000)	($49,431)	$118,934	$128,834	$135,174	$136,954	$139,834	$142,714	$144,954	$147,179	
Income Taxes at 34%		$17,000	$16,807	($40,438)	($43,804)	($46,959)	($46,564)	($47,544)	($48,523)	($49,285)	($50,041)	
Net Income		($33,000)	($32,624)	$78,496	$85,030	$88,215	$90,390	$92,290	$94,191	$95,670	$97,138	
Add Back Depreciation			$29,431	$41,066	$31,166	$24,826	$23,046	$20,166	$17,286	$17,046	$12,821	
Investment in Fixed Assets (Table 8.7 to 8.9)	($300,000)	($500,000)	$0	$0	$0	$0	$0	$0	$0	$0	$0	
Investment in Working Capital (Table 8.7 to 8.9)	$0	($5,000)	($14,000)	($29,000)	$0	$0	$0	$0	$0	$0	$0	
After-Tax Cash Flow	($300,000)	($538,000)	($17,193)	$90,562	$116,196	$114,041	$113,436	$112,456	$111,477	$110,716	$109,959	$45,360
PV Factor	1.000	0.9091	0.8668	0.7880	0.7164	0.6512	0.5920	0.5382	0.4893	0.4448	3.0307	0.1351
Present Value	($300,000)	($489,096)	($14,903)	$71,363	$83,243	$74,263	$67,154	$60,524	$54,546	$49,246	$333,253	$71,112
Net Present Value	$60,705											

all involved in projecting information that is used in the estimation of costs and benefits. The capital investment analyst has the job of bringing together information from numerous sources to prepare a single profitability analysis.

While the provision of expertise in each of the areas that might provide input to the profitability analysis of a capital investment is obviously beyond the scope of this or any other single book, it is useful to review the basic tools that are widely used in preparing forecasts.

Forecasting Sales

If a capital investment is expected to result in increased revenues, sales forecasts are an integral part of the capital budgeting process. Sales forecasting is a specialty field of its own, and there are many excellent books on the topic. Some of the more widely used sales forecasting methods are discussed in the following paragraphs.

Trend Analysis. Trend analysis consists of the study of past revenue growth to predict future revenue. Typically, past growth is fitted to a standard trend pattern such as one of those in Figure 8.1. The dangers from mistaking the trend shape are illustrated by a series of bankruptcies in the Florida condominium market in the 1976–1980 period and among Texas savings and loans in the 1980s. In both cases, a growth curve like (c) in Figure 8.1 was mistaken for a curve like (b). As a result, loans to fund construction exceeded future demand for buildings.

Example. Chrysler Corporation was considering the addition of pickup truck capacity in 1987, because pickup trucks had become increasingly popular as personal-use vehicles. Compact pickup truck sales grew at an annual rate of 44 percent from 1980 through 1986, while automobile sales grew at 4 percent a year. Compact pickup truck sales in the United States for the past 20 years are shown as the dots in Figure 8.2. Naturally, it is difficult to fit the growth precisely to any curve because of other events affecting sales. Line I is based on the assumption of compound growth, while line II is based on the assumption that sale of pickup trucks for personal use will follow the product life-cycle curve, with converts to pickup trucks slacking off and some drivers returning to automobiles. The resulting sales forecasts are radically different, depending on which assumption is made, so it is imperative that Chrysler gain additional information to help in identifying the type of growth trend that is occurring.

Study of Potential Purchasers. Potential customers can be studied in several ways. Chrysler Corporation may, for example, conduct surveys to determine how many automobile drivers expect to buy a truck, how many truck drivers intend to buy another truck, and so forth. Studies of the characteristics of truck buyers may give an indication of the maximum possible number of truck drivers. This information could be combined with analysis of recent trends to forecast truck sales.

Test marketing is another way to predict consumer response, although this may be difficult for pickup trucks. Nestle can sell a new coffee flavor in several

| FIGURE 8.1 COMMON TREND PATTERNS

This figure shows four types of sales trends widely observed in practice; k, a, and b are the constants defining a particular trend.

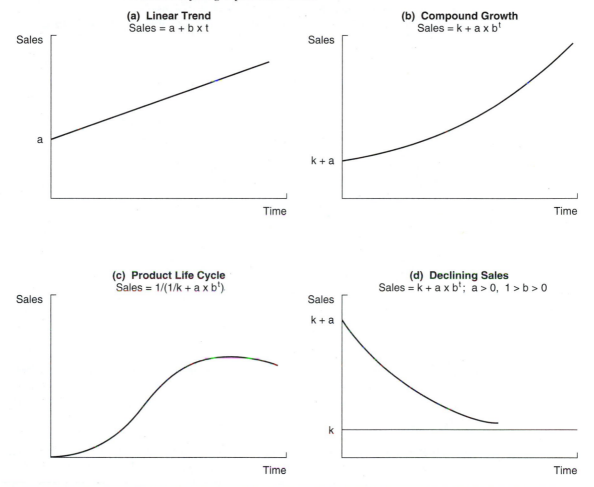

(a) Linear Trend
Sales = a + b x t

(b) Compound Growth
Sales = k + a x b^t

(c) Product Life Cycle
Sales = 1/(1/k + a x b^t)

(d) Declining Sales
Sales = k + a x b^t; a > 0, 1 > b > 0

test markets to find out how many people will buy the product. Test markets also provide the opportunity to test different approaches to pricing, packaging, advertising, and so forth. This allows managers to choose the marketing mix that generates the greatest net present value.

Derived Demand. Demand for some products is derived from other activities, often beyond the control of the manufacturer. Sales by USX (previously U.S. Steel), for example, are affected by automobile production, construction, and the general growth of the economy. Housing demand is affected by the overall health of the economy and the costs of mortgage money as well as the rate of family formation.

| FIGURE 8.2 SALES OF PICKUP TRUCKS IN THE UNITED STATES

The dots represent historical sales. Line I is based on the assumption of compound growth, while line II is based on the assumption that sale of pickup trucks for personal use will follow the product life-cycle curve.

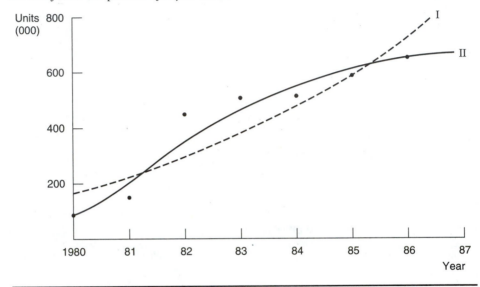

Demand for John Deere farm equipment depends on the health of the farm economy. For products of this type, the emphasis is on forecasting the factors from which demand is derived and studying the relationship between demand and those factors. Professional economists are often useful in these cases.

Other Revenue Forecasting Methods. There are numerous other specialized revenue forecasting methods. Studies of demographic trends are the key to forecasting school enrollment and nursing home demand. Government budgets are used to predict demand for military equipment and roads. Panels of experts are sometimes assembled when other specific forecasting methods cannot be used.

Forecasting Costs

Capital investments that generate revenue generally result in increased costs as well. Other capital investments are acquired with the expectation of reducing costs. Some companies can forecast costs with considerable accuracy. If Kitchenaid develops a new dishwasher, for example, production managers will be able to estimate production costs accurately based on their long experience in production of similar products, supported by a good cost accounting system. In other cases, cost forecasts are extremely difficult, as evidenced by Union Electric's spending $2.4 billion on a nuclear power plant, when the original forecast was for an expenditure of $1.05 billion. With errors of this magnitude, efforts to improve the accuracy of cost forecasts are worthwhile.

Engineers and production managers often develop cost estimates for specific tasks or operation of specific machinery. Costs will include energy, repairs, labor, etc. Personnel specialists can provide estimates of future costs per hour of labor. Purchasing agents can estimate costs of materials and components that must be purchased in order to produce a product. Marketing managers can prepare budgets for marketing and distribution.

In most cases, costs can be divided between fixed and variable portions. Variable costs depend on the level of output while fixed costs do not change over wide ranges of output. Once we decide to fly from New York to Paris, for example, 90 percent of the costs are fixed. Variable costs include meals, commissions to travel agents, very small increases in fuel costs, etc. At the other extreme, a small construction contractor may find that 90 percent of costs are variable, primarily in the form of material and labor. Cost accountants help by estimating fixed costs and by estimating variable costs per unit of output.

Fixed costs are only fixed over some specific time period and over some range of output. A factory can always be closed, so factory overhead is not fixed forever. Furthermore, demand in excess of factory capacity may lead to construction of a new factory, and additional fixed overhead. The new financial reporting system Pacific Resources, Inc., of Honolulu, acquired for $800,000 will not be made obsolete by the addition of one more small business unit, but with enough expansion the system will become inadequate, requiring replacement.

Example. Managers at Chrysler Corporation can estimate raw material, labor, and other direct production costs per pickup truck with considerable accuracy. The company can also estimate the fixed costs of having a factory open. Estimation of administration overhead is more difficult, though. Figure 8.3 shows

| **Figure 8.3**   **Administrative Costs at Chrysler Corporation**

This figure shows the relationship between sales revenue and administrative costs over time at Chrysler Corporation.

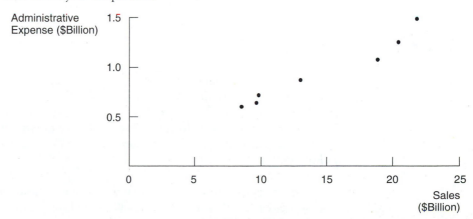

the relationship between sales and administrative expense for Chrysler Corporation in recent years. This relationship can be used to forecast the administrative cost impact of an increase in sales. Using regression analysis on these numbers, for example, we estimate the following relationship between sales and administrative/marketing costs:

$$\text{Admin. \& marketing costs} = \$139 \text{ million} + .05 \cdot \text{Sales}$$

Given this relationship, we might expect administrative and marketing costs to increase by 5 percent of the sales increase.

Forecasting Working Capital Needs

Working capital investments are an important and frequently overlooked part of the relevant cash outlays required for a capital investment. Increased working capital requirements come from transaction cash needs, accounts receivable, inventory, and prepaid expenses. These needs are somewhat offset by increases in accounts payable and accrued expenses; the required increase in net working capital is a relevant cash cost. Inventory managers and credit managers can often be relied upon to generate estimates of needs in these important categories. Alternately, relationships between levels of these categories of assets and the level of sales can be studied for the same or similar products in past periods, in a manner similar to what was done with sales and administrative costs in Figure 8.3. Studies of past relationships or the terms of purchase for specific needed inputs can be used to estimate prepaid expenses, accounts payable, and accrued expenses.

Identification of relevant cash flows and computation of net present values are the culmination of the process of study and consultation with people in many fields of responsibility. The quality of the final decisions can be no better than the quality of the information that is generated from various sources within the business in the process of analyzing a proposed investment. The need to integrate information from many sources in the decision process is one reason degree requirements in business schools include courses in a broad range of topics, not just a narrow specialty.

SUMMARY |

Capital investment analysis is based on relevant cash flows rather than accounting income or other measures of profitability. Cash flow is used because, unlike income, it is what is actually available to spend or reinvest. Cash flow analysis provides the necessary basis for choosing between benefits at different times.

For purposes of capital investment analysis, relevant cash flows are defined as follows:

■ A relevant cash outflow is a cash outflow that will be caused by the course of action, a cash inflow that will be eliminated, or an increase in claims by suppliers of capital that will be created.

■ A relevant cash benefit is a cash inflow that will be caused by the course of action, a cash outflow that will be avoided, or claims by suppliers of capital that will be avoided.

■ An irrelevant cash flow is a cash flow that will occur whether or not the proposed course of action is taken.

Following are the major types of relevant cash costs and benefits at the beginning of an asset's life.

Capital Costs: Purchase and installation price of fixed assets, plus costs of licenses and patents.

Expenses: Training, advertising, legal, and other expenses associated with start-up, less the income tax savings resulting from these expenses.

Working Capital: Increases in current assets required at or near the beginning of a new activity, less current liabilities (accounts payable and accrued expenses) generated at or near the beginning of the activity.

Estimating the cash flows from a potential project is no small undertaking and it requires the help of engineers, cost analysts, marketing personnel, and others. We have broken the process into the following steps:

Estimating the Income Statement

1. Estimate the relevant revenues and/or expenses you expect to receive from the project.
2. Assemble these revenues and expenses into a preliminary income statement making an appropriate calculation of the after-tax income.

Estimating the Balance Sheet

3. Determine all of the balance sheet accounts that are impacted by the project.
4. Estimate the initial size of the investment in these balance sheet accounts. In particular, estimate the incremental investment in fixed assets, such as buildings and equipment, and working capital items, such as cash balances, accounts receivable, and inventory.
5. Determine size and growth of these accounts after the project is operational.

Rolling the Income Statement and Balance Sheet into a Cash Flow Statement

6. Calculate the depreciation charge flowing from the fixed assets into the balance sheet each year.
7. Estimate the life of the project.
8. Determine the terminal values for fixed assets and the disposition values of working capital (net of taxes).
9. Roll all of this information together into a projected cash flow statement.

Making the Decision

10. Calculate the net present value of the project using the appropriate discount rate.[5]
11. Make the appropriate accept or reject decision.

[5]Determination of the appropriate discount rate given the risk for the project is discussed in the risk section of the book, Chapters 11 to 15.

The forecasting of relevant costs and benefits frequently involves the expertise of many people inside and outside the business. The forecasting of benefits often starts with sales forecasts, which may be based on market research, economic analysis, etc. The projection of costs may use the skills of cost accountants, engineers, production managers, and regulatory environment analysts as well as financial analysts. Thus, the capital budgeting process brings together the expertise of people throughout the business to identify and evaluate all of the relevant costs and benefits of a capital investment. The quality of the final decisions will depend on the quality of the information generated from these various sources.

QUESTIONS

8–1. Define, in your own words, the meaning of the phrases *relevant cash cost* and *relevant cash benefit*.

8–2. Why is an increase in working capital considered a relevant cash cost?

8–3. For a movie producer, give an example of sunk costs that might exist when the release of a new picture is being considered.

8–4. An airline is considering a new promotional campaign to attract college students by offering them the right to fly stand-by at low prices when seats are not otherwise filled. List several examples of relevant and irrelevant costs from the airline's point of view.

8–5. A shirt manufacturer is considering the addition of a line of neckties. Give examples of joint costs that might be encountered. How should these joint costs be considered in the decision process?

8–6. Why is interest expense not treated as a relevant cash cost in the capital budgeting process?

8–7. A broadcasting company is considering the offering of a new 24-hour sports news service. Who in the company may be involved in estimating the relevant costs and benefits?

8–8. In which of the following three categories would the following cash flows belong? (It is possible for a cash flow to go in more than one category.)
Categories: Initial Outlay, Yearly Cash Flows, Disposition Cash Flows
a. The cost of training existing workers to use a new piece of equipment.
b. The incremental revenue generated from the project.
c. The proceeds of a "going out of business" sale.
d. The freight on the new piece of equipment.
e. The difference in the sale price of the old equipment and the trade-in allowed on the old equipment.
f. The cost of advertising the grand opening of the new business.
g. The cost of adding an indoor playground to the neighborhood McDonald's.

8–9. (Applications) There has been an explosion in the popularity of rotisserie cooked chicken. Even the country singer Kenny Rogers recognized the enthusiasm and opened his own chain of chicken outlets. Please list five initial outlay cash flows, three variable operating cash flows, three fixed operating cash flows, and three disposition cash flows. Note if cash flows are positive (inflows) or negative (outflows).

8–10. (**Applications**) Wal-Mart Corporation has announced its intention to expand its movement into groceries through the construction of Super-Wal-Marts. In many cities, they are replacing the existing Wal-Mart discounted hard goods store with a much larger Super-Wal-Mart that sells discount groceries, meats, produce, and an expanded line of hard goods carried in the traditional store. For this situation, list three sunk costs, three indirect costs, and three indirect benefits.

PROBLEMS |

8–1. Fort Wayne Corporation expects the following revenues, cash expenses, and depreciation charges as a result of its recent opening of an affiliated store in Lansing:

Year	1	2	3	4	5
Revenues	$16,000	$20,000	$38,000	$48,000	$35,000
Cash Expenses	$ 8,000	$ 5,000	$14,000	$19,000	$19,000
Depreciation	$ 3,000	$ 4,000	$ 3,000	$ 3,000	$ 3,000

Fort Wayne is in the 40 percent tax bracket. Please compute the after-tax cash flows from this investment in the Lansing store.

8–2. Right before opening the Lansing store discussed in problem 1, you have discovered that Fort Wayne forgot to budget 10 percent of revenues as a cash balance, 20 percent of cash expenses as an inventory balance, and 10 percent of cash expenses as an accounts payable balance. All of these balances would be needed at the beginning of each year and are estimated from the year-end annual estimates of revenues and cash expenses given above. Please recalculate the cash flows for the Lansing store investment.

8–3. Payson Corporation purchased a copying machine for $15,600 and placed it into service on January 1, Year 1. This machine is expected to last for 5 years, during which it will produce approximately 200,000 copies each year. Copies will sell for an average of 6 cents each. Material, labor, and other variable costs will be approximately 3 cents a copy. Working capital needs will be negligible, as copying with this machine will be almost all on a cash basis and current liabilities will offset the supplies inventory need. The copier will be disposed of at the end of 5 years for $0. Please calculate the net present value of this copy machine investment using a 40 percent tax rate and a 10 percent cost of capital.

8–4. A new investment in inventory being considered by Quincy Corporation requires an initial outlay of $100,000 on January 1, Year 1. The inventory is expected to be liquidated at the end of five years for $80,000. At a 40 percent income tax rate and a 10 percent required return, is the investment attractive?

This investment is expected to generate the following additional revenues and expenses:

Year	1	2	3	4	5
Revenues	$6,000	$10,000	$28,000	$38,000	$25,000
Expenses	$3,000	$ 5,000	$14,000	$19,000	$19,000
Liquidation loss					$20,000

8–5. You may have observed the increased popularity of "fashionable" pool halls. These pool halls are nothing like their often violent and smoke-filled predecessors. These establishments target an upscale clientele who like to meet for pool rather than dancing or some other activity. Assume that you build one of these establishments and spend $500,000 for the building and $100,000 for equipment (tax life of 5 years) and place it into service on January 1. The pool hall will bring in $5,000 per week in revenue and cost $2,300 per week in cash expenses. Assume a 50-week year. The building will be sold for $400,000 at the end of the fifth year, and the equipment will be sold for $10,000 at the end of the fifth year. No other cash flows will occur during the 5 years of operation. What is the net present value at a 15 percent interest rate?

8–6. Muncie Manufacturing is increasing its collection period by 25 days in hopes of attracting additional sales. Muncie currently has annual sales of $500,000. They expect revenues to increase by $25,000 per year and expenses to increase by $10,000 per year. Muncie believes that an additional $3,000 will go uncollected each year as a result of this change in policy. This $3,000 loss will have to be replaced each year to keep the accounts receivable balance at the increased 25-day level. They project that they will be able to collect 90 percent of the outstanding balance at the end of year 4 (after replacement). Using a four-year life, a 40 percent tax rate, and a 10 percent required return, is the investment attractive?

8–7. Myles Corporation is considering a new computer that can be purchased for $14,800. Delivery will cost $300 and setup will cost $500. What is the initial depreciable cost of the computer machine?

8–8. Terre Haute Cola Distribution can purchase a new executive airplane for $2,300,000. Delivery will cost $10,000 and fitting out after delivery will cost $130,000. The plane has a tax life of 5 years and the plane will be depreciated using the MACRS tables introduced in the chapter. The airplane will be used to transport its executives and it will physically last for 10 years (even though it was depreciated over 5 years). At the end of 10 years the plane will have no salvage value. Wages, repairs, fuel, and so on to operate the airplane are expected to total $250,000 a year. The airplane is expected to save 4,000 hours of management time a year. The managers involved receive salary and benefits that average $115 an hour. The company has a 40 percent tax rate and a 12 percent required return. Is the airplane an attractive investment?

8–9. A new broad-spectrum blood analyzer will allow Lafayette Clinic to earn additional test fees of $30,000 a year for the analyzer's estimated 8-year technical life. The analyzer will cost $100,000, including delivery and installation, and will have a 7-year depreciation life. There is space available in the laboratory that has no other use, and the laboratory technician can do the tests in about the same time it presently takes to send out the samples. The technician earns $20 an hour and will spend 5 percent of his time using this machine. It will be necessary to send the technician to a school to operate the new machine. The school costs $1,000, and a temporary replacement must be hired for the period at a cost of $1,200. The clinic has a 40 percent tax rate and a 12 percent required return. Is the analyzer attractive? (Assume January 1 installation.)

8–10. South Bend Building Services needs to replace a worn-out floor stripping machine. A machine similar to the one being replaced costs $3,000. A new type of machine would cost $4,000, but would be more efficient to operate, reducing labor expense by $500 a year. Unfortunately, the new machine also requires some special maintenance tools that would cost $2,000. The tools will not wear out, so they are expected to last indefinitely and could be used for a large number of these machines. The company has 19 additional stripping machines that must be replaced within the next year. Either the old-style or the new-style machine will be placed in service January 1 and will last for 5 years, with no salvage value. Either machine will be depreciated using the depreciation rates discussed in the chapter. At a 40 percent tax rate, and a 10 percent required return, which machine should the company acquire? (Assume a 7-year tax life.)

8–11. Tom Yeager, a college student, is presently working 16 hours a week (50 weeks a year) at a menial job paying the minimum wage. He can get a job making deliveries for a pizza company in Ames at a $2 increase in his hourly wage, but he must have his own car. A used Chevette is for sale for $3,600. Insurance, gasoline, and maintenance would cost $1,000 a year. Tom would use the car only for business so that he could treat the car as a capital investment for tax purposes. Tom would place the car in service on December 31, 1999, and would use the car for this purpose through the end of 2002, at which time it would have an estimated market value of $1,000. Tom is in a 15 percent tax bracket and could otherwise invest at a rate of 10 percent after tax. Should Tom keep his current job or deliver pizzas?

8–12. Campus Dry-Cleaning has an on-campus location with 10 years to go on the lease. An existing dry-cleaning machine will last for the 10-year duration of the lease, at which time it will be worn out and worthless. A new machine will be more efficient and allow the company to handle a broader range of fabrics. As a result, the new machine will increase revenues by $1,500 a year and decrease operating costs other than depreciation by $600 a year. The old machine, which is fully depreciated, could be sold for $6,000 today. The new machine will cost $20,000. The lease is not renewable, and the new machine is expected to have a salvage value of $5,000 in 10 years. Campus Dry-Cleaning is in a 34 percent tax bracket and the required return on new investments is 10 percent. Should Campus Dry-Cleaning acquire the new machine?

8-13. For the new dry-cleaning machine in problem 12, redo the analysis assuming the lease can be renewed indefinitely and the new machine will last 15 years with no salvage value at the end of 15 years.

8-14. Central Telephone Company is considering the addition of a new type of call-waiting service for its customers. The service can be offered with present hardware, but new software must be purchased at a cost of $1 million. The software will be placed in service January 1, 1993, and depreciated over the estimated 5-year life of the equipment, using the straight-line method. Monthly fees for the service will be $2 initially and will increase 5 percent a year thereafter. An estimated 10,000 customers will sign up for the service in the first year, with the number increasing at 4 percent a year thereafter. The advertising expense for the service will be $100,000 at the time of introduction and $5,000 a month thereafter. The only variable cost will be bad debt expense, equal to 1 percent of revenue. The only significant working capital item is accounts receivable, and the average collection period will be 73 days. Because of uncertainty about developing technology, management wants to assume that the service will not be offered after the 5-year life of the existing hardware. The telephone company has a 12 percent required return. Is the call-waiting service an attractive offering?

8-15. Cedar Falls Menswear is considering the addition of a line of shirts and ties. After-tax cash outlays and after-tax benefits each year for the 10-year planning horizon are shown below. The required return is 10 percent, and no salvage values are anticipated. Should the company invest in either or both lines?

	Shirts	Ties	Shirts & Ties
Initial outlay	$5,000,000	$1,000,000	$5,900,000
Annual after-tax revenue	6,000,000	800,000	7,000,000
Annual after-tax outlays	5,000,000	700,000	5,800,000
Annual net cash flow	$1,000,000	$100,000	$1,200,000

8-16. (Applications) Several years ago Sears realized that it could not compete with the local Wal-Mart by carrying the same merchandise and advertising the same low price. By their very nature, most Sears stores were located as anchors to malls and as such paid higher rents than the stand-alone Wal-Marts. A corporate decision was made to differentiate the product offering at Sears from the product offering at the typical Wal-Mart. Assume that restocking the typical Sears store had the following cost (in thousands):

- $1,000 in losses on the sale of discontinued merchandise (Year 0)
- $50 in additional advertising to introduce the new stores (Year 0)
- $30 in training to sell the new higher-margin merchandise (Year 0)
- $2,000 in additional inventory of higher-margin merchandise (Years 1–5)
- $3,000 in additional sales (Years 1–5)
- $1,500 in additional cost of merchandise sold (Years 1–5)
- $200 in additional loss of inventory due to obsolescence or other reasons (Years 1–5)
- $750 in additional loss from the liquidation sale (at the end of Year 5)

Using a 5-year time horizon and a 12 percent cost of capital, what is the net present value of this strategic shift?

8–17. (**Applications**) One of Dell Computers' major competitive advantages is the production system that allows them to produce a computer to order for each customer per individual specifications. A side benefit of this system is the ability of Dell to hold substantially fewer dollars in parts and finished goods inventories than competitors like Compaq Computers that produce models and then sell these at retail stores. There is a new production system proposal that would cost $100,000,000 immediately and would yield the following reductions in inventory balances:

- Inventory reduction at the end of Year 1—$20,000,000
- Inventory reduction at the end of Year 2—$95,000,000
- Inventory reduction at the end of Year 3—$15,000,000
- Thereafter—$0

Assume that 60 percent of the new system could be written off as a 5-year asset for tax purposes. Using a 10 percent cost of capital, calculate the net present value of this project.

8–18. Mason James Corporation expects to install a $100,000 machine in 1999 and another $120,000 machine in 2002. The first machine has a 5-year tax life and the second machine has a 7-year tax life. What is the total expected depreciation expense for these two machines in 2004?

CASE PROBLEM |

Walton Medical Laboratory

Margaret Walton spent 10 years working in the laboratory at City Hospital. During that time, she advanced to the position of director of the laboratory and completed an MBA degree. She felt that opportunities for further advancement at the hospital were limited and was looking for a new challenge. She took a course in entrepreneurship and was fascinated by the idea of starting her own business. Walton decided that she would open an independent laboratory to provide medical tests for independent medical practices. She believed that she could help physicians reduce both their capital requirements and administrative chores, as well as provide more accurate testing.

Walton began assembling information. She discovered a piece of land available near a number of independent medical practices. The land could be purchased for $100,000, and a suitable building would cost approximately $400,000. The building would have a useful life of approximately 40 years. Laboratory equipment would cost $1 million. The equipment would have a life of 7 years for tax purposes, but would actually last 10 years. Although the business could continue indefinitely, Walton wanted to do the analysis based on the assumption of a life similar to that of the laboratory equipment: 10 years.

In addition to fixed assets, working capital such as cash, supplies, receivables, and payables would be needed. Walton wanted to maintain a minimum cash balance of $20,000. She estimated that $100,000 of supplies would be needed initially, and accounts receivable would rise to $20,000 within a month of starting the business. She estimated initial accounts payable at $40,000. She estimated that the cash, supplies, receivables, and payables categories would double at the end of the first year and would not increase thereafter.

Walton predicted revenue of $600,000 during the first year and $1,200,000 each year thereafter. She estimated that labor expenses, including a salary for her equal to what she was now earning, of $300,000 in the first year and $480,000 each year thereafter. She estimated a supplies expense of $120,000 in the first year and $190,000 each year thereafter. She estimated overhead expense, other than depreciation, of $100,000 a year.

Looking ahead, Walton estimated that the equipment would have a negligible value in ten years, while the building would have lost one-fourth of its value and the land would still be worth $100,000. She guessed that supplies inventory could be sold for half its cost, and other working capital items would be settled at their book values.

Walton turned her attention to financing. She had limited capital of her own and would need to seek outside investors. She had heard enough horror stories about problems that occurred when companies could not make payments on debts, and she wanted to avoid those troubles. Thus, she wanted to try to arrange all equity financing, and use a bank line of credit only for temporary needs. Walton decided on a plan involving ten wealthy investors, preferably senior physicians who would then serve on the board of directors and give their business to the laboratory. She would fund the project by creating 11 shares—one share free to herself as a founder's share and one share to each of the investors. Each investor would then invest 10 percent of the capital requirements.

Walton tentatively discussed the project with several senior physicians to see what would be required. They viewed this as an investment of moderate risk and indicated that they would want a 12 percent after-tax return from an investment of this type. While several investors encouraged her to continue, they were naturally unwilling to make a commitment without a proposal and a thorough financial analysis. Walton began to develop a profitability analysis and a proposal. She had to choose between the corporate tax form and an S form. She estimated that most investors would be in 28 percent tax brackets. All funds not needed internally would be paid out to the shareholders. She thought she could be ready to start by the first of the year, so assets would be considered placed in service in January.

CASE QUESTIONS

1. Identify all cash flows on the assumption the business is taxed at a 28 percent tax rate.
2. Prepare a net present value analysis.
3. Does this investment provide a satisfactory rate of return to investors?
4. Is it fair and reasonable for Walton to get one-eleventh of the company without putting up equity capital of her own?
5. Is it ethical for a doctor to be a shareholder in a lab that is also used by the doctor?

SELECTED REFERENCES

Ang, James S., Jess H. Chua, and Ronald Sellers. "Generating Cash Flow Estimates: An Actual Study Using the Delphi Technique." *Financial Management* 8 (Spring 1979): 64–67.

Barnett, F. William. "Four Steps to Forecast Total Market Demand." *Harvard Business Review* 88 (July-August 1988): 28–30+.

Brown, Keith C. "A Note on the Apparent Bias of Net Revenue Estimates for Capital Investment Projects." *The Journal of Finance* 29 (September 1974): 1215–1216.

Brunton, Nancy M. "Evaluation of Overhead Allocation." *Management Accounting* 70 (July 1988): 22–26.

Dhavale, Deleep G. "Overhead and CIMS: Indirect Costs Take on Greater Importance and Require New Accounting Methods." *Industrial Engineering* 20 (July 1988): 41–43.

Enrich, Norbert L. *Marketing and Sales Forecasting: A Quantitative Approach*, rev. ed. Melbourne, Fla.: Krieger Publishing, 1979.

Howe, Keith M. "Does Inflationary Change Affect Capital Asset Life?" *Financial Management* 16 (Summer 1987): 63–67.

Hurwood, Donald L. *Sales Forecasting*. New York: The Conference Board, 1978.

Kroll, Yoram. "On the Differences between Accrual Accounting Figures and Cash Flows: The Case of Working Capital." *Financial Management* 14 (Spring 1985): 75–82.

McLean, Lawrence B., and A. William Worthman. "Methodology Aids Forecasting with Limited Information." *Industrial Engineering* 20 (February 1988): 18–23.

Pan, Judy, Donald R. Nichols, and O. Maurice Joy. "Sales Forecasting Practices of Large U.S. Industrial Firms." *Financial Management* 6 (Fall 1977): 72–77.

Schall, Lawrence D. "Taxes, Inflation, and Corporate Financial Policy." *The Journal of Finance* 39 (March 1984): 105–126.

Seitz, Neil E. *Business Forecasting: Concepts and Microcomputer Applications*. Englewood Cliffs, N.J.: Prentice-Hall, 1984.

Statman, Meir, and Tyzoon T. Tyebjee. "Optimistic Capital Budgeting Forecasts." *Financial Management* 14 (Autumn 1985): 27–33.

CHAPTER 9 |

TAXES AND FOREIGN INVESTMENTS

After completing this chapter you should be able to:

1. Understand the adjustments that need to be made for corporate taxes at the capital acquisition stage, the operating or asset usage stage, and the disposal stage.

2. Describe the difference between accrual book basis accounting and accrual tax basis accounting.

3. Grasp the meaning of the terms: *capital gains, depreciation, Modified Accelerated Cost Recovery System, Alternative Minimum Tax, loss carry-back, loss carry-forward,* and *S corporation.*

4. Ascertain the depreciation method or combination of depreciation methods that result in the highest net present value given the firm's projected income.

5. Explain the dividend exclusion rule as it applies to dividends paid between corporations.

6. Understand the different tax treatments for proprietorships, partnerships, S corporations, and regular corporations as they relate to the capital budgeting decision.

7. Evaluate the impact that many additional business taxes have on the capital budgeting decision such as state income tax, local income tax, excise taxes, social security taxes, unemployment compensation tax, and others.

8. Show that net present value is still the optimal decision criterion even when taxes are introduced.

9. Understand the proper tax treatment when an asset is replaced and there is a trade-in allowance involved.

10. Describe the important factors that need to be considered in evaluating an international capital investment.

11. Understand the cash flow implications of international capital budgeting projects.

J. R. Vingo, vice president for finance of Alaska Air Group, faced a problem after the tax reform act of 1986. The firm needed 10 additional commuter aircraft for its fleet. Unfortunately, the tax reform act, passed six months earlier, decreased the attractiveness of such capital investments by stretching depreciation lives, eliminating the investment tax credit, and imposing an alternate minimum tax.

Vingo looked for a way to minimize the impact of the tax reform act. The company ended up leasing the airplanes from United Technologies, which in turn leased them from United Pacificorp, a utility holding company in Portland, Oregon. Vingo estimated that Alaska Air Group would save as much as $4 million in taxes by this method of dealing with tax law changes.[1]

Vingo is not the only manager whose attention is frequently drawn from managing the business to managing tax liabilities. Uncle Sam (the U.S. government) is a major participant in business, receiving over a third of the typical large company's income in the form of taxes. Uncle Sam is also picky about when and how his share is calculated and paid. The federal income tax laws and accompanying Internal Revenue Service Regulations, for example, covered over 12,000 pages before being expanded by "tax simplification." If you always meant to read Shakespeare and never found the time, bear in mind that his complete works are one-fortieth of that length. The volume of laws and regulations pales, though, when compared to the administrative and court rulings that are used to determine tax implications of specific actions. In addition, state and local governments have their own tax laws. There could be an end in sight: in mid-1997 the U.S. House of Representatives voted to abolish the tax code in the year 2004. Whether this happens and what will replace it remain to be seen.

In the meantime, the voluminous tax laws and regulations must be considered in estimating capital investment cash flows; otherwise, you may overestimate or underestimate cash flows by 100 percent or more. Equally important, a knowledge of taxes allows you to take advantage of opportunities to reduce taxes and, thereby, increase the profitability of capital investments. Businesses often employ tax experts because the average manager cannot keep up with the massive and ever-changing tax code. However, managers involved in capital investment decisions must understand at least the general principles that will allow them to estimate the tax implications of their decisions and work toward reduction of taxes.

Fortunately, the massive volumes of tax laws and regulations are mostly applications of some general principles to specific situations. These principles have remained steady over time, even though details of the tax code have changed frequently. The focus of this chapter is on the application of general principles of taxation to capital budgeting, with current laws as an illustration.

The income tax is the basis of the tax system in the United States and the major tax affecting capital budgeting.[2] Following an overview of the general prin-

---

[1]Lee Berton, "Surprise Loophole: Firms Expect Leasing to Save Them Millions under New Tax Law," *Wall Street Journal* (Wednesday, March 11, 1987): 1+.

[2]Other taxes include property tax, social security tax, and excise taxes. These taxes must also be considered in that they affect cash flows. Many of the non-income taxes are levied by state and local governments and vary by jurisdiction.

ciples of income taxation, we will trace the implications of income taxes over the life cycle of a capital investment, from acquisition to disposition. Businesses are assumed to be ordinary corporations in this discussion unless otherwise noted. Some differences for businesses not taxed as corporations are covered later in this chapter.[3]

ACCRUAL BOOK BASIS INCOME VERSUS ACCRUAL TAX BASIS INCOME

Income was defined in the last chapter as revenues less expenses. The meaning is the same here except that the timing and recognition of revenues and expenses for tax purposes may be different than the definition and timing of revenues and expenses for accrual accounting book purposes. The tax law defines what is recognized as revenues and expenses for tax purposes and for the most part this is the same as what is recognized for accrual accounting purposes. The difference lies in the timing and amounts to be recognized. For example, corporations typically want to show a higher level of income to their shareholders than to the IRS. They can do this by electing to use straight-line depreciation to depreciate their fixed assets for book purposes and by using the much more rapid Modified Accelerated Cost Recovery System (MACRS), discussed in Chapter 8, for calculating their taxable income. Using different book basis rules to calculate a higher income for the shareholder and tax basis rules to show a lower income to the IRS is known as tax avoidance rather than tax evasion. Knowing the difference between the two is critical. Tax avoidance is typically smart management because you can defer taxes until future years and pay them in cheaper dollars. Tax evasion is illegal and typically carries a federal prison sentence (if convicted).

Example. To illustrate the difference between accrual book basis income and accrual tax basis income, consider the activities of Merrill Corporation summarized in Table 9.1. The company bought a $100 machine in 1999 that had a 3-year tax life but a 10-year economic life. Revenues were $500 each year and cash expenses were $300 each year. The company uses the MACRS rates discussed in Chapter 8 to depreciate for tax purposes and the straight-line method[4] for accounting purposes. The asset is placed into service on January 1, 2000, and Merrill is in the 40 percent marginal tax bracket.

The example in Table 9.1 demonstrates the differences between income, deferred taxes payable, and cash flow that result under tax basis accounting and those that result with accrual book basis accounting. In this example Merrill reported

---

[3]The reader who wants a more in-depth understanding of tax issues can start by acquiring one of the many detailed tax guides such as the *Federal Tax Course*, published annually by Commerce Clearing House.

[4]The straight-line method involves taking the acquisition cost and subtracting the expected disposal value and dividing the difference by the expected life of the asset. Sometimes this number is divided by 2 to adjust to a mid-year convention In this case, the $100 acquisition cost less the salvage value of $0 leaves a difference of $100. Dividing this by 10 we arrive at a yearly depreciation of $10.

| **TABLE** **9 . 1** | COMPARISON OF ACCRUAL BOOK BASIS ACCOUNTING AND ACCRUAL TAX BASIS ACCOUNTING |

This table illustrates the differences in net income, the balance sheet, and the cash flow statement using accrual tax basis accounting and accrual book basis accounting.

INCOME STATEMENT (USING ACCRUAL TAX BASIS ACCOUNTING)

Year	2000	2001	2002	2003
Revenue	$500	$500	$500	$500
Cash expenses	(300)	(300)	(300)	(300)
Depreciation expense (MACRS)	(33)	(45)	(15)	(7)
Taxable income	167	155	185	193
Taxes	(67)	(62)	(74)	(77)
Net income	100	93	111	116

BALANCE SHEET (USING ACCRUAL TAX BASIS ACCOUNTING)

Year	2000	2001	2002	2003
Deferred taxes payable	$0	$0	$0	$0

CASH FLOW STATEMENT (USING ACCRUAL TAX BASIS ACCOUNTING)

Year	2000	2001	2002	2003
Revenue	$500	$500	$500	$500
Cash expenses	(300)	(300)	(300)	(300)
Depreciation expense (MACRS)	(33)	(45)	(15)	(7)
Taxable income	167	155	185	193
Taxes	(67)	(62)	(74)	(77)
Net income	100	93	111	116
Add back depreciation	33	45	15	7
Add (sub.) changes in deferred taxes	0	0	0	0
Cash flow	133	138	126	123

a higher income to the owners than to the Internal Revenue Service in the first three years. The reason is that depreciation expense is not the same for tax and accounting purposes.[5] These differences in income do not imply dishonesty. The accelerated depreciation rates presently used by the Internal Revenue Service are for the purpose of encouraging investment, not for the purpose of recognizing the actual rates at which assets wear out. The income tax expense on the book basis income statement is approximately the tax that would have been paid if the income reported to the owners was also reported to the Internal Revenue Service. The difference between the tax expense reported to owners and the tax actually paid is treated as a deferred tax liability. The reason for this treatment is a belief that taxes being avoided through accelerated depreciation will be paid later when tax depreciation is lower than accounting depreciation. In this example this reversal begins in 2003 when MACRS depreciation is $7 and straight-line depreciation is $10.

[5]Companies may also use different inventory valuation methods, warranty methods, pension methods, and receivable methods for tax and book accounting.

| TABLE 9.1 | COMPARISON OF ACCRUAL BOOK BASIS ACCOUNTING AND ACCRUAL TAX BASIS ACCOUNTING (*CONT.*)

INCOME STATEMENT (USING ACCRUAL BOOK BASIS ACCOUNTING)

Year	2000	2001	2002	2003
Revenue	$500	$500	$500	$500
Cash expenses	(300)	(300)	(300)	(300)
Depreciation expense	(10)	(10)	(10)	(10)
Taxable income	190	190	190	190
Taxes	(76)	(76)	(76)	(76)
Net income	114	114	114	114

BALANCE SHEET (USING ACCRUAL BOOK BASIS ACCOUNTING)

Year	2000	2001	2002	2003
Change in deferred taxes	$9	$14	$2	$(1)
Deferred taxes payable	9	23	25	24

CASH FLOW STATEMENT (USING ACCRUAL BOOK BASIS ACCOUNTING)

Year	2000	2001	2002	2003
Revenue	$500	$500	$500	$500
Cash expenses	(300)	(300)	(300)	(300)
Depreciation expense (MACRS)	(10)	(10)	(10)	(10)
Taxable income	190	190	190	190
Taxes	(76)	(76)	(76)	(76)
Net income	114	114	114	114
Add back depreciation	10	10	10	10
Add (sub.) changes in deferred taxes	9	14	2	(1)
Cash flow	133	138	126	123

The differences between book basis accounting and tax basis accounting are adjusted in the construction of the cash flow statement. When book basis accounting is used to construct the income statement, an adjustment for any increase or decrease in deferred taxes must be made in the cash flow statement. This annual increase or decrease in deferred taxes will be roughly the difference in the taxes owed using tax basis accounting and the taxes owed using book basis accounting.

TAX RATES |

ORDINARY CORPORATE INCOME TAX RATES

Ordinary income tax rates for corporations rise until the corporation reaches a plateau income. Currently that plateau is approximately $18,000,000 in taxable income. Beyond this amount, corporate income is taxed at a flat 35 percent. The particular tax rates and plateau amounts change periodically, but the principle has remained the same for many years. For the problems at the end of the chapter we will assume a 40 percent tax rate. This assumption is based on a 35 percent federal income tax rate and an average state income tax rate of roughly 5 percent.

RATES ON CAPITAL, 1245, AND 1250 GAINS AND LOSSES

Capital gains occur when certain financial instruments that are typically not bought or sold in the ordinary course of business are sold at a price higher or lower than the original purchase price or adjusted basis.

1245 gains (and losses) occur when depreciable assets other than real estate are sold for more (or less) than their remaining basis.[6] 1250 gains (and losses) occur when real estate assets are sold for more (or less) than their remaining basis.

For the typical corporation (identified in the tax code as a "C" corporation) there is presently no difference in the tax rate on capital gains, 1245 gains, 1250 gains, or ordinary income. There is and will probably always be talk of reinstating or changing this section of the tax code. If the past is used as an example for future tax proposals then there will likely be different treatment for the different classes of property. The actual calculation of these gains is explained in some detail in the section on asset disposal.

For partnerships, individuals, and "S" corporations, there are special rates and gain calculations that apply. Since we are dealing with corporations in this text, we refer you to a tax book or sound tax counsel for these specific cases. In the following paragraphs, we will illustrate the application of federal income tax laws over the life cycle of a capital investment, from acquisition through use and eventual disposal.

TAXES APPLYING TO CAPITAL INVESTMENT ACQUISITION |

Capital investments may be in the form of fixed assets such as land, buildings, machinery, airplanes, and furniture, short-term assets such as inventory, or expenses such as advertising campaigns and research. Many capital investments, such as the introduction of a new product, are combinations of a variety of smaller investments. The tax implications of a capital investment at the time of acquisition depend on the type of investment being acquired and are discussed in the following sections.

OUTLAYS TREATED AS INVESTMENTS

Capital investments involving the acquisition of actual assets—land, building, machinery, inventory, securities, etc.—are generally not treated as expenses for tax purposes. The same treatment is applied for certain intangible assets, such

---

[6]Remember from Chapter 8 that the remaining basis is the initial cost of the asset less depreciation taken to date.

as licenses, patent rights, and purchased goodwill. Most of these assets are used up or wear out over time, and the use or wearing out is recognized as a depreciation or amortization expense that reduces taxes. The acquisition cost itself, though, is simply viewed as a change from one type of asset to another, such as from cash to fixed assets, and has no immediate tax implications.

Overhauls. An overhaul extends the life of an existing asset. The overhaul is treated as a capital expenditure for tax purposes and depreciated accordingly. A repair, on the other hand, is treated as an expense for tax purposes.

Investment Tax Credits. Governments periodically introduce investment tax credit programs to spur investment. An investment tax credit reduces the company's tax liability by some percent of the cost of the capital investment. The investment tax credit has come and gone several times in the United States. It was repealed again in 1986.

OUTLAYS TREATED AS EXPENSES

Some capital investments are treated in the tax code as expenses that reduce taxable income in the period of expenditure even if benefits are anticipated over several years. Training programs and advertising expenses fall in this category, as do many research and development expenses. For example, a retail store that is starting a new department spends $12,000 on training and $18,000 on advertising. If the company faces a marginal tax rate of 34 percent, these costs will result in a tax savings of ($12,000 + $18,000).34 = $10,200, and the after-tax expenditure will be $19,800.

Example. Taxes and cash flows associated with the opening of Gainesville Discount Drug Center are summarized in Table 9.2. The land will cost $250,000, the building will cost $1 million, fixtures will cost $200,000, and inventory will cost $1 million. Advertising and training prior to opening will cost $100,000. The company's marginal tax rate is 34 percent. The only expenditures with an immediate tax implication are the advertising and training,[7] which reduce taxes by .34 × $100,000 = $34,000.

TAXES APPLYING TO THE OPERATING STAGE |

During the years in which a capital investment is being used, income tax is affected. Tax rules are similar whether income is being taxed as corporate income or the income of the owner, but there are differences. The treatment of income under corporate tax rules is treated here. Differences in tax treatment when income is taxed as the income of the owner are discussed later in this chapter.

---

[7]If the store is placed in service at or near the end of the company's tax year, depreciation tax savings may occur almost immediately, further reducing the net outlay. These depreciation benefits are discussed in association with tax treatment of ongoing operations.

| **TABLE   9.2**   **CASH OUTLAY FOR GAINESVILLE DISCOUNT DRUG CENTER TO BEGIN OPERATIONS**

This example reflects the various cash outlays at the time of acquisition and the tax savings associated with acquisition, which arise from those items categorized as expenses for tax purposes.

Land	$(250,000)
Building	(1,000,000)
Fixtures	(200,000)
Inventory	(1,000,000)
Advertising & training	(100,000)
Tax savings	34,000
Total cash flow	$(2,516,000)

The accrual tax basis approach to measuring taxable income was explained earlier in this chapter and applies to taxation during the use of a capital investment. If the investment results in increased revenue, the taxable income from the investment each period is the increase in revenue, minus any increase in expenses. Some capital investments result in no new revenue but result in a net decrease in expenses. The reduction of expenses also increases taxable income, in most cases.

DEPRECIATION

Depreciation is a particularly important expense for capital investment analysis. It was introduced in the prior chapter but we will review depreciation in greater detail here as it applies to taxes. Assets that wear out over time and are not bought or sold in the normal course of business are depreciated. Depreciation is a process of recognizing this wearing out, and the resultant loss of value, as an expense each period. This expense reduces taxable income. Depreciation has been a part of the tax law since 1913, with each type of asset assigned a life and then depreciated over that life using one of several approved formulas. Depreciation rates for most assets are currently governed by the Modified Accelerated Cost Recovery System that was introduced and discussed in Chapter 8.

Example. In Table 9.2, the tax and cash flow implications of the opening of Gainesville Discount Drug Center were developed. That same store can be used to summarize taxation during an asset's useful life. Assume the store was placed in service January 1, 1999, and sales were $1 million in 1999. The cost of goods sold was $700,000 and other expenses, excluding depreciation, were $100,000. The building is a 39-year asset, and the fixtures are 7-year assets. Depreciation on the building and fixtures for 1999 was therefore:

Building: $\$1,000,000(11.5/12)(1/39) = \$24,572$

Fixtures: $\$ 200,000 \times .1429 = 28,580$

Earnings before tax from operations for 1999 were therefore:

Sales	$1,000,000
Cost of goods sold	700,000
Operating expenses	100,000
Depreciation—Building	24,572
Depreciation—Fixtures	28,580
Earnings before tax	$ 146,848

If the company was taxed at 34 percent, the income tax owed would be .34 × $146,848 = $49,928.

Note from Table 9.2 that advertising and training expenses of $100,000 reduced taxes by $34,000 at opening time. The advertising and training expenses would affect either 1998 or 1999 taxes, depending on the year in which the expenditures occurred. Taxes associated with acquisition and taxes over the operating life are separated for convenience of discussion, not necessarily because the taxes occur in different years. It is, for example, possible that the $49,928 tax liability for the first year of operations and the $34,000 tax savings from start-up expenditures both occur in the same tax year, meaning the *net* tax for the first year is $49,928 − $34,000 = $15,928.

Other Depreciation Rules. Assets acquired prior to the enactment of each new tax law continue to be depreciated under the rules in effect at the time of acquisition. The tax code also specifies alternate depreciation rules that result in slower depreciation. These rules, which may be used if the company desires, are required in certain situations, such as when an asset is used outside the country for more than half of the year. For depreciation under these other rules, see a specialized tax guide, such as the *Federal Tax Course*, published annually by Commerce Clearing House.

CHOOSING A DEPRECIATION METHOD

When there is a choice between depreciation methods, you will prefer the method that maximizes the present value of depreciation tax savings. If the tax rate is expected to be the same each year, MACRS depreciation will be preferred over straight line because the MACRS method provides the depreciation tax savings sooner. If the tax rate is expected to increase in the future, the depreciation methods should be compared on a present value basis.

Example. Jacksonville Machine Tool will acquire a special cutting die for $10,000 on January 1, 1999. The die will have a 3-year life for tax purposes. The company's marginal tax rate is expected to be 15 percent in 1999 and 2000, but is expected to be 34 percent in later years. Depreciation amounts and their present values are shown in Table 9.3. The company's required return is 10 percent. Tax payments are treated as year-end payments for simplicity. Because the tax rate will be higher in later years, the present value of depreciation tax savings is maximized in this case by choosing the straight-line method.

In this example, it is $321 better (in present value terms) for Jacksonville Machine Tool to use straight-line depreciation than the quicker MACRS depreciation. This is due to the fact that in the first two years Jacksonville will have a lower tax rate than in the later two years.

ALTERNATE MINIMUM TAX

The alternate minimum tax (AMT) is a special aspect of the Tax Reform Act of 1986. Essentially, the AMT law requires corporations to compute two incomes: regular income and alternate minimum income. A corporation earning over $18,333,333 is taxed at the higher of:

- 35% of regular income, or
- 20% of alternate minimum income

| TABLE 9.3 ANALYSIS OF STRAIGHT-LINE AND MACRS DEPRECIATION

Present values of depreciation tax savings for a $10,000 asset are computed using both straight-line and MACRS depreciation. The company's tax rate is expected to be 15 percent in the first two years and 34 percent in the second two years. Required return is 10 percent.

Year	Straight-Line Depreciation	Tax Savings	Present Value Factor	Present Value
1999	(1/6)10,000 = 1,667	1,667(.15) = 250	.9091	$227
2000	(1/3)10,000 = 3,333	3,333(.15) = 500	.8264	413
2001	(1/3)10,000 = 3,333	3,333(.34) = 1,133	.7513	851
2002	(1/6)10,000 = 1,667	1,667(.34) = 567	.6830	387

Present value of depreciation tax savings: $1,878

Year	MACRS Accelerated Depreciation	Tax Savings	Present Value Factor	Present Value
1999	(.3333)10,000 = 3,333	3,333(.15) = 500	.9091	$455
2000	(.4444)10,000 = 4,444	4,444(.15) = 667	.8264	551
2001	(.1482)10,000 = 1,482	1,482(.34) = 504	.7513	379
2002	(.0741)10,000 = 741	741(.34) = 252	.6830	172

Present value of depreciation tax savings: $1,557

The alternate minimum income is computed by adding certain items, called *tax preferences*, to regular income. There are over a dozen preference items, but the ones of particular interest for capital investment are:[8]

- Excess of accelerated cost recovery depreciation over the Alternative Depreciation System (ADS).
- Seventy-five percent of the excess of adjusted current earnings (book income) over alternative minimum tax income.

The Alternative Depreciation System is less accelerated than regular (MACRS) depreciation and is based on longer asset lives.

The alternate minimum tax provides a good example of how companies modify plans to minimize taxes. The leasing plans of Alaska Air Group, cited at the beginning of this chapter, were motivated by the alternate minimum tax. W. H. Sparrow, treasurer of CSX Corporation, estimates that the company saves $1,000 a year in taxes for every boxcar it leases instead of purchases. A statement by Mr. Nevitt of Bank Ameri-lease further highlights the importance of this type of planning to American business: "We're normally slack this time of year, but because of leasing volume to avoid the new tax act, six of our leasing specialists have had to cancel their ski vacations."[9]

OPERATING LOSS CARRY-BACK AND CARRY-FORWARD

If a company experiences negative ordinary income some year, the loss can be carried back 3 years and then carried forward for up to 15 years or just carried forward for 15 years to offset taxable income.

Example. The ordinary income and taxes on that income for Atlanta Southern Corporation follow. The company paid income tax in the first three years, using a 15 percent tax rate. Then, the company had negative ordinary income of $100,000 in 2002. The company first used $30,000 of the 2002 loss to offset 1999 income. Next, it used $20,000 to offset 2000 income and another $20,000 to offset 2001 income. As a result, the company qualified for a refund of the tax paid in those three years: $10,500. The total ordinary income for those three years was $70,000, so $30,000 of the 2002 loss remains unused. That amount can be carried forward for a maximum of 15 years and subtracted from ordinary income for future years, until it is used up, to reduce tax liabilities in those years.

---

[8]Others include difference between accelerated cost recovery depreciation and straight-line depreciation for real estate, excess of expensed R&D over R&D if amortization is used, deferred income under completed-contract method of accounting for long-term contracts, excess of percentage depletion over the adjusted basis of the property, net corporate capital gains not otherwise included, tax-exempt interest, profit deferred by using the installment method of accounting, untaxed appreciation on charitable contributions, and excess of financial institution bad-debt deduction over that allowed under experience method.

[9]Berton, "Surprise Loophole."

Year	1999	2000	2001	2002
Taxable ordinary income	$30,000	$20,000	$20,000	−$100,000
Income tax	4,500	3,000	3,000	−10,500

TAXES APPLYING TO THE DISPOSITION STAGE |

The final stage in the life cycle of a capital investment is the liquidation or sale of assets. Like every other stage in the life cycle, taxes are an important part of the picture and must be taken into account. Taxes differ somewhat between disposition under corporate taxation and disposition if the business income is treated as personal income of the owners, partners, and S corporation shareholders. Corporate taxation is treated here, and personal taxation is covered later.

CAPITAL GAINS AND LOSSES

The major types of capital gains and losses are summarized in Table 9.4.

For individuals, there is a $3,000 annual capital loss allowance. For corporations, capital losses can only be subtracted from capital gains. 1250 losses must be matched first against 1250 gains and then against capital gains. And 1245

| TABLE 9.4   TYPES OF GAINS AND LOSSES

This table summarizes the categories of capital gains and losses under current tax law.

GAINS	LOSSES
Capital Gains	**Capital Losses**
Excess of sale price over cost for non-depreciable assets not regularly bought or sold in the course of business, such as stock, bonds, and land.	Amount by which sale prices of these same assets fall below cost.
1250 Gains	**1250 Losses**
Excess of sale price over remaining basis for real estate.	Amount by which the sale price falls below cost for real estate used in the business.
1245 Gains	**1245 Losses**
Excess of sale price over original basis for depreciable assets other than real estate used in the business.	Amount by which the sale price falls below cost for depreciable assets other than real estate used in the business.

losses are treated the same way. In the end everything is rolled into a capital gain or loss category. If capital losses exceed capital gains in any year, the excess must be carried back three years to offset past capital gains. If there are not enough prior capital gains in the prior three years, the excess capital loss can be carried forward for a maximum of five years.[10]

Example. Boca Raton Development placed a copier (a 5-year asset) in service in 1999, with an original basis of $100,000. The asset was then sold for $110,000 at the beginning of 2001. Common stock of another corporation which had been purchased for $50,000 was sold for $30,000 in 2001, and the company had no other gains or losses on the sale of assets. The tax implications are as follows:

Copier		Common Stock	
Original basis for copier	$100,000	Sale price	$30,000
−1999 depreciation	20,000	Purchase price	50,000
−2000 depreciation	32,000	Capital loss	$20,000
=Remaining basis	$ 48,000		
1245 gain ($110,000 − $48,000)	$ 62,000		

Of the capital loss on the stock sale, $20,000[11] can be used to offset the 1245 gain on the copier sale. Because capital losses can eventually be offset against 1245 gains, the company must pay regular income tax on $42,000 of additional income.

TRADE-INS

When an asset is traded in on a like-kind new asset rather than being sold, no immediate tax consequences occur. The basis of the new asset is the remaining basis (original cost − depreciation) of the asset traded in, plus the additional amount paid.

Example. Athens Corporation bought a machine several years ago for $100,000. Since then, the company has claimed $56,270 of MACRS depreciation expense. The machine is now traded in on a new model. The new model was priced at $170,000, but the dealer will give a trade-in allowance of $60,000. The basis for the new machine is determined as follows:

---

[10]When an asset is traded in a like-kind exchange rather than being sold at the end of its life, no taxable gains or losses are created.

[11]The Revenue Reconciliation Act of 1993 allowed for the exclusion of 50 percent of the gain on the sale of stock of certain "qualified small business stock." This stock must be issued after August 10, 1993, and at the time of issuance the corporation cannot be larger than $50,000,000 in gross assets. There are many additional requirements that must be met to qualify for this treatment.

$$\text{Payment in addition to trade-in} = 170,000 - 60,000 = \$110,000$$

$$+ \text{ Remaining basis for trade-in} = 100,000 - 56,270 = \underline{\quad 43,730}$$

$$= \text{ Basis for the new machine} \qquad \underline{\underline{\$153,730}}$$

If the new machine has a 7-year life for tax purposes, application of the MACRS depreciation rates in the prior chapter gives acquisition-year depreciation of:

$$.1429 \times \$153,730 = \$21,968.$$

REPLACEMENT DECISIONS IN THE PRESENCE OF TAXES |

Replacement decisions must be treated carefully because of their unique cash-flow implications. Replacement decisions fall in three general categories:

a. Replacement of a worn-out asset that has a sale value.
b. Replacement of a worn-out asset that has a trade-in value different from the sale value.
c. Replacement of a usable asset with another asset.

Decisions in category (a) present no new problems. If an asset can no longer be used, but can be sold, that sale price is available whether or not a new asset is acquired, and therefore does not meet the definition of a relevant cash flow. Categories (b) and (c) are discussed in the following sections.

REPLACEMENT WITH A TRADE-IN VALUE DIFFERENT FROM THE SALE VALUE

In some cases, though, there is an opportunity to trade in the asset for a higher value than would be available with a simple sale. The difference between the trade-in value and the sale value, adjusted for tax implications, would be a reduction in the relevant cost of the new asset.

Example. Quincy Excavation has a worn-out, fully depreciated back-hoe that can be sold for scrap at a price of $1,000. Alternately, a dealer will allow a $1,200 trade-in on the cost of a new $20,000 back-hoe. The new back-hoe will have a physical life of 10 years, but will be depreciated on a straight-line basis (using a mid-year convention) over a 5-year period for tax purposes. It will generate earnings before depreciation and tax of $5,000 a year, and will have an estimated salvage value of $0. Straight-line tax depreciation is used for simplicity of illustration. The new back-hoe will be placed in service December 31, 1999, so an immediate depreciation tax savings would occur. Quincy Excavation's marginal income tax rate is 34 percent. The relevant cash flows are shown in Table 9.5.

REPLACEMENT OF ONE USABLE ASSET WITH A NEW ASSET

Replacement of a usable asset with a new asset can present complications, particularly if the new asset has a life different from the remaining life of the existing usable asset. The trick in solving these problems is not in identifying marginal cash costs, but in deciding which alternatives should be assigned which costs. Errors often occur when the sale price of the old asset is deducted from the cost of the new asset, rather than being treated as an opportunity cost of using the old asset. The principles of cost assignment for those problems were developed in Chapter 7. The following example extends that analysis by treating the tax implications in such settings.

Example. Muncie Corporation has an old, fully depreciated machine that can be sold for $7,500 or repaired at a cost of $500 and used another three years, after which it will be worthless. Operating costs will be $1,000 a year. The

| TABLE 9.5 RELEVANT CASH FLOWS FOR A BACK-HOE PURCHASE

A back-hoe can be purchased for $20,000. The old, fully depreciated back-hoe can be sold outright for $1,000 or traded in for a trade-in allowance of $1,200. A back-hoe will generate earnings before depreciation and tax of $5,000 and the company is in a 34 percent tax bracket.

Year	1999	2000–2003	2004	2005–2008
Earnings before dep. and tax	0	$5,000	$5,000	$5,000
−Depreciation[a]	1,880	3,760	1,880	
=Earnings before tax	−1,880	1,240	3,120	5,000
−Income tax payments		422	1,061	1,700
+Income tax savings	639			
Net income	−1,241	818	2,059	3,300
+ Depreciation	1,880	3,760	1,880	
Cash flow	639	4,578	3,939	3,300
Purchase price	$20,000			
Less trade-in allowance	1,200			
Net cost	18,800			
Plus forgone sale of old[b]	660			
Net acquisition outlay[c]	19,460			
Net relevant cash flow	−$18,821	$4,578	$3,939	$3,300

[a]Basis for depreciation is $18,800 paid, plus the remaining basis of the asset traded in (+ $0 in this case).

[b]$1,000 − .34 × $1,000.

[c]Although all 1999 cash flows are shown in one column, this does not imply that all 1999 cash flows occur at the same time. The acquisition flows will generally precede operating cash flows, and those timing differences must be taken into account in the present value calculations.

| TABLE 9.6 ANALYSIS OF A REPAIR OPTION FOR MUNCIE CORPORATION

A fully depreciated asset can be sold today for $7,500 or repaired for $500 and used for 3 years, after which it will be worthless. Operating costs will be $1,000 each year. The required return is 10 percent.

Year	0	1-3
Operating expense		$1,000
Tax savings from operating expense		340
Net operating expense		660
Forgone sale price	$7,500	
Less tax on sale	2,550	
Forgone net proceeds from sale	4,950	
Repair cost	500	
Tax savings from repair	170	
Net repair cost	330	
Relevant cash costs	$5,280	$ 660
Present value factor	1.0000	2.4869
Present value	5,280	1,641
Total present value = $6,921		

relevant cash costs and net present value (at a 10 percent required return assuming year-end cash flows) to use this machine for three years are shown in Table 9.6. Muncie is in the 34 percent tax bracket.

As an alternative, Muncie Corporation can buy a new machine for $10,000. The entire cost of the new machine will be recognized as an expense in the year of acquisition as allowed under current tax law for very small businesses (and to simplify the illustration). The new machine will last for 12 years, will cost $900 a year to operate, and will have no salvage value at the end of 12 years. The relevant cash flows and net present value are as follows:

Year	0	1-12
Operating cost		$900
Tax savings		306
Net operating cost		594
Cost of the new machine	$10,000	
Tax savings from purchase	3,400	
Net cost to purchase	6,600	
Relevant cash costs	$6,600	$594
Present value factor	1.0000	6.8137
Present value	6,600	4,047
Total present value = $10,647		

The present values of the net costs for the repair and replacement alternatives are $6,921 and $10,647 respectively. We assume for this example that the benefits are the same, and we are simply considering two ways of achieving those benefits. We also assume that services of these types will be needed in the future so that the repaired item can be replaced with a new machine (or another similar used machine) at the end of its three-year life. With these assumptions, the equivalent annuity can be used to find an annual cost of providing whatever service these machine alternatives provide:

Alternative	PV of net costs ÷ PVAI$_{n,10\%}$ = Equivalent Annual cost
Repair	$6,921 ÷ 2.4869 = \$2,783$
Replace	$10,647 ÷ 6.8137 = \$1,563$

Assuming a long-term need for the service of the asset, the replacement alternative is more attractive than the repair alternative because, if it were repeated on a continual basis, it would result in a lower present value of total cost.

As a rule we replace an asset when the net present value to the firm of continuing with the present asset is less than the net present value to the firm of acquiring and using the new asset. The existing asset can have value but it is replaced if this value is less than the value added by the new asset. In the previous example the equivalent cost of running the old asset was $2,783 while the equivalent cost of the replacement was $1,563. The present value of the firm is increased by the replacement of the old asset.

To see the importance of proper cost and benefit allocation, suppose we had subtracted the sales price of the old asset from the cost of the new asset. The equivalent annuities for the repair and replacement alternatives would then be:

$$\text{Repair:} \ [330 + (660 \times 2.4869)]/2.4869 = \$793$$

$$\text{Replace:} \ [(10,000 - 7,500).66 + (594 \times 6.8137)]/6.8137 = \$836$$

We would erroneously choose the repair over the replacement alternative even though its annual cost is almost twice as high when properly evaluated. A way to look at this problem that leads to the right assignment of relevant costs is to assume that the old machine was not owned now, but could be bought for $7,500. This is not economically different from the use of a machine that could be sold for $7,500.

CORPORATE INCOME AND TAXATION OF OWNERS |

A corporation is a separate entity for tax purposes and pays taxes on its income as previously discussed. The owners are not taxed on their shares of the company's income and cannot deduct their shares of the company's losses from their taxable income. Owners are only required to recognize the dividends they receive as taxable income.

An exception to the above rule, known as the **dividend exclusion rule**, occurs when one corporation holds the stock of another corporation. Under this rule a corporation holding less than a 20 percent share of another corporation can exclude from income 70 percent of the dividend income received. Corporations holding 20 to 79 percent of another corporation's stock can exclude 80 percent of the dividend income received. If the company has 80 percent or more ownership, 100 percent is excluded from the receiving corporation's taxable income.

The owners of a business that is earning profits and retaining most of the profits to finance further growth would generally prefer that the business be taxed as a corporation because owners are not required to pay personal taxes on any of the income that is retained by the company. If the company is paying all its profits to the shareholders in the form of dividends, double taxation occurs; corporate income tax is paid on the income, then the remainder is taxed again as dividend income of the owners. In this situation, the owners would prefer a form that caused the income to be taxed only once. In addition, the owners of a corporation that suffers losses cannot deduct those losses from their other income and might, therefore, prefer a form of organization that allows them to take advantage of the company's losses. The organization forms discussed in the following paragraphs avoid corporate tax by requiring the owners to be taxed on all of the businesses' income, but also allow the owners to deduct the losses of the businesses from their personal income from other sources.

BUSINESSES NOT TAXED AS CORPORATIONS |

Several business forms that avoid corporate income tax are discussed in this section. Following this, the tax rules for income treated as personal income of the owners are outlined. Then, considerations leading to a choice of tax form are discussed.

OTHER ORGANIZATIONAL FORMS OF BUSINESS

Proprietorship. If you decide to go into business and will be the sole owner of the business, the proprietorship form of organization can be used. The business is not recognized as a separate entity for tax purposes. The profits or losses of the business are simply treated as your personal income or losses as owner, and taxed accordingly.

Partnership. The partnership form of business is similar to the proprietorship, except that the business has more than one owner. The owners do not apply for a corporate charter, which would give the business legal status as a separate entity. For tax purposes, the income and losses of the business are divided equally or by some other formula agreed to by the owners. The owners then pay tax on their shares of the business income (or have their taxable income reduced by the amount of their share of the losses), regardless of whether any income is actually distributed to them. The partnership form is attractive for a business that is expected to suffer losses in its early years.

Limited Partnership. A disadvantage of the partnership is that partners are fully liable for claims against the business in the event of its failure. In a limited partnership, certain investors, designated limited partners, put up money but take no part in running the business. In the event of default, these limited partners are not liable to creditors, and cannot lose more than their original investment. However, the limited partners are still able to deduct their share of the losses of the business from their other personal income. Real estate ventures and other businesses commonly referred to as "tax shelters" are generally set up as limited partnerships, with the general partner being a corporation.[12]

S Corporations. An S corporation has a charter from the state, like any other corporation, but is treated like a partnership for income tax purposes. This arrangement allows owners of a business to enjoy the benefits of limited personal liability offered by a corporation while enjoying the tax benefits of a partnership. An S corporation can have no more than thirty-five shareholders, so this form is generally limited to relatively small businesses. Many businesses are started as S corporations so that early losses can be used to reduce the taxable income of investors holding the stock, and then converted to regular "C" corporation tax status when they become profitable.

TAXATION OF PERSONAL INCOME

Personal tax rules are important for both investment and financing decisions of businesses. Partnership, proprietorship, and S corporate income is taxed at personal tax rates. Furthermore, the tax status of investors is important if you are planning the financing mix for a regular C corporation. The major components of taxable income for an individual (or household paying tax as a unit) are shown in Table 9.7.

Like corporations, individuals face a progressive tax structure, with the tax *rate* rising as income rises. Current tax laws have an initial 15 percent rate that increases to 28 percent and 31 percent and tops out at 39.6 percent on income over approximately $250,000. For income above $250,000, a 3.6 percent (10 percent of 36 percent) surtax is applied. This was the much-talked-about "millionaire's" tax. The actual tax brackets applicable for each percentage have been adjusted for inflation yearly since 1988.

Taxation of Gains and Losses on Sale of Assets. Gains or losses on the sale of assets are treated slightly differently for individuals than for corporations. Gains on the sale of depreciable assets held for more than twelve months are subject to the recapture of MACRS depreciation. Losses are not subject to recapture.

---

[12]In the Tax Reform Act of 1986, the losses from many partnerships are classified as "passive losses." These losses can be used only to offset income from similar activities.

| **TABLE** **9.7** **CALCULATION OF PERSONAL TAXABLE INCOME**

This table summarizes the components of taxable personal income under current tax law.

Wages
+ Interest and dividend income
± Taxpayer's share of profit or loss from a partnership or proprietorship
+ Other categories of income such as rents and royalties
= Gross income
− Qualified deductions
= Adjusted gross income
− Personal exemptions
− Itemized deductions[a] or standard deduction, whichever is greater
= TAXABLE INCOME

[a]Primarily interest expense for a home mortgage, charitable contributions, medical expenses beyond some percent of income, and some taxes paid to state and local governments.

Most of these gains and losses receive capital gains treatment. The maximum capital gains tax rate for individuals is currently 20 percent. But this is scheduled to decrease in steps in the coming years. Capital losses can be used to offset capital gains. Any net capital loss, after netting against capital gains, can be deducted from ordinary income up to a maximum of $3,000 per year. Any remaining amount can be carried forward indefinitely.

STATE AND LOCAL INCOME TAXES |

Many state and municipal governments levy income taxes in addition to the federal income tax. These taxes are hardly trivial, as evidenced by the $325 million in tax concessions Toyota negotiated in developing plans for an automobile factory in Kentucky. State and local income taxes are generally a percentage of income taxable for federal tax purposes. State and local taxes other than sales tax are deducted in arriving at taxable income for federal taxes, so the *effective* state and local income tax rate is the state and local income tax rate multiplied by (1 − federal tax rate).

NON-INCOME TAXES |

Businesses are subject to a number of taxes besides income tax. Property taxes levied by state and local governments must often be considered when evaluating capital investments, as must excise taxes (taxes based on amount sold), extraction taxes levied on mineral removal, and personnel-related taxes such as social security, unemployment, and workmen's compensation. These taxes vary by state and locality as well as by type of business, so generalization is difficult. If one is moving into a new locale or type of business, information about local and industry-specific taxes must be obtained. This frequently means turning to tax experts in the area.

CHOICE OF TAX FORM |

Organizational form, like depreciation methods, can be chosen to minimize the present value of taxes. Taxes are computed for both a corporate and a personal tax form, and then the form with the lower present value of taxes is chosen.

Example. C. Jones is starting a new business on January 1, 1999. His income from other sources is such that Jones's marginal tax rate is 28 percent. Jones has a choice between setting up the business as an ordinary C corporation or an S corporation. Jones, who will be the sole stockholder, plans to plow all profits back into this business for the foreseeable future. Income before tax and taxes paid using the S form and corporate form are in Table 9.8. Year-end cash flows are assumed, and the required return is 10 percent.

In this example, the benefit of being able to use the 1999 loss to reduce personal income tax is more than offset by the higher tax rate that Jones must pay on later income; the present value of taxes is lower using the corporation tax form.

| TABLE 9.8 CORPORATE AND PERSONAL INCOME TAX EXAMPLE

This table is a present value comparison of taxes that would be paid on the income from a business if taxed as corporate income and if taxed as personal income.

PERSONAL TAX—S CORPORATION

Year	1999	2000	2001	2002	2003
Income before tax	−50,000	0	30,000	40,000	80,000
Personal income tax on income	−14,000	0	8,400	11,200	22,400
Present value factor	.9091	.8264	.7513	.6830	.6209
Present value	−12,727	0	6,311	7,650	13,908
Total present value of income tax = $15,142					

CORPORATE TAX—C CORPORATION

Year	1999	2000	2001	2002	2003
Income before tax	−50,000	0	30,000	40,000	80,000
Tax loss carry-forward	—	—	30,000	20,000	—
Taxable income	—	—	—	20,000	80,000
Income tax paid	—	—	—	3,000	15,450
Present value factor				.6830	.6209
Present value				$2,049	$9,593
Total present value of income tax = $11,642					

Another alternative is available though. Jones could start the company as an S corporation and convert to regular C corporation tax in 2001. Using this approach, the taxes would be as follows:

Year	1999	2000	2001	2002	2003
Income before tax	−50,000	0	30,000	40,000	80,000
Personal income tax	−14,000				
Corporate income tax			4,500	6,000	15,450
Present value factor	.9091	.8264	.7513	.6830	.6209
Present value	−12,727	0	3,381	4,098	9,593
Total present value = $4,345					

Using present value analysis, the best choice in this example is to start out as an S corporation and then switch to regular C corporate tax form by 2001.

TIMING OF TAX PAYMENTS |

The exact timing of tax payments is sometimes important for present value analysis. Corporations are required to make estimated tax payments on the 15th day of the fourth, sixth, ninth, and twelfth months of their fiscal year (April 15, June 15, September 15, and December 15 for calendar-year payers). These payments must generally be equal in size and total the lesser of 100 percent of the prior year's taxes or 100 percent of the current year's taxes.

Individuals paying tax on a calendar-year basis must make estimated tax payments on April 15, June 15, September 15, and then January 15 of the following year. These payments, combined with income tax withheld from wages, must generally be equal and must generally total 90 percent of the tax liability for the year or 100 percent of the prior year's tax liability, with the balance due April 15 of the following year. For individuals earning over $150,000, the floor is raised to 110 percent of the prior year's taxes.

Tax payments and benefits are sometimes delayed because of disputes with the Internal Revenue Service. It took Herb Alpert and Lani Hall 10 years, for example, to get a court ruling in their favor for the depreciation schedule for their Hyatt Hotel near the Los Angeles Airport.[13]

FOREIGN CAPITAL INVESTMENT |

Tax rates differ markedly from country to country, and businesses sometimes operate multinationals to take advantage of tax rate differences. Some countries give tax incentives to attract business, and companies may be able to allocate in-

[13]*Wall Street Journal* (April 1, 1987): 1.

come among countries by changing the price at which goods they produce in one country are sold to a division in another country: for example, engines built in Mexico and imported to the United States for assembly into cars. In addition, import duties are avoided by producing in the country in which the goods are to be sold. The Honda plant in Marysville, Ohio, allows Honda to avoid shipping costs and import duties as well as decreasing exchange rate risk and improving its public image. It is estimated by a tax study group, for example, that over a third of the jobs in Puerto Rico are accounted for by companies moving there to get breaks on their federal taxes.

TAXES AND INTERNATIONAL INVESTMENT ANALYSIS

Corporations doing business in more than one country typically pay tax in each country. Taxation by the U.S. government of multinational corporation income is treated first, followed by taxation by foreign countries.

Taxation by the U.S. Government. If foreign activities of a U.S. corporation are carried out through a division that is not separately incorporated, all income is taxed as U.S. income, just as if it were earned in the United States. Foreign subsidiaries are frequently used for this reason. The U.S. corporation is then simply a stockholder—possibly the only stockholder—of a foreign corporation. Income is taxed in the United States only when it is paid to the U.S. parent in the form of dividends. Unlike income received by a corporation from another domestic corporation, dividends from the foreign subsidiary are not eligible for dividend exclusion and are fully taxable income.[14]

Taxation by Foreign Countries. It is more difficult to summarize taxation by foreign countries. Virtually all countries tax income of foreign companies operating in their country. But methods of measuring income and methods of deciding what income was earned in what country vary widely. Developed countries charge higher tax rates while less developed countries often charge lower tax rates to encourage business. Property tax, sales tax, etc., are also common. Value added tax is common in Europe. The value added tax is similar to a sales tax, except that it is applied to the increase in value rather than total value. If you buy bicycle parts for a total cost of $50 and sell the finished bicycle for $120, you pay a value added tax on $70.

Coordination of Taxes between Countries. When a U.S. corporation pays income tax to a foreign government, its U.S. tax on that income is reduced by the amount paid to the foreign government. Suppose, for example, that a corporation earns $1 million in Malaysia and pays Malaysian income tax of $300,000. The company's U.S. tax on that income would be $340,000. But U.S. tax is reduced by the $300,000 paid to Malaysia, so only $40,000 is paid to the U.S. government.

---

[14]In some cases, the domestic corporation will be required to pay tax on unrepatriated income of the subsidiary. This results from rules designed to discourage use of foreign subsidiaries solely to avoid tax.

Similar provisions apply to dividends received from foreign subsidiaries, but property taxes, sales taxes, etc., are not offset. The United States has treaties with many countries governing the amount of tax collected from corporations by each country.

ESTIMATING CASH FLOWS FROM INTERNATIONAL CAPITAL INVESTMENTS

The estimation of cash flows from international capital investments is not essentially different from that of domestic investments. In both cases, we are looking for increases in revenue, expense, and balance sheet accounts. Additional considerations faced when computing the cash-flow effects of international capital investments include exchange rate changes and restrictions on capital flows. We will consider both of these aspects of international investment analysis in the following paragraphs.

Exchange Rates and International Cash-Flow Analysis

A U.S. corporation must evaluate capital investments in terms of their ultimate ability to generate cash flows for stockholders in the United States, and exchange rates are a key factor in that evaluation. Once cash flows from a foreign business are forecasted in the currency of the foreign country, they can be converted to U.S. dollars based on the expected exchange rate. In today's newspaper, the South Korean won is valued at $0.001237. Thus, 1 billion won would be converted to 1 billion × .001237 = $1,237,000 today. Unfortunately, exchange rates are highly volatile, and it is extremely difficult to predict future exchange rates. Thus, prediction of the dollar value of future cash flows is difficult. Methods of analyzing and dealing with exchange rate risk are treated in the next chapter.

Repatriation and International Cash-Flow Analysis

The analysis is sometimes confused by uncertainty as to whether cash flows for a capital investment will be reinvested in the foreign country or repatriated. As long as there are no restrictions on cash flows, though, analysis of a capital investment does not depend on the country in which earnings from that investment will be used. A new investment in Italy will be equally attractive whether funded by dollars that could be converted to lira or lira that could be converted to dollars.

Example. American International Motors (AIM) is an American corporation that specializes in automobile dealerships in foreign countries. AIM is considering a Cadillac dealership in Riyadh, Saudi Arabia, to be incorporated as a wholly owned subsidiary. The dealership will require a capital outlay of 17.5 million riyal. The current exchange rate is $0.2667 per riyal, and the riyal is expected to increase in value 5 percent a year against the dollar. Sales are expected to be 37.5 million riyal a year, and cash flow after Saudi tax is expected to be 15 percent of sales. This cash flow will be paid to the U.S. parent corporation as year-end dividends, and then taxed at the 34 percent tax rate. Management wants to use a 5-year planning horizon and a 15 percent required return. It is assumed that the after-tax salvage value, after all taxes, will be $3 million. The present value analysis of this investment appears in Table 9.9.

Suppose AIM anticipates starting another dealership in Jidda within a few years. Cash flows from the Riyadh dealership could be used to fund the Jidda dealership, but that possibility does not affect the attractiveness of the Riyadh dealership. The analysis of the Jidda dealership is the same whether based on riyal that could be converted to dollars or dollars that will be converted to riyal.

The picture is more complicated when there are restrictions on repatriation of profits. These restrictions may be absolute or may be in the form of taxes to discourage repatriation. In these cases, the attractiveness of investments still depends on cash flows for the company's stockholders, given these restrictions. An absolute, permanent restriction on repatriation makes a foreign investment worthless. In the case of taxes or temporary restrictions, cash flow going into a country must be evaluated in light of the expected cash flows back out of that country. This may force investments to be interrelated when they would otherwise be independent.

Example. Suppose that Saudi Arabia places restrictions on capital flows such that funds cannot be taken out of the country before 2004. The Riyadh dealership would then be evaluated based on the present value of cash flows in 2004. To complete this analysis, it is necessary to make an assumption about rates of return that can be earned when cash flows from the dealership are reinvested in

| TABLE 9.9 PRESENT VALUE ANALYSIS OF RIYADH AUTOMOBILE DEALERSHIP

This table shows the present value analysis of an automobile dealership in Riyadh, assuming a 5 percent annual increase in the value of the riyal (numbers are in thousands).

	1999	2000	2001	2002	2003	2004
Riyal value	$0.2667	$0.2800	$0.2940	$0.3087	$0.3242	$0.3404
Sales (riyal)	37,500	37,500	37,500	37,500	37,500	
Outlay (riyal)	17,500					
Riyal flow	(17,500)	5,625	5,625	5,625	5,625	5,625
Dollar flow	($4,667)	$1,575	$1,654	$1,737	$1,823	$1,915
U.S. tax		536	562	590	620	651
Salvage						3,000
U.S. flow	($4,667)	$1,040	$1,092	$1,146	$1,204	$4,264
P.V. factor (15%)	1.0000	0.8696	0.7561	0.6575	0.5718	0.4972
Present value	($4,667)	$904	$825	$753	$688	$2,120

NPV = $624

Saudi Arabia. Suppose the opportunity rate is expected to average 6 percent. The net present value is then determined as follows.

2004 riyal = 5,625FVA|$_{5yrs,6\%}$ =	31,709 Riyal
2004 value of riyal	$\times$ .3403
2004 dollars	$10,790
−U.S. tax (.34 × 10,790)	3,669
+Salvage value	3,000
Total 2004 dollar flow	$10,121
Present value at 15%	5,032
−Original outlay	4,667
Net present value	$ 365

The temporary restriction on repatriation is not sufficient to make this investment unattractive, but it does cut the net present value almost in half.

SUMMARY

This chapter is a distillation of thousands of pages of laws, regulations, and rulings that focus on the main tax principles affecting capital investments.

At the time a capital investment is made, the investment itself is generally not treated as an expense for tax purposes. This rule holds for both long-term physical assets and working capital. It also holds for intangibles, such as patent rights. The only items that can generally be treated as expenses are things normally recognized as ongoing expenses of a business, such as advertising and training.

During the use life of a capital investment, increases in sales or other revenues are typically the major sources of increased taxable income. Expenses that reduce taxable income include materials, labor, overhead costs, interest, rent, and depreciation. Depreciation is a recognition of the wearing out of an asset and is computed based on guidelines provided by the Internal Revenue Service.

When an asset used in a business is sold at its cost—remaining basis for depreciable assets—the sale generally has no tax implications. When an asset used in a business is sold for more than its remaining basis, the gain is generally an increase in taxable income. If an asset is sold for less than the remaining basis, the loss is a decrease in taxable income.

Companies face many opportunities to control their tax expense. Based on expected income patterns, they can choose between MACRS accelerated and straight-line depreciation. They can choose between being taxed as corporations or having income treated as if it were income of the owners. They can also control the timing of asset sales, and therefore the year in which gains or losses are recognized. The loss carry-back and carry-forward is another of the provisions that can be used in planning. The general objective of a value-maximizing business is to choose the set of tax treatments that maximizes net present value.

Replacement decisions require special care in the identification of relevant cash flows. When an asset is actually worn out, the potential salvage value is not a relevant cost because the asset will be sold regardless. If replacement of a used but usable asset is being considered, the forgone sale price of that asset is a relevant cost of its use.

International capital investments are evaluated in the same general way as domestic capital investments. The primary difference is that the ultimate measure of cash flow is the cash flow that can be repatriated to the home country, in the currency of that home country. The equity residual cash-flow method (discussed in Chapter 4) can be used to evaluate foreign investments because it provides a relatively easy way to deal with the variety of tax differences and exchange rate changes that affect foreign investments.

QUESTIONS

9–1. What are the major additions to the income of a business?

9–2. What are the major expenses that serve to reduce the income of a business?

9–3. Summarize the main tax considerations at the time an asset is acquired.

9–4. What are the tax implications if working capital is liquidated at cost? below cost? above cost?

9–5. If a piece of machinery is sold for more or less than its remaining basis, what are the tax implications?

9–6. Briefly explain the loss carry-back and carry-forward provisions. What types of businesses are helped by these provisions?

9–7. If a corporation pays 40 percent income tax as a corporation, what portion of its income is treated as income of the owners? How could this double taxation of income be avoided?

9–8. Under what conditions would it be preferable to avoid taxation as a corporation and have the income of a business considered income of the owners?

9–9. What are some of the main types of taxes, other than income taxes, that are levied on businesses?

9–10. Under what conditions is the trade-in value of an existing asset relevant in the analysis of a new asset?

PROBLEMS

9–1. Macon Corporation spent $30,000 on training and advertising expenses as part of its development of the new business activity. Dixon Corporation did not spend any money on training and advertising related to it new business activity. Both Macon and Dixon earned $60,000 before training and advertising expenses and both are in the 40 percent tax bracket. What are Macon's taxable income, net income, and cash flow? What are Dixon's taxable income, net income, and cash flow? How much did the $30,000 in training and advertising actually cost Macon in terms of cash flow?

9–2. Pocatello Corporation had sales of $100,000. The cost of goods sold was $60,000, administrative expenses were $20,000, and depreciation was $10,000. What were Pocatello's taxable income, net income, and cash flow?

9–3. Lewiston Corporation placed a $100,000 piece of equipment in service on January 1, 1999. This equipment has a five-year life for tax purposes. The company's marginal income tax rate is 40 percent. By how much will depreciation reduce 1999 income tax?

9–4. Albion Corporation is taxed on the accrual basis. The company buys inventory for $100 in 1999 and pays for the inventory in 2000. The company spends $50 on advertising in 2000, which results in the sale of the inventory for $200. The inventory is sold on credit, and payment is actually received in 2001. What is the taxable income from these actions in each year?

9–5. Charleston Corporation has a choice between using five-year MACRS depreciation or straight-line depreciation at the rate of $200,000 per year for the acquisition of a new $1,000,000 computer system. The system will be placed in service in 1999. Charleston expects the marginal tax rates shown below. Using a 10 percent required return, which depreciation method should be chosen?

Year	1999	2000	2001	2002	2003	2004
Marginal tax rate	15%	15%	40%	40%	40%	40%

9–6. Fairmont Stores began operations on January 1, 1999 (assets are considered to be placed in service on that date). The store cost $1 million, fixtures cost $200,000 (with a seven-year tax life) and the land cost $200,000, all paid for in 1998. Inventory was acquired on credit terms in 1998 at a cost of $500,000, with payment actually made in 1999. During 1999, additional inventory of $300,000 was acquired, with $200,000 of that inventory actually paid for in 1999. Sales in 1999 were $1 million, with $900,000 of payment actually received; the balance was still due on charge accounts. There was $200,000 worth of inventory still on hand at the end of 1999. Fairmont experienced labor, utility, maintenance, advertising, and insurance expenses totaling $100,000 in 1999, with 90 percent of these expenses paid during the year and the balance still owed. The company is to be taxed as a corporation. Please prepare the 1999 year-end abbreviated balance sheet, income statement, and cash flow statement for Fairmont using accrual tax basis accounting. (Hint: The value of inventory sold during the year equals beginning inventory, plus purchases, minus ending inventory.)

9–7. Sales for Fairmont (problem 6) increase to $1.2 million in 2000, with cost of goods sold being the same percentage of sales as before. Other operating expenses, except depreciation, remain at $100,000. Accounts payable for inventory was $120,000, ending inventory was $220,000, $100,000 in accounts payable for operating expenses, and inventory purchases were $149,000. Please prepare the 2000 year-end abbreviated balance sheet, income statement, and cash flow statement for Fairmont using accrual tax basis accounting.

9–8. In early 2001, Fairmont (problem 6) decided that it needed all new fixtures. Two of the old fixtures were sold for $60,000. What are the tax implications of this sale?

9–9. Suppose the fixtures in problem 8 had been sold for $250,000. What would be the tax implications of the sale?

9–10. Urbana Cleaning Service, Inc., a C corporation, bought its own building for $200,000 on January 1, 1999. Urbana sold the building on January 1, 2002, a year in which Urbana was in the 40 percent marginal tax bracket. What would be the tax implications if the building was sold for $100,000? $150,000? $250,000?

9–11. Carbondale Corporation places a $100,000, five-year piece of equipment into service on December 31, 1999. The asset was sold for $20,000 on January 1, 2003, a year in which Carbondale was in the 40 percent marginal tax bracket. What are the tax implications of this sale?

9–12. Interstate Airlines started business in 1999. Taxable income in 1999 through 2003 is shown below, before adjusting for loss carry-back and carry-forward. Determine the income tax that would be paid by Interstate in each year using a 40% tax rate.

Year	1999	2000	2001	2002	2003
Taxable income	−100,000	−20,000	50,000	100,000	200,000

9–13. Suppose Interstate (problem 12) was organized as an S corporation with stock held by individuals in 28 percent tax brackets.
   a. Compute the tax implications each year for the stockholders.
   b. Suppose, further, that the company did not intend to pay out any dividends in the foreseeable future. Should it change from S to regular corporate status during this five-year period? If so, when?

9–14. DeKalb-Normal Corporation received taxable income of $100,000 from its operations in 1999. In addition, the company received dividends of $40,000 from an investment in the stock of another corporation. Compute DeKalb-Normal's income tax liability for 1999. (Assume 50 percent ownership and a 40 percent tax bracket.)

9–15. Peoria Industries, Inc., has income of $100,000 a year. The company is in a state that applies a 5 percent tax to all corporate income over $25,000 and pays state income tax accordingly. What is Peoria's total federal income tax for the year? What is Peoria's marginal income tax rate?

9-16. The average holder of Peoria Industries stock (problem 15) is in a 33 percent combined federal and state income tax bracket and holds stock in a number of other companies. Peoria pays out all of its after-tax income in the form of dividends. What is the total of federal and state income tax, both corporate and personal, on Peoria's income? What could Peoria do to reduce this tax burden?

9-17. A farmer near Bloomington owns a combine and uses it to provide harvesting service to other farmers. He receives revenue of $40,000 a year, plus the avoidance of $2,000 in fees he would have to pay someone else to harvest his wheat if he did not own the machine. Fuel and repairs are $10,000 a year and the farmer does not have another profitable use for the time he spends harvesting wheat. Unfortunately, the existing combine is worn out and fully depreciated. It can be sold for its $1,000 spare parts value, but a dealer will allow $5,000 as a trade-in allowance on a new $100,000 combine. The new combine will last for an estimated 10 years, after which it will have a negligible salvage value. The farmer is in a 28 percent tax bracket and requires 10 percent after-tax return on investments. Is the new combine an attractive investment? (Assume January 1 installation.)

9-18. Campus Dry-cleaning has an on-campus location with 10 years to go on the lease. An existing dry-cleaning machine will last for the 10-year duration of the lease, at which time it will be worn out and worthless. A new machine will be more efficient and allow the company to handle a broader range of fabrics. As a result, the new machine will increase revenues by $1,500 a year and decrease operating costs other than depreciation by $600 a year. The old machine, which is fully depreciated, could be sold for $6,000 today. The new machine will cost $20,000. The lease is not renewable and the new machine is expected to have a salvage value of $5,000 in 10 years. Campus Dry-cleaning is in a 34 percent tax bracket and the required return on new investments is 10 percent. Should Campus Dry-cleaning acquire the new machine?

9-19. For the new dry-cleaning machine in problem 18, redo the analysis assuming the lease can be renewed indefinitely and the new machine will last 15 years with no salvage value at the end of 15 years.

9-20. A rental house in Iowa City can be purchased for $40,000, with closing to occur on January 1, 1993. Closing costs will be $2,000, half of which will be treated as expenses and half of which will be treated as capital investments. The house can be rented for $450 a month. Insurance, maintenance, etc., are expected to average $100 a month. The house will be held for five years and is not expected to increase or decrease in value. Is this an attractive investment for an investor in a 33 percent tax bracket who wants to earn a 10 percent after-tax return?

9-21. For the rental house in problem 20, assume the investor will use $6,000 of his own money and borrow the remaining $36,000 at a 12 percent annual interest rate. The loan has a 30-year maturity and calls for payments of $370.30 at the end of each month. Is the investment attractive if the investor wants to earn a 15 percent return on his equity investment?

9–22. A capital investment costs $1 million New Zealand dollars today and will generate cash flow of $2 million New Zealand dollars in five years. The New Zealand dollar is presently worth U.S. $0.5772. Assuming the U.S. company making this investment has a 10 percent cost of capital and does not hedge the exchange rate risk, what is the net present value for each of the following prices of the New Zealand dollar in five years?

   a. $0.5772

   b. $0.75

   c. $0.40

9–23. An investment in the United States will cost $1 million and will generate after-tax cash flows of $500,000 at the end of each year for three years, after deducting income tax of $100,000 a year. By investing in a foreign country, taxes can be cut in half. The cost of capital is 10 percent and exchange rate risk will not be hedged. The value of a unit of the foreign currency in the spot market is $0.50. What is the minimum average value of the foreign currency over the next three years that will make the foreign investment more profitable than the domestic alternative?

9–24. At the present time, 7.8 Hong Kong dollars are worth one U.S. dollar. An asset costs $1 million Hong Kong dollars. What is the cost in U.S. dollars?

9–25. The Philippine peso is currently worth $0.04871. A capital investment costs one million pesos and provides two million pesos at the end of five years. If the exchange rate does not change, what is the internal rate of return for a U.S. company acquiring this asset? If the peso declines to .04 by the end of five years, what is the internal rate of return for a U.S. company acquiring this asset?

9–26. (**Ethical considerations**) Section 162(m) of the Revenue Reconciliation Act of 1993 sets a $1 million limit on the deductibility of compensation paid to the chief executive officer and the next four highest-paid managers. This tax does not apply to commissions based on performance, bonuses paid for attaining performance goals approved by the shareholders, and payments to a qualified retirement plan.

   a. Assume that there is a competitive market for executives, and that the average compensation package is in excess of $1 million. In terms of wealth, will this provision in the tax law create wealth or shift wealth among the stakeholders? Explain.

   b. As a result of this provision, many corporations are placing performance measures in their proxy statements so that bonuses are "performance based" and, thus, exempt from the new provision. Assuming that the performance measures are set at levels at or below current performance, is it ethical for the corporation to include these performance measures in the proxy statements?

   c. Is this an ethical role for government or should this be the responsibility of outside directors on the board of directors? Explain.

CASE PROBLEM |

B and F Computer Repair (A)

Jane Burns and Carl Foster started a computer store several years ago. The first couple of years were excellent, but then they began to feel the pressure of increasing competition; volume and profit margins plummeted. After paying themselves $20,000 salaries each, they were just breaking even.

Burns and Foster noticed, though, that the computer repair business was not nearly as competitive. Most retailers wanted to sell computers and considered repair an annoyance. Burns and Foster considered leaving the retail business and starting a repair business. They would handle the management and marketing, hiring technicians to do the repairing, primarily on-sight. There were several technical schools offering training in computer repair, so they did not anticipate difficulty in finding trained technicians.

Burns and Foster hired a consultant to help them prepare forecasts and a feasibility study. The consultant charged $3,000 for a study that provided most of the numbers they would need for their final decision.

The test equipment and inventory for each technician would cost approximately $15,000 and $7,000, respectively. The technicians would be required to own their own vehicles. An office and small repair shop space could be rented in an industrial area for $1,000 a month, including rent and utilities. Special inventory and special test equipment at that location would cost $20,000 and $15,000 respectively. This special inventory and test equipment would have a five-year tax life and could support up to two dozen technicians. Technicians could be hired for $2,000 a month, including fringe benefits and social security tax. The company could bill $50 per hour for a technician's time and could probably bill 30 hours per week per technician. Parts sales would be $20 per hour of billed time and the cost of parts sold would average 60 percent of sale price. Average collection period on revenues would be 55 days. Prepaid expenses would be 5 percent of revenue. Inventory would be purchased for cash. Accounts payable and accrued expenses would be 4 percent of revenue. Cash balances will be $10,000.

Burns and Foster expected to hire four technicians immediately, four more at the end of the first full year of operation, eight at the end of the second year, and four more at the end of the third year. They did not expect demand to grow beyond those twenty technicians.

The lease on the store ended December 31, so they could use that as their closing date, starting the new business on January 1. This would give them the next several months to start contacting businesses to sell the repair service, and to start hiring technicians. They could run the repair business out of the retail store until the end of the year and be fully operational by January 1. Repair revenue during the transition period would probably cover marginal costs for the period.

One area of concern was the loss they would suffer in closing the old store. Inventory valued at $135,000 would be sold at a going-out-of-business sale for no more than $100,000. Fixtures in the store had a remaining book value of $20,000 for accounting purposes and $12,000 for tax purposes. These fixtures would be worthless and would be written off. In addition, closing the old store would force them to repay their only debt—a $50,000 bank loan secured by the inventory.

Burns and Foster wanted to use a 15 percent required return and a 10-year time horizon with no salvage value for fixed assets to evaluate the investment. They did not want to assume a perpetual life in such a volatile field. The business would be set up as a subchapter S corporation. Burns and Foster were both in 28 percent tax brackets due to other family income.

CASE QUESTIONS

1. What is the significance of the loss on closing the old store?
2. Identify all relevant cash flows.
3. Compute the net present value.
4. What are some of the things that could go wrong in this business?
5. Should Burns and Foster switch from retail sales to computer repair?

SELECTED REFERENCES

Amoako-Adu, Ben, and M. Rashid. "Corporate Tax Cut and Capital Budgeting." *The Engineering Economist* 35 (Winter 1990): 115–128.

Ang, James. "Tax Asymmetries and the Optimal Investment Decision of the Firm." *The Engineering Economist* 32 (Winter 1987): 135–161.

Ben-Horim, Moshe, Shalom Hochman, and Oded Palmon. "The Impact of the 1986 Tax Reform Act on Corporate Financial Policy." *Financial Management* 16 (Autumn 1987): 29–35.

Caks, John. "Sense and Nonsense about Depreciation." *Financial Management* 10 (Autumn 1981): 80–86.

Claire Crutchley, Enyang Guo, and Robert S. Hansen. "Stockholder Benefits from Japanese-U.S. Joint Ventures." *Financial Management* 20 (Winter 1991): 22–30.

Cooper, Ian, and Julian R. Franks. "The Interaction of Financial and Investment Decisions When the Firm Has Unused Tax Credits." *Journal of Finance* 38 (May 1983): 571–583.

Dammon, Robert M., and Lemma W. Senbet. "The Effect of Taxes and Depreciation on Corporate Investment and Financial Leverage." *Journal of Finance* 43 (June 1988): 357–373.

Emery, Douglas R., Wilbur G. Lewellen, and David C. Mauer. "Tax-Timing Options, Leverage, and the Choice of Corporate Form." *The Journal of Financial Research* 11 (Summer 1988): 99–110.

Gordon, Roger H. "Can Capital Income Taxes Survive in Open Economies?" *Journal of Finance* 47 (July 1992): 1159–1180.

Graham, Edward M., and Paul R. Krugman. *Foreign Direct Investment in the United States.* Washington, D.C.: Institute for International Economics, 1991.

Heaton, Hal. "On the Bias of the Corporate Tax against High-Risk Projects." *Journal of Financial and Quantitative Analysis* 22 (September 1987): 365–371.

Hodder, James E. "Evaluation of Manufacturing Investments: A Comparison of U.S. and Japanese Practices." *Financial Management* 15 (Spring 1986): 17–24.

Hoffman, Michael J. R., and Bart P. Hartman. "Recent Changes in Tax Law and the Uncertainties in Capital Budgeting Decisions." *Business Horizons* 30 (January–February 1987): 12–19.

John, Kose, Lemma W. Senbet, and Anant K. Sundaram. "Cross-Border Liability of Multinational Enterprises, Border Taxes, and Capital Structure." *Financial Management* 20 (Winter 1991): 54–67.

Kim, Ji Soo, Il Geon Yoo, and Ju Chull Park. "Valuation of Income Producing Assets with Income Tax Consideration." *The Engineering Economist* 35 (Spring 1990): 173–190.

Malony, Kevin J., and Thomas I. Selling. "Simplifying Tax Simplification: An Analysis of Its Impact on the Profitability of Capital Investment." *Financial Management* 14 (Summer 1985): 33–42.

McCarty, Daniel E., and William R. McDaniel. "A Note on Expensing Versus Depreciating under the Accelerated Cost Recovery System: Comment." *Financial Management* 12 (Summer 1983): 37–39.

Oblak, David J., and Roy J. Helm, Jr. "A Survey and Analysis of Capital Budgeting Methods Used by Multinationals." *Financial Management* 9 (Winter 1980): 37–41.

Porcano, Thomas M. "Factors Affecting the Foreign Direct Investment Decision of Firms from and into Major Industrialized Countries." *Multinational Business Review* 1 (Fall 1993): 26–36.

Pruitt, Stephen W., and Lawrence J. Gitman. "Capital Budgeting and the Fortune 500." *Financial Management* 16 (Spring 1987): 46–51.

Remer, Donald S., and Yong Ho Song. "Depreciation and Tax Policies in the Seven Countries with the Highest Direct Investment from the U.S." *The Engineering Economist* 38 (Spring 1993): 193–208.

Shapiro, Alan C. "Capital Budgeting for the Multinational Corporation." *Financial Management* 7 (Spring 1978): 7–16.

Stanley, Marjorie T., and Stanley B. Block. "A Survey of Multinational Capital Budgeting." *Financial Review* 19 (March 1984): 36–54.

Stultz, R. M. "A Model of International Asset Pricing." *Journal of Financial Economics* 9 (December 1981): 383–406.

CHAPTER 10

INFLATION AND CAPITAL INVESTMENT ANALYSIS

After completing this chapter you should be able to:

1. Describe why inflation is important to capital budgeting.
2. Calculate the constant dollar equivalent price for a stream of cash flows.
3. Recognize the difference between nominal and real interest rates and be able to adjust from one to the other.
4. Identify the influence that inflation has on inventory values.
5. Explain how inflation impacts taxes, debt repayment, and overall economic risk to possibly change shareholder's wealth.
6. List and describe some of the gauges used to measure inflation.
7. Describe how the equivalent annuity technique can be used to choose between mutually exclusive investments in an inflationary environment.
8. Understand the influence that different inflation rates in other countries may have on the cash flows from a foreign subsidiary to the parent company.

The history of Butte, Montana, is closely linked with the copper ore that underlies the area. Prices of copper, like many other commodities, fluctuate with inflation rates and exchange rates. As a result, Butte has experienced numerous booms, followed by busts. The latest nadir of the cycle hit in the mid-1980s. Low inflation rates and a strong dollar drove the price of copper below the cost of bringing it out of the ground. Anaconda Minerals, a major local employer, had closed its last mine by 1986 and was getting out of copper.

By 1988, the dollar had weakened and copper had recovered from $0.60 to $1.10 a pound. Anaconda's mine was reopened by a new owner, who had originally purchased the mine to sell off the scrap equipment. Butte began another cycle of its copper-related history. Civic leaders of Butte also began restructuring the economy to become less dependent on price changes.[1]

Butte and Anaconda are not alone in finding the success of their investments strongly affected by changing prices. They are also not alone in their efforts to predict the impacts of price changes and decrease the sensitivity of their investments to price movements. The issues discussed in this chapter are of interest to most managers who are involved in capital budgeting. This chapter begins with explanations of inflation terminology, including price indexes, current prices, constant dollar prices, nominal return, and real return. Then, the impact of inflation on income and cash flow is discussed. Finally, capital budgeting in the face of inflation is discussed.

Inflation Defined

Inflation is defined as an increase in average prices. Inflation is generally expressed as a percent; if average prices increase from $100 to $106 over the course of a year, the inflation rate is 6 percent. Inflation is often measured using the consumer price index (CPI), which is the price of a "market basket" of goods and services purchased by a typical consumer, stated as a percent of the price at some base period. Numerous other indexes are also used, including the producers' price index and Gross National Product deflator.

Sometimes 1983 is used as a base period for the CPI, and the CPI of 158.6 at the end of 1996 meant that the price of the "market basket" was then 158.6 percent of (1.586 times) the average price in 1983. The consumer price index was 161.3 at the end of 1997. The inflation *rate* for 1997 was therefore $(161.3 - 158.6) \div 158.6 = 1.7$ percent.

Inflation rates have varied sharply from year to year and from country to country. During the early 1930s, the United States and many other countries actually suffered deflation, with average prices declining. Less than a decade later, inflation in Germany was so high that workers demanded pay for the morning's work at noon so that they could spend the money before its value was eroded by the afternoon's inflation. The inflation history of the United States appears in Figure 10.1.

Inflation is, of course, the rate of change in average prices. As the earlier copper example illustrated, prices do not all change at the same rate. The price of ethylene rose faster than the inflation rate in 1987 because of insufficient production capacity. The drought of 1988 caused beef prices to fall during the summer, as farmers culled their herds, and then rise during the winter, as fewer cattle came to market. Walter F. Williams, chairman of Bethlehem Steel Corp., was expecting increased profits in 1988, even though tonnage sales were expected to decline. One reason for optimism was an anticipated increase in the price of steel, relative to the prices of other goods.

[1] *Business Week* (July 16, 1988).

| **F I G U R E 1 0 . 1**   **INFLATION HISTORY OF THE UNITED STATES**

Both inflation rates and levels of the consumer price index appear. These illustrate the instability of inflation rates as well as the long-term effects on prices.

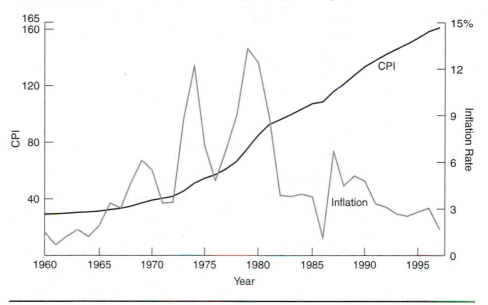

CURRENT AND CONSTANT DOLLAR PRICES |

The *current price* is the price at which an item could be purchased today. The *constant dollar price* is the current price adjusted to buying power at some base time. The constant dollar price, expressed in base year b buying power, is:

$$\text{Constant dollar price} = \frac{\text{Current price}_t}{PI_t \div PI_b} \qquad \text{(10-1)}$$

where PI_t is the price index in year t and PI_b is the price index in year b.

Example. In 1977, Ralston-Purina purchased the floriculture assets of Stratford of Texas for $35 million plus a $10 million, 10-year noninterest-bearing note. The consumer price index in 1977 was 61.1, in relation to the 1983 base of 100. By 1987, the consumer price index was 116.0. The value of the 1987 payment, expressed in 1977 purchasing power, was:

$$\frac{\$10,000,000}{116.0 \div 61.1} = \underline{\$5,267,241}$$

The inflation from 1977 to 1987 reduced the constant dollar cost substantially for Ralston-Purina.

Example. The Dow-Jones Industrial Average (DJIA), a closely followed stock price index, increased from 995 in 1966 to 7,910 in late 1997, while the consumer price index increased from 32.4 in 1966 to 161.3 in late 1997. The 1997 level of the DJIA, expressed in 1966 dollars, was:

$$\text{1997 DJIA (in constant 1966 dollars)} = 7,910 \div (161.3 \div 32.4) = 1,589$$

In buying-power terms, the DJIA actually increased almost 600 points over the 31-year period. Dividends provided additional return so that investors gained even more over the 31-year period. A history of the DJIA, in current and constant dollars, appears in Figure 10.2. Failure to consider inflation gives a misleading picture of the profitability of common stock investments.

Constant and current dollar concepts are also used to forecast future cash flows generated by capital investments. Cash outlays and benefits are often forecasted in constant dollars, and then adjusted to estimate current dollars for future periods.

Example. In 1999 Lawrence Electronics was considering an expansion of its repair shop, to be placed in service on January 1, 2000. Revenue forecasts have been prepared without considering inflation and are, therefore, stated in 1999

| FIGURE 10.2 CURRENT AND CONSTANT DOLLAR STOCK PRICES

This figure shows the Dow-Jones Industrial Average in current dollars and constant (1974) dollars.

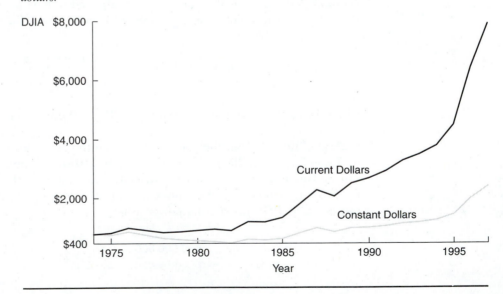

dollars. The revenue forecasts reflect a 5 percent growth in the number of repairs. Assuming the consumer price index averaged 144.1 for 1999, managers expect inflation to average 4 percent a year. Constant (1999) dollar cash flow projections follow, along with projections of the consumer price index. These are used to estimate current dollar revenue for future periods. For example, the expected CPI for 2001 is $144.1(1.04)^2 = 155.9$, and the current dollar revenue forecast for 2001 is:

2001 Current dollar revenue = $105,000(155.9 \div 144.1)$ = **$113,598**

Year	2000	2001	2002	2003
Revenue in 1999 dollars	$100,000	$105,000	$110,250	$115,763
Consumer price index	149.9	155.9	162.1	168.6
Current dollar revenue	$104,000	$113,598	$124,022	$135,445

Using only four years and a fairly modest inflation rate of 4 percent, revenue forecasts would be substantially underestimated if inflation were ignored.

REAL AND NOMINAL INTEREST RATES

Interest rates and required returns in general rise when the inflation rate is expected to be high. The explanation of the increase in interest rates lies in the concept of real and nominal interest rates. The *nominal* interest rate is based on dollar interest paid or expected, and represents a percentage increase in dollars. The *real* interest rate is the percentage increase in buying power achieved when considering the interest rate and inflation. Suppose, for example, a one-year treasury bill pays interest of 12 percent. If you invest $1,000 today, you will have $1,120 in one year. If prices increase 5 percent over the year, goods that cost $1.00 at the beginning of the year will cost $1.05 at the end. You could have used the $1,000 to buy 1,000 units at the beginning of the year. You can use the $1,120 to buy $1,120/$1.05 = 1,066.67 units at the end of the year. Your purchasing power has, therefore, increased $(1,066.67 - 1,000)/1,000 = 6.67$ percent. In other words, the real interest rate was 6.67 percent. The real interest rate (R_{real}) can be computed with a simple formula:[2]

---

[2]The real interest rate is sometimes defined as $R_{nom} - Inf$. This gives a close approximation to the true real interest rate because Equation 10-2 can be rearranged to give:

$$R_{nom} = R_{real} + Inf + R_{real} \, Inf$$

$R_{real}Inf$ is small if inflation rates are modest—for a real interest rate of 6.67 percent and an inflation rate of 5 percent, $R_{real}Inf = .0033$. Ignoring this small term and rearranging the remaining terms gives:

$$R_{real} - R_{nom} - Inf$$

$$R_{real} = \frac{1 + R_{nom}}{1 + Inf} - 1 \qquad\qquad (10\text{-}2)$$

where R_{nom} is the nominal interest rate and *Inf* is the inflation rate. Applying this formula to the example in the previous paragraph, the real interest rate is:

$$R_{real} = \frac{1 + .12}{1 + .05} - 1 = 6.67 \text{ percent}$$

Example. Alabama Power issued new 10 percent bonds in 1997. With an inflation rate of around 3 percent at the time, the real interest rate was:

$$R_{real} = \frac{1 + .10}{1 + .03} - 1 = 6.80 \text{ percent}$$

It is important to differentiate between expected and realized real rates. The *expected* real interest rate or rate of return is computed using the expected nominal rate and the expected inflation rate. The *realized* real rate is based on the nominal rate that has already been earned and the inflation that has already occurred.

Some economic theories are based on the assumption that the real interest rate will be stable, with the nominal rate adjusting to reflect inflation. The idea behind this theory is that both borrowers and lenders will base their negotiations on the real (buying power) impact of their loan contracts. In practice, nominal interest rates do respond strongly to increases in expected inflation, although the correlation between expected inflation and nominal interest rates is not perfect. Uncertainty is one reason the relationship is not perfect. Loan contracts are drawn in light of *expected* inflation, while actual inflation may be substantially different. Furthermore, inflation does not affect all prices equally, and economic activity is affected by inflation. Therefore, risks to both borrowers and lenders increase. Consequently, supply and demand for credit change, with resulting changes in real interest rates. However, real rates, both expected and realized, fluctuate much less than nominal interest rates, as shown in Figure 10.3.

When a business raises money for the purpose of making a capital investment, the return required by investors reflects the inflation expected by those investors. If inflation is ignored in forecasting the benefits from the investment, there will often be substantial errors in the estimates of benefits.

Expected inflation is even more important when the company is considering foreign capital investment because differences in inflation rates between the parent and subsidiary country will impact the exchange rate used to compute the cash flow to the parent. In this next section, we will first examine domestic inflation and then conclude with a discussion of the impacts of inflation on exchange rates and consequently cash flow to the parent.

| **FIGURE 10.3** **REAL AND NOMINAL INTEREST RATES**

This figure shows interest rate history in the United States, based on U.S. Treasury bill interest rates. These rates are adjusted using the consumer price index to give realized real interest rates.

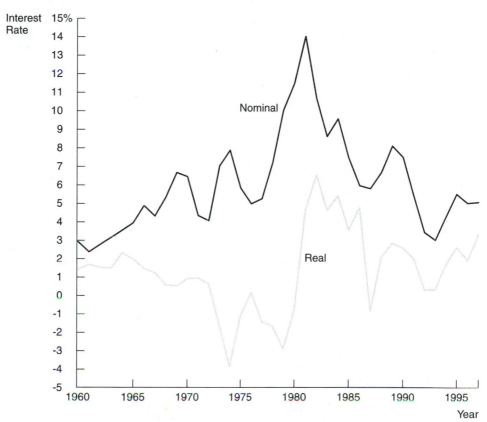

INFLATION AND INCOME |

The relationship between inflation and income is important because reported income matters to investors, because taxes are based on income, and because income statements are often used to develop cash flow estimates. Unfortunately, inflation does not affect income in a simple, direct way. Some prices change by more or less than inflation. Some costs, such as depreciation and interest, are fixed when the asset is acquired, and do not respond to inflation. Some prices tend to lead overall inflation, and some price changes tend to lag behind inflation. Methods of valuing inventory are particularly important in determining the impact of inflation on income.

Inventory Valuation. New Deal stereo store can be used to illustrate the accounting treatment of inventory. New Deal started carrying the RX2 CD player in December 1999. Purchases and sales of the RX2 during the first three months were as follows:

Month		Dec, 99	Jan, 00	Feb, 00
Purchases	Units	1	1	
	Price	$100	$120	
Sales	Units			1
	Price			$130

What was the profit on the February sale? With *first in, first out* (FIFO) accounting, the cost of goods sold is the price of the oldest unit of inventory: $100. With *last in, first out* (LIFO) accounting, the cost is the price of the most recently purchased unit: $120. Profits and value of remaining inventory with FIFO and LIFO are as follows:

	FIFO	LIFO
Sales	$130	$130
Cost of goods sold	100	120
Earnings before tax	30	10
Value of remaining inventory	$120	$100

With either LIFO or FIFO, inflation will increase profit because the cost of goods sold represents a past cost of inventory, not the current cost. FIFO uses an older inventory cost, so the increase will be more pronounced with FIFO. LIFO is generally used for tax purposes because it results in lower reported income, and is often used for public reporting because it is believed to more accurately reflect actual profitability.

Example. For a broader look at inflation and income, consider Topeka Corporation in Table 10.1. There was no inflation in year 1, and inflation is expected to be 10 percent a year thereafter. Topeka sells one unit a year. The sale price will be $1,000 in year 1, and will increase at the general inflation rate each year thereafter. The company keeps two units in stock, and buys a replacement immediately when a unit is sold. The purchase price increases at the inflation rate, and the company uses LIFO inventory accounting. Therefore, the cost of goods sold is the previous year's purchase price. Labor is $200 a year, and increases proportionally with inflation. Depreciation is $100 a year, and is not affected by inflation.

| **TABLE 10.1** FINANCIAL STATEMENTS FOR TOPEKA CORPORATION

There is no inflation in year 1, and inflation is 10 percent in each year thereafter. LIFO inventory valuation is used, and inventory is purchased one year before sale.

Year	1	2	3	4
Sales	$1,000	$1,100	$1,210	$1,331
Cost of goods sold	600	600	660	726
Labor	200	220	242	266
Depreciation	100	100	100	100
Earnings before tax	100	180	208	239
Tax	34	61	71	81
Net income	$ 66	$ 119	$ 137	$ 158

The delay between purchase and sale of inventory is exaggerated in this example to simplify the analysis and highlight the impacts of inflation. The delay between purchase and sale of a unit of inventory is much less than a year for most companies, so inventory valuation does not affect income as dramatically as in this example. However, the direction of change in income is the same as in this example.

While individual companies may experience leads or lags in prices of inputs purchased or output sold, net leads and lags for companies as a group are likely to be small. One company's fixed cost through a long-term contract is often another company's fixed revenue. Furthermore, net leads and lags across all sectors of the economy will be zero; a net lag across the economy would mean a lower inflation rate, for example.

If a company experiences no leads or lags in prices of inputs or outputs, and experiences no changes in volume of output, the effect of inflation is likely to be a growth in income from existing assets that is greater than the inflation rate. Inventory valuation methods increase income, and depreciation expense does not increase with inflation after the asset is acquired.

Accountants have attempted to adjust for the impact of inflation by producing income statements using replacement costs instead of historical costs to compute depreciation and the cost of goods sold. Table 10.2 shows the 1977 return on equity using historical and replacement cost for some sample companies. The inflation was approximately 7 percent in 1977. These numbers clearly illustrate the potentially large magnitude of the impact of inflation, although it should be noted that these are mostly capital-intensive companies for which the impact of inflation on income is greater than average.

Even if inflation increases a company's income, the company is not necessarily better off. First, the increase in income depends on unit sales volume remaining at least constant. High rates of inflation can cause disturbance to the economic system and, therefore, lead to decreased sales volume. Additionally, increased income does not necessarily mean increased cash flow. Replacement inventory must be purchased at ever-higher costs, for example. Finally, inflation

| TABLE 10.2 RETURN ON EQUITY USING HISTORICAL AND REPLACEMENT COST

Returns on equity using historical and replacement cost are shown for 1977, a year in which the inflation rate was 7 percent.

	Historical	Replacement
Alcoa	10.9%	14.6%
Ashland Oil	19.3	9.5
Consolidated Edison	11.7	4.3
General Telephone and Electric	15.0	6.8
Georgia-Pacific	17.1	9.6
Lockheed	25.1	9.3
Missouri Pacific Corporation	23.7	2.4
Procter & Gamble	17.6	10.2
Tenneco	15.0	7.3
Teledyne	29.2	18.1

Source: *Forbes* (June 12, 1978).

causes discount rates to increase and, therefore, decreases the present value of future benefits. We look at cash flow impacts of inflation in the next section and then look at the impact of inflation on value.

INFLATION AND CASH FLOW |

For a given capital investment, cash flows resulting from inflation follow primarily from income changes and working capital changes. These effects can be illustrated by continuing with the previous example of Topeka Corporation from Table 10.1. The company purchases inventory on 1-year credit terms and sells its product on 1-year credit terms. The annual cash flows are shown in Table 10.3. Inventory value represents one original unit at $600, plus one unit bought at the current price. Accounts payable represent the one unit of inventory bought at current prices, and accounts receivable represent the sale price of one unit. Net cash flow is then net income plus depreciation, minus the increase in working capital.

The Topeka Corporation example illustrates the main cash flow issues with regard to inflation and existing capital investments. Net income will generally be expected to increase. However, cash flow may either increase or decrease, depending on how working capital for the particular company is affected. This depends, in turn, on inventory turnover and credit terms for both sales and purchases. Of course, some or all of the working capital may be recovered at the end of the asset's life, but a dollar in the future is less valuable than a dollar today.

The cash flow analysis was performed for existing capital investments. If the outlay for a capital investment is spread over several years, and the price is not

| TABLE 10.3 TOPEKA CORPORATION CASH FLOW ANALYSIS

The company uses LIFO inventory valuation and maintains two units of inventory, with a new unit acquired immediately when a unit is sold. Both purchase and sale are on 1-year credit terms.

Year	1	2	3	4
Sales	$1,000	$1,100	$1,210	$1,331
Cost of goods sold	600	600	660	726
Labor	200	220	242	266
Depreciation	100	100	100	100
Earnings before tax	100	180	208	239
Tax	34	61	71	81
Net income	$ 66	$ 119	$ 137	$ 158
+ Depreciation	100	100	100	100
Inventory	1,200	1,260	1,326	1,399
Accounts receivable	1,000	1,100	1,210	1,331
Accounts payable	600	660	726	799
Net working capital	1,600	1,700	1,810	1,931
− Change in net working capital	0	100	110	121
= Net cash flow	$ 166	$ 119	$ 127	$ 137

contractually determined, the outlay will probably be affected by inflation. Furthermore, the analysis focused on a single capital investment. If an asset is to be replaced at the end of its life, the replacement cost will be higher because of inflation and will, therefore, further reduce cash flows to owners.

DOES INFLATION INCREASE SHAREHOLDER WEALTH? |

The relationship between inflation and shareholder wealth has been studied extensively, with ambiguous results.[3] Reasons for ambiguous results can be understood by reference to Table 10.3. Assuming that the required return increases with an increase in inflation, it is necessary that cash flows increase by enough to provide the same net present value using a higher discount rate. Given constant unit sales, the cash flows may or may not increase, depending on working capital effects. Furthermore, a company is an ongoing concern and must replace assets as they wear out. The higher replacement costs mean that more earnings must be retained in the business to maintain the existing asset level, and the cash flow to owners is reduced.

[3]See the selected references at the end of this chapter for a listing of many of these studies.

Taxes. Taxes are an important issue in determining the value of a company in an inflationary environment. As illustrated in Table 10.3, taxes often rise during inflation periods, even if cash flows decline. Both cost of goods sold and depreciation expenses are based on historical cost, not replacement cost. Therefore, the expense allowed for tax purposes is not sufficient to cover the cash flow for replacement.

Debt. Interest rates for many long-term loans are fixed when the loans are first arranged. Thus, interest expense is a fixed cost once an asset is acquired. If inflation increases unexpectedly after an asset is acquired, and market interest rates rise accordingly, the value of existing debt declines. Shareholders potentially gain at the expense of creditors. Whether this gain is sufficient to offset negative impacts of inflation depends on the characteristics of the particular company.

Economic Distortion. Inflation often leads to economic distortion, with growth slowed for the entire economy or growth increasing in some sectors while decreasing in others. At a minimum, increased inflation results in increased uncertainty. As a result, unit sales may increase or decrease for a particular business when inflation increases. These changes also affect cash flows.

From a review of these various factors, we can draw the firm conclusion that inflation may increase or decrease the value of a particular company. The characteristics of the particular company as well as overall economic conditions are important in predicting whether the value of a particular company will increase or decrease. Empirical studies during recent periods of high inflation suggest that, on average, the value of common stock has declined with increases in inflation rates. This does not mean that the values of all companies decline or that all capital investments become less attractive. The impact of inflation must be considered separately for each proposed investment.

RECOGNIZING INFLATION IN CAPITAL BUDGETING |

To properly deal with inflation, you must recognize expected inflation in the projection of future cash flows and use a discount rate that reflects investors' expectations of future inflation. When your company raises money for the purpose of making a capital investment, the returns required by investors are stated in terms of nominal rates of return. The required returns are affected by interest rates in the financial markets and, therefore, reflect investors' expectations of inflation. Thus the required return should be applied to the actual cash flows expected, not the cash flows adjusted to base period buying power. The required return itself includes the adjustment for buying power loss.

Example. Wichita Corporation purchases an automatic pressure valve for $10,000 on December 31, 1999. The valve has a 5-year tax life and 5-year actual life. The asset will reduce labor expense by $2,800 a year at mid-1999 prices, and labor expense is expected to increase 4 percent a year due to inflation. The required return is 10 percent, which reflects investors' expectations of inflation. Ignoring inflation, the net present value from the investment would be as shown in Table 10.4.

The investment is unattractive because the net present value is negative. But if inflation is recognized in forecasting labor savings, the picture changes. In Table 10.5, expected labor savings are increased by 4 percent each year because the same hours of labor being saved would cost more each year in the future.

| TABLE 10.4 NET PRESENT VALUE ANALYSIS IGNORING INFLATION

Net present value analysis for a $10,000 automatic pressure valve with a 5-year life that will reduce labor expense by $2,800 a year. The required return is 10 percent and the annual cash flows are treated as if they occur at year-end.

Year	1999	2000	2001	2002	2003	2004
Labor savings		$2,800	$2,800	$2,800	$2,800	$2,800
Depreciation	($2,000)	(3,200)	(1,920)	(1,152)	(1,152)	(576)
Change in earnings before tax	(2,000)	(400)	880	1,648	1,648	2,224
Change in tax	680	136	(299)	(560)	(560)	(756)
Change in net income	(1,320)	(264)	581	1,088	1,088	1,468
+ Depreciation	2,000	3,200	1,920	1,152	1,152	576
− Initial outlay	(10,000)					
Net cash flow	(9,320)	2,936	2,501	2,240	2,240	2,044
P.V. factor	1.0000	0.9091	0.8264	0.7513	0.6830	0.6209
Present value	($9,320)	$2,669	$2,067	$1,683	$1,530	$1,269
Net Present Value	($102)					

| TABLE 10.5 NET PRESENT VALUE RECOGNIZING INFLATION

Net present value analysis of the automatic pressure valve analyzed in Table 10.4, recognizing that the $2,800 labor savings are at mid-1999 prices and inflation of wages is expected to be 4 percent a year.

Year	1999	2000	2001	2002	2003	2004
Labor savings		$2,912	$3,028	$3,150	$3,276	$3,407
Depreciation	($2,000)	(3,200)	(1,920)	(1,152)	(1,152)	(576)
Change in earnings before tax	(2,000)	(288)	1,108	1,998	2,124	2,831
Change in tax	680	98	(377)	(679)	(722)	(962)
Change in net income	(1,320)	(190)	731	1,319	1,402	1,869
+ Depreciation	2,000	3,200	1,920	1,152	1,152	576
− Initial outlay	(10,000)					
Net cash flow	(9,320)	3,010	2,651	2,471	2,554	2,445
P.V. factor	1.0000	0.9091	0.8264	0.7513	0.6830	0.6209
Present value	($9,320)	$2,736	$2,191	$1,856	$1,744	$1,518
Net Present Value	$725					

   This investment is attractive when the impact of inflation on future benefits is properly recognized. A profitable investment would be erroneously rejected if inflation were ignored in the analysis.

INFLATION AND CASH FLOW PROJECTION

To project cash flows in light of inflation, you must forecast the inflation rate and estimate the impact of inflation on each component of cash flows. Forecasting the inflation rate is an economic problem well beyond the scope of this book. There are many economic forecasting services that forecast the inflation rate, and methods of forecasting inflation are covered in economics texts.[4] It must be said, though, that accurate forecasts are hard to come by. The following quote from *Forbes* illustrates the problem.

   Monetarist economists and their followers in business and Wall Street have the public half crazy with fears of runaway inflation. Look at how fast the money supply is growing, they say; look how the Fed keeps pushing up interest rates.
   Forbes, whose approach to economics is eclectic rather than doctrinaire, says: "Yes, inflation is higher than it should be but it will slow down in the second half—along with the economy . . . the U.S. is not heading into 8 percent inflation, whatever the money supply figures seem to show."[5]

   This forecast was published in July 1978, and inflation for the second half of 1978 was at almost exactly an 8 percent rate, followed by an unprecedented 13 percent rate in 1979! Inflation rates are directly affected by policies of the central banking system, which are, in turn, responses to economic conditions, political pressures, demographics, and international events. Predicting these various factors and the responses of the central banking system is extremely difficult. A so-called naive forecast, based on average inflation rates in the past, may be as accurate as the results of sophisticated models.
   Once you have acquired an inflation rate forecast, you must estimate the impacts of inflation on various components of cash flow. The relationships between various cash flows and inflation can be summarized as follows:

Unaffected. Some cash flows are totally unaffected by inflation. Depreciation tax shields, for example, are determined by the cost of the asset and the depreciation rules in effect at the time of acquisition, and are unaffected by later inflation. Likewise, a long-term fuel contract, a labor contract, or the purchase of a commodity in the forward markets may lock in the pres-

---

[4]See, for example, Geoffrey H. Moore, *Business Cycles, Inflation, and Forecasting,* 2nd ed. (Cambridge, Mass.: Ballinger Publishing Co., 1983).

[5]"Why Monetarists Are Wrong," *Forbes* (July 10, 1978): 103.

ent price, thereby making other components of cash flow independent of inflation.

Partially affected. Some benefits and costs may increase with inflation, but at a rate less than the inflation rate. Wages in many industries, for example, tend to rise at or above the inflation rate when the inflation rate is low to moderate, but rise at less than the inflation rate when inflation rates are high.

Fully affected. The prices of many consumer products, for example, can be expected to increase at approximately the inflation rate. Material costs can often be expected to respond in a similar way.

Leads and lags. Another important aspect of estimating the impact of inflation is the recognition of leads and lags. Some revenues and expenses may increase by the same percentage as inflation, but not at the same time. Public utility rates, for example, tend to move with the inflation rate, but with lags of six months to a year as the utility companies must apply to public utility commissions for permission to raise their rates.

INFLATION AND THE EQUIVALENT ANNUITY

The value of the equivalent annuity as a ranking tool for mutually exclusive investments with unequal lives was demonstrated in Chapter 7. The equivalent annuity can be used in inflationary environments if inflation over the long term is recognized in the computations. Recall that the equivalent annuity can be defined as the annual cash flow in perpetuity that would have a net present value the same as the net present value of the investment in question if that investment were repeated at the end of its life in perpetuity. Looked at from the other direction, the equivalent annuity can be defined as the present value with perpetual repetition, multiplied by the required return, k.

We assume, for the following analysis, that a constant inflation rate of Inf will occur. Assume the net present value of an investment has been computed with inflation recognized, as was done in Table 10.5, and NPV is used to signify that net present value. Now, place our decision maker at the end of the project's life. If the project is to be repeated, all costs and benefits will have risen, and the new net present value will be $NPV(1 + Inf)^n$ where n is the life of the investment. The equivalent annuity (EA) with perpetual repetition is then:[6]

$$EA = [NPV + NPV(1 + Inf)^n/(1 + k)^n + NPV(1 + Inf)^{2n}/(1 + k)^{2n} + . .]k \qquad \text{(10-3)}$$

which can be simplified, with a little rearrangement of terms, to:

[6]If this statement is not intuitively appealing, go to Table 10.5 and assume a repeat with the capital investment now costing $10,000(1 + .10)^5 = \$16,105.10$ and all other costs and benefits likewise adjusted for expected inflation. The net present value will work out to be $\$1,130(1.10)^5 = \$1,820$.

$$EA = NPV\{1 + 1/[(1 + k_{real})^n - 1]\}k \qquad (10\text{-}4)$$

where k_{real} is the required return in real terms:[7] $k_{real} = (1 + k)/(1 + Inf) - 1$. The equivalent annuity for the investment in Table 10.5 is therefore:

$$EA = 725\{1 + 1/[(1 + .05769)^5 - 1]\}.10 = \$296$$

Thus, in an inflationary environment, the equivalent annuity adjusted for inflation can be used for choosing between mutually exclusive investments in the same manner the equivalent annuity was used in the absence of inflation.

INFLATION, EXCHANGE RATES, AND INTERNATIONAL CAPITAL PROJECTS |

Earlier in the chapter we illustrated the relationship between expected inflation and nominal interest rates. In this section we will explore the relationship between prices, inflation, interest rates, and the existing and expected exchange rates between countries. Portions of this material were introduced in Chapter 4 to illustrate the role of arbitrage in setting the value of a currency. This material is repeated here for completeness in the discussion of the influence that inflation has on expected exchange rates and consequently expected cash flows.

Exchange rates have fluctuated over wide ranges in recent years, as Figure 10.4 illustrates, and four theories are used to explain these movements: purchasing power parity theory, capital market equilibrium theory, expectation theory, and interest rate parity theory. Purchasing power parity is discussed first.

PURCHASING POWER PARITY THEORY

Purchasing power parity theory states that equilibrium exchange rates between two countries will result in identical goods selling at identical prices. If a hotel room rents for 22,484 yen in Tokyo and $154 in Seattle, the purchasing power parity price of the yen is $.00685 so that 22,484 yen can be exchanged for $154. If the inflation rate over the course of a year is .5 percent in Japan and 3 percent in the United States, prices of hotel rooms will increase to 22,596 yen and $158.62 respectively. For purchasing power parity to hold, the value of a yen will increase to $158.62/22,596 = $.00702. The inflation rates summarized in Table 10.6

---

[7]To begin, $(1 + Inf)^n/(1 + k)^n = 1/[(1 + k)^n/(1 + Inf)^n] = 1/(1 + k_{real})^n$. Consequently, equation 10-3 can be rewritten:

$$EA = [NPV + NPV/(1 + K_{real})^n + NPV/(1 + k_{real})^{2n} + NPV/(1 + k_{real})^{3n} + ..]k$$

From the value of a perpetuity formula, this can be rewritten:

$$EA = \{NPV + NPV/[(1 + k_{real})^n - 1]\}k = NPV\{1 + 1/[(1 + k_{real})^n - 1]\}k$$

| FIGURE 10.4   EXCHANGE RATE MOVEMENTS

This figure shows the history of exchange rates between the U.S. dollar and three other currencies: the German mark, the Japanese yen, and the Italian lira. This history illustrates the variability of exchange rates in recent years. The exchange value of the mark is expressed in U.S. dollars, while the values of the other two currencies are stated in U.S. pennies.

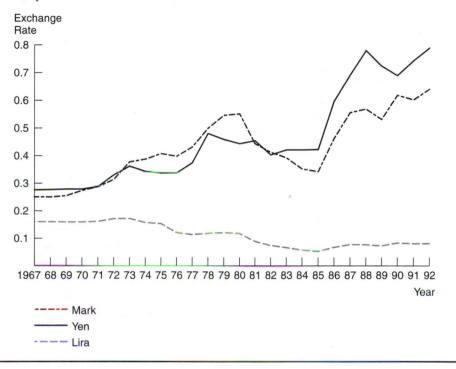

would lead us to expect large fluctuations in exchange rates, and as expected, large fluctuations have occurred.

If purchasing power parity theory holds, the movements of exchange rates can be reduced to a simple formula:

$$ER_t = ER_{t-1}(1 + INF_D)/(1 + INF_F) \qquad \text{(10-5)}$$

where ER_t is the exchange rate at the end of period t expressed as the price of one unit of the foreign currency, INF_D is the domestic inflation rate for the period, and INF_F is the inflation rate in the foreign country for the period. We can confirm this formula by finding the end-of-period value of the yen for the previous example:

$$ER_t = .00685(1 + .03)/(1 + .005) = .00702$$

| TABLE 10.6 INFLATION RATES IN SAMPLE COUNTRIES

	United States	Canada	Japan	France	Germany	Italy	United Kingdom
1980	13.5%	10.1%	7.9%	13.5%	5.2%	21.3%	17.9%
1981	10.3%	12.5%	4.7%	13.3%	6.5%	19.3%	12.0%
1982	6.2%	10.9%	2.8%	12.1%	5.2%	16.3%	8.5%
1983	3.2%	5.8%	1.8%	9.4%	3.4%	14.9%	4.6%
1984	4.3%	4.4%	2.3%	7.7%	2.4%	10.6%	5.0%
1985	3.6%	3.9%	2.0%	5.8%	2.0%	8.6%	6.0%
1986	1.9%	4.1%	0.7%	2.5%	−0.1%	6.1%	3.4%
1987	3.6%	4.4%	0.1%	3.3%	0.2%	4.6%	4.2%
1988	4.1%	4.1%	0.8%	2.7%	1.3%	5.0%	4.9%
1989	4.8%	5.0%	2.2%	3.6%	2.7%	6.6%	7.8%
1990	5.4%	4.8%	3.1%	3.3%	2.7%	6.1%	9.5%
1991	4.2%	5.6%	3.2%	3.0%	3.5%	6.3%	5.9%
1992	3.0%	1.5%	2.0%	2.9%	4.1%	5.4%	4.2%

Purchasing power parity theory does not always hold in practice though. Differences in interest rates and perceived safety between countries can increase demand for one currency and decrease demand for the other. Market forces are not strong enough to ensure rapid movement to equilibrium. Japanese will not rush to Seattle for vacation to take advantage of the price disparity in hotel rooms, for example. Nevertheless, movements in exchange rates over the long run are strongly influenced by differences in inflation rates.[8]

CAPITAL MARKET EQUILIBRIUM THEORY

A general theory of interest rates, called the *Fisher Effect*,[9] suggests that interest rates in any country will adjust to inflation so that the real rate—the increase in buying power—remains constant. The idea behind the Fisher Effect is that investors and borrowers will compute the cost and benefit of interest in terms of purchasing power effect rather than nominal dollar effect. The specific formula for the real interest rate is:

$$R_{Real} = (1 + R_{Nom})/(1 + INF) - 1 \qquad (10\text{-}6)$$

[8]For additional reading, see Richard Roll, "Violations of the 'Law of One Price' and Their Implications for Differentially Denominated Assets," in *International Finance and Trade,* ed. M. Sarnat and G. Szego (Cambridge, Mass.: Ballinger Press, 1979); and Rita Maldonado and Anthony Saunders, "Foreign Exchange Futures and the Law of One Price," *Financial Management* 12 (Spring 1983): 19–23.

[9]Irving Fisher, *The Theory of Interest* (New York: Macmillan, 1930).

where R_{Real} is the real interest rate, which is the percent increase in buying power after adjusting interest for inflation. R_{Nom} is the nominal interest rate, which is the interest rate actually paid, and INF is the inflation rate. International capital market equilibrium theory—the international version of the Fisher Effect— states that real interest rates will be the same in all countries and that nominal rate differences will reflect differences in expected inflation. Unfortunately, the Fisher Effect does not hold very well in domestic markets or international markets. Both supply and demand of credit are affected by increased inflation. And the changes in supply and demand may lead to different real interest rates in different countries. In the United States, for example, real interest rates were negative during the high-inflation years in the 1970s. Nevertheless, nominal interest rates are strongly correlated with inflation rates.[10]

EXPECTATION THEORY

Expectation theory says that forward exchange rates are unbiased estimates of future spot rates. This is an efficient market theory in that contracts for future exchange involve no investment, and are therefore expected to provide zero return on average. The argument that someone would receive a positive return for risk-bearing is mitigated by the fact that each party to the contract may be using it to hedge other positions, and there may be no party identified as accepting risk for another party.

Expectation theory holds well in practice,[11] so you will not make money *on average* by speculating on future exchange rates. Likewise, you will not decrease expected return by hedging against exchange rate changes. This is important because it means you can hedge to eliminate exchange rate risk without sacrificing expected return. Specific hedging techniques typically involve options or option-type contracts so further discussion of hedging is delayed until Chapter 15 when pricing of options is explained.

INTEREST RATE PARITY THEORY

Interest rate parity theory, which predicts a specific relationship between spot exchange rates, forward exchange rates, and interest rates, follows from the no-arbitrage-profit principle that is central to so much finance theory. Investors will always search for opportunities to make a risk-free investment at a superior rate

---

[10]For additional reading, see Fisher Black, "International Capital Market Equilibrium with Investment Barriers," *Journal of Financial Economics* 1 (December 1974): 337–352; R. M. Stultz, "A Model of International Asset Pricing," *Journal of Financial Economics* 9 (December 1981): 383–406; and Alex Kane, Leonard Rosenthal, and Greta Ljung, "Tests of the Fisher Hypothesis with International Data: Theory and Evidence," *Journal of Finance* 38 (May 1983): 539–551.

[11]See, for example, Bradford Cornell, "Spot Rates, Forward Rates and Exchange Market Efficiency," *Journal of Financial Economics* 5 (1977): 55–65; and R. M. Levich, "Tests of Forecasting Models and Market Efficiency in the International Money Market," in *The Economics of Exchange Rates: Selected Studies*, ed. A. Frenkel and H. G. Johnson (Reading, Mass.: Addison-Wesley, 1978).

of return. Suppose interest rates on risk-free government securities are higher in the United States than in Japan. You can convert yen into dollars, and buy the dollar-denominated securities. You can make this a risk-free investment by also entering into a futures contract to repurchase yen at the maturity date for the dollar-denominated security. The futures contract makes this a risk-free investment. If the investment provides a return above the domestic risk-free rate, numerous investors will join you in seeking to take advantage of the opportunity and will drive the return back into equilibrium. For the foreign investment to provide the same return as the domestic investment, the relationship between interest rates and exchange rates must be as follows:

$$R_{Foreign} = (ER_{Spot}/ER_{Forward})(1 + R_{Domestic}) - 1 \qquad \text{(10-7)}$$

where $R_{Foreign}$ and $R_{Domestic}$ are the foreign and domestic nominal risk-free interest rates, respectively. ER_{Spot} and $ER_{Forward}$ are the spot and forward exchange rates, respectively. The exchange rate is expressed as the price of the foreign currency in terms of the domestic currency.

To illustrate the use of Equation 10-7, we return to the yen which was experiencing an inflation rate of .5 percent while the dollar inflation rate was 3 percent. Assume the spot exchange rate is $.00685 per yen, and the 1-year forward contract rate is $.00702 per yen. The risk-free interest rate in dollar-denominated securities is 5.5 percent. The equilibrium interest rate in yen-denominated securities is therefore:

$$R_{Foreign} = (.00685/.00702)(1 + .055) - 1 = 2.94\%$$

There are powerful forces at work to enforce interest rate parity. You can make deposits in a Japanese bank in any one of a number of currencies, with all of these deposits being virtually risk-free with regard to interest and principal payments. At the same bank, you can exchange one currency for another and enter into a futures contract. Given the Bank of Japan's .5 percent interest rate, it is easy to take advantage of any violation of interest rate parity theory, and investors will respond quickly to these money-making opportunities, bidding rates back into equilibrium.[12]

Interest rate parity theory can be used to understand how a government can temporarily drive exchange rates out of purchasing power equilibrium. Suppose the exchange and interest rates between Japan and the United States are in equilibrium as previously defined. The spot and 1-year forward exchange rates are

[12]For additional discussion, see T. Agmon and S. Bronfield, "The International Mobility of Short-Term Covered Arbitrage Capital," *Journal of Business Finance and Accounting* 2 (Summer 1975): 269–278; J. A Frenkel and R. M. Levich, "Covered Interest Arbitrage: Unexploited Profits?" *Journal of Political Economy* 83 (April 1975): 325–338; F. X. Browne, "Departures from Interest Rate Parity: Further Evidence," *Journal of Banking and Finance* 7 (June 1983): 253–272; and Ian H. Giddy, "An Integrated Theory of Exchange Rate Equilibrium," *Journal of Financial and Quantitative Analysis* 11 (December 1976): 883–892.

$.00685 and $.00702 respectively. The interest rate is 2.94 percent in Japan, and the U.S. federal reserve bank decreases the money supply, driving interest rates up to 8 percent. The Japanese government, on the other hand, commits itself to a monetary policy that will maintain the 2.94 percent interest rate. Investors view these disturbances as temporary, so the future contract exchange rate does not change. For interest rate parity to hold, it is necessary for the spot rate to change as follows:

$$2.94 = (ER_{Spot}/.00702)(1 + .08) - 1; ER_{Spot} = .006691$$

The increase in interest rates in the United States drives the relative value of the yen down and the relative value of the dollar up. This change violates purchasing power parity, but it can be maintained at least temporarily through a high interest rate policy. Relationships between exchange rates and U.S. interest rates are summarized in Figure 10.5.

In summary, we know from observations that inflation rates are the primary determinants of exchange rate changes over the long run, but there are numerous

| **FIGURE 10.5** **EXCHANGE RATES AND INTEREST RATES**

The exchange rate is the trade-weighted average of the exchange rate of the dollar against foreign currencies, with 100 being the March 1973 base value. The interest rate is the real (inflation-adjusted) interest rate on 10-year treasury bonds.

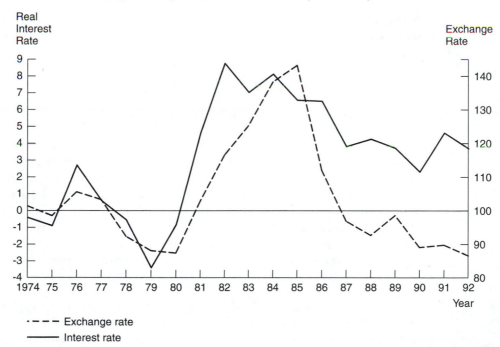

disturbances to the purchasing power parity relationships. For example, the banking crisis in Indonesia, Thailand, and Japan in 1998 caused concern about Asian stability and there was a rush to the U.S. dollar as a safe-haven currency, temporarily driving up the value of the dollar. We also know that exchange rates are sensitive to monetary policy, because monetary policy affects interest rates. Thus, theory and observations tell us that we can expect sharp fluctuations in exchange rates. Fortunately, evidence supporting expectation theory also tells us that companies can use hedging to decrease exchange rate risk without decreasing expected return.

SUMMARY

Inflation is defined as an increase in average prices. The inflation *rate* is the percentage change in a *price index,* which is the price of some representative market basket as a percent of its price in a specified base period. The *current price* is the price at which an item could be purchased today. The *constant dollar price* is the current price adjusted to buying power at some base time. The constant dollar price, expressed in year b buying power, is:

$$\text{Constant dollar price} = \text{Current price}_t \div (PI_t \div PI_b) \qquad (10\text{-}1)$$

where PI_t is the price index in year t and PI_b is the price index in year b.

The *nominal* interest rate is the interest actually paid. The *real* interest rate is the percentage increase in buying power achieved when considering the interest rate and inflation. The formula for the real interest rate or rate of return (R_{real}) is:

$$R_{real} = (1 + R_{nom})/(1 + Inf) - 1 \qquad (10\text{-}2)$$

where R_{nom} is the nominal interest rate and *Inf* is the inflation rate.

Inflation often increases income more than proportionally. Some costs, like depreciation and interest, are fixed. In addition, inventory accounting procedures mean that the cost of goods sold lags behind inflation. Cash flows are another matter, though. The cost of an existing asset is not affected by subsequent inflation, but working capital needs often rise with inflation, so net cash flow may actually decrease with increased inflation, even though income increases. Whether a particular company gains or loses with an increase in inflation depends on a number of complicated considerations, including the state of the economy, the extent to which the inflation was anticipated through interest rates, and the extent to which prices for that company's inputs and outputs lead or lag inflation.

Inflation can dramatically affect the attractiveness of specific capital investments. The inflation rate expected by investors affects required return in the financial marketplace and is, therefore, incorporated in the required return. Failing to consider the impact of inflation in estimating cash flows can lead to serious errors, either overestimation or underestimation of cash flows. Therefore, ignoring inflation can lead to the acceptance of unprofitable investments and the rejection of profitable investments.

There is no simple relationship between inflation and cash flows for specific investments. Some cash flows are unaffected, some are partially affected, and some are fully affected by inflation. Net cash flows may even be negatively affected by inflation, particularly when the impact of taxes and replacement costs is considered. Furthermore, some cash flow effects occur at the same time as inflation while others lead or lag inflation. Because of these complications, it is necessary to study each component of cash flow independently to determine the impact of inflation on that component. A complete cash flow projection considering inflation must be based on summaries of the impact of inflation on the individual components of cash flow. We know from observations that inflation rates are the primary determinants of exchange rate changes over the long run, but there are numerous disturbances to the purchasing power parity relationships. We also know that exchange rates are sensitive to monetary policy, because monetary policy affects interest rates. Thus, theory and observations tell us that we can expect sharp fluctuations in exchange rates. These same theories and observations can sometimes allow us to predict the long-run direction of the exchange rate. Without some estimate of the direction of the exchange rate, it is difficult to estimate the after-translation cash flows to the parent company and consequently the net present value of the foreign project.

QUESTIONS |

10–1. Define the terms *inflation* and *consumer price index.*

10–2. Suppose the consumer price index is 345.3 on a certain date, using 1983 as the base year. What does this mean?

10–3. Explain the difference between *current* and *constant dollar* price.

10–4. Explain the meaning of the terms *real* and *nominal* interest rate.

10–5. What factors may cause income to increase more than proportionally with an increase in inflation?

10–6. What factors may cause cash flow from a capital investment to decrease with an increase in inflation even if income increases?

10–7. Why is it *not* necessary to adjust the required return for expected inflation when evaluating capital investments in an inflationary environment?

10–8. Give examples of cash flows that are
  a. Unaffected by inflation
  b. Partially affected by inflation
  c. Fully affected by inflation

10–9. Give examples of cash flows that lead and lag inflation.

10–10. (Applications) Peru's annual inflation rate for 1990 was 7,650 percent, an all-time high for this country. In 1991 the annual rate dropped back to approximately 140 percent. In September 1993, the annual rate was at approximately 20 percent, the lowest in 17 years. Given the high rate in 1990, is it possible to make a long-term capital investment in this environment? Given the scenario above, if you were to make a capital investment, what are the characteristics that would be most important to you? Address financing, pricing, cost of inputs, and any other factors.

10-11. (**Ethical considerations**) Recently a large regulated utility which supplied natural gas to residential customers filed for bankruptcy because managers had incorrectly predicted a large increase in the price of natural gas and a large decrease in price occurred. Prior to bankruptcy, they had locked in suppliers to very long contracts, thinking the price would move up. At the time of the filing, this company was still viable but decided to file early to keep from draining the resources of the company.

a. Is it ethical to use bankruptcy in this manner?

b. Who benefited and who lost?

Can you think of other business or personal situations that might result in a rash of bankruptcy filings if rapid inflation or deflation occurs?

10-12. Describe each of the following theories. Indicate the extent to which each theory holds in practice.

a. Purchasing power parity theory

b. Capital market equilibrium theory

c. Expectation theory

d. Interest rate parity theory

PROBLEMS |

10-1. A capital investment generates cost savings of $1,000 in 1999. Assuming these costs increase with inflation, and the inflation rate is 4 percent, what will be the cost savings in 2009?

10-2. The consumer price index was 158.6 at the end of 1996 and 153.9 at the end of 1995. What was the inflation rate for 1996?

10-3. The consumer price index was 161.3 at the end of 1997. At a 3 percent inflation rate, what would be the consumer price index at the end of 1998? At the end of 2007?

10-4. The consumer price index was 161.3 at the end of 1997, measured against a base year of 1983. A portable television that sold for $99 in 1967, when the consumer price index was 33.3, could be purchased for $89 at the end of 1997. Restate the 1997 price in 1967 dollars. Comment on the rate of inflation in the price of portable televisions.

10-5. The consumer price index averaged 59.2 in 1977 and 160.6 in 1997. For an asset that cost $100,000 in 1997, express the price in 1977 dollars. For an asset that cost $100,000 in 1977, express the price in 1997 dollars.

10-6. The interest rate on Treasury bills was 5.07 percent in 1997. If the inflation rate for 1997 was 1.70 percent, what was the real interest rate for 1997?

10–7. Emporia Supply Corporation began stocking the new Superaid in January 1999. One unit was purchased in January for $100; one unit was purchased in February for $110, and one unit was sold in March for $120. What was the profit on this sale if the company used FIFO accounting? LIFO accounting?

10–8. Kansas City Corporation began operation on December 31, 1999. The company bought two units of inventory initially for $1,000 each. The company will sell one unit of inventory each year for $2000 in 1999 dollars and immediately replace that unit. Depreciation will be $400 a year, and labor expenses will be $500 a year in the absence of inflation. Sale price and inventory purchase price will rise with inflation. Depreciation will remain fixed and labor expense will lag one year behind inflation due to labor contracts. The company's tax rate is 34 percent. Assume the inflation rate will be 0 percent in 2000 and 10 percent a year thereafter. Using FIFO, show net income for 2000, 2001, 2002, and 2003.

10–9. For Kansas City Corporation in problem 8, inventory is purchased for cash and sold for cash. Show the annual cash flows for 2000, 2001, 2002, and 2003.

10–10. For Kansas City Corporation in problem 8, assume inventory is sold for cash, but purchased on one-year credit terms. Show the cash flow each year for 2000 through 2003.

10–11. Pittsburg Corporation has sales of $100,000 a year, and the sale price will increase with inflation. Inventory valuation is such that the effective cost of goods sold is the purchase price three months prior to sale. Depreciation is fixed, and other operating costs increase proportionately with inflation. The company sells on terms of net 30 and buys inventory on terms of net 60. All other purchases are for cash. Shown below is a financial statement for the first year of operation, with no inflation. Show the income for the following year, with a 10 percent inflation rate.

Sales	$100,000
Cost of goods sold	80,000
Depreciation	5,000
Other operating expenses	10,000
Earnings before tax	5,000
Tax	1,700
Net income	$ 3,300

10–12. For Pittsburg Corporation in the previous problem, goods are sold for cash. Inventory will be $50,000 with no inflation and $51,000 with 10 percent inflation. Accounts payable will be $30,000 with no inflation and $33,000 with 10 percent inflation. Show the cash flow with and without inflation.

10–13. Richmond Corporation can buy a new asset with a 5-year depreciation life for $10,000 at the end of 1999. The asset will reduce material waste by $3,000 a year, in mid-1999 prices. The inflation rate is expected to average 4 percent a year, and the cost of materials is expected to increase at the inflation rate. Materials are purchased for cash within a few days of their actual use, so there is no significant lag of cost behind inflation. The asset is expected to have a six-year operating life. The required return is 10 percent and the company is in a 34 percent tax bracket. Compute the net present value for this investment.

10–14. A capital investment of $100,000 at the end of 1999 will be required if Frankfort Corporation is to introduce a new product. The capital investment will have a ten-year operating life and a five-year life for tax purposes. In addition, inventory must be purchased for $50,000 at the end of 1999. The inventory will be sold for cash one year after purchase for $100,000 in 1999 prices, and replaced immediately. Other operating costs (excluding depreciation) will be $20,000 a year in 1999 prices. The product is expected to have a ten-year market life, and inflation is expected to be 6 percent a year over the next ten years. Inventory cost, sale price, and operating costs are expected to increase at the inflation rate. The required return is 12 percent, and the tax rate is 34 percent. Is the investment attractive?

10–15. Investment A has a five-year life and a net present value, considering inflation, of $100,000. Investment B has a ten-year life and a net present value, considering inflation, of $150,000. The required return is 16 percent, and the inflation rate is 6.48 percent. Investments A and B both use the same scarce resource. Both investments A and B can be repeated at the end of their life. Which investment do you recommend?

10–16. In problem 5-17, an investment in an MBA degree was evaluated. Rework the analysis for a 3 percent inflation of wages after the MBA is completed.

10–17. The Japanese yen is currently priced at $.00685. Suppose an apartment that would rent for $2,000 a month in New York is renting for 260,000 yen in Tokyo. Does this relationship violate purchasing power parity theory? Are there any market forces that would bring the prices in line?

10–18. The Russian ruble is currently priced at $.1598. A dress that would sell for $120 in Chicago is in a store in Moscow. What price for the dress would be consistent with purchasing power parity theory?

10–19. The value of country A's currency is $.50 on January 1 and $.60 on January 1 of the following year. Inflation over the period was 10 percent in the United States and 30 percent in country A. Is the change in currency value consistent with purchasing power parity theory?

10–20. Suppose the rate on 1-year U.S. Treasury securities is 12 percent and the inflation rate for the year is 9 percent. Is this consistent with the Fisher Effect if 3 percent is viewed as the equilibrium real interest rate?

10–21. The 1-year risk-free interest rates in countries A and B are 10 percent and 15 percent respectively. The anticipated inflation rates for countries

A and B are 8 percent and 12 percent respectively. Are these relationships consistent with international capital market equilibrium?

10–22. The spot rate and 6-month forward rate for the Japanese yen are 146.25 yen per dollar and 142.41 yen per dollar respectively. The interest rate per 6-month period is 2.75 percent in the United States and .25 percent in Japan. Are these relationships consistent with interest rate parity theory?

CASE PROBLEM |

MidCity Center (B)

The MidCity Center (A) case appears in Chapter 5. In that case, the board was considering two energy conservation proposals.

One member of the board pointed out that the assumption of no fuel price increase was unrealistic. She suggested that a 5 percent increase in fuel price each year was a conservative estimate. Another member objected, noting that fuel prices had actually declined in recent years.

Assuming a 5 percent inflation rate, answer the following questions.

CASE QUESTIONS

1. Using a 10 percent discount rate, compute the net present value of the storm window investment with and without a new furnace.
2. Using a 10 percent discount rate, compute the net present value of the furnace investment with and without storm windows.
3. Which investments, if any, should the board accept?

CASE PROBLEM |

B and F Computer Repair (B)

B and F Computer Repair (A) appears at the end of Chapter 9. In that case, Burns and Foster did not consider the impact of inflation.

Burns attended a seminar on the economic outlook, and one of the speakers talked about the possibility of an increase in inflation. Burns suggested to Foster that they should consider the possible impact of inflation before making a decision. After considerable discussion, they made the following set of assumptions.

1. There would be no inflation in the first year, and inflation would be 5 percent a year thereafter.

2. The number of hours and parts would not be affected by inflation.
3. Hourly charges and the sale price of parts would both change proportionally with inflation.
4. Labor expense increases would lag six months behind inflation.
5. Because of LIFO inventory valuation, the average accounting cost of a part would be the purchase price three months earlier.
6. Because of LIFO accounting, three-fourths of inventory would be valued at original cost while one-fourth would reflect approximately the current price.
7. Other costs would rise with inflation.
8. Because of the anticipated inflation, a 20 percent required return should be used in evaluating the investment.

CASE QUESTIONS

1. Prepare income statements for each year.
2. Identify the changes in working capital for each year.
3. Identify cash flow for each year.
4. Compute the net present value with inflation considered.
5. Should Burns and Foster enter the computer repair business?

SELECTED REFERENCES

Adler, Michael, and Bernard Dumas. "Exposure to Currency Risk: Definition and Measurement." *Financial Management* 13 (Summer 1984): 41–50.

Bailey, Andrew D., Jr., and Daniel L. Jensen. "General Price Level Adjustments in the Capital Budgeting Decision." *Financial Management* 6 (Spring 1977): 26–31.

Bernard, Victor L. "Unanticipated Inflation and the Value of the Firm." *Journal of Financial Economics* 15 (March 1986): 285–321.

Bjerksund, Petter, and Steiner Ekern. "Managing Investment Opportunities under Price Uncertainty: From 'Last Chance' to 'Wait and See' Strategies." *Financial Management* 19 (Autumn 1990): 65–83.

Brenner, Menachem, and Seymour Schmidt. "Asset Characteristics and Systematic Risk." *Financial Management* 7 (Winter 1978): 33–39.

Browne, F. X. "Departures from Interest Rate Parity: Further Evidence." *Journal of Banking and Finance* 7 (June 1983): 253–272.

Chang, Eric C., and J. Micheal Pinegar. "Risk and Inflation." *Journal of Financial and Quantitative Analysis* 22 (March 1987): 89–99.

Chang, Rosita P., and S. Ghon Rhee. "Does the Stock Market React to Announcements of the Producer Price Index?" *Financial Review* 21 (February 1986): 125–134.

Chen, Andrew H., and James A. Boness. "Effects of Uncertain Inflation on the Investment and Financing Decisions of a Firm." *Journal of Finance* 30 (May 1975): 53–63.

Cooley, Philip L., Rodney L. Roenfeldt, and It-Keong Chew. "Capital Budgeting Procedures under Inflation." *Financial Management* 4 (Winter 1975): 18–27.

Ezzell, John R., and William A. Kelly, Jr. "An APV Analysis of Capital Budgeting under Inflation." *Financial Management* 13 (Autumn 1984): 49–54.

Fama, Eugene F. "Stock Returns, Real Activity, Inflation and Money." *American Economic Review* 71 (September 1981): 545–565.

Fama, Eugene F., and G. William Schwert. "Asset Returns and Inflation." *Journal of Financial Economics* 5 (November 1977): 115–146.

Feldstein, Martin A. "Inflation and the Stock Market." *American Economic Review* 70 (December 1980): 839–847.

Findlay, Chapman M., et al. "Capital Budgeting Procedures under Inflation: Cooley, Roenfeldt, and Chew vs. Findlay and Frankle." *Financial Management* 5 (Autumn 1976): 83–90.

Fisher, Irving. *The Theory of Interest.* New York: Macmillan, 1930.

Hasbrouck, Joel. "Stock Returns, Inflation, and Economic Activity: The Survey Evidence." *Journal of Finance* 39 (December 1984): 1293–1310.

Hochman, Shalom, and Oded Palmon. "The Irrelevance of Capital Structure for the Impact of Inflation on Investment." *Journal of Finance* 38 (June 1983): 785–794.

Kane, Alex, Leonard Rosenthal, and Greta Ljung. "Tests of the Fisher Hypothesis with International Data: Theory and Evidence." *Journal of Finance* 38 (May 1983): 539–551.

Kim, Moon. "Inflationary Effects in the Capital Investment Process: An Empirical Examination." *Journal of Finance* 34 (September 1979): 941–950.

Lease, Ronald C., John J. McConnell, and James S. Schallheim. "Realized Returns and the Default and Prepayment Experience of Financial Leasing Contracts." *Financial Management* 19 (Summer 1990): 11–20.

Metha, Dileep R., Michael D. Curley, and Hung-Gay Fung. "Inflation, Cost of Capital, and Capital Budgeting Procedures." *Financial Management* 13 (Winter 1984): 48–54.

Moore, Geoffrey H. *Business Cycles, Inflation, and Forecasting,* 2nd ed. Cambridge, Mass.: Ballinger Publishing Co., 1983.

Nelson, Charles R. "Inflation and Capital Budgeting." *Journal of Finance* 31 (June 1976): 923–931.

Pindyck, Robert S. "Risk, Inflation, and the Stock Market." *American Economic Review* 74 (June 1984): 335–351.

Rappaport, Alfred, and Robert A. Taggart, Jr. "Evaluation of Capital Expenditure Proposals under Inflation." *Financial Management* 11 (Spring 1982): 5–13.

Roll, Richard. "Violations of the 'Law of One Price' and Their Implications for Differentially Denominated Assets," in *International Finance and Trade,* ed. M. Sarnat and G. Szego. Cambridge, Mass.: Ballinger Press, 1979.

Schwert, William G. "The Adjustment of Stock Prices to Information about Inflation." *Journal of Finance* 36 (March 1981): 15–29.

Soldofsky, Robert M., and D. F. Max. "Stock and Bonds as Inflation Hedges." *Michigan State University Business Topics* 26 (Spring 1978): 17–24.

Van Horne, James C. "A Note on Biases in Capital Budgeting Introduced by Inflation." *Journal of Financial and Quantitative Analysis* 8 (January 1971): 653–658.

Walter, James E. "Investment Planning under Variable Price Change." *Financial Management* 1 (Winter 1972): 36–50.

Williams, R. "Forecasting Inflation and Interest Rates." *Business Economics* 14 (January 1979): 57–60.

INTEGRATIVE CASE FOR PART III |

Machine Tool Corporation (A)

Machine Tool Corporation was searching for ways to increase productivity and decrease costs. The company began to look at the use of robots. One possible use of robots was in gear hobbing. A gear-hobbing machining center consisted of four machines operated individually by semiskilled human operators. Two sets of machines operated in the shop. Depending upon production requirements, either the four-spindle hobbing machine and shaving machine (low volume) or the eight-spindle hobbing machine and shaving machine was used. Major operator functions involved loading gear blanks, cutting gear profiles, stacking semi-finished parts, and trimming the gears on the shaving machine. The cleaning and inspection operations, subsequent to shaving, were also done manually.

The existing workstation could be modified so that a single robot could perform all loading and unloading operations. Stacking the parts on incoming and outgoing trays, inspection, and overall supervision of the workstation could then be done by one operator, instead of the four operators required for the previous setup. The operator who remained would then be responsible for

1. programming and starting the robot,
2. arranging parts on the incoming tray,
3. periodic inspection of the finished parts,
4. unloading finished parts and stacking on the outgoing tray, and
5. general maintenance of the work center.

Special tools, to support the operation, were designed and the best robot for the use was identified. The layout of the modified workstation and specifications of robots available in the market were taken into consideration in identifying the best robot. Using the technical specifications of this robot, a time study was conducted and the cycle time for the operation was determined (88.1 seconds). From the cycle time, the production capacity of the robotized plant was determined. The production capacity of the human-operated work center was 800 units per day; for the robotized plant, the production capacity would be 1,315 units per day.

ECONOMIC FEASIBILITY STUDY

Once the technical feasibility study was completed, an economic analysis from the company's perspective was performed to justify the investment (robot). To simplify the analysis, the following assumptions were made:

| TABLE IIIA.1 INITIAL EXPENDITURE DUE TO ROBOT INSTALLATION

Cost Description	Amount ($)
Cost of robot (base)	$80,000
Special holders and tools	3,000
Installation cost	
Rearrangement cost	1,280
Installation cost	1,500
Feedback & interface devices	5,000
Feasibility study	300
Rearrangement cost	
Conveyor cost	4,362
Fence	670
Feeders & trays	2,000
Special tooling cost	
Grippers	4,000
Special arbor & fixtures	2,000
Control locks & safety	5,000
Total Expenditure	$109,112

1. The company is unable to meet the demand due to low production capacity of the human-operated work center. The additional capacity, due to robot installation, can be sold without any difficulty.
2. The life period of the robot installation is ten years, with a salvage value of $10,000.
3. The interest rate is 12 percent per year.
4. All retraining costs are borne by the company.
5. The displaced employees, permanently unemployed, are not compensated by the company.
6. The effect of inflation can be ignored.
7. Working capital is not affected.
8. The company's required return is 25 percent.

Changes in the cash flow of the company due to robotization were estimated by identifying various costs and savings involved. The relevant costs and savings are described briefly:

1. Robot and accessories cost—includes cost of the robot, special tools, test equipment, etc.
2. Installation cost—labor and materials for the site, floor and foundation preparations, utilities and interface devices between the robot and fixtures.

| **TABLE IIIA.2**   CHANGES IN THE ANNUAL CASH FLOW OF THE COMPANY

Description of the Cash Flow	Amount ($/year)
Maintenance and service labor cost for the robot work center	$6,000
Operating supplies	3,000
Training cost of the technician ($3,000 is distributed over 10 years using the 12 percent interest rate)	530
Tax and insurance (2.5%)	2,721
Increase in pay due to job upgrading of technician	5,000
Other miscellaneous costs	1,000
Total variable cost/year	$18,251
Savings due to labor displacement (20,000/year/displacement)	$60,000

3. Rearrangement cost—labor and material cost for the installation of the safety fence, conveyors, etc.
4. Special tooling costs—including costs of special end-of-arm devices and changes in the fixture design, clamps, limit switches, sensors, etc.
5. Indirect labor costs—repair and maintenance costs.
6. Operating supplies cost—annual cost of utilities and services used by the robot and the support equipment.
7. Maintenance supplies cost.
8. Launching costs—work stoppage due to installation costs.
9. Taxes and insurance.
10. Savings through reduced scrap, increased productivity, and other credits.
11. Savings in direct labor.

CASE QUESTIONS

1. Identify after-tax cash flows for the investment.
2. Find the net present value.
3. Find the internal rate of return.
4. Is the investment attractive from the company's perspective?
5. A 10-year life was assumed. What is the minimum life needed for the investment to be attractive?

Machine Tool Corporation (B)

The economic analysis was expanded to include cost and revenue changes in the government's cash flow and to determine if it was still economically desirable to install the robot.

Robot installation would lead to the unemployment of three workers. This would cause changes in the cash flows to and from the government. Most changes were due to tax losses; additional costs were due to unemployment compensation, welfare, etc. If the employees were relocated to different jobs, tax revenues would be altered due to change in income. Increased profit from selling additional capacity, however, increases tax revenue to the government. These cash flows were not considered in the conventional economic analysis.

The following changed the cash flow of the government:
Federal corporate tax
State corporate tax
City and corporate franchise tax
Tangible property tax
Sales tax (due to increased sales)
Federal individual tax
State and city individual tax
Social security paid by the employees
Social security paid by the employer
Payroll tax
Unemployment compensation paid by the government
Welfare
Other miscellaneous taxes and expenditures

Taxes were computed from tax tables and forms provided by the various tax agencies (since local and state taxes vary widely, the final outcome can be significantly influenced). In this case study, taxes were calculated on the basis of the tax laws of the state of Ohio.

When determining changes in the cash flow of government, two different cases were examined:
Case 1: Displaced workers are permanently unemployed.
Case 2: Displaced workers are relocated.

Case 1. The displaced workers depend on unemployment compensation and welfare from the government. This change in their status alters the cash flow of the government. Various taxes paid by the employees stop. Also, some taxes paid by the employer stop. Government's expenses at the same time increase.

The increased productivity and labor savings, on the other hand, increase the company's profit. This profit, in turn, generates tax revenues to the government. The investment (robot) also increases the GNP.

Table IIIB.1 shows the additional revenues received by the government as the result of robotization. These were generated from the taxes due to increased employer's savings and sales. The various costs to the government as the result of worker displacement are shown in Table IIIB.2. These costs were mainly due to losses in tax revenue, expenses on unemployment compensation, and welfare.

Case 2. In this case, it was assumed that the workers can be transferred to a different location in the company, but without retraining since the new jobs require the same levels of skills. It was also assumed that the three workers, once relocated, will earn the same salary.

Impact of Robot Installation on GNP

GNP (gross national product) is the yardstick of an economy's performance. It is the measure of overall annual flow of goods and services in the economy and consists of three major components:

1. Personal consumption expenditure (65% of GNP)
2. Government expenditure on goods and services (18% of GNP)
3. Gross private domestic investment (17% of GNP)

| TABLE IIIB.1 CHANGES IN THE REVENUES OF THE GOVERNMENT

Item	Amount ($/year)
Federal corporation tax	18,930.84
State corporation tax	1,509.75
City tax	823.08
Corporate franchise tax (CFT)	5,864.88
Tangible property tax (TPT)	507.96
Sales tax	256.53
Indirect gain due to productivity and other sources	1,394.65
Total Revenue/Year	$29,287.69

| TABLE IIIB.2 CASH FLOW LOST BY THE GOVERNMENT DUE TO THE ROBOT

Item	Amount ($/year)
Federal individual income tax (20.7% of company's profit)	$4,143.00
State income tax	549.33
City income tax	400.00
Social Security paid by the employee (SSI)(7%)	1,400.00
Payroll tax paid by the employer	1,240.00
Social Security paid by the employer (SSI)(7%)	1,400.00
Unemployment compensation paid by the government to the unemployed	7,000.00
Other governmental cost (10% of the above)	1,613.23
Total cost/year/employee	$17,745.56
Total cost/yr. = $17,745 × 3 workers = $53,235	

In the present case study, the personal consumption expenditure of each displaced worker was expected to change depending on his new income. If the worker remained unemployed, the reduction in personal consumption expenditure would be:

$$[1 - (7,000 \div 20,000)] \times 100 = 65$$

where $7,000 is the unemployment compensation and $20,000 is the original income. This is approximately 3.95×10^{-11} of the GNP (as of April 1984 the GNP was $3,541.6 billion). Since in this case study, three workers were displaced, the GNP was lowered by 11.85×10^{-11} percent. However, the increase in GNP due to investment (investment on robot installation was $109,112) was 31.06×10^{-11} percent. It appears that in this case, there is a net increase in GNP. If we assume the total displacement nationwide of three million workers by robots by the year 1990, the net change in GNP will be a decrease of approximately 2 percent. If the worker is relocated instead of being unemployed, the change in the GNP is mainly due to the investment.

CASE QUESTIONS

1. Assuming displaced workers are permanently unemployed, is the new investment attractive from the perspective of the government?
2. Assuming displaced workers are relocated, is the new investment attractive from the perspective of the government?
3. How should conflicts between government and company interests be dealt with in the company's decision-making process?

Machine Tool Corporation (C)

Managers at Machine Tool Corporation want to consider the possibility of inflation in analyzing the robot investment. A 5 percent annual increase in all costs is assumed for this purpose. Assume that the company's required return already reflected anticipated inflation.

CASE QUESTIONS

1. Identify the annual after-tax cash flows to the company considering inflation.
2. Compute the net present value.

PART IV

RISK AND INVESTMENT CHOICE

In the previous chapters, risk considerations were eliminated with the assumption that all of the company's investments were riskless or at least in the same risk class. In this part of the book, risk differences are incorporated into the analysis. General insights into decision making under risk are discussed in Chapter 11. Methods of recognizing risk from the perspective of an isolated investment are treated in Chapter 12. Method of recognizing risk from the perspective of the top management of the company, including diversification issues, are dealt with in Chapter 13. In Chapter 14, the mean-variance capital asset pricing model is used to consider risk from the perspective of a fully diversified shareholder. In Chapter 15, arbitrage pricing theory and the option pricing model are used as additional methods of considering risk from the perspectives of shareholders and other affected parties. These chapters cover methods of measuring risk, methods of reducing or controlling risk, and methods of choosing investments in the face of risk.

Upon completing these chapters, you will have an understanding of the general principles of risk analysis as well as a good kit of tools for risk analysis.

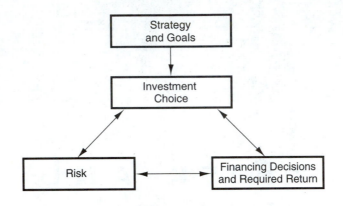

CHAPTER 11

INTRODUCTION TO RISK ANALYSIS

After completing this chapter, you should be able to:

1. Apply basic probability rules to determine the probability of an outcome or range of outcomes.
2. Describe the various ways of measuring risk.
3. Describe and compute each summary measure of a central tendency like expected value, median, mode, and geometric mean.
4. Calculate and understand the various measures of dispersion such as variance, standard deviation, coefficient of variation, and semivariance.
5. Determine and explain the meaning of a risk-return indifference curve.
6. Explain the implication of the statement that someone is an expected utility maximizer.
7. Understand the importance of each of the five risk perspectives introduced in this chapter and developed in this section of the book.

Jim Burke, CEO of Johnson and Johnson, likes to tell the story of one of his earlier experiences in risk taking. He suggested that the company start a new products division, and was hired to head the fledgling unit. One of his first products was a chest rub for children. Unfortunately, the product was a complete failure.

Burke was called to the office of General Robert Wood Johnson, then chairman of the board. "Are you the one who just cost us all that money?" the General asked. Burke confirmed his guilt, while wondering if he was about to be fired. The General said, "Well, I just want to congratulate you. If you are making mistakes, that means you are making decisions and taking risks. And we won't grow unless we take risks."[1]

[1]John Steinbreder, "Taking Chances at J&J," *Fortune* (June 6, 1988): 60.

Risk is inherent in most long-term decisions, especially capital budgeting decisions. Both costs and benefits must be predicted for periods from a few years to a few decades in the future. Customers, suppliers, competitors, and governments all affect future cash flows, as do weather conditions and the activities of businesses, consumers, and nations having no direct dealings with the company. Businesses that fail to consider the risks to which they expose themselves will not be around long. On the other hand, like the proverbial turtle, you cannot make progress without sticking your neck out. Appropriate methods of dealing with risk are, therefore, essential for successful capital budgeting.

The objective of this chapter is to develop a foundation for capital budgeting in the face of risk. One characteristic of a risky investment is that there is more than one possible outcome. We developed the net present value as a way to compare cash flows occurring at different times, and we must also develop desirability measures that allow us to evaluate an investment characterized by a range of possible cash flows. The first tasks we face are defining and measuring risk. Then, we need to develop some understanding of how humans respond to risk. Thus, we begin this chapter with some definitions, and then turn our attention to measurement tools used in the face of risk. The definitions and measurement tools provide the background for understanding utility theory, which is the next topic. Utility theory summarizes much of our understanding about how people decide when faced with risk. Since risk measures and investment choices are affected by our choices of the person(s) whose welfare is being maximized, this chapter ends with a discussion of whose perspective to use in decision making. The topics covered in this chapter provide the foundation for the various approaches to risky investment choice discussed in Chapters 12 through 15.

SOME DEFINITIONS |

Terminology is important, in that many long-standing debates boil down to nothing more than the combatants using the same word to mean two different things. A brief overview of some widely used terminology may help to avoid such problems.

Risk. *Risk* is used in common language to mean exposure to the chance of an injury or loss. In finance, the term *risk* is used in general to refer to the chance of the loss of money. Risk may also refer to the chance of getting back less than was expected, less than the rate of return on a sure thing such as a Treasury bill, or less than would have been received from some other risky investment.

Probability. The probability of an occurrence is the likelihood of an event, expressed as a ratio. It is the expected relative frequency of the event when the number of observations is very large. If you flip a coin, for example, the probability of a head is $\frac{1}{2}$; if the coin is flipped many times, we would expect heads half of the time. If a die is rolled, the probability of an even number less than six is $\frac{1}{3}$ (a 2 or a 4 will satisfy these criteria, and there are six possible, equally likely, outcomes).

Risk vs. uncertainty. Risk is sometimes used to identify only the situation in which the probabilities of all outcomes are known. When the term is used in this way, *uncertainty* is used to identify situations in which the probabilities of outcomes are not known. This is an unfortunate terminology choice for two reasons. First, the term *risk* is used in everyday conversation to refer to any situation involving the possibility of an undesired outcome, whether or not probabilities are known. Second, there is hardly ever a real-world environment other than the gaming table in which probabilities are known. Real-world decision making involves a continuum, with one end reflecting a high degree of confidence in probability estimates and the other end reflecting a low degree of confidence. In this book, we will use both *risk* and *uncertainty* in the more general sense, to cover situations in which the outcomes are not known with certainty, whether or not probabilities are known.

Probability distribution. A probability distribution is a set of all possible occurrences and their associated probabilities. With a *discrete* probability distribution, the number of possible occurrences is finite. Some probability distributions are *continuous* and, therefore, cover an infinite number of possible occurrences. The probability distribution of return on assets for General Electric is infinite, for example; for any two values of return on assets, it is possible to have a value between those two. Continuous distributions are generally defined by a mathematical function, and we generally talk about the probability of an occurrence within a particular range rather than the probability of any single occurrence.

Subjective vs. objective probability. Objective probability is probability that can be measured or otherwise computed. If we have determined that a pair of dice is fair, for example, we can objectively determine the probability of a total score of seven on any roll. *Subjective probability* is an estimate based on someone's opinion. The probability that Nike's jogging shoe sales will increase 5 percent or more next year is a subjective probability. While the estimate of the jogging shoe sales growth may be based on extensive analytical work, it often depends on the analyst's judgment concerning which information is important in arriving at a probability estimate.[2]

Variation vs. event risk. In common language, risk is often associated with the chance of a specific undesired event. Risk of ruin, such as the risk of bankruptcy, is one such event risk in business. The possible failure of Monsanto's new herbicide to pass Environmental Protection Agency tests could be another event risk. By way of comparison, a range of possible levels of jogging shoe sales rather than one known sales level is an example of variation risk. This latter type of risk is often described in terms of some measure of the variability of future cash flows, such as the standard deviation of the probability distribution, which is discussed later in this chapter.

---

[2]The most famous subjective estimate may be that of Murray Wiedenbaum, then chairman of the Council of Economic Advisors. In what David Stockman described as "the belly slap heard round the world," Wiedenbaum justified his pessimistic economic forecast by touching his midsection and saying "it comes from here."

Diversifiable vs. nondiversifiable risk. Diversifiable risk is risk that can be eliminated by combining one investment with other investments. Nondiversifiable risk, also referred to as systematic risk or portfolio risk, relates to factors that tend to affect all investments and consequently cannot be reduced by combining investments in portfolios. We can diversify away the risk that Nike's jogging shoes will be unpopular by buying stock in all running shoe companies. We can diversify away the risk of jogging shoes declining in favor of other recreation goods by buying the stocks of a broad range of recreation companies. A general downturn in the economy will, however, affect the sales of virtually all companies, and this risk cannot be diversified away. Nondiversifiable risk can be avoided only by investing in risk-free investments, which generally means accepting a lower expected return.

PROBABILITY RULES |

Basic probability rules involving multiple events are often used in the analysis of risk. The most frequently used rules are discussed in this section.

MUTUALLY EXCLUSIVE EVENTS

Events are mutually exclusive if the occurrence of one eliminates any possibility of the occurrence of the other(s). Suppose developers in the downtown area and two suburbs of St. Louis are competing to have their sites chosen for the stadium for a new NFL football team. These are mutually exclusive choices because the team cannot simultaneously play at two stadiums. The probability of an occurrence from a set of mutually exclusive events is simply the sum of the probabilities of the individual events in the set. Suppose there is a .5 probability the stadium will be built in the northern suburb site and a .25 probability the southern suburb site will be approved. The probability of a suburban site being chosen is:

$$P(\text{Suburban}) = P(\text{North}) + P(\text{South}) = .50 + .25 = \underline{\underline{.75}}$$

where $P(\cdot)$ is the probability of the event(s) within parentheses. P(North), for example, is the probability of the northern site being chosen.

INDEPENDENT EVENTS

Two events are independent if the probability of one event is not affected by the outcome of the other event. The probability that Texaco's new well in the Bourbon field will produce oil is not affected by results from its well in the Arctic field. Let $P(A)$ be the probability of event A and $P(B)$ be the probability of event B. Since probabilities must sum to 1.0, the probability of A not occurring is $[1 - P(A)]$ and the probability of B not occurring is $[1 - P(B)]$. The probability of both A and B occurring is:

$$P(A \cap B) = P(A)P(B) \tag{11-1}$$

where ∩ means intersection in set theory terminology, so P(A∩B) is the probability of both A and B occurring.

There are four possible combinations of outcomes, and their probabilities are as follows:

	Event B occurs	Event B does not occur
Event A occurs	P(A)P(B)	P(A)[1 − P(B)]
Event A does not occur	[1 − P(A)]P(B)	[1 − P(A)][1 − P(B)]

Example. For Texaco, the probability that the Arctic well will be successful is .7, and the probability that the Bourbon well will be successful is .4. The projects are independent, so the probabilities of the possible combinations of outcomes are as follows:

	Bourbon is successful	Bourbon is unsuccessful
Arctic is successful	.7 × .4 = .28	.7 × .6 = .42
Arctic is unsuccessful	.3 × .4 = .12	.3 × .6 = .18

Each of the four combinations is mutually exclusive; a well cannot both succeed and fail. Therefore, the probability that one or more well will be successful can be found by adding probabilities:

$$P(\text{at least one well succeeds}) = .28 + .42 + .12 = \underline{\underline{.82}}$$

The probability of at least one investment succeeding could have also been found as follows:

$$P(\text{at least one investment succeeds}) = 1 - P(\text{both fail}) = 1 - .18 = \underline{\underline{.82}}$$

DEPENDENT EVENTS

Suppose that the probability of B depends on whether or not A occurs. B is then dependent on A, and the rules of conditional probability must be applied. The probability that both A and B will occur is then:

$$P(A \cap B) = P(B|A)P(A) \tag{11-2}$$

where P(B|A) is the probability of B occurring, given that A has occurred.

This basic conditional probability rule can be extended to chains of events in which the probability of an event depends on the occurrence of two or more previous events. If event C is dependent on events A *and* B, the formula is:

$$P(A \cap B \cap C) = P(C|A \cap B)P(A \cap B) \qquad (11\text{-}3)$$

where $P(A \cap B \cap C)$ is the probability of A, B, and C all occurring, and $P(C|A \cap B)$ is the probability of C occurring, given that A and B have occurred.

Example. Suppose the northern suburb of St. Louis will put a bond issue on the ballot to fund a new stadium. There is an .8 probability that the bond issue will pass. The probability that the northern site will be approved depends on whether the bond issue passes, as follows:

1. If the bond issue passes, the probability of the northern site being selected is .6.
2. If the bond issue fails, the probability of the northern site being selected is .3.

The probabilities for the various possible outcomes are as follows:

	North selected	North rejected
Bond issue passes	.8 × .6 = .48	.8 × .4 = .32
Bond issue fails	.2 × .3 = .06	.2 × .7 = .14

Because each of the combinations is mutually exclusive, we can find the probability that the northern site will be selected:

$$P(\text{North selected}) = .48 + .06 = \underline{\underline{.54}}$$

These various probability rules will be applied in the following chapters when analyzing capital investments under conditions of risk.

MEASURING RISK |

Risk is a complex and many-faceted problem. While there have long been attempts to reduce risk to concrete measures, we are not yet to the point where any one measure adequately describes risk in every situation. Various risk measures are discussed in the following paragraphs, and each risk measure has its own information content. Managers often look at more than one risk measure in the process of describing risk, seeking ways to eliminate or control risk, and making investment decisions in the face of risk.

The simplest risk analysis is *descriptive* and *subjective*. Things that might go wrong are identified, and the decision makers are left to their own judgment as to the importance of these things in terms of either likelihood of occurrence or significance of consequences. The most basic risk analysis, then, may simply involve statements such as "we might be overly optimistic about the rate of demand growth" or "competitors may cut their prices too."

SENSITIVITY ANALYSIS

Sensitivity analysis is a method of quantifying uncertainty without having to estimate probabilities. You simply estimate the consequences of different levels of one or more variables that affect the investment. You can, for example, assess the importance of a slower-than-anticipated growth rate in sales of 3M's new paper fastener by computing the net present value at various growth rates. Break-even analysis is one of the tools that has been useful in this regard, not just to measure risk but to consider approaches that can improve the profitability-risk trade-off. Despite the development of more sophisticated approaches, sensitivity analysis and break-even analysis continue to be useful tools and are discussed in more detail in Chapter 12.

EVENT PROBABILITY

A limitation of sensitivity analysis is that it shows us the profitability at different levels of some variable, but tells us nothing about the likelihood of each level occurring. Thus, the next step is to attach probabilities to various outcomes. In a simple analysis, probability assessment may be attempted for only one or a few possible events. The statement that "there is a one-out-of-ten probability of bankruptcy if this strategy is followed" is a simple event probability assessment. At the other extreme, probabilities may be attached to each of a large number of possible events.

Beyond event probability, risk is often measured using summary statistics for the probability distribution of outcomes, such as the expected value and variance. These measures are covered in the next section.

SUMMARY MEASURES OF PROBABILITY DISTRIBUTIONS |

If each possible amount of annual cash flow from Hewlett-Packard's factory investment is considered an event, the number of outcomes may be measured in the billions. Stating each possible outcome and its probability would be overwhelming. Some way to summarize the probability distribution of outcomes is needed. Distributions are frequently summarized with measures of central tendency and dispersion. Discussion of these measures follows. Capital investment decisions are often made using a measure of the central tendency as the index of desirability and a dispersion measure as the measure of risk.

MEASURES OF CENTRAL TENDENCY

The most widely used measures of central tendency are the expected value, the median, the mode, and the geometric mean. Each of these gives some indication of the likely result of an action.

EXPECTED VALUE

The expected value is also called the arithmetic mean or simply the mean of the probability distribution. For a probability distribution with n possible outcomes, the expected value, $E(X)$, is defined as follows:

$$E(X) = \sum_{i=1}^{n} p_i X_i \qquad (11\text{-}4)$$

where p_i is the probability of amount X_i occurring. Suppose, for example, Alcoa is considering a capital investment with the following probability distribution of net present values:

NPV	100	200	300	400	500
Probability	.1	.2	.4	.2	.1

The expected net present value is:

$$E(NPV) = (.1 \times 100) + (.2 \times 200) + (.4 \times 300) + (.2 \times 400) + (.1 \times 500) = \underline{\$300}$$

If Alcoa could repeat the investment an infinite number of times, the expected net present value of $300 is the expected average net present value per investment.

MEDIAN

There is an equal probability of an outcome greater or less than the median value. The median for the Alcoa example is $300; there is a .3 probability of a lower net present value and a .3 probability of a higher net present value.

MODE

The mode is the outcome with the highest probability. In the Alcoa example, the mode is $300 because the highest probability (.4) is associated with $300.

The mean, median, and mode are equal in this particular example, because the probability distribution is symmetrical; the probability of outcomes above the mean equals the probability of outcomes below the mean. Non-symmetrical distributions are shown in Figure 11.1, with expected value, median and mode identified.

GEOMETRIC MEAN

In finance, the geometric mean is associated with rates of return and represents the expected long-run growth rate of money, given repeated investments with the same probability distribution of returns. The formula for the geometric mean return, GM, is:

$$GM = (1 + R_1)^{P_1}(1 + R_2)^{P_2}(1 + R_3)^{P_3} \ldots (1 + R_n)^{P_n} \qquad \text{(11-5)}$$

where R_1 through R_n are the possible rates of return, and P_1 through P_n are the associated probabilities.

| FIGURE 11.1   NONSYMMETRICAL PROBABILITY DISTRIBUTIONS OF NET PRESENT VALUE

This figure illustrates the location of the expected value, median, and mode for nonsymmetrical distributions. The area under the curve between any two values, as a proportion of the total area under the curve, represents the probability of an outcome within that range.

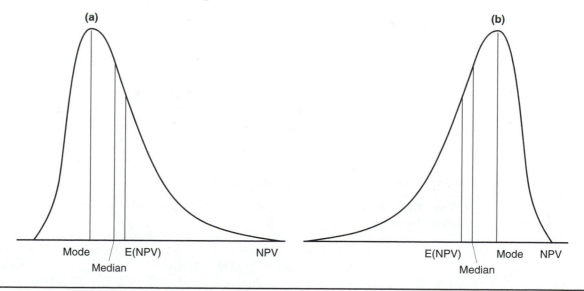

Example. An investment at Omaha Packing has the following probability distribution of annual rates of return:

Return	−.6	0	.2	.3	.5
Probability	.1	.2	.4	.2	.1

The expected return is:

$$E(R) = .1 \times (-.6) + .2 \times 0 + .4 \times .2 + .2 \times .3 + .1 \times .5 = \underline{\underline{.13}}$$

The geometric mean return is:

$$GM = (1 - .6)^{.1}(1 + 0)^{.2}(1 + .2)^{.4}(1 + .3)^{.2}(1 + .5)^{.1} = \underline{1.077}$$

In other words, wealth committed to this investment can be expected to grow at an annual rate of $1.077 - 1 = 7.7$ percent over the long term.

The expected return for the previous example is 13 percent, but because of variability, the long-term growth rate of wealth is only 7.7 percent. This illustrates one disadvantage of variability. The long-term growth rate from a sure-thing with an expected return of 13 percent is greater than the long-run growth rate from an investment with a 13 percent expected return and variability around that expected return. If the decrease in long-term growth were the only reason for disliking variability, the geometric mean might serve as a single measure of desirability combining risk and return. But variability has disadvantages in the short run as well as in the long run. Therefore, expected value is widely used as the central tendency measure, along with one of the following measures of dispersion.

MEASURES OF DISPERSION |

Dispersion measures are summary statistics of the way possible outcomes are spread around some measure of central tendency, generally the expected value. The most widely used measures are the variance and its square root, the standard deviation.

VARIANCE AND STANDARD DEVIATION

When there are a number of possible outcomes, each with an associated probability, the *variance* is:

$$\sigma_x^2 = \sum_{i=1}^{n} p_i [X_i - E(X)]^2 \qquad \text{(11-6)}$$

where p_i is the probability of value X_i and $E(X)$ is the expected value of X, as defined in Equation 11-4. The *standard deviation* is simply the square root of the variance.

Lotus 1-2-3 will calculate a variance and standard deviation. Simply list the observations, go to an empty cell, and type @ VAR (Range) for the variance of a population range. Type @ STD (Range) for the standard deviation of a range.

Example. In Table 11.1, variance and standard deviation are illustrated with the Alcoa investment that was used to illustrate expected return, median, and mode.

The standard deviation, in particular, is a widely used measure of risk. It is preferred over the variance because it is expressed in the same units as the original problem, such as dollars, rather than in squared dollars, and is therefore easier to interpret. The standard deviation can combine hundreds of possible outcomes and probabilities in a single risk statistic. The standard deviation is helpful in stating probabilities of occurrences within various ranges, particularly if the probabilities of outcomes are approximately normally distributed, as illustrated in Figure 11.2.

The normal distribution was first recognized by scientists in the 18th century, who observed an amazing degree of regularity in the distribution of errors of measurement. Nature and people have produced many things that are normally distributed. For example, the distributions of intelligence quotients and machined part diameters are approximately normal. Even when samples are drawn from a nonnormal distribution, the distribution of sample means tends toward normality as the sample size becomes large. If events can be categorized according to success or failure, the probability distribution of the number of successes approaches normality as the number of trials becomes large.[3]

| TABLE 11.1 PROBABILITY DISTRIBUTION OF NET PRESENT VALUES FOR A SAMPLE ALCOA INVESTMENT

The investment has five possible net present values, with probabilities as indicated. Expected net present value, variance, and standard deviation are computed from this information.

Net Present Value	100	200	300	400	500
Probability	.1	.2	.4	.2	.1

$E(NPV) = .1 \times 100 + .2 \times 200 + .4 \times 300 + .2 \times 400 + .1 \times 500 = \underline{300}$

$\sigma_{npv}^2 = .1(100-300)^2 + .2(200-300)^2 + .4(300-300)^2 + .2(400-300)^2 + .1(500-300)^2$

$\quad = \underline{12,000}$

$\sigma_{npv} = \sqrt{12,000} = \underline{\underline{110}}$

[3]If there are n trials and the probability of success on any one trial is p, the expected value and variance are $E(V) = np$ and $\sigma_{npv}^2 = np(1 - p)$.

| **FIGURE 11.2** **THE NORMAL CURVE**

The area under the curve between any two values, as a proportion of the total area under the curve, represents the probability of an outcome within that range.

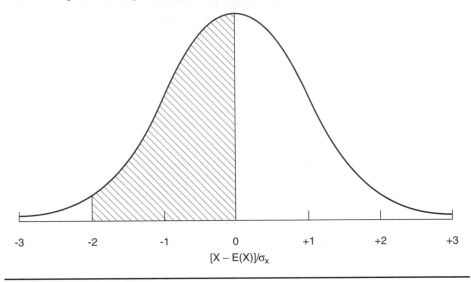

We cannot always count on normality, though. One characteristic of a normal distribution is that it is symmetrical; an outcome more than 20 percent below the mean equals the probability of an outcome more than 20 percent above the mean, for example. If return from a portfolio each year is drawn from a symmetrical distribution, the probability distribution of terminal wealth will not be symmetrical. Suppose, for example, return each year is +80 percent or −80 percent, each with a .5 probability. This is a symmetrical distribution with an expected value of 0 percent. The four equally likely outcomes over a 2-year period, with a beginning investment of $100, are:

Year 1	Year 2	Terminal wealth
+80%	+80%	324
+80%	−80%	36
−80%	+80%	36
−80%	−80%	4

This expected terminal wealth is $100, but the probability distribution is clearly not symmetrical around that expected value. Since symmetry can be destroyed in this way, and normal distributions are symmetrical, normality can be destroyed. Therefore, it is wise to check for normality rather than assuming its existence. Tests are explained in any elementary statistics book.

The normal distribution table in Appendix B can be used to find the probability of an outcome within any range if the expected value and standard deviation are known. Appendix B contains the probability of an occurrence between the expected value and the specified number of standard deviations on *one* side of the expected value. For example, the value for 2.00 in Appendix B is the shaded area in Figure 11.2, as a percent of the total area under the curve; it is the probability of an outcome being between the expected value and two standard deviations on one side of the expected value. Since the normal distribution is symmetrical, doubling the probability from the table gives the probability of an outcome within a certain distance above or below the expected value. To find the probability of being more than some specified number of standard deviations to one side of the expected value, simply find the probability of being between the mean and that value, then subtract that probability from .50. A similar procedure is used to find a value within a range, such as between 1.5 and 2.0 standard deviations below the mean.

Example. The probability distribution of net present values[4] for an investment at Lexington Corporation is normally distributed with an expected value of $300 and a standard deviation of $110. We want to find the probability of a net present value less than $150. To do this, we complete the following steps:

1. Note that ($150 − $300)/110 = − 1.36, so $150 is 1.36 standard deviations below the mean. The probability of a net present value between $150 and $300 is the probability associated with 1.36 in Appendix B: .4131.
2. The probability of a net present value between $150 and $300 is .4131.
3. The probability of a net present value less that $150 is .5000 − .4131 = <u>.0869</u>. A graphical summary of the solution follows, with P representing probability within a range.

Example. With an expected net present value of $300 and a standard deviation of $110, managers at Murray Corporation want to know the probability of a net

---

[4]In a strict sense, an investment has only one net present value, which is the amount by which the value of the probability distribution of future benefits exceeds the value of the probability distribution of outlays. Thus, net present value is the change in wealth when an investment is selected. Subsequent changes in wealth as uncertainty is resolved are not changes in the net present value. While it is true in this sense that an investment has only one net present value, a commonly used approach to risk analysis is to compute a net present value for each possible outcome. The probability of a negative net present value has meaning, for example, in that it is the probability that the subsequent cash flows will not be sufficient to provide investors a fair rate of return that compensates for risks taken.

present value between $150 and $250. A graphical summary of the solution follows this paragraph. First we find the probability of being between each of these values and $300, using Appendix B:

$$(\$150 - \$300)/110 = -1.36; P(150 < NPV < 300) = .4131$$

$$(\$250 - \$300)/110 = -0.45; P(250 < NPV < 300) = .1736$$

The probability of a value between $150 and $250 is then:

$$P(150 < NPV < 250) = P(150 < NPV < 300) - P(250 < NPV < 300) =$$
$$.4131 - .1736 = \underline{.2395}$$

The variance and standard deviation allow a description of risk in one statistic, and can be converted to statements of probability with regard to various ranges.

COEFFICIENT OF VARIATION

One problem with the variance and standard deviation is that they are not adjusted for scale. Using the standard deviation, an investment with an expected net present value of $1 million and a standard deviation of $11,000 would be viewed as more risky than an investment with an expected net present value of $1,000 and a standard deviation of $10,000.

The coefficient of variation restates the standard deviation in relation to the scale of the project. The formula for the coefficient of variation (CV) is:

$$CV = \sigma_X/E(X) \qquad \qquad (11\text{-}7)$$

For an investment with an expected net present value of $300 and a standard deviation of $110, the coefficient of variation is:

$$CV = 110/300 = .367$$

Using the coefficient of variation, this investment would be viewed as less risky than an investment with an expected net present value of $100 and a standard deviation of $50; the latter investment would have a coefficient of variation of .50.

SEMIVARIANCE

Another problem with the standard deviation is that it treats outcomes above and below the expected value in the same way. This is not likely to cause difficulty with a *symmetrical* distribution, such as that illustrated in Figure 11.2, for which the probability of being a certain amount above the expected value is the same as the probability of being that amount below. But problems arise if distributions are nonsymmetrical, such as those illustrated in Figures 11.1(a) and 11.1(b). The expected value and standard deviation are the same for each distribution, but the risk characteristics are quite different. These are called *skewed* distributions because one tail of each distribution is longer than the other. Figure 11.1(a) is skewed to the right because the long tail is on the right side, and distribution 11.1(b) is skewed to the left. There is a significant probability of large losses in the case of 11.1(b), but not in the case of 11.1(a).

The semivariance can be used to compare risk between projects when the probability distributions are skewed. The semivariance is computed in the same manner as the variance, except that only outcomes below the expected value are considered in its calculation. For the investment analyzed in Table 11.1, the semivariance is:

$$\text{Semivariance} = .1(100-300)^2 + .2(200-300)^2 = 6,000$$

The *semi–standard deviation* is the square root of the semivariance:

$$\text{Semi–standard deviation} = \sqrt{6,000} = \underline{77.46}$$

To make the semivariance and variance comparable in scale, the semivariance can be adjusted by doubling; it will then equal the variance if the distribution is symmetrical. The adjusted semi–standard deviation is the square root of the doubled semivariance. For the investment in Table 11.1, the adjusted semi–standard deviation is:

$$\text{Adjusted semi–standard deviation} = \sqrt{2 \times 6,000} = 110$$

The adjusted semi–standard deviation will be the same as the standard deviation if the probability distribution is symmetrical, greater than the standard deviation if the distribution is skewed to the left, and less than the standard deviation if the distribution is skewed to the right. Any of these measures can also be divided by the expected value to convert them to coefficients adjusted for project size, as was done with the coefficient of variation.

ALTERNATE PROFITABILITY MEASURE AND RISK |

With the exception of the geometric mean return, the risk measures discussed in this chapter are stated in terms of risk related to net present value. All of the same risk statistics can be computed in relation to the internal rate of return, payback, equivalent annuity, or most other measures that might be used for capital investment evaluation. It should be noted, though, that the limitations of specific desirability measures come along as unwanted baggage when these measures are carried into the risk analysis arena. A higher internal rate of return or shorter payback is not always better, for example, as illustrated with the following example.

Example. A capital investment at Bowling Green Corporation requires an outlay of $100 and will generate cash flows of $20 a year forever, if successful. An alternate outcome is a $125 inflow at the end of the first year, and nothing thereafter. Given a 10 percent required return, the two net present values and internal rates of return are:

Outcome	Success	Alternate
Cash flow per year	$ 20	$125
Number of years cash flow is received	∞	1
Present value of inflow	$200	$113.64
Net present value	$100	$ 13.64
Internal rate of return	20%	25%

In this example, the higher internal rate of return is associated with a less desirable outcome, in net present value terms. Likewise, the less desirable outcome has a shorter payback period. Therefore, decisions based on the probability distribution of internal rate of return or payback period may lead to erroneous capital investment decisions.

COMPREHENSIVE EXAMPLE |

Suppose you are a production manager for Treac, a manufacturer of floppy disk drives. Three production methods are available to meet increased demand and are summarized in Table 11.2.

| TABLE 11.2 PRODUCTION METHODS FOR MANUFACTURING DISK DRIVES

Production Method	Manual	Semi-automated	Fully automated
Expected net present value	$300,000	$400,000	$500,000
σ_{npv}	300,000	400,000	700,000
Coefficient of variation	1.00	1.00	1.40
Adjusted semi–standard deviation	300,000	350,000	700,000
P(NPV < 0)	.1587	.1271	.2389

If there were no risk, you would choose the fully automated method because it has the highest net present value. However, the standard deviation suggests that you can increase the net present value only by increasing risk. The coefficient of variation, on the other hand, adjusts the standard deviation for project scale and suggests the semiautomated method is not more risky than manual production. Skewness is recognized with the adjusted semi–standard deviation, which is lowest as a ratio to NPV for semiautomated production.

You would prefer the semiautomated method over the manual method because it has a higher expected net present value and lower risk. Whether you would be willing to accept the higher risk of the fully automated method in exchange for higher expected net present value is a more difficult question, depending on your own preferences. If you will face a postaudit, for example, you may want to choose the semiautomated method to minimize the probability of negative net present value. Your stockholders' and superiors' preferences will depend on their utility functions, which brings us to our next topic.

UTILITY THEORY—PERSPECTIVE ON RISK TAKING |

Utility theory is basic to much study of economic decision making. Utility is often referred to in economics as a measure of the degree of satisfaction received. In our analysis of decision making under uncertainty, we only need to define utility as an index to measure the relative desirability of monetary payoffs of varying degrees of uncertainty.

Use of utility theory in valuing risky alternatives was suggested by Daniel Bernoulli in 1738,[5] following his demonstration of the futility of using expected value as a guiding rule for evaluating gambles.[6] Bernoulli suggested that people choose between risky alternatives so as to maximize expected utility. Expected utility, $E(U)$, is defined as:

$$E(U) = p_1 U(X_1) + p_2 U(X_2) + p_3 U(X_3) + \ldots\ldots \quad \text{(11-8)}$$

where p_1 is the probability of outcome 1, X_1 is the payment received if outcome 1 occurs, and $U(X_1)$ is an index which turns out to reflect the relative attractiveness of payment X_1 in relation to other possible payments. Widespread use of expected utility concepts followed rigorous development of the theory by

[5]D. Bernoulli, "Specimen Theoriae Novae de Mensura Sortis" (St. Petersburg, 1738). English translation: *Econometrica* (1954): 23–36.

[6]This demonstration, called the St. Petersburg paradox, involves a game in which a coin is flipped until it comes up heads. The payoff is $\$2^n$ where n is the number of flips until a head occurs. The expected value is:

$$E(V) = \$2(1/2) + \$4(1/4) + \$8(1/8) + \ldots = \infty$$

The expected value rule leads to the ludicrous conclusion that even the richest person would trade all of his or her wealth for a gamble with the probability of a payoff in excess of $16 being $\frac{1}{16}$.

Von Neumann and Morgenstern[7] and a pioneering application in finance by Markowitz.[8]

The reason for the use of expected utility is that choices consistent with expected utility maximization are rational, while other choices are not rational. The essential characteristic of rational choice is that if A is preferred over B and B is preferred over C, then A must be preferred over C; if rational people prefer Ford over Chevrolet and prefer Chevrolet over Chrysler, they will prefer Ford over Chrysler. This essential characteristic also implies that rational decision makers who are indifferent between A and B, and also indifferent between B and C, will be indifferent between A and C. A rational decision maker will be able to rank alternatives in this way whether A, B, and C are certain payments or gambles.

As a second characteristic, rational decision makers will not be fooled by method of presentation; a rational decision maker will be indifferent between a .25 probability of receiving $10 and a .5 probability of winning a free play in a coin-flip game that pays $10 if the coin comes up heads and $0 if it comes up tails.

To begin exploring the meaning of the expected utility criterion, take M. Clark, a rational decision maker who is considering a gamble that pays $5 or nothing, with the probability of a $5 payoff being h. The gamble can be shown graphically as follows, with p representing event probability.

$$p = h \qquad \$5$$
$$p = 1 - h \qquad \$0$$

Suppose we present Clark with numerous choices, each involving a certain $3 or the gamble with a different value of h. We find that Clark chooses the gamble whenever h is greater than .85 and chooses the certain $3 whenever h is less than .85. Clark is indifferent between a certain $3 and the gamble with h of .85.

By repeating the questioning of Clark for other certain amounts, we can find Clark's indifference level of h for each certain amount between $0 and $5. The results of the questioning of Clark appear in Figure 11.3.

What happens if we decide to use the values of h as indexes of relative desirability? Let H be the total amount of h from a set of payments and E(H) be the expected H from a gamble involving various possible payments. Suppose we want to know how Clark will respond to gamble A, which has a payment of $2 or $4, with probabilities of .4 and .6 respectively:

$$p = .6 \qquad \$4$$
$$p = .4 \qquad \$2$$

---

[7]John Von Neumann and Oskar Morgenstern, *Theory of Games and Economic Behavior,* 2nd ed. (Princeton, N.J.: Princeton University Press, 1947).

[8]Harry Markowitz, "Portfolio Selection," *Journal of Finance* 7 (March 1952): 77–91.

| **FIGURE 11.3**   **INDIFFERENCE CURVE FOR M. CLARK**

For each dollar amount, this curve shows the value of h such that the investor would be indifferent between the certain amount and a probability h of receiving $5 (with a probability 1 − h of receiving $0).

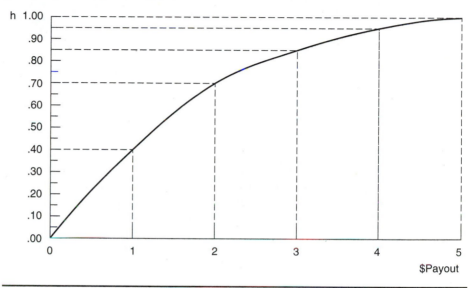

The expected value of H for this gamble, using the h values for $2 and $4 from Figure 11.3, is:

$$E(H) = .4(.7) + .6(.95) = .85$$

Since .85 is the value of h associated with a certain $3, Clark will be indifferent between a certain $3 and gamble A, if Clark wishes to maximize E(H).

We see the choice that results from deciding so as to maximize E(H), but is that the right choice? Based on Clark's previously stated preferences, we can demonstrate that the choice that resulted from using E(H) as the guideline is rational, while any other choice is irrational. To show this, we first note that Clark previously expressed the following indifferences:

Certain amount	Gamble toward which decision maker was indifferent
$2	.7 probability of $5 and .3 probability of $0
$4	.95 probability of $5 and .05 probability of $0

Given these indifferences and our definition of rational choice, these gambles can be substituted into gamble A in place of the certain payoffs of $2 and

$4, without changing the desirability of gamble A. Therefore, a gamble that is equally attractive to gamble A is as follows:

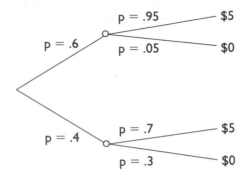

Rather than having a .6 probability of a $4 payoff, this gamble has a .6 probability of receiving another gamble that is of equal value to a certain $4 payoff for the decision maker, etc. For this new gamble, the payouts and probabilities can be summarized as follows:

$$\text{Probability of receiving } \$5 = .6(.95) + .4(.7) = .85$$

$$\text{Probability of receiving } \$0 = .15$$

In other words, Clark will be indifferent between gamble A and a gamble that is as desirable as a certain $3. Concluding that gamble A was either more or less desirable than a certain $3 would be inconsistent with E(H) maximization. Concluding that gamble A was either more or less desirable than a certain $3 would also be inconsistent with previously stated preferences and, therefore, irrational.

With the previous example, we demonstrated that the decisions based on E(H) are consistent with rational behavior, while decisions inconsistent with E(H) maximization are inconsistent with rational behavior. But what has this to do with maximization of expected utility? Recall that utility was defined as an index of the worths of monetary payoffs of varying degrees of uncertainty. Thus, the values of h meet the definition of a utility function.

Utility, like temperature, is only a relative measure. We can assign any arbitrary numbers to the freezing and melting points of water and then describe all other degrees of warmth in relation to those two points. Likewise, we can assign any arbitrary values to $0 and $5, then define the utilities of other payouts in relation to those two points. Mathematically, this is equivalent to saying that our decision maker's choices are consistent with any utility function for which utility, U, is:

$$U = a + bh \tag{11-9}$$

where a and b are constants. Letting $a = 0$ and $b = 1$ is equivalent to making the utility of $0 equal to 0.0 and the utility of $5 equal to 1.0 for Clark. The utility of any payout is then the value of h associated with that payout, and Figure 11.3 then represents the decision maker's utility function. Rational choice among risky alternatives is identical to choice that maximizes expected utility.

To further clarify the meaning of expected utility, the decision maker's beginning position must be clarified. In the previous examples, we were implicitly assuming Clark started with wealth of $0 and was choosing between certain and uncertain additions to wealth. Now suppose Clark has $3. A gamble will either increase wealth by $1, with a probability of .7, or decrease wealth by $1, with a probability of .3. The utility of $3 of wealth is .85, while the expected utility of the gamble is:

$$E(U) = .3U(\$2) + .7U(\$4) = .3(.7) + .7(.95) = .875$$

The gamble is attractive because expected utility is increased, by .025.

This same gamble could have been evaluated using marginal utility. In the case of a loss, wealth is decreased to $2, and the change in total utility is .70 − .85 = −.15. In the case of a win, total wealth increases to $4, and total utility increases by .95 − .85 = .10. The expected increase in total utility is:

$$E(\text{increase in total utility}) = .3(-.15) + .7(.10) = .025$$

From this example, we note that the desirability of a gamble depends on the decision maker's beginning wealth level. Depending on the shapes of their utility functions, decision makers may become more or less willing to accept gambles as their wealth increases.

TYPES OF UTILITY FUNCTIONS

Figure 11.4 includes three types of utility curves. Curve A shows declining marginal utility, the type illustrated in the previous example. Each additional dollar of wealth provides less utility than the previous dollar. As illustrated in the previous example, you will be *risk-averse* if you have this type of marginal utility curve. You will need payoffs with expected values sufficiently in excess of cost if you are to be induced to take risks. Line B is a utility curve for which each new dollar of wealth has a utility equal to the utility of the last dollar. The decision maker with this curve would be *risk-neutral*. This decision maker will be indifferent about a gamble with an expected value equal to its cost, and will accept all gambles for which expected value exceeds cost, no matter how small the excess. Curve C is one for which the marginal utility of each new dollar is higher than the marginal utility of the previous dollar. This person is a *risk-seeker*, and would be willing to accept some gambles for which the expected value is less than the cost; this person may be found at the gaming tables in Las Vegas or Monte Carlo.

Evidence suggests that most decision makers are risk-averse and will, therefore, gamble only when expected value exceeds cost by a sufficient amount. People

| **FIGURE 11.4** **UTILITY OF WEALTH CURVES**

Curve A is the total utility curve for a risk-averse decision maker. Line B is the total utility curve for a risk-neutral decision maker, and Curve C is the total utility curve for a risk-seeker.

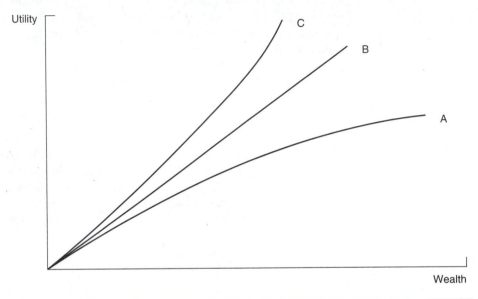

regularly buy insurance, for example, even though the expected payout is the insurance premium *minus* the insurer's administrative costs and profits. Bond issues considered risky must pay higher interest rates to compensate investors for risk. Expected returns from common stock portfolios are higher than those for U.S. government bonds, because investors will take risks only if they can improve their expected returns.

Not everyone requires compensation to accept risk though. We have observed many people buying lottery tickets or visiting gaming tables, thereby giving up expected return to get risk. We have also observed people simultaneously buying insurance and lottery tickets, both paying to reduce risk and paying to obtain risk. Gambling may be explained by utility curves with increasing marginal utility of wealth. Simultaneous purchase of lottery tickets and insurance policies may be explained by utility functions that reflect increasing marginal utility in one range and decreasing marginal utility in another.[9]

[9]This explanation was first suggested by Friedman and Savage. See Milton Friedman and L. J. Savage, "The Utility Analysis of Choices Involving Risk," *Journal of Political Economy* (1948): 279–304.

USING UTILITY THEORY

In theory, we could question people about their preferences among various gambles and use this information to map their utility of wealth functions. This information could then be used to choose the risk-return trade-off they would prefer. This has been done, but as a practical matter it is not done frequently. Measurement of utility functions in this manner is extremely time-consuming and the utility functions appear to change frequently.

Furthermore, there is the question of whose utility function to use for business decisions. Should we measure the utility function of the project manager, the chief executive officer, or the owner? If we want to use the owner's utility function, which owner should we use when the stock is held by thousands of people?

There is another important reason for not measuring managers' utility functions. Managers generally want to make the major decisions of the organization based on input from analysts rather than giving input to analysts who then make the major decisions. Once the manager's utility function is measured and the manager expresses his or her beliefs with regard to payoffs and probabilities, the analyst can make the optimal decision based on the input from the manager. This process is exactly the opposite of that desired by most managers.

Why spend all of this time on utility theory if utility functions are seldom measured? Recall the no-arbitrage profit principle, which says that two assets with identical payoff characteristics must sell at identical prices in an efficient market. The expected utility criterion is analogous in that it is simply a result of the assumption that decision makers will act rationally and will, therefore, attach identical values to sets of payoffs toward which they have expressed indifference. Thus, expected utility theory is simply the theory of rational choice. Expected utility theory is the basis for many models for the analysis of investments under risk, such as the mean-variance capital asset pricing model. An understanding of utility theory is, therefore, essential for the understanding of financial decision making under conditions of risk. We will apply utility theory in later chapters, most directly in Chapters 14 and 15, to develop specific rules for capital budgeting in the face of risk.

CHOICE OF A RISK PERSPECTIVE |

Regardless of the risk measure used, there are five general alternatives with regard to a perspective from which to view risk. Risk can be viewed from the perspective of:

1. A *single investment* in isolation
2. An investment's contribution to the riskiness of a *portfolio of the company's assets*
3. An investment's contribution to the riskiness of the *portfolio of a shareholder*

4. An investment's contribution to the riskiness of the various *contingent claims* against the company
5. An investment's contribution to the riskiness of the *overall economy*

There are reasons for considering each perspective, and as a result, the risk of an investment is often considered from more than one perspective. Reasons for considering each perspective are outlined in the following paragraphs.

Single-project perspective. A manager responsible for a single project will probably be evaluated in terms of that project's *outcome*, not the nature of the probability distribution when the decision was made. Therefore, that manager will be concerned about the project's total risk, not its contribution to the company's risk. Furthermore, many managers are far removed from the executive suite, and do not have information about how other segments of the company are expected to respond to various economic conditions. Additionally, the dynamics of corporate decision making often mitigate in favor of the single-project view of risk. Final approval or recommendation is often made by a capital budgeting committee whose members are top-level managers with other full-time duties and varying levels of financial training. Investment proposals are generally reviewed one at a time so it is difficult to consider, in other than general terms, how they will fit together in a portfolio. Methods of single-project risk analysis are covered in Chapter 12.

Company portfolio perspective. Top managers are responsible for the overall performance of the company, and their compensation is generally tied to overall company performance. They will almost certainly care about the company's overall risk. In other words, top managers will view the company as a portfolio of capital investments, and they will be interested in how a particular investment contributes to the riskiness of that portfolio. Recognition of risk from the company perspective is covered in Chapter 13.

Shareholder portfolio perspective. Shareholder wealth maximization is a commonly cited goal of the firm. Acquisition of an asset by a company adds that asset to the shareholders' portfolios of assets. From the viewpoint of the shareholders, the important risk is that risk which cannot be diversified away. If investors have well-diversified portfolios, the only risk that cannot be diversified away is sensitivity to factors affecting returns on all investments. The general approach to recognizing risk from the shareholder perspective is to adjust required return for nondiversifiable risk. These adjustments are developed in Chapters 14 and 15.

Contingent claims perspective. Shareholders, creditors, and managers all have claims against the company which are contingent on future events. Bondholders, for example, will receive principal and interest payments only if the company can earn enough money to make the payments. A change in riskiness of capital investments can change the value of various claims against the company, even if it does not change the total value of the company. Option pricing models are used in Chapter 15 to measure the impact of risk on the relative values of claims against the company. These changes in relative values can be important for capital investment decision making.

Total economy perspective. Government policy makers may be interested in looking at the riskiness of the overall economy, and may want to encourage or discourage particular types of capital investments based on considerations of impact on the country's economy. A diversified shareholder's returns are closely correlated with the overall health of the economy in the long run, so the contribution of a capital investment to the riskiness of the shareholder's portfolio is similar to the contribution to the riskiness of the overall economy. The relationship is not perfect because of externalities, taxes, insurance, and government programs like crop and flood insurance. Nevertheless, the relationship is close enough that an understanding of the shareholder portfolio perspective is useful for thinking about a total economy perspective.

Numerous parties are involved in the typical capital investment decision, from the project's proponent to the capital budgeting committee and chief executive. In addition, capital investments frequently affect the welfare of workers and investors who do not participate in the decisions. Consequently, risk analysis frequently includes analysis from several different perspectives. Thus, the risk analysis methods discussed in Chapters 12 through 15 are often complementary rather than competing.

SUMMARY

This chapter has focused on the general principles underlying the consideration of risk in the analysis of capital investments. Methods of defining risk are often quite helpful in decision making. Risk analysis may consist of qualitative statements about uncertainties, sensitivity analyses, statements about the probability of some failure, or summaries of the probability distribution of outcomes. Expected value is the most common measure of the central tendency of a distribution of possible outcomes. The most widely used dispersion measures are the variance, standard deviation, coefficient of variation, and semivariance. Methods will be developed in the following chapters for using these risk measures when analyzing capital investments.

Utility theory forms the basis of much of our understanding of decision making under risk. The fundamental assumption needed to justify the use of utility theory in evaluating risky alternatives is that decision makers are rational. It is generally believed that most decision makers have declining marginal utility of wealth functions and are therefore risk-averse; they will accept risk only if compensated with a sufficient increase in expected return.

QUESTIONS |

11–1. Is risk a common or rare problem in capital budgeting? Explain.

11–2. Define the following terms: (a) risk, (b) probability, (c) probability distribution, (d) subjective probability, (e) objective probability, (f) risk-averse, (g) diversifiable risk, (h) nondiversifiable risk.

11–3. Explain the strengths and weaknesses of the variance and standard deviation as risk measures.

11–4. What weakness of the standard deviation is overcome through the use of the coefficient of variation?

11–5. What weakness of the standard deviation is overcome through the use of the semivariance?

11–6. Is it believed that the marginal utility of wealth for most decision makers increases or decreases with each additional dollar of wealth?

11–7. What types of utility curves (increasing, decreasing, or constant marginal utility of wealth) are generally associated with each of the following attitudes toward risk: (a) risk-averse, (b) risk-neutral, (c) risk-seeking?

11–8. Why are the utility functions of individuals not measured frequently in the process of risk analysis?

11–9. What are the justifications for viewing risk from the perspective of:
a. Contribution to the riskiness of a shareholder's diversified portfolio?
b. Contribution to the risk of the company's portfolio of assets?
c. A single project in isolation (total project risk)?

11–10. (**Ethical considerations**) Many research labs of major corporations are cutting back on their expenditures on "pure" or "basic" research. Instead they have shifted the expenditures to product development. These managers believe in funding only research that shows promise of generating a profit. An example of "pure" or "basic" research is the Supercollider project that attempts to answer the question "What happens when atoms collide?" NEC has made the corporate decision to continue to invest in pure research regardless of how remote the probability of a profitable return.
a. List several ethical arguments for NEC's continued investment in "pure" or "basic" research.
b. List several ethical arguments for the more popular policy to discontinue funding for "pure" or "basic" research.

PROBLEMS |

11–1. A die is fair in that there is an equal probability of it landing on each of its six sides. If a value of 1, 2, or 3 appears on the face of the die, the player receives $50. If a 4 appears, the player receives $150. If a 5 or 6 appears, the player receives $300. What is the expected value from a single roll? Would a risk-averse investor be willing to pay the expected value for the opportunity to play?

11–2. When an exploratory oil well is drilled, there is a .1 probability of finding oil. If two exploratory wells are drilled in different parts of the country, what is the probability that (a) oil will be found in both wells, (b) oil will be found in neither well, (c) oil will be found in one well?

11–3. If oil is found in an exploratory well, there is a .5 probability that the field will prove commercially viable. If the probability of finding oil in an exploratory well is .1, what is the probability that oil will be found in the exploratory well *and* the field will prove to be commercially viable?

11–4. If competitors do not respond to a new product, there is a .9 probability of a positive net present value. If competitors do respond, there is a .4 probability of a positive net present value. There is an .8 probability that competitors will respond. What is the probability of a positive net present value?

11–5. Possible net present values and associated probabilities for a new investment are as follows. What is the probability of a positive net present value?

NPV	−100	−50	0	50	100	200
Probability	.10	.10	.20	.20	.30	.10

11–6. For the investment in problem 5, what is the (a) expected value, (b) median, (c) mode?

11–7. An investment costs $100 today and has a one-year life. There is a .5 probability of receiving $120 at the end of the year and a .5 probability of receiving $90 (in other words, a return of +20 percent or −10 percent). What is the geometric mean return?

11–8. The net present values and associated probabilities for an investment, designated investment H, follow. Compute the expected value for the probability distribution.

NPV	0	200	400	600	800	1,000	1,200	1,400
Probability	.05	.1	.1	.2	.25	.15	.1	.05

11–9. Compute the variance and standard deviation for the probability distribution for investment H in problem 8.

11–10. Compute the coefficient of variation for the probability distribution for investment H in problem 8.

11–11. Compute the semivariance for the probability distribution for investment H in problem 8.

11–12. Compute the adjusted semi–standard deviation and the coefficient of adjusted semi–standard deviation for investment H in problem 8. Is the distribution skewed to the left or to the right?

11–13. Investment J has the probability distribution of net present values cited below. Is this investment preferable to investment H discussed in problem 8?

Net present value	0	200	500	800	1,000
Probability	.1	.1	.6	.1	.1

11–14. The possible net present values for investment K are normally distributed with a mean of $100,000 and a standard deviation of $50,000. What is the probability of a negative net present value? a net present value above $150,000?

11–15. The expected net present value for investment L is $180,000 and the standard deviation is $100,000. The probability distribution is normal. What is the probability of a negative net present value? If we are primarily concerned about the risk of a negative net present value, which investment is riskier, K (in problem 14) or L?

11–16. D. Morton has been asked to choose between certain payments and gambles, with a probability h of receiving $10 (and a probability of 1 − h of receiving $0). Morton's indifference values of h for various certain amounts are as follows:

Certain Amount	0	1	2	3	4	5	6	7	8	9	10
h	0	.289	.458	.578	.671	.744	.812	.867	.916	.960	1

Morton has starting wealth of $0. Morton is asked to choose between a certain $5 and a gamble. The gamble has a .5 probability of a $6 payoff and a .5 probability of a $4 payoff. Morton chooses the gamble. Is this rational?

11–17. Morton (problem 16), whose preferences were revealed above, has starting wealth of $0. Morton is offered a gamble with a .7 probability of a $7 payoff and a .3 probability of a $2 payoff. Morton will be indifferent between the gamble and what certain payment?

11–18. Morton (problem 16), whose preferences were revealed above, has beginning wealth of $5. A gamble involves a .5 probability of losing $1 and a .5 probability of gaining $2. In other words, the probabilities of ending wealth of $4 and $7 are each .5. If Morton is rational, will the gamble be chosen?

11–19. K. Nielsen makes decisions so as to maximize expected utility and has a utility function that is approximately as shown below over the relevant range:

$$\text{Total utility} = W - .0000001W^2$$

where W represents total wealth. Nielsen has $100,000 of total wealth and has the opportunity to spend that wealth on a gamble with a .5 probability of receiving nothing and a .5 probability of receiving $225,000. Would Nielsen be willing to take the gamble? Would Nielsen be willing to pay $1 million (if Nielsen had $1 million) in exchange for a gamble with a .5 probability of $2.25 million and a .5 probability of $0?

11–20. An expected utility-maximizing decision maker with $1 of wealth is indifferent between keeping a dollar or taking a gamble with a .5 probability of receiving $5 and a .5 probability of receiving nothing. For convenience, we can assign utility of 0.0 to $0 and 1.0 to $1. What is the utility of $5? Is this person risk-averse, risk-neutral, or risk-seeking?

11–21. (**Applications**) Several studies have reported that the historical rate of return in the stock market, as measured by an index like the Standard and Poor's 500, has averaged 15 percent per year from 1981 to 1997. The standard deviation of these annual returns during this same period was 12 percent. Assume that the past is indicative of the future and that the returns are distributed normally. What is the probability that the return in the stock market will exceed a 3 percent return on a savings account?

SELECTED REFERENCES |

Bernoulli, D. "Specimen Theoriae Novae de Mensura Sortis." St. Petersburg, 1738. English translation: *Econometrica* (1954): 23–36.

Carlson, Phillip G. "An Argument for 'Generalized' Mean-Coefficient of Variation Analysis: Comment." *Financial Management* 10 (Autumn 1981): 87–88.

Chow, Edward H., Wayne Y. Lee, and Michael E. Solt. "The Economic Exposure of U.S. Multinational Firms." *Journal of Financial Research* 20 (Summer 1997): 191–210.

Crum, R. L., and F. G. J. Derfinderen. *Capital Budgeting under Condition of Uncertainty.* Boston: Martinus Nijhoff, 1981.

Crum, Roy L., Dan J. Laughhunn, and John W. Payne. "Risk-Seeking Behavior and Its Implications for Financial Models." *Financial Management* 10 (Winter 1981): 20–27.

Forham, David R., and S. Brooks Marshall. "Tools for Dealing with Uncertainty." *Management Accounting* 79 (September 1997): 38–43.

Harris, Milton, and Artur Raviv. "The Capital Budgeting Process, Incentives, and Information." *Journal of Finance* 51 (September 1996): 1139–1174.

Latané, Henry A., and Donald L. Tuttle. "Criteria for Portfolio Building." *Journal of Finance* 22 (September 1967): 359–373.

Lintner, John. "The Valuation of Risk Assets and Selection of Risky Investments in Stock Portfolios and Capital Budgets." *Review of Economics and Statistics* (February 1965): 13–37.

Markowitz, Harry M. "Investment for the Long Run: New Evidence for an Old Rule." *Journal of Finance* 31 (December 1976): 1273–1286.

———. "Portfolio Selection." *Journal of Finance* 7 (March 1952): 77–91.

May, Don O. "Do Managerial Motives Influence Firm Risk Reduction Strategies?" *Journal of Finance* 50 (September 1996): 1291–1308.

Morgan, George Emir. "Risk Aversion in the Approximate and in the Exact Forms." *Engineering Economist* 37 (Winter 1992): 137–144.

Morrin, Roger A., and A. Fernandez Suarez. "Risk Aversion Revisited." *Journal of Finance* 38 (September 1983): 1201–1216.

Sharpe, William F. "Capital Asset Prices: A Theory of Market Equilibrium under Conditions of Risk." *Journal of Finance* 19 (September 1964): 425–442.

Swalm, Peter O. "Utility Theory—Insights into Risk Taking." *Harvard Business Review* (November–December 1966): 123–136.

Thakor, Anjan V. "Game Theory in Finance." *Financial Management* 20 (Spring 1991): 71–94.

Von Neumann, John, and Oskar Morgenstern. *Theory of Games and Economic Behavior,* 2nd ed. Princeton, N.J.: Princeton University Press, 1947.

Young, W., and R. Trent. "Geometric Mean Approximations of Individual Security and Portfolio Performance." *Journal of Financial and Quantitative Analysis* 4 (June 1969): 179–199.

CHAPTER 12

SINGLE INVESTMENT RISK ANALYSIS

After completing this chapter you should be able to:

1. Explain why it is important to look at risk exposure from the perspective of a single project.
2. Conduct a simple sensitivity analysis and understand the results.
3. Grasp the role that earnings break-even point and net present value break-even play as indicators of risk.
4. Calculate a break-even point and know how changes in fixed cost, variable cost, and selling price influence the break-even point.
5. Calculate the expected value and describe what it means.
6. Discern between perfectly correlated, uncorrelated, and perfectly negatively correlated cash flows.
7. Describe how simulation works.
8. Diagram a decision tree and calculate the resulting probabilities.
9. Understand some of the ways probability estimates are developed in practice.
10. Explain some of the ways in which risk is managed.
11. List several ways in which projects are selected when risky cash flows are involved.

Recognition Equipment of Irving, Texas, is a good example of the small high-technology companies that have accounted for much recent growth in the economy of the United States. With their small size and entrepreneurial spirit, these companies can respond rapidly to a dynamic marketplace.

Managers at Recognition Equipment knew the importance of flexibility. They also knew the importance of achieving cost-effective production through automation. Unfortunately, a capital investment in automated production equipment could tie up large amounts of capital and could, therefore, sharply reduce future flexibility. Inability to respond to sudden changes in markets or technology could mean missed opportunities, or worse. Managers assessed the risks to the company that were associated with various alternatives and sought ways to achieve their productivity goals while limiting their risk exposure. They settled on a strategy involving used automation equipment.[1]

Managers at Recognition Equipment are typical in that assessing and dealing with risk are important aspects of their capital budgeting programs. A complete evaluation of a proposed capital investment requires that risk be considered from the perspectives of numerous parties: the manager proposing the investment, the senior executives, the shareholders, and others affected by the company's actions. The assessment of risk often begins with *single investment risk* analysis, an examination of the investment's total risk as a stand-alone unit. There are five reasons for starting with single investment risk analysis:

1. The manager proposing a capital investment in a large organization often lacks comprehensive information about the company and its plans that would be needed to measure the investment's contribution to the riskiness of the company.
2. The manager proposing a capital investment is likely to be evaluated on the performance of that investment. In such cases, the proposing manager is concerned about total risk, not contribution to the risk of the total company or its shareholders.
3. Single investment risk analysis is useful in developing ways to eliminate or decrease risk without proportional decreases in expected return.
4. Analysis of single investment risk often serves as the basis for understanding the investment's contribution to the company's risk, the shareholder's risk, and so forth.
5. Capital investments in many organizations are considered one at a time by a capital budgeting committee. The members seldom have the time or the background to fully consider interactions with all other investments being held or considered by the company or its shareholders.

This chapter begins with a survey of single investment risk measurement methods: sensitivity analysis, break-even analysis, and probability-based methods, including simulation and decision trees. These tools are used to help managers develop a clear picture of the risks to which they are exposed. A variety of tools are discussed because no one tool fits every situation. Sensitivity analysis and break-even analysis are simple to use and the results are easy to explain, but the simplicity is gained at the expense of an understanding of the probabilities of the

---

[1]Ward Chartier and Mike Moline, "Selective Automation Can Be Profitable in a Small Factory," *Industrial Engineering* 20 (April 1988): 28–34.

various outcomes. Simulation and decision trees provide more insight into probabilities, but are more difficult (therefore more expensive and time consuming) to use. An extensive simulation study would probably be appropriate for the evaluation of a proposed second canal across Central America, but we would not go beyond simple sensitivity analysis for the choice between copy machines at a neighborhood real estate office. Consequently, each risk-measurement tool has its place.

Once you have measured risk, you can begin to think of ways to control risk, decreasing or even eliminating some sources of uncertainty. Finally, you must decide if the expected profitability justifies the risks involved. Following the discussion of risk measurement methods, we will consider methods of controlling risk and capital investment choice in the face of risk.

SENSITIVITY ANALYSIS |

The first question that arises in discussing the riskiness of an investment is often "what can go wrong?" followed by "what are the critical variables?" Both of these questions can be answered through sensitivity analysis. *Sensitivity analysis is the computation of present value or other profitability measures for multiple values of at least one variable that will affect the investment.* Suppose, for example, a capital investment is affected by sales volume and salvage value. Net present value would be computed for numerous combinations of sales volumes and salvage values.

Example. Rediform Concrete is considering a $5 million capital investment for a factory to manufacture formed concrete products, such as patio stones, mobile home stairs, and lawn decorations. The proposed factory will generate annual sales between $2 million and $5 million. After-tax fixed costs are $500,000 and after-tax variable costs are 50 percent of sales. Annual after-tax cash flow is determined as follows:

$$\text{After-tax cash flow} = (.5 \times \text{Sales}) - \$500,000$$

The expected life is 5 years, and the salvage value depends on land prices at the end of 5 years. The factory would be built on Palmetto Road, near the Sunshine Expressway. A new freeway exit is being planned for the Sunshine Expressway. If the exit is built at Palmetto Road, the salvage value of the factory will be $3 million. If the exit is located on one of the two competing roads, the salvage value will be $1 million. To consider the risks involved, managers compute the net present value for various combinations of sales and salvage value, as illustrated in Table 12.1. For example, using Rediform's 10 percent required return, the net present value with sales of $4 million and salvage value of $3 million is:

$$\begin{aligned} \text{NPV} &= [(.5 \times 4,000,000) - 500,000]\text{PVA}|_{5\text{yrs},10\%} + 3,000,000/1.10^5 - 5,000,000 \\ &= \underline{\$2,549,000} \end{aligned}$$

| TABLE 12.1 SENSITIVITY ANALYSIS OF THE REDIFORM CONCRETE FACTORY

Net present values of the proposed formed concrete factory, letting revenue and salvage value vary. The net present values were computed using a Lotus 1-2-3 sensitivity analysis table.

	A	B	C	D	E	F	G	H
1				Sales ($000)				
2	Salvage							
3	Value	2,000	2,500	3,000	3,500	4,000	4,500	5,000
4	($000)							
5								
6	1,000	−2,484	−1,536	−588	359	1,307	2,255	3,202
7	3,000	−1,242	−294	654	1,601	2,549	3,497	4,444

The critical variables are often seen more easily with graphical sensitivity analysis. Figure 12.1 summarizes the information from Table 12.1 in graphical form.

It is relatively easy to carry out sensitivity analysis. Computer programs like Lotus 1-2-3 and Excel have built-in functions for performing sensitivity analysis on one specified factor or two specified factors with both allowed to vary simultaneously. If sensitivity analysis is done using either of the packages or a similar spreadsheet program, a graph such as that in Figure 12.1 can be readily produced with a few more keystrokes.

As illustrated in Table 12.1 and Figure 12.1, sensitivity analysis gives managers an easily understood picture of possible outcomes. Important variables can be identified, as can the levels of those variables needed for project success. Managers may attempt to objectively determine the probability of each outcome or to use their own subjective assessments of the probability of each outcome. Frequently, managers rely on their own judgment to decide if the risk is acceptable, without explicitly using probability. Managers may also decide to take some risk-reduction action, such as choosing another site or leasing rather than purchasing the land, to reduce uncertainty about the salvage value.

BREAK-EVEN ANALYSIS |

Sensitivity analysis is helpful in identifying key variables, and sales are often one of those key variables. Earnings or cash flow break-even analysis focuses on the relationship between sales and profitability or cash flow. NPV break-even extends cash flow break-even and looks at the relationship between sales, cash flow, interest rate, and net present value.

| **FIGURE 12.1**   **SENSITIVITY ANALYSIS OF THE REDIFORM CONCRETE FACTORY**

This graph shows the sensitivity of net present value to sales and salvage value, drawn from the results from Table 12.1 and produced by Lotus 1-2-3.

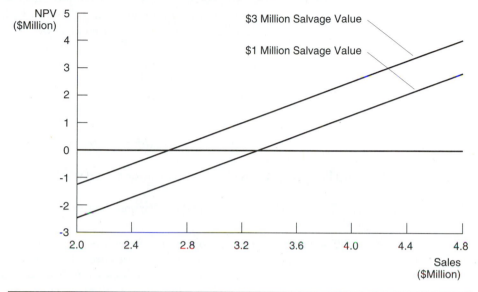

To understand break-even we need to remember that in this analysis all costs are viewed as either variable or fixed cost. A variable cost is one that changes in total amount as the level of unit sales change but is usually assumed to stay constant in per-unit amount or percentage as sales units change. For example, a variable cost for Wendy's Hamburgers would be the "beef" they so proudly talk about in their commercials. As Wendy's sells one more hamburger at 99 cents they incur the cost of one more patty of beef at 10 cents. This cost varies in total dollars. As Wendy's sells more hamburgers the total amount spent on hamburger patties will increase. This cost stays constant in per-unit amount or percentage because as Wendy's sells more hamburgers, 10 cents per hamburger sold or roughly 10 percent of the sales price is spent on this variable cost, hamburger patties.

Fixed costs are costs that remain constant in total dollars as the sales level in units changes but decrease in per-unit amount as the volume increases within some range. The salary of the manager of a business would be an example of a fixed cost. To extend the Wendy's example, assume that a manager is paid $40,000 per year excluding any bonus. If Wendy's has the capacity to sell between 0 and 500,000 hamburgers under this manager's supervision then the total dollar management cost of selling 160,000 hamburgers is $40,000, or $40,000/160,000 or 25 cents per hamburger. At 500,000 hamburgers the total dollar management cost is still $40,000 (thus the name *fixed*), or $40,000/500,000 or 8 cents per hamburger. It is not coincidental that the fixed cost per unit is lowest when the business is using the asset (the manager in this case) at its capacity. This is one of the reasons break-even analysis is a good measure of the risk of a single project. Depending on where you expect sales to be and the variation in the level of sales, break-even analysis determines the sales level necessary to cross over from negative earnings to positive earnings or, in other words, break even.

The earnings or cash flow *break-even point* is the level of sales necessary to produce a profit or cash flow of $0. From this point on, to simplify the discussion, we are going to assume that all variable and fixed expenses are paid in cash in the period that the sale takes place. By doing this we can assume that earnings and cash flow are equal. The cash flow break-even point in quantity sold (BEP_q) is:

$$BEP_q = \text{Fixed cost/(Price} - \text{Variable cost per unit)} \qquad (12\text{-}1)$$

The cash flow break-even point in dollar sales ($BEP_\$$) is:

$$BEP_\$ = \text{Fixed cost/(}1 - \text{Variable cost as a percent of dollar sales)} \qquad (12\text{-}2)$$

Example. Assume variable costs for Rediform Concrete are 50 percent of sales, and fixed costs for accounting purposes are $1 million. In unit terms, the price per cubic yard is $40 and variable costs are $20 (note that accounting costs in this case are assumed to equal cash outflows). The earnings break-even points in terms of quantity sold and dollar sales are:

$$BEP_q = \$1,000,000/(40 - 20) = \underline{50,000} \text{ cubic yards}$$
$$BEP_\$ = \$1,000,000/(1 - .5) = \underline{\$2,000,000} \text{ sales}$$

To extend the analysis and calculate an NPV break-even, recall that cash flow for Rediform is $(.5 \times \text{Sales}) - \$500,000$, the required return is 10 percent, and salvage value will be either $1 million or $3 million. The break-even sales levels in terms of net present value are as follows:

Salvage value of $1 million:

$$NPV = [(.5 \times \text{Sales}) - 500,000]PVA1_{5yrs,10\%} + 1,000,000/1.10^5 - 5,000,000 = 0$$
$$\text{Sales} = \underline{\$3,306,000}$$

Salvage value of $3 million:

$$NPV = [(.5 \times \text{Sales}) - 500,000]PVA1_{5yrs,10\%} + 3,000,000/1.10^5 - 5,000,000 = 0$$
$$\text{Sales} = \underline{\$2,655,000}$$

The earnings break-even point gives us the sales level necessary to report an income of $0. This may be of interest if, for example, debt covenants result in some loss of control if the company does not earn a profit. The cash flow break-even tells us the level of sales necessary to earn $0 in cash flow, a number that is useful in predicting our ability to meet future cash obligations. In general, though, the NPV break-even point would be the most interesting for capital budgeting purposes. It tells us the sales level above which wealth is created for the shareholders.

Managers occasionally want to know the break-even sales level in terms of earning a risk-free return. This would indicate the sales level below which we would have been better off leaving the money in some risk-free asset such as Treasury bills. For a risk-free rate of 6 percent after tax, the sales level that just provides the risk-free return with a $3 million salvage value is found as follows:

$$NPV = [(.5 \times Sales) - 500,000]PVA_{5yrs,6\%} + 3,000,000/1.06^5 - 5,000,000 = 0$$

$$Sales = \underline{\$2,310,000}$$

Break-even analysis is often presented graphically. Since the horizontal axis in Figure 12.1 is sales, Figure 12.1 is a graphical presentation of break-even analysis.

A limitation of sensitivity analysis, including break-even analysis, is that it generally shows the relationship between profitability and only one or two variables while holding all other variables constant. A table of net present values for ten levels of each of six factors would have one million entries, for example, and a graphical presentation would be virtually impossible. Thus, sensitivity analysis is useful for identifying one or two key factors and measuring sensitivity to those factors *in isolation*, or for considering a limited number of scenarios. Probability-related methods are often more time-consuming to use, but give an improved *overall* understanding of risk, particularly when the project is subject to numerous sources of uncertainty.

RISK ANALYSIS METHODS BASED ON PROBABILITY

In Table 12.1, the net present value for the formed concrete plant could be between -$2,484,000 and +$4,444,000. The next question likely to be asked by managers is: "What is the probability of each outcome?" This question may be answered by computing the parameters of the probability distribution of net present value—expected net present value, standard deviation, etc.—or it could be answered by computing the probabilities of specific events. We first deal with methods of computing the expected net present value and standard deviation based on the probability distributions of future cash flows. Next, we look at Monte Carlo simulation, a process for combining large amounts of information in the form of a probability distribution of outcomes. Finally, we look at decision trees, a tool for computing the probabilities of specific outcomes when some decisions can be delayed until more information is available.

EXPECTED PRESENT VALUE

If expected cash flows for each future year are known, the expected present value of those flows is simply:

$$E(PV) = E(CF_0) + E(CF_1)/(1 + k)^1 + E(CF_2)/(1 + k)^2 + \ldots \qquad (12\text{-}3)$$

where $E(CF_1)$ is expected cash flow at time 1, and k is the required return. This formula is valid whether cash flows are perfectly correlated, partially correlated, or uncorrelated from year to year.[2] Unfortunately, a similar rule does not hold for the internal rate of return.[3]

The standard deviation of the present value of a series of cash flows depends on correlation between year-to-year cash flows. Cash flows are correlated from period to period if the probability distribution cash flow for one period is related to actual cash flows in prior periods. We begin by looking at the two extremes, perfect correlation and no correlation at all, and then look at ways to deal with the more typical case of partial correlation.

STANDARD DEVIATION OF THE PRESENT VALUE OF PERFECTLY CORRELATED CASH FLOWS

Cash flows are perfectly correlated from period to period if cash flows after the first period are completely determined by cash flows in the first period. In other words, all uncertainty about future cash flows is eliminated when the first cash flow occurs. If a series of cash flows are perfectly correlated, the standard deviation of the present value of those flows, σPV, is:[4]

---

[2]We should note that when the life of an asset is uncertain, use of the expected life—the expected value from the probability distribution of life—will result in an inaccurate estimate of net present value. When life is uncertain, the net present value should be based on expected cash flow for each year, with the probability of the investment still operating in that year being used in the computation of expected cash flow.

[3]For methods of estimating the standard deviation of the probability distribution of internal rate of return under some conditions, see William Fairley and Henry D. Jacoby, "Investment Analysis Using the Probability Distribution of the Internal Rate of Return," *Management Science* 21 (August 1975): 1428-1437. But recall the limitations of this measure discussed in Chapter 11.

[4]Equation 12-4 follows directly from basic rules of statistics. The standard deviation of the sum of n perfectly correlated variables is

$$\sigma_{sum} = \sqrt{\sum_{t=1}^{n}\sum_{j=1}^{n}\sigma_{t,j}} = \sqrt{\sum_{t=1}^{n}\sum_{j=1}^{n}\sigma_t\sigma_j} = \sqrt{\left(\sum_{t=1}^{n}\sigma_{t,j}\right)^2} = \sum_{t=1}^{n}\sigma_t$$

where $\sigma_{t,j}$ is covariance between variables t and j (variance when t = j), and σ_t is the standard deviation of variable t. The expression following the first = sign is the standard statistical formula for the variance of the sum of any series of variables. The expression following the second = sign reflects the facts that $r_{t,j}\sigma_t\sigma_j = \sigma_{t,j}$ where $r_{t,j}$ is the correlation coefficient between variables t and j (all $r_{t,j}$s are 1.0 for perfectly correlated numbers). The expressions following the third and fourth = signs are each mathematically equivalent to the prior expression. Since the standard deviation of any variable multiplied by a constant is that constant multiplied by the standard deviation of the variable, $\sigma CF_t/(1 + k)^t$ can be substituted for each σ_t to give the standard deviation of present value.

$$\sigma_{PV} = \sum_{t=1}^{n} \sigma_{CF_t}/(1 + k)^t \qquad (12\text{-}4)$$

where σCF_t is the standard deviation of the probability distribution of cash flows for year t, and k is the required return.

STANDARD DEVIATION OF THE PRESENT VALUE OF UNCORRELATED CASH FLOWS

If cash flows are uncorrelated, the cash flows in any one year are independent of the cash flows in previous years. At the end of the first year, for example, we would not be able to use knowledge of actual cash flows for the first year to revise our estimates of cash flows for the second year. If a series of cash flows are uncorrelated, the formula for the standard deviation of the present value of those flows is:[5]

$$\sigma_{PV} = \sqrt{\sum_{t=1}^{n_2} \sigma F_t/(1 + k)^{2t}} \qquad (12\text{-}5)$$

Example. Possible annual sales levels and cash flows for Rediform Concrete's proposed new factory are shown in Table 12.2 (in thousands):

Expected annual cash flow and standard deviation of annual cash flow are as follows. The numbers are in $ thousands.

$$E(CF) = .05(500) + .10(750) + .20(1,000) + .30(1,250) + .20(1,500)$$
$$+ .10(1,750) + .05(2,000)$$
$$= \$1,250$$

$$\sigma_{CF} = [.05(500 - 1,250)^2 + .10(750 - 1,250)^2 + .20(1,000 - 1,250)^2$$
$$+ .30(1,250 - 1,250)^2 + .20(1,500 - 1,250)^2 + .10(1,750 - 1,250)^2$$
$$+ .05(2,000 - 1,250)^2]^{\frac{1}{2}}$$
$$= \$362$$

| TABLE 12.2 | REDIFORM CONCRETE: POSSIBLE ANNUAL SALES LEVELS AND CASH FLOWS |

Sales	2,000	2,500	3,000	3,500	4,000	4,500	5,000
Cash flow	500	750	1,000	1,250	1,500	1,750	2,000
Probability	.05	.10	.20	.30	.20	.10	.05

[5]This follows from the standard statistical property that the variance of the sum of a series of independent variables equals the sum of the variances.

If cash flows are perfectly correlated from year to year, the standard deviation of the present value of annual cash flows in thousands is:

$$\sigma_{PV} = \$362 PVA|_{5yrs,10\%} = \underline{\$1,372}$$

If cash flows are uncorrelated, on the other hand, the standard deviation of the present value of annual cash flows in thousands is:

$$\sigma_{PV} = \sqrt{362^2/1.1^2 + 362^2/1.1^4 + 362^2/1.1^6 + 362^2/1.1^8 + 362^2/1.1^{10}}$$
$$= \underline{619}$$

If the probability of a $1 million salvage value is .4, the expected salvage value and the standard deviation of the salvage value in thousands are:

$$E(\text{Salvage value}) = .4(\$1,000) + .6(\$3,000) = \underline{\$2,200}$$

$$\sigma_{\text{Salvage}} = \sqrt{.4(1,000 - 2,200)^2 + .6(3,000 - 2,200)^2} = \underline{\$980}$$

The expected present value of the salvage value and the standard deviation of the present value of the salvage value in thousands are then:

$$E(\text{PV of salvage}) = \$2,200/1.10^5 = \underline{\$1,366}$$

$$\sigma_{\text{PV of salvage}} = \$980/1.10^5 = \underline{\$609}$$

The salvage value is uncorrelated with the annual operating cash flows, so we can apply the basic statistical rule that the variance of the sum of independent events equals the sum of the variances. Since the initial outlay is known, we can compute the expected net present value and the standard deviation of net present value under both the assumptions of no correlation from year to year and perfect correlation from year to year (in thousands):

$$E(\text{NPV}) = 1,250 PVA|_{5yrs,10\%} + 2,200/1.1^5 - 5,000 = \underline{\$1,105}$$

Perfect correlation from year to year:

$$\sigma_{\text{NPV}} = \sqrt{1,372^2 + 609^2} = \underline{\$1,501}$$

Uncorrelated from year to year:

$$\sigma_{\text{NPV}} = \sqrt{619^2 + 609^2} = \underline{\$868}$$

Perfect correlation and complete lack of correlation are extreme positions that we rarely see in practice. Partial correlation is much more common, with there being some relationship between cash flows in one year and cash flows in the following year. If sales are less than expected during the first year, for example, forecasts for the second year will probably be scaled down as well, but knowledge of sales in the first year will not eliminate all uncertainty about future sales.

The analysis of the two extremes is useful in the case of partial correlation. If cash flows are partially correlated, the standard deviation of net present value is somewhere between the two extremes, between $868,000 and $1,501,000 for the Rediform example. Judgment can be used, estimating a standard deviation close to $868,000 if correlation is believed to be low, and close to $1,501,000 if correlation is believed to be high. Alternately, various authors have contributed analytical methods of computing the stan-dard deviation of net present value in particular situations involving partial correlation.[6]

Once expected net present value and standard deviation have been computed, managers can use the information in decision making, either applying judgment or developing policy guidelines for acceptable trade-offs between profitability and risk. We will discuss decision making after explaining simulation and decision tree analysis, which are additional tools for studying the probability distribution of profitability.

SIMULATION

A *simulation model* is a model of a system that can be manipulated to learn how the real system would react in various situations. Some models are physical, such as the small-scale models of boat hulls that are tested in tanks to predict how the actual boats will perform. Most models, though, are constructed as a series of mathematical equations.

Like the man who had written prose all his life without knowing it, many people have used simulation models without knowing it. If you have ever set up a pro-forma financial statement in Lotus 1-2-3 and then changed sales or accounts receivable turnover to see how profit and cash flow were affected, you have constructed a simulation model and performed a simulation experiment on that model.

As a simple example of a simulation model, consider the Rediform Concrete factory again. The capital investment can be described as a series of equations, as illustrated in Table 12.3.

This model can easily be entered into a computer using Lotus 1-2-3 or any number of other software packages. The simulation experiment then consists of changing the input values in the first five equations to determine the impacts of various combinations of these input variables on net present value. Suppose, for example, you are uncertain about sales level, salvage value, and the variable cost

---

[6]Frederick Hillier, "The Derivation of Probabilistic Information for the Evaluation of Risky Investments," *Management Science* 9 (April 1963): 443–457; Frederick Hillier, *The Evaluation of Risky Interrelated Investments* (New York: American Elsevier Publishing Company, 1969); Roger Bey and J. Clay Singleton, "Autocorrelated Cash Flows and the Selection of Capital Assets," *Decision Sciences* 9 (October 1978): 640–657.

| **Table 12.3** | **The Rediform Concrete Factory Described as a Mathematical Model** |

The Rediform Concrete factory is described as a simple mathematical model. The first five equations are simply input variables, while the last two equations explain how these variables interact in generating a net present value.

Cost = $5,000,000
Sales = $3,000,000
Variable Cost Ratio = .5
Fixed Cost = $500,000
Salvage Value = $3,000,000
Cash Flow = Sales(1 − Variable Cost Ratio) − Fixed Cost
Net Present Value[a] = Cash Flow × $PVA1_{5yrs,10\%}$ + Salvage Value/1.1^5 − Cost

[a]The present value of an annuity formula would generally be entered directly into the computer: $PVA1_{life,10\%} = (1 − 1/1.10^{life})/.10$.

ratio. You can construct a table of net present values as was done in Table 12.1 for uncertain sales and salvage values. The computer simply speeds up what would otherwise be some very tedious calculations.

If you are beginning to suspect that there is little difference between simulation analysis and simple sensitivity analysis, you are right. The difference is primarily one of scale. A simulation model, being a set of equations programmed into a computer, can describe a much more complex situation and can be used to examine the impacts of numerous variables changing in conjunction with one another. Monte Carlo simulation differs, though, in that probability is incorporated directly in the simulation model.

Monte Carlo Simulation

Monte Carlo simulation is a simulation technique that has been used for over two decades in capital investment analysis. The technique draws its name from the use of values that are randomly drawn, but with probability of each draw controlled to approximate the actual probability of occurrence.

To explain how Monte Carlo simulation works, consider the Rediform Concrete factory capital investment described in Table 12.3. Assume management is uncertain about sales, salvage value, and the variable cost ratio. Possible values of each variable are shown in Table 12.4 (in $ thousands), with probabilities in parentheses.

To perform a Monte Carlo simulation for this problem, we could set up three roulette wheels, one for each of the variables about which we are uncertain. These are illustrated in Figure 12.2. Take the variable cost ratio wheel, for example. One-fourth of that wheel represents a variable cost ratio of .4, one-half of the wheel represents a ratio of .5, and one-fourth of the wheel represents a

| TABLE 12.4 OUTCOMES AND PROBABILITIES FOR REDIFORM CONCRETE

Sales and salvage value are in $ thousands, and variable costs are cash. Probabilities are in parentheses.

	2,000	2,500	3,000	3,500	4,000	4,500	5,000
Sales	2,000	2,500	3,000	3,500	4,000	4,500	5,000
Probability	(.05)	(.10)	(.20)	(.30)	(.20)	(.10)	(.05)
Salvage value	1,000	3,000					
Probability	(.40)	(.60)					
Variable cost ratio	.40	.50	.60				
Probability	(.25)	(.50)	(.25)				

| FIGURE 12.2 SIMPLE MONTE CARLO SIMULATION FOR REDIFORM CONCRETE
(IN $ THOUSANDS)

A simple Monte Carlo simulation model to incorporate probability distributions with regard to sales, salvage value, and the variable cost ratio in the analysis of a capital investment.

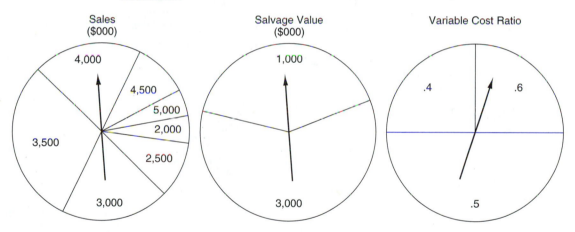

Cost = $5,000,000

Sales =

Salvage value =

Variable cost ratio =

Fixed cost = $500,000

Cash flow = Sales (1 − Variable cost ratio) − Fixed cost

Net present value = Cash flow x PVA1 $_{5yr., 10\%}$ + $\dfrac{\text{Salvage value}}{1.1^5}$ − Cost

ratio of .6, to correspond with the probability distribution of variable costs. When the wheel is spun, the probability of it stopping on a particular variable cost ratio is the same as the actual probability of that ratio occurring. Each of the wheels is spun once, to provide values for sales, salvage value, and the variable cost ratio. Based on these three values, a net present value is computed. The three wheels are each spun again, and a new net present value is computed based on the new sales, salvage value, and variable cost ratio. This procedure is repeated several hundred times, with each repetition referred to as an *iteration*.

After a large number of iterations, the proportion of iterations that result in a particular net present value (or range of net present values) approximately equals the probability of that net present value (or range) occurring. One thousand iterations of the above model were carried out, and the results are summarized in Figure 12.3. Those results can be used for the same types of risk-return decision making used with probability distributions of net present value obtained in other ways.

| **Figure 12.3** **Results of Monte Carlo Simulation Analysis of the Rediform Concrete Factory (in $ thousands)**

A summary of the results from 1,000 iterations of the simulation model shown in Figure 12.2. Dollar amounts are in thousands.

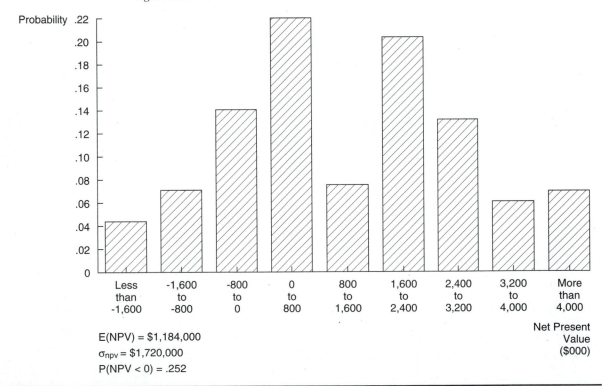

E(NPV) = $1,184,000

σ_{npv} = $1,720,000

P(NPV < 0) = .252

The Monte Carlo simulation gives managers a more detailed view of risk than the earlier-discussed probability methods. In addition to expected net present value and standard deviation, managers get a graphical picture of the probability distribution of net present value and the probability of a negative net present value. This more detailed picture of risk is often helpful in making capital investment decisions.

Naturally, it would be a bit tedious to go through a thousand iterations of even this simple model, and it would be much more tedious to perform numerous iterations on a complex model. This is where the computer comes in. The iterations reported in Figure 12.3 were actually carried out on a personal computer using a Basic language program, and could have been carried out using Lotus 1-2-3. A random-number generator was used instead of roulette wheels.[7] The random-number generator used for this purpose generates a random number between 0 and 1, with all values being equally likely. For example, the variable cost ratio is assigned as follows:

Value of random number	less than .25	.25 through .75	over .75
Variable cost ratio	.40	.50	.60

New random numbers were chosen for both sales and life so that the three variables were treated as uncorrelated items.

Some commercially available financial planning model packages, such as *Interactive Financial Planning System,* have built-in capabilities for performing Monte Carlo simulation. Using one of these packages basically involves two steps. First, a model is written as a series of equations, as was done in Table 12.3. Second, information about the nature of the probability distribution is provided for each input variable about which there is uncertainty. Given this information, the program then takes over and carries out the Monte Carlo simulation on its own.

Probability Distribution Shapes. For the example, it was assumed that the variables could have only a limited number of values, that is, sales could be $2 million or $2.5 million, but not $2.3 million. This was done for simplicity in the illustration, but is not necessary. Virtually any probability distribution shape can be accommodated. Random-number generators are available for a number of widely used probability distribution shapes, and any distribution can be approximated by a set of discrete values with probabilities assigned.

Dealing with Correlation. In the example, we assumed no correlation between variables about which we were uncertain. If two variables are perfectly correlated, one is treated as a random variable, and the other is simply made a function of the random variable. One way to handle partial correlation is to specify

[7]Random-number tables can also be used for this purpose.

a relationship with random coefficients. Suppose, for example, that sales are partially correlated from year to year. The relationship may be stated in a simple formula such as:

$$\text{Sales}_t = \alpha + b \cdot \text{Sales}_{t-1},$$

where Sales_t = sales for the year t, and α and b are random variables, with a probability distribution and "roulette wheels" established for each. Simple regression might be used to develop estimates of α and b by studying the pattern of sales growth and sales in the past. The regression analysis will provide confidence ranges for α and b that can be used in developing information about the probability distributions of those variables.

Disadvantages of Simulation. Simulation analysis overcomes the limitations of many of the other risk analysis methods discussed in this chapter, but simulation has its disadvantages too. Data for a simulation model can be expensive to construct because probability distribution estimates must be developed for a number of variables, then a model must be constructed, programmed into the computer, and verified. This can cost many thousands of dollars in the time of skilled people, and it can delay decision making.

Critics also point out that Monte Carlo simulation does not separate out the nondiversifiable risk that is really of concern to investors. This is true of Monte Carlo simulation as well as the other techniques discussed in this chapter, but as discussed in Chapter 11, many decision makers are personally concerned about total risk. Thus, they want to consider total risk as well as risk to diversified investors. Monte Carlo simulation can be supplemented with the analysis methods discussed in Chapters 13 through 15 that do focus on diversification and investor perspectives. In fact, Monte Carlo simulation can be used to generate inputs for some of those methods. Finally, Monte Carlo simulation shares with the other techniques discussed in the chapter the lack of a firm decision rule. Managers must still use their own judgment in deciding if the combination of benefits and risk summarized through the Monte Carlo simulation is attractive.

Decision Trees

Decision trees are particularly helpful when dealing with sequential decisions, such as the Boeing 7J7 project, in which $100 million was spent on preliminary development for a fuel-efficient airliner prior to a decision to commit $3 billion to go ahead with production. A sequential decision might also involve an opportunity to expand or abandon a factory depending on sales during the first year.

Example. Rediform can be used to explain decision tree analysis. Recall that annual cash flow for Rediform Concrete was (.5 × Sales) − $500,000, and that the salvage value at the end of the 5-year life would be either $1 million or $3 million, depending on where the freeway exit was built. We extend the problem by adding the following assumptions:

1. Sales will be either $2 million or $4 million a year, with probabilities of .3 and .7, respectively.
2. Whatever sales occur in the first year will also occur in later years.
3. The factory can be sold for $3.5 million at the end of the first year, when the location of the freeway exit is still unknown.
4. There is a .4 probability of a $1 million salvage value at the end of year 5, and a .6 probability of a $3 million salvage value at that time.

The problem facing management is summarized in Figure 12.4. A square with lines branching out is a decision node, with each line representing an alternative; the square labeled A represents the original decision point: to build or not to build? A circle with lines branching out is an outcome node; given the

| **FIGURE 12.4** **DECISION TREE ANALYSIS OF THE REDIFORM CONCRETE FACTORY**

The squares represent decision nodes and the circles represent outcome nodes. The numbers in parentheses are probabilities. This figure represents a factory investment with sales to be either $2 million or $4 million a year, and with an opportunity to abandon for $3.5 million after one year. Dollar amounts are in thousands.

	Sales		Salvage Value	NPV	Probability
			Abandon	-1,364	.30
		C	$1,000 (.4)	-2,484	X
	$2,000 (.3)	E	$3,000 (.6)	-1,242	X
Build	B				
A	$4,000 (.7)		Abandon	-454	X
Not Build		D	$1,000 (.4)	1,307	.28
		F	$3,000 (.6)	2,549	.42
				0	1.00

decision that took us to that node, each branch represents a possible outcome. Arrival at node B occurs only if the factory is built, and the lines branching out from that node represent possible sales. Numbers in parentheses are probabilities, given arrival at that node, so there is a .3 probability that sales will be $2 million a year and a .7 probability that sales will be $4 million a year. The square labeled C is the decision node at the end of the first year if sales are $2 million. Management has a choice between receiving the $3.5 million salvage value or continuing for 4 more years and accepting an uncertain salvage value. The square labeled D is the decision node if sales are $4 million. The choice at point D is between the $3.5 million salvage value or continuing for 4 more years and accepting an uncertain salvage value.

Decision tree problems are solved by starting at the right-hand side and working backward, choosing the optimal decision at each decision node.[8] At decision node C, the company faces a choice between $3.5 million in abandonment value and sales of $2 million a year for 4 years, with an uncertain abandonment value in 5 years. The expected net present value from continuing is:

$$E(NPV_{Continue}) = .4(-2,484) + .6(-1,242) = -\underline{\$1,739}$$

If sales turn out to be $2 million, management will abandon the factory at the end of the first year. An X is placed in the probability columns for the outcomes resulting from continuance, to show that the continuance path will not be taken.

The analysis is continued in a similar way for sales of $4 million. It is clear that the investment would not be abandoned in this case since net present value with either salvage value at the end of the fifth year is higher than net present value with abandonment.

Given the decisions that will be made at the end of the first year, there are only three possible net present value outcomes for the investment. The expected net present value is therefore:

$$E(NPV) = .3(-1,364) + .28(1,307) + .42(2,549) = \underline{\$1,027}$$

Of course, the decision not to build results in a certain net present value of $0. Standard deviation, coefficient of variation, and so forth can also be computed from the probability distribution, and a graph similar to Figure 12.3 can be prepared. The internal rate of return can also be computed for each possible path, and the probability distribution of internal rates of return can be analyzed in the same manner.

Decision tree analysis, like other risk measurement methods, does not tell the managers which choice they should make. This tool does, however, give a clearer picture of the possible consequences of the decisions faced by the managers at Rediform. They can use this information to consider ways to control risk or to decide if the potential benefits are worth the risk.

---

[8]We classify decision trees as a risk analysis tool because they are primarily used in risk settings, but they can actually be used to analyze sequential decision problems with no uncertainties involved.

For the illustration of decision tree analysis, we reduced the number of possible sales levels to two, from seven used in the simulation analysis. This was done only for simplicity of presentation. We could have used seven different sales levels by having seven branches instead of two at outcome node B. Computer programs are available for analyzing large, complex decision trees.

Decision trees can be combined with Monte Carlo simulation. We might, for example, conduct simulation studies given arrival at decision nodes C and D, to help managers decide what they would do at those points. Once decision rules at all later nodes are determined, a Monte Carlo simulation can be run for the entire proposed investment, incorporating the decision rules established for each decision node after the initial investment decision. Figure 12.5 shows the results of a simulation study of the Rediform factory assuming the probability distributions in Table 12.3. Results in this figure differ from Figure 12.3 in that

| **FIGURE 12.5** **MONTE CARLO SIMULATION COMBINED WITH DECISION TREE ANALYSIS FOR REDIFORM (IN $ THOUSANDS)**

This figure extends the simulation result from Figure 12.3 to assume management will abandon the factory for $3.5 million at the end of the first year if

1. *sales are $2 million;*
2. *sales are $2.5 million and the variable cost ratio is .5 or .6; or*
3. *sales are $3 million and the variable cost ratio is .6.*

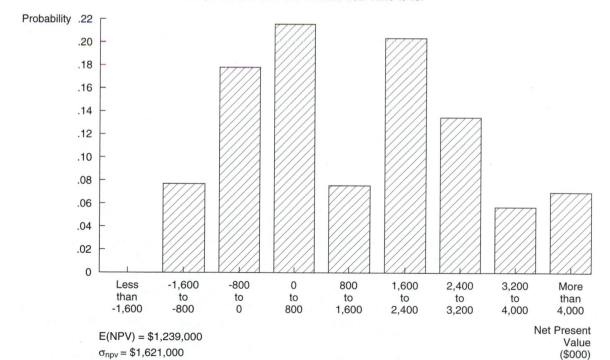

E(NPV) = $1,239,000

σ_{npv} = $1,621,000

P(NPV < 0) = .252

managers have decided they will abandon the investment for $3.5 million at the end of the first year if

1. sales are $2 million;
2. sales are $2.5 million and the variable cost ratio is .5 or .6; or
3. sales are $3.0 million and the variable cost ratio is .6.

Monte Carlo simulation combined with decision tree analysis gives us a more specific view of risk and profitability than either tool used in isolation. Managers can now consider ways to reduce risk and reach their own decision as to whether the expected profitability is worth the risk.

DISCOUNT RATES AND RISK ANALYSIS

It is frequently argued that the appropriate discount rate for computing the probability distribution of net present value is the after-tax risk-free rate. The reason for this position can be summarized with a simple example. The investment used for this example is affected by the level of sales. Net present values for each sales level using 6 percent, 9 percent, and 12 percent required returns are as follows:

Outcome	Low sales	Medium sales	High sales
NPV at 6%	$1,000	$2,000	$3,000
NPV at 9%	−500	500	1,500
NPV at 12%	−1,500	−500	500

At a 6 percent discount rate, there is no possibility the project will be unsuccessful. Assuming each outcome is equally likely, the probability of failure is $\frac{1}{3}$ with a 9 percent discount rate and $\frac{2}{3}$ with a 12 percent discount rate. Thus, the measured risk is affected by the discount rate, which is itself often affected by risk. It is often argued that the only way to compare the riskiness of investments is to use the after-tax risk-free rate as the discount rate for the risk analysis.[9]

Nevertheless, managers gain important insights from risk analysis carried out using higher discount rates, particularly the company's cost of capital. We will argue in subsequent chapters that the cost of capital for a project is primarily the return necessary to compensate investors for the use of their money and for the acceptance of nondiversifiable risk, which typically accounts for only a small portion of total project risk. If managers want to know the probability that the returns from a capital investment will not be high enough to compensate investors for risks taken, a probability distribution of net present values using the appropriate cost of capital answers the question. If the objective is to determine

[9]This point is discussed in more detail in Wilbur G. Lewellen and Michael S. Long, "Simulation Versus Single-Value Estimates in Capital Expenditure Analysis," *Decision Science* 3 (October 1972): 19–33.

the probability that a return less than the risk-free rate will be earned, then a probability distribution of net present values based on the risk-free rate will answer the question. Other questions could lead to other discount rates.

DEVELOPING PROBABILITY ESTIMATES FOR RISK ANALYSIS

The risk analysis methods simply start with probability information for input variables and work forward to probability distributions of outcomes. Finding the probability information about inputs is a major part of the task. The three primary ways of developing these probability estimates are study of historical data, experimentation, and judgment.

History. If you want to know variance of temperature or stock prices, you can compute the historical variance. If you want to estimate the probability of a recession in any future year you might look to the number of years in which there were recessions in the past. When we run a regression analysis on past relationships between variables, we receive information about the variance of the probability distribution of each regression coefficient. These variances can be used as the variances in a Monte Carlo simulation model. To estimate a probability distribution from historical observations, it is necessary that the probability distribution has remained stable for a sufficient number of periods, and will remain stable in the future. These requirements do limit the use of the historical approach. However, history is often useful in estimating probabilities.

Experiments. Test markets and pilot production facilities are common types of experiments that lead to information about probabilities. If Procter & Gamble test-markets its new laundry soap in six cities, the test market results can be used to estimate the probability distribution of sales for the general market. Procter & Gamble may divide the test market into cells and vary the packaging or price slightly in each cell. Not only does the company end up with expected results and risk information, but it ends up with information about how the nature of the offering affects those characteristics.

Judgment. Knowledgeable people are often queried with regard to their estimates. This approach is particularly popular for forecasting future technology. For example, a knowledgeable person may be asked for the expected number of years until half the population has high-resolution television. A probability distribution can be estimated based on this information. There is an extensive literature on eliciting subjective probability estimates, and the method is widely used in certain fields.[10]

---

[10]See, for example, Irwin Kabus, "You Can Bank on Uncertainty," *Harvard Business Review* (May–June 1976): 95–105; Rakesh Kumar Sarin, "Elicitation of Subjective Probabilities in the Context of Decision Making," *Decision Sciences* 9 (January 1978): 37–48; and James S. Ang, Jess H. Chua, and Ronald Sellers, "Generating Cash Flow Estimates: An Actual Study Using the Delphi Method," *Financial Management* (Spring 1979): 64–67.

MANAGING RISK |

In addition to measuring risk, there are important opportunities to change the desirability of proposed investments by changing their risk-return characteristics. You may succeed in reducing risk without a commensurate decrease in expected benefits. You may even use tools like decision tree analysis to develop strategies that increase expected benefits while decreasing risk. On a less ambitious but still important scale, you may reduce the risk so that managers are willing to take the personal risks associated with sponsoring the investment.[11] Some methods of controlling risk are discussed in the following paragraphs.

FIXED COST AND VARIABLE COST CHANGES

One of the more common ways to affect the risk of an investment is to change the mix of fixed costs and variable costs. Ford Motor Company, for example, made only $1.2 billion in 1979. By restructuring to lower its break-even point, Ford earned $3 billion on the same volume in 1986.[12] Buying components as needed instead of manufacturing them makes the entire cost of those components variable, whereas manufacturing the components requires fixed costs. The net effect of a buy decision may be higher costs under normal conditions, but the absence of fixed costs during a slowdown will reduce risk.

Example. When computer companies like Hewlett-Packard first developed laser printers, they had a choice between designing printers from scratch or modifying existing personal copiers. Suppose cash outlays required for the two alternatives were as shown in Table 12.5 (we ignore taxes for simplicity). Assume further that the computer company had a 10 percent required return, the investment was expected to have a life of 5 years, the printers could be sold for $2,000 each,

| TABLE 12.5 CASH OUTLAYS FOR TWO ALTERNATIVES AT HEWLETT PACKARD

	Modify Copier	Design from Scratch
Design cost	$10,000,000	$20,000,000
Cost to convert factory	20,000,000	30,000,000
Fixed annual production cost	500,000	1,000,000
Fixed administrative and marketing cost	1,000,000	1,000,000
Variable production cost per unit	1,000	800
Variable administration and marketing cost per unit	200	200

[11]Risk reduction of this last type is generally not thought of as contributing to shareholder wealth, but shareholder wealth will be improved if managers are persuaded to accept wealth-creating investments they would have otherwise rejected.

[12]"Ford Continues to Outearn GM and Chrysler Combined," *Business Month* (June 1987): 10.

and the salvage value for the production facilities would be negligible. The net present value break-even points for the two alternatives are as follows.

Modified copier:

$$NPV = -30,000,000 + PVAI_{5years,10\%}[Q(2,000 - 1,000 - 200) - 1,500,000] = 0$$

$$Q = 11,767 \text{ printers a year}$$

Design from scratch:

$$NPV = -50,000,000 + PVAI_{5years,10\%}[Q(2,000 - 800 - 200) - 2,000,000] = 0$$

$$Q = 15,190 \text{ printers a year}$$

We note that design from scratch increases the NPV break-even point by 30 percent, increases the initial investment by two-thirds, and increases annual fixed costs by 33 percent. Furthermore, demand must be greater than 28,880 units a year—2.5 times the modified design break-even point—before net present value is higher with design from scratch.[13] The break-even analysis tells us that the modified design approach is less risky, unless managers are certain that sales will be greater than 28,880 units a year. Managers must still rely on their judgment to decide which combination of expected benefits and risk is preferred. The decision was to reduce risk by taking advantage of existing copier designs.

Fixed and variable cost trade-offs occur in areas other than production. Banks, for example, commonly borrow on shorter terms than they lend, hoping to reduce their cost of funds in that way. But they also accept the risk that the interest rate they are paying may go above the rate charged on existing loans. Thus, they accept costs that vary, although the variance is not caused by changes in the volume of business. When considering a new loan product, the risk/return characteristics of the capital investment can be affected significantly by the funding decision. Likewise, farmers have a choice between taking a chance on market prices of their products at harvest time or locking in the price at planting time with a futures contract. A three-year wage contract with the United Autoworkers Union makes Ford's costs more predictable than a one-year contract, etc.

PRICING STRATEGY

For many companies, pricing strategy is an important aspect of risk management. A lower price increases potential demand, but also increases the break-even point. This is one reason computer companies first bring their models out at a high

---

[13]The net present value equations for the modified copier and design from scratch are set equal to each other and solved for Q:

$$-30,000,000 + PVAI_{5years,10\%}[Q(2,000 - 1,000 - 200) - 1,500,000]$$
$$= -50,000,000 + PVAI_{5years,10\%}[Q(2,000 - 800 - 200) - 2,000,000]; Q = \underline{28,880}$$

price and then reduce the price after a few months. If it turns out that the product only meets a few specialized needs, those with the specialized needs are probably willing to pay the higher price, and getting the higher price on some units decreases the break-even point. Sensitivity analysis and simulation are again helpful in evaluating the riskiness of various pricing alternatives.

Example. If demand for laser printers had turned out to be limited to a few specialized uses, those with the specialized needs would probably be willing to pay the higher price, and the higher price would decrease the break-even point. Suppose the computer company developing the laser printer decided to use a modified copier and chose the following pricing strategy:

Year	1	2	3–5
Unit price	$4,000	$3,000	$2,000

Managers believed that this price pattern would level out demand, and unit sales would be held constant through the price reduction. The net present value break-even point in annual sales would then be found as follows:

$$\text{NPV} = -30,000,000 - \text{PVAI}_{5yrs,10\%} \times 1,500,000 + Q[(4,000 - 1,200)/1.1$$
$$+ (3,000 - 1,200)/1.1^2 + (2,000 - 1,200)/1.1^3 + (2,000 - 1,200)/1.1^4$$
$$+ (2,000 - 1,200)/1.1^5] = 0$$

$$Q = \underline{6,286} \text{ printers a year}$$

This pricing strategy decreases risk by reducing the break-even quantity by 47 percent.

SEQUENTIAL INVESTMENT

In many situations, there is a choice between starting large or starting small and then expanding if demand is sufficient. Economies of scale are such that the total cost of achieving a particular capacity level will generally be lower with a single, large investment than with smaller, sequential investments. But the risk is also greater. Decision tree analysis or simulation analysis for each alternative provides information about the risk/return characteristics of each option.

EXTENT OF ANALYSIS

Additional study and experimentation, such as General Electric's $1 million expenditure for a pilot plant for its Ultem plastic, can decrease uncertainty. For many capital investments, a decision must be made as to how much analysis to do. This is itself a risk/return decision, because additional study can often improve predictability. Additional test marketing and testing of production technology in small-scale facilities are ways to reduce risk, but the direct cost and the opportunity cost from delayed action can be considerable. The analysis is similar to that for sequential investment. Decision trees are one way to evaluate the potential benefit of additional study. By deciding how they would respond to both positive and negative information, managers can often decide if the information is worth the cost.

FINANCIAL LEVERAGE

We have discussed the mix of fixed and variable operating costs. Financial leverage is another way to affect risk. Financial leverage refers to the use of fixed cost financing: debt, preferred stock, and leasing. The use of financial leverage increases the return on equity if an investment is successful, but it also creates another set of fixed costs that must be met even in times of difficulty. Typically, companies that otherwise face high risks use less financial leverage, and vice versa. Financial leverage is covered in detail in Part IV of this book.

DIVERSIFICATION

Diversification is the reduction of risk by combining assets in portfolios. When investments are combined in a portfolio, the investments generally will not all respond in the same way to all changes in the environment. Therefore, the risk of the portfolio is often less than the sum of the risks of the assets in that portfolio. Diversification is the main topic of the next chapter.

PROJECT SELECTION UNDER RISK

Once all of the investments and risk/return alternatives have been identified and measured, you must still make a decision. There are five primary ways to incorporate risk in the decision process: judgment, adjustment of required return, certainty equivalents, a payback period requirement, and arbitrage valuation.

JUDGMENT

When judgment is used, managers consider the information about the risk and return characteristics of an investment and then make an accept/reject decision without formally defined selection standards. The decisions are often made by vote of a capital budgeting committee, an executive committee, or a board of directors. If judgmental decision making seems haphazard, consider how most of us make the most important personal decisions of our lives. Few of us select a career or a spouse by starting with a predefined selection formula and then running each alternative through that formula to look for the highest score; we apply judgment instead.

REQUIRED RETURN ADJUSTMENT

Many companies use higher required returns for more risky investments. Some companies make judgmental adjustments to the required return based on how risky a particular investment appears to be. Other companies use different required returns for capital investments in different divisions, based on the perceived riskiness of each division.

Many companies adjust the required return for the type of investment being considered, as follows:

Cost reduction investments are given the lowest required return because costs and benefits are fairly predictable.

Volume expansion projects in existing product lines are treated as intermediate risk investments. Cash flow forecasts depend on product demand forecasts, but the company does have experience with the product line. A required return intermediate between low and high risk projects is used.

New product lines are considered the highest risk products, and are assigned the highest required return. Cash flow forecasts depend on product demand forecasts in an area in which management has no prior experience.

The problem with assigning required return in this way is that the distinction between diversifiable and nondiversifiable risk is not recognized. Most of the extra risk associated with a new product line results from the company's lack of experience. Much of Armco's loss in insurance business—over half a billion dollars—can probably be attributed to Armco's lack of experience in insurance, a risk that can be readily diversified away by shareholders. Current finance theory suggests that required return should be adjusted only for risks that cannot be readily diversified away by the shareholders. Formal procedures for adjusting the required return in response to risk are explained in Chapters 14 and 15.

CERTAINTY EQUIVALENTS

Another approach to risky capital investment decision making is to convert uncertain future cash flows to certainty equivalents. As generally used in capital budgeting, a *certainty equivalent* is defined as a certain dollar amount at time t which, if discounted to the present at the risk-free rate, is the amount you would be willing to pay today in exchange for the uncertain cash flow that will occur at time t. Suppose, for example, a capital investment will generate cash flows in year 5 with an expected value of $1,000 and a standard deviation of $500. The risk-free rate is 6 percent, and the company uses a 10 percent required return for investments with this level of risk. The certainty equivalent (CE) that would lead to the same present value as that computed using the risk-adjusted discount rate can be found as follows:

$$\frac{1,000}{(1 + .10)^5} = \frac{CE_t}{(1 + .05)^5}$$

Solving $CE_5 = \$1,000(1.05/1.10)^5 = \underline{\$792}$

We can generalize from this example to say that the certainty equivalent (CE_t) gives the same net present value as the risk-adjusted discount rate if:

$$CE_t = E(CF_t)[(1 + r_f)/(1 + k)]^t \qquad \text{(12-6)}$$

where r_f is the risk-free rate, $E(CF_t)$ is expected cash flow at time t, and k is the risk-adjusted required return. Some authors argue in favor of the certainty equivalent approach because the risk-adjusted discount rate method implicitly assumes a specific certainty-equivalent factor: $[(1 + r_f)/(1 + k)]^t$. They argue that it is better to use an explicit certainty-equivalent factor that can be specified for each period, according to the riskiness of that period's cash flows.[14]

A problem with certainty equivalents is the question of whose certainty equivalent to use. If we can instruct managers to consider only shareholder interest, there are some ways to compute certainty equivalents, and these are discussed in Chapter 15. If a decision maker wants to consider total project risk, though, the certainty equivalent is relevant only if it is a certainty equivalent that will be accepted by the decision maker. The decision maker must be willing to make numerous hypothetical choices so that certainty equivalent values can be based on this person's preference function.

The problem of mapping preference functions quickly explodes in complexity. If the decision maker is indifferent between an immediate payment from the probability distribution described in the previous example and an immediate payment of $800, does it follow that the decision maker is indifferent between a payment from the probability distribution in 10 years or a certain $800 in 10 years? There is reason to believe that the general answer is *no*, because the decision maker cannot develop an optimal pattern of consumption over time when future wealth is not known. Therefore, development of the utility function mapping needed to find the certainty equivalent would be extremely time-consuming.

PAYBACK PERIOD REQUIREMENT

Some companies use net present value analysis as a project profitability criterion, but use payback period as a risk control criterion. If an investment is considered more risky, a shorter payback period is required for its acceptance, even if the net present value is positive. This approach is based on the assumption that risk is primarily related to the period of time until benefits are received. Recognition Equipment, discussed in the opening paragraphs of this chapter, used the payback criterion as part of its planning to control risk.

The longer we have to wait for payment, the greater is our uncertainty about economic conditions and other variables that change over time. Therefore, there is some relationship between risk and time until benefits are received. The shortened payback requirements are frequently used, for example, by companies investing in politically unstable countries. However, risk is related to things other than passage of time in most cases, and control of payback period is therefore an incomplete method of controlling risk exposure.

---

[14]See, for example, Harold Bierman, Jr., and Seymour Schmidt, *The Capital Budgeting Decision*, 7th ed. (New York: Macmillan Publishing Co., 1988).

ARBITRAGE VALUATION

Arbitrage valuation is based on the principle that two identical streams of expected cash flows, with identical risk characteristics, will have identical values. A publicly traded security portfolio that will provide the same expected cash flows and risks as the capital investment under consideration is constructed. A capital investment is desirable if it costs less than this substitute portfolio. Arbitrage methods in general are covered in Chapter 15. The mean-variance capital asset pricing model is a widely used application of the arbitrage concept, and is covered in Chapter 14.

CHOOSING HOW TO CHOOSE

In considering these project selection methods in the face of risk, it is helpful to distinguish between policies and decision support systems. For the hundreds or thousands of small capital-budgeting decisions faced each year, senior managers must establish policies that allow middle- and lower-level managers to make the right decisions without extensive project-by-project inputs from top management. A positive net present value requirement based on a risk-adjusted required return is often used for these purposes, sometimes supplemented with a payback requirement. Although the rules are often arbitrary, top managers can control risk exposure through policy without having to examine each individual investment proposal.

For the major investments in which senior managers are involved, decision support systems are needed. A decision support system must provide information about proposed investments, and *may* also include predetermined decision rules. If certainty equivalents or discount rates adjusted for total project risk are used, the decision support system includes some specific decision rules based on the manager's prior preference statements. If judgment is used as the decision method, the decision support system does not include predetermined decision rules; in comparing alternatives, the manager decides which combination of benefits and risks is more attractive. While some predetermined criteria may be used, managers have shown a preference for using judgment in the final decision process. This is why capital budgeting committees exist.

RISK ANALYSIS OF INTERNATIONAL INVESTMENTS

Risk analysis is more extensive for international investments than for domestic investments. Risk encountered include project risk, political risk, and exchange rate risk.

Project risk is the same fundamental risk faced in domestic capital investments. We may experience technical difficulties with the product or production process, competitors may enter and force prices down, or customers may simply reject the product. Economic changes, climate changes, etc. may affect the profitability of the project. While these are the same risks faced in domestic business, they are often heightened in the international arena. Because managers are less familiar with the environment in the foreign country, they have more difficulty in predicting outcomes. For a Cadillac dealership in Saudi Arabia, project risks include an economic decline due to falling oil prices and a strong preference for Mercedes instead of Cadillacs.

Political risk refers to political events that might be unfavorable to the investment. These range from increased taxation or controls on repatriating earnings to political upheaval and outright expropriation of assets. The stability and dependability of the government is a major consideration in risk analysis. A Persian Gulf war and an anti-Arab foreign policy tilt in Washington could completely wipe out the investment. Recent events in Indonesia with the resignation of the Suharto government illustrate the tremendous impact the government has on the economic well-being of the country. Models have been developed for the prediction of government stability and there are services that monitor government stability.[15]

Exchange rate risk adds a new dimension to risk. The exchange rate between two currencies is the number of units of one currency that must be given in exchange for a unit of another. As an illustration, the deutsche mark was worth $0.3787 early in 1984 and $0.5753 early in 1994. Suppose Krup, a German company, made an investment in 1984 with the expectation of receiving $1 million in 1994, and did not anticipate a change in the exchange rate. The expected and actual deutsche mark payments would be as follows.

$$\text{Expected amount} = \$1,000,000/.3787 = 2,640,613 \text{ D.M.}$$

$$\text{Actual amount} = \$1,000,000/.5753 = 1,738,224 \text{ D.M.}$$

In other periods, major currencies have lost value in relation to the dollar, and U.S. companies suffered losses.

Assume that a Cadillac dealership in Saudi Arabia was based on a 5 percent annual increase in the value of the riyal in relation to the dollar. If the value of the dollar increased 5 percent a year against the riyal instead, the net present value would turn from a positive $624,000 to a *minus* $282,000. This further illustrates the importance of exchange rate risk. Chapter 9 introduced exchange rates, this chapter mentions the risk exposure, and Chapter 15 discusses some of the ways exchange rate risk can be managed with the use of futures, swaps, and options.

Stanley and Block surveyed the largest multinational firms in the United States, and provided us with important insights concerning capital budgeting practices for multinational investments.[16] One finding was that risk analysis is

---

[15]For additional discussion of political risk, see Pravin Banker, "You're the Best Judge of Foreign Risks," *Harvard Business Review* 61 (March–April 1983): 157–165.

[16]Marjorie T. Stanley and Stanley B. Block, "A Survey of Multinational Capital Budgeting," *Financial Review* 19 (March 1984): 36–54.

of critical importance in multinational capital budgeting, and 62 percent of the respondents used some risk adjustment technique. Over half used a different risk analysis method for foreign investments than for domestic investments. Respondents were evenly divided in their choices between discount rate adjustment and cash flow adjustment.

SUMMARY |

This chapter has focused on risk analysis from the total project perspective. Covered in this chapter were methods of defining risk, methods of controlling risk, and investment decision making in the face of risk. Methods of defining risk were divided between those depending on probability and those not depending on probability.

Sensitivity analysis, including break-even analysis, is the primary method of defining risk without using probability. The objective in probability-related analysis is to develop a description of the probability distribution of profitability. Simulation and decision tree analysis are popular tools for this purpose.

Risk management is another important part of the problem. Managers have available to them numerous actions that can change the risk/return characteristics of an investment, possibly making it more desirable. Alternatives available to management include changing the fixed cost/variable cost mix, selection of the amount of study before the decision, making the investment commitment in stages, choice of pricing strategy, choice of financial leverage, and diversification.

Decision making under risk: once all the analysis is completed, someone has to make a decision, considering both risk and profitability. For small projects, predetermined standards such as risk-adjusted required returns and shortened payback periods are used. For large investments, certainty equivalents are possible, but many companies rely on judgment rather than predetermined rules.

Risk analysis of foreign investments begins with analysis of project risk, which is the same risk faced with domestic investments. Political risk is an additional risk and refers to various political events that might be unfavorable to the investment. Exchange rate risk adds another dimension to risk analysis in that it increases uncertainty with regard to the number of dollars the company will finally end up with. There are four main ways of managing exchange rate risk: (1) currency futures contracts, (2) swaps, (3) options, and (4) balance sheet hedging. The first three are discussed in Chapter 15 and balance sheet hedging is discussed in the financing section of the text.

The methods covered in this chapter focus primarily on total investment risk. Total risk is certainly important to managers making the investment decision, and total risk analysis is an important information source for risk management. However, risks viewed from the perspectives of the company's asset portfolio and an investor's investment portfolio are at least equally important. Risk analysis from these perspectives is covered in Chapters 13 through 15.

QUESTIONS |

12–1. As a tool for risk analysis, what are the advantages and disadvantages of sensitivity analysis?

12–2. One reason for numerous risk analysis techniques is that each one fits different types of problems. What are the characteristics for which each of the following techniques would be appropriate? What are the disadvantages of these methods?

a. Decision trees.

b. Monte Carlo simulation.

12–3. What is the difference between sensitivity analysis and simulation without probability?

12–4. List several examples of cash flows that would

a. be highly correlated from period to period.

b. have little or no correlation from period to period.

12–5. What are the restrictions in a Monte Carlo simulation with regard to the probability distribution characteristics that can be included?

12–6. Can a Monte Carlo simulation handle correlation between variables? Explain.

12–7. What are the guidelines for choice of a discount rate to use in simulation and the other risk analysis methods discussed in this chapter?

12–8. How can probability estimates for the input variables to a risk analysis be developed?

12–9. Discuss the methods available to alter the risk/return characteristics of a capital investment.

12–10. What methods do companies use to make capital investment decisions after risk analysis has been completed?

12–11. (**Ethical considerations**) You are a management consultant in the middle of what has turned out to be a rather long term engagement. You have just uncovered the following facts:

■ Charris, the founder of a successful plastics company, sold the company to his banker, Rassie, five years ago for $250,000 but retained a substantial portion of the company's stock with a book value of $2,500,000. He has since died and left the stock to his widow who has very little business knowledge. The widow has hired an attorney to represent her.

■ For a number of years, Rassie and his managers have been diverting money from the company mainly by starting and investing in negative net present value projects that are actually hobbies for Rassie.

■ The local accounting firm audit fails to call attention to the diversion of funds into these hobbies and simply reports that the core plastics firm is unprofitable.

■ After years of mismanagement, the firm is reporting a loss and the shares held by the widow have a book value of $300,000. Checks drawn on the plastics firm's account have paid for Rassie's condominiums, luxury cars, and a horse-breeding ranch which is in his mother's name.

- The widow, thinking the plastics firm is unprofitable, is persuaded on the advice of her attorney to sell her shares in the firm to Rassie for pennies on the dollar.
- Rassie puts the plastics business up for sale and a competitor pays $10,000,000 for the assets of the plastics firm.
- Rassie pockets most of this gain but also spreads two million around to the senior executives who participated in the diversion of funds.
- The business is operated by the new owners and is generating $500,000 a month in income.

Given the facts above, clearly Rassie benefited at the widow's expense.

a. Was there an ethical violation from the viewpoint of the local CPA firm?

b. Was there an ethical violation from the viewpoint of the lawyer representing the widow?

c. Assume there is a 15 percent chance that the local CPA firm will admit to its mistake and a 25 percent chance that the lawyer will admit to his mistake. If either of these two parties comes forward, Rassie will probably have to return the $10,000,000 to the widow as well as go to jail for the diversion of funds. From Rassie's point of view, what is the expected value of the $10,000,000 payoff?

12-12. (Application) Blockbuster Video has been extremely profitable in the past. Suppose you were considering the opening of a video store in your town.

a. Describe the process you would go through to evaluate the risk of such a store.

b. Describe how you would go about collecting the data needed for your analysis.

c. Using your own numbers, calculate a break-even and be prepared to explain how you arrived at your numbers. Illustrate another method besides break-even to analyze the proposal.

d. What are the two most important variables, under your control, to the success of a video store?

PROBLEMS |

12-1. Athens Development Corporation is considering a new product that will be sensitive to both economic conditions and competitor response. The product manager has decided to focus on three economic conditions: weak economy, normal economy, and strong economy. Competitors either will or will not respond with a competitive product, and competitor response is unlikely unless economic conditions turn out to be strong. Annual cash flows for each of these conditions appear below. The product has a five-year life and will require an initial cash outlay of $100,000.

The cost of capital is 10 percent. Should Athens invest in this product? Explain.

Competitor Response	Weak Economy	Normal Economy	Strong Economy
Yes	$10,000	$20,000	$30,000
No	20,000	30,000	40,000

12–2. Define a weak economy as no growth, a normal economy as 3 percent growth, and a strong economy as 6 percent growth. Prepare a graphical sensitivity analysis for the new product investment in problem 1.

12–3. Denver Doughnuts is considering a new store location. For accounting purposes, fixed operating costs for a store are $23,500 a year, and variable costs are 40 percent of sales. Compute the break-even sales level for a store location.

a. If average revenue per customer is $1.40, how many customers must be served each hour to break even in earnings? (The stores are open twenty-four hours a day, 365 days a year.)

b. If the price (only) is raised 10 percent, what will be the new earnings break-even point?

12–4. For Denver Doughnuts (problem 3), fixed cash outlays are $18,750 a year at each location, and variable cash outlays are 40 percent of sales. A store requires an initial outlay of $60,000, and the company uses a 14 percent required return. Because of changing neighborhood characteristics, the company does its analysis based on a 10-year store life. Since the locations are leased, the terminal value is minimal.

a. What annual sales volume will be needed to generate a net present value of $0?

b. The after-tax risk-free interest rate is 6 percent. What annual sales value will be needed to generate a net present value of $0 using a 6 percent discount rate?

12–5. Salt Lake Systems is a small company started by two recent college graduates to market a small-business inventory management system they developed and patented as a class project. The system requires a special hard-disk drive that plugs into a microcomputer.

Buy and Modify Alternative: With this alternative Salt Lake Systems would buy standard hard-disk systems at $2,200 and then modify them at a cost of $900 each. Annual fixed cash outlays for the modification operation would be $50,000. Capital investment requirements will be $30,000 to modify.

Build Alternative: Under this alternative Salt Lake Systems would construct the special hard-disk system from scratch. Component parts can be readily purchased, and the production process is not complex. The variable cost to build each special hard-disk system would be $2,000.

Annual fixed cash outlays for the building alternative would be $100,000. Capital investment requirements will be $60,000 to build.

Salt Lake Systems plans to price the systems at $4,995 each because they have a patent and proprietary software. The partners estimate that they can complete 100 units a year, either building or modifying. Potential demand could be for thousands of units a year, but could also be only a fraction of capacity. The partners do not have enough information to estimate probabilities and cannot afford market research. They recognize that technology changes rapidly and, therefore, use a 3-year life for analysis. The cost of capital is 12 percent, and the partners are not subject to income tax. Use net present value break-even analysis to recommend a production method.

12–6. Upscale Home Fashions of Burlington pays fees to a delivery service that amount to an after-tax cost of 2 percent of revenue. Sales have averaged approximately $1.5 million, but have been as low as $1 million and as high as $2 million in the past decade. Upscale could buy its own delivery truck for $30,000, after tax, eliminating the need for the delivery service. The truck would last eight years, with a negligible salvage value. Salary for a driver and other operating costs would result in an after-tax cash outlay of $20,000 a year. The company has a 10 percent cost of capital. Prepare a graphical sensitivity analysis, showing the relationship between net present value for the truck investment and sales for the store. Would you recommend acquisition of the truck?

12–7. For the delivery truck investment in problem 6, assume that expected sales are $1.5 million and the standard deviation of the probability distribution of sales is $300,000. Compute the expected net present value and standard deviation of net present value under the assumption that the cash flows are perfectly correlated.

12–8. Rework problem 7 on the assumption that cash flows are uncorrelated from year to year.

12–9. A rental property with a 20-year life can be purchased for $100,000. Net cash benefits per year have an expected value of $15,000 and a standard deviation of $5,000. At a 10 percent required return, compute the expected net present value and standard deviation of net present value under the assumption of

a. perfect correlation from year to year.

b. no correlation from year to year.

12–10. National Bank is considering a new loan product. Initial costs to design and introduce the product will be $200,000 (all numbers in this example are after-tax). Managers are confident of achieving interest income of $1 million per year, but are not sure how much promotion will be needed to achieve that volume. They estimate promotion expense of $60,000 a year, with a standard deviation of $30,000. The initial market response will carry forward to future years, so perfect correlation is assumed. Managers are also uncertain about bad debt expense. The estimate is $50,000 a year, with a standard deviation of $20,000, and perfect correlation from year to year is assumed. Interest expense depends on interest rate movements and is also uncertain. The expected annual interest expense is $600,000, with a standard deviation of $100,000, and is treated as having no correlation from year to year. Other operating expenses will be $180,000 a year, and can be estimated with virtual certainty. The product will be evaluated over a three-year time horizon because competitors will come in by that time and squeeze profit margins down to the point where the bank will just earn its 15 percent required return.

a. Find the expected net present value.

b. Find the standard deviation of present value for interest expense, bad debt expense, and promotion expense.

c. Assume independence between the three components analyzed in part b. Recognizing that the variance equals the sum of the variances, find the standard deviation of net present value.

12–11. An apartment house can be purchased for $200,000. Rent is expected to be $30,000 a year in the first year and is expected to grow at 5 percent a year. The standard deviation of cash flow is expected to be $3,000 in the first year and is also expected to grow at 5 percent a year. Rental income from year to year is expected to be perfectly correlated. Operating expenses are expected to be $8,000 a year, with a standard deviation of $2,000, and are expected to be uncorrelated from year to year. The salvage value after 10 years is estimated to be $300,000, with a standard deviation of $50,000. The various components of cash flow are uncorrelated, and the required return is 10 percent.

a. Compute the expected net present value.

b. Compute the standard deviation of present value for each component of cash flow.

c. Assuming independence between components, the present values of components are independent variables. Recognizing that the variance of the sum of a series of independent variables equals the sum of the variances, find the standard deviation of net present value.

12–12. A capital investment requires a cash outlay of $60,000 and has a three-year life. It provides cash inflows of $30,000 with a probability of .3 or $40,000 with a probability of .7. At a 10 percent required return, find the possible net present values and their probabilities, assuming

a. perfect correlation from year to year.

b. no correlation from year to year.

12–13. For problem 12, find the expected internal rate of return.

12–14. An investment costs $5,000, after tax considerations, and will generate cash flows of $1,000 a year over its life. The capital investment will last 8, 9, or 10 years, with probabilities of .4, .4, and .2 respectively. At a 10 percent required return, compute the expected net present value and standard deviation of net present value.

12–15. A capital investment requires an initial outlay of $1,000. In the first year, it will provide cash flows of $300 with a probability of .3, or $600 with a probability of .7. If cash flows in the first year are $600, they will be $700 or $800 in the second year, with a .5 probability of each outcome. If cash flows are $300 in the first year, they will be $300 in the second year. At a 10 percent required return, find each possible net present value and its associated probability. Is this investment attractive?

12–16. Cincinnati Express is a small regional airline. To open a new route, the airline must buy two commuter airplanes at an estimated cost of $3 million dollars, after tax. Other start-up costs are estimated to be $500,000, after tax. Annual operating costs are expected to be $600,000 a year, after tax. Costs are largely fixed, and do not depend on revenue. As with many new routes into smaller towns, demand is uncertain until the service has actually been offered. Demand after the first year is expected to be very similar to that in the first year, though. A discrete approximation to the probability distribution for demand follows:

Probability	.10	.20	.40	.20	.10
Revenue (after tax)	700,000	900,000	1,200,000	1,500,000	2,000,000

If the route turns out to be unprofitable, the airplanes can be sold at the end of one year for an estimated market value of $2.5 million, after tax. The airplanes will last approximately 10 years, after which the estimated salvage value is $250,000, after tax. A 10-year horizon is used for decision making, and the company uses a 10 percent required return for decision making. Use decision tree analysis to evaluate this capital investment opportunity.

a. Would you recommend the capital investment for a small commuter airline that has only one other route, with that route being of similar size and marginally profitable?

b. Would you recommend the capital investment for a large commuter airline with dozens of profitable routes?

c. How would your recommendation be changed if any airline entering the route must continue the route for ten years?

12–17. Harvey Publishing Company, a small publisher in Columbus, is considering a new book. Typesetting and related costs to prepare for production are $10,000. It will cost $2.00 per copy to produce the book. If additional copies are needed at a later time, the set-up cost will be $5,000 and the cost per copy will again be $2.00. The book will sell for $14.00 a copy. Royalties, commissions, shipping costs, etc. will be $4 a copy. If the book gets good reviews, it can be expected to sell 5,000 copies a year for 3 years. If it gets bad reviews, sales will be 2,000 copies in the first year, and will then cease. There is a .3 probability of a favorable review. Sally Harvey, president, faces a choice between ordering an immediate production run of 15,000 copies or a production run of 5,000 copies, followed by an additional production run at the end of the first year if the book is successful. All production runs must be in increments of 5,000 copies. Harvey uses a 10 percent required return for evaluating new investments. She will pay no taxes because of previous losses, and her capital is very limited. Use decision tree analysis to recommend a production schedule and decide whether to publish the book.

12–18. For the situation described in problem 17, some new information about demand has become available. If the book is successful in the first year, selling 5,000 copies, demand in the second and third years will be 5,000. If the book is unsuccessful in the first year, though, there is still a .2 probability of it catching on, with sales of 3,000 copies in the second year and 5,000 copies in the third year. Use decision tree analysis to develop a production plan.

12–19. Jane Engle, a new college graduate, wants to go into business and is considering a copy center in a small, new office park in San Jose. It will cost $100,000 after tax to open the business. Fixed costs are expected to be $50,000 a year, including her salary, and variable costs are expected to be 40 percent of revenue. Assume all costs are cash, for simplicity. She decided to limit the risk analysis to ten years because changing technology could make this kind of business obsolete. She uses a 15 percent required return (the risk-free rate is 10 percent) and estimates that she will be in a 30 percent marginal tax bracket. Revenue is expected to be $90,000 a year. Model this business as a series of equations.

12–20. Jane Engle (problem 19) is uncertain about demand for the proposed copy center. She will be given the exclusive right to operate a copy center at the office park. If many small offices move in, demand will be large. But if a few large organizations take over the space, they will use their own facilities, and demand will be limited. She has estimated a probability distribution of revenues as follows:

Probability	.25	.50	.25
Annual Revenue	100,000	140,000	170,000

Use a Monte Carlo simulation with 10 iterations to analyze the problem. Instead of a random-number generator or roulette wheel, you may flip two coins for each iteration. If both come up tails, use revenue of $100,000. If both come up heads, use revenue of $170,000. If there is one head and one tail, use revenue of $140,000.

12–21. Using a computer and random-number generator, rework problem 20 using 100 iterations.

12–22. Please use the data from problem 5 to complete this problem. You have concluded that the two most influential variables on your NPV are changes in taste and preferences towards playing pool and the degree of competition. Before investing in this pool hall you would like to run several different scenarios to test the sensitivity of the NPV to these variables. You estimate that there are three different market responses, either early death after 2 years, a five-year life, or a seven-year life. Salvage values for building and equipment (after taxes) would be $450,000 at the end of two years, $380,000 at the end of five years, and $250,000 at the end of seven years. Competitive responses are very intense, normal, and weak. With a very intense competitive response the revenues per week would be only $3,500, with a normal competitive response the revenues would be $5,000 per week, and with a weak competitive response the revenues per week would be $6,500. All other numbers in the problem remain the same. Please complete the following table.

Net present value for nine scenarios:

	Two-year life	Five-year life	Seven-year life
Intense competition			
Normal competition			
Weak competition			

CASE PROBLEM |

Scandinavian Styles

Peter Nielsen and Jens Andersen moved to the United States as sales representatives for a Danish furniture manufacturer. Nielsen had the southeast territory and Andersen had the midwest territory, but they met several times a year and talked frequently on the phone to coordinate shipments. After several years of selling to retail stores that carried numerous styles, the two decided to start their own store specializing in Scandinavian furniture.

Nielsen and Andersen continued in their jobs for another year while they organized the business. They knew the demographic characteristics of Scandinavian furniture buyers from company studies and their own experience. Upper middle income and under forty-five best described the group. Thus, they chose to locate in an upper-middle-income section of Springfield. Knowing that furniture was hardly a convenience good, and knowing they needed adequate display space, Nielsen and Andersen leased a 10,000-square-foot area in a small strip shopping center that had fallen on hard times due to the opening of a large shopping center several blocks away. The rent was low, and the space was adequate for their display needs. They thought they could generate customer traffic through advertising more effectively than by counting on an expensive location.

The major decisions of Nielsen and Andersen proved to be right. Despite a few mistakes and rocky periods, the business thrived. Within two years, business was suffering from severe space limitations. To control shipping costs, it was necessary to place large orders. Most of the furniture came "knocked down" and required final assembly. Thus, both storage and work space was needed. They handled the space needs temporarily by renting a small warehouse. This, however, was unsatisfactory as many customers wanted to take their purchases with them. A separate warehouse also created control problems. By the time they had been in business 5 years, the partners decided to build a new store, giving them adequate display, storage, and assembly space at one location. Again, the decision proved to be profitable.

Looking toward further growth, Nielsen and Andersen decided they would have to expand outside of the Springfield area. They decided on Oak Hill, a suburb in Andersen's old sales territory. The primary appeal of this location was that Andersen knew the area and market better than any other. Andersen would run the new store while Nielsen would stay in the old store. They decided to evaluate the expansion opportunity using a 10-year horizon; style changes or balance of payments problems could end their business.

A developer was in the process of building some store space that would be within the right rent range for a furniture store. Space could be had for $10 per square foot per year, and a 10-year lease was required. Nielsen and Andersen could cancel the lease at any time, but there would be a penalty of 20 percent of the remaining lease payments. The location looked good, but the question was how much space to rent.

Nielsen and Andersen agreed that 10,000 square feet was the optimal sales space. Andersen was in favor of taking 15,000 square feet of space so they would have 5,000 square feet for a storage and assembly area on site. Nielsen wanted to take a more conservative approach, using weekly drop-shipments from the Springfield location to deliver inventory to Oak Hill. The distance was over 500 miles, and this would add approximately 15 percent to the cost of the furniture, but risk would be reduced substantially, and the need for 5,000 square feet of space could be eliminated.

Andersen pointed out that if the store was successful, they would quite likely find themselves facing the necessity of buying their way out of the lease within 2 years to get warehouse and assembly space. An 8-year lease on 15,000 square feet would probably cost $12 a square foot by then. Nielsen was more concerned about buying out of a 15,000-square-foot lease after 1 year if the store was unsuccessful. Both partners agreed to study the alternatives some more over the weekend and to make a decision on Monday.

From their past experience and observations, Nielsen and Andersen believed the big risks in opening a store of this type occurred in the first year. They projected sales in the second year to be double those in the first year and predicted little growth beyond that. For purposes of analysis, the partners decided to concentrate on two cases with regard to first-year sales: weak and successful. Weak sales would be $250,000 the first year, and successful sales would be $600,000. The probabilities were estimated to be .7 for success and .3 for weak sales.

The primary up-front costs were promotion and miscellaneous expenses of $30,000 without the warehouse/assembly space and $50,000 with the warehouse/assembly space. These expenses would result in an immediate 28 percent tax savings. Inventory would cost $200,000 with the warehouse/assembly area and $100,000 without. It was estimated that the inventory could be liquidated at cost if or when the store was closed. There would be no accounts receivable because most customers used credit cards, and arrangements would be made with a finance company for those needing credit. Other current assets and current liabilities would also be negligible. Depreciation and noncash expenses would be minimal, so income and cash flow would be the same.

As a general guideline, Nielsen and Andersen estimated a cost of goods sold with on-site assembly at 60 percent of sales. Other variable costs would be 10 percent of sales. They estimated fixed costs other than rent of $4 a year for every square foot of space in either sales space or warehouse/assembly space. The partners faced 28 percent tax rates and used a 10 percent required return in their analysis.

CASE QUESTIONS

1. Compute a net income break-even point for the smaller and larger facilities.
2. Find the sales level (after the first year) that will result in a net present value of $0. Remember that sales the first year will be half of those after the first year.
3. Prepare a decision tree analysis of the alternatives.
4. Prepare a graphical sensitivity analysis showing the relationship between sales level and net present value for each size alternative.
5. Should they lease space of 10,000 or 15,000 square feet? Why?

SELECTED REFERENCES

Aggarwal, Raj, and Luc A. Soenen. "Project Exit Value as a Measure of Flexibility and Risk Exposure." *Engineering Economist* 34 (Fall 1989): 39–54.

Bjerksund, Petter, and Steiner Ekern. "Managing Investment Opportunities under Price Uncertainty: From 'Last Chance' to 'Wait and See' Strategies." *Financial Management* 19 (Autumn 1990): 65–83.

Chiu, Chui-Yi, and Chan S. Park. "Fuzzy Cash Flow Analysis Using Present Worth Criterion." *Engineering Economist* 39 (Winter 1994): 113–138.

Eschenbach, Ted G., and Robert J. Gimpel. "Stochastic Sensitivity Analysis." *Engineering Economist* 35 (Summer 1990): 305–322.

Eschbenbach, Ted G., and Lisa S. McKeague. "Exposition on Using Graphs for Sensitivity Analysis." *Engineering Economist* 34 (Summer 1989): 315–333.

Hertz, David B. "Investment Policies That Pay Off." *Harvard Business Review* (January–February 1968): 96–108.

———. "Risk Analysis in Capital Investment." *Harvard Business Review* (January–February 1964): 95–106.

Hurley, W. J., and L. D. Johnson. "Capital Investment under Uncertainty: Calculating the Present Value of the Depreciation Tax Shield When the Tax Rate Is Stochastic." *Engineering Economist* 41 (Spring 1996): 243–251.

Jones, P. C., W. J. Hopp, and J. L. Zydiak. "Capital Asset Valuation and Depreciation for Stochastically Deteriorating Equipment." *Engineering Economist* 38 (Fall 1992): 19–30.

Joy, O. Maurice, and Jerry O. Bradley, "A Note on Sensitivity Analysis of Rates of Return." *Journal of Finance* 28 (December 1973): 1255–1261.

Keeley, Robert, and Randolph Westerfield. "A Problem in Probability Distribution Techniques for Capital Budgeting." *Journal of Finance* 27 (June 1972): 703–709.

Kensinger, John W. "Adding the Value of Active Management into the Capital Budgeting Equation." *Midland Corporate Finance Journal* 5 (Spring 1987): 31–42.

Kulatilaka, N. and A. J. Marcus. "Project Valuation under Uncertainty: When Does DCF Fail?" *Journal of Applied Finance* 5 (1992): 92–100.

Lambert, R. "Executive Effort and Selection of Risky Projects." *The Rand Journal of Economics* 17 (Spring 1986): 77–86.

Lin, Edward Y. H., and James R. Buck. "Measuring Conditional Partial Expected Loss under Uniformly Distributed Uncertain Timing." *Engineering Economist* 33 (Fall 1988): 61–78.

Markowitz, Harry M. "Investment for the Long Run: New Evidence for an Old Rule." *Journal of Finance* 31 (December 1976): 1273–1286.

McConkey, Dale. "Planning for Uncertainty." *Business Horizons* 30 (January–February 1981): 40–45.

Meimban, Julian J., III, John S. Morris, and Robert L. Govett. "The Evaluation of Wood-Fired Cogeneration Investments Using Monte-Carlo Simulation." *Engineering Economist* 37 (Winter 1992): 115–136.

Moore, William T., and Son-Sam Chen. "Implementing the IRR Criterion When Cash Flow Parameters Are Unknown." *Financial Review* 19 (November 1984): 351–358.

Murphy, K. "Corporate Performance and Managerial Remuneration: An Empirical Analysis." *Journal of Accounting and Economics* 7 (April 1985): 11–42.

Noble, Donald J. "Using Simulation as a Tool for Making Financial Decisions in a Uncertain Environment." *Industrial Engineering* 20 (January 1988): 44–48.

Osteryoung, Jerome S., Elton Scott, and Gordon S. Roberts. "Selecting Capital Projects with the Coefficient of Variation." *Financial Management* 6 (Summer 1977): 65–70.

Quederni, Bechir N., and William G. Sullivan. "A Semi-Variance Model for Incorporating Risk into Capital Investment Analysis." *Engineering Economist* 36 (Winter 1991): 83–106.

Robichek, Alexander A. "Interpreting the Results of Risk Analysis." *Journal of Finance* 30 (December 1975): 1384–1386.

Schnabel, Jacques A. "Uncertainty and the Abandonment Option." *Engineering Economist* 37 (Winter 1992): 172–177.

Schrieves, Ronald E., and John M. Wachowicz, Jr. "Proper Risk Resolution in Replacement Chain Analysis." *Engineering Economist* 34 (Winter 1989): 91–114.

Shashua, Leon, and Yaagov Goldschmidt. "Break-even Analysis under Inflation." *Engineering Economist* 32 (Winter 1987): 79–88.

Sick, Gordon A. "A Certainty-Equivalent Approach to Capital Budgeting." *Financial Management* 15 (Winter 1986): 23–32.

Thompson, Robert A., and Gerald J. Thuesen. "Application of Dynamic Criteria for Capital Budgeting Decisions." *Engineering Economist* 32 (Fall 1987): 59–87.

Trigerorgis, Lenos, and Scott P. Mason. "Valuing Managerial Flexibility." *Midland Corporate Finance Journal* 5 (Spring 1987): 14–21.

Tufekci, Suleyman, and D. B. Young. "Moments of the Present Worths of General Probabilistic Cash Flows under Random Timing." *Engineering Economist* 32 (Summer 1987): 303–336.

Wachowicz, John M., Jr., and Ronald E. Schiieves. "An Argument for 'Generalized' Mean-Coefficient of Variation Analysis." *Financial Management* 9 (Winter 1980): 51–58.

Weiss, Harry H. "An Accuracy Range System of Uncertain Appraisal." *Engineering Economist* 32 (September 1987): 197–216.

Whisler, William D. "Sensitivity Analysis of Rates of Return." *Journal of Finance* 31 (March 1976): 63–69.

Williams, Joseph T. "Trading and Valuing Depreciable Assets." *Journal of Financial Economics* (June 1985): 283–308.

Yoon, Kwangsun Paul. "Capital Investment Analysis Involving Estimate Error." *Engineering Economist* 35 (Fall 1990): 21–30.

CHAPTER 13 |

RISK FROM THE COMPANY PERSPECTIVE: CAPITAL BUDGETING WITH CONSIDERATION OF FIRM RISK REDUCTION EFFECTS

After completing this chapter you should be able to:

1. Explain why the total firm risk is important to some shareholders, management, other employees, customers, suppliers, present and potential competitors, and others.
2. List what market imperfections lead to the importance of measuring total firm risk.
3. Understand the risk-reducing response the firm experiences when it adds non-perfectly correlated projects to its existing portfolio of projects.
4. Explain why diversification reduces total risk.
5. Calculate the correlation coefficient, the beta coefficient, and the covariance between the firm and a proposed capital project.
6. Apply the mean-variance method to a project and make the accept-reject decision.
7. Characterize the problems associated with the use of the mean-variance method.
8. Understand how sensitivity analysis is used in evaluating possible project combinations within the firm.
9. Present the arguments for and against firms diversifying their portfolio when it can be done by the shareholder.

Executives at Martin Marietta might have been depressed when NASA announced its contract awards for the $6.5 billion space station, and Martin was left on the ground. But a day earlier, Martin had been chosen by the Defense Department to build an air defense system worth up to $4 billion. The same day, Martin got a $608 million Air Force contract. Martin was also managing the FAA's attempt to modernize the air-traffic system and headed a team bidding for a multibillion dollar contract to overhaul the federal government's phone and data system.

It is "received wisdom" that diversification by companies does not help the shareholders because the shareholders can diversify on their own. But you might have trouble convincing Martin's president, Norman Augustine, that their diversification strategy was not worthwhile. As Augustine put it, "Like squirrels, we wanted to bury a lot of acorns." By not putting all their eggs in one basket, managers at Martin were able to move ahead virtually unfazed after losing out on a major contract. Several years earlier, Marietta had been forced to add $1 billion of debt in order to fight off a takeover attempt by Bendix. Failure to secure the space station contract might have led to another takeover attempt had it not been for Martin's strategy of diversifying within its area of expertise.[1]

In a perfect market, the firm perspective would not be worth a chapter in a capital budgeting book. In reality, market imperfections, such as transaction cost, bankruptcy cost, and goal incongruence, operate to make the market less than perfect. These imperfections have the disadvantage of making reality hard to model, but they also create an opportunity for positive net present value projects for those who identify and exploit these imperfections. In this chapter, we will first look at how market imperfections make it important to view risk from a total firm perspective. Covariance among existing projects is discussed next. Then the calculation of covariance and the application of mean-variance analysis in a capital budgeting setting is discussed. Problems with the application of the mean-variance model follow. Other selection techniques are explained and the chapter concludes with a discussion of the cost and benefits of diversification. An Appendix is attached that describes the development of the mean-variance portfolio construction method.

MARKET IMPERFECTIONS AND THE IMPORTANCE OF TOTAL FIRM RISK IN CAPITAL BUDGETING |

A completely rational manager, having just learned about risk reduction in an MBA finance course, once stood in front of a group of executives and asked: What difference does it make if I carry fire insurance for my firm? One answer is that the firm should not carry fire insurance if it believes that the only stakeholders important to the company are several thousand well-diversified shareholders who can afford the cost of the fire. For employees and nondiversified stockholders on the other hand, the fire may be catastrophic.

---

[1]Tim Smart, with Seth Payne, "Diversity Is the Secret Weapon," *Business Week* (December 14, 1987): 36.

DIVERSIFICATION—IT'S THE SIZE OF THE BET THAT COUNTS!

Imagine someone asking you to flip a coin 50 times for a dollar bet each time. Knowing that you can afford to lose a dollar and knowing that a fair coin should leave you with the same amount of money that you came with, you might accept this bet. On the other hand, if someone asked you to flip a coin once for $50, you would probably decline the offer. In this second case, you would either leave $50 ahead or $50 dollars down. This second bet is much like the position of management in many corporations. Most senior managers, who also decide the acceptance and rejection of capital projects, have a disproportionate share of their present or potential wealth tied to the corporation. Compensation plans designed to tie management success to stockholder success increase the proportion of the manager's wealth that depends on the company's success. To expect these managers to divorce all personal interest from the capital budgeting decision and take the position of a diversified shareholder is naive.

OTHER STAKEHOLDERS' PERSPECTIVES

The firm's total risk is important because many of the firm's stakeholders would pay large transaction or liquidation costs if the firm exposed itself to excessive risk. Several of these perspectives are discussed next.

All other things being equal, a manager's marketability probably decreases as her age increases. This can be observed by the difficulty many displaced managers from "right-sizing" firms are having replacing their income. This has capital budgeting connotations in that a risky project may not be proposed if it increases the manager's exposure to termination. In addition, signaling may operate in the employment market to the extent that a manager released after a failed project may not be as employable as one released after a string of small successes, even though the failed employee created more wealth.

As a manager is awarded stock options and other performance-based incentives over time, the manager's wealth becomes concentrated in the firm. A manager with this store of wealth in a firm may reduce the risk of the firm (and his portfolio) by selecting slow growing, safe projects rather than projects with a higher net present value and higher risk. This is especially true when the forgone projects are not observable by the shareholder.

Suppliers have an interest in the total risk of the customer company and price their product accordingly. This is especially true when suppliers are capital intensive and redeployability of excess capacity is limited. Suppliers also worry about total company risk when they extend sizable amounts of credit to the firm.

Many customers and purchasing managers have vested interests in a supplier's total firm risk. Chrysler, in the past, has had to guarantee the debt of some of its suppliers to keep them as reliable sources of supply. This type of reliance will probably increase with the adoption of just-in-time inventory techniques by more firms. By its very nature, just-in-time usually means using only one supplier. This consequently increases the importance of the risk exposure of the supplier company. An unstable supplier may not even be allowed to bid for business.

Lenders and bond-rating agencies evaluate total company risk when estimating the ability of the company to repay. In addition, some lenders have an interest in total company risk because they are not adequately diversified across borrowing companies. A potentially profitable firm could fail because cash flows are deficient in a specific period, causing a liquidity crisis that the firm may not survive.

Companies are also interested in their competitors' overall risk exposure. Where risk exposures are similar for all companies, the industry as a group might weather a bad outcome. Where they are different, the competitors may create situations to increase the other firms' exposure to the identified risk. This was probably the case when profitable and small People's Express purchased Frontier Air in the 1980s. Prior to this purchase, People's was a small nuisance to the big carriers. After the purchase and the debt associated with the purchase, People's had a much higher financial risk exposure and was vulnerable to price wars. This new exposure combined with some sustained price wars ultimately led to the demise of People's Express.

If these perspectives are rationalized away by the assumption of an efficient and competitive market, it is hard to explain the billions of dollars spent each year in aggregate on property and casualty insurance by virtually every corporation, even though many are owned by well-diversified shareholders. Our main mission here is not to answer why the risk reduction is practiced, but rather to model and measure the risk so it can be managed. Luckily, some of this risk reduction comes at a relatively inexpensive price through the addition of new projects that increase wealth and, at the same time, reduce total company risk.

CORRELATION AND COMPANY RISK |

Every firm currently in existence can be considered a group, or *portfolio,* of ongoing projects. The correlation between these projects will lie somewhere between perfectly positively correlated (+1) and perfectly negatively correlated (−1). We will calculate this correlation after discussing its meaning. Perfect positive correlation as described in the last chapter means that the occurrence of one cash flow predicts the size and occurrence of the other cash flow. The word "positive" indicates the direction of the relationship; the word "perfect" indicates the degree of the relationship. A positive relationship should exist between the sale of hamburgers and the sale of French fries at McDonald's.

Many projects are positively correlated, but few are perfectly positively correlated. An example of something approaching perfect positive correlation would be the relationship between the revenue from hamburgers and the variable cost of the meat, bun, and condiments.

A negative correlation occurs when the payoff from one project is often matched with a loss on another project. You can construct an example of a negative correlation by betting with one individual that the St. Louis Cardinals will beat the Chicago Cubs in an upcoming game and betting with another individual that the Cubs will beat the Cardinals in the same game. If you bet the same amount with each individual, you have a perfectly negatively correlated relationship (with no profit).

By recognizing the natural risk position of the firm and acquiring an offsetting project that is negatively correlated with this natural position you can reduce risk and create wealth at the same time. The trick to creating wealth is to generate a positive NPV on the combined natural position and the risk-reducing project.

As an example, Transamerica Corporation owns both Transamerica Financial Services, the fourth-largest finance company in the United States, and Transamerica Life Companies, the eighth-largest life insurance company. A large risk exposure for the finance company is that it will not be able to find sources for the money it needs to provide loans to its customers. The life insurance company faces the risk that it will not be able to find enough worthwhile investments paying more than the actuarially determined required rate of return. Although there is significant regulation regarding the commingling of funds, the two businesses appear to reduce each other's risks while meeting their own needs.

In the problems at the end of the chapter, we will illustrate some of the other ways management reduces the total risk of the firm. First, we need to understand how an additional project affects the risk of the firm.

EXISTING FIRM RISK AND THE CORRELATION BETWEEN THE FIRM AND A PROPOSED PROJECT

The total risk of a company can be influenced by selection of an additional project or projects. An additional project's influence on the total risk of an existing firm is a function of the project's size, the variance of its probability distribution of benefits, and the correlation between the company and project. Naturally, with everything else being equal, large projects will have a greater influence than smaller ones.

If the firm is not currently in existence, it is possible to construct a portfolio of projects that would maximize the return for a given level of risk (as measured by the standard deviation of returns). Starting with a nonexistent firm is typically not the position of most managers making capital budgeting decisions. Therefore, marginal impacts on an existing firm are discussed here, and optimal portfolio selection without a starting position is illustrated in Appendix 13-A at the end of the chapter.

Where you have an existing firm, this firm will have a total firm risk based on the correlation between ongoing projects that have been accepted in the past. To stretch the coin-flipping analogy further, your past decisions may have glued your coins together as is the case if past projects were perfectly positively correlated. For example, if you are now flipping rolls of glued-together coins, you will either lose the roll of coins or win another roll of coins. There is not much risk reduction or diversification benefit in accepting highly positively correlated projects.

What is more common over time is that the firm has accepted projects that are correlated to some degree. Because the projects are not perfectly correlated, some risk reduction occurs. The purchase of Kelly Springfield Tire Corporation by Goodyear Tire Corporation, to add a low-priced tire line to its offering without "cheapening" the Goodyear name, is an example of a total firm risk-reducing project. Returns for the two tire companies are correlated, but they are not perfectly correlated because people will often turn to the cheaper tire line in difficult economic times.

Negatively correlated projects are hard to find because the revenues of most projects are influenced by the economy in general. If you could find enough negatively correlated projects, it would be possible to eliminate risk altogether. An additional problem with finding negatively correlated projects is that in a competitive market the price would be so high that it would drive the return on a risk-free combination of projects to a low interest rate such as that paid on U.S. Treasury bills.

Example. As a numerical example of how the acceptance of a negatively correlated project can reduce the risk, consider the returns of Green Thumb Vegetable Seed Company when it expands into the flower seed business. The returns of the existing company and a proposed flower seed project are summarized in Table 13.1. The returns, which vary according to the state of the economy, reflect a tendency for gardeners to grow vegetables during times of economic difficulty and flowers when the economy is strong. As you can see, the existing vegetable seed company and the proposed flower seed project are more risky when considered alone. But when an equal amount is invested in the flower seed project, the resulting company is less sensitive to economic conditions than before the acceptance of the project.

MEAN-VARIANCE PORTFOLIO PRINCIPLES |

In this section, we will extend the general concepts of correlation and risk reduction to the specific problems of measuring risk and return, and applying those measures to the construction of portfolios. In the mean-variance approach, risk

| TABLE 13.1 ILLUSTRATION OF DIVERSIFICATION BENEFITS FOR GREEN THUMB SEED COMPANY

Rates of return in the vegetable seed company and the proposed flower seed project are shown. Combined return assumes an equal investment in the flower seed project.

| | | STATE OF THE ECONOMY | |
	Stagnation	Moderate Expansion	Strong Expansion
Existing Vegetable Seed Company	50%	24%	−20%
Proposed Flower Seed Project	−30%	30%	72%
Combined Return	10%	27%	26%

is measured by the variance or standard deviation of the probability distribution of expected returns. In the following section, we will apply those concepts to capital budgeting.

MEASURING HOLDING PERIOD RETURN

Return is generally measured as holding period return:

$$\frac{\text{Ending value} - \text{Beginning value} - \text{Cash inflow during period}}{\text{Beginning value}} \qquad \text{(13-1)}$$

If a capital investment requires an initial outlay of \$1,000, requires an additional outlay of \$200 during the period, and has a value of \$1,300 at the end of the period, the holding period return is:

$$\text{Holding period return} = (1,300 - 1,000 - 200) \div 1,000 = 10\%$$

MEASURING THE CORRELATION COEFFICIENT, BETA, AND COVARIANCE

We will use R to represent holding period return, but the mathematics of covariance is the same, for the most part, if R represents some other measure of profitability, such as the net present value, profitability index, or internal rate of return.

The key risk measures are those that capture the relationships among the existing company and the proposed project in a form that allows us to predict the variance of the total company after the acceptance. The key risk measure used in mean-variance analysis is the covariance. Letting the company be represented as "A," and the potential project represented as "B," the covariance of returns $(\sigma_{A,B})$ is:[2]

$$\sigma_{A,B} = \sum_{i=1}^{m} p_i[R_{A,i} - E(R_A)][R_{B,i} - E(R_B)] \qquad \text{(13-2)}$$

where p_i is the probability of state of nature[3] i occurring, m is the number of possible states, $R_{A,i}$ and $R_{B,i}$ are the holding period returns on A, the company, and B, the proposed project if state i occurs. $E(R_A)$ and $E(R_B)$ are the expected holding period returns on A, the company, and B, the proposed project.

---

[2] In more general terms, we can say that $\sigma_{A,B} = E\{[R_A - E(R_A)][R_B - E(R_B)]\}$.

[3] A state of nature is a set of conditions that might occur, and which are beyond the control of the decision maker. For example, a 3 percent economic growth rate and a 4 percent inflation rate might be one state.

Other closely related measures are the correlation coefficient ($r_{A,B}$) and the beta ($\beta_{A,B}$):

$$r_{A,B} = \sigma_{A,B}/(\sigma_A \sigma_B) \tag{13-3}$$

$$\beta_{A,B} = \sigma_{A,B}/\sigma_B^2 \tag{13-4}$$

where $\beta_{A,B}$ is the beta of the company with regard to the proposed project B,[4] and σ_A and σ_B are the standard deviations of the probability distributions of expected returns for the company and the proposed project, respectively.

Example. For the Green Thumb example appearing in Table 13.1 and in Figure 13.1, the measures of expected return, variance, $\beta_{A,B}$, and correlation, assuming each economic condition is equally likely, are:

$$E(R_A) = (1/3)(.50) + (1/3)(.24) + (1/3)(-.20) = \underline{.180}$$

$$E(R_B) = (1/3)(-.30) + (1/3)(.30) + (1/3)(.72) = \underline{.240}$$

$$\sigma_A = \sqrt{(1/3)(.50 - .18)^2 + (1/3)(.24 - .18)^2 + (1/3)(-.20 - .18)^2} = \underline{.289}$$

$$\sigma_B = \sqrt{(1/3)(-.30 - .24)^2 + (1/3)(.30 - .24)^2 + (1/3)(.72 - .24)^2} = \underline{.419}$$

$$\sigma_{A,B} = (1/3)(.50 - .18)(-.30 - .24) + (1/3)(.24 - .18)(.30 - .24)$$

$$+ (1/3)(-.20 - .18)(.72 - .24)$$

$$= \underline{-.117}$$

$$\beta_{A,B} = -.117/.419^2 = \underline{-0.666}$$

$$r_{A,B} = -.117/(.289 \times .419) = \underline{-.966}$$

A GRAPHIC REPRESENTATION OF THE CORRELATION

Figure 13.1, which is based on the data in Table 13.1, can be used to illustrate these three measures of relationships. The vertical axis represents returns for the existing vegetable seed company A while the horizontal axis represents return for possible flower seed project B. Each dot represents a combination of return for company A and return for project B. For simplicity of explanation, we assume that this set of dots represents all possible combinations, and that each of these combinations is equally likely. These combinations could be developed from actual combinations of returns that occurred in past periods or from expected returns for each investment in a number of different states. We would usually have many more than three combinations, but these three allow us to illustrate the basic principles without unnecessary complications.

The horizontal line in Figure 13.1 passes through the vertical axis at the expected return for the existing company (A). The variance for company A (σ_A^2) is

---

[4]Note from Equation 13-4 that $\beta_{A,B} = \beta_{B,A}$ only if $\sigma_A = \sigma_B$.

| FIGURE 13.1 RELATIONSHIP BETWEEN RETURNS FOR THE EXISTING GREEN THUMB VEGETABLE SEED COMPANY AND A PROPOSED FLOWER SEED DIVISION

The dots represent equally likely combinations of returns for the company A and the proposed project B. The horizontal line was drawn through the expected return for company A. The sloping line was drawn so as to minimize the average squared vertical distance from the dots to the sloping line; this is the standard method for fitting a line in linear regression analysis.

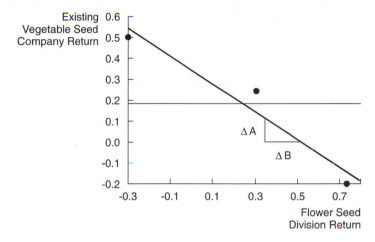

the average squared vertical distance from the dots to the horizontal line. The sloping line is the straight line drawn so as to minimize the average squared vertical distance from the dots to the line, which is the standard method for fitting a line in linear regression analysis. The slope of that line is $\beta_{A,B}$. Note the small triangle with the vertical side marked ΔA and the horizontal side marked ΔB. $\beta_{A,B}$ is $\Delta A \div \Delta B$. The beta of -0.666 means that we would expect a 30 percent increase in returns for division B (flowers) to be associated with a 20 percent decrease in returns for the existing vegetable seed business A.

The correlation coefficient measures how well the sloping line fits the dots. The correlation coefficient is positive if $\beta_{A,B}$ is positive (the line slopes up to the right) and vice versa. A correlation of $+1$ for an upward slope (or -1 for a downward slope) means that all the dots are precisely on the sloping line. A correlation coefficient of 0 means that there is no relationship between A and B. A correlation coefficient between 0 and 1 (or 0 and -1 for a negative slope) means that the situation is similar to that of Figure 13.1, in which the sloping line explains some, but not all, of the variation in A. The correlation coefficient close to -1 indicates that the two investments are highly negatively correlated; all three dots would lie close to the downward sloping line.

The covariance does not have as simple and direct a graphical interpretation. It is not constrained between $+1$ and -1 as is the correlation coefficient, but it will be 0 if the correlation coefficient is zero and, otherwise, will have the same sign as the correlation coefficient. Although the covariance does not have a simple, intuitive interpretation, we will see that its mathematical properties are important for portfolio construction.

Two Asset Mean-Variance Portfolio Construction

The principles of mean-variance portfolio construction were developed by Harry Markowitz.[5] We will use these principles with a two-asset portfolio here, and extend them to the general case in Appendix 13-A. The two-asset case is itself useful for capital budgeting.

Total Company Risk Reduction from Adding a Project

To simplify the measurement of the risk reduction resulting from the addition of a project to the present portfolio of projects, we will assume that the profitability measure is in terms of profitability per dollar of investment. It could, for example, be holding period return, internal rate of return, profitability index, or accounting rate of return. For a two-asset portfolio, the expected return, $E(R_p)$, and standard deviation of the probability distribution of expected returns, σ_p, are:[6]

$$E(R_p) = W_A E(R_A) + W_B E(R_B) \tag{13-5}$$

$$\sigma_p = \sqrt{W_A^2 \sigma_A^2 + W_B^2 \sigma_B^2 + 2W_A W_B \sigma_{A,B}} \tag{13-6}$$

where W_A is the proportion of total funds invested in asset A, etc; W_A plus W_B must equal one in this case since only two assets are being considered. The other terms are as previously defined.

Note from Equation 13-3 that $\sigma_{A,B} = r_{A,B} \sigma_A \sigma_B$. Using this relationship, Equation 13-6 can be rewritten:

$$\sigma_p = \sqrt{W_A^2 \sigma_A^2 + W_B^2 \sigma_B^2 + 2W_A W_B r_{A,B} \sigma_A \sigma_B} \tag{13-6'}$$

In Equation 13-6A, the risk positions that can be obtained by combining two assets depend on the standard deviations of the two assets and the correlation coefficient between the two assets. The impact of the correlation coefficient is illustrated graphically in Figure 13.2, with the existing vegetable seed company,

---

[5]Harry Markowitz, "Portfolio Selection," *Journal of Finance* 7 (March 1952): 77–91.

[6]To derive these expressions, assume there are m possible states of nature, with probability of state j being P_j. All Σs signify summation from j = 1 through j = m.

$E(R_p) = \Sigma\, P_j[W_A R_{Aj} + W_B R_{Bj}] = W_A E(R_A) + W_B E(R_B)$

$\sigma_p^2 = \Sigma\, P_j\{[W_A R_{Aj} + W_B R_{Bj}] - [W_A E(R_A) + W_B E(R_B)]\}^2$. Rearranging terms,

$\sigma_p^2 = W_A^2 \Sigma P_j[R_{Aj} - E(R_A)]^2 + W_B^2 \Sigma P_j[R_{Bj} - E(R_B)]^2 + 2W_A W_B \Sigma[R_{Aj} - E(R_A)][R_{Bj} - E(R_B)]$

$\qquad = W_A^2 \sigma_A^2 + W_B^2 \sigma_B^2 + 2W_A W_B \sigma_{A,B}$

| **FIGURE 13.2** | **CORRELATION AND DIVERSIFICATION BENEFITS FOR GREEN THUMB SEED COMPANY** |

Dots A and B represent the risk-return characteristics of the two divisions. The lines connecting those dots represent risk-return combinations that would be available by combining various proportions of these two divisions in portfolios, depending on the degree of correlation between the two assets.

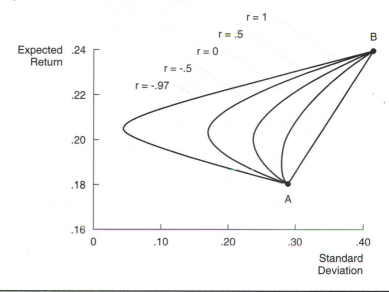

Green Thumb Seed Company, again used as an example. Division A, represented by the lower dot, has an expected return of .180 and a standard deviation of .289. Division B, the proposed flower seed division, represented by the upper dot, has an expected return of .240 and a standard deviation of .419. The set of lines connecting the dots represents the risk-return combinations that could be achieved by combining investments in these two divisions in portfolios, depending on the correlation coefficient. The line farthest to the left is for the actual correlation of −.970, while the other lines show the opportunities that would exist with other degrees of correlation. Movement along one of these lines is achieved by changing the proportion of funds invested in each division—assuming, again, that all funds are invested in some combination of these two divisions.[7] The lower (or more negative) the correlation coefficient, the lower is the risk that can be achieved at each level of expected return. If correlation is low or negative, a risk-averse, rational investor will prefer some combination of A and B over pure investment in A, because some combinations provide more

[7]If the two assets are securities, the short sale of X in order to invest over 100 percent of one's money in Y would allow the line to be continued on past point Y to positions with higher risk and higher expected return.

expected return *and* less risk than A. An investor may also prefer some combination of A and B over pure investment in B, but that will depend on the individual investor's preferences since a trade-off between risk and expected return is involved.

Borrowing, Lending, and Portfolio Choice

Suppose we were to invest some of our money in a risky portfolio with expected return and standard deviation of $E(R_p)$ and σ_p. Suppose we invest the rest of our money in a risk-free asset such as U.S. Treasury bills, with a return of R_f. The expected return would be:

$$\text{Expected return} = X \cdot E(R_p) + (1 - X)R_f \qquad (13\text{-}7)$$

where X is the proportion of our money invested in the risky portfolio; we could also use leverage by borrowing so that X would be greater than 1.

Note from Equation 13-6A that if the standard deviation for asset B is 0, the standard deviation of a portfolio consisting of assets A and B is simply $W_A\sigma_A$. Since the Treasury bills are risk-free, their standard deviation is 0. The standard deviation for the combination of Treasury bills and a risky portfolio is:

$$\text{Standard deviation} = X\sigma_p \qquad (13\text{-}8)$$

We can choose from a number of risky portfolios, and we can combine any portfolio with risk-free lending or borrowing. Therefore, we would prefer the portfolio that gives the greatest increase in expected return for each increase in risk as we increase the proportion of our money that is invested in the portfolio. This will be the portfolio that maximized the reward to variability ratio:

$$\text{Reward to variability ratio} = [E(R_p) - R_f]/\sigma_p \qquad (13\text{-}9)$$

For Green Thumb, with a correlation of -0.97, we can find the optimal combination of the two divisions by a bit of trial and error. We simply compute the reward to variability ratios for various combinations of A and B. Assuming a risk-free rate of 10 percent, trial and error leads us to the optimal combination of 59 percent of their money in division A and 41 percent in division B for a reward to variability ratio of:

$$\frac{(.59 \cdot .18 + .41 \cdot .24) - .10}{\sqrt{.59^2 \cdot .289^2 + .41^2 \cdot .419^2 + 2 \cdot .59 \cdot .41 \cdot (-0.97) \cdot .289 \cdot .419}} = 2.494$$

To apply the model to a company, we simply treat the company as the portfolio of assets being analyzed. GE could have used this approach, for example, to evaluate the then-proposed acquisition of Kidder Peabody, a large financial services company unrelated to the main thrust of GE's business.

For smaller investments, the beta between the investment and the company's existing portfolio can be used as a risk measure for incremental decision making. GE might use this approach for a new kitchen appliance, for example. The investment will improve the company's reward to variability ratio if:[8]

$$[E(R_a) - R_f]/\beta_{a,c} > E(R_c) - R_f \qquad \text{(13-10)}$$

where $E(R_a)$ is the expected return for the asset, $E(R_c)$ is the expected return for the company as it exists, and $\beta_{a,c}$ is the beta between the asset and the company $(\sigma_{a,c}/\sigma_c^2)$. Of course, this approach requires the estimation of $\beta_{a,c}$. The development of inputs such as $\beta_{a,c}$ is considered following the discussion of the use of mean-variance analysis for strategic assessment.[9]

Example. Expected return for Beckman Corporation's existing portfolio of assets is 18 percent. Beckman finances part of its assets with debt, at an after-tax interest rate of 6 percent. A new product that would be less than 1 percent of Beckman's assets has an expected return of 20 percent. By looking at the new product and the existing company in a number of possible states of nature, $\beta_{a,c}$ of 1.4 was estimated. Thus, the investment in the new product will not improve the company's reward to variability ratio:

$$(.20 - .06)/1.4 < .18 - .06$$

[8]*Proof:* Define W as the proportion of funds invested in asset a, with the rest invested in the company's existing portfolio. The expected return and standard deviation of the portfolio thus created are:

$$E(R_p) = WE(R_a) + (1 - W)E(R_c) \text{ and } \sigma_p = [W^2\sigma_a^2 + (1 - W)^2\sigma_c^2 + 2W(1 - W)\sigma_{a,c}]^{1/2}$$

The derivatives of these two equations, evaluation at W=0, are

$$\partial E(R_p)/\partial W|_{W=0} = E(R_a) - E(R_b) \text{ and } \partial\sigma_p/\partial W|_{W=0} = [\sigma_{a,c} - \sigma_c^2]/\sigma_c.$$

We evaluate these two expressions at W=0 to find the marginal impact as we start adding asset a to the existing portfolio. The risk-return trade-off from a small increase in W at W=0 is therefore:

$$[\partial E(R_p)/\partial W]/[\partial\sigma_p/\partial W] = [E(R_a) - E(R_c)]/[(\sigma_{a,c} - \sigma_m^2)/\sigma_m]$$

The existing risk-return trade-off by borrowing or lending is $[E(R_c) - R_f]/\sigma_c$, so the new asset is desired if it provides an improved risk-return trade-off. Rearranging the terms in this inequality condition yields Inequality 13-10.

[9]Another approach is to use betas in relation to some index which measures the common factor(s) affecting all investments, such as the change in gross national product. Assuming that sensitivity to the index captures all nondiversifiable risk, the standard deviation of a well-diversified portfolio is:

$$\sigma_p = \sum_{i=1}^{n} W_i\beta_{i,I}\sigma_I$$

where $\beta_{i,I}$ is the beta of asset i in relation to the index and σ_I is the standard deviation of the index. If the company's portfolio is well diversified, a new asset will improve the reward to variability ratio if:

$$[E(R_a) - R_f]/\beta_{a,I} > [E(R_c) - R_f] \div \beta_{c,I}.$$

Mean-Variance Models and Strategic Assessment

The mean-variance model can be used to allocate funds among the company's main divisions. GE might, for example, use a mean-variance portfolio model to allocate money among its dozen or so major product areas. To use the model in this way, it is only necessary to estimate expected return for each division, variance for each division, and covariance between divisions.

Example. Diversified Energy Corporation has three main divisions: oil, coal, and fast-food restaurants. Expected return, standard deviation, and correlation coefficients for the three divisions are as follows. (Subscripts o, c, and r represent oil, coal, and restaurants respectively.)

$$E(R_o) = .20 \qquad E(R_c) = .15 \qquad E(R_r) = .15$$

$$\sigma_o = .20 \qquad \sigma_c = .15 \qquad \sigma_r = .20$$

$$r_{o,c} = .50 \qquad r_{o,r} = .00 \qquad r_{c,r} = .20$$

The company can borrow at an after-tax interest rate of 6 percent, and management wants to allocate funds between the three divisions so as to maximize the reward to variability ratio. The optimal allocation could be found using methods described in Appendix 13-A, which simply extends the logic of two-asset portfolio selection. The optimal allocation is:

Division	Oil	Coal	Fast-food restaurants
Proportion of assets	.43	.29	.28

With this allocation, the expected return is 17.15 percent, the standard deviation is 13.45 percent, and the reward to variability ratio is .8287. This is the optimal allocation, given the mean-variance criterion, and managers will move to the risk-return position they prefer by deciding the amount of debt to use in the capital structure.

Special Problems in Applying the Mean-Variance Model to Capital Budgeting |

To apply the mean-variance portfolio model to capital budgeting, we must first recognize that we are analyzing risk from the perspective of the company and its managers, not from the perspective of diversified shareholders. If shareholders are well diversified in their own portfolios, we would expect them to be concerned only about an asset's contribution to nondiversifiable risk for a broadly based portfolio, and mean-variance analysis of the company's portfolio is not needed for that purpose. Problems encountered by managers in applying mean-variance portfolio theory include the indivisibility of assets, the problem of choosing an appropriate holding period for the analysis, choice of the appropriate interest rate, and assembly of large amounts of data. The following discussion of these problems is based on the perspective of the company and its managers.

INDIVISIBILITY OF ASSETS

Full mean-variance portfolio analysis is based on the assumption that securities are infinitely divisible, while capital investments often come in very large, indivisible units. When George Steinbrenner set out to build two cruise ships for the Hawaiian market, for example, he had a couple of choices with regard to size, but he knew that .82 of a ship would sink rather quickly. Fortunately, the lack of divisibility can be handled with integer quadratic programming, which forces the selection of only whole units of specified investments. Constraints can also be used to limit the choice between zero and one unit.

HOLDING PERIOD CHOICE

We could use mean-variance analysis to find the portfolio of capital investments that has the highest net present value for each level of risk, where risk is measured as the standard deviation of the net present value. We could do the same thing with the profitability index or the internal rate of return. Unfortunately, though, the efficient frontiers that result are difficult to interpret because asset lives are not all identical. GE, for example, would generally expect an investment in a new consumer product for this year's Christmas market to have a much shorter life than an investment in its power systems area. Thus, cash flows from some assets will be freed up for other investments, with possible additional diversification benefits. To avoid ambiguity caused by unequal lives, we usually measure return over some holding period. The choice of a holding period is discussed in the following paragraphs.

One alternative is to use a long holding period, such as the life of the longest-life asset being considered. To measure portfolio risk and return over this holding period, though, it is necessary to identify all assets that will be selected between now and the end of the holding period. In addition, there is no date at which the lives of all assets to be acquired both now and later will end, unless the company plans to liquidate. Therefore, some terminal value estimates will be required as well. Beyond these difficulties of application, there is a serious conceptual problem. Risk analysis based on the results over a multiyear holding period does not give a complete picture of risk because it ignores fluctuations during the holding period. Problems like the risk of not being able to meet financial obligations during a bad year are missed when a long holding period is used, so the long holding period gives an incomplete picture of risk.

These problems are avoided by using a short holding period, such as a year, and using the present value of remaining cash flows as the value of each asset at the end of the holding period. Present value of remaining cash flows would be used instead of market value because many profitable capital investments cannot really be sold after such a short holding period, without suffering a large loss. Unfortunately, the lack of opportunity to sell an asset for the present value of its cash flows limits our ability to modify the portfolio at the end of the holding period. This disadvantage is not assigned a specific value by the model, so the short holding period also gives an incomplete picture of risk and return.

Because of the problems in choosing a holding period, we must recognize the possibility that we have missed some aspects of risk and return in creating the efficient frontier. This does not mean that the model cannot be helpful to managers choosing portfolios, but it suggests that managers will want supplemental information. If a long time horizon is being used, for example, information about risk in the intermediate periods may also be considered as a check on the desirability of the efficient portfolios that have been identified. Alternately, managers may want to check for consistency by using several different holding period lengths to select optimal portfolios. Once again, we find that our analytical tools provide insights, but they do not completely automate the decision process.

DEFINING THE BORROWING-LENDING RATE

The interest rate depends on the maturity of the debt, and the only risk-free interest rate for a holding period is that for debt with a maturity equal to the holding period. For a long holding period, the rate on long-term bonds can be used. For a short holding period, a short-term rate would be appropriate. However, the possibility of entering into long-term loan agreements must be recognized, even if a short holding period is used for the analysis. One way to recognize the potential for long-term borrowing is to treat long-term debt as a risky asset in which a negative position can be taken. The long-term debt is risky over a short holding period because the terminal value of that asset will depend on the interest rate prevailing at the end of the holding period.

If market interest rates increase over the period, for example, the long-term debt can be retired for less than its face value, at least partially offsetting the decrease in the present value of future cash flows from other assets that result from a higher interest rate.

DATA NEEDS

Another problem with the use of mean-variance portfolio analysis for capital budgeting is the tremendous amount of data required. Covariance estimates are needed for each asset in relation to every other asset. The number of covariance terms needed (excluding variances which are covariances of an asset with itself) is $.5N^2 - .5N$ where N is the number of assets being considered. Including expected return and standard deviation for each asset, the total number of terms needed is $.5N^2 + 1.5N$. If 1,000 capital investments are being considered,

501,500 risk and return measures must be estimated. The estimation is made more difficult by the fact that covariances and correlation coefficients are not the types of measures for which the average manager will be prepared to make judgmental estimates.

OTHER SELECTION TECHNIQUES |

While maximizing the return for any level of risk measure in the mean-variance context is one method of deciding the acceptability of a proposed capital project, several other methods are available. Two models provide methods of responding to skewness while one responds to alternate utility function shapes.

MODELS RECOGNIZING SKEWNESS

The problem of skewness was discussed in Chapter 11. As shown in Figure 11.1, a skewed distribution has one tail that is longer than the other. A long tail to the right increases the standard deviation as much as a long tail to the left. Methods using skewness as an additional criterion are based on the assumption that decision makers like expected return, dislike variance, like positive skewness, and dislike negative skewness. Portfolio models using skewness have been proposed.[10] There are, however, technical difficulties in the development of mathematical programming models to select portfolios using skewness. Those problems have limited the popularity of models incorporating skewness.

 Semivariance was discussed in Chapter 12. It is computed the same way as the variance, except that only values below the expected value are considered. Semivariance may be a more reasonable measure of risk than variance, and several people have applied semivariance to portfolio selection.[11] Unfortunately, though, technical problems have been encountered in the construction of mathematical programming models to select the portfolio that minimizes semivariance for each level of expected return. Mathematical programming models using standard deviation, on the other hand, are readily available.

GROWTH-OPTIMAL (GEOMETRIC MEAN) MODEL

The formula for and use of geometric mean return as a single measure combining risk and return was discussed in Chapter 11. The geometric mean criterion is based on the assumption that the objective of the decision maker is to maximize

---

[10]Alan Kraus and Robert H. Litzenberger, "Skewness Preference and the Valuation of Risky Assets," *Journal of Finance* 31 (September 1976): 1085–1100.

[11]See, for example, Timothy J. Nantell and Barbara Price, "An Analytical Comparison of Variance and Semivariance Capital Market Theories," *Journal of Financial and Quantitative Analysis* 14 (June 1979): 221–242; and Colin G. Hoskin, "Capital Budgeting Decision Rules for Risky Projects Derived from a Capital Market Model Based on Semivariance," *Engineering Economist* 23 (1978): 211–222.

the expected long-term growth rate of wealth. The geometric mean criterion is also consistent with a logarithmic utility function for wealth. If the probability distribution of holding period return is the same each period, the portfolio with the highest geometric mean return provides the highest long-run growth rate of wealth. The geometric mean method has been suggested for at least two decades and has a number of academic supporters.[12] However, it has never gained the broad recognition accorded the mean-variance model. The use of the geometric mean in capital budgeting has been suggested, but the geometric mean has never been widely used for this purpose.

STATE-PREFERENCE MODELS

State-preference models are based on the assumption that the value of a particular return to a decision maker depends on the conditions at the time the return is received. A dollar received in a recession may be more valuable than a dollar received during a strong economy, for example. A dollar received during a nuclear holocaust may be of no value at all if the potential recipient expects to be vaporized. State-preference models assume a different utility function of wealth in each possible state of nature, with decisions based on the state-dependent preferences.

Because we do not have a method for finding utility functions for each possible state of nature, the practical application of the state-preference model has been limited. It has, however, received some increased use in indirect form because state-preference theory is consistent with the arbitrage pricing model discussed in Chapter 15.[13]

OTHER DECISION RULES IN PRACTICE

Some managers have a minimum acceptable return number, and they want to minimize the chances of falling below that number. A decision rule meeting this objective would be to accept projects that reduce the probability that the firm will earn less than the assigned minimum. Suppose, for example, a firm is considering projects Z and S shown below. If the minimum rate of return is 10%, then the firm with the addition of project Z is preferred over the existing firm, and the firm with project S is preferred over both.

---

[12]See, for example, Henry A. Latane' and Donald L. Tuttle, "Criteria for Portfolio Building," *Journal of Finance* 22 (September 1967): 359–373; Harry M. Markowitz, "Investment for the Long Run: New Evidence for an Old Rule," *Journal of Finance* 31 (December 1976): 1273–1286; and Mark Rubinstein, "The Strong Case for the Generalized Logarithmic Utility Function as the Premier Model of Financial Markets," *Journal of Finance* 31 (May 1976): 551–571.

[13]For additional information on state-preference theory, see Jack Hirshleifer, "Investment Decisions under Uncertainty: Choice Theoretic Approaches," *Quarterly Journal of Economics* (November 1965): 509–536; Jack Hirshleifer, *Investment, Interest, and Capital* (Englewood Cliffs, N.J.: Prentice-Hall, 1970); and Chapter 5 of Thomas E. Copeland and J. Fred Weston, *Financial Theory and Corporate Policy*, 3d ed. (Reading, Mass: Addison-Wesley, 1988).

	Existing Firm	Firm with Project Z	Firm with Project S
Mean Return	15%	22%	13%
Standard Deviation	7%	6%	1%

You will see in the next chapter that this approach is weak when risk can be diversified away by the shareholder. You can also see why it might be preferred by a manager who has a substantial portion of her present and future wealth in the company. The manager will be particularly tempted to take S when the shareholders are not aware of the existence of project Z.

SENSITIVITY-RELATED COMPANY PORTFOLIO RISK ANALYSIS

While various portfolio models have been widely suggested and occasionally used, sensitivity analysis is more widely used in practice to apply portfolio concepts. The general approach is to identify possible states of nature, and then to predict the performance of the company in each state, with and without the proposed investment. Alternately, sensitivity of the company to some critical variable, with and without the proposed investment, can be studied with graphical sensitivity analysis, as was explained for a single investment in Chapter 12. Break-even analysis can also be performed for the company, with and without the proposed investment.

Sensitivity analysis can be extended to recognize probabilities. If probabilities are assigned to the states of nature, then expected return, standard deviation, and other probability-related measures can also be computed for the company, with and without the proposed investment. Likewise, Monte Carlo simulation can be used to develop a probability distribution of returns for the company, with and without the proposed investments.

One limitation of these sensitivity-related techniques is that the analysis is generally carried out on an incremental basis, considering the addition of one asset to the company's existing portfolio of assets. If hundreds of proposals are being considered, the analysis of each *combination* would be prohibitively time-consuming. Thus, sensitivity-related techniques are generally applied only to large investments that will have a significant impact on the overall company. Smaller investments are then analyzed in isolation, or their required returns are adjusted for risk using a method such as a company beta or one of the models described in Chapters 14 and 15.

Example. Phoenix Corporation presently has fixed costs, other than interest, of $100,000, and variable costs are 60 percent of sales. Long-term debt is $80,000 and equity is $80,000. A proposed new division will require additional long-term debt of $40,000 and new equity of $40,000. Fixed costs, other than interest, for the division will be $60,000 and variable costs for the division will be 40 percent of sales. Assume, for simplicity of illustration, that all costs are cash and

| TABLE 13.2 PHOENIX CORPORATION

This table shows cash flows in three economic conditions for Phoenix as presently structured, for a proposed division, and for Phoenix if the division is acquired.

Economy Probability	Weak .25	Moderate .50	Strong .25
Sales for existing company	$200,000	$300,000	$400,000
Variable costs	120,000	180,000	240,000
Fixed costs	100,000	100,000	100,000
CASH FLOW	−20,000	20,000	60,000
Sales for proposed division	50,000	125,000	200,000
Variable costs	20,000	50,000	80,000
Fixed costs	60,000	60,000	60,000
CASH FLOW	−30,000	15,000	60,000
COMBINED CASH FLOW	−50,000	35,000	120,000

the company pays no taxes. Sales for the company and the proposed division in each of three states of nature are shown in Table 13.2, along with estimation of cash flows.

Expected cash flow for the existing company is .25(−20,000) + .50(20,000) + .25(60,000) = $20,000. This provides a return on capital (long-term debt plus equity) of $20,000/$160,000 = 12.5 percent. Expected cash flow for the new division is $15,000, and the expected return on capital is $15,000/$80,000 = 18.75 percent. Thus, the new division increases the expected profitability of the company.

The expected investment also increases risk. Rather than having to cover a $20,000 negative cash flow in a weak economy, Phoenix Corporation would have to cover a $50,000 negative cash flow if this division were added. Adding the division also increases the standard deviation of cash flow, the standard deviation of return on capital, the coefficient of variation of cash flow, and the coefficient of variation of return on capital. The coefficient of variation of return on capital, for example, increases from 1.41 to 1.71. The required return for the division can be adjusted for risk, as explained in the following chapter, but an adjustment of required return answers only part of the question. In studying its risk exposure, management will look at such things as sources of cash flows available in a weak economy to decide if they will be able to meet the potential cash flow requirement of the division. Such things as lines of credit available and assets that can be sold will be important in this analysis.

Use of Financial Planning Models. Many large companies maintain financial planning models, which describe the entire company as a series of equations. These models can be used to predict the impacts of changes in capital structure, price and product mix, economic conditions, etc. These models are generally deterministic; one set of conditions is specified by the user and one set of outputs is obtained, generally in the form of a set of pro forma financial statements for several years or more into the future. To consider other scenarios, new input is provided by the user, and the model is run again. For a major capital investment, the financial planning model of the company can be run with and without acquisition of the investment, for various assumptions about conditions affecting the company and the investment. The results can be compared to determine the risk contribution of the particular investment being considered.

DOES DIVERSIFICATION PAY?

There has been a long-running debate on the benefits of corporate diversification programs. The fundamental argument for diversification is that it decreases risk, while the fundamental argument against diversification is that shareholders can enjoy the same benefits by diversifying their portfolios. Proponents of diversification counter the homemade diversification argument by noting that many investors are not diversified. They also discuss other advantages of stability achieved through diversification. Product warranties may be more valuable to consumers if the risk of bankruptcy declines, and ability to attract employees may be enhanced by stability. Frequent-flier points, for example, are not much of a sales tool if investors worry that the issuing airline is on the verge of bankruptcy. Long-range, strategic planning is made easier if the company's earnings are stabilized by a diversification program. Critics can respond to these supposed advantages with adequate examples of companies that have gotten in trouble through ill-advised diversification.

We have available hundreds of examples of successful and unsuccessful diversification. Martin Marietta, used to introduce this chapter, can be used as an example of success. ARMCO, on the other hand, can be used as an example of failure. With the steel business on the decline, Chairman C. William Verity led the company in diversifying into such unrelated areas as insurance. To quote a Merrill Lynch analyst, Verity's diversification drive "turned out to be a gigantic mistake."[14] While some companies have succeeded in diversification, others have failed. Still other companies have remained highly profitable by staying in their own market niches. To quote *Changing Times,* "McDonalds and Federal Express have resisted all urges to deliver pizzas or carry passengers."[15]

Proponents and opponents of diversification can find support for their views in the experiences of one company or another. It is interesting, therefore, to look at more systematic evidence concerning the success of diversification activities. Unfortunately, systematic studies of corporate diversification have also yielded

[14]"Smeltdown at ARMCO: Behind the Steelmaker's Long Slide," *Business Week* (February 1, 1988): 48–49.

[15]"Cornering the Market on Tennis-ball Fuzz," *Changing Times* (July 1988): 37–40.

mixed results.[16] Some studies have shown that diversification in existing or related lines of business makes a greater contribution to wealth than acquisitions in unrelated lines of business. Others, though, have found the opposite to be true. Thus, managers must make their diversification decisions without firm answers to empirical questions involved.

RISK PERSPECTIVE |

One criticism of the mean-variance portfolio model is that it is based on risk viewed from the perspective of the company. Shareholder wealth maximization is frequently cited as the goal of the firm, and shareholder wealth maximization would result in risk being viewed from the perspective of an equity investor. Risk analysis from the shareholder's perspective is covered in Chapters 14 and 15. Survey evidence, though, suggests that managers consider total project risk and company portfolio risk as well as shareholder portfolio risk.

SUMMARY |

This chapter has focused on diversification and portfolio effects, which are important tools for risk management. Diversification benefits occur because investments do not all respond in the same way to factors affecting return. The major focus in this chapter was on mean-variance portfolio concepts. Alternate approaches were also described.

The mean-variance portfolio concept begins with the assumption that investors like expected return and dislike risk. It is further assumed that the perceived risk of a portfolio can be approximated by the standard deviation of the probability distribution of expected returns. The expected return and standard deviation of a portfolio depend on expected returns and standard deviation of assets in the portfolio, plus covariances between those assets.

Mathematical programming procedures are available for searching out the lowest standard deviation portfolio for each level of expected return, or the highest expected return portfolio for each level of standard deviation. The choice of a portfolio from among the set with the highest expected return for their level of risk may simply be a matter of judgment. If, however, one can borrow or lend at the risk-free interest rate, the optimal portfolio is the one that maximizes the reward to variability ratio (RV):

$$RV = [E(R_p) - R_f]/\sigma_p$$

---

[16]See, for example, Neil W. Sicherman and Richard H. Pettway, "Acquisition of Divested Assets and Stockholders' Wealth," *Journal of Finance* 42 (December 1987): 1261–1273; and Allen Michel and Israel Shaked, "Does Business Diversification Affect Performance?" *Financial Management* 13 (Winter 1984): 18–25.

where R_f is the risk-free borrowing and lending rate, and $E(R_p)$ and σ_p are the expected return and standard deviation of the portfolio.

Several special problems are encountered when mean-variance portfolio theory is applied to capital budgeting. Because many investments are integer in nature, constraints must be added to the mathematical programming model so that these investments are either accepted or rejected in their entirety. Also, the choice of a holding period leads to problems. If a long holding period is used, the importance of year-to-year fluctuations is ignored. If a short holding period is used, the inability to liquidate capital investments each period is ignored. In addition, the amount of data needed to conduct a full mean-variance analysis of all existing and proposed capital investments is often staggering.

Modified applications of portfolio theory are possible for capital budgeting. One such approach is incremental analysis, simply looking at how a proposed investment will affect the risk-return characteristics of the company, given the company's existing portfolio of assets. Another alternative is to use the full mean-variance portfolio model only to allocate capital between a few major divisions. A final alternative is to examine portfolio benefits more informally by applying sensitivity analysis, looking at how the company will perform in each state of nature, with and without a proposed asset.

Developing inputs for analysis can be extremely time-consuming and expensive. One way to get the risk measures needed is to identify a number of relevant states of nature and then compute return for each proposed investment in each state. Monte Carlo simulation is sometimes useful for this purpose.

The methods discussed in this chapter are used to examine risk from the perspective of the total company. These techniques are extended in the next chapter to examine risk from the perspectives of outside investors.

QUESTIONS

13-1. Describe a project that might be undertaken to reduce firm-specific risk for a newspaper.

13-2. Define the following terms: (a) *covariance*, (b) *correlation coefficient*, and (c) *beta*.

13-3. What value of the correlation coefficient between two investments gives the greatest benefits from diversification? What range of correlation coefficient values gives some benefit from diversification?

13-4. A Fortune 200 company just spent a lot of money having its transformers replaced as the result of an order by the EPA to reduce PCB emissions. This company now leases the new transformers. In a capital budgeting context, what risky cash flow was passed to the writer of the lease?

13-5. Which one of the following real combinations results in the greatest total-firm risk reduction?
   a. Rubbermaid's ownership of Lil Tykes Toys
   b. General Mills' ownership of Red Lobster
   c. Wrigley's ownership of the Chicago Cubs

13–6. Is it ever wise to accept a project that is more risky than the existing firm? Why or why not?

13–7. Summarize the ways in which applying the mean-variance portfolio model to a company's capital budgeting differs from application of the model to security selection.

13–8. What are the information need problems encountered in using the mean-variance portfolio model for capital budgeting? How can those problems be overcome?

13–9. List the portfolio approaches that a company could use as alternatives to the mean-variance model.

13–10. As top manager of a company, would you be interested in both total project risk and company portfolio risk? Why?

13–11. (**Ethical considerations**) Your firm currently has two projects in process that are expected to have the range of cash flows given below, based on the condition of the economy over the following year. You are considering the addition of one or both of these projects.

Economy	Good	Average	Bad
Existing company's net present value	$450	$435	$410
Existing company's year-end cash flow	$65	$50	$25
Project 1's net present value	$10	$5	$2
Project 1's year-end cash flow	$35	$25	$10
Project 2's net present value	−$25	−$30	−$45
Project 2's year-end cash flow	$125	$100	$75

a. Given that you are very concerned about your career and the ability to pay back a $100 debt at the end of the year, which project should you accept and why?

b. What do you believe is more observable by the market, the net present value decrease that may result from the acceptance of a bad project or the rating agency downgrades that result from the missed loan payment? What is the ethical dilemma in your selection above? What did it cost the shareholder?

c. What can the firm do to reduce these conflicts in the future?

PROBLEMS |

13–1. You are an insurer who currently writes "rain-out" policies for event sponsors. These policies pay the event sponsor $1,000 if it rains, to reduce some of the lost revenue. The company is considering adding a rain policy to be sold to farmers who have invested in seed and labor, and need rain. The present "rain out" policies are sold for $600 and pay $1,000 to the sponsor if it rains. You are considering the offering of new farming policies, which can be sold for $600 and pay the farmer $1,000 if it does not rain. The sponsors' locations and the farms are in the same area, and there is a 50% chance of rain tomorrow. (a) How risky is your present firm measured by the standard deviation of possible returns? (b) How profitable is the existing firm measured by the expected value? (c) What happens to the riskiness or standard deviation of possible returns if the farm rain insurance project is added? (d) What happens to the expected return with the addition of the farm rain insurance project?

13–2. Your firm and a possible project have the following cash flows:

	COMPANY		PROJECT	
Economy	Good	Bad	Good	Bad
Year 0	−200	−200	−50	−50
Year I	100	50	20	60
Year 2	120	60	30	50
Year 3	110	55	40	90
Year 4	90	45	35	70

    a. Given an 8 percent discount rate, a 60 percent chance of a good economy over the next four years, and a 40 percent chance of a bad economy, what are the expected net present value and standard deviation of net present value for the company?

    b. for the project?

    c. for the combination of the company and the project?

13–3. An asset will cost $1,000. During the next year, it will generate cash flows of $100. At the end of the year, the asset will be worth either $900 or $1,100. Compute the holding period return for each ending value.

13–4. For the asset in problem 3, there is a .5 probability of each ending value. Compute the expected holding period return and standard deviation.

13–5. There are four possible, equally likely states of nature. Returns for the existing company and a proposed project in each state are shown below. Compute the expected return and standard deviation for the existing company and project B.

State of Nature	Very Bad	Bad	Good	Very Good
Return for the company	.00	.06	.18	.24
Return for project B	.15	.09	.06	.05

13–6. Compute the covariance and correlation coefficient for the combination of the company and the project in problem 5. Compute the beta of the project in relation to the company. Do these measures indicate an opportunity for diversification benefits?

13–7. For the company and project in problem 5, draw a graph showing the combinations of risk and return that can be achieved with various divisions of your investment funds between the existing company and project B.

13–8. Compute the covariance and correlation coefficient for the following combinations of the existing company and differing project sizes based on the data in problem 5:

Size of the Firm	$1,000	$1,000	$1,000	$1,000	$1,000
Size of the Project	$ 0	$ 250	$ 500	$ 750	$1,000

13–9. For problem 13-7, add lines to the graph to include correlation coefficients of -1.0, 0, .5, and 1.0.

13–10. Investments E and F each have the same expected return: .20. They also have the same standard deviation: .30. For a portfolio consisting of one-half of your funds in each asset, compute the expected return and standard deviation for correlation coefficients of -1, 0, .5, and 1.0.

13–11. Two investments, designated C and D, have the expected returns and standard deviations shown below. The correlation coefficient between the two is $-.50$. Compute the standard deviations for portfolios consisting of the following proportions of assets invested in C (the remainder must be invested in D): 0, .25, .50, .75, 1.0. Use these results to plot a graph similar to Figure 13.2.

	Expected return	**Standard deviation**
Investment C	.25	.25
Investment D	.10	.05

13–12. Assume the only two investments available to an investor are those in problem 11. Is it possible that a rational investor would choose to invest all of his or her funds in C? in D? Explain.

13–13. A risky portfolio has an expected return of 15 percent and a standard deviation of 20 percent. The risk-free rate is 8 percent. What is the expected return and standard deviation if 60 percent of your funds are invested in the risk-free asset, and 40 percent are invested in the risky portfolio?

13–14. The risk-free rate is 10 percent. Portfolios J and K have expected returns of 20 percent and 25 percent respectively. These two portfolios have standard deviations of 15 percent and 20 percent respectively. Compute the reward to variability ratio for each portfolio. If you can borrow and lend at the risk-free rate, which portfolio would you prefer? Why?

13–15. A company's existing portfolio of assets has an expected return of 20 percent, and the risk-free rate is 6 percent. A small, new investment is being analyzed on an incremental basis. The proposed investment has a company-related beta of 1.5 and has an expected return of .25. Is it desirable?

13–16. If a company wishes to consider 100 capital investments, how many co-variance terms are needed? Including expected return for each asset and the standard deviation for each asset, how many terms are needed in total?

13–17. There are three possible levels of economic growth and two possible in-terest rates, as indicated below. The interest rate is partially dependent on the rate of economic growth. The conditional probability of each out-come is in parentheses beside that outcome. Expected returns for assets L and M in each outcome are given below. Compute the probability of each of the six possible states of nature. Compute the expected return and standard deviation for each asset and the covariance between the two assets. Find the expected return and standard deviation of a port-folio of funds divided evenly between the two assets.

Economic Growth	Interest Rate	EXPECTED RETURN	
		L	M
Strong(.20)	high(.6)	.20	.00
	low(.4)	.25	.03
Moderate(.60)	high(.4)	.12	.20
	low(.6)	.15	.16
Weak(.20)	high(.3)	.06	.30
	low(.7)	.12	.25

13–18. The company considering the investments in problem 17 has the fol-lowing expected returns for its existing assets:

Economic Growth Rate	High Interest Rate	Low Interest Rate
Strong	.21	.13
Moderate	.17	.11
Weak	.10	.15

The company presently has total assets of $1 million. Each of the in-vestments proposed in the previous problem would cost $100,000. All re-turns are after tax, and the after-tax risk-free rate is 8 percent. Compute the expected return, standard deviation, and reward to variability ratio for the company, the company with investment L added, the company with investment M added, and the company with investments L and M both added. Which investment(s) should the company add to its existing port-folio of assets?

13–19. Wyoming Processing has expected annual sales of $1,200,000. Fixed cash costs are $100,000 and variable cash costs are 70 percent of sales. A new capital investment with a 10-year life will require an after-tax cash out-lay of $100,000. The result will be a change in production methods that increases fixed cash costs to $200,000 a year and reduces variable cash costs to 60 percent of sales. The required return is 10 percent and all cash flows are after tax. (Assume year-end cash flow for simplicity.)

a. Does the capital investment have a positive net present value?

b. Find the cash flow break-even analysis for the company, with and without the capital investment.

13–20. For the previous problem, assume that the standard deviation of the probability distribution of expected sales is $400,000. What is the probability of a sales level below the break-even point, with and without the new investment? Would you recommend acceptance of the new investment? (Assume sales are normally distributed.)

13–21. (Ethical considerations) Kmart Corporation owned the following businesses: approximately 2,000 Kmart stores, approximately 1,300 Waldenbook outlets, approximately 150 Builders Square (hardware and lumber) outlets, a number of Payless Drug stores, and a number of Sports Authority stores. List at least three risks that were reduced by assembling this portfolio of companies. For each of these three risks, be prepared to give your opinion concerning why you think this risk reduction is a good or bad idea. Even with this combination of companies, Kmart was still exposed to some risk. Please list and explain two remaining risks.

CASE PROBLEM |

Houston Disbursement

Betsy Cotner went to work for a title company after graduating from college. The department she worked in provided disbursement advice to banks with regard to oil/gas-related loans. When a bank granted a construction loan, the money was paid out according to progress made. Someone had to monitor the project and authorize disbursement of cash under the loan agreement. While most banks monitor progress themselves, a few rely on outside firms to do the monitoring, and this is what Cotner's department did.

Cotner spent nearly a decade learning the business and working her way up to assistant manager of the department. Then a recession caused a decline in profits for the title company. The title company decided to get out of oil/gas disbursement, and the department manager decided to retire.

Cotner thought that there was still enough business to make a decent living for herself if she did not have to bear the overhead cost of the title company. As she informed the lenders of the title company's decision, she also informed them that she would be opening her own office. She had developed an excellent personal reputation, and several major lenders indicated a willingness to continue doing business with her. Thus, Houston Disbursement was born.

As the recession ended, Cotner's business picked up substantially, but she began to worry about the vagaries of the oil business. She decided to diversify into general commercial construction in the Houston area. She hired Brent Ross, a young loan officer in the commercial construction field, with the understanding that he could eventually buy an interest in Houston Disbursement.

Cotner soon came to realize that she had gained little from diversification. A drop in oil prices caused the entire Houston economy to turn down, even when the national economy was strong. Based on her experiences, Cotner prepared an estimate of revenue and profits for Houston Disbursement for both a strong and a weak economy, and for both high and low oil prices. Her estimates are summarized in Table 13.3. While the analysis focuses on earnings before tax, this is approximately the same as cash flow because capital investments were limited to office furniture, and net working capital was negligible. Net working capital was kept negligible by the practice of collecting retainer fees from banks at the start of a construction project. Cotner's salary, based on her estimate of what she could get if she were working for another company, is included in the cost figures. The business was organized as a Subchapter S corporation and Cotner was in a 28 percent tax bracket.

To diversify, Cotner decided to open a second office. She would go to the new location and promote Ross to manager of the Houston office. Two possibilities that would take advantage of her current contacts were a commercial construction disbursement office in San Francisco and an oil business disbursement office in Alaska. Cotner was quite willing to move to either area.

Cotner's estimates of profitability appear in Table 13.4. The costs include a fair wage for Cotner; there would be no significant wage savings at the Houston office because a replacement for Cotner would be needed.

Cotner considered high and low oil prices equally likely. However, she believed the probability of a strong economy was twice that of a weak economy. She did not believe a weak economy was likely to last more than two years. Low oil prices, on the other hand, could continue for at least five years. Oil prices and the economy were both strong at the moment.

| **TABLE 13.3**   **HOUSTON DISBURSEMENT PROFITABILITY**

Profitability of Houston Disbursement in various economic conditions. Variable wages are 40 percent of revenue, and variable operating costs are 20 percent of revenue.

ECONOMY:	WEAK ECONOMY		STRONG ECONOMY	
Oil prices:	Low	High	Low	High
Total revenue	$200,000	$300,000	$250,000	$400,000
Variable wages	80,000	120,000	100,000	160,000
Variable operating costs	40,000	60,000	50,000	80,000
Fixed wages	50,000	50,000	50,000	50,000
Fixed operating costs	45,000	45,000	45,000	45,000
Earnings before tax	($ 15,000)	$ 25,000	$ 5,000	$ 65,000

| **TABLE 13.4**   **PROFITABILITY ESTIMATES FOR NEW OFFICE LOCATIONS**

This table contains profitability estimates for two possible locations for a new office of Houston Disbursement. Profitability for each is estimated using both strong and weak national economies and high and low oil prices.

ALASKA

ECONOMY:	**WEAK ECONOMY**		**STRONG ECONOMY**	
Oil prices:	**Low**	**High**	**Low**	**High**
Total revenue	$50,000	$300,000	$75,000	$400,000
Variable wages	20,000	120,000	30,000	160,000
Variable operating costs	10,000	60,000	15,000	80,000
Fixed wages	30,000	30,000	30,000	30,000
Fixed operating costs	30,000	30,000	30,000	30,000
Earnings before tax	($ 40,000)	$ 60,000	($ 30,000)	$100,000

CALIFORNIA

ECONOMY:	**WEAK ECONOMY**		**STRONG ECONOMY**	
Oil prices:	**Low**	**High**	**Low**	**High**
Total revenue	$200,000	$200,000	$250,000	$250,000
Variable wages	80,000	80,000	100,000	100,000
Variable operating costs	40,000	40,000	50,000	50,000
Fixed wages	40,000	40,000	40,000	40,000
Fixed operating costs	35,000	35,000	35,000	35,000
Earnings before tax	$ 5,000	$ 5,000	$ 25,000	$ 25,000

It would cost approximately $75,000 to open an office in either San Francisco or Alaska. The costs would be primarily development costs and would be expensed for tax purposes. Fixed assets included in this cost would be under $10,000, and a provision of the tax law allowed expensing up to $10,000 of fixed asset acquisitions. Cotner had approximately $200,000 invested in U.S. government securities earning 9 percent, so she would have no difficulty in getting the $75,000.

CASE QUESTIONS

1. Compute expected return and standard deviation of annual return for each alternative separately.
2. Compute covariance of annual returns between the Alaska and Houston offices, and between the California and Houston offices.
3. Compute the expected return and standard deviation for each of the two combinations.
4. Prepare pro forma statements for each new office combined with the Houston office, using each of the four possible conditions.
5. What would you recommend to Cotner? Why?

A p p e n d i x   1 3 - A

MEAN-VARIANCE PORTFOLIO CONSTRUCTION WITH MORE THAN TWO ASSETS

This appendix extends the mean-variance portfolio model to more than two assets. When more than two assets are being considered, the expected return and standard deviation formulas—Equations 13-5 and 13-6—are extended to become:[17]

$$E(R_p) = \sum_{i=1}^{n} W_i E(R_i) \qquad (13\text{-}11)$$

$$\sigma_p = \sqrt{\sum_{i=1}^{n} \sum_{j=1}^{n} W_i W_j \sigma_{i,j}} \qquad (13\text{-}12)$$

Example. Three assets, designated A, B, and C, have expected returns of .10, .15, and .20. Their variances and covariances are as follows:

	A	B	C
A	.01	0	.015
B	0	.04	−.06
C	.015	−.06	.09

For example, $\sigma_{A,C} = .015$ and $\sigma_B^2 = .04$. For a portfolio consisting of 50 percent of funds in asset A, 30 percent in asset B, and 20 percent in asset C, the expected return and standard deviation are:

$$E(R_p) = .50(.10) + .30(.15) + .20(.20) = \underline{.135}$$

$$\sigma_p = [(.50)(.50)(.01) + (.50)(.30)(0) + (.50)(.20)(.015) +$$

$$(.30)(.50)(0) + (.30)(.30)(.04) + (.30)(.20)(-.06) +$$

$$(.20)(.50)(.015) + (.20)(.30)(-.06) + (.20)(.20)(.09)]^{1/2}$$

$$= \underline{.0742}$$

[17]Note from the definition of covariance in Equation 10-1 that the covariance of something with itself is its variance: $\sigma_{i,i} = \sigma_i^2$.

| **FIGURE 13A.1** **PORTFOLIO OPPORTUNITY SET AND EFFICIENT FRONTIER**

The shaded area represents the risk-return combinations that can be achieved by creating portfolios from some set of assets. The solid line is the efficient frontier, consisting of portfolios with the highest return for their level of risk or the lowest risk for their level of return.

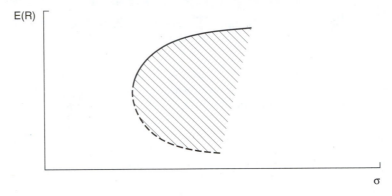

Figure 13A.1 illustrates the risk-return opportunity set when numerous investments are available and can be combined in a portfolio in any desired combination. The shaded area represents the complete set of risk-return positions that could be achieved. Many of these, though, are not desirable. An *efficient* portfolio provides the highest expected return for its level of risk or the lowest risk for its level of expected return. The solid line running along the upper-left perimeter of the shaded area represents the set of efficient portfolios and is referred to as the *efficient frontier*.

Once we know how diversification reduces risk, we are still left with the problem of *finding* the efficient frontier. It is clearly not feasible to examine an infinite number of possible combinations. Fortunately, there are available a number of commercially produced computer software packages that use quadratic programming to search efficiently for the set of portfolios that constitutes the efficient frontier for any set of assets, given that the expected returns, standard deviations, and covariances have been determined.

UTILITY THEORY AND PORTFOLIO CHOICE

Once the efficient frontier has been identified, the next step is to choose a portfolio from among those on the efficient frontier. If decision makers are risk-averse and standard deviation of the probability distribution of return is a complete measure of risk, the choice process is illustrated in Figure 13A.2.

The efficient frontier is the same as that shown in Figure 13A.1. The three curves marked I_1, I_2, and I_3 are indifference curves of some decision maker. Each curve represents a set of risk-return combinations about which the decision maker would be indifferent. The line is curved upward, indicating that ever-increasing

| **FIGURE 13A.2 INDIFFERENCE CURVES AND PORTFOLIO CHOICE**

The lines marked I_1, I_2, and I_3 are a particular decision maker's indifference curves. Each curve represents combinations of risk and return about which the decision maker is indifferent. The optimal portfolio is at the point where the highest attainable indifference curve is tangent to the efficient frontier.

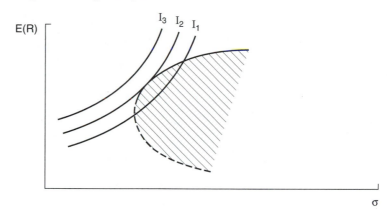

amounts of expected return are needed to compensate for increased standard deviation. A higher indifference curve is preferred over a lower one, because a higher curve provides more return at each level of risk. The optimal portfolio, from the perspective of this decision maker, is at the point where the efficient frontier is tangent with the highest attainable indifference curve.

LENDING, BORROWING, AND THE OPTIMAL PORTFOLIO

A problem with the portfolio selection process illustrated in Figure 13A.2 is that the portfolio choice depends on the indifference curves of the individual decision maker. Fortunately, consideration of opportunities to borrow and lend allows us to identify an optimum portfolio that all decision makers would prefer.

Note from Equation 13-6A that if the standard deviation for asset B is zero, the standard deviation of a portfolio consisting of assets A and B is simply $W_A\sigma_A$. Suppose we construct a new portfolio by investing proportion W_p of funds in some portfolio on the efficient frontier and the remainder at the risk-free rate. (A W_p greater than 1.0 implies investing over 100 percent of one's funds in the risky asset and, therefore, implies borrowing at the risk-free rate.) The expected return and standard deviation will be:

$$E(R_{W_p}) = W_p E(R_p) + (1 - W_p)R_f$$

$$\sigma W_p = W_p \sigma_p$$

The risk-return combinations achieved by varying W_p would fall on a straight line in Figure 13A.3 connecting the risk-free rate and the risky asset portfolio

| **FIGURE 13A.3** **PORTFOLIO CHOICE WITH BORROWING AND LENDING**

This figure contains the same investment opportunity set and indifference curves as those in Figure 13A.2, and it also contains the opportunity set created by dividing funds between the risk-free asset and a particular portfolio, designated portfolio p.

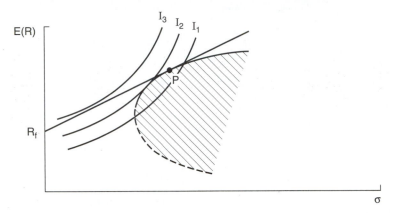

in which investment was made. Figure 13A.3 contains the same information as Figure 13A.2, plus a straight line connecting the risk-free rate of return with a particular portfolio on the efficient frontier, designated portfolio p. That line is the risk-return opportunity set available by investing various proportions, W_p, of your money in portfolio p and the rest in the risk-free rate. A similar line can be drawn from the risk-free rate to every other portfolio, giving risk-return combinations from dividing funds between any other portfolio and the risk-free rate. Straight lines between the risk-free rate, R_f, and every other portfolio will be below this line and will, therefore, provide less expected return at each level of risk.

Tobin, who first developed this application of borrowing and lending at the risk-free rate,[18] referred to it as the *separation theorem* because the choice of a portfolio is separated from the choice of a risk-return position. Every decision maker who could borrow and lend at the risk-free rate would prefer portfolio p to any other risky portfolio. Each individual investor would choose a value of W_p consistent with his or her own utility function. The optimal value of W_p generates the point on the line from R_f through point p, where that line is tangent to the highest attainable indifference curve. Note in this case that the decision maker could only get to indifference curve 2 by investing in portfolios on the efficient frontier, but can reach indifference curve 3 by splitting the investment between portfolio p and the risk-free asset.

Portfolio p has two important characteristics. First, it is the portfolio at the point where a line drawn through the risk-free rate is tangent to the efficient

[18]The originator of this method is James Tobin, "Liquidity Preference as a Behavior toward Risk," *Review of Economic Studies* 67 (February 1958): 65–86.

frontier. Second, compared to any other risky portfolio, portfolio p has the highest reward to variability ratio (RV):

$$RV = [E(R_p) - R_f]/\sigma_p \qquad (13\text{-}13)$$

The reward to variability is, therefore, used as a standard of comparison; the optimal risky portfolio is the portfolio with the highest reward to variability ratio, regardless of the individual decision maker's degree of risk aversion.

UNEQUAL BORROWING AND LENDING RATES

The separation of risky asset portfolio choice from the decision maker's utility function depends on the availability of both borrowing and lending at the risk-free rate. Almost everyone can lend at the risk-free rate by purchasing U.S. Treasury bills or investing in a money market fund, but very few companies can borrow at the risk-free rate.[19] The analysis is complicated by differences between borrowing and lending rates.

Fortunately, the problem of unequal borrowing and lending rates may be less severe for capital budgeting than for other portfolio selection activities. The majority of companies have at least some debt in their capital structures, indicating a decision to move to the right of p by borrowing. If we know in advance that the company will borrow rather than lend, we simply use the company's borrowing rate instead of R_f in asset selection. As discussed in the following section, other problems are more difficult to handle when the mean-variance portfolio model is applied to capital budgeting.

PROBLEMS |

13–A–1. The variances and covariances for investments G, H, and I appear below. The expected returns are .10, .20, and .30 respectively. Compute the expected return and standard deviation of a portfolio in which one-third of the funds are invested in each asset.

	G	H	I
G	.01	.01	−.015
H	.01	.04	0
I	−.015	0	.09

13–A–2. For the investments in problem A-1, find the minimum variance portfolio assuming negative investments are not allowed. (This problem can be solved using a Lotus 1-2-3 data table or quadratic programming.)

[19]If a company happens to be holding risk-free assets, selling those assets would be equivalent to borrowing at the risk-free rate.

13–A–3. For the investments in problem A-1, find the optimal reward to variability portfolio for a 6 percent risk-free rate.

SELECTED REFERENCES |

Amihud, Y., and B. Lev. "Risk Reduction as a Managerial Motive for Conglomerate Mergers." *Bell Journal of Economics* 12 (Autumn 1981): 605–617.

Bauman, Joseph, Steve Saratore, and William Liddle. "A Practical Framework for Corporate Exposure Management." *Journal of Applied Corporate Finance* 7 (Fall 1994): 66–72.

Bjorklund, Glenn J. "Planning for Uncertainty at a Public Utility." *Public Utilities Fortnightly* 120 (October 15, 1987): 15–21.

Chen, Chia Lin, Saeed Maghsoodloo, and Chan S. Park. "A Method for Approximating Semivariance in Project Portfolio Analysis." *Engineering Economist* 37 (Fall 1991): 33–60.

Comment, Robert, and Gregg A. Jarrell. "Corporate Focus and Stock Returns." *Journal of Financial Economics* 37 (January 1995): 67–87.

Findlay, M. Chapman, III, Arthur E. Gooding, and Wallace Q. Weaver, Jr. "On the Relevant Risk for Determining Capital Expenditure Hurdle Rates." *Financial Management* 5 (Winter 1976): 9–16.

Gilson, Stuart C. "Management Turnover and Financial Distress." *Journal of Financial Economics* 25 (December 1989): 241–262.

Harris, Robert S., Thomas J. O'Brien, and Doug Wakeman. "Divisional Cost-of-Capital Estimation for Multi-Industry Firms." *Financial Management* 18 (Summer 1989): 74–84.

Hirshleifer, Jack. "Investment Decisions under Uncertainty: Choice Theoretic Approaches." *Quarterly Journal of Economics* (November 1965): 509–536.

———. *Investment, Interest, and Capital.* Englewood Cliffs, N.J.: Prentice-Hall, 1970.

Hoskin, Colin G. "Capital Budgeting Decision Rules for Risky Projects Derived from a Capital Market Model Based on Semivariance." *Engineering Economist* 23 (1978): 211–222.

Kraus, Alan, and Robert H. Litzenberger. "Skewness Preference and the Valuation of Risky Assets." *Journal of Finance* 31 (September 1976): 1085–1100.

Latane', Henry A., and Donald L. Tuttle. "Criteria for Portfolio Building," *Journal of Finance* 22 (September 1967): 359–373.

Markowitz, Harry M. "Investment for the Long Run: New Evidence for an Old Rule." *Journal of Finance* 31 (December 1976): 1273–1286.

———. "Portfolio Selection." *Journal of Finance* 7 (March 1952): 77–91.

Michel, Allen, and Israel Shaked. "Does Business Diversification Affect Performance?" *Financial Management* 13 (Winter 1984): 18–25.

Nantell, Timothy J., and Barbara Price. "An Analytical Comparison of Variance and Semivariance Capital Market Theories." *Journal of Financial and Quantitative Analysis* 14 (June 1979): 221–242.

Rubinstein, Mark. "The Strong Case for the Generalized Logarithmic Utility Function as the Premier Model of Financial Markets." *Journal of Finance* 31 (May 1976): 551–571.

Sicherman, Neil W., and Richard H. Pettway. "Acquisition of Divested Assets and Stockholders' Wealth." *Journal of Finance* 42 (December 1987): 1261–1273.

Stein, Jeremy C. "Internal Capital Markets and the Competition for Corporate Resources." *Journal of Finance* 52 (March 1997): 111–133.

Tobin, James. "Liquidity Preference as a Behavior toward Risk." *Review of Economic Studies* 67 (February 1958): 65–86.

Van Horne, James C. "Capital Budgeting Decisions Involving Combinations of Risky Investment." *Management Science* (October 1966): B84–92.

Young, W., and R. Trent. "Geometric Mean Approximations of Industrial Security and Portfolio Performance." *Journal of Financial and Quantitative Analysis* 4 (January 1969): 179–199.

CHAPTER 14

RISK FROM THE SHAREHOLDERS' PERSPECTIVE: USING CAPM IN CAPITAL BUDGETING

After completing this chapter you should be able to:

1. Understand the three inputs into the Capital Asset Pricing Model.
2. Explain why the Capital Asset Pricing Model is an appropriate tool to estimate the required rate of return for a well-diversified shareholder.
3. Know what the beta coefficient measures.
4. List some of the sources of published betas for publicly traded companies.
5. Explain why an adjustment needs to be made in estimating the beta for a company with leverage different than the proxy company.
6. Detail the steps necessary to adjust from published betas for like (proxy) companies to a project, divisional, or company beta.
7. List common sources for estimating the expected return on the market portfolio.
8. Explain the reasons for using a long-term risk-free rate of return.
9. Characterize the assumptions and the criticisms of the Capital Asset Pricing Model.
10. Use the Capital Asset Pricing Model to determine a required return for a risky investment.
11. Summarize the advantages and disadvantages of international diversification.

When AT&T was ordered to divest itself of the regional telephone companies and the "Baby Bells" were born, these new orphans faced a number of problems that had previously been handled by their New York parent. Among other things, they were responsible for determining their own required returns and making their own capital investment decisions. The problems of the Baby Bells were complicated by expansion into unregulated business. Southwestern Bell, for example, became a nationwide publisher of yellow-page business directories while other regional telephone companies entered into businesses as diverse as insurance and real estate development. These forms of expansion made necessary the estimation of required returns for the regulated telephone business and several lines of unregulated business.

The mean-variance capital asset pricing model (CAPM) was one of the tools that was called into play to deal with these problems. The CAPM provided a method of estimating the overall required returns for these telephone companies as well as a method for determining a required return that was appropriate for each of the diverse areas of business into which they were expanding. The CAPM also proved useful in the regulatory arena, in which regulators were required to set telephone rates based on required return standards.

The usefulness of the CAPM has not been limited to public utilities. The CAPM has proved to be a durable tool for considering risk in capital budgeting. The dominance of the CAPM for more than two decades follows from two features. First, the model focuses on risk from the perspective of the stockholders, who are the owners of the company. Second, the model provides a simple way to adjust for risk by adjusting the required return. Long before they were aware of the CAPM, managers required higher rates of return for investments perceived to be more risky than average. Just as present value analysis provides an objective application of the general principle that a dollar later is less attractive than a dollar now, the CAPM provides an objective application of the general principle that a higher expected return is required as compensation for accepting additional risk.

This chapter begins with an explanation of the mean-variance capital asset pricing model. Then, empirical evidence about the model is presented. Next, the model is applied to the risk-adjusted required return for a company, a division, and an individual capital investment. The final topic covered is comprehensive risk analysis, considering shareholder risk, company risk, and total project risk.

THE MEAN-VARIANCE CAPITAL ASSET PRICING MODEL (CAPM)

The mean-variance capital asset pricing model was originally developed to explain the relationship between risk and required returns in securities markets.[1]

---

[1]The model was developed by William F. Sharpe, "Capital Asset Prices: A Theory of Market Equilibrium under Conditions of Risk," *Journal of Finance* 20 (September 1964): 425–442, and John Lintner, "The Valuation of Risk Assets and the Selection of Risky Investments in Stock Portfolios and Capital Budgets," *Review of Economics and Statistics* (February 1965): 13–37, based on earlier contributions by Harry Markowitz, "Portfolio Selection," *Journal of Finance* 7 (March 1952): 77–91, and James Tobin, "Liquidity Preference as a Behavior toward Risk," *Review of Economic Studies* (February 1958): 65–86.

Like most financial models, the CAPM is a simplified approximation of a complex system. If some of the assumptions on which the model is based seem unrealistic, remember that these are justified only as simplifications used in approximating the actual behavior of the financial markets. The test of the model is not the realism of the simplifying assumptions, but the ability of the model to predict the returns required by investors as compensation for risk. We will see that the predictions are not perfect, but have been accurate enough to justify use until someone develops a better model.

The CAPM was developed when people wondered how the investment markets would behave if all investors made their investment decisions as suggested by mean-variance portfolio theory. Under this theory the investor's goal is to build the portfolio that maximizes his or her utility by putting together combinations of projects or stocks that increase return for a given level of risk or decrease risk for a given level of return. When all securities are considered, an optimal portfolio emerges. Understanding the development of mean-variance portfolio theory is not necessary to utilize CAPM in capital budgeting. More details of portfolio theory are presented in the Appendix at the end of Chapter 13. The CAPM is based on the following set of assumptions:

1. All investors are single-period decision makers who wish to maximize their expected utility of terminal wealth, and whose choices among portfolios depend on the expected return and standard deviation of the probability distribution of expected returns.
2. All investors agree on both the expected returns and standard deviations of all assets and also agree on covariances of returns between all pairs of assets.
3. All investors can borrow or lend unlimited amounts of money at the risk-free interest rate.
4. There are no taxes.
5. All investments are completely divisible, can be bought or sold without delay or difficulty, and can be bought or sold without transaction costs.
6. No investor holds a large enough portfolio to individually affect prices of investments by buying or selling.
7. The quantities of all investments are fixed.

Assumption number 1 is another way of saying that investors use the mean-variance portfolio construction principles.[2] Mean-variance decision makers with unlimited ability to borrow or lend at the risk-free rate will choose the portfolio that maximizes the reward to variability ratio:

$$RV_p = [E(R_p) - R_f]/\sigma_p \qquad (14\text{-}1)$$

---

[2]Several authors have demonstrated that the CAPM can be developed under much less restrictive assumptions. See, for example, Young K. Kwon, "Derivation of the Capital Asset Pricing Model without Normality or Quadratic Preference," *Journal of Finance* 40 (December 1985): 1505–1509.

where $E(R_p)$ is the expected return for the portfolio, σ_p is the standard deviation of the probability distribution of expected returns for the portfolio, and R_f is the risk-free rate. The implication of assuming all investors agree about risk and expected return is that all investors perceive the same efficient frontier and, therefore, choose the same risky asset portfolio. Portfolio m in Figure 14.1 is the portfolio that every investor would choose and is referred to as the *market portfolio*. Each individual would acquire portfolio m and would then borrow or lend, thereby moving up or down the straight line labeled CML to adjust for his or her own degree of risk aversion. Thus, the straight line represents the highest expected return that can be achieved at each level of portfolio risk and is referred to as the *capital market line* (CML).

In security markets equilibrium, all investments in the fixed supply of investments must be held by someone. Since everyone would want to hold the market portfolio, the market portfolio must contain all investments in proportions such that no investments are left over. If, for example, the value of General Motors stock was 1 percent of the value of all investment assets available, then 1 percent of the value of the market portfolio must be in General Motors stock. Otherwise, there will be either an excess demand or insufficient demand for General Motors stock, and the financial markets will not be in equilibrium.

For a portfolio to be as desirable as the market portfolio, it must provide as much expected return as could be achieved by moving to the same risk level on the capital market line. If the portfolio does not provide that much expected return, investors would be better off acquiring the market portfolio and adjusting

| F I G U R E   1 4 . 1   ILLUSTRATION OF THE MEAN-VARIANCE CAPITAL ASSET PRICING MODEL

The curved line is the efficient frontier as perceived by all investors, R_f is the risk-free borrowing and lending rate, and m is the market portfolio which all investors will want to hold. Investors can move up and down the capital market line (CML) from point m by buying the market portfolio and borrowing or lending.

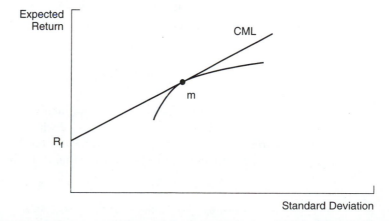

for risk by borrowing or lending. This requirement can be expressed as an equation with subscript m used to represent the market portfolio:

$$[E(R_p) - R_f]/\sigma_p = [E(R_m) - R_f]/\sigma_m \qquad \text{(14-2)}$$

Equation 14-2 has long been used as a standard for measuring the performance of managed portfolios, such as mutual funds.[3] The market portfolio is represented by some broad-based market index such as the Standard and Poor's 500 stock index. If the reward to variability ratio, measured using realized holding period returns over some historical period (after deducting management fees), is higher for the mutual fund than for the market index, the portfolio managers are judged to have earned their pay.

Optimal portfolios are interesting, but a capital investment or the stock of a company is just an asset in a portfolio. Thus, the required return for a company's equity capital or a single capital investment depends on the required return for a single asset, not a fully diversified portfolio. The required return for a single asset is, therefore, an important implication of the CAPM for capital budgeting. The CAPM provides a simple, easily used estimate of required return for a single asset.

In Chapter 13, we showed that addition of an asset would improve the reward to variability ratio of the company's asset portfolio if:

$$[E(R_a) - R_f]/\beta_{a,c} > E(R_c) - R_f \qquad \text{(13-5)}$$

where the subscript a signifies a specific asset and the subscript c signifies the existing company portfolio. It also follows that addition of the asset will decrease the reward to variability ratio if the inequality sign is reversed and will leave the reward to variability ratio unaffected if the inequality sign is replaced with an equal sign.

This same relationship holds if the market portfolio is substituted for the company portfolio. In equilibrium, there is no incentive to increase or decrease holding of a particular asset, so the inequality sign must be replaced by an equal sign. Substituting m for c and rearranging terms, the equilibrium expected return for an asset is:

$$E(R_a) = R_f + \beta_{a,m}[E(R_m) - R_f] \qquad \text{(14-3)}$$

This relationship is illustrated graphically in Figure 14.2. The straight line in Figure 14.2, referred to as the *security market line* (SML), shows the expected return that is required for each level of risk in Equation 14-3. For corporation finance and capital investment analysis, Equation 14-3 is the key

---

[3]See, for example, Jack L. Treynor, "How to Rate Management of Investment Funds," *Harvard Business Review* (January–February 1965).

| FIGURE 14.2 ILLUSTRATION OF THE SECURITY MARKET LINE

This figure illustrates the relationship between required return and risk for a single asset, as specified in Equation 14-3.

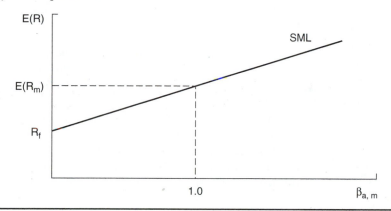

conclusion from the CAPM. The conclusion is that the required return on an investment is a function of the risk-free rate, the expected returns on the market portfolio, and the sensitivity of the investment to factors affecting returns on investments in general. After evidence concerning the accuracy of the CAPM is summarized, applications to risk-adjusted capital investment analysis will be discussed.

EVIDENCE ON THE ACCURACY OF THE CAPM |

The ideal way to measure the accuracy of the CAPM would be to observe investors' perceptions of the betas and expected returns for a sample of securities as well as the expected return for the market portfolio. The return investors expected for each investment could then be compared to the equilibrium expected return predicted by the CAPM. Unfortunately, information on what investors expect is quite sketchy.

Researchers have substituted historical data for expectations when testing the CAPM. A general index of common stock returns, such as the Standard and Poor's 500 stock index is chosen to represent the market portfolio. Holding period returns, generally for periods of one month, are computed for some number of past periods for both the index and individual securities. Realized return for each security, realized return for the index, and beta between each security and the index are computed for the study period. These data are then substituted for investor expectations. If expected returns over shorter periods are not biased estimates, then realized returns over the long run will average out to be the same as expected returns.

Once the returns and betas have been computed using historical data, the standard test consists of a linear regression[4] analysis comparing betas of securities to historical realized returns for those securities, as follows:[5]

$$R_i = a + b\beta_{i,m} + e_i \qquad (14\text{-}4)$$

where a and b are the intercept and slope generated by the regression analysis, R_i is realized return for security i over the study period, and $\beta_{i,m}$ is the beta of security i with regard to the market portfolio. The term e_i is a random term associated with security i and accounts for factors like differences between realized and expected return that leave some variation in realized return unexplained by the regression analysis.

If the CAPM implications of Equation 14-3 hold completely, then a in Equation 14-4 will equal the risk-free rate and b will equal $(R_m - R_f)$ where R_m is the realized return for the market portfolio. The results of empirical tests in relation to these expectations are then the basis for evaluation of the accuracy of the CAPM. The complete set of standards for comparison is:

1. R_m should be greater than the risk-free rate. Otherwise, no premium for risk is being earned.
2. The term b should be positive and should not be significantly different from $Rm - R_f$.
3. The term a should not be significantly different from the risk-free rate.
4. The relationship should be linear; that is, variations on beta such as $B_{i,m}^2$ should not give better explanatory power if substituted for beta in the regression.[6]
5. There should not be other factors, such as total variance of return for security i or size of the company represented by security i, that affect R_i.
6. The model should explain a significant portion of the variation in returns among securities.

---

[4]Linear regression is the mathematical process of fitting a straight line to the relationship between an independent variable, x, and a dependent variable, y, so that the average squared difference between the straight line and the observed values of y is minimized. The straight line can be defined with two coefficients. The intercept coefficient (a or o) is the value of y predicted by the line when x is zero. The slope coefficient (b or B) was computed in Chapter 13 for the relationship between two assets, and in general equals $\sigma_{x,y}/\sigma_x^2$.

[5]For technical reasons having to do with changes in the risk-free rate over the study period, the actual test form is generally

$$R_i - R_f = a + b\beta_{i,m} + e_i$$

With this formulation, the value of a will be zero if the CAPM is correct.

[6]More generally, standard regression tests can be applied to the e_i to check for evidence of nonlinearity.

There have been hundreds of tests of the CAPM, and the general conclusions will be discussed instead of attempting to discuss each study.[7] The results discussed in the following paragraphs can be summed up by saying that the CAPM does explain differences in return between assets with different risk levels, but it does not explain all differences.

Standard 1 is met when empirical tests are conducted; the realized return on the market portfolio over the long term is greater than the risk-free rate. When empirical tests are conducted, b in Equation 14-4 is greater than zero. This indicates a positive relationship between beta and return, and the relationship appears to be linear. However, b is generally observed to be less than $R_m - R_f$ while a is generally observed to be greater than the risk-free rate. These results suggest that the CAPM may not be a complete model of the relationship between risk and return.

There appear to be factors in addition to beta that affect return. Variance—total risk for the security—appears to have explanatory power in addition to beta in some cases. The small-firm effect is a widely recognized phenomenon in which securities of small firms tend to provide returns greater than would be suggested by their betas. More recent studies have indicated that this size effect may be linked to the calendar effect since most of the abnormal return occurs in the first part of January. Some arbitrage pricing theory studies, discussed in more detail in Chapter 15, have suggested that returns may be affected by three to five or more factors. These results would suggest that the CAPM is not a complete model of the relationship between risk and return.

Finally, the correlation coefficients tend to be low when regression tests are conducted using Equation 14-5, suggesting that beta does not explain a very high percentage of the variance in returns among securities. This result is not surprising, however, in light of studies showing that 70 percent or more of total variance of return for securities is diversifiable (unsystematic) risk, which would not lead to a higher required return. The majority of year-to-year fluctuations in profits at MGM, for example, depend on the box-office success of performers like Goldie Hawn and Sylvester Stallone, not fluctuations in overall economic conditions.

In reviewing the empirical evidence, two important problems must be kept in mind. First, the studies substitute historical results for expectations, on the assumption that on average historical results will equal expected results in the

---

[7]See, for example, Ralph Banz, "The Relationship between Return and the Market Value of Common Stocks," *Journal of Finance* 36 (March 1981): 3–18; Irwin Friend and Marshall Blume, "Measurement of Portfolio Performance under Uncertainty," *American Economic Review* (September 1970): 561–575; Marshall Blume and Irwin Friend, "A New Look at the Capital Asset Pricing Model," *Journal of Finance* 28 (March 1973): 19–34; Eugene F. Fama and James MacBeth, "Risk, Return and Equilibrium: Empirical Test," *Journal of Political Economy* (May–June 1973): 607–636; D. Deim, "Size-Related Anomalies and Stock Return Seasonality: Further Empirical Evidence," *Journal of Financial Economics* (June 1983): 13–32; Robert H. Litzenberger and Krishna Ramaswamy, "The Effects of Dividends on Common Stock Prices: Tax Effects or Information Effects?" *Journal of Finance* 37 (May 1982): 429–444; Douglas DeJong and Daniel W. Collins, "Explanation for the Instability of Beta: Risk-Free Rate Changes and Leverage Effect," *Journal of Financial and Quantitative Analysis* 20 (March 1985): 73–94.

long run. If this is so, the long run is indeed long. Certainly, investors who bought stock in the 1960s did not do so with the expectation that twenty years later the average stock price would be unchanged in nominal terms and would have declined by two-thirds in real (buying power) terms.

An even more troubling problem with the tests was pointed out by Roll.[8] He showed that the failure to find the anticipated risk-return relationship may simply be the result of selecting an inefficient market index to represent the market portfolio. Since a theoretically correct index would incorporate every asset, including real estate, rare stamps, etc., it is unlikely that a truly accurate market index can ever be identified. Thus, observed deviations from the CAPM predictions may result both from inaccuracy of the model and inaccuracy of the tests.

To the extent that the empirical tests have validity, they suggest that the CAPM explains some of the variation in return among securities, but not all. This is what we would expect from a simplified model. It appears that more complex models, such as multi-factor capital asset pricing models and the arbitrage pricing model, can explain a higher proportion of variation in security returns. However, these other models are more difficult to use, and you would incur greater costs in applying them.

While the CAPM is apparently not a perfect model of the relationship between risk and return, it is a relatively simple model that can be applied. For these reasons, the CAPM, despite reservations about its accuracy, is more widely used than any competing model. The use of this model can be attributed, at least in part, to the fact that if you reject this model because of incompleteness and lack of perfect accuracy, you may be left with no usable model at all. Some objective estimate of the required return needed to compensate for additional risk may be better than a completely subjective estimate or no estimate at all. This situation may change as additional empirical evidence is gathered with regard to the arbitrage pricing model discussed in Chapter 15, and guidelines for applying that model are further developed. But, for now, the CAPM appears to be the model of choice in practice.

APPLICATION OF THE CAPM TO CAPITAL BUDGETING |

The basic implication of the CAPM in conjunction with use of the shareholder wealth maximization goal is that the required return should be adjusted for non-diversifiable risk from the perspective of a shareholder. When Eastman Kodak bought Sterling Drug, for example, the required return for the investment included compensation for the degree to which Sterling is affected by those factors affecting stocks in general. The required return would not, based on the CAPM, include an adjustment for risks unique to the drug industry or to Sterling.

---

[8]Richard Roll, "A Critique of Asset Pricing Theory's Tests," *Journal of Financial Economics* (March 1977): 129–175.

In this section, general guidelines are developed for using the CAPM to estimate required returns for companies, divisions, and individual capital investments. Then, the specific data problems faced in application are discussed. Finally, an example of the application of the technique is presented.

A PROBLEM IN HOLDING PERIODS

One of the assumptions underlying the CAPM is that all investors make decisions for a single-period horizon and can revise their portfolios at the end of that horizon. The length of the holding period is not specified, but it is generally treated as a short period, such as a month. Capital investments, on the other hand, provide returns over a number of years, and are not marketable along the way, at least for an amount close to what they are really worth in operation.

A number of people have worked on multiperiod capital asset pricing models, particularly with regard to implications for capital budgeting.[9] It has been shown that the required return computed using the single-period CAPM can be applied to multiperiod capital budgeting if the risk-free rate, the market price of risk (the increase in expected return per unit increase in risk), and the systematic risk of the capital investment remain constant over the life of the capital investment. These assumptions are consistent with standard capital budgeting practice, in which the same required return is applied to cash flows in all future periods. A constant discount rate is routinely assumed in practice to make the basic net present value technique workable, so the simplified assumptions needed to apply the CAPM to capital budgeting are not radically different from those routinely applied in practice.

RISK-ADJUSTED REQUIRED RETURN FOR A COMPANY

Risky capital investments must provide expected returns that are sufficient to compensate investors for accepting the risks involved. Otherwise, the investments will decrease the wealth of the shareholders. To measure the return necessary to compensate investors for the riskiness of a particular company's assets, we use the weighted average cost of capital, which was first introduced in Chapter 5.[10]

---

[9]See, for example, M. C. Bogue and Richard R. Roll, "Capital Budgeting of Risky Projects with 'Imperfect' Markets for Physical Capital," *Journal of Finance* 29 (May 1974): 601–613; D. T. Breeden, "An Intertemporal Asset Pricing Model with Stochastic Consumption and Investment Opportunities," *Journal of Financial Economics* (September 1979): 265–296; G. Constantinides, "Admissible Uncertainty in the Intertemporal Asset Pricing Model," *Journal of Financial Economics* (March 1980): 71–86; Eugene F. Fama, "Risk-Adjusted Discount Rates and Capital Budgeting under Uncertainty," *Journal of Financial Economics* (August 1977): 3–24; R. Merton, "An Intertemporal Asset Pricing Model," *Econometrica* (September 1973): 867–888; R. Stapleton and M. Subrahmanyam, "A Multiperiod Equilibrium Asset Pricing Model," *Econometrica* (September 1978): 1077–1096; and R. Stapleton, "Multiperiod Equilibrium: Some Implications for Capital Budgeting," *TIMS Studies in Management Sciences* 11 (1979): 233–248.

[10]Recall that the weighted average cost of capital is an average of the required returns of the various suppliers of capital—bondholders, stockholders, etc.—weighted according to the proportion of the total value of capital provided from each source.

Creditors' required returns are observable, but estimation of common stock-holders' required returns has proved to be difficult. The CAPM provides a solution to this problem.

To apply the CAPM, you will need the beta for the company's stock in relation to the market portfolio as well as the risk-free rate and expected return for the market portfolio. You can then determine the required return for the stock of the company using Equation 14-3. Methods of obtaining the necessary data follow.

ESTIMATING THE BETA FOR THE COMPANY'S STOCK

There are three generally used ways to estimate a company's beta. One approach is to compute the beta using historical holding period returns for the company's stock and the market portfolio. If historical data for the company are not available, or are not relevant because the characteristics of the company are changing, historical betas for comparable companies can be used. If it is not possible to rely on historical data for your own company or comparable companies, a state of nature approach can be used. Each of these three approaches is illustrated in the following paragraphs.

Beta Based on Historical Returns. Using Equation 14-3, the formula for beta between the company's common stock and the market portfolio $\beta_{s,m}$ is $\sigma_{s,m}/\sigma_m$ where the subscript s identifies the company's common stock and the subscript m identifies the market portfolio. $\sigma_{s,m}/\sigma_m$ is the slope coefficient of the return for the security regressed on return for the market portfolio. To avoid a bias introduced by changing risk-free rates, the regression equation is generally:

$$R_s - R_f = a + \beta_{s,m}(R_m - R_f) \tag{14-5}$$

where R_s is the holding period return on the company's stock. A typical beta computation would use monthly holding period returns for the security and the market portfolio for a period of three to five years, with R_f being the risk-free rate for a particular month as well.

Example. Monthly holding period returns (HPRs) and monthly risk-free rates for Alcoa's stock and the market portfolio are shown in Table 14.1. To simplify the illustration, 12 observations are used instead of the typical 36 to 60. The estimated beta for Alcoa is then:

$$\beta_{s,m} = .0596/.0723 = \underline{\underline{.82}}$$

As a practical matter, you can obtain betas for most publicly traded stocks from publishers such as Value Line, Moody's, Standard and Poor, and others. The published sources rely on historical data to compute their betas and often do not agree. This disagreement can be the result of differing lengths of the measurement period, more recent measurement, or some other unique practice of the analyzing firm.

| TABLE 14.1 HOLDING PERIOD RETURNS FOR ALCOA AND STOCKS IN GENERAL

Monthly holding period returns (R_s), holding period returns for the S&P Composite Index (R_m), and the monthly interest rate on U.S. Treasury bills (R_f) are shown, along with the calculations needed for the beta. A letter with an overbar (such as $\bar{e}$) represents the average value for that column.

	(a)	(b)	(c)	(d)	(e)	(f)	(g)
	R_s	R_m	R_f	$R_s - R_f$	$R_m - R_f$	$(e - \bar{e})^2$	$(d - \bar{d})(e - \bar{e})$
Jul	0.3387	0.0762	0.0047	0.3340	0.0715	0.0063	0.0250
Aug	−0.1434	0.0107	0.0050	−0.1485	0.0056	0.0002	−0.0022
Sep	0.1307	−0.0218	0.0053	0.1254	−0.0272	0.0004	−0.0021
Oct	0.0110	−0.2149	0.0051	0.0058	−0.2200	0.0451	0.0027
Nov	−0.2903	−0.0823	0.0047	−0.2951	−0.0870	0.0063	0.0249
Dec	0.0625	0.0760	0.0048	0.0577	0.0711	0.0062	0.0031
Jan	−0.1166	0.0434	0.0048	−0.1214	0.0386	0.0021	−0.0065
Feb	0.1402	0.0447	0.0047	0.1355	0.0400	0.0023	0.0056
Mar	−0.0695	−0.0303	0.0048	−0.0743	−0.0351	0.0007	0.0025
Apr	0.0155	0.0124	0.0049	0.0106	0.0075	0.0002	−0.0001
May	0.0484	0.0062	0.0052	0.0432	0.0010	0.0001	0.0002
Jun	0.1576	0.0463	0.0054	0.1522	0.0409	0.0024	0.0065
Sum				0.2251	−0.0931	0.0723	0.0596
Sum/12				0.0188	−0.0078	0.0060	0.0050

With any use of betas based on historical periods, questions of stability must be kept in mind. Numerous studies have provided evidence that betas change over time.[11] One reason for changing betas is a change in financial leverage. Procedures to be explained shortly can be used to adjust historical betas for changes in financial leverage. Betas can also change because the nature of the business changes. If this is the case, or historical data are not available, it may be necessary to rely on betas for comparable companies.

Betas for Comparable Companies. A beta for your company can be estimated by reference to other companies if those companies have similar risk characteristics to your own. There is no magic formula for choosing similar companies, and the general approach is to choose companies with similar products, market positions, and so forth. When TWA decided to invest in hotels, for example, it could use the betas for several publicly traded hotel chains to estimate the degree of nondiversifiable risk in the hotel business. When TWA set out to create a reservation network for use by all travel agents and airlines, there was no simple category of publicly owned reservation systems.

[11]See, for example, Douglas V. DeJong and Daniel W. Collins, "Explanations for the Instability of Equity Beta: Risk-Free Rate Changes and Leverage Effects," *Journal of Financial and Quantitative Analysis* 20 (March 1985): 73–94.

One problem with using betas for other companies is that companies may be similar in product characteristics, but differ in financial leverage. Since return to stockholders is affected by financial leverage, betas are affected by leverage, and accuracy may be improved by compensating for these differences. The most widely used formula for this purpose is that developed by Hamada, based on the assumption that debt is riskless:[12]

$$\beta_l = \beta_u[1 + (1 - T)D/E] \tag{14-6}$$

where β_l is the leveraged beta in relation to the market portfolio. The amount of leverage is represented by the debt to equity ratio (D/E). β_u is the beta with no leverage and T is the company's tax rate. The market values of debt and equity should be used in determining debt to equity ratios for computing leveraged and unleveraged betas. The use of market value eliminates distortion caused by accounting rules that focus on historical cost rather than on the actual values of assets and liabilities.[13]

Example. The stock of Microsoft, a producer of software for microcomputers, was first publicly traded in March of 1986. If managers at Microsoft wanted to estimate their beta without waiting 5 years, they could have looked to the two leading competitors who had been publicly traded for enough years to have measurable market betas. Beta and market value debt to equity ratios at that time for two leading companies that produce microcomputer software follow:

	Beta	Debt to Equity Ratio
Ashton Tate	1.55	.012
Computer Associates	1.50	.054

Assuming 35 percent tax rates, the estimated unleveraged betas for the two companies would then be:

Ashton Tate: $\beta_u = 1.55/[1 + (1 - .35).012] = 1.54$

Computer Associates: $\beta_u = 1.50/[1 + (1 - .35).054] = 1.45$

---

[12]For the derivation, see Robert Hamada, "The Effect of the Firm's Capital Structure on the Systematic Risk of Common Stocks," *Journal of Finance* 27 (May 1972): 435–452.

[13]The formula developed by Hamada was later modified by Conine to accommodate risky debt:

$$\beta_l = \beta_u[1 + (D/E)(1 - T) + (P/E)] - \beta_D(1 - T)(D/E) - \beta_P(P/E)$$

where P and E are the market values of preferred and common stock respectively, and β_P is the beta of the preferred stock. Bond betas can be estimated using the bond's yield to maturity of the bond for $E(R_a)$ in Equation 11-14. If the risk-free rate is known and expected return for the market has been estimated, the only unknown is $\beta_{a,m}$ which is the implied beta for the bond. For more details, see Thomas E. Conine, Jr., "Corporate Debt and Corporate Taxes: An Extension," *Journal of Finance* 35 (September 1980): 1033–1037; Thomas E. Conine, Jr., "Debt Capacity and the Capital Budgeting Decision: A Comment," *Financial Management* 9 (Spring 1980): 20–22; Thomas E. Conine, Jr., and Maurry Tamarkin, "Divisional Cost of Capital Estimation: Adjusting for Leverage," *Financial Management* 14 (Spring 1985): 54–58.

The average unleveraged beta for the two companies would therefore be $(1.54 + 1.45)/2 = 1.495$.

Microsoft had a market value debt to equity ratio of approximately .035. Assuming a 35 percent tax rate, the estimated leveraged beta for Microsoft would be:

$$\beta_l = 1.495[1 + (1 - .35).035] = \underline{1.53}$$

Once the leveraged beta for Microsoft has been estimated, Equation 14-3 can be used to estimate the required return on equity. The weighted average cost of capital computation can then be carried out.

State of Nature Models for Beta Estimation. If beta for your company or comparable companies cannot be used because of changing risk characteristics or lack of data, you may be able to apply a state of nature model. With a state of nature model, return for the market portfolio and holding period return for the company's stock are both estimated under a variety of conditions. The estimates are then used to compute a covariance and a beta.

Example. Five sets of economic conditions are being considered. Expected return for the market and expected return for Taylor Corporation's common stock in each state are as follows:

State	1	2	3	4	5
Probability	.10	.20	.40	.20	.10
Return on market portfolio	−10%	0%	10%	20%	30%
Percent change in value of owners' claim	−14	−5	11	25	40

The expected returns, variance, and covariance are then:

$$E(R_m) = .1(-.10) + .2(0) + .4(.10) + .2(.20) + .1(.30) = \underline{.10}$$

$$E(R_s) = .1(-.14) + .2(-.05) + .4(.11) + .2(.25) + .1(.40) = \underline{.11}$$

$$\sigma_m^2 = .1(-.10 - .10)^2 + .2(0 - .10)^2 + .4(.10 - .10)^2 + .2(.20 - .10)^2$$
$$+ .1(.30 - .10) = \underline{.012}$$

$$\sigma_{s,m} = .1(-.10 - .10)(-.14 - .11) + .2(0 - .10)(-.05 - .11)$$
$$+ .4(.10 - .10)(.11 - .11) + .2(.20 - .10)(.25 - .11)$$
$$+ .1(.30 - .10)(.40 - .11) = \underline{.0168}$$

The estimated beta for Taylor is therefore $\beta_{s,m} = .0168/.012 = \underline{1.4}$

EXPECTED RETURN FOR THE MARKET PORTFOLIO

Attempts to measure the expected return on the market portfolio have been based on both historical study and expectation surveys. The most widely cited historical studies are those by Ibbotson and Sinquefield. For the period 1926 through 1989, they found that the long-run growth rate of value for a broadly diversified, representative stock portfolio was 9.8 percent, which exceeded the long-term growth rate from investment in U.S. government bonds by 5.7 percent, while average annual return on stocks exceeded average annual return on U.S. government bonds by 7.5 percent.[14] Unfortunately, there is also a substantial amount of variation, as illustrated in Figure 14.3.

| FIGURE 14.3 HOLDING PERIOD RETURN FOR TIME HORIZONS OF VARIOUS LENGTHS

This figure shows a frequency distribution of average annual returns over 10-year time periods from 1926 through 1986.

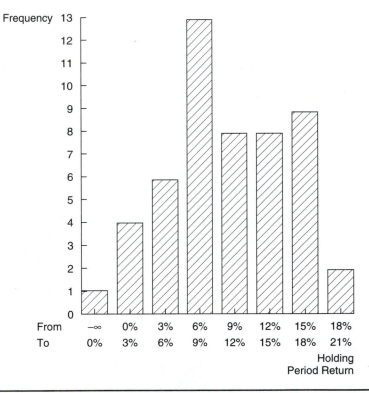

---

[14]R. Ibbotson and R. A. Sinquefield, *Stocks, Bonds, Bills, and Inflation: 1990 Yearbook* (Chicago: Ibbotson Associates, Inc., 1986).

In two recent studies, Harris and Marston[15,16] took a completely different approach and arrived at a similar result. Harris used currently available stock price and dividend data combined with surveys of security analysts' expectations about future growth. With this information he computed a required return using the formula for the present value of a continually growing stream of payments introduced in Chapter 3:

$$PV = PMT_1/(k - g) \tag{3-8}$$

where PV is present value (price in this case), PMT_1 is the dividend expected at the end of period 1, k is the required return, and g is the expected growth rate of dividends.

Harris and Marston examined analysts' forecasts on a monthly basis for the years 1982 through 1991. They found that the expected returns, on average, exceeded the rate on long-term U.S. Treasury bonds by 6.47 percent. Like researchers substituting historical results for expectations, Harris and Marston found that the risk premiums changed significantly, from a low of 4.78 percent to a high of 7.24 percent during the period of study. We do not yet have a good understanding of the factors that cause general market risk premiums to vary, but we do have some estimates of average risk premiums.

To estimate the required return for the market portfolio, the general approach is to add the estimated risk premium to the risk-free rate. These studies suggest an average market risk premium in the neighborhood of 6.5 percent. If the rate on long-term U.S. government bonds is currently 6 percent, the implied expected return for the market portfolio would be 12.5 percent.[17]

As another source, *Quantitative Analysis*, published monthly by Merrill Lynch, includes an estimate of expected return for the market portfolio based on discounted cash flow analysis.

RISK-FREE RATE

Returns on U.S. Treasury securities are generally used as the risk-free rate. The main question is the appropriate maturity to use. There may be a substantial difference between the interest rate on 13-week Treasury bills and the rate on long-term Treasury bonds.

The appropriate risk-free rate would be the rate for a holding period. The holding period for each cash flow from a capital investment will typically be the

---

[15]Robert S. Harris, "Using Analysts' Growth Forecasts to Estimate Shareholder Required Rates of Return," *Financial Management* 15 (Spring 1986): 58–67.

[16]Robert S. Harris and Felicia C. Marston, "Estimating Shareholder Risk Premia Using Analysts' Growth Forecasts," *Financial Management* 21 (Summer 1992): 63–70.

[17]For a discussion of issues involved in estimating market risk premiums, see Richard J. Sweeney and Arthur D. Warga, "The Possibility of Estimating Risk Premia in Asset Pricing Models," *Financial Review* 21 (May 1986): 299–308.

time from acquisition of the investment until receipt of the cash flow. This would imply a different risk-free rate for each cash flow: the rate for U.S. Treasury bonds maturing when that cash flow is received. For simplicity, we generally use a single risk-free rate in order to use a single cost of capital for each investment. Since capital investments are long-term in nature, the interest rate for long-term, U.S. Treasury bonds would be preferred.

To look at the problem of risk-free rate choice another way, remember that the objective of the CAPM application is to find the required return for the company's stock. The stock is a long-term investment in that dividend returns are expected over an indefinite number of future periods. If the stock or the capital investments were risk-free, we would expect them to have required returns similar to other long-term, risk-free assets: U.S. Treasury bonds. If a stock were just slightly risky, its required return would be just slightly more than the long-term risk-free rate. The same progression would continue with each increment of risk. Thus, the appropriate risk-free rate for evaluating long-term investments is the rate on long-term risk-free securities, generally U.S. Treasury bonds.[18]

For a further argument in favor of using a long-term risk-free rate, recall that a constant risk-free rate is implicitly assumed when the single-period CAPM is applied to multiperiod capital investments. Expectation theory of the relationship between interest rates and maturity tells us that the long-term rate is a measure of market participants' expectations of average short-term rates over the time period involved.[19]

SAMPLES OF REQUIRED RETURN ON EQUITY

Table 14.2 contains betas for a sample of companies, as well as the estimates of required return on equity for those companies. The required returns on equity are based on a U.S. Treasury bond rate of 6 percent and an estimated market portfolio risk premium of 6.5 percent.

---

[18]Many authors argue that the Treasury bill rate should be used as the risk-free rate in CAPM analysis, but consider the consequences of such an approach in a typical situation. Suppose the Treasury bill rate is 8 percent, the rate on U.S. government bonds is 12 percent, and expected return for the market portfolio is 18 percent. If a stock were risk-free, it would be a long-term, risk-free asset by definition and it would have a return of 12 percent in equilibrium. Now, if some stock has a very small amount of risk, say a beta of .1, using the short-term risk-free rate would lead to the conclusion that this stock had a required return of

$$E(R_s) = .08 + .1(.18 - .08) = 9\%$$

Thus, by using the short-term rate as the risk-free rate to which to add a risk premium, we come to the conclusion that the required return for a long-term investment *falls* sharply in response to a small increase in risk. If the required return falls in response to an increase in risk, the CAPM and much of the rest of finance theory is wrong.

[19]Fred C. Yeager and Neil E. Seitz, *Financial Institution Management,* 2nd ed. (Englewood Cliffs, N. J.: Prentice-Hall, 1985), 102.

| **TABLE 14.2** | **BETAS AND ESTIMATES OF REQUIRED RETURN ON EQUITY FOR A SAMPLE OF U.S. CORPORATIONS** |

Company	Beta	Req. Ret. on Equity
Aluminum Company of America	1.15	13.5%
American Express	1.45	15.4
BankAmerica	1.55	16.1
Bell Atlantic Corporation	0.90	11.9
Bristol-Myers	1.05	12.8
Caterpillar	1.15	13.5
CBS	0.95	12.2
Disney	1.25	14.1
Dow Chemical	1.25	14.1
Eastman Kodak	1.10	13.2
General Motors	1.10	13.2
IBM	0.95	12.2
May Department Stores	1.35	14.8
UAL	1.40	15.1
Winn-Dixie Stores	1.05	12.8
California Federal Bank*	2.15	20.0
Kloof Gold Mining*	−0.05	5.7

*Highest and lowest found.
Source: *Value Line.*

RISK-ADJUSTED REQUIRED RETURN FOR A PROJECT OR DIVISION OF A COMPANY

The risk-adjusted required return for the company is appropriate for projects of average risk. Decision making will be improved if adjustment is made for proposed investments with above- or below-average risk. One way to do this is to decide that all projects in a particular business category or division have similar nondiversifiable (systematic) risk characteristics. A company that both drills for oil and refines oil might, for example, assign one risk-adjusted required return to all oil-drilling investments and another risk-adjusted required return to all refining operations.

The required return for a division can be estimated by treating the division as if it were a separate company. This approach is referred to as the *pure play* approach. The general approach was applied to air mail operations of the U.S. Postal Service by Gordon and Halpern.[20] Theoretical and empirical advances

[20]Myron Gordon and P. Halpern, "Cost of Capital for a Division of a Firm," *Journal of Finance* 29 (September 1974): 1153–1163.

to make the technique applicable were contributed by Hamada,[21] Fuller and Kerr,[22] Conine and Tamarkin,[23] and Boquist and Moore,[24] as well as a score of others.

With the pure play approach, companies similar to each division are identified. The unleveraged beta for each division is assumed to be the same as the average unleveraged beta for companies similar to that division. The company that was both drilling for and refining oil would, for example, attempt to identify a group of pure drilling companies and another group of pure refining companies for this purpose.

Once an unleveraged beta for each division or project is determined using Equation 14-6, the same procedure followed to find a company required return is used to find a required return for each division or project. The only difference is that a project or division beta is used instead of a company beta. The steps are therefore as follows:

1. Identify a company or companies similar to the division.
2. Compute the average unleveraged beta for companies similar to the division.
3. Compute a leveraged beta for the division, based on average unleveraged betas for similar companies.
4. Compute a division cost of equity using the leveraged beta and Equation 14-3.
5. Compute the division weighted average cost of capital.

A division debt ratio is needed to compute a division cost of capital. It is generally assumed that the division debt to total asset ratio and cost of debt is the same as that of the total company of which it is a part. An alternative is to allocate debt and equity of the company among the divisions in a way that approximates the amount of debt and equity the divisions would carry as independent companies.

Example. Edson Oil Company has a refining and a drilling division. The company wants to estimate a risk-adjusted required return for each division. Edson has a debt to equity ratio of 1.5. Edson's borrowing cost is 10 percent before tax and 6.5 percent after tax; Edson's debt has a beta of .25. The risk-free rate is

---

[21]Hamada, "The Effect of the Firm's Capital Structure."

[22]R. Fuller and H. Kerr, "Estimating the Divisional Cost of Capital: An Analysis of the Pure-Play Technique," *Journal of Finance* 36 (December 1981): 997–1009.

[23]Conine, "Debt Capacity and the Capital Budgeting Decision"; Conine, "Corporate Debt and Corporate Taxes"; and Conine and Tamarkin, "Divisional Cost of Capital Estimation."

[24]John A. Boquist and William T. Moore, "Estimating the Systematic Risk of an Industry Segment: A Mathematical Programming Approach," *Financial Management* 12 (Winter 1983): 11–18.

8.0 percent and the expected return on the market portfolio is estimated to be 14.5 percent. Other relevant data are:

	Refining	Drilling
Total assets ($ millions)	$3.0	$1.0
Unleveraged betas for similar companies	0.8	1.2

Based on this information, and using the debt to equity ratio, the leveraged betas for the two divisions are:

$$\text{Refining: } \beta_1 = 0.8[1 + (1 - .35)1.5] = 1.58$$

$$\text{Drilling: } \beta_1 = 1.2[1 + (1 - .35)1.5] = 2.37$$

The required return on equity for each division is therefore:

$$\text{Refining: } k_e = .08 + 1.58(.145 - .08) = 18.27\%$$

$$\text{Drilling: } k_e = .08 + 2.37(.145 - .08) = 23.41\%$$

These required returns can be combined with the cost of debt to develop a weighted average cost of capital for each division. The weighted average cost of capital for each division will, therefore, reflect the riskiness of that division. Thus, new capital investments in drilling will be evaluated using a higher required return than that applied to refining.

The pure play approach requires that there be an observable company specializing in one particular area of business. In some cases, this will not be possible. There may be no close competitors, or close competitors may also be divisions of larger companies. Earnings betas have been used as substitutes for betas based on holding period returns in some cases, and additional research on economic and accounting data that affect beta has been conducted.[25] It is, therefore, possible to estimate a pure play beta in the absence of a comparable company in the marketplace.

A pure play approach can be used for a division or a major capital investment, but a pure play analysis is time-consuming and therefore expensive.[26] The approach may not be feasible for a smaller capital investment. If Marriott is considering a new automatic elevator system at its Hong Kong hotel, for example,

[25]See, for example, Menachem Brenner and Seymour Smidt, "Asset Characteristics and Systematic Risk," *Financial Management* 7 (Winter 1978): 33–39; Robert G. Bowman, "The Theoretical Relationship between Systematic Risk and Financial (Accounting) Variables," *Journal of Finance* 34 (June 1979): 617–630; Kee S. Kim, "Comment," *Journal of Finance* 36 (June 1981): 747–748; and Don M. Chance, "Evidence on a Simplified Model of Systematic Risk," *Financial Management* 11 (Autumn 1982): 53–63.

[26]A recent quote for completing a pure play analysis for a three-division company was $50,000.

it cannot find companies that specialize in selling elevator rides in hotels. On the other hand, the risks unique to the elevator are probably diversifiable. The systematic risks are related to further investment in the hotel system, so required return for the hotel business is appropriate.

In the case of a large capital investment involving a new line of enterprise, though, a pure play approach can be used for the individual investment. Suppose Marriott is considering the purchase of a cruise ship. A pure play required return for the cruise ship business can be used for that investment. If a comparable company is not available, a state of nature model can be used, as illustrated on page 453.[27]

EVIDENCE OF USE OF THE CAPM IN CAPITAL BUDGETING

Surveys of business practice have shown that adjusting the required return is a widely used response to risk in capital budgeting.[28] Many companies make the adjustments on a judgmental basis, and it is not clear from the survey results how many companies use the CAPM to make this adjustment. But the CAPM is consistent with the widely used approach of adjusting required return and is dominant in the literature as a consistent method of making those adjustments. In addition, we have the evidence of numerous published articles and business cases documenting the application of the CAPM in determining a risk-adjusted required return. Public utilities are in a unique position in that their costs of capital are the subject for public debate and regulatory proceedings. Use of the CAPM has been documented with some frequency in that arena.[29] Thus, the overall evidence suggests extensive applications.

COMPREHENSIVE RISK ANALYSIS USING THE CAPM

Surveys of business practice have shown that managers want more information about a capital investment than a single number. This is true regardless of whether risk or return is being considered. Just as length, width, and height are combined to give a complete description of the size of a box, risk is measured from the perspectives of the single project, the company, and the shareholders. The various measures of risk covered in this and the previous chapters can, therefore, be viewed as complementary rather than competing information. Managers will usually want the complete picture before making a decision.

---

[27]There is a risk of a biased estimate of beta with the state model for a single capital investment. See Stuart C. Myers and S. M. Turnbull, "Capital Budgeting and Asset Pricing Model: Good News and Bad," *Journal of Finance* 32 (May 1977): 321–332.

[28]Meir J. Rosenblatt and James V. Jucker, "Capital Expenditure Decision/Making: Some Tools and Trends," *Interfaces* (February 1979): 63–69.

[29]Philip Cooley, "A Review of the Use of Betas in Regulatory Proceedings," *Financial Management* 10 (Winter 1981): 75–81.

The importance of more than one risk measure is further emphasized when the capital budgeting process is considered. The capital investment proposal process often starts with a project proponent, who first identifies the opportunity. If risk from the proponent's perspective is not acceptable, the proponent will not forward the proposal for further consideration. The proponent's perspective will usually be that of total project risk. Higher managers would be expected to view the proposal in terms of nondiversifiable risk from their perspectives, at least for projects large enough to have an important impact on the company. At the top management level, the project's impact on the overall risk of the company will be a major area of concern. In addition, the senior executives must be concerned about providing a return sufficient to compensate investors for nondiversifiable risk from the perspective of a diversified stockholder. Each of the perspectives on risk is important in some part of the capital budgeting process.

When numerous individuals have the opportunity to kill specific capital investment proposals based on their own risk perspective, how can we be sure that the company makes consistent, optimal capital investment decisions? The answer is that we cannot. Unfortunately, though, nobody has come forward with a better, workable solution. There has been work on realigning compensation so that the welfare of individual managers is more closely aligned with the welfare of the company and its shareholders. However, these reward systems must be weighed against the advantages of compensating managers according to performance in their own areas of responsibility. As long as the proponent of a major capital investment will be held accountable for that investment's performance, that proponent is going to consider total risk. As long as chief executives are held accountable for the company's performance, they will be concerned about total company risk.

If we were not dealing with human beings, we could simply instruct managers not to consider risk from perspectives other than that of the shareholders. However, ideas are formed in minds, not on paper, so a monitoring system to assure that only shareholder risk is considered must begin inside the heads of all employees. It is doubtful that we will ever have a way of assuring that each individual evaluates each of his or her ideas without a moment's reflection on self-interest. It is also doubtful that we will develop a reward system that perfectly aligns the interests of all employees with those of the shareholders. Therefore, we must anticipate that risk will continue to be viewed from more than one perspective. The risk analysis methods discussed in this and the previous chapters can at least contribute to objective, consistent ways of measuring risk and, therefore, contribute to objective decision making.

ALTERNATIVE MARKET MODELS AND CAPITAL BUDGETING |

It is possible to construct portfolio theories from wide varieties of assumptions about the preferences of individuals. Many such portfolio theories have been developed, and many theories of capital asset pricing have likewise evolved. These include the semivariance model, a three-moment model that recognizes skewness as well as standard deviation, the growth-optimal model, option pricing models, state preference models, and the arbitrage pricing model. Most of these models have not gained wide support. But arbitrage pricing theory is of growing importance and may supplant the CAPM as the most widely used model. Option pricing models are also gaining in recognition as tools for valuing specific claims against risky assets. Arbitrage pricing theory and option pricing models are discussed in Chapter 15.

INTERNATIONAL DIVERSIFICATION |

Our discussion would not be complete if we did not look at the influence of international diversification on risk and return to the stockholder. As illustrated in Figure 14.4, risk can be reduced more rapidly through diversification when risky investments are spread across countries. This is because economic activity is not perfectly correlated from country to country. Benefits of international diversification have been demonstrated in terms of variance and systematic risk.

There is, then, evidence that a given level of expected return can be achieved through internationally diversified investment with less risk than would be necessary with only domestic diversification. However, it is often difficult for an individual investor to achieve the benefits of international diversification. Investors are frequently not familiar with foreign financial markets, and the transaction costs may be inordinately high.

| **Figure 14.4** **International Diversification and Risk Reduction**

This figure illustrates that the variance of a portfolio decreases as the number of assets increases, and the rate of decrease is greater if international investments are included in the portfolio.

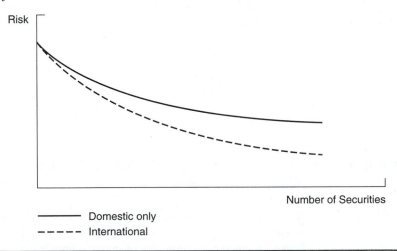

Investors can achieve international diversification by purchasing shares of internationally diversified mutual funds or internationally diversified companies. The benefits of both internationally diversified mutual funds[30] and internationally diversified companies[31] have been demonstrated. Internationally diversified mutual funds are a practical route to international diversification, but they are limited primarily to securities that can be purchased domestically or in foreign financial markets.

International diversification by investing in multinational corporations has several advantages. First, the management fees and load charges associated with a mutual fund are avoided. Second, a potentially broader range of investments and countries can be included. Your mutual fund may not be able to buy shares in a Mexican automobile manufacturer, but you can buy shares in General Motors, which has Mexican production facilities. Third, managers can reduce total company risk, not just systematic risk, through international diversification. For example, 17 percent of multinationals responding to a survey indicated that their debt capacity was increased by international diversification.[32] Finally, other benefits of international operations may be combined with diversification, thereby increasing value beyond that achieved with an internationally diversified stock portfolio.

SUMMARY

The mean-variance capital asset pricing model (CAPM) is widely used in finance and is used in capital budgeting as a method of adjusting the required return for risk. The CAPM is based on the assumption that all investors are single-period decision makers who like expected return and dislike variance of the probability distribution of expected returns. The CAPM is further based on the assumption of a fixed quantity of securities being traded in an efficient capital market—a market with perfect liquidity, perfectly divisible investments, no one investor big enough to individually affect price, and no taxes. It is further assumed that unlimited borrowing and lending at the risk-free rate is possible, and that all investors agree about the outcomes for all investments. Given these assumptions, the primary conclusion of the CAPM that affects capital budgeting can be mathematically derived:

$$E(R_a) = R_f + \beta_{a,m}[E(R_m) - R_f] \tag{14-3}$$

---

[30]Dennis Proffitt and Neil Seitz, "The Performance of Internationally Diversified Mutual Funds," *Midwest Finance Journal* 12 (1983).

[31]Ali M. Fatemi, "Shareholder Benefits from Corporate International Diversification," *Journal of Finance* 39 (December 1984): 1325–1344.

[32]Marjorie T. Stanley and Stanley R. Block, "A Survey of Multinational Capital Budgeting," *Financial Review* 19 (May 1984): 36–54.

where $E(R_a)$ is the equilibrium expected return for an asset, R_f is the risk-free rate, $\beta_{a,m}$ is the asset's beta in relationship to the market portfolio, and $E(R_m)$ is the expected return for the market portfolio.

For capital budgeting, the CAPM can be used to find the required return for a company, a division, or a single asset. The *pure play* approach can be used to find the risk-adjusted required return on equity for a division of a company or a single asset. The first step in applying the pure play approach is to identify one or more companies that have risk characteristics similar to the division or asset. The average of the betas for these companies is then used as the surrogate beta for the division or asset, generally with adjustments for differences in financial leverage. This beta is used to compute a required return on equity and then a weighted average cost of capital for the division or asset.

Data needs. In order to use the CAPM to estimate the risk-adjusted required return, it is necessary to have a beta, the risk-free rate, and the expected return for the market portfolio. Beta is generally computed on historical returns for a security and the market portfolio; betas for many stocks are computed and published by investment advisory services. An alternative is to use a state of nature model. The long-term U.S. government bond rate is recommended as the risk-free rate. Expected return on the market portfolio is based on either surveys of expectations or the use of historical realized returns as surrogates for expectations. Studies of both types have led to estimates of the expected return for the market portfolio, averaging a little more than 6 percent over the risk-free rate.

The CAPM is not a perfect model, but it does provide a method for adjusting required return in response to risk. Furthermore, it is a technique that can be readily applied with information that is currently available. Arbitrage pricing theory, discussed in Chapter 15, has the potential for overcoming some of the limitations of the CAPM and may eventually supplant the CAPM for these purposes when sufficient information for its application is available. For the time being, though, the CAPM is an important tool for capital budgeting and has been for some time.

Because economic activity is not perfectly correlated from country to country, international diversification by capital investment in many different countries may reduce the risk or beta of the corporation. Given the other strategic advantages of international operations discussed in Chapter 2 combined with the diversification advantage discussed in this chapter, multinational firms may be increasing value to the stockholder beyond that achieved with an internationally diversified stock portfolio.

QUESTIONS

14-1. For each of the assumptions underlying the CAPM, comment on the degree to which the assumption describes the actual investment world.

14–2. Several of the assumptions underlying the CAPM are unrealistic. What is the justification for using unrealistic assumptions in constructing a model of this type?

14–3. What standard must a portfolio meet to be superior to the market portfolio in the context of the CAPM?

14–4. What standard must a security meet to be superior in the context of the CAPM?

14–5. In general, how is the CAPM tested?

14–6. Summarize briefly the results of tests of the CAPM.

14–7. What was Roll's criticism of the tests of the CAPM?

14–8. How is expected return for the market determined when the CAPM is applied in capital budgeting?

14–9. How are stock betas determined when the CAPM is applied to capital budgeting?

14–10. How can the beta for debt be inferred when debt instruments are not publicly traded?

14–11. How might shareholders benefit from a company's international diversification efforts?

14–12. (**Ethical considerations**) You are a financial analyst in the corporate office of a food-processing company, and you own stock in that company. Recently, you worked on an assignment during which you found out the company was going to take on additional debt and start an airline. You are thinking about selling your stock prior to the announcement.

   a. What do you think will happen to the beta for this company after the announcement?

   b. What do you think will happen to the price of the stock given your answer to part a?

   c. Ethically, what are the consequences if you decide to sell before the announcement and if you do not sell?

   d. What would you do?

14–13. (**Applications**) There are several publishers who will provide a beta for a company, including Moody's, Standard and Poor's, Value Line, and others.

   a. If you saw three different betas for the same company that ranged from 1.0 to 1.7, how would you explain this difference to a local investment club gathering?

   b. Some services report an "up beta" and a "down beta" indicating how the company stock does in either a bull or a bear market. For this same investment club, which beta would you tell them to use today?

PROBLEMS |

14–1. Kim National, a mutual fund, has earned an annual return of 16 percent with a standard deviation of 10 percent over a historical period. Over the same historical period, the risk-free rate was 6 percent. Compute the reward to variability ratio for Kim National.

14–2. For Kim National in the previous problem, the annual return on the market portfolio over the same period was 15 percent, and the standard deviation was 6 percent. Did Kim outperform the market?

14–3. A diversified portfolio has a standard deviation of 20 percent, and the standard deviation for the market portfolio is 13 percent. The risk-free rate is 6 percent, and the expected return for the market portfolio is 12.5 percent. What is the required return for the portfolio?

14–4. The risk-free rate is 6 percent, the expected return for the market portfolio is 12.5 percent, and the standard deviation for the market portfolio is 20 percent. For a portfolio consisting of $1,000 invested at the risk-free rate, and $3,000 invested in the market portfolio, what is the expected return and standard deviation?

14–5. The risk-free rate is 6 percent, and the expected return for the market portfolio is 12.5 percent. Wilson Corporation has a beta of .8. What is the required return for the equity of Wilson?

14–6. The stock of Lansing Corporation has a beta of 1.2. Lansing earned an annual return of 14 percent during a period when the return on the market portfolio was 12.5 percent. If the risk-free rate was 6 percent, did Lansing outperform the market on a risk-adjusted basis?

14–7. Boston Corporation has a debt to equity ratio of 1.5 and a beta of 2.0. Boston's borrowing cost is 8 percent and the risk-free rate is 6 percent. Boston has a 35 percent tax rate. Compute the unleveraged beta.

14–8. A company similar to Burlington Corporation has an unleveraged beta of .8. Burlington has $2 million of debt and $1 million of equity. Burlington pays 8 percent interest on its debt, and the risk-free rate is 6 percent. Burlington's tax rate is 34 percent. Estimate Burlington's leveraged beta.

14–9. Providence Corporation is not publicly traded. The company has total debt of $1 million and total equity of $1 million. A company with comparable risk characteristics, other than capital structure–related risks, has a beta of 1.5. That company has debt of $1 million and equity of $2 million. Each company has a tax rate of 34 percent. The risk-free rate is 6 percent and the expected return on the market portfolio is 12.5 percent. Estimate the required return on equity for Providence.

14–10. Dover Corporation is not publicly traded. However, a company that produces the same product has a beta of 1.5 and a debt to equity ratio of .8. The competitor has a tax rate of 34 percent and pays interest of 8 percent on its debt. Dover has debt of $1 million and equity of $1.5 million. Dover pays a 34 percent tax rate and pays 7.5 percent interest on its debt. The expected return for the market portfolio is 12.5 percent, and the risk-free rate is 6 percent. Compute the cost of equity capital for Dover.

14–11. Martin Corporation has two divisions, one specializing in production and one specializing in shipping. Two companies similar to the production division in nonfinancial risk characteristics have unleveraged betas of 1.0 and 1.2. Martin has total debt of $20 million and total equity of $30 million. The interest on Martin's debt is 8 percent and the risk-free rate is 6 percent, and Martin's tax rate is 34 percent. Compute the required return on equity for the production division. Return on a market portfolio is 12.5 percent.

14–12. A company with nonfinancial risk characteristics similar to the shipping division of Martin (previous problem) has an unleveraged beta of .6. Compute the required return on equity for the shipping division.

14–13. Rather than assuming each division has the same debt ratio, Martin (previous two problems) assumes that the production division is financed with $10 million of debt and $20 million of equity, while the shipping division is financed with $10 million of debt and $10 million of equity. Compute the required return on equity for each division.

14–14. The risk-free rate is 6 percent. Based on information about average market risk premiums presented in this chapter, estimate the expected return on the market portfolio.

14–15. The risk-free rate is 6 percent and the debt of Burner Corporation has a yield of 9 percent. What is the implied beta for the debt? (See footnote 13.) Return on a market portfolio is 12.5 percent.

14–16. Klemkosky is considering the acquisition of a privately held company. The company's equity can be purchased for $1.2 million in cash and is expected to generate after-tax cash flows of $250,000 a year for ten years, with no terminal value. The acquisition candidate is financed with 60 percent debt and 40 percent equity. The interest on the debt is 8 percent and the risk-free rate is 6 percent. The tax rate is 34 percent. Companies in the same industry as the acquisition candidate have unleveraged betas of .90. Should Klemkosky make the acquisition? Return on a market portfolio is 12.5 percent.

 14–17. Monthly holding period returns are shown for Portland Corporation and the market portfolio. The risk-free rate for each month is also shown. Compute the company's beta. Is the number of observations large enough to provide a really meaningful estimate of the beta?

Month	1	2	3	4	5	6
Portland HPRs	.011	.014	.010	.015	.018	.020
Market HPRs	.009	.015	.010	.012	.010	.015
Risk-free rate	.005	.006	.007	.008	.006	.005

14–18. Did Portland Corporation in problem 17 outperform the market or underperform the market?

14–19. Bronx Corporation has assets of $50 million and is financed entirely with equity. The risk-free rate is 6 percent and expected return for the market portfolio is 12.5 percent. The expected return, beta, and standard deviation for the company's equity are .16, 1.2, and .20, respectively. A new $5 million project has a beta of 1.0, an expected return of .15, and a standard deviation of −.50. The correlation coefficient ($r_{a,c}$) between the project and the company's existing assets is .5. Is the new asset attractive

from the perspective of
a. the shareholders?
b. the company's chief executive?
c. the project manager?

14–20. HiPoint Corporation cannot find independent companies similar to its new division. Management has identified six possible market conditions. Based on history, return for the market portfolio has been estimated for each condition. Using the company's financial planning model, management has also estimated returns for investment in the new division in each condition. Estimate the beta for the new division. If the risk-free rate is 6 percent, what is the required return on equity for the new division?

Inflation	Low			High		
Economic growth	Low	Normal	High	Low	Normal	High
Probability	.125	.250	.125	.125	.250	.125
Expected return on market	0	.150	.300	−.050	.080	.150
Expected return for division	−.100	.200	.400	−.200	.100	.200

CASE PROBLEM |

DeKalb AgResearch Cost of Capital

Anyone who drives through America's heartland in the summer months is familiar with the DeKalb corn test plots that dot the landscape. Possibly less well known is DeKalb's second line of business: exploration and production of oil and gas.

For a company in two such divergent industries, it is important that the cost of capital properly reflect differences in risk. If the same cost of capital is used for both industries, the capital allocation process will be biased toward the risky industry because high expected return tends to be associated with high risk. Thus, investments in the risky industry may be accepted even though they do not provide a sufficient return to compensate for the risk of that industry. Likewise, investments in the low-risk industry may be rejected even though they provide more than enough return to compensate for the low risk of the industry. In other words, capital budgeting will not maximize value.

A pure play approach is one way to come up with risk-adjusted required return for each division of the company. Table 14.3 contains data about companies in the industries in which DeKalb operates.

The interest rate on corporate debt ranged from 10 percent to over 12 percent at the time, while the interest rate on long-term U.S. government bonds was approximately 9 percent. Naturally, the safest companies were able to borrow money at a 10 percent cost, while companies viewed as risky would have to pay rates of 12 percent or more. Bond and stock rating agencies place DeKalb about in the middle of the risk range. The corn-related companies tended to be considered medium risk by rating agencies while the oil companies were at the high-risk end. DeKalb or one of the corn-related companies could probably borrow in the range of 10.9 percent, while an oil-related company would probably have to pay around 12.1 percent. The marginal corporate income tax rate was 46 percent.

Financial statement information about DeKalb appears in Table 14.4. Of the total revenues, $158.9 million were generated by oil and gas operations, and the rest was generated by agriculture operations. DeKalb's stock was selling at $24 a share, for a price-earnings ratio of 14.8. The tax rate was then 46 percent.

| TABLE 14.3 DATA ON COMPANIES IN THE INDUSTRIES IN WHICH DEKALB OPERATES

This table contains data for five companies primarily in corn-related businesses and five companies primarily in oil exploration and production. Dollar amounts are in millions. The equity and long-term debt are at estimated market values.

Company	Business	Revenue	Long Term Debt	Equity	Beta
Pioneer Hi-Bred	Corn and other seeds	$821.1	$18.3	$1,089.8	.80
Am. Maize Prod.	Corn processor	433.2	93.8	84.1	.90
Staley Corp.	Corn processor	2,139.8	512.4	868.9	1.20
Archer-Daniels	Corn & other food processor	4,738.8	532.3	3,047.7	1.05
CPC Int'l	Corn & other food processor	4,209.9	462.9	3,114.2	.81
Apache Corp.	Oil & gas exploration & prod.	128.5	103.4	205.7	1.30
Forest Oil Co.	Oil & gas exploration & prod.	133.1	235.9	112.9	.90
Noble Affiliates	Oil & gas exploration & prod.	170.0	90.1	495.5	1.35
Texas Int'l	Oil & gas exploration & prod.	95.6	278.3	123.9	1.50
Wainoco	Oil & gas exploration & prod.	42.8	80.1	72.7	1.20

| **TABLE 14.4** **DEKALB FINANCIAL STATEMENTS** |

Income statement for the fiscal year ending August 31, 1985, and balance sheet of DeKalb AgResearch, as of the company's fiscal-year closing date, August 31, 1985. All numbers but per-share data in $ millions.

Earnings

Operating revenues	$569.9
Operating profit	44.3
Earnings before tax	30.3
Income tax	10.2
Net income	$20.1
Earnings per share	$1.62

Capital Structure

Long-term debt:	
12.3% notes due in installments 1991 through 1993	$ 50.0
10.55% notes due in 1990	50.0
9 1/8% notes due in installments through 1998	24.4
Capitalized lease obligations at interest rates of	
6% – 7 1/4%, payable through 2007	11.3
Other debt	33.8
Less current maturities	4.9
Total long-term debt	164.6
Total shareholders' equity	375.6

CASE QUESTIONS

1. Find the unleveraged beta for each company in Table 14.3.
2. Estimate the unleveraged betas for the agriculture and oil divisions of DeKalb.
3. Estimate the leveraged beta for each division of DeKalb.
4. Compute the required return on equity capital for each division.

Appendix 14-A

PRESENT VALUES
OF RISKY OUTFLOWS |

Some capital budgeting decisions are based solely on analysis of cash outflows. Replacement of a worn-out air-conditioning compressor in a New Orleans movie theater is one such example. Unless closing the theater is a serious option, there is no need to estimate all future theater revenues; the only question is which compressor to buy. The company will choose between various combinations of initial cash outlay and future operating costs. Lease vs. buy analysis, treated in Chapter 21, is another type of analysis in which streams of cash outlays are compared. If those future cash outflows are uncertain, a risk-adjusted present value must be determined.

If the future cash outflows are risky, we need to choose an appropriate risk-adjusted discount rate to use in finding their present values. Having introduced the CAPM, we now have a vehicle with which to develop rules for the evaluation of risky outflows. The basic principle of valuation for risky outflows is straight-forward: *The present value of a series of cash outflows is the same as the present value of a series of cash inflows with identical characteristics.*

For an intuitive justification for this statement, note that one person's cash outflow is another person's cash inflow. In an equilibrium capital market, the present value of a series of outflows is the present value of those flows to the person receiving them. A CAPM-based proof and a state-preference-based proof as well as a more general example are available in an article by Laurence D. Booth.[33] The following examples demonstrate the validity and application of this principle.

Example. For this simple example, assume a one-period capital investment and a world in which there are only two possible outcomes, each with a probability of .5. Information about the investment and the market portfolio follows.

State	State I	State II	Expected Amount
Market portfolio value	100	130	115
Cash inflows	100	130	115
Cash outflows	80	110	95
Net cash flows	20	20	20

To round out the information needed, the market portfolio is currently priced at $100 and the risk-free rate is 10 percent. Since the expected value of the market portfolio at the end of the period is $115, the expected return on the market portfolio is 15 percent.

Because the cash inflows from the capital investment are identical to ending market portfolio value,[34] the equilibrium present value of the risky inflow stream equals the value of the market portfolio: $100. The net cash flows are

[33]Laurence D. Booth, "Correct Procedures for the Evaluation of Risky Cash Outflows," *Journal of Financial and Quantitative Analysis* 27 (June 1982), 287–300.

[34]We made the cash flows for the capital investment identical to the ending value of the market portfolio solely to simplify the example. This saves a step in finding a combination of the market portfolio and risk-free borrowing or lending that duplicates the cash inflows from the capital investment.

the same in either state and are, therefore, risk-free. The present value of a risk-free $20 payment is that amount discounted at the risk-free rate: $20 ÷ 1.10 = $18.18. Therefore, the equilibrium present value of the outflows (PV_{out}) is:

$$PV_{out} = \$100.00 - \$18.18 = \$81.82$$

The equilibrium required return for the expected cash outflows (k_{out}) is then:

$$\$81.82 = \$95/(1 + k_{out}); k_{out} = \underline{16.11\%}$$

We can then confirm that this is the same risk-adjusted discount rate that would be applied to a series of cash inflows with the same characteristics. The two possible end-of-period outflows, measured as returns on the original present value, are:

$$(80 - 81.82)/81.82 = -.0222 \text{ and } (110 - 81.82)/81.82 = .3444$$

Beta is the slope coefficient for the relationship between returns for some asset and return for the market portfolio. The market portfolio return is 0.0 in State I and .30 in State II. The beta for the outflows is:

$$\beta_{out,m} = [.3444 - (-.0222)]/[.30 - 0.0)] = 1.222$$

Using the standard CAPM required return formulation, the required return associated with this beta is:

$$K_{out} = .10 + [1.222(.15 - .10)] = \underline{16.11\%}$$

Thus, equilibrium risk-adjusted discount rate is the same whether the cash flows are costs or benefits.

As another example, consider the case in which cash outflows move in the opposite direction from general market returns and, therefore, increase risk. Cash flows in each state are shown below.

State	State I	State II	Expected Amount
Market portfolio value	100	130	115
Cash inflows	100	130	115
Cash outflows	110	80	95
Net cash flows	−10	50	20

It is necessary to solve jointly for the present value of the net cash flows (PV_{net}), the beta of the net cash flows ($\beta_{net,m}$), and the required return for the net cash flows (k_{net}):

$$PV_{net} = 20/(1 + k_{net})$$

$$k_{net} = .10 + \beta_{net,m}(.15 - .10)$$

$$\beta_{net,m} = [(50 - PV_{net})/PV_{net} - (-10 - PV_{net})/PV_{net}]/(.30 - .00)$$

$$= 200/PV_{net}$$

Substituting,

$$PV_{net} = 20/[1 + .10 + (200/PV_{net})(.15 - .10)]; PV_{net} = \$9.09$$

The present value of the cash outflows is therefore $100 - \$9.09 = \$90.91$, and the implied discount rate is:

$$\$90.91 = \$95/(1 + k_{out}); k_{out} = 4.5\%$$

The reader can confirm that the beta for these cash outflows is -1.1. Using the CAPM, the required return for this beta is $.10 - [1.1(.15 - .10)] = 4.5\%$. Again, the risk-adjusted present value of the outflows is the same present value that would be found for risky inflows with identical characteristics.

SUMMARY |

In summarizing these examples, note that a positive beta on a cash outflow means that the outflow tends to move with revenues, and the variability of the outflow, therefore, decreases risk. A risk-averse decision maker would prefer variable outflows that *decrease* risk over a known cost with the same expected amount. The higher discount rate applied to risky outflows means a smaller present value of the outflow, which is consistent with the risky outflow being preferred over a riskless outflow. Likewise, a cash outflow with a negative beta increases risk and, therefore, is less desirable than a riskless outflow. The low discount rate and resulting high net present value reflect the undesirability of the increased risk.

Finally, we should note that this appendix does not negate the approach of discounting net cash flows at a discount rate appropriate for the risk of the net cash flows. The guidelines in this appendix are designed to assure that if components of net cash flow are discounted separately, the sum of the present values will equal the present value of the net cash flows.

PROBLEMS |

14-A-1. A hotel that is financed entirely with equity must add a new elevator system. The hotel's equity has a beta of 1.5, the risk-free rate is 6 percent, and expected return on the market portfolio is 12.5 percent. Two solutions to the elevator problem are being compared. What is the appropriate discount rate if the beta for the elevator cash flows is -1.0? 0.0? 1.5?

14–A–2. Cash flows related to an asset in each of two possible (equally likely) states of nature are shown. The appropriate discount rate for the net cash flows is 15 percent. The appropriate discount rate for the cash inflows, if analyzed separately, would be 10 percent. What is the appropriate discount rate for the outflows? Does the variability of the outflows serve to increase or decrease risk?

State	I	II
Cash inflow	1,000	2,000
Cash outflow	800	1,200
Net cash flow	200	800

SELECTED REFERENCES |

Adler, Michael, and Bernard Dumas. "International Portfolio Choice and Corporation Finance: A Synthesis." *Journal of Finance* 38 (June 1983): 925–984.

Banz, Ralph. "The Relationship between Return and the Market Value of Common Stocks." *Journal of Finance* 36 (March 1981): 3–18.

Black, Fischer. "A Simple Discounting Rule." *Financial Management* 17 (Summer 1986): 7–11.

Blume, Marshall, and Irwin Friend. "A New Look at the Capital Asset Pricing Model." *Journal of Finance* 28 (March 1973): 19–34.

Bogue, M. C., and Richard R. Roll. "Capital Budgeting of Risky Projects with 'Imperfect' Markets for Physical Capital." *Journal of Finance* 29 (May 1974): 601–613.

Booth, Laurence D. "Correct Procedures for the Evaluation of Risky Cash Outflows." *Journal of Financial and Quantitative Analysis* 27 (June 1982): 287–300.

Boquist, J., R. Racette, and G. Schlarbaum. "Duration and Risk Assessments for Bonds and Common Stocks." *Journal of Finance* 30 (December 1975): 1360–1365.

Boquist, John A., and William T. Moore. "Estimating the Systematic Risk of an Industry Segment: A Mathematical Programming Approach." *Financial Management* 12 (Winter 1983): 11–18.

Bowman, Robert G. "The Importance of Market Value Measurement of Debt in Assessing Leverage." *Journal of Accounting Research* 17 (Spring 1980): 242–254.

———. "The Theoretical Relationship between Systematic Risk and Financial (Accounting) Variables." *Journal of Finance* 34 (June 1979): 617–630.

Breeden, D. T. "An Intertemporal Asset Pricing Model with Stochastic Consumption and Investment Opportunities." *Journal of Financial Economics* (September 1979): 265–296.

Brenner, Menachem, and Seymour Smidt. "Asset Characteristics and Systematic Risk." *Financial Management* 7 (Winter 1978): 33–39.

Brown, Keith C., W. V. Harlow, and Seha M. Tinic. "How Rational Investors Deal with Uncertainty (or, Reports of the Death of Efficient Markets Theory Are Greatly Exaggerated)." *Journal of Applied Corporate Finance* 2 (Fall 1989): 45–58.

Chance, Don M. "Evidence on a Simplified Model of Systematic Risk." *Financial Management* 11 (Autumn 1982): 53–63.

Chung, Kee H., and Charlie Charoenwong. "Investment Options, Assets in Place, and the Risk of Stocks." *Financial Management* 20 (Autumn 1991): 21–33.

Conine, Thomas E., Jr. "Corporate Debt and Corporate Taxes: An Extension." *Journal of Finance* 35 (September 1980): 1033–1037.

———. "Debt Capacity and the Capital Budgeting Decision: A Comment." *Financial Management* 9 (Spring 1980): 20–22.

Conine, Thomas E., Jr., and Maurry Tamarkin. "Divisional Cost of Capital Estimation: Adjusting for Leverage." *Financial Management* 14 (Spring 1985): 54–58.

Constantinides, G. "Admissible Uncertainty in the Intertemporal Asset Pricing Model." *Journal of Financial Economics* (March 1980): 71–86.

Cooley, Philip. "A Review of the Use of Betas in Regulatory Proceedings." *Financial Management* 10 (Winter 1981): 75–81.

Crutchley, Claire, Enyang Guo, and Robert S. Hansen. "Stockholder Benefits from Japanese-U.S. Joint Ventures." *Financial Management* 20 (Winter 1991): 22–30.

Daniel, Kent, and Sheridan Titman. "Evidence on the Characteristics of Cross Sectional Variations in Stock Returns." *Journal of Finance* (March 1997): 1–33.

Deim, D. "Size-Related Anomalies and Stock Return Seasonality: Further Empirical Evidence." *Journal of Financial Economics* (June 1983): 13–32.

DeJong, Douglas, and Daniel W. Collins. "Explanations for the Instability of Equity Beta: Risk-free Rate Changes and Leverage Effects." *Journal of Financial and Quantitative Analysis* 20 (March 1985): 73–94.

Dhalimal, D. "Measurement of Financial Leverage in the Presence of Unfunded Pension Obligations." *Accounting Review* 61 (October 1986): 651–661.

Erhardt, Michael C., and Yatin N. Bhagwat. "A Full-Information Approach for Estimating Divisional Betas." *Financial Management* 20 (Summer 1991): 60–69.

Eun, Cheol S., and Bruce G. Resnick, "Exchange Rate Uncertainty, Forward Contracts, and International Portfolio Selection." *Journal of Finance* 43 (March 1988): 197–215.

Fama, Eugene F. "Risk-Adjusted Discount Rates and Capital Budgeting under Uncertainty." *Journal of Financial Economics* (August 1977): 3–24.

Fama, Eugene F., and Kenneth R. French. "The CAPM Is Wanted, Dead or Alive." *Journal of Political Economy* 51 (December 1996): 1947–1958.

———. "Multifactor Explanations of Asset Pricing Anomalies." *Journal of Finance* 51 (March 1996): 55–84.

Fama, Eugene F., and James MacBeth. "Risk, Return and Equilibrium: Empirical Test." *Journal of Political Economy* (May–June 1973): 607–636.

Fatemi, Ali M. "Shareholder Benefits from Corporate International Diversification." *Journal of Finance* 39 (December 1984): 1325–1344.

Friend, Irwin, and Marshall Blume. "Measurement of Portfolio Performance under Uncertainty." *American Economic Review* (September 1970): 561–575.

Fuller, R., and H. Kerr. "Estimating the Divisional Cost of Capital: An Analysis of the Pure-Play Technique." *Journal of Finance* 36 (December 1981): 997–1009.

Gordon, Myron, and P. Halpern. "Cost of Capital for a Division of a Firm." *Journal of Finance* 29 (September 1974): 1153–1163.

Hamada, Robert. "The Effect of the Firm's Capital Structure on the Systematic Risk of Common Stocks." *Journal of Finance* 27 (May 1972): 435–452.

Harris, Robert S. "Using Analysts' Growth Forecasts to Estimate Shareholder Required Rates of Return." *Financial Management* 15 (Spring 1986): 58–67.

Harris, Robert S., and Felicia C. Marston. "Estimating Shareholder Risk Premia Using Analysts' Growth Forecasts." *Financial Management* 21 (Summer 1992): 63–70.

Kahn, Arshad M., and Donald Fiorino. "The Capital Asset Pricing Model in Project Selection: A Case Study." *Engineering Economist* 37 (Winter 1992): 145–160.

Khaksari, Shahriar, and Neil Seitz. "A Real Return Test of International Capital Market Efficiency." *In The Changing Environment of International Financial Markets: Issues and Analysis*, Dilip K. Ghosh and Edgar Ortiz, ed. 189–200. New York: St. Martin's Press, 1994.

Kim, Kee S. "Comment," *Journal of Finance* 36 (June 1981): 747–748.

Kwon, Young K. "Derivation of the Capital Asset Pricing Model without Normality or Quadratic Preference." *Journal of Finance* 40 (December 1985): 1505–1509.

Ibbotson, R., and R. A. Sinquefield. *Stocks, Bonds, Bills, and Inflation: 1990 Yearbook*. Chicago: Ibbotson Associates.

Lee, Jae Ha, and William T. Moore. "Application of the Bootstrap to Assess the Precision of Industry Risk Measures." *Engineering Economist* 34 (Fall 1988): 51–60.

Lintner, John. "The Valuation of Risk Assets and the Selection of Risky Investments in Stock Portfolios and Capital Budgets." *Review of Economics and Statistics* (February 1965): 13–37.

Litzenberger, Robert H., and Krishna Ramaswamy. "The Effects of Dividends on Common Stock Prices: Tax Effects or Information Effects?" *Journal of Finance* 37 (May 1982): 429–444.

Markowitz, Harry. "Portfolio Selection." *Journal of Finance* 7 (March 1952): 77–91.

Merton, R. "An Intertemporal Asset Pricing Model." *Econometrica* (September 1973): 867–888.

Miller, Edward. "On the Systematic Risk of Expansion Investment." *Quarterly Review of Economics and Business* 28 (Autumn 1988): 67–77.

Myers, Stuart C., and S. M. Turnbull. "Capital Budgeting and Asset Pricing Model: Good News and Bad." *Journal of Finance* 32 (May 1977): 321–332.

O'Brien, Thomas J. "Operating Leverage in Cost Reduction Capital Budgeting Proposals." *Engineering Economist* 34 (Summer 1989): 305–314.

Proffitt, Dennis, and Neil Seitz. "The Performance of Internationally Diversified Mutual Funds." *Midwest Finance Journal* 12 (1983).

Roll, Richard. "A Critique of Asset Pricing Theory's Tests." *Journal of Financial Economics* (March 1977): 129–175.

Roll, Richard, and Stephen A. Ross. "On the Cross-sectional Relation between Expected Returns and Betas." *Journal of Finance* 49 (March 1994): 101–121.

Rosenblatt, Meir J., and James V. Jucker. "Capital Expenditure Decision/Making: Some Tools and Trends." *Interfaces* (February 1979): 63–69.

Sharpe, William F. "Capital Asset Prices: A Theory of Market Equilibrium under Conditions of Risk." *Journal of Finance* 20 (September 1964): 425–442.

Stapleton, R. "Multiperiod Equilibrium: Some Implications for Capital Budgeting." *TIMS Studies in Management Sciences* 11 (1979): 233–248.

Stapleton, R., and M. Subrahmanyam. "A Multiperiod Equilibrium Asset Pricing Model." *Econometrica* (September 1978): 1077–1096.

Sweeney, Richard J., and Arthur D. Warga. "The Possibility of Estimating Risk Premia in Asset Pricing Models." *Financial Review* 21 (May 1986): 299–308.

Tobin, James. "Liquidity Preference as a Behavior toward Risk." *The Review of Economic Studies* (February 1958): 65–86.

Treynor, Jack L. "How to Rate Management of Investment Funds." *Harvard Business Review* (January–February 1965): 63–75.

Uppal, Raman. "A General Equilibrium Model of International Portfolio Choice." *Journal of Finance* 48 (June 1993): 529–553.

CHAPTER 15

ARBITRAGE PRICING THEORY, OPTION PRICING THEORY, AND CAPITAL BUDGETING

. After completing this chapter you should be able to:

1. Differentiate between the arbitrage pricing theory (APT) model and the capital asset pricing model (CAPM).
2. Apply APT to calculate a risk-adjusted required return.
3. List the four economic activity measures identified by Chen, Roll, and Ross as highly correlated with APT factors.
4. Apply state-based arbitrage analysis to value a stream of cash flows.
5. Define option terms.
6. Identify embedded calls and puts when they exist in a capital project.
7. Explain the role that options play in the selection of financing.
8. Explain the role that stock options play in motivating managers to accept risk.
9. Estimate the value of an option using the Black-Scholes pricing model.
10. Know the variables that influence the value of an option and the relationship of each to the value of a call option.
11. Describe several of the methods used by managers to manage exchange rate risk.

When Boeing Corporation started to work on the 7J7 jet design, the total investment was estimated at $3 billion, and the risks to the company were monumental. Shifting demand could leave the entire investment sitting high and dry. The risks of shifts were substantial because the development effort alone would require several years.

Management at Boeing was certainly interested in moving ahead while limiting its risk exposure. In addition, management did not want to undertake the investment unless its expected returns were sufficient to compensate stockholders for the risks involved. Arbitrage pricing models, discussed in the first part of this chapter, provide a way to evaluate expected benefits in relation to risk. Option pricing models, discussed in the second half of this chapter, are valuable tools for viewing and controlling risk in projects of this type. The $100 million Boeing spent on development over three years can be viewed as the purchase of an option giving the company an opportunity to make the full $3 billion investment if later conditions justified the action. The option approach allowed Boeing to move forward while limiting risk to an acceptable level.

Arbitrage pricing models and option pricing models use similar sets of assumptions to value different types of assets. Both models assume perfect markets in which there are no taxes, no transaction costs, and no restrictions on short sales. The two models apply these assumptions to different types of assets.

ARBITRAGE PRICING THEORY |

Arbitrage is the process of increasing returns at no cost by taking advantage of inefficient price relationships. The classic example of an arbitrage opportunity involves a security trading at different prices on east coast and west coast exchanges. An arbitrage profit can be had by simultaneously buying in the low-price market and selling in the high-price market. It is, of course, necessary that there be no restrictions on trading so that it is possible to take advantage of the inefficient price relationship. An arbitrage opportunity also exists if one set of securities costs less than another set of securities that provides the same benefits in each possible state of nature; a short-sale[1] of the high-cost set and a purchase of the low-cost set are used in this case.

Investors taking advantage of arbitrage opportunities will quickly eliminate those opportunities. The high-priced set of assets will be bid down in price while the opposite will happen to the low-priced assets. Thus, countless investors seeking even the smallest arbitrage opportunity keep price and return relationships efficient. Arbitrage pricing theory is simply a theory of relationships among investment returns in a market in which arbitrage opportunities have been eliminated.

As a simple example of an arbitrage situation, consider three "securities," each of which will pay off after the flip of a single coin. The prices and payoffs are shown in Table 15.1.

An investor who is currently holding security A is searching for an arbitrage opportunity. The investor notes that 24 shares of security B will provide $60 if

---

[1]A short-sale consists of borrowing a security and then selling that security. The short-seller repurchases the security at a later time and returns it to the owner. The short-seller's gain or loss depends on whether the security can be repurchased for less or more than the sale price. The short-seller must also pay the lender any dividends that would have been received.

| TABLE 15.1 PRICE AND RETURNS FOR THREE SECURITIES

Each security makes one payoff after a coin is flipped, as indicated. Market prices, it turns out, are not in equilibrium.

Security	Price	PAYOFF	
		Heads	Tails
A	100.00	60	160
B	1.00	2.50	0
C	1.00	0	2.50

the coin comes up heads, and 64 shares of security C will provide $160 if the coin comes up tails. For $88, the investor can buy a combination of B and C that will exactly duplicate the returns from A. No rational investor would hold A in this situation. Investors attempting to sell A in order to purchase B and C will quickly bid the prices back into equilibrium.

One advantage of arbitrage pricing theory is that it does not rest on a set of complex and/or unrealistic assumptions about investor preferences. The general principle is based only on the assumptions that investors prefer more wealth to less wealth and that investors are risk-averse in a general way. However, market efficiency is assumed in that the absence of arbitrage profit opportunities is assumed. Furthermore, specific required return implications are based on assumptions about behavior of security returns, such as linear relationships between returns for individual investments and factors affecting returns for all investments. Finally, restrictions on the use of short-sale proceeds are assumed away, just as taxes and transaction costs are assumed away when constructing the mean-variance capital asset pricing model. Like the taxes and transaction costs, restrictions on the use of short-sale proceeds are part of the practical investment world. Since you sell short by borrowing shares, the lender of those shares typically requires a security deposit which uses up the short-sale proceeds. Only very large institutions may be able to avoid these restrictions on the use of short-sale proceeds. The ultimate tests of these models are not in the reality of assumptions, but in accuracy and usefulness. After exploring arbitrage pricing in some detail, we will turn to the questions of accuracy and usefulness.

THE STANDARD ARBITRAGE PRICING THEORY (APT)

There are many possible arbitrage pricing models, depending on things like assumptions about behavior of security returns. The arbitrage pricing model that has gained wide recognition is the linear model developed by Ross.[2] We follow

[2]Stephen Ross, "The Arbitrage Theory of Capital Asset Pricing," *Journal of Economic Theory* (December 1976): 341–361.

convention in using the acronym APT to refer to the Ross model. The APT is based on the assumption of perfectly competitive, frictionless markets. The result of this assumption is that securities are priced so that there are no arbitrage profit opportunities. Furthermore, the APT is based on the assumptions that returns for assets are linearly related to certain overall factors and that the number of investments being considered is much larger than the number of factors. In other words, the APT is based on the assumption that the return for a particular asset during a particular period ($R_{s,t}$) is determined as follows:

$$R_{s,t} = E(R_s) + \beta_{s,1}F_{1,t} + \beta_{s,2}F_{2,t} + \ldots + \beta_{s,n}F_{n,t} + e_{s,t} \tag{15-1}$$

where

$E(R_s)$ = expected return for asset s

$\beta_{s,n}$ = the sensitivity of return for asset s to factor n from a set of factors common to returns for all assets

$F_{n,t}$ = factor n of a set of factors common to returns for all assets, with each factor having an expected value of 0

$e_{s,t}$ = a random-noise term for security s, with an expected value of 0

Ross showed that if relationships described in Equation 15-1 hold, and arbitrage profit opportunities have been eliminated, then the expected return for an asset is:

$$E(R_s) = R_f + [E(R_1) - R_f]\beta_{s,1} + [E(R_2) - R_f]\beta_{s,2} + \ldots + [E(R_n) - R_f]\beta_{s,n} \tag{15-2}$$

where

R_f = the risk-free interest rate

$E(R_n)$ = the expected return on a portfolio with unitary sensitivity[3] to factor n and zero sensitivity to all other factors

$\beta_{s,n}$ = the sensitivity of asset s to factor n

A formal derivation of Equation 15-2 is a bit tedious,[4] but a simple example can be used to illustrate why Equation 15-2 must hold in equilibrium. Assume that there are two factors, and three securities (a, b, and c) are to be combined in a portfolio. Information about the securities and unitary sensitivity portfolios follows:

---

[3]In a linear regression analysis between the factor and return for the portfolio, the beta would be 1.0.

[4]See Ross, "Arbitrage Theory," for a proof.

Unitary sensitivity portfolios	Security sensitivities		
$E(R_1) = .15$	$\beta_{a,1} = 1$	$\beta_{b,1} = 2$	$\beta_{c,1} = 1$
$E(R_2) = .20$	$\beta_{a,2} = 2$	$\beta_{b,2} = 1$	$\beta_{c,2} = 3$

Using Equation 15-2, and assuming a 10 percent risk-free rate, the equilibrium expected returns for these three securities are:

$$E(R_a) = .10 + 1(.15 - .10) + 2(.20 - .10) = .35$$

$$E(R_b) = .10 + 2(.15 - .10) + 1(.20 - .10) = .30$$

$$E(R_c) = .10 + 1(.15 - .10) + 3(.20 - .10) = .45$$

To demonstrate that the expected return determined with Equation 15-2 must be the expected return in equilibrium, we construct a portfolio with zero elasticity for both factor 1 and factor 2. This involves solving three simultaneous equations:

$$1W_a + 2W_b + 1W_c = 0$$

$$2W_a + 1W_b + 3W_c = 0$$

$$1W_a + 1W_b + 1W_c = 1$$

where W_a is the proportion of funds invested in security a, etc. The first two equations require that portfolio sensitivity to factors 1 and 2 be zero, while the third equation requires that these three securities comprise the entire portfolio. Solving these simultaneous equations gives the solution $W_a = 5$, $W_b = -1$, and $W_c = -3$. Negative proportions for securities b and c imply short-sales of those assets.

The portfolio constructed with these proportions is risk-free, because risk is captured through sensitivity to factors. Since the portfolio is risk-free, it must provide the risk-free return. We see that this condition is satisfied:

$$E(R_p) = 5(.35) - 1(.30) - 3(.45) = \underline{\underline{.10}}$$

An increase or decrease in the expected return of any security that takes it away from the expected return specified in Equation 15-1 allows us to create a risk-free portfolio paying a return other than the risk-free rate. Suppose, for example, the expected return for security a is 40 percent. The expected return for the risk-free portfolio is therefore:

$$E(R_p) = 5(.40) - 1(.30) - 3(.45) = \underline{\underline{.35}}$$

A risk-free portfolio paying more or less than the risk-free return cannot exist in equilibrium,[5] so in equilibrium no security can have an expected return that violates Equation 15-2.

If you are left with a nagging doubt about the possibility of some other, unimagined, equilibrium involving offsetting violations of Equation 15-2 by more than one security, see Ross's previously cited article for a formal derivation of Equation 15-2 as the only possible equilibrium position.

Equation 15-2 depends on the existence of unitary sensitivity portfolios, and people considering the APT for the first time are sometimes concerned about the existence of such portfolios in the real world. The creation of such portfolios simply involves a simultaneous equation problem. For the previous example, the three securities can be combined to create unitary sensitivity portfolios for each factor. The unitary sensitivity portfolio for factor 1 is found by simultaneously solving the following set of equations:

$$1W_a + 2W_b + 1W_c = 1$$
$$2W_a + 1W_b + 3W_c = 0$$
$$1W_a + 1W_b + 1W_c = 1$$

Solving these simultaneous equations gives the portfolio with unitary sensitivity to factor 1, and no sensitivity to factor 2: $W_a = 3$, $W_b = 0$, and $W_c = -2$. A portfolio with unitary sensitivity to factor 2 can be created with equal ease. To create unitary sensitivity portfolios in practice, the only requirement is that there be one more nonredundant security than there are factors for which unitary sensitivity portfolios are needed. A security is nonredundant if its characteristics— betas with regard to all factors—cannot be duplicated by some combination of the other securities being considered.[6]

Like the CAPM, the APT provides a statement of the relationship between equilibrium expected return and sensitivity to certain factors affecting return. The APT is, therefore, an alternative to the CAPM for determining a risk-adjusted required return for capital investment analysis. Its relevance is the same as that of the CAPM in that they both provide information about the same vari-

---

[5]Had the expected return for security a been less than the equilibrium required return, the portfolio would be risk free and would have a return below the risk-free rate. Short-selling of this portfolio would be a way to borrow below the risk-free rate.

[6]A set of nonredundant assets can be constructed step-wise. Following the selection of any asset as the starting position, assets are added one at a time, with each potential new asset checked for redundancy through an attempt to replicate that asset's characteristics with some combination of assets already selected. Security c in the example would be redundant to a and b if there was a solution to the simultaneous equation problem:

$$1W_a + 2W_b = 1$$
$$2W_a + 1W_b = 3$$
$$W_a + W_b = 1$$

able: risk-adjusted required return. The choice between the two depends on accuracy and ease of use.

Note that if there is only one factor, and the portfolio with unitary sensitivity to that factor is the market portfolio, Equation 15-2 reduces to the CAPM formula for the relationship between beta for an investment and required return for that investment. The general form of the APT, though, makes no assumption about the number of factors, economic nature of the factors, or the portfolios with unitary sensitivity to those factors. In fact, the factors are generally constructed using the statistical tool of factor analysis[7] applied to returns for past periods. The objective of factor analysis is to explain variances in individual observations (security returns in our case) by statistically searching out a limited number of factors that explain a high percentage of variance. These factors may be thought of as indexes, in the same way we think of stock price indexes or consumer price indexes, because a single factor may capture a whole set of influences. A factor does not necessarily correlate with any single real economic variable, such as stock market returns or interest rates, although it is generally assumed that the factors represent real economic variables.[8]

To determine a risk-adjusted required return, the APT can be applied using securities that have been publicly traded over a historical period of sufficient length. The process is somewhat analogous to that using the CAPM with historical data, but more time-consuming. First, a sample set of securities is selected. Then, returns are collected for each security in the sample for each of a number of historical holding periods. Factor analysis of the data is then performed using a commercially available computer program. The result is a set of factors that are common to returns for all securities.

Once the factor analysis is completed, the same sample set of securities, or a different sample set, is used to construct a unitary sensitivity portfolio for each factor. The first step in constructing these portfolios is to compute $\beta_{s,n}$s relating each security to each factor. The construction of these unitary sensitivity portfolios is a simultaneous equation problem, as previously illustrated, that can be solved using matrix algebra.

Once the unitary sensitivity portfolios are constructed, the difference between historical return for each portfolio and the historical risk-free return is used as the risk premium for that factor: $[E(R_n) - R_f]$. Alternately, expected return for each portfolio could be estimated from published forecasts of returns for the assets in the portfolio. This latter approach has been used for the market portfolio in mean-variance CAPM tests, but no studies of this type have yet appeared in the APT literature.

The $\beta_{s,n}$s for an investment that is being considered can be constructed using historical data or can be estimated by analysts who attempt to predict how

[7]See, for example, T. W. Anderson, *An Introduction to Multivariate Statistical Analysis,* 2nd ed. (New York: John Wiley and Sons, 1984).

[8]The assumption that factors represent real economic variables is made strongly by Richard Roll and Stephen A. Ross in "A Critical Reexamination of the Empirical Evidence on the Arbitrage Pricing Theory: A Reply," *Journal of Finance* 39 (June 1984): 347–350.

the particular asset will respond to factors affecting each unitary sensitivity portfolio. If one is attempting to develop a risk-adjusted required return for a company, the historical $\beta_{s,n}$s may be used. If one is attempting to develop a risk-adjusted required return for a division, nonpublic company, or major capital investment, the pure play approach discussed in Chapter 14 can be used. One or more companies that are believed to have similar characteristics can be identified and their $\beta_{s,n}$s can be used as the estimated $\beta_{s,n}$s. State-based analysis can also be used. Return for each unitary sensitivity portfolio and return for the asset can be estimated in each state of nature, then the $\beta_{s,n}$s can be computed as was explained for a single beta in Chapter 14. Once the $\beta_{s,n}$s for the asset of interest are determined, the required return is then computed using Equation 15-2.

The APT has potential accuracy advantages over the CAPM in that it is based on less restrictive assumptions about investor preferences. The APT also has the advantage of being a directly testable theory.[9]

TESTS OF THE APT

On the critical question of accuracy, the evidence is still incomplete. Evidence that the APT is a more accurate predictor of returns than the CAPM for public utility stocks has been presented by Roll and Ross,[10] by Bower, Bower, and Logue,[11] and by Pettway and Jordan.[12] Chen also found that the firm size effect that often shows up as a disturbance in CAPM models was eliminated when using APT.[13] In considering these test results, it is important to keep in mind that the tests suffer from some of the same problems that plague the CAPM tests. Specifically, both sets of tests rely on historical returns and relationships as surrogates for expected returns and expected relationships.

The validity of most tests of the APT has been called into question. Conway and Reinganum observed that empirical tests of the APT have used the same

[9]See, for example, Adam K. Gehr, Jr., "Some Tests of the Arbitrage Pricing Theory," *Journal of the Midwest Finance Association* (1975): 91–105; Richard Roll and Stephen Ross, "An Empirical Investigation of the Arbitrage Pricing Theory," *Journal of Finance* 35 (December 1980): 1073–1103; Nai-Fu Chen, "Some Empirical Tests of the Theory of Arbitrage Pricing," *Journal of Finance* 38 (December 1983): 1393–1414; P. Dhrymes, Irwin Friend, and B. Gultekin, "A Critical Reexamination of the Empirical Evidence on the Arbitrage Pricing Theory," *Journal of Finance* 39 (June 1984): 323–346, and a reply to Dhrymes et al. by Roll and Ross in the same volume.

[10]Richard Roll and Stephen Ross, "Regulation, the Capital Asset Pricing Model, and the Arbitrage Pricing Theory," *Public Utilities Fortnightly* (May 26, 1983): 22–28.

[11]D. Bower, R. Bower, and D. Logue, "Arbitrage Pricing Theory and Utility Stock Returns," *Journal of Finance* 39 (September 1984): 1041–1054.

[12]Richard H. Pettway and Bradford D. Jordan, "APT vs. CAPM Estimates of the Return-Generating Function Parameters for Regulated Public Utilities," *Journal of Financial Research* 10 (Fall 1987): 227–238.

[13]Chen, "Some Empirical Tests of the Theory of Arbitrage Pricing."

sample of securities to create factors and measure the relationship between return and factor sensitivity. Conway and Reinganum performed a cross-validation test in which the model was tested on a sample different from that used to identify factors. They found only one factor that affected required return. This raises questions about earlier studies in which required return was found to be affected by sensitivity to numerous factors.[14]

We discover again that there are no free-lunches. The generality and possible increased accuracy of the APT are only achieved at a cost. A multifactor APT model is more difficult and expensive to use than the CAPM. Instead of estimating one market beta or simply looking up the beta in a published source, it is necessary to go through factor analysis of a large number of securities to develop $\beta_{s,n}$s. Instead of estimating the risk premium for the market portfolio, it is necessary to construct a set of unitary sensitivity portfolios and then estimate a required return for each portfolio. Using CAPM to estimate the required return on equity for a company with a published beta requires only a few minutes. Using APT to estimate the required return for the same company may take months.

In addition to simply requiring substantially more effort, and therefore expense, the APT's appeal is limited by difficulties in giving economic interpretation to the factors. It may be difficult to estimate the sensitivity of a nontraded security or capital investment to a factor or a unitary sensitivity portfolio when the factor has not been given economic interpretation, and there is no obvious logic to the unitary sensitivity portfolio. A model in which required return is determined by sensitivity to undefined factors may be tough to sell to practicing managers.

The problems cited in the last two paragraphs are current information problems and may be subject to solution through empirical research. The lack of economic interpretation for the factors has been and is being addressed by researchers. The general approach is to attempt to find economic series such as Gross National Product growth, stock market returns, and inflation rates that are highly correlated with historically determined factors. If such surrogates are found, they simplify the problem of computing $\beta_{s,n}$s and constructing unitary sensitivity portfolios. The identification of surrogates also makes it easier to predict the response of a new capital investment to factor movements. An analyst may feel reasonably comfortable in predicting a capital investment's response to Gross National Product change, while predicting sensitivity to an unknown statistical construct called factor three is impossible. Last, but not least, the identification of surrogate economic variables allows a logical economic interpretation of the model that should greatly increase the acceptance by practitioners.

Important work on the identification of economic surrogates for factors has been and is being conducted. Empirical research in this area consists of first carrying out the factor analysis as previously described, and then searching for economic series that are highly correlated with individual factors. In a widely

---

[14]Delores A. Conway and Marc R. Reinganum, "Capital Market Factor Structure: Identification through Cross Validation," University of Chicago Graduate School of Business Working Paper #183, July 1986.

cited study, Chen, Roll, and Ross found four factors[15] and found those factors to be highly correlated with the following economic variables:

1. Industrial production or the return on the market portfolio.
2. Changes in the risk premium indicated by the difference between Aaa and Baa corporate bonds.
3. The slope of the yield curve, represented by differences between yields to maturity on long-term and short-term government bonds.
4. Unanticipated inflation.[16]

Numerous other studies are being and have been carried out with the objective of identifying economic counterparts of factors.[17] Unfortunately, the studies carried out to date have not resulted in anything approaching a consensus on either the number of priced factors or their economic counterparts.

As an understanding of the number of factors and their economic counterparts is developed, it will become easier to compute historical $\beta_{s,n}$s and to estimate $\beta_{s,n}$s for assets that do not have a history of holding period returns from public trading. In a few years, a practitioner may turn to *Value Line Investment Survey* and find listed below the market beta a series of betas relating securities to key economic variables. Just as research has given us indications of the required return for the market portfolio, empirical research can provide indications of the required returns as risk premiums for sensitivity to other economic variables. When information of this type becomes available through empirical research, the APT may provide superior estimates of value and required return while being nearly as easy to use as is the CAPM at present.

STATE-BASED ARBITRAGE ANALYSIS OF CAPITAL INVESTMENTS

Ross suggested a direct valuation of capital investments by finding a portfolio that would provide identical cash flows to the proposed capital investment in all conditions. The net present value is the cost of the asset subtracted from the cost of the portfolio of publicly traded securities that will replicate its cash flows.[18]

---

[15]Dhrymes, Friend, and Gultekin ["Critical Reexamination," and "New Tests of the APT and Their Implications," *Journal of Finance* 40 (July 1985): 659–675] took strong exception to the conclusion that there are only a few priced factors. They argued that the empirical studies suffered from insufficient sample size and other problems.

[16]Nai-Fu Chen, Richard W. Roll, and Stephen A. Ross, "Economic Forces and the Stock Market: Testing the APT and Alternative Asset Pricing Theories," UCLA Working Paper #20-83, December 1983.

[17]See, for example, Conway and Reinganum, "Capital Market Factor Structure"; S. Kandel and G. Huberman, "A Size Based Stock Returns Model," working paper, University of Chicago Graduate School of Business; and J. Shanken and M. I. Weinstein, "Testing Multifactor Pricing Relationships with Prespecified Factors," working paper, University of Southern California Graduate School of Business.

[18]Stephen A. Ross, "A Simple Approach to the Valuation of Risky Streams," *Journal of Business* (July 1979): 254–286.

To apply Ross's suggestion, Gehr demonstrated the use of a set of discrete states of nature that approximate the continual distribution of returns.[19] When managers at Sohio were considering the purchase of North Slope oil leases, for example, they could have used several economic growth scenarios along with two OPEC cartel scenarios—success or collapse of the price control mechanism—to create a set of six discrete states for analysis. The discrete state approach is an extension of the approach used at the beginning of this chapter to value payoffs from a coin toss. The discrete state method avoids assumptions of linear relationships and may be easier to apply in some cases.

To apply the discrete state approach to a capital investment, m states of nature and m nonredundant alternate investments are identified. The investments can, for example, be publicly traded securities. Cash flow per dollar invested for each alternative investment in each state of nature is estimated. The portfolio that will duplicate the cash flow from the proposed capital investment in each state of nature is found by solving for the a_m in the simultaneous equation problem:

$$a_1 r_{1,1} + a_2 r_{1,2} + \ldots + a_m r_{1,m} = CF_1$$

$$a_1 r_{2,1} + a_2 r_{2,2} + \ldots + a_m r_{2,m} = CF_2$$

$$\vdots \qquad\qquad\qquad \vdots \qquad\quad \vdots$$

$$a_1 r_{m,1} + a_2 r_{m,2} + \ldots + a_m r_{m,m} = CF_m \qquad\qquad (15\text{-}3)$$

where $r_{i,m}$ is the estimated cash flow per dollar invested in asset m if state of nature i occurs, a_m is the amount invested in asset m, and CF_i is the expected cash flow from the candidate capital investment if state i occurs; each column represents an investment and each row represents a state of nature. Each equation requires that the portfolio provide the same cash flow as the capital investment in one state of nature. The sum of the a_js is the amount that must be invested in the alternate assets to duplicate the returns from the candidate capital investment. The cost of the proposed capital investment is subtracted from the cost of this portfolio to find the net present value of the capital investment.

Example. Assume Findlay Industries uses four states of nature in estimating annual cash flows from investments:

State	Description
1	Expanding economy and rising inflation
2	Expanding economy and decreasing inflation
3	Recession and decreasing inflation
4	Recession and increasing inflation

---

[19]Adam K. Gehr, Jr., "Risk-Adjusted Capital Budgeting Using Arbitrage," *Financial Management* 10 (Winter 1981): 14–19.

Those states include the primary factors that affect Findlay's success. Managers at Findlay perform risk analysis by determining each year's expected cash flow from a proposed capital investment in each state, rather than relying on a single estimate of annual cash flows. To apply arbitrage valuation, managers selected four industry common stock indexes to represent portfolios of common stock, and computed year-end cash flow in each state of nature per dollar invested in each portfolio at the beginning of the year (effectively assuming that the factors that affect returns on these broad-based industry portfolios are stable from year to year). Annual cash flows from a capital investment in each state, as well as year-end cash flow per dollar invested in each state, appear in Table 15.2.

Recall that the objective in arbitrage valuation is to find the amount that must be invested elsewhere to duplicate the cash flows from this capital investment. Let V_t be the total amount that must be invested in the alternate portfolios at the beginning of year t to duplicate cash flows from the proposed capital investment in each state at the end of year t. This amount can be found by solving Equations 15-3 once for each year. Taking year 3, for example, we would solve the following set of simultaneous equations:

$$1.50a_1 + 1.09a_2 + 1.25a_3 + 0.60a_4 = 20,000$$

$$0.40a_1 + 1.65a_2 + 1.65a_3 + 1.65a_4 = 30,000$$

$$1.26a_1 + 1.15a_2 + 0.55a_3 + 0.45a_4 = 20,000$$

$$1.65a_1 + 0.35a_2 + 0.35a_3 + 0.85a_4 = 10,000$$

The solution to this set of equations is $a_1 = \$1,344$, $a_2 = \$14,653$, $a_3 = 138$, and $a_3 = 3,065$. Therefore:

$$V_3 = \$1,344 + \$14,653 + \$138 + \$3,065 = \underline{\underline{\$19,200}}$$

The alternate portfolio will cost $19,200 at the beginning of year 3.

| **TABLE 15.2** **CAPITAL INVESTMENT INFORMATION FOR FINDLAY INDUSTRIES**

This table contains expected annual cash flows from a capital investment in each state as well as year-end cash flow per dollar invested in each state for four common stock portfolios.

	CASH FLOW FROM CAPITAL INV.			**YEAR-END IND. PORTFOLIO CASH FLOWS***			
State	**Year 1**	**Year 2**	**Year 3**	**Port. 1**	**Port. 2**	**Port. 3**	**Port. 4**
1	15,000	18,000	20,000	1.50	1.09	1.25	0.60
2	24,000	27,000	30,000	0.40	1.65	1.65	1.65
3	16,000	17,000	20,000	1.26	1.15	0.55	0.45
4	8,000	9,000	10,000	1.65	0.35	0.35	0.85

*Per $1 invested at the beginning of the year.

The amount that must be invested today in order to buy the alternate portfolio at the beginning of year t is then $V_t/(1 + R_f)^{t-1}$, where R_f is the risk-free interest rate. If the risk-free rate is 9 percent, the amount that must be invested elsewhere today in order to duplicate the capital investment's cash flows at the end of year 3 is:

$$19,200/1.09^2 = \underline{\$16,160}$$

This process can then be repeated for the other two years to generate the amount that must be invested today to duplicate all future cash flows from the proposed investment. The net present value is the initial outlay for the proposed capital investment, subtracted from the amount that must be invested elsewhere to duplicate that investment's cash flows.

A problem with this approach is tedium. For a 30-year investment, it is necessary to solve the set of simultaneous equations 30 times, and the process must be repeated for each proposed capital investment. Fortunately, the process can be speeded up by finding the amount that must be invested at the start of a year to generate cash flow of $1 at the end of the year if state i occurs, and nothing if any other state occurs. Repeating this for each state gives us a set of factors to multiply directly against state-dependent cash flows to avoid repeated solutions of simultaneous equations. For example, the amount that must be invested at the start of a year to receive $1 at the end of the year if state 1 occurs, and nothing otherwise, is found by modifying the right-hand side of Equations 15-3 as follows:

$$1.50a_1 + 1.09a_2 + 1.25a_3 + 0.60a_4 = 1$$

$$0.40a_1 + 1.65a_2 + 1.65a_3 + 1.65a_4 = 0$$

$$1.26a_1 + 1.15a_2 + 0.55a_3 + 0.45a_4 = 0$$

$$1.65a_1 + 0.35a_2 + 0.35a_3 + 0.85a_4 = 0$$

The solution to this set of equations is $a_1 = \$0.276580$, $a_2 = -\$0.663653$, $a_3 = \$1.462383$, and $a_3 = -\$0.865780$. Letting A_i be the amount that must be invested at the beginning of a year to generate $1 at the end of the year if state i occurs, and nothing otherwise:

$$A_1 = \$0.276580 - \$0.663653 + \$1.462383 - \$0.865780 = \$0.209530$$

This process is repeated for each of the other states by changing the row in which 1 appears on the right-hand side of Equations 15-3, to give us the set of factors:

$$A_1 = \$0.209530$$

$$A_2 = \$0.368550$$

$$A_3 = \$0.055874$$

$$A_4 = \$0.283564$$

These factors can now be multiplied directly against the capital investment's cash flows at the end of year t to provide the amount that must be invested elsewhere to duplicate those cash flows. The net present value becomes:

$$NPV = (\sum_{t=1}^{n} A_1 CF_{t,1} + A_2 CF_{t,2} + \ldots + A_m CF_{t,m})/(1 + R_f)^{t-1} - I_o \qquad (15\text{-}4)$$

where m is the number of states being used, $CF_{t,m}$ is cash flow from the capital investment in year t if state m occurs, and I_o is the initial outlay required. If Findlay is considering several hundred capital investments, the same A_ms can be used for all of the capital investments. It is only necessary to estimate cash flow for each investment each year in each state.

Findlay's capital investment costs $40,000, so the net present value is:

NPV = (15,000 × .209530 + 24,000 × .368550 + 16,000 × .055874 + 8,000
    × .283564) + (18,000 × .209530 + 27,000 × .386550 + 17,000
    × .055874 + 9,000 × .283564)/1.09¹ + (20,000 × .209530 + 30,000
    × .386550 + 20,000 × .055874 + 10,000 × .283564)/1.09² − 40,000
    = $7,113

The state-based arbitrage approach has several appealing features. Many risk analysis methods currently in use rely on identifying a set of scenarios and estimating return in each scenario. This approach is, therefore, an extension of familiar techniques. In addition, many managers are uncomfortable with the probability estimates necessary to go beyond scenario analysis and compute the expected values or standard deviations needed for some risk analysis methods. This approach avoids the problem of estimating probabilities. Some estimates of probabilities by the investing public are implied in the prices of the various securities, but these probabilities need not be discovered to perform an arbitrage valuation of a capital investment using the state approach. This approach is also free of the assumptions about linear relations to factors that are used in the APT. As with other arbitrage analysis forms, the state-based approach is free from assumptions about utility functions or degrees of risk aversion.

ARBITRAGE PRICING AND CERTAINTY EQUIVALENTS

The choice between certainty equivalents and risk-adjusted discount rates as practical capital budgeting tools has been debated for years. With risk-adjusted discount rates, expected cash flows are discounted to the present using a discount rate appropriate for the degree of risk involved. The use of risk-adjusted discount rates is usually based on the assumption of constant systematic risk, so that the same discount rate can be used for each future period, and this assumption is not always justified. Use of certainty equivalents avoids this problem. The year t *certainty equivalent* is the certain amount at the end of year t which, if discounted at the risk-free rate, is as desirable as the probability distribution of cash flows for year t. No assumptions about stability of risk for the proposed investment are needed to justify the certainty equivalents. Unfortunately, though, application of the certainty-equivalent approach has been hampered by the lack of a method for measuring the certainty equivalent.

Arbitrage pricing principles provide a way to measure certainty equivalents. In the Findlay Industries example, V_t was the amount that must be invested in the alternate portfolios at the *beginning* of year t to duplicate the year t cash flows from the proposed investment. The amount that must be invested today to duplicate those cash flows is therefore $V_t/(1 + R_f)^{t-1}$. The certainty equivalent for year t (CE_t) is the certain amount at the *end* of year t, which, when discounted to the present at the risk-free rate, is as attractive as the probability distribution of cash flows for the proposed investment at the end of year t. Therefore:

$$CE_t = V_t(1 + R_f)$$

and

$$NPV = CE_t \sum_{t=1}^{n} /(1 + R_f)^t - I_o$$

Arbitrage pricing models offer distinct advantages over the mean-variance capital asset pricing model in that they do not depend on restrictive assumptions and can easily handle multiperiod cash flows involved in capital investment analysis. The primary disadvantages of the arbitrage pricing model, relative to the mean-variance capital asset pricing model, are related to questions that may be answered with additional empirical research. As the nature of the underlying factors becomes better understood, arbitrage pricing models may replace the mean-variance capital asset pricing model for much decision making.

OPTION PRICING MODELS (OPMs)

An *option* is a contract giving the holder the right to buy or sell an asset for a predetermined price. Interest in options was heightened in 1973 when the Chicago Board of Trade began organized trading in options on specified common stocks. Options have special characteristics which result in the need for special valuation tools. A widely recognized option pricing model was developed in that year by Black and Scholes.[20] It was soon recognized that common stock and debt share important characteristics with options.

---

[20]Fisher Black and Myron Scholes, "The Pricing of Options and Corporate Liabilities," *Journal of Political Economy* 81 (May–June 1973): 637–654.

OPMs are complementary to the mean-variance capital asset pricing model and arbitrage pricing models. The other two models focus on sensitivity to factors affecting returns on investments in general. OPMs focus on the role of total risk in valuing various claims against the stream of cash flows. Changes in nonsystematic risk often change the value of claims—debt and equity—even if they do not affect the overall value of the company. If capital budgeting is carried out with the objective of maximizing shareholder wealth, these changes in relative values are important. Thus, OPMs provide useful insights for capital budgeting, financing of capital investments, and management compensation.

This section begins with some basic definitions. Then, a two-state OPM is used to develop the basic principles of option valuation. Following this, the more general Black-Scholes OPM is explained. Empirical evidence on the model is surveyed and application of the model to selection and financing of capital investments is covered.

SOME BASIC TERMINOLOGY

To move along with minimum difficulty, it is helpful to provide a brief glossary of terminology at the outset.

Call option: an option to buy an asset.

Put option: an option to sell an asset.

Exercise of an option: the buying or selling of the asset as provided for in the option contract.

Exercise price (striking price): the price at which the asset can be bought or sold, as stated in the option contract.

Expiration date: the last day on which the option may be exercised. Most option contracts are not open-ended, and have a specific expiration date.

European option: an option that can be exercised only on the expiration date.

American option: an option that can be exercised at any time prior to its expiration date.

Writer: the person who sells an option contract to another, thereby granting the buyer an option to buy or sell the asset at the exercise price under the terms specified in the contract.

OPTIONS ILLUSTRATED

An options theoretician finds options everywhere. Many financial contracts are not called options, but have the major characteristics of options. Direct options and financial contracts that behave as options are discussed in the following paragraphs.

Publicly traded options. The options most widely recognized in the public press are options on common stocks. While options on common stocks have existed in limited supply for many years, public trading of these options began on the Chicago Board of Trade in 1973 and spread rapidly to other exchanges. In addition to providing a market for buying and selling, the Chicago Board of Trade standardized options in terms of exercise price and maturity. This greatly enhanced trading.

On October 5, 1993, IBM stock was trading for $43.75 a share. The prices of twelve different IBM options on that same day follow:

| | Strike price | CALL OPTION PRICES | | | PUT OPTION PRICES | | |
Maturity:		Oct.	Nov.	Jan.	Oct.	Nov.	Jan.
	40	$3\frac{3}{4}$	$4\frac{1}{8}$	5	$\frac{1}{16}$	$\frac{5}{8}$	$1\frac{1}{4}$
	45	$\frac{5}{16}$	$1\frac{1}{4}$	$2\frac{1}{4}$	$1\frac{5}{8}$	$2\frac{7}{16}$	$3\frac{1}{2}$

We will focus on the January option with a $45 striking price. If IBM stock is selling for more than $45 on the January expiration date, the call option will be valuable because the holder can buy IBM stock below the prevailing market price; otherwise the option will be worthless. The price of the option today reflects investors' assessments of the likelihood of its having value on the expiration date. The January put option will be valuable on the expiration date if the price of IBM stock is less than $45; the put option allows the holder to sell stock above the prevailing market price in that case. Writers and buyers of options may be investors with different expectations, different risk-return utility functions, or different risks against which they want to hedge.

If you own IBM stock on October 5, and want to reduce risk, you can write a $45 January call option and receive $2.25. If the price of the stock falls or only increases moderately, you improve your income for the 3-month period by $2.25. The tradeoff is that if the stock is over $45, the option buyer will exercise the option and buy the stock from you for $45, thereby limiting your profits. The option buyer may be a speculator who hopes for a high return. If the price of IBM stock rises to $60 by expiration date, for example, the option buyer exercises the option by buying the stock for $45, and then immediately resells the stock for $60. The speculator's profit is the gain on the stock sale, minus the cost of the option: $15 − $2.25 = $12.75. The return on the original option investment is $12.75 ÷ $2.25 = 567 percent.

Many option contracts do not involve publicly traded securities. When Delta entered into a contract with McDonnell-Douglas for 140 MD11s, Delta contracted to purchase some of the airplanes and received options on the rest. This gave Delta a predictable cost structure for the completion of its fleet and the income McDonnell-Douglas received for selling the contracts decreased its risk exposure by helping with the recovery of development costs.

Options are commonly used in real estate development. A developer will often purchase an option on land, then work out detailed plans and secure financing. This arrangement limits the developer's risk exposure and capital requirements during the planning phase while also avoiding the risk that the land will not be available on acceptable terms after the planning is completed. The land owner is, of course, allowed to keep the amount paid for the option if the purchase is not completed. Furthermore, the land owner can probably get a higher price through the option arrangement than a developer would be willing to pay for a direct purchase.

OTHER ASSETS AS OPTIONS

Assets such as corporate debt also have the characteristics of options. Capital structure and capital investment decisions can often be improved by taking advantage of the option characteristics of the assets. Many other contracts can be usefully analyzed as options.

Common stock. This is considered to be an option on the firm itself. If the firm is worth more than the amount owed when debt matures, the stockholders exercise their option to repay the debt and keep the residual value for themselves. If the firm is worth less than the amount of debt at maturity, the stockholders turn the firm over to the creditors. Companies like Wickes, LTV, and Continental Airlines have taken this latter course. These actions do not necessarily result in liquidation because the creditors may decide the firm is worth more as a going concern than it is worth in liquidation. Because common stock is effectively an option, options written on common stock are therefore options on options.

Debt. If common stockholders effectively hold an option, then creditors effectively purchased the firm and wrote an option in the form of common stock. Whirlpool's creditors, for example, put up $850 million of their own money and turned over control of the company to the stockholders who paid $1,350 million for their option to buy the company back from the creditors for $850 million. In an equilibrium market in which arbitrage profits are not possible, the value of the debt is the value of the firm, minus the value of the option in the form of common stock. Later in this chapter, we will use an option pricing model to determine the required interest rate on risky debt.

Contingent claims. Many investments and contracts call for payment if certain conditions occur. Even if these contracts are not strictly options, they can be valued as substitutes for options with the same payment characteristics. For example, the bulk of Lee Iaccoca's $21 million income for 1986 was a result of contract provisions making his income dependent on the success of Chrysler Corporation. A manager's position may be perceived as paying a fixed amount plus a percent of profits if profit exceeds a satisfactory level, and zero otherwise—managers can be fired for unsatisfactory performance. The impact of a change in unsystematic risk on the value of the manager's contract may be entirely different from the impact on the value of the common stock. Later in this chapter, the use of an option pricing model to design a management compensation contract will be illustrated.

Capital investments. Many capital investments have option characteristics. Research programs and test-marketing of new products are classic examples of investments which create the opportunity to make additional, larger investments. Boeing's development efforts for the 7J7 airplane are an example. Rather than committing to a $3 billion production plan, the company committed to a $100 million, 3-year development program. This $100 million capital investment gave Boeing the option to acquire a $3 billion investment. As it turned out, management decided not to exercise the option, and did not go into production.

GRAPHICAL VIEW OF OPTIONS

Figure 15.1 graphically illustrates the nature of a call option. The area under the curve represents the entire probability distribution of values of the asset as of the option expiration date. The exercise price is the maximum that can be received by the person who owns the asset and wrote an option. The net amount received by the option buyer on the expiration date is the amount by which the value of the asset on that date exceeds the exercise price. Thus, a call option is simply the sale of part of the probability distribution of returns. Specifically, the shaded area to the right of the exercise price is the portion of the distribution that has been sold. Let P in Figure 15.1 be the exercise price of a put option. The holder of the IBM stock who writes a put option will be assured of receiving at least price P for the stock. Buying a put option, then, consists of paying someone to accept the risk of value being in some lower portion of the distribution.

| **FIGURE 15.1** **GRAPHICAL REPRESENTATION OF AN OPTION CONTRACT**

The area under the curve is the entire probability distribution of the asset's value on the option's expiration date. The shaded area is the portion of probability distribution of value that has been sold via the call option contract.

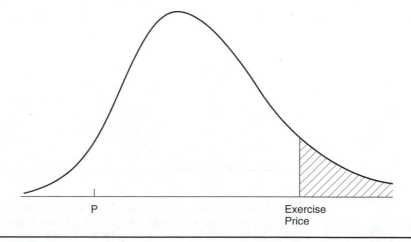

A TWO-STATE OPTION PRICING MODEL

A two-state option model is helpful in understanding the general principles of option valuation, and the implications of the OPM for capital budgeting and financing decisions.[21] This model assumes that there is only one period (however that period is defined) and there are only two possible values of the underlying asset at the end of that period—the option's expiration date. In addition, this model incorporates the assumptions inherent in some more general option pricing models:

1. The financial markets are frictionless, with no transaction costs and with information freely available to all.
2. There are no restrictions on short-sales.
3. There are no dividends or other cash disbursements to the owners of the asset prior to the option's expiration date.
4. There are no opportunities for arbitrage profits; specifically, there are no opportunities to make risk-free investments earning above the risk-free rate.

To develop the price of a call option in a two-state world, we use a share of stock. The present price of the stock (S_o) is $50 a share. At the end of one period, the stock will have one of two values. The value if the stock goes up (S_u) is $60 and the value if the stock goes down (S_d) is $40. This situation is presented graphically in Figure 15.2.

| **FIGURE 15.2** **STOCK PRICES IN A SIMPLE TWO-STATE MODEL**

S_o is the present price of the stock. S_u and S_d are the two possible prices at the end of the single period.

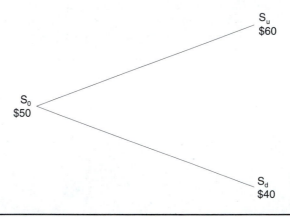

---

[21]The two-state model was developed by John C. Cox, Stephen A. Ross, and Mark Rubinstein, "Option Pricing: A Simplified Approach," *Journal of Financial Economics* 7 (September 1979): 229–263; and by Richard J. Rendleman, Jr., and Brit J. Bartter, "Two-State Option Pricing," *Journal of Finance* 34 (December 1979): 1093–1110.

Suppose a holder of one share of this stock decides to write (sell) call options against this stock. The stockholder writes q options and receives an amount of C per option. The options have an exercise price (E) of $45. If stock price S_d occurs, the option is worthless and the stockholder keeps stock worth $40. If stock price S_u occurs, the stockholder can sell the stock for $45 or buy back the options. The options will then be worth $(S_u - E)$ or $15 each. The stockholder's wealth will be the same whether she buys back the options or honors at least some of them by selling stock for $45. The initial investment and ending value amounts for the stockholder are summarized in Figure 15.3.

We want to find C, the market-clearing price of an option. To do this, we find the number of options the stockholder must write to create a risk-free investment. Specifically, we decide how many options the stockholder must write to receive the same amount whether S_u or S_d occurs. To do this, we first set wealth with S_u and S_d equal to each other:

$$S_u - q(S_u - E) = S_d$$

Then, we rearrange terms to solve for q:

$$q = (S_u - S_d)/(S_u - E) \tag{15-5}$$

For the example, $q = (60 - 40)/(60 - 45) = 1\frac{1}{3}$; writing $1\frac{1}{3}$ options will provide the same value in either state.

If the investment is to be risk-free, and arbitrage profits are not possible, the risk-free rate must be earned in either state. A risk-free return if S_d occurs means S_d must be greater than the initial net investment by the risk-free rate:

| **F I G U R E   1 5 . 3** | **RETURNS TO AN OPTION WRITER IN A SIMPLE TWO-STATE MODEL** |

The amount invested, after deducting the amount received for writing options, is shown on the left. The amount on the upper right is the amount received if the options are repurchased and the stock is sold for S_u. The amount on the lower right is the amount received for the stock with the options expiring unexercised.

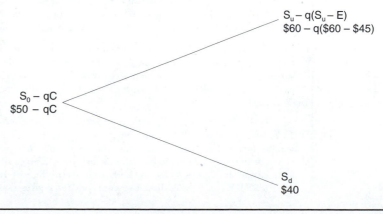

$S_u - q(S_u - E)$
$60 - q(\$60 - \$45)$

$S_0 - qC$
$50 - qC$

S_d
$40

$$(S_o - qC)(1 + R_f) = S_d$$

Rearranging terms gives:

$$C = \frac{S_o - S_d/(1 + R_f)}{q}$$

Substituting in for the value of q, as determined in Equation 15-5, the equilibrium value of the call option is:[22]

$$C = [S_o - S_d/(1 + R_f)](S_u - E)/(S_u - S_d) \tag{15-6}$$

Applying this formula to the example, the value of a call option is:

$$C = [50 - 40/1.1](60 - 45)/(60 - 40) = \$10.227$$

The beginning and ending wealth positions are then:

$$\text{Beginning net investment} = 50 - (4/3)10.227 = \$36.36$$

$$\text{Value in the case of } S_u = 60 - (4/3)(60 - 45) = \$40$$

$$\text{Value in the case of } S_d = \$40$$

Thus, the stockholder earns a risk-free return of 10 percent in either case.

If the investment were risk-free and did not earn a 10 percent return, the markets would not be in equilibrium and arbitrage opportunities would exist. An investor could earn infinite profits while accepting no risk by simply exploiting the arbitrage opportunity.[23]

Applying the same logic, the value of a put option is:[24]

$$P = [S_u/(1 + R_f) - S_o](E - S_d)/(S_u - S_d) \tag{15-7}$$

---

[22]We can confirm that if the call option is priced as indicated, the risk-free rate is also earned if S_u occurs. But confirmation is unnecessary because the value of the call was derived under the requirement that the amount received be the same whether S_u or S_d occurred.

[23]If the option is overpriced, for example, an investor would buy all the stock that was available and write call options against the stock. The investor would be able to borrow at a risk-free rate to support the investment since the position would be riskless. The positions would be reversed if the call option was underpriced. Thus, the investor could earn virtually unlimited returns with virtually no capital.

[24]To develop the price of a put option, we use the same terminology as used in Figures 15.1 and 15.2, adding the term P to represent the value of a put option. Assuming $S_d < E < S_u$, the initial amount invested by someone who buys the asset and buys q put options is $S_o + qP$. The amount received at the end of the period is either S_u or $S_d + q(E - S_d)$. To earn the same return in either state, it is necessary that $S_u = S_d + q(E - S_d)$. To earn the risk-free rate, it is necessary that $S_u = (S_o + qP)(1 + R_f)$. Solving these two equations for P gives Equation 15-6.

The simple two-state model can be used to identify the main factors that determine the value of an option. These factors can all be seen in Equations 15-6 and 15-7. The variables are:

- the starting price of the stock
- the two possible ending prices of the stock
- the risk-free rate
- the exercise price of the option

For a more general model, the two ending stock prices are replaced with the variance of the stock's probability distribution of returns and time until expiration of the option.

THE BLACK-SCHOLES OPTION PRICING MODEL

The Black-Scholes OPM allows valuation of an option when the underlying asset has a range of possible future values rather than just two possible values.[25] The Black-Scholes OPM uses the assumptions underlying the two-state model except that it substitutes a continuous distribution for a two-outcome discrete distribution of terminal asset values and allows the expiration date to be more than one period away. In addition to assuming frictionless markets, unrestricted short-selling, no cash payments on the underlying asset prior to option maturity, and no arbitrage profits, the Black-Scholes OPM requires the following additional assumptions:

1. The risk-free rate remains constant over time.
2. Assets are traded continuously.
3. Asset returns obey a stationary stochastic process over time[26] which results in asset return being lognormally distributed[27] for any finite period.

The Black-Scholes model focuses on European options, which can be exercised only at maturity; extensions of the model deal with American options and alternate patterns of price movement.[28] Black and Scholes employed the same

---

[25]Black and Scholes, "The Pricing of Options."

[26]A stationary stochastic returns process over time results in the mean and variance of the probability distribution of returns being the same for each period.

[27]In other words, the logarithms of the returns are normally distributed.

[28]See, for example, John C. Cox and Stephen A. Ross, "The Valuation of Options for Alternative Stochastic Processes," *Journal of Financial Economics* 3 (January–March 1976): 145–166; Robert Geske, "The Valuation of Compound Options," *Journal of Financial Economics* 7 (March 1979): 63–81; Robert Geske and Richard Roll, "On Valuing American Call Options with the Black-Scholes European Formula," *Journal of Finance* 39 (June 1984): 443–455; and Robert E. Whaley, "Valuation of American Futures Options: Theory and Empirical Tests," *Journal of Finance* 41 (March 1986): 127–150.

general approach used to value options in the two-state model. They determined the conditions necessary for a risk-free investment to provide the risk-free return. Given the set of assumptions and the requirement that a risk-free combination of securities and options must provide the risk-free rate of return, they derived the value of an option as:

$$C = S_o N(d_1) - [E \div e^{R_f T}]N(d_2) \qquad \text{(15-8)}$$

where

S_o is the current price of the stock

E is the exercise price of the option

R_f is the risk-free rate, continuously compounded

$N(d_i)$ is the value from the table of the normal distribution representing the probability of an outcome less than d_i

$d_1 = [\ln(S_o/E) + (R_f + .5\sigma_s^2)T]/(\sigma_s\sqrt{T})$

$d_2 = d_1 - (\sigma_s\sqrt{T})$

σ_s = standard deviation or the continuously compounded annual rate of return for the stock

T = time in years or fractions of years until the expiration date of the option e is 2.71828 . . . , the base of the natural logarithm

Although a proof of the Black-Scholes option pricing model is exceedingly time-consuming,[29] we can see the general characteristics by studying the components of Equation 15-8. For this purpose, it is helpful to adopt the perspective of a person who is choosing between an investment in the stock and purchase of the option. First, we note that the price of the option will increase with an increase in the price of the stock. This makes sense because a higher stock price means the option buyer saves more money by using the option to acquire a claim against future returns. Likewise, a higher interest rate increases the value of the option by increasing the advantage of spending only the cost of the option now and waiting to exercise the option if the stock price rises sufficiently. A higher variance of returns for the stock also increases the value of the option because a higher variance increases the probability that the ending stock price will be above the exercise price of the option. A higher variance also means a higher probability of a very low price, but that is the problem of the stockholder, not the option buyer. The value of an option also increases with an increase in

---

[29]For the proof of this model see Black and Scholes "The Pricing of Options," or James R. Garven, "A Pedagogic Note on the Derivation of the Black-Scholes Option Pricing Formula," *Financial Review* 21 (May 1986): 337–344.

the time until expiration. The longer the time until expiration, the greater the probability that the stock price will rise above the exercise price, and the greater the advantage of waiting to make the investment required to buy the stock. Finally, a lower exercise price makes an option more valuable for obvious reasons. The direction of relationship between each of these five factors and option price can be developed by armchair thought about options. Black and Scholes went the next step to develop the precise mathematical relationships between these five factors and option prices based on a specific set of assumptions about stock price movements.

Example. The stock of Howe Corporation is presently priced at $100 a share. A call option with nine months until expiration and an exercise price of $120 is currently available. The risk-free interest rate is 10 percent a year, continuously compounded. Month-end prices for the previous thirteen months appear in Table 15.3, along with the standard deviation of continuously compounded monthly returns. The value of the option is found as follows:

| **TABLE 15.3** STANDARD DEVIATION OF MONTHLY RETURNS

Month-end prices for Howe Corporation stock are shown for thirteen months. The continuously compounded monthly return for month t is $\ln(price_t/price_{t-1})$.* The standard deviation of monthly returns is then the standard deviation of the numbers in column 3.

(1)	(2)	(3)
Month	Month-end Price	Continuously Compounded Monthly Return
1	100	
2	120	0.18232
3	110	−0.08701
4	90	−0.20067
5	110	0.20067
6	120	0.08701
7	150	0.22314
8	120	−0.22314
9	120	0
10	130	0.08004
11	140	0.07411
12	130	−0.07411
13	120	−0.08004
Standard deviation		0.14420

*If dividends had been paid during month t, the holding period return would be $\ln[(price_t + dividend_t)/price_{t-1}]$. For the reasons for using the natural logarithm, see Equation 2-A-3 and the related discussion.

Standard deviation of continuously compounded annual return $= .144\sqrt{12} = .50$

$$d_1 = [\ln(100/120) + (.1 + .5 \times .5^2).75]/(.5\sqrt{.75}) = -.03134$$

$$d_2 = -.03134 - (.5\sqrt{.75}) = -.4644$$

$$N(d_1) = .4875$$

$$N(d_2) = .3212$$

$$C = 100(.4875) - [120 \div e^{.10 \times .75}].3212 = \underline{\$12.99}$$

EMPIRICAL EVIDENCE CONCERNING THE BLACK-SCHOLES OPM

To test or apply the option pricing model, it is necessary to find values for each of the variables. The risk-free rate, the exercise price, and the time until expiration are known, and the beginning stock price is known for a publicly traded stock. The unknown variable is the variance. The variance can be estimated by studying the variance of holding period returns for the stock for past periods, just as the beta is routinely estimated from past holding period returns for the mean-variance capital asset pricing model.

Numerous tests of the Black-Scholes OPM have been conducted,[30] and some biases have been found in tests of the model. Black and Scholes, for example, found that the model underpriced options on low-variance stocks and overpriced options on high-variance stocks. These results were confirmed by other authors, although the bias with regard to in-the-money and out-of-the-money options appeared to have changed over time.

Biases in the model may arise from misspecification, difficulty in developing the variance measure, or some unknown cause. The Black-Scholes OPM is based on options that can only be exercised at maturity and is based on the assumption that the underlying asset generates no cash flows—i.e., dividends prior to the expiration date. Some of the biases have been explained by using the Roll-Geske[31] dividend-adjusted model and some of the biases have been explained by

[30]See, for example, Fisher Black and Myron Scholes, "The Valuation of Option Contracts and a Test of Market Efficiency," *Journal of Finance* 27 (May 1972): 399–418; Fisher Black, "Fact and Fancy in the Use of Options," *Financial Analysts Journal* (July–August 1975): 61–72; James D. Macbeth and Larry J. Merville, "An Empirical Examination of the Black-Scholes Call Option Pricing Model," *Journal of Finance* 34 (December 1979): 1173–1186; James D. Macbeth and Larry J. Merville, "Tests of the Black-Scholes and Cox Option Valuation Models," *Journal of Finance* 35 (May 1980): 285–300; Mark Rubinstein, "Nonparametric Tests of Alternative Option Pricing Models Using All Reported Trades and Quotes on the 30 Most Active CBOE Option Classes from August 23, 1976, through August 31, 1978," *Journal of Finance* 40 (June 1985): 455–480; W. Sterk, "Tests of Two Models for Valuing Call Options on Stocks with Dividends," *Journal of Finance* 37 (December 1982): 1229–1237; and Whaley, "Valuation of American Futures Options."

[31]Richard A. Roll, "An Analytic Valuation Formula for Unprotected American Call Options with Known Dividends," *Journal of Financial Economics* 5 (November 1977): 251–258, and Robert Geske, "A Note on the Analytical Valuation Formula for Unprotected American Call Options on Stocks with Known Dividends," *Journal of Financial Economics* 7 (December 1979): 375–380.

using improved measures of variance. Securities priced out of equilibrium in an arbitrage context imply the opportunity for large profits, and nobody has been able to demonstrate superior profits by trading based on prices that are biased according to the Black-Scholes OPM.

USING OPTION PRICING MODELS IN THE SELECTION AND FINANCING OF CAPITAL INVESTMENTS

To apply OPMs to selection and financing of capital investments, we should recognize that a company's capital investments are the assets underlying the various financial claims against the company: common stock, preferred stock, debt, warrants, convertible bonds, etc. All the claims against the company are combinations of the asset (the total stream of cash flows generated by the asset, to be more precise), risk-free debt, call options, and put options. It will be demonstrated for the two-state case, and can be shown for the continuous case as well, that the risky debt of the company could be made risk-free by selling call options. Therefore, risky debt is effectively a combination of riskless debt and the purchase of call options. Stock is a call option giving the stockholders the right to reclaim the company from the creditors. Convertible bonds are combinations of bonds and call options. Warrants are pure call options.

The set of capital investments (the company itself) can be valued using present value analysis of cash flows, possibly applying the mean-variance capital asset pricing model or arbitrage theory to adjust for risk. The values of the individual claims can then be determined by breaking the claim down to components consisting of pure claims against the asset, risk-free debt, call options, and put options. If the objective in choosing and financing assets is to maximize shareholder wealth, it is necessary to consider both the impact of a capital investment on the total value of the company and the impact of the combined investment and financing decisions on the wealth of the shareholders. The use of the OPM in this context is illustrated in the following examples. The two-state model is used to simplify the illustrations, but the same conclusions could be reached with one of the continuous distribution OPMs.

Debt

One question when selecting assets is how those assets will affect the required returns on the various sources of capital. The mean-variance CAPM and arbitrage pricing theory were used to determine a required return for equity of an unleveraged company. Given a value of the total (unleveraged) company, the OPM can be used to determine the required interest rate on debt.

Suppose a company will be worth $1,950 if it is successful and $550 if it fails. The total (unleveraged) value of the company is currently $1,600. That value may simply be observed in the marketplace or it may have been determined by a method such as assigning probabilities to each of the possible outcomes and finding the present value of expected cash flows using the mean-variance capital asset pricing model to adjust for systematic risk. We do not need to know how the current value was determined though; we just need to know what it is.

The risk-free rate is 10 percent and the company wants to issue debt of $1,000. If the company issues debt, the creditors' position is the same as if they bought the company for $1,600 and sold an option to the stockholders for $600. The stockholders have the right to buy back the company if it is successful by paying off the debt. The exercise price of the option is the amount that must be paid to the creditors at the end of the period to eliminate their claims.

The call option price is the amount invested by the stockholders—the value of the company minus the amount of debt, or $600. The call price and other known factors are substituted into Equation 15-6, leaving only the exercise price unknown:

$$600 = [1,600 - 550/1.1](1,950 - E)/(1,950 - 550)$$

Solving for E gives $1,186. In other words, an equilibrium-priced debt contract will require the company to pay the creditors $1,186 if is successful, and the creditors will receive $550 if the company fails. Since this is a one-period model, the interest rate on the debt is therefore $(1,186 - 1,000)/1,000 =$ 18.6 percent for the period. Note that 18.6 percent is not the creditors' expected return, but the interest rate paid on the debt *if* the company does not default.

Stockholder Wealth and Risk Changes

OPMs are also useful for considering changes in risk. Suppose that after issuing the debt in the previous example, the company replaces one of its capital investments, changing its risk posture such that the value is $2,100 in the case of success and $400 in the case of failure. Suppose further that this change in risk posture increases systematic risk and therefore decreases the total value of the company to $1,550. The risk change decreases total value—the new asset has a negative net present value using normal capital budgeting methods. But the situation is different when viewed solely from the position of a stockholder.

Remembering that the stock is a call option, the value of the stock would increase to:

$$C = [1,550 - 400/1.1](2,100 - 1,186)/(2,100 - 400) = \$638$$

Since the total value of the company declined to $1,550 and the value of the stockholders' claim increased to $638, this implies that the value of the creditors' claim decreased to $1,550 - $638 = $912.[32]

---

[32]If the risk had been nonsystematic, so that it did not affect the total value of the company, the value of the shareholders' claim would have increased sharply to $665, and the value of the debt would have declined to $935.

As another example, consider a company that has a current total value of $1,000. The principal and interest due to the creditors at the end of one period is $500. The risk-free rate is 10 percent and the standard deviation of continuously compounded return for the company for the period is 50 percent. The stock is a call option against the company and is valued as follows:

$$d_1 = [\ln(1,000/500) + (.1 + .5 \times .5^2)1]/(.5\sqrt{1}) = 1.8363$$

$$d_2 = 1.8363 - .5\sqrt{1} = 1.3363$$

$$N(d_1) = .9668$$

$$N(d_2) = .9093$$

$$C = 1,000(.9668) - (500 \div e^{.1}).9093 = \underline{\$555}$$

The current value of the stock is therefore $555 while the current value of the debt is then $445. The coupon rate on the debt is then:

$$(500 - 445)/445 = 12.4\%$$

Suppose, now, the company changes its risk so that total value remains unchanged but the standard deviation of continuously compounded return increases to .60. Reworking the problem, the new value of C is $565. The change in standard deviation, while not changing the value of the company, increases the value of the stock by $10 and therefore decreases the value of the debt by $10. The required yield to maturity on the debt increases to $(500 - 435)/435 = 14.9$ percent.

The increased riskiness of the company hurts the creditors because the amount they receive if the company is successful remains unchanged while the probability of default increases and the amount they receive in the case of default decreases. Since the debt is already outstanding, the creditors cannot demand a higher interest rate from the company as compensation for the extra risk. The stockholders are in the opposite position: the amount they receive in the case of default remains at $0 while the amount they receive in the case of success increases. Thus, a capital investment may benefit the stockholders even if it decreases the value of the company.

Motivating Managers to Take Risks

The OPM can also be used to consider the motivation of managers to make capital investment and financing decisions. For the company in the two previous two-state examples, suppose the manager receives a salary of $100 if the company is successful and $0 if it fails; the manager is fired for failure. (The stated value of the company in the case of success is after paying the manager.) We start by looking at the beginning and possible ending values of the stockholders' claim in each case:

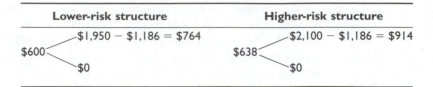

To determine if the manager would be happy with this change, we again look at the risk-free position. In this case, the manager can achieve a risk-free position through short-sales. With the low-risk structure, the manager could short-sell shares equal to $100/764 = 13$ percent of the value of the company. The manager would receive $.13 \times 600 = \$78$ immediately. In the case of success, the $100 salary would be just sufficient to settle the short position. In the case of failure, short-sold stock would be worthless; the manager would receive no salary and would not have to spend money to cover the short position. Thus, the present value of the compensation package is $78. Applying the same analysis to the high-risk situation, the present value of the compensation package is $(100/914)638 = \$70$. Even though the high-risk structure is better for shareholders, the manager is not likely to voluntarily make changes that will decrease the present value of the compensation package from $78 to $70.

To design a compensation package that will encourage the manager to choose the risk-return positions preferred by the shareholders, the present value of the compensation package must rise and fall with the present value of the shareholders' claim. With the low-risk structure, the present value of the combined owners' and manager's claims are $600 + $78 = $678; in other words, the manager's claim is worth $78/678 = 11.5$ percent of the combined owners' and manager's claims. If the fixed salary were replaced with ownership of 11.5 percent of the stock, the manager would still have a compensation package with a present value of $78 with the low-risk structure, but the value would rise or fall with actions that caused the value of the stock to rise or fall. The manager would then be motivated to move to the high-risk structure preferred by the shareholders. The OPM illustrates the importance of designing contracts with managers so as to motivate them to make the choices preferred by shareholders.

As these examples illustrate, even nonsystematic risk can be important in that risk changes the relative values of claims against an income stream. Thus, nonsystematic risk and OPMs have important implications for capital budgeting, financing of capital investments, and the design of compensation arrangements. If these issues are not considered, management decisions will not lead to maximization of shareholder wealth.

The conclusions from OPM analysis may appear to negate the principles developed through the first fourteen and one-half chapters of this book. Prior to the OPM, value was affected only by systematic risk in the various models considered. The adjustments of required return for risk using asset pricing models did not take into consideration the role of risk in allocation of asset value among claimants. Management contracts that include stock options suggest that the implications of OPMs are widely used by companies in designing management contracts. The wide use of net present value and internal rate of return analysis by companies suggests that the ability to exploit existing creditors is not a major factor in most capital investment decision making. Restrictive bond covenants and the necessity of maintaining a good credit rating limit these opportunities. However, there are cases in which the position of one set of claimants relative to another is a key part of capital investment decision making, and option pricing models are important in these cases.

MANAGING EXCHANGE RATE RISK USING FUTURES, SWAPS, AND OPTIONS |

Managing exchange rate risk is given a separate section in this chapter because it is an important part of international investment analysis. Fluctuations in exchange rates increase risk that can be decreased or eliminated with various hedging techniques."[33] Currency futures, options, and swaps are tools used to manage this risk. To truly understand the difference in these methods requires an understanding of the option instruments discussed previously in this chapter.

There are two types of exchange rate risk. *Translation* risk is the risk that reported income will fluctuate because of fluctuating exchange rates. Translation risk is a serious problem in a world in which accounting income matters, but it is only a risk of accounting numbers. *Transaction* risk is the risk that actual cash flows will fluctuate because of fluctuating exchange rates. Currency futures, options, and swaps are used to manage short-term transaction risk while balance sheet hedging is used to manage translation risk and longer-term transaction risk. Discussion of the first three methods of managing exchange rate risk follows. Balance sheet hedging is discussed in the financing section of the text.

CURRENCY FUTURES

A currency future is simply a contract to exchange a specific amount of one currency for a specific amount of another currency at a designated future date. By agreeing to these conditions ahead of time, you can effectively eliminate exchange rate risk for a transaction.

Suppose, for example, you sign a contract to purchase a shipment of computer chips from Japan. Delivery and payment are to occur in 90 days, and you agree to pay 100 million yen. The spot exchange rate is 102.8 yen to the dollar, so you are agreeing to pay $972,763 at today's exchange rate. If the dollar falls in price to 95 yen by the end of 90 days though, the chips will cost you $1,052,632. This increase in price may completely wipe out your profits, but you can protect yourself with a futures contract. The 90-day forward rate is 102.5,

---

[33]For a detailed argument for the use of hedging, see Gunter Dufey and S. L. Srinivasulu, "The Case for Corporate Management of Foreign Exchange Risk," *Financial Management* 12 (Winter 1983): 54–62.

so you can contract today to buy the 100 million yen in 90 days at a cost of $975,610. This reduces your risk by locking in the dollar cost of the chips.

Unfortunately, contracts are actively traded for only a half-dozen major currencies, and most contracts are for delivery 6 months or less in the future; a year is about the outer limit. Consequently, futures contracts cannot be used to hedge against the impacts of exchange rate fluctuations for capital investments generating cash flows over a period of 20 or 30 years.

CURRENCY SWAPS

A currency swap is a spot transaction in one direction offset by a futures contract in the opposite direction. We exchange one currency for another today, agreeing to reverse the transaction at a specified future date. The forward exchange rate is fixed, but may not be the same as the exchange rate for the spot transaction. Swaps may be used when futures contracts are not available. There are no listed futures contracts for the Indian rupee, for example, but a swap may be arranged. Swaps are sometimes made available by governments wishing to stabilize the currency.

OPTIONS

Futures contracts and swaps can be used to manage exchange rate risk when there is a known future need for a currency. Suppose, though, you are bidding to buy wool from Australians, with payment to be in Australian dollars. You must bid today, but it will be 2 months before you find out if your bid has been accepted. To avoid exchange rate risk, you can purchase Australian dollar currency options for the number of Australian dollars in the contract. If your offer is accepted, we have already locked in the U.S. dollar cost with the option contract. If your offer is rejected, you need not exercise the option (although you can resell the option at a profit if the Australian dollar has increased in value).

Like futures contracts, options are limited to a handful of leading currencies and have short lives; actively traded currency options do not extend beyond three months. They are available as both put and call options, though, so it is possible to lock in either a buying or a selling price of the foreign currency.

SUMMARY |

This chapter has focused on two approaches to valuation under risk: arbitrage pricing theory and option pricing models. Arbitrage pricing theory is related to the mean-variance capital asset pricing model in that it is used to find the required return or value of a risky investment, based on systematic risk. Option pricing models focus on the values of claims against a risky investment, rather than just the investment itself. Option pricing models emphasize the importance of total risk in determining the values of the various claims against returns from investments.

Arbitrage pricing theory is not based on specific assumptions about utility functions of investors. Arbitrage pricing theory is based on the assumption of perfectly competitive, frictionless markets in which there are no restrictions on short-sales, and there are therefore no arbitrage profit opportunities. The standard arbitrage pricing theory is based on the assumptions that returns for assets are related to certain overall factors in a linear form and that the number of investments being considered is much larger than the number of factors.

Arbitrage pricing theory can be used to determine required return as was done with the mean-variance CAPM, and it is possible to use arbitrage pricing models to directly value cash flows from a capital investment. Direct arbitrage valuation is based on finding the cost of a publicly traded portfolio that will duplicate the cash flows from the proposed capital investment. State-based arbitrage models are one alternative to the more widely recognized APT form for capital budgeting.

Option pricing models (OPMs) focus on the values of claims against an asset rather than the value of the asset itself. The option models consider the impact of systematic risk as well as nonsystematic risk, and they give insights with regard to how changes in risk change the values of the various claims against an income stream.

OPMs are based on the assumptions that there are no restrictions on short-sales and that financial markets are frictionless, with information freely available to all. The Black-Scholes model for European options is based on the additional assumptions that options cannot be exercised until their expiration date and that there are no cash distributions to holders of the underlying asset prior to the option's expiration date. The Black-Scholes model is also based on the assumptions that the risk-free rate remains constant over time, assets are traded continuously, and asset returns obey a stationary stochastic process over time. Other extensions allow for the possibility of exercise before maturity.

OPMs are particularly useful for examining the values of claims against a company because all claims, whether debt, equity, or hybrid, are combinations of the underlying asset, risk-free debt, call options, and put options. OPMs can be used to determine the required interest rate on debt, to examine how a change in risk will change the relative values of the debt and equity claims against a company, and to determine the compensation contracts that will align the interests of managers and stockholders.

Exchange rate risk—translation risk and transaction risk—adds another dimension to risk analysis in that it increases uncertainty with regard to the number of dollars the company will finally end up with. We discussed three ways of managing exchange rate risk: (1) currency futures contracts, (2) swaps, and (3) options.

Questions

15–1. Compare the assumptions underlying arbitrage pricing theory with those underlying the mean-variance capital asset pricing model. Which set of assumptions seems more realistic to you? Why?

15–2. What conditions are necessary for the APT to reduce to the CAPM formula for the relationship between beta for an investment and required return for that investment?

15–3. Give examples of economic factors for which a higher expected return may be required as compensation for sensitivity.

15–4. Summarize the current state of empirical evidence with regard to arbitrage pricing theory.

15–5. What problems can arise in the application of discrete state arbitrage pricing theory to capital budgeting?

15–6. Define the following terms: (a) option, (b) call option, (c) put option, (d) European option, (e) American option, (f) exercise, (g) exercise price, (h) striking price, (i) exercise date.

15–7. Why is total risk important in option pricing models whereas only systematic risk is important in models such as the mean-variance capital asset pricing model?

15–8. Describe the characteristics of stocks and bonds in the context of option analysis.

15–9. What are the assumptions underlying the Black-Scholes option pricing model?

15–10. Summarize the empirical evidence with regard to the Black-Scholes option pricing model.

15–11. What are the general implications of option pricing theory for the design of management reward systems?

15–12. **(Application)** Several years ago one of the big three automakers began marketing a diesel-powered minivan. The aftermarket for these vans turned out to be disastrous.

    a. In terms of options, what is the difference between the outright purchase of an asset like this minivan and the leasing of the minivan?

    b. In option terminology, what do you call the option at the end of the lease to turn the minivan over to the dealer?

    c. Would you consider this lease more like a European or an American option?

    d. With low market value after only a 3-year life, was leasing a good idea?

15–13. **(Ethical considerations)** Recent television commercials have encouraged people to get out of low-earning savings accounts and into collateralized mortgage obligations (CMOs). The way CMOs work is a group of mortgages is pooled and usually the federal government guarantees it will return the principle and accrued interest should the original borrower default. The mortgage borrowers have the right to repay their mortgages if interest rates fall so that they can refinance at a lower interest rate. The risk with a CMO is that general interest rates will fall and borrowers will exercise this option.

    a. Knowing what you know about options and the fact the borrower can and is likely to refinance when interest rates decline, why are these securities losing their popularity?

b. Would you market these 20-year securities to the elderly?

c. What are the ethical ramifications involved in selling these securities?

15–14. (**International**) Explain the difference between translation risk and transaction risk.

15–15. (**International**) Explain how the following are used to reduce exchange rate risk. What types of exchange rate risks are they typically used to reduce:

    a. Currency futures?

    b. Currency options?

    c. Swaps?

15–16. (**International ethical considerations**) There is a school of thought which states that over a long period, gains in the currency market will be offset by losses in the currency market and that an unhedged position is just as profitable as a hedged position. Assume that shareholders are expecting to earn a higher rate of return for a given level of risk by purchasing stock in companies with significant international exposure. At the same time many of the managers at these companies are hedging this exposure at a significant cost with currency futures, swaps, and options. They do this to reduce the volatility on the balance sheet equity account because many bonuses are based on return on equity. Is there an ethical concern here? What is it and how can the situation be improved? If you were the manager, would you hedge your exposure?

PROBLEMS |

15–1. A company evaluates its capital investments with regard to four factors. Information with regard to two capital investments and the four factors appears below. The risk-free rate is 6 percent. Find the required return for each capital investment.

Factor	Expected Return for a Unitary Sensitivity Portfolio	Factor Betas for the Capital Investments	
		A	B
GNP	10 percent	1.5	0.5
Bond Risk Premiums	8 percent	0.5	2.0
Yield Curve	7 percent	0.5	2.0
Inflation	7 percent	0.75	0.25

Compute the required returns for capital investments A and B.

15–2. Shown in the following table are betas for three securities with regard to each of two factors. Use this information to construct a unitary sensitivity portfolio with regard to each factor.

Security	A	B	C
Sensitivity to Factor 1	1.00	.50	0
Sensitivity to Factor 2	.50	.75	1.25
Expected return	.12	.10	.10

15–3. Compute the expected return for each unitary sensitivity portfolio in problem 2.

15–4. An investment has betas of 1.5 and −0.5 with regard to factors 1 and 2 respectively from problem 2. The risk-free rate is 6 percent. Based on the expected returns for unitary sensitivity portfolios computed in problem 3, what is the required return for this investment?

15–5. There are two possible states of nature. Cash flows per dollar invested for each of two securities in each state appear below, along with cash flow from a proposed capital investment. The capital investment costs $50,000. What is the net present value?

	Security A	Security B	Capital Investment
State 1	.20	.30	$20,000
State 2	.50	.20	10,000

15–6. There are three possible states of nature. Cash flows per dollar invested for each of three securities in each state appear below, along with cash flows for a proposed capital investment. If the capital investment costs $50,000, what is the net present value?

	Security A	Security B	Security C	Capital Investment
State 1	.20	.30	.30	$20,000
State 2	.50	.20	.20	10,000
State 3	.10	.40	.60	12,000

15–7. Managers at Midwest Grain Exporters believe that their profitability depends on the productivity of the world economy, and world grain output. They decide to use four states of nature, including high and low levels of world economic growth and world grain output. They have identified four portfolios of alternate investments which are sensitive to these variables. The rate of return expected from each portfolio in each state is as follows. Determine the value, at the start of a year, of the portfolio that will provide $1 at the end of the year in each of the states, while providing nothing in the other states.

WORLD ECONOMIC GROWTH	LOW		HIGH	
World Grain Production	**Low**	**High**	**Low**	**High**
Portfolio 1	.10	.15	.16	.12
Portfolio 2	.12	.13	.14	.18
Portfolio 3	.15	.11	.13	.10
Portfolio 4	.09	.18	.11	.18

15–8. Managers at Midwest Grain Exporters (problem 7) are considering a new shipping facility. Cash flows each year will depend on the state of nature that occurs that year, as follows. At a 13 percent risk-free rate, what is the maximum price Midwest can afford to pay for the shipping facility?

World Econ.	Low		Low	
Wheat Prod.	**Low**	**High**	**Low**	**High**
Year				
1	$5,000	$1,000	$7,000	$4,000
2	5,250	1,050	7,350	4,200
3	5,513	1,103	7,718	4,410
4	5,788	1,158	8,103	4,631
5	6,078	1,216	8,509	4,862
6	6,381	1,276	8,934	5,105
7	6,700	1,340	9,381	5,360
8	7,036	1,407	9,850	5,628
9	7,387	1,477	10,342	5,910
10	7,757	1,551	10,859	6,205

15–9. A stock priced at $20 a share will be worth either $30 or $10 at the end of one period. A call option has an exercise price of $25 at the end of the period, which is also the expiration date. The risk-free rate is 6 percent.

    a. A person could achieve a risk-free position by buying the stock and writing how many options?

    b. What is the equilibrium price of a call option?

    c. What would be the value of a put option with an exercise price of $25?

15–10. A company is worth $100,000. At the end of the period, the company will be worth either $200,000 or $30,000. The risk-free rate is 10 percent. How much can the company borrow based on a promise to repay $60,000 if the company is successful, and to turn the company over to the creditors if it is unsuccessful?

15–11. A company is worth $500,000. The company will be worth $1 million at the end of one period if it is successful and $100,000 if it fails. The risk-free rate is 10 percent. The company wants to borrow $200,000 that will be repaid at the end of the period. What must be the effective interest rate?

15–12. A company is worth $10 million now. The company will be worth $20 million at the end of one period if it is successful and $1 million otherwise. These values are before deducting the value of the manager's compensation. The manager receives $100,000 if the company is successful, and $0 otherwise. The company has debt with a face value of $5 million. The $5 million plus interest is due at the end of one period, and the risk-free rate is 8 percent. What is the equilibrium coupon interest rate on the debt?

15–13. For the company in problem 12, a change in risk structure leaves the beginning total value of the company unchanged, but changes the ending value to $30 million if successful and $500,000 otherwise. Would the shareholders prefer this change? Would the manager voluntarily change the company in this way?

15–14. For the company in problems 12 and 13, design a compensation program that would give the manager and shareholders identical attitudes toward risk.

15–15. The price of a company's stock is currently $50. A call option with an exercise price of $60 will expire in six months. The risk-free rate is 10 percent, and the standard deviation of the rate of the continuously compounded annual return for the stock is 50 percent. What is the value of the call option?

15–16. The stock of Manhattan Products Corporation is presently selling for $50 a share. A call option with an exercise price of $70 will expire in six months. The risk-free interest rate is 8 percent a year, compounded continuously. The standard deviation of the continuously compounded annual return for the stock is 60 percent. What is the value of the call option?

15–17. Month-end prices for Lawrence Corporation for thirteen recent months appear below. The company paid no dividends during that period, and the most recent price of the stock is $120. Options with one year until maturity and an exercise price of $140 are currently available. The risk-free rate is 10% a year, continuously compounded. What is the value of the call option?

Month	Month-end price	Month	Month-end price
1	120	8	140
2	110	9	100
3	130	10	120
4	120	11	110
5	130	12	100
6	150	13	120
7	160		

15–18. Norman Services has a total value of $1 million. The principle and interest owed to creditors at the end of one year is $600,000. The standard deviation of continuously compounded annual return for the company is .50. The risk-free rate is 10 percent continuously compounded. What are the market values of debt and equity? What is the contract (coupon) interest rate on the debt?

15–19. Suppose the standard deviation for Norman Services (problem 18) decreased to .40 and the value of the company increased to $1,050,000. What would this do to the values of debt and equity? Would shareholders be in favor of this change?

15–20. Arlington Gas has common stock with a $\beta_{s,m}$ of 1.1 and a market price of $100 a share. The standard deviation of continuously compounded annual returns is .50. Options maturing in one year have a market price of $30 and an exercise price of $90. The risk-free rate is 10 percent. What is the beta of the options?

15–21. We are preparing to sign an agreement to import clothing from France. The price is 100,000 francs and payment is due in 90 days. We have a contract to sell the goods for $18,000. The 90-day forward exchange rate is .1646. What will be our profit if we eliminate exchange rate risk with a forward exchange contract?

15–22. We have placed a bid for Canadian wheat for 1.2 million Canadian dollars. If our bid is accepted, we can resell the wheat for 1 million U.S. dollars. We will know if the bid has been accepted in thirty days. A thirty-day option to buy Canadian dollars for 0.78 U.S. dollars each can be purchased for $0.0012 U.S. per Canadian dollar. What will be our profit if we buy options and the bid is accepted? What will be our loss if we buy options and the bid is rejected (assuming the options expire without being exercised)?

CASE PROBLEM |

GRQ Properties

GRQ Properties was a small family partnership established for the purpose of investing in residential properties. The partnership started out by purchasing several single-family homes as rental properties. The partners studied the rental market carefully before investing, and chose houses in areas that turned out to have both strong rental demand and decent price appreciation. However, the partners discovered that identifying and keeping good tenants was difficult. Growth of the partnership was halted for several years until income stabilized and the managing partner, Joyce Green, learned more about dealing with tenants.

During this stabilization period, the tax law changed. The profitability of the partnership was satisfactory and relationships between the partners were harmonious, but the attractiveness of additional rental property purchases had declined because rents had not risen by enough to offset the new tax law changes.

Green, the managing partner, was eager to expand the business and began looking for other opportunities. She found a small one-office mortgage broker-age company for sale and proposed this to the partners as a new investment. The basic job of a mortgage broker of this type was to attract mortgage applicants and complete the mortgage application process. A mortgage banker actually made the loans, and then sold them to investors such as pension funds and savings and loans. The owner of the mortgage brokerage company wanted to retire, but was willing to work for several more years until Green learned the business. Green would quit her full-time job to manage the mortgage brokerage office. The business was for sale for $500,000.

Walter Ransom, one of the partners and a brother of Green, worked with Green to examine the investment proposal. The owner of the business provided audited financial statements to estimate the cash flow from the business, after deducting salaries, in each of four representative states of nature. These states included two rates of GNP growth and two levels of mortgage interest rates:

State	GNP Growth Rate	Interest Rate	Annual Cash Flow
I	0%	12%	−$100,000
II	0	6	100,000
III	5	12	100,000
IV	5	6	200,000

Ransom decided that an appropriate way to evaluate this business was to compare it with returns that could be earned elsewhere. He would be selling mu-tual fund shares to pay his part of the $500,000 cost, so he considered common stocks as the alternative. He estimated the annual return (cash flow per dollar invested) for four stock price indexes in each of the four states of nature by study-ing past performance of these indexes. He used the Standard and Poor's indus-trials, utilities, transportation, and financial indexes. His estimates of the returns for each index in each state follow.

State	Industrials	Utilities	Transportation	Financials
I	.04	.06	.04	−.05
II	.15	.13	.15	.16
III	.03	.03	.04	.02
IV	.14	.09	.16	.12

Based on this information, Ransom felt that he should be able to make a de-cision about the desirability of the mortgage brokerage business investment. In the back of his mind, though, was the fact that harmonious family relations were at stake, in addition to his financial well-being.

CASE QUESTIONS

1. Set up the simultaneous equation problem needed to find out how much must be invested in common stocks represented by these indexes to duplicate the cash flows from the mortgage brokerage business.
2. Solve the simultaneous equation problem (*hint:* Lotus 1-2-3 can be used to solve these equations in only a couple of minutes).
3. Do you recommend investment in the proposed mortgage brokerage business?

SELECTED REFERENCES

Abuaf, Niso. "Foreign Exchange Options: The Leading Edge." *Midland Corporate Finance Journal* 5 (Summer 1987): 51–58.

Adler, Michael, and Bernard Dumas. "Exposure to Currency Risk: Definition and Measurement." *Financial Management* 13 (Summer 1984): 41–50.

Agmon, T., and S. Bronfield. "The International Mobility of Short-Term Covered Arbitrage Capital." *Journal of Business Finance and Accounting* 2 (Summer 1975): 269–278.

Bakshi, Gurpid, Charles Cao, and Zhiwu Chen. "Empirical Performance of Alternative Option Pricing Models." *Journal of Finance* 52 (December 1997): 2003–2049.

Bansal, Ravi, David A. Hseih, and S. Viswanathan. "A New Approach to International Arbitrage Pricing." *Journal of Finance* 48 (December 1993): 1719–1747.

Black, Fisher. "Fact and Fancy in the Use of Options." *Financial Analysts Journal* (July–August 1975): 61–72.

Black, Fisher, and John C. Cox. "Valuing Corporate Securities: Some Effects of Bond Indenture Provisions." *Journal of Finance* 31 (May 1976): 351–367.

Black, Fisher, and Myron Scholes. "The Pricing of Options and Corporate Liabilities." *Journal of Political Economy* 81 (May–June 1973): 637–654.

Blattacharya, Mihir. "Empirical Properties of the Black-Scholes Formula under Ideal Conditions." *Journal of Financial and Quantitative Analysis* (December 1980): 1081–1106.

Bower, Dorothy H., Richard S. Bower, and Dennis E. Logue. "Arbitrage Pricing Theory and Utility Stock Returns." *Journal of Finance* 39 (September 1984): 1041–1054.

Burmeister, Edwin, and Marjory B. McElroy. "Joint Estimation of Factor Sensitivities and Risk Premia for the Arbitrage Pricing Theory." *Journal of Finance* 43 (July 1988): 721–735.

Chang, Jack S. K., and Latha Shanker. "Option Pricing and the Arbitrage Pricing Theory." *Journal of Financial Research* 10 (Spring 1987): 1–16.

Chen, Nai-Fu. "Some Empirical Tests of the Theory of Arbitrage Pricing." *Journal of Finance* 38 (December 1983): 1393–1414.

Chen, Nai-Fu, Richard W. Roll, and Stephen A. Ross. "Economic Forces and the Stock Market: Testing the APT and Alternative Asset Pricing Theories." UCLA Working Paper #20-83, December 1983.

Cho, D. Chinhyung. "On Testing the Arbitrage Pricing Theory: Inter-Battery Factor Analysis." *Journal of Finance* 39 (December 1984): 1485–1502.

Chung, Kee H., and Charlie Charoenwong. "Investment Options, Assets in Place, and the Risk of Stocks." *Financial Management* 20 (Autumn 1991): 21–33.

Conway, Delores A., and Marc R. Reinganum. "Capital Market Factor Structure: Identification through Cross Validation." University of Chicago Graduate School of Business Working Paper #183, July 1986.

Cox, John C., and Stephen A. Ross. "The Valuation of Options for Alternative Stochastic Processes." *Journal of Financial Economics* 3 (January–March 1976): 145–166.

Cox, John C., Stephen A. Ross, and Mark Rubinstein. "Option Pricing: A Simplified Approach." *Journal of Financial Economics* 7 (September 1979): 229–263.

Dhrymes, P., Irwin Friend, and B. Gultekin. "A Critical Reexamination of the Empirical Evidence on the Arbitrage Pricing Theory." *Journal of Finance* 39 (June 1984): 323–346.

————. "New Tests of the APT and Their Implications." *The Journal of Finance* 40 (July 1985): 659–675.

Dixit, Avinash, and Robert Pindyck. "The Options Approach to Capital Investment." *Harvard Business Review* 73 (May–June 95): 105–126.

Dufey, Gunter, and S. L. Srinivasulu. "The Case for Corporate Management of Foreign Exchange Risk." *Financial Management* 12 (Winter 1983): 54–62.

Dybvig, Philip H., and Stephen A. Ross. "Yes, the APT Is Testable." *Journal of Finance* 40 (September 1985): 1173–1188.

Erhardt, Michael C. "Arbitrage Pricing Models: The Sufficient Number of Factors and Equilibrium Conditions." *Journal of Financial Research* 10 (Summer 1987): 111–120.

Frenkel, J. A., and R. M. Levich. "Covered Interest Arbitrage: Unexploited Profits?" *Journal of Political Economy* 83 (April 1975): 325–338.

Froot, Kenneth A. "A Framework for Risk Management." *Journal of Applied Corporate Finance* 7 (Fall 1994): 22–32.

Garven, James R. "A Pedagogic Note on the Derivation of the Black-Scholes Option Pricing Formula." *Financial Review* 21 (May 1986): 337–344.

Gehr, Adam K., Jr. "Risk-Adjusted Capital Budgeting Using Arbitrage." *Financial Management* 10 (Winter 1981): 14–19.

————. "Some Tests of the Arbitrage Pricing Theory." *Journal of the Midwest Finance Association* (1975): 91–105.

Geske, Robert. "A Note on the Analytical Valuation Formula for Unprotected American Call Options on Stocks with Known Dividends." *Journal of Financial Economics* 7 (December 1979): 375–380.

————. "The Valuation of Compound Options." *Journal of Financial Economics* 7 (March 1979): 63–81.

Geske, Robert, and Richard Roll. "On Valuing American Call Options with the Black-Scholes European Formula." *Journal of Finance* 39 (June 1984): 443–455.

Glen, Jack, and Philippe Jorion. "Currency Hedging for International Portfolios." *Journal of Finance* 48 (December 1993): 1865–1886.

Huberman, Gur, Schmuel Kandel, and Robert Stambaugh. "Mimicking Portfolios and Exact Arbitrage Pricing." *Journal of Finance* 42 (March 1987): 1–9.

Ingersoll, J. E., and Stephen Ross. "Waiting to Invest: Investment and Uncertainty." *Journal of Business* (January 1992): 1–29.

Jacob, David P., Graham Lord, and James A Tilley. "A Generalized Framework for Pricing Contingent Cash Flows." *Financial Management* 16 (Autumn 1987): 5–14.

Jamshidian, F. "An Exact Bond Option Formula." *Journal of Finance* 44 (March 1989): 205–209.

Kandel, S., and G. Huberman. "A Size Based Stock Returns Model." University of Chicago, Graduate School of Business, working paper.

Kaufold, Howaard, and Michael Smirlock. "Managing Corporate Exchange and Interest Rate Exposure." *Financial Management* 15 (Autumn 1986): 64–78.

Lee, Moon. "Valuing Finite-Maturity Investment Timing Options." *Financial Management* 26 (Summer 1997): 58–67.

Macbeth, James D., and Larry J. Merville. "An Empirical Examination of the Black-Scholes Call Option Pricing Model." *Journal of Finance* 34 (December 1979): 1173–1186.

———. "Tests of the Black-Scholes and Cox Option Valuation Models." *Journal of Finance* 35 (May 1980): 285–300.

Majd, Saman, and Robert S. Pindyck. "Time to Build, Option Value, and Investment Decisions." *Journal of Financial Economics* 18 (March 1987): 7–27.

Maldonado, Rita, and Anthony Saunders. "Foreign Exchange Futures and the Law of One Price." *Financial Management* 12 (Spring 1983): 19–23.

Maloney, Peter J. "Managing Currency Exposure: The Case of Western Mining." *Journal of Applied Corporate Finance* 2 (Winter 1990): 29–34.

McCulloch, Robert, and Peter E. Rossi. "Posterior, Predictive, and Utility-Based Approaches to Testing the Arbitrage Pricing Theory." *Journal of Financial Economics* 28 (November–December 1990): 7–38.

McDonald, R., and D. Siegel. "The Value of Waiting to Invest." *Quarterly Journal of Economics* (November 1986): 707–727.

Miller, Edward. "A Problem in Textbook Arbitrage Pricing Theory Examples." *Financial Management* 18 (Summer 1989): 9–10.

Pettway, Richard H., and Bradford D. Jordan. "APT vs. CAPM Estimates of the Return-Generating Function Parameters for Regulated Public Utilities." *Journal of Financial Research* 10 (Fall 1987): 227–238.

Phelan, Steven E. "Exposing the Illusion of Confidence in Financial Analysis." *Management Decision* 35 (January–February 1997): 163–169.

Reisman, Haim. "Reference Variables, Factor Structure, and Approximate Multibeta Representation." *Journal of Finance* 47 (September 1992): 1303–1314.

Rendleman, Richard J., Jr., and Brit J. Bartter. "Two-State Option Pricing." *Journal of Finance* 34 (December 1979): 1093–1110.

Roll, Richard A. "An Analytic Valuation Formula for Unprotected American Call Options with Known Dividends." *Journal of Financial Economics* 5 (November 1977): 251–258.

Roll, Richard, and Stephen A. Ross. "A Critical Reexamination of the Empirical Evidence on the Arbitrage Pricing Theory: A Reply." *Journal of Finance* 39 (June 1984): 347–350.

———. "Regulation, the Capital Asset Pricing Model, and the Arbitrage Pricing Theory." *Public Utilities Fortnightly* (May 26, 1983): 22–28.

Ross, Stephen. "The Arbitrage Theory of Capital Asset Pricing." *Journal of Economic Theory* (December 1976): 341–361.

———. "An Empirical Investigation of the Arbitrage Pricing Theory." *Journal of Finance* 35 (December 1980): 1073–1103.

———. "A Simple Approach to the Valuation of Risky Streams." *Journal of Business* (July 1979): 254–286.

———. "Uses, Abuses, and Alternatives to the Net Present Value Rule." *Financial Management* 23 (Autumn 1994): 96–102.

Rubinstein, Mark. "Nonparametric Tests of Alternative Option Pricing Models Using All Reported Trades and Quotes on the 30 Most Active CBOE Option Classes from August 23, 1976, through August 31, 1978." *Journal of Finance* 40 (June 1985): 455–480.

Shankin, Jay. "The Arbitrage Pricing Theory: Is It Testable? *Journal of Finance* 37 (December 1982): 1129–1140.

———. "The Current State of the Arbitrage Pricing Theory." *Journal of Finance* 47 (September 1992): 1569–1574.

———. "Multi-Beta CAPM or Equilibrium-APT: A Reply." *Journal of Finance* 40 (September 1985): 1189–1196.

Siegel, Daniel R., James L. Smith, and James L. Paddock. "Valuing Offshore Oil Properties with Option Pricing Models." *Midland Corporate Finance Journal* 5 (Spring 1987): 22–30.

Smith, C., Jr., and J. Zimmerman. "Valuing Employee Stock Option Plans Using Option Pricing Models." *Journal of Accounting Research* 14 (Autumn 1976): 357–364.

Sterk, W. "Tests of Two Models for Valuing Call Options on Stocks with Dividends." *Journal of Finance* 37 (December 1982): 1229–1237.

Stultz, R. M. "A Model of International Asset Pricing." *Journal of Financial Economics* 9 (December 1981): 383–406.

Trigeorgis, L. "A Conceptual Options Framework for Capital Budgeting." *Advances in Futures and Options Research* 3 (1988): 145–167.

Whaley, Robert E. "Valuation of American Futures Options: Theory and Empirical Tests." *Journal of Finance* 41 (March 1986): 127–150.

INTEGRATIVE CASE FOR PART IV

Callaway (A)

Union Electric (UE) joined the Nuclear Age in 1973 when it ordered two nuclear reactors from Westinghouse. The reactors, to be installed on a site in Callaway County, Missouri, were expected to cost a total of $1.05 billion, and were expected to produce a total of 2,300,000 kilowatts of electricity. UE derived 90 percent of its power from coal in 1973. The plan was to use 60 percent coal and 36 percent nuclear power by 1985.

The nuclear plant was expected to solve several problems. First, it would provide the additional capacity that was needed to meet projected demand. Second, it would avoid dependence on oil, which had become scarce and expensive in the wake of the OPEC oil embargo. Third, it would eliminate acid rain and other air pollution that was produced by coal-powered plants. Finally, nuclear energy was expected to be a low-cost source of energy that would be important in developing the industrial base in UE's service area, which included substantial portions of Missouri, and smaller areas of Illinois and Iowa.

An electric utility differs from the local 7-Eleven store in several important ways. First, the 7-Eleven store can get a new delivery of Pepsi in a few hours, but it takes years—often more than a decade—for a nuclear plant to add generating capacity. Second, the 7-Eleven store can tell its customers it is out of Pepsi, but the electric company must maintain adequate capacity to provide all the electricity wanted by all of its customers during the highest-demand hour of the year.[1] Finally, electricity is so important in industrialized economies that the entire welfare of a region is affected by its availability and cost of electricity.

Peak-demand history and capacity for UE are shown in Table IV.1. Based on these data and other information, a 6.2 percent growth rate in demand was

| TABLE IV.1   DEMAND AND CAPACITY HISTORY FOR UNION ELECTRIC

Year	Peak-time demand	Peak-time capability
1963	2,891,000 kW	3,098,000 kW
1966	3,257,000	3,495,000
1967	3,438,000	3,840,000
1968	3,830,000	4,171,000
1969	4,078,000	4,611,000
1970	4,362,000	5,078,000
1971	4,503,000	5,682,000
1972	4,994,000	5,663,000

This table shows the actual peak-time demand and actual peak-time capacity of UE by year, taken from the company's annual reports.

[1]Generally between 1 P.M. and 3 P.M. on the hottest day in August.

forecasted. This meant that the company would need to add approximately 4.2 million kilowatts of electrical capacity over the next 10 years. New coal-powered plants which were to come on-line were as follows.

Labadie, Mo.	1973	600,000 kW
Rush Island, Mo.	1976	600,000
Rush Island, Mo.	1977	600,000

Thus there was a need for an additional 2.4 million kilowatts of capacity. The 2.3 million kilowatts anticipated from the two Callaway units would provide the bulk of this need, although some additional capacity would still be needed. Other capacity was also needed to carry the company through until 1981, when the first Callaway unit would become operational. In addition, at least one anti-quated plant would be shut down, again necessitating additional capacity.

The economic justification for the Callaway plant was fairly simple in con-cept. Construction cost per kilowatt capacity was estimated to be $315 for a coal plant and $456 for a nuclear plant. Offsetting the higher construction cost was a major savings in fuel cost. A pound of "yellowcake" uranium fuel costing $7 could produce as much electricity as several tons of coal, and the price per ton of coal was higher than the price per pound of yellowcake. A ton of coal would produce approximately 2,000 kilowatts of electricity. We can work with an as-sumed hourly output of 4,380 hours per year for either plant.

Antinuclear groups objected to UE's plans on grounds of both safety and cost. First and foremost, an accident could cause thousands of deaths. In addi-tion, it was necessary to find a way to store spent fuel for periods of up to 200,000 years. The economic benefits depended on relative construction costs, relative fuel costs, and electricity demand. Critics argued that earlier nuclear plants had incurred large cost overruns, and UE, having agreed to cost-plus contracts, could expect similar problems. Discovery of new uranium ore had begun to decline in the late 1960s, so the antinuclear groups argued that nuclear fuel costs could be expected to rise rapidly in the future as supplies became increasingly scarce. Finally, the most optimistic estimate called for the plant to be placed in service 8 years after the order was placed. Since construction of a nuclear plant required many more years than a coal plant, the economic viability of the whole project rested on an unproved ability to forecast long-term demand growth.

UE was able to point out that there had never been a serious nuclear acci-dent, and nuclear reactors did not pollute the air or cause acid rain, as was the case with coal. The possibility of new pollution-control requirements made the cost of coal-powered plants unpredictable as well, and the price of coal in fu-ture periods was unknown. On the other hand, UE was able to lock in the cost of nuclear fuel by signing a 21-year fuel supply contract with Westinghouse. This was important because inflation was approximately 6 percent in 1973.

Charges to customers for construction in progress are an interesting aspect of public-utility rate setting. In setting rates, public utilities were allowed to include a fair return on invested capital. Invested capital included both operating plants and plants under construction. Thus UE was allowed to charge customers each year for a fair return on the amount that had already been spent on the nuclear plants, even though they were not yet producing electricity.

CASE QUESTIONS

To focus on the areas of greatest interest, ignore taxes and assume that the primary objective is to produce electricity at the lowest possible cost. Also assume a 10 percent cost of capital. Assume that either plant will last 30 years and will have no salvage value, assume a 3-year period to build a coal-powered plant and an 8-year period to build a nuclear plant.

1. Given the figures available in 1973, compare coal to nuclear fuel in terms of cost per kilowatt to the customer after the plant is completed. Assume that the price of coal is $7.20 per ton in 1973, and increases at a rate of 6 percent a year.
2. Given the figures available in 1973, compare coal to nuclear fuel considering both electricity cost after completion and amounts paid during construction.
3. Prepare a sensitivity analysis table for the proposed nuclear plants, considering variations in construction cost and fuel prices.
4. The general market prices of coal and yellowcake will depend on supply and demand for both fuels. Coal supplies are probably well known, but price will vary with demand. The supply of uranium is probably less certain, and the demand depends on the number of plants that are built. Thus the prices of both coal and yellowcake may vary. Furthermore, the cost of a coal-powered plant can vary, depending on changes in air pollution regulation. Discuss the diversification considerations affecting the decision from the point of view of (a) UE, (b) the customers, and (c) the stockholders.
5. Given the situation prevailing in 1973, would you recommend construction of the nuclear reactors?

Callaway (B)

By the end of 1977 the nuclear power situation looked substantially different. In September 1975, Westinghouse announced unilateral cancellation of its nuclear contracts, accusing producers of price fixing. By 1976, the price of yellowcake was $42 a pound and still rising. UE's average coal cost was $15.04 in 1976 and $17.86 in 1977.

In November 1976, Missouri voters approved Proposition 1, which required that the cost of the new plant not be included in the rate base until the plant was in operation. This meant that the cumulative cost of funds over the construction period would be included in the asset base when the plant was placed in service.

Cost overruns were a concern in 1977. The cost estimate for the two Callaway units was raised to $1.8 billion in 1975. By 1977, the total construction cost estimate for Callaway was $2.385 billion, plus $262 million for an initial fuel charge in unit 1. Two specific reasons for cost overruns were changes in safety requirements and the addition of the cost of funds to the cost of the project rather than charging those costs to customers during construction. Nuclear plants being constructed by other utilities had often experienced cost overruns of 100 percent or more, and large numbers of orders had been canceled. Kay Dry, an antinuclear activist, asked, "Is even a reasonable ballpark estimate [of construction cost] possible?"

The starting dates had been delayed to 1982 for unit 1, partly because of Proposition 1. Demand for electricity had also slacked off, as shown in Table IV.2. This was at least partly the result of higher energy costs, but slower demand was also affected by a regional growth rate substantially below the growth rates in other parts of the country, such as the Southwest.

Safety issues were also causing increased concern. Indeed, changing policy on the part of the Nuclear Regulatory Commission was cited as one of the chief reasons for cost overruns. Since the construction contract was on a cost-plus basis, all cost increases were absorbed by UE.

In late 1977, calls for abandonment of the Callaway project were being made. Abandonment would mean stranding the investment of $224 million that had already been made, but it would avoid the additional $2.25 billion cost that was then being estimated for completion of the two projects. Abandonment would also necessitate the construction of coal-powered plants, and the cost of coal-powered plants had nearly doubled because of pollution requirements.

Abandonment now would involve minimal shutdown costs because the generators had not yet been loaded with nuclear fuel. Closing down at the end of the plant's operating life could be expensive because of the radioactivity involved. Estimates of the closing costs ranged from 5 percent to 30 percent of initial construction cost.

CASE QUESTIONS

1. How would each of the following be expected to affect UE's beta?

  a. A nuclear power plant involves increased fixed costs with the objective of reducing variable (fuel) costs.

TABLE IV.2 UE's ELECTRICITY DEMAND FROM 1973 THROUGH 1977		
Year	Peak-time demand	Peak-time capability
1973	5,138,000 kW	6,963,000 kW
1974	5,318,000	6,660,000
1975	5,363,000	6,474,000
1976	5,582,000	6,913,000
1977	5,837,000	6,891,000

    b. Construction costs are uncertain.

    c. Fuel costs are uncertain.

2. How should the risk of a nuclear accident be factored into the decision making?

3. What is the significance of the eventual spent-fuel storage problem?

4. Considering the situation at the end of 1977, would abandonment be in the interest of customers? stockholders?

5. Suppose that contract cancellation fees must be paid to contractors. How would these affect the decision making?

PART VI

FINANCING DECISIONS AND REQUIRED RETURN

In the previous chapters the financing decisions were taken as given, and the focus was on the optimal use of money for capital investments. Financing and investment decisions are often intertwined, if for no other reason than that the cost of capital is affected by the company's financing decisions. In addition, the cost of capital may depend on which assets were selected. Financing decisions are analyzed directly in this part, and relationships between financing decisions and investment decisions are examined. Both the practice and theory of financing decisions are covered, and these topics are related to capital budgeting. Topics covered in this section include cost of capital, capital structure theory and practice, dividend policy, joint investment-financing decisions, leasing, and capital rationing.

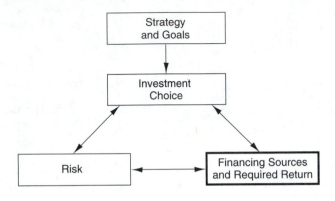

CHAPTER 16

COST OF CAPITAL

After completing this chapter you should be able to:

1. Explain to a classmate why a company must earn its cost of capital.
2. Identify the typical sources of existing and additional capital.
3. Calculate the after-tax cost of existing debt and new debt.
4. Compute the cost of existing and new preferred stock.
5. Determine the cost of existing equity using the capital asset pricing model, the earnings yield model, and the dividend growth model.
6. Calculate the cost of new equity using the earnings yield model and the dividend growth model.
7. Discuss the advantages and disadvantages of the three possible weighting practices: book weights, market weights, and target weights.
8. Analyze the liability side of an actual balance sheet to determine the market weights of each component in the capital structure.
9. Describe the role that deferred taxes, accounts payable, accruals, short-term debt, leases, convertibles, and depreciation play in calculating the weights.
10. Calculate the weighted average cost of capital for an actual corporation for increasing levels of investment.
11. Utilize the weighted average cost of capital in judging potential capital projects and existing operations.
12. Calculate the cost of capital for an international capital investment.

Opponents of nuclear power have traditionally focused their attention on safety, but they are turning their attention to the cost of capital. The essential economic characteristic of a nuclear power plant is that it costs more to build than a coal- or oil-powered plant, but is expected to produce electricity at a lower operating cost per unit after construction. The pivotal question is whether the future savings justify the present cost.

The cost of capital has become a key consideration in the decision process. In a recent study, George Yarrow found that nuclear electricity was 29 percent less expensive than coal-produced energy at a 5 percent discount rate, but was more expensive than coal at a 10 percent discount rate.[1] The nuclear debate may finally be settled by reference to the cost of capital.

A company's *capital* structure is its mix of long-term financing sources, including debt, common stock, and preferred stock. The *cost of capital* is an average of the returns required by the various providers of capital to the business, weighted according to the proportion of capital coming from each source. The cost of capital links together many aspects of financial management because shareholder wealth is maximized through the process of arranging financing so as to minimize the cost of capital and choosing capital investments so as to maximize net present value, using the cost of capital as the required rate of return.[2]

In this chapter, the cost of capital concept is developed and procedures for estimating a company's cost of capital are explained. After learning the material in this chapter, you will be able to make a reasonable estimate of the cost of capital for an actual company. In the following chapters, the relationship between capital structure and the cost of capital is examined.

COST OF CAPITAL CONCEPT |

The cost of capital is an *opportunity cost*. Money is a scarce resource, and when money is used for a capital investment, it is diverted from other productive uses. For a capital investment to be justified, the return on money used must be at least as great as the returns from alternate opportunities of equal risk. In most situations, money invested by a company must be raised from investors who could invest elsewhere. The cost of capital—the minimum acceptable rate of return— is the return that investors could earn in opportunities of equal risk. We will first apply this concept with a simple example in which the company raises money from only one source, and then develop the cost of capital when multiple sources of capital are used.

Pacific Corporation is a new company that is going to raise money only from creditors; it will have no equity. For simplicity, assume that Pacific pays no taxes. Investors who would consider loaning money to Pacific could invest their money at 10 percent in other loans of equal risk. Thus, they would be willing to loan money to Pacific only if they could expect a return of at least 10 percent. Managers at Pacific are considering an investment that will cost $1,000, will have a 1-year life, and will provide cash inflows of $1,150 at the end of the year. The amount the lenders would be willing to provide in exchange for a payment of $1,150 in 1 year is the present value (PV) of the $1,150:

$$PV = \$1,150/1.1 = \$1,045.45$$

[1]"The 10% Solution," *The Economist* (July 6, 1988): 63.

[2]While the general objective is to minimize the cost of capital, strategic issues such as flexibility or the ability to withstand a price war may cause the wealth-maximizing capital structure to differ from that with the lowest average cost of funds.

In other words, Pacific could borrow $1,045.45 today in exchange for a promise to pay $1,150 in 1 year.[3] Suppose Pacific borrowed $1,045.45 and used $1,000 for the investment. The proceeds from the $1,000 investment would be exactly enough to repay the loan, and the remaining $45.45 would be an immediate increase in wealth. Thus, the net present value of the investment is $45.45. The cost of capital is the return required to satisfy providers of funds, and the net present value is the amount of money investors would be willing to supply in exchange for the future cash flows from the investment, less the initial outlay.

THE WEIGHTED AVERAGE COST OF CAPITAL CONCEPT

In the previous example, capital was raised from only one source. However, capital is typically raised from a combination of sources in an effort to reduce the average required return. The *weighted average cost of capital* (WACC) is the rate of return that must be earned on assets in order to provide an expected return to all suppliers of funds equal to what they could expect from alternate investment opportunities of equal risk. This required return is an average of the required returns for the various sources, weighted according to the proportion of total capital raised from each source.

As an example, consider again Pacific's opportunity to invest $1,000 and receive $1,150 in 1 year. However, assume Pacific will be financed $\frac{3}{4}$ with debt and $\frac{1}{4}$ with equity. Lenders require an 8 percent return while the equity holders require a 12 percent return. The equity holders require a higher return because they get paid from the money left after satisfying the creditors, so their investment is more risky. Suppose Pacific raises $1,000, with $750 from debt and $250 from equity. If we continue to assume no taxes, the return Pacific must earn to satisfy both groups is:

$$\frac{(\$750 \times .08) + (\$250 \times .12)}{\$1,000} = \frac{\$90}{\$1,000} = 9\%$$

The 9 percent required return is Pacific's weighted average cost of capital.

A shorthand way to express the weighted average cost of capital is to use the formula:

$$\text{WACC} = \sum_{i=1}^{m} w_i k_i \qquad (16\text{-}1)$$

where w_i is the proportion of capital coming from source i, k_i is the required rate of return for source i, and m is the number of different sources of capital used. Applying this formula to Pacific:

[3] The effective interest earned by the investors would be:

$$\frac{1,150 - 1,045.45}{1,045.45} = \frac{104.55}{1,045.45} = 10\%$$

$$\text{WACC} = .75 \times .08 + .25 \times .12 = 9\%$$

The answer is the same as that obtained previously, but the computation is easier when there are numerous sources of capital.

The Marginal Cost of Capital Concept

In capital budgeting and cost of capital analysis, we follow the same principles used in most business analysis: we compare marginal benefits with marginal costs. The *marginal cost of capital* is the rate of return that must be earned on a new investment to satisfy investors. To illustrate the marginal cost of capital concept, suppose Pacific Corporation acquired the previously discussed $1,000 asset and the managers are now considering a new investment. The managers believe that the optimal capital structure consists of $\frac{3}{4}$ debt and $\frac{1}{4}$ equity. However, interest rates have risen so that Pacific must pay 9 percent interest on any new debt instead of the 8 percent rate being paid on existing debt. Equity holders can now expect a 16 percent return if they are to make new investments today in assets of equal risk to Pacific's stock. The marginal cost of capital is the weighted average cost of capital that must be earned on new investments:

$$\text{WACC} = .75 \times .09 + .25 \times .16 = \underline{10.75\%}$$

The old 9 percent WACC was the marginal cost of capital when the earlier investment was acquired. The marginal cost of capital increased because the general level of interest rates increased.

We should pause here to explain why the rate paid on the funds actually raised for a new capital investment may not be the appropriate discount rate for you to use in capital budgeting. Suppose managers at Pacific, which previously had $750 of debt and $250 of equity, decide to finance a new $1,000 investment entirely with debt. The higher debt ratio makes Pacific more risky, and therefore increases the required returns on both debt and equity; the required interest rate on debt jumps from 9 percent to 10 percent and the required return on equity jumps from 16 percent to 20 percent. The existing debt must be refinanced at the higher interest rate because debt covenants do not allow a debt to total assets ratio greater than .75. The amount that must be earned changes as follows:

New interest expense:	$.10 \times 1750 = \$175$
New required earnings for equity:	$.20 \times 250 = \underline{\$\ 50}$
Total new required earnings	$\$225$
Old interest expense:	$.09 \times 750 = \$\ 67.50$
Old required earnings for equity:	$.16 \times 250 = \underline{\ 40.00}$
Total old required earnings	$\$107.50$
Increase in required earnings:	$225 - 107.50 = \underline{\$117.50}$

The marginal cost of capital is the change in required earnings divided by the increase in total capital:

$$\text{WACC} = \frac{117.50}{1,000} = 11.75\%$$

Even though the interest rate paid on the new debt is only 10 percent, the marginal cost is 11.75 percent because the required return on other funds is increased by the addition of more debt. Use of the 10 percent direct borrowing cost as the cost of capital gives a false picture of the true costs from the change in financial structure.

It is important to note that we generally assume that the company is at its optimal debt-equity mix, and that any new capital will be raised in the same proportion as existing capital. If an increased ratio of debt to total capital would decrease the weighted average cost of capital because the company is not presently at the optimal mix, then the marginal cost of new debt might appear to be quite low. However, a new investment should not be justified by the benefits of moving to an optimal capital structure. The benefit of moving to an optimal capital structure can be had by raising more of one type of capital and using the proceeds to retire another, without making new investments.

The marginal cost of capital concept also applies if your company has funds on hand and is trying to decide whether to invest those funds or return them to the lenders and stockholders. Current market rates of return are still relevant in this situation. In the case of debt, for example, an alternative for old bonds with interest rates far below current interest rates is to buy back the old bonds at the low market price, effectively providing the company a yield to maturity[4] similar to current market interest rates. Thus, the benefit of having issued bonds when interest rates were lower can be fully realized without making a new capital investment.

Flotation costs may raise the cost of new capital a small amount above the cost of existing capital. Flotation costs are the costs associated with a new issue of debt or equity, such as the fees paid to investment bankers for handling the sale. Likewise, the administrative costs associated with buying back outstanding bonds may decrease the marginal required return necessary to justify continued use of those funds.

COST OF CAPITAL COMPONENTS

Now that the general cost of capital principles have been developed, the next step is to determine the costs of the various components of capital so that these can be tied together in a single weighted average cost. Identification of the individual component costs is covered in this section.

[4]The yield to maturity is the internal rate of return based on the current price and the stream of interest and principal payments.

COST OF DEBT

If your company has no excess funds on hand and is considering new investments, the component cost of debt is the effective interest rate on new debt, adjusted for taxes. The interest rate on new debt can be estimated by talking to potential lenders and investment bankers. Alternately, the estimation can begin with observation of market interest rates on debt of similar risk such as bonds the rating agencies have assigned to the same risk class as your company's bonds. Another alternative is to use the effective interest rates earned by holders of the company's existing marketable debt.

IBM bonds maturing in 2013 pay annual interest of 7.5 percent of face value. The bonds were selling for $1,087.50 for every $1,000 of face value in early 1998. IBM must provide investors with a rate of return at least equal to the yield to maturity on the existing bonds if it is to sell new debt. The yield to maturity on the existing bonds can be found using the procedures discussed in Chapter 3 for finding the internal rate of return.[5] Applying the internal rate of return approach, and assuming year-end interest payments for simplicity, the yield to maturity on the IBM bond is 6.57 percent. This yield to maturity can be confirmed by noting that $\$1087.50 = \$75PVA1_{15yrs,6.57\%} + \$1,000/1.0657^{15}$. Investors would not be interested in buying new bonds of this company at this time unless they could expect a return of at least 6.57 percent.[6]

When a company issues new debt, there are often administrative costs, fees to investment bankers, and other flotation costs that can raise the effective interest cost. Suppose, for example, IBM issues new bonds promising annual interest of $65.70 on each $1,000 bond. Flotation costs are $25 per bond, so IBM will net only $975. The effective interest cost to IBM is the yield to maturity or internal rate of return at the $975 price. If the new bonds have a 15-year maturity, the yield to maturity at a $975 price is 6.84 percent. This can be confirmed by noting that $65.70PVA1_{15yrs,6.84\%} + 1,000/1.0684^{15} = \$975$. Thus, the before-tax cost of the new debt for IBM is 6.84 percent.

After-Tax Cost of Debt

Interest expense and flotation costs are tax-deductible expenses in that they reduce taxable income. Thus, the after-tax cost of existing debt (k_d) is approximately:

$$k_d = YTM \ (1 - tax\ rate) \tag{16-2}$$

---

[5]An easily applied approximation formula can be used:

YTM = [Annual interest payment + (maturity value − market value)/n] ÷
      [(maturity value + market value)/2]
    = [75 + (1,000 − 1,087.5)/15] ÷ [(1,000 + 1,087.5)/2] = 6.63%

[6]Timing of tax payments may cause the required yield to maturity on new debt to be a bit different from the yield to maturity on existing debt. With IBM's 7.5 percent, 15-year bonds, the after-tax yield to maturity (YTM*) for an investor in a 28 percent tax bracket is:

$$1,087.5 = 75(1 - .28)PVA1_{15yrs,YTM*} + [1,000 - (1,000 - 1,087.5).28]/(1 + YTM*)^{15}$$

Solving with trial-and error or other procedures, YTM* = 4.82 percent. For a new bond selling at par to provide the same after-tax return, the interest rate must be .0482/(1 − .28) = 6.69%.

where YTM is the *yield to maturity* (effective interest rate) on existing debt. For a corporate tax rate of 35 percent and bonds with a yield to maturity of 6.57 percent, the cost of existing debt is approximately:[7]

$$k_d = .0657 \, (1 - .35) = 4.27\%$$

To justify the use of funds on hand, the component cost of debt is 4.27 percent.

Flotation costs are also a tax-deductible expense, so the after-tax cost of new debt (k_{nd}) is approximately:

$$k_{nd} = YTM_n \, (1 - \text{tax rate}) \qquad \text{(16-3)}$$

where YTM_n is the yield to maturity on the new debt, based on the net proceeds to the borrower. For a company with a 6.84 percent before-tax cost of new debt and a 35 percent marginal tax rate, the after-tax cost of new debt is approximately:[8]

$$k_{nd} = .0684 \, (1 - .35) = 4.45\%$$

To justify borrowing more money, the component after-tax cost of debt is 4.45 percent.[9]

---

[7]The exact after-tax cost must take into consideration the timing of tax savings. For the 7.5 percent bond with 15 years until maturity, selling at $1,087.5, the after-tax cost to retire early is $1,087.5 + .35(1,000 − 1,087.5) = $1,056.88. The after-tax annual interest payment avoided is $75(1 − .35) = $48.75, and the avoided principal payment in year 15 is $1,000. The discount rate that equates the avoided future payments with the after-tax outlay to retire the bond now is 4.35 percent. Management should not retire existing debt as long as a 4.35 percent component after-tax cost of debt can be justified by investment opportunities.

[8]The timing of tax savings from flotation costs can affect the after-tax cost of debt because flotation costs are paid up-front, but are amortized over the life of the bond for tax purposes. This raises the required return for IBM slightly:

Initial inflow = $1,000 − $25 = $975.00

Annual outflow = $65.70 − ($65.70 × .35) − ($25 ÷ 15).35 = $42.12

Cash outflow in year 10 to retire the bond = $1,000

The discount rate that equates these cash flows is 4.44%. In this case, the two approaches give answers that differ by only one one-hundredth of a percent.

[9]An alternative to adjusting the required return for flotation cost is to deduct the flotation cost as an initial cash outlay for the investment. The choice between the two approaches that assures wealth-maximizing decisions depends on the life of the company's competitive advantage, which is ultimately the source of a positive NPV. If funding is for longer than the life of the proposed capital investment, which is typically the case with equity financing, allocating all the flotation cost to the first use of those funds overstates the cost of funding for that project while understating the cost of funds for later projects. Suppose, for example, you are raising long-term funds for a one-year investment, with the expectation of rolling over that 1-year investment indefinitely. By deducting flotation cost as a cash outflow, you are assigning all flotation costs to the first year. This may cause you to reject a series of profitable investments because the entire flotation cost for the series cannot be absorbed by the first use of funds. If you expect your competitive advantage to last for only the life of the initial investment, on the other hand, then flotation costs must be recovered over the life of that investment in order to make wealth-maximizing choices.

COST OF PREFERRED STOCK

Preferred stock pays a fixed dividend and generally has no maturity date. The dividends are not, of course, contractual like the interest on debt. The main problems caused by a decision not to pay a preferred dividend are that the company's reputation is damaged, preferred stockholders may gain voting rights, and most preferred stock is cumulative, meaning that missed dividends must be made up before dividends can be paid to common stockholders. These problems are sufficient to keep most companies paying their preferred dividends unless they are in severe financial difficulty. The effective rate of return earned by a buyer of preferred stock is simply the dividend divided by the price. If your company has funds on hand, and is facing the question of whether to invest in new projects or return money to investors, the component cost of existing preferred stock (k_p) is the return earned by an investor:

$$k_p = D_p/P_p \qquad \qquad \text{(16-4)}$$

where D_p is the annual dividend per share for existing preferred stock and P_p is the price per share of existing preferred stock. This is the opportunity cost because one alternative use of available funds is the purchase of the preferred stock in the marketplace at the current price of P_p, thereby saving perpetual dividends of D_p. There is no adjustment for taxes because dividends do not result in a decrease in the company's income tax.

The effective cost to a company issuing new preferred stock is the dividend per year (D_{np}), divided by the amount the company can expect to net for a share after paying flotation costs (P_{np}). In other words, the cost of new preferred stock (k_{np}) is:

$$k_{np} = D_{np}/P_{np} \qquad \qquad \text{(16-5)}$$

Example. General Motors' $1.98 preferred stock was selling for $26.125 a share in early 1998. The component cost of this preferred stock is:

$$k_p = 1.98/26.125 = 7.58\%$$

If General Motors has funds on hand, it can buy back the preferred stock in the marketplace for $26.125 a share. The $1.98 a year in dividends saved results in an opportunity cost of 7.58 percent. If General Motors needs to raise additional funds, however, the effective cost rises. In order to sell new $100 preferred stock at its par value of $100, a dividend of $7.58 per year would be required. If flotation costs for General Motors will be 3 percent of new preferred stock issued, the net amount received per share will be $97. The component cost of new preferred is therefore:

$$k_{np} = 7.58/97 = 7.81\%$$

COST OF COMMON STOCK

The principle of required return for common stock is the same as that for debt and preferred stock. The required return is an opportunity cost based on returns investors can expect from alternative investments of equal risk. For bonds and preferred stock, the current price was related to the promised series of payments in order to compute the rate of return expected by investors. However, there is no promised payment for common stockholders, and there is no direct way to observe the returns stockholders expect to earn on investments of equal risk. Thus, estimation procedures must be used.

In order to estimate the required return on common equity, it is necessary to know something about the nature of common stock itself. Common stock, like preferred stock, pays dividends. In the absence of stock repurchase, acquisition, or voluntary liquidation, the only thing shareholders will ever receive is dividends. A particular investor may receive money by selling stock to some other investor, but as a group investors receive nothing but dividends. The value of a share of stock, therefore, is the present value of the stream of future dividends. In other words:

$$P = \frac{D_1}{(1 + k_e)^1} + \frac{D_2}{(1 + k_e)^2} + \cdots \tag{16-6}$$

where P is the price of the stock, D_t is the dividend at the end of the period t, and k_e is the required return on equity.

If the stream of future dividends were known, the discount rate that made the present value of dividends equal the stock's current price would be the investors' required return. However, future dividends are not known with certainty and in many cases are extremely difficult to predict. Various methods have been applied to overcome these problems and estimate the required return in different situations. The three most widely used methods are the constant growth dividend valuation model, the earnings yield model, and the mean-variance capital asset pricing model. The appropriate method depends on the information available, and more than one method is often used as a check. The three most widely used methods are discussed here.

Constant Growth Dividend Valuation Model

In Chapter 3, we showed that if cash flows grow at a constant rate of g per period, Equation 16-6 can be reduced to:

$$P = D_1/(k_e - g) \tag{16-7}$$

With a little rearrangement of terms, Equation 16-7 can be rewritten as:

$$k_e = (D_1/P) + g \tag{16-7a}$$

As an example, suppose Davenport Corporation has just paid an annual dividend of $3.50 per share, and dividends are expected to grow 4 percent a year. The dividends after one year (D_1) are therefore expected to be $3.50 \times 1.04 = 3.64$. If the stock has a current price of $50 a share, this implies that the return expected by investors is:[10,11]

$$k_e = 3.64/50 + .04 = \underline{\underline{11.3\%}}$$

The dividend growth model analysis began with an observed price and last year's dividend, so the only item difficult to estimate is the dividend growth rate. If dividends have grown steadily in the past and there is reason to believe that pattern will continue, the historical growth rate can be used as g. Unfortunately, historical dividend growth is seldom that steady. In other cases, surveys of security analysts or published forecasts like those in *Value Line* are used to estimate g. Many public utilities survey hundreds of security analysts in preparation for rate hearings to determine analysts' estimates of dividend growth.

Another approach to estimating the dividend growth rate is based on the dividend payout ratio and the reinvestment rate. If dividends remain a constant percentage of earnings, the dividend growth rate will be:[12]

$$g = \text{return on reinvested equity} \times \text{retention rate}$$

For example, a company that retains 40 percent of earnings for reinvestment and is able to earn a return of 10 percent on the equity portion of funds reinvested in the company will have a dividend growth rate of:

$$g = .10 \times .40 = \underline{\underline{4.0\%}}$$

To apply this approach, it is necessary that the rate earned on additional equity investment in the company be known and steady, that earnings from existing investments be steady, and that the dividend payout ratio be constant. The growth rate can be estimated using Equation 16-7 only if these conditions are approximated.

There are many cases in which a company is not currently paying dividends, although dividends are expected at some future time. There are other cases in

---

[10]Dividends are often paid quarterly rather than annually. Suppose, instead, that a quarterly dividend of $0.85 has just been received and dividends are expected to grow at 1 percent a quarter. The return per quarter expected by investors is $(.85 \times 1.01)/50 + .01 = .02717$. The annual required return is then $(1.02717)^4 - 1 = 11.32\%$.

[11]If the required return is being computed 1/q of a period after the last dividend, rather than immediately after the last dividend, Equation 13-6 is rewritten $P = [D_1/(k_e - g)](1 + k_e)^{1/q}$. This equation can be solved for k by trial and error, as was done for the internal rate of return.

[12]*Proof*: Assuming that existing assets are invested at a constant rate of return, growth in earnings per share comes from reinvestment of earnings as follows:

$$EPS_{t+1} = EPS_t + \text{reinvestment rate} \times \text{retention rate} \times EPS_t$$

This equation can be rewritten $EPS_{t+1}/EPS_t - 1 = \text{reinvestment rate} \times \text{retention rate}$.

which dividends are being paid, but growth is erratic. In these cases, it is necessary to turn to some other method to estimate the return required by common equity investors.

Earnings Yield Model

Managers sometimes use their company's earnings yield (earnings per share, price per share) as the required return on equity. The rationale for this measure is that the price per share is the amount that will be received from selling a new share and earnings per share are the amount that must be earned on the additional equity to avoid a dilution of earnings per share for the existing shareholders.

A problem with the earnings yield model is that it is based on accounting income rather than cash flow. Furthermore, it is based on earnings per share for a past period while the stock price is affected by investors' expectations of future performance. For this reason, earnings yields based on early 1998 stock prices ranged from 1 percent for American Financial to 100 percent for Mercury Financial, two companies in the financial services industry. The earnings yield model is consistent with the cash flow approach used in the dividend growth model only if accounting earnings are the same as cash flow, and any retained earnings are reinvested at the required return on equity. If investors expect the company to have future investment opportunities with positive net present values, the earnings yield is not a good estimate of shareholders' required return.

Mean-Variance Capital Asset Pricing Model

The mean-variance capital asset pricing model approach differs from the cost of equity approaches previously discussed in that it focuses on market returns for investments of similar risk rather than investor response to a particular security. Thus, it can be used when earnings and dividends are unstable and when the stock is not publicly traded so there is no market price. As shown in Chapter 14, the mean-variance capital asset pricing model leads to the conclusion that the required return on equity is:

$$k_e = R_f + \beta_{s,m}(R_m - R_f) \tag{16-8}$$

where R_f is the current interest rate on risk-free investments; R_m is the expected return for investments in general, commonly referred to as expected return for the market portfolio; $\beta_{s,m}$ is the stock's beta (systematic risk) in relation to the market portfolio; and $R_m - R_f$ is therefore the risk premium for investments in general. The risk premium for a particular investment is then its beta multiplied by the general market risk premium.

Risk-free interest rates are widely published, with the interest rates on U.S. government bonds being commonly used as the risk-free rate. Betas for the stocks of publicly traded companies are computed using historical data and published in various investment advisory services such as *Value Line*. Alternately, betas can be computed directly from historical data as illustrated in Chapter 14. If the company's stock is not publicly traded, meaning there is no market price to use in computing holding period returns, betas for publicly traded companies believed to have similar risk characteristics can be used. Expected return for investments in general (R_m) is estimated from historical returns or surveys of investor expectations. Measurement issues are discussed in more detail in Chapter 14.

Example. The stock of Harley Davidson had a beta of 1.20, according to *Value Line*. The interest rate on long-term U.S. government bonds was 6 percent, and the estimated market risk premium was 6.5 percent. The required return for equity investors of Harley Davidson was therefore:

$$k_e = .06 + 1.20(.065) = \underline{\underline{13.80\%}}$$

By way of comparison, the required return under these conditions for a stock of average risk would be:

$$k_e = .06 + 1.00(.065) = \underline{\underline{12.50\%}}$$

These various methods of estimating the cost of common equity exist primarily because it is impossible to observe directly the return investors are expecting from investments of similar risk. The choice of an appropriate measure in a particular situation depends primarily on the type of information that is available. In public utility rate cases, where cost of equity is critically important and decision making is done in public, the traditional method has been the dividend growth model, but the mean-variance capital asset pricing model has gained in popularity, and new methods such as the arbitrage pricing model have been used as well. With further research efforts, we will probably improve our ability to estimate the required return on equity, with or without direct observation of investor expectations.

Cost of Existing Equity (Retained Earnings)

Once the return required by investors is determined, this return must be converted to a return required by the company to satisfy investors. The equity investors' required return is often used directly as the component cost of the equity portion of existing funds. Some authors, however, argue that there is an important tax issue involved. Equity funds on hand for investment often arise from retained earnings. If earnings are paid out in the form of dividends, many investors must pay taxes on the dividends, and therefore have less money to use or invest. If the earnings are reinvested internally instead of being paid out, the increase in earnings may cause the stock price to rise, and the gain would be taxed only when the stock was sold. Some authors suggest that the cost of existing equity funds is therefore the return required by shareholders, multiplied by (1 − the marginal tax rate of the average shareholder).

We estimated the required return of Harley Davidson shareholders to be 13.80 percent. If the average shareholder were in a 28 percent tax bracket, the opportunity cost of existing equity (k_e) using this approach would be:

$$k_e = .1380(1 - .28) = \underline{9.94\%}$$

A problem with basing the opportunity cost of existing equity on the share-holders' tax rates is that tax rates vary among shareholders. Charitable endowment funds, pension funds, IRA accounts, and other personal pension accounts invest in common stock and pay no income tax. Stocks also are held by people in low marginal tax brackets, including retirees and young people who received stock as gifts. Therefore, taxes on dividend income are minimal or nonexistent for many shareholders. Furthermore, companies can use at least part of their retained earnings to buy back stock rather than paying dividends, thereby returning money to shareholders without the tax consequences of dividend payments. Consequently, most authors suggest the use of the equity investors' required return as the cost of existing equity capital, without adjustment for investors' tax rates.

Some authors use the term *cost of retained earnings* rather than cost of existing equity. One reason they use this terminology is that the existing equity choice facing a company is often between reinvesting this year's earnings and paying them out as dividends. However, companies without good investment opportunities can buy back common stock or even liquidate completely, so the term *existing equity* gives a more comprehensive view of the choices you face as a manager.

On the balance sheet, the common equity account is often broken into three categories: common stock, paid-in capital in excess of par, and retained earnings. These divisions exist for accounting purposes, but all common equity is money of the common stockholders being used in the company. Retained earnings do not have an opportunity cost different from the opportunity costs of shareholders' funds categorized in other common equity accounts.

Cost of New Equity

If your company has no funds available and must turn to outside sources, the return earned must be higher than that required by investors in order to cover flotation costs and still provide investors with their required return.

If all earnings are being paid out in the form of dividends, a commonly used formula for the cost of new common equity is:

$$k_{ne} = k_e/(1 - f) \tag{16-9}$$

where f is flotation cost as a percent of market price. Suppose, for example, Harley Davidson was going to sell new common stock and investors had a required return of 13.8 percent. If the stock was selling at $30 a share and the company would receive a net amount per share of only $27 from the sale of a new issue, the percentage flotation cost, f, would be 3/30 = .10 and the cost of new equity would be:

$$k_{ne} = .1380/(1 - .10) = \underline{15.33\%}$$

If some earnings are being retained, resulting in anticipated dividend growth, the impact of flotation costs is decreased. This decrease occurs because the total amount of equity capital made available through the new issue includes both the money raised directly through the new issue and the retention of earnings on that money. The cost of new equity with dividend growth anticipated declines to:[13]

$$k_{ne} = D_1/[P(1 - f)] + g \qquad\qquad (16\text{-}10)$$

Again taking Harley Davidson as an example, the annual dividend was $0.16 a share, and investors had a required return of 13.8 percent. If the stock price was $30, Equation 16-7a could be used to estimate an implied growth rate:

$$.1380 = 0.16(1 + g)/30 + g; \text{ therefore } g = .1320$$

The estimated cost of new equity would therefore be:

$$k_{ne} = 0.16(1.1320)/[30(1 - .10)] + .1320 = \underline{13.87\%}$$

WEIGHTS FOR THE WEIGHTED AVERAGE COST |

To combine the previously determined component costs in a weighted average cost of capital, it is necessary to determine what percentage of total capital comes from each source. Assuming, for the moment, that the company is at what its managers consider to be its optimal capital structure (optimal mix of debt, equity, and other capital sources), the company will then continue to raise money in the same proportions. There will probably be small variations from these proportions because of economies of scale in raising money; if General Electric needs $100,000, the company will not raise that small amount with combination of debt and equity issues because the flotation costs would exceed the amount raised. However, small movements around the optimal capital structure need not be of concern for the purpose of our analysis.

Example. Tyler Corporation has no excess funds on hand. It maintains what management considers to be an optimal capital structure of 40 percent long-term debt,

---

[13]Each of these formulas for the cost of new equity depends on the assumption that cash inflows from the investment, other than the cash flows paid out as dividends, can be reinvested at k_{ne}. With Equation 16-9, this assumption is satisfied if the investment is a perpetuity. With Equation 16-10, this assumption is justified if a series of new investment opportunities paying k_{ne} is anticipated. To take another extreme position, assume the capital investment being financed has only a 1-year life, after which the funds must be invested at k_e. To justify selling new equity in this case, k_{ne} must equal $(1 + k_e)/(1 - f) - 1$ so that the flotation cost is completely recovered in the first year. Thus, the precise cost of new equity depends on the life of the investment being considered and investment opportunities available in the future.

10 percent preferred stock, and 50 percent common equity. The after-tax costs of new funds in these three categories are 8 percent, 12 percent, and 15 percent, respectively. The proportion of the optimal capital structure represented by each source is multiplied by the cost of that source in determining a cost of capital. Using Equation 16-1, the weighted average cost of capital is therefore:

$$WACC = (.40 \times .08) + (.10 \times .12) + (.50 \times .15) = 11.9\%$$

The same computation is often set up in table form for convenience:

Source	Weight (Proportion)	Cost	Weighted Cost
Debt	.40	.08	.032
Preferred Stock	.10	.12	.012
Common Stock	.50	.15	.075
Weighted average cost			.119

A choice must be made between weights (proportions) based on market values and weights based on the book values of capital sources. The conclusion that net present value measures the increase in shareholder wealth is based on the assumption that the capital structure remains unchanged; that is, the *value* of each component of capital remains a constant proportion of the total *value* of capital. The total value of capital, in turn, is the present value of future cash flows from the company's investments, and the value of each component of capital is then the present value of cash flows to that component. If markets are efficient, market values will equal present values of cash flows. Book values, on the other hand, represent historical cost. Therefore, market values appear to be a superior basis for developing weights.

Despite this conclusion, many companies use book value weights for what they view as practical considerations. Market weights change on an hourly basis, as stock prices change, and managers like to fix their eyes on more stable targets. Book weights, although inconsistent with the theoretical justification for net present value, are stable.

The market values of stocks and bonds can generally be determined by reference to the financial press. For untraded bonds or for long-term debt not in the form of marketable securities, the market value can be estimated by finding the present value of remaining principal and interest payments, discounted at the yield to maturity for similar instruments that are publicly traded, possibly increasing the required interest somewhat to compensate investors for lack of marketability. Current maturities of long-term debt, which appear in the current liabilities section of the balance sheet, would generally be considered part of the debt capital used to finance fixed assets, as would the current portion of capital lease obligations.

The market value of common stock is the value of the common stockholders' total claims, which equals the number of shares outstanding, multiplied by the market price per share. The shareholders' claims are represented on the balance sheet by several separate accounts, including common stock, paid-in-capital in excess of par, and retained earnings. The various common stock accounts do not, however, have separate values and costs in the cost of capital analysis. For untraded common stock, a value estimate can be made by such methods as computing the present value of the expected stream of future dividends at the required return on equity or referral to the price-earnings ratios of traded stocks of similar companies.

If a company is not at its optimal capital structure, but is in the process of working toward that target structure, then it makes sense to evaluate new projects with a cost of capital as it will be in the target capital structure. The target capital structure is used to determine the weights, and the costs of the various components are adjusted for estimates of what they will be when the optimal capital structure is realized.[14]

MARGINAL COST OF CAPITAL SCHEDULE |

As defined earlier in this chapter, the marginal cost of capital is the weighted average cost, assuming that new funds used for the investment will be in the same proportion as the company's existing capital structure. However, the marginal cost depends on whether internally generated funds are being used or capital is being raised from outside sources. If internally generated funds are adequate for all attractive investments, the marginal cost is the weighted average cost of existing funds. If funds must be raised externally, then flotation cost must be recognized in computing weighted average cost.

Example. Corvallis Corporation maintains a capital structure of 60 percent debt and 40 percent equity. The component costs of capital are as follows:

	Debt	Equity
Cost of existing funds	6%	14%
Cost of new funds	7	16

The managers anticipate having $50,000 of income available for reinvestment in the business over the next year. Depreciation, a noncash expense, of $30,000 will be deducted in computing income, so the managers anticipate a total of $80,000 in internally generated funds.

---

[14]Impacts of changes in leverage on beta are discussed in Chapter 14.

If Corvallis makes only $30,000 of new capital investments, no new capital will be raised, and the marginal cost of capital will be the weighted average cost of existing funds:

$$\text{WACC}_1 = .6 \times .06 + .4 \times .14 = \underline{9.2\%}$$

If only $30,000 is invested, all income can be paid out as dividends, and the proportions of debt and equity in the capital structure will remain unchanged.

If the managers decide to invest more than $30,000, the company will retain some income. To maintain the optimal capital structure, though, the company must raise $1.50 of new debt for each dollar of income retained. The total amount of debt the company can raise while using retained earnings for the equity portion is determined as follows:

$$\text{debt} = .60 \ (\text{debt} + \text{equity})$$
$$\text{debt} = .60 \ (\text{debt} + 50{,}000)$$
$$\text{debt} = 75{,}000$$

The weighted average cost in this range is based on the cost of *new* debt and *existing* equity:

$$\text{WACC}_2 = .6 \times .07 + .4 \times .14 = \underline{9.8\%}$$

Thus, the marginal cost of the first $30,000 of investment capital is 9.2 percent, and the marginal cost of the next $125,000 ($75,000 of debt + $50,000 of retained earnings) is 9.8 percent. Beyond this, both new debt and new equity must be raised, and the weighted average cost becomes:

$$\text{WACC}_3 = .6 \times .07 + .4 \times .16 = \underline{10.6\%}$$

This schedule of costs can be plotted graphically as a marginal cost of capital schedule, which is illustrated in Figure 16.1. The marginal cost of capital schedule in Figure 16.1 is shown as stable at 10.6 percent for all amounts above $155,000. It is possible that the cost would rise further if large amounts of money were raised and this lead investors to perceive Corvallis as more risky because of its rapid growth.

An investment opportunity schedule for Corvallis is also shown in Figure 16.1. To simplify the discussion of investment opportunities, we assume that there are no mutually exclusive projects and no multiple internal rate of return projects, so that all investments with internal rates of return above the weighted average cost of capital will be accepted. With these assumptions, we can use the internal rate of return to define the investment opportunity schedule, as illustrated in Figure 16.1. In this case, a total of $120,000 is invested and all projects with internal rates of return above the 9.8 percent marginal cost of capital

| **Figure 16.1** **Marginal Cost of Capital and**
Investment Opportunity Schedules

This figure shows a rising cost of capital schedule based on use of internal and external funds. The investment opportunity schedule represents the internal rates of return available on capital investments.

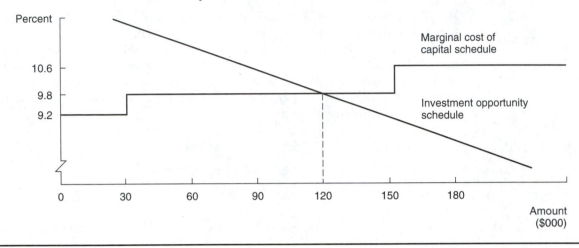

are accepted. Corvallis would finance the $120,000 by using $30,000 of internally generated funds other than income, by retaining income of .4 × $90,000 = $36,000, and by issuing new debt in the amount of $54,000.

To provide an indication of the actual sizes of the steps in a marginal cost of capital schedule, Table 16.1 summarizes flotation costs as a percent of issue

| **Table 16.1** **Flotation Costs as a Percent of Issue**

This table shows flotation costs as a percent of issue, and therefore gives an indication of the sizes of steps in the weighted average cost of capital schedule. Total flotation costs include the underwriter's commission and other expenses, such as legal fees.

Size of Issue (in $ millions)	Bonds	Preferred Stock	Common Stock
0.0–0.5			23.7
0.6–0.9			20.9
1.0–1.9			16.9
2.0–4.9	6.2		12.4
5.0–9.9	3.2	2.6	8.1
10.0–19.9	1.9	1.8	5.9
20.0–49.9	1.4	1.7	4.6
50.0–99.9			4.2
100 and over	1.1	1.1	3.5

size. Because percentage issue costs decline as the size of the issue increases, the sizes of the steps will be inversely related to the size of the company.

SOME ADDITIONAL ISSUES IN COST OF CAPITAL ANALYSIS |

DEFERRED TAXES

Deferred taxes are often a substantial item on the liability side of the balance sheet, and may initially appear to be a cost-free source of funds with which to acquire new investments. Upon examination, however, it becomes clear that deferred taxes are *not* a source of investment capital. Deferred taxes appear on the balance sheet primarily because assets are being depreciated less rapidly for public reporting purposes than for tax purposes. These differences in depreciation cause income reported to the public to exceed income used by the Internal Revenue Service to determine the tax liability. The income tax expense on the income statement is the tax that would have been paid if publicly reported income was what the government taxed. The excess of the income tax expense on the income statement over the income tax actually paid to the government is treated as an addition to the deferred tax liability on the balance sheet. Deferred tax reflects the fact that if no new assets are acquired the income reported to the government will eventually be higher than the income reported to the public, and consequently, the income tax paid will be greater than the tax expense shown on the income statement.

For capital budgeting, we use projected cash flows, not income statement numbers. To forecast cash flows, we deduct taxes that will be paid, not the income tax expense on the public financial statements. Thus, the deferred tax, being nothing but a means of reconciling the financial statements with the actual cash flows, is not a source of cash with which to acquire capital investments.

ACCOUNTS PAYABLE AND ACCRUED EXPENSES

The logic applied to accounts payable, accrued expenses, and other spontaneous current liabilities is similar to that for deferred taxes. If the capital investment analysis is carried out on a cash flow basis, the payment of wages, material costs, and so on are recognized for capital investment analysis purposes when the payments are made, not when the liabilities are incurred. An account payable or an accrued expense is a forewarning that a cash payment is required, not a source of funds for making cash payments.

SHORT-TERM DEBT

Short-term debt is a potential source of confusion and controversy in determining a cost of capital. Short-term borrowing may be used to meet temporary needs, such as a seasonal inventory buildup, or it may be used as permanent funding.

In the latter case, the company finances part of its permanent needs with what is technically short-term debt, hoping thereby to reduce overall financing costs. Some companies, for example, borrow in the commercial paper market, with each individual issue of commercial paper maturing within 9 months and being repaid with the proceeds of a new issue. In other cases, companies may borrow from banks on a demand basis, but with the loans actually remaining outstanding for years even though they are technically callable on a moment's notice.

When short-term debt is used as permanent financing, it is clearly part of the company's permanent capital in substance, if not in form, and should be treated like other long-term debt in the cost of capital analysis. A decision to finance a long-term investment with short-term funds is a decision to speculate on interest rate movements. A long-term investment that is not profitable when financed with long-term sources of funds should not be justified by hopes of successful speculation on interest rate movements. After all, a manager with the exceedingly rare ability to forecast interest rates over the life of a capital investment can profit from that ability by trading in financial futures, without being distracted by capital investments. A simple and reasonable approach is to carry out capital budgeting assuming long-term investment will be financed from long-term sources of funds, and then make a separate decision about whether to speculate on interest rate movements.

When short-term borrowing is actually used for short-term needs, such as seasonal inventory buildups, the problem is a little more difficult. This financing is not part of the company's permanent capital, but the cost must be recognized somewhere in the analysis of a capital investment. One approach is to forecast the amount of short-term borrowing that will be used for a particular investment's seasonal working capital buildups, and compute net cash flow to capital after deducting cash flows to (or adding cash flows from) short-term creditors. This is appropriate if the short-term debt does not decrease the optimal amount of long-term debt in the capital structure.

A second possible approach to recognizing temporary short-term debt is to determine the average amount outstanding over the year and use that as an amount of debt, to be added to any long-term debt to arrive at total debt. This latter approach can be justified if the average amount of short-term debt directly decreases the optimal amount of long-term debt in the capital structure.

LEASES

Leases are frequently used as an alternative to debt. Instead of signing a loan agreement calling for a fixed series of principal and interest payments, the company signs a lease agreement calling for a fixed series of lease payments over all or most of the asset's life. Accountants recognize the similarity of leasing and borrowing by classifying those leases that are close substitutes for borrowing as *financial leases*,[15] also called *capital leases*, and requiring the present values of

---

[15]Financial leases are defined in Chapter 21.

the lease payments for those leases to appear as assets and long-term liabilities on the balance sheet. If a lease has the same economic consequences as debt, the present value of contractual lease payments should be treated as part of the long-term debt in cost of capital analysis as well. As a practical matter, the present value of lease payments appears on the balance sheet. As with debt, it is necessary to include the current portion of the lease obligation as well as the present value of payments on operating and capital leases that are due more than a year in the future.

The effective rate of return for a new lease contract can be found by computing an internal rate of return, with the lease payments being outflows and the avoided purchase price of the asset being a benefit. The effective rate of return is typically very close to that of the company's other long-term debt. For an existing lease, it is generally assumed that the required return (k_d) is the same as that for the long-term debt. The present value of the lease payments, discounted at the yield to maturity of existing debt, may be used as a substitute for the market value of the lease payments in determining weights for the weighted average cost of capital. Other aspects of lease analysis will be discussed in Chapter 21.

CONVERTIBLES

Convertible bonds and convertible preferred stock can be exchanged for a specified number of shares of common stock at the option of the holder. These securities are effectively combinations of fixed-income securities and options. These securities, and their cost of capital implications, were examined using the option pricing models discussed in Chapter 15. A simpler approach is to estimate the market value of the convertible security without the conversion feature, then assume that the difference between market value and value as a nonconvertible security is an option investment. The beta for the call option can be computed as was explained in Chapter 15. Then, the mean-variance capital asset pricing model can be used to compute the required return on the option investment.

Example. Excel Corporation has 10-year, 8 percent convertible bonds outstanding. The bonds are selling for $1,100, or $100 over their par value. The interest rate on nonconvertible bonds of this type is 10 percent, so the value as a nonconvertible bond is:

$$80 \text{PVAI} \mid_{10 \text{yrs}, 10\%} + 1,000/1.1^{10} = \underline{\underline{\$877}}$$

Thus, each bond represents an $877 pure debt instrument and an option valued at $1,100 − $877 = $223. For computation of the weighted average cost of capital, the $877 is added to the market value of debt and the $223 is added to the market value of a source of funding category called *options*.

DEPRECIATION-GENERATED FUNDS

A simple approximation to cash flow from operations is net income plus depreciation. Use of this form of cash flow approximation in forecasting benefits of capital investments often leads to controversy with regard to the role of depreciation and the cost of so-called depreciation-generated funds. If cash flows from operations exceed income, it is because assets have decreased or spontaneous liabilities have increased, and depreciation is just one of the ways in which the value of assets can decrease. Thus, there is nothing unique about depreciation-generated funds. It would be more appropriate to talk in general about "internally generated funds in excess of earnings," which can arise from decreases in assets or increases in spontaneous liabilities. These funds are simply existing funds available for reinvestment and have a cost equal to the weighted average cost of existing funds.

COSTS OF CAPITAL FOR INTERNATIONAL CAPITAL INVESTMENTS

A general principle of capital investment analysis is that the discount rate should reflect the marginal cost of capital, which may be affected by the characteristics of that particular project. For domestic investments, risk is the most important characteristic in this regard. For multinational capital investments, the opportunity to take advantage of international capital markets must be considered as well.

If the foreign investment is to be financed in the United States, an approach similar to the pure-play approach of Chapter 14 can be used. If an equity beta for overseas operations of this type can be estimated, a cost of capital can be estimated as was done for division costs of capital in Chapter 14.

Example. American International Motors (AIM), an automobile dealership in Riyadh, arranges all of its funding in the United States. AIM uses $\frac{2}{3}$ equity and $\frac{1}{3}$ debt in its capital structure. While AIM is not publicly traded, betas for domestic automobile makers are slightly over 1.0. An international mutual fund with similar systematic risk characteristics to AIM has a beta of 1.877 though. AIM borrows at 10 percent, the risk-free rate is 7 percent, and the average risk premium in the market is 6.5 percent. AIM pays a U.S. income tax rate of 34%. Given this information, the required return for the Riyadh dealership investment is found as follows:

$$k_e = .07 + 1.877 \times .065 = .1920$$

$$\text{WACC} = (2/3).1920 + (1/3).10(1 - .34) = .15$$

If world capital markets are truly integrated, there is no benefit to overseas financing and the divisional cost of capital approach is all that is needed for net present value analysis of an overseas investment. But there are restrictions on cash flows so that the world capital markets do not operate as a single unit. When part of the cost of an asset is funded overseas, imbalances between capital markets must also be considered. Foreign interest rates must be considered, along with implications of foreign taxes. The impact of foreign debt on the company's overall optimal debt ratio must also be considered.

Example. Suppose that American International Motors (AIM) can arrange dollar-denominated borrowing in Riyadh at an interest rate of 7 percent for the debt portion of its financing. The interest expense would reduce taxable income, which is being taxed at an effective 20 percent marginal rate in Saudi Arabia, after considering various tax benefits available, and then taxed at 34 percent in the United States. This financing opportunity would decrease the cost of capital as follows, and further increase the attractiveness of the investment:

$$\text{WACC} = (2/3).1920 + (1/3).07(1 - .20)(1 - .34) = 14.03\%$$

One way to simplify the analysis of foreign investments is to use the equity residual approach discussed in Chapter 20. To briefly preview that approach, cash flow to the equity holders, after deducting interest expense, is forecast, and the present value of those cash flows is computed using the cost of equity as the discount rate.[16]

As in the case of industrial revenue bonds for domestic investments, special financing may be provided as an incentive to invest in a particular country. The special financing may be substantially more than the proportion of debt normally used by the company. The treatment of these special financing arrangements is not essentially different from that discussed for domestic investments in Chapter 20. The interest saved is essentially a subsidy to the project, and can be treated as an additional cash flow to be discounted at the appropriate discount rate.

Example. Suppose the Saudi government is willing to provide a loan of 17.5 million riyals for 5 years with no interest, to encourage American International Motors to open a dealership. Suppose the riyal interest rate is 7 percent, and the marginal Saudi tax rate is 20 percent. The effect of this financing is then an additional cash flow of $.07 \times 17.5(1 - .20) = .98$ million riyals a year for 5 years. The cash flow saved from the special financing is discounted at a rate appropriate for its risk.

A COMPREHENSIVE EXAMPLE

The balance sheet of Toys "R" Us is summarized in Table 16.2.[17] Deferred liabilities, such as deferred taxes, can be ignored because they reconcile reported income with cash flow and, thus, do not constitute sources of funds for capital

---

[16]For additional reading, see Alan C. Shapiro, "Financial Structure and Cost of Capital in the Multinational Corporation," *Journal of Financial and Quantitative Analysis* 13 (June 1978): 211–226.

[17]Estimates in this example were prepared by the author from publicly available information and do not necessarily reflect estimates by Toys "R" Us management.

| TABLE 16.2 SUMMARY OF THE BALANCE SHEET OF TOYS "R" US, INC.
(DOLLAR FIGURES ARE IN MILLIONS)

Current liabilities	$1,588
Deferred taxes	176
Long-term debt	660
Obligation under capital leases*	10
Common stock, including excess over par value	345
Retained earnings	2,530
Translation adjustments	14
Total common stockholders' equity	2,889
Total liabilities and stockholders' equity	$5,323

*In this case the obligation under capital leases is such a very small source of funding that it is ignored. When it is material, it should be included both in the cost of funding and in the weighting as described earlier in the chapter.

investment. Likewise, the current liabilities can be ignored because an examination of the details of the financial report did not reveal any substantial amount of short-term borrowing that is effectively permanent. Only the costs of long-term debt, leases, and common equity are included in the weighted average cost of capital.

An examination of the footnotes reveals that the average maturity of the long-term debt is approximately 20 years and the average coupon interest rate on the long-term debt is approximately 8.22 percent.[18] The average yield to maturity on the company's bonds, found by checking the current financial press, was approximately 7.23 percent. At the then-prevailing 34 percent marginal tax rate, this implies an after-tax cost of debt of:

$$k_d = .0723 (1 - .34) = \underline{4.77\%}$$

For a typical 20-year, 8.22 percent, $1,000 bond paying interest annually (for simplicity) and providing a yield to maturity of 7.23 percent, the price will be the present value of the principal and interest payments, discounted at 7.23 percent: $82.20PVA1$_{20yrs,7.23\%}$ + $1,000/1.0723^{20}$ = $\underline{\$1,103}$.

In other words, the debt has a market value equal to 110.3 percent of its book value, or $1.103 \times \$660 = \underline{\$728\ million}$.

According to *Value Line Investment Services*, the beta of Toys "R" Us common stock was 1.35 at that time. The risk-free rate, represented by U.S. Treasury bonds, was approximately 6.0 percent. Using a market risk premium esti-

[18]It is becoming more common to disclose the fair market value of the outstanding long-term debt in the footnotes to the financial statements. If it is disclosed, you may not have to recalculate the market value if conditions have not changed since the balance sheet date.

mate of 6.5 percent,[19] the required return on equity can be estimated with the mean-variance capital asset pricing model to be:

$$k_e = .06 + 1.35(.065) = \underline{14.78\%}$$

The market price per share of common stock was reported to be $40. With 298 million shares outstanding, the total market value of the equity would therefore be $40 × 298 million = $\underline{\$11,920 \text{ million}}$.

The weighted average cost of *existing* capital for Toys "R" Us would therefore be determined as follows:

Source	Market Value	Weight (Proportion)	Required Return	Weighted Cost
Debt	728	.0576	.0477	.0027
Equity	11,920	.9424	.1478	.1393
Weighted average cost of existing capital (WACC₁) =				.1420 or 14.20%

If Toys "R" Us is to raise additional outside capital, the company will face flotation costs. If debt flotation costs are 2.25 percent, this raises the before-tax cost of new debt to 7.46 percent, for an after-tax cost of new debt of .0746(1 − .34) = 4.92 percent.

Assume that after flotation costs the cost for new equity is 15.48 percent. Toys "R" Us has never paid a dividend and is not expected to in the near future given the pool of projects available to management.

The Toys "R" Us statement of cash flows showed that $136 million in addition to income was generated from operations—primarily from decreases in asset values through depreciation. The required return for these $136 million of internally generated funds is the weighted average cost of existing capital: 14.20 percent. We assume a similar amount available in the upcoming year.

Toys "R" Us also had an income of $437 million, with nothing paid out in the form of dividends. If the same pattern continued over the next year, the company would have $437 million of retained earnings to reinvest. This equity would be matched with an amount of debt so that equity would remain 94.24 percent of total capital. The amount of new capital that can be supported using retained earnings as the equity portion is:

$$\text{Retained earnings} = .9424 \times \text{new capital}$$

$$\text{New capital} = \text{retained earnings}/.9424 = \$437/.9424 = \underline{\$464 \text{ million}}$$

[19]See chapter 14 for a discussion of market risk premiums.

In this range, the required return on equity is the cost of existing equity, but the required return on debt is the cost of new debt. The weighted average cost of capital (WACC) for this $464 million is therefore:

$$WACC_2 = .0576 \times .0492 + .9424 \times .1478 = \underline{14.21\%}$$

If the company wants to expand beyond this point, both debt and equity must be raised externally. The weighted average cost of capital then becomes:

$$WACC_3 = .0576 \times .0492 + .9424 \times .1548 = \underline{14.87\%}$$

Summarizing, Toys "R" Us' marginal cost of capital schedule is as follows:

Amount	First $136 million	Next $464 million	Additional capital
Cost	14.20%	14.21%	14.87%

Assume Toys "R" Us has the following investment opportunities available:[20]

Investment	A	B	C	D	E
Cost ($ millions)	300	150	125	20	200
Internal rate of return	15.25%	15.00%	14.75%	14.50%	14.25%

Figure 16.2 summarizes the marginal cost of capital schedule and investment opportunity schedule for Toys "R" Us. Given this hypothetical investment opportunity set, Toys "R" Us would maximize value for the shareholders by investing in projects A, B, C, and D. The marginal cost of capital that these projects must satisfy is therefore $WACC_2 = 14.21$ percent.

SUMMARY |

The cost of capital is an *opportunity cost*, determined by the returns that could be expected by investors from other investments of equal risk. Since companies typically raise money through both debt and equity, the cost of capital is a weighted average of the costs of these various sources.

The *marginal cost of capital* is the cost of the next dollar invested: It is the change in after-tax required payment to keep all providers of capital satisfied, divided by the change in total capital invested. Assuming that the company is at

[20]To justify a simple ranking according to internal rate of return, we again assume that each investment has only one internal rate of return and that there are no mutually exclusive investments.

| **FIGURE 16.2** | **MARGINAL COST OF CAPITAL AND HYPOTHETICAL INVESTMENT OPPORTUNITY SCHEDULE FOR TOYS "R" US** |

The cost of capital schedule is estimated from publicly available data, and the investment opportunity schedule is hypothetical. In this case, Toys "R" Us would invest $595 million. Additional investment would require acceptance of investments with negative net present values when evaluated at the marginal cost of capital.

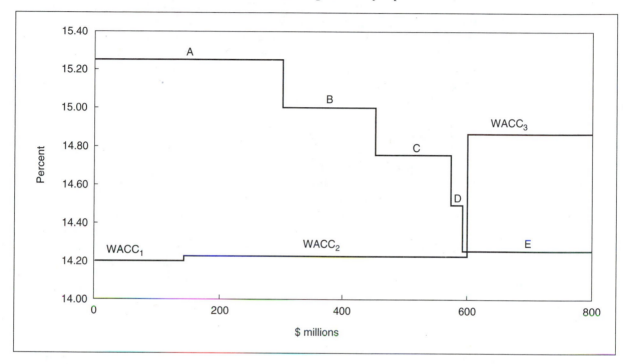

its target capital structure and that the target capital structure is measured in terms of the market value of each form of capital in proportion to the total, the marginal cost of capital is a weighted average of the costs of the various components used. If an investment has a positive net present value when evaluated at the marginal cost of capital, then that investment will increase the wealth of the shareholders.

In order to determine the marginal cost of each component of capital, one must determine if that component is available from internal sources or must be raised externally. The cost of existing debt is generally the yield to maturity on existing bonds, adjusted for the tax deductibility of interest. Once the component costs of capital have been determined, a marginal cost of capital curve can be constructed. The marginal cost in each range is the weighted average cost of the funds, either external or internal, that would be used in that range. Assuming the company is at its optimal or target mix, the proportions used in the weighted average cost of capital analysis should be the market value of each capital component, as a percent of the total market value of capital.

A capital investment is attractive if the net present value is positive at the marginal cost of capital for the funds that must be raised if that investment is to be accepted.

QUESTIONS |

16–1. For what purposes is the cost of capital used?

16–2. Explain the meanings of the expressions (a) weighted average cost of capital, (b) marginal cost of capital.

16–3. What do we mean when we say the cost of capital is an opportunity cost?

16–4. Why do companies raise funds from a combination of sources?

16–5. Why is the effective interest rate on debt multiplied by $(1 - \text{tax rate})$ when similar adjustments are not made to the required return on preferred stock and common stock?

16–6. Why are several formulas often used to estimate the cost of common equity instead of *the* right formula?

16–7. Why are market value weights used instead of book value weights in computing a weighted average cost of capital?

16–8. Why would a company face a marginal cost of capital schedule instead of a single weighted average cost of capital?

16–9. How should the following be treated in the estimation of the cost of capital? (a) deferred taxes, (b) accounts payable, (c) accrued expenses, (d) short-term debt, (e) depreciation-generated funds.

PROBLEMS |

16–1. Midwest Electric's bonds will mature in 20 years. The coupon interest rate on the bonds is 7 percent, paid at the end of each year. The bonds have maturity values of $1,000 each and are currently selling at a market price of $744.59. What is the yield to maturity? (Solve by finding the internal rate of return.) If the company's marginal tax rate is 35 percent, what is the after-tax cost of existing debt?

16–2. Midwest Electric's preferred stock has a par value of $100 a share and a market price of $80 a share. Dividends per year are $10. What is the cost of existing preferred stock?

16–3. In order to sell new $100 par-value preferred stock at a price of $100, Midwest Electric must pay a dividend that will provide a dividend yield equal to the cost of preferred stock determined in problem 2. Flotation costs would be $5 a share. What is the cost of new preferred stock?

16–4. Midwest Electric is expected to pay a dividend of $5 per share over the next year, and the stock is currently selling for $50 a share. If dividends are expected to grow at 5 percent a year, what is the cost of existing common stock?

16–5. Flotation costs for a new issue of common stock in problem 4 would be $3 a share. What is the cost of new equity for Midwest Electric?

16–6. The 10-year bonds of Indiana International have a yield to maturity of 9.186 percent. The company can sell new 10-year bonds to provide this same interest rate, but flotation costs will be 5 percent of issue price. The company has a 35 percent marginal tax rate. What is the after-tax cost of existing debt and new debt?

16–7. Michigan Corporation is expected to have earnings per share of $10 over the next year. Dividends are expected to be kept at 60 percent of earnings, and retained earnings are expected to be reinvested at a 14 percent rate of return. The price of the stock is presently $40. What is the anticipated growth rate of dividends, and what is the cost of existing equity? (*Hint:* remember that g = return on reinvested equity × retention rate.)

16–8. American Services Corporation's common stock has a beta of 1.30. The interest rate on U.S. Treasury bonds is 8 percent, and the interest rate on U.S. Treasury bills is 6 percent. Assuming an average market risk premium of 6.5 percent, use the mean-variance capital asset pricing model to estimate the cost of existing common equity for American.

16–9. American Service Corporation's common stock (see problem 8) has a price of $20 a share, and dividends are expected to be $2 a share for the next year. What is the implied growth rate of dividends? If flotation costs would be $2 a share, what is the cost of new equity?

16–10. CalMark is a privately held company, so there is no information about beta available. However, a company in the same business with a debt to equity ratio the same as that of CalMark is publicly traded and has a beta of 1.2. If the risk-free rate is 9 percent, and the average market risk premium is 6.5 percent, what is the estimated cost of existing equity for CalMark?

16–11. Annual dividends for Adams Mills are shown below. The price of Adams Mills' stock was around $14 at the end of 1994, and earnings per share for 1994 were $1.28. The risk-free rate was 7 percent and, according to *Value Line*, the beta was .90. Estimate the cost of equity using the dividend growth model, the earnings yield model, and the mean-variance capital asset pricing model (assume a 6.5 percent market risk premium). Why are the answers not the same for each method of computation? Which cost of equity estimate should the company use?

Year	1984	1985	1986	1987	1988	1989	1990	1991	1992	1993	1994
Dividend	.00	.10	.10	.10	.10	.10	.10	.12	.15	.17	.21

16–12. Return on market value of equity for Adams Mills (problem 11) was 9.14 percent. The dividends were 16.4 percent of income. What is the implied dividend growth rate? Given a 1994 dividend of $0.21 and a 1994 year-end price of $14, what is the cost of equity?

16–13. Contal Corporation has equity with a market value of $1 million, debt with a market value of $2 million, and a financial lease calling for payments of $100,000 a year for 10 years. The cost of equity is 15 percent, the interest rate on debt is 10 percent, and the tax rate is 35 percent, so the after-tax cost of debt is 6.5 percent. The lease is of similar risk to the debt, so the value of the lease payments can be found by discounting them at the interest rate on the debt. What is the weighted average cost of capital?

16–14. Several recent college graduates are planning to open a computer service business. Each person must invest $20,000 to provide the necessary equity capital. Kirsten Maull is considering joining the group and wants to determine what would be a reasonable opportunity cost for equity invested in this way. All such businesses are small, so there are no publicly traded companies to use for comparison. Ms. Maull talked to an accounting professor who was considered an expert on small business valuation, and he indicated that a typical small service business would sell for about five times earnings. She looked at the stock market to consider alternatives. Smaller companies being traded on the over-the-counter stock market had price-earnings ratios averaging about six. The higher-risk companies traded on the organized exchanges had betas of 2.0 and above. Ms. Maull guessed that this investment would be of similar risk to investment in a stock with a beta of 2.0. The risk-free rate at the time was 8 percent, and Ms. Maull believed, from her finance studies, that the market risk premium was about 6.3 percent. What required return should Ms. Maull use in evaluating the business opportunity being considered?

16–15. Texal Corporation has $4 million of long-term debt, $1 million of preferred stock, and $5 million of common stock on its balance sheet. The market value of the debt is 80 percent of book value, the market value of preferred stock is 70 percent of book value, and the market value of common stock is 130 percent of book value. The after-tax costs of existing debt, existing preferred stock, and existing common stock are 6 percent, 9 percent, and 15 percent, respectively. What is the marginal cost of existing capital?

16–16. Carolina Corporation has a capital structure consisting of 60 percent debt and 40 percent equity. The cost of existing equity is 14 percent and the cost of new equity is 16 percent. The cost of existing debt is 7 percent and the cost of new debt is 8 percent. Over the next year, net income is expected to be $1 million and management will not consider dividends of less that $400,000. Funds from operations other than income are expected to be $300,000. Prepare a marginal cost of capital schedule for Carolina Corporation.

16–17. A major private university is considering new insulated windows for one of its buildings. The risk-free rate is 8 percent, and the university can borrow for 10 percent a year. The benefit from the windows depends on energy prices. Oil-exploring companies also depend on energy prices, and have betas of 1.3. The average risk premium for common stock investments is 6.5 percent. The university could use endowment fund money currently invested in common stock. What is the appropriate required return for this investment?

16–18. KanAg Corporation has a marginal cost of capital schedule as follows:

	Weighted Average Cost
First $1 million	12%
Second $2 million	13%
Amounts above $3 million	15%

The company is considering the following assets:

			NET PRESENT VALUE AT WACC OF		
Asset	Cost	IRR	12%	13%	15%
A	$1,000,000	17%	$400,000	$350,000	$250,000
B	900,000	16	200,000	190,000	150,000
C	600,000	15	200,000	180,000	0
D	500,000	14	100,000	60,000	−50,000
E	500,000	13.8	150,000	80,000	−70,000
F	500,000	13.5	80,000	30,000	−100,000

In which asset should the company invest?

16–19. The balance sheet of Wisconsin Dairy Products, in millions of dollars, is shown below.

Current assets	$100	Current liabilities	$ 50
Fixed assets	400	Long-term debt	200
		Deferred taxes	50
		Common stock	100
		Retained earnings	100
Total assets	$500	T L & NW	$500

The debt consists of 20-year, 8 percent, $1,000 bonds, presently selling at $701.25. Flotation costs on new bonds would raise the effective before-tax interest cost to 0.5 percent above the yield to maturity on existing debt. The company has 10 million shares of common stock outstanding, with a market price of $30 a share. The stock has a beta of 1.5. The risk-free rate is 10 percent and the average market risk premium is 6.5 percent. Flotation costs would raise the effective cost of new equity by 1 percent over the cost of existing equity. Over the next year, which is the company's capital investment planning period, the company expects to have $20 million of internally generated funds in addition to net income of $30 million. At least half of the net income must be paid out in dividends. The company faces a 35 percent marginal tax rate. Prepare a marginal cost of capital schedule.

16–20. **(Application)** Coca-Cola states in its 1992 annual report: "Over the last five years, Economic Profit has increased at an annual compound rate of 27 percent, resulting in Economic Value Added of $952 million." If economic profit is calculated by subtracting the dollar cost of capital (percent times capital in use) from the net operating income after taxes, discuss two ways management can increase the economic profit.

16–21. **(Application)** The following information was taken from the Chrysler and Ford 1992 annual reports (some pooling of accounts was necessary; amounts in millions as of 12-31-92):

	Chrysler	Ford
Accounts Payable	$ 5,798	$ 26,813
Short-Term Debt and Current Portion of Long-Term Debt	2,117	35,242
Accrued Liabilities	4,090	9,983
Long-Term Debt	13,434	63,262
Accrued Pension or Post-retirement Obligations	4,187	15,714
Common Equity	7,538	14,752
Other Pooled Accounts (not considered capital by the writers)	3,489	14,779
Total Liabilities and Equities	$40,653	$180,545

a. Using book values, what is the value of total capital for Chrysler and Ford?

b. Assume that all the book values above are approximate market values, with the exception of common equity, which is selling for $52 per share for Chrysler, with 295,892,000 shares outstanding, and for $58 per share for Ford, with 486,500,000 shares outstanding. Please recompute the total capital for Chrysler and Ford.

c. In 1992 Ford reduced its Common Equity account by $7.54 billion to reflect its existing obligation for post-retirement benefits other than pensions. Chrysler decided to delay recognition of its $4.7 billion obligation until 1993. In 1993 Chrysler will reduce equity by the estimated after-tax cost of $4.7 billion by reporting a large loss on the income statement in the same manner that Ford reported a large loss in 1992. What impact does this have on the weights in percentage terms used for debt and equity in calculating the cost of capital?

d. Given your answer to the previous question, is it better to use market values or book values when calculating the weightings for debt and equity in the capital structure?

16–22. **(Ethical considerations)** It is fashionable today to report an "Economic Profit" amount to your shareholders in the annual report when management is discussing performance. Assume that economic profit is reported income plus interest (capital × WACC). Assume that you had been given the task to calculate the "economic profit" for McDonald's 1992 annual report and were presented with the following information:

	At Book	**At Market**
Long-Term Debt	3,446,000,000	3,646,000,000
Preferred Stock	680,000,000	751,000,000
Common Equity	6,635,000,000	17,706,000,000
After-Tax Cost of Debt		6%
Cost of Preferred Stock		7%
Cost of Common Stock (using the dividend growth model)		11%
Cost of Common Stock (using the earnings yield model)		5%
Cost of Common Stock (using the capital asset pricing model)		12%
After-Tax Income plus Interest Expense		$1,205,000,000

a. If you use book values and the dividend growth model, what is McDonald's economic profit or loss?
b. If you use market values and the dividend growth model, what is McDonald's economic profit or loss?
c. What additional method will show the greatest economic profit?
d. Calculate and justify what you believe is the fairest representation of McDonald's 1992 economic profit or loss.

CASE PROBLEM |

Wal-Mart Cost of Capital

Wal-Mart, with $55 billion in sales in 1992, is the world's largest retailer.[21] It operates nearly 2,000 Wal-Mart discount stores in the United States, approximately 200 Sam's Clubs membership-warehouse stores, and a specialty distribution segment that serves 30,000 convenience stores and independent grocers. Discount stores' sales accounted for 73 percent of 1992 sales. Membership club sales were the second-largest area, accounting for 22 percent of 1992 sales. The remaining 5 percent of Wal-Mart's sales were accounted for by McLane & Western convenience store and independent grocer supply division. Thus, Wal-Mart was one of the companies that had resisted the trend toward diversifying into everything from aardvarks to zymometers.

[21]This analysis, along with necessary estimates, was prepared by the author and does not represent the views of managers at Wal-Mart.

Concentration did not mean lack of growth, however. New capital expenditures in 1992 alone were $3.5 billion, plus an associated investment in working capital of $1.8 billion. If Wal-Mart was to make optimal capital investment decisions, it was clear that an accurate estimate of the cost of capital was needed.

Wal-Mart presently had 2.3 billion shares of common stock outstanding. The stock had a beta of 1.3 and was selling at $30 a share in 1992. The yield to maturity on U.S. Treasury bonds was 6.5 percent, and Treasury bills were selling to yield 3 percent in 1993. Based on dividends to date, dividends per share during the year 1993 were expected to be $.12. Historical dividends per share and earnings per share were as follows:

Year	1982	1983	1984	1985	1986	1987	1988	1989	1990	1991	1992
Dividends	.01	.01	.01	.02	.02	.03	.04	.06	.07	.09	.11
Earnings	.06	.09	.12	.15	.20	.28	.37	.48	.57	.70	.87

Wal-Mart's balance sheet, of January 31, 1993, summarizes the company's financial structure (Table 16.3). Most of the company's debt was not actively traded. However, the company disclosed in a note to the financial statements that long-term debt with a book value of $3.073 had a fair market value of $3.357 billion. Assuming the average stated rate on outstanding securities was 7.5 percent, the yield to maturity would be 6.87 percent. It was assumed that other long-term debt would sell at a similar yield to maturity if the debt were publicly sold.

Wal-Mart was a heavy user of commercial paper with an average daily balance outstanding for 1992 of $1.184 billion. The weighted average before tax interest rate on this paper was 3.5 percent.

Wal-Mart has $1.818 billion in capital lease obligations on the balance sheet. In the footnote there is a historical 8 to 14 percent imputed discount rate used in calculating this obligation. Given the overall decline in interest rates, the lower end of the range, or 8 percent, is probably the better estimate of what future leases will cost. Details of the long-term capitalized lease obligations and additional operating lease obligations are as follows:

Year	Aggregate Minimum Lease Payments Due (in $ millions)
1993	$ 486
1994	476
1995	470
1996	475
1997	464
Thereafter	5,316

| **TABLE 16.3** WAL-MART BALANCE SHEET

Amounts stated are in millions of dollars, and the date of the balance sheet is January 31, 1993.

Assets

Current assets	$10,197
Property, plant, and equipment	9,794
Other assets	574
TOTAL ASSETS	$20,565

Liabilities and Equities

Current liabilities:	
Accounts payable	$ 3,873
Commercial paper	1,588
Accrued expenses and taxes	1,233
Long-term debt maturing within 1 year	13
Capital lease obligations due within 1 year	46
Long-term Liabilities:	
Long-term debt	3,073
Capital lease obligations	1,772
Deferred income taxes	207
Shareholder equity:	
Common stock	230
Capital in excess of par	527
Reinvested earnings	8,003
TOTAL LIABILITIES AND STOCKHOLDERS' EQUITY	$20,565

The "thereafter" amount is assumed to be due at $443 million per year for the next 12 years from 1998 to 2009. The market rate of interest to be used to find the market value of these lease obligations is assumed to be 8 percent.

There were no shares of preferred stock outstanding. Wal-Mart had a 37 percent combined federal and state marginal tax rate in 1992.

CASE QUESTIONS

1. Estimate the market value of each component of the capital structure.
2. Estimate the required return for each component of the capital structure.
3. Estimate the weighted average cost of capital for Wal-Mart.
4. In which area of your analysis is there the greatest potential for error? Why? Is there anything that could be done to improve estimates in this area?

SELECTED REFERENCES |

Adler, Michael. "The Cost of Capital and Valuation of a Two-Country Firm." *Journal of Finance* 29 (March 1974): 119–132.

Arditti, Fred D. "The Weighted Average Cost of Capital: Some Questions on Its Definition, Interpretation, and Use." *Journal of Finance* 28 (December 1973): 1001–1007.

Arditti, Fred D., and Milford S. Tysseland. "Three Ways to Present the Marginal Cost of Capital." *Financial Management* 2 (Summer 1973): 63–67.

Boudreaux, Kenneth J., et al. "The Weighted Average Cost of Capital: A Discussion." *Financial Management* 8 (Summer 1979): 7–23.

Bower, Richard S., and John P. Jenks. "Divisional Screening Rates." *Financial Management* 4 (Autumn 1975): 42–49.

Brennan, Joseph F., and Paul R. Moul. "Does the Constant Growth Discounted Cash Flow Model Portray Reality?" *Public Utilities Fortnightly* 121 (January 21, 1988): 24–29.

Brigham, Eugene F., and Louis G. Gapenski. "Flotation Cost Adjustments." *Financial Practice and Education* 1 (Fall/Winter 1991): 29–34.

Brown, Robert J., and Mukund S. Kulkarni. "Duration and the Risk Adjustment of Discount Rates for Capital Budgeting." *Engineering Economist* 38 (Summer 1993): 299–307.

Conine, Thomas E., Jr., and Maurry Tamarkin. "Divisional Cost of Capital Estimation: Adjustment for Leverage." *Financial Management* 14 (Spring 1985): 54–58.

Constantinides, G. "Warrant Exercise and Bond Conversion in Competitive Markets." *Journal of Financial Economics* (September 1984): 371–398.

Diamond, Douglas W., and Robert E. Verrecchia. "Disclosure, Liquidity, and the Cost of Capital." *Journal of Finance* 46 (September 1991): 1325–1359.

"Division Hurdle Rates and the Cost of Capital." *Financial Management* 18 (Spring 1989): 18–25.

Dumas, Bernard, and Bruno Solnik. "The World Price of Foreign Exchange Risk." *Journal of Finance* 50 (June 1995): 445–479.

Fama, Eugene F., and Kenneth R. French. "Business Conditions and Expected Returns on Stocks and Bonds." *Journal of Financial Economics* 25 (November 1989): 23–49.

Frankel, Jeffrey A. "The Japanese Cost of Finance: A Survey." *Financial Management* 20 (Spring 1991): 95–127.

Fuller, Russell J., and Halbert S. Kerr. "Estimating the Divisional Cost of Capital: An Analysis of the Pure-Play Technique." *Journal of Finance* 36 (December 1981): 997–1009.

Gallinger, George W., and Glenn V. Henderson, Jr. "Public Utility Cost of Capital Models: An Examination of Assumptions." *Engineering Economist* 34 (Spring 1989): 177–184.

Gitman, Lawrence J., and Vincent A. Mercurio. "Cost of Capital Techniques Used by Major U.S. Firms: Survey and Analysis of Fortune's 1000." *Financial Management* 11 (Winter 1982): 21–29.

Gup, Benton E., and Samuel W. Norwood III. "Divisional Cost of Capital: A Practical Approach." *Financial Management* 11 (Spring 1982): 20–24.

Harris, Robert S., and Felicia C. Marston. "Estimating Shareholder Risk Premia Using Analysts' Growth Forecasts." *Financial Management* 21 (Summer 1992): 63–70.

Harris, Robert S., Thomas J. O'Brien, and Doug Wakeman. "Divisional Cost-of-Capital Estimation for Multi-Industry Firms." *Financial Management* 8 (Summer 1979): 74–84.

Harris, Robert S., and John J. Pringle. "Risk-Adjusted Discount Rates − Extensions from the Average-Risk Case." *Journal of Financial Research* 8 (Fall 1985): 237−244.

Henderson, Glenn V., Jr. "In Defense of the Weighted Average Cost of Capital." *Financial Management* 8 (Autumn 1979): 57−61.

Howe, Keith M. "A Note on Flotation Costs and Capital Budgeting." *Financial Management* 11 (Winter 1982): 30−33.

Howe, Keith M., and James H. Patterson. "Capital Investment Decisions under Economies of Scale in Flotation Cost." *Financial Management* 14 (Autumn 1985): 61−69.

Hubbard, Carl M. "Flotation Costs in Capital Budgeting: A Note on the Tax Effect." *Financial Management* 13 (Summer 1984): 38−40.

Hubbard, Jeff, and Roni Michaely. "Do Investors Ignore Dividend Taxation? A Reexamination of the Citizens Utilities Case." *JFQA* 32 (March 1997): 117−135.

Ingersoll, J. "A Contingent Claims Analysis of Convertible Securities." *Journal of Financial Economics* (May 1977): 289−322.

Jakque, Andrea S., and Gabriel Hawawini. "Myths and Realities of the Global Capital Market: Lessons and Myths for Financial Managers." *Journal of Applied Corporate Finance* 6 (Fall 1993): 81−90.

Kalotay, A. J. "Sinking Funds and the Realized Cost of Debt." *Financial Management* 11 (Spring 1982): 43−54.

Kester, W. Carl, and Timothy A. Luehrman. "What Makes You Think U.S. Capital Is So Expensive?" *Journal of Applied Corporate Finance* 5 (Summer 1992): 29−41.

Lee, Inmoo, Scott Lochhead, Jay Ritter, and Quanshui Zhao. "The Costs of Raising Capital." *Journal of Financial Research* 19 (Spring 1996): 59−74.

Linke, Charles M., and J. Kenton Zumwalt. "Estimation Biases in Discounted Cash Flow Analysis of Equity Capital Cost in Rate Regulation." *Financial Management* 13 (Autumn 1984): 15−21.

Petry, Glenn H. "Empirical Evidence on Cost of Capital Weights." *Financial Management* 4 (Winter 1975): 58−65.

Riener, Kenneth D. "A Pedagogic Note on the Cost of Capital with Personal Taxes and Risky Debt." *Financial Review* 20 (May 1985): 229−235.

Shapiro, Alan C. "Financial Structure and Cost of Capital in the Multinational Corporation." *Journal of Financial and Quantitative Analysis* 13 (June 1978): 211−226.

Siegel, Jeremy J. "The Application of the DCF Methodology for Determining the Cost of Equity Capital." *Financial Management* 14 (Spring 1985): 46−53.

Spiro, Peter S. "Should the Discount Rate Change If an Electric Utility Is Privatized?" *Engineering Economist* 36 (Fall 1990): 1−10.

Stein, Jeremy C. "Internal Capital Markets and the Competition for Corporate Resources." *Journal of Finance* 52 (March 1997): 111−133.

Stulz, Ren M. "Globalization of Capital Markets and the Cost of Capital: The Case of Nestlé." *Journal of Applied Corporate Finance* 8 (Fall 1995): 19−29.

Taggart, Robert A., Jr. "Allocating Capital among a Firm's Divisions: Hurdle Rates vs. Budgets." *Journal of Financial Research* 10 (Fall 1987): 177−189.

———. "Consistent Valuation and Cost of Capital Expressions with Corporate and Personal Taxes." *Financial Management* 20 (Autumn 1991): 8−20.

Thakor, Anjan V. "Strategic Issues in Financial Contracting: An Overview." *Financial Management* 18 (Summer 1989): 39−58.

CHAPTER 17 |

CAPITAL STRUCTURE AND VALUE

After completing this chapter you should be able to:

1. Explain to a fellow student why changing the capital structure cannot create value for the shareholder when perfect markets exist.

2. List the market imperfections that exist in reality and explain the influence these imperfections have in determining the "optimal" capital structure of a specific firm.

3. Understand the role of bankruptcy cost and liquidation cost in setting an upper boundary on the level of debt in the capital structure.

4. Comprehend the role that corporate and individual taxes play in determining the level of debt versus equity financing for corporations in general.

5. Recognize the influence that the Alternative Minimum Tax rates, other tax shields, and other corporate-specific factors play in the capital structure decision.

6. Justify differing capital structures using an agency cost of debt and the agency cost of equity argument.

7. Demonstrate how the presence of one information set for managers and a different information set for outsiders can have a signaling influence in the capital structure choice.

8. Describe the influence that differences in personal borrowing and corporate borrowing have on the capital structure decision.

9. Cite the results of several of the more important empirical tests of the linkage between capital structure choice and value.

General Electric gradually reduced its debt over the past decade to the point where long-term creditors have provided 2 cents for each dollar provided by the owners. Caterpillar, on the other hand, has increased its long-term debt over the same period so that long-term creditors now provide $1.60 for each dollar provided by the owners. Why do companies choose such divergent approaches to capital structure? In this chapter and the next, we will be looking at the use of capital structure in creating value, particularly focusing on the role of market imperfections.

The capital structure of a firm is its set of long-term sources of funds. The proportion of funds financed by debt and by equity is one important part of capital structure planning, but specific methods of raising debt and equity capital are also important. Risk, value, and the attractiveness of capital investments can be affected by capital structure decisions.

The optimal capital structure is often thought of as the financing mix that maximizes the value of the firm. In the absence of market imperfections, this optimal capital structure will also minimize the weighted average cost of capital. In searching for the optimal capital structure, it is necessary to consider interest rates, tax rates, bankruptcy costs, agency relations, and information asymmetries between managers and investors. This chapter is devoted to the theory of capital structure and value. The theory is applied to capital structure decisions in Chapter 18.

Please do not cringe at the thought of a chapter on theory. Theory is not an idle exercise of academics, but a framework for analysis leading to practical decision making. Theory is particularly useful in areas in which direct observation and measurement is difficult. Direct measurement of the impacts of changes in capital structure is difficult, and we often refer to theory to predict the effects of a capital structure change.

This chapter begins with an analysis of how capital structure affects value and required return in an idealized, perfect capital market setting. This may seem like a fruitless approach to developing implications for decision making in an imperfect world, especially when capital structure turns out to be irrelevant in a perfect market setting. But the idealized perfect market setting proves to be a useful foundation for analysis. If capital structure does not matter in a perfect market, then capital structure decisions must be responses to market imperfections. Perfect market assumptions are replaced one by one with more realistic descriptions of the environment, and the implications for the relationship between capital structure and value are developed. In the following chapter, the principles developed in this chapter are applied to capital structure choice in a real-world setting.

PERFECT MARKETS AND CAPITAL STRUCTURE IRRELEVANCE

The pioneer work in capital structure analysis was carried out by Modigliani and Miller (M&M).[1] They began with a set of idealized market assumptions:

---

[1]Franco Modigliani and Merton H. Miller, "The Cost of Capital, Corporation Finance, and the Theory of Investment," *American Economic Review* 48 (June 1958): 261–297; Franco Modigliani and Merton H. Miller, "Corporate Income Taxes and the Cost of Capital: A Correction," *American Economic Review* 53 (June 1963): 433–442; and Franco Modigliani and Merton H. Miller, "Reply to Heins and Sprenkle," *American Economic Review* 59 (September 1969): 592–595.

1. Perfect capital markets exist: investors are rational; information is freely available to all; securities are infinitely divisible; there are no transaction costs for investors buying and selling securities and no flotation costs for companies issuing securities.
2. There are no income taxes.
3. Firms can be divided into risk classes, and each firm within a risk class has the same amount of business risk.[2] (This assumption is used only for convenience in exposition.)
4. The future operating earnings of the firm are random variables, and all investors agree about the expected values of the probability distributions.
5. There is no bankruptcy.
6. Corporations and individuals can borrow and lend at the same market interest rate. In the absence of bankruptcy risk, this rate is a risk-free rate.

Based on these assumptions, M&M concluded that the value of the firm was unaffected by capital structure choice. As explained in the following paragraphs, theirs was fundamentally an arbitrage argument. The net operating income represents the benefits created by the assets of the firm, and capital structure is simply a way to divide claims against future cash flows among different claimants. The mix of debt and equity cannot affect the total amount of cash that can be paid to suppliers of funds. The only way capital structure could increase value would be if investors were willing to pay a premium to have the same cash flow stream split up among claimants in a particular way.

Given the M&M assumptions, investors can use *homemade leverage*.[3] In other words, they can create the mix of debt and equity they prefer, regardless of the capital structure decision of the company. Suppose, for example, the company issues only equity and you prefer to invest in a company financed with one-half debt and one-half equity. You can buy common stock of the company using a dollar of borrowed money for each dollar of your own money. You will receive the same stream of cash flows that could be realized by investing in a company financed with one-half debt and one-half equity.

Example. Hershey Corporation had net operating income of $563 million in 1998. Hershey had $685 million of debt, with an estimated interest rate of 8 percent. In the absence of earnings retention and taxes, the stockholders would receive:

$$\$563 \text{ million} - .08 \times \$685 \text{ million} = \$508 \text{ million}$$

Suppose Hershey decided to sell another $685 million of stock and use the proceeds to retire debt. Existing stockholders could re-create the old debt position

---

[2] In this context, business risk refers to the variability of the stream of net operating income generated by the firm.

[3] In general, leverage means the substitution of fixed costs for variable costs. The payment to creditors is fixed, while the payment to equity holders is variable, depending on earnings. Thus, leverage is used here to refer to debt financing.

by borrowing $685 million at 8 percent and using the loan proceeds to buy the newly issued shares. The income of the stockholders before and after the issuance of new stock can be summarized as follows.

Hershey net operating income	$563	$563
Interest paid to creditors of Hershey	55	0
Earnings to stockholders	508	563
Interest paid by stockholders	0	55
Net income of stockholders	$508	$508

In the absence of taxes, the stockholders end up with the same income whether they borrow or Hershey borrows.

An investor who prefers a company financed exclusively with equity can undo corporate borrowing with equal ease. An inventor buying all of Hershey's debt and equity in the previous example would receive the same cash flow that would be realized by purchasing all of the equity of a Hershey financed entirely with equity.

To summarize, investors can create any leverage position they desire. Therefore, the value of a company can be affected by financial leverage only if financial leverage changes the total cash flows that can be paid to investors. In the absence of taxes, the total stream of cash flows is not affected. Therefore, the total values of the securities of companies in the same risk class must be the same (per dollar of expected net operating income), regardless of the capital structure.

If the total price of the securities of one company was less than the total price of the securities of another company with the same risk and the same expected net operating income, an arbitrage opportunity would exist for investors in the higher-priced company. Those investors could sell their investments in the higher-priced company and invest in the lower-priced company, borrowing or buying debt instruments to create their own preferred mix of debt and equity. By moving from the higher- to the lower-priced company, the investors could buy the same series of expected future cash flows at a lower price, thereby increasing their return with no increase in risk. More complex transactions also could be used, such as short-selling[4] the stock of the high-priced company and buying stock of the low-priced company to earn a risk-free return with no capital invested. The pressure of these attempts to take advantage of an arbitrage profit opportunity would instantaneously eliminate any differences in value in a perfect market.

[4]Short-selling consists of borrowing shares and selling them. In reality there is usually a substantial margin requirement that must be kept on deposit with the broker. This reduces the funds available for arbitrage. In addition the short-seller must pay the lender of the shares any dividends that would have been received until the short-seller purchases identical shares and returns them to the lender of the shares.

The value of a company is the present value of the future cash flows, based on an overall discount rate commonly referred to as the weighted average cost of capital.[5] If the value of the company cannot be changed by capital structure decisions in the idealized world of M&M, then it follows necessarily that the weighted average cost of capital is not affected by capital structure decisions.

Example. This example begins with one company financed entirely with equity, and another, otherwise identical, company financed with a mix of debt and equity. As shown in Table 17.1, expected annual net operating income for each company is $1,000. Company A has no debt, while company B has $6,000 of debt, financed at the current market interest rate of 6 percent. For company A, the required return on equity is 10 percent, and the value is therefore $10,000. The theoretical equilibrium value of equity for company B is then $10,000 minus the amount of debt, or $4,000. Suppose, though, that the value of company B's equity is higher, say $5,000. This implies that the required return on equity for company B is 640/5,000 = 12.8 percent, and implies that the weighted average cost of capital for company B is 1,000/11,000 = 9.09 percent. By altering its debt to equity ratio, company B has increased its value and decreased its weighted average cost of capital. We will see though, that this situation cannot exist in equilibrium, and the differential between the two companies will be eliminated instantly in a perfect market.

Suppose you are an investor holding both the stock and debt instruments of company B. The total market value of your investment is $11,000 and your ex-

| TABLE 17.1 DISEQUILIBRIUM VALUE BASED ON CAPITAL STRUCTURE

Companies A and B have identical expected net operating incomes. Company A is financed entirely with equity, while company B has $6,000 of debt, at a 6 percent interest rate. The values of the two companies are not in equilibrium because company B has a higher market value than company A.

Company	A	B
Net operating income	$1,000	$1,000
Interest expense	0	360
Net income	1,000	640
Market value of debt	0	6,000
Market value of equity	10,000	5,000
Total market value of company	10,000	11,000
Implied required return on equity	10.00%	12.80%
(net income ÷ market value of equity)		
Implied weighted average cost of capital	10.00%	9.09%
(net operating income ÷ total market value)		

[5]Modigliani and Miller called this statement Proposition I.

pected cash inflow is $1,000 a year. You can sell both the stock and the debt instruments for a total of $11,000, purchase the stock of company A for $10,000, and receive the same future cash flows plus a one-time gain of $1,000. All investors would simultaneously attempt to sell their interests in company B for the same purpose. However, nobody would be interested in buying B's stock as long as the price was above $4,000. Therefore, the price would be instantaneously driven back to the point where the values of the two companies were equal.

The same arbitrage process works for an investor who prefers a leveraged position. Suppose you own the stock of company B, but not the debt, because you prefer a company financed partly with debt. You are looking for an arbitrage opportunity, a way to increase your wealth with no increase in risk. You sell your stock in company B for $5,000 and buy the stock of company A, using $4,000 of your own money and $6,000 of money borrowed at a 6 percent interest rate. The expected cash flow to you after interest expense is the same you were receiving from company B: $640. But you sold your stock in B for $5,000 and used only $4,000 of your own money to generate the identical cash flow from a leveraged investment in company A.

You can make an arbitrage profit from this situation even if you do not own the stock of either company. You can short-sell the stock of company B for $5,000, thereby making a commitment to pay an expected $640 a year. You then use $4,000 of the short-sale proceeds and $6,000 of borrowed money to buy $10,000 worth of stock in company A. The cash flows after interest from the investment in company A will be sufficient to pay the amount owed each year as a result of the short-sale. However, the investment in company A is $1,000 less than the proceeds from the short-sale. You make a riskless profit of $1,000 with no capital investment. Short-selling would be another pressure bringing down the price of company B's stock.[6]

The same arbitrage opportunities would exist if the stock of company B was priced at less than $4,000. For example, an investor who did not want leverage could sell her holdings in company A and buy both debt and equity of company B to maintain the same stream of cash flows with a smaller investment.

Arbitrage opportunities such as these do not exist in a perfect market. Investors will respond to such opportunities quickly, selling the overpriced security and buying the underpriced security. This buying and selling drives the prices back into equilibrium. Therefore, the total values and the weighted average costs of capital will be the same for the two companies; the mix of debt and equity will not affect value or required return.

In the previous example, the equilibrium weighted average cost of capital for company B must be the same as that for company A. This does not imply that the component costs are the same for both companies. If the adjustment to move to equilibrium is going to occur in the price of company B, then the equilibrium

---

[6]Practical limitations on short-selling limit the price pressure from this source. For example, short-sellers must place on deposit with the stockbroker either cash or securities equal to half of the value of the securities short-sold, and the short-seller does not have full use of the sale proceeds while the position is open.

value of the equity is $4,000. Since the net income is $640 a year, the implied required return on equity is 640/4,000 = 16 percent.[7] This results in a weighted average cost of capital for B of:

$$\text{WACC}_B = .6(6\%) + .4(16\%) = 10\%$$

which is the same as the weighted average cost of capital for company A.

Figure 17.1 illustrates the pattern of debt costs, equity costs, and weighted average costs of capital under the M&M assumptions as the debt to total assets ratio of a firm changes. The required return on debt stays constant because the riskiness of the debt does not increase in the absence of bankruptcy risk. The cost of equity increases, but the proportion of funds coming from the lower-cost debt source also increases, so the weighted average cost of capital remains unchanged.[8] If the weighted average cost of capital were to change with a change in capital structure, the previously illustrated arbitrage process would instantly return the weighted average cost of capital to its equilibrium level.

M&M assumed the existence of risk classes. This assumption makes the analysis simpler and avoids the necessity of assuming any specific utility function shapes. But the assumption of risk classes is not necessary. The irrelevance of capital structure has also been proved under M&M's idealized conditions with the mean-variance capital asset pricing model substituted for the risk-class assumption.[9] The necessary equilibrium relationships between debt and equity can also be determined using option pricing theory, as was demonstrated in Chapter 15. The conclusion is robust with regard to definition of the actual pricing process, as long as markets are perfect.

The perfect market analysis of capital structure has important implications for the real world. If capital structure matters, it is because of imperfections, and the selection of an optimal capital structure must then come as a response to imperfections. Implications of imperfections are discussed in the following paragraphs. Taxes, bankruptcy costs, agency problems, and information asymmetry between managers and investors are the primary imperfections affecting capital structure.

---

[7]Modigliani and Miller's Proposition II is the formula for the required return on equity for a leveraged firm (k_{eL}) in relation to the required return for an unleveraged firm (k_{eu}):

$$k_{eL} = k_{eu} + (k_{eu} - k_d)(D/E)$$

where k_d is the cost of debt and (D/E) is the debt to equity ratio. For the example:

$$k_{eL} = .10 + (.10 - .06)(60,000/40,000) = \underline{.16}$$

[8]A constant weighted average cost of capital can also be demonstrated with risky debt. All that changes is who receives compensation for accepting risk.

[9]See Robert S. Hamada, "Portfolio Analysis, Market Equilibrium, and Corporation Finance," *Journal of Finance* 24 (March 1969): 13–19; and Jack Becker, "General Proof of Modigliani-Miller Propositions I and II Using Parameter-Preference Theory," *Journal of Financial and Quantitative Analysis* 13 (March 1978): 65–69.

| **FIGURE 17.1** **LEVERAGE AND COST OF CAPITAL UNDER THE M&M ASSUMPTIONS**

Both the cost of debt (K_d) and the cost of equity (K_e) increase with a higher debt ratio, but the no-arbitrage condition requires that the weighted average cost of capital (K_o) remain unchanged. The increasing costs of the components are offset by increased use of the lower-cost component, debt, to leave the weighted average cost of capital unchanged.

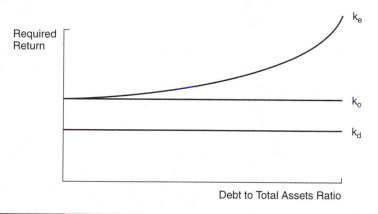

TAXES AND CAPITAL STRUCTURE |

Taxes are one of the more important imperfections. Corporate earnings used to pay interest are taxed only once, as income of the lender or bondholder. Earnings used to pay dividends are first taxed as corporate income, and then taxed again as income of the stockholder. The tax advantages of corporate debt can be seen by again looking at companies A and B from Table 17.1. Assume, though, that both companies have total market values of $10,000 so an investor with $10,000 can buy all of the stock of company A or the stock and debt instruments of company B. Also assume a 40 percent income tax rate for both corporations and investors. As shown in Table 17.2, the total after-tax cash flow to the investor is $360 from company A, which is financed only with equity, and $446 from company B, which issues debt and equity securities. Capital structure can affect total cash flow and value in this case.

The advantage of corporate borrowing also holds for an investor who wants a leveraged investment. An investor with $4,000 can either buy the stock of company B or borrow $6,000 to buy the stock of company A. That investor also benefits from company B's borrowing. The reader can rework the numbers in Table 17.1 to confirm that the after-tax cash flow to the investor is $144 if the investor borrows and $230 if the company borrows. Homemade leverage is not effective in this tax situation because the investor must pay interest from income on which the corporation has already paid tax. The value of the same stream of net operating income increases as the company's debt ratio increases, and the weighted average cost of capital therefore decreases.

| **TABLE 17.2** ILLUSTRATION OF THE TAX ADVANTAGES OF CORPORATE DEBT

*Companies A and B have identical expected net operating incomes. An investor with $10,000 can buy either the stock of company A or the stock and debt instruments of company B. Both the companies and the investor have 40 percent tax rates.**

Company	A	B
Net operating income	$1,000	$1,000
Interest expense	0	360
Income before tax	1,000	640
Corporate income tax	400	256
Net income (paid to investor)	600	384
Interest paid to investor	0	360
Total payment to investor	600	744
Investor's income tax	240	298
Net cash flow to investor	$ 360	$ 446

*Note from the example that if corporations and their creditors have identical tax rates, while stockholders do not pay taxes, there is no tax advantage to corporate debt. Therefore, some writers prefer to talk about the tax disadvantage of equity rather than the tax advantage of debt.

Figure 17.2 shows the increase in value as the debt ratio is increased with constant tax rates.

Figure 17.2 suggests that the optimal capital structure is almost entirely debt. This, of course, runs contrary to capital structure practice. Either managers are irrational or some pieces of the puzzle are still missing. We will see that additional considerations lead to capital structure implications more in line with observed practice.

DIFFERENTIAL TAX RATES AND THE OPTIMAL CAPITAL STRUCTURE

The previous analysis with taxes was based on the assumption that income to an investor was taxed at the same rate whether the investor held stock or debt securities. Miller pointed out that our conclusions about the impact of taxes on optimal capital structure are drastically altered if differential tax rates exist.[10] The total value of a corporation is the present value of the cash flows to investors. When a dollar of net operating income is paid out as interest, the corporation does not pay tax on that operating income. If an investor's personal tax rate on interest income is T_p, the after-tax cash flow to an investor is $(1 - T_p)$ times the interest payment. Net income not used for interest payments is taxed

[10]Analysis with two different individual tax rates was developed by Merton Miller, "Debt and Taxes," *Journal of Finance* 32 (May 1977): 261–275. The model was extended to include corporate taxes by Harry DeAngelo and Ronald W. Masulis, "Optimal Capital Structure under Corporate and Personal Taxation," *Journal of Financial Economics* 8 (March 1980): 3–30.

| FIGURE 17.2   LEVERAGE AND VALUE WITH CONSTANT TAX RATES

With a constant tax rate, the cash flow to investors increases with all increases in the debt to total assets ratio.

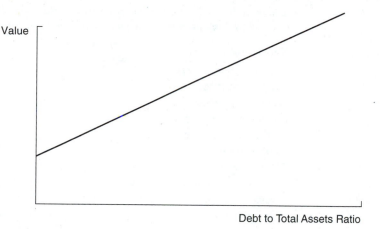

at the corporate tax rate, T_c. The amount left after corporate tax is paid to an equity investor who is then taxed again, at a rate applicable to equity income: T_g. The after-tax cash flow to the equity investor is $(1 - T_c)(1 - T_g)$ times the net operating income not used for interest payments. The total after-tax cash flow to investors (TCF) is therefore:

$$TCF = I(1 - T_p) + (NOI - I)(1 - T_c)(1 - T_g) \qquad (17\text{-}1)$$

where NOI is net operating income, and I is interest expense. Total cash flow will be increased through the use of debt if:

$$(1 - T_p) > (1 - T_c)(1 - T_g) \qquad (17\text{-}2)$$

Example. Suppose the corporations examined in Table 17.2 can shelter a substantial portion of their income from taxes, so the effective corporate tax rate is 25 percent. Suppose investors pay 30 percent income tax on interest income and 10 percent on equity income. One reason the effective tax on equity income is often lower is that part of the income is in the form of capital gains, and tax on the gains can be avoided until many years in the future, when the stock is sold. After-tax cash flow to investors with and without corporate borrowing is shown in Table 17.3.

The net cash flow from Table 17.3 can also be found using Equation 17-1:

$$\text{Without debt: TCF} = \$1{,}000(1 - .1)(1 - .25) = \$675$$

$$\text{With debt: TCF} = \$360(1 - .30) + (\$1{,}000 - \$360)(1 - .1)(1 - .25) = \$684$$

| **Table 17.3** | **Illustration of the Tax Advantages of Corporate Debt** |

Company A and B have identical expected net operating incomes. An investor with $10,000 can buy either the stock of company A or the stock and debt instruments of company B. Each company has a 25 percent tax rate while investors pay a 30 percent income tax rate on interest income and 10 percent income tax rate on equity income.

Company	A	B
Net operating income	$1,000	$1,000
Interest expense	0	360
Income before tax	1,000	640
Corporate income tax	250	160
Net income (paid to investor)	750	480
Interest paid to investor	0	360
Total payment to investor	750	840
Investor's tax on interest income	0	108
Investor's tax on equity income	75	48
Net cash flow to investor	$ 675	$ 684

Financing with debt increases total cash flow, and therefore increases value. In fact, the company would want as high a debt to total assets ratio as possible.

Tax Clientele Effect

A clientele effect occurs when the tax rates of all investors are not identical. Suppose that there are two potential investors. The first investor has $6,000 to invest and has the tax rate previously described. The second investor pays a tax rate of 40 percent on interest income and 10 percent on equity income. The positions of the two investors are as follows:

	First Investor	**Second Investor**
Tax on interest income	30%	40%
Tax on equity income	10%	10%
After-tax cash flow per dollar of net operating income used for:		
Interest income	$.700	$.600
Equity income	.675	.675

The first investor is better off with interest income, while the second investor is better off with equity income. In this case, the company will maximize its value by creating a financial structure to accommodate both investors. Specifically, it will have $6,000 of debt in its capital structure, borrowed from the first investor, with the second investor holding equity. The optimal capital structure, then, is the capital structure that recognizes the needs of each "client."

The "clientele effect" established in the previous example can be extended to companies in general. Suppose all companies have identical tax rates, but investors differ with regard to the tax rates each pays on income to equity and income to debt. Such variance can readily occur in practice. For example, an investor with interest expense in excess of investment income because of limited partnership losses can avoid taxes on interest and dividend income, but may still pay taxes on capital gains from stock investments. For other investors, tax on interest and dividends must be paid immediately, while taxes on capital gains can be delayed or avoided. A corporation holding the stock of another corporation pays tax on only 20 percent of dividend income, but pays tax on all interest income.

If tax rates are not the same for all individuals, Equation 17-2 leads to the conclusion that companies as a group would maximize value by issuing enough debt to accommodate those investors for whom $(1 - T_p) > (1 - T_c)(1 - T_g)$. This implies an optimal amount of debt for the economy as a whole, but not for an individual company. Figure 17.3 illustrates the supply and demand for loans in this situation. If all corporations have the same tax rate, the demand for loans is completely elastic; below some interest rate, r, all companies would want to issue debt because they could decrease their cost of capital by doing so. If decreasing the weighted average cost of capital by adding debt seems inconsistent with the earlier M&M analysis, note that an interest rate below r is a disequilibrium condition, and the earlier M&M analysis was based on the assumption of equilibrium. The supply schedule for loans is based on the number of investors whose after-tax return on debt is higher than their after-tax return on equity

| **FIGURE 17.3** **SUPPLY AND DEMAND FOR LOANS, WITH CONSTANT CORPORATE TAX RATES**

With a constant tax rate for corporations, and varying tax rates for interest income, the demand for loans is perfectly elastic and the supply of loans is upward sloping with regard to interest rate.

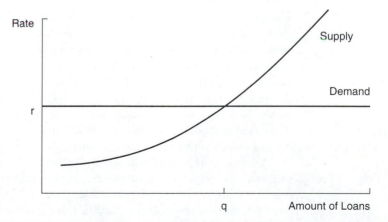

income at each interest rate (assuming some given return on equity). The interest rate on debt would adjust to r through the issuance of a total amount of debt q.

The only way a company could increase value by issuing additional debt or equity would be if the amount of total debt outstanding in the economy was more or less than the optimal amount. A disequilibrium of this type could occur because of shifts in relative tax rates caused by things like rising or falling interest rates and stock prices. Investors would then bid interest rates on debt above or below the equilibrium price, creating an opportunity to reduce the weighted average cost of capital by issuing more debt or more equity.

Differential Tax Rates among Corporations

The previous examples assumed individuals with different tax rates, but did not allow for differences in corporate tax rates. Although the official corporate income tax rate is 35 percent for most large corporations under current federal law, this does not assure that the *marginal* tax rate (the tax rate on the last dollar of income) will be the same for all corporations. State taxes and foreign taxes for multinational corporations are part of the total income tax picture, and these taxes vary by area. Some corporations pay the Alternative Minimum Tax of 20 percent rather than the regular corporate rate of 35 percent. A corporation that suffers an overall loss pays no tax on a marginal increase in income (decrease in loss). A corporation that lost money in the past can take advantage of tax loss carry-forward provisions to avoid taxes, but a dollar of extra income means consumption of the loss carry-forward and a reduction of the time until taxes are paid. Thus, the tax expense is the present value of a future payment in this case.

The higher the corporation's tax rate, the greater the savings from interest. Thus, the equity holders of some corporations can benefit from issuing debt at a higher interest rate than can others. The demand schedule for loans is then downward sloping with regard to interest rates, like that in Figure 17.4.

Decreasing Marginal Tax Rates of Individual Corporations

The factors that lead to different tax rates for different corporations also suggest decreasing marginal tax rates for an individual corporation as the amount of income sheltered by interest increases. Increased debt may decrease taxable income to $0 or to the Alternative Minimum Tax rate of 20 percent. In addition, increased debt increases the probability that part of the tax shield cannot be used in the future, thereby reducing the *expected* tax savings per dollar of interest expense as total interest expense increases. In a tax-loss carry-forward situation, decreased taxable income increases the time until taxes must be paid, again reducing the effective marginal tax rate as more debt is added.

A single corporation will generally not be big enough to affect the marginal interest rate required by investors, so the individual corporation faces a horizontal supply schedule for loans, like that in Figure 17.5. But the interest rate at which the corporation can benefit from issuing debt decreases as the amount of debt issued by the corporation increases (and its marginal tax rate therefore decreases). Thus, the optimal amount of debt for that corporation is the amount at which the two schedules intersect.

| **FIGURE 17.4**   **SUPPLY AND DEMAND FOR LOANS, WITH DIFFERENT CORPORATIONS HAVING DIFFERENT TAX RATES**

With tax rates varying among corporations, and varying tax rates for interest income and equity income to investors, the demand for loans is downward sloping with regard to interest rates and the supply of loans is upward sloping with regard to interest rate.

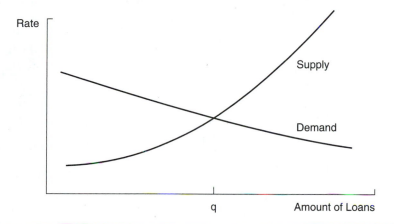

| **FIGURE 17.5**   **OPTIMAL AMOUNT OF DEBT FOR A CORPORATION WITH A MARGINAL TAX RATE THAT DECLINES AS IT ISSUES MORE DEBT**

If the corporation's marginal tax rate declines as it issues additional debt, the amount of debt the corporation will be willing to issue increases as the interest rate decreases. If the corporation is not big enough to affect overall market conditions, it faces a horizontal supply schedule for loans.

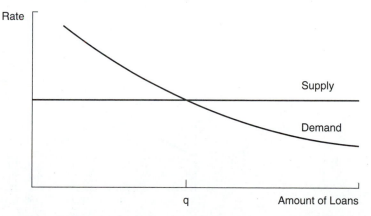

Figure 17.5 implies a relationship between value and capital structure. Value is maximized by issuing quantity q of debt, which corresponds to debt ratio d_1 in Figure 17.6. Value decreases if either too much or too little debt is issued.

VALUE MAXIMIZATION, SHAREHOLDER WEALTH, AND EQUILIBRIUM INTEREST RATES

We can confirm that shareholders benefit from value-maximizing capital structure and gain some additional insights by looking at equilibrium in relation to tax-free interest rates. Suppose there are tax-free investments, such as municipal bonds, paying an interest rate of R_{mun}, and having the same risk as the corporate debt. An investor in debt instruments would buy a corporation's debt only if the after-tax interest was at least as high as the interest on tax-free investments of equal risk. In other words, the interest rate on corporate debt, R_c, must be such that:

$$R_c(1 - T_p) \geq R_{mun} \qquad \text{(17-3)}$$

where R_{mun} is the interest rate on tax-free investments of equal risk, typically municipal bonds.

An equity investor in a corporation would benefit from the corporation issuing debt only if:

$$R_{mun} \geq R_c(1 - T_c)(1 - T_g) \qquad \text{(17-4)}$$

| **FIGURE 17.6** **LEVERAGE AND VALUE WITH VARYING TAX RATES**

If a corporation faces a decreasing marginal tax rate as income increases, this can result in an amount of debt that maximizes the total value of the corporation. That optimal amount of debt with varying tax rates corresponds to debt to total assets ratio d_1.

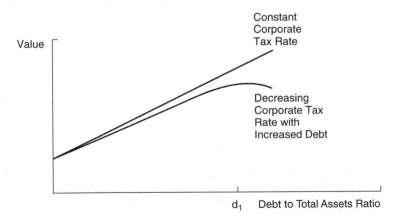

To see that Inequality 17-4 is an appropriate requirement, recognize that with a given set of assets, a corporation increases debt by borrowing and then decreasing equity by returning the amount borrowed to the shareholders. If Inequality 17-4 holds, the after-tax cost to an equity holder from the corporation's interest payment is less than or equal to what the equity holder can earn from investing the money returned by the corporation in tax-free debt. Thus, additional corporate borrowing would give the equity holder an opportunity to increase after-tax cash flow with no change in risk.

Since companies would issue debt as long as equity holders could benefit, and holders of tax-free debt would switch to corporate debt as long as they could benefit, the equilibrium relationship between interest rates and *marginal*[11] tax rates is:

$$R_c(1 - T_p) = R_{mun} = R_c(1 - T_c)(1 - T_g) \qquad \text{(17-5)}$$

Because all corporations face the same potential investors, all face the same marginal investor tax rates. R_c and R_{mun} are also the same for all corporations in this model because all debt is riskless in the absence of bankruptcy. A particular corporation, then, will continue increasing the debt ratio until T_c declines to the point where Equation 17-5 is satisfied. This does not imply that all corporations will have the same debt ratio; the debt ratio necessary to bring the marginal tax rate to T_c will be affected by the return earned on assets and the availability of other forms of tax shelters, such as accelerated depreciation, available to the corporation.

If Equation 17-5 is simplified by the normal rules of algebra, the interest rate terms fall out and what is left is:

$$(1 - T_p) = (1 - T_c)(1 - T_g) \qquad \text{(17-6)}$$

Note from Inequality 17-2 that this is also the condition that makes it impossible to increase the total value of the corporation by increasing or decreasing debt. Thus, the capital structure that maximizes the value of the corporation also maximizes the wealth of the shareholders. Going one step further, we are still assuming risk-free corporate debt, so the interest rate on corporate debt is market-determined, and the corporation cannot affect the wealth of the creditors. Therefore, any change in wealth, from a change in total value to a change in capital structure, must accrue to the shareholders.

BANKRUPTCY COSTS AND CAPITAL STRUCTURE

The analysis thus far has assumed no possibility of bankruptcy. Bankruptcy itself does not decrease value because bankruptcy is merely a process of realigning claims against a given stream of cash flows. However, friction costs associ-

---

[11]For this purpose, the marginal tax rate is the tax rate on the last dollar of income for the marginal investor—the investor who would be the first to sell the security if there was any decrease in after-tax benefits.

ated with bankruptcy do decrease wealth. As discussed in the option pricing part of Chapter 15, bankruptcy is the situation in which the corporation is worth less than the amount owed to the creditors and is, therefore, turned over to the creditors. Bankruptcy is not the same as liquidation. Bankruptcy transfers ownership status to the creditors whereas the liquidation decision is based on the conclusion that the present value of future cash flows from operations is less that the sale price of the assets. The possibility of a transfer of ownership through bankruptcy increases as the amount of debt increases, but this does not change value if it does not change the probability distribution of operating cash flows. The probability of bankruptcy affects value only if there are specific costs associated with bankruptcy.

The direct costs associated with bankruptcy are of two varieties: legal costs and disruption costs.[12] Bankruptcy proceedings can cost millions of dollars in legal and administrative fees. More seriously, business is disrupted by the uncertainty surrounding the bankruptcy, and this uncertainty may continue for some time as bankruptcy proceedings frequently drag on for years. Long-range planning and new capital investments are often curtailed during the process, and many employees may leave because of the uncertainty. These disruptions can reduce cash flows and substantially reduce the value of the firm.

Customers may also be lost when the probability of bankruptcy increases, or the company may be forced to accept lower prices to compensate potential customers for the increased risk.[13] One thing government guarantees did for Chrysler was provide assurance that the company would be in existence long enough to honor its warranties.

As the amount of debt increases, the expected bankruptcy cost—the cost of bankruptcy times the probability of bankruptcy—increases and the value of the firm correspondingly decreases, other things being equal. Figure 17.7 extends the analysis of Figure 17.6 to include the value-reduction impact of expected bankruptcy cost as the amount of debt increases. The optimal capital structure will include less debt than if there were no bankruptcy costs.

INFORMATION PROBLEMS AND CAPITAL STRUCTURE |

Information is another key factor affecting capital structure. Investors are limited in their knowledge of what managers are doing and what managers expect. The lack of complete, free information about what managers are doing leads to

---

[12]For detailed discussions for the theory related to bankruptcy costs, see N. Baxter, "Leverage, the Risk of Ruin, and the Cost of Capital," *Journal of Finance* 22 (September 1967): 395–403; Joseph Stiglitz, "Some Aspects of the Pure Theory of Corporate Finance: Bankruptcies and Takeovers," *Bell Journal of Economics and Management Science* (Autumn 1972): 458–482; Alan Kraus and Robert Litzenberger, "A State-Preference Model of Optimal Financial Leverage," *Journal of Finance* 28 (September 1973): 911–922; and E. Han Kim, "A Mean Variance Theory of Optimal Capital Structure and Corporate Debt Capacity," *Journal of Finance* 33 (March 1978): 45–64.

[13]This point is developed in more detail by S. Titman, "The Effect of Capital Structure on a Firm's Liquidation Decision," Ph.D. thesis, Graduate School of Industrial Administration, Carnegie-Mellon University, 1981.

| **FIGURE 17.7** **LEVERAGE AND VALUE WITH VARYING TAX RATES AND BANKRUPTCY COSTS**

This figure shows the relationship between capital structure and value with constant tax rates and with varying tax rates, plus the relationship between value and capital structure with varying tax rates and bankruptcy costs.

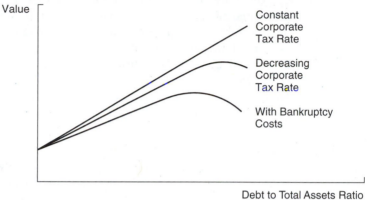

an agency problem. It is necessary to find a way to motivate managers to voluntarily act in the interests of shareholders. Capital structure can be part of a system designed to assure that managers maximize their own wealth by acting in the interests of the shareholders. In addition investors do not know the true value of the firm because they have less information about the company than the managers have. This *information asymmetry* problem may be overcome through signaling mechanisms. Capital structure can be part of a signaling process. Use of capital structure to solve agency and information asymmetry problems is covered next.

AGENCY PROBLEMS AND CAPITAL STRUCTURE

An agency problem arises whenever one person hires another person to do something. Adam Smith observed very early that agents may not behave as diligently as would a principal whose own wealth was at stake. The managers of a modern corporation serve as agents for a number of people. They manage the funds provided by the creditors and by the equity investors. Consumers can also be thought of as people who hire managers to bring together the necessary resources to produce a product for them. The importance of these agency relationships for capital structure decisions has received widespread attention as a result of the work of Jensen and Meckling.[14] The practical importance of these relationships is highlighted by a series of advertisements from NCR, stressing its "stakeholder" approach to management.

[14]Michael Jensen and W. Meckling, "Theory of the Firm: Managerial Behavior, Agency Cost, and Ownership Structure," *Journal of Financial Economics* (October 1976): 305–360.

Agency Costs of Debt

The creditors of a corporation entrust their money to the managers, generally on the belief that the riskiness of their debt securities will not increase substantially. But it was demonstrated in Chapter 15 that managers could increase the wealth of the shareholders at the expense of the creditors by moving to a more risky asset structure. If the total amount owed by the company is small in relation to the value of its assets,[15] the risks to creditors are small. For companies with higher debt ratios, the possibility of usurping creditor wealth through a change in capital structure increases. It becomes necessary to establish elaborate contracts and then spend considerable time in monitoring the company to insure compliance. The increased agency costs of debt as the debt to total assets ratio increases are shown in Figure 17.8. Creditors will demand an interest rate that provides an equilibrium return *after* agency costs.

Agency Costs of Equity

Shareholders also face an agency problem in that their agents, the managers, may not act diligently on their behalf. Managers may be slothful and they may consume excessive wages or excessive perquisites such as travel. In addition, managers may be too conservative or too aggressive in their investment strategy. The smaller the proportion of the equity owned by managers, the greater is the incentive for managers to act in their own self-interest at the expense of the shareholders, and the greater the agency cost. If the size of the company and the size of management's equity investment are fixed, the *proportion* of equity owned by management increases as the debt ratio increases. As shown in Figure 17.8, agency costs of equity steadily decline as the debt ratio increases.

Total agency costs—the sum of debt and equity agency costs—decrease as some debt is added, but then begin to increase as the debt ratio increases further. Other things being equal, the optimal capital structure would be at the point where total agency costs were minimized.[16]

A limitation in the agency cost argument develops when large firms are involved. H.J. Heinz Corporation has total capital of $4.7 billion. Suppose management has an equity position of $5 million. If the company is financed exclusively with equity, management owns 0.11 percent of the equity. If Heinz is financed with one-half debt, management's ownership increases to only 0.22 percent of equity, and the cost of $100 of perquisite consumption increases from 11 cents to 22 cents. Since the cost to management is still miniscule in this situation, it is doubtful that increased debt has significant impact on agency costs of equity. Agency costs would then increase with all increases in debt.

---

[15]The protection of the creditors comes from the amount of debt in relation to the *market value* of the assets, not the book value. This point is stressed by J. H. Scott, "Bankruptcy, Secured Debt, and Optimal Capital Structure," *Journal of Finance* 32 (March 1977): 1–19.

[16]For a proof, see Jensen and Meckling, "Theory of the Firm."

| **F I G U R E 1 7 . 8 Leverage and Agency Costs**

Agency costs of debt, agency costs of equity, and total agency costs are shown. Other things being equal, the optimal capital structure is the capital structure that minimizes agency costs.

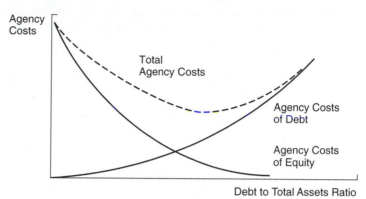

Figure 17.9 shows the relationship between capital structure and value with agency costs considered. Figure 17.9 shows the relationship when agency costs of equity can be affected by capital structure.[17]

Agency considerations extend to the maturity as well as the amount of debt. A key consideration is the possibility of risky asset substitution, the borrowing of money for one implied purpose, and then the acquisition of more risky assets after the investors have committed their funds. Several scholars have noted the importance of debt maturity in addressing this problem. Short- and intermediate-term debt requires the company to repeatedly return to the lenders so that asset substitution can be monitored and punished quickly. Thus, companies for which investors see a risk of risky asset substitution can reduce their cost of capital by issuing short- or intermediate-term debt to allay these fears.[18]

Before leaving the topic of agency costs, we should note that agency theory has its detractors as well. Fama noted that the value of a manager's human capital will be affected by the quality of management provided.[19] If a manager changes jobs, the salary that manager can obtain will depend on previously

[17]A curve can be drawn as easily for a company that can only reduce agency costs of debt through capital structure, and an optimal capital structure will occur in either case. With only agency costs of debt affected, the optimal debt ratio will be below that without agency costs.

[18]See, for example, Hayne E. Leland and Klaus Bjerre Toft, "Optimal Capital Structure, Endogenous Bankruptcy, and the Term Structure of Credit Spreads," *Journal of Finance* 51 (July 1996): 987–1019; and Jose Guedes and Tim Opler, "The Determinants of the Maturity of Corporate Debt Issues," *Journal of Finance* 51 (December 1996): 1809–1833.

[19]Eugene Fama, "Agency Problems and the Theory of the Firm," *Journal of Political Economy,* (April 1980): 288–307.

| **FIGURE 17.9**   **LEVERAGE AND VALUE WITH VARIABLE TAX RATES, BANKRUPTCY COSTS, AND AGENCY COSTS**

Variable tax rates lead to an optimal capital structure. Bankruptcy costs modify the picture to result in a lower optimal debt to total assets ratio. Inclusion of agency costs reduces the optimal debt ratio further in this case, although agency costs could shift the optimal debt ratio either up or down.

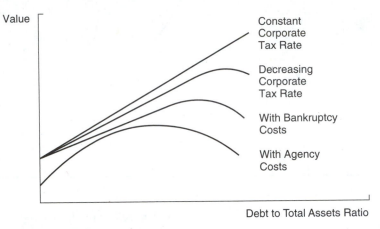

observed work. The discipline of the labor market depends on (1) the quality of the manager's work being observable and (2) the manager being submitted to the discipline of the labor market. Managers of many large corporations are not selected by the stockholders—new candidates for the board of directors are nominated by existing managers, not shareholders—and managers of many of these corporations never change jobs. This limits the discipline of the labor market in many cases. On the other side, takeover artists like Carl Ichan bring some discipline by acquiring companies and replacing existing managers when they believe managers are not maximizing value.

INFORMATION ASYMMETRY AND INCENTIVE SIGNALING

Managers typically have more information about the prospects of the corporation than do shareholders. A company's stock will be underpriced if managers are not able to convey good news to the stockholders in a believable manner. The underpricing means earnings dilution as more new shares must be sold to raise money than would otherwise be necessary. It would be nice if managers could simply tell shareholders what they expected, but managers who expect their company to perform poorly in the future may delay the passing of this news to investors. The making of such announcements is unpleasant and may threaten managers' jobs. Furthermore, there have been cases in which managers acted illegally to sell their shares before the truth became known. What is needed is a way to be sure managers are telling the truth.

Ross showed how capital structure could serve as a vehicle for signaling investors about management expectations.[20] The main conditions for a signal to be sent are (1) managers are restricted from selling their shares or buying additional shares for some specified period of time, and (2) managers are heavily penalized if their company goes bankrupt. An increased debt ratio is viewed as a signal of a good outcome being expected, and vice versa. Results of debt ratio signals for each type of expected outcome are summarized as follows:[21]

	EXPECTED RESULT	
Signal	**Good outcome**	**Bad outcome**
Increased debt ratio	Greater value for manager because of less earnings dilution	Greater probability of bankruptcy
Decreased debt ratio	NA (No motive to signal a bad outcome when none is expected.)	More earnings dilution, but decreased probability of bankruptcy

Recent studies have extended the asymmetry analysis to include debt maturity. Goswami, Noe, and Rebello extend the asymmetry analysis to debt maturity. They show that if information asymmetry is around long-term cash flows, firms finance with long-term debt that partially restricts dividends. If asymmetry is concentrated around near-term cash flows and there is considerable refinancing risk, firms finance with long-term debt that does not restrict dividends. If asymmetry is distributed evenly across dates, firms use short-term debt.[22] Flannery shows that in information assymetry, strong firms that cannot completely convey their strengths to the investors will think of their long-term debt as requiring an interest rate that is too high, and will thus avoid long-term debt while weaker companies will want to issue long-term debt.[23]

Figure 17.10 illustrates a situation in which signaling is considered along with other market conditions. The optimal capital structure would not be at the

---

[20]Stephen Ross, "The Determination of Financial Structure: The Incentive Signaling Approach," *Bell Journal of Economics and Management Science* (Spring 1977): 23–40.

[21]Haugen and Senbet suggest the use of put and call options as part of the signaling process. Managers can use a combination of put and call options to narrow the range of stock prices over which they will profit, and thereby send a more precise signal. R. A. Haugen and Lemma W. Senbet, "New Perspectives on Informational Assymetry," *Journal of Financial and Quantitative Analysis* 14 (November 1979): 671–694.

[22]Gautam Goswami, Thomas Noe, and Michael Rebello, "Debt Financing under Asymmetric Information," *Journal of Finance* 50 (June 1995): 633–659.

[23]Mark J. Flannery, "Asymmetric Information and Risky Debt Maturity Choice," *Journal of Finance* 41 (March 1986): 19–37.

| FIGURE 17.10   VARIABLE TAX RATES, BANKRUPTCY COSTS, AGENCY COSTS, SIGNALING COSTS, AND THE OPTIMAL CAPITAL STRUCTURE

Information asymmetry costs associated with issuing less than the amount of debt that send the appropriate signal are combined with other previously discussed costs to show the capital structure that maximizes value with all of these costs recognized.

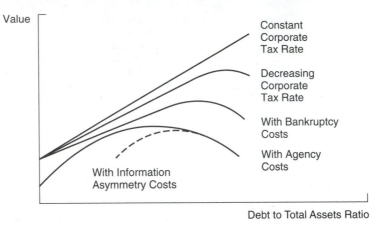

point where signaling costs are minimized, but at the point where total value is maximized, with signaling cost being one of the capital structure–related costs that decrease value.

OTHER CONSIDERATIONS AND CAPITAL STRUCTURE CHOICE |

The analysis thus far has assumed that investors can substitute their own borrowing for that of the corporation. There are several problems with this assumption in practice, and these problems increase the attractiveness of corporate debt.

UNEQUAL COSTS OF CORPORATE AND PERSONAL BORROWING

In the previous analysis, it was assumed that individuals and corporations could borrow at the same rate. This is, however, frequently not true. Among other things there are economies of scale involved; the corporation may borrow hundreds of millions of dollars while each individual would borrow only a few thousand dollars instead. Administrative costs for these small loans may be high, making the effective interest cost higher for the individual than for the corporation. Cost differentials of this type would lead to a higher optimal amount of corporate debt.

RISK ASSOCIATED WITH PERSONAL DEBT

If you buy the stock of a leveraged corporation you cannot lose more than the amount you invested because stockholders are not liable for the corporation's debts. If you use homemade leverage instead, you can lose the equity capital invested and have to pay off the loan as well. This discourages homemade leverage and therefore increases the attractiveness of corporate leverage.

INSTITUTIONAL RESTRICTIONS ON HOMEMADE LEVERAGE

Margin requirements set by the Federal Reserve system limit how much an investor can borrow to purchase common stock. The margin requirements, which are 50 percent of value now, do not depend on the amount of debt used by the company, so a company that has debt in its capital structure increases the financial leverage opportunities available to investors. Again, inclusion of debt in the capital structure can increase value.

Many institutional portfolio managers are not allowed to borrow money. These limitations are generally designed to protect the portfolio from undue risks. But these same limitations do not stop the portfolio manager from buying the stock of a company with a large amount of debt in its capital structure. The portfolio manager can generally unleverage by buying the stock and debt instruments, but cannot create a debt to equity ratio higher than that chosen by the company. These institutional restrictions again increase the desirability of corporate debt.

Portfolio Effects. Suppose that a firm decides to issue only equity or decides to issue almost all debt. If there are restrictions on homemade leverage, then the all-equity company cannot appeal to all investors. An extremely high debt ratio may lead to earnings and dividends being so unstable that some institutional portfolio managers are not allowed to hold the stock. Extremely low leverage excludes investors, including some portfolio managers, who prefer a leveraged position but cannot borrow effectively for some reason. If some investors are excluded, other investors must hold a disproportionately large amount of that stock in their portfolios. This means that investors will require a return that includes compensation for accepting risk that could otherwise be diversified away. Thus, portfolio considerations may be another factor affecting the optimal capital structure.

EMPIRICAL EVIDENCE |

Numerous empirical studies have been conducted in attempts to confirm or reject the theories of capital structure choice. Several studies have focused on the costs of bankruptcy, and the question of whether those costs are high enough to be significant. Warner found that direct bankruptcy costs for a sample of railroads were only 1 percent of the market value of assets 7 years before the bankruptcy.[24] Altman studied indirect bankruptcy costs for a group of retailers and industrial companies. He concluded that indirect bankruptcy costs were 8 percent of market value 3 years before the bankruptcy.[25] A 1 percent bankruptcy cost may be insignificant if there is a small probability of bankruptcy. On the other hand, 8 percent may be sufficient to affect capital structure decisions. Alderson and Betker discovered that firms with high liquidation costs tend to emerge from Chapter 11 with relatively low debt ratios,[26] which appears to be direct evidence that bankruptcy costs are a consideration in capital structure choice.

Bradley, Jarrell, and Kim focused on cross-sectional analysis of corporate capital structures. They found the following relationships between financial variables and financial leverage:[27]

Variable	Correlation with amount of financial leverage
1. Earnings volatility (proxy for bankruptcy risk)	Negative
2. Advertising and R&D as a proxy for assets that cannot be used as collateral	Negative
3. Other tax shields/earnings	Positive

The directions of correlation for the first two variables are consistent with the theory, while the direction of correlation for the third variable is not.[28] In another study, Long and Malitz found nondebt tax shields to be negatively correlated with capital structure, as expected.[29] With conflicting results from the two studies, the validity of the theory is still not confirmed.

---

[24]J. Warner, "Bankruptcy Costs: Some Evidence," *Journal of Finance* 32 (May 1977): 337–347.

[25]E. Altman, "A Further Empirical Investigation of the Bankruptcy Cost Question," *Journal of Finance* 39 (September 1984): 1067–1089.

[26]Michael J. Alderson and Brian L. Betker. "Liquidation Costs and Capital Structure," *Journal of Financial Economics* 39 (September 1995): 45–69.

[27]M. Bradley, G. Jarrell, and E. Han Kim, "On the Existence of an Optimal Capital Structure: Theory and Evidence," *Journal of Finance* 39 (July 1984): 857–878.

[28]Dammon and Senbet suggest that unexpected signs on this variable can be explained if firms adjust for changing nondebt tax shields through investment decisions instead of financing decisions: Robert M. Dammon and Lemma W. Senbet, "The Effects of Taxes and Depreciation on Corporate Investment and Financial Leverage," *Journal of Finance* 43 (June 1988): 357–373.

[29]M. Long and I. Malitz, "Investment Patterns and Financial Leverage," in *Corporate Capital Structure in the United States*, ed. Friedman (University of Chicago Press, 1985). Cited in Thomas E. Copeland and J. Fred Weston, *Financial Theory and Corporate Policy*, 2nd ed. (Reading, Mass.: Addison-Wesley, 1988).

Numerous announcement-effect studies have been conducted on exchange offers and seasoned security issues that change the firm's capital structure.[30] The general conclusion is that those actions that increase leverage increase stock value, and vice versa. This pattern of behavior could be attributed to leverage preferences, or to the belief that increased leverage signals management optimism. The latter explanation would be consistent with the theory.

Kaley and Shimrat confirmed other studies that found that stock price fell, on average, with the announcement of a new equity issue. However, they went one step further to look at what happened to bond prices when new equity issues were announced. Bond prices fell as well. This is inconsistent with theories that suggest stock prices fall because bondholders are gaining from the increased safety or that stock prices fall because of temporary increased supplies of stock. However, Kaley and Shimrat's observations are consistent with the view that issuance of stock conveys to investors a management belief that the stock is overpriced in relation to the company's prospects.[31]

Friend and Lang studied the relationship between managerial equity holdings and the use of debt financing, and found that the amount of debt decreased as the proportion of equity owned by managers increased. Their results were consistent with a management self-interest hypothesis because the risks arising from debt financing are not diversifiable to managers. This would suggest that the resolution of agency problems is important in capital structure analysis.[32]

Empirical evidence continues to accumulate. Klock and Thies find evidence that debt in the capital structure offsets any desire of management of low profitability firms to overinvest, because of the cash flow requirements to repay debt.[33] This is further evidence that debt serves to reduce agency problems. Shah finds that increased leverage appears to lower investors' assessment of risk of the firm's stock, but does not appear to change expected cash flows. Leverage-decreasing offers appear to lower expectations of cash flows, but do not change risk assessment.[34] This again suggests that debt can relieve information asymmetry problems.

[30]See, for example, R. Masulis, "The Effects of Capital Structure Changes on Security Prices: A Study of Exchange Offers," *Journal of Financial Economics* (June 1980): 139–178; R. Masulis and A. Korwar, "Seasoned Equity Offerings: An Empirical Investigation," *Journal of Financial Economics* (January–February 1986): 91–118; W. Mikkelson and W. Partch, "Valuation Effects of Security Offerings and the Issuance Process," *Journal of Financial Economics* (January–February 1986): 31–60; P. Asquith and David Mullins, Jr., "Equity Issues and Offering Dilution," *Journal of Financial Economics* (January–February 1986): 61–90; and R. Kolodny and D. Suhler, "Changes in Capital Structure, New Equity Issues, and Scale Effects," *Journal of Financial Research* 8 (Summer 1985): 127–136.

[31]Avner Kaley and Adam Shimrat, "Firm Value and Seasoned Equity Issues," *Journal of Financial Economics* 19 (September 1987): 109–126.

[32]Irwin Friend and Larry H. P. Lang. "An Empirical Test of the Impact of Managerial Self-Interest on Corporate Capital Structure," *Journal of Finance* 43 (June 1988): 271–281.

[33]Mark Klock and Clifford F. Thies, "A Test of Stulz's Overinvestment Hypothesis," *Financial Review* 30 (August 1995): 387–398.

[34]Kshitij Shah, "The Nature of Information Conveyed by Pure Capital Structure Changes," *Journal of Financial Economics* 36 (August 1994): 89–126.

Roden and Lewellen find evidence that agency, bankruptcy costs, and taxes all affect capital structure decisions.[35] Rajan and Zingales confirm some of these same observations with international data.[36]

With theoretical models identifying numerous factors affecting capital structure, it is difficult to use existing empirical evidence to choose between theories. In the absence of conclusive empirical evidence, theory is particularly important because theories are logical extensions from what we do know to produce estimates of how various factors will affect capital structure choice. Theory is, therefore, useful for practical decision makers who cannot wait to make capital structure decisions until empirical researchers have answered all of their questions. Chapter 18 is devoted to capital structure choice, based on existing theories and evidence.

SUMMARY

Capital structure choice does not affect firm value in an idealized world devoid of taxes and market imperfections. Thus, capital structure decisions are responses to market imperfections.

The primary factors believed to affect the relationship between leverage and value are:

- Tax rates of businesses and investors
- Bankruptcy costs
- Agency costs
- Information asymmetry and signaling problems

Taxes are a common type of market imperfection. Specifically, a company can increase its value by choosing debt financing as long as there are investors still available for whom:

$$(1 - T_p) > (1 - T_c)(1 - T_g)$$

where T_p is the investor's marginal tax rate on interest income, T_c is the corporation's marginal income tax rate, and T_g is the investor's tax rate on equity income. Tax rates of both companies and investors vary. This suggests an optimal amount of debt for the economy and may suggest an optimal amount of debt for individual companies.

Bankruptcy results in direct legal expenses, and also results in disruption costs. The tax savings resulting from increased debt are partially offset by in-

[35]Dianne M. Roden and Wilbur G. Lewellen, "Corporate Capital Structure Decisions: Evidence from Leveraged Buyouts," *Financial Management* 24 (Summer 1995): 76–87.

[36]Raghuram G. Rajan and Luigi Zingales, "What Do We Know about Capital Structure? Some Evidence from International Data," *Journal of Finance* 50 (December 1995): 1421–1460.

creases in expected bankruptcy costs as the debt ratio increases. Agency costs present yet another consideration. Increased debt results in increased agency costs of debt, while increased equity may result in increased agency costs of equity. The optimal capital structure will be at the point where the sum of agency costs, tax costs, and expected bankruptcy costs is minimized.

Finally, information asymmetry and signaling enters the picture. Investors do not have the management's information about the company and may use the capital structure as a signal of management's expectations. Failure to choose the capital structure that sends the appropriate signal can result in an information asymmetry cost. This cost must be added to the previously considered costs in choosing a capital structure that minimizes costs.

It is also important to note that it is much easier to reduce the solution to a neat formula than it is to plug values into the formula. Marginal tax rates, expected bankruptcy costs, agency costs, and responses to signals are extremely difficult to measure and predict. We can, however, use these principles as general guidelines as we look at capital structure decision making. The primary topic of Chapter 18 is the application of these principles in a world of uncertainty and incomplete information.

QUESTIONS

17-1. What is an optimal capital structure?

17-2. With perfect markets, no taxes, no probability of bankruptcy, and both corporations and individuals able to borrow at the same interest rate, how is the optimal capital structure of a firm determined?

17-3. Explain the concept of homemade leverage. What are the implications for capital structure choice?

17-4. If the only violation of the M&M assumptions is a constant tax rate for both corporations and investors, what is the implication for the optimal capital structure of a corporation?

17-5. If the only violation of the M&M assumptions is that investors face one tax rate for interest income and another tax rate for equity income, what is the implication for the optimal capital structure of a corporation?

17-6. With regard to capital structure choice, what is the tax clientele effect?

17-7. If investors face different tax rates for interest income and equity income, and the corporation's tax rate declines as taxable income declines, what are the implications for capital structure choice?

17-8. For capital structure choice, what are the implications of
  a. bankruptcy costs?
  b. agency costs?

17-9. What type of capital structure change would managers use to signal their expectations of improved profitability?

17-10. What would discourage managers, expecting declining performance, to send false signals to investors via a change in capital structure?

Problems

17–1. Corporations X and Y each have net operating incomes of $1,200. Corporation X has no debt, and corporation Y has debt of $4,000, on which the interest rate is 10 percent. The total value of corporation X's stock is $10,000 and the total value of corporation Y's stock is $7,000. Is this an equilibrium price, given the M&M assumptions and no taxes? If not, what would the equilibrium price of corporation Y's stock be if nothing else changed? Would the prices move to equilibrium?

17–2. Richards Corporation is financed entirely with equity. The company has net operating income of $10,000 and stock valued at $80,000. Richards has $30,000 of debt in its capital structure, with an interest rate of 10 percent. Assuming the M&M conditions hold and there are no taxes, what is Richards' weighted average cost of capital if its stock is priced at equilibrium?

17–3. For corporations X and Y in problem 1, what would be the total cash flow to investors in each company if there was a 40 percent tax rate for both companies and investors?

17–4. Rework problem 3 on the assumption that each company's tax rate is 40 percent and investors are taxed at a 20 percent rate.

17–5. Alpha and Beta corporations each have net operating income of $100,000. Alpha corporation is financed entirely with equity, and the common stock is valued at $360,000. Beta corporation has $200,000 of debt paying interest of 6 percent a year. The value of Beta's stock is $160,000. Your tax rate and the tax rates of both corporations are 40 percent. You are holding the stock of Alpha corporation and prefer an unleveraged investment. Is there an arbitrage opportunity available?

17–6. Draper Corporation has a marginal tax rate of 25 percent, and needs total capital of $1 million. There are two potential investors, one with $500,000 and a tax rate on interest income of 30 percent. Another investor has a million dollars available, and has a tax rate of 50 percent on interest income. Each investor has a tax rate of 10 percent on equity income. How much debt and how much equity would the company issue to maximize value?

17–7. The interest rate on municipal bonds is 6 percent. An investor pays tax of 30 percent on interest income. What is the minimum interest rate that investor would accept on corporate debt of equal risk?

17–8. The interest rate on municipal bonds is 8 percent. What is the maximum interest rate Burger Corporation can pay if Burger's marginal tax rate is 30 percent and shareholders' marginal tax rate on equity income is 20 percent (assuming equal risk)?

17–9. Chapel Hill Corporation has a marginal tax rate on corporate income of 20 percent. Investors' marginal tax rates on equity and interest income are 10 percent and 40 percent respectively. The interest rate on municipal bonds is 6 percent. What is the equilibrium interest rate on corporate debt? Can Chapel Hill Corporation increase shareholder wealth by changing its capital structure? How will Chapel Hill Corporation know when it has the optimal amount of debt in its capital structure?

17–10. Greenville Corporation operates in a world in which taxes are not a consideration. The company does face bankruptcy risk, agency costs of debt, and agency costs of equity. It does not face information asymmetry costs. Draw a figure showing the relationship between debt to total asset ratio and value for this corporation.

17–11. Athens Corporation has a marginal tax rate of 35 percent. If the company issues over $40,000 of debt, the marginal tax rate declines to 30 percent. If the company issues over $80,000 of debt, the marginal tax rate declines to 20 percent. If the company issues over $100,000 in debt, the marginal tax rate declines to $0. Investors face tax rates of 33 percent on interest income and 20 percent on equity income. How much debt should the company issue?

17–12. For Athens Corporation (problem 11), suppose the interest rate on municipal bonds is 6 percent. What is the maximum interest rate the company can pay on corporate debt at each debt level if shareholders are to benefit from leverage?

17–13. (**Application**) Two of the changes resulting from the passage of the Revenue Reconciliation Act of 1993 were:

- The corporate tax rate was raised from 34 percent to 35 percent for firms earning over $18,333,333 in income.
- The highest tax rate was raised from 31 percent to 39.6 percent for married individuals filing a joint return.

a. Taken one at a time, what impact do you believe these changes will have on the value of the company?

b. What impact do you think these changes will have on the capital structure decision?

c. You pay out 100 percent of earnings and are in the top tax brackets for both corporate and personal income. For each $100 of income before corporate taxes, what was the cash flow to the shareholder after corporate and personal taxes before and after the new act?

17–14. Some financial analysts watch the buying or selling activities of corporate insiders as a guide to the direction of the future stock price.

a. Why might the selling by insiders of 20 percent of the outstanding stock in a particular company be viewed as a negative signal by the market?

b. What are some of the legitimate reasons an insider might be liquidating a portion of his or her stake in the company?

c. What factors would you look at to determine the degree to which this is a negative signal versus a normal liquidation of an insider's interest?

SELECTED REFERENCES |

Aivazian, Varouj A., and Jeffrey L. Callen. "Miller's Irrelevance Mechanism: A Note." *Journal of Finance* 42 (March 1987): 169–180.

Alderson, Michael J., and Brian L. Betker. "Liquidation Costs and Capital Structure." *Journal of Financial Economics* 39 (September 1995): 45–69.

Altman, Edward. "A Further Empirical Investigation of the Bankruptcy Cost Question." *Journal of Finance* 39 (September 1984): 1067–1089.

Asquith, P., and David Mullins, Jr. "Equity Issues and Offering Dilution." *Journal of Financial Economics* (January–February 1986): 61–90.

Baxter, N. "Leverage, the Risk of Ruin, and the Cost of Capital." *Journal of Finance* 22 (September 1967): 395–403.

Becker, Jack. "General Proof of Modigliani-Miller Propositions I and II Using Parameter-Preference Theory." *Journal of Financial and Quantitative Analysis* 13 (March 1978): 65–69.

Benston, G. "The Self-Serving Management Hypothesis: Some Evidence." *Journal of Accounting and Economics* 7 (April 1985): 67–84.

Bhagast, Sanjai, James Brinckley, and Ronald C. Lease. "Incentive Effect of Stock Purchase Plans." *Journal of Financial Economics* 14 (June 1985): 195–215.

Boquist, John A., and William T. Moore. "Inter-Industry Leverage Differences and the DeAngelo-Masulis Tax Shield Hypothesis." *Financial Management* 13 (Spring 1984): 5–9.

Bradley, M., G. Jarrell, and E. Han Kim. "On the Existence of an Optimal Capital Structure: Theory and Evidence." *Journal of Finance* 39 (July 1984): 857–878.

Campbell, Tim, and William A. Kracaw. "The Market for Managerial Labor Services and Capital Market Equilibrium." *Journal of Financial and Quantitative Analysis* 20 (September 1985): 277–297.

Dammon, Robert M., and Lemma W. Senbet. "The Effect of Taxes and Depreciation on Corporate Investment and Financial Leverage." *Journal of Finance* 43 (June 1988): 357–373.

Davis, Alfred H. R. "Effective Tax Rates as Determinants of Canadian Capital Structure." *Financial Management* (Autumn 1987): 22–28.

DeAngelo, Harry, and Ronald W. Masulis. "Optimal Capital Structure under Corporate and Personal Taxation." *Journal of Financial Economics* 8 (March 1980): 3–30.

Fama, Eugene. "Agency Problems and the Theory of the Firm." *Journal of Political Economy* (April 1980): 288–307.

Flannery, Mark J. "Asymmetric Information and Risky Debt Maturity Choice." *Journal of Finance* 41 (March 1986): 19–37.

Friend, Irwin, and Larry H. P. Lang. "An Empirical Test of the Impact of Managerial Self-Interest on Corporate Capital Structure." *Journal of Finance* 43 (June 1988): 271–281.

Fries, Steven, Marcus Miller, and William Perraudin. "Debt in Industry Equilibrium." *Review of Financial Studies* 10 (Spring 1997): 39–67.

Goswami, Gautam, Thomas Noe, and Michael Rebello. "Debt Financing under Asymmetric Information." *Journal of Finance* 50 (June 1995): 633–659.

Guedes, Jose, and Tim Opler. "The Determinants of the Maturity of Corporate Debt Issues." *Journal of Finance* 51 (December 1996): 1809–1833.

Hamada, Robert S. "Portfolio Analysis, Market Equilibrium, and Corporation Finance." *Journal of Finance* 24 (March 1969): 13–19.

Haugen, Robert, and Lemma W. Senbet. "Bankruptcy and Agency Costs: Their Significance in the Theory of Optimal Capital Structure." *Journal of Financial and Quantitative Analysis* 23 (March 1988): 27–38.

———. "Corporate Finance and Taxes: A Review." *Financial Management* 15 (Autumn 1986): 5–21.

Jensen, Michael, and W. Meckling. "Theory of the Firm: Managerial Behavior, Agency Cost, and Ownership Structure." *Journal of Financial Economics* (October 1976): 305–360.

Jensen, Michael, and C. Smith, Jr. "Stockholders, Manager, and Creditor Interests: Application of Agency Theory." In *Recent Advances in Corporate Finance*, ed. E. Altman and M. Subrahmanyam. Homewood, Ill.: Richard D. Irwin, 1985.

Kaley, Avner, and Adam Shimrat. "Firm Value and Seasoned Equity Issues." *Journal of Financial Economics* 19 (September 1987): 109–126.

Kim, E. Han. "A Mean Variance Theory of Optimal Capital Structure and Corporate Debt Capacity." *Journal of Finance* 33 (March 1978): 45–64.

Klock, Mark, and Clifford F. Thies. "A Test of Stulz's Overinvestment Hypothesis." *Financial Review* 30 (August 1995): 387–398.

Kolodny, R., and D. Suhler. "Changes in Capital Structure, New Equity Issues, and Scale Effects." *Journal of Financial Research* 8 (Summer 1985): 127–136.

Kose, John. "Risk-Shifting Incentives and Signaling through Corporate Capital Structure." *Journal of Finance* 42 (July 1987): 623–641.

Kraus, Alan, and Robert Litzenberger. "A State-Preference Model of Optimal Financial Leverage." *Journal of Finance* 28 (September 1973): 911–922.

Leland, Hayne E. "Corporate Debt Value, Bond Covenants, and Optimal Capital Structure." *Journal of Finance* 49 (September 1994): 1213–1252.

Leland, Hayne E., and Klaus Bjerre Toft. "Optimal Capital Structure, Endogenous Bankruptcy, and the Term Structure of Credit Spreads." *Journal of Finance* 51 (July 1996): 987–1019

Long, M., and I. Malitz. "Investment Patterns and Financial Leverage." In *Corporate Capital Structure in the United States*, ed. Friedman. Chicago: University of Chicago Press, 1985.

Masulis, R. "The Effects of Capital Structure Changes on Security Prices: A Study of Exchange Offers." *Journal of Financial Economics* (June 1980): 139–178.

Masulis, R., and A. Korwar. "Seasoned Equity Offerings: An Empirical Investigation." *Journal of Financial Economics* (January–February 1986): 91–118.

Mikkelson, W., and W. Partch. "Valuation Effects of Security Offerings and the Issuance Process." *Journal of Financial Economics* (January–February 1986): 31–60.

Miller, Merton. "Debt and Taxes." *Journal of Finance* 32 (May 1977): 261–275.

Modigliani, Franco, and Merton H. Miller. "Corporate Income Taxes and the Cost of Capital: A Correction." *American Economic Review* 53 (June 1963): 433–442.

———. "The Cost of Capital, Corporation Finance, and the Theory of Investment." *American Economic Review* 48 (June 1958): 261–297.

———. "Reply to Heins and Sprenkle." *American Economic Review* 59 (September 1969): 592–595.

Myers, Stuart C., and Nicholas S. Majluf. "Corporate Financing and Investment Decisions When Firms Have Information That Investors Do Not Have." *Journal of Financial Economics* 13 (June 1984): 187–221.

Narayanan, M. P. "Debt versus Equity under Assymetric Information." *Journal of Financial and Quantitative Analysis* 23 (March 1988): 39–51.

Rajan, Raghuram G., and Luigi Zingales. "Debt, Folklore, and Cross-Country Differences in Financial Structure." *Journal of Applied Corporate Finance* 10 (Winter 1988): 102–107.

———. "What Do We Know about Capital Structure? Some Evidence from International Data." *Journal of Finance* 50 (December 1995): 1421–1460.

Roden, Dianne M., and Wilbur G. Lewellen. "Corporate Capital Structure Decisions: Evidence from Leveraged Buyouts." *Financial Management* 24 (Summer 1995): 76–87.

Ross, Stephen. "The Determination of Financial Structure: The Incentive Signaling Approach." *Bell Journal of Economics and Management Science* (Spring 1977): 23–40.

Scherr, Frederick C. "A Multiperiod Mean-Variance Model of Optimal Capital Structure." *Financial Review* 22 (February 1987): 1–31.

Schooley, Diane K., and L. Dwayne Barney, Jr. "Using Dividend Policy and Managerial Ownership to Reduce Agency Costs." *Journal of Financial Research* 17 (Fall 1994): 363–373.

Scott, J. H. "Bankruptcy, Secured Debt, and Optimal Capital Structure." *Journal of Finance* 32 (March 1977): 1–19.

Shah, Kshitij. "The Nature of Information Conveyed by Pure Capital Structure Changes." *Journal of Financial Economics* 36 (August 1994): 89–126.

Stiglitz, Joseph. "Some Aspects of the Pure Theory of Corporate Finance: Bankruptcies and Takeovers." *Bell Journal of Economics and Management Science* (Autumn 1972): 458–482.

Titman, S. "The Effect of Capital Structure on a Firm's Liquidation Decision." Ph.D. thesis, Graduate School of Industrial Administration, Carnegie-Mellon University, 1981.

Warner, J. "Bankruptcy Costs: Some Evidence." *Journal of Finance* 32 (May 1977): 337–347.

CHAPTER 18 |

CAPITAL STRUCTURE DECISIONS

After completing this chapter you should be able to:

1. Differentiate between how capital structure decisions are made when there is asymmetrical information and when the participants are well informed.
2. List four sources used by management to judge the market's response to a proposed issuance.
3. Discuss the merits and demerits of generalizing from other offerings.
4. Explain the difference between judging an issuance of debt based on earnings volatility and judging it based on debt capacity.
5. Calculate an income break-even point and an earnings per share crossover point using differing financing alternatives.
6. Compute the probability of default in a recession.
7. Recommend and discuss several of the tools used by managers to reduce the probability of default.
8. Describe at least three qualitative reasons managers might chose one form of financing over the other.

Long before the current rash of buyouts and restructurings of corporate America, conglomerate RapidAmerica Corporation was a pioneer in expanding the limits of corporate debt. Following the academic arguments of people like Gordon Donaldson, chairman Malchusem Ricklis focused his attention on the ability to service debt rather than ratios of debt to total assets. When he was questioned about the use of large amounts of debt in assembling RapidAmerica, Ricklis responded that he could count on being dead before most of the debt was due.

Ricklis's witty response actually underlies a serious approach to practical capital structure decisions, an approach that focuses on cash flows needed and cash flows available under various conditions. In this chapter, we will consider cash flow analysis and other practical approaches to capital structure decisions. We currently have no way to be sure that we have the optimal capital structure, but we nevertheless have tools that help us to make capital structure decisions.

Like capital investment decisions, capital structure decisions are often viewed from the perspective of their effect on shareholder wealth. In the previous chapter, four major costs were considered:

1. Taxes
2. Bankruptcy costs
3. Agency costs
4. Information asymmetry costs

The optimal capital structure will minimize the sum of these four costs, minus any benefit that can be gained from taking advantage of other market imperfections. As explained in Chapter 17, the optimal capital structure will thereby maximize the wealth of the shareholders.

In attempting to find the optimal capital structure, the problem of information asymmetry can be treated separately from the other considerations. If investors are as well informed as the managers about prospects for future profitability, then the optimal capital structure will result in the highest stock price right now. If we do not face information asymmetry, the focus of capital structure decision making is on the immediate impact on stock price; a movement toward the optimal capital structure will result in an immediate increase in stock price, and vice versa. If managers are better informed than investors, it is necessary for managers to go beyond immediate investor response to consider future profitability and risk. Capital structure choice with well-informed investors is considered in the first part of this chapter, followed by a discussion of tools that are useful when information asymmetry makes it impossible to rely on investor responses.

CAPITAL STRUCTURE CHOICE WITH INVESTORS INFORMED OF FUTURE PROSPECTS |

To the extent that the investments and strategies of a business are well known, investors may be as good as managers at forecasting profitability. This claim particularly makes sense when we consider the role of security analysts, who spend years becoming experts on one industry and focus all of their energy on predicting profitability of companies in that industry. Information asymmetries are more likely to occur when the company is changing its strategy, and keeping that strategy secret for competitive reasons. Thus, the assumption of informed investors is appropriate for many capital structure decisions.

In theory, the optimal capital structure with well-informed investors is the capital structure that maximizes immediate stock price; this structure will also minimize the weighted average cost of capital. The problem in practice is that there is no precise way to identify the exact capital structure that will maximize stock price. Fortunately, managers are seldom asked to identify the precise optimal capital structure anyway; they are asked to make incremental financing decisions. Choosing between debt and equity financing to build a new plant or pay off a maturing bond issue is easier than choosing the optimal capital structure. The guidelines developed in this section will be helpful in estimating the impact of an incremental financing decision and, therefore, moving toward the optimal capital structure.

When facing difficulties in predicting investor response, we can take some comfort in realizing that the greatest difficulty occurs when the company is near its optimal capital structure. As shown in Figure 17.10, value becomes less and less sensitive to changes in capital structure as the company approaches the optimal capital structure. Estimation is more difficult near the optimal capital structure precisely because the cost of being wrong is smaller.

Estimates of investor response can be based on (1) studying market response to other offerings, (2) surveying and talking to key participants in the financial markets, and (3) evaluating possible disequilibrium conditions in the financial markets. Combining these three modes of inquiry can result in reasoned judgments with regard to the best financing alternative.

STUDY OF MARKET RESPONSE TO OFFERINGS

One approach to studying market response is to simply observe what happens when new issues either increase or decrease financial leverage. You can observe responses to your own company or companies with similar risk. Companies with similar risk are often found in the same industry. If a similar company announces a new financing that changes its financial leverage, a rise in stock price is a positive response and a decrease in stock price is a negative response. Of course, the market response to a change in capital structure must be evaluated in terms of the starting financial structure. A positive response to an increase in leverage by a competitor more heavily leveraged than your company, for example, suggests that addition of debt to your capital structure would increase share value.

In considering market responses to changes in other companies' capital structures, it is necessary to measure their leverage relative to our own. Ratios such as the debt to total assets ratio and times interest earned ratio can be used for this purpose:

Debt to total assets:

$$\text{Total debt} \div \text{Total assets}$$

Times interest earned:

$$\text{Earnings before interest and tax} \div \text{Interest expense}$$

The debt to total assets ratio is a measure of the proportion of the historically based cost of assets that is financed with debt. The times interest earned ratio is one measure of the income of the company in relation to the interest expense. The times interest earned ratio gives some indication of the likelihood that the income will be high enough to take advantage of the tax savings from interest expense. Additional ratios as well as other methods for assessing the risk associated with a particular capital structure are discussed later in this chapter.

In interpreting market responses, related conditions must be kept in mind. For example, a company with a high marginal tax rate would be expected to improve its value by issuing more debt, and vice versa. An industry leader is likely to have a more stable earnings pattern, and therefore have the ability to carry relatively more debt than smaller, less stable companies. In addition, a change in marginal tax rates of investors since the last observed financing may negate the information content of that financing. Investors responded favorably to a sharp increase in debt ratio voluntarily undertaken at Ralston-Purina. On the other hand, Litzenberger found no value creation when Phillips Petroleum and Unocal were forced by takeover attempts to sharply increase their debt ratios.[1] Because financial market conditions change frequently, the information value of a market response decreases rapidly with time since the event occurred.

STUDY OF MARKET RESPONSE TO DIFFERENT CAPITAL STRUCTURES

In many cases, there are not enough recent changes in financial structure among similar companies to draw conclusions about market responses to a change in capital structure. Additional insights can be gained by computing the weighted average costs of capital for companies with similar operating characteristics and different capital structures. Again, debt to total assets, times interest earned, and risk analysis methods discussed later in this chapter can be used to identify companies with similar risk.

Example. Scott Corporation has total assets of $100 million and needs $5 million to finance a new plant. The company must choose between debt and equity financing. Financial information about Scott and five competitors appears in Table 18.1. The costs of capital of the five competitors were estimated using publicly available information.[2]

The weighted average cost of capital for these five companies appears to decline with increased debt, up until some point at which increased risk causes the cost to begin to rise again. This is consistent with the theories summarized in Figure 17.10. Scott has the second-lowest debt ratio and the highest times interest earned. Thus, Scott appears to be in a stronger position to handle debt

---

[1]Robert H. Litzenberger, "Some Observations on Capital Structure and the Impact of Recent Recapitalizations on Share Prices," *Journal of Financial and Quantitative Analysis* 21 (March 1986): 59–71.

[2]In analyzing the end-of-chapter case, you will observe at least some relationships of this type in practice.

| TABLE 18.1 FINANCIAL LEVERAGE AND COST OF CAPITAL

Debt-related ratios and weighted average cost of capital estimates for Scott Corporation and five competitors are shown. These data can be used to estimate the market response to an increase in Scott's debt level.

Company	1	2	3	4	5	Scott
Debt to total assets	.20	.32	.37	.40	.55	.25
Times interest earned	9.30	6.77	3.60	6.50*	2.73	9.33
Weighted average cost of capital	10.00%	9.97%	9.80%	10.02%	10.54%	9.94%

*Company 4 has a high times interest earned despite a high debt ratio because it is more profitable than its competitors.

than are those companies that have more debt and lower costs of capital. Financing the incremental $5 million with debt would still leave Scott with a strong position and, based on the other companies in the industry, could be expected to decrease the weighted average cost of capital.

When looking at competitors, managers often find little variation in capital structure or no clear relationship between capital structure and cost of capital or value. Lack of variation in capital structure may reflect the general skill of financial managers in using available information, such as input from market participants, to stay near their optimal capital structure. Lack of a clear relationship between capital structure and cost of capital also may be due to intervening influences, such as differences in systematic risk among competitors.

INFORMATION FROM KEY PARTICIPANTS IN THE FINANCIAL MARKETS

Managers often confer directly with key participants in the financial markets as part of the process of estimating response to changes in capital structure. Investment bankers are one of the more helpful groups in this regard. Investment bankers specialize in aiding companies in the sale of additional securities and generally guarantee the company that it will be able to sell the securities by providing underwriting.[3] Investment bankers must, therefore, be well informed regarding investor preferences. Based on their study of other recent issues and their discussions with other market participants, the investment bankers can often give managers a good estimate of how the markets will respond to any type of new issue.

Bond ratings are another useful source of information. Rating agencies such as Moody's and Standard and Poor's set their ratings based on their assessment of riskiness. These ratings affect interest cost, as illustrated in Figure 18.1, as

[3]The investment banker guarantees that the company will be able to sell the issue, but the investment banker does not guarantee the quality of the issue to the eventual purchasers.

| **FIGURE 18.1** BOND RATINGS AND INTEREST RATES

This figure shows interest rates for Aaa (low risk) and Baa (medium risk) corporate bonds over the business cycle.

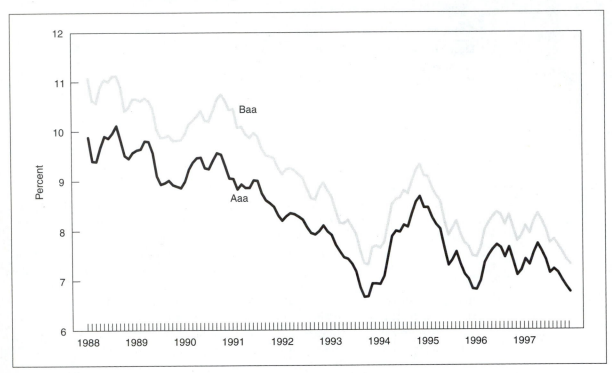

well as the availability of debt capital. Consequently, managers can study the relationship between bond rating and weighted average cost of capital in the industry, if all companies in the industry do not have identical bond ratings. While rating agencies will not tell managers how much debt they can issue without changing their rating, managers study past decisions of rating agencies to estimate how much debt they can issue without hurting their rating.

Many companies use maintenance of a particular bond rating as part of capital structure policy. For example AT&T's capital structure policy prior to the split-up called for maintenance of an Aaa rating. One reason for this policy was the necessity of raising large amounts of money regardless of financial market conditions. In contrast, Ralston-Purina purposely decided to accept a downgraded debt rating as part of a capital structure reorganization plan developed at a time when investors seemed to be responding favorably to highly leveraged capital structures and risky debt issues. Each policy was based on the corporation's peculiar financing needs and its assessment of likely market response to its security issues.

Security analysts are also important sources of information. A security analyst specializes in one particular industry, and continually studies the companies in that industry. Many investors and portfolio managers rely heavily on security analysts for advice on which securities to purchase. Thus, the responses of security analysts to a change in capital structure are important. Fortunately, input can be obtained from security analysts in two ways. Many security analysts publish their opinions, and it is also possible to talk to security analysts directly. Many security analysts will give an indication of their assessment of various aspects of management. Thus, the likely responses of security analysts and investors who rely on security analysts can be obtained.

Portfolio managers make investment decisions for mutual funds, pension fund portfolios, charitable trusts, and a number of other portfolios. As such, they are a growing influence in the financial markets. As with security analysts, it is possible to get inputs from portfolio managers with regard to what types of issues they would and would not respond to favorably. In fact, security issues are often custom-designed in cooperation with a particular portfolio manager who then acquires the entire issue.

Naturally, investment bankers have a good understanding of the bond rating process, as well as continual contact with security analysts and portfolio managers. Many companies rely on investment bankers rather than attempting to maintain individual contact with the market participants on their own. Regardless of whether the information is obtained directly or through investment bankers, inputs from key market participants can be combined with observed market responses to estimate the effect of a change in capital structure.

CONSIDERING DISEQUILIBRIUM

Financial market equilibrium with regard to supply and demand for debt and equity instruments can easily be disturbed. Suppose, for example, stock prices decline one year. This decreases capital gains and therefore decreases the marginal tax rate on equity income. Likewise, a rise or fall in interest rates or general incomes can affect the marginal tax rate on interest income. A government deficit financed in the debt markets can push up interest rates on debt and decrease the relative attractiveness of that source of financing.

These disequilibrium positions would be eliminated immediately in the absence of barriers; companies would issue the favored type of security and use the proceeds to retire the other type. But the transactions costs to retire one security and issue another may be greater than the benefit from taking advantage of disequilibrium. As a result, disequilibrium may continue for some time, and a company may be able to increase value by taking advantage of disequilibrium in its financing choices.

We often hear talk of new bond issues being favored, the equity markets having dried up, and so on. These are the investment bankers' ways of saying there are imperfections in the market that make the issuance of one particular type of security attractive at the present time. While an investment banker may not be able to identify a precise optimal capital structure, an investment banker may be able to give your company a very good idea of the *relative* attractiveness of various alternatives for raising money at a particular time.

In addition, a particular company may not be at an equilibrium position. Recall from Chapter 17 that the tax rate relationships in equilibrium without agency or bankruptcy costs are:

$$(1 - T_p) = (1 - T_c)(1 - T_g)$$

where T_p and T_g are the marginal personal tax rates on interest and equity income respectively, while T_c is the corporation's marginal tax rate. If a corporation's tax rate increases without the other rates changing, as might be the case if a particular corporation's profitability increases, that corporation would be in a disequilibrium position, and would increase value by issuing debt. The reverse would be true if the tax rate of the corporation fell with no other changes in tax rates. As a result of disequilibrium and the cost of moving to an equilibrium condition, it is sometimes possible to observe a range of capital structures and, consequently, a range of costs of capital.

As mentioned earlier, investment bankers are one of the important sources of information about disequilibrium in the marketplace. The investment bankers will be aware of growth in demand for one type of security or the other and can give the company important advice in this regard. Combining direct analysis of investor responses with information from investment bankers and assessment of possible market disequilibrium can provide the basis for a reasoned judgment as to the appropriate financing method for the company's incremental financing needs.

INFORMATION ASYMMETRY AND CAPITAL STRUCTURE DECISIONS |

When investors are not well informed, managers cannot rely on immediate investor response. Managers must then make their own assessments of alternate capital structures with regard to future profitability and the two main types of risk: earnings variability and bankruptcy risk. Pro forma analysis is the general basis for profitability and risk analysis. Debt capacity analysis, discussed later in this chapter, is an extension of pro forma analysis. After completing various types of pro forma analysis, managers then make their own choice of capital structure considering future profitability and risk.

Although the focus of this section is on information asymmetry, some of the techniques can be applied if investors are well informed. To consider the responses of well-informed investors, it is often necessary to make a judgment about the relative riskiness of different companies with different capital structures. Furthermore, managers may limit their risk exposure even if they believe well-informed investors would respond favorably to increased financial leverage. Examples of why rational managers may behave this way were given in Chapter 15. Some of the methods developed in this section will serve as supplements to simple ratios like times interest earned and debt to total assets for that purpose.

PRO FORMA ANALYSIS OF CAPITAL STRUCTURE ALTERNATIVES

Pro forma analysis is the construction of financial statements as they are expected to appear in future periods. By preparing pro forma financial statements for alternate financial structures, you can assess the impacts of financing alternatives on key performance measures. Key performance measures include return on equity and earnings per share. As we will see when discussing risk, pro forma analysis also can be used to access bankruptcy risk and the risk of not having enough income to take advantage of interest tax shields. This is useful information for choosing an optimal capital structure following the principles established in Chapter 17.

Example. The actual 1998 and expected 1999 financial statements of Knoxville Corporation appear in Table 18.2. The company presently has assets of $1,500,

| **TABLE 18.2** | KNOXVILLE CORPORATION PRO FORMA FINANCIAL STATEMENTS

This table shows the actual 1998 and expected 1999 financial statements of Knoxville Corporation. Expected financial statements for three ways of financing a $1,000 expansion are shown.

		PROJECTED 1999		
Financing Arrangement	**1998**	**No Debt**	**Half Debt**	**All Debt**
Sales	$ 700	$1,000	$1,000	$1,000
Variable costs	300	400	400	400
Fixed operating costs	250	300	300	300
Earnings before interest & tax	150	300	300	300
Interest expense	0	0	50	100
Earnings before tax	150	300	250	200
Tax (34%)	51	102	85	68
Net income	99	198	165	132
Earnings per share	$ 0.99	$ 0.99	$ 1.10	$ 1.32
Return on equity	9.90%	9.90%	11.0%	13.2%
Current assets	$ 500	$1,000	$1,000	$1,000
Fixed assets	1,000	1,500	1,500	1,500
Total assets	$1,500	$2,500	$2,500	$2,500
Current liabilities	$ 500	$ 500	$ 500	$ 500
Long-term debt	0	0	500	1,000
Equity	1,000	2,000	1,500	1,000
Total liabilities & equity	$1,500	$2,500	$2,500	$2,500
Number of shares[*]	100	200	150	100

[*]Number of shares = old shares + [(funds needed − new debt) ÷ price per share]. With half debt, for example, the number of shares is 100 + [(1,000 − 500) ÷ 10] = 150.

and needs an additional $1,000 for the investments that are expected to increase sales and income to the levels shown in Table 18.2. The company can finance the expansion with debt carrying a 10 percent interest rate, with equity, or with a mix of one-half debt and one-half equity. Knoxville Corporation presently has 100 shares of stock outstanding, and new shares can be sold for $10 a share.

Knoxville Corporation will maximize its return on equity and earnings per share by financing the $1,000 expansion entirely with debt. This would suggest that debt is the preferred form of financing and will increase share price if risk is not a problem. Risk will be treated in some detail after the concepts of favorable and unfavorable leverage are defined.

In the previous paragraph it was suggested that financial leverage—the use of debt financing—was favorable to Knoxville Corporation. *Favorable financial leverage* is financial leverage that improves the return on the shareholders' investment. Be warned, though, that this is a limited definition because the focus is on accounting income, not shareholder wealth. A small increase in earnings per share achieved by accepting a large increase in risk may decrease stock price and shareholder wealth. Thus, improved earnings per share must be evaluated in relation to risk.

RISK ANALYSIS AND CAPITAL STRUCTURE

Risk comes in two general forms: income variability and bankruptcy risk. Income risk is seen in the form of unstable earnings, with resulting unstable dividends and lower stock price. Bankruptcy risk, also referred to as default risk, is the risk of being unable to meet obligations to creditors, and therefore being forced into bankruptcy or some other undesired position, such as loss of control. Methods of measuring both types of risk are discussed in the remainder of this chapter.

Ratio Measures of Capital Structure–Related Risk

Ratio measures of risk are some of the easiest measures to apply. Some of the more widely used ratios for this purpose are:

$$Debt\ to\ total\ assets = Total\ debt \div Total\ assets$$

$$Debt\ to\ equity = Total\ debt \div Total\ stockholders'\ equity^4$$

$$Long\text{-}term\ debt\ to\ total\ capitalization = \frac{Long\text{-}term\ debt}{Total\ long\text{-}term\ sources\ of\ funds}$$

$$Long\text{-}term\ debt\ to\ fixed\ assets = Long\text{-}term\ debt \div Fixed\ assets$$

$$Times\ interest\ earned = \frac{Earnings\ before\ interest\ and\ tax}{Interest\ expense}$$

[4]Total stockholders' equity includes common stock, paid-in capital in excess of par, and retained earnings.

Fixed charge coverage =

$$\frac{\text{Earnings before interest and tax} + \text{Depreciation} + \text{Lease payments}}{\text{Interest payments} + \text{Lease payments} + [\text{Annual principal repayment}/(1 - T_c)]}$$

where T_c is the corporation's marginal tax rate.

The debt to total assets ratio and debt to equity ratio are redundant to each other, in that they are two different ways of measuring the proportion of assets financed with debt. Long-term debt to total capitalization focuses on the proportion of permanent capital needs funded with debt. In responding to surveys, many corporate managers have indicated that they use the long term debt to total capitalization ratio as a guideline. Long-term debt to fixed assets is another supplementary measure in that it gives an indication of the amount of long-term debt in relation to the fixed assets. The balance sheet ratios serve two purposes. First, they can be used for general comparisons between companies. Second, they can give an indication of the protection of creditors in the event of bankruptcy.

Going beyond balance sheet ratios, a company's debt capacity depends on the ability to make principal and interest payments. The times interest earned ratio is a measure of income in relation to interest expense. Thus, it gives an indication of the cushion available to handle any decreases in profitability. A times interest earned ratio of 5 means that earnings before tax could decrease to 20 percent of the current level and there would still be enough income to cover interest expenses, and therefore receive tax benefits from interest expense.

Another critical question is whether there is enough *cash flow* to meet both principal and interest payments. The fixed charge coverage ratio is a measure of cash flows in relation to commitments against those cash flows for principal and interest payments. The concept considered in the fixed charge coverage ratio is extended later in this chapter to develop a more general approach to the assessment of bankruptcy risk.

Example. Three possible capital structures for Knoxville Corporation were shown in Table 18.2. Included in the company's fixed operating costs are depreciation expenses of $100 a year. The company has no lease payments and debt must be repaid in ten equal annual installments. The key ratios for each financial structure are shown in Table 18.3.

Ratio analysis does not give an exact measure of risk because no measure of instability of earnings or cash flows is incorporated in the ratios, but a general indication of relative riskiness is provided. Considering Knoxville Corporation, for example, the highest expected return on equity and earnings per share are achieved by financing the expansion entirely with debt. But the ratio analysis in Table 18.3 indicates that financing the expansion exclusively with debt would place the company among the higher-risk companies in its industry. Using no debt would be extremely conservative compared to the rest of the industry. Using one-half debt would place the company just above the industry median with regard to riskiness.

| TABLE 18.3   KNOXVILLE CORPORATION RATIO ANALYSIS

This table shows 1999 financial ratios with three alternate financial structures, and industry average ratios. The financial statements of Knoxville Corporation appear in Table 18.2. The company has no lease payments, and depreciation expense of $100 a year is included in fixed operating costs.

	KNOXVILLE CORP.			INDUSTRY[a]		
Financing Arrangement	**No Debt**	**Half Debt**	**All Debt**	**Lower Quartile**	**Median**	**Upper Quartile**
Debt to total assets	.20	.40	.60	.50	.38	.28
Debt to equity	.25	.67	1.50	1.00	.61	.39
Long-term debt to total capitalization	0	.25	.50	.38	.23	.11
Long-term debt to fixed assets	0	.33	.67	.50	.30	.13
Times interest earned	∞	6.00	3.00	4.00	6.67	15.00
Fixed charge coverage[b]	∞	3.18	1.59	1.84	3.08	6.91

[a]Upper and lower quartile are in terms of strength rather than absolute value of a ratio. The lowest quartile would be the most risky, measured by that ratio.

[b]For example, the fixed charge coverage with one-half of the expansion financed with debt is:

$$\frac{300 + 100}{50 + [50/(1 - .34)]} = 3.18$$

Managers would probably want to use some debt because of the potential improvement in earnings per share. But financing the expansion entirely with debt would mean going against consensus within the industry on how much debt can be handled. As a manager, you may decide to go against the industry consensus, particularly if you believe your company has more stable income and cash flows than other companies in the industry. But you must consider the possibility that investors will respond negatively to what they perceive as a more risky position than that of the industry, and that this will cause a decrease in stock price.

Ratio analysis does provide a crude indication of relative riskiness, and is important because investors compare companies using leverage ratios. But ratios are a crude measure, and improved insights into risk can be gained by combining ratio analysis with other methods discussed in the balance of this chapter.

Break-Even Analysis and Crossover Analysis

The *break-even point* is the sales level below which the company has a loss instead of income. Identification of the break-even point with each type of financing can give additional insights into riskiness. The formula for the break-even point is:

$$\text{Break-even point} = \frac{\text{Fixed operating costs} + \text{Fixed financing costs}}{1 - \text{Variable costs as a percent of sales}} \tag{18-1}$$

The break-even point for Knoxville Corporation with each of the financing methods is:

$$\text{All equity: BEP} = (300 + 0) \div (1 - .4) = \$500$$

$$\text{One-half debt: BEP} = (300 + 50) \div (1 - .4) = \$583$$

$$\text{All debt: BEP} = (300 + 100) \div (1 - .4) = \$667$$

Break-even analysis can be used to develop a general view of riskiness. Alternately, break-even analysis can be combined with probability to develop more specific measures of risk.

Suppose the expected sales level for Knoxville Corporation is $1,000 and the standard deviation is $275; furthermore, assume that sales variation is the only significant source of income variability. If the probability distribution is approximately normal, the probability of a sales level below the break-even point can be found using Appendix B at the end of this book. The probabilities of a negative net income with each alternative for financing the expansion are as follows:[5]

$$\text{All equity: Z} = (500 - 1,000) \div 275 = -1.82;$$

$$P(Z < -1.82) = .50 - .4656 = \underline{.0344}$$

$$\text{Half debt: Z} = (583 - 1,000) \div 275 = -1.52;$$

$$P(Z < -1.52) = .50 - .4357 = \underline{.0643}$$

$$\text{All debt: Z} = (667 - 1,000) \div 275 = -1.21;$$

$$P(Z < -1.21) = .50 - .3869 = \underline{.1131}$$

The probabilities of being below the break-even point illustrate two points. First, there is some probability of being below the break-even point even with no debt. Second, the probability of being below the break-even point increases at an increasing rate as the debt ratio increases. Assuming a 10 percent financing cost, Figure 18.2 shows the probability of being below the break-even point cost as the ratio of debt to total capital increases. This is consistent with Figure 17.10, in which expected bankruptcy cost increases at an increasing rate as the debt ratio increases.

The probability of negative net income increases at an increasing rate. Therefore, the expected tax shield per dollar of interest *decreases* at an increasing rate as the amount of interest expense increases. Expected tax savings for each additional dollar of interest decrease because the probability of being below the break-even point and, therefore, having no income to shelter from taxes, increases. The expected tax shield also may decrease because of a decrease in marginal tax rate as expenses rise, and taxable income declines.

---

[5]Refer to Chapter 11 if you need a refresher on using the normal distribution table.

| **FIGURE 18.2** **DEBT LEVEL AND PROBABILITY OF NEGATIVE NET INCOME**

This figure shows the relationship between the long-term debt to total capital ratio and the probability of a sales level below the break-even point for Knoxville Corporation. The basic financial statements for Knoxville Corporation are in Table 18.1.

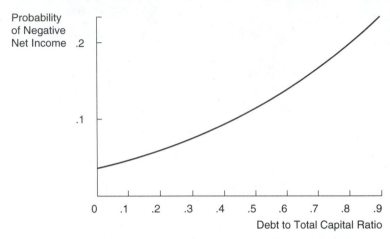

Knowledge of the probability of being below the break-even point with each possible debt level gives managers additional input to use in making a decision, even though the need to apply judgment is not eliminated. The acceptable probability of a loss depends on what happens if a loss occurs. If management's control of the company is shaky and a loss might mean a shift in control, the probability of a loss will be held very low. Debt capacity analysis, taken up later in this chapter, will supplement break-even analysis for this purpose.

The previous example was based on the assumption that variability of sales was the only significant source of uncertainty. Suppose managers were also uncertain about various components of costs. Monte Carlo simulation, discussed in Chapter 12, can be used to develop a distribution of earnings or cash flows and, therefore, a probability of negative earnings or negative cash flows.

Crossover Point Analysis

The *crossover point* is the sales level or earnings before interest and tax level at which the company would earn the same earnings per share with either debt or equity financing. Using sales, the earnings per share (EPS) are:

$$\text{EPS} = \frac{[\text{Sales}(1 - \text{VC}) - \text{FOC} - \text{Interest}](1 - \text{Tc}) - \text{Preferred dividends}}{\text{Number of shares}} \qquad \textbf{(18-2)}$$

where VC is variable costs as a percent of sales and FOC is fixed operating costs. The crossover point is where earnings per share are the same for the two methods of financing.

In Table 18.2, the crossover point between financing the expansion with all debt and all equity is found by first setting the earnings per share formulas for the two financing methods equal to each other:[6]

$$\frac{[\text{Sales}(1 - .4) - 300 - 0](1 - .34)}{200} = \frac{[\text{Sales}(1 - .4) - 300 - 100](1 - .34)}{100}$$

Solving this equation for sales gives the sales level at the crossover point: $833. If sales are above $833, earnings per share will be higher with debt financing, and vice versa.

Crossover analysis can be enhanced in a couple of ways. One enhancement is a graph relating sales to earnings per share for each financing method, as illustrated in Figure 18.3. Figure 18.3 confirms the earlier crossover point computation and shows the earnings per share at each sales level with each financing method. The figure also shows the break-even points. Thus, this graph is useful for summarizing a good deal of information.

| FIGURE 18.3 CROSSOVER ANALYSIS OF KNOXVILLE CORPORATION

This graph shows the earnings per share for Knoxville Corporation at each sales level with three different financing methods. This analysis is based on the financial statements for Knoxville Corporation in Table 18.2.

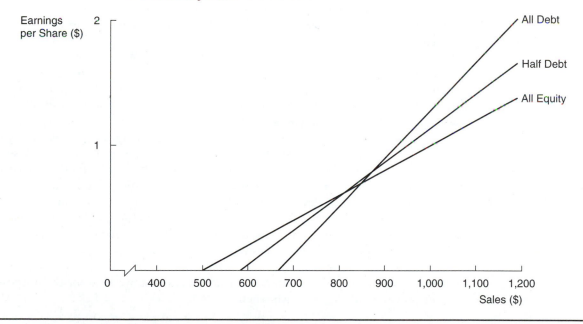

---

[6]It should be noted that the crossover point depends on the stock price. In the example, the stock price was $10 per share. At a price of $15 a share, for example, the crossover point would be $917.

Another enhancement is to compute the probability of being above and below the crossover point, as was done with the break-even point. With a standard deviation of sales at $275, the probability of being below the crossover point is found as follows.

$$Z = (833 - 1,000)/275 = -0.61; P(Z < -0.61) = (.50 - .2291) = .27$$

Thus, there is a .73 probability that debt financing will increase earnings per share.

Crossover analysis addresses risk in terms of earnings impacts, but it does not address the risk of defaulting on debt obligations. Debt capacity analysis is needed for that purpose.

Debt Capacity Analysis

Debt capacity analysis focuses on the ability of the firm to meet cash flow obligations with various amounts of debt. This approach to evaluating debt was first developed by Gordon Donaldson.[7] The approach has been endorsed by many business people, including Ricklis in the first paragraph of this chapter, who have argued that capital structure analysis should focus on cash flows. Debt capacity can be defined in terms of the probability of default or in terms of some scenario.

A scenario analysis describes the worst case through which managers want to plan for survival. Donaldson defined a scenario in terms of a recession. You might, for example, decide that you want your company to survive through the most severe recession that has occurred in the last forty years. For a particular company, though, the problem may be something other than a recession. John Deere Corporation, for example, will be harmed more by worldwide food surpluses than by overall economic recessions, because farmers do not buy new equipment when food prices are low. In developing a scenario through which the company wants to survive, it is important to recognize that survival in all possible conditions cannot be guaranteed. Even with an all-equity capital structure, a company will go bankrupt if a depression is long enough and deep enough.

Once a scenario is defined, the net cash flow of the company in that scenario is predicted using pro forma analysis. A probability distribution of cash flows in the scenario may be developed if there is substantial uncertainty with regard to possible cash flows in the conditions specified in the scenario.

Estimation of net cash flows is only the first step though. The next step is the development of an inventory of resources available to meet a negative cash flow. Commonly available resources to offset negative cash flows follow:

Reserves: cash on hand and marketable securities that are held for the purpose of providing additional cash when needed.

---

[7]Gordon Donaldson, "New Framework for Corporate Debt Capacity," *Harvard Business Review* 40 (March–April 1962): 117–131; Gordon Donaldson, "Strategy for Financial Emergencies," *Harvard Business Review* 47 (November–December 1969): 67–79.

External financing: lines of credit available, lenders who can be counted on to provide credit, possible sale of bonds and equity.

Reduction of outflows: cancellation or delay of expansion plans, research and development, new product introductions, dividend payments, and so on.

Sale of assets: divisions, factories, specific pieces of equipment, and so on.

Each of the resources must be evaluated in terms of how soon it can be available. Cash reserves are immediately available and marketable securities can be sold almost instantly. An existing line of credit can also be drawn on with very little notice. Arranging a new loan or selling securities may take months, if it is possible to raise money this way during a downturn. Reduction of planned outflows may require some lead time as contracts for equipment, advertising, etc. are well in advance of the actual expenditure. Eastern Airlines will order new airplanes months before delivery, and Kaiser will be forced to make some commitments years in advance when it constructs a new aluminum processing plant. Sale of assets also may require considerable time. This is particularly true for major assets, such as a factory or division.

Once the net cash flows and resources have been analyzed, pro forma financial statements for the key scenario are prepared. If survival is not possible with a given debt structure, then the amount of debt must be reduced or the method of debt financing must be changed. For example, change in maturity of debt can reduce the cash flow commitment per dollar of debt and thereby increase the probability of survival for a given debt level.

Example. The summary of a debt capacity analysis of Knoxville Corporation appears in Table 18.4. The first column contains the financial statements of a normal year of operations. The second two columns represent projected financial statements in a severe 2-year recession. Management wants to be able to handle a severe 2-year recession without default. These statements are based on the following set of assumptions.

1. The company finances the expansion with $1,000 of long-term debt.
2. Knoxville Corporation's sales decline 25 percent a year during the recession.
3. Variable costs continue to be 40 percent of sales and fixed operating costs continue to be $300.
4. Days receivables outstanding are 73 days under normal conditions, and will rise to 85 days during a recession.[8]
5. Because it is difficult to reduce inventory in the face of a sales decline, inventory will just hold steady during the first year of recession and decline modestly to $500 during the second year.
6. Tax liability at the end of a year is approximately one-fourth of the tax expense for the year. If a tax refund is due because of a loss, it is not received until the year following the loss.

[8]Days receivable outstanding is defined as (accounts receivable/sales) × 365.

| TABLE 18.4 DEBT CAPACITY ANALYSIS OF KNOXVILLE CORPORATION

Pro forma financial statements for Knoxville Corporation were prepared for a two-year severe recession. The purpose is to determine if the company will be able to meet its cash obligations in a recession.

	Normal Year	First Year of Recession	Second Year of Recession
Sales	$1,000	$ 750	$ 563
Variable costs	400	300	225
Fixed operating costs	300	300	300
Net operating income	300	150	38
Interest expense	100	90	80
Earnings before tax	200	60	−42
Income tax	80	24	−17
Net income	$ 120	$ 36	$ −25
Cash	$ 200	$ 47	$ −55
Accounts receivable	200	185	139
Inventory	600	600	500
Tax refund due	0	0	17
Current assets	1,000	832	601
Fixed assets	1,500	1,450	1,450
Total assets	$2,500	$2,282	$2,051
Accounts payable	$ 470	$ 340	$ 240
Tax liabilities	30	6	0
Current liabilities	500	346	240
Long-term debt	1,000	900	800
Equity	1,000	1,036	1,011
Total liability & equity	$2,500	$2,282	$2,051

7. Fixed assets can be reduced to $1,450 in the first recession year by replacing assets at a rate slower than depreciation, but fixed assets cannot be reduced further without halting production entirely.
8. The company pays no dividends, so equity increases or decreases by the amount of income or loss.

In preparing the pro forma financial statements, all other items on the balance sheet were forecast, and cash was found by subtracting other assets from total liabilities and equity. The negative cash in year 2 means that the company will not be able to meet its cash obligations in year 2 of a severe recession if it finances the expansion entirely with debt. A 2-year source and use of funds statement is an alternate way to do this analysis.

Knoxville Corporation has a number of alternatives. The most straightforward approach is to reduce the amount of leverage, financing only half of the expansion with debt. An alternate approach is to focus on the lesson of debt capacity analysis: it is the cash flow commitment, not the absolute amount of debt, that determines debt capacity. If Knoxville Corporation could negotiate a loan with a balloon payment[9] or with payments spread over twenty years instead of ten years, it would be able to meet its cash obligations in a recession while financing the expansion entirely with debt. Knoxville Corporation can also turn to other ways of assuring cash flow in a recession, such as maintaining additional reserves or arranging a line of credit. Thus, debt capacity analysis allows the company to go beyond simply deciding how much debt it can safely carry to identify ways it can carry the same amount of debt with decreased risk.

Banks use an approach very similar to debt capacity analysis, which is called *earnings at risk*. They define a maximum acceptable decline in net income, given certain unfavorable interest rate movement scenarios. They then adjust the relative maturities of their assets and liabilities, as well as the amount of equity, to seek maximum profitability, subject to the constraint on the net income decline they are willing to accept if interest rates shift.

Modeling ideas similar to those developed by Donaldson have enjoyed renewed interest. Opler, Sharon, and Titman recently published a model to simulate the effects of various capital structure choices over various economic conditions.[10] Mayer and Triantis have studied the impacts of production and financing flexibility on debt capacity.[11]

OTHER CONSIDERATIONS |

Future financing needs are often an important consideration in choosing a financial structure. There have been many incidents of managers of rapidly growing companies deciding that their stock was underpriced in light of their future growth, and therefore financing entirely with debt, expecting to issue equity next time they needed money. A number of these managers have found themselves effectively shut off from new sources of capital because they financed with as much debt as possible and found market conditions had changed to the point that sale of stock was virtually impossible the next time they needed money.

Flexibility was inferred in the previous paragraph, but is a broader issue than simply dealing with future growth plans. Managers may need to change various aspects of the company's operations quickly in response to changing market conditions. Restrictive covenants associated with debt issues have often limited the

---

[9]A balloon payment loan is not completely paid off by installments over its life. A single large payment of all or part of the amount borrowed is made at maturity. For example, a ten-year, $100,000 loan might call for principal payments of $5,000 a year for 10 years with a balloon payment of $50,000 at the end of ten years.

[10]Tim C. Opler, Michael Sharon, and Sheridan Titman, "Designing Capital Structure to Create Shareholder Value," *Journal of Applied Corporate Finance* 10 (Spring 1997): 21–32.

[11]David C. Mayer, and Alexander J. Triantis, "Interactions of Corporate Financing and Investment Decisions: A Dynamic Framework," *Journal of Finance* 49 (September 1994): 1253–1277.

alternatives available to managers, for example. The call provision on bonds is one example of designing financing to maintain flexibility. Almost all corporate bonds have *call provisions* which allow the corporation to retire the debt early if management should choose to do so.

Control issues often affect capital structure decisions. If managers have a very narrow margin of voting control, they will be hesitant to issue additional shares that will place voting rights in the hands of additional investors. On the other hand, debt also places some aspects of control in the hands of others. Creditors frequently require the company to agree to meet certain standards as a condition for receiving credit. Approval of the creditors may be required to expand further, issue additional debt, sell assets, etc. Thus, the choice between debt and equity financing involves trade-offs between different types of external control.

Hedging means arranging the maturity of funding sources to be similar to the maturity of assets. Matching of maturities can reduce the risks of getting caught by rapidly fluctuating interest rates. This is particularly important for companies like financial institutions that pay interest to one group and collect interest from another group.

Strategy considerations also affect capital structure decisions. Attempts to increase market share often trigger strong responses from competitors, and lead to periods of low profitability. A strong financial position allows a company to take aggressive actions to increase or maintain market share. A strong financial position may discourage competitors from aggressive action. People's Express airline was forced out of business when competitors attacked its low price/low cost strategy with low prices of their own. People's Express was vulnerable because it had huge amounts of debt in the capital structure. Had People's Express had the capital structure to withstand a sustained period of price-cutting, the other airlines may have never attacked. In addition, Opler and Titman observe that highly leveraged firms lose market share to more conservatively financed competitors during an industry downturn.[12]

WHAT MANAGERS SAY AND DO

In light of the considerations that have been discussed in the last two chapters, a survey of management attitudes is of interest. Blume, Friend, and Westerfield surveyed the managers of some of the largest corporations in the United States with regard to factors they believed to be important in choosing the level of long-term debt.[13] Results from that survey are summarized in Table 18.5.

In a survey of NYSE firms published in 1997, Kamath found that managers were more likely to use a hierarchy of financing sources, what Stuart Myers dubbed a "pecking order," than to pursue a target debt ratio. In other words,

---

[12]Tim C. Opler, and Sheridan Titman, "Financial Distress and Corporate Performance," *Journal of Finance* 49 (July 1994): 1015–1040.

[13]M. E. Blume, Irwin Friend, and R. Westerfield, "Impediments to Capital Formation," Rodney White Center for Financial Research, December 1980.

| TABLE 18.5 SURVEY OF MANAGERS CONCERNING THE LEVEL OF LONG-TERM DEBT

This table summarizes the responses of managers of some of the largest companies in the United States with regard to the factors they considered important in establishing the level of long-term debt.

	Very Important	Moderately Important	Not Important
Level of current and prospective profitability	49%	47%	4%
Stability of profits	41	53	6
Continuity of dividends	26	45	29
Need for investment funds	78	16	6
Tax considerations	29	55	16
Stockholder and creditor attitudes	58	40	2
Management attitudes	45	49	6
Credit ratings	86	12	2

managers would use the first choice until it was exhausted, then go to the second choice, and so forth. Retained earnings was the clear first choice, followed by straight debt. Convertible debt was the third choice, followed by direct sale of additional common stock.[14]

The fact that capital structure was important to these managers is consistent with the existence of market imperfections as discussed in Chapter 17. It is not surprising that the amount of debt was heavily influenced by the need for investment funds. Beyond this, though, it is interesting to note that the two most important considerations were investor attitudes and credit ratings. These considerations would be most important if managers believed investors were generally well informed about the company. Of course, these considerations are also important if investors are not well informed, and investor attitudes affect the ability of the company to raise money. The importance of the present profit, future profit, and stability of profit suggests that managers do go beyond investor response to look at the profitability and debt capacity issues discussed in this chapter. The low ranking of tax considerations is also interesting. Recall from Chapter 17 that tax considerations will be unimportant if the tax shelter from debt is correctly priced in the marketplace.

Studies of capital structure behavior have suggested that industry is one of the primary factors explaining capital structure differences.[15] This is not surprising as many of the factors identified by managers would vary from industry to

[14]Ravindra R. Kamath, "Long-Term Financing Decisions: Views and Practices of Financial Managers of NYSE Firms," *Financial Review* 32 (May 1997): 331–356.

[15]Michael Bradley, Gregg A. Jarrell, and E. Han Kim, "On the Existence of an Optimal Capital Structure: Theory and Evidence," *Journal of Finance* 39 (July 1984): 857–878.

industry. Long-term debt and net worth as a percent of total assets for some sample industries appear in Table 18.6.

SUMMARY |

Capital structure decisions are generally evaluated in terms of their impact on shareholder wealth. The major considerations are taxes, bankruptcy costs, agency costs, information asymmetry, and other market imperfections. The optimal capital structure will minimize the sum of costs related to these factors, minus any benefit that can be gained from taking advantage of market imperfections. The optimal capital structure will thereby maximize the wealth of the shareholders.

If investors and managers have the same information, the anticipated responses of equity investors to a capital structure change—in the form of an increase or decrease in stock price—is a sufficient guideline for decision making. Estimates of investor response to debt or equity offerings can be based on (1) study of market response to other offerings, (2) surveying and talking to key participants in the financial markets, and (3) evaluating possible disequilibrium conditions in the financial markets. Study of market response may include prior offerings of the same company, offerings by similarly positioned companies, or simply a study of companies with different capital structures.

If managers believe that they are better informed than investors, they must rely on their own analysis rather than inputs from investors. Specifically, they

| TABLE 18.6 CAPITAL STRUCTURE BY INDUSTRY

Shown in this table are average ratios of long-term debt and equity as a percent of total assets for large companies in each industry.

	LTD	NW
Cable TV operators	50.9	25.9
Pharmaceutical manufacturers	17.9	44.7
Household appliance manufacturers	13.8	45.5
Optical equipment manufacturers	3.7	63.4
Commercial printers	25.8	35.1
Tire wholesalers	7.0	34.1
Clothing retailers	13.0	46.0
Automobile dealers	6.8	21.0
Advertising agencies	5.3	18.6
Airlines	24.0	18.5
Bowling centers	50.5	15.4
Movie producers	17.6	28.1

Source: RMA Annual Statement Studies, 1997.

must make their own estimates of profitability and risk with alternate capital structures. Pro forma analysis is one useful tool for this purpose. Return on equity and earnings per share can be predicted in various possible future conditions for each capital structure alternative.

Risk analysis—income risk and bankruptcy risk—is a critical part of capital structure evaluation. *Income risk* is seen in the form of unstable earnings, with resulting unstable dividends and lower stock price. *Bankruptcy risk*, also referred to as default risk, is the risk of being unable to meet obligations to creditors, and therefore being forced into bankruptcy or some other undesired position, such as loss of control.

Ratio analysis provides one way to estimate risk. Break-even analysis and crossover analysis are additional tools for examining the riskiness of debt in terms of earnings impact. *Debt capacity analysis* focuses directly on the ability of the company to service its debt during periods of distress. The primary technique is development of pro forma financial statements for possible scenarios through which the company wants to plan for survival. By changing debt terms, arranging lines of credit, holding reserves, etc. a company can substantially reduce risk for any given level of debt.

In addition to investor response, profitability, and risk, managers weigh a number of other considerations in their capital structure decisions. These include future financing needs, flexibility, control, hedging, and strategy.

Questions

18–1. What are the major considerations in determining the optimal capital structure?

18–2. If investors are well informed, what are the general guidelines for choosing a capital structure?

18–3. How can managers estimate investor response to a change in capital structure using information from other companies?

18–4. What market participants can provide information to managers with regard to likely market response to a change in capital structure?

18–5. What types of financial market disequilibrium can cause one type of financing to be preferred over another?

18–6. In what conditions is it more likely that there will be information asymmetries between managers and investors?

18–7. Define the following terms:
   a. Break-even point
   b. Crossover point
   c. Debt capacity

18–8. What are the two major types of risk encountered in capital structure choice?

18–9. What are the major determinants of a company's debt capacity?

18–10. In addition to costs and risk, what are some other considerations that affect capital structure decisions?

PROBLEMS |

18–1. Memphis Corporation, a company with total assets of $100 million, is considering financing alternatives for a $10 million expansion. Investors are believed to be generally well informed. Information about Memphis Corporation and four other companies in the industry appears below. Would you recommend debt or equity financing for Memphis Corporation?

Company	1	2	3	4	Memphis
Debt to total assets	.30	.40	.45	.50	.47
Times interest earned	8.32	6.41	5.83	5.23	4.98
Weighted average cost of capital	12.23%	10.67%	11.56%	12.68%	13.12%

18–2. Orlando Technology Corporation has total assets of $100 million and needs $5 million for expansion. Investors are believed to be well informed. Information about Orlando and companies in the same industry appears below. How do you recommend that Orlando finance the expansion?

Company	1	2	3	4	Orlando
Debt to total assets	.30	.41	.45	.52	.25
Times interest earned	12.73	8.25	8.74	7.78	6.32
Weighted average cost of capital	10.86%	10.67%	10.76%	11.12%	11.12%

18–3. Tampa Consolidated has total assets of $100 million, and needs $50 million for a major expansion. Management estimates that the expansion will increase net operating income by $9 million a share, and investors are aware of this profitability. Tampa's existing balance sheet and income statement appear below.

Net operating income	$ 15,000
Interest	2,000
Earnings before tax	$ 13,000
Total assets	$100,000
Accounts payable	$ 20,000
Long-term debt	20,000
Equity	60,000

Information about competitors follows.

Company	1	2	3	4	5
Debt to total assets	.33	.37	.41	.43	.45
Times interest earned	8.53	7.74	7.64	7.85	5.31
Weighted average cost of capital	14.38%	13.49%	13.27%	13.27%	15.51%

The interest rate on new debt will be 10 percent. What types(s) of financing do you recommend?

18–4. Gainesville Corporation has total assets of $100,000 and needs an additional $3 million for expansion. Management estimates that the marginal investor tax rates for interest income and equity income are 33 percent and 10 percent respectively. Gainesville's expected tax savings per dollar of interest expense is $.25. Should Gainesville expand with debt or with equity?

18–5. For Gainesville Corporation (problem 4), what is the highest expected tax savings per dollar of interest at which equity financing is preferred over debt financing? Is it possible for the rate to be that low under the current tax structure?

18–6. Sunshine Corporation of Boca Raton has expected sales of $1 million a year. Variable costs are expected to be 30 percent of sales and fixed operating costs are $400,000 a year. Total capital is presently $600,000 and must be expanded to $900,000 to generate the anticipated sales level. The company presently has no debt outstanding, and 60,000 shares of stock. Additional common stock could be sold for $10 a share. The interest rate on new debt would be 10 percent and the tax rate is 34 percent. Compute the return on equity and earnings per share assuming the expansion is financed
  a. exclusively with debt.
  b. exclusively with equity.
  c. with one-half debt and one-half equity.

18–7. In problem 6, would Sunshine Corporation be using favorable financial leverage if it issued debt? Answer this question with regard to both earnings per share and return on equity.

18–8. Recompute the answers to problem 6 on the assumption that stock can be sold at $30 a share.

18–9. For the company in problem 6, what is the lowest stock price at which issuance of stock would improve earnings per share?

18–10. Jacksonville Health Centers is presently financed entirely with equity. The company's financial statements follow. The company is considering issuing debt, at an interest rate of 10 percent, to replace part of the equity. The company has 100,000 shares of stock outstanding and shares could be repurchased in the marketplace for $8.00 a share. Would the company enjoy favorable financial leverage with regard to return on equity? earnings per share?

Sales	$500,000
Variable costs	200,000
Fixed operating costs	200,000
Net operating income	100,000
Interest expense	0
Earnings before tax	100,000
Income tax	34,000
Net income	$ 66,000
Current assets	$400,000
Fixed assets	500,000
Total assets	$900,000
Current liabilities	$200,000
Long-term debt	0
Owners' equity	700,000
Total liabilities & equity	$900,000

18–11. For the company in problem 10, suppose the stock can be repurchased for $12 a share.
   a. Would the company enjoy favorable financial leverage in terms of return on equity?
   b. Would the company enjoy favorable financial leverage in terms of earnings per share?

18–12. For the company in problem 10, what is the highest stock price at which the company will enjoy favorable financial leverage in terms of return on equity? earnings per share?

18–13. Industry data for companies in the same business as Jacksonville Health Centers (problem 10) follow. Use ratio analysis to determine an amount of debt that would give Jacksonville Health Centers a risk position similar to that of the rest of the industry. Depreciation for Jacksonville Health Centers is $50,000 a year, and any long-term debt must be repaid in ten equal annual installments.

	INDUSTRY		
Financing Arrangement	**Lower Quartile**	**Median**	**Upper Quartile**
Debt to total assets	.61	.44	.33
Debt to equity	1.57	.80	.50
Long-term debt to total capitalization	.50	.29	.14
Long-term debt to fixed assets	.70	.40	.20
Times interest earned	2.57	5.00	11.00
Fixed charge coverage	2.29	3.98	8.35

18–14. For Jacksonville Health Centers (problem 10), what is the break-even point if the company uses $200,000 of long-term debt?

18–15. For Jacksonville Health Centers (problem 10), assume sales are normally distributed with a standard deviation of $100,000. What is the probability of being below the break-even point if the company issues $200,000 of long-term debt?

18–16. Assume Jacksonville Health Centers (problems 10 and 15) issues $200,000 of long-term debt. Depreciation is $100,000 a year and debt must be repaid at the rate of $20,000 a year. What is the probability of operating cash flow being below the level necessary to service debt?

18–17. For Jacksonville Health Centers (problems 10 and 16) what is the maximum amount of debt the company can issue without the probability of falling below the break-even point exceeding 5 percent? 1 percent?

18–18. Prepare a crossover chart for Jacksonville Health Centers (problem 10) for financing with no long-term debt and financing with $200,000 of long-term debt.

18–19. Jacksonville Health Centers (problem 10) wants to be able to survive during a two-year period in which revenues decline 20 percent each year. Current assets presently include $20,000 of cash. Current assets other than cash cannot be decreased by more than 10 percent a year even if revenues decline at a faster rate. Current liabilities will remain at the same percent of revenue as that which currently exists. Tax liabilities and tax refunds due were considered in making these estimates of current assets and current liabilities. The company cannot reduce fixed assets because it must respond to changing technology. With $200,000 of long-term debt, will the company be able to meet its obligations in a downturn?

18–20. After considering debt capacity as suggested in problem 19, managers at Jacksonville Health Centers decided to do an inventory of resources available in a financial emergency. The company had an unused $50,000 line of credit, for which it paid an annual fee of .25 percent of the unpaid balance. The bank could withdraw the line with ninety days' notice though. Half of current assets other than cash were primarily in the form of accounts receivable. These were not pledged as security, and it was estimated that a secured loan equal to half of the receivables could be obtained even in a downturn. While estimated revenues in the second year of a severe downturn were $320,000, the standard deviation of the probability distribution of sales in year two of a severe downturn would be approximately $50,000. Starting with $200,000 of long-term debt, will Jacksonville Health Centers have a 90 percent probability of surviving a severe two-year downturn?

18–21. (**Applications**) On the 1992 balance sheets for the software giant Microsoft and hardware manufacturer Compaq Computers there appears no long-term debt. Statistics for others in the industry are:

	LTD/Assets	Cash Flow (Operations) (millions)	Capital Spending (millions)
Microsoft	0%	+907	−642
Compaq	0%	−59	−230
IBM	44%	+6,274	−5,878
Intel	9%	+1,635	−1,479
Cray Research	11%	+186	−147

a. Using what you know about Microsoft and the very limited data above, why do you think that Microsoft has no debt in its capital structure?

b. If you were the Vice President of Finance at Microsoft, what are some of the ways you could alter the capital structure?

c. What information is necessary to determine if it is financially beneficial to add debt to Microsoft's capital structure? Describe the variables and the process you would use to make such a determination.

18–22. **(Ethical considerations)** Stuart Myers observed and reported in the early 1980s that there is a "pecking order" in the way managers actually finance additional capital investments. They first use money generated internally and then turn to the debt markets for additional funding. They rarely use the equity market. This ordering appears to hold true in the early 1990s as well. One reason suggested for this ordering is that there is information asymmetry between the information sets of the managers and the information sets of the stockholders.

a. Assuming that this asymmetrical relationship is true, under what conditions is it advantageous for the existing shareholders for managers to refrain from the issuance of new stock? (When they believe it to be overpriced by the market or when they believe it to be underpriced?)

b. Whose responsibility is it to reduce information asymmetry?

c. What are some of the actions that would reduce this asymmetry?

d. Suppose you have a $200 million positive net present value project but you believe it will take time for the market to realize the merits of the investment. During this time you believe the market will discount the $2 billion market value of the company by 15%. Upon realization you believe market value will recover and approach $2.5 billion in two years. Would you accept this project? Is it ethical to "walk away" from this project?

CASE PROBLEM |

Brand-Name Corporation (A)

Brand-name Corporation was a producer of a broad line of men's and women's clothing. However, Brand-name was not widely recognized by the public because its products almost always carried someone else's name. Brand-name sold to major department store chains, with the label reflecting the name of the department store. Almost half of Brand-name's sales went to two department store chains, with the other half of sales being divided among several dozen smaller contracts. While Brand-name had maintained its major sales relationships for over two decades, there were no long-term contracts. The customers could, in theory, shift to a new supplier with no obligations other than contracts calling for delivery over a period of no more than a year.

The apparel industry had experienced sales growth averaging 11 percent a year and net income growth averaging 17 percent a year for the past 5 years. As a result, stock prices of many companies in the industry had increased sharply in recent years. Unfortunately, the stock market had been less kind to Brand-name. As shown in Table 18.7, Brand-name's price-earnings ratio had generally been below the industry average. Lackluster stock market performance was of great concern to the executives at Brand-name.

A modernization program was part of management's plan to increase stock price. A plant modernization would allow Brand-name to price aggressively and be more profitable in the highly competitive markets in which it operated. The modernization would not add significantly to capacity. To complete the modernization program, Brand-name needed $20 million of new external capital. The

| **TABLE 18.7** | SEVEN-YEAR HISTORY OF THE FINANCIAL PERFORMANCE OF BRAND-NAME (IN $ MILLIONS) |

Year	1986	1987	1988	1989	1990	1991	1992
Sales	591,823	607,812	572,988	582,688	589,101	501,997	484,823
Net op. inc.	33,046	47,330	49,868	44,270	44,138	47,197	55,575
Interest	8,772	8,674	8,676	14,950	15,378	7,601	7,430
Other expenses	20,704	25,403	25,386	9,851	9,985	8,355	10,959
Earn bef. tax	3,570	13,253	15,806	19,469	18,775	31,241	37,186
Tax	29	4,758	4,916	4,906	3,473	10,154	13,201
Net income	3,541	8,495	10,890	14,563	15,302	21,087	23,985
Depreciation	8,521	8,368	9,176	9,198	8,903	9,911	10,487
Cur. assets	223,472	224,086	224,982	201,539	222,467	181,889	203,865
Fixed assets	84,025	64,716	67,670	67,799	69,463	77,116	92,565
Total assets	307,497	288,802	292,652	269,338	291,930	259,005	296,430
Current liab.	167,272	148,486	145,082	50,739	71,801	60,576	74,249
L.T. debt	60,771	55,683	56,414	116,132	123,784	67,713	70,192
Equity	79,454	84,633	91,156	102,467	96,345	130,716	151,989
TL&NW	307,497	288,802	292,652	269,338	291,930	259,005	296,430
Earnings per share	0.35	0.78	1.05	1.35	1.49	1.82	2.05
Dividends per share	0.13	0.13	0.13	0.28	0.35	0.44	0.55
Price-earnings ratio	9.28	4.31	5.89	7.58	5.42	6.87	14.1
PE/Industry[a]	1.23	0.83	1.05	0.94	0.69	0.56	0.82

[a]Brand-name's price-earnings ratio divided by the industry average price-earnings ratio.

| TABLE 18.8 ANALYSIS OF COMPETING APPAREL MANUFACTURERS

Data in this table are based on the 1992 financial statements of the major competitors.

Company	Beta	Pfd.	Debt	TIE[a]	Book Value/ Share	Market/ Book Value	EPS[b]	P-E[c] Ratio	WACC[d]	Sales Growth[e]
			% OF CAPITAL SALES							
A	0.91	0.00	0.47	3.70	10.81	1.26	1.29	10.59	10.98	29%
B	1.36	0.00	0.36	1.70	12.21	1.81	0.71	31.21	14.56	21
C	0.64	0.00	0.12	9.70	22.37	0.96	0.96	22.35	12.05	−13
D	1.01	0.00	0.18	7.80	17.51	1.43	1.20	20.81	13.87	3
E	1.34	0.00	0.00	NA	5.62	7.03	2.00	19.74	17.37	53
F	1.04	0.02	0.43	NA	13.61	1.03	(0.10)	NA	11.31	−8
G	0.81	0.00	0.44	2.70	8.60	1.56	0.58	23.19	11.24	17
H	0.94	0.00	0.12	6.40	12.21	1.19	0.93	15.68	13.89	1
I	0.86	0.00	0.10	9.50	27.24	1.41	3.00	12.82	13.60	1
J	1.06	0.00	0.13	20.50	6.34	2.44	1.08	14.32	14.90	11
K	0.91	0.06	0.02	22.00	21.01	1.36	2.65	10.79	14.19	4
L	0.74	0.16	0.14	0.10	8.49	1.11	1.35	7.01	11.94	6
M	0.61	0.00	0.36	1.30	17.16	0.73	0.50	24.97	9.64	3
N	1.06	0.01	0.26	10.30	5.78	2.73	1.32	11.94	14.33	4
O	1.01	0.00	0.16	13.70	11.26	2.74	2.05	15.03	14.55	12

[a]Times interest earned (earnings before interest and tax ÷ interest expense).
[b]Earnings per share.
[c]Price-earnings ratio.
[d]Weighted average cost of capital.
[e]Average annual growth rate per year for the past three years.

modernization was expected to increase net operating income by $5 million and increase depreciation by $1 million, with no increase in sales.

Managers wanted to choose a financing method that would have the most favorable impact on the company's stock price. Brand-name company could raise money by selling twenty-year bonds at an interest rate of 9.8 percent before tax. The new bonds would be retired through equal annual payments over the 20-year period. The existing long-term debt was selling at par for a yield to maturity of 8.9 percent, and was being repaid at a rate of $5 million a year. The interest rates on U.S. Treasury bills and Treasury bonds were 5.76 percent and 7.11 percent respectively. Brand-name could sell common stock at a price of $25 a share, after flotation costs. Brand-name had a beta of 1.10.

In preparing for a financing decision, the treasury department at Brand-name prepared a study of competitors, which is summarized in Table 18.8. They computed an estimated cost of capital for each competitor, using the capital asset pricing model and the market yield on the competitor's debt. These weighted average cost of capital estimates also appear in Table 18.8.

CASE QUESTIONS

1. Compare Brand-name to the industry with regard to times interest earned and long-term debt to total capital ratios for both the debt and equity financing alternatives. Would either of the financing alternatives place Brand-name outside of industry norms?

2. Suppose there is no change in sales from 1992. Assume no change in ratios of current assets and current liabilities to sales. Assume the new equipment is placed in service at the beginning of 1993. What level of net operating income is needed to meet the financial obligations if debt financing is used? if equity financing is used?

3. Find the crossover point in net operating income (the net operating income level above which earnings per share will be higher with debt financing and below which earnings per share will be higher with equity financing).

4. Estimate the marginal cost of capital for the $20 million, for both debt and equity financing.

5. Study the relationships between financial leverage and weighted average cost of capital for the apparel industry. Based on this information, what conclusions can you reach concerning investor response to capital structure in this industry?

6. Study the profitability trends at Brand-name. Indicate any positive or negative trends you observe.

7. Should Brand-name use debt or equity financing?

SELECTED REFERENCES

Blume, M. E., Irwin Friend, and R. Westerfield. "Impediments to Capital Formation." Rodney White Center for Financial Research, December 1980.

Bradley, Michael, Gregg A. Jarrell, and E. Han Kim. "On the Existence of an Optimal Capital Structure." *Journal of Finance* 39 (July 1984): 857–878.

Donaldson, Gordon. "New Framework for Corporate Debt Capacity," *Harvard Business Review* 40 (March–April 1962): 117–131.

———. "Strategy for Financial Emergencies." *Harvard Business Review* 47 (November–December 1969): 67–79.

Ederington, Louis H., Jess B. Yawitz, and Brian E. Roberts. "The Information Content of Bond Ratings." *Journal of Financial Research* 10 (Fall 1987): 211–226.

Gehr, Adam K., Jr. "Financial Structure and Financial Strategy." *Journal of Financial Research* 7 (Spring 1984): 69–80.

Glascock, John L., Wallace N. Davidson III, and Glenn V. Henderson, Jr. "Announcement Effects of Moody's Bond Rating Changes on Equity Returns." *Quarterly Journal of Business and Economics* 26 (Summer 1987): 67–78.

Kamath, Ravindra R. "Long-Term Financing Decisions: Views and Practices of Financial Managers of NYSE Firms." *Financial Review* 32 (May 1997): 331–356.

Kim, Wi Saeng, and Eric H. Sorensen. "Evidence on the Impact of the Agency Costs of Debt on Corporate Policy." *Journal of Financial and Quantitative Analysis* 21 (June 1986): 131–144.

Kolodny, Richard, and Diane Rizzuto Suhler. "Changes in Capital Structure, New Equity Issues, and Scale Effects." *Journal of Financial Research* 8 (Summer 1985): 127–136.

Litzenberger, Robert H. "Some Observations on Capital Structure and the Impact of Recent Recapitalizations on Share Prices." *Journal of Financial and Quantitative Analysis* 21 (March 1986): 59–71.

Malitz, Ileen. "On Financial Contracting: The Determinants of Bond Covenants." *Financial Management* 15 (Summer 1986): 18–25.

Mauer, David C., and Wilbur G. Lewellen. "Debt Management under Corporate and Personal Taxation." *Journal of Finance* 42 (December 1987): 1275–1291.

Mayer, David C., and Alexander J. Triantis. "Interactions of Corporate Financing and Investment Decisions: A Dynamic Framework." *Journal of Finance* 49 (September 1994): 1253–1277.

Myers, Stuart C. "The Search for the Optimal Capital Structure." *Midland Corporate Finance Journal* 1 (Spring 1983): 6–16.

Opler, Tim C., Michael Sharon, and Sheridan Titman. "Designing Capital Structure to Create Shareholder Value." *Journal of Applied Corporate Finance* 10 (Spring 1997): 21–32.

Opler, Tim C., and Sheridan Titman. "Financial Distress and Corporate Performance." *Journal of Finance* 49 (July 1994): 1015–1040.

Perry, Larry G., Glenn V. Henderson, Jr., and Timothy P. Crowan. "Multivariate Analysis of Corporate Bond Ratings and Industry Classifications." *Journal of Financial Research* 7 (Spring 1984): 27–36.

CHAPTER 19 |

DIVIDEND POLICY AND INVESTMENT DECISIONS

After completing this chapter you should be able to:

1. Explain why dividend policy does not matter in a perfect market.
2. Describe how market imperfections, such as transaction cost, flotation cost, and taxes, influence dividend policy.
3. Discuss the role that information asymmetry and agency costs play in setting dividend policy.
4. List and discuss at least five firm-specific variables that can influence dividend policy.
5. Recognize and discuss four common dividend policies used in practice.
6. Qualify the differences, advantages, and disadvantages of stock repurchases and stock dividends.

The dividend histories of Delta Airlines and Southwest Airlines, summarized in Figure 19.1, make an interesting study. The managers at Delta increased dividends in response to both increases and decreases in earnings. Likewise, they decreased dividends in response to both increased and decreased earnings. Southwest, on the other hand, maintained a stable policy, increasing dividends only when earnings increased and primarily holding dividends constant. Possible reasons for such disparate policies are covered in this chapter.

A dividend is a payment of part of the corporation's earnings to the stockholders. We will see that in a world with no taxes, no transactions costs, perfect information, and so on, dividend policy does not affect the wealth of the shareholders or the investment policy of the firm. But taxes, limited information, and other *market imperfections* create the possibility that shareholder wealth can be affected by dividend policy. The right dividend policy may increase the value of the company's stock, thereby reducing the cost of equity capital. A lower cost of

| **FIGURE 19.1** **DIVIDENDS FOR DELTA AIRLINES AND SOUTHWEST AIRLINES**

Dividends per share (DPS) in relation to earnings per share (EPS) are compared for Delta Airlines and Southwest Airlines.

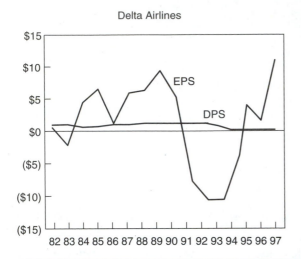

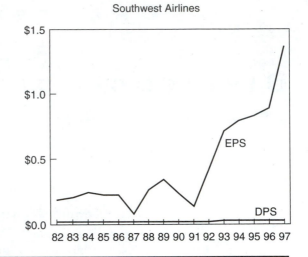

Source: *Value Line.*

capital increases the net present values of investments and makes some investments profitable when they would otherwise be rejected.

Dividend policy may also affect the amount of money available to invest. Because of market imperfections, some companies do not have the ability to sell new equity and are limited in growth by the amount of equity available through retained earnings. These companies must make trade-offs between the value that can be generated by new investments and the value that can be created by dividend policy. Thus, dividend policy has implications for investment decisions in a wide variety of businesses.

It should be stressed at the outset that this chapter will not end with a formula for the optimal dividend policy. Our current knowledge allows us to make general statements that should provide guidance in setting dividend policy, but does not allow the derivation of a formula for the exact optimal policy in light of all factors affecting dividend decisions.

PERFECT MARKETS AND DIVIDEND IRRELEVANCE |

In 1961, Merton Miller and Franco Modigliani (M&M) published an article on dividend policy using a line of reasoning similar to that applied in their previously cited analysis of capital structure decisions.[1] M&M's work is critical for es-

[1]Merton H. Miller and Franco Modigliani, "Dividend Policy, Growth, and the Valuation of Shares," *Journal of Business* 34 (October 1961): 411–433.

tablishment of dividend policy, not because of their particular conclusions, but because of the foundation they laid for understanding the role of dividends. Most of the arguments for specific dividend policies arise from changing the assumptions used by M&M.

M&M began with the following set of assumptions:

1. Perfect capital markets exist: investors are rational; information is freely available to all; securities are infinitely divisible; no investor is large enough to affect price; there are no transaction costs for investors buying and selling securities and no flotation costs for companies issuing securities.
2. There are no taxes.
3. The investment policy of the firm is given.

Based on these assumptions, M&M concluded that dividend decisions do not affect shareholder wealth or the cost of capital. Theirs was fundamentally an arbitrage argument. If your company decides to reinvest all earnings and some shareholder wants cash flow, that shareholder can simply sell a portion of his or her shares to receive the desired amount of cash. Likewise, a shareholder who receives dividends and prefers to leave the money invested in the company can purchase additional shares. Since shareholders can create the cash flow pattern they prefer regardless of dividend policy, the company cannot create or destroy value through dividend policy.

The value of the company equals the present value of future cash flows; the total value of those cash flows is not affected by whether they are financed by retained earnings or the sale of new stock. Likewise, the proportion of that value owned by a particular investor is not affected by dividend policy since that investor can increase his or her investment by reinvesting dividend money in the company, and can reduce his or her investment by selling shares. Thus, neither the value of the company nor the wealth of the shareholders is affected by dividend policy.

In the following paragraphs, the conclusions of M&M will be developed in a bit more detail. The M&M analysis is based on a predetermined investment set for the firm. To simplify the discussion, assume that the proportion of assets financed with debt and with common stock has been determined. The assumption of a given debt and equity mix decision does not result in any loss in generality because capital structure and dividend decisions can be made independently. Movement to any desired debt-equity mix can be achieved by buying back or selling stock, with that action offset by additional borrowing or debt repayment. Thus, dividend policy need not affect the mix of debt and equity.

In Chapter 4, the value of a share of stock was established as the present value of all future dividends. If the value at time zero (P_0) is the present value of all dividends at time zero, and the value at time one (P_1) is the present value of all dividends at time one, then the value at time zero can also be stated as:

$$P_0 = (P_1 + D_1)/(1 + k) \qquad (19\text{-}1)$$

where D_1 is the dividend per share at time one (with no dividends between time zero and time one) and k is the required return for investments of this risk level.

To again simplify the discussion, by focusing on only one dividend decision, assume that additional capital investments will be made at time one, but that all earnings will be paid out as dividends after that time. The value of a share of stock at time one is:

$$P_1 = V_1/(n + m) \tag{19-2}$$

where V_1 is the present value at time one of all future dividends to the shareholders that will be generated by the company's predetermined set of investments, n is the number of shares outstanding at time zero, and m is the number of shares that must be issued at time one to raise capital for predetermined new investments. The number of new shares issued at time one is based on the source and use of funds identity (assuming the debt ratio is not affected by dividend decisions):

$$Y_1 + mP_1 = I_1 + nD_1 \tag{19-3}$$

where I_1 is the amount of new equity required for capital investment at time one, Y_1 is the amount of income available at time one, before paying dividends, and D_1 is the dividend per share at time one. Simultaneously solving Equations 19-2 and 19-3 gives:

$$P_1 = (V_1 - I_1 + Y_1)/n - D_1 \tag{19-4}$$

Substituting Equation 19-4 into Equation 19-1 gives:

$$P_0 = [(V_1 - I_1 + Y_1)/n - D_1 + D_1]/(1 + k) \tag{19-5}$$

Simplifying gives:

$$P_0 = [(V_1 - I_1 + Y_1)/n]/(1 + k) \tag{19-5a}$$

The important thing to note is that dividends have disappeared in Equation 19-5a; the value of a share of stock and the total value of the company depend on the stream of future cash flows generated by the company from a given investment policy, not on the proportion of those cash flows used for dividends in any particular period.

If dividend policy matters, it can only be because M&M's proof is in error or because some of their assumptions are violated in practice. Their proof has been examined many times, and can be accepted as valid, given their assumptions. But assumptions of perfect capital markets and no taxes do not describe the real world. If dividend policy matters, it is because of these imperfections. In the following paragraphs, imperfections that would cause dividend policy to affect value are discussed. If dividend policy affects value, it also affects capital investment decisions.

DIVIDEND POLICY AND VALUE |

Factors that may make dividend policy relevant in the real world can be lumped into four broad categories: (1) friction costs, which include, transaction costs, flotation costs, and taxes; (2) use of dividend policy to signal stockholders about future profitability; (3) portfolio considerations; and (4) use of dividend policy to resolve agency problems.

FRICTION COSTS

Transaction Costs. Transaction costs to investors are one possible reason dividend policy may affect value. In the M&M analysis, it was assumed that shareholders could simply sell a few shares if the dividends they wanted were not paid, or buy a few shares if unwanted dividends were paid. However, investors must pay brokerage fees when they buy or sell stock; when a few shares are bought or sold, the brokerage fees can be a substantial portion of the value of the stock involved. Therefore, a dividend policy that pays the amount of cash investors want may increase value to the investor.

Many companies handle the possibility they are paying more dividends than investors want by offering automatic reinvestment services. With these services, dividends that would otherwise be paid out are used to buy additional shares for any stockholders requesting the service. These transactions are generally handled at no cost to the stockholder, and shares can be held in the name of a fund so a fraction of a share can be purchased by an individual investor. Some companies even offer a small discount of 2 or 3 percent on the price of stock purchased in this way. Acme Electric goes one step further, giving a 10 percent discount on stock purchased through its dividend reinvestment plan.

Flotation Costs. The floatation costs involved in selling new common stock can run to 10 percent or more of the amount raised. There are also some processing costs involved in paying dividends. Other things being equal, these costs would cause a value-maximizing company that needed equity capital for new investments to retain earnings rather than selling new stock.

Lack of access to capital markets is the extreme case of high flotation costs. Many smaller companies have no access to a public market in which they can sell additional equity, or could only accomplish a sale with exorbitantly high flotation costs. In a recent study, Ritter found that the costs of going public averaged 22.22 percent of the realized market value of securities issued with underwriting by the investment bankers and 31.87 percent for best-efforts offers.[2] Needless to say, companies often decide not to expand rather than face costs of this magnitude. The only alternatives generally available for these companies are to sell out to a larger company, rely on retained earnings for new equity, or forgo growth.

---

[2]Jay R. Ritter, "The Cost of Going Public," *Journal of Financial Economics* 19 (December 1980): 269–281.

Taxes. Taxes are one of the most obvious violations of the M&M assumptions. Under current law, the maximum capital gains rate is 28 percent while the highest tax rates for individuals, heads of household, and married filers is 39.6 percent. In addition, taxes on dividends must be paid immediately while taxes on capital gains need not be paid until the stock is sold, possibly decades in the future. Consider, for example, an investor in a 40 percent combined federal and local tax bracket who buys $100 worth of stock in a company that earns 10 percent annual return on its equity. If the company reinvests all earnings, the investor's stock will grow in value over a twenty-year period to:

$$\$100(1 + .10)^{20} = \$672.75$$

After paying a 40 percent tax on the price increase, the investor will have:

$$\$672.75 - .40(\$572.75) = \$443.65$$

If the company paid out all its earnings in dividends each year, and the investor used after-tax dividends to buy new shares, the investment would grow to:

$$\$100[1 + .10(1 - .40)]^{20} = \$320.71$$

Thus, capital gains have a tax advantage due to the flexibility offered the recipient.

The previous example assumes capital gains actually occur. Suppose, though, a company pays dividends and the stock declines in value by an amount equal to the dividends. The total wealth of the stockholders is unchanged before tax, but they pay taxes on the dividends, and they do not generally get a tax savings from the price decline. Again, tax considerations make dividends undesirable.

These examples would suggest that dividends should be avoided because of the tax structure. But, *clientele effects* may offset general tax disadvantages of dividends in some cases. A clientele effect arises if some investors want dividends and some do not, regardless of the reason. Taxes are a widely cited reason for a clientele effect.[3] For example, an investor with interest expense in excess of investment income can deduct the interest expense from dividends, thereby making the dividends tax-free; that investor would prefer dividends over capital gains. Investors experiencing capital losses from other investments would prefer capital gains because offsetting losses would cause the gains to be tax-free. As pointed out earlier, other investors would prefer capital gains taxes at a later time over taxes on dividends today, and would not want dividends.[4]

---

[3]Transaction costs can also lead to a clientele effect. An investor who needs cash for consumption purposes on a regular basis may find that selling a few shares of stock at a time results in prohibitively high transaction costs; that investor will seek a certain amount of dividend income.

[4]Some investors avoid dividend taxation by methods such as holding stock in tax-free retirement funds. For further discussion of the ways in which investors avoid taxation of dividends, see Merton H. Miller and Myron S. Scholes, "Dividends and Taxes," *Journal of Financial Economics* 6 (December 1978): 333–364.

The tax clientele effect taken in isolation would suggest an optimal amount of dividends for the economy, based on the number of investors preferring dividend income over capital gain income, but would not suggest a dividend policy for a particular company. Dividend policy would affect value only if the optimal amount of dividends was not being paid out by companies as a whole.[5]

In a 1978 article, Lewellen, Stanley, Lease, and Schlarbaum presented evidence of a significant clientele effect, but the effect was small in magnitude. These authors divided stocks into 10 groups according to dividend yield. The highest dividend yield group provided a dividend yield close to 8 percent, and the lowest yield group paid no dividends. There was a tendency for investors in higher tax brackets to hold stocks with lower dividend yields, but the range was narrow. The average tax rate was 35 percent for holders of the highest dividend yield stocks and 41 percent for holders of the lowest dividend yield stocks.[6] Papaioannou and Savarese confirmed in 1994 that dividend payout does indeed respond logically to changes in tax rates.[7]

Combining Friction Cost Considerations. If friction costs were the only violation of the M&M assumptions, a *residual dividend policy* would be implied. The company would invest internally all funds for which it could earn a high enough return to justify reinvestment, and would pay the rest out as dividends. The return required to justify reinvestment would be based on consideration of investors' opportunities outside the company as well as the tax rates and transactions costs to which investors would be subjected. Flotation costs would be minimized because the company would not pay dividends and sell new shares during the same period.

Example. Mitchell Corporation has a risk level such that equity investors can earn 12 percent before personal income tax elsewhere in investments of equal risk. Further suppose that the average investor is in a 30 percent tax bracket, does not need cash for consumption purposes, and must pay transaction costs equal to 3 percent of any amount invested. Stockholders of this company tend to hold their stock for long periods, so capital gains taxes are delayed; the effect is approximately the same as if capital gains were taxed immediately at 20

[5]For further discussion of the clientele effect, see Fischer Black and Myron Scholes, "The Effects of Dividend Yield and Dividend Policy on Common Stock Prices and Returns," *Journal of Financial Economics* 1 (May 1974): 1–5; Edwin J. Elton, Martin J. Gruber, and Joel Rentzler, "The Ex-Dividend Day Behavior of Stock Prices; a Re-Examination of the Clientele Effect: A Comment," *Journal of Finance* 39 (June 1984): 551–561; and R. H. Litzenberger and K. Ramiswamy, "The Effects of Dividends on Common Stock Prices: Tax Effects or Information Effects?" *Journal of Finance* 37 (May 1982): 429–444.

[6]Wilbur G. Lewellen, Kenneth. L. Stanley, Ronald C. Lease, and Gary G. Schlarbaum, "Some Direct Evidence on the Dividend Clientele Phenomenon," *Journal of Finance* 33 (December 1978): 1385–1399.

[7]George J. Papaioannou and Craig M. Savarese, "Corporate Dividend Policy Response to the Tax Reform Act of 1986," *Financial Management* 23 (Spring 1994): 56–63.

percent.[8] If the company pays \$100 in dividends, the average investor will pay \$30 in taxes, leaving \$70 to reinvest. Transaction costs will be $.03 \times \$70 = \$2.10$, so the amount actually invested will be \$67.90. If the \$67.90 is invested at 12 percent, the annual income will be $.12 \times \$67.90 = \$8.148$. Because the effective tax rate on capital gains is 20 percent, the effective tax on \$100 of retained earning is \$20, and the amount left to invest is \$80. Thus, the company can justify reinvestment if investors can earn 12 percent elsewhere, and the company can earn at least $\$8.148/\$80 = 10.2$ percent from internal investments.

The process illustrated in the previous example can be reduced to the formula:

$$\text{Required return} = R_a(1 - T_D)(1 - TC)/(1 - T_g) \tag{19-6}$$

where R_a is the return that can be earned on investments of equal risk, T_D is the tax rate applied to dividend income, TC is transaction cost to the stockholder as a percent of amount invested, and T_g is the effective tax rate on capital gains. Using residual dividend policy, earnings would be paid out as dividends only if they could not be reinvested to earn the required return defined in Equation 19-6. Applying Equation 19-6 to the previous example:

$$\text{Required return} = .12(1 - .30)(1 - .03)/(1 - .20) = 10.2\%$$

Application of residual dividend theory is complicated by several factors. First, shareholders are not all in the same tax brackets, and not all shareholders hold the stock for the same amount of time. Therefore, the effective tax rates for dividends and capital gains are not clear. Furthermore, portfolio considerations, information signaling, agency, and other problems must be considered in establishing dividend policy. These other problems are considered in the following paragraphs.

[8]The effective tax rate on capital gains can be found as follows: Assume an amount of \$1 is invested at a return of R for n years, with the increase in value taxed at the rate T when the asset is sold at the end of n years. The terminal wealth is:

$$TW = \$1(1 + R)^n - [\$1(1 + R)^n - \$1]T$$

Now, suppose the tax law changes so that a tax rate of T_g is paid each year on the return earned that year. The terminal wealth would then be:

$$TW = \$1[1 + R(1 - T_g)]^n$$

Setting these two equations for terminal wealth equal to each other and solving for T_g gives:

$$T_g = 1 - \{[(1 - T)(1 + R)^n + T]^{1/n} - 1\}/R$$

Thus, T_g is the tax rate which, if paid on gains in value each year as they occur, provides the same terminal wealth as a tax rate of T paid on gains when the asset is sold in n years. Assume, for example, T is .3, the rate of return is 12 percent, and the stock will be held for 11 years. T_g is then:

$$T_g = 1 - \{[(1 - .30)(1 + .12)^{11} + .30]^{1/11} - 1\}/.12 = .20$$

Stockholders would be indifferent over paying a tax rate of 30 percent on capital gains at sale time and paying a rate of 20 percent on gains each year, whether or not the asset is sold.

PORTFOLIO CONSIDERATIONS

Portfolio considerations must be weighed against the implications of friction costs, especially clientele effects. The presumed result of residual dividend policy would be some companies that paid dividends and some companies that did not. Stock of the dividend-paying companies would be held by those who could shelter dividends from taxes, and stock of nondividend companies would be held by those who could not shelter dividends from taxes. Clientele effects would therefore result in investors not holding the market portfolio, and possibly not achieving optimal diversification. Feldstein and Green have demonstrated that value maximization requires each firm to attract both types of investors, and, therefore, requires each firm to pay out a portion of its income as dividends.[9] While elimination of one company from the portfolio may not seriously decrease diversification, a dividend policy followed by all companies in an industry may eliminate that industry from some portfolios, with consequent decreases in diversification benefits.

INFORMATION SIGNALING

Information signaling is another possible reason for paying dividends. Investors receive earnings reports, but the variety of allowable accounting choices makes the reported earnings suspect. Furthermore, investors may not know what future income managers expect. Thus, investors may not have complete information, and complete information is clearly desired.

Ross first developed the theoretical analysis of dividends as a signaling device.[10] In order to signal stockholders about future prospects, managers must have strong incentives to send accurate signals. It must be difficult for an unsuccessful firm to mimic the signal of a successful firm, and the signal must be of some easily observed future event so the accuracy of the signal can be confirmed later.

Companies tend to raise dividends only if they believe the new, higher dividend level can be sustained. Likewise, companies tend to decrease dividends only if sustained lower income is expected. Dividends are not easily raised by unsuccessful companies because the unsuccessful companies are often short of cash. In addition, future earnings and dividends are readily observable as time passes, so the accuracy of the signal can be confirmed. Therefore, dividends are a potentially useful part of the signaling process.

Managers may be motivated to send honest signals for a couple of reasons. First, management compensation may be designed so that managers' wealth is maximized by sending an accurate signal. Most top managers, for example, have stock options and direct stock ownership that tie their wealth to the future value of the company's stock. A false signal may increase the price of the stock

---

[9]Martin Feldstein and Jerry Green, "Why Do Companies Pay Dividends?" *American Economic Review* (March 1983): 17–30.

[10]Stephen Ross, "The Determination of Financial Structures: The Incentive Signaling Approach," *Bell Journal of Economics* 8 (Spring 1977): 23–40.

immediately, but lead to an even greater decline when later events show the signal to be false and investors lose confidence. In addition, management reputation developed over time may serve as a basis for evaluating the dividend signal. Managers may be motivated to send accurate signals because their own value in the marketplace will decline if the signals they send turn out to be false.[11]

Empirical evidence supports the view of dividends as a signaling device. Watts found that high dividends do tend to be followed by abnormally high earnings, and vice versa.[12] Thus, dividend policy appears to provide signals to investors in a world with incomplete information.[13]

Risk Reduction. It is sometimes suggested that managers can reduce shareholder risk through dividend policy because a predictable dividend stream makes one portion of the return to shareholders known. But examination of Equation 19-4 makes it clear that the terminal value of a share of stock goes down one dollar for each dollar of dividends paid on that share. Therefore, dividend policy does not affect the variance of the shareholders' terminal wealth. Only a reduction in the variability of V_1 would reduce risk.[14] This point can be extended to a multiperiod analysis as well, as long as the investment policy of the company and the amount invested in the company by the shareholder are not affected by dividend policy.

Suppose, though, that dividends do provide information about management expectations. The risk to a shareholder is based on the *shareholder's* uncertainty about future events. That uncertainty may result from unpredictable world events or from not having the same information that is available to managers. Suppose an increase in dividends serves as an effective way for managers to tell shareholders that uncertainty concerning the company's future cash flows has declined. The increased dividend then provides information that decreases the shareholders' uncertainty about future cash flows.

AGENCY CONSIDERATIONS

Rozeff suggested that dividends may also play a role in resolving agency problems between managers and shareholders. A company that funds its growth through internally generated capital needs to deal with its shareholders only through mailing of annual reports and dividend checks. If there is no risk of a takeover or a

---

[11]See Eugene Fama, "Agency Problems and the Theory of the Firm," *Journal of Political Economy* (April 1980): 288–307.

[12]Ross Watts, "The Information Content of Dividends," *Journal of Business* 46 (April 1973): 191–211.

[13]For additional discussion of signaling issues, see Sudipto Bhattacharya, "Imperfect Information, Dividend Policy, and 'The Bird in the Hand Fallacy,'" *Bell Journal of Economics* 10 (Spring 1979): 259–270; and Nils H. Hakansson, "To Pay or Not to Pay," *Journal of Finance* 37 (May 1982): 415–428.

[14]For additional discussion, see Bhattacharya, "Imperfect Information"; and John Kose and Joseph Williams, "Dividends, Dilution, and Taxes: A Signaling Equilibrium," *Journal of Finance* 40 (September 1985): 1053–1070.

proxy battle, pressures from outside investors are minimal. Retaining all earnings increases the likelihood of this comfortable situation for managers.

Payment of dividends, on the other hand, increases the probability that managers will have to face investment bankers, the Securities and Exchange Commission, and potential new investors. The discipline of the marketplace will force managers to conduct business in a way that will stand close scrutiny when they go to the markets for additional capital. Managers wanting to sell additional securities may also be required to furnish additional information, which can be used by existing shareholders as well as potential new investors.

These offsetting costs are summarized in Figure 19.2. Note that transaction costs increase with all increases in dividend payments, while the agency costs of equity decrease with all increases in dividend payments. The result is a minimum level of total costs, which represents the optimal dividend policy. Rozeff found support for this theory in an empirical study of dividend policy.[15]

OTHER PRACTICAL CONSIDERATIONS

Friction costs, signaling, and agency problems provide reasons dividend policy may affect value. A number of practical considerations that may affect dividend decisions also have been suggested. Some of these considerations relate to value, and some do not. These other reasons are discussed in the following paragraphs.

| **FIGURE 19.2 AGENCY COSTS AND DIVIDENDS**

This figure shows the agency costs associated with equity, which decrease with increases in dividends, and transactions costs, which increase with increases in dividends.

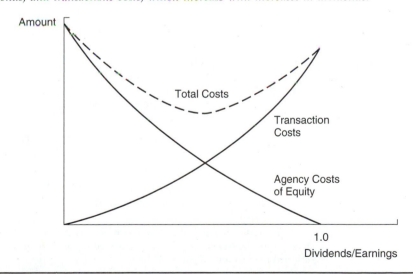

[15]Michael S. Rozeff, "Growth, Beta and Agency Costs as Determinants of Dividend Payout Ratios," *Journal of Financial Research* 5 (Fall 1982): 249–259.

INVESTMENT OPPORTUNITIES

In the previous analysis, it was assumed that companies had internal investment opportunities available. Some companies, though, generate more cash than they can invest profitably. For these companies, the choice is between paying dividends, changing the capital structure by retiring debt, or finding alternatives to dividends for distributing money to shareholders. Since payment of dividends does not result in flotation costs of new equity for these companies, they are likely to pay higher dividends than companies with more profitable internal investment opportunities.

INSTITUTIONAL RESTRICTIONS

Traditionally, many portfolio managers were restricted to common stocks of companies that had not skipped or reduced dividends for a specified number of years. Rules of this type have declined, but another type of restriction is quite common. Many trust portfolios, including some large charitable trusts, are required to protect the investment principal, and can only spend investment income.[16] For common stock investments, this means that only dividends can be spent. When Medicine Shoppe, Inc., announced its first-ever dividend in 1988, a spokesperson said that one of the reasons was to make the stock attractive to portfolio managers who could invest in only dividend-paying stocks.

Richardson, Sefcik, and Thompson looked at stock volume when companies first paid dividends for evidence of clientele effects, which could result from tax differences or institutional restrictions. They found small clientele effects.[17] The managers of these portfolios are often under pressure to provide both income and growth. They will therefore prefer stocks that pay at least some dividends. A dividend policy that eliminates this set of investors from the potential set of stockholders decreases demand for the stock and may therefore decrease price.

LEGAL REQUIREMENTS

Various legal and contract requirements can set upper and lower limits on dividend policy. These are discussed in the following paragraphs.

Restrictive Covenants. Many companies have equity positions on their balance sheets consisting of small amounts of common stock and large amounts of retained earnings. Lenders tend to view the entire equity position as their protection in the event of bankruptcy. Therefore, lenders often require borrowers to sign restrictive covenants saying that dividends will be paid only from earnings

---

[16]The author has served on the board of a trust that gives money to programs to "benefit the poor." The will establishing the trust specified expenditure of income only, and that restriction has affected the investment policy of the trust.

[17]Gordon Richardson, Stephen Sefcik, and Rex Thompson, "A Test of Dividend Irrelevance Using Volume Reactions to a Change in Dividend Policy," *Journal of Financial Economics* 17 (December 1986): 313–333.

subsequent to the date of the loan. In some cases, restrictive covenants go further to limit the proportion of income that can be paid out as dividends until the debt has been reduced to some specified level. These restrictive covenants set upper limits on the amount of dividends that can be paid.

Income Rules. Various state laws are designed to assure that a company does not distribute all its assets to the shareholders while leaving the creditors holding the bag. The *net profits rule* says that dividends can be paid only from past or present earnings. The *capital impairment rule* prohibits the payment of dividends from capital; capital in this context is defined as the par value of the common stock in some states and par value plus paid-in surplus in other states. The *insolvency rule* prohibits dividends when the company is insolvent or when the dividends would lead to insolvency. Insolvency may be defined as liabilities in excess of assets or inability to meet payment obligations.

Tax on Improperly Accumulated Earnings. Companies, particularly closely held companies, may decide to retain earnings solely as a means of avoiding taxes, even if the companies have no investments for those earnings. In such cases, the funds are held as cash or invested in securities. If the Internal Revenue Service can prove that there is no legitimate business reason for retaining the funds held in cash or invested in securities, a tax on improperly accumulated earnings can be applied. The effect is to establish minimum dividends for some companies by restricting retained earnings to those amounts for which they have legitimate business needs.

Because the burden of proof is on the Internal Revenue Service, many small corporations have held substantial amounts of money in securities. Potential justifications include liquidity needs, precautionary balances, and the accumulation of funds to move from a leased to an owned office building.

Cash Flow

Cash is needed to pay cash dividends, and a company may have income but no cash. Asset expansion, particularly working capital growth, may have eaten up all available cash. Debt repayment can also consume cash inflows. In addition, the company may need to maintain cash simply to handle its liquidity needs over the annual cycle or business cycle. Therefore, earnings do not necessarily translate into cash available to pay dividends. The amount of cash available to pay dividends sets an upper limit on dividends unless the company is willing to borrow or sell additional shares.

Management Interests

The M&M analysis focuses on the impact of dividend policy on shareholder wealth. But managers may be concerned about other problems as well. Considerations of particular interest to managers are discussed in the following paragraphs.

Control. For smaller companies, selling additional shares often means placing stock in the hands of investors who are not currently owners. This means that voting rights and at least some control will be in the hands of a new group. Even for some major corporations, the family of the founder still holds controlling interest, and the sale of new shares may disturb a delicate balance of power. Such companies may limit expansion to that which can be funded without the sale of additional common stock. Dividends will be held low to allow as much new investment as possible.

Takeover Defense. Takeover defense is another type of control problem. Top managers are concerned about unfriendly takeovers that may break their control of the company and threaten their jobs. Dividend policy responses depend on the relative positions of the company and potential acquirers. If it is anticipated that an acquisition attempt will be in the form of an offer to exchange shares, a high dividend may be chosen. Because investors are often unwilling to accept an exchange that reduces their dividends, a high dividend may force the acquiring company to increase its dividend as well, and may therefore discourage a takeover attempt. If management controls a large block of stock, dividends may be held low to avoid selling new shares that could be purchased by a potential acquirer. If stock ownership is widely dispersed, on the other hand, managers may want to flood the market with new shares so that the company attempting a takeover will have to acquire a larger number of shares.

Management Attitudes toward Risk. Managers may consider their own attitudes toward risk in developing dividend policy. Managers who are risk-averse may want to minimize debt, maximize liquid reserves, and minimize commitments to pay cash. Managers may find it impossible to sell new stock for the purpose of reducing risk because investors would not be attracted by the low profitability. But stockholder permission is not needed to retain earnings, and retained earnings can be accumulated over time to reduce risk.

Management Growth Preferences. Managers have often been accused of preferring growth over shareholder wealth maximization—growing by going beyond the set of profitable opportunities to invest in projects that are paying returns below their required returns. As lackluster earnings continue to be reported, stock price declines. (Managers in these situations often express frustration because their stock price is "low" despite their impressive growth.) Sale of additional shares at a low price to fund growth would further decrease earnings per share and further depress price. In these situations, growth is often financed with retained earnings. It is true that retained earnings could have been returned to investors to earn higher returns elsewhere, but the retention of earnings does not *directly* result in decreased earnings per share.

Example. To illustrate the effects of retaining earnings to fund projects of low profitability, consider a company financed entirely with equity, represented by 100 shares of common stock. Cash flow is $3,000 a year, or $30 a share, and this level of cash flow will continue indefinitely if the company does not expand. The investors' required return is 10 percent. If cash flows each year are paid out as a single annual dividend payment, the value of a share immediately *after* a dividend payment is:

$$V = \$30/.10 = \$300$$

Managers want to expand, but have no investment opportunities paying 10 percent; the best investment available pays only 6 percent. If they sell five new shares and invest the $1,500 proceeds at 6 percent, total cash flow in each future year will be:

$$\text{Total cash flow} = \$3,000 + (.06 \times \$1,500) = \$3,090$$

Cash flow per share will decline to $3,090 ÷ 105 = $29.43, and the value of a share will decline to:[18]

$$V = \$29.43 \div .10 = \$294.30$$

To expand faster than can be justified, and avoid the resulting decline in stock price, the managers decide to rely on retained earnings, cutting dividends in half to raise the $1,500. Cash flow per share would then increase to $3,090 ÷ 100 = $30.90, and the value of a share of stock immediately after the dividend payment would then *increase* from $300 to:

$$V = \$30.90 \div .10 = \$309$$

Before congratulating these managers for the clever way of increasing stock price with a low profitability investment, we should note that the $9 gain in stock value came at the expense of a $15 reduction in dividends. The wealth of the shareholders therefore decreased by $6 a share, and the benefit of using retained earnings to justify otherwise unjustifiable expansion is purely illusory.

DIVIDEND POLICY: A SYNTHESIS

The current state of knowledge does not make it possible to identify the exact dividend policy that will maximize value. But it is possible to develop some general guidelines.

First, legal requirements set upper and lower limits on dividend policy. Second, tax considerations taken in isolation would suggest that dividends be minimized. A company with substantial internal investment opportunities would

---

[18]Assuming the new shares could be sold for $300. If the new shareholders understand what is happening, the new shares will be sold at a lower price, and the dilution of earnings for the old shareholders will be even greater.

minimize friction costs by paying no dividends. But payment of regular dividends and avoidance of dividend reductions will make the stock accessible to a broad group of portfolio managers. Furthermore, an identifiable, stable dividend policy allows managers to signal shareholders about future prospects through changes in dividends. Finally, payment of dividends may help to reduce agency costs.

To simultaneously consider these various factors affecting dividends, most companies establish dividend policies involving payment of some target percentage of earnings as dividends. The target percentage is dependent on internal investment opportunities, with rapidly growing companies sometimes paying only a few percent of earnings in dividends and mature companies paying out most of their earnings in dividends. Although dividend policy is often based on a target percentage of earnings, the actual amount paid during any period is a function of dividends in the last period, earnings in the present period, and expected earnings in future periods. If possible, dividends will be at least as high as dividends for the prior period. If earnings for the present period are above historical levels, dividends will be raised, but only if this level of earnings is expected to continue in the future. When earnings rise sharply, it tends to take several years for dividends to fully adjust to the new earnings level.

Figure 19.3 graphically illustrates a mixed dividend policy of the type suggested in the previous paragraph. In the years prior to year N_1, the company had numerous attractive internal investment opportunities. A low payout ratio was used to avoid flotation costs. During this period, the company maintained a target dividend level of 20 percent of earnings. However, earnings fluctuated considerably and a stable dividend was desired. Therefore, dividends were increased

| **FIGURE 19.3** **MIXED DIVIDEND POLICY**

A target payout ratio is used, with the ratio itself adjusted over time in light of internal investment opportunities. Dollar stability is also pursued, with slow adjustments to changes in earnings.

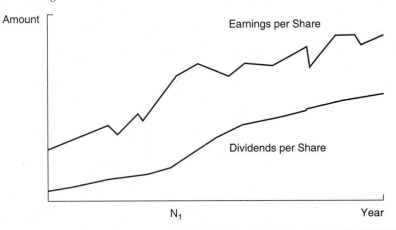

only after a new, higher earnings level had proved sustainable. Temporary decreases in earnings did not lead to reductions in dividends.

After time N_1, the company's growth rate and investment opportunities declined. The target payout ratio was raised to 60 percent of earnings. Again, the move toward a higher dividend was made only when it appeared that the new dividend level was sustainable, and dividends were not reduced as a result of short-term earnings fluctuations.

The mixed policy is consistent with observations in a study by Fama and Babiak. They observed that dividend increases depended on the number of times earnings had increased and how recently they had increased. Fama and Babiak also found that firms tended on average to move about one-third of the way from their previous position to their target dividend in any one year.[19] Watts found that dividends tended to be related to past dividends, present earnings, and future earnings.[20] Jensen and Johnson found that a dividend reduction marks the end of a firm's decline, but theorized that the negative response may reflect predictions that actions being taken by the firm will impair its long-run competitive position.[21] There is also evidence that unanticipated dividend changes do provide information about future prospects.[22]

In addition to being consistent with theory (when market imperfections are recognized), a mixed dividend policy is consistent with empirical evidence on investors' responses to dividends. Despite numerous studies of the impact of dividend payout ratios on value, there is no clear empirical evidence about preferred payout ratios. There is not even clear evidence with regard to whether dividends are preferred or not preferred, although the bulk of the evidence seems to be that higher returns are required from companies with high dividends.[23] This lack of clear preference is consistent with our conclusion that the optimal payout ratio for a particular company depends on factors such as friction costs and internal investment opportunities, not on some arbitrary ratio. Investors would be expected to respond positively to dividend increases by some companies and negatively to dividend increases by others.

[19]Eugene F. Fama and Harvey Babiak, "Dividend Policy: An Empirical Analysis," *Journal of the American Statistical Association* 63 (December 1968): 1132–1161.

[20]Watts, "The Information Content of Dividends."

[21]Gerald R. Jensen and James M. Johnson, "The Dynamics of Corporate Dividend Reductions," *Financial Management* 24 (Winter 1995): 31–51.

[22]See, for example, Watts, "The Information Content of Dividends"; J. Aharony and I. Swary, "Quarterly Dividend and Earnings Announcements and Stockholder Returns: An Empirical Analysis," *Journal of Finance* 35 (March 1980): 1–12; and C. Kwan, "Efficient Market Tests of the Informational Content of Dividend Announcements: Critique and Extension," *Journal of Financial and Quantitative Analysis* 16 (June 1981): 193–206.

[23]For examples of these studies, see Black and Scholes, "The Effects of Dividend Yield and Dividend Policy"; Litzenberger and Ramiswamy, "The Effects of Dividends on Common Stock Prices:"; Roger H. Gordon and David F. Bradford, "Taxation and the Stock Market Valuation of Capital Gains and Dividends: Theory and Empirical Results," *Journal of Public Economics* 14 (October 1980): 109–136; and Merton H. Miller and Myron S. Scholes, "Dividends and Taxes: Some Empirical Evidence," *Journal of Political Economy* (December 1983): 1118–1141.

The mixed dividend policy combines characteristics of three pure dividend policies. A *residual dividend policy* consists of paying out only those earnings that cannot be invested at a rate above the required return; dividend payout could fluctuate between 0 percent of earnings and 100 percent or more of earnings from period to period. A pure residual dividend policy would be the optimal policy if the M&M assumptions were correct except for the existence of friction costs. A *constant dollar policy* simply specifies a dollar dividend per share and holds that amount constant forever. A *constant payout ratio policy* calls for a constant percent of earnings being paid as dividends each period; dividends rise and fall with income. By combining these three policies as previously suggested, the company is able to respond to friction costs, internal investment opportunities, institutional restrictions, and information problems.

A fourth dividend policy consists of stable-dollar *regular dividends plus special dividends*. A typical application of this policy involves regular, stable quarterly dividends, with a special dividend each year depending on actual profitability during the year. The hope is that the shareholders will not come to anticipate the special dividends, and therefore will not respond negatively if special dividends are cut or omitted. Unfortunately, a dividend cut by any name is still a dividend cut. A company may pay a special dividend once and avoid expectations of future payments by explaining the situation that lead to the availability of excess funds on this one occasion. But if you have been receiving special dividends each year, you are likely to respond to a cut in special dividends about like you would respond to a cut in any other dividends. Brickley found that investors did respond to special dividends in ways that suggested expectations of future cash flows were being increased by those dividends.[24]

In addition to considering the welfare of the stockholders, managers may alter the dividend payout policy to fund their own growth desires, to help protect themselves from takeover, to reduce their personal risks, and to grow at rates faster than those justified by an objective of shareholder wealth maximization.

The considerations discussed thus far in this chapter can be used to suggest whether a particular company should be paying out a high or a low proportion of its earnings in the form of dividends. Unfortunately, the state of our knowledge is not such that we can tell a company to change from paying out 62 percent of earnings to paying out 63 percent of earnings with any degree of confidence in the accuracy of the decision.

OTHER DIVIDEND ACTIONS |

Only the payment of cash dividends has been discussed thus far, and there are a number of other related actions and ways to return money to stockholders. These actions are used in conjunction with cash dividends to maximize value and minimize required return.

---

[24]J. A. Brickley, "Shareholder Wealth, Information Signaling, and the Specially Designated Dividend," *Journal of Financial Economics* 12 (August 1983): 187–210.

STOCK DIVIDENDS

When a company pays stock dividends, it gives the investors additional shares instead of cash. With a 5 percent stock dividend, for example, the company would give each investor five additional shares for each one hundred shares held. To issue additional shares, the company simply mails pieces of paper to the shareholders. The stock dividend is often viewed as a way to give the shareholders something at no cost. Unfortunately, though, it turns out to be a way to give nothing at some cost.

If you owned 1 percent of the company before receiving a stock dividend, you will own 1 percent of the company after the stock dividend, with the 1 percent ownership represented by more pieces of paper. If the company still has the same assets and the same debt, we would expect the total value of your claims to remain unchanged after a stock dividend. Your claim is simply represented by more pieces of paper. If 100 shares were worth $5,000 before a 5 percent stock dividend, 105 shares will be worth $5,000 after a 5 percent stock dividend; the price of a share would be expected to decline from $50 to $47.62. Other things being equal you will be worse off because stocks are generally bought and sold in round lots of 100 shares, and the shares gained through the stock dividend may necessitate selling an odd lot, defined in stock trading terms as a number of shares less than one hundred. Transaction costs are considerably higher for odd-lot transactions. Furthermore, the company may have incurred several hundred thousand dollars of administrative and mailing costs in issuing the stock dividend.

Stock dividends may be important as conveyors of information about future cash dividends though. Phillips, Baker, and Edelman found that abnormal returns were negative, but not statistically significant on the day of an announcement of a discontinuance of stock dividends.[25] Rankine and Stice found that companies choose stock dividends based on expectations of future earnings growth, but do not choose stock splits for similar reasons.[26]

Many companies and investors believe there is a preferred price range for stocks, and a price above that range discourages trading. Stock dividends are one way to bring the price of the stock back into what is considered a preferred trading range. Stock splits—replacing each existing share of stock with two or more shares of stock—are another way to achieve the same purpose. Attempts to move down to an optimal trading price also may be interpreted as good news about the company's future earnings expectations. Stock dividends could also be important if there was some group of investors who were irrational, and thought they received something when the ownership of the company was represented by more pieces of paper. For whatever reasons, stock dividends remain popular enough that *Moody's Dividend Record* identified approximately 400 companies

[25]Aaron L. Phillips, H. Kent Baker, and Richard B. Edelman, "The Market Reaction to Discontinuing Regular Stock Dividends," *Financial Review* 32 (November 1997): 801–819.

[26]Graeme Rankine and Earl K. Stice, "The Market Reaction to the Choice of Accounting Method for Stock Splits and Large Stock Dividends," *Journal of Financial and Quantitative Analysis* 32 (June 1997): 161–182.

that paid stock dividends in the first ten months of 1988, and a like number of stock splits.[27]

STOCK REPURCHASE

Repurchase of stock is an alternative to dividends as a way to return money to stockholders. One advantage of repurchase is that the payment goes to someone who wants it because each stockholder can decide whether or not to sell. Second, the cash payment is often taxed favorably. Suppose, for example, an investor bought the stock for $20 a share and the price is now $30 a share. If the company buys back that share for $30, the investor is taxed only on the $10 gain. If $30 were distributed in dividends instead, the entire $30 would be taxed. The repurchase in lieu of dividends would be expected to result in a higher price for the remaining shares, but that gain will not be taxed until the shares are sold.

Stock repurchase may also be used when a company has excess funds from a one-time event like the sale of a division. A large dividend may lead to the expectation of continued large dividends, and to a decline in price when continued large dividends are not forthcoming. Rather than increasing dividends based on a one-time cash flow, a company can buy back stock. The repurchase does not necessarily create the expectation of future cash disbursements.

Stock repurchase often results from a management belief that the stock is underpriced.[28] If managers mean that the stock is underpriced in relation to future income, stock repurchase can make sense, assuming managers are right and investors are wrong.[29]

Example. To see the effect of stock repurchase for an undervalued stock, consider Boston Corporation, which has had some poor years but will earn a return of 10 percent on its assets in every future year; all income will be distributed as dividends. The company currently has $1 million of assets and 100,000 shares of stock. Earnings per share and dividends per share with the current structure are shown in the first column of numbers below. If the required return is 10 percent, the value of a share is $10. Suppose, though, that investors are not yet convinced of the future prosperity, so the stock is actually selling at $5 a share. The second column illustrates the position of the company if it uses $400,000 to buy back 80,000 shares.

---

[27]Immune Response may have the record, with a 100-to-1 stock split in 1988.

[28]Share repurchases are often accompanied by announcements to the effect that the company is investing in itself because it is optimistic about its future. This is an odd line of reasoning when we realize that buying back shares is really a way of returning money to the shareholders. Managers who are extremely optimistic about the company will presumably buy back all of the shares, thereby liquidating and going out of business.

[29]Stock repurchase may also be used as part of a takeover defense strategy. For a discussion of the phenomenon, see Larry Y. Dann and Harry DeAngelo, "Corporate Financial Policy and Corporate Control," *Journal of Financial Economics* 20 (January–March 1988): 87–127.

	Current Structure	After Stock Repurchase
Total assets	$1,000,000	$600,000
Rate of return	10%	10%
Income/dividends	100,000	60,000
Number of shares	100,000	20,000
Earnings per share	$1	$3

If the company does not buy back stock, the price of the stock will adjust to $10 as investors come to realize the new profitability level. With repurchase, the price of the stock will adjust to $30 a share.

Note that this maneuver does not create wealth. Assuming adjustment of expectations immediately after the potential repurchase date, the total value of all stock is $1 million without repurchase and $600,000 with repurchase; the other $400,000 of wealth was distributed to stockholders through repurchase. Although the repurchase did not create wealth, it did increase the wealth of those who held the stock at the expense of those who voluntarily sold their stock to the company and would have otherwise enjoyed price appreciation.

Managers often view stock repurchase as a way to decrease their attractiveness as a takeover candidate by driving up price and decreasing the takeover company's opportunity to make quick changes that will increase price. In addition to increasing price by increasing earnings per share, managers expect to increase price by increasing short-term demand through the repurchase program.

DIVIDEND PATTERNS IN THE UNITED STATES

Figure 19.4 illustrates the history of dividend payments for all companies in the United States. The payment pattern does reflect the mixed dividend policy suggested in this chapter. Dividends overall moved with earnings, but were much more stable than earnings. Dividends were even held stable during periods of sharp earnings declines. As a result, dividend payout ratios have fluctuated significantly from year to year.

Table 19.1 shows dividend practices for several major industries. Note that the overall pattern reflects attempts to maintain stable dividends in the face of erratic earnings. Note also that dividend payout ratios vary from industry to industry. This variation depends, among other things, on earnings stability and the need for new capital for expansion.

SUMMARY

In a world with no taxes, no transactions costs, perfect information, and so on, dividend policy does not affect the wealth of the shareholders or the investment policy of the firm. But taxes, limited information, and other market imperfections

| **FIGURE 19.4** **DIVIDENDS OF CORPORATIONS IN THE UNITED STATES**

This figure illustrates a mixed dividend policy for corporations as a whole. Dividends are more stable than earnings, and are not decreased during periods of temporary declines.

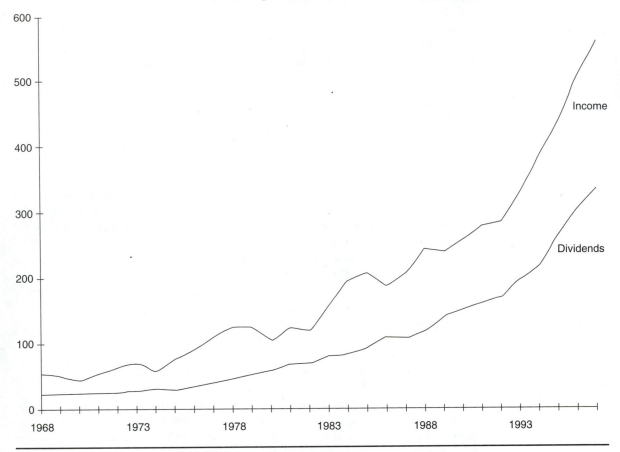

Source: *Economic Report of the President.*

lead to situations in which shareholder wealth can be affected by dividend policy. In these situations, availability of funds, the cost of capital, and therefore the investment decisions of the firm are affected by dividend policy.

Based on the assumption of perfect markets, no taxes, and a given investment policy for the firm, Miller and Modigliani (M&M) showed that dividend policy does not matter. The essential part of the M&M argument is that shareholders can create the cash flow pattern they prefer by buying and selling shares, regardless of dividend policy. Dividend policy matters only because M&M's assumptions do not hold in the real world.

Market imperfection responses that may make dividend policy relevant in the real world can be lumped into four broad categories: (1) friction costs, which include transaction costs, flotation costs, and taxes; (2) portfolio considerations, (3) use of dividend policy to signal stockholders about future profitability; and

| TABLE 19.1 EARNINGS AND DIVIDENDS BY INDUSTRY |

Net profits (in $ millions) and the percent of profits paid out as dividends are shown for each of ten industries for the years 1991 through 1993.

	1991		1992		1993	
	Profit	Payout Ratio	Profit	Payout Ratio	Profit	Payout Ratio
Auto Parts (Original Equip.)	$ 163	122%	$ 361	57%	$ 550	40%
Computers	4,916	61	3,745	82	4,700	67
Environmental	1,468	30	1,518	31	1,620	30
Food Processing	6,400	39	6,700	41	7,600	38
Medical Supplies	4,856	31	5,366	32	5,555	33
Integrated Petroleum	22,091	76	20,818	79	21,500	70
Restaurants	1,269	19	1,380	18	1,600	19
Publishers	1,516	58	1,722	55	1,810	56
Textiles	102	45	212	28	250	28
Toiletries/Cosmetics	890	40	1,063	36	1,180	36

(4) use of dividend policy to resolve agency problems. In addition, dividend policy is affected by the capital investment opportunities available to the company, institutional restrictions on holding the stock of companies that cut or omit dividends, restrictive covenants associated with debt, state laws, federal tax laws, cash flow considerations, and management interests. Management interests include control, takeover defense, risk, and growth preferences.

To simultaneously consider these various factors affecting dividends, most companies establish mixed dividend policies involving a target payout ratio. The target payout ratio is dependent on internal investment opportunities, with rapidly growing companies having low payout ratios. Although dividend policy is often based on a target percentage of earnings, the actual amount paid during any period is a function of dividends in the last period, earnings in the present period, and expected earnings in future periods. If possible, dividends will be at least as high as dividends for the prior period. If earnings for the present period are above historical levels, dividends will be raised, but only if this level of earnings is expected to continue in the future. When earnings rise sharply, it tends to take several years for dividends to fully adjust to the new earnings level.

The mixed dividend policy combines characteristics of three pure dividend policies. A *residual dividend policy* consists of paying out only those earnings that cannot be invested at a rate above the required return. A *constant dollar policy* simply specifies a dollar dividend per share and holds that amount constant forever. A *constant payout ratio policy* calls for a constant percent of earnings being paid as dividends each period. An additional possible dividend policy consists of stable regular dividends plus special dividends depending on profitability.

Alternatives to cash dividend include stock dividends and stock repurchase. Stock dividends are used to send a signal about future profitability while preserving present cash. Stock repurchase is used to distribute funds without the tax disadvantages of dividends or the creation of expectations with regard to future dividends.

QUESTIONS |

19–1. Define the terms (a) dividend, (b) clientele effects, (c) residual dividend policy, (d) net profits rule, (e) capital impairment rule, (f) insolvency rule.

19–2. A number of characteristics of perfect capital markets were listed. Which of these are likely to hold in practice? Which are not?

19–3. In the Miller and Modigliani analysis, why are dividends irrelevant?

19–4. In Chapter 4, the value of a share of stock was defined as the present value of the future dividend stream. Yet Miller and Modigliani concluded that dividend policy did not matter. Can these two views be reconciled?

19–5. What are the implications of the following considerations for dividend policy? (a) friction costs, (b) portfolio considerations, (c) signaling theory, (d) agency problems, (e) institutional and legal restrictions, (f) management interests.

19–6. Explain how a mixed dividend policy works.

19–7. Explain the following dividend policies: (a) residual dividend policy, (b) constant dollar dividend policy, (c) constant payout ratio policy, (d) regular dividend plus special dividend policy.

19–8. What are the advantages and disadvantages of paying stock dividends?

19–9. What are the advantages and disadvantages of stock repurchase as an alternative to cash dividends?

19–10. (**Applications**) In 1992, nearly one-half of the 5,100 companies represented on the New York Stock Exchange, the American Stock Exchange, and the National Market System of the over-the-counter market did not pay a dividend.
  a. How would you explain this behavior?
  b. During this same time approximately 500 of the 5,100 companies paid dividends that exceeded the respective company's earnings. How would you explain this behavior?

19–11. (**Ethical considerations**) As a result of several recent proxy battles waged against entrenched management of firms like Texaco and others, assets were sold and very large one-time dividends were paid to the shareholders. Often this was promised by the existing management prior to the shareholders voting for new board members. Is there an ethical concern here? If so, what is it?

PROBLEMS |

19–1. Miller and Modigliani's assumptions hold for Rochester Corporation. The company is in a risk class such that investors require a 10 percent return on equity investments. The company presently has total equity of $100,000, on which it earns a 10 percent return forever. At the end of year 1, the company will make a new investment of $10,000 on which it will earn 12 percent a year forever. After year 1, the company will make no new investments and will pay out all income as dividends. The company will pay dividends of $10,000 and then sell $10,000 worth of new equity.

   a. What is the total value of the equity at the end of year 1 (after dividends have been paid and new shares have been sold)?

   b. What will be the price of a share at the end of year 1 (after payment of dividends)?

   c. How many new shares must be sold?

   d. What is the price of a share at the beginning of year 1?

19–2. Rework problem 1 on the assumption that income of $10,000 was retained at the end of year 1 and used for the new investment. Compare the results to those obtained in problem 1. What are the implications for dividend policy?

19–3. Buffalo Corporation can earn a return of 10 percent after corporate income tax on new equity capital. The stock presently has a value of $100 a share. An investor in a 30 percent tax bracket for both capital gains and regular income owns one thousand shares and intends to sell the stock in 10 years. Ignore transaction costs and problems involved in purchasing fractions of a share.

   a. How much will the investor have after paying tax on the capital gain at the end of 10 years if the company reinvests all earnings?

   b. Suppose the company pays out all income in the form of dividends and the investor uses the dividends to buy additional stock. How much will the investor have at the end of 10 years?

19–4. For Buffalo Corporation in problem 3, suppose a particular investor can avoid tax on dividends because of unrelated interest expense but must pay taxes of 30 percent on capital gains. How much will that investor have at the end of 10 years if all income is retained for reinvestment in the company and if all income is paid out in the form of dividends and then reinvested in the company?

19–5. For Buffalo Corporation in problem 3, another investor must pay taxes of 30 percent on dividends but can avoid taxes on capital gains because of losses on other stocks. How much will that investor have at the end of 10 years if all income is retained for reinvestment in the company and if all income is paid out in the form of dividends and then reinvested in the company?

19–6. For the three investors identified in problems 3, 4, and 5, compute the effective annual after-tax return (internal rate of return) earned on the investment, with and without dividends.

19–7. Rework problem 3 on the assumption that transaction costs are 2 percent of the amount invested when the after-tax proceeds from dividends are reinvested in the company.

19–8. Albany Corporation can earn 10 percent after corporate income tax on new equity. Other opportunities of equal risk available to the investors pay 12 percent before personal income tax. The average stockholder pays a 30 percent tax rate on regular income. Because of delays in payment, the effective tax rate on capital gains is 20 percent. Transaction costs are 2 percent of any amounts invested. Should this company retain earnings or pay dividends?

19-9. Queens Corporation follows a residual dividend policy. The company has income for the next year of $500,000. The company is financed with 50 percent debt and 50 percent equity. The after-tax cost of debt is 7 percent. Equity investors can earn 12 percent on investment opportunities of equal risk that will generate income taxed at a 40 percent rate. The average investor pays an effective tax rate of 40 percent on dividends and 20 percent on capital gains. Transaction costs are nominal. Investment opportunities anticipated over the next year follow. (The investments are perpetuities.) How much in dividends should Queens pay out?

Investment	Amount	Internal Rate of Return
A	$100,000	12.0%
B	100,000	10.0
C	100,000	9.0
D	100,000	8.5
E	100,000	7.5
F	100,000	6.5

19-10. For Queens Corporation in problem 9, assume dividends and capital gains are taxed at the same rate. How much should the company pay in dividends?

19-11. Brooklyn Corporation anticipates net income of $1 million for the next year. The company has 100,000 shares of stock outstanding. Dividends were $5 per share last year and are always paid at year-end. If dividends are $5 per share again, it is expected that the price-earnings ratio will be 12 immediately before dividends are paid, and the price will decline $5 when dividends are paid. If dividends are increased to $6, a price-earnings ratio of 12.2 is anticipated immediately before dividends are paid. If dividends are eliminated, a price-earnings ratio of 11.8 is anticipated. The company needs $1 million of new equity for an investment that will generate $200,000 a year of net income forever. Flotation costs are 5 percent of any new equity raised. Any new shares will be issued at the end of the year, immediately after dividend payments.

a. For each of the dividend alternatives, what will be the price of the stock at the end of year 1, after dividend payments?

b. For each of the dividend alternatives, how many new shares must be issued?

    c. For each of the dividend alternatives, what will be the price of a share at the end of year 2 (before dividend payments) assuming a price-earnings ratio of 12?

19-12. Which dividend policy should Brooklyn Corporation (problem 11) choose? Why?

19-13. Long Island Sound Corporation has 100,000 shares of common stock outstanding. Earnings per share are $2 and the price-earnings ratio is 10. Suppose a 5 percent stock dividend is declared.

    a. Find the value of a share before and after the dividend.

    b. Sam Shapiro had 100 shares before the stock split. What is the total value of Shapiro's holdings before and after the split?

19-14. Managers at Stony Brook Industries believe that the price of a share of stock immediately after a dividend payment is:

$$\text{Price} = 9\text{EPS}_t + 1\text{DPS}_t + 2(\text{DPS}_t - \text{DPS}_{t-1})$$

where EPS_t and DPS_t are earnings and dividends for the most recent period. Earnings per share have been stable at $10 a share and dividends have been stable at $6 a share. Dividends are paid at the end of each year and a dividend has just been paid. A 5 percent stock dividend would be interpreted correctly as a signal of increased cash dividends because investors would not expect a decrease in dividends per share. Investors require a 10 percent return.

    a. What is the value of a share in 1 year (after dividend payment), with and without a stock dividend?

    b. Should the company pay the stock dividend?

19-15. Rochester Corporation is financed entirely with equity. The company has assets of $1 million, and has 100,000 shares of stock outstanding. The company has lost money for the past several years. However, the company anticipates earning a 12 percent return on assets next year, which is the required return of the shareholders. Shareholders have not responded to the improved prospects, and the stock is still selling for $3 a share. Managers are considering the repurchase of 50,000 shares at $3 a share. Compute the earnings per share at the end of the first successful year, with and without the repurchase. Who wins and who loses from the repurchase? Is total wealth increased through the repurchase? Explain.

19-16. An investor can reinvest funds at a rate of 15 percent, and pays a combined federal and state tax of 34 percent on either capital gain or dividend income. However, capital gains tax is delayed until the investor sells, and this particular investor does not plan on selling the stock for 10 years. What is the effective tax rate on capital gains? (*Hint*: see footnote 8.)

19-17. Cosmic Corporation, which is financed entirely with equity, has 1,000 shares of stock outstanding, and generates income of $50,000 a year. This level of income will continue indefinitely if the company does not expand. Investors require a 10 percent return, so the stock is selling at

$500 a share. Management wants to invest $40,000 in a new product line, but the investment is expected to provide a return of only 8 percent on the equity portion of capital. Friction costs are not a significant factor. Show the impact of the investment on stock price and shareholder wealth assuming that

a. the investment is financed with the sale of additional stock, at $500 a share immediately after dividends are paid.

b. the investment is financed with retained earnings.

CASE PROBLEM |

Brand-name Corporation (B)

The price earnings ratio for Brand-name Corporation had remained consistently below the industry average in recent years, and managers were searching for a way to improve the price of the stock. Dividend policy was being examined as part of an overall review of company policy. As shown in Table 18.7, Brand-name Corporation had followed a policy of paying a stable dividend equal to about one-fourth of earnings. Managers had increased dividends in response to increased earnings only when they were confident that the higher earnings would continue. Although this seemed like a sound policy, all policies were up for consideration as frustration about low stock prices grew.

Opinions about dividend policy were sharply split. The controller, Mark Johnson, was of the opinion that the company should cut out dividends entirely. He noted that dividends resulted in immediate taxes while capital gains would not be taxed until the investor sold the stock. He based his opinions primarily on the information in Tables 18.8 and 19.2. He noted that company C reduced its dividend in 1992, and the stock price did not decline. He also observed that two companies had paid no dividends in recent years, and both companies had relatively high price-earnings ratios. In light of the need for an additional $20 million of capital, he recommended that the company end its policy of paying cash dividends and begin paying stock dividends instead.

Karen Miller, the treasurer, disagreed. She agreed that the companies that had never paid dividends seemed to get by without harm, but cutting dividends was another matter. While the stock price did not fall for the company that reduced dividends, stock prices increased for most companies in the industry. The company that reduced its dividend suffered a decline in *relative* price. Investors were expecting a dividend, and the price of Brand-name's stock would almost certainly fall if dividends were cut.

Miller also examined the relationship between dividend payout ratio and price. She excluded the two companies that paid no dividends because they probably appealed to a special investor group that did not want dividends. She noted that the seven companies paying out less than a third of their earnings in divi-

| **TABLE 19.2** | DIVIDEND PATTERNS IN THE APPAREL INDUSTRY | | | | | | | |

This table contains dividends and earnings per share for the past 7 years for the 15 leading competitors in the apparel industry.

Company		1986	1987	1988	1989	1990	1991	1992
A	EPS	0.61	0.38	0.39	0.75	1.17	1.07	1.29
A	DPS	0.10	0.10	0.10	0.12	0.15	0.17	0.21
B	EPS	0.64	0.99	1.11	2.24	2.51	1.78	0.71
B	DPS	NA	NA	NA	0.33	0.77	0.88	0.88
C	EPS	2.10	2.91	2.51	3.32	3.63	1.71	0.96
C	DPS	0.67	0.83	1.00	1.00	1.20	1.20	0.75
D	EPS	1.17	1.40	1.59	1.91	2.09	2.10	1.20
D	DPS	0.43	0.48	0.54	0.61	0.75	0.85	0.90
E	EPS	0.17	0.26	0.34	0.53	0.99	1.42	2.00
E	DPS	0.01	0.00	0.00	0.00	0.10	0.16	0.23
F	EPS	1.21	2.43	1.78	2.67	0.20	−2.21	−0.10
F	DPS	0.24	0.24	0.25	0.26	0.27	0.23	0.20
G	EPS	−0.97	−1.14	−2.61	0.29	0.02	0.58	0.58
G	DPS	0.20	0.00	0.00	0.00	0.00	0.00	0.00
H	EPS	0.47	0.74	1.42	1.96	2.17	0.64	0.93
H	DPS	0.18	0.20	0.23	0.30	0.36	0.42	0.45
I	EPS	0.90	1.27	1.54	2.94	2.44	2.54	3.00
I	DPS	0.30	0.30	0.30	0.33	0.40	0.40	0.40
J	EPS	0.55	0.64	0.56	0.68	0.70	0.74	1.08
J	DPS	0.10	0.12	0.13	0.14	0.15	0.15	0.16
K	EPS	1.69	1.94	1.89	2.29	2.09	2.47	2.65
K	DPS	0.59	0.67	0.67	0.74	0.76	0.76	0.76
L	EPS	0.04	1.03	0.60	0.56	−0.38	−0.32	1.35
L	DPS	0.05	0.10	0.10	0.10	0.10	0.10	0.10
M	EPS	1.49	0.62	0.86	0.99	−0.20	0.37	0.50
M	DPS	0.00	0.00	0.00	0.00	0.00	0.00	0.00
N	EPS	0.43	0.56	0.70	0.81	0.54	0.66	1.32
N	DPS	0.09	0.12	0.14	0.18	0.21	0.23	0.28
O	EPS	0.64	0.81	1.41	1.82	1.96	2.25	2.05
O	DPS	0.21	0.26	0.33	0.43	0.52	0.58	0.66

dends had price-earnings ratios averaging 12.8. The three companies paying out at least three-fourths of their earnings in dividends had price-earnings ratios averaging 24.8. She suggested an immediate increase in dividends in pursuit of a new target payout ratio of three-fourths of earnings.

CASE QUESTIONS

1. Describe the relationship between dividend payout ratios and price-earnings ratios for the apparel industry. Consider the importance of factors such as capital structure, sales growth, earnings per share growth, and return on equity in this analysis.
2. Describe the relationship between dividend payout ratios and market to book value ratios for the apparel industry. Consider the importance of factors such as capital structure, sales growth, earnings per share growth, and return on equity in this analysis.
3. Look at companies that either increased or decreased dividends. Does there appear to be any relationship between these changes and price-earnings ratios? Consider the importance of factors such as capital structure, sales growth, earnings per share growth, and return on equity in this analysis.
4. Look at companies that either increased or decreased their dividend payout ratios. Does there appear to be any relationship between these changes and price-earnings ratios? Consider the importance of factors such as capital structure, sales growth, earnings per share growth, and return on equity in this analysis.
5. What dividend policy do you recommend for Brand-name Corporation?

SELECTED REFERENCES

Ambarish, Ramasastry, John Kose, and Joseph Williams. "Efficient Signaling with Dividends and Investments." *Journal of Finance* 4 (June 1987): 301–320.

Asquith, Paul, and David W. Mullins, Jr. "Signaling with Dividends, Stock Repurchases, and Equity Issues." *Financial Management* 15 (Autumn 1986): 27–44.

Baker, H. Kent, Gail E. Farrelly, and Richard Edelman. "A Survey of Management Views on Dividend Policy." *Financial Management* 14 (Autumn 1985): 78–84.

Bierman, Harold, Jr., and Jerome E. Hass. "Investment Cut-off Rates and Dividend Policy." *Financial Management* 12 (Winter 1983): 19–24.

Black, Fischer, and Myron Scholes. "The Effects of Dividend Yield and Dividend Policy on Common Stock Prices and Returns." *Journal of Financial Economics* 1 (May 1974): 1–5.

Brickley, J. A. "Shareholder Wealth, Information Signaling, and the Specially Designated Dividend." *Journal of Financial Economics* 12 (1983): 187–210.

DeAngelo, Harry. "Corporate Financial Policy and Corporate Control." *Journal of Financial Economics* 20 (January–February 1988): 87–127.

DeAngelo, Harry, Linda DeAngelo, and Douglas Skinner. "Dividend Signaling and the Disappearance of Sustained Earnings Growth." *Journal of Financial Economics* 40 (March 1996): 341–371.

Eades, Kenneth M., Patrick J. Hess, and E. Hahn Kim. "Market Rationality and Dividend Announcements." *Journal of Financial Economics* 14 (December 1985): 581–604.

Elton, Edwin J., Martin J. Gruber, and Joel Rentzler. "The Ex-Dividend Day Behavior of Stock Prices; a Re-Examination of the Clientele Effect: A Comment." *Journal of Finance* 39 (June 1984): 551–561.

Fama, Eugene. "Agency Problems and the Theory of the Firm." *Journal of Political Economy* (April 1980): 288–307.

Feldstein, Martin, and Jerry Green. "Why Do Companies Pay Dividends?" *American Economic Review* (March 1983): 17–30.

Gordon, Roger H., and David F. Bradford. "Taxation and the Stock Market Valuation of Capital Gains and Dividends: Theory and Empirical Results." *Journal of Public Economics* 14 (October 1980): 109–136.

Grinblatt, Mark S., Ronald W. Masulis, and Sheridan Titman. "The Valuation Effects of Stock Splits and Stock Dividends." *Journal of Financial Economics* 13 (December 1984): 461–490.

Hubbard, Jeff, and Roni Michaely. "Do Investors Ignore Dividend Taxation? A Reexamination of the Citizens Utilities Case." *Journal of Financial and Quantitative Analysis* 32 (March 1997): 117–135.

Impson, Michael. "Market Reaction to Dividend-Decrease Announcements: Public Utilities vs. Unregulated Industrial Firms." *Journal of Financial Research* (Fall 1997): 407–422.

Jensen, Gerald R., and James M. Johnson. "The Dynamics of Corporate Dividend Reductions." *Financial Management* 24 (Winter 1995): 31–51.

Kalay, Avner, and Uri Loewenstein. "The Informational Content of Dividend Announcements." *Journal of Financial Economics* 16 (July 1986): 373–388.

———. "Predictable Events and Excess Returns: The Case of Dividend Announcements." *Journal of Financial Economics* 14 (September 1985): 423–449.

Kose, John, and Joseph Williams. "Dividends, Dilution, and Taxes: A Signaling Equilibrium." *Journal of Finance* 40 (September 1985): 1053–1094.

Kwan, C. "Efficient Market Tests of the Informational Content of Dividend Announcements: Critique and Extension." *Journal of Financial and Quantitative Analysis* 16 (June 1981): 193–206.

Litzenberger, Robert H., and Krishan Ramiswamy. "The Effects of Dividends on Common Stock Prices: Tax Effects or Information Effects?" *Journal of Finance* 37 (May 1982): 429–444.

Madden, Bartly J. "Make Shareholders a Partner in the Dividend Payout Decision." *Midland Corporate Finance Journal* 5 (Summer 1987): 39–45.

Menartzi, Shlomo, Roni Michaely, and Richard Thaler. "Do Changes in Dividends Signal the Future or the Past?" *Journal of Finance* 52 (July 1997): 1007–1034.

Michaely, Roni, Richard H. Thaler, and Kent L. Womack. "Price Reactions to Dividend Initiations and Omissions: Overreaction or Drift?" *Journal of Finance* 50 (June 1995): 573–608.

Miller, Merton H., and Franco Modigliani. "Dividend Policy, Growth, and the Valuation of Shares." *Journal of Business* 34 (October 1961): 411–433.

Miller, Merton H., and Kevin Rock. "Dividend Policy under Asymmetric Information." *Journal of Finance* 40 (September 1985): 1031–1051.

Miller, Merton H., and Myron S. Scholes. "Dividends and Taxes." *Journal of Financial Economics* 6 (December 1978): 333–364.

Moore, William T., and William L. Sartoris. "Dividends and Taxes: Another Look at the Electric Utility Industry." *Financial Review* 20 (February 1985): 1–20.

O'Brien, Thomas J., and Paul A. Vanderheiden. "Empirical Measurement of Operating Leverage for Growing Firms." *Financial Management* 16 (Summer 1987): 45–53.

Papaioannou, George J., and Craig M. Savarese. "Corporate Dividend Policy Response to the Tax Reform Act of 1986." *Financial Management* 23 (Spring 1994): 56–63.

Peterson, Pamela P., David P. Peterson, and James S. Ang. "Direct Evidence on the Marginal Rate of Taxation on Dividend Income." *Journal of Financial Economics* 14 (June 1985): 267–282.

Peterson, Pamela P., David P. Peterson, and Normal H. Moore. "The Adoption of New-Issue Dividend Reimbursment Plans and Shareholder Wealth." *Financial Review* 22 (May 1987): 221–232.

Phillips, Aaron L., H. Kent Baker, and Richard B. Edelman. "The Market Reaction to Discontinuing Regular Stock Dividends." *Financial Review* 32 (November 1997): 801–819.

Prezas, Alexandros P. "Effects of Debt on the Degrees of Operating and Financial Leverage." *Financial Management* 16 (Summer 1987): 39–44.

Rankine, Graeme, and Earl K. Stice. "The Market Reaction to the Choice of Accounting Method for Stock Splits and Large Stock Dividends." *Journal of Financial and Quantitative Analysis* 32 (June 1997): 161–182.

Richardson, Gordon, Stephen E. Sefcik, and Rex Thompson. "A Test of Dividend Irrelevance Using Volume Reactions to a Change in Dividend Policy." *Journal of Financial Economics* 17 (December 1986): 313–333.

Ross, Stephen. "The Determination of Financial Structures: The Incentive Signaling Approach." *Bell Journal of Economics* 8 (Spring 1977): 23–40.

Rozeff, Michael S. "Growth, Beta and Agency Costs as Determinants of Dividend Payout Ratios." *Journal of Financial Research* 5 (Fall 1982): 249–259.

Schooley, Diane K., and L. Dwayne Barney, Jr. "Using Dividend Policy and Managerial Ownership to Reduce Agency Costs." *Journal of Financial Research* 17 (Fall 1994): 363–373.

Shefrin, Hersh M., and Meir Statman. "Explaining Investor Preference for Cash Dividends." *Journal of Financial Economics* 13 (June 1984): 253–282.

Stock, Duane. "Dividend Changes of Financially Weak Firms." *Financial Review* 21 (November 1986): 419–431.

Williams, Joseph. "Efficient Signaling with Dividends, Investment, and Stock Repurchases." *Journal of Finance* 43 (July 1988): 737–747.

C H A P T E R   2 0 |

INTERACTIONS BETWEEN INVESTMENT AND FINANCING DECISIONS

After completing this chapter you should be able to:

1. Explain to a friend the separation principle in regard to wealth created from investing in positive net present value projects versus wealth transferred or created from changing the capital structure (or financing mix).
2. Differentiate between projects that transfer wealth from one financing source to another, ones that create wealth, and ones that do both.
3. Describe how certain projects can change the overall risk of the firm in such a way that the optimal mix of debt and equity may change and the cost of debt and/or equity may change.
4. Recognize projects that have special financing attached to them and which should be considered when evaluating their acceptability.
5. Calculate an Arditti-Levy net present value that adjusts for a change in the financing mix.
6. Compute a Myers adjusted net present value.
7. Determine an equity residual net present value.
8. Recognize situations that may have an investment and financing interaction.

The state of Massachusetts wanted to attract new business to a state that was losing its traditional industrial base. Under the leadership of governor and presidential aspirant, Michael Dukakis, the state provided $500 million of low-interest financing in 1987 for companies willing to expand in Massachusetts.

For reasons discussed in the following paragraphs, we generally operate under the assumption that capital budgeting decisions can be separated from capital structure decisions. This assumption does not hold, though, if you are choosing between factory sites in Connecticut and sites in Massachusetts. The interest savings from the choice of a Massachusetts site must be factored into the decision. Similar circumstances occur when lease options are available or when manufacturers offer incentive financing. Decision making when financing and investment decisions interact are covered in this chapter.

THE SEPARATION PRINCIPLE |

The *separation principle* is one of the traditional bases for capital budgeting. The separation principle states that the attractiveness of a capital investment is independent of how that particular investment is financed. A review of the reasons for the separation principle creates the foundation for dealing with exceptions. The separation principle gained prominence in capital budgeting as a response to often erroneous attempts to make undesirable investments look desirable by tying them to debt financing. Suppose, for example, Pitt Corporation, a company with $1 million of capital, is financed with 40 percent debt and 60 percent equity. The after-tax costs of debt and equity are 15 percent and 8 percent, respectively, so the weighted average cost of capital is:

$$\text{WACC} = .6(.15) + .4(.08) = 12.2\%$$

A manager at Pitt is trying to justify a proposed $200,000 capital investment, but the investment has an internal rate of return of only 12.1 percent. The manager tries to justify the investment by saying that the project can be financed entirely with debt.

To see the fallacy of this justification and the importance of the separation principle, consider what happens if Pitt invests in this project. Assume the company was previously at its optimal capital structure, that the cost of equity will rise to 16 percent with the increased leverage, and the cost of debt will rise to 9 percent. The weighted average cost of capital after the new asset is acquired with all-debt financing will be:

$$\text{WACC} = .5(.16) + .5(.09) = 12.5\%$$

To find the marginal cost of capital if the investment is financed exclusively with debt, recognize that Pitt must earn an after-tax return of 12.5 percent on $1,200,000 of assets, whereas the previous requirement was that it earn 12.2 percent on $1,000,000 of assets. Thus, the required after-tax benefit increases by:

$$\text{Increase in required benefit} = .125(\$1,200,000) - .122(\$1,000,000) = \$28,000$$

This means that the marginal cost of capital is $28,000/$200,000 = 14%.

If your company is at its optimal capital structure, it minimizes its marginal cost of capital for a new project by financing with the existing mix. If your company is not at its optimal capital structure, you need not make a capital investment to get to the optimal structure. You can gain the benefit of moving to the optimal capital structure by issuing one type of security and buying back the other. Thus, the company will maximize the wealth of the shareholders by applying the separation principle. The shareholder wealth-maximizing company will create the capital structure that minimizes the weighted average cost of capital, then choose investments with internal rates of return above that weighted average cost of capital.

Because of flotation costs and economies of scale, in securities issues, a company may move around the optimal capital structure, issuing debt one time it needs money and issuing equity the next time. The separation principle still holds in these cases because any movement away from the optimal capital structure is purely temporary and only for the purpose of minimizing transaction costs. You would not maximize value by selecting 9 percent return projects one month because it was the month you were issuing debt, knowing you would be turning down 14 percent return investments the next month because you would be issuing equity that month.

EXCEPTIONS TO THE SEPARATION PRINCIPLE

The separation principle is an important response to what can otherwise be erroneous decisions. But, like most rules, it can be carried too far. There are situations in which the separation principle does not hold. An investment may transfer wealth from creditors to stockholders, or vice versa, and that wealth transfer must be considered in capital budgeting. Alternately, the capital investment may change the risk characteristics of the firm, and change the optimal debt ratio. Some investments also create the opportunity for special financing such as industrial revenue bonds, and those benefits must be recognized. This chapter is devoted to dealing with these exceptions to the separation principle.

WEALTH TRANSFERS AND CAPITAL INVESTMENT DECISIONS

Litzenberger documented wealth transfer effects in his study of the Unocal and Phillips Petroleum restructurings.[1] To see how a wealth transfer might occur, assume that the Pitt Corporation from the previous example has $400,000 of long-term debt and $600,000 of equity outstanding. The company can issue $200,000 of new debt without refinancing the old debt. The increased debt ratio makes old debt more risky—the required return increases and the price falls—but Pitt need not pay the higher required return because the interest rate is already contractually set. The existing creditors simply lose wealth. The necessary after-tax benefit before the expansion was:

$$.15(\$600,000) + .08(\$400,000) = \$122,000$$

The necessary after-tax benefit after financing a new $200,000 asset entirely with debt is:

$$.16(\$600,000) + .08(\$400,000) + .09(\$200,000) = \$146,000$$

---

[1]Robert H. Litzenberger, "Some Observations on Capital Structure and the Impact of Recent Recapitalizations on Share Prices," *Journal of Financial and Quantitative Analysis* 21 (March 1986): 59–71.

The marginal cost of capital for a $200,000 investment is therefore:

Marginal Cost of Capital = ($146,000 − $122,000) ÷ $200,000 = 12.0%

With wealth transfer from creditors to shareholders, the marginal cost of capital is 12 percent, below the weighted average cost of capital at the optimal capital structure. Thus, the wealth transfer effect may make an otherwise undesirable capital investment attractive. If it was necessary to pay the higher interest rate to all creditors, the all-debt financing would result in a 14 percent marginal cost of capital, well above the 12.2 percent cost at the optimal capital structure.

Other considerations often negate the wealth transfer effect. First, one must be cautious in assigning the benefit of wealth transfer to a particular investment by decreasing the marginal cost of capital for that investment. If you can issue debt and buy back equity, the same wealth transfer can be achieved independent of investment decisions. Even if wealth transfer can be achieved only through acquisition of assets, the benefit will generally be available regardless of which asset is acquired. Consequently, the marginal cost of capital based on wealth transfer must generally be applied to all proposed investments in choosing the appropriate investments. Consequently, the wealth transfer effect generally results in a cost of capital schedule such as that in Figure 20.1 rather than a lower cost of capital for a specific investment. Furthermore, the stepped cost of capital curve illustrated in Figure 20.1 occurs only if it is not possible to issue additional debt to buy back equity.

The wealth transfer benefit would accrue to a particular investment only if there was some characteristic of that investment that meant that it alone could be used to capture the wealth transfer benefit. This could be the case

| **FIGURE 20.1** **COST OF CAPITAL SCHEDULE WITH WEALTH TRANSFER**

This shows a lower cost of capital up to some amount of money that results from a wealth transfer action, with the marginal cost of capital being above the old costs of capital beyond that amount.

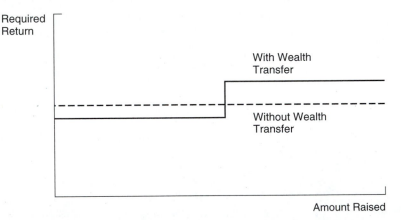

if, for example, one particular investment created the opportunity for secured financing.

Second, restrictive covenants associated with debt issues are specifically designed to limit the potential for wealth transfers of this type. If the old debt has restrictive covenants limiting total debt to 40 percent of capital, Pitt must retire the old debt and replace it with new debt costing 9 percent after-tax. This eliminates the opportunity for wealth transfer and means that the marginal cost of capital is minimized by staying at the old debt ratio.

Future financing needs are an important consideration in wealth transfer situations. When the old debt matures, you must either issue higher interest rate debt or change the capital structure to minimize the cost of capital again. Asset acquisition in future periods also results in increased needs for financing. The past manipulations may affect the reputation of your company and affect the future cost of funds. Thus, the weighted average cost of capital for each future period must be considered in the analysis.

Example. For the previous example, assume that Pitt Corporation's existing assets will generate a perpetuity of $122,000. The proposed new asset will generate an after-tax cash flow of $83,413 at the end of each year for 3 years. The debt with an 8 percent after-tax interest rate must be repaid over the first 2 years. If Pitt takes advantage of the wealth transfer opportunity now, its reputation will be affected. Investors will believe the company intends to finance with one-half debt even if it temporarily lowers the debt ratio. Therefore, the required interest rate on new debt will be 9 percent after tax, and the required return on equity will be 16 percent, even if the company lowers its debt ratio. As a result, the optimal capital structure in the future is half debt after Pitt has once moved to that position. The present values of all future cash flows are shown in Table 20.1 for both the all-debt financing of the expansion and financing of the expansion using 40 percent debt.

In examining the present values in Table 20.1, note that discount rates change from period to period with the changed leverage alternative. Applying present value principles for changing interest rates that were developed in Chapter 3, the present values are:

$$\text{Year I flow: } \frac{204,413}{1.121} = \$182,348$$

$$\text{Year 2 flow: } \frac{204,413}{1.121 \cdot 1.121} = \$162,666$$

$$\text{Year 3 flow: } \frac{204,413}{1.121 \cdot 1.121 \cdot 1.125} = \$144,594$$

At the start of year 4, Pitt will have an annuity of $122,000 a year forever. With the changed leverage, the value of that annuity, as of the end of year 3 or the start of year 4, is $122,000 ÷ .125 = $976,000. With changed leverage, the value of that annuity, as of now, is:

| **TABLE 20.1** PRESENT VALUE WITH AND WITHOUT A CAPITAL STRUCTURE SHIFT

This table shows the present value of all future cash flows for Pitt Corporation with and without an attempt by managers to transfer wealth from existing creditors by increasing the debt ratio.

Year	1	2	3	$4 - \infty$
CASH FLOWS				
Existing assets	$122,000	$122,000	$122,000	$122,000
New asset	83,413	83,413	83,413	=
Total cash flow	$205,413	$205,413	$205,413	$122,000
UNCHANGED LEVERAGE:				
Required return	12.2%	12.2%	12.2%	12.2%
Total cash flow	$205,413	$205,413	$205,413	$122,000
Present value	$183,078	$163,171	$145,428	$707,981
Total present value = $1,199,658				
CHANGED LEVERAGE:				
Required return	12.1%	12.1%	12.5%	12.5%
Present value	$183,242	$163,462	$145,300	$690,377
Total present value = $1,182,380				

$$Present\ value\ of\ annuity = \frac{976,000}{1.121 \cdot 1.121 \cdot 1.125} = \$690,377$$

For the particular example in Table 20.1, the higher cost of capital later offsets the benefit of a lower initial cost of capital. Wealth was transferred away from existing creditors, but the wealth transfer was not sufficient to offset the longer-term detrimental effects of the leverage change. Likewise, the proposed capital investment is not attractive because it was attractive only if the marginal cost of capital could be brought below 12.1 percent.

If Pitt were able to refinance at the end of year three and return to a 12.2 percent cost of capital, a different picture would emerge. Likewise, existing debt with very long maturity would increase the attractiveness of the change in capital structure. On the other hand, a need for additional funds for other new investments would further decrease the attractiveness of the capital structure change if it was not possible to return to the old capital structure later.

INFORMATION ASYMMETRY AND WEALTH TRANSFER

Wealth transfer can also occur because investor expectations differ from those of management. Suppose, for example, that Garden Corporation has annual income of $100 and has 100 shares of stock, so the earnings per share are $1.00.

Income is distributed as dividends, and investors expect this level of income to continue indefinitely. Investors require a 20 percent return, so the price of a share of stock is $5.00.

Management at Garden Corporation knows that investors are wrong. Earnings and dividends will double next year with no new investment, and will stay at that same level forever. Once investors see the new earnings, the price of the stock will double to $10.

Garden Corporation also has a new investment opportunity requiring $100 of new equity, and promising perpetual income and dividends of $30 a year. With a 20 percent required return, the investment obviously has a positive net present value. The investment must be made now, and investors do not know that the new investment will provide superior returns, so 20 additional shares of stock must be sold at $5.00 a share. After earnings from existing assets double, the earnings per share and anticipated stock price will be as follows:

$$\text{Earnings per share} = \$230 \div 120 = \$1.92$$

$$\text{Anticipated stock price} = \$1.92 \div .20 = \$9.60$$

Because investors are uninformed, and the current stock price is unchanged by the investment, the stock price a year later is depressed. Wealth is created by the new investment, but that wealth and more is transferred from old to new stockholders.[2] This analysis would suggest that an otherwise profitable investment should be forgone. Before carrying this point too far, it is important to note that managers frequently overestimate their prospects.[3]

INVESTMENTS THAT CHANGE THE RISK CHARACTERISTICS OF THE FIRM |

In Chapters 14 and 15 we focused on how systematic risk and other sensitivities to overall market conditions affect required return for an individual capital investment. Now that capital structure principles have been developed, we can combine concepts from portfolio theory and capital structure theory to also consider the impact of nonsystematic risk on required return for an individual capital investment. This section begins with investments that change the optimal mix of debt and equity, but do not change the component costs of either of these sources of capital. The analysis is then extended to consider investments that change both component costs and optimal mix.

[2]The problem that arises when investors do not correctly recognize future investment opportunities is developed further in John C. Woods and Maury R. Tandall, "The Net Present Value of Future Investment Opportunities: Its Impact on Shareholder Wealth and Implications for Capital Budgeting Theory," *Financial Management* 18 (Summer 1989): 85–92.

[3]David I. Levine, "Do Corporate Executives Have Rational Expectations?" *Journal of Business* 66 (April 1993): 271–293.

Investments that Change the Optimal Debt Ratio

Recall from Chapter 13 that the variance of returns for a portfolio depends on the variances of the assets in that portfolio, and on their covariances. If the correlation between two assets is less than perfect, combining those two assets may result in a portfolio with less variance than either of the assets considered alone. This benefit of diversification is not closely related to systematic risk, which is sensitive to one or more overall market conditions. Thus, two investments may have identical betas, and still result in a portfolio with less variance than that possessed by either investment independently. Portfolio effects were measured in terms of returns in Chapter 13, but can also be measured in terms of cash flows.

Recall from Chapter 17 that the optimal amount of debt is affected by the risk of not being able to take advantage of tax savings from interest and by the risk of bankruptcy. These risks can be reduced, and the optimal debt ratio increased, by increasing the stability of income and cash flow. Therefore, an investment that has a low correlation with the company's existing assets can increase the optimal debt ratio even if systematic risk is not affected.

In the simplest case of changing debt capacity, the component costs remain unchanged, but the optimal debt ratio increases due to low or negative correlation between cash flows for the investment and cash flows for the company's existing assets. In this case, the marginal cost of capital (MCC) for the investment is based on the increase in the total optimal amount of debt if the investment is accepted:

$$MCC = \frac{k_d \times \textit{Increased debt} + k_e \times \textit{Increased equity}}{\textit{Total investment required}} \qquad \text{(20-1)}$$

where k_d and k_e are respectively the after-tax costs of debt and equity.

Example. Pitt Corporation in the previous examples had a capital structure consisting of $400,000 of debt and $600,000 of equity before expansion, and this was believed to be optimal for the existing asset base. The after-tax costs were 8 percent and 15 percent respectively. Pitt was considering a new $200,000 capital investment. Suppose that this investment would improve stability of cash flow and profit, so the optimal debt ratio with this new investment would be 0.45. This means that:

$$\text{new debt} = .45(\$1,200,000) - .40(\$1,000,000) = \$140,000$$

and new equity will therefore be $200,000 - $140,000 = $60,000.

In other words, the marginal financing for the investment will be 70 percent debt and 30 percent equity. Assuming the component costs do not change, the required return for this investment is

$$MCC = .7(.08) + .3(.15) = \underline{10.1\%}$$

INVESTMENTS THAT CHANGE THE OPTIMAL DEBT RATIO AND COMPONENT COSTS

It is quite likely that an investment that changes the company's optimal debt ratio will also change the component costs of funds. In this case, the marginal cost of capital is again the guideline. In the absence of an opportunity to transfer wealth from creditors to shareholders, the marginal cost of the increase in debt as a result of adding a new asset is:

$$\text{Marginal cost of debt} = \frac{k_{dn}\text{Debt}_n - k_{do}\text{Debt}_o}{\text{Debt}_n - \text{Debt}_o} \qquad (20\text{-}2)$$

where k_{do} and k_{dn} are respectively the costs of debt at the old and new optimal debt ratios. Debt_o and Debt_n are the optimal amounts of debt before and after acquisition of the asset.

The marginal cost of equity is defined in a similar manner:

$$\text{Marginal cost of equity} = \frac{k_{en}\text{Equity}_n - k_{eo}\text{Equity}_o}{\text{Equity}_n - \text{Equity}_o} \qquad (20\text{-}3)$$

where k_{eo} and k_{en} are respectively the costs of equity before and after acquisition of the new asset. Equity_o and Equity_n are the optimal amounts of equity before and after acquisition of the new asset.

Example. For Pitt Corporation in the previous examples, assume again that there is no opportunity to transfer wealth from existing creditors to stockholders, or vice versa. Assume again that the proposed new asset will increase the optimal debt ratio from .40 to .45. With acquisition and optimal financing of the new asset, the after-tax cost of debt will decrease to 7.9 percent and the cost of equity will increase to 15.2 percent. The marginal costs of debt and equity are therefore:

$$\text{Marginal cost of debt} = \frac{.079 \times 540{,}000 - .08 \times 400{,}000}{540{,}000 - 400{,}000} = 7.614\%$$

$$\text{Marginal cost of equity} = \frac{.152 \times 660{,}000 - .15 \times 600{,}000}{660{,}000 - 600{,}000} = 17.200\%$$

Since the $200,000 increase in assets results in an increase of $140,000 in the optimal amount of debt, the debt ratio for the investment is .7, and the marginal cost of capital for the investment is:

$$\text{MCC} = .7 \times .07614 + .3 \times .1720 = 10.490\%$$

You can find the same marginal cost of capital without finding component costs. First, find the required earnings (after tax but before interest) with and without the new asset. Then, express the required earnings as a percent of the increases in assets:

MCC =

$$\frac{(.079 \times 540,000 + .152 \times 660,000) - (.08 \times 400,000 + .15 \times 600,000)}{1,200,000 - 1,000,000}$$

$$= 10.490\%$$

In looking at the marginal cost of capital in this way, it is important to stress again the difference between an asset that changes the optimal amount of debt and the decision to finance an asset in a certain way even if the asset does not change the optimal amount of debt. The company might actually finance one asset entirely with debt, recognizing economies of scale in raising money and realizing that it will move back to its optimal debt ratio by issuing equity to finance another project next month. This type of incremental financing does not change the marginal cost of capital for the investment.

The difficulty in applying the marginal cost of capital concept with changing debt capacity should not be underestimated or trivialized. Estimation of investor response to both a new asset and a new financing mix is hardly a trivial process. As discussed in Chapter 17, though, there are methods available for making estimates. Making decisions based on the best estimates available is better than simply ignoring the possible impact of a new asset on the company's optimal capital structure and component costs of capital.[4]

SPECIAL FINANCING OPPORTUNITIES AND CAPITAL INVESTMENT EVALUATION |

Some investments generate special financing opportunities that would not be available if the asset were not acquired. Low interest rate incentive financing for the purchase of automobiles is the most visible example. Use of industrial revenue bonds to provide low-interest loans, such as the $1 billion provided to businesses by the state of New Jersey, is another example. Likewise the bonds sold by the Dade County (Florida) Port Authority on behalf of Eastern Airlines provided low-cost financing for investments made at a specific location. Real estate

---

[4]For additional work on the marginal cost of capital for an investment with changes in the optimal capital structure, see Stewart C. Myers, "Interactions of Corporate Financing and Investment Decisions—Implications for Capital Budgeting," *Journal of Finance* 29 (March 1974): 1–25; John D. Martin and David F. Scott, Jr., "Debt Capacity and the Capital Budgeting Decision," *Financial Management* 5 (Summer 1976): 7–14; Thomas E. Conine, Jr., "Debt Capacity and the Capital Budgeting Decision: Comment," *Financial Management* 9 (Spring 1980): 20–22; John D. Martin and David F. Scott, Jr., "Debt Capacity and the Capital Budgeting Decision: A Revisitation," *Financial Management* 9 (Spring 1980): 23–26; and S. Ghon Rhee and Franklin L. McCarthy, "Corporate Debt Capacity and Capital Budgeting Analysis," *Financial Management* 11 (Summer 1982): 42–50.

investors often find that the type and availability of financing depend on the particular property being acquired. Leases are another example of special financing, and those are discussed in Chapter 21.

Special financing can be recognized through adjustment to the weighted average cost of capital, but proper specification of the weighted average cost of capital is difficult because the amount and maturity of the financing may not coincide with the optimal financing mix for the investment. Calculations can be simplified and risk of error reduced if the net present value of the project is first computed as if special financing were not available. Then, the net advantage of the special financing (NAF) is added to the net present value to give an adjusted net present value. This approach is particularly easy to use if the investment's risk is the same as the average risk of the company or a division for which the weighted average cost of capital has already been determined.

The net advantage of financing is the present value of the difference between the after-tax principal and interest payments for special financing and what would be required for regular financing with the same maturity. We assume special debt financing since that is the type generally observed. The formula for the net advantage of special financing (NAF) is:

$$\text{NAF} = \text{Amount of special financing} - \left[\sum_{t=1}^{n} \frac{P_t + \text{Int}_t(1 - T_c)}{(1 + k_d)^t} \right] \quad \text{(20-4)}$$

where P_t and Int_t are the principal and interest payments on the special financing. T_c is the corporate tax rate and k_d is the cost of the corporation's regular debt.[5]

Example. Philadelphia Corporation has a weighted average cost of capital of 12 percent. The corporate tax rate is 35 percent and the company can borrow at an interest cost of 10 percent. The company is considering a new plant that would cost $8 million and generate year-end cash flows of $1 million after tax but before considering interest. The plant would have the same average risk as the company's other assets and would have a 20-year life. The net present value is therefore:

$$\text{NPV} = \$1,000,000 \text{PVA}|_{20\text{yrs},12\%} - \$8,000,000 = -\$530,556$$

The investment is, therefore, unattractive.

However, the community is willing to provide a $6 million loan with a 6 percent interest rate and the entire principal due in 10 years. The net advantage of the special financing is $6 million, minus the present value of the principal payment and after-tax interest payments, discounted at the after-tax cost of the company's regular debt:

[5]The amount of special financing is used in the formula instead of the present value of principal and interest payments on regular debt because the present value of after-tax principal and interest payments on regular debt, discounted at the after-tax cost of debt, always equals the amount borrowed.

$$\text{NAF} = \$6,000,000 - \$6,000,000 \times .06 \times (1 - .35)\text{PVA}|_{10\text{yrs},6.5\%} - \$6,000,000/1.065^{10}$$

$$= \underline{\underline{\$1,121,458}}$$

The net present value with special financing (NPVF) is then:

$$\text{NPVF} = \text{NPV} + \text{NAF} = -\$530,556 + \$1,121,458 = \$590,902$$

The special financing achieves the community's objective. The capital investment is unattractive without special financing, but becomes attractive with special financing. The investment will increase shareholder wealth.

SOME ALTERNATE METHODS FOR DEALING WITH FINANCING MIX |

While the net present value has been espoused throughout this book, alternatives, such as the internal rate of return and payback, also were included because they are used in practice. Likewise, there are several formulations of the net present value that recognize the impact of leverage. Each of these is used in practice, and is therefore worthy of note.[6]

STANDARD NET PRESENT VALUE

The alternate methods should be compared to the standard net present value method, which uses a weighted average cost of capital to discount future cash flows. To put everything in comparable terms, the net present value method using the weighted average cost of capital—the method used throughout this book—is:[7]

$$\text{NPV(WACC)} = \sum_{t=1}^{n} \frac{\text{EBIT}_t(1 - T_c) + \text{Dep}_t - I_o}{(1 + k_o)^t} \qquad \textbf{(20-5)}$$

where EBIT_t is earnings before interest and tax in period t, Dep_t is depreciation in period t, T_c is the corporate tax rate, and I_o is the initial investment. Depreciation is added in arriving at cash flow because it was deducted in arriving at EBIT even though it was not a cash expense. The marginal cost of capital applicable to the investment, k_o, is based on the weighted average cost of capital concept. This will be the weighted average cost of capital for the firm unless the investment changes the optimal debt ratio or the component costs. In these cases, the marginal cost of capital will be determined as explained earlier in this chapter.

---

[6]For a more detailed discussion of these alternate approaches, see Donald R. Chambers, Robert S. Harris, and John J. Pringle, "Treatment of Financing Mix in Analyzing Investment Opportunities," *Financial Management* 11 (Summer 1982): 24–41.

[7]To simplify the discussion, we abstract from other cash flows, such as change in net working capital.

It should be noted that k_o incorporates both the risk of the investment and the financing mix. It is generally assumed that k_o remains constant over the life of the investment, although this assumption is not required. For k_o to remain constant, it is generally necessary that the debt ratio and risk remain constant over the life of the investment.

ARDITTI-LEVY NET PRESENT VALUE

An alternate to the standard net present value has been supported by Arditti and Levy.[8] This approach is often used by public utilities; Southwestern Bell Telephone company used this method until recently. The Arditti-Levy net present value formula, NPV(AL) is:

$$NPV(AL) = \sum_{t=1}^{n} \frac{(EBIT_t - Int_t)(1 - T_c) + Dep_t + Int_t - I_o}{(1 + k_{AL})^t} \tag{20-6}$$

where $k_{AL} = wk_d/(1 - T_c) + (1 - w)k_e$. In this equation, $k_d/(1 - T_c)$ is the before-tax marginal cost of debt for the investment. Int_t is the increase in interest expense as a result of the investment, and k_e is the marginal cost of equity for the project.

The difference between the Arditti-Levy method and the standard weighted average cost of capital approach is that the tax saving from interest is recognized in the numerator rather than the denominator. The Arditti-Levy method gives the same net present value as the standard net present value if the debt is held at a constant percent of value throughout the asset's life.

Public utility commissions, which set prices, aim for net present values of zero, based on the Arditti-Levy method. After the commissions estimate k_{AL}, they set rates so that their estimate of k_{AL} can be achieved. The regulated utilities then evaluate investments using k_{AL} and Equation 20-6.

ADJUSTED PRESENT VALUE

The adjusted present value method was developed by Myers to consider interactions between investment and financing decisions.[9] The formula for the adjusted present value is:

$$APV = \sum_{t=1}^{n} \frac{EBIT_t(1 - T_c) + Dep_t}{(1 + k_u)^t} - I_o + \sum_{t=1}^{n} \frac{T_c Int_t}{(1 + R_d)^t} \tag{20-7}$$

where k_u is the required return appropriate for an unleveraged investment, and R_d is the interest rate on the corporation's debt:

[8]Fred D. Arditti and Haim Levy, "The Weighted Average Cost of Capital as a Cutoff Rate: A Critical Examination of the Classical Textbook Weighted Average," *Financial Management* 6 (Fall 1977): 24–34.

[9]Myers, "Interactions of Corporate Financing and Investment Decisions."

$$R_d(1 - T_c) = k_d$$

With a little manipulation, it can be seen that the cash flows discounted in the adjusted present value are the same as those discounted in the Arditti-Levy approach. The difference is that one required return is used for the interest tax shield and another is used for other cash flows. The adjusted present value is different from the standard net present value and the Arditti-Levy net present value, except under special conditions. The adjusted present value avoids the necessity of assuming that debt remains a constant percent of value. Unfortunately, it requires estimation of the debt ratio for each future period to estimate interest expense in future periods. This may be difficult because interest expense is not limited to debt specifically used to finance the investment, but depends on the investment's contribution to the corporation's debt capacity each period. The model also appears to be based on an implied assumption that debt results in tax shields, but that there are no other costs or benefits associated with debt. In other words, agency costs and bankruptcy costs are assumed to be unaffected by debt. The adjusted present value would increase with all increases in the ratio of debt to total assets.

A modified version of the adjusted present value is used in Chapter 21 for lease analysis.

EQUITY RESIDUAL NET PRESENT VALUE

The equity residual method treats financing alternatives by focusing entirely on the cash flows to equity holders. The formula for the equity residual net present value, NPV(ER), is:

$$NPV(ER) = \sum_{t=1}^{n} \frac{(EBIT_t - Int_t)(1 - T_c) + Dep_t + (B_t - B_{t-1})}{(1 + k_e)^t} - (I_o - B_o) \qquad \text{(20-8)}$$

where B_t is the amount of debt supported by the investment at time t, and B_o is the initial amount of debt used to finance the investment.

The equity residual method has intuitive appeal in that it focuses on the cash flows to shareholders. The equity residual net present value method is the same as the standard net present value if debt is a constant percent of value throughout the asset's life. Like the adjusted present value, the equity residual net present value provides a method for dealing with changes in capital structure over the life of an asset. It also provides a method of dealing with differences in contribution to debt capacity between assets.

The equity residual method is particularly popular with financial institutions. They tend to view borrowed money as their basic raw material rather than a component of a capital structure. Also, new regulations set equity capital requirements that vary by type of asset held. Consequently, bank managers are turning from a return on total assets focus to a return on equity focus. Of course, use of the equity residual method does not change the general principles with regard to the marginal amount of debt and equity assigned to a particular project. The equity residual method should not be used as a justification for the type of erroneous analysis that was illustrated at the beginning of this chapter.

Example. Fullerton Corporation is considering a new $1 million automated cutter. For simplicity, assume the cutter will last for only 2 years and will have no salvage value. Depreciation will be $500,000 a year. The cutter will generate earnings before interest and tax of $150,000 a year. Fullerton maintains debt equal to 75 percent of value, using the present value of future cash flows to represent value. Fullerton can borrow at 12 percent, and the required return on equity is 15 percent. The tax rate is 35 percent, and the weighted average cost of capital is therefore:

$$\text{WACC} = .75(.12)(1 - .35) + .25(.15) = \underline{.0960}$$

The annual cash flow and standard net present value is (numbers are expressed in thousands):

$$\text{Annual cash flow} = \$150(1 - .35) + \$500 = \underline{\$597.50}$$

$$NPV(WACC) = \frac{\$597.50}{1.096} + \frac{\$597.50}{1.096^2} - 1,000 = \underline{\$42.58}$$

To find the Arditti-Levy net present value, we need to know the amount of debt outstanding each period. Fullerton's policy is to have debt equal 75 percent of the value of remaining cash flows. The resulting debt schedule is in Table 20.2.

The discount rate and Arditti-Levy net present value are then:

| **TABLE 20.2** DEBT SCHEDULE FOR FULLERTON CORPORATION

This table shows the debt and interest payments each period, based on the assumption that Fullerton maintains debt equal to 75 percent of the present value of future cash flows. (Dollar amounts are in thousands.)

Year	0	1	2
Cash flow	−1,000.00	597.50	597.50
Present value of remaining cash flows (k_o = 9.6%)	1,042.58	545.16	0
Debt at end of period	781.94	408.87	0
Interest (12% of debt at the end of previous period)	93.83	49.06	

$$k_{AL} = .75(.12) + .25(.15) = .1275$$

$$NPV(AL) = \frac{(150 - 93.83)(1 - .35) + 500 + 93.83}{1.1275}$$

$$+ \frac{(150 - 49.06)(1 - .35) + 500 + 49.06}{1.1275^2} - 1,000$$

$$= \underline{\$42.58}$$

To find the adjusted present value, it is necessary to have a cost of capital for an unleveraged firm. Assume that cost of capital would be 12.7787 percent. The adjusted present value is then:

$$APV = \frac{150(1 - .35) + 500}{1.127787} + \frac{150(1 - .35) + 500}{1.127787^2} + \frac{.35(93.83)}{1.12}$$

$$+ \frac{.35(49.06)}{1.12^2} - 1,000$$

$$= \underline{\$42.58}$$

The equity residual net present value is then found as follows:

$$NPV(ER) = \frac{(150 - 93.83)(1 - .35) + 500 + (408.87 - 781.94)}{1.15}$$

$$+ \frac{(150 - 49.06)(1 - .35) + 500 + (0 - 408.87)}{1.15^2} - (1,000 - 781.94)$$

$$= \underline{\$42.58}$$

The standard net present value, Arditti-Levy net present value, and equity residual net present value are all the same as long as debt remains a constant proportion of the present value of future cash flows from the project, with the present value of future cash flows determined using the standard net present value formulation. The adjusted present value provides the same answer only with a specific assumption about the relationship between leveraged and unleveraged cost of capital.

These examples stress the importance of assumptions underlying capital budgeting. The justification for the standard net present value method is based on the assumptions that risk and optimal capital structure are not affected by the investment under consideration and remain constant in future periods. To justify the standard net present value, we further assume that debt remains a constant percentage of the remaining *value* of cash flow throughout the life of the assets. If these assumptions hold, the standard net present value equals the Arditti-Levy net present value and the equity residual net present value. However, the adjusted present value is consistent with the standard net present value only with an additional assumption about the relationship between the leveraged and unleveraged cost of capital. When the assumptions needed to justify the net present value are not met, it is necessary to consider the interactions between the investment and financing decisions of the firm in capital budgeting.

SUMMARY

The separation principle states that the selection of capital investments is independent of the selection of financing methods. There are sound reasons for this principle, as a general principle, but there are situations in which an investment affects the optimal debt ratio and/or the component costs of capital. In those cases, the financing implications of the investment must be considered in the capital budgeting process.

Wealth transfer situations are one case in which the separation principle does not hold. Some capital investments can transfer wealth from creditors to stockholders. A classic example is a project that increases total risk, thereby decreasing the value of existing debt. These investments can be analyzed using a marginal cost of capital analysis that recognizes the benefit of not having to pay a higher interest rate on existing debt. The immediate wealth increase benefits must, however, be weighed against a possible higher weighted average cost of capital in future periods when new financing is needed, and the firm is perceived as more risky.

Investments that change the optimal debt ratio without changing the component costs of capital are a special type of consideration. An investment can increase the optimal debt ratio by having less variability of earnings and cash flows, or by having low correlation with the other assets of the firm. In these cases, the marginal cost of capital for the investment depends on the optimal amounts of debt and equity that will be added as a result of the investment.

In many cases, both the optimal debt ratio and the component costs of capital are changed by the acceptance of the project. The marginal cost of capital in these cases is the total increase in earnings after tax, but before interest, necessary to service the debt and equity financing that will be used to finance the investment and move the company to its new optimal capital structure, divided by the amount of investment.

Instead of using a marginal cost of capital approach based on the weighted average costs to deal with interactions between investment and financing decisions, some companies choose other methods. The Arditti-Levy method focuses on cash flows, including interest tax shield, and finds the present value with a discount rate based on the required return on equity and before-tax cost of debt. The adjusted present value approach discounts earnings after tax and before interest at the appropriate discount rate for an unleveraged firm, and then discounts interest tax shields at the interest rate for debt. The equity residual method identifies cash flows after principal and interest payment, and then finds the present value using the marginal cost of equity as the discount rate. The standard net present value, Arditti-Levy net present value, and the equity residual net present value are identical if debt is held at a constant proportion of value and cost of capital is estimated using as weights the amount of each component as a percent of value. Managers have found each of the methods to be useful in particular situations.

QUESTIONS |

20–1. What is the separation principle?

20–2. Why has the separation principle been important in capital budgeting?

20–3. What are the main exceptions to the separation principle?

20–4. Explain how a change in capital structure might transfer wealth from creditors to stockholders.

20–5. Explain how a capital budgeting decision might transfer wealth from creditors to stockholders.

20–6. As a business manager, what is your ethical responsibility when you have an opportunity to transfer wealth from creditors to stockholders?

20–7. What are the characteristics of an investment that would cause it to increase the firm's optimal debt ratio?

20–8. Why might special low-cost financing be available for a specific investment but not available for other investments being considered by the firm?

20–9. What are the advantages and disadvantages of the adjusted present value in comparison to the standard net present value as a capital budgeting tool?

20–10. What are the advantages and disadvantages of the equity residual net present value in comparison to the standard net present value as a capital budgeting tool?

20–11. What are the conditions necessary for the net present values to be identical using the standard net present value, the Arditti-Levy net present value, and the equity residual net present value?

PROBLEMS |

(For simplicity, assume year-end cash flows.)

20–1. San Diego Corporation has debt of $1 million and equity of $1 million. The after-tax costs of debt and equity are 6 percent and 14 percent respectively. A proposed $200,000 capital investment has an internal rate of return of 9 percent. The project proponent has suggested that the investment is attractive as long as it is financed entirely with debt. An increase in the debt ratio would increase the after-tax cost of all debt to 7 percent and would increase the cost of equity to 14.25 percent. What is the marginal cost of capital if the investment is financed entirely with debt? Should the company invest in the new asset?

20-2. For San Diego Corporation (problem 1), assume that the existing debt has a very long maturity, so the higher interest cost applies only to the new debt. The company does not anticipate expansion beyond this $200,000 investment.
   a. Will the change in the debt ratio increase shareholder wealth?
   b. Should San Diego Corporation invest in this asset if it is the only way the debt ratio can be increased?
   c. Should San Diego Corporation invest in this asset if an alternative is to increase the debt ratio by issuing debt and buying back common stock?

20-3. Palo Alto Corporation has existing assets that will generate a perpetuity of $200,000 a year. The company has $1 million of debt and $1 million of equity outstanding. The after-tax costs are 7 percent and 14 percent respectively. The company is considering a new capital investment that will cost $200,000 and will generate cash flows of $20,000 a year in perpetuity. The company can finance the asset entirely with debt, but this will raise the after-tax costs of debt and equity to 8 percent and 14.25 percent, respectively.
   a. Is the investment attractive if existing debt is a perpetuity, with the interest rate already determined by contract?
   b. Is the investment attractive if existing debt must then be refinanced at an after-tax cost of 8 percent, in order to issue the new debt?

20-4. Davis Corporation is financed with $1 million of debt and $1 million of equity. The interest rate on debt is 10 percent, and the required return on equity is 16 percent. The tax rate is 40 percent.
   a. What is the weighted average cost of capital?
   b. Suppose Davis adds $100,000 of debt. As a result of this change in capital structure, the required interest rate on debt rises to 11 percent, and the required return on equity increases to 17 percent. The higher interest rate must be paid on all existing debt as well as new debt. What is the marginal cost of this additional $100,000 of debt?

20-5. For Davis Corporation (problem 4), assume that existing debt is a perpetuity, and it will therefore be necessary to pay the higher interest rate only on new debt. What is the marginal cost of the additional $100,000 of debt?

20-6. The existing assets of San Francisco Corporation generate cash flows of $100,000 a year, with a standard deviation of $50,000. A proposed capital investment will generate cash flows of $40,000 a year, with a standard deviation of $10,000. Cash flows from the new investment are uncorrelated with those from existing investments. Cash flow to service debt is 10 percent of the amount of debt outstanding. Cash flows are normally distributed and San Francisco Corporation defines its debt capacity as the amount of debt it can carry and have not more than a 5 percent probability of having inadequate cash flow to service debt. What is the contribution of the new investment to the company's optimal amount of debt?

20-7. Los Angeles Corporation has a capital structure consisting of $500,000 of debt and $500,000 of equity. The after-tax costs of debt and equity are 8 percent and 12 percent respectively. A new $200,000 capital investment will increase the optimal debt ratio to 0.55, with no change in component costs. What is the marginal cost of capital for this investment?

20–8. Riverside Corporation has a capital structure consisting of $1 million of debt and $1 million of equity. After-tax costs of debt and equity are 7 percent and 15 percent respectively. A proposed $1 million capital investment will increase the optimal debt ratio to .6, with component costs of debt and equity increasing to 7.1 percent and 15.2 percent respectively. There is no opportunity to transfer wealth from existing creditors to stockholders. What is the marginal cost of capital for this new investment?

20–9. Lodi Corporation has a weighted average cost of capital of 10 percent. The company is considering a new facility near Bakersfield. The facility will cost $10 million and will generate after-tax cash flows of $2 million a year for 7 years. The local government is willing to provide a $3 million, 5-year balloon payment loan with an after-tax interest rate of 5 percent paid annually and the entire principal paid at maturity. The after-tax cost of debt for Lodi Corporation is otherwise 7 percent. Is the investment attractive

a. without the special financing?
b. with the special financing?

20–10. The city of Berkeley wants to encourage the location of a research center in the community. The center will create high-paying jobs and will not generate pollution. The center is a nonprofit organization and therefore does not pay taxes. Another community has offered to provide a $10 million, 20-year 5 percent loan, to be repaid in equal annual installments of $802,426. Otherwise, the center would have to pay interest of 8 percent on its financing. Instead of offering low-cost financing, Berkeley may offer free land. How much must the land be worth for the value of Berkeley's incentive package to be the same as that of the competing city?

20–11. A $1 million investment will generate earnings before interest and tax of $110,000 a year for its 5-year life. Depreciation will be $200,000 a year, and the company's tax rate is 40 percent. The company maintains a capital structure of one-half debt and one-half equity. The interest rate on debt is 10 percent and the required return on equity is 14 percent. The company will repay debt so that debt remains at 50 percent of the present value of remaining cash flows. Compute the standard net present value.

20–12. For the investment in problem 11, compute the Arditti-Levy net present value.

20–13. For the investment in problem 11, compute the equity residual net present value.

20–14. For the investment in problem 11, the discount rate for an unleveraged investment is 12 percent. Compute the adjusted present value.

20–15. Valley Public Service, a regulated utility, has a marginal tax rate of 40 percent. The company is financed with 40 percent debt and 60 percent equity. The interest rate on debt is 10 percent and the cost of equity is 14 percent. The company needs to expand to meet customer demand. The expansion will require a capital investment of $50 million. The asset life is ten years. For simplicity, assume ten-year straight-line depreciation with a full year's depreciation in the first year of operation. The debt portion of financing will be repaid in 10 equal annual installments, so that debt always equals 40 percent of the present value of remaining payments. Operating expenses other than interest and depreciation will be $15 million a year. The public service commission wants to set a rate that will generate enough revenue to provide a net present value of $0. How much revenue is needed if revenue will be the same each year?

20–16. Sunset Bank, one of the major banks on the West Coast, is considering a new loan product. The cost of equity is 16 percent, and the bank does not believe the product will change the cost of equity. Initial development costs will be $1 million, but these are tax-deductible expenses. It is estimated that an average loan balance of $50 million will be generated, and the product will have a life of 5 years. Approximately 95 percent of the loan portfolio will be financed with debt, costing 8 percent, and the rest will be financed with equity. The average interest rate on the loans will be 14 percent, and operating costs will be 3 percent of loan balance. Use the equity residual net present value to determine if the loan product is desirable.

20–17. Sunset Bank (problem 16) is also considering a new automatic teller machine (ATM) network. The ATMs will be financed with one-half debt and one-half equity. The debt will carry an interest rate of 10 percent and will be repaid in 8 equal annual installments. The total cost of the system will be $5 million, and the depreciation life will be seven years, using depreciation rates explained in Chapter 8. Operating costs other than depreciation will be $1 million a year and the system will generate additional fee revenue of $2 million a year over its anticipated 8-year life. Use the equity residual net present value method to determine if the asset is attractive.

20–18. (**Applications**) The following list of events took place in the 1990s:

   a. Goodyear Tire and Rubber Co. sold its Scottsboro, Alabama, polyester tire cord and fabric plant to Akzo for $105 million. The proceeds were to be used to reduce Goodyear's $3.7 billion debt.

   b. MCI board authorized the repurchase of as many as 15 million shares of the 262 million shares outstanding. The repurchased shares will be used for its employee benefit program.

   c. Wal-Mart agreed to buy a number of Pace Wholesale stores from K-Mart. This move decreased K-Mart's warehouse club exposure and increased the number of warehouse clubs owned by Wal-Mart to approximately 200.

    d. Mercedes Benz chose Alabama as the site for its new auto plant after huge tax concessions and up-front incentives were given by the state.

    e. Reynolds Metal was negotiating the sale of its Eskimo Pie Corp. to Nestlé USA. Reynolds would use the proceeds to invest in its other businesses. Required for each event:

        I. State weather you believe wealth was created, shifted, or both created and shifted between the financing sources for each firm. (Make whatever assumptions are necessary.)

        II. List the parties to whom wealth accrued and the parties from whom wealth was lost for each firm.

        III. Discuss the shifting of risk, if any, between the parties in each firm.

20–19. (**Ethical considerations**) In the late 1980s Kolhberg, Kravis, Roberts and Company took RJR Nabisco private for approximately $23 billion in debt. Prior to this RJR Nabisco was approximately a $10 billion company with $2 billion in long-term debt. Several pension plans and insurance companies held a sizable portion of the long-term debt prior to the leveraged buyout. After the buyout many of these debt-holders sued to try and recover what was reported in the press as a $200 million loss in market value for the existing bonds. Because there were no put options (giving the debt-holder the right to sell the debt to the corporation) attached to the existing debt, all of this debt remained outstanding after the leverage buyout.

    a. In terms of risk and required rate of return, why did the market value of the outstanding debt decrease with the announcement of the leveraged buyout?

    b. In terms of wealth, was wealth created or transferred with this leveraged buyout? Explain.

    c. Please comment on the ethical responsibilities of management in relation to the debt-holders and stockholders in this situation.

CASE PROBLEM |

Black Shoe Company

The shoe industry is labor intensive, and shipping costs are modest, so the shoe industry in the United States has been severely hurt by foreign competition. Shoe manufacturing in the United States had been concentrated in large factories in Northern industrial cities, and labor costs were at least several times those available in countries such as Taiwan. Abandoned shoe factories became symbols of the rust belt: a northern tier dotted by the hulks of dying industries.

    Black Shoe Company was one of the leading shoe companies in the United States. It produced and distributed a wide range of shoes for both men and women, priced in the middle and upper-middle ranges. Black had been forced to follow the national trend in relying increasingly on overseas production. Black had followed this policy with some regret, because management had a strong preference for manufacturing in the United States. Nevertheless, overseas sources seemed to be necessary for survival. Black built several overseas factories and contracted with other overseas manufacturers to build shoes of its design.

Despite success with overseas sources, management was interested in finding a way to keep at least some manufacturing in the United States. National pride, advertising advantages, and protection from fluctuating exchange rates were their primary motives. Automation was one way to reduce labor costs, but opportunities for increased automation were limited by constant changes in style. Thus, lower labor costs appeared to be essential if any manufacturing was to be kept in the United States.

A strategy task force was put together to work on ways to manufacture in the United States, and the Clear Spring, Missouri, proposal resulted. The fundamental strategy was to build small factories in rural areas where wages were low and unemployment was high. It was envisioned that one large factory would be replaced by ten small, rural factories employing approximately 400 people each. The Clear Spring proposal was the prototype for this strategy.

Clear Spring was a town of 2,500 in the Ozark region of southern Missouri. With surrounding towns and rural populations included, 12,000 people lived within a 12-mile radius of Clear Spring. The primary industries in the area were forestry and agriculture, and both were marginal. The hillsides were too steep for farming, while the soil in the valleys was thin and stony. Forestry consisted of harvesting naturally growing trees for low-grade lumber use such as railroad ties, pallets, and firewood. Railroad construction had slowed dramatically, plastic pallets were replacing wood for many uses, and it was uneconomical to truck firewood to major cities such as St. Louis.

By official estimates there were 4,800 people in the Clear Spring area labor force, with 10 percent of those unemployed. The potential labor pool for the factory was much higher than 480 though. Many of the employed worked poor farms, held seasonal jobs in lumbering, or drove 60 miles to jobs in Cape Girardeau. Furthermore, as many as 1,200 women who were not considered part of the work force, because they had not applied for jobs recently, would be happy to work if good job opportunities were available. When American Hat opened a small factory 30 miles away at Honesty, they had been flooded with applications.

The proposed factory would consist of an 80,000-square-foot, one-story building. Land would cost $40,000 and the building would cost $1,600,000. Most of the equipment would be transferred from a large factory that had been shut down because it could not compete with foreign producers. Installation of existing equipment and purchase of a small amount of new equipment would cost approximately $600,000. The expenditure would be capitalized and depreciated over 7 years for tax purposes, although the equipment would last ten years. If all-new equipment was used instead, the cost would be $1,800,000, and the new equipment would last for 20 years, although it would be depreciated over 7 years. The equipment would be placed in service January 1, and Black had a 34 percent tax rate. Net working capital requirements would be no greater, and possibly a little less, than those required to have the shoes produced overseas under contract. Design and start-up costs, which would not be capitalized, were estimated to be $300,000, but those costs would be cut in half if additional small factories were built.

It was estimated that the factory would produce 1.4 million pairs of shoes a year. Labor costs would be $5.7 million a year; materials would cost $4.3 million a year. Utilities, insurance, and other miscellaneous expenses, excluding depreciation, would cost $1.1 million a year. Black could purchase the same shoes under contract with a Taiwanese firm for $8.64 a pair, including shipping. However, the price could rise or fall sharply with a change in exchange rates. Through its distribution system, Black could sell the shoes at a wholesale price averaging $10.44, while incurring sales costs of 10 percent of sale price. Headquarters overhead was allocated to the divisions at 5 percent of sales.

Black Shoe's financial structure consisted of 30 percent debt and 70 percent equity. The yield to maturity on long-term U.S. government bonds was 8.13 percent, and Black's common stock had a beta of 1.1. The yield to maturity on Black's existing bonds was 9.76 percent. The mayor of Clear Spring had offered to donate the land and sell industrial revenue bonds to cover the $1,600,000 cost of the building. The industrial revenue bonds would carry an interest rate of 7.32 percent, and would be repaid in installments of $80,000 a year for 20 years.

CASE QUESTIONS

1. How should the industrial revenue bonds be treated in the analysis?
2. Compute the net present value of the Clear Spring plant.
3. Discuss the risks involved with building the factory and not building the factory.
4. Should Black build the Clear Spring factory? Why or why not?

SELECTED REFERENCES

Arditti, Fred D., and Haim Levy. "The Weighted Average Cost of Capital as a Cutoff Rate: A Critical Examination of the Classical Textbook Weighted Average." *Financial Management* 6 (Fall 1977): 24–34.

Bergman, Yaacov Z., and Jeffrey L. Callen. "Opportunistic Underinvestment in Debt Renegotiation and Capital Structure." *Journal of Financial Economics* 29 (March 1991): 137–171.

Berkovitch, Elazar, and M. P. Narayanan. "Timing of Investment and Financing Decisions in Imperfectly Competitive Financial Markets." *Journal of Business* 66 (April 1993): 219–248.

Bohl, Alan, and Frederic H. Murphy. "The Effect of the Mix of Equity and Debt on the Selection of Projects." *Engineering Economist* 37 (Fall 1991): 61–74.

Brigham, Eugene F., and T. Craig Tapley. "Financial Leverage and Use of the Net Present Value Investment Criterion: A Reexamination." *Financial Management* 14 (Summer 1985): 48–52.

Chambers, Donald R., Robert S. Harris, and John J. Pringle. "Treatment of Financing Mix in Analyzing Investment Opportunities." *Financial Management* 11 (Summer 1982): 24–41.

Cooper, Ian., and Julian R. Franks. "The Interactions of Financing and Investment Decisions When the Firm has Unused Tax Credits." *Journal of Finance* 38 (May 1983): 571–583.

Fries, Steven, Marcus Miller, and William Perraudin. "Debt in Industry Equilibrium" *Review of Financial Studies* 10 (Spring 1997): 39–67.

Golbe, Devra L., and Barry Schachter. "The Net Present Value Rule and an Algorithm for Maintaining a Constant Debt-Equity Ratio." *Financial Management* 14 (Summer 1985): 53–58.

Greenfield, Robert L., Maury R. Randall, and John C. Woods. "Financial Leverage and Use of the Net Present Value Investment Criterion." *Financial Management* 12 (Autumn 1983): 40–44.

Howe, Keith M. "A Note on Flotation Costs and Capital Budgeting." *Financial Management* 11 (Winter 1982): 30–33.

Howe, Keith M., and James H. Patterson. "Capital Investment Decisions under Economies of Scale in Flotation Cost." *Financial Management* 14 (Autumn 1985): 61–69.

Kamath, Ravindra R. "Long-Term Financing Decisions: Views and Practices of Financial Managers of NYSE Firms." *Financial Review* 32 (May 1997): 331–356.

Kensinger, John W., and John D. Martin. "Project Financing: Raising Money the Old-Fashioned Way." *Journal of Applied Corporate Finance* 1 (Fall 1988): 69–81.

Laber, Gene. "Bond Covenants and Forgone Opportunities: The Case of Burlington Northern Railroad Company." *Financial Management* 21 (Summer 1992): 71–77.

Levine, David I. "Do Corporate Executives Have Rational Expectations?" *Journal of Business* 66 (April 1993): 271–293.

Litzenberger, Robert H. "Some Observations on Capital Structure and the Impact of Recent Recapitalizations on Share Prices." *Journal of Financial and Quantitative Analysis* 21 (March 1986): 59–71.

Martin, John D., and David F. Scott, Jr. "Debt Capacity and the Capital Budgeting Decision." *Financial Management* 5 (Summer 1976): 7–14.

———. "Debt Capacity and the Capital Budgeting Decision: A Revisitation." *Financial Management* 9 (Spring 1980): 23–26.

Myers, Stewart C. "Interactions of Corporate Finance and Investment Decisions—Implications for Capital Budgeting." *Journal of Finance* 29 (March 1974): 1–25. Also, see comment and reply in *Journal of Finance* 32 (March 1977): 211–220.

Ravid, S. Abraham. "On Interactions of Production and Financial Decisions." *Financial Management* 17 (Autumn 1988): 87–99.

Rhee, S. Ghon, and Franklin L. McCarthy. "Corporate Debt Capacity and Capital Budgeting Analysis." *Financial Management* 11 (Summer 1982): 42–50.

Ruback, Richard S. "Calculating the Market Value of Riskless Cash Flows." *Journal of Financial Economists* 15 (March 1986): 323–339.

Taggart, Robert A., Jr. "Capital Budgeting and the Financing Decision: An Exposition." *Financial Management* 6 (Summer 1977): 59–64.

Woods, John C., and Maury R. Tandall. "The Net Present Value of Future Investment Opportunities: Its Impact on Shareholder Wealth and Implications for Capital Budgeting Theory." *Financial Management* 18 (Summer 1989): 85–92.

CHAPTER 21 |

LEASE ANALYSIS

After completing this chapter you should be able to:

1. Differentiate between the lessee and the lessor.
2. Discuss the differences between an operating lease, a financial lease, a leveraged lease, and a sale and leaseback.
3. List and explain eight reasons for leasing.
4. Know who receives the tax benefits (depreciation expense) from the leased asset.
5. Calculate and compare the net present value of purchasing an asset with the net present value of leasing an asset.
6. Recognize a situation where an otherwise negative net present value project may become positive with lease financing.
7. Identify the appropriate interest rate to use when discounting the cash flows from a leased asset.
8. Adjust your analysis when comparing the performance of a leased asset with the performance of a purchased asset.
9. Describe the different financial disclosures necessary for a capital lease versus an operating lease.
10. List the conditions that separate a capital lease from an operating lease.
11. Identify and discuss some of the factors or reasons for the popularity of leasing in practice.

Steven F. Udvar-Hazy and Louis L. Gonda met in college and, being airplane buffs, decided to start a commuter airline. The airline, funded with $100,000 of capital from their Hungarian immigrant families, failed. As part of their effort to dispose of the airplanes, the two friends leased a DC-8 to Aeromexico. One lease lead to another and the business was transformed into International Lease Finance Corp. (ILC). Although no longer owning an airline, the two friends are among the world's leading owners of airplanes.

In 1988, ILC placed the largest airplane purchase order in history. They ordered $5 billion worth of airplanes from Boeing and Airbus Industries. All of the airplanes were to be leased to airlines, reflecting the airlines' growing reliance on leasing as a method for acquiring airplanes.[1] The airlines are not alone. Leasing has grown in popularity as a means of acquiring a wide variety of assets, including automobiles, computers, offices, and factories.

A *lease* is a contract by which the owner of property gives someone else the right to use that property for a specified time period in exchange for specified payments. In this chapter, we focus on the choice between leasing and purchasing as a means of acquiring the use of an asset. Present value of cash flows and financial statement impact are considered, along with other factors that bear on the choice between leasing and owning. Based on this analysis, the impact of a lease alternative on the desirability of a capital investment is considered. The analysis of a capital investment also is considered for situations in which the asset cannot be purchased, and the only alternative is leasing.

OVERVIEW OF LEASES |

The two parties to a lease are the lessor and the lessee; if you rent an apartment, the landlord is the *lessor* and you are the *lessee*. An overview of types of assets leased, types of lessors and lessees, and types of lease contracts is provided in the following paragraphs.

Types of Assets Leased. Leasing first became popular in connection with real estate: land and buildings. Those of us who have lived in apartments or rented houses have been lessees. In recent decades, leasing has expanded to serve as a method of acquiring a broad variety of assets. Motor vehicle leasing is a well-established industry, and leasing of equipment ranging from computers to factory machinery and total factories has also become popular. Leasing was originally limited to assets that could be transferred to other users if the lessee defaulted, but leasing of user-specific assets has become increasingly popular.

GTE Corporation provides us with an example of the growing use of leases as a means of acquiring an ever-increasing range of assets. When GTE wanted to place its $248 million Spacenet 3 satellite transponder in orbit, it arranged for a group of investors to buy the transponder, and then signed an agreement to lease the transponder from the investors. This particular transaction fell through when the rocket carrying the satellite malfunctioned and was destroyed shortly after takeoff in Kourou, French Guiana.[2] While the enthusiasm of the insurance companies may have suffered, enthusiasm for leasing was not dampened. Leasing is

---

[1]"An Order of Wings to Go," *Business Week* (May 30,1988): 32.

[2]This example and numerous other examples cited in this chapter come from "Top 10 Lease Transactions of 85 Total $4.1 billion." *Pension and Investment Age* (April 14, 1986): 31+; and M. Douglas Dunn and Bernard C. Topper, Jr., "Terms and Conditions for Electric Utility Success with Leveraged Leases," *Public Utilities Fortnightly* 119 (April 16, 1987): 14–23.

being used to acquire an ever-growing variety of assets. It is possible to go into business today by leasing a building, leasing the production machinery, leasing the office furniture, and leasing the motor vehicles needed to transport products. Several companies are even offering to lease employees.

Lessees include individuals, businesses, nonprofit organizations, and governments. Individuals regularly lease homes, automobiles, computers, and even furniture. Land, buildings, and equipment are leased by businesses, nonprofit organizations, and governments.

Lessors are divided into two broad groups: those interested in selling a product and those interested only in providing financing. Computer companies, for example, view the lease as a way to persuade customers to acquire a product they may be unwilling to buy. Banks, commercial finance companies, leasing companies, and wealthy individuals, on the other hand, purchase assets and lease those assets to others as an alternative to lending money or investing in stock. As real estate limited partnerships decreased in popularity after tax reform, leasing limited partnerships such as Atel Cash Distribution Fund and Phoenix Leasing Capital Assurance Fund, grew. Investment bankers often aid in packaging complex lease transactions.

There are four widely used lease arrangements: operating leases, financial leases, leveraged leases, and sale and leaseback. These are discussed in the following paragraphs.

OPERATING LEASE

An operating lease, also called a *service lease* or *service contract,* commits the lessor to provide and maintain the asset. These leases, which date back to at least the leasing of Model T Fords in 1918, gained popularity in the computer business. People were unfamiliar with computers, and the operating lease assured them that the manufacturer was committed not just to delivering and setting up the equipment, but also to assuring its continued serviceability. Operating leases are widely used for computers and other office equipment, and for motor vehicles. Portland General Electric signed an operating lease contract to sell its Boardman power plant while continuing to use the electricity generated there.

Operating leases often do not run for the life of the asset. Automobile leases, for example, are often for a period less than half of the average life of an automobile. Furthermore, many operating leases include a provision allowing the lessee to cancel the agreement before the end of the lease, normally with a cancellation penalty. Thus, the lessor is generally at risk with regard to the terminal value of the asset at the end of the lease period. TRAC (Terminal Rental Adjustment Clause) leases, often used for motor vehicle financing, transfer terminal value risk to the lessee by requiring the lessee to guarantee a specified market value of the asset at the end of the lease.[3]

---

[3]Many automobile leases that sound too good to be true are based on the lessee guaranteeing a high market value at the end of the lease. Tax law penalizes terminal rental adjustment clauses in leases for assets other than motor vehicles and trailers.

FINANCIAL LEASE

A financial lease, also called a *capital lease,* is purely a method of financing. The lessor neither maintains the equipment nor otherwise assures its serviceability. Furthermore, a financial lease is often for all or most of the service life of the asset so that the lessor has minimal risk with regard to the later value of the asset, unless the lessee defaults. The lessor in a financial lease is, therefore, in a position similar to that of a secured creditor.

In a typical financial lease arrangement, the lessee selects the asset and negotiates the price. The lessee also negotiates independently with a bank, commercial finance company, or leasing company that will serve as lessor. The lessor buys the asset and simultaneously leases the asset to the lessee. Typically, the asset moves from the manufacturer to the lessee, with the lessor taking title but not physical possession. From the perspective of both the lessor and lessee, the lease is simply an alternative to a loan.

LEVERAGED LEASE

A leveraged lease is a lease in which the lessor uses borrowed money to acquire the asset to be leased. As an example of a leveraged lease, consider a steam and electric plant leased by PSE Corporation. GE Credit became the owner (and lessor) of the $233 million plant by putting up $80 million. The remainder was provided in the form of loans by a group of banks. This lease also qualifies as a financial lease as long as PSE remains responsible for maintenance and operation. Lease payments from the lessee go to a trustee, who uses the bulk of the payments to pay the lenders. The lessor, as owner of record, gets the benefits of depreciation tax savings and investment tax credits, if any. The lessor may be a bank, leasing company, wealthy individual, or limited partnership. The lender may be a life insurance company, charitable trust, or other investor in a low tax bracket. In some cases, such as El Paso Electric's lease for its Palo Verde Nuclear plant, a public bond issue is used for the debt portion of the financing. The leveraged lease allows assignment of cash flows and tax benefits among parties according to their particular tax situations, and, therefore, reduces the cost of the lease.

The tax law with regard to leveraged leases has been tightened somewhat in recent years. The lessor must now expect to make a profit independent of tax considerations in order for the tax deductions to be allowed.

SALE AND LEASEBACK

With a sale and leaseback arrangement, the owner of an asset contracts to sell the asset and to lease it from the buyer, typically under a financial lease arrangement. Thus, the financial lease is an alternative to borrowing against an asset already owned. The sale and leaseback is a way to raise money based on an asset while continuing to use the asset. An example is Tuscon Electric's sale of its Springerville generating plant for $850 million, while simultaneously agreeing to lease the plant back from the new owner. To keep terminology straight, a *direct lease* involves leasing an asset not previously owned by the lessee while a sale and leaseback involves leasing an asset that was previously owned by the lessee.

REASONS FOR LEASING |

The growth in leasing must be attributed to real or perceived advantages of leasing over other methods of financing the acquisition of an asset. Some of the major reasons generally given for leasing are discussed in the following paragraphs.

Increased Availability of Financing. In the event of default, a lessor can often reclaim the leased asset faster and easier than would be the case for a secured lender. Therefore, lessors are often willing to provide assets through a lease when the company's credit rating would not be strong enough to induce a creditor to make money available. The creditor compensates for risk by financing only part of the cost of the asset, while leases often provide close to 100 percent financing.[4] Furthermore, the lessor is also often willing to arrange for lease payments over the entire life of the asset, while creditors will want to protect themselves by requiring that the loan be completely repaid well before the end of the asset's life. Because of the increased protection of the lessor, an organization that needs an asset can often arrange a lease faster than a loan, and with divulgence of less information.

Leasing is also used when restrictive covenants limiting additional borrowing have been accepted as part of past financings. Since a lease is not technically a loan, a lease can sometimes be used when additional borrowing is not allowed. CBI Corporation listed debt covenants as one of the reasons it was seeking off-balance-sheet financing when it arranged an operating lease for its air exchange plant, according to its treasurer, Buell T. Adams. This opportunity has been decreased because many loan agreements now include covenants limiting leases as well as additional borrowing.

Shift of Ownership Risk. The purchaser of an asset faces uncertainty with regard to serviceability, obsolescence, and residual value of the asset at the end of its use life. Leases can be a tool for decreasing or shifting those risks. When an asset is purchased, there is an agency-type problem in that the buyer must often rely on the seller's word and reputation with regard to asset quality. While there may be a warranty, the burden of enforcing the warranty falls on the buyer. With an operating lease, the lessor promises not just the asset, but the service. The lessee has the option of ceasing lease payments if the asset is not serviceable. While there is the potential for a lawsuit when payments are stopped, the burden of enforcing the contract is shifted to the lessor. Thus, the operating lease is a method of assuring quality.

---

[4]Business Aircraft Finance is one company that provides 100 percent financing to counter lessors ["To Finance or Lease," *Business Monthly* (August 1987): 72+].

Obsolescence risk is not eliminated by the lease, but a lease is often a method of transferring that risk. Many leases give the lessee the option to cancel before the end of the lease, normally with some cancellation penalty. A cancellation option transfers the risk of obsolescence to the lessor. Likewise, the lessor is generally the party at risk with regard to the residual value of the asset at the end of the lease. Needless to say, these risks are still borne by someone, and the lease will be priced so that the lessor is compensated for risk bearing. As with other insurance, though, the lessee may feel that the reduction of risk is worth the cost incurred.

Flexibility. Flexibility is another advantage of leasing. Particularly with a cancellation provision,[5] the lessee can respond quickly to changing market conditions. A St. Louis marketer of photocopy machines advertises a cancellation clause in its lease that can be used if the customer's needs change. This is probably a more appealing scenario to the customers than the search for a buyer for a used copying machine.

Tax Advantages. Depreciation tax savings are of little use to nonprofit organizations and companies not making profits. Furthermore, the tax reform act of 1986 sets limits on the amount of income that can be sheltered from taxes through the use of accelerated depreciation. A lease transfers depreciation tax benefits to the lessor. If the lessor is in a better position to use these benefits, the lease may be less expensive than the purchase. General Electric Credit received an immediate $35 million of tax benefits in 1985 from its position as lessor of PSE's electric and steam generating plant.[6] In other cases, a lease for less than the tax depreciation life of the asset effectively allows a more rapid write-off for tax purposes than would be possible with a purchase.

Accounting Benefits. When assets and debt are placed on the company's books, the debt to equity ratio increases, and ratios measuring the efficiency of asset usage decline.[7] In addition, the combined interest and depreciation expenses cause income to decline. Accounting rules discussed later in this chapter require a financial lease to be treated on the accounting statements as if the asset were purchased. An operating lease, on the other hand, results in no change to the balance sheet and may result in lower reported expenses than would occur if the asset were purchased. When CBI Corporation of Oak Brook, Illinois, sold an $18 million air-separation plant to GATX Corporation, it simultaneously signed a 15-year operating lease contract. As a result, CBI moved $18 million of assets off its balance sheet, freed up $18 million of cash to expand or repay debt, and still maintained use of the plant. A sale and leaseback may also generate one-time

---

[5]See Thomas E. Copeland and J. Fred Weston, "A Note on the Evaluation of Cancelable Operating Leases," *Financial Management* 11 (Summer 1982): 60–67.

[6]Immediate tax benefits were decreased by the Tax Reform Act of 1986, but tax benefits still exist.

[7]These ratios include sales to total assets (turnover) and sales to fixed assets.

accounting income gains, such as the $79 million gain recognized by Oglethorpe Power Corporation through a sale and leaseback of its Sherer coal-fired Unit 2. The financial statement impacts of leases are covered later in this chapter.

Circumvent Decision Process. The purchase of an asset often requires a lengthy capital expenditure approval process. In some cases, though, acquisition of an asset through a lease is not subjected to the same decision process. Thus, a manager may be able to acquire an asset quickly through a lease when a request to purchase would be time-consuming, and the response to the request would be uncertain. Circumvention of the company's decision process will not generally contribute to shareholder wealth maximization, but leases are sometimes used for this purpose anyway.

Reimbursement. Some organizations, such as hospitals, are reimbursed based on expenses incurred. When assets are leased, the lease payments are allowed as expenses. When assets are purchased, depreciation is allowed as an expense. If a cost of money is not also allowed with the purchase, reimbursement will generally be greater with a lease.[8] Electric utilities sometimes use leases to delay rate increases by smoothing cost recovery evenly across an asset's life.

Lower Cost. Other things aside, a lease will be attractive if the present value of the net cash outflows to lease is less than the present value of the net cash outflows to buy. The net result of many of the considerations previously discussed may be that the lease is a lower-cost alternative to the purchase. To the extent a lease results in less cash outflow than a loan, it also decreases the probability of default and bankruptcy.

TAXES AND LEASING

In general, the lessor receives the tax benefits of ownership. The lessor reports the lease payment as income and reports the depreciation on the asset as an expense in computing taxable income. The lessee reports the lease payment as an expense in computing taxable income.

The main tax complication is with regard to the question of whether a contract is really a lease, or an installment sale masquerading as a lease. If the Internal Revenue Service is successful in upholding its opinion that a particular contract is really an installment sale, the lease payments are treated as principal and interest payments on a loan while the lessee is treated as the owner of the asset for tax purposes.

To decide if a contract is a genuine lease, the fundamental question is *who bears the risks of ownership*? The IRS *may* decide to challenge a lease contract if *some* of the following guidelines are violated:

---

[8]See Rodney Roenfeldt and Jerome S. Osteryoung, "Lease-Cost Measurement of Hospital Equipment," *Financial Management* 8 (Spring 1979), 24–35.

1. The term of the lease must not exceed 30 years.
2. The remaining useful life of the asset after the end of the lease must be at least 20 percent of the original estimated useful life, and the asset must be potentially useful to others besides the lessee.
3. The lease payments must provide the lessor a reasonable rate of return apart from tax benefits.
4. The lease should not include a bargain option to buy the asset or renew the lease.
5. The lease should not have early payments that are substantially higher than later payments.
6. The lease agreement should not limit the lessee's right to issue debt or equity.

CASH FLOW ANALYSIS FOR LEASE VS. BUY DECISIONS |

The choice between leasing and purchasing often boils down to a pure cost question: Is the present value of the net cash outflows to lease greater or less than the present value of the net cash outflows to purchase?

The cost to lease an asset is generally the present value of the after-tax lease payments. For a lease covering n periods, the general formula for the cost is:[9]

$$\text{Cost to lease} = \sum_{t=0}^{n} \frac{(1 - T)L_t}{(1 + k_d)^t} \qquad (21\text{-}1)$$

where T is the tax rate, L_t is the lease payment in period t, and k_d is the company's after-tax cost of debt.

The cash flows to lease are clear, at least in principle, but the reasons for using the after-tax cost of debt as the discount rate may need a bit of clarification. The appropriate discount rate for present value calculations in general is the rate of return available on alternatives of equal risk. The stream of payments for a lease is a set of contractual, fixed payments,[10] generally substituted for a set of fixed payments on debt. Therefore, the lease payments are as certain as the payments on debt; either type of payment will be made unless the company defaults. Likewise, the tax savings are as likely to occur as the tax savings that would result from interest expense on debt. Consequently, the after-tax lease payments are as risky as the after-tax debt payments they supplant, and should be discounted at the after-tax cost of debt to compare lease with purchase.

---

[9]This formula assumes that tax benefits occur at the same time as lease payments. Frequently, lease payments are at the beginning of each year, while the tax reduction is spread over the year. In these cases, the present value of the lease payments and tax savings should be computed separately so that the timing of each can be accurately recognized.

[10]For variable lease payments, see Stewart D. Hodges, "The Valuation of Variable Rate Leases," *Financial Management* 14 (Spring 1985): 68–74.

Example. Kellnor Corporation needs a new computer system. The computer system can be leased for $21,000 at the *beginning* of each year for 7 years. Kellnor's marginal income tax rate is 35 percent, and the company can borrow money at an interest rate of 12.31 percent. The after-tax cost of debt is, therefore, $.1231(1 - .35) = 8$ percent. Assuming tax savings occur at approximately the same time as lease payments, the cost of leasing is determined by finding the after-tax lease payment and then multiplying by the present value of $1 at the beginning of each year for 7 years:[11]

$$\text{Cost of leasing} = \$21,000(1 - .35)5.6229 = \$76,753$$

The cost to buy an asset is generally the present value of the after-tax cash flows to purchase:[12]

$$\text{Cost to buy} = I_o + \sum_{t=0}^{n} \frac{(1 - T)OC_t - T \times Dep^t}{(1 + k_d)^t} - \frac{\text{Net terminal value}}{(1 + k_o)^n} \qquad \textbf{(21-2)}$$

where I_o is the initial outlay; OC_t is expected operating cost in period t that will be borne by the user if the asset is purchased, but not if it is leased; net terminal value is the terminal value of the asset, less any tax or other expense associated with the sale; and k_o is the company's weighted average cost of capital.

For the analysis of the purchase decision, the discount rates are again based on risk. Depreciation tax savings are generally felt to be low-risk cash flows, and the general practice is to use the after-tax cost of debt, effectively assuming these flows have a degree of predictability similar to debt payments and their associated tax savings.

Readers are occasionally concerned about discounting depreciation tax savings at the after-tax cost of debt when these same cash flows were discounted at the weighted average cost of capital in the original capital budgeting analysis. When net cash flows are being analyzed, a discount rate for average risk can be used, but when cash flow components are being analyzed individually, as is done in lease analysis, discount rates appropriate for those particular components should be used.[13,14]

If operating costs are highly predictable, they are discounted at the after-tax cost of debt, as illustrated in Equation 21-2. Many operating costs associated

---

[11]The present value factor for $1 at the *beginning* of each year for 7 years is $(1.08)PVA1_{7years,8\%} = 5.6229$.

[12]This formula again assumes that tax savings occur at the same time as expenses. If this is not the case, operating costs and resulting tax savings should be found separately to recognize the actual timing of these flows.

[13]See Appendix 14-A for a demonstration of the consistency between discounting total cash flows for average risk and discounting components at rates appropriate for those components.

[14]Despite these assurances, we must take seriously the concerns of practitioners like Roger L. Carson, who expresses concern about using multiple discount rates in practical settings. Roger L. Carson, "Leasing, Asset Lines, and Uncertainty: A Practitioner's Comments," *Financial Management* 16 (Summer 1987): 13–16.

with fixed assets are certain or have only nonsystematic risk and should, therefore, be discounted at the after-tax cost of debt. Uncertain operating costs require another discount rate, though. As pointed out in Appendix 14-A, an operating cost that is positively correlated with the company's cash inflows is discounted at a discount rate higher than the cost of debt, and vice versa. If operating costs tend to increase proportionally with the company's other cash flows, as would frequently be the case when operating costs depend on the level of activity, the weighted average cost would be the appropriate discount rate for operating costs.

The net terminal value is usually an uncertain amount,[15] and the general practice is to assume it has a risk similar to the average risk of the other cash flows of the company. The weighted average cost of capital is, therefore, used as the discount rate. The required return can be adjusted using methods described in Chapters 14 and 15 if it is believed that the systematic risk associated with net terminal value is greater or less than the systematic risk for the company as a whole, or option pricing models can be applied.[16]

In computing the cost of owning, the present value of the after-tax principal and interest payments on a loan that is displaced by the lease is sometimes substituted for the cost of the asset itself. But the present value of the after-tax payments on a loan (principal payments, plus interest payments, minus tax savings from interest payments), discounted at the after-tax cost of debt, equals the amount borrowed. This relationship holds as a matter of definition because the after-tax cost of debt is the internal rate of return relating after-tax principal and interest payments with net loan proceeds.[17] Therefore, substituting the present value of the loan payments results in considerably more calculation and the same cost of buying.

A common error in comparing lease with purchase is to recognize the original cost, as is done in Equation 21-2, and also add the present value of interest payments on a loan. Because I_o equals the cost and also equals the present value of after-tax principal and interest payments, adding the present value of interest payments again is clearly a case of double counting.

Example. Kellnor Corporation, in the previous example, can purchase a computer system for $100,000, with the system to be placed in service on January 1. The system will have a 5-year tax life and a 7-year use life. At the end of 7 years, the system will have a salvage value, net of taxes and removal costs, of $20,000. If Kellnor purchases the system, it must provide maintenance that would otherwise

---

[15]Salvage value and other lease-related cash flows are affected by inflation as well as other uncertainties. For a discussion of the role of inflation in lease analysis, see Shalom Hochman and Ramon Rabinovitch, "Financial Leasing under Inflation," *Financial Management* 13 (Spring 1984): 17–26.

[16]Wayne Y. Lee, John D. Martin, and Andrew J. Senchak, Jr., "The Case for Using Options to Evaluate Salvage Values in Financial Leases," *Financial Management* 11 (Autumn 1982): 33–41.

[17]The interested reader can confirm this for any loan amount, any interest rate, any payment sequence, and any tax rate desired.

be provided by the lessor. The maintenance cost is $6,000 at the end of each year for 6 years, with a fixed-price maintenance contract. Kellnor will use straight-line depreciation. The after-tax cost of debt is 8 percent and the weighted average cost of capital is 12 percent.[18] The cost of buying is the present value of all the cash flows associated with owning. The cost of buying is computed in Table 21.1.

The cost of buying the computer system was $82,069 while the cost of leasing was $76,753. Therefore, leasing would be preferred.

The net advantage of leasing over owning (NAL) can be found by subtracting the cost of leasing from the cost of owning. Subtracting Equation 21-1 from Equation 21-2 gives the NAL:[19]

$$\text{NAL} = I_o + \sum_{t=0}^{n} \frac{(1 - T)OC_t - T \times \text{Dep}^t}{(1 + k_d)^t} - \frac{\text{Net terminal value}}{(1 + K_o)^n} -$$

$$\sum_{t=0}^{n} \frac{(1 - T)L_t}{(1 + k_d)^t} \qquad \textbf{(21-3)}$$

Example. For the previously considered computer system, the net advantage of leasing is:

| **TABLE 21.1** **COST OF BUYING CALCULATION** |

The cost of buying calculation is illustrated for a $100,000 asset with a 5-year tax life and 7-year useful life. Contractual maintenance expense of $6,000 a year can be avoided with a lease. The after-tax cost of debt is 8 percent and the weighted average cost of capital is 12 percent. The net salvage value at the end of 7 years is $20,000.

Year	0	1	2–5	6	7
Purchase	100,000				
Maintenance		6,000	6,000	6,000	
		× (1 − .35)	× (1 − .35)	× (1 − .35)	
After-tax maintenance		3,900	3,900	3,900	
Depreciation[a]		10,000	20,000	10,000	
		× .35	× .35	× .35	
Depreciation tax savings		3,500	7,000	3,500	
Net salvage value					20,000
Net cash outflow	100,000	400	−3,100	400	−20,000
Present value factor[b]	1.0000	.9259	3.0668	.6302	.4523
Present value	100,000	370	−9,507	252	−9,046
Cost of Owning = $82,069					

[a]Current tax law requires depreciation during acquisition year to be based on the assumption the asset was acquired at mid-year.

[b]Note that the discount rate is 12 percent for the salvage value and 8 percent for all other cash flows.

[18]Assume for simplicity that taxes also occur at year end.

[19]For a detailed analysis of lease valuation, see John J. McConnel and James S. Schallheim, "Valuation of Asset Leasing Contracts," *Journal of Financial Economics* 12 (August 1983): 237–261.

$$\text{NAL} = \$82{,}069 - \$76{,}753 = \$5{,}316$$

Since the net advantage of leasing is positive in this case, leasing would be preferred over owning, other things being equal.

LEASING AND CAPITAL INVESTMENT DECISIONS |

In the previous examples, the choice was between leasing and buying; we assumed that the asset would be acquired one way or the other. There are, however, situations in which lease terms may be attractive enough to turn the net present value of an investment from negative to positive. The capital budgeting implications of attractive leasing terms are treated in the following paragraphs.

It is interesting to note that changing the signs of all the cash flows in Equation 21-3 gives the net advantage to the lessor. If all markets were perfectly efficient and the lessor was in the same tax bracket as the lessee, we would expect the equilibrium lease payment to be such that the net advantage of leasing would be zero, and there would be no financial advantage or disadvantage to leasing. However, imperfections do exist. The lessor may have better access to the capital markets, and may therefore have a lower cost of funds. The lessor may also be in a higher tax bracket, thereby reducing after-tax costs. The lessor may be the manufacturer, and may be willing to lease at a lower cost to encourage acquisition of assets, or the lessor may be in a better position to dispose of the asset at the end of the lease term. Thus, there are numerous reasons why the net advantage of leasing may be positive, and may make an otherwise undesirable investment attractive.

The net present value if the asset is leased is simply the net present value if the asset is purchased, plus the net advantage of leasing. Suppose, for example, the net present value of the investment analyzed in Table 21.1 was −$3,000, determined by the normal capital budgeting methods described in Chapter 5. The investment proposal would be rejected. But the net advantage of leasing is $5,316, so the net present value with leasing is −$3,000 + $5,316 = $2,316.

CAPITAL BUDGETING WHEN AN ASSET CAN ONLY BE LEASED |

Some capital investments are assets that cannot be purchased. Many retail locations, for example, are only available on a lease basis, and departments in retail stores are being leased with increased frequency. If a retail store in leased space at one location is being compared to a store in purchased space at another location, a meaningful method of comparison must be developed.

Companies will sometimes deduct the lease payments from the benefits to arrive at net cash flows, and then discount the net cash flows at the weighted average cost of capital or the cost of equity. This, though, is equivalent to discounting the lease payment as well as the project cash flows at the weighted average cost of capital or cost of equity rather than the after-tax cost of debt. As illustrated in the next example, this form of analysis is biased in favor of the leased asset.

If the lease payment is purely a financing cost, we can discount the after-tax lease payment at the after-tax cost of debt, and discount all other cash flows at the weighted average cost of capital. More typically though, the lease payment includes compensation for various costs and benefits: the use of money, operating expenses, and depreciation tax savings, to name a few. If the lease payments replace fixed costs, the cash flows left after deducting the lease payments may be more risky than the net cash flows from ownership. An alternative that will generally categorize the riskiness from various cash flows correctly is to estimate the cost of the asset if it could be purchased, and use that cost in the analysis.

Example. Oceanside Corporation can lease an asset for $75,000 at the end of each year for the asset's 10-year life. The asset will generate earnings before depreciation and tax of $100,000 a year, and all cash flows occur at year-end. The company has a 35 percent tax rate, pays a 10 percent interest rate on debt, and has a 12 percent weighted average cost of capital. The asset cannot be purchased, but it is estimated that an asset of this type would be worth approximately $500,000 if it could be purchased. Assuming depreciation of $50,000 a year, annual cash flows to purchase and to lease are as follows:

	Buy	Lease
Earnings before depreciation and tax	$100,000	$100,000
− Depreciation	50,000	0
− Lease payment	0	75,000
Earnings before tax	$ 50,000	$ 25,000
Tax	17,500	8,750
Net income	$ 32,500	$ 16,250
+ Depreciation	50,000	0
= Cash flow	$ 82,500	$ 16,250

Using the first approach, the investment is attractive because the net present value is positive:[20]

$$\$16,250 PVA\vert_{10yrs,12\%} = \underline{\$91,816}$$

[20]Discounting the $16,250 at the cost of equity might seem to be appropriate, but it is not. A lease that provides 100 percent financing will have a positive NPV at any discount rate as long as the *expected* cash flows after deducting the lease payments are positive. Thus, there is no effective way to adjust for risk through the choice of a discount rate when the net cash flow is the cash flow after deducting lease payments.

Discounting lease payments at the after-tax cost of debt, the net present value is substantially lower:

$$100,000(1 - .35)PVAI_{10yrs,12\%} - 75,000(1 - .35)PVAI_{10yrs,6.5\%} = \underline{\$16,809}$$

Using the estimated purchase price, the net present value to purchase is:

$$NPV_{purchase} = 82,500PVAI_{10yrs,12\%} - 500,000 = -\underline{\$33,857}$$

and the net advantage of leasing is:

$$NAL = 500,000 - .35 \times 50,000 \times PVAI_{10yrs,6.5\%} - (1 - .35)75,000PVA_{10yrs,6.5\%}$$

$$= \underline{\$23,740}$$

The net present value with the leasing option is:

$$NPV = -\$33,857 + 23,740 = -\underline{\$10,117}$$

The net present value in this example ranged from plus $91,816 to minus $10,117. This range occurred despite the fact that the same *net* annual cash flow of $16,250 was used in each analysis. The only thing that changed was the discount rate being applied to each component of cash flow. Obviously, the discount rate choice is critical for the analysis, and the discount rate depends on the riskiness of each component of cash flow when evaluating an asset that can only be leased. Correctly assessing the risks of those cash flows is, therefore, critical.

FINANCIAL STATEMENT IMPACTS OF LEASES |

While the main focus of the analysis is on cash flows, it is unrealistic to ignore financial or capital statement impacts of capital investments. Management reward systems are often based on reported income, and financial statements are the information available to lenders and stockholders. Although it seems unlikely that sophisticated investors would be fooled, many managers seem to place a value on "window dressing" which is the name applied to activities designed purely to improve the appearance of the financial statements. Financial statement impacts are examined in the following paragraphs.

Accountants recognize two types of leases: operating leases and financial leases. The treatment of a lease on the financial statements depends on which type of lease it is. Accountants classify a lease as a financial lease if it meets one of the following tests, and as an operating lease otherwise:

1. The lease transfers ownership of the property to the lessee at the end of the lease term.

2. The lease contains a *bargain* purchase option.
3. The lease term is 75 percent or more of the estimated economic life of the leased property.
4. At the beginning of the lease term, the present value of the minimum lease payment equals or exceeds 90 percent of the fair market value of the asset. The minimum lease payment is the smallest possible lease payment if the lease payments depend on some future events; for a fixed-cost lease, the contractual lease payment is the minimum lease payment.

If a lease is considered an operating lease, the lease payment is treated as an expense on the income statement and the balance sheet is not affected.

Accountants consider a financial lease to be a close substitute for acquisition of the asset through an installment loan. The accountants attempt to show financial leases on the financial statements as if they were purchases. An asset equal to the present value of the lease payments is placed on the balance sheet and offset by a loan on the liability side equal to the present value of all future lease payments. The lease payments are then treated as principal and interest payments on a loan. The lease payment does not appear as an expense on the income statement, but interest on the implied loan and depreciation on the implied asset do appear on the income statement. The treatment of a lease on the financial statements can substantially affect the company's reported profitability.

Example. San Diego Industries is required to install new pollution-control equipment. The equipment will be acquired on January 1, 1999. The equipment will have a 10-year life for accounting purposes and a 5-year life for tax purposes. The equipment can be bought for $200,000, and financed with a 10 percent installment loan; payments would be $32,549 at the end of each year for 10 years. Alternately, the asset could be acquired through a lease, with payments of $32,549 at the end of each year for 10 years.

If the lease is considered an operating lease, San Diego will show a lease expense of $32,549 on the income statement, and the balance sheet will be unaffected. If the lease is considered a financial or capital lease, the accountants will first find the present value of the lease payments, discounted at the company's 10 percent borrowing cost:

Present value of lease payments = 32,549PVA $|_{10yrs,10\%}$ = $200,000. This $200,000 is the implied asset value.

With the financial lease, the income statement will not reflect a lease payment, but will show depreciation on the implied asset and interest on the implied loan. Straight-line depreciation is often used for accounting purposes, so the depreciation will be $200,000 \div 10 = $20,000$ and interest for 1988 will be another $.10 \times $200,000 = $20,000$. Even though the series of payments for all three methods of acquisition are the same, the financial lease or purchase would result in $40,000 of expenses on the income statement, while the operating lease would result in only $32,549 of expenses.

Turning to the balance sheet at the end of 1999, the operating lease would not have any impact. The purchased asset, though, would have a book value of $200,000, minus one year's accounting depreciation, or $180,000. Thus, total assets would increase by $180,000. The same thing would be true for the financial lease. Assuming no changes in other assets and no changes in equity, reported debt would also be $180,000 greater at the end of 1999 with either the purchase or financial lease.

The financial statements for San Diego Industries appear in Table 21.2. The first column is the actual 1998 statement. The second column is the pro-forma 1999 financial statement with an operating lease. The third column is the pro-forma 1999 financial statement with a purchase or financial lease. Since the pollution-control equipment generates no revenue, profitability goes down regardless of the method of acquisition. But the impact of a financial lease or pur-

| **TABLE 21.2** FINANCIAL STATEMENT IMPACTS OF PURCHASE, OPERATING LEASE, AND FINANCIAL LEASE FOR SAN DIEGO INDUSTRIES

This table illustrates the impacts of three methods of acquiring an asset that can be purchased for $200,000, with installment loan financing, or acquired through lease payments with a present value of $200,000.

| | | PRO-FORMA 1999 | |
	1998	Operating Lease	Purchase or Financial Lease
Sales	$1,000,000	$1,000,000	$1,000,000
Cost of goods sold	600,000	600,000	600,000
Admin. expense	140,000	140,000	140,000
Depreciation	60,000	60,000	80,000
Lease payments	0	32,549	0
Interest expense	40,000	40,000	60,000
Earnings before tax	160,000	127,451	120,000
Tax (35%)	56,000	44,608	42,000
Net income	$ 104,000	$ 82,843	$ 78,000
Total assets	$1,000,000	$1,000,000	$1,180,000
Debt	$ 400,000	$ 400,000	$ 580,000
Equity	600,000	600,000	600,000
Total liabilities and equity	$1,000,000	$1,000,000	$1,180,000
Profit margin (net income/sales)	10.4%	8.3%	7.8%
Return on assets (net income/total assets)	10.4%	8.3%	6.6%
Return on equity (net income/equity)	17.3%	13.8%	13.0%
Debt to total assets	.40	.40	.49

chase is substantially worse than the impact of an operating lease. The profit margin on sales, return on assets, return on equity, and debt to total assets ratios are all lower with the financial lease or purchase than with the operating lease.

It should be noted that the net advantage of leasing is −$11,031 in this situation, indicating that the purchase is preferred over the lease[21] on a present value basis. But managers may not choose to purchase. Concern over what is reported may override concern about the actual cash flows generated, and lead to the choice of the operating lease if that alternative is available.

The objective of accountants in the treatment of financial leases is to accurately report the economic nature of the contract, and to discourage decision-making aimed at distorting the information reported through financial statements. Further changes in accounting rules would be needed to remove the financial statement advantages of an operating lease over a financial lease.

CURRENT LEASING PRACTICE |

Several surveys of leasing practice have been conducted, and several studies have been aimed at finding out why some companies use leases more than others. With regard to decision techniques, evaluation of after-tax lease payments using an after-tax cost of debt, as discussed in this chapter, is common practice.[22] Ang and Peterson found that companies that used substantial amounts of borrowing also used substantial amounts of leasing,[23] which is consistent with the explanation that leases are used to extend debt capacity. Sharpe and Ngyun found that leases are more common with lower-rated, cash-poor firms, the types of companies that tend to have high borrowing costs.[24] Krishnan and Moyer found evidence that companies are more likely to lease if the likelihood of bankruptcy and the associated costs of bankruptcy are high in the industry.[25]

Smith and Wakeman found that, as would be expected, the tax rates of lessors and lessees were important factors in determining who acted as lessors and

---

[21]The net advantage of leasing was found using Equation 21-3. Note that the after-tax cost of debt is 6.5 percent and accelerated tax depreciation for a 5-year asset is used to find the NAL:

$Dep_1 = .2 \times 200,000 = \$40,000$, $Dep_2 = .4 \times 160,000 = \$64,000$, and so on:

$NAL = 200,000 - .35(40,000)/1.065 - .35(64,000)/1.065^2 - .35(38,400)/1.065^3 -$
$.35(23,040)/1.065^4 - .35(23,040)/1.065^5 - .35(11,520)/1.065^6 -$
$(1 - .35)32,549 PVAI_{10yrs,6.5\%}$

$= -\$11,031$

[22]T. J. O'Brien and B. H. Nunnally, Jr., "A 1982 Survey of Corporate Leasing Analysis," *Financial Management* 12 (Summer 1983): 30–39.

[23]James Ang and Pamela Peterson, "The Leasing Puzzle," *Journal of Finance* 39 (September 1984): 1055–1065.

[24]Steven A. Sharpe and Hien H. Nguyen, "Capital Market Imperfections and the Incentive to Lease," *Journal of Financial Economics* 39 (December 1995): 271–294.

[25]V. Sivarama Krishnan and R. Charles Moyer, "Bankruptcy Costs and the Financial Leasing Decision," *Financial Management* 23 (Summer 1994): 31–42.

lessees. Smith and Wakeman also observed eight factors which appeared to make the decision to lease more likely:

1. The value of the asset is less sensitive to use and maintenance decisions. This decreases the agency problems associated with the contract.
2. The asset is not specialized to the firm. An asset that can be used by others generates fewer risks for the lessor.
3. The expected period of use is short relative to the useful life of the asset. The lessor is often in a better position to find a new user than is the lessee.
4. Corporate bond contracts contain specific financial policy covenants. As explained earlier, a lease can sometimes be used to acquire an asset when additional borrowing is not allowed.
5. Management compensation contracts contain provisions specifying payoffs as a function of the return on invested capital. In these cases, leases reduce the asset base on paper while still giving the company the same assets to use in generating income.
6. The firm is closely held so that risk reduction is important. Leases transfer risks such as obsolescence risk and nonperformance risks to people or organizations who may be able to diversify away those risks.
7. The lessor has market power. In some cases, lessors make assets available only on a lease basis. This way, they can control how the assets are used. Only lessors with market power can do this, because competition would otherwise force them to offer sale contracts as well.
8. The lessor has a competitive advantage in asset disposal. If the lessor is also the manufacturer or dealer, for example, the lessor can capitalize on a network of sales contacts to sell or re-lease an asset when another user would have difficulty finding a buyer.[26]

The factors which seem to affect the leasing decision in practice are consistent with the general reasons for leasing cited earlier in this chapter and also are consistent with the principles of lease analysis developed in this chapter.

SUMMARY

A *lease* is a contract by which the owner of property gives someone else the right to use that property for a specified amount of time in exchange for specified payments. In a lease contract, the owner is called the *lessor* and the party who has the use of the asset in exchange for payments is called the *lessee*. An operating lease, also called a *service lease* or *service contract,* commits the lessor to provide and maintain the asset. A *financial lease* is purely a method of financing. The lessor neither maintains the equipment nor otherwise assures its serviceability. A *leveraged lease* is a lease in which the lessor uses borrowed money to acquire

[26]Clifford W. Smith, Jr., and L. MacDonald Wakeman, "Determinants of Corporate Leasing Policy," *Journal of Finance* 40 (July 1985): 896–910.

the asset to be leased. With a *sale and leaseback* arrangement the owner of an asset contracts to sell the asset and to lease it from the buyer, typically under a financial lease arrangement.

Reasons for Leasing. The primary reasons generally cited for leasing are (1) increased availability of financing, (2) shift of ownership risk, (3) flexibility, (4) tax advantages, (5) accounting benefits, (6) opportunity to circumvent the capital investment decision process, (7) reimbursement formulas, and (8) lower cost.

Cash Flow Analysis of Lease vs. Buy Decisions. A lease can be compared to a purchase based on the present value of the cash flows to lease and the present value of the cash flows to own. The net advantage of leasing is the difference between the present value of cash flows to own and cash flows to lease.

Leasing and Capital Budgeting. The sum of the net present value of a purchased asset and the net advantage of leasing is the net present value if the asset is leased. An asset that has a negative net present value if purchased is still attractive if the net advantage of leasing is larger than the amount of negative net present value.

Financial Statement Impacts of Leases. If accountants classify a lease as an operating lease, the lessee shows the lease expense on the income statement, and the balance sheet is not affected. If the accountants classify a lease as a financial lease, an asset with a value equal to the present value of the lease payments is implied, and the lease payments are treated as payments on an installment loan for the implied asset. The lease payment is replaced on the income statement by implied interest expense and implied depreciation. The implied asset and implied debt are placed on the balance sheet. An operating lease often looks better on the financial statements than a purchase or a financial lease.

QUESTIONS |

21–1. Define the terms (a) lease, (b) lessor, (c) lessee, (d) financial lease, (e) operating lease, (f) leveraged lease, and (g) sale and leaseback.

21–2. What types of assets can be leased?

21–3. What types of organizations act as lessors? as lessees?

21–4. What are the main advantages of leasing that may cause companies to choose that method of acquiring assets?

21–5. What are the conditions that may cause the Internal Revenue Service to treat a lease as if it were a purchase?

21–6. What happens if the Internal Revenue Service treats a lease as if it were a purchase?

21–7. What conditions may make it possible for a lessor to offer a lease that would yield a smaller present value of cash costs than a purchase?

21–8. What conditions cause accountants to consider a lease to be a financial or capital lease?

21-9. How does the accounting treatment of a financial lease differ from that of an operating lease?

21-10. Why is the depreciation tax shield discounted at the after-tax cost of debt in computing the net advantage of leasing when it was discounted at the weighted average cost of capital in other capital budgeting analysis?

PROBLEMS |

21-1. Booth Corporation is considering a minicomputer that can be leased for $2,000 a year for 5 years. The company's marginal tax rate is 35 percent and the yield to maturity on the company's debt is 9.23 percent. Compute the cost to lease if lease payments and associated tax savings are at the
a. beginning of each year.
b. end of each year.

21-2. For the asset in problem 1, lease payments are at the beginning of each year, and tax payments are spread over the year. Assume, for simplicity, that tax payments occur at mid-year. Compute the cost of leasing.

21-3. A dental x-ray machine can be leased for $1,000 at the beginning of each month for four years. The dental clinic's borrowing rate is 10.769 percent and the tax rate is 35 percent. For simplicity, treat both the lease payments and the associated tax savings as if they arrived at year-end. What is the cost to lease?

21-4. A $30,000, 12.308 percent loan will be paid off in 3 years. At the end of each year, a $10,000 principal payment will be made, plus an interest payment of 12.308 percent of the amount owed at the beginning of the year. The borrower faces a 35 percent marginal tax rate.
a. Ignoring taxes, find the present value of the principal and interest payments, discounted at the interest rate on the debt.
b. Find the present value of the after-tax principal and interest payments, discounted at the after-tax cost of debt.

21-5. Hodges Corporation is considering a new asset that can be purchased for $100,000. Maintenance costs will be $5,000 a year for the asset's 8-year actual life, and are highly predictable. The asset will be depreciated over an 8-year life for tax purposes, using depreciation of $12,500 a year (for simplicity). The asset will be placed in service on January 1. The asset will have no salvage value. Assume all cash flows other than the initial purchase are year-end, the tax rate is 34 percent, and the after-tax cost of debt is 6 percent. What is the cost to buy?

21-6. Ann Arbor salvage needs a new compactor that can be purchased for $100,000. The asset will last for 10 years, but has a tax life of 5 years. Operating costs, excluding depreciation, will be $20,000 a year. The asset will be placed in service January 1 and depreciated using the straight-line method. The estimated salvage value, before tax, is $10,000. The tax rate is 34 percent, the after-tax cost of debt is 6 percent, and the weighted average cost of capital is 12 percent. Assume the operating costs are highly predictable and that all cash flows occur at year-end. What is the cost to own?

21–7. For the asset in problem 6, assume the operating costs are highly correlated with (have the same beta as) the company's net cash flows. Find the cost to own.

21–8. Las Cruces Printing is considering a new press. The press can be purchased on January 1 for $24,000. The press has an 8-year actual life and a 5-year tax life. Depreciation will be straight-line, and the estimated salvage value is $6,000, before tax. Operating expenses will be $2,000 a year, and are not correlated with any other activity. Instead of purchasing, the company can lease the asset for $5,250 at the *beginning* of each year for 8 years. Operating costs will be paid by the lessor. Assume all cash flows except the lease payments and initial purchase price occur at year-end. The tax rate is 34 percent, the weighted average cost of capital is 12 percent, and the after-tax cost of debt is 6 percent. Should the company lease or buy?

21–9. For the press in problem 8, what is the minimum salvage value for the purchase to be preferred over the lease?

21–10. For the press in problem 8, what is the maximum acceptable lease payment if the lease is to be preferred over the purchase?

21–11. You want a new status automobile for personal use. Neither depreciation nor interest payments will be tax-deductible. You can buy the automobile for $23,450, with a $5,000 down payment and a 12 percent, 40-month loan. The monthly payments will be $561.91. Alternately, you can lease the automobile with only a $500 refundable security deposit and lease payments of $499 at the beginning of each month for 40 months. Using a 12 percent annual required return to evaluate the salvage value, what must the car be worth at the end of 40 months for the purchase to be more attractive than the lease?

21–12. Lansing Electric is considering a new automatic test unit. The asset can be purchased on January 1 for $45,000. The asset has a 6-year actual life, a 5-year tax life, and no anticipated salvage value. Depreciation will be $9,000 a year (for simplicity) if the asset is acquired. The asset will generate earnings before tax of $6,600 a year. The company has a 35 percent tax rate, a 10 percent weighted average cost of capital, and a 6 percent after-tax cost of debt. Assume benefits and taxes occur at year-end.

a. Is this an attractive investment?

b. The asset can also be leased for $7,500 at the beginning of each year for six years. What should the company do?

21–13. Milwaukee Supply is considering asset A, which can be leased for $30,000 at the beginning of each year for 10 years and would be placed in service on January 1. The lease is a financial lease arrangement, not providing for any maintenance. This asset will generate earnings before lease payments and taxes of $45,000 a year for 10 years. The company has a 34 percent tax rate. The company has a 10 percent before-tax cost of debt and a 10 percent weighted average cost of capital. Although the asset is not available for purchase, it is estimated that an asset of this type would sell for approximately $215,000, would have a 5-year tax life, and would have no salvage value. Should it be leased?

21–14. Asset A in problem 13 is mutually exclusive with regard to asset B. Asset B can only be purchased—for $215,000. Asset B will generate earnings before depreciation and tax of $50,000 a year for its 10-year life. The asset will be placed in service on January 1, and straight-line depreciation will be used for a 5-year tax life. The asset is not expected to have a salvage value. Should the company choose asset A, asset B, or neither asset?

21–15. Rochester Human Services Association needs a new blood-storage unit. A blood-storage unit can be purchased for $100,000. The asset has a 5-year tax life and a 6-year actual life. The asset will be placed in service on January 1 and is expected to have no salvage value. Both the association and the potential lessor can borrow at 10 percent. The lessor is in a 40 percent tax bracket and the association pays no income tax. The lessor will also provide maintenance services worth $5,000 a year. What is the maximum lease payment the association would be willing to make, and what is the minimum lease payment the lessor would be willing to accept?

21–16. Athens Technology can purchase a needed asset for $100,000 or lease it for $30,000 at the end of each year for 5 years. The lease would be considered an operating lease and the asset would have a 5-year life for accounting purposes. The company would finance the purchase with a 10 percent loan, and has a 34 percent tax rate. Show the impact of the purchase and the lease on accounting income for the first year.

21–17. The balance sheet for Athens Technology follows. Show how the balance sheet would look immediately after acquiring the asset in the previous problem
  a. through a purchase.
  b. through an operating lease.

Current assets	$200,000	Current liabilities	$100,000
Fixed assets	400,000	Long-term debt	200,000
Total assets	$600,000	Owners' equity	300,000
		Total liab. & o. e.	$600,000

21–18. A lease calls for payments of $20,000 at the beginning of each year for 5 years. The lease is considered a financial lease by the accountants. The company pays a 10 percent interest rate on debt. What is the implied asset value and the implied first-year interest? What are the total first-year implied interest and depreciation expenses? What would be the total first-year expense if the lease were considered an operating lease?

21–19. A needed asset can be purchased by Jackson Bearing Service on January 1 for $50,000, and placed in service on January 1. The asset has a 6-year actual life and a 5-year tax life. The company's tax rate is 35 percent. The after-tax cost of debt is 6 percent, the before-tax cost of debt is 9.23 percent, and the weighted average cost of capital is 10 percent. Alternately, the asset can be leased for $10,700 at the beginning of each year for 6 years. The asset is expected to have a $10,000 salvage value. Consider both the cash flows and the financial statement impacts. Should the company purchase or lease the asset?

21–20. (**Applications**) The Limited, Inc., is a specialty retailer with nearly $7 billion in sales in 1992. They operate The Limited, Lerner, Lane Bryant, Victoria's Secret, Structure, Bath & Body Works, and several specialty stores under different names. In total they had 4,425 stores at the end of 1992. In the 1992 annual report they reported no capitalized lease obligations. In the footnotes to the same annual report they reported minimum rent commitments under noncancelable leases of:

1993	$ 527,000,000
1994	524,600,000
1995	508,300,000
1996	490,800,000
1997	466,800,000
Thereafter	$2,636,000,000

The Limited, Inc., had the following capital structure disclosed in the balance sheet:

Long-Term Debt	$ 541,639,000
Stockholders' Equity (at book value)	2,267,617,000

They had 362,648,000 shares outstanding with a market price of $23 each. Their beta was 1.5 and the cost of existing equity using the CAPM was 15 percent. The before-tax cost of debt was approximately 7.5 percent with an after-tax cost of 4.6 percent.

a. Assuming the $2,636,000,000 labeled "thereafter" equals $439,000,000 for the next 5 years (1998 to 2002) and $441,000,000 in the sixth year (2003), what is the present value of the lease commitments for The Limited?

b. Calculate the weighted average cost of capital without the lease commitments and then with the lease commitments.

c. For a project that involves the opening of a new store by signing a lease for the store, which discount rate is more appropriate?

21–21. (**Ethical considerations**) Within the last five years, the practice of leasing people has become more and more popular in practice. Under the typical agreement, an employment agency hires the individuals and takes care of the payroll duties and the required labor reporting. As the client businesses need additional staff, the individuals are contacted by the employment agency and told where to report for work. Some of these workers are hired by the client business if the demand is expected to continue and the leased worker is "working out" in the job. When demand is not sufficient to maintain the leased person, the business notifies the employment agency, and the person is either reassigned, furloughed, or terminated.

a. In a purely financial sense, leasing people has some of the same benefits and disadvantages as leasing any other asset. From the corporate perspective, what are the benefits and disadvantages of leasing employees?

b. Ethically, who assumes most of the risk under the set-up described above? Given that managers should have the best information concerning the employment needs of the organization and a fiduciary responsibility to the shareholders and other parties, comment on the ethical issues surrounding the leasing of employees. Describe the situations in which you feel leasing people is acceptable and where you feel it is unacceptable.

c. Do you expect this practice to increase or decrease in popularity in the future? Why?

CASE PROBLEM |

National Petrochemical

National Petrochemical was a producer of various chemicals, primarily based on petroleum. Security analysts had been critical of National for several reasons. First and foremost, return on equity was low and declining. National had a profit margin on sales similar to the rest of the industry, but National had a lower total asset turnover ratio and used less financial leverage than the industry. While asset turnover and profit margin had improved slightly in the past year, operating costs had increased faster than sales and total asset turnover had declined. None of these trends seemed healthy. National's operating results for 1993 and 1994 are shown in Table 21.3.

For comparison, average ratios for a sample of six similar companies were as follows:

Ratio	1993 Competitor Averages
Sales/total assets	1.3
Net income/sales	4.00%
Net income/total assets	5.20%
Debt/total assets	50.53%
Return on equity	11.34%

| TABLE 21.3 FINANCIAL STATEMENTS FOR NATIONAL PETROCHEMICAL

All dollar amounts are in thousands. 1993 statements are actual and 1994 statements are forecast, based on results for the first three quarters.

Year	1993	1994
Sales	$561,225	$572,250
Cost of goods sold	470,675	477,925
Gross profit	90,550	94,325
Operating costs	44,875	46,750
Net operating income	45,675	47,575
Interest expense	11,850	11,325
Earnings before tax	33,825	36,250
Income tax	14,771	16,947
Net income	$ 19,054	$ 19,303
Current assets	$199,575	$203,225
Fixed assets	186,925	224,825
Other assets	86,050	76,925
Total assets	$472,550	$504,975
Current liabilities	$104,000	$131,500
Long-term debt	76,350	68,350
Other liabilities	43,175	56,725
Common equity	249,025	248,400
Total liab. & net worth	$472,550	$504,975

Profitability problems were on the mind of the controller, Irene Watson, when she began to analyze two proposals for a new telephone system for the company's headquarters. There was no question about the need for a new system, but the choices available would affect the company's financial position differently. The impact of a communication system was small compared to something like a new factory. But Watson knew that performance would be improved by doing a lot of small things right, not by one or two dramatic actions. She was, therefore, determined to make a communication system decision that would move the company in the right direction.

One system consisted of a central telephone switch located on National's premises. This switch would cost $4,832,000, including installation. A parts inventory would cost $223,680 and would have no salvage value. Maintenance was estimated at $343,267 a year. The system would be placed in service for tax purposes on December 31, 1994, and would have a depreciation life of seven years. However, National's lease on its headquarters building only had 5 years to run, and it was not anticipated that the system would have any salvage value if National moved at the end of 5 years. The system would be financed with a 5-year term loan requiring equal annual payments. Space, insurance, and electricity costs would be approximately $110,000 a year.

The regional telephone company had proposed an alternate system, using the telephone company's local switching office. That system would require service contract payments of $1,800,000 a year. Payments would be made at the beginning of each month.

National had a weighted average cost of capital of 13 percent and a borrowing rate of 10 percent. Including state and local taxes, National expected to have a 40 percent marginal tax rate in 1994 and later years although the historical average rate was higher for reasons not relevant to this case.

CASE QUESTIONS

1. Compute the present value of the cash flows to own over a 5-year period.
2. Compute the present value of the cash flows for 5 years with the telephone company service contract.
3. Assume the 1995 financial statement is the same as the pro-forma 1994 statement, except for tax rates, and the impact of the new telephone system.
   a. Show the financial statement impacts of the purchase.
   b. Show the financial statement impacts of the service contract.
4. Should National purchase the equipment or enter into a service contract?

SELECTED REFERENCES

Ang, James S., and Pamela P. Peterson. "The Leasing Puzzle." *Journal of Finance* 39 (September 1984): 1055–1065.

Athanasopoulos, Peter J., and Peter W. Bacon. "The Evaluation of Leveraged Leases." *Financial Management* 9 (Spring 1980): 76–80.

Bayless, Mark E., and David J. Diltz. "Capital Leasing and Corporate Borrowing." *Engineering Economist* 32 (Summer 1987): 281–302.

_____. "An Empirical Study of Debt Displacement Effects of Leasing." *Financial Management* 15 (Winter 1986): 53–60.

Bierman, Harold, Jr. "Buy Versus Lease with an Alternative Minimum Tax." *Financial Management* 17 (Winter 1988): 87–91.

Carson, Roger L. "Leasing, Asset Lines, and Uncertainty: A Practitioner's Comments." *Financial Management* 16 (Summer 1987): 13–16.

Copeland, Thomas E., and Fred J. Weston. "A Note on the Evaluation of Cancelable Operating Leases." *Financial Management* 11 (Summer 1982): 60–67.

Crawford, Peggy J., Charles P. Harper, and John J. McConnel. "Further Evidence on the Terms of Financial Leases." *Financial Management* 10 (Autumn 1981): 7–14.

Dunn, M. Douglas, and Bernard C. Topper, Jr. "Terms and Conditions for Electric Utility Success with Leveraged Leases." *Public Utilities Fortnightly* 119 (April 16, 1987): 14–23.

Franks, Julian R., and Stewart D. Hodges. "Lease Valuation When Taxable Earnings Are a Scarce Resource." *Journal of Finance* 42 (September 1987): 987–1007.

Grimlund, Richard A., and Robert Capettini. "A Note on the Evaluation of Cancelable Operating Leases." *Financial Management* 11 (Summer 1982): 68–72.

Hartman, Joseph C., and Jack R. Lohman. "Multiple Options in Parallel Replacement Analysis: Buy, Lease, or Rebuild." *Engineering Economist* 42 (Spring 1997): 223–248.

Heaton, Hal. "Corporate Taxation and Leasing." *Journal of Financial and Quantitative Analysis* 21 (September 1986): 351–359.

Hochman, Shalom, and Ramon Rabinovitch. "Financial Leasing under Inflation." *Financial Management* 13 (Spring 1984): 17–26.

Hodges, Stewart D. "The Valuation of Variable Rate Leases." *Financial Management* 14 (Spring 1985): 68–74.

Idol, Charles R. "A Note on Specifying Debt Displacement and Tax Shield Borrowing Opportunities in Financial Lease Valuation Models." *Financial Management* 9 (Summer 1980): 24–29.

Krishnan, V. Sivarama, and R. Charles Moyer. "Bankruptcy Costs and the Financial Leasing Decision." *Financial Management* 23 (Summer 1994): 31–42.

Lease, Ronald C., John J. McConnell, and James S. Schallheim. "Realized Returns and the Default and Prepayment Experience of Financial Leasing Contracts." *Financial Management* 9 (Summer 1980): 11–20.

Lee, Wayne Y., John D. Martin, and Andrew J. Senchak, Jr. "The Case for Using Options to Evaluate Salvage Values in Financial Leases." *Financial Management* 11 (Autumn 1982): 33–41.

Levy, Haim, and Marshall Sarnat. "Leasing, Borrowing, and Financial Risk." *Financial Management* 8 (Winter 1979): 47–54.

Mukherjee, Tarun K. "A Survey of Corporate Leasing Analysis." *Financial Management* 20 (Autumn 1991): 96–107.

Roenfeldt, Rodney L., and Jerome S. Osteryoung. "Analysis of Financial Leases." *Financial Management* 2 (Spring 1973): 74–87.

_____. "Lease-Cost Measurement of Hospital Equipment." *Financial Management* 8 (Spring 1979): 24–35.

Schall, Laurence D. "Analytical Issues in Lease vs. Purchase Decisions." *Financial Management* 16 (Summer 1987): 17–20.

Sharpe, Steven A., and Hien H. Nguyen. "Capital Market Imperfections and the Incentive to Lease." *Journal of Financial Economics* 39 (December 1995): 271–294.

Smith, Bruce D. "Accelerated Debt Repayment in Leverage Leases." *Financial Management* 11 (Summer 1982): 73–80.

Smith, Clifford W., Jr., and L. MacDonald Wakeman. "Determinants of Corporate Leasing Policy." *Journal of Finance* 40 (July 1985): 895–910.

Steele, Anthony. "Difference Equation Solutions to the Valuation of Lease Contracts." *Journal of Financial and Quantitative Analysis* 19 (September 1984): 311–328.

Weingartner, H. Martin. "Leasing, Asset Lives, and Uncertainty: Guides to Decision Making." *Financial Management* 16 (Summer 1987): 5–12. Also see "Rejoinder" on pages 21–23.

CHAPTER 22

CAPITAL RATIONING

After completing this chapter you should be able to:

1. Explain how the capital markets may influence a firm to ration capital.
2. Criticize and/or justify a management policy limiting the amount of capital to be invested in a specific time period.
3. Differentiate between single-period capital rationing and multiple-period capital rationing.
4. Describe how some companies use the internal rate of return to ration capital and the conditions necessary for a wealth-maximizing decision when ranking with the internal rate of return.
5. Calculate the profitability index and understand what this measures.
6. Select between mutually exclusive investments within a capital rationing framework.
7. List resources, other than cash, that can be the limiting or rationed resource in deciding among mutually exclusive investments.
8. Prepare a presentation to an executive committee detailing why your firm should ration capital.

In January 1988, William H. Sullivan, Jr., found himself in imminent danger of losing his New England Patriots football team, while his son Charles was in imminent danger of losing the stadium. The junior Sullivan bought the Patriots' stadium in 1981 and then invested heavily in a new electronic scoreboard and luxury boxes. He also invested in a harness racing track and a deal to license products associated with a Michael Jackson tour. He was saddled with $40 million of debt on a stadium for which he had paid only $5 million. In the meantime, the senior Sullivan invested heavily in players and gave an option to acquire the team in order to secure debt financing. He then tried to sell stock to buy back the option, but investors were not interested. By early 1988, the creditors were preparing to exercise their option, and Charles Sullivan was in default on $20 million of debt.[1]

[1]*Business Week* (January 25, 1988): 40.

The Sullivans' problems illustrate the difficulties that can follow uncontrolled expansion. If the expansion appears to be uncontrolled or unprofitable, the investing public declines to furnish equity under terms that managers will accept. Expansion is then financed with debt, at increasingly higher interest rates and with increasingly onerous conditions attached. It may be argued that the Sullivans' underlying problem was that they made capital investments that did not have positive net present values. However, unprofitable investments are more likely to occur when expansion is uncontrolled. One way to control expansion and avoid problems of this type is to use capital rationing. Capital rationing occurs when the total capital budget is limited, forcing rejection of some capital investments that have positive net present values.

Survey results suggest that most companies operate under capital rationing at least part of the time,[2] so a reasonable basis for decision making under capital rationing is needed. The goal of maximizing wealth is still the main capital budgeting criterion when we face capital rationing, but future investment opportunities and future availability of funds must be considered in selecting investments to achieve that goal.

Capital rationing differs from the mutually exclusive investment decisions discussed in Chapter 7. Mutually exclusive investments are generally competing methods of achieving the same goal or competing uses of a scarce resource other than money. When two investments are mutually exclusive, there are often physical reasons why both cannot be chosen. Competitors under capital rationing are competing uses of the same scarce money.

This chapter begins with a discussion of why capital rationing occurs. Then, a general model for capital budgeting under capital rationing is developed. Next, a usable approach is developed under some reasonable simplifying assumptions. Finally, we will consider the joint problems of capital rationing and mutually exclusive investments.

REASONS FOR CAPITAL RATIONING |

The numerous explanations for capital rationing that have been cited fall into one of two broad categories: management policy and capital market conditions.

CAPITAL MARKET–IMPOSED RATIONING

Rationing never occurs in theoretical perfect markets because companies can always raise money if they have attractive investments. But information limits and transaction-related costs can lead to capital rationing in real markets. Capital markets impose capital rationing when investors and lenders absolutely refuse to provide capital beyond some specific amount. Market-imposed rationing also

---

[2]Larry J. Gitman and J. R. Forrester, Jr., "A Survey of Capital Expenditure Techniques Used by Major U.S. Firms," *Financial Management* 6 (Fall 1977): 66–71; J. W. Petty, D. F. Scott, and M. M. Bird, "The Capital Expenditure Decision-Making Process of Large Corporations," *Engineering Economist* 20 (Spring 1975): 159–172; and Marc Ross, "Capital Budgeting Practices of Twelve Large Manufacturers," *Financial Management* 15 (Winter 1986): 15–22.

occurs when the marginal cost of capital rises vertically as more capital is sought. Both types of rationing can be dealt with using the same model because absolute refusal to furnish more funds is an extreme case of a vertically rising marginal cost of capital.

Figure 22.1 illustrates market-imposed capital rationing. Up to amount A, the company's marginal cost of capital is 10 percent. Above amount A, the cost rises to 12 percent. *Friction costs* are one common reason for a rising cost of capital schedule. The cumulative amount represented by A may be provided from internally generated funds, for example, while amounts beyond A must be raised externally. The cost of internally generated capital is the return that could be earned outside the firm if the funds were returned to shareholders and lenders, *minus* taxes and other friction costs that would be incurred if funds were returned to investors. The cost above A would then be the return that could be earned outside the firm by shareholders and lenders, *plus* flotation costs associated with raising new capital. The estimation of these costs was treated in Chapter 16.

In Figure 22.1, 12 percent and 10 percent are sometimes referred to as the "borrowing" and "lending" rates. The company has available amount A. The company can "lend" some of that money at 10 percent by buying back its own securities or buying similar securities. If the company wants to "borrow" by raising additional funds, it must pay 12 percent. For a large company with publicly traded stock, the jump at A may be as small as a fraction of 1 percent. A small, privately held company wanting to sell its stock to the public for the first time may experience flotation costs in excess of 30 percent of the market value of the new capital. Companies of this type will experience substantial vertical segments of their marginal cost of capital schedules.

In Figure 22.1, the investment opportunity schedule represents the investments being considered by the company.[3] (For simplicity, assume investments precede benefits and each investment has only one internal rate of return.) The company could earn a 15 percent return on the last dollar invested if it invested only small amounts. If the company invested amount A, though, it would earn a return of 11 percent on the last investment. Beyond amount A, the company would be raising money at a cost of 12 percent to invest in assets earning less than 11 percent. Given this set of investment opportunities, the company will maximize wealth by investing amount A and rejecting some investments providing returns above 10 percent.

Even if the marginal cost of capital schedule has vertical segments, capital rationing may not occur. Capital rationing occurs only if the investment opportunity schedule intersects a vertical segment of the cost of capital schedule. A

---

[3]In practice the curve is not smooth, but consists of steps because of lumpiness; many investments must be taken in their entirety or not at all. Lumpiness is a potential problem for the projects near the intersection with the cost of capital schedule. Because of lumpiness, it may not be necessary to carry over some money from one year to the next in short-term investments. Lumpiness is not an important problem for large firms considering making hundreds or thousands of capital investments every year. Methods of expanding the analysis to deal with lumpiness where this is a problem are taken up later.

| **FIGURE 22.1** **INVESTMENT OPPORTUNITY AND COST OF CAPITAL SCHEDULE**

Amount A can be raised internally at a 10 percent cost of capital. If the company wants to raise additional funds, the cost will rise to 12 percent because of flotation costs. The highest-return investment opportunity available to the company is 15 percent, and to invest an amount greater than A, the company must accept investments with returns below 11 percent.

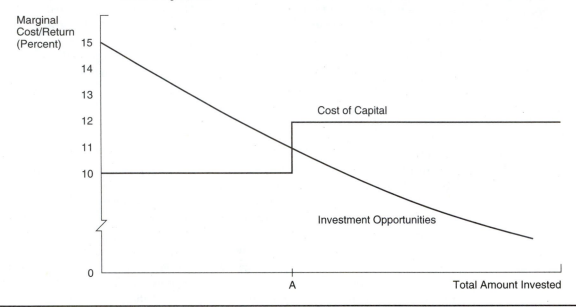

sufficient shift of the investment opportunity schedule to either the left or the right in Figure 22.1 would move this company out of capital rationing. This can explain why companies report capital rationing in some years and not in others.

The greater the increase in the marginal cost of capital at quantity A, the greater the likelihood of market-imposed capital rationing. If the marginal cost of capital rose to infinity at A—an absolute refusal to supply more than amount A to the company—there would be a high probability of market-imposed capital rationing occurring. Absolute refusal could occur because of problems like information asymmetry. Suppose, for example, that potential investors are much less optimistic than management about investment opportunities. Suppose, for example, that potential investors believe that proposed new capital investments will force the company into bankruptcy. Since lenders do not expect to receive either principal or interest payments, there is no level of promised interest payment that will compensate them for their risk. Whited suggests that information asymmetry may be a particularly important source of capital restraint for distressed companies.[4]

[4]Toni M. Whited, "Debt, Liquidity Constraints, and Corporate Investment: Evidence from Panel Data," *Journal of Finance* 47 (September 1992): 1425–1460.

Some prefer to define capital rationing as the absolute refusal of investors to provide funds at any price.[5] The reason for using a broader definition of capital rationing here is that the decision problems are similar whether investors absolutely refuse to provide more money or the marginal cost of capital schedule is vertical at its intersection with the investment opportunity schedule. In either case, the company will reject investments that have positive net present values when evaluated using the marginal cost of capital for the last dollar used.

CAPITAL RATIONING AS MANAGEMENT POLICY |

Capital rationing as management policy occurs when managers set an upper limit on the total amount of capital investment for a period, even if additional funds could be raised and investments with positive net present values are being rejected. An example of capital rationing by managers would be a decision to limit investment to an amount less than A in Figure 22.1.

Capital rationing may be used as a method of management control. If all investments with positive net present values are accepted in a large organization, this leaves the choices of both rate and direction of growth in the hands of managers well down in the organization; there will be no strategy.

Capital rationing is one way to implement strategy and avoid uncontrolled growth. The executives can set a total capital budget amount for the year, which then defines the target rate of asset growth. Then, the capital budget can be allocated among divisions based on strategic decisions about areas of growth. Additional rounds of allocation may take place within divisions in a similar manner. Finally, the individual capital investment proposals in each responsibility area compete for the capital budget allocated to that area, assuming the supply of attractive proposals is adequate. With this approach, top executives know the direction of growth, amount of growth, and amount of new money they must raise. While rejecting positive net present value investments may seem like an expensive way to implement controls, managers often find this approach more workable than any known alternatives.[6] In a survey of major corporations, Klammer,

---

[5]Brigham and Gapinski, for example, define capital rationing as occurring when the "size of the [capital] budget is less than the investment called for by the NPV (or IRR) criterion." [Eugene F. Brigham and Louis C. Gapinski, *Intermediate Financial Management* (Hinsdale, Ill.: Dryden Press, 1985), 404.] A in Figure 22.1 is the amount called for by the net present value criterion, given the cost of capital and investment opportunity schedules, so the problem illustrated in that figure would not meet Brigham and Gapinski's definition of capital rationing. Bierman and Smidt, on the other hand, identify differences between "lending" and "borrowing" rates as one of the causes of capital rationing. [Harold Bierman, Jr., and Seymour Smidt, *The Capital Budgeting Decision*, 7th ed. (New York: Macmillan Company, 1988), 191–196.]

[6]For additional discussion of these problems, see Robert H. Litzenberger and O. Maurice Joy, "Decentralized Capital Budgeting Decisions and Shareholder Wealth Maximization," *Journal of Finance* 30 (September 1975): 993–1002.

Koch, and Wilner found that 72 percent of the responding companies start with a predetermined capital budget amount rather than funding all positive net present value investments.[7]

Closely related to management control is the problem of risk control. The faster a company grows, the greater the portion of its business that is untested, the greater the number of people who are not well known, and so on. Thus, rapid growth and risk often go hand in hand. It was rapid growth, especially the purchase of MGM's library of classic films for $1.5 billion on the heels of several other expansionary ventures, that forced Ted Turner to give up part of his control of his TBS broadcasting empire in order to secure an equity infusion when things did not work out as well as expected.

Because of problems like those encountered by Turner, rapid growth and management comfort are often in opposition. Wright has suggested that some top managers are uncomfortable with a range of responsibility that increases too rapidly and, therefore, use capital rationing as a tool for limiting growth.[8]

Managers also use capital rationing because they are unhappy with the conditions under which additional funds would be furnished from outside sources. Myers' pecking order hypothesis suggests that managers prefer debt over equity, and will only resort to equity when they cannot borrow more.[9] An extension of this view may be an unwillingness to invest beyond amounts that can be funded with internally generated funds and new debt. There is usually not a clear point at which debt becomes absolutely unattainable. More typically, the restrictions imposed by lenders may become increasingly unacceptable as the debt level rises. Managers may be willing to limit the company's growth and give up some wealth rather than accept outside interference.

Management-imposed capital rationing may be used as a surrogate method for dealing with other scarce resources, such as a shortage of middle managers. More wealth would probably be created by seeking to maximize net present value subject to a constraint on the number of middle-level managers used, but a constraint on total capital may be simpler to implement.

Some managers use capital rationing with the anticipation that competition for limited funds will separate good investments from bad. A manager may, for example, be tempted to use overly optimistic projections to get a pet project approved. If acceptance of one investment means rejection of another, though, assumptions and forecasts will be vigorously challenged. This may discourage managers from being overly optimistic as well as flushing out any overly optimistic projections that are made. This motivation for capital rationing is supported by a study showing a tendency for capital investment proposals to be overly opti-

[7]Thomas Klammer, Bruce Koch, and Neil Wilner, "Capital Budgeting Practices—A Survey of Corporate Use," University of North Texas, mimeo, 1988.

[8]F. K. Wright, "Project Evaluation and the Managerial Limit," *Journal of Business* (April 1964): 179–185.

[9]Stewart C. Myers, "The Capital Structure Puzzle," *Journal of Finance* 39 (July 1984): 575–592.

mistic.[10] Some top managers also believe that subordinates are kept on their toes by competition for capital investment dollars.

A MODEL FOR CAPITAL RATIONING |

Regardless of whether capital rationing is chosen by managers or imposed by capital markets, the company has a fixed amount of capital available for some period, referred to as the *capital rationing period*. The appropriate objective for a wealth-maximizing firm working with a fixed pool of capital is to use that fixed pool of capital to maximize future wealth over the time that capital is available for use. To maximize wealth in the face of capital rationing, we can, therefore, decide to maximize wealth as of the end of the capital rationing period. We will illustrate the application of this principle with single-period capital rationing, and then move to a more general model.

SINGLE-PERIOD CAPITAL RATIONING

Single-period capital rationing occurs when capital rationing is not expected to occur after the initial period. In this situation, we can reasonably assume that any funds not invested in the proposed set of investments will be invested elsewhere at the company's cost of capital. As illustrated below, wealth will be maximized if the company simply acts to *allocate scarce capital so as to maximize net present value.*

Example. GNW Corporation has $1,000 available to invest and has two investments available. GNW is experiencing single-period capital rationing and has a 10 percent cost of capital. GNW wants to maximize wealth as of the end of the single capital rationing period. The cash flows for the proposed investments are as follows (I_o is the initial outlay and CF_t is cash flow at the end of year t):

Inv.	I_o	CF_1	CF_2	CF_3
A	700	300	200	500
B	500	400	200	100

GNW can choose only one of these investments with its budget constraint, and unused funds will be invested at the 10 percent cost of capital. The company's wealth as of the end of the first period is the cash it has on hand at the end of the first period, plus the present value of cash flows to be received later. Year-end wealth for each investment alternative follows.

---

[10]Meir Statman and Tyzoon T. Tyebjee, "Optimistic Capital Budget Forecasts," *Financial Management* 14 (Autumn 1985): 27–33.

A: $(\$1,000 - \$700)(1 + .10) + \$300 + \$200/(1 + .10) + \$500/(1 + .10)^2 =$
$$\$1,225.04$$

B: $(\$1,000 - \$500)(1 + .10) + \$400 + \$200/(1 + .10) + \$100/(1 + .10)^2$
$$= \$1,214.46$$

If neither A or B is chosen, the \$1,000 would be invested at 10 percent and the company would have \$1,100 at the end of the year. Therefore, investment A will *increase* wealth at the end of the rationing period by \$1,225.04 − \$1,100.00 = \$125.04, and B will increase wealth at the same time by \$114.46; A is preferred. The net present value is the present value of the amount by which the terminal wealth is increased:

$$NPV_A = \$125.04/(1 + .10) = \$113.67$$

$$NPV_B = \$114.46/(1 + .10) = \$104.05$$

Note that the net present value computed in this way for the single-period rationing case is identical to the traditionally computed net present value:

$$NPV_A = \$300/1.1 + \$200/1.1^2 + \$500/1.1^3 - \$700 = \underline{\$113.67}$$

$$NPV_B = \$400/1.1 + \$200/1.1^2 + \$100/1.1^3 - \$500 = \underline{\$104.05}$$

Thus, allocation of scarce capital so as to maximize net present value will maximize wealth in the face of single-period capital rationing.

Multiperiod Capital Rationing

Multiperiod capital rationing is more complicated because it is necessary to estimate investment opportunity rates in future periods. Recall that the objective is to use the fixed pool of money available for the capital rationing period to maximize wealth as of the end of the rationing period. Going back to GNW, assume that capital rationing will last for 2 years. Any funds not used at the beginning can be invested for the 2-year period at a 20 percent annual return. Funds available at the end of year 1 can be invested at 15 percent for the remaining year of capital rationing.

If GNW chooses neither investment A nor B, the amount it will have at the end of the 2-year rationing period is $\$1,000(1 + .20)^2 = \$1,440$. If GNW invests only in project A, \$300 will still be invested for 2 years at 20 percent. Wealth at the end of the capital rationing period will be:

$$300(1 + .20)^2 + 300(1 + .15) + 200 + 500/(1 + .10) = \underline{\$1,431.55}$$

The investment in project A will, therefore, *decrease* terminal wealth by \$1,440.00 − \$1,431.55 = \$8.45.

This method of analysis can be summarized graphically as follows:

Time 0	I	2	C	C + I	C + 2	N

The process can also be reduced to a formula for the increase in wealth as of the end of the capital rationing period:

$$TW_c = \sum_{t=1}^{c} CF_t(1 + R_t)^{c-t} + \sum_{t=c+1}^{n} CF_t/(1 + k)^{t-c} - I_0(1 + R_0)^c \qquad (22\text{-}1)$$

where

TW_c = contribution to wealth as of the end of the capital rationing period

$\quad c$ = the number of periods capital rationing will occur

$\quad n$ = the number of years until the end of the investment's life

$\quad R_t$ = the rate of return at which funds available at time t can be reinvested until the end of the capital rationing period

$\quad k$ = the cost of capital

Returning to GNW, the terminal wealth contribution of investments A and B are:

$$A: TW_c = 300(1 + .15) + 200 + 500/(1 + .10) - 700(1 + .20)^2 = -\$8.45$$

$$B: TW_c = 400(1 + .15) + 200 + 100/(1 + .10) - 500(1 + .20)^2 = \$30.91$$

Note that A was preferred with single-period capital rationing, but A is unattractive and B is preferred with this capital rationing scenario.

Although terminal wealth maximization leads to the optimal choice, managers often prefer to talk about net present value impact. The net present value impact is simply the present value of the terminal wealth increase. The net present value of terminal wealth (NPV_{TW})[11] is found by dividing Equation 22-1 by $(1 + k)^c$:

---

[11]We assumed that money available at time t could be reinvested until the end of the capital rationing period at rate R_t. If funds available at the end of period t can be invested for only one period at rate R_t, then Equation 19-2 must be rewritten as:

$$NPV_{TW} = \frac{\sum_{t=1}^{c} CF_t(1 + R_t)(1 + R_{t+1}) \cdots (1 + R_{c-1})}{(1 + k)^c} + \sum_{t=c+1}^{n} Cf_t/(1 + k)^t$$

$$- \frac{I_0(1 + R_t)(1 + R_{t+1}) \cdots (1 + R_{c-1})}{(1 + k)^c}$$

Applying this formula to GNW's investment A:

$$NPV_{TW} = \frac{300(1 + .15) + 200}{(1 + .10)^2} + \frac{500}{(1 + .10)^3} - \frac{700(1 + .20)(1 + .10)}{(1 + .10)^2} = \$27.72$$

$$NPV_{TW} = \frac{\sum_{t=1}^{c} CF_t(1 + R_t)^{c-t}}{(1 + k)^c} + \sum_{t=c+1}^{n} CF_t/(1 + k)^t - \frac{I_0(1 + R_0)^c}{(1 + k)^c} \qquad (22\text{-}2)$$

For GNW's investment alternatives, the net present value impacts are:

$$\text{A: } NPV_{TW} = \frac{300(1 + .15) + 200}{(1 + .10)^2} + \frac{500}{(1 + .10)^3} - \frac{700(1 + .20)^2}{(1 + .10)^2} = \underline{\$6.99}$$

$$\text{B: } NPV_{TW} = \frac{400(1 + .15) + 200}{(1 + .10)^2} + \frac{100}{(1 + .10)^3} - \frac{500(1 + .20)^2}{(1 + .10)^2} = \underline{\$25.54}$$

The example was simplified by assuming that an unlimited amount could be invested at a 20 percent return in the first year. Often, though, the company faces an investment opportunity schedule such as that in Figure 22.1, so that the marginal rate of return declines as the amount of new investment increases. The example was also simplified by assuming that the cost of capital was the same in each future period; the company may face a different cost of capital in each future period. These complications make it necessary to jointly select the set of present and future investments. Given the necessary forecasts of future cash flows and investment opportunities, this can be done using mathematical programming procedures explained in Chapter 24.Unfortunately, the analysis is further complicated if investment opportunities in future periods are unknown.

If you do not know how to forecast investment opportunities 10 years from now, and are discouraged at the thought of developing a complex mathematical programming model, take heart. Equation 22-2 can be simplified and a complex multiperiod joint solution can be avoided if you are willing to make the following simplifying assumptions:

1. capital rationing will continue as long as the lives of the investments currently being considered;[12]
2. the marginal cost of capital, k, will be the same for each period;
3. the reinvestment opportunity rate, R, will be the same for each period; and
4. lumpiness is not a significant problem. Lumpiness refers to the fact that certain assets and sources of funds can be acquired only in units of some minimum size. Ford cannot, for example, build an efficient $100,000 automobile factory or raise $7,000 by selling new equity to the public.

With this set of assumptions, Equation 22-2 simplifies to:

$$NPV_{TW} = \left[\sum_{t=1}^{n} CF_t/(1 + R)^t\right][(1 + R)^c/(1 + k)^c] - I_0(1 + R)^c/(1 + k)^c \qquad (22\text{-}3)$$

[12]Alternately, as will be seen, a simple solution is available if capital rationing is only expected to last for one period.

The term $(1 + R)^c/(1 + k)^c$ is a multiplier that will be the same for all investments. Therefore, we can factor out that multiplier and choose investments so as to maximize:

$$NPV_R = \sum_{t=1}^{n} CF_t /(1 + R)^t - I_0 \qquad (22\text{-}4)$$

where NPV_R is the net present value computed with the internal reinvestment opportunity rate rather than the cost of capital. Note that like the original net present value, NPV_R measures the increase in wealth given the set of assumptions used to derive NPV_R.

Looking at Figure 22.1, the assumptions to justify use of Equation 22-4 could be fulfilled by assuming that conditions in the future will be the same as now: the cost of capital, k, will be 10 percent and the reinvestment opportunity rate, R, will be the rate at the intersection of the two schedules: 11 percent.

With these simplifying assumptions, optimal investment selection under capital rationing is again a problem of choosing the set of investments that will maximize net present value. The only difference is that the reinvestment opportunity rate is used instead of the cost of capital as the discount rate. Many companies use this simplified assumption approach because they believe future cost of capital and investment opportunity schedules are too uncertain to justify the use of mathematical programming techniques. Furthermore, investment decisions are decentralized and spread through the year so that a joint decision is not feasible.

Example. Oakland Corporation anticipates having $1 million of internally generated funds available this year, at a 10 percent cost of capital. Oakland is privately owned at present and raising additional capital would require turning to outside markets. Investment bankers indicate that the markets are not currently receptive to new issues, so the marginal cost of externally generated capital would be 15 percent. Management decides that a conservative assumption of a 12 percent reinvestment rate should be used for planning since large amounts can be invested at that rate. The company has the investment opportunities listed in Table 22.1.

If Oakland Corporation expects capital rationing to continue in future years, it will choose investments so as to maximize net present value with a 12 percent discount rate, subject to a constraint of no more than $1 million being invested this year. The combination A, B, D provides the maximum possible net present value using a 12 percent discount rate: $137,000.

THE INTERNAL RATE OF RETURN AND CAPITAL RATIONING |

Some companies use the internal rate of return as a selection method under capital rationing. The internal rate of return ranking will lead to selection of the wealth-maximizing set of investments if lumpiness is not a problem, capital

| TABLE 22.1   INVESTMENT OPPORTUNITY SCHEDULE FOR OAKLAND CORPORATION

The capital investments described in this table represent the investment opportunities currently available to Oakland Corporation. The company has $1 million to invest.

Opportunity	Cost	Life	IRR	NPV(10%)	NPV(12%)
A	$ 500,000	5 years	20%	$134,000	$103,000
B	400,000	5 years	15	52,000	30,000
C	100,000	3 years	14	7,000	3,000
D	100,000	10 years	13	13,000	4,000
E	100,000	20 years	12.5	17,000	3,000
F	1,000,000	10 years	12	87,000	0
G	2,000,000	20 years	10	0	−245,000

rationing will continue as long as the lives of investments currently being considered, all proposed investments have the same risk, and the reinvestment rate, R, meets the following conditions:

1. R will be the same each period,
2. R will exceed the marginal cost of capital for the last dollar used, and
3. R is the return on the highest-return opportunity that would be rejected with an internal rate of return ranking.

Using Table 22.1, an internal rate of return ranking would lead to selection of investments A, B, and C. The highest-return rejected project would be D, with an internal rate of return of 13 percent. Choice of A, B, and C would maximize wealth if the investment opportunity rate in future periods was 13 percent, because these are the only investments with positive net present values at a 13 percent discount rate.[13] Therefore, given these assumptions, the internal rate of return ranking leads to the same choice as NPV_R.

Choosing investments according to internal rate of return ranking will also maximize wealth if the cash inflows from each project can be reinvested for the planning horizon at a rate equal to the internal rate of return for that project.[14] This is, however, a somewhat questionable assumption. Would it not make more sense, for example, to assume that marginal cash inflows can be reinvested at the internal rate of return of the lowest-return project being accepted, or the highest-return project being rejected?

[13]We know from Chapter 6 that an investment with an internal rate of return above the discount rate has a positive net present value, and vice versa.

[14]Robert Dorfman, "The Meaning of Internal Rates of Return," *Journal of Finance* 36 (December 1981): 1011–1021.

MULTIPLE INTERNAL RATES OF RETURN AND CAPITAL RATIONING

Dorfman has shown that when a company is facing capital rationing and an investment has more than one internal rate of return, the highest internal rate of return is the rate at which a starting capital base will grow if all cash flows from the project are invested in projects with the same internal rate of return. If this assumption about the reinvestment opportunity rate does not seem reasonable, the problem can be avoided by choosing according to net present value using the assumed reinvestment opportunity rate.

THE PROFITABILITY INDEX AND CAPITAL RATIONING |

The profitability index (previously defined in Chapter 6) is sometimes suggested as a method of selecting investments under capital rationing. However, a study of Table 22.1 will make it clear that a profitability index ranking using the cost of capital will *not* lead to the optimal decision. On the other hand, a profitability index ranking using the 12 percent opportunity rate expected for future periods will lead to the wealth-maximizing choice in the absence of lumpiness.[15] As an example of why lumpiness causes problem, suppose a company with $100,000 to allocate has the following investment opportunities, each of which must be taken in its entirety or not at all:

Investment	Cost	NPV	Profitability Index
H	$ 10,000	$ 5,000	1.5
I	100,000	20,000	1.2

A profitability index ranking would lead to the choice of H and the rejection of I; this choice would not maximize wealth.[16] An initial ranking by profitability index followed by checking of projects near the cut-off point is usually sufficient to pick up these problems and make the necessary adjustments. In summary, the profitability index using the reinvestment rate is not an alternative to Equation 22-4, but a way to apply Equation 22-4.

[15]For this purpose, the profitability index should be computed using only the initial cash outlay in the denominator, not the present value of all capital outlays for the investment as is sometimes done in other settings. The reason for this measurement method is that we are trying to find the set of investments that lead to the maximum attainable wealth creation, given the $1 million constraint on initial capital.

[16]If leftover funds are invested at the weighted average cost of capital, the $90,000 left over after investment in asset H creates additional net present value of $0.

SELECTION AMONG MUTUALLY EXCLUSIVE INVESTMENTS UNDER CAPITAL RATIONING |

A general model for choice among mutually exclusive investments under capital rationing requires the use of mathematical programming, illustrated in Chapter 24. However, the forecasting problems associated with these models can often be avoided by using the assumptions of constant values of R and k in future periods if some simplifying conditions exist.

One simplifying condition is *the company has enough capital this period to accept all investments with returns above R,* the future investment opportunity rate. In this case, the most desirable of the mutually exclusive investments is the one that maximizes net present value over the life of the scarce resource, using R to compute the net present value as was done in Equation 22-4. If the lives of mutually exclusive investments differ, and the constraining resource can be reused, the equivalent annuity is used. The only change from use of the equivalent annuity in the absence of capital rationing is that R is used instead of k in the computations.

If there is not enough capital to accept all non–mutually exclusive investments with returns above R this period, the choices become a bit more complex. The analysis is still based on the net present value over the constraining resource's life for each possible use of the resource. In this case, though, it is necessary to consider any possible paths of usage that involve a less capital-intensive use of the resource in the beginning, followed by a more capital-intensive use later. It is also necessary to consider the possibility of not using the scarce resource at all. The total set of investments, including one of the mutually exclusive investments, is chosen so as to maximize total net present value.

Example. Basin Corporation operates under capital rationing and has $10,000 to invest this year. The assumed investment opportunity rate in future years is 12 percent. Basin is considering the three capital investment proposals summarized below. Investments A and B are mutually exclusive because they use the same scarce resource: a dock. The dock can be reused indefinitely, but it is not possible to add a second dock. It is possible to acquire more than 1 unit of C.

Investment	Cost	Life	NPV$_R$	Equivalent Annuity
A	$ 5,000	5 years	$ 767.64	$212.95
B	10,000	10 years	1,300.45	230.16
C	5,000	5 years	600.00	166.45

The alternatives available and their net present values are summarized in Table 22.2. If delayed use of the scarce resource is feasible, the best alternative

| TABLE 22.2   ANALYSIS OF CAPITAL INVESTMENT ALTERNATIVES
FOR BASIN CORPORATION

The 5 alternatives and their net present values are summarized. Investments A and B are mutually exclusive.

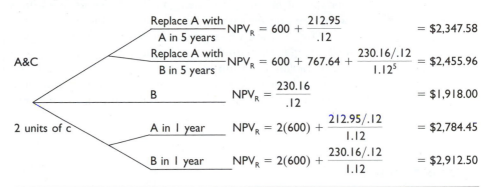

$$\text{Replace A with A in 5 years} \quad NPV_R = 600 + \frac{212.95}{.12} \qquad = \$2,347.58$$

$$\text{Replace A with B in 5 years} \quad NPV_R = 600 + 767.64 + \frac{230.16/.12}{1.12^5} = \$2,455.96$$

$$B \qquad NPV_R = \frac{230.16}{.12} \qquad = \$1,918.00$$

$$\text{A in 1 year} \quad NPV_R = 2(600) + \frac{212.95/.12}{1.12} \qquad = \$2,784.45$$

$$\text{B in 1 year} \quad NPV_R = 2(600) + \frac{230.16/.12}{1.12} \qquad = \$2,912.50$$

A&C

2 units of c

is to acquire 2 units of C now and acquire B in 1 year. If delayed use is not feasible, the best alternative is to acquire A and C now, and then replace A with B in 5 years.

SUMMARY |

Capital rationing occurs when a company limits the total capital budget, thereby forcing it to choose between capital investments with positive net present values. Capital rationing may be imposed by the capital markets or may be the result of management decisions.

Capital market–imposed rationing may be the result of (1) friction costs or other problems resulting in vertical segments in the cost of capital schedule or (2) absolute inability to raise additional capital.

Managers may use capital rationing as a means of controlling the amount and direction of growth. Capital rationing also is viewed as a way to control risk. Managers may use capital rationing as a surrogate method for dealing with other scarce resources such as management time. Managers may use capital rationing because they are unhappy with control problems or other unfavorable aspects of new funds acquisition. Capital rationing also forces competition for scarce resources, and may result in better investment proposals working their way through the decision process.

A general wealth-maximizing solution under capital rationing requires the identification of the set of investments that maximizes terminal wealth, given the investment opportunities this period and every other period. Since the returns on marginal cash flows in future periods generally depend on the amount of cash flow in those periods, a complex joint selection problem is involved, and mathematical programming is generally required.

Fortunately, selection according to the net present value using the reinvestment opportunity rate as the discount rate leads to wealth maximization under reasonable simplifying assumptions. The profitability index and internal rate of return rankings, if properly applied, can lead to rankings that maximize value under capital rationing by leading to the choice of the same set of investments that would be chosen using the net present value criterion directly.

After a wide variety of capital investment selection problems have been considered, the conclusion is that a properly computed net present value is the superior criterion when the various criteria give conflicting rankings. It has also been demonstrated that when internal rate of return and net present value signals conflict under capital rationing, the net present value signals are correct.

QUESTIONS |

22–1. What is meant by the expression *capital rationing?*

22–2. Why would managers voluntarily ration capital?

22–3. What conditions could lead to capital market–imposed capital rationing?

22–4. What is the capital budgeting objective when capital rationing is experienced?

22–5. What simplifying assumptions are necessary for the optimal investment set under capital rationing to be the set that maximizes net present value, using the investment opportunity rate as the required return? Are these assumptions reasonable enough to use in practical decision making?

22–6. If capital rationing is not expected to occur after selection from the current set of proposed projects in the current period, what is the appropriate method for capital investment selection?

22–7. Under what conditions will an internal rate of return ranking give the optimal set of capital investments under capital rationing?

22–8. If the internal rate of return is being used in a capital rationing situation, which internal rate of return is the appropriate one when there is more than one internal rate of return?

22–9. Discuss the usefulness of the profitability index in a capital rationing situation.

22–10. What assumption is necessary to use Equation 22-4 when both capital rationing and mutual exclusiveness problems are encountered?

PROBLEMS |

22–1. Athens Product Company has $1 million of internally generated funds available, at a required return of 10 percent. To raise additional external funds, friction costs would increase the required return to 14 percent. The company has available the following investments:

Investment	Amount	IRR
A	$500,000	20%
B	500,000	15
C	500,000	12
D	500,000	10

a. Will the company experience capital rationing?

b. How much will the company invest?

22–2. Bowling Green Corporation has $1 million of internally generated funds available to invest. The required return on these funds is 12 percent, and friction costs will increase the required return on new capital to 16 percent. The company has the investment opportunities shown below.

Investment	Amount	IRR
A	$500,000	20%
B	500,000	18
C	500,000	19
D	500,000	15

a. Will the company experience capital rationing?

b. How much will the company invest?

22–3. Cleveland Consolidated is expecting capital rationing to last for the next 3 years. The company's cost of capital is 10 percent, and that cost of capital is expected to continue indefinitely. Cash flows available prior to year 3 are expected to earn a rate of return of 20 percent a year until the end of capital rationing. A proposed capital investment costs $100,000 and is expected to generate cash flows of $30,000 at the end of each year for 6 years. Is the investment attractive? Why?

22–4. For Cleveland Consolidated (problem 3), a mutually exclusive investment to the investment in the previous problem has a cost of $100,000 and generates cash flows of $50,000 at the end of each year for 3 years. Which investment is preferred? Why?

22–5. Akron Transportation Service is operating under capital rationing, and expects to be in a capital rationing environment for 3 years. The cost of capital is 10 percent. A $100,000 capital investment will provide cash flows of $30,000 at the end of each year for 5 years. Funds not used immediately can be invested until the end of the capital rationing period at a 20 percent annual return. Funds available at the end of the first year can be invested at 18 percent until the end of the rationing period, and funds available at the end of the second year can be invested for 1 year at 15 percent. Is that capital investment attractive? Why?

22–6. Oxford Supply has $1 million available to invest this period. The cost of capital is 10 percent, and is expected to remain at 10 percent in future periods. The company faces capital rationing and will not be able to raise additional funds. The capital rationing is expected to last for 2 years. Funds available at year 1 can be invested to earn 20 percent for the remaining year. Any idle funds not invested in capital investments now can be invested in temporary money market securities at an 8.3 percent return for 1 year. The company is considering one investment. The investment will require an initial outlay of $1,000,000. This investment will provide cash flows of $400,000 after 1 year and $800,000 after 2 years. Is the investment attractive?

22–7. Toledo Electrosensor has $1 million available to invest this year. The company is experiencing capital rationing and expects to experience capital rationing for 2 years. The weighted average cost of capital is 10 percent and is expected to remain at 10 percent. Funds not used for capital investment this year can be temporarily invested to earn the cost of capital for a 1-year period. Funds available at the end of 1 year can be invested to earn 15 percent return for the following year. Initial outlays and year-end cash inflows for investments being considered by Toledo Electrosensor are summarized as follows:

Investment\Year	0	1	2
A	−500,000	300,000	350,000
B	−500,000	200,000	550,000
C	−1,000,000	300,000	1,140,000

Which investment(s) should the company choose?

22–8. For Toledo Electrosensor in the previous problem, suppose that cash flows available at the end of 1 year could be invested at a return of 25 percent for the following year. Which investment(s) should be chosen in this case?

22–9. Cincinnati Technology is facing capital rationing. The company has $1,000 of cash on hand for investment this year and is expecting an additional $1,000 from existing operations at the end of 1 year. At the end of 2 years, capital rationing will no longer be a problem. Initial outlays and year-end cash inflows from projects available now and at the end of one year follow.

Investment\Year	0	1	2	3
A		−1,000	1,200	
B	−500	0	1,000	
C		−1,000	1,300	
D		−2,000	1,200	1,500

The company's cost of capital is 10 percent. If part of the $1,000 currently available is not used, it can be invested for a year at a 6 percent risk-free interest rate. Select the optimal set of investments.

22–10. Marietta Stoneware is operating under capital rationing, and that situation is expected to continue for 5 years. The cost of capital is presently 10 percent and is not expected to change. The investment opportunity rate is 20 percent and is not expected to change for the next 5 years. A proposed capital investment costs $1 million and will provide cash flows of $300,000 at the end of each year for 5 years. Is the investment attractive? Why?

22–11. Lexington Linotype has $1 million to invest and is operating under capital rationing. The cost of capital and investment opportunity rate are 10 percent and 25 percent, respectively; neither is expected to change over the next 5 years. Initial outlays and year-end cash flows for three investment alternatives follow. Which investments, if any, should Lexington Linotype select? Why?

Investment\ Year	0	1	2	3	4	5
A	−500,000	100,000	100,000	200,000	200,000	400,000
B	−500,000	200,000	200,000	100,000	100,000	100,000
C	−1,000,000	300,000	300,000	300,000	300,000	300,000

22–12. Louisville Foods is operating under single-period capital rationing. The company, which has $100,000 to invest and has a 10 percent cost of capital, is considering two $100,000 investments. The first investment provides cash flows of $20,000 at the end of each year for 10 years. The second investment provides cash flows of $30,000 at the end of each year for 5 years. Which investment should be chosen? Why?

22–13. Boone Corporation faces capital rationing and is considering the following mutually exclusive investments either of which will require an outlay of $500,000. The cost of capital is 10 percent.

Investment	NPV(10%)	NPV(20%)	IRR
A	$100,000	$50,000	25%
B	150,000	10,000	21

a. Which investment should be chosen if the capital rationing is expected to occur only in the current period?

b. Which investment should be chosen if the capital rationing is expected to continue, and the reinvestment opportunity rate is 20 percent?

22–14. For the capital investments in problem 13, which capital investment should be chosen if the proceeds from either capital investment can be reinvested at the same rate of return as was earned by that investment?

22–15. Hazard Corporation is operating under capital rationing and expects to be in that condition indefinitely. Year-end cash flows for two mutually exclusive investments follow. The scarce resource can be reused for a similar investment at the end of the life of either asset. The cost of capital is 10 percent, and the investment opportunity rate is 15 percent. Which investment should be chosen?

Investment\Year	0	1	2	3	4
A	−1,000	400	400	400	400
B	−500	275	275	275	

22–16. A company facing capital rationing is considering the following capital investments:

Investment	Cost ($ thousands)	IRR	NPV(10%)	NPV(12%)	NPV(20%)
A	500	15.24%	$ 69	$ 41	($51)
B	300	22.11	98	79	14
C	200	14.98	28	16	(23)
D	100	15.00	13	8	(11)
E	100	17.28	11	7	(3)
F	100	12.47	14	2	(28)
G	100	11.84	9	(1)	(30)

The company has $1 million available from internal sources, and a return of 10 percent is required on these funds to satisfy investors. The company could raise up to $1 million more externally, but the cost would be 20 percent.

a. Management believes that the internal rate of return on the highest IRR project that is rejected represents the reinvestment rate that will be available in future periods. Which investments should be selected?

b. Management wants to use a more conservative reinvestment rate assumption: 12 percent. Which investments should be selected?

22–17. For the set of investments in problem 16, assume the company has $1.1 million of internal funds available. Which investments would be chosen with each of the following management decisions?

a. Management believes that the internal rate of return on the highest IRR project that is rejected represents the reinvestment rate that will be available in future periods.

b. Based on a study of investments available today, management decides to base decisions on a more conservative reinvestment rate assumption: 12 percent.

c. Management decides to base the decision on an even more conservative reinvestment rate assumption: 10 percent.

22–18. Investments C and D in problem 16 are mutually exclusive. Investment C has a life of 6 years and investment D has a life of 4 years. The company assumes a 12 percent reinvestment opportunity rate in future years. If the company has $1 million to invest this period, which investments should be chosen under each of the following assumptions?

a. The scarce resource cannot be reused, and it must be used this period or not at all.

b. The scarce resource cannot be reused, but its use can be delayed until next year.

c. The scarce resource can be reused, it is possible to switch from investment type D to investment type C at the expiration of D, and the resource must be used in the current period or not at all.

d. Conditions described in (c) hold, except that the use of the resource can be delayed until next year.

22–19. (**Applications**) In late 1993, Boston Chicken, Inc., a fast-food restaurant specializing in meals of rotisserie roasted chicken, fresh vegetables, salads, and other side dishes, made an initial public offering of 1,900,000 shares or 11 percent of the company at an offer price of $20 a share. By the end of the first day of trading the stock price had reached $48. It was one of the hottest offerings in that year.

At the time of the offering Boston Chicken owned and operated 28 stores in Boston, Detroit, New York, Denver, Philadelphia, and Toledo. They had 147 stores operating under various franchise agreements and 612 stores committed to franchise agreements. Management believed that "rapid penetration in areas of dominant influence" was critical to the company.

Franchising can be considered a useful strategy to alleviate many of the constrained or rationed resources discussed in this chapter. Boston Chicken could have chosen to slow the expansion of it outlets. Instead, it opted for franchise agreements that require, on average, a franchise fee of $35,000 per store and 5 percent of gross revenue. The existing stores averaged $850,000 in sales in 1993 and this is assumed to continue with the new stores.

Use the following assumptions in answering the questions below:

- All expansion is in the form of franchised outlets.
- New stores open at a rate of 200 stores per year and this number grows at a rate of 10 percent per year until 4,000 stores are opened. (This is approximately how many Taco Bells there were at the end of 1992.)
- Cash expenses consume 91 percent of the "5 percent of revenue" so 9 percent of the fee will be cash profit.

- There is a 15 percent cost of equity with an all equity financed firm.
    a. Using the assumptions above, calculate the net present value of Boston Chicken, Inc.
    b. What is 11 percent of the company worth? Why do you think the price differs from the $91,200,000 value set by the market at the end of the first day ($48 × 1,900,000 shares)?
    c. Discuss the reasons you believe franchising was used by the management of Boston Chicken, Inc.

22–20. **(Ethical considerations)** You are the newly promoted Director of Strategic and Financial Planning. Part of your new job is to recommend a capital budgeting dollar level for the following year. You have put together the following list of investments along with the probability of success for each. In the past you have observed that most of the managers that have been promoted have a string of successes to their credit and no failures. The net present value of each of the investments in the list is high enough to give each a positive expected net present value. Your preliminary listing is as follows:

	Cost	Probability of Success
Replacement of current equipment	1,000,000	100%
Expansion of existing products in existing markets	500,000	75%
Introduction of new product into new markets	500,000	30%
Introduction of existing products into new markets	500,000	50%
Automation of existing plant & delivery processes	500,000	85%

   a. At what level would you recommend cutting off capital investment for the coming year, given the investment listing above? What is the personal ethical dilemma here?
   b. What personal or corporate limiting factors might cause you to change your decision towards capital rationing or towards accepting all of the investments?
   c. If marketing is the only limiting factor and the investments all have an equal expected net present value, which investments would you recommend and in which order?

CASE PROBLEM |

Heritage Corporation

Harold Gray started Heritage Corporation as a one-man carpentry shop in Lansing, Michigan, in 1892, and gradually expanded to 80 employees by the time of his retirement in 1928. Gray maintained a conservative growth pattern, rarely using debt and never turning to outside sources of equity. As a result, he handed a debt-free company to his son, John, on what turned out to be the eve of the Great Depression.

The depression was an extremely difficult time for the furniture business, although fine furniture was not hit as hard as the lower-priced lines. Many furniture companies that had grown more rapidly, with high debt and high fixed costs, went bankrupt. John credited the survival of Heritage to business skill, low fixed costs, and no debt.

John retired in 1954, turning the business over to his son, Fred, who joined other furniture companies in moving to North Carolina in 1958. This move had been under consideration since the early 1950s because labor costs in Lansing were high and the supply of prime Michigan hardwood was declining. In the following years, the firm benefited from the Baby Boom and a growing number of affluent Americans. Fred took advantage of this position to maintain a sound growth policy through the 1960s and 1970s. By the time of his retirement in 1980, Heritage had become one of the major producers of fine furniture. Furthermore, this position had been obtained without selling outside equity and with the addition of very little debt. Because Heritage was privately owned, there was no clamor for dividends, and Fred had been able to pour nearly 90 percent of earnings back into the business. The primary debt of the company was in the form of industrial revenue bonds provided by communities as incentives for factory expansion.

Fred's retirement marked the end of an era. There was no family member to take over the business, so the reins passed to Lynn Shelby, who had come up through the marketing side of the business. The influence of the family was hardly lost in this transition. The stock was held entirely by family members, who comprised the board of directors. The family members wanted to continue the tradition of maintaining little or no debt and funding equity growth through retained earnings, but the family also wanted some dividend income. Specifically, they wanted a total dividend payment of $5 million a year. Based on the company's pro-forma financial statements (Table 22.3), it appeared that $31,453,000 would be available for investment over the next year. The remaining problem was the choice of specific capital investments.

Proposed Capital Investments

Management was considering six capital investment proposals. (All dollar amounts and rates of return for these projects are after-tax.)

1. Invest $6.4 million in an efficiency improvement program at the Greenhill plant. The efficiency program was expected to generate after-tax cash flows of $1,364,000 at the end of each year for 10 years.
2. Buy a small, specialty furniture company for $23.6 million. The company would complement Heritage's existing products, and marketing could be

| TABLE 22.3 PRO-FORMA FINANCIAL STATEMENTS FOR HERITAGE CORPORATION

Sales	$432,731	Current assets	$122,437
Net operating income	30,499	Fixed assets	239,439
Interest expense	2,816	Total assets	$361,876
Earnings before tax	27,683		
Income tax	8,392	Current liabilities	$ 64,138
Net income	19,291	Long-term debt	44,865
		Deferred taxes	13,596
− Dividends	5,000	Common stock	239,277
+ Depreciation	15,485	Total liabilities & net worth	$361,876
+ Deferred tax increase	1,677		
= Cash flow	$ 31,453		

handled by Heritage's existing sales organization. Cash flow was expected to be $2.58 million at the end of the first year, and was expected to grow at 3 percent a year thereafter.

3. Build a new mill at Bernwood. The project would require two years for completion. Outlays of $5.2 million would be required immediately and another $5.8 million would be required in 1 year. Operation would begin in Year 3. Cash flows would then be $2.8 million at the end of each year for 10 years, with an estimated terminal value of $5 million, after tax.

4. Invest $3 million in a new design and development center. Operating costs for the center would then be $460,000 at the end of each year. While improved designs were expected, there was no identifiable cash flow benefit.

5. Purchase tracts of young hardwood for $400 an acre. Maintenance costs would be $12 an acre, payable at the end of each year, for 15 years. The hardwood could be harvested and sold to produce cash flow of $3,100 an acre. Immediately after harvest, the land would have a value of $200 an acre. At least 200,000 acres of young hardwood were available, in plots of almost every possible size. Timberland is easily bought and sold at any state of maturity to provide the owners the same rate of return regardless of how long it is held.

6. Invest in 1 year U.S. government securities yielding 7.1 percent after tax, or buy 5-year U.S. government securities yielding 8.9 percent after tax.

Due to uncertainty in the business, Heritage generally used a 10-year planning horizon for evaluating new investments. However, exceptions were made in certain cases, such as purchase of timber stands. It was impossible to evaluate these investments unless a longer life was considered. Heritage had a weighted average cost of capital of approximately 13 percent.

Shelby knew that nothing could be done about the board's capital rationing policy immediately, but saw modification of this policy as an important objective.

Shelby decided to work under the assumption that it would take 5 years to persuade the board to change its policy. Capital rationing would be eliminated if the policy was changed, although the cost of capital was not expected to change significantly.

CASE QUESTIONS

1. What combination of investments will maximize shareholder wealth?
2. What combination of investments would maximize shareholder wealth if no investments earning more than the weighted average cost of capital would be available after the initial investment decision?
3. Assume existing investment opportunities other than the acquisition can be postponed until the end of the 5-year rationing period, but no other investments with returns above the weighted average cost of capital will be available. Identify the investment choices and timing that will maximize shareholder wealth.

SELECTED REFERENCES

Barbarosoglu Güulay, and David Pinhas. "Capital Rationing in the Public Sector Using the Analytical Hierarchy Process." *Engineering Economist* 40 (Summer 1995): 315–341.

Borun, Victor M., and Susan L. Malley. "Total Flotation Costs for Electric Utility Company Equity Issues." *Public Utilities Fortnightly* 117 (February 20, 1986): 33–39.

Burton, R. M., and W. W. Damon, "On the Existence of a Cost of Capital under Pure Capital Rationing." *Journal of Finance* 29 (September 1974): 1165–1173.

Dorfman, Robert. "The Meaning of Internal Rates of Return." *The Journal of Finance* 36 (December 1981): 1011–1021.

Forsyth, J. D., and D. J. Laughhunn. "Rationing Capital in a Telephone Company." *Financial Management* 3 (Autumn 1974): 36–43.

Gahlon, James M., and Roger D. Stover. "Debt Capacity and the Capital Budgeting Decision: A Caveat." *Financial Management* 8 (Winter 1979): 55–59.

Gitman, Larry J., and J. R. Forrester, Jr. "A Survey of Capital Expenditure Techniques Used by Major U.S. Firms." *Financial Management* 6 (Fall 1977): 66–71.

Klammer, Thomas, Bruce Koch, and Neil Wilner. "Capital Budgeting Practices—A Survey of Corporate Use." University of North Texas, mimeo, 1988.

Litzenberger, Robert H., and O. Maurice Joy. "Decentralized Capital Budgeting Decisions and Shareholder Wealth Maximization." *Journal of Finance* 30 (September 1975): 993–1002.

Martin, John D., and David F. Scott, Jr. "Debt Capacity and the Capital Budgeting Decision." *Financial Management* 5 (Summer 1976): 7–14.

———. "Debt Capacity and the Capital Budgeting Decision: A Revisitation." *Financial Management* 9 (Spring 1980): 23–26.

Myers, Stewart C. "The Capital Structure Puzzle." *Journal of Finance* 39 (July 1984): 575–592.

Petty, J. W., D. F. Scott, and M. M. Bird. "The Capital Expenditure Decision-Making Process of Large Corporations." *Engineering Economist* 20 (Spring 1975): 159–172.

Rhee, S. Ghon, and Franklin L. McCarthy. "Corporate Debt Capacity and Capital Budgeting Analysis." *Financial Management* 11 (Summer 1982): 42–50.

Ross, Marc. "Capital Budgeting Practices of Twelve Large Manufacturers." *Financial Management* 15 (Winter 1986): 15–22.

Statman, Meir, and Tyzoon T. Tyebjee. "Optimistic Capital Budget Forecasts." *Financial Management* 14 (Autumn 1985): 27–33.

Weingartner, H. Martin. "Capital Rationing: Authors in Search of a Plot." *Journal of Finance* 32 (December 1977): 1403–1431.

Whited, Toni M. "Debt, Liquidity Constraints, and Corporate Investment: Evidence from Panel Data." *Journal of Finance* 47 (September 1992): 1425–1460.

Wright, F. K. "Project Evaluation and the Managerial Limit." *Journal of Business* (April 1964): 179–185.

INTEGRATIVE CASE FOR PART V: |

IBM

International Business Machines, commonly referred to as IBM or Big Blue, was one of the great long-term success stories in American business. The company was formed in 1911 as Computing-Tabulating-Recording Company, and went on to become the country's dominant producer of information handling equipment, including computers and office typewriters. After seven decades in business, the company was still growing at over 15 percent a year.

IBM's stock had been an extremely profitable investment over the years. However, there were still critics who suggested that wealth could be increased more rapidly by a more aggressive approach to capital structure and dividend policy. This debate was particularly relevant in 1984 as competition was heating up in the rapidly expanding microcomputer market and IBM was considering its first acquisition in 20 years.

IBM's financial statements for years prior to 1984 appear in Table V.1. These are supplemented by a 10-year history of stock-related information in Table V.2. Table V.3 includes a detailed breakdown of long-term debt. Most notable are an extremely conservative balance sheet and a declining dividend payout ratio. It is hard to compare a company like IBM to any peer group, but the average large competitor maintained a debt ratio of approximately 54 percent and a dividend payout ratio of approximately 41 percent. Times interest earned ratios of leading competitors were less than half that of IBM.

The critics of IBM focused on three facts:

1. The company held almost $5 billion dollars in marketable securities, accounting for 13 percent of total assets. With short-term interest rates under 9 percent, it was argued that this money should be invested in the company, paid out in the form of dividends, or used to repurchase common stock.
2. The debt ratio was far below the industry average, despite IBM being the industry leader. It was argued that IBM should be able to carry more debt than other companies in the industry and, therefore, was not at its optimal capital structure. This meant higher taxes and less advantage of leverage for the stockholders.
3. The declining dividend payout ratio was criticized in light of the falling debt ratio and the growing balance of marketable securities. As shown in Table V.2, most companies had increased their payout ratios over the 10-year period, while IBM's payout ratio had declined. Likewise, price-earnings ratios had increased for other companies and decreased for IBM during the period. Money was available to pay dividends, and failure to increase dividends may have signaled shareholders that declines in earnings growth were coming, resulting in lower price-earnings ratios than had occurred in the early 1970s.

TABLE V.1 IBM FINANCIAL STATEMENTS (IN $ MILLIONS)				
	1980	**1981**	**1982**	**1983**
Sales	$10,919	$12,901	$16,815	$23,274
Rentals	10,869	10,839	11,121	9,230
Services	4,425	5,330	6,428	7,676
Total revenue	$26,213	$29,070	$34,364	$40,180
Cost of sales	4,238	5,162	6,682	9,748
Cost of rentals	3,841	4,041	3,959	3,141
Cost of services	2,187	2,534	3,047	3,506
Selling & admin.	8,094	8,383	9,286	10,614
Research & devel.	2,287	2,451	3,042	3,582
Interest expense	273	407	454	390
Other income	430	368	328	741
Inc. before tax	5,723	6,460	8,222	9,940
Income tax	2,326	2,850	3,813	4,455
Net income	$ 3,397	$ 3,610	$ 4,409	$ 5,485
Cash dividends	2,008	2,023	2,053	2,251
Cash		$ 454	$ 405	$ 616
Marketable sec.		1,575	2,895	4,920
Notes & accts rec.		4,382	4,976	5,735
Other accts rec.		410	457	645
Inventory		2,803	3,492	4,381
Prepaid exp.		685	789	973
Total CA		10,309	13,014	17,270
Rental machines		9,252	9,117	6,812
Plant & equip.		7,545	8,446	9,330
Other assets		2,001	1,964	3,831
Total assets	$26,381	$29,107	$32,541	$37,243
Tax liabilities		$ 2,412	$ 2,584	$ 3,220
Loans payable		773	529	532
Wages payable		1,556	1,959	2,450
Other current liab.		2,585	3,137	3,305
Total CL		7,326	8,209	9,507
Deferred inv. tax cr.		252	323	713
Pension plan reserves		1,184	1,198	1,130
Long-term debt	2,099	2,669	2,851	2,674
Stockholders equity	16,578	17,676	19,960	23,219
TL & NW	$26,381	$29,107	$32,541	$37,243

| TABLE V.2 | STOCK HISTORY OF IBM AND THE S&P 500 |

IBM*	1974	1975	1976	1977	1978	1979	1980	1981	1982	1983
EPS	3.12	3.34	3.99	4.58	5.32	5.16	6.10	5.63	7.39	9.04
DPS	1.39	1.63	2.00	2.50	2.88	3.44	3.44	3.44	3.44	3.71
Payout	0.45	0.49	0.50	0.55	0.54	0.67	0.56	0.61	0.47	0.41
PE ratio	16.5	15.3	16.6	14.5	12.7	13.9	10.4	10.3	9.4	12.7
S&P 500 averages										
PE ratio	8.6	10.9	11.2	9.3	8.3	7.4	7.9	8.4	8.6	12.5
Payout	0.39	0.47	0.42	0.43	0.44	0.41	0.42	0.43	0.50	0.55

*IBM information taken from *Value Line*.

IBM had 610,724,261 shares of common stock outstanding at the beginning of 1984, with a market price of $120 a share. The beta for IBM was close to 1.0, and IBM's bonds were rated Aaa. Interest rates were as follows in early 1984.

3-month Treasury bills	8.93%
Aaa corporate bonds	12.20%
Long-term U.S. government bonds	11.67%
Baa corporate bonds	13.65%

The computer marketplace was in the midst of two revolutions in 1984. One revolution started with the introduction of PCs. By 1984, IBM was winning the battle to set the industry standards. It was becoming increasingly clear that competitors would be forced to follow the operating standards set by IBM. Unfortunately, though, competitors were doing this entirely too well. Low-priced clones were a formidable source of competition and were squeezing profit margins.

| TABLE V.3 | DETAILS OF IBM'S LONG-TERM DEBT (IN $ MILLIONS) |

9.5% notes, due 1986	$ 500
$9\frac{3}{8}$% sinking fund notes, due 1985–2003	500
10.80% notes, due 1984–1986	240
12.9% notes, due 1984–1992	678
11.6% notes, due 1984–1992	249
Foreign-denominated notes	755
Total	2,922
Current maturities	248
Total long-term debt	$2,674

Finding a way to set standards while maintaining market share and profitability in this important area would be a major challenge.

At the other end of the market, a bitter battle was shaping up for the automated office. The automated office would have an information processing system with a telecommunications system at its center. Both voice communications and communications between computers are handled through this same nerve system. AT&T, the leader in telecommunications systems, had expanded into computer lines and was prepared to offer a complete integrated system. IBM had the advantage in computers, but had yet to develop a telecommunications system to use in offering an integrated package. An acquisition of another company to gain a strong position in telecommunications could easily cost $1 billion.

CASE QUESTIONS

1. What are the possible reasons for holding almost $5 billion in marketable securities? Should the level of marketable securities be changed?

2. Does IBM have excess debt capacity? In answering this question, consider stability of cash flow in relation to debt repayment obligations as well as cash reserves, access to capital markets, and IBM's competitive position in the industry.

3. Plot IBM's earnings per share and dividends per share on a graph. Identify the dividend policy followed as well as any possible change in dividend policy. What would be the possible reasons for changes in dividend policy?

4. Compute the weighted average cost of capital for IBM, given its 1983 capital structure.

5. Recommend a policy with regard to capital structure, dividends, and marketable securities.

PART VI

SPECIAL TOPICS

Several topics of growing importance do not fit neatly into any of the first five parts of this book. Chapter 23 focuses on the special problems of nonprofit organizations. These organizations, including hospitals, schools, governments, and charities, account for a growing percentage of all capital investments. Since their motive is not to create wealth for shareholders, they face especially complex trade-offs when making capital investment decisions. Chapter 24 uses linear programming to deal with capital budgeting problems involving multiple goals and multiple constraints. It applies to complex problems in wealth-seeking corporations and also applies to the problems of nonprofit organizations. Chapter 25 deals with mergers, which are an important category of capital investment that are of particular importance today.

CHAPTER 23 |

CAPITAL BUDGETING IN NONPROFIT ORGANIZATIONS

After completing this chapter you should be able to:

1. Understand the importance that nonprofit organizations play in society and the peculiarities associated with capital budgeting for these organizations.
2. List similarities and differences in strategic planning between nonprofit organizations and for-profit businesses.
3. Judge the net present value of a project within a nonprofit environment with particular attention to identifying the nonquantitative or qualitative benefits and costs.
4. Adjust for the roles that taxes and tax-exempt status play in nonprofit capital budgeting.
5. Explain the cash flow peculiarities associated with capital budgeting for hospitals and the government.
6. Justify a cost of capital rate for a nonprofit organization.
7. Explain the variables that influence the capital structure of nonprofit organizations.

THE IMPORTANCE OF NONPROFIT ORGANIZATIONS |

Recently, management scholar Peter F. Drucker wrote that: "America needs a new social priority: To triple the productivity of the nonprofits and double the share of gross personal income—now just under 3 percent—they collect as donations. Otherwise the country could face social polarization in just a few years."[1] Drucker cites the success that nonprofits have had as an efficient

[1] *Wall Street Journal* (December 19, 1991): 14, column 3.

means of achieving social goals. In fact he asserts that "virtually every success the U.S. has achieved in solving social problems has been because of nonprofits."[2]

IMPORTANCE MEASURED BY THE SIZE OF DONATIONS

One way to measure the importance that nonprofits play in society is to measure the amount given to these institutions. In 1996, $150.7 billion was donated to nonprofit organizations, up 35 percent from 1990.[3] The breadth of support for nonprofits is another way to measure their importance. Over two-thirds of the population of the United States gives money to charities each year. In addition, 49 percent of individuals donated time to nonprofits in 1995.[4] Another source reports that 90 million Americans work, on average, three hours per week for a nonprofit organization.[5]

Donated time and money represent only the tip of the nonprofit iceberg. Nonprofit organizations, such as hospitals and universities, sell their services to those in need of healing or education. Governments in the United States collect over a trillion dollars in taxes each year and spend the money to provide services requested by citizens, ranging from building inspections to education to defense.

IMPORTANCE IN FULFILLING SOCIETAL MISSIONS

Nonprofits exist for many reasons. People form and join groups to achieve goals or benefits that they either cannot achieve on their own or they cannot achieve efficiently on their own. A library can be thought of as an efficient way to obtain the use of books. The goals or benefits provided by nonprofits can be broken down into three groupings: benefit to the members, either individually or collectively; promotion of an ideal or belief; and provision of a product or service. Many nonprofits serve more than one of these goals. Table 23.1 provides a listing of some of the nonprofits by broad classification.

Governments, including their various agencies and subdivisions, are an important group of nonprofit organizations. Governments are unique among nonprofit organizations primarily because they are involuntary organizations; street gang membership may also be involuntary. Citizens do not individually volunteer to provide money to governments in most cases. In terms of meeting needs, though, governments provide streets, and possibly safety in the streets, as well as education, medical care, and a court system for resolving disputes.

[2]Ibid.

[3]*The World Almanac and Book of Facts 1998* (Mahwah, N.J.: World Almanac Books, 1998), 720.

[4]*Statistical Abstract of the United States* (Washington, D.C.: U.S. Government Printing Office, 1998), 391.

[5]*Wall Street Journal* (December 19, 1991): 14, column 3.

| **TABLE 23.1** **CLASSIFICATIONS OF NONPROFIT ORGANIZATIONS**

The table provides a summary of the various types of nonprofit organizations that currently exist, along with examples of each classification.

Class Example	Organizations
Benefits to members	
Community Service	Neighborhood improvement or protection groups
Self-Improvement	Boy Scouts, Girl Scouts, YMCA, YWCA
Educational	Teacher's aides, PTO, PTA, honorary societies
Information	Libraries, public awareness groups
Consumer Welfare	Consumers Union
Professional	Professional associations, AICPA, AMA, ABA
Occupational	AFL-CIO, UAW
Leisure	Little League, community arts groups
Deviant	Street gangs, terrorist groups
Ideal or belief	
Disadvantaged or Minority	NAACP
Political Action	Citizens for the American Way, United We Stand
Environmental	Greenpeace
Religion	Churches
Provision of service	
Health	Hospitals, mental health centers
Education	Grade schools, high schools, trade schools, universities
Social Welfare	Big Brother, Big Sister
Fund Raising	United Way, March of Dimes

STRATEGY IN NONPROFIT ORGANIZATIONS |

Competition plays as important a role in the life of a nonprofit organization as it does in the life of a business. The nonprofit provides services. It seeks direct fees for its services and/or it seeks funds from others who see those services as consistent with their values and, therefore, desirable. The nonprofit typically faces competition as vigorous as that faced by the most enthusiastic profit-seeking business. It would be difficult to think of a nonprofit organization that does not face a competitor when it offers its services or seeks funds from contributors. The buyers of nonprofits' services face multiple providers, just as do the buyers of products offered by businesses. In fact, many of the services offered by nonprofits, such as health care and social connections, are also offered by businesses. Buyers will seek out the best value; those providing the best value will prosper, and others will wither. Likewise, contributors can be likened to investors. They want to use their money to achieve desired goals, and they will invest their contributions in the organizations that show the greatest success in reaching toward those goals.

A membership organization such as a YWCA might think of its activities as being completely different from those of a business and, therefore, not subject to the same strategy considerations. However, the YWCA offers a bundle of services to members in exchange for their fees, and TWA faces a similar problem in choosing member services to provide through its Ambassador Club lounges. Likewise, Diners Club faces a similar problem in choosing the package of services that will induce people to sign up for a Diners Club card, when they can get a Visa card for a smaller annual fee. Our friends at the YWCA may argue that they are different because they are not driven by profit, but the difference in their actions may be smaller than they think. Like a business, the YWCA faces the prospect of a new competitor coming along to offer the same service for less, or to offer an improved service. This is hardly an idle threat. The new recreation center at the local university may, for example, begin selling memberships to its alumni, some of whom are YWCA members. Likewise, dozens of for-profit health clubs spring up to compete by offering the latest in exercise equipment. While the YWCA may prefer not to think of its services in dollar-and-cents terms, it has little choice but to ask itself whether an investment in modern exercise equipment will be justified by increasing revenues from its members. If it does not allocate resources in these ways, it will eventually be forced out of existence by organizations, either business or nonprofit, that provide better benefits per dollar spent.

COMPETITIVE ADVANTAGE

A nonprofit organization must go through the same strategic planning process used by a business. It must identify a need and position itself to meet that need with a service that provides an outstanding value in relation to the cost. This requires that it analyze its industry, that it position itself successfully in relation to its competitors, and that it allocate its resources efficiently.

Industry. As with a business, the nonprofit operates as one of a category of service providers, which would be called an industry in the for-profit world. The degree of competitive vigor in that industry will have a direct impact on the success of the nonprofit. Numbers of players, closeness of substitutes, costs of competitors, motives of competitors, information available to users of services, and preferences of users of services are all important considerations, just as they are in the for-profit world. Our friends at the YWCA may find that competition for service quality is quite vigorous and that for-profit competitors even have a cost advantage.

Product (Service) Advantage. A nonprofit hospital typically finds itself competing with several other nonprofit hospitals, and may also find that Humana, Inc., has a hospital down the street. Each organization will probably attempt to differentiate its product in terms of features such as range of service, quality factors such as room comfort, and so on. In order to raise money from contributors, an organization must also show that its service has especially desirable features from the perspective of those contributors. Universities have often been able to stress the values held by their graduates as part of their case for support from contributors.

Cost Advantage.   Nonprofits are in no way excused from cost pressures, and a cost advantage can be as powerful in a nonprofit organization as in a business. The YWCA can successfully compete with the university recreation center and Vic Tanny, Inc., if it can provide the same level of service at a lower cost. Likewise, potential donors are going to be much more receptive if they believe their money is not only being used for the right goal, but is being used efficiently for that goal.

Management guru Peter Drucker, speaking at an awards ceremony he sponsored to honor successful nonprofits, urged the boards, staff, and volunteers of all nonprofit organizations to ask themselves, "What is our mission?" and "What is our plan?"[6] Nonprofits appear to have received the message of the importance of delineating their mission. According to a survey of 800 nonprofits by Independent Sector, the priorities of nonprofits in order of importance were mission, leadership, effective fund-raising, and a good board of directors.

Goals and Feedback for Nonprofits

Operating goals for nonprofits can be categorized as service goals, cash inflow goals, and cash outflow goals. Attainment of service goals can be measured by customer satisfaction surveys, donations per member, the number of new donations, the increase in memberships, or any other statistic that can be tracked over time. The purpose of these measurements is to provide management and the board with an indication of the perception of the audience from which it draws its support. This in not unlike the customer satisfaction cards found on the tables at most Wendy's establishments. The feedback to Wendy's management will probably occur much quicker in the form of lost or increased sales. The cards help management to identify the reasons. In nonprofits there may be years between the time of the initial donations, or the government subsidy that initially funded the program, and the time at which the program is up for refunding or seeking additional support. The signals or feedback received at the time of refunding may be too late for management to take corrective action.

Feedback is more important for nonprofits for several reasons:

1. The nonprofit may not receive the lost or increased sales feedback like forprofits. Charities that do not charge for their services will probably not see much of a reduction in the use of their service as a result of poor service.
2. The source of cash inflows may not be the recipient of the service. For example, a food bank may be funded by a church or business donor while the recipients are the poor.

[6]*Wall Street Journal* (November 11, 1993): 1, column 5.

3. A change in cash inflow may lag years behind a change in satisfaction. Professional associations and schools with large endowments can lose members or students for years before a financial crisis forces them to address their problems.

Cash-inflow financial goals or measurements include grants or donations pledged, grants or donations received, and delinquent donations. These financial measurements differ from the service measurements that are nonfinancial in nature. One could argue that in the end the best indication of members' satisfaction is when they continue to give to the organization. In other words, money talks the loudest.

Cash-outflow financial goals and measurements include cost per client, cost per service, cost per member, operating cost, salaries, and fringes, as well as others. Again, it is every bit as important for the nonprofit to measure expenses as it is for the for-profit enterprise.

By gauging the success of the nonprofit in these three areas, the manager is measuring his or her organization's effectiveness in meeting "fundable" societal objectives, raising funds, and controlling expenses. In business, the firm that best identifies the wants of the market, produces the service, charges an appropriate price, and does so at the lowest cost per unit of output is the most profitable, a potential long-run survivor, and a good investment. The same is true for nonprofit organizations. To paraphrase the statement at the beginning of the chapter, it is in society's interest to have efficient and effective nonprofit organizations.

MANAGEMENT AND GOVERNANCE OF NONPROFITS |

Agency problems, as discussed in Chapter 1, occur when managers and board members place their self-interest above that of the organization, its owners, or its beneficiaries. Agency costs are the costs of monitoring managers or accepting deviations from the preferred behavior. If managers deviate too much from shareholder desires, the shareholders step in through proxy battles or outside board members to either rework the contract with existing board member and managers, or to relieve those individuals of their duties. In nonprofits, there are no active shareholders, only board members, management, employees, contributors, and various beneficiaries of the organization. It is hoped that the board is made up of individuals who have donated a substantial amount of their financial or human capital to the nonprofit and are actively interested in its survival.

Financial statements prepared according to generally accepted accounting principles, and audited by independent accountants, are an important tool of the stockholders in monitoring a business corporation. In addition to not having shareholders who are expecting profits on a quarterly basis, nonprofits have had very little guidance from the accounting standard-setting bodies. As a result, even if nonprofits do calculate a profit (usually called an increase in the fund balance), this number would be subject to very wide interpretation. Many nonprofits, including the federal government and many state governments, lack the accounting sophistication to measure income using the accrual accounting method that is commonly used by businesses, and which recognizes such non-cash expenses as depreciation. Instead, they simply report on cash inflows and outflows. One problem with this cash approach is that capital investments are not differentiated from expenses. An example of the distortion caused by these accounting deficiencies is the popularity of leasing among government agencies. The lease allows the agency to recognize the cost of the asset over its life, just as a business would do if it purchased the asset, rather than recognizing all of its cost as an expense during the acquisition year.

The United Way provides a recent example of the difficulty in balancing the social goals of the nonprofit with the individual goals of the management and board members. In theory the United Way exists with the goal of gaining economies of scale in the collection of money for other nonprofits. In principle, organizations like the Boy Scouts should concentrate on scouting and not on fund raising. The United Way was formed so that every nonprofit would not have to conduct duplicate calls on each donating organization to raise money. In 1992, it came to light that William Aramony, president of the United Way, received a salary in excess of $400,000, hired his friend as Chief Financial Officer, and purchased a first-class ticket with donated funds. As a result Aramony resigned, the board was enlarged from 37 to 45 members to increase the representation by local United Way leaders, and the lax accounting that was in place was improved.

Fortunately, competitive pressures on the nonprofit organization serve to keep managers focused. A nonprofit that does not work vigorously to provide a valued service as efficiently as possible will be supplanted by its competitors. People will buy services elsewhere and donors, like stockholders, will invest elsewhere. Managers who do not respond to competitive pressures by seeking to provide valued services efficiently are likely to have relatively short careers.

Compensation plans provide evidence of the degree of competition and control faced by managers of nonprofit organizations. While the leading managers of nonprofit organizations can earn incomes in the hundreds of thousands, the multimillion-dollar executive compensation packages sometimes found in business do not seem to exist in nonprofit management. The absence of these multi-million-dollar packages might be evidence of the extent of competitive pressure and external control on nonprofit organizations. Roughly one-third of the non-profits studied in a recent survey offered employees annual cash awards based on their performance. These cash award plans are gaining in popularity in the for-profit sector and are highly touted as better because they link pay to some measure of performance. Once again, we find substantial evidence of compensation arrangements consistent with the existence of competitive pressure as an important force controlling management decisions.

CAPITAL BUDGETING IN NONPROFITS |

From the prior discussion of competitive advantage, one might suspect that capital budgeting in a nonprofit organization shares many characteristics with capital budgeting in a business. Businesses are forced to allocate resources efficiently in order to compete for capital and compete with other businesses for customers. Likewise, nonprofits are forced to operate efficiently in order to sell their services or attract alternate sources of resources such as contributions. The nonprofit world is very similar to the business world in that new competitors continually arise to offer similar services, and only the efficient producers of valued services will survive. The uniqueness of your mission will not protect you because a competitor will arise to achieve the same mission at a lower cost if you are inefficient. For a nonprofit organization, the competitors may be other nonprofits or business.

Table 23.2 further highlights the similarities between types of investments made by businesses and nonprofits. Efficiency investments such as an efficient furnace or automated equipment are essentially the same whether they are being purchased by a nonprofit or a business. They are justified by comparing the present values of benefits to costs. Likewise, investments expected to generate increased payment for products or services are essentially the same in either type of organization. Like a business, a nonprofit will not be able to attract resources if it does not provide those services efficiently. Comparing the present value of benefits to cost is still the standard way to measure efficiency.

The final group of services consists of those paid for by third parties, whether private or government, that support the nonprofit's activity because they believe it is desirable in its own right rather than in exchange for perceived personal

| **TABLE 23.2** | **CLASSIFICATIONS OF CAPITAL INVESTMENTS IN NONPROFITS AND BUSINESSES** |

With the exception of actions paid for because of a general perception of value, capital investment categories for nonprofits are the same as those for business.

	Nonprofit Examples	**Business Examples**
Efficiency	High-efficiency furnace in a school	High-efficiency furnace in a hotel
	Automated blood analyzer in a university hospital	Automated blood analyzer at a Humana Corp. hospital
	Computerized accounting system at a church	Automated assembly line at General Motors
Increased sales/service		
Payment for product or service	Course tuition	Automobile sales
	Medical fees	Airline ticket sales
Payment for service package	Health maintenance organization membership	American Express membership
	YMCA/YWCA membership	Airline executive lounge membership
Payment based on general perception of value	Food kitchens	None
	Political action groups	

benefit. Charitable support of a soup kitchen or university research project could fall in this category. An important characteristic of these organizations is that the benefit may be quantities, as in number of people fed or premature babies saved. It does not have a value that can be measured in dollar-and-cent terms. Thus, qualitative factors must be considered.

Kamath and Oberst in a survey of 427 hospitals found that over 95 percent of those responding indicated that qualitative factors entered into the hospital's capital budgeting decisions. In another study, over 97 percent responded in the same manner.[7] When asked to rank the qualitative factors in order of importance, facility need, physician demand, and community need were ranked the three most important qualitative factors considered. Overall, over 25 percent of the responding hospitals reported that qualitative factors "determine the acceptance decision more than 75 percent of the time."[8] This percentage was 77 percent at government-affiliated hospitals.

These so-called qualitative factors do not provide any relief from the need to be efficient that is central to all capital budgeting. While organizations feeding the homeless will typically not face business competitors, they will compete with numerous other potential providers, some of whom may exactly match their mission statement, and they must demonstrate their efficiency to survive. It may be impossible and unnecessary to attach dollar amounts to benefits—what is the value of saving the life of a premature baby?—but it is still necessary to show that the benefit was provided more efficiently than by competitors. It would be difficult to think of a cause for which there are not multiple competitors offering to use the public's contributions to address that cause.

Given the similarities between businesses and nonprofits, how do we know if a nonprofit capital investment is attractive? When a project has dollar benefits, it is attractive if the present value of the dollar inflows is greater than the present value of the dollar outflows. When the organization is using its resources primarily to pursue a nonfinancial goal, the best allocation of resources is that allocation that makes the greatest contribution toward the goal. When comparing alternate approaches, the one that achieves the goal with the lowest present value of costs is best; the organization not choosing that alternative risks being forced out of existence by a competing provider. Thus, net present value rules in the nonprofit as well as the profit world.

Example. Indiana College, with an endowment of $40 million and a cost of capital of 12 percent, is considering the following projects:

a. A new business building with a cost of $2 million. It is projected that successful business alumni will contribute to this cause, that this upgrading will attract additional students, and that this new building will improve the aesthetics of the campus.

---

[7]See Ravindra Kamath and J. Elmer, "Capital Investment Decisions in Hospitals: Survey Results," *Health Care Management Review* 37 (Spring 1989): 45–56.

[8]See Ravindra Kamath and Eugene R. Oberst, "Capital Budgeting Practices of Large Hospitals," *Engineering Economist* 37 (Spring 1992): 203–232.

Business Building Option	Amount	Present Value (assuming a 40-year life)
Initial outlay	−$2,000,000	−$2,000,000
Projected donations	+1,000,000 per year over two years	+1,690,051
Income from additional students	+40,000 per year indefinitely	+333,333
Increase in aesthetics of the campus	Nonquantifiable	
Net present value		+23,384

b. A new sports complex for the students. The cost is $4 million. Additional donations will be attracted, the health and morale of the students and faculty will be increased, and more students will be attracted to the school.

Sports Complex Option	Amount	Present Value (assuming a 40-year life)
Initial outlay	−$4,000,000	−$4,000,000
Projected donations	+1,000,000 per year over 4 years	+3,037,349
Income from additional students	+60,000 per year indefinitely	+500,000
Increase in health and morale of the students	Nonquantifiable	
Net present value		−462,651

c. Additional faculty to reduce class size and advising loads. Annual cost is $200,000 per year indefinitely. Benefits include additional enrollment, better student morale, better faculty morale, and more effective teaching in smaller classes.

Additional Faculty Option	Amount	Present Value (assuming a 40-year life)
Initial outlay	0	0
Cost of additional faculty	−$200,000 per year indefinitely	−1,666,667
Income from additional students	+20,000 per year indefinitely	+166,667
Increase in student and faculty morale	Nonquantifiable	
Increase in student learning	Nonquantifiable	
Net present value		−1,500,000

The new business building option appears to be the best project with a net present value of $23,384. But the accept/reject decision may consider the large qualitative benefits and costs. In particular, the smaller class size option seems to be much more in line with the educational purpose of the school than the sports complex option.

Hospitals have attempted to quantify the social healthcare cost for a community so that they can use this information to apply for money for capital projects. For projects they have funded, they attempt to quantify as many benefits as possible so that it improves their performance toward the mandated percentage of services they are required to perform on a charitable basis to retain their tax-exempt status.

Taxes and the Nonprofit Cash Flows

Nonprofits are divided into public charities and private charities under section 501(c)(3) of the tax code. Table 23.3 lists seven types of organizations the IRS considers to be public charities. In addition to this list, the IRS publishes a list of names of charities that qualify under code section 501.

To maintain their tax-exempt status, it is important for these organizations to refrain from allowing for-profit subsidiary activities from becoming too large a percentage of their operation. The code does not define a specific percentage and it is hard to tell if the nonprofit is exceeding the boundary until the IRS informs the nonprofit of the excess. Recently the IRS informed several nonprofit hospitals that they were about to lose their tax-exempt status. These hospitals had entered into joint ventures with physicians that rewarded these physicians for referring patients to hospitals.[9]

Sometimes the mission of the nonprofit may be called into question by the IRS. The restaurant owners in Burlington, Vermont, were conspicuous in their use of a nonprofit for personal gain. They established Westward Ho with the mission of encouraging vagrants to leave the area by giving them one-way tickets to Oregon. As often happens, a sobering hand interferes. The IRS entered and ruled that this mission was not honorable enough for Westward Ho to be awarded a charitable exemption under tax law.[10] On average, a little over 70 percent of the organizations seeking tax exemption are approved by the IRS.

There are several changes under the Revenue Reconciliation Act of 1993 that affect tax-exempt charitable nonprofits. Under the act, any charity must itemize the amount of any donation that renders a service or product to the contributor. For example if an art society is selling dinner theater seats for $80 a ticket, they need to tell the purchaser the amount of the $80 ticket price that is considered the cost of the dinner. This rule applies for all donations or charges over $75.

A second provision requires the contributor to receive a receipt for all cash donations of $250 or more, prior to filing a return. Of more substance is the new

[9]*Wall Street Journal* (December 9, 1991).

[10]*Wall Street Journal* (April 15, 1992): 1, column 5.

| **TABLE 23.3 ORGANIZATIONS CONSIDERED BY THE IRS TO BE PUBLIC CHARITIES**

1. Church or a convention or association of churches.
2. Educational organization that normally maintains a regular faculty and curriculum and a regularly enrolled body of students.
3. Hospitals and medical research organizations.
4. Organizations supported by the government that are organized to administer property to or for the benefit of a college or university as described in no. 2.
5. Governmental units.
6. A U.S. corporation, trust, or community chest, fund, or foundation organized and operated exclusively for religious, charitable, scientific, literary, or international amateur sports competition, or for the prevention of cruelty to children or animals.
7. Private foundations that distribute substantially all of their income for the conduct of charitable purposes.

rule allowing contributors who donate art, stocks, bonds, real estate, and other property to value these donations at fair market value. This should benefit museums, universities, and other nonprofits because it in effect lowers the taxes paid to the government by an amount equal to the increased contribution.

Example. Phil Lanthropy, a wealthy individual, has stock that he purchased for $500,000 dollars and that now has a market value of $2 million. He is considering the following options: He can sell the stock and donate the proceeds, or he can donate the stock immediately.

$$\text{Sell the Stock: Net Proceeds} = \$2,000,000 - [(\$2,000,000 - 500,000) \times .28]$$
$$= \$1,580,000$$

$$\text{Donate the Stock: Net Proceed} = \$2,000,000$$

By choosing to donate the stock, Phil can forward $420,000 more by avoiding the 28 percent maximum capital gains tax. Note that there are many other ways to structure a donation that allows additional benefits to the donor in the form of timing and life income.

RISK AND NONPROFITS

Like the revenues of for-profit organizations, year to year cash inflows of nonprofits are uncertain. Demand for services may fluctuate for any number of reasons. Donations probably have an income elasticity like that of luxury goods and, as such, donations may magnify the business cycle. One way to reduce the volatility of donations is to diversify across as many individuals as possible. Unfortunately even a church that is supported by the donations of several thousand individuals will probably suffer if most of these individuals are affected by a catastrophe, such as area-wide flooding.

Adjustment for risk can be made in the capital budgeting process, also. In the previously cited Kamath and Oberst study, they found that 34 percent of the responding hospitals account for risk in making their capital budgeting decisions. The most popular method was to do a sensitivity analysis assuming several scenarios. Shortening the payback period and using a risk-adjusted discount rate were also popular methods.

Rush–Presbyterian–St. Lukes Hospital, in Chicago, adjusts for risk by adding an additional 10 percent to the initial outlay to offset the risk of underestimating by their in-house architects. Another practice used by other nonprofits to isolate risk is to set up the high-risk projects as subsidiaries, when possible, to limit the nonprofit's exposure.

SURVEYS OF NONPROFIT CAPITAL BUDGETING AND OTHER FINANCIAL DECISIONS

Zeitlow surveyed 47 independent religious foreign mission agencies and found that 47 percent of the respondents used payback analysis in making capital budgeting decisions. Only 10 percent used either internal rate of return or net present value. He attributed this to the often nonquantitative backgrounds of the people who typically run these agencies.

Kamath and Oberst studied the capital budgeting practices at 427 large hospitals and found that 65 percent of the hospitals responding subjected more than half of their capital projects to some form of formal evaluation. The most popular method used by the responding hospitals was the payback method, with 29 percent using payback as their primary tool. Net present value and internal rate of return were tied for second with approximately 18 percent of the respondents using each method as their primary tool. In addition, they found that approximately 80 percent of the hospitals used some discounted cash flow method, when secondary methods were considered.

These nonprofit practices are typical of what was seen in business two or three decades earlier. It would be reasonable to expect these organizations to become more sophisticated about the allocation of their resources as well and for those who allocate resources efficiently to have a survival edge.

Nonprofits do use operating budgets. A recent survey of nonprofit service-giving charities, independent schools, professional associations, housing associations, and grant-making trusts found that 92 percent of the respondents use budgets. This is further evidence that they are pressured to use resources in ways similar to those used by businesses.

ACCOUNTING RULES FOR NONPROFITS |

In normal business, the excess of revenue over expense is called a profit. In the nonprofit setting, this excess is called an increase in the fund balance. Nonprofit revenues can come from taxes, a one-time large donation, a series of donations, or from fees charged for the services performed. No nonprofit organization can exist without a source of revenue, and none can survive for a long duration without revenue exceeding the expenses. Table 23.4 illustrates in equation form the difference between for-profit businesses and nonprofit organizations.

One difference noted in Table 23.4 is that most for-profits earn revenue from the sale of merchandise or a service while many nonprofits receive their cash inflows from donations or taxes. A second difference is in the nomenclature. Where for-profit businesses call the excess of revenues over expenses *profit,* the nonprofits call the excess an *increase in the fund balance.* The last difference is that most nonprofits apply for and are granted a tax-exempt status from the Internal Revenue Service, and these nonprofits do not pay federal income taxes.[11] The important point to remember is that the long-run survival of any nonprofit depends on that nonprofit generating enough of a surplus in donations or fees over expenses to add to or at least not exhaust the fund balances.

Nonprofits have long been a haven for the "creative" accountant. Throughout the 1970s and the 1980s, there has been an undeclared turf war of sorts between the accounting bodies over who should dictate appropriate accounting procedure for nonprofit organizations. For years, the Internal Revenue Service has placed the greatest accounting constraints on the nonprofits by dictating the conditions necessary to retain the tax-exempt status of the nonprofit. More recently the Governmental Accounting Standards Board was established to delineate the cost accounting procedures to be used by for-profit and nonprofit organizations doing business with or receiving funding from the government. In 1990, the Office of Management and Budget entered the accounting/regulatory picture by issuing Circular A-133, detailing the organization-wide audit and test of the internal control structure that must be conducted by a certified public accountant to assess the control risk of the organization.

Circular A-133 by the Office of Management and Budget is basically to ensure that the funds allocated to these nonprofits are spent on the objectives

T A B L E 2 3 . 4	**Differences in the Operating Statements of Business and Nonprofit Organizations**

Both types of organizations have a "bottom line," which is revenue minus expense. Both have an economic profit, which is the amount left after deducting the opportunity cost of funds used.

For-Profit Business	Nonprofit Organization
Revenue or sales	Donations, fees, or taxes
Less: Expenses	Less: Expenses
Income before taxes	Increase or decrease in the fund balance
Less: Taxes	
Income or profit	

[11]For further analysis, see Burton A. Weisbrod, *The Nonprofit Economy* (Cambridge, Mass.: Harvard University Press, 1988).

for which they were appropriated and not stolen or misappropriated by individuals. In 1993 and 1994, the Financial Accounting Standards Board (FASB) passed SFAS No. 116 and SFAS No. 117 governing the accounting for donations and the preparation of financial statements by nonprofit institutions. The FASB statements were effective for large nonprofits in 1994 and for all other nonprofits in 1995. The reason for and the major benefits of the statements are to force nonprofits to account for their revenues (cash inflows) on more of an accrual basis, and to recognize the restrictive nature of certain donations in fund balances.

For example, Phil Lanthropy donated $3 million dollars to a local school under the condition that the money would be set aside in an irrevocable trust until Phil's death and that Phil would receive all income from the trust until his death. Prior to the new rules, there was a lot of latitude on how this donation would be booked. Some would book it as income immediately at the full $3 million amount and show it as an increase in the assets and the fund balance or endowment of the school. The new rules are quite clear in stating that this would be booked to income because it is an irrevocable trust. The amount to be booked would be the present value of the $3 million dollars using some reasonable discount rate and life expectancy for the donor. In addition, the present value of the $3 million dollars is not booked to a generic endowment fund but is instead segregated as temporarily or permanently restricted net assets of the school. If Phil later decided to donate the income from the trust, this income would be booked yearly to contributed income.

CAPITAL STRUCTURE AND NONPROFITS |

The capital structure question for a nonprofit is quite similar to that for a business: What portion of the assets should be financed with debt? Businesses rely on a combination of debt and equity to fund their assets. Nonprofits rely on a combination of debt, retained income, and contributions. Nonprofits are often significant users of debt. In 1980, Trigeorgis found that hospitals in the United States had borrowed between 70 and 80 percent of total capital compared with 50 percent for utilities and 30 percent for manufacturing firms.

Debt capacity, the ability to repay debt, is an important consideration for each type of organization. However, the method of determining debt capacity is somewhat different. First, where for-profits rely on a history of sales or service revenues to generate the cash flow necessary to repay the loan, many nonprofits rely on pledges of future donations. The bank or potential lender will need to appraise the likelihood that pledges will materialize. The privacy concerns of the potential donors may impede the disclosure of the information necessary to obtain the loan. Secondly, in many nonprofits such as churches, the assets that could normally be pledged as collateral are held in trusts for the religious denominations and, therefore, cannot be pledged. Court cases have backed the national denominations' claims to the local chapters' assets.

NONPROFIT HOSPITALS AS A CAPITAL STRUCTURE EXAMPLE

Each nonprofit makes its debt decision considering its mission, its debt capacity, and numerous other considerations. Often, unusual debt structure decisions can be traced back to peculiar institutional considerations. The high levels of debt that Trigeorgis found in hospitals is not hard to understand when we consider the reimbursement mechanism presented in Table 23.5.

Example. Hospital A invests $1,200,000 in a Magnetic Resonance Imaging (MRI) machine. This hospital is reimbursed over the years by billing for cost as the machine is depreciated on a 5-year straight-line basis. Assume a 10 percent cost of capital.

	Cash Flow	Present Value
Initial Cash Flow Reimbursement	−$1,200,000	−1,200,000
Year 1	240,000	218,182
Year 2	240,000	198,347
Year 3	240,000	180,316
Year 4	240,000	163,923
Year 5	240,000	149,021
Net Present Value		−290,211

Example. Hospital B invests $1,200,000 in an MRI machine and finances the purchase with a zero-coupon, 6 percent note maturing in 5 years. This hospital is reimbursed over the 5 years by billing for cost as the machine is depreciated on a 5-year straight-line basis. The interest is also passed through in the cost of the service.

	Cash Flow	Present Value
Initial Cash Flow Reimbursement	0	0
Year 1	240,000	218,182
Year 2	240,000	198,347
Year 3	240,000	180,316
Year 4	240,000	163,923
Year 5	240,000	149,021
Balloon Payment—Year 5	−1,200,000	−745,106
Net Present Value		164,683

It is evident from the preceding examples that in the presence of cost-plus pricing for hospital services, a negative net present value project can become a

| TABLE 23.5 PECULIARITIES ASSOCIATED WITH HOSPITALS' CASH FLOWS

The reimbursement mechanism changes the motivation of hospitals with regard to capital structure.

1. Hospitals typically apply for a certificate of need before making a large capital expenditure. Failure to do so may result in the exclusion of reimbursement for depreciation on the machine in billings for service to the government.
2. The IRS requires that the money for a project must be borrowed within 18 months after the project is placed in service or 3 years after the expenditure, whichever comes first.
3. Hospitals are typically reimbursed by the government and private insurers for the cost of a procedure. Included in this cost is a depreciation charge of the use of capital equipment.
4. Since 1979, hospitals that apply for federal money for new construction under the Hill Burton Act are required to provide charity care for 20 years after completion of construction. This care must be the smaller of 10 percent of a hospital's federal construction funds or 3 percent of the annual operating cost.
5. Until 1969, the IRS had a "community benefit" standard that required nonprofit hospitals to give 5 percent of revenue as charity care. Recently, there is no firm percentage in the rules, and some hospitals have begun to report uncollectible accounts as charity care.
6. Many states are now linking funding to charity care. For property tax exemption in Pennsylvania, a hospital must spend 51 to 75 percent of the previous year's profits on uncompensated care.

positive net present value project with appropriate financing.[12] The astute observer might assert that the second project is more risky than the first because debt is involved, and the government might change its method of reimbursement. It is possible for the government to change its reimbursement policies, but most hospitals are comforted by the fact that they applied for and received a certificate of need from the funding authorities or the state before making the expenditure. In all likelihood the government would still have to cover these obligations.

Wedig, Sloan, Hassan, and Morrisey conducted a cross-sectional study of hospitals and support the conclusion of the preceding cost reimbursement examples. They found that hospitals with a higher percentage of their revenue based on a cost-plus basis take on more debt. In addition they found that those hospitals that had more of their assets in tangible form had higher ratios of debt, and those with newer assets also had higher debt levels.

GOVERNMENT LEASES AS A CAPITAL STRUCTURE EXAMPLE

The lease payments for real property leased by the U.S. government were over $1 billion dollars in 1988. Given the exempt status of federal debt, one might inquire why the government leases so much.

---

[12]For a more complete proof, see Lenos Trigeorgis and Paul Brindamour, "Distortions in Capital Asset Acquisition and Financing under Cost-Based Reimbursement," *Financial Review* 28 (August 1993): 417–429.

Example. Dutchtown, Missouri, needs a post office, and the cost of construction is $175,000 dollars. Henry Fry, a local businessman who is in the process of building a strip mall, is informed of the post office's desire to lease a building and have a say in the design of the post office. Henry feels that a new post office at the end of his strip mall would have a positive impact on traffic flow for the rest of the mall, and he places a bid to construct and lease a post office to the government. Henry is in the 40 percent tax bracket and plans to depreciate the building for tax purposes over the required 39-year period. The government may sign a 40-year lease with an escape clause requiring that the lease be renewed once a year. The lease payment would be $22,700 per year, and the post office portion of the strip mall would cost $175,000 to construct. The local post office has two options: it can borrow the money from Washington or it can lease the building. The current rate on government agency debt is 6.5 percent, and the cost of capital for United Parcel Service (a competitor of the post office) is 9 percent. The net present values of these options are presented below:

BORROW AND BUILD OPTION		
	Cash Flow	Present Value
Initial Outlay	−$175,000	−175,000
Net Present Value		−175,000

LEASE THE BUILDING OPTION		
	Cash Flow	Present Value at 9 percent
Initial Outlay	0	0
Lease Payments for Years 1 to 40	−22,700 per year	−244,192
Net Present Value at 9 percent		−244,192

The borrow and build option is clearly the best option for the post office, but several factors contribute to the post office choosing the lease option over the build option. The Anti-Deficiency Act requires that all government agencies obtain appropriations for the amount of money to be spent over the life of a contract before entering into the contract. If the building option is chosen, the post office would have to ask Congress for the entire $175,000. By wording the lease as a 1-year lease with the option to renew 40 times, the post office needs only to ask for $22,700. Under the Graham-Rudman-Hollings Act, which targets a balanced budget, it is easier for a government agency to request the amount of a costlier annual lease obligation than money for a less expensive capital expenditure.

The loss is even greater to the government when the present value of the taxes avoided by Henry through depreciation are considered. If Henry depreciates the building over 39 years, his annual depreciation will be $4,487. In the 40 percent tax bracket, this works out as a savings to him of $1,795 per year in taxes. Using the Treasury's cost of funds of 6.5 percent, the net present value of the loss of this income to the Treasury is $25,391. The post office lost

$244,192 − 175,000, or $69,192, by choosing to lease the building, and the Treasury lost $25,391 in tax revenue from depreciation allowances on the leased asset. In total, the government lost $94,583. The post office, being basically a cost-plus operation, will pass the higher cost to the postal patron, and the loss to the Treasury is inconsequential to the post office because it is an independent agency of the government.

The reader might suggest that enterprising individuals should be attracted to this market and drive the lease payments down to the level where the government would not lose on a lease transaction. Several factors keep this from happening. First, the owner of the building is accepting some risk in agreeing to these 1-year renewable leases, and this risk is present regardless of the lessor. Second, the building owner is subject to sales tax and other taxes on the building from which a government owner would be exempt. Finally, the cost of funds will be higher for any lessor because he or she is not as creditworthy as an agency of the government.

In 1982, the Navy proposed to a congressional subcommittee the leasing of 13 ships at a net present value cost of $1,836 million in lease payments plus $751 million in lost taxes, for a total cost to lease of $2,587 million. The cost to build these ships would have been $2,217 million, or a savings of $370 million.

With government lease payments running in excess of $1 billion yearly on real estate alone, the logical conclusion is that the government agencies have found a way to acquire the use of assets without the scrutiny of a budget appropriation hearing.

COST OF CAPITAL IN NONPROFIT ORGANIZATIONS |

To compare future benefits with present costs, a required return must be determined. The opportunity cost principle applied to business can also be applied to nonprofit organizations, but the method of application is different. A weighted average cost of capital for a business is determined by investment opportunities outside the firm. Many nonprofit corporations have debt outstanding and can compute a cost of debt. These organizations do not, however, have an observable cost of equity. Most nonprofit organizations have a fund balance or net worth, in that assets exceed liabilities, but there is no market for this fund balance in which a required return can be observed. Thus, computation of a weighted average cost of capital is often impossible for a nonprofit organization.

When a weighted average cost of capital cannot be observed directly, the opportunity cost principle can be applied directly by studying investment opportunities outside the organization.

Example. Midcity Center was a community service organization used in Chapter 5 to illustrate capital budgeting principles. The directors were considering the addition of storm windows and a new furnace to reduce energy costs. The center had an endowment portfolio earning 10 percent, so one possible opportunity cost was the rate of return being earned on the endowment portfolio. However, the endowment portfolio would not have the same risk characteristics as the furnace and storm window investment. A more appropriate opportunity cost would be the expected return from a portfolio of energy stocks, which would tend to have a high return when energy costs were high, and vice versa.

State governments are a special application of the opportunity cost principle. The state of Pennsylvania, for example, may be able to raise money at an interest rate several percentage points below the interest rate on U.S. Treasury bonds because the interest received on the bonds issued by the state is free of federal income tax, and the bonds are secured by the general taxing ability of the state. The state is limited with regard to how much debt it can issue without lowering its credit rating, though, so the state must allocate a limited supply of funds among investment opportunities. The appropriate discount rate, therefore, is the return that could be earned on other investments of equal risk. If a state is considering the use of bonds to finance an industrial park, for example, the appropriate discount rate might be based on returns available in the private sector on real estate developments of similar risk. If the opportunity cost principle is applied, the required return for an investment by a nonprofit organization will be similar to the required return if the same investment were made by a profit-seeking firm. The major difference between the two would be in tax treatment of revenues and expenses.

U.S. government agencies typically have a very low cost of capital. Agency debt is extremely marketable and usually free from state income taxes. The implied backing of the government allows these agency securities to trade at interest rates very near that of the government's debt securities.

Nonprofits can raise money by issuing tax-exempt bonds in a manner similar to the method used by municipals. Since the issue is not backed by a municipality, there is very poor liquidity for those who attempt to resell these securities. In 1991, these issues were selling to yield 9.5 percent to 11 percent while at the same time 30-Year Treasuries were yielding 8.3 percent. A recent innovation to increase liquidity of these issues was the establishment of the first mutual fund to invest in the tax-exempt bonds and notes issued by the Massachusetts Bond Issuing Authority on behalf of hospitals and other nonprofit organizations. This fund, called the Massachusetts Health & Education Tax-Exempt Trust, raised $30 million in its initial offering of 2.67 million shares. The increased liquidity and lower cost of issue is the result of the pooling of these debt offerings and the listing of these shares on the American Stock Exchange.

CAPITAL RATIONING |

Where there are more projects than money, management and the board can artificially limit the amount they will spend or they can rank-order the proposals they are considering. It is in this rank ordering that the capital budgeting techniques discussed in the prior chapters apply. The American Cancer Society has recently been criticized for moving money out of service for cancer patients and into holdings of cash, securities, land, and buildings.[13] This dilemma is not unique to the American Cancer Society but is a concern of any nonprofit that has an endowment or large fund balance or is in the process of building a large fund balance.

Example. Assume that you are the president and administrator of a $40 million endowment fund for a private college. The first question is a capital budgeting question and involves the difficult choice of how much of the endowment (if any) you are going to spend on current operations or expansion of current service. The second question is a portfolio management question involving the choice of the level of risk and return you are willing to accept in investing the fund balance.

The common-law Prudent Man Rule has been cited in court cases as the guiding premise for the second decision, but interpreting what is prudent is very difficult. For example, is it prudent for a university endowment to be placed in high-yield or junk securities? By doing so, the interest and capital appreciation may allow the university to grow to a higher level than if the endowment is placed in government securities. The answer to this portfolio management question appears to be to diversify across securities so that an appropriate level of risk is assumed. But the second portfolio management question cannot be answered because it depends on the cash flow projected from answering the capital budgeting question. For example, you might not want to lock in long-term illiquid securities if the capital budget calls for draining part of the endowment for upcoming expansion in services.

How much to spend today for services, how much to invest for increased donations or service revenue in the future, and how much to invest for interest income or capital appreciation are all interrelated questions. The answer lies in a well-defined mission statement and having an understanding of the market of potential donors or service recipients.

EXAMPLES OF SOCIAL RESPONSIBILITY BY CORPORATIONS |

Nonprofit organizations are not the only organizations that pursue social goals or good. There are numerous examples of for-profit organizations spending money or accepting negative net present value projects for the benefit of society. Listed below are eight examples making the news.[14]

- General Electric donated its 50-story former headquarters to Columbia University.
- American Cyanamid's Laderle Laboratories donated 2 million nicotine patches to the poor.

[13]*Wall Street Journal*, (March 13, 1992).

[14]Taken from various issues of the *Wall Street Journal*.

- Pfizer established "Sharing the Care" to provide free prescription drugs to 1 million needy patients at an annual cost of $15 to $20 million.
- International Paper donated 20,000 acres worth $5 to $6 million in New York State to establish a recreation and wildlife management region.
- NationsBank created a $100,000 million housing fund to provide investment money to fund 70 to 100 low-income housing developments.
- Scott Paper raised over $5 million for the Ronald McDonald houses from 1986 to 1990. These "houses" help the families of seriously ill children.
- Coors Brewery spent $40 million teaching 500,000 illiterate American adults to read in 1990.
- A. Finki and Sons, a steel producer, plants trees to absorb a comparable amount of carbon dioxide that is emitted from its facilities. From 1989 to early 1993 the company has planted 800,000 trees.

Some skeptics say that these actions are merely an attempt to associate the company's name with a good feeling or thought in much the same way as you would purchase the representation of an athlete or model to promote your product. Others forward the notion that unless for-profit organizations act in socially responsible ways, their very existence is in question. Maybe they are just Good Samaritans.

SUMMARY

Nonprofits play an important role in society. A large amount of money and time is devoted to nonprofits. The missions of nonprofits can range from health to terrorism. Some provide opportunities for play, affiliation, self-fulfillment; some ease social integration; others promote an ideal or belief; while others provide health care, education, and other services or products. It is the role of the board to insure that management is focused on the mission of the organization and not on self-enrichment at the expense of the nonprofit.

Just as profit is important to ordinary organizations, an excess of cash inflows from donations, interest, or fees over cash outflows is important to nonprofits. To insure that this excess continues, the nonprofit must identify its competitive advantage, the life cycle of its service or product, and continually collect feedback from potential donors, members, and customers. The nonprofit organization faces competitive pressures similar to those of businesses, and those that do not provide a valued service efficiently will eventually be driven out of existence.

Qualitative factors have a large impact on the capital budgeting decisions of nonprofits. A defined mission and strategy will be of great benefit in weighing alternatives with large qualitative benefits and large quantitative cost. The net present value method is still the best tool to quantify the benefits and cost of different alternatives for nonprofits. The correct procedure is to quantify as many of the costs and benefits that can be quantified and judge the qualitative residual factors in relation to the nonprofit's mission. In practice, religious organizations do not use sophisticated capital budgeting techniques, but hospitals report that 80 percent use some form of discounted cash flow technique.

Taxes impact nonprofits in several ways. The IRS places constraints on the nature of the business, the amount of charitable care donated by tax-exempt hospitals, and sometimes the salaries of key executives. Since most nonprofits operate as tax-exempt organizations, their debt is not tax deductible but donations, a major source of their cash inflows, are.

Accounting rules had been lax for nonprofits but have improved. Accounting bodies have passed rules to bring the accounting procedures for nonprofits more in line with the accrual accounting procedures used in for-profit businesses by reducing the latitude or freedom that once existed in booking donations and in preparing financial statements.

The capital structure decision would seem to be easy for nonprofits: In the absence of taxes, nonprofits should be all-equity financed. Hospitals use large amounts of debt financing due, in part, to the way they are reimbursed for their capital projects. The U.S. government has lease payments in excess of $1 billion because it is more politically expedient to obtain budget approval for a short-term lease and renew that lease than it is to obtain approval for capital expenditures.

Almost all nonprofits are subjected to some form of capital rationing. A difficult decision is to determine the rate at which the nonprofit established for social good should deplete or enlarge its endowment or fund balance.

QUESTIONS

23–1. Identify the primary service and the competitors for each of the following nonprofit organizations:
   a. Boy Scouts
   b. street gangs
   c. libraries
   d. the United Mine Workers
   e. your university

23–2. If you were the president of the nonprofit organizations listed in question 1, what feature or features do you think are most important to the success and survival of the organization?

23–3. For the organizations listed in question 1, identify at least one external threat to their continued existence or continued growth.

23–4. What are the qualitative benefits of investing in social security rather than education?

23–5. What are some of the ways that a nonprofit university can monitor its effectiveness in meeting the mission of the school? How would you monitor its effectiveness in raising money?

23–6. Why do you think nonprofits use less-sophisticated capital budgeting methods, like payback?

23–7. Why are taxes important to the typical nonprofit organization?

23–8. Why do some nonprofits use debt in their capital structure even though debt is not tax deductible to tax-exempt nonprofits?

23–9. What qualitative benefits accrue to a corporation that invests in hiring and promoting disadvantaged groups?

23–10. Is it socially responsible for the government to pass laws that encourage capital investment in labor-saving equipment if one of the side effects is an increase in unemployment and a decrease in the amount of taxes that can be collected?

23–11. (**Applications**) Workers of Rural Kentucky (WORK) is a nonprofit organization with the purpose of making loans to low-income individuals to help them get off of welfare. Teresa Bolwes opened a T-shirt shop with a $19,000 loan in 1992 in Booneville, Kentucky. What are the non-financial goals that should be considered in this situation?

23–12. (**Ethical considerations**) There is a practice used by some charities to inflate the financial position of the charity by inflating the value of donated property. For example, a local business donated three parcels of land valued at $300,000 to the Founders Society of a local college. The land was valued using the fair market value of a $100,000 roadside parcel that just sold. What the public and the IRS do not know is that the $100,000 parcel that sold was the only one that was presently marketable. For the donated land to become marketable the city must build a road and run utilities to the land. This road and utility installation will also help the donating corporation, who owns additional adjacent property.
   a. Why do you think the manager of the Founders Society would "play along" with this overvaluation?
   b. Why do you think the donating business did this?
   c. If the goal of the Founders Society is to make the college more effective in educating students and more accessible to financially disadvantaged students, is it ethical to further their goals by inflating the value of donations?
   d. You are asked to account for the transfer of wealth from the different parties from the information above. From where and to where was wealth transferred?

PROBLEMS

23–1. Please review question 11. Assume that WORK is submitting a proposal for state funding of an initial endowment from which it hopes to continue to operate. WORK believes that it can help 15 people per year off of welfare, and this number will grow by 3 people per year up to a maximum of 30 people per year. Assume that each welfare recipient is currently costing the state of Kentucky $6,500 per year and that the state calculates a 9 percent cost of capital for this proposal. What is the maximum the state should forward to WORK in the form of an initial endowment so that it can complete its mission? Assume a 50-year time frame.

23–2. In all likelihood the state would not fund WORK with the initial endowment calculated in problem 1, but instead, it would ask for progress reports and that additional requests be submitted in the future. Why do you think the state would do this? If the resubmissions for funding are performed every 5 years, why is it important for WORK to obtain feedback on its performance in the meantime?

23–3. In 1993 the expenses of the U.S. Postal Service exceeded its revenues by approximately $1 billion. One way managers hope to make up the deficit is to increase the rates on the mail of nonprofit organizations from $.02 per item to $.04 per item. Assume that the United Way mails 200 million pieces of mail each year and that volume is expected to continue for the next 20 years. How much would this cost the United Way in net present value terms? Assume a 9 percent cost of capital.

23–4. How long would it take a small school with a $40 million endowment to go out of business if it receives $6,000 per student per year in revenue, has variable expenses of $1,500 per student per year, and has $5,100,000 per year in fixed expenses? Assume that the endowment is earning 8 percent and that enrollment is now 880 students and is decreasing at the rate of 40 students per year starting next year. Will the school run out of students or money first?

23–5. It is estimated that it costs on average $25,000 per year to imprison a criminal. Assume, for simplicity's sake, that the typical criminal begins breaking the law at the age of 16 and has 8 crime-filled years before he is incarcerated for the remainder of his life, which is expected to be 40 additional years. How much could the government spend during the 8 years in turning around this individual, assuming its only motive is avoidance of the cost of prison? Assume an 8 percent cost of capital.

23–6. In some societies, elderly people do not receive medical treatment if there is not a significant chance that they will return to the work force and pay back society through productive labor. Use an 8 percent discount rate for the following situations:

a. An attorney falls ill and the cost of medical treatment is $1 million. When he recovers, he will return to work for 25 years and earn $125,000 per year.

b. A medical student becomes ill and medical attention will cost $80,000. When she recovers, she will work for 45 years and earn $145,000 per year.

c. A retired autoworker is ill and medical care will cost $35,000. When he gets better he intends to go fishing and live off his social security for the next 10 years at $8,500 per year.

From an extremely cold-hearted point of view, which of these situations should the government fund? Ethically, what is wrong with this logic? Do you think your opinion might change as you age?

23–7. Using the information in problem 6, how would your answer change if the lawyer is given a 60 percent chance of survival after the medical care, the medical student is given a 5 percent chance, and the autoworker is given a 100 percent chance?

23–8. The local YWCA has the following three projects for consideration:

   a. Hire a full-time child-care professional for $25,000 per year to staff a day care for parents while they exercise. This is expected to add 66 new members with annual membership dues of $300. Since the YWCA is not at capacity, there are no additional costs.

   b. Hire one day-care professional for $25,000 and three assistants at $6,000 to open an educational preschool for the children of members. In addition, $45,000 per year in fixed costs would be incurred, and $1.50 per day over a 250-day year will be incurred per child. It is expected that 20 new members will join with one child each and 30 existing members will enroll in the preschool. Assume that the existing members would continue as members even if the pre-school is not opened. The parents will be charged $4.50 per day for the service.

   c. Spend $1 million on a pool and exercise room. Annual operating cost will be $60,000 and 560 new members will join with dues of $300 each.

   Assuming a 9 percent cost of capital and a 40-year life for each project, which project should be accepted?

23–9. Somebody has proposed that you charge a fee per user to recover the negative net present value for any of the three options rejected in problem 8. If such a fee were used, what would you have to charge per person on an annual basis?

23–10. Hot Meals runs a soup kitchen for the poor and homeless out of an old warehouse. Recently, they received word that the warehouse would have to be retrofitted with ramps and other devices to be in compliance with the Americans with Disabilities Act. The estimated cost of these improvements is $150,000. Hot Meals does not have any money to speak of and is thinking about approaching the city council for the money. They serve 285 people three meals per day that would otherwise cost these individuals $2 per meal. Prepare the financial analysis you would present to the city council. Assume an 8 percent cost of capital.

23–11. In addition to the quantitative benefits of Hot Meals in problem 10, what are some of the qualitative benefits you would present to the council?

23–12. The United States Army Defense Mapping Agency recently signed a lease to rent 196,000 square feet of a building for $12 per square foot per year. It was estimated that a comparable building could be constructed for $16 million. Operating cost will be the same under the lease and build options. Using a 7 percent cost of capital, was it better for the mapping agency to build or lease the building? Assume the lease is a 20-year lease that is renewable each year.

23–13. Give some reasons the mapping agency (problem 12) might lease rather than buy.

23–14. Assume the lessor (the owner of the building) in problem 12 depreciates the $16 million building over 40 years using straight-line depreciation. If she is in the 42 percent tax bracket, and the U.S. Treasury has a 7 percent cost of capital, what is the present value of the loss to the U.S. Treasury?

23–15. Saint Everywhere Hospital has an approved certificate of need to build an addition to the emergency wing at a total cost of $5 million dollars. It can finance the expansion in one of three ways: it can use equity, it can borrow and pay interest and equal annual principal payments of $1 million per year for 5 years, or it can pay interest over the life of the loan and one balloon payment of $5 million at the end of 5 years. The interest and depreciation will be passed on to the users of the emergency wing. Which of the options will result in the highest net present value for the hospital? Assume a 12 percent cost of capital.

23–16. Urban University was recently given close to $1 million to beautify its campus. Part of the beautification specified by the owner was the construction of a very ornate fountain complete with a water pond and surrounding garden. In the days when tuition is rising at Urban University what are the advantages and disadvantages of accepting this donation?

23–17. Upward University recently spent $200,000 on a very elaborate boardroom complete with chandeliers, kitchen, and adjoining offices. Speculation is that the reasoning behind this move is that potential contributors are more likely to "get out their checkbook" and become part of a school that looks like it is prospering. Upward University has no existing endowment and currently omitted annual raises for nonfaculty support staff. If the school has a cost of capital of 10 percent, by how much would annual contributions need to increase to pay for this decision? What are the likely nonquantitative advantages and disadvantages resulting from the decision to build the boardroom?

23–18. A crowded university recently constructed a $12 million, 1,200-space parking garage to alleviate the parking problems that existed at the school. Operating cost for this garage is $60,000 per year. After construction, the faculty and staff were told that the parking that previously was free will now cost $400 a year, and this amount will be withheld on an after-tax basis from their respective paychecks. In addition, the student fee was increased from $75 per year to $400 per year. Assume that 1,200 faculty and staff people and 8,800 students were affected by this fee increase. Before the garage, the $75 parking fees just covered the operating expenses and these expenses are not expected to change. How long will it take to pay off the garage if the cost of capital for the university is 8 percent? If the parking garage lasts 20 years, was this a good investment?

23–19. The state government was considering an investment in a new $200 million bridge, which would create a more direct route across the Mississippi River and save the residents $20 million a year in driving costs and lost time. Maintenance costs for the bridge would be $1 million a year, and the bridge would have an estimated life of 30 years. The highway department had prepared a proposal that showed the bridge to be a highly desirable investment. In completing this analysis, the highway department discounted the benefits at the state's 7.1 percent borrowing cost, which was well below the rate on U.S. Treasury bonds because state bonds were exempt from federal taxes and were guaranteed by the general taxing ability of the state. Opponents suggested that the residents of the state would actually benefit more if the state were to sell $200 million worth of 7.1 percent bonds and invest the proceeds in U.S. Treasury bonds earning 10 percent. The opponents went on to suggest that the savings were speculative and that the bridge investment was at least as risky as the average investment of a public utility. In recent rate hearings, the public utility commission had allowed the telephone company a return on equity of 15.5 percent. Opponents also argued that the bridge would destroy a delicate area of ecological significance. The highway department countered that its original analysis had, in fact, underestimated the benefit by not considering inflation, which was projected to be 5 percent. Construction companies and labor unions argued that the bridge would give a major boost to the local economy. Should the state invest in this new bridge?

CASE PROBLEM |

Blessing & Saint Mary's Hospital

Quincy, Illinois, had been serviced by two hospitals for as long anybody in the town could remember, and the town, the doctors, and others were concerned about the proposed merging of these two nonprofit institutions. Blessing Hospital was a community hospital operated for the benefit of the community by a board of trustees and was generally perceived by the community as the more progressive if not slightly more expensive hospital. Saint Mary's Hospital, owned by the Sisters of the Franciscan Order of the Catholic Church, had a local operating board for many years but due to recent financial difficulty, most of the decision making had been taken back to the central office in New York. Saint Mary's was more conservative, austere, and perceived as less expensive.

In the 10 years prior to 1987 several large industries like Motorola had closed up shop in Quincy and the population base of the town was shrinking. Talk of the merging of the two hospitals began in earnest in 1987 with a filing with the Justice Department. Since these were the only two hospitals to serve Quincy and the surrounding population there was at least the appearance that the combining of these two competing nonprofits would reduce competition, decrease service, and/or increase price. The reasons cited in the filing for the merger were to better manage cost, to increase cost-effectiveness, to improve the availability of service, and to improve the quality of service. According to the rules, the

Justice Department had 30 days to make a review and respond in a negative manner with a "cause for concern" hearing. Nothing implied that the action was acceptable. Because this transaction involved hospitals, the Health Facilities Planning Board and other government regulators were informed of the intent to merge.

In early 1988, Saint Mary's had a book value of $13 million. Under the proposed merger a new board would be formed that would run both hospitals as one. This board was to be composed of 4 individuals of Blessing's choosing and 4 individuals of the Sisters' choosing. The immediate mission of the board was to work out the details of the merger. Until such an agreement could be reached, the hospitals would continue to operate independently. The new board could not agree on a new name but it was implied that the Sisters would be compensated by the new entity for the assets given to the merged entity. From 1988 to 1992, the new board met and nothing progressed. As might be expected, board votes were split four to four. In the same time period Saint Mary's Hospital became less and less profitable, and the Sisters in New York were rethinking the feasibility of running a hospital in Quincy. On April 1, 1993, a sale/merger was consummated. The Sisters agreed to sell Saint Mary's Hospital to Blessing for $18 million.

CASE QUESTIONS

1. The nonprofit mission of Saint Mary's Hospital was to provide health care to Catholic and other members of the community in Quincy. This mission would be adopted by Blessing with the acquisition of Saint Mary's. From a philosophical point of view, what should have been the purchase price for Saint Mary's?
2. Assume that Blessing will now have to recover the $18 million paid for Saint Mary's. If Blessing has a 12 percent cost of capital, what annual dollar amount of savings is necessary to recover this cost in 40 years?
3. One of the benefits of the merger will be the elimination of duplicate services. Rather than each hospital operating an emergency room and a maternity ward, the combined Blessing will run just one. List at least two nonquantitative or qualitative disadvantages and advantages from the patient's perspective. List two nonquantitative or qualitative advantages and disadvantages from the hospital board's perspective.
4. As a result of the acquisition, Blessing now has two hospital buildings located 8 blocks from each other and the following projects:
   a. Connect the two buildings with fiber-optic cable to facilitate the transfer of patient records to and from the buildings in which the service is performed, the doctors' offices, billing, and other functions. The cost is $1,200,000 and the benefit is expected to be $50,000 savings annually in actual inter-building transfer expenses. Nonquantitative benefits are the timeliness and accuracy that will accrue to the automated system.
   b. One helicopter will be used by both hospital buildings where previously only one hospital had helicopter service.

c. Assume that 120 people earning on average $48,000 per year will be released because they are deemed to be employed in services that were previously duplicated at both hospitals. Severance pay is expected to average $10,000 per worker. Assume year-end cash flows for both severance and payroll savings.

Assuming a 12 percent cost of capital, which of the projects should be accepted?

SELECTED REFERENCES

Anthony, Robert N. "The Foolishness of FASB's Nonprofit Classes." *Management Accounting* 74 (July 1993): 53–57.

Ashford, Ken. "Management Accounting Practices in Nonprofit Organizations." *Management Accounting—London* 25 (December 1989): 36–37.

Barbarosoglu, Güulay, and David Pinhas. "Capital Rationing in the Public Sector Using the Analytical Hierarchy Process." *Engineering Economist* 40 (Summer 1995): 315–341.

Blose, Laurence, and John D. Martin. "Federal Government Leasing: Costs, Incentives, and Effects." *Public Budgeting & Finance* 23 (Summer 1989): 66–75.

Bowe, Thomas. "A Med Center's Intensive FM Care." *Facilities Design and Management* 16 (March 1989): 52–55.

Brinckerhoff, Peter. "What Is Capital, and Why Is It Important Anyway?" *Nonprofit World* 8 (September/October 1993): 17–21.

Brown, Victor H., and Susan E. Weiss. "Toward Better Not-for-Profit Accounting and Reporting." *Management Accounting* 74 (July 1993): 48–52.

Burda, David. "Charity Care: Are Hospitals Giving Their Fair Share?" *Modern Healthcare* 12 (June 15, 1992): 22–29.

Byrnes, Nanette. "The Nonprofit Business." *Financial World* 19 (August 3 1993): 68.

Copeland, T. E., and K. V. Smith. "An Overview of Nonprofit Organizations." *Journal of Economics and Business* 23 (Winter 1978): 147–154.

"Corporate Giving: Who Spends Most, and for What?" *Across the Board (CBR)* 15 (May 1990): 30–33.

Crump, Roberts. "Bottom-Line Budgeting Based on Estimated Cash Flow Needs." *Healthcare Financial Management* 5 (April 1992): 86–87.

Edkels, Timothy, and Julie Trocchio. "Model Refines Quantification of Community Service." *Healthcare Financial Management* 5 (February 1992): 34–38.

Fama, E. F., and Michael Jensen. "Organizational Forms and Investment Decisions." *Journal of Financial Economics* 23 (1985): 101–119.

Forrester, Robert. "Are Your Not-for-Profit Clients Ready for Compliance Auditing?" *Journal of Accountancy (JAC)* 173 (July 1990): 70–76.

Herzlinger, R. "Managing the Finances of Nonprofit Organizations." *California Management Review* 12 (Spring 1979).

Hildebrant, Dean. "Planning Rewards." *Association Management* (May 1991): 97–101.

Kamath, Ravindra, and J. Elmer. "Capital Investment Decisions in Hospitals: Survey Results." *Health Care Management Review* 37 (Spring 1989): 45–56.

Kamath, Ravindra, and Eugene R. Oberst. "Capital Budgeting Practices of Large Hospitals." *Engineering Economist* 37 (Spring 1992): 203–232.

Langer, Steven. "Who's Being Paid What—And Why." *Nonprofit World* 5 (November/December 1990): 20–22.

Mandel, Michael, and Paul Magnusson. "What Crime Is Costing Us Every Year." *Business Week* (December 13, 1993): 72–81.

Oldenburg, Don. "Big Companies Plug Big Causes for Big Gains." *Business & Society Review (BUS)* 9 (Fall 1992): 22–23.

Paige, Kenneth L. "Do Nonprofits Use Management Accounting Properly?" *Management Accounting* 74(January 1992): 56–58.

Pallarito, Karen. "Mutual Fund Will Let Hospitals, Charities in Mass. Gain Access to Funds for Small Projects." *Modern Healthcare* (August 2, 1993): 36.

"Statement of Financial Accounting Standards No. 116—Accounting For Contributions Received and Contributions Made." *Journal of Accountancy* 176 (November 1993): 127–131.

"Statement of Financial Accounting Standards No. 117—Financial Statements of Not-for-Profit Organizations." *Journal of Accountancy* 176 (December 1993): 109–113.

Taylor, Kevin W. "How to Prepare Loan Proposals for Not-for-Profit Clients." *Journal of Accountancy* 177 (January 1994): 68–71.

Thomassen, Henry. "Capital Budgeting for a State." *Public Budgeting and Finance* 7 (Winter 1990): 72–86.

Topping, Sharon, Carolyn Carroll, and James T. Lindley. "The Impact of Health Care Reform on Capital Acquisition for Hospitals." *Financial Review* 32 (November 1997): 751–778.

Trigeorgis, Lenos. "Why Cost-Reimbursed Not-for-Profits use Debt Financing Despite the Absence of Tax Incentives." *Financial Accountability and Management* 7 (Winter 1991): 229–238

Trigeorgis, Lenos, and Paul Brindamour. "Distortions in Capital Asset Acquisition and Financing under Cost-Based Reimbursement." *Financial Review* 28 (August 1993): 417–429.

Umapathy, Srinivasan. "Financial Risk Management: The Board's Responsibility." *Nonprofit World* 8 (September/October 1993): 10–15.

Wacht, R. F. "A Financial Management Theory of the Nonprofit Organization." *Journal of Financial Research* 41 (Spring 1984): 37–45.

Wedig, Gerald, Frank A. Sloan, Mahmud Hassan, and Michael A. Morrisey. "Capital Structure, Ownership, and Capital Payment Policy: The Case of Hospitals." *Journal of Finance* 43 (March 1988): 21–37.

Weisbrod, Burton A. *The Nonprofit Economy*. Cambridge, Mass.: Harvard University Press, 1988.

CHAPTER 24

MULTICRITERIA CAPITAL BUDGETING AND LINEAR PROGRAMMING

After completing this chapter you should be able to:

1. Describe the role that linear programming plays in solving capital budgeting problems when there is more than one constraining factor.
2. Calculate an optimal solution using linear programming.
3. Explain the significance that shadow prices or dual values have in interpreting the optimal solution.
4. List some of the common constraints in the typical capital budgeting linear programming problem.
5. Solve a capital rationing problem using linear programming.
6. Describe situations where integer programming, goal programming, chance constrained programming, and quadratic programming would be preferred over typical linear programming.

Emerson Electric is typical of American corporations in stating multiple goals. Emerson Electric identified growth and profitability goals, as well as a desire to maintain a growth rate of R&D expenditures that exceeded the growth rate of sales. In addition, management wanted to maintain a 30-year tradition of increased dividends and maintain a strong financial position, exemplified by an AAA bond rating.[1]

Emerson cannot meet all of these goals by using a simple net present value criterion in its capital budgeting. Managers must develop decision-making tools that allow them to choose capital investments in light of contribution to these

[1]Emerson Electric, 1986 annual report.

various, often conflicting goals. Finding the optimal set of investments for Emerson in light of these various considerations is especially difficult. Fortunately, linear programming provides a tool for dealing with these problems.

Linear programming, a widely recognized tool for decision making with numerous constraints and considerations, is applied to capital budgeting in this chapter. The chapter begins with an introduction to linear programming. Next, linear programming is applied to general capital budgeting problems involving multiple considerations and constraints. Then, linear programming is applied to the special problem of capital rationing. Finally, extensions of linear programming and alternatives to linear programming are briefly introduced.

Introduction to Linear Programming |

Linear programming is a mathematical technique for choosing the optimal combination from a set of alternatives. The optimal combination depends on the objectives and constraints. The optimal combination will maximize the objectives—those things you want to achieve—given the limitations set by the constraints. We begin with a simple problem in which a company must deal with some constraints in seeking to maximize net present value. The analysis is then extended to include other objectives.

Santa Cruz Corporation faces one-time capital rationing; the company is subject to capital rationing now, but capital rationing is not anticipated in future years. Santa Cruz has two divisions and must allocate capital between those two divisions. For every dollar invested in division one, $0.20 of net present value is created, and for every dollar invested in division two, $0.30 of net present value is created. The variables x_1 and x_2 represent the amounts invested in divisions one and two respectively; they are called the decision variables. The total effectiveness (net present value in this case) of any particular allocation of capital is:

$$E = .2x_1 + .3x_2 \qquad (24\text{-}1)$$

Equation 24-1 is called the objective function. It is a linear function, which is required for linear programming.[2] The objective function is illustrated in Figure 24.1. The amount invested in division one is measured on the horizontal axis, and the amount invested in division two is measured on the vertical. Each of the downward sloping lines represents combinations of x_1 and x_2 that will result in a particular value of E. Thus, net present value of $300 can be achieved by the following combinations (among others):

x_1	$1,500	$ 0	$300
x_2	0	1,000	800

[2] Examples of nonlinear functions are $E = .2x_1 + .3x_2{}^2$ and $E = .2x_1 + .3x_2 + .1x_1x_2$. Methods for dealing with specific nonlinear functions are pointed out at the end of this chapter.

Since Santa Cruz Corporation prefers as much net present value as possible, it would want to be on the highest line possible, that is, the farthest toward the "northeast" in Figure 24.1. In the absence of constraints, there is no limit on how high a line can be drawn, and the company will choose a position resulting in an infinite net present value. If constraints are introduced, the company will seek to be on the highest attainable line, which represents the highest attainable net present value.

Few of us live without constraints. For Santa Cruz Corporation, total investment opportunities in division one are limited to $3,000, and total investment opportunities in division two are limited to $2,000. A byproduct from division one is used in division two, so investment in division one must be at least twice the investment in division two. This last constraint, in mathematical terms, is:

$$x_1 \geq 2x_2$$

| **FIGURE 24.1** SANTA CRUZ CORPORATION CAPITAL BUDGETING PROBLEM

Each of the downward sloping lines represents combinations of x_1 and x_2 that will result in a particular value of E. x_1 and x_2 are amounts invested in divisions one and two, respectively. E is the effectiveness—total net present value in this case.

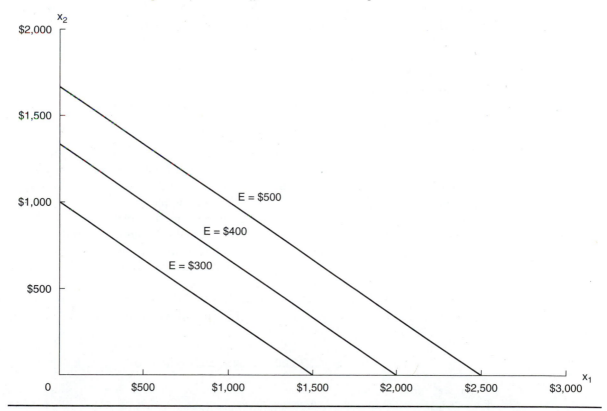

Rearranging terms for convenience:

$$-x_1 + 2x_2 \leq 0$$

One set of implied constraints must be recognized. Negative investment is not allowed, so both x_1 and x_2 must be greater than or equal to zero. This is, in fact, a general characteristic of the mathematical procedures used to solve linear programming problems. Only nonnegative (zero or greater) values of the decision variables are considered.[3]

Bringing the objectives and constraints together, the problem faced by Santa Cruz Corporation is:

Maximize	$.2x_1 + .3x_2$
Subject to	$x_1 \leq \$3,000$
	$x_2 \leq \$2,000$
	$-x_1 + 2x_2 \leq \$0$
	$x_1 \geq \$0$
	$x_2 \geq \$0$

The constraints are illustrated graphically in Figure 24.2. The lines in Figure 24.2 are drawn by converting each of the inequality constraints to an equality. The shading on one side of the line then indicates the side of the line that is allowed by the inequality constraint. The limit of $2,000 for investment in division two is represented by the horizontal line, and the shading below the line indicates that investment of less than $2,000 is allowed. The constraint that investment in division one cannot exceed $3,000 is represented by the vertical line, with the shading again pointing to the side of the line that is allowed. The upward sloping line represents the constraint that investment in division one must be at least twice the investment in division two.

The constraints define the feasible region. The shaded area in Figure 24.3 is the feasible region for Santa Cruz Corporation's problem. The company wants to choose from the feasible region the combination that leads to the maximum attainable net present value. The downward sloping parallel lines in Figure 24.3 are repeats of the three levels of the objective function in Figure 24.1. Since each line represents combinations of investment in divisions one and two that result in a particular net present value, the objective is to be on the highest attainable line. The highest attainable line will always touch the feasible region at one of the region's corners. In this case, the highest attainable line is reached by investing $3,000 in division one and $1,500 in division two. x^*_i is used in linear programming terminology to represent the optimal value of x_i, so we can say $x^*_1 = \$3,000$, $x^*_2 = \$1,500$, and:

$$E = .2(\$3,000) + .3(\$1,500) = \$1,050$$

---

[3]There are ways to overcome the nonnegativity assumption. See a linear programming text such as Jay E. Strum, *Introduction to Linear Programming* (San Francisco: Holden-Day, 1972).

| FIGURE 24.2   CONSTRAINTS FOR THE SANTA CRUZ CORPORATION CAPITAL BUDGETING
PROBLEM

The lines with shading on one side represent the constraints. The shaded side of each line is the area that is allowed with that constraint.

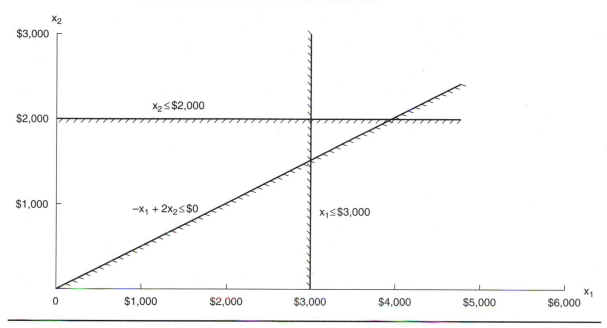

The graphical method of finding the optimal combination is cumbersome and time-consuming. Furthermore, the graphical method cannot be used with more than two decision variables. Fortunately, there are mathematical procedures available that follow the same principles applied in the two-variable case. The mathematical methods can be difficult to use, but fortunately these algorithms are available in the form of packaged computer programs. To use linear programming, it is only necessary to state the problem in terms of a linear objective function and linear constraints, and to interpret the results after the computer program is run.

THE GENERAL LINEAR PROGRAMMING PROBLEM |

The general linear programming problem is stated as follows.

| Maximize | $E = a_{0,1}x_1 + a_{0,2}x_2 + \cdots + a_{0,n}x_n$ | (24-2) |

Subject to	$a_{1,1}x_1 + a_{1,2}x_2 + \quad + a_{1,n}x_n \leq C_1$	(24-3)
	$a_{2,1}x_1 + a_{2,2}x_2 + \quad + a_{2,n}x_n \leq C_2$	(24-4)
	$\vdots$	
	$a_{m,1}x_1 + a_{m,2}x_2 + \quad + a_{m,n}x_n \leq C_m$	(24-5)
	$x_i \geq 0 \text{ for all } I$	(24-6)

| **FIGURE 24.3** **THE COMPLETE SANTA CRUZ CORPORATION CAPITAL BUDGETING PROBLEM**

The shaded area is the feasible region. The downward sloping parallel lines represent the objective function.

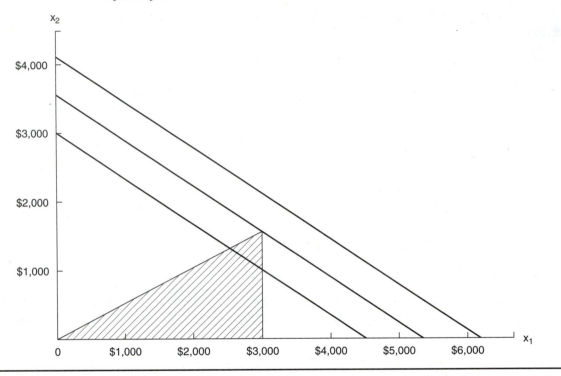

The $a_{i,j}$s and C_is are constants, provided by the analyst, while the x_is are found through linear programming. In a typical capital budgeting problem, x_i is the amount invested in project i while $a_{o,i}$ is the net present value per dollar invested in asset i. If all $a_{1,i}$s equal 1 and C_1 is the amount of money available to invest, Inequality 24-3 expresses the capital constraint. The other constraints represent additional limitations. For example, C_2 may be the amount of floor space available, while $a_{2,i}$ is the amount of floor space per dollar invested in asset i. A surprisingly wide variety of capital budgeting problems can be expressed in this form by a skilled analyst, although not every capital budgeting problem can be solved with linear programming.

We should note several important characteristics of all linear programming problems. First, it is important to reiterate that both the objective function and constraints must be in linear form for the linear programming algorithms to function. There are techniques, such as quadratic programming, that can handle certain types of nonlinearity, and these techniques are discussed briefly at the end of this chapter. Second, the decision variables are generally constrained to values equal to or greater than zero. Third, the optimal solution in Figure 24.3 was found at the intersection of two of the constraint lines. This was not a coincidence. These intersections on the edges of the feasible region are corner points, and the optimal solution will always be at a corner point. The optimal solution could be found by computing the value of E at each corner point, but this could be an extremely tedious process for a large problem. Linear programming algorithms are simply efficient ways of searching among the corner points to find the optimal solution.

In applying the linear programming algorithms, certain additional considerations should be kept in mind. These are discussed in the following paragraphs.

Minimization problems. Linear programming can be used to either maximize or minimize some objective function. Suppose, for example, we are considering inputs to the production process and wish to select the combination that minimizes the present value of costs. Most of the computer programs that are used for linear programming ask whether the objective function is to be maximized or minimized. The necessary adjustments to achieve minimization are handled with no further input from the user.

Alternate constraint forms. Except for the requirement that the solution not require negative amounts of any decision variable, all the constraints used in the example problem required linear functions of the decision variables to be less than or equal to some value. Equality constraints and greater than or equal to constraints can also be used. In the example problem, one constraint was:

$$-x_1 + 2x_2 \leq 0$$

In other circumstances, the constraint could be:

$$-x_1 + 2x_2 \geq 0 \text{ or } -x_1 + 2x_2 = 0$$

Most linear programming computer programs do the necessary adjustments so that the user need only indicate which constraints are equality constraints, which are greater than or equal to constraints, and which are less than or equal constraints. Constraints must, however, be in linear form.

DUAL VALUES IN LINEAR PROGRAMMING

Dual values, also referred to as shadow prices, provide important additional information about the nature of the optimal solution. Most packaged computer programs for linear programming automatically compute the dual values. There is a dual value associated with each constraint. In general, the dual value is the amount by which the objective function would be changed if the constraint limit were changed by one unit and the resources were then reallocated optimally. For Santa Cruz Corporation, the dual values for the three constraints are:

Constraint		Dual Value (Shadow Price)
x_1	$\leq \$3,000$	$\$0.35$
x_2	$\leq \$2,000$	0.00
$-x_1 + 2x_2 \leq \$0$		0.15

To see the meanings of these dual values, consider what would happen if the first constraint were increased to 3,001. From Figure 24.3, we can see that the optimal solution would still be found at the intersection of the lines for the first and third constraints, but the line for the first constraint would be higher. The new optimal solution is $x_1 = \$3,001$ and $x_2 = \$1,500.50$. The value of E increases from $\$1,050$ to $.2(\$3,001) + .3(\$1,500.50) = \$1,050.35$. Raising the constraint one unit increases E by .35, so the shadow price of that constraint is 0.35.

Raising the second constraint would make no difference at all, so the shadow price of that constraint is zero. If the third constraint were raised one unit, this would allow no increased investment in division two, but would allow investment in division one to be increased by $0.50. This would increase net present value by $0.15, so the shadow price is $0.15.

The shadow price for any one constraint depends on the other constraints remaining fixed. If the second constraint were decreased below $1,500, its shadow price would become positive while the shadow price of the third constraint would go to zero.

Shadow prices are often helpful for planning. Managers can examine constraints with high shadow prices to see if there is some way to ease those constraints. Suppose, for example, Continental Airlines is attempting to plan routes so as to maximize net present value and finds gate space at the Denver airport to be a constraint with a high shadow price. Managers can then focus on ways to increase gate space or increase the efficiency of gate usage in Denver.

SENSITIVITY ANALYSIS

Sensitivity analysis is also reported by many computer programs for linear programming. Sensitivity analysis tells how much a particular constraint can change, with all other constraints held constant, before its shadow price will change. For Santa Cruz Corporation, the ranges within which the shadow price for each constraint will remain unchanged are:

Constraint 1	between $0 and $4,000
Constraint 2	between $1,500 and infinity
Constraint 3	between −$3,000 and +$1,000

These ranges can be confirmed by inspection of Figure 24.3. Sensitivity analysis can also be performed on the objective function by finding out how much each coefficient can change before the optimal allocation changes.

Sensitivity analysis is useful when you are unsure of some of the estimates used in developing the model. Sensitivity analysis allows you to identify the factors to which the solution is most sensitive so that additional attention can be given to those factors. Suppose, for example, that Continental Airlines finds its optimal route plan to be very sensitive to landing fees. Additional efforts could then be focused on improving estimates of future landing space fees.

MULTIPLE GOALS AND CONSTRAINTS IN CAPITAL BUDGETING |

Linear programming became a capital budgeting tool because multiple considerations are commonly encountered in capital budgeting. Multiple considerations may be observed in the form of multiple goals or multiple constraints. These two types of considerations are discussed in the following paragraphs.

MULTIPLE GOALS

Accounting income is often an important consideration in addition to net present value. Limits on information available to shareholders play a key role in making accounting income important. While it may be true that the net present values of cash flows are of paramount concern, shareholders do not know what cash flows managers expect from capital investments. Thus, investors must make their decisions based on the information they do have. Income is regularly reported to the public and is confirmed by certified public accountants. When Digital Equipment announced on March 8, 1988, that earnings per share would be $2.50 rather than the $2.55 to $2.70 expected by analysts, the stock immediately fell in price by $4.00 a share. The lower price meant that if Digital Equipment wanted to raise more capital for investment purposes, it would be forced to give up a larger proportion of ownership than before the disappointing earnings announcement. Thus, long-term shareholder wealth maximization in an imperfect world may necessitate the consideration of the accounting impacts of capital investments.

Management reward systems are often tied to accounting income rather than cash flow. In addition, the ability of managers to maintain control of the company may depend on reported income. Falling or unstable income may, for example, make the company vulnerable to an unfriendly takeover. Therefore, managers considering their own interest will also be interested in reported income. Earnings per share, growth of earnings per share, and stability of earnings per share are often the most important income considerations. IC Industries, for example, has a goal of 6 percent annual earnings growth, net of inflation. In its 1986 annual report, Colgate-Palmolive specified a goal of achieving a 15 percent return on capital by 1991. Citicorp's goals include 20 percent return on equity and a 15 percent earnings per share growth.

Managers may also be interested in cash flow over and above its impact on net present value. Cash flow increases liquidity and decreases risk. The importance of cash flows may be captured by having a payback period goal as well as a net present value goal and an income goal.

Managers are also interested in growth. Growth may be measured in earnings per share, income, sales, total assets, share of market, and so on. Growth of one type or another is included in the set of objectives for many companies. Recall that above-average growth was one of Emerson Electric's goals.

MULTIPLE CONSTRAINTS

We work without constraints only in an idealized world, and even in that world there is a limit on the number of profitable investments available. In many cases, companies experience other constraints as well. Capital rationing is a particularly important constraint and is of sufficient importance to be treated in a separate section of this chapter. Other constraints are discussed in the following paragraphs.

Resource constraints are an important type of limitation. The May Company cannot readily increase overall size of its downtown store, so it must allocate available floor space among competing uses. The supply of trained personnel may also act as a constraint. It takes time to locate and train competent people in many specialty fields, and the problem is common enough that some companies have regular human resource planning offices as an adjunct to the personnel function. Availability of raw materials also serves as a constraint in many cases.

Input-output relationships represent an important type of resource constraint. Suppose, for example, that wood scraps are a byproduct of a pallet yard in the Ozarks. A charcoal plant is a capital investment that could make use of the wood scraps. But the volume of wood scraps available depends on the demand for pallets and the capacity of the pallet yard.

Market size represents another type of constraint. If Monsanto is considering four new broad-leaf weedkillers, it is considering four alternatives for serving the same market. Total production is limited by the overall market size and the share of that market that Monsanto can expect to capture.

Constraints can be handled by simply including the limitations in the constraint set for the linear programming formulation of the capital budgeting problem, as long as the constraints are linear. The only problem is the risk of there being no feasible region after all of the constraints are introduced. Multiple goals can present more difficult problems though.

HANDLING MULTIPLE GOALS AND CONSTRAINTS

To see the potential problems in dealing with multiple goals, recall that Emerson Electric wants to increase sales along with other objectives. The net present value and annual sales per dollar invested in each of two assets are as follows:

	Asset 1	Asset 2
Net present value per dollar invested	$ .20	$ .30
Sales per dollar invested	1.50	1.00

If the board of directors likes a dollar of net present value as well as a dollar of sales, the objective function is:

$$E = (\$.20 + \$1.50)x_1 + (\$.30 + \$1.00)x_2 = \$1.70x_1 + \$1.30x_2$$

Suppose, though, that the board likes a dollar of net present value 10 times as much as it likes a dollar of sales. The objective function must then be rewritten:[4]

$$E = (10 \times \$.20 + \$1.50)x_1 + (10 \times \$.30 + \$1.00)x_2 = \$3.50x_1 + \$4.00x_2$$

Writing the objective function is not a problem, but choosing the weights is difficult. Managers may be concerned about net present value and sales, but find it extremely difficult to assign relative weights to the two measures of investment desirability. Furthermore, there is a question of whose weights should be used. Shareholder wealth maximization is the assumed goal of the firm, but we do not have adequate information about shareholders' preferences.

An alternative that avoids assignment of weights is the conversion of goals to constraints. For example, the objective of maximizing net present value can be recognized in the objective function while a desire to increase sales by at least $1 million can be recognized in the constraints:

$$\text{Maximize } E = .2x_1 + .3x_2$$

$$\text{Subject to } \$1.50x_1 + \$1.00x_2 \geq \$1,000,000$$
$$x_1 \geq \$0$$
$$x_2 \geq \$0$$

This approach requires that some minimum level of sales increase be specified. The dual value on the minimum sales constraint tells managers how much net present value is being sacrificed for each dollar of sales increase. Sensitivity analysis can be performed by altering the minimum acceptable net sales increase to determine the impact on net present value.

Example. Giant National Bank managers must decide on the amount of expansion in each of their three divisions: consumer, commercial, and international lending. Managers want to maximize net present value, but they are also concerned about accounting income and risk. The benefits and costs associated with a dollar of assets added in each division are summarized in Table 24.1.

In addition to wanting to maximize net present value, managers want the return from the portfolio of new assets to be at least 75 basis points in the first year and 90 basis points thereafter. To control risk, new international investments must not exceed $500 million and must not exceed one-half of total new assets.

---

[4]Note that multiplying the net present value by 2 would lead to the same investment decision as dividing the net income by 2. Multiplying the objective function by any positive value does not change the optimal solution.

| TABLE 24.1 COSTS AND BENEFITS FOR GIANT NATIONAL BANK

Development costs, income, and net present value per dollar of assets in each division are shown. bp stands for basis point. A basis point is one-hundredth (.01) of 1 percent.

Division	One-time Development Cost	Income[a]	Net present value
Consumer	100 bp	110 bp	.012
Commercial	20	93	.006
International	0	85	.003

[a]Before subtracting development costs.

Letting x_1 be the amount of new consumer loans, x_2 be the amount of new commercial loans, and x_3 be the amount of new international loans, the objective function is:

$$\text{Maximize } E = .012x_1 + .006x_2 + .003x_3$$

The requirement that return on the new assets average 75 basis points during the first year can be written as:

$$(110 - 100)x_1 + (93 - 20)x_2 + 85x_3 \geq 75(x_1 + x_2 + x_3)$$

This inequality can be rewritten as:

$$65x_1 + 2x_2 - 10x_3 \leq 0$$

The requirement that the average return on assets be at least 90 basis points after the first year can be written as:

$$110x_1 + 93x_2 + 85x_3 \geq 90(x_1 + x_2 + x_3)$$

This inequality can be simplified as:

$$-20x_1 - 3x_2 + 5x_3 \leq 0$$

The requirements that international investment not exceed $500 million or half of total new investment can be written as:

$$x_3 \leq \$500 \text{ million}$$

$$-x_1 - x_2 + x_3 \leq 0$$

Adding the constraints that none of the investment amounts can be negative, the investment problem is:

$$\text{Maximize E} = .012x_1 + .006x_2 + .003x_3$$

$$
\begin{aligned}
\text{Subject to} \quad 65x_1 + 2x_2 - 10x_3 &\leq \$0 \\
-20x_1 - 3x_2 + 5x_3 &\leq \$0 \\
x_3 &\leq \$500 \\
-x_1 - x_2 + x_3 &\leq \$0 \\
x_1, x_2, x_3 &\geq \$0
\end{aligned}
$$

Solving the problem via a computer linear programming routine, the optimal solution is:

$$x^*_1 = 0 \qquad x^*_2 = 2{,}500 \text{ million} \qquad x^*_3 = 500 \text{ million}$$

The optimal expansion decision will result in $3 billion of new assets, with $2.5 billion going to commercial loans and $500 million going to international loans. The value of the objective function is E = $16.5 million, so the optimal solution will increase net present value by $16.5 million dollars. The dual values for the constraints are:

Constraint #	Constraint Definition	Dual value (Shadow price)
1	First year return	.003
2	Second year return	0
3	International investment $\leq$ 500	.033
4	International investment $\leq$ half of total investment	0

The dual value for the first constraint means that if the bank was willing to accept a decrease in first-year return on assets of 1 basis point (.01 of 1 percent), it could increase net present value by .003 million, or $3,000. From the shadow price for constraint three, the bank could increase net present value by .033 million or $33,000 by investing an additional million overseas. Note that the shadow price of the third constraint is substantially higher than the net present value from simply investing $1 million overseas. The ability to invest more money overseas would allow the company to invest more in commercial or consumer loans as well, since international loans are needed to offset low profitability from these other loans in the first year. Constraints two and four could be removed without changing the solution.

The bank example is fairly simple in that only three investments and four constraints were being considered. But even with this simple problem, the identification of the optimal solution and critical constraints would be quite difficult without using linear programming. It took less than 10 minutes to turn on the computer, load the program, enter the data, and solve this linear programming problem.

The bank example introduces a particularly helpful application of linear programming. Decentralized companies often select investments by focusing on the characteristics of each investment in isolation. But individual investments should be consistent with strategy. In this example, linear programming was used to identify the amount of expansion to pursue in each area. This allocation decision will then guide the development of policies and an annual operating plan to guide managers in selection of specific assets.

CAPITAL RATIONING |

Capital rationing occurs when a company limits the total capital budget, thereby forcing it to choose among competing capital investments, each of which has a positive net present value. Survey results suggest that most companies operate under capital rationing at least part of the time.[5] Reasons for capital rationing were discussed in Chapter 22, and a general objective of maximizing the terminal wealth or net present value of terminal wealth was specified. A simple decision rule was developed under the following assumptions:

1. Capital rationing will continue as long as the lives of the investments currently being considered.
2. The marginal cost of capital will be the same for each period.
3. The reinvestment opportunity rate will be the same for each period.
4. Lumpiness is not a serious problem.

With these assumptions, the optimal set of investments could be identified by simply using the reinvestment opportunity rate instead of the cost of capital in the net present value analysis.

Projects with lives longer than the capital rationing period can be handled without linear programming, and a cost of capital that changes over time can also be handled conveniently. Changing investment opportunity rates in future periods are a more serious problem though. The specific complication is that the opportunity cost of funds in future periods depends on the amount of money available to invest in future periods. The amount of money available to invest in future periods depends in turn on the investments chosen in each prior period. Joint selection of present and future investments is therefore required, and this calls for mathematical programming.

There are two general approaches to solving capital rationing problems with linear programming. One approach is to compute net present value, based on a first estimate of future investment opportunity rates, and then redo the analy-

[5]Lawrence J. Gitman and J. R. Forrester, Jr., "A Survey of Capital Budgeting Techniques Used by Major U.S. Firms," *Financial Management* 6 (Fall 1977): 66–71; J. W. Petty, D. F. Scott, and M. M. Bird, "The Capital Investment Decision-Making Process of Large Corporations," *Engineering Economist* 20 (Spring 1975): 159–172; Marc Ross, "Capital Budgeting Practices of Twelve Large Manufacturers," *Financial Management* 15 (Winter 1986): 15–22.

sis substituting the shadow prices of the budget constraints for the required returns. This may require numerous iterations before the resulting shadow prices match the investment opportunity rates used in computing the net present value.[6]

To solve the problem without an interactive linear programming procedure, consider the essence of the capital rationing problem: We start with a fixed pool of money and we want to end up with as much wealth as possible. Thus, we try to maximize value as of some time horizon. This is referred to as the horizon model approach. The horizon may be at the end of the life of the longest-life project currently under consideration. The horizon may also be at the end of the period for which capital rationing is expected to occur. The value at the end of the time horizon equals the cash flow on hand at that time, plus the present value (at the end of the horizon) of expected future cash flows.

Example. Stelco Corporation is currently operating under capital rationing, and managers expect to be under capital rationing until the end of the third year. Cash flows for Stelco's investment opportunities are shown in Table 24.2, along with capital available each year (other than that generated by investments being considered).

With a horizon model, the objective is to maximize cash flow at the end of Year 3, plus the present value of cash flow after Year 3. For this company, the cost of capital is expected to be 10 percent after the capital rationing period, so the $1.98 at the end of Year 4 is worth $1.80 at the end of Year 3 ($1.98 ÷ 1.10 = $1.80). The objective function is therefore:

| **TABLE 24.2** **CASH FLOWS FOR EXISTING AND PROPOSED INVESTMENTS AT STELCO**

Cash flows per dollar invested in each of six investments are shown. The capital limit is the annual cash flow from existing investments.

Asset	YEAR				
	0	**1**	**2**	**3**	**4**
1	−$1.00	$0.50	$.50	$.50	
2	−1.00			2.00	
3		−1.00			$1.98
4	−1.00	1.10			
5		−1.00	1.20		
6			−1.00	1.20	
Capital Limit	$1,000,000	$500,000	$400,000	NA	NA

[6]Difficulties in applying this method were explored by W. J. Baumol and R. E. Quandt, "Investment and Discount Rates under Capital Rationing—A Programming Approach," *Economic Journal* (June 1965): 317–329.

$$\text{Maximize } E = \$0.50x_1 + \$2.00x_2 + \$1.80x_3 + \$0.00x_4 + \$0.00x_5 + \$1.20x_6$$

where x_i is the amount invested in project i. The constants in the objective function are cash flows in Year 3, plus the present values (as of Year 3) of cash flows after Year 3, per dollar invested in each project. In specifying the objective function, it was unnecessary to add cash flows received in earlier periods. Those cash flows would be used to invest in some other asset, which generates cash flows in Year 3, and that reinvestment opportunity is expressed in the constraints on investment after the initial period. Cash flows will not be held idle; they will at least be invested in some temporary security. Projects one through three may be viewed as capital investments, while projects four through six are 1-year investments of idle funds.

The constraints have to do with the amount of money available. The limit set by the $1,000,000 available initially can be specified as follows:

$$\$1.00x_1 + \$1.00x_2 + \$1.00x_4 \leq \$1,000,000$$

In period 1, total capital investment cannot exceed the sum of cash flows from investments made initially, plus $500,000:

$$\$1.00x_3 + \$1.00x_5 \leq \$.50x_1 + \$1.10x_4 + \$500,000$$

Rearranging terms:

$$-\$.50x_1 + \$1.00x_3 - \$1.10x_4 + \$1.00x_5 \leq \$500,000$$

Similarly, the budget constraint for Year 2 is:

$$1.00x_6 \leq .50x_1 + 1.20x_5 + 400,000$$

or

$$-.5x_1 - 1.20x_5 + 1.00x_6 \leq 400,000$$

The entire capital rationing problem can then be summarized as follows:

Maximize $E = \quad 0.50x_1 + 2.00x_2 + 1.80x_3 + 0.00x_4 + 0.00x_5 + 1.20x_6$

Subject to
$$
\begin{array}{llll}
1.00x_1 + 1.00x_2 & + 1.00x_4 & \leq \$1,000,000 \\
-0.50x_1 & + 1.00x_3 - 1.10x_4 + 1.00x_5 & \leq \$\ 500,000 \\
-0.50x_1 & - 1.20x_5 + 1.00x_6 & \leq \$\ 400,000 \\
& x_1, x_2, x_3, x_4, x_5, x_6 \geq \$\qquad 0
\end{array}
$$

Solving this problem with a linear programming computer program, the optimal values are:

$$x^*_1 = \$0 \qquad x^*_2 = \$1,000,000 \qquad x^*_3 = \$500,000$$

$$x^*_4 = \$0 \qquad x^*_5 = \$0 \qquad x^*_6 = \$400,000$$

Thus, Stelco would invest \$1 million in asset 2 at the outset. The company would then invest \$500,000 in asset 3 in Year 1. Finally, the company would invest \$400,000 in asset 6 in Year 2. The optimal value of the objective function (terminal wealth) is E = \$3,380,000. From the same computer program, the shadow prices of the three constraints are:

Constraint	Shadow price
Initial budget	\$2.00
Year 1 budget	1.80
Year 2 budget	1.20

The shadow price on constraint 1 is the same as the coefficient on x_2 in the objective function. This follows because an additional dollar available at the beginning would be invested in project 2, and would increase terminal wealth by \$2. A similar interpretation applies to the other two constraints in this example.[7]

The capital constraint can be readily combined with other constraints in this process. Suppose, for example, management at Stelco is also concerned about the use of skilled personnel. There are 100 skilled personnel available immediately, and another 50 will be available at the end of the first year. Investment 1 requires .0001 people per dollar invested, investment 2 requires .0002 people per dollar invested, and investment 3 requires .0005 people per dollar invested. The limitation on personnel leads to the following constraints being added.

$$.0001x_1 + .0002x_2 \qquad\qquad \le 100$$

$$.0001x_1 + .0002x_2 + .0005x_3 \le 150$$

Solving the problem with these additional constraints yields the revised optimal solution:

$$x^*_1 = \$1,000,000 \qquad x^*_2 = \$0 \qquad x^*_3 = \$100,000$$

$$x^*_4 = \$0 \qquad x^*_5 = \$900,000 \qquad x^*_6 = \$1,980,000$$

From the same computer program, the shadow prices of the three constraints are:

[7]If asset 1 had been part of the optimal solution instead of asset 2, the shadow price for the first constraint would not have been the same as the coefficient for asset 1 in the objective function. The increase in terminal wealth for an additional dollar invested in asset 1 is not just the cash flow from the asset in year 3, but it also includes the terminal values from reinvesting the cash flows received during earlier years.

Constraint	Shadow price
Initial budget	1.584
Year 1 budget	1.440
Year 2 budget	1.200
Initial personnel limit	1,640
Year 1 personnel limit	720

The availability of one additional skilled person at the beginning would increase terminal value by $1,640, if other variables are unchanged. From the shadow prices, an additional dollar at the beginning would increase terminal value by $1.584, if other variables are unchanged. The shadow prices for Year 1 and Year 2 budget constraints have similar interpretations. The shadow prices are effectively the returns that could be earned over a period of time if more money were available. An extra dollar invested at the beginning will result in an extra $1.584 of terminal wealth at the end of period 3, which is an annual rate of return of $(1.584/1.000)^{1/3} - 1 = 16.6$ percent. Managers at Stelco may want to reconsider the capital constraint in light of this information. They may, for example, seek alternative methods of funding in light of these rate of return opportunities.

The horizon value approach is a straightforward solution to capital rationing. It follows a simple decision rule and therefore results in solutions that maximize value and make sense to decision makers. It does not require the iterative development of estimates of marginal opportunity costs as is required with an opportunity cost net present value approach. Since linear programming routines are readily available, application of the technique is relatively easy.[8]

OTHER MATHEMATICAL PROGRAMMING TECHNIQUES |

Linear programming is one of the more widely recognized mathematical tools for decision making in the face of complex considerations. It is relatively easy to use, and computer programs for its application are widely available. Linear programming has limitations, though, and several extensions are therefore useful.[9]

---

[8]For additional discussion, see Stephen Bradley and Sherwood C. Frey, Jr., "Equivalent Mathematical Programming Models of Pure Capital Rationing," *Journal of Financial and Quantitative Analysis* 13 (June 1973): 345–361; L. H. Ederington and W. R. Henry, "On Costs of Capital in Programming Approaches to Capital Budgeting," *Journal of Financial and Quantitative Analysis* 19 (December 1979); J. R. Freeland and M. J. Rosenblatt, "An Analysis of Linear Programming Formulations for the Capital Rationing Problem," *Engineering Economist* 24 (Fall 1978); Reuven Levary and Neil Seitz, *Quantitative Analysis for Capital Investment Decisions* (Cincinnati: Southwestern Publishing Company, 1989); H. Martin Weingartner, *Mathematical Programming and the Analysis of Capital Budgeting Problems* (Englewood Cliffs, N.J.: Prentice-Hall, 1963); H. Martin Weingartner, "Capital Rationing: n Authors in Search of a Plot," *Journal of Finance* 32 (December 1977): 1403–1431.

[9]Linear programming and the various extensions are discussed in detail in Levary and Seitz, *Quantitative Analysis for Capital Investment Decisions.*

INTEGER PROGRAMMING

Integer programming is one extension of linear programming that is particularly applicable to capital budgeting. In many cases, a capital investment must be either accepted or rejected in its entirety. If Holland-America Cruise Lines attempts to sail 2.74 ships, for example, a disaster at sea can be anticipated. Likewise, Kellogg cannot profitability operate 3.4 factories. Integer programming also is useful when there are large fixed costs associated with entry into a business area. Integer programming is used in the same way as linear programming, except that some investments being considered are constrained to take on only whole number values. Computer programs to carry out integer programming are available.

Zero-one integer programming is a variant of linear programming that is potentially useful for capital budgeting. With this technique, each investment is either accepted or rejected in its entirety. In other words, the factory either is or is not acquired.

The advantages of integer programming are partially offset by disadvantages. Computer programs to do integer programming are more expensive than linear programming routines, and they use considerably more computer time, more than one hundred times as much in some cases.[10] In addition, integer programming routines incorporate heuristics—techniques that probably lead to an optimal or near-optimal solution—rather than techniques that are certain to lead to the optimal solution.

Frequently, it is possible to avoid integer programming by using standard linear programming and then rounding the values of the decision variables to the nearest whole number. If only a few investments must be taken or rejected in their entirety, linear programming can be used to find the optimal allocation of resources to combine with each possible set of integer-constrained investments. The optimal set of integer-constrained investments and allocation of the remainder can then be chosen.

GOAL PROGRAMMING

Goal programming is an extension of linear programming especially for dealing with multiple goals. The technique could be used if, for example, managers want to generate a 10 percent growth rate while maintaining a positive net present value. With goal programming, the objective is to minimize deviation from each goal. The goal programming algorithm treats the goals in priority fashion, first attempting to minimize deviation from priority 1 goals, then moving on to priority 2 goals, and so on. Within each priority group, weights can be assigned to each goal to specify the relative emphasis to be placed on each goal. Furthermore, the user can specify whether deviations in either direction or just one direction from each goal are to be minimized.

[10]Richard H. Pettway, "Integer Programming in Capital Budgeting: A Note on Computational Experience," *Journal of Financial and Quantitative Analysis* (September 1973): 665–672.

The procedure used in goal programming is to reduce the feasible region to the area that satisfied priority 1 goals, then move on to repeat the process for priority 2 goals, and so on. When goals in a particular priority group cannot be satisfied, then the solution that comes as close as possible to satisfying those goals is found.[11]

Example. As an example of a goal programming problem with zero-one integer choices, consider Nickle Corporation, which has the following six projects available. The company wants to achieve a net present value of at least $90,000. However, it also wishes to stay within certain budget constraints. It is very important to stay within the Year 1 budget constraint. However, it is less important to stay within the Year 2 and Year 3 constraints. The $90,000 net present value standard is more important than the Year 2 and Year 3 budget constraints, as indicated by the greater weight.[12]

		PROJECT						Goal Value (in $000)	Weight (Importance)
		1	2	3	4	5	6		
Expected	Year 1	7	9	2	12	3	5	30	Very high
outlay	Year 2	4	2	4	8	3	0	15	3
(in $000)	Year 3	2	3	5	1	10	4	15	1
Expected NPV (in $000)		15	7	12	20	4	10	90	8

A computer solution results in the selection of projects 1, 3, 4, 5, and 6. The net present value with this solution is $61,000; $90,000 cannot be achieved while satisfying the Year 1 budget constraint. The Year 1 budget constraint is satisfied, but the Year 2 and Year 3 constraints are exceeded by $4,000 and $7,000 respectively. A straight linear programming solution would have maximized net present value while satisfying the Year 2 and Year 3 constraints, resulting in satisfaction of those constraints and a smaller net present value.

CHANCE-CONSTRAINED PROGRAMMING

Chance-constrained programming is an extension of linear programming that is used to deal with risk. Using regular linear programming, the optimal solution will not violate any constraints. With chance-constrained programming, there is

---

[11]For additional details on goal programming, see John J. Clark, Thomas J. Hindelang, and Robert E. Pritchard, *Capital Budgeting: Planning and Controlling Capital Expenditures*, 2nd ed. (Englewood Cliffs, N.J.: Prentice-Hall, 1984); C. A. Hawkins and R. A. Adams, "A Goal Programming Model for Capital Budgeting," *Financial Management* 3 (Spring 1974): 52–57; J. P. Ignizio, *Goal Programming and Extensions* (Lexington, Mass.: Lexington Books, 1976); and Levary and Seitz, *Quantitative Analysis for Capital Investment Decisions*.

[12]This example first appeared in Reuven Levary and Neil Seitz, *Quantitative Methods for Capital Budgeting* (Cincinnati: Southwestern Publishing Co., 1990), 210–212.

at least one constraint for which some probability of violation is acceptable. To use chance-constrained programming, we identify the factors determining the probability that a constraint will be violated and establish constraints to control the levels of those factors.[13]

Example. Managers at Las Vegas Corporation will accept no more than a .10 probability of negative net income. The probability distribution of net income for each investment is normal, and the investments are perfectly correlated. Using the normal distribution (Appendix B), we can determine that expected net income must be at least 1.282 times the standard deviation of net income.[14]

Data on the two projects follows:

Project	Expected Net Income	Standard Deviation
1	.30	.20
2	.35	.30

The necessary condition is then:[15]

$$\frac{\text{Expected net income}}{\text{Standard deviation}} = \frac{.30x_1 + .35x_2}{.20x_1 + .30x_2} \geq \$1.282$$

Rearranging terms, we get:

$$.0436x_1 - .0346x_2 \geq 0$$

One of the major limitations of chance-constrained programming is that the problem often turns out to be nonlinear. The constraint would have been nonlinear in the previous example if the projects were not perfectly correlated. When the problem is nonlinear, it is difficult if not impossible to develop an efficient method of searching for the optimal solution.

---

[13]For additional reading on chance-constrained programming, see R. Byrne et al., "A Chance-Constrained Programming Approach to Capital Budgeting," *Journal of Financial and Quantitative Analysis* 2 (December 1967): 339–364; Clark, Hindelang, and Pritchard, *Capital Budgeting*; F. S. Hillier, "A Basic Model for Capital Budgeting of Risky Interrelated Investments," *Engineering Economist* 17 1–30; and Levary and Seitz, *Quantitative Analysis for Capital Investment Decisions*.

[14]1.282 is the value of z in Appendix B that is associated with a probability of .4 of an outcome between z and the expected value. Thus, it is necessary that the expected net income $\geq 0 +$ 1.282 × standard deviation of net income.

[15]Based on the fact that the standard deviation of the sum of two perfectly correlated variables is the sum of the standard deviations.

QUADRATIC PROGRAMMING

Quadratic programming can be used with specific types of nonlinear objective functions, specifically quadratic objective functions. In a quadratic equation, one of the variables is multiplied by itself or another variable. The widest use of quadratic programming has been in association with the mean-variance portfolio selection model discussed in Chapter 13. The standard mean-variance portfolio selection model is of the form:

$$\text{Maximize } E = \sum_{I=1}^{n} a_i x_i - A \sum_{i=1}^{n} \sum_{j=1}^{n} x_i x_j \sigma_{i,j} \tag{24-7}$$

$$\text{Subject to } \sum_{i=1}^{n} x_i = 1 \tag{24-8}$$

$$x_i \geq 0 \text{ for all I} \tag{24-9}$$

where x_i is the proportion of funds invested in asset i. The variable a_i is the measure of profitability of asset i, typically either a rate of return or a net present value per dollar invested. The variable A is a coefficient reflecting the investor's attitude toward risk; the higher the value of A, the more risk-averse the investor. The variable $\sigma_{i,j}$ is the covariance between the profitability of asset i and the profitability of asset j.

By specifying a value of A representing his or her utility function, an investor can find the preferred portfolio of assets. By finding the optimal portfolio for a number of different values of A, you can identify the highest profitability portfolio for each level of risk. This set of portfolios was referred to as the efficient frontier in Chapter 13. Quadratic programming has been used primarily for portfolio selection, but can be used for capital budgeting.

BUSINESS USE OF MATHEMATICAL PROGRAMMING TECHNIQUES |

A frequent question about advanced techniques such as mathematical programming is "Does anyone use this stuff?" The answer is yes. Surveys have been conducted on an irregular basis since 1959, when 5 percent of the responding firms indicated that they used linear programming in capital budgeting. Approximately 8 percent of the firms responding to a 1964 survey indicated that they used linear programming in capital budgeting, as did 17 percent of the firms responding to a 1970 survey.[16] In 1986, Petty and Bowlin published a survey of financial executives who were Financial Management Association members. While these managers were probably more sophisticated than average, 25 percent of those responding said that they were using linear programming. Integer pro-

---

[16]T. Klammer, "Empirical Evidence on the Adoption of Sophisticated Capital Budgeting Techniques," *Journal of Business* (July 1972): 387–397.

gramming and goal programming were being used much less, though. Just 7.8 percent of the respondents said they were using goal programming and only 7.4 percent said they were using integer programming.[17] In other words, the degree of use of integer and goal programming was similar to the use of linear programming 10 or 15 years earlier.

SUMMARY |

A simple capital investment decision involves only cash flows now and cash flows in the future, using the company's cost of capital as the discount rate. Numerous complications pop up in practice, though, and it is often necessary to balance numerous considerations. There may, for example, be limits on the amounts of various resources, including capital, and you may be concerned about performance measures such as net income, earnings per share, and sales growth, in addition to net present value. Investments may also be interrelated in that the profitability of one investment, or even the ability to acquire the investment, depends on whether some other investment is acquired. Risk is another complication and was considered in earlier chapters.

Linear programming is the primary tool for dealing with complex considerations in capital budgeting. Linear programming is a mathematical technique for choosing the optimal amount of each of a set of decision variables. A linear programming problem consists of an objective function and a set of constraints. The objective function and the constraints must be linear functions of the decision variable. The decision variables might, for example, be amounts invested in various projects. The objective may be to maximize net present value, while constraints might include a limit on raw material or limits on trained personnel, for example.

Linear programming problems are generally solved using computer programs. The computer programs find the optimal levels of the decision variables, subject to the constraints. The computer programs also find the total value of the objective function that can be attained and compute the dual values. The dual values, also called shadow prices, are associated with the constraints. Each dual value is the amount by which the objective function would change if the constraint was changed by one unit. Sensitivity analysis is also generated by many programs. Sensitivity analysis tells how much each constraint can be changed without changing the optimal solution.

Capital rationing is a particular type of constraint problem. Capital rationing occurs when a company limits the total capital budget, thereby forcing managers to choose between capital investments with positive net present values. In the case of capital rationing, project selection is complicated by the fact that the cost of capital as an opportunity cost must be jointly determined with the asset selection. To simplify the decision process, it is possible to select investments with

---

[17]J. W. Petty and Oswald Bowlin, "The Financial Manager and Quantitative Decision Models," *Financial Management* (Winter 1986): 32–41.

the objective of maximizing wealth as of some time horizon, given a constraint on beginning wealth.

There are a number of other mathematical programming techniques in addition to linear programming, but few companies have adopted these models for capital budgeting. Linear programming is used for capital budgeting by a substantial minority of companies, and use of some other mathematical programming methods is being observed.

QUESTIONS

24–1. With regard to linear programming, define the terms (a) decision variable, (b) objective function, (c) shadow price, and (d) feasible region.

24–2. What characteristics must a problem have if it is to be solvable via linear programming?

24–3. For each of the characteristics identified in answering question 2, is there a mathematical programming technique that can be used if the problem does not have that characteristic?

24–4. What types of constraints are commonly encountered in capital budgeting?

24–5. Why would companies face multiple goals in practice when it has been demonstrated that maximization of net present value is consistent with maximization of shareholder wealth?

24–6. What difficulties are encountered in dealing with multiple goals in linear programming? How can the difficulties be overcome?

24–7. Why would a company face capital rationing?

24–8. Under what conditions would linear programming be an appropriate tool for capital budgeting under capital rationing?

24–9. What difficulties are encountered in choosing a discount rate for net present value analysis when using linear programming for capital rationing? How can the problem be overcome?

24–10. How can shadow prices be used in the process of decision making related to capital investments?

24–11. (**Ethical considerations**) Increasingly, companies are being encouraged to pursue a more ethical presence in their capital investments. For each of the following situations list at least one additional constraint that would be imposed to restrain the maximizing of the net present value.

    a. Coca-Cola plans to spend $1 billion on contracts for food and services supplied by businesses owned by minorities and women.

    b. Wal-Mart is constructing an "environmentally considerate" store in Lawrence, Kansas, that will include solar power, trash recycling bins, and other features.

    c. First Fidelity pledges $65.6 million for reinvestment in local communities across the state of New Jersey.

    d. Kansas Power and Light and Illinois Power are setting aside wildlife and recreation areas.

Which of these actions do you think will have the smallest impact on net present value. Do you agree that business should engage in these actions? Would your answer differ if you were a bondholder in one of the above listed corporations? What if you were a stockholder?

PROBLEMS

24–1. Burlington Products is considering expansion of its two factories. Net present value per dollar of expansion at factory one is $0.25 while net present value per dollar invested in factory two is $0.15. Factory one uses input from factory two, so expansion of factory one cannot exceed expansion of factory two. Because of limits on market size, total expansion of factory two cannot exceed $100,000. Set this up as a linear programming problem and solve it graphically.

24–2. For problem 1, find and interpret the shadow price for each constraint.

24–3. New Haven Corporation can expand either its computer business or its fast-food franchise business. Net present value per dollar invested is $0.10 in the computer business and $0.05 in the fast-food business. The growth of the computer business is limited by the availability of skilled technicians. Over the next year, not more than $20 million can be effectively invested in the computer business. Personnel are not a limitation in the fast-food business, but the home office staff cannot be expanded by more than 100 people in the upcoming year without risk of losing control. One home office person is required for each $1 million invested in the computer business, and two home office people are required for each $1 million invested in the fast-food business. To control risk, managers do not want the amount invested in either division to be more than twice the amount invested in the other. Set this up as a linear programming problem and solve it graphically.

24–4. Find and interpret the shadow prices for the constraints in problem 3.

24–5. Amherst Corporation has three divisions. Net present value per dollar invested in the divisions are $0.10, $0.20, and $0.30 respectively. Total market size is such that no more than $100,000 can be invested in division three. Division three uses input from division two, so investment in division two must be at least half of investment in division three. To control risk, the board of directors will not allow more than half of new capital investment to be in any one division. The company has $200,000 available to invest. Set this up as a linear programming problem.

24–6. Solve the linear programming problem identified in problem 5 and interpret the results.

24–7. Providence Express has a moving company division, an intercity trucking business, and an air express business. Net present values per dollar invested in the three divisions are $.30, $.20, and $.25, respectively. Net incomes per dollar invested in each of the three divisions are $0.05, $0.10, and $0.15. Management wants to maximize net present value, but wants net income of at least 12 percent of the amount invested. Because of external restrictions, no more than $50 million can be invested in the air freight business. Set this up as a linear programming problem.

24-8. Solve problem 7 and interpret the results.

24-9. Urbana Corporation is considering three capital investments. Information about the investments follows.

	INVESTMENT		
	1	2	3
Net present value per unit	$100	$200	$ 50
Use of resource A	100	50	100
Use of resource B	100	200	0
Use of resource C	0	100	50

The total amounts of resources A, B, and C are 10,000, 20,000, and 5,000 respectively. Solving this problem with linear programming, the optimal values are $x^*_1 = \$75$, $x^*_2 = \$50$, and $x^*_3 = \$0$. The dual values for constraints A, B, and C are $1.00, $0, and $1.50 respectively. Interpret this information for someone without knowledge of linear programming.

24-10. Information about benefits per dollar invested for four proposed capital investments follows.

	INVESTMENT			
	1	2	3	4
Net present value	$.10	$.15	$.20	$.25
Income in year 1	.10	.05	.04	0
Income in year 2	.05	.10	.05	.15
Income in year 3	.00	.10	.15	.15

Managers at Chicago Corporation want to maximize net present value, but also have certain income objectives. The company wants income of at least $5,000 in year one, $8,000 in Year 2, and $10,000 in Year 3. The company has a total of $100,000 available to invest. Solving this problem with linear programming, the optimal solution was $x^*_1 = \$26,667$, $x^*_2 = \$20,000$, $x^*_3 = \$33,333$, and $x^*_4 = \$20,000$. The dual value for the total budget constraint was $0.575. The dual values for the Year 1, 2, and 3 income constraints were $4.167, $1.167, and $1.000 respectively. Interpret this information for someone without knowledge of linear programming.

24–11. Lorie and Savage contributed to our interest in capital rationing through a now-famous problem. They dealt with a company that wanted to maximize net present value, given a budget constraint. The company had available for investment $50 in period 1 and $20 in period 2. Net present values and cash flows required each period are as follows.[18] Set this up as a linear programming problem.

Project	Net present value	CASH OUTFLOW Period 1	CASH OUTFLOW Period 2
1	$14	$12	$ 3
2	17	54	7
3	17	6	6
4	15	6	2
5	40	30	35
6	12	6	6
7	14	48	4
8	10	36	3
9	12	18	3

24–12. Solve problem 11 using linear programming.
24–13. Orono Corporation faces capital rationing and wants to maximize terminal wealth at the end of Year 2. The company has $2,000 to invest now and is expecting an additional $1,000 of cash flow from existing operations at the end of Year 1. Cash flows per dollar invested for two proposed investments are as follows:

Project	YEAR 0	YEAR 1	YEAR 2
A	−$1.00	$0.50	$1.00
B	0	−1.00	1.60

Set this up as a linear programming problem and solve it graphically.
24–14. Find and interpret the dual values for problem 13.
24–15. Cleveland Corporation faces capital rationing. Based on existing operations, the company will generate cash flows of $10,000 a year for investment. The company wants to maximize terminal wealth as of the end of Year 3. Five capital investments are being considered, and cash flows per dollar invested follow:

[18]J. J. Lorie and L. J. Savage, "Three Problems in Rationing Capital," *Journal of Business* 28 (October 1955): 229–239.

Project	YEAR			
	0	**1**	**2**	**3**
A	−$1.00	$ .50	$ .50	$ .50
B	−1.00	0	0	2.00
C	−1.00	1.10	0	0
D	0	−1.00	1.12	0
E	0	0	−1.00	1.10

Set this up as a linear programming problem.

24–16. Solve and interpret the linear programming problem set up in problem 15.

24–17. For the capital rationing problem set up in problem 15, the company also is concerned about income. The company wants minimum income of $550 in Year 1, $600 in Year 2, and $700 in Year 3. Income per dollar invested in each project follows. Expand the linear programming problem set up in problem 15 to include these new constraints.

Net Income	PROJECT				
	A	**B**	**C**	**D**	**E**
Year 1	$.20	$.05	$.10	$ 0	$ 0
Year 2	.20	.05	0	.12	0
Year 3	.20	.50	0	0	.10

24–18. Solve the linear programming problem set up in problem 17.

24–19. Baltimore Corporation faces capital rationing, and wants to maximize value at the end of Year 3. The company has $5,000 on hand and anticipates cash flows of $5,000 a year from its existing assets. Cash flows per dollar invested in each available project are as follows:

Cash Flow	PROJECT					
	1	**2**	**3**	**4**	**5**	**6**
Year 0	−$1.00	−$1.00	−$1.00	$ 0	$ 0	$ 0
Year 1	0	0	1.10	−1.00	−1.00	0
Year 2	1.00	0	0	0	1.10	−1.00
Year 3	1.00	2.40	0	1.80	0	1.10

This problem was set up and solved as a linear programming problem, using Year 3 cash flow as the objective function. The optimal solution was $x^*_2 = \$5,000$, $x^*_4 = \$5,000$, and $x^*_6 = \$5,000$. The dual values for the year zero, year one, and year two budget constraints were $2.40, $1.80, and $1.10 respectively. Interpret this information for someone without knowledge of linear programming.

24–20. Baltimore Corporation (problem 19) is also concerned about income. The minimum acceptable income from new capital investments is $800 in year one, $1,600 in year two, and $2,400 in year three. Income per dollar invested for each project follows:

	PROJECT					
Net Income	1	2	3	4	5	6
Year 1	$.20	$.15	$.10	$ 0	$ 0	$ 0
Year 2	.20	.15	0	.20	.10	0
Year 3	.20	.30	0	.30	0	.10

When the problem was solved with these additional constraints, the solution was $x^*_1 = \$1,000$, $x^*_2 = \$4,000$, $x^*_4 = \$5,000$, $x^*_6 = \$6,000$. The dual values for the constraints were as follows:

Constraint	Cash flow	Income
Year 1	$3.30	$6.00
Year 2	1.80	0
Year 3	1.10	0

Interpret this information for someone who has no knowledge of linear programming.

24–21. The right to operate the only gambling casino in the shadow of the Arch in downtown St. Louis is viewed as a very positive net present value project. The city will award only one license and five bidders have submitted proposals. These bidders have proposed everything from building a certain number of housing units for the poor, hiring a certain percentage of the workforce from the ranks of the poor to work in the casino, pledging donations to the neighboring school systems, and agreeing to award a specific percentage of the new construction to minority-owned construction companies. The single contract to be awarded will probably go to the bidder with the "best" package of benefits as perceived by the Board of Aldermen of St. Louis. In general terms, how would you set up this problem as a goal programming problem?

CASE PROBLEM |

Family Services Corporation

A. Duncan, the controller of Family Services Corporation, faced a problem that has plagued thousands of managers of companies both large and small. Duncan had become convinced that capital investment decisions should be based on a time-adjusted return method, such as net present value, rather than accounting measures. But Family Services was a victim of accounting rules.

Family Services Corporation was a rapidly growing provider of consumer products and services. The company's major capital investments involved expansion of its four product lines, and accounting income per dollar invested varied among the product lines. Because of current accounting rules, losses during the early years among some lines could be a significant drag on income. Start-up costs, and their impacts on earnings, were substantial because of Family Services' rapid growth rate.

The result of these accounting rules was that it was possible to see stock prices declining because of short-term bookkeeping impacts of otherwise excellent investment decisions. Duncan had always suspected that these problems could be overcome if there was just some way to communicate to the shareholders what management was expecting in terms of the long-run earnings impacts of their investment decisions. But management had not been able to find an effective way to communicate this information. The CEO had often said that the company was being held captive by accounting rules.

While Duncan would have liked to use net present value for evaluating capital investments, this seemed impossible because of accounting problems. As a result, the company relied on the accounting rate of return. The limitations of this approach frequently came up for discussion in the finance committee because Family Services sometimes selected projects that later turned out to be unprofitable. Furthermore, Family Services still suffered considerable income variability, which resulted in unsatisfactory price-earnings ratios. The only reason for sticking with an investment analysis system that had all of these problems was that the alternatives looked even worse.

The situation described above was the state of affairs when Mary Kilpatrick joined Family Services as manager of capital investment analysis. She had spent the three years since completing her MBA working in the area of capital investment analysis for a large manufacturer. The manufacturer had been relying on net present value for years, and Kilpatrick was brought to Family Services with the hope that she could find a way to implement an improved capital budgeting procedure.

The controller explained the problem with reported income and told Kilpatrick that if she could find a way to solve these problems, everyone would be delighted. Her experience with the manufacturer provided no solution. The manufacturer had a modest growth rate so that start-up costs were easily absorbed. Kilpatrick went back to her college finance texts, but could find little that was useful. The texts simply rejected accounting income as a factor of little significance. Kilpatrick knew better. As one who "played" the stock market a little bit, she knew how important earnings per share could be.

Kilpatrick decided she had to find a solution without the help of her textbooks. She started by writing down what she wanted to achieve:

1. Maximize net present value
2. Report a satisfactory profit level to the shareholders each year

Her first thought was that she could meet these two objectives by requiring projects to meet both a net present value requirement and an accounting rate of return requirement. Experimentation quickly proved the futility of this approach. Accounting rate of return averaged profit over the life of the project and, therefore, added almost nothing to net present value alone as a method for assuring that earnings were smoothed out.

Kilpatrick decided to collect information on some sample projects to see if she could develop an evaluation method to solve these problems. After studying a number of capital investment requests that involved expansion of one of the product lines, she decided that the major capital investment decision was really one of how much to expand each product line. Within each product line, net present value per dollar invested, start-up time, and start-up cost tended to be quite similar. Shown below are the net present values per dollar invested in each product line as well as the annual income each year for the first 4 years per dollar invested in each product line. She chose 4 years as a cut-off for income measurement because all of the projects would pass through the start-up phase by the end of 4 years.

Product Line	A	B	C	D
NPV per $1 invested	$.20	$.18	$.25	$.30
Income in year				
1	.20	−.20	.10	−.30
2	.20	−.10	.10	−.20
3	.20	−.10	.10	−.10
4	.20	.50	.30	.70

Kilpatrick had to make some attempt to define a satisfactory profit level. She knew that the capital budget was limited to a total of $50 million this year, although capital rationing in later years was not anticipated. She knew that management would accept somewhat lower reported income from new projects in early years but would want to see some income from the new projects right away. She made an arbitrary decision that the minimum acceptable profit each year was as follows:

Year	Minimum Acceptable Profit
1	$4,000,000
2	5,000,000
3	6,000,000
4	7,000,000

In addition, a steady increase in profit would be required. For example, $6 million in Year 1 and $5 million in Year 2 would not be acceptable. She decided that a 10 percent increase in profit each year would satisfy management.

Kilpatrick sat down with this information to try to work out a satisfactory capital investment selection model.

CASE QUESTIONS

1. Assuming reported income was not an issue, what would be the optimal allocation of the $50 million?
2. Set up the problem described by Kilpatrick as a linear programming problem.
3. Solve the linear programming problem for the optimal allocation of capital.
4. By how much do income considerations decrease net present value?
5. Interpret the dual values from the linear programming solution.

SELECTED REFERENCES |

Andrews, Victor L. "Sterile Assumptions in Corporate Capital Theory." *Financial Management* 8 (Winter 1979): 7–11.

Barbarosoglu, Gülay, and David Pinhas. "Capital Rationing in the Public Sector Using the Analytical Hierarchy Process." *Engineering Economist* 40 (Summer 1995): 315–341.

Bierman, Harold Jr. "A Reconciliation of Present Value Capital Budgeting and Accounting." *Financial Management* 6 (Summer 1977): 52–54.

Boucher, Thomas O., and Elin L. MacStravic. "Multiattribute Evaluation within a Present Worth Framework and Its Relation to the Analytic Hierarchy Process." *Engineering Economist* 37 (Fall 1991): 1–32.

Bradley, Stephen, and Sherwood C. Frey, Jr. "Equivalent Mathematical Programming Models of Pure Capital Rationing." *Journal of Financial and Quantitative Analysis* 13 (June 1973): 345–361.

Byrne, R., et al. "A Chance-Constrained Programming Approach to Capital Budgeting." *Journal of Financial and Quantitative Analysis* 2 (December 1967): 339–364.

Ederington, L. H., and W. R. Henry. "On the Costs of Capital in Programming Approaches to Capital Budgeting." *Journal of Financial and Quantitative Analysis* 19 (December 1979): 1049–1058.

Falkner, Charles H., and Saida Benhajla. "Multi-Attribute Decision Models in the Justification of CIM Systems." *Engineering Economist* 35 (Winter 1990): 91–114.

Findlay, M. Chapman, III, and G. A. Whitmore. "Beyond Shareholder Wealth Maximization." *Financial Management* 3 (Winter 1974): 25–35.

Freeland, J. R., and M. J. Rosenblatt. "An Analysis of Linear Programming Formulations for the Capital Rationing Problem." *Engineering Economist* 24 (Fall 1978): 49–61.

Grossman, S. J., and J. E. Stiglitz. "On Value Maximization and Alternative Objectives of the Firm." *Journal of Finance* 32 (May 1977): 389–402.

Hartman, Joseph C., and Jack R. Lohman. "Multiple Options in Parallel Replacement Analysis: Buy, Lease, or Rebuild." *Engineering Economist* 42 (Spring 1997): 223–248.

Hawkins, Clark A., and Richard A. Adams. "A Goal Programming Model for Capital Budgeting." *Financial Management* 3 (Spring 1974): 52–57.

Kim, Hong H., and Venkat Srinivasan. "Evaluating Interrelated Capital Projects: An Alternate Framework." *Engineering Economist* 33 (Fall 1987): 13–30.

Keown, Arthur J., and John D. Martin. "An Integer Goal Programming Model for Capital Budgeting in Hospitals." *Financial Management* 5 (Autumn 1976): 28–35.

Klammer, T. "Empirical Evidence on the Adoption of Sophisticated Capital Budgeting Techniques." *Journal of Business* (July 1972): 387–397.

Kumar, P. C., and Trami Lu. "Capital Budgeting Decisions in Large Scale, Integrated Projects: Case Study of a Mathematical Programming Application." *Engineering Economist* 36 (Winter 1991): 127–150.

Lee, Sang M., and A. J. Lerro. "Capital Budgeting for Multiple Objectives." *Financial Management* 3 (Spring 1974): 58–66.

Levary, Reuven, and Neil Seitz. *Quantitative Analysis for Capital Investment Decisions.* Cincinnati: Southwestern Publishing Company, 1989.

Liggett, Hampton R., and William G. Sullivan. "Multi-Attribute Evaluation of Local Area Network Topologies." *Engineering Economist* 37 (Winter 1992): 91–114.

Logue, Dennis E., and T. Craig Tapley. "Performance Monitoring and the Timing of Cash Flows." *Financial Management* 14 (Autumn 1985): 34–40.

Lorie, J. J., and L. J. Savage. "Three Problems in Rationing Capital." *Journal of Business* 28 (October 1955): 229–239.

Myers, Stewart C. "A Note on Linear Programming and Capital Budgeting." *Journal of Finance* 27 (March 1972): 89–92.

Myers, Stewart C., and Gerald A. Pogue. "A Programming Approach to Corporate Financial Management." *Journal of Finance* 29 (May 1974): 579–599.

Narayanan, M. P. "Managerial Incentives for Short-Term Results." *Journal of Finance* 40 (December 1985): 1469–1484.

Pettway, Richard H. "Integer Programming in Capital Budgeting: A Note on Computational Experience." *Journal of Financial and Quantitative Analysis* (September 1973): 665–672.

Sealey, C. W., Jr. "Financial Planning with Multiple Objectives." *Financial Management* 7 (Winter 1978): 17–23.

Thompson, Howard E. "Mathematical Programming, the Capital Asset Pricing Model and Capital Budgeting of Interrelated Projects." *Journal of Finance* 31 (March 1976): 125–133.

Wacht, Richard F., and David T. Whitford. "A Goal Programming Model for Capital Investment Analysis in Nonprofit Hospitals." *Financial Management* 5 (Summer 1976): 37–47.

Weingartner, H. Martin. "Capital Rationing: n Authors in Search of a Plot." *Journal of Finance* 32 (December 1977): 1403–1431.

———. *Mathematical Programming and the Analysis of Capital Budgeting Problems.* Englewood Cliffs, N.J.: Prentice-Hall, 1963.

Walls, Michael R. "Integrating Business Strategy and Capital Allocation: An Application of Multi-Objective Decision Making." *Engineering Economist* 40 (Spring 1995): 247–266.

CHAPTER 25 |

MERGERS

After completing this chapter you should be able to:

1. List some of the more common reasons that firms merge.
2. Distinguish between a horizontal, vertical, and conglomerate merger.
3. Recognize the difference between shareholder value-related reasons for merging and management-related reasons.
4. Describe the merger process and define the common terminology used in reference to mergers.
5. Calculate an acquisition price using capital budgeting techniques.
6. Recognize the difference between the pooling of interest accounting method and the purchase accounting method for mergers.
7. Understand the circumstances in which pooling-accounting is beneficial over purchase-accounting.
8. Calculate the impact that a merger will have on the income statement and the earnings per share of the combined company.
9. Describe the conditions necessary to perform a successful leveraged buyout.
10. Define a spin-off or divestiture and the reasons for these actions.

Howard Love and National Intergroup illustrate the good, bad, and ugly sides of the several thousand mergers that occur each year in the United States. When Love was promoted to chief executive of National Steel in 1980, the steel industry was being battered by foreign competition. Love decided that the solution was to diversify by buying other companies. By 1987, National Steel had been renamed National Intergroup. In addition to steel, it was involved in the disparate fields of financial services, oil, drug distribution, and five-and-dime stores.

Love's success in diversification was not matched by success on the bottom line. Love had been able to report a profit in only 1 year and was forced to sell assets to satisfy creditors. Ironically, diversification principles worked. Disappointing performance of the acquisitions was offset by improved conditions in the steel industry. As a result, National's stock price declined only 20 percent in a 7-year period in which stock prices in general more than doubled.

Mergers can be a source of increased wealth and decreased risk. But as illustrated by Howard Love's experience, mergers can also have the opposite effect. Successful merger activity requires careful attention to the basics. The basic fact is that acquiring another company is a capital budgeting decision, an alternative to the slower process of acquiring assets individually. In this chapter, we will focus on the analysis of acquisitions and mergers as capital budgeting decisions.

A *merger* is the forming of one economic unit from two independent units. A merger may have the characteristics of a marriage, in which two partners come together to form a new unit. Alternately, the merger may be in the form of an *acquisition*, in which one company buys another, generally paying in cash or securities.[1] To apply capital budgeting principles, we will focus on the acquisition problem, in which one company is considering a capital investment that consists of buying another company. The same principles of analysis can be applied if both parties are equals; namely, that managers wishing to maximize shareholder wealth will enter into a merger only if the value of cash flows to their stockholders is at least as great as it would be without the merger.

Mergers may be vertical, horizontal, or conglomerate. A *vertical* merger involves integration forward or backward in the chain from customer to raw material. A beer company may buy a beer distributor, or an automobile manufacturer may buy a steel producer, for example. A *horizontal* merger involves expansion within a particular business line, such as the purchase of Pacific Telesis by Southwestern Bell Corporation (SBC). A *conglomerate* merger involves the companies in unrelated business lines, such as the acquisition of a ski resort by packaged goods producer Ralston Purina. The first part of this chapter is an overview of reasons for mergers, the second part deals with methods of acquisition, and the final part is devoted to the financial analysis of an acquisition as a capital budgeting decision.

REASONS FOR MERGERS

Reasons for mergers can be divided into two broad categories: value-related and management-related. A merger is *value-related* if it is expected to increase the wealth of the shareholders. A *management-related* merger is motivated by managers' desires to achieve objectives other than maximization of shareholder wealth, such as sales growth or job security. Value-related reasons for mergers are discussed first, followed by management-related motives for mergers.

VALUE-RELATED REASONS FOR MERGERS

Synergism, taxes, information asymmetry, and agency problems are the four most widely cited reasons for value-related mergers. *Synergism* occurs when the whole is worth more than the sum of its parts, generally because the resources of the

---

[1]Some writers differentiate the two by using the term *merger* to represent only a marriage of equals.

two companies can be used more effectively after an acquisition or merger. *Tax benefits* occur when total tax payments by two companies or their owners are reduced by a merger. *Information asymmetry* motives occur when investors are not as well informed as the acquirer with regard to the true value of the acquisition candidate, causing the acquisition candidate to be underpriced. *Agency* problems can be resolved in a number of ways through acquisition, with the most common way being the use of an acquisition to dislodge unproductive managers. These value-related reasons for acquisitions and mergers are discussed in the following paragraphs.

Synergism

In the merger boom of the late 1960s, synergism was used to justify virtually any imaginable business combination. The idea that any big company could be managed more efficiently than any small company seemed to be sufficient justification. Synergism got a bad name from overuse, but we can sometimes increase total profitability by combining two companies.

Mercedes-Benz's proposed acquisition of Chrysler is an example of an acquisition based on an expectation of synergistic benefits. Chrysler has productive capacity and a well-trained work force, but its car designs were not selling as well as they could be and in many studies Chrysler's quality and engineering ranked third among the "big three" U.S. automakers. Mercedes-Benz, on the other hand, has a quality, design, and engineering team that ranks it among the top in the world. By purchasing Chrysler, Mercedes-Benz gets productive capacity and the opportunity to use its design staff to design cars for Chrysler and its engineering and production specialists to improve the quality of Chrysler's offering.

Economies of scale are one type of synergistic benefit. If a business has both fixed and variable costs, we would expect a decrease in total cost per unit as output increases. The merger of NationsBank and BankAmerica is an example of a merger in which economy of scale benefits were anticipated. There is, however, some point beyond which management becomes more difficult and marginal cost per unit begins to increase.[2] In a perfectly competitive economy, the number of companies in existence in a particular industry will be such that the cost per unit produced is minimized. If there are too many companies, some will be forced out of existence as all companies attempt to expand to the optimal size. The optimal size often changes as technology changes. The existence of modern data processing equipment seems to have increased the optimal size of a bank, for example.

Movement to optimal size can occur through the failure of some companies and the growth of others. Alternately, companies can move to the optimal size through mergers. The choice of expansion method is a capital budgeting decision, which depends on the costs and benefits from acquisition of another company and from expanding by purchasing assets individually. In some cases, acquisition is the only allowed means of expansion. The major banks in the United States have not been allowed to expand across state lines by opening branches

---

[2]If there were no limitations on economies of scale in management, we would probably see the highest levels of output in planned economies.

or subsidiary banks. They have, however, been allowed to expand by acquiring failed institutions.

Economies of scope occur when one company can carry out two or more activities more profitably than two separate companies could carry out the same activities. Economies can result from the production of similar products or from integration. Backward integration occurs when a company increases its control over the inputs to its productive process—acquisition of a steel company by an automobile manufacturer, for example. Forward integration occurs when a company moves its control one step closer to the customer. Disney's purchase of the ABC network's parent company, Capital Cities, is an example of economies of scope. This purchase allowed Disney one more venue for its production company's product. To the extent that there are economies of scope to be had, those benefits can be achieved by either expanding through asset acquisition or expanding through company acquisition. Again, the choice is a capital budgeting decision.

Economies of financing occur because as a general rule, large companies can raise funds more economically than small companies. One reason for lower costs is that there are many fixed costs associated with a new security issue; the more money raised, the lower is the administrative cost per dollar raised. Another reason is that investors prefer securities that can be sold again if they should need money. A small company's stock may not be traded on any organized exchange, so the holder would be forced to search for a private buyer. Holders of the stock of large companies, on the other hand, are virtually certain of being able to sell their stock within a few minutes if they should need money. Owners of small companies often sell out to larger companies when they reach a point where they are unable to expand without raising equity capital from the general public.

Mergers result in *risk reduction*. Portfolio theory suggests that mergers will not decrease systematic risk. Mergers will reduce unsystematic risk, but we would not expect reduction of unsystematic risk to decrease required return. There are, however, conditions in which reduction of unsystematic risk may increase value. A merger that reduced unsystematic risk would generally reduce expected bankruptcy cost, for example. If your company acquires a supplier, you may end up with less unsystematic risk than the sum of the unsystematic risks experienced by the two companies separately. Merger will allow sharing of information that you and your supplier previously withheld from each other in order to strengthen your bargaining positions.

Market power is another consideration leading to mergers. A company with a large share of a market is generally able to exercise some control over price. Economic theory suggests that there is less incentive to decrease price to the break-even level in a market dominated by a few large competitors than in a market divided among innumerable small competitors. To increase market share by taking business away from competitors is a long, expensive process; expansion by buying a competitor is much easier.[3] When harp-maker Les Arts Mecanique of Switzerland bought Lyons and Healy in 1987, it ended up with 80 percent of

---

[3]It is possible, though, that the merger will be challenged by the Justice Department, based on potential anticompetitive effects.

the world harp market. The route to market dominance without an acquisition would have been long and expensive, if not impossible. While market power may motivate some mergers, it obviously does not motivate all mergers because many mergers are across industries.

Taxes

A merger may result in taxes paid by the combined companies being less than the total of taxes paid by the two companies as independent units. A list of some possible reasons for tax benefits follows.

1. The acquiring company has substantial cash flows and limited opportunities for internal investment. If the money is distributed via dividends, those payments will be taxed as income to the stockholders. If the money is used to acquire another company, that payment is not considered income to someone else.
2. There may be an opportunity to revalue assets that had been fully depreciated and, therefore, gain new depreciation benefits. These may be offset by capital gains tax later, but a delayed tax is better than tax paid now.
3. One company may be earning a profit while the other company is suffering a temporary loss. This often happens with new companies that require several years or more to begin showing a profit. The tax loss carry-forward provisions may allow the company to offset present losses against *future* income. An acquiring company could offset present losses against *present* income, though, and save taxes now instead of at an uncertain future date.[4]
4. The alternate minimum tax may encourage mergers, as explained in the following example.
5. Diversification through a merger may increase debt capacity, thereby increasing interest tax deductions.

Example. Financial statements for Adams Corporation and Barnes Corporation appear in Table 25.1. Recall from Chapter 9 that companies are required to pay the higher of the regular tax or the alternate minimum tax. Because Adams has added fixed assets at a rapid rate, its tax is sharply reduced by accelerated depreciation. Taxable income using the alternate minimum tax approach (using straight-line depreciation) is high enough that the alternate minimum tax rate of 20 percent is paid. Thus, Adams's tax liability is $120. Barnes Corporation, on the other hand, has older assets and can depreciate its assets only at the straight-line rate. Because Barnes has no tax preference items, it pays the 35 percent tax rate on its ordinary income. As Table 25.1 illustrates, the total income tax of the two companies is $120 + $210 = $330 as separate entities, but only $280 if merged.

Information Asymmetry

Managers sometime justify acquisitions by explaining that the company was available at a "bargain price." A conclusion of this type might be justified by assuming investors underestimate the company's prospects because they are not using

---

[4]The ability to reduce income for losses of the acquired company that occurred before the acquisition has been sharply curtailed by the Tax Reform Act of 1986.

| TABLE 25.1 TAX SAVINGS THROUGH MERGER

This table illustrates how the total tax paid can be reduced when two companies merge to avoid the imposition of the alternate minimum tax.

Company	Adams		Barnes	Merged	
	Regular Tax	AMT	Regular Tax	Regular Tax	AMT
Earnings before depreciation & tax	$1,000	$1,000	$1,000	$2,000	$2,000
Accelerated depreciation	800			1,200	
Straight-line depreciation		400	400		800
Taxable income	200	600	600	800	1,200
Regular tax	70		210*	280*	
Alternate minimum tax		120*			240

*Tax that would actually be paid in each situation.

the information they have available. A more plausible justification, though, would be that the acquiring company has information that is not generally available. In such cases, it may be possible to create value by buying bargains. The actual frequency of bargain purchases is undocumented. It is more likely that information asymmetry mergers would take place when competitors within industries merge. In those types of situations the competitors will probably know each other and their common situations better than the market in general.

Agency

We have discussed divergence between management and shareholder interests at several points in this book. If managers are acting in their own interest, value is not being maximized, and there is an opportunity to improve shareholder wealth. Removal of managers through proxy battles is extremely difficult. Furthermore, the costs of the battle are often borne by a handful of dissidents while any benefits are spread across all stockholders. An acquisition is often easier than a proxy battle, and the acquirer can enjoy a larger share of the benefits of any value creation.

Carl Icahn is one of a number of current acquisition artists who see their role as bringing management focus back to shareholder wealth. Icahn's acquisition of TWA was followed by substantial restructuring aimed at increasing the value of the company. Researchers have provided evidence that elimination of nonproductive assets and refusing the business are frequent reasons for takeovers.[5]

[5]Amar Bhide, "The Causes and Consequences of Hostile Takeovers," *Journal of Applied Corporate Finance* 2 (Summer 1989): 36–59; Paul M. Healy, Krishna G. Palepu, and Richard S. Ruback, "Does Corporate Performance Improve after Mergers?" *Journal of Financial Economics* 31 (April 1992): 135–175; Andrei S. Schleifer and Robert W. Vishny, "The Takeover Wave of the 1980s," *Journal of Applied Corporate Finance* 4 (Fall 1991): 49–56.

The prospect of future takeover attempts has caused some managers to work more vigorously toward shareholder wealth maximization. Jensen argues that manufacturing productivity soared during the 1980s primarily as a result of pressure from the takeover market.[6] Other managers concentrated their efforts on gaining so-called "golden parachute" contracts which protect their income if a takeover occurs, or on poison pills and other forms of takeover defense.

Mergers may also decrease agency problems by eliminating free cash flow. Managers of companies with cash flow in excess of profitable investment opportunities may be tempted to invest those funds unwisely. An acquisition that uses up those funds forces managers to submit their plans to investors in order to raise additional capital. The prospect of having to justify a project to investors is often sufficient to discourage managers from attempting frivolous investments.

MANAGEMENT-RELATED REASONS FOR MERGERS

Managers potentially benefit from mergers in several ways that do not directly affect stockholders. These include reduction of unsystematic risk, reduction of takeover risk, and realization of management benefits directly related to size.

Reduction of unsystematic risk. Suppose you own an automobile manufacturer. The profitability of the automobile industry is dependent on oil prices, and high oil prices will hurt your business. An oil company with substantial reserves gains from increased oil prices, on the other hand. By merging with an oil company, you can decrease your unsystematic risk. The merger of the gold mining and real estate development companies would not be expected to decrease risk for the shareholders. After all, the shareholders could divide their capital between gold mining and real estate companies if they desired. But the managers may benefit from the diversification. The merger reduces the likelihood of earnings fluctuations that might result in stockholders' dissatisfaction, a takeover attempt, or even a proxy battle. Furthermore, incomes of managers are often tied to income of the company so a merger that stabilizes company income also stabilizes management income.

Takeover risk. This type of management risk can also be reduced through a merger. If you believe that your company is a potential acquisition target and you want to protect yourself from a takeover attempt, you might try to acquire another company simply to increase your size and, therefore, become harder to swallow. If your company is an attractive acquisition candidate because it has a lot of cash, you can decrease its attractiveness by using the cash to buy some other company. Mergers may also allow a company to protect itself from takeover through the use of antitrust legislation. For example, Goodrich Tire Company purchased a trucking company when it was being pursued by Northwest Industries, which owned a railroad line. This made it possible to delay the takeover attempt by raising a claim that the acquisition of Goodrich would be anticompetitive because the two companies were competitors in the freight-hauling business.

---

[6]Michael C. Jensen, "Corporate Control and the Politics of Finance," *Journal of Applied Corporate Finance* 4 (Summer 1991): 13–33.

Size preference. Finally, some managers prefer growth, whether or not the growth results in increased shareholder wealth. In some cases, this is simply a matter of ego. Most chief executive officers want to be head of the biggest company in the industry, for example. Management interest in growth may be motivated by other personal interests as well. Evidence suggests that incomes of top managers are more closely related to company size than to company profitability. Therefore, a top manager may very well expect to increase personal income by increasing the size of the company. In an efficient labor market, higher salaries for running larger organizations would occur only if different skills were required to run larger organizations, and the CEO with those skills could presumably go to a larger organization instead of increasing the size of an existing organization through merger. Since management labor is specialized and probably unique, labor markets may be imperfect enough that the best way to get a larger company to manage is through merger.

Mergers motivated by management interest often decrease shareholder wealth. We know from reading about option pricing theory in Chapter 15 that reduction of risk through a merger will transfer wealth from the stockholders to the creditors. Actions that discourage takeover attempts hurt the shareholders' chance of selling their stock at a profit; we might expect shareholder-wealth maximizing managers to structure their company to fetch the highest possible price in takeover rather than discouraging takeover. Finally, growth hurts the shareholders when it is achieved by making capital investments, including mergers, that do not have positive net present values.

Regardless of whether mergers are motivated by management's or shareholders' interests, there are several ways in which mergers are carried out. Merger processes are described in the next section.

MERGER PROCESS |

Merger activity is generally initiated by the acquiring company, although there are cases in which a company seeks an acquirer. Once an acquisition candidate— called a *target company*—has been selected, the critical question is whether the acquisition attempt will be *friendly* or *hostile*. A friendly acquisition is carried out by negotiation with the board of directors of the target company. A hostile acquisition is carried out by going directly to the stockholders; hostile means being friendly with the owners rather than with the managers.

FRIENDLY TAKEOVERS

If a friendly takeover is anticipated, management of the acquiring company contacts the board of directors of the target company. Initial contact may be handled discreetly by a third party, such as an investment banker, or it may take the form of a simple phone call from one chief executive to another. Following this initial contact, negotiations are carried out between the two boards. The target company often gives the acquiring company access to more detailed financial information than that available to outside investors. Negotiations focus on price, but other terms are also of interest.

Roles of the managers of the acquired company are often a critical part of the negotiations. In many cases, the existing management will be left in place at the target company following the acquisition. Managers are often given employment contracts to decrease their concerns about being removed. Managers may also be concerned about the welfare of communities and employees. When Mobil Oil attempted to acquire Marathon Oil, for example, Marathon managers stood to lose their Findlay, Ohio, headquarters, and their jobs. Marathon managers succeeded in arranging a rescue in the form of an acquisition by U.S. Steel, a company that was not in the oil business and would still need Marathon's management organization.

Once the two companies have succeeded in negotiating terms, the proposal is submitted to the target company's shareholders. If the merger is approved by the shareholders—mergers generally are approved if recommended by management—the shareholders of the target firm receive the amount agreed to. The agreement may call for cash payment at a specific price per share, or it may call for payment in the form of securities. The simplest security payment consists of a specified number of shares of the acquiring company for the shares of the target company. Offers are often more complex, though, with debt instruments and preferred stock also being issued.

HOSTILE TAKEOVERS

A hostile takeover is often attempted when management of the target company rejects a friendly overture. The initial attempt may be hostile if it is anticipated that management will not respond favorably. By starting with a hostile attempt, the acquiring company avoids giving the target advance warning.

A hostile attempt often begins with the surreptitious acquisition of shares in the target company. The shares are usually held in the names of brokerage firms to disguise the action and hide the identity of the acquirer. After a substantial block of stock is acquired, a tender offer is made. Shareholders are invited to *tender* their shares (offer their shares for sale) to the acquiring company. The tender offer specifies a price, a number of shares in the acquiring company, or amounts of other securities to be paid per share.

Management of the acquiring firm can only move a certain distance along the acquisition route in secret. Once a substantial block of the target's stock is acquired, the identity of the acquirer must be made public, even if the stock is technically held in the names of stock brokerage firms. Furthermore, management and the SEC[7] must be given notice of an attempted acquisition 30 days before the attempt. The acquiring firm will attempt to have all other details taken care of so that management of the target will not have more than 30 days in which to develop a defense.

---

[7]Securities and Exchange Commission.

As discussed in the following paragraphs, managers of the target firm will often act vigorously to fight off the takeover attempt. The result is often delay through court action and solicitation of bids from other companies. The original tender offer may be modified several times in the process of attempting to complete the acquisition. If enough shareholders finally tender their shares, the merger is completed in the same manner as if the acquisition had been friendly. The difference is that the target's management will generally stay in place after a friendly takeover and will generally be fired after a hostile takeover.

TAKEOVER DEFENSE |

Managers have many reasons to want to avoid takeovers. They may believe that they can create more wealth for the shareholders as an independent company. They may prefer to be in charge of their own operation rather than being in charge of someone else's subsidiary. Or they may fear that they will be fired if there is a takeover. Regardless of the motive for fighting an acquisition attempt, the development of defenses has become a modern art form.

For many corporations, the first lines of takeover defense are constructed when there are no immediate threats of takeover. The board, often dominated by the company's executives, gives the executives employment contracts commonly referred to as *golden parachutes*. These contracts require payments, often in millions of dollars, if executives are dismissed following a takeover. The golden parachute decreases the attractiveness of the company as a takeover candidate, but its main effect is to comfort managers in the event their takeover defense fails.

A recent variation of the golden parachute is an employment condition guarantee offered to most or all of the company's employees. These so-called "tin parachutes" are a more potent takeover defense in that they substantially decrease the ability of the acquiring company to make changes after the acquisition. These "tin parachutes" are of questionable legality, but they do add to confusion and difficulty for the acquiring company.

Managers also attempt to change the corporate charter in order to make a takeover more difficult. Movements toward voting and nonvoting common stock are examples. Staggering the terms of the directors so that only a third of the directors are up for election each year is another way to make it difficult for the acquiring company to gain control. Various "poison pill" arrangements have also become popular. For example, managers may renegotiate terms of a large debt issue so that it becomes payable immediately on any change in management. When watching managers develop these defenses, it is sometimes difficult to remind oneself that they are acting in the interest of their shareholders.

Companies also change their structures so as to be less attractive. A large cash position or a small amount of debt makes a company more attractive as a takeover candidate. Thus, getting rid of excess cash and maintaining a highly leveraged capital structure helps managers to protect themselves from acquisitions. Acquiring other companies is one way to get rid of excess cash, add debt, and make the company more difficult to acquire.

Once a hostile takeover attempt has been announced, the defensive actions become intense. Managers begin with a publicity campaign, attempting to convince stockholders that the acquisition is bad. If the acquisition offer is for a cash price, managers try to convince their shareholders that the price is much less than the company is really worth. This is difficult because the tender offer is usually for substantially more than the previous price of the stock. But the board can take other actions like immediately voting an increase in dividends to convince the shareholders to reject the tender offer. If the offer is for stock or securities, management tries to convince shareholders that their position will be weakened through problems, such as excess debt of the acquiring company.

Managers also turn to the legal arena. They attempt to show that the merger will be anticompetitive, they attempt to show that the acquirer did not adequately inform investors, etc. Managers of target companies have been helped substantially by state laws in recent years. The state laws are designed primarily to protect the local community from any harmful effects and, therefore, set restrictions on tender offers that might potentially hurt citizens of the state. These laws primarily serve to slow down the acquisition process. But slowing the process is often sufficient. If managers of the target company can buy enough time, the merger attempt may fizzle.

Greenmail is another alternative available to management of the target company. In a typical greenmail scenario, the acquiring company has already purchased a number of shares of the target company's stock. Managers of the target offer to buy back the stock, at a price that gives the would-be acquirer a substantial profit. Through greenmail, millions of dollars in profit can be had from a takeover attempt, even if the attempt fails. Since money is not created from thin air, someone loses, and the losers in a greenmail situation are the stockholders of the target company. Their money was used to pay someone else to abandon an attempt to buy their shares.

Greenmail has been discouraged by the Tax Reform Act of 1986. Neither the amount paid to repurchase stock nor the related administrative expenses are tax deductible. This restriction on tax deductibility also applies to money paid for so-called "standstill agreements," in which the potential acquirer agrees not to acquire any more of the target company's stock for a specified period of time.

The final action available to managers of a target company is the search for a *white knight*. A white knight is another company that will acquire the target company, thereby protecting it from the unwanted suitor. The ideal white knight will pay at least as much per share as the unwanted suitor and will also allow the existing managers to continue running the company. As noted earlier, Marathon Oil is an example of a company that was successful in finding a white knight.

With greenmail and white knights around, the pain of failure is often bearable. Paul Bilzerian failed in five takeover attempts from 1985 through 1987: H. H. Robertson, Cluett Peabody, Hammermill Paper, Allied Stores, and Pay 'N Pak Stores. The agony of defeat was somewhat softened by the $50 million gain he recognized when selling his shares in those companies.

POST-ACQUISITION FORM |

If an acquisition attempt is successful, several post-acquisition forms of organization are possible. The acquirer may simply hold all of the shares of the acquired company and operate the company as a subsidiary. Alternately, the target company may be genuinely merged onto the acquirer, losing its identity as an independent corporation. In many cases, a holding company is used as the vehicle for ownership.

A *holding company* is a corporation whose major assets are the shares of subsidiary corporations. The holding company arrangement is particularly popular when mergers involve unrelated business lines. The holding company makes it easy to bring new acquisitions into the organization and also makes it easy to sell off a company that does not work out as well as expected. Holding companies were widely used in the merger boom of the 1960s and are widely used today in some industries. Banks expanding across the country often organize as holding companies and carry out their acquisitions by setting up numerous subsidiary corporations. Holding companies may allow the company to increase its debt capacity because the holding company can borrow money based on its ownership of stock in companies that, in turn, borrow money.

CAPITAL BUDGETING ANALYSIS OF AN ACQUISITION CANDIDATE |

Mergers have social and economic implications sufficient to fill several books. The analysis of acquisition candidates as capital investments is just one issue, but it is the issue of primary concern for the financial analysts assigned to evaluate an acquisition candidate. In many cases, it is necessary to consider the acquisition in terms of both cash flows and financial statement impacts. Cash flow analysis of an acquisition is treated first.

Cash flow evaluation of an acquisition is similar to cash flow evaluation for any other capital investment. First, it is necessary to forecast cash flows. The cash flows of importance are, as always, the marginal cash flows that will be caused by the investment decision. If the target company is to be operated as an independent business, the analyst can focus on its cash flows. If the target is to be integrated into the operations of the acquiring company, then economies from the combination must also be considered in the analysis.

The first step in cash flow analysis is generally the preparation of pro-forma financial statements—income statements and balance sheets—for the business. Preparation of pro-forma statements requires forecasts of sales, costs, and asset requirements. Once the pro-forma statements are prepared, cash flows are estimated and present values are computed.

Net cash flows for an acquisition can be measured in the same ways used to measure net cash flows for any other capital investment. Alternately, the equity residual method discussed in Chapter 20 can be used. Net cash flow, also called after-tax cash flow to capital, is the cash flow generally used in capital budgeting. With a constant tax rate, and letting EBIT represent earnings before interest and tax, net cash flow is:

$$\text{EBIT} \times (1 - \text{tax rate})^8$$

\+ depreciation and other noncash expenses[9]
− acquisition of new assets
\+ increases in liabilities other than long-term debt

= Net cash flow

Equity residual cash flow can be measured as follows:

Net income
− preferred dividends
\+ depreciation and other noncash expenses
− acquisition of new assets
\+ increases (−decreases) in liabilities
\+ increases (−decreases) in preferred stock

= Equity residual cash flow

To easily grasp the concept of net cash flow, note that if no new assets are acquired and liabilities other than long-term debt do not change, net cash flow is generally EBIT $\times$ (1 − tax rate) + depreciation. This is the same after-tax cash flow we have used for capital investment analysis throughout this book. The relationship between the two measures can be illustrated by adjusting equity residual cash flow to estimate net cash flow:

Equity residual cash flow
\+ preferred dividends
\+ interest expense $\times$ (1 − tax rate)
− increases (+ decreases) in long-term debt
− increases in (+ decrease) in preferred stock

= Net cash flow

Carrying the pro-forma analysis out to infinity is generally not feasible, even though most companies are expected to stay in business indefinitely. Pro-forma analysis is typically carried out for a limited time horizon, such as five or ten years. It is then assumed that cash flows stabilize after that time period, either

---

[8]If tax rates are not constant, EBIT $\times$ (1 − tax rate) can be replaced with the net income the company would have if it had no interest expense. This often equals:

net income + interest expense $\times$ (1 − marginal tax rate)

[9]We generally think of depreciation and amortization as the major noncash expenses. Payment of less income tax than the income tax expense item on the income statement, for example, is picked up by adding the increases in income tax due or deferred income tax on the liability side of the balance sheet to cash flow.

remaining constant or growing at a constant rate. Fortunately, errors in forecasting distant events are not critical because the present values of distant amounts are quite small.

Once the cash flows are identified, the final step is computation of a present value. This, of course, requires the choice of a discount rate. As discussed in Chapters 14 and 15, the discount rate should reflect the risk of the business being acquired, not the risk of the existing assets of the acquiring company. The acquisition target's beta can be used with the mean-variance capital asset pricing model as a method of estimating a required return. The procedure is essentially the same as the methods used to find the cost of capital for a division of a firm.

After the cash flows and required return are estimated, the remaining step is the mechanical process of computing a present value. Sensitivity analysis is often carried out as well, with pro-forma statements and net present value estimated for each of several different scenarios. Based on the present value analysis and an estimate of what the target company's stockholders will accept, a decision is made as to whether to attempt the acquisition.

Example. Portland Corporation is an acquisition candidate being considered by Seattle Corporation. Actual and pro-forma financial statements for Portland Corporation appear in Table 25.2. Portland Corporation had ceased growing under present management, and Seattle Corporation's managers believe that they could give the company additional growth for several years through their market connections. The pro-forma financial statements reflect the sales that Seattle Corporation expects if the acquisition occurs. Cash flow to equity holders and net cash flow were both estimated from the pro-forma statements.

It is estimated that there will be no further growth after 2003, and that new asset acquisition will approximately equal depreciation. Therefore, cash flow will be the same as income after 2003, and income after 2003 will be the same as income in 2003.

Having identified cash flows, the next step is to estimate a required return. Companies in Portland's industry, with similar capital structures, had betas averaging 1.5. The interest on U.S. government bonds was 7 percent, and the average risk premium was estimated to be 6 percent for stocks in general. This implies a required return on equity of:

$$\text{Required return on equity} = .07 + 1.5(.06) = 16 \text{ percent}$$

Recall that Portland's cash flow to equity after 2003 is expected to be the same as 2003 net income. Assuming year-end cash flows, the value of Portland's equity at the end of 2003 is:

$$V_{2003} = 14,178/.16 = \$88,613$$

Using an equity residual valuation method and continuing to assume that cash flows occur at year-end, the value of Portland Corporation is:

| TABLE 25.2 FINANCIAL STATEMENTS FOR PORTLAND CORPORATION

Actual and pro-forma financial statements for a potential acquisition are shown. Net cash flows and equity residual cash flows are also shown.

Year	Actual 1999	PRO-FORMA 2000	2001	2002	2003
Sales	$100,000	$110,000	$121,000	$133,100	$146,410
Cost of goods sold	60,000	66,000	72,600	79,860	87,846
Gross profit	40,000	44,000	48,400	53,240	58,564
Depreciation	4,600	5,000	5,200	5,400	5,600
Administrative costs	20,000	21,800	23,764	25,907	28,246
Net operating income	15,400	17,200	19,436	21,933	24,718
Interest	2,400	2,520	2,644	2,773	2,906
Earnings before tax	13,000	14,680	16,792	19,160	21,812
Income tax	4,550	5,138	5,877	6,706	7,634
Net income	$ 8,450	$ 9,542	$ 10,915	$ 12,454	$ 14,178
Current assets	$ 30,000	$ 33,000	$ 36,300	$ 39,930	$ 43,923
Fixed assets	50,000	52,000	54,000	56,000	58,000
Total assets	$ 80,000	$ 85,000	$ 90,300	$ 95,930	$101,923
Current liabilities	$ 15,000	$ 16,500	$ 18,150	$ 19,965	$ 21,962
Long-term debt	24,000	25,200	26,440	27,724	29,056
Deferred taxes	5,000	5,500	6,050	6,655	7,320
Common equity	36,000	37,800	39,660	41,586	43,585
TL&NW	$ 80,000	$ 85,000	$ 90,300	$ 95,930	$101,923

Cash Flow to Equity

Net income		$ 9,542	$10,915	$12,454	$14,178
+ depreciation		5,000	5,200	5,400	5,600
+ increased long-term debt		1,200	1,240	1,284	1,332
+ increased deferred tax		500	550	605	665
− increased net working capital		1,500	1,650	1,815	1,997
− purchases of fixed assets		7,000	7,200	7,400	7,600
= Equity residual flow		$ 7,742	$ 9,055	$10,528	$12,178

Net Cash Flow

= Equity residual flow		$ 7,742	$ 9,055	$10,528	$12,178
+ interest × (1 − .35)		1,638	1,719	1,802	1,889
− increased long-term debt		1,200	1,240	1,284	1,332
= Net cash flow		$ 8,180	$ 9,534	$11,046	$12,735

•

$$\text{Equity residual value} = \frac{7{,}742}{1.16^1} + \frac{9{,}055}{1.16^2} + \frac{10{,}528}{1.16^3} + \frac{12{,}178}{1.16^4} + \frac{88{,}613}{1.16^4}$$

$$= \$75{,}814$$

To use the net cash flow method, the weighted average cost of capital must first be determined. The value of the equity has been estimated to be $75,814. Assuming, for simplicity, that the market value and book value of the long-term debt are the same, the ratio of debt to total capital is:

$$\text{Debt to total capital} = 24{,}000/(24{,}000 + 75{,}814) = .2404$$

The borrowing rate is 10 percent, so the after-tax borrowing cost is $.10(1-.35) = .065$. The weighted average cost of capital is therefore:

$$\text{WACC} = .2404(.065) + .7596(.16) = .1372$$

Net cash flow after 2003 will be net income plus after-tax interest expense: $14,178 + $2,906\ (1 - .35) = $16,067$. The value of capital at the end of 2003 is then $16,067/.1372 = $117,106$. The value of Portland Corporation's net cash flows is therefore:

$$\text{Capital value} = \frac{8{,}180}{1.1372^1} + \frac{9{,}354}{1.1372^2} + \frac{11{,}046}{1.1372^3} + \frac{12{,}735}{1.1372^4} + \frac{117{,}106}{1.1372^4}$$

$$= \$99{,}713$$

Since the purchaser of the company also accepts a $24,000 debt obligation, the value of the equity is then $99,713 - $24,000 = $75,713$. The small difference between the value of equity using the equity residual cash flow and net cash flow results from rounding in the cost of capital calculation and the fact that debt as a percent of the total market value of capital does not remain exactly constant over the life of the company. Recall from Chapter 16 that the standard weighted average cost of capital method assumes a constant debt ratio, in market value. These differences are small, however, in relation to the differences that are likely to result from varying assumptions about future cash flows and/or interest rates.

The maximum Seattle Corporation would be willing to pay for the equity of Portland is around $75.7 thousand. Naturally, a lower price would be preferred. Management at Seattle Corporation needs to make some estimate of the lowest price the shareholders will accept. A study of financial statement impacts, discussed in the following sections, gives some insight into the lowest price shareholders might accept. Financial statement impacts are also important to the managers of Seattle Corporation in that they must be concerned about accounting issues like reporting income.

Accounting for Mergers |

To consider the financial statement impacts of mergers, it is first necessary to summarize the accounting rules for preparing financial statements after a merger. There are two accounting methods available for the treatment of a merger: *pooling of interest* and *purchase*.

Balance Sheet Impacts of the Pooling of Interest Method of Accounting

The pooling of interest method can be used only if payment for the acquired company is made in the form of stock in the acquiring company. Furthermore, the acquiring company must get at least 90 percent of the stock of the acquired company. In addition, the acquired firm's stockholders must maintain an ownership position in the combined firm, asset accounting policies of the acquired firm must remain unchanged, and the combined companies must not dispose of significant portions of the assets for two years after the acquisition. With the pooling of interest method, the merger is viewed as simply the adding up of two previously independent companies.

Balance sheet impacts of a pooling of interests treatment are illustrated in Table 25.3. Company A acquired company T in that example. The post-merger balance sheet is simply the sum of the balance sheet items from companies A and T.

Balance Sheet Impacts of the Purchase Method of Accounting

With the purchase method of accounting, the acquisition is viewed as a capital investment. The purchase method can be used whether the company is purchased for cash, stock, or other securities. If the price paid for the acquired company is the same as the net asset value (book value of assets minus total liabilities), the balance sheet treatment is the same as with a pooling of interest.

| **Table 25.3** | Balance Sheet Impacts of Pooling of Interest Accounting |

This table illustrates the pooling of interest method of accounting for a merger. Company A acquires company T, and the resultant balance sheet is simply the sum of the balance sheets of the two companies.

Company	A	T	Merged A
Current assets	$100	$ 50	$150
Fixed assets	200	100	300
Total assets	$300	$150	$450
Debt	$100	$ 50	$150
Common equity	200	100	300
Total liabilities and net worth	$300	$150	$450

If the net asset value is greater than the purchase price, the assets of the acquired company are written down to the point where the net asset value is the same as the price. This requires an appraisal of the assets in order to decide which assets to write down.

If the net asset value is less than the purchase price, the assets will be appraised and adjusted to an estimate of their current market values. If the net asset value is still less than the purchase price, the difference is assigned to an asset called *goodwill*. The use of goodwill is justified by the assumption that a price in excess of net asset value is justified by something else of value, such as the general reputation of the company.

Balance sheet impacts of purchase accounting are illustrated in Table 25.4. The post-merger balance sheets are shown with three different acquisition prices; the price may be in cash, or in stock or other securities with a market value equal to the specified price. Note that with a price of $100—equal to the net asset value—the balance sheet is the same as it was with pooling of interests in Table 25.3. With a price of $80, the assets were written down in value by $20, the difference between the purchase price and the net asset value. The decision to write down fixed assets instead of current assets was based on appraisal to determine which assets were worth less than book value. With a price of $150, assets were first appraised and adjusted to their estimated market value. The purchase price was $50 over net asset value, and the appraisal only increased asset values by $30, so the remaining $20 was treated as an addition to goodwill.

INCOME STATEMENT IMPACTS OF MERGERS

With a pooling of interest, the income of the combined companies will be the sum of the incomes of the two companies as independent organizations, assuming no change in activity following the merger. The situation is somewhat more complex with the purchase method of accounting, though. Depreciation will

| TABLE 25.4 BALANCE SHEET IMPACTS OF PURCHASE ACCOUNTING

This table illustrates the purchase method of accounting for a merger. Company A acquires company T, and the resultant balance sheet depends on the price paid for T.

Company	A	T	Merged A		
Price paid for company T			$ 80	$100	$150
Current assets	$100	$ 50	$150	$150	$150
Fixed assets	200	100	280	300	330
Goodwill					20
Total assets	$300	$150	$430	$450	$500
Debt	$100	$ 50	$150	$150	$150
Common equity	200	100	280	300	350
Total liabilities and net worth	$300	$150	$430	$450	$500

change if the values of the fixed assets are adjusted, and the cost of goods sold will change if the value of inventory is adjusted. Last but not least, goodwill must be amortized over a period not to exceed 40 years. The amortization of goodwill reduces reported income, and usually reduces taxable income.

To illustrate the income impacts of purchase and pooling of interest, the income statements for the previously analyzed mergers between companies A and T are presented in Table 25.5. It is assumed that company T is purchased with shares of company A. Since inventory was not revalued in the example, the cost of goods sold is simply the sum of the costs of goods sold for the independent companies. Depreciation is $30 with pooling of interest or purchase at net asset value. With purchase for other than net asset value, fixed assets changed and depreciation also changed. For the example, it was assumed that depreciation was simply one-tenth of asset value.

Amortization of goodwill arises only if the purchase price is higher than the net asset value, and higher than the net asset value after assets are appraised at market value. The amortization of goodwill reduces income. For acquisition after August 1993, goodwill can be amortized over 15 years and deducted in the computation of taxable income. Amortization for book purposes can be over a period of as long as forty years, but twenty years was used in the example.

Earnings per share after the acquisition depend on the number of shares in company A previously outstanding, plus the number of shares issued to acquire company T. Even though the net income with pooling does not depend on the

| TABLE 25.5 | INCOME STATEMENT IMPACTS OF PURCHASE AND POOLING OF INTEREST

This table illustrates income statement impacts of the purchase and pooling of interest methods of accounting for a merger. Income statements are for the companies whose balance sheets were examined in Tables 25.3 and 25.4. The impact of a purchase is shown for three different purchase prices.

| | Company | | MERGED COMPANY A | | | |
| | A | T | Purchase Price Paid for Co.T | | | Pooling |
			$80	$100	$150	
Sales	$300	$200	$500	$500	$500	$500
Cost of goods sold	200	130	330	330	330	330
Administrative exp.	40	30	70	70	70	70
Depreciation	20	10	28	30	33	30
Interest expense	10	5	15	15	15	15
Earnings before tax	30	25	57	55	52	55
Income tax	12	10	23	22	21	22
Earnings after tax	18	15	34	33	31	33
Goodwill amortization					1	
Net income	$ 18	$ 15	$ 34	$ 33	$ 30	$ 33

number of shares, the earnings per share are affected. Company A had 10 shares of stock outstanding prior to the merger, and earnings per share were, therefore, $18/10 = $1.80. The stock was selling for $10 a share. Earnings per share after the merger are shown in Table 25.6 with both purchase and pooling of interest.

Table 25.6 again drives home the point that the financial statement impacts are the same with purchase and pooling if the purchase price equals the net asset value. If the purchase price is less than the net asset value, income will generally be higher with purchase accounting. If the purchase price is greater than net asset value, income will generally be higher using the pooling method.

Acquisition year income is particularly affected by the method of accounting for the merger. If the purchase method of accounting is used, the acquiring company can include in its annual income statement only the income of the acquired company from the date of acquisition. With a pooling of interest, the acquired company's income for the entire year will be shown, regardless of when during the year the acquisition occurs. A company that wants to cover its own weak earnings for the year with earnings gained through acquisition will certainly prefer the pooling method of accounting.

In general, the pooling method of accounting is preferred. As previously discussed, though, there are restrictions on its use. Thus, it is often impossible to construct a merger to satisfy the requirements for pooling.

INCOME-BASED ANALYSIS OF MERGERS

Two companies will merge only if both sides gain. In general, this means that shareholders of both firms must gain, although some evidence suggests that mergers often benefit the stockholders of the acquired company at the expense of the stockholders of the acquiring company. We proceed under the assumption that the goal is to maximize the wealth of shareholders. We look at earnings per share

| **TABLE 25.6** EARNINGS PER SHARE IMPACTS OF PURCHASE AND POOLING OF INTEREST

This table illustrates the post-merger earnings per share impacts of the purchase and pooling of interest methods of accounting for a merger. The price of company A's stock was $10 before the merger, and earnings per share were $1.80.

	PURCHASE			**POOLING**		
Price Paid for Co. T	**$80**	**$100**	**$150**	**$80**	**$100**	**$150**
Net income	$ 34	$ 33	$ 30	$ 33	$ 33	$ 33
Number of old shares	10	10	10	10	10	10
Shares issued	8	10	15	8	10	15
Total shares	18	20	25	18	20	25
Earnings per share	$1.89	$1.65	$1.20	$1.83	$1.65	$1.32

impacts first, and then consider price and earnings per share simultaneously. We focus on pooling of interest mergers to simplify the discussion, although the principles can be easily extended to other mergers.

We prefer to focus on cash flows and carry out a proper capital budgeting analysis. The fact is, though, that managers spend a good deal of time worrying about accounting income impacts; any CEO who has faced an angry shareholders' meeting after reporting an earnings drop does not relish the thought of repeating the experience. Therefore, income and earnings per share analysis are likely to remain a part of merger analysis.

EARNINGS PER SHARE AND MERGERS

One way each party to a merger can benefit is if each party has a claim to income that is at least as great as its claim to income before the merger. The shareholders of each company must, therefore, end up owning a proportion of the post-merger company at least equal to:

Income of their company before merger ÷ Income of merged company

The exchange ratio is the number of shares of the acquiring company that will be given for each share of the target company. For the shareholders of the target company to maintain the amount of income to which they had a claim before the merger, the exchange ratio must be at least:[10]

$$ER_T = \frac{(S_A/S_T)NI_T}{NI_M - NI_T} \qquad (25\text{-}1)$$

where

ER_T = the minimum number of shares the acquiring company must give for each share of the target company
S_A = the number of acquiring company shares outstanding before the merger
S_T = the number of target company shares outstanding before the merger
NI_T = the net income[11] of the target company before the merger
NI_M = the net income of the combined companies after the merger

---

[10]In order for the shareholders of the target company to have a claim to income equal to that which they had before the merger, their proportion of post-merger shares must be such that $S_g/(S_g + S_A) = I_T/I_M$. In this equation, S_g is the number of shares given to shareholders of the target company in exchange for all of their shares. The other terms are defined in the body of the text. Rearranging terms, $S_g = S_A NI_T/(NI_M - NI_T)$. The exchange ratio is S_g/S_T, so dividing this equation by S_T gives Equation 25-1.

[11]If there is preferred stock outstanding, earnings available to common shareholders (net income less preferred dividends) should be used instead of net income.

By similar logic, the maximum number of shares the acquiring company will be willing to give for each share in the acquiring company (ER_A) is:[12]

$$ER_A = (S_A/S_T)(NI_M - NI_A)/NI_A \qquad (25\text{-}2)$$

where NI_A is the net income of the acquiring company before the merger.

Example. In the previous examples, the acquiring company had net income of $18, and the target company had net income of $15; if there were no synergistic benefits, post-merger income would be $33. If each company had 10 shares of stock outstanding before the merger, the minimum exchange ratio would equal the maximum exchange ratio:

$$ER_T = (10/10)15/(33 - 15) = .8333$$

$$ER_A = (10/10)(33 - 18)/18 = .8333$$

Assume there are synergistic benefits, so the post-merger income of the combined companies will be $40. Each company had 10 shares of stock before the merger. Therefore, the minimum acceptable exchange ratio from the perspective of the shareholders of the target company is:

$$ER_T = (10/10)15/(40 - 15) = .60$$

The maximum acceptable exchange ratio from the perspective of the shareholders of the acquiring company is:

$$ER_A = (10/10)(40 - 18)/18 = 1.222$$

A range of possible exchange ratios exists because of the synergistic benefits of the merger. If both parties agree about the synergistic benefits, any exchange ratio between .60 and 1.222 is possible. If T's stockholders are not willing to bet on synergy, any ratio over .8333 is potentially acceptable to them.

In present nomenclature, when a merger is expected to increase earnings per share for the acquiring company, it is said to be accretive. Mergers that decrease earning per share for the acquiring company are said to be dilutive.

SUMMARY OF VALUE AND EXCHANGE RATIO CONSIDERATIONS

In determining a price or exchange ratio, numerous considerations must be weighed. These include the following:

---

[12]The shareholders of the acquiring company must also end up with as much claim to income as they had before the acquisition. Therefore, the minimum proportion of post-merger shares they will accept is such that $S_A/(S_A + S_g) = NI_A/NI_M$. Rearranging terms, $S_g = S_A(NI_M - NI_A)/NI_A$. The exchange ratio is S_g/S_T, so dividing the prior equation by S_T gives Equation 25-2.

Market price: The target company's shareholders generally will not accept an offer unless they receive cash or securities with a market price higher than that of their existing stock.

Earnings per share: The acquiring company will be very interested in increasing earnings per share for its stockholders, and the target company's shareholders may also want to avoid dilution of their claim on income. Synergistic benefits may be considered in forecasting earnings per share impacts, especially by the acquiring company.

Dividends per share: If the target company shareholders are to receive stock in exchange for their existing shares, they will often be concerned that their dividend income remain as high as it was before the merger.

Present value: Both parties will want the present values of their cash flows to be higher than before the merger. Again, the acquiring company may be more willing to consider synergistic benefits in this analysis.

Example. Information about the acquiring company (A), the target company (T), and the likely performance of the merged companies follows. Some of this information was presented in the earlier analysis of these two companies. Using this information, we can compute a maximum acceptable exchange ratio for A and a minimum acceptable ratio for T, based on each consideration. These ratios are shown in Table 25.7 and their explanations follow.

	A	T	Merged
Number of shares	10	10	
Price per share	$ 10	$ 8	
Net income	$ 18	$15	$ 40
Earnings per share	$ 1.80	$ 1.50	
Dividends per share	$ 1.00	$ 0.70	$1.00
Present value of equity residual cash flows	$100	$80	$ 240

Market price: If neither set of stockholders is willing to have the market price of their claim decreased, and the merger will not increase total market value, only one exchange ratio is possible. By giving .8 shares per share of T, company A will be giving the shareholders of T stock worth the same market price as their existing shares.

Earnings per share: The maximum and minimum acceptable exchange ratios for earnings per share with and without synergistic benefits were previously computed.

Dividends: The minimum acceptable ratio for dividends is based on the assumption that A will not increase dividends per share, and stockholders in T will not want their dollar dividends reduced. For each share of T, 0.7 shares of A would be required.

| TABLE 25.7 EXCHANGE RATIO RANGES

Minimum and maximum acceptable exchange ratios for a merger of acquiring company A and target company T are shown. The maximum is the greatest number of shares A would give per share of T, while the minimum is the smallest number of shares T's shareholders would accept for each share of their stock.

	Maximum A Can Give	Minimum T Can Accept
Current market price per share	0.8000	0.8000
Earnings per share		
ignoring synergy	0.8333	0.8333
with synergy	1.2222	0.6000
Dividends	NA	0.7000
Equity residual present value		
ignoring synergy	0.8000	0.8000
with synergy	1.4000	0.5000

Present value: The equity residual present value exchange ratios are based on the requirement that neither set of investors reduce their equity residual present value from its present level. With synergism, stockholders of A must end up holding at least 100/240 of the combined company, while stockholders in T must end up with at least 80/240. If T's stockholders get 1.4 shares of A for each share of their stock, A will end up with 10 out of 24 total shares, or 41.67 percent. If T's stockholders get 0.5 shares of A per share of T, they will end up with 5 out of 15 shares, or 33.33 percent of the combined company. Thus, an exchange ratio between 0.5 and 1.4 would meet the present value requirement.

There is no exchange ratio that would leave each group better off on every measure. If management of A is willing to base the decision on an assumption of synergistic benefits, though, any exchange ratio below 1.2222 would be satisfactory. Holders of T's stock may be less willing to assume synergistic benefits, though. Ignoring synergistic benefits, T's shareholders will gain in all categories at any exchange rate above .8333. It is not essential that all shareholders gain in every category, but each side must gain by most measures of factors important to them.

There is a substantial range between the minimum and maximum exchange ratios, so there is an opportunity for a successful merger here. The exact price or exchange rate is uncertain, though; a ratio as high as 1.4 or as low as 0.5 is possible. If cash is being offered, the minimum possible price would be the $8 market price of T, while the maximum price would not exceed $14. (At $14 a share, the shareholders in T would receive the entire $140 increase in present value expected to result from the acquisition.) The exchange ratio or price will depend on the bargaining skills of the two parties, the number of other companies interested in acquiring T, the eagerness of both parties, and so on. The range

| **TABLE 25.8** MERGER OF EXCHANGE-LISTED COMPANIES IN THE UNITED STATES

This figure shows the rise and fall of merger activity in the United States. As can be seen, mergers follow a wave pattern.

Year	Mergers	Year	Mergers	Year	Mergers
1960	11	1970	45	1980	90
1961	12	1971	40	1981	102
1962	18	1972	32	1982	97
1963	38	1973	44	1983	78
1964	43	1974	42	1984	120
1965	39	1975	24	1985	135
1966	57	1976	44	1986	169
1967	101	1977	71	1987	167
1968	118	1978	96	1988	176
1969	70	1979	116	1989	173
				1990	173

Source: J. R. Franks and R. S. Harris, "Merger Waves: Theory and Evidence" (University of North Carolina working paper, Chapel Hill, 1986). Data after 1984 estimated from the *Statistical Abstract of the United States.*

of possible exchange ratios at which both sides can gain explains why the final exchange ratio may be as much as twice as high as the original offer.

STUDIES OF MERGER ACTIVITY |

Studies of merger activity have focused on why mergers occur and how mergers affect value. Merger activity has followed a wave pattern through the years, as illustrated in Figure 25.8. Although numerous explanations have been offered, the reasons for these periodic waves are not well understood.[13] Merger activity seems to move with the overall business cycle and with stock prices; companies use acquisition of another company as an alternative to growing through direct asset acquisition. However, there is no clear theory as to why the benefits of merger would be greater in one part of the business cycle than in another. In 1997, the seventh year of an expanding business cycle, over $183 billion exchanged hands in the 3,533 mergers that were consummated during the year.

The question of how mergers affect value lends itself to more direct study, and numerous studies of the impacts of merger announcements have been conducted. These studies show that the shareholders of the target company enjoy

[13]D. J. Ashton and D. R. Atkins, "A Partial Theory of Takeover Bids," *Journal of Finance* 39 (March 1984): 167–183; and J. Fred Weston and K. S. Chung, "Some Aspects of Merger Theory," *Midwest Finance Journal* 12 (1983): 1–38.

an average increase of 20-30 percent in the value of their investment when the acquisition offer is announced. The gains to shareholders of the target company reflect the typical terms of offers. If the offer is not above the previous market price of the target's stock, there will be no incentive to tender shares. Therefore, the offer will be for cash or securities in excess of the previous value of the target's stock. The immediate increase in the price of the target's stock depends on investors' perceptions of the likelihood of a completed agreement and the possibility of higher bids from other companies.

The shareholders of the acquiring company are not quite as fortunate. Numerous studies have provided mixed evidence about the immediate stock price response to an acquisition announcement.[14] Clearly, there is no large gain, and some studies suggest a small average loss. Agrawal et al. provide evidence that the price of the acquirer's stock declines relative to non-acquiring companies over the five-year post-merger period.[15]

It is difficult to determine if mergers improve shareholder wealth in the long run. An adequate test requires the holding of other variables constant, and this means matching a sample of companies that did merge with an otherwise identical sample of companies that did not merge. Finding a sample like this to examine over long periods is extremely difficult.

LEVERAGED BUYOUTS

A leveraged buyout and going private are not forms of merger, but are frequently used by managers to avoid being acquired. When managers set out to buy all of a company's shares, we say they are *going private*. If outside investors and large amounts of debt are used, we call the transaction a *leveraged buyout*. Borg-Warner used a leverage buyout to avoid a takeover by GAF, for example. Assets of the company may be sold to finance part of the purchase, as was done in the case of Southland Corporation (7-11 stores). Leveraged buyouts have grown in popularity in recent years.

[14]See Paul Asquith and E. Han Kim, "The Impact of Merger Bids on the Participating Firms' Security Returns," *Journal of Finance* 37 (December 1982): 1209–1228; Julian Franks, Robert Harris, and Sheridan Titman, "The Postmerger Share-Price Performance of Acquiring Firms," *Journal of Financial Economics* 29 (March 1991): 81–96; Eugene Furtado and Vijay Karan, "Causes, Consequences, and Shareholder Wealth Effects of Management Turnover: A Review of the Empirical Evidence," *Financial Management* 19 (Summer 1990): 60–75; P. J. Halpern, "Corporate Acquisitions: A Theory of Special Cases? A Review of Event Studies Applied to Acquisitions," *Journal of Finance* 38 (May 1983): 297–317; Paul M. Healy, Krishna G. Palepu, and Richard S. Ruback, "Does Corporate Performance Improve after Mergers?" *Journal of Financial Economics* 31 (April 1992): 135–175; Gregg A. Jarrell and Annette B. Poulsen, "The Returns to Acquiring Firms in Tender Offers: Evidence from Three Decades." *Financial Management* 18 (Winter 1989): 12–19; and Claudio Loderer and Kenneth Martin, "Corporate Acquisitions by Listed Firms: The Experience of a Comprehensive Sample," *Financial Management* 19 (Winter 1990): 17–33.

[15]Anup Agrawal, Jeffrey F. Jaffe, and Gershon N. Mandelker, "The Post-Merger Performance of Acquiring Firms: A Re-examination of an Anomaly," *Journal of Finance* 47 (September 1992): 1605–1621.

In a typical leveraged buyout, a group including the top management of the company offers to buy the shares of the company from the existing shareholders for a price well above the existing market price so that stockholders will accept the offer. All shares may be purchased by a newly formed corporation, or most of the shares may be bought back by the company itself, with the rest bought by management and the outside investors who will be part of the new ownership group. The company may end up with debts equal to 90 percent or more of total assets. The debt, often referred to as junk bonds (now called high-yield bonds), is considered risky and carries high interest rates. Southland Corporation ended up paying 18 percent on funds used to finance its leveraged buyout in 1987. The lenders may also be members of the new ownership group.

To qualify as a leveraged buyout candidate, a company must have competent managers, a strong position in its industry, and stable earnings. Otherwise, lenders would be unwilling to provide the large amounts of debt needed. Leveraged buyout candidates are typically capital-intensive companies because those companies have a substantial asset base to pledge for collateral. The company should also have very little debt and very few assets that have been pledged as collateral for debt. A strong liquidity position helps too. Lenders generally like to see cash flow that is 1.5 times the interest on the debt used to finance the buyout.[16]

There are several potential benefits of a leveraged buyout. Freedom from public reporting policies required of publicly owned companies is one advantage. A privately held company may be able to enhance its value by keeping its financial position and strategy a secret from competitors. Furthermore, compliance with public reporting requirements involves substantial administrative costs. Avoiding public reporting has yet another advantage: it allows managers to focus on cash flows rather than on the accounting reports that are read by public shareholders. GAF Chairman Samuel Heyman identified public accounting rules as an important reason for using a leveraged buyout.

An agency problem is also solved by the leveraged buyout in that managers who are substantial owners will have a greater motivation to manage the company for the benefit of the shareholders. Tax savings are often one of the most important benefits of a leveraged buyout. The addition of an extremely large amount of debt decreases taxable income and increases the amount of money to be distributed among providers of funds.

Because of these benefits, substantial profits have been made using leveraged buyouts and then selling the shares to the public again after 5 years or so when the benefits of the leveraged buyout decision are reflected in higher earnings. DeAngelo, DeAngelo, and Rice found an average stock price jump of 30 percent with the announcement a company was going private or entering into a leveraged buyout.[17] Wesray Investment Group did a little better than average. They invested $265 million in cash in a leveraged buyout of Avis in 1986, re-

---

[16]*Business Week* (September 21, 1987): 31.

[17]H. DeAngelo, L. DeAngelo, and E. Rice, "Going Private: Minority Freeze-outs and Stockholder Wealth," *Journal of Law and Economics* (October 1984): 367–401.

covered the initial investment quickly through asset sales, and got another $750 million by selling Avis to the employees in 1987.[18]

SPIN-OFFS AND DIVESTITURES

To wrap up the chapter on corporate marriages, we should briefly discuss those times when the happy family splits up. A *spin-off* occurs when a part of a business is set up as a subsidiary corporation, and the shares of that subsidiary are distributed pro rata to the parent's shareholders. A *divestiture* occurs when part of the firm is sold to outsiders. PepsiCo's spin-off to the stockholders of Taco Bell, KFC, and Pizza-Hut into a new company called Tricon Global Restaurants is an example of a firm recommitting itself to it core business, soda pop in this case.

Spin-offs and divestitures are essentially abandonment decisions. A spin-off or divestiture is justified when managers decide that the components of the business are worth more separately than together. A spin-off may occur when a particular piece of the business no longer fits into the overall strategy. A divestiture will be used if the component being disposed of can be sold for more than its estimated value as a stand-alone unit. Otherwise a spin-off will be used.

SUMMARY

A *merger* is generally used to mean the forming of one economic unit from two independent units. An *acquisition* is a form of merger in which one company buys another, generally paying in cash or securities. Reasons for mergers can be divided into two broad categories: value-related and management-related. A value-related acquisition decision, for example, is a capital investment decision that the present value of cash flows achieved through the acquisition is more than the present value of cash flows acquired with an equal expenditure on individual assets. Synergism, taxes, information asymmetry, and agency problems are the four most widely cited reasons for value-related mergers. A management-related merger decision is motivated by managers' desires to achieve some objective other than maximization of shareholder wealth. Management interests include risk reduction, protection from takeover, and desire for a larger size.

A merger generally begins with an offer from the acquiring company to the target company. A *friendly* offer is made to management of the target company, while a *hostile* attempt involves an appeal directly to the shareholders. The offer may be for cash, stock, or other securities. Several offers are often made before one is accepted.

Capital investment analysis of a potential acquisition follows the same principles used for other capital investments. The most direct form of analysis is a cash flow analysis, in which the present value of cash flows generated is compared to the price that must be paid. This generally requires the construction of pro-forma financial statements to identify cash flows, the determination of a required return, and the computation of a present value. This present value is the maximum the acquiring company would be willing to pay.

[18]"When You Own the Company, You Try Harder," *Business Week* (September 28, 1987): 32–33.

Financial statement impacts must also be considered when evaluating a potential acquisition. Of particular concern are net income and earnings per share. The financial statement impact depends on whether the merger is considered a pooling of interest or a purchase. With a *pooling of interest*, the financial statements of the two companies are simply added together. With a *purchase*, the assets of the acquired company are appraised and restated at current market values. If the price paid is above the value of the assets, a goodwill account is created. Depreciation based on market value and amortization of goodwill can decrease reported income. Certain conditions must be met to qualify for pooling of interest treatment. Included in these conditions are the requirement that the target company be purchased in exchange for stock of the acquiring company, and that the stockholders of the acquired company continue to hold an interest in the combined company.

Terms of merger depend on a number of factors; the acquiring company is interested in the present value of cash flows as well as the impact on accounting income and earnings per share. The target company shareholders will accept the offer only if they expect to gain. For the target company shareholders, the gain may come in the form of an immediate increase in wealth because they are offered cash or stock with a value in excess of the market value of their shares. Target company shareholders will also be interested in their claim to earnings after the merger as well as their anticipated dividends after the merger. Naturally, both parties expect to gain. Evidence suggests that on average both parties do gain in the short run, but whether the shareholders of the acquiring company gain in the long run is difficult to determine.

QUESTIONS |

25–1. Define the terms: (a) *merger*, (b) *acquisition*, (c) *synergism*, (d) *leveraged buyout*, (e) *divestiture*, and (f) *spin-off*.

25–2. What are the main reasons that a merger may increase value?

25–3. Discuss the various reasons why mergers may lead to value creation through synergism.

25–4. How can agency problems be resolved through a merger?

25–5. How can information asymmetry problems be resolved through a merger?

25–6. Discuss ways in which managers can benefit from a merger.

25–7. Explain the difference between a friendly and a hostile acquisition attempt.

25–8. What can the managers of a target company do if they want to fend off a hostile acquisition attempt?

25–9. Explain the difference between purchase and pooling of interest accounting for a merger.

25–10. In deciding whether or not to accept the acquiring company's offer, what are some of the things the target company's shareholders will consider?

25–11. In general, have shareholders benefited from mergers?

25–12. (Applications) Merrill Lynch reported that the number of mergers and acquisitions fell in 1991 to 1,877 from 2,058 in 1990. Listed below are some of these mergers and acquisitions and others in later years:

a. AT&T Universal Card buys Utah Financial Services (a small industrial-loan company) to expand its credit card business with corporate accounts.

b. The Weather Channel buys the Travel Channel from Trans World Airlines.

c. Gillette purchases Duracell International for $7.7 billion.

d. Seagram (the liquor concern) announces its intention to buy up to a 15 percent interest in Time Warner (the movie and magazine concern).

e. Boeing purchases McDonnell-Douglas for $13.3 billion.

f. Newmont Mines buys a 50 to 75 percent interest in 125 square miles of mining claims in Nevada from Galactic Resources and Cornucopia Resources, Ltd.

g. Blockbuster Video (movie rental and record store concern) increases its stake in Viacom, the ultimate purchaser of Paramount Entertainment (movie and television concern).

h. DuPont purchases 15,400 acres in Georgia from Union Camp Corporation to mine the mineral sands.

Please classify these mergers as horizontal, vertical, or conglomerate mergers. Do you think a vertical, horizontal, or conglomerate merger is more likely to generate a positive net present value? Why? Which of these do you think will be most likely to generate a positive net present value? Why?

PROBLEMS

25–1. Honolulu Corporation has earnings before tax of $1 million, after deducting accelerated depreciation of $2 million. Anchorage Corporation has earnings before interest and tax of $1 million, after deducting accelerated depreciation of $500,000. For each corporation, straight-line depreciation is one-half of accelerated depreciation. Considering the alternative minimum tax, could the two corporations reduce their taxes by merging? (Taxes = 34 percent.)

25–2. Tuscaloosa Corporation is considering the acquisition of Montgomery Corporation. Montgomery Corporation generates earnings before interest and tax of $1 million a year, and asset replacement cost approximately equals depreciation. Alternative minimum tax is not an issue, there are no synergistic benefits, and cash flows are not expected to grow in the future. Assuming a 35 percent tax rate and a 10 percent after-tax required return, what is net cash flow? Assuming year-end cash flows, what is the value of Montgomery Corporation's capital? If Montgomery Corporation has long-term debt of $3 million, what is the value of the equity of Montgomery Corporation?

25–3. Normal Corporation is considering the acquisition of Auburn Corporation. Auburn Corporation has earnings before interest and tax of $1 million, and asset replacement cost approximately equals depreciation. Efficiencies gained through the merger will reduce Auburn's operating costs by $200,000. Cash flows occur at year-end.

a. Assuming a 35 percent tax rate and a 12 percent required return, what is the value of Auburn's capital without a merger?

b. Assuming a 35 percent tax rate and a 12 percent required return, what is the value of Auburn's capital after a merger?

25–4. Flagstaff Corporation is considering the acquisition of Tempe Corporation. Without the merger, cash flow to capital is expected to be $2 million next year and is expected to grow at 3 percent a year thereafter. With a merger, the growth rate will be increased to 4 percent. The tax rate is 35 percent and the after-tax required return is 10 percent. Assume year-end cash flows.

a. What is the value of Tempe's capital if Tempe is not acquired?

b. What is the value of Tempe's capital if Tempe is acquired?

25–5. Phoenix Corporation is considering the acquisition of Tucson Corporation. Following are past and pro-forma financial statements assuming the merger occurs. No growth is anticipated after 1992, and depreciation is expected to approximately equal asset replacement cost after 1992. Assuming a 10 percent required return and year-end cash flows, what is the value of the company's capital? (Tax = 34 percent.)

		PRO-FORMA		
Year	**Actual 1989**	**1990**	**1991**	**1992**
Sales	$200,000	$220,000	$242,000	$266,200
Cost of goods sold	120,000	132,000	145,200	159,720
Gross profit	80,000	88,000	96,800	106,480
Depreciation	9,200	10,000	10,400	10,800
Administrative costs	40,000	43,600	47,528	51,814
Net operating income	30,800	34,400	38,872	43,866
Interest	4,800	5,040	5,288	5,544
Earnings before tax	26,000	29,360	33,584	38,322
Income tax	8,840	9,982	11,418	13,029
Net income	$ 17,160	$ 19,378	$ 22,166	$ 25,293
Current assets	$ 30,000	$ 33,000	$ 36,300	$ 39,930
Fixed assets	50,000	52,000	54,000	56,000
Total assets	$ 80,000	$ 85,000	$ 90,300	$ 95,930
Current liabilities	$ 15,000	$ 16,500	$ 18,150	$ 19,965
Long-term debt	24,000	25,200	26,440	27,724
Deferred taxes	5,000	5,500	6,050	6,655
Common equity	36,000	37,800	39,660	41,586
TL&NW	$ 80,000	$ 85,000	$ 90,300	$ 95,930

25–6. For Tucson Corporation in problem 5, what is the total value of capital if net cash flow is expected to grow at 3 percent a year each year after 1992?

25–7. Monticello Corporation is considering the acquisition of Pine Bluff Corporation. Pine Bluff Corporation generates sales of $20 million a year, and sales are not expected to grow. The net profit margin (net income ÷ sales) is 5 percent. Depreciation approximately equals asset replacement cost, and the amount of debt is not expected to change. Required return on equity for a company in this risk class is 15 percent. Assuming year-end cash flows, what is the value of Pine Bluff's equity?

25–8. Suppose the merger between Monticello and Pine Bluff (problem 7) would decrease Pine Bluff's operating expenses by $100,000 a year. Assuming a marginal tax rate of 35 percent, what is the post-merger value of the equity?

25–9. Jonesboro Corporation is considering the acquisition of Fayetteville Corporation. Net income is expected to be $1 million in the first year and is expected to grow at a rate of 5 percent a year. Half of the net income must be reinvested in the company to support this growth level. The required return on equity for companies in this risk class is 15 percent. Assuming year-end cash flows, what is the value of Fayetteville's equity?

25–10. The required return on equity for a company similar to Tucson Corporation (problem 5) is 15 percent. Find the cash flows to equity and find the value of the equity based on those year-end cash flows.

25–11. For Tucson Corporation (problem 5) year-end cash flow to the equity holders is expected to increase 5 percent each year after 1992. If the required return for equity investments in this risk class is 15 percent, what is the value of Tucson's equity?

25–12. Santa Barbara Corporation is interested in acquiring Chico Corporation. Each company has a 6 percent after-tax cost of debt. Santa Barbara Corporation has debt and equity with market values of $1 million and $2 million respectively. Santa Barbara Corporation has a beta of 1.0. Chico Corporation has debt and equity with market values of $500,000 and $1,500,000 respectively, and this is believed to be the optimal capital structure for a company in Chico's industry. Chico has a beta of 2.0. The average market risk premium is 6 percent, and the risk-free rate is 9 percent. If we want to find the total value of Chico's capital to Santa Barbara Corporation, net cash flows to capital should be discounted using what required rate of return?

25–13. Suppose Santa Barbara Corporation (problem 12) wants to focus on equity residual cash flows. What required rate of return should be used in finding the present value of Chico's equity residual cash flows?

25–14. The balance sheets of Stanford Corporation and Boulder Corporation appear below. Stanford Corporation has 100,000 shares of stock outstanding and Boulder Corporation has 50,000 shares of stock outstanding. Stanford Corporation acquires Boulder Corporation by issuing one new share of Stanford for each four shares of Boulder. The merger is treated as a pooling of interest. Show the balance sheet of the combined companies as it would appear after the merger.

	Stanford	Boulder
Current assets	$1,000,000	$200,000
Fixed assets	2,000,000	500,000
Total assets	$3,000,000	$700,000
Current liabilities	$ 500,000	$100,000
Long-term debt	1,000,000	300,000
Equity	1,500,000	300,000
Total liab. & equity	$3,000,000	$700,000

25–15. The income statements for Stanford Corporation and Boulder Corporation (problem 14) follow. Show the post-merger income statement assuming a pooling of interest and no synergistic benefits.

	Stanford	Boulder
Sales	$5,000,000	$2,000,000
Cost of goods sold	4,000,000	1,700,000
Administrative expense	200,000	150,000
Depreciation	200,000	50,000
Net operating income	600,000	100,000
Interest	100,000	30,000
Earnings before tax	500,000	70,000
Income tax	170,000	23,800
Net income	$330,000	$46,200
Earnings per share	$3.30	$0.92

25–16. The shares of Stanford Corporation (problem 14) are priced at $30 each, and the shares of Boulder Corporation are priced at $7 each. Stanford acquires Boulder by paying one share of Stanford for each four shares of Boulder; Stanford effectively pays $375,000. The acquisition is treated as a purchase. On appraisal, the value of the current assets is found to be the same as their book value, but the value of the fixed assets is found to be $50,000 greater than book value. Show the balance sheet of the merged companies.

25–17. As described in problem 16, Stanford Corporation purchases the equity of Boulder Corporation by paying one share of Stanford stock for each four shares of Boulder stock and treats the transaction as a purchase. Depreciation each year is one-tenth of beginning asset value and goodwill is depreciated over a 20-year period. Show the income statement for the year following merger, assuming no synergistic benefits, a 34 percent tax rate, and goodwill that is not tax deductible.

25–18. For Stanford Corporation and Boulder Corporation, as described in problems 14 and 15, assume that the merger is by pooling of interest, that there are no synergistic benefits, and that both parties want to avoid a dilution in their claim on earnings. What exchange ratio(s) will satisfy the requirement of no dilution in claim on income for either set of shareholders?

25–19. For Stanford Corporation and Boulder Corporation, as described in problems 14 and 15, assume that the merger is by pooling of interest. There are synergistic benefits in that administrative costs for the two combined companies are $50,000 less than the sum of these costs for the independent companies. What exchange ratio(s) are possible, given that neither set of shareholders is willing to decrease the amount of income to which it has claim? (Taxes = 34 percent.)

25–20. For Stanford Corporation and Boulder Corporation, as described in problems 14 and 15, assume that the merger is by pooling of interest. The shares of Stanford Corporation are priced at $30 each, and the shares of Boulder Corporation are priced at $7 each. There are synergistic benefits in that administrative costs for the two combined companies are $50,000 less than the sum of these costs for the independent companies. What exchange ratio(s) are possible, given that the shareholders of Boulder must receive stock with a market value at least as great as the market value of their present stock, and given that Stanford Corporation stockholders want to increase their earnings per share through the transaction? (Taxes = 34 percent.)

25–21. (**Ethical considerations**) The following leveraged buyouts and prices were reported in a March 5, 1990, article in *Business Week*:

a. Frostmann Little & Co. paid $650 million for Dr Pepper Inc. in 1984. They sold assets for $462 million and the rest was sold to several investors in 1986 for $416 million.

b. Frostmann Little purchased all of the outstanding stock of Topps (the baseball card concern) for $98 million in 1984. After two public offerings in later years Frostmann received $204 million and still owns 55 percent of the company.

The typical Frostmann-style leveraged buyout awards 20 percent of the company to remaining management, raises 40 to 50 percent through the sale of securities (usually subordinated debt), and borrows the rest from banks. Assume that management took a 20 percent interest in the leveraged buyouts of Dr Pepper and Topps. What is the ethical dilemma concerning existing management taking a 20 percent interest in a leveraged buyout? What price will they want to pay to take the company private? Does this contradict the fiduciary responsibility to increase shareholders' wealth? What is the net present value to management in 1984 of a 20 percent interest in the Dr Pepper deal? Assume year-end cash flows and a 10 percent required return.

CASE PROBLEM |

First Federal

Banking was one of the most heavily regulated industries in the United States. State laws limited banks to operations within one state and limited the abilities of banks to open branches in their state of operation. Furthermore, banks were not allowed to enter into any line of business not closely related to their primary banking purpose. As a consequence, the United States had 14,000 banks while financial markets in many other large countries were dominated by a half-dozen major banks.

Seeds of a new philosophy, trusting in competition to regulate financial markets, were planted in the late 1960s. The seeds grew in the 1970s with deregulation of security broker commissions, deregulation of some interest rates, and authorization of savings and loans to offer checking accounts. The process blossomed with the Financial Institution Deregulation and Monetary Control Act of 1980, which phased out regulation of interest rates paid by banks and interest rates charged on mortgage loans. This same law gave savings and loans the power to make a limited number of loans for purposes other than the purchase of a home. Thus, savings and loans evolved from limited institutions accepting long-term deposits and making home mortgage loans into institutions offering consumers a full range of financial services.

The move toward deregulation occurred against a background of rising inflation and rising, unstable interest rates. Savings and loans held portfolios of fixed interest rate mortgages, accumulated over decades in a low interest rate environment, and were forced to pay ever-higher interest rates with little change in their interest income. As a result, many savings and loans were in serious difficulty when the Garn–St. Germain Act was passed in 1982. An important aspect of this act was that it allowed banks to cross state lines to buy troubled savings and loans, with the permission of regulators. The Garn–St. Germain Act accelerated the race among banks to dominate the national market for consumer financial services.

The rapidly developing competition for national dominance was in the minds of managers at Commerce Bank when they were examining First Federal Savings and Loan in early 1983. First Federal had lost so much money that it had a negative net worth and had been taken over by the regulators. The regulators were now looking for a buyer, and several major out-of-state banks were expected to bid vigorously for this opportunity to enter a state from which they were otherwise proscribed. Commerce, on the other hand, was the leading bank in the same city in which First Federal operated. State law allowed savings and loans to branch state-wide, while banks were not allowed to have branches at all.

Commerce was the leading commercial bank in the city, focusing primarily on service to businesses. The acquisition would allow Commerce to instantly achieve a major position in financial service to individuals. Equally important, the acquisition would stall attempts by the leading banks in the country to enter the state.

The analysis of First Federal began with an examination of its financial statements, shown in Table 25.9. The negative net worth was one of the first items on which managers focused. The regulators would require that the net worth be brought up to 5 percent of total assets immediately after acquisition and maintained at that level. The income statement revealed negative income, and an examination of the loan portfolio showed that low profitability was likely to continue for some time in the future.

Interest income for First Federal could be increased by replacement of existing assets as they matured and by expansion of the asset base.

A vigorous expansion was anticipated if the acquisition was completed. New managers would be recruited from the consumer banking industry, and new products would be introduced, including credit cards, expanded checking account services, and nonmortgage loans. Total assets were expected to remain constant during the first year, as operations were consolidated, then grow at 20 percent a year for 5 years, before stabilizing. Assuming stable interest rates in the marketplace, interest income as a percent of total assets was expected to increase as shown in Table 25.10. Interest expense was expected to be 8.3 percent of total assets in 1983 and thereafter, based on interest rates early in 1983. The expansion program would require development expenses of $10 million in the first year and $5 million a year for the following 4 years. Physical asset investments would be minimal as First Federal already had an extensive branch system and certain processing operations would be combined with those of Commerce. Projected operating expenses, other than development expense and credit loss (labeled noninterest expense), are shown in Table 25.10. The expansion program would result in an increase in fee income, from checking accounts and credit cards. Projections of fee income as a percent of total assets are also shown in Table 25.10. Bad debt expense as a percent of total assets was expected to remain unchanged

| **TABLE 25.9** | 1982 FINANCIAL STATEMENTS OF FIRST FEDERAL SAVINGS AND LOAN |

Income Statement		Balance Sheet	
Interest income	$ 506,762	Cash	$ 162,991
Interest expense	528,841	Investment securities	1,029,887
Net int. expense	−22,079	Loans	3,367,438
Non-interest income	26,612	Other assets	336,920
Non-interest expense	71,507	Total assets	$4,897,236
Bad debt loss	22,527		
Earnings before tax	$ −89,501	Deposits	$3,664,728
Tax	41,171	Borrowed funds	1,065,447
Net income	$ −48,330	Other liabilities	203,843
		Owners' equity	−36,782
		Total liabilities	
		& net worth	$4,897,236

TABLE 25.10	PROJECTED PERFORMANCE OF FIRST FEDERAL SAVINGS AND LOAN MEASURED AS A PERCENT OF TOTAL ASSETS								
Year	83	84	85	86	87	88	89	90	91	92
Interest inc.	10.7	10.8	11.1	11.3	11.5	11.7	11.8	11.8	11.7	11.7
Nonint. inc.	0.6	0.7	0.7	0.8	0.8	0.8	0.8	0.7	0.6	0.6
Nonint. exp.	1.8	2.0	2.0	2.0	2.0	1.9	1.8	1.8	1.8	1.8

from 1981. Because noncash expenses were minimal, income after tax would be very close to cash flow.

In looking at First Federal, management noted several potential problems. First, the acquisition analysis was based on a stable interest rate assumption. If interest rates rose, interest expense would increase more rapidly than interest income. Likewise, a decline in interest rates would cause interest expense to fall more rapidly than interest income. The spread between interest income and interest expense as a percent of total assets had been as low as 1 percent during periods of rising interest rates.

Management was also concerned about credit losses. The company would be introducing new loan products, and credit control could be a problem. Other institutions had experienced credit losses approaching 1 percent of total assets in the first several years of a rapid expansion.

Finally, the ability to earn excess profits would decline as the industry matured. A reasonable expectation was that the industry would mature within 10 years, and profits would then decline to the opportunity cost of capital, approximately a 15 percent return on equity. Management thought that its opportunity to reduce costs by combining processing operations might allow it to earn 16 percent return on equity after maturity, though.

The regulators would try to attract enough interest that someone would pay them for First Federal. At a minimum, though, the regulators hoped to find someone who would accept ownership of First Federal without requiring a subsidy from the government. The income tax rate was 46 percent at the time.

CASE QUESTIONS

1. Identify all cash flows to and from Commerce as a result of the acquisition.
2. Find the present value of those flows using the 15 percent opportunity cost of equity capital.
3. Should Commerce accept ownership of First Federal with no subsidy from the government?
4. Bearing in mind the competitive environment and strategic considerations, prepare a sealed bid for First Federal. The bid may be positive, or it may require a government subsidy.

SELECTED REFERENCES |

Agrawal, Anup, Jeffrey F. Jaffe, and Gershon N. Mandelker. "The Post-Merger Performance of Acquiring Firms: A Re-examination of an Anomaly." *Journal of Finance* 47 (September 1992): 1605–1621.

Ashton, D. J., and D. R. Atkins. "A Partial Theory of Takeover Bids." *Journal of Finance* 39 (March 1984): 167–183.

Asquith, Paul, and E. Han Kim. "The Impact of Merger Bids on the Participating Firms' Security Holders." *Journal of Finance* 37 (December 1982): 1209–1228.

Bhide, Amar. "The Causes and Consequences of Hostile Takeovers." *Journal of Applied Corporate Finance* 2 (Summer 1989): 36–59.

Bierman, Harold, Jr. "A Neglected Tax Incentive for Mergers." *Financial Management* 14 (Summer 1985): 29–32.

Bruner, Robert F. "The Use of Excess Cash and Debt Capacity as a Motive for Merger." *Journal of Financial and Quantitative Analysis* 23 (June 1988): 199–217.

Clayton, Ronnie J., and William Beranek. "Disassociations and Legal Combinations." *Financial Management* 14 (Summer 1985): 24–28.

Davidson, Wallace N., III, Sharon Hatten Garrison, and Glenn V. Henderson, Jr. "Examining Merger Synergy with the Capital Asset Pricing Model." *Financial Review* 22 (May 1987): 233–247.

DeAngelo, H., L. DeAngelo, and E. Rice. "Going Private: Minority Freeze-outs and Stockholder Wealth." *Journal of Law and Economics* (October 1984): 367–401.

Dennis, Debra K., and John J. McConnell. "Corporate Mergers and Security Returns." *Journal of Financial Economics* 16 (June 1986): 143–187.

Eger, Carol Ellen. "An Empirical Test of the Redistribution Effect in Pure Exchange Mergers." *Journal of Financial and Quantitative Analysis* 18 (December 1983): 547–572.

Franks, Julian, Robert Harris, and Sheridan Titman. "The Postmerger Share-Price Performance of Acquiring Firms." *Journal of Financial Economics* 29 (March 1991): 81–96.

Furtado, Eugene P. H., and Vijay Karan. "Causes, Consequences, and Shareholder Wealth Effects of Management Turnover: A Review of the Empirical Evidence." *Financial Management* 19 (Summer 1990): 60–75.

Halpern, Paul. "Corporate Acquisitions: A Theory of Special Cases? A Review of Event Studies Applied to Acquisitions." *Journal of Finance* 38 (May 1983): 297–317.

Haugen, Robert A., and Terence C. Langetieg. "An Empirical Test for Synergism in Merger." *Journal of Finance* 30 (September 1975): 1003–1014.

Healy, Paul M., Krishna G. Palepu, and Richard S. Ruback. "Does Corporate Performance Improve after Mergers?" *Journal of Financial Economics* 31 (April 1992): 135–175.

Hearth, Douglas, and William T. Moore. "Voluntary Corporate Divestitures and Value." *Financial Management* 13 (Spring 1984): 10–16.

Holderness, C., and D. Sheehan. "Raiders or Saviors? The Evidence on Six Controversial Investors." *Journal of Financial Economics* 14 (1985): 555–588.

Huang, Yen-Sheng, and Ralph A. Walking. "Target Abnormal Returns Associated with Acquisition Announcements: Payments, Acquisition Form, and Managerial Resistance." *Journal of Financial Economics* 19 (December 1987): 329–349.

Jarrell, Gregg A., and Annette B. Poulsen. "The Returns to Acquiring Firms in Tender Offers: Evidence from Three Decades." *Financial Management* 18 (Winter 1989): 12–19.

Jensen, M. "Agency Costs of Free Cash Flow, Corporate Finance, and Takeovers." *American Economic Review* (May 1986): 323–329.

Jensen, Michael C. "Corporate Control and the Politics of Finance." *Journal of Applied Corporate Finance* 4 (Summer 1991): 13–33.

Lam, Chun H., and Kenneth J. Boudreaux. "Conglomerate Merger, Wealth Redistribution and Debt: A Note." *Journal of Finance* 39 (March 1984): 275–281.

Lang, Larry H. P., René M. Stulz, and Ralph A. Walking. "Managerial Performance, Tobin's Q, and the Gains from Successful Tender Offers." *Journal of Financial Economics* 24 (September 1989): 138–154.

_____. "A Test of the Free Cash Flow Hypothesis." *Journal of Financial Economics* 29 (October 1991): 316–335.

Law, Warran A. "A Corporation Is More Than Its Stock." *Harvard Business Review* 64 (May–June 1986): 80–83.

Lee, Winson B., and Elizabeth S. Cooperman. "Conglomerates in the 1980s: A Performance Appraisal." *Financial Management* 18 (Spring 1989): 45–54.

Lewellen, Wilbur G., and Michael G. Ferri. "Strategies for the Merger Game: Management and the Market." *Financial Management* 12 (Winter 1983): 25–35.

Lichtenberg, Frank R., and Donald Siegel. "The Effect of Control Changes on the Productivity of U.S. Manufacturing Plants." *Journal of Applied Corporate Finance* 2 (Summer 1989): 60–67.

Loderer, Claudio, and Kenneth Martin. "Corporate Acquisitions by Listed Firms: The Experience of a Comprehensive Sample." *Financial Management* 19 (Winter 1990): 17–33.

Malatesta, P. H. "The Wealth Effect of Merger Activity and the Objective Functions of Merging Firms." *Journal of Financial Economics* (April 1983): 155–181.

Markowitz, Zane. "Aquiring the Right Company." *Journal of Business Strategy* 9 (September–October 1988): 43–46.

McCardle, Kevin F., and S. Viswanathan. "The Direct Entry versus Takeover Decision and Stock Price Performance around Takeovers." *Journal of Business.* 67 (January 1994): 1–44.

Melnik, A., and M. A. Pollatschek. "Debt Capacity, Diversification and Conglomerate Mergers." *Journal of Finance* 28 (December 1973): 1263–1273.

Merville, Larry J., and Lee A. Tavis. "A Generalized Model for Capital Investment." *Journal of Finance* 28 (March 1973): 109–118.

_____. "Long-Range Financial Planning." *Financial Management* 3 (Summer 1974): 56–63.

Opler, Tim, and Sheridan Titman. "The Determinants of Leveraged Buyout Acitivity: Free Cash Flow versus Financial Distress Costs." *Journal of Finance* 48 (December 1993): 1985–1999.

Reinganum, Marc R., and Janet Kiholm Smith. "Investor Preference for Large Firms: New Evidence on Economies of Size." *Journal of Industrial Economics* 32 (December 1983): 213–242.

Romano, Roberta. "Rethinking Takeover Regulation." *Journal of Applied Corporate Finance* 4 (Fall 1992): 47–57.

Rosenfeld, James D. "Additional Evidence on the Relation between Divestiture Announcements and Shareholder Wealth." *Journal of Finance* 39 (December 1984): 1437–1448.

Roy, Asim. "Partial Acquisition Strategies for Business Combinations." *Financial Management* 14 (Summer 1985): 16–23.

Schleifer, Andrei S., and Robert W. Vishny. "The Takeover Wave of the 1980s." *Journal of Applied Corporate Finance* 4 (Fall 1991): 49–56.

Shick, Richard A. "The Analysis of Mergers and Acquisitions." *Journal of Finance* 27 (May 1972): 495–502.

Shick, Richard A., and Frank C. Jen. "Merger Benefits to Shareholders of Acquiring Firms." *Financial Management* 3 (Winter 1974): 45–53.

Song, Mooh H., and Ralph A. Walking. "The Income Impact of Managerial Ownership on Acquisition Attempts and Target Shareholder Wealth." *Journal of Financial and Quantitative Analysis* 28 (December 1993): 439–457.

Stoughton, Neal M. "The Information Content of Corporate Merger and Acquisition Offers." *Journal of Financial and Quantitative Analysis* 23 (June 1988): 175–197.

Wamsley, James H., Rodney L. Roenfeldt, and Philip L. Cooley. "Abnormal Returns from Merger Profiles." *Journal of Financial and Quantitative Analysis* 18 (June 1983): 149–162.

Wamsley, James H., William R. Lane, and Ho C. Yang. "Abnormal Returns to Acquired Firms by Type of Acquisition and Method of Payment." *Financial Management* 12 (Autumn 1983): 16–22.

Weston, J. Fred. "Do Mergers Make Money?" *Mergers and Acquisitions* (Fall 1983): 40–48.

Weston, J. Fred, and K. S. Chung. "Some Aspects of Merger Theory." *Midwest Finance Journal* 12 (1983): 1–38.

Yagil, Joseph. "An Exchange Ratio Determination Model for Mergers: A Note." *Financial Review* 22 (February 1987): 195–202.

APPENDIX A |

MATHEMATICAL TABLES

TABLE A.1 FUTURE VALUE OF A SINGLE PAYMENT OF $1 = (1 + k)^n

PERCENT (k)

Periods (n)	1%	2%	3%	4%	5%	6%	7%	8%	9%	10%	12%	14%	15%	18%	20%	25%
1	1.0100	1.0200	1.0300	1.0400	1.0500	1.0600	1.0700	1.0800	1.0900	1.1000	1.1200	1.1400	1.1500	1.1800	1.2000	1.2500
2	1.0201	1.0404	1.0609	1.0816	1.1025	1.1236	1.1449	1.1664	1.1881	1.2100	1.2544	1.2996	1.3225	1.3924	1.4400	1.5625
3	1.0303	1.0612	1.0927	1.1249	1.1576	1.1910	1.2250	1.2597	1.2950	1.3310	1.4049	1.4815	1.5209	1.6430	1.7280	1.9531
4	1.0406	1.0824	1.1255	1.1699	1.2155	1.2625	1.3108	1.3605	1.4116	1.4641	1.5735	1.6890	1.7490	1.9388	2.0736	2.4414
5	1.0510	1.1041	1.1593	1.2167	1.2763	1.3382	1.4026	1.4693	1.5386	1.6105	1.7623	1.9254	2.0114	2.2878	2.4883	3.0518
6	1.0615	1.1262	1.1941	1.2653	1.3401	1.4185	1.5007	1.5869	1.6771	1.7716	1.9738	2.1950	2.3131	2.6996	2.9860	3.8147
7	1.0721	1.1487	1.2299	1.3159	1.4071	1.5036	1.6058	1.7138	1.8280	1.9487	2.2107	2.5023	2.6600	3.1855	3.5832	4.7684
8	1.0829	1.1717	1.2668	1.3686	1.4775	1.5938	1.7182	1.8509	1.9926	2.1436	2.4760	2.8526	3.0590	3.7589	4.2998	5.9605
9	1.0937	1.1951	1.3048	1.4233	1.5513	1.6895	1.8385	1.9990	2.1719	2.3579	2.7731	3.2519	3.5179	4.4355	5.1598	7.4506
10	1.1046	1.2190	1.3439	1.4802	1.6289	1.7908	1.9672	2.1589	2.3674	2.5937	3.1058	3.7072	4.0456	5.2338	6.1917	9.3132
11	1.1157	1.2434	1.3842	1.5395	1.7103	1.8983	2.1049	2.3316	2.5804	2.8531	3.4785	4.2262	4.6524	6.1759	7.4301	11.642
12	1.1268	1.2682	1.4258	1.6010	1.7959	2.0122	2.2522	2.5182	2.8127	3.1384	3.8960	4.8179	5.3503	7.2876	8.9161	14.552
13	1.1381	1.2936	1.4685	1.6651	1.8856	2.1329	2.4098	2.7196	3.0658	3.4523	4.3635	5.4924	6.1528	8.5994	10.699	18.190
14	1.1495	1.3195	1.5126	1.7317	1.9799	2.2609	2.5785	2.9372	3.3417	3.7975	4.8871	6.2613	7.0757	10.147	12.839	22.737
15	1.1610	1.3459	1.5580	1.8009	2.0789	2.3966	2.7590	3.1722	3.6425	4.1772	5.4736	7.1379	8.1371	11.974	15.407	28.422
16	1.1726	1.3728	1.6047	1.8730	2.1829	2.5404	2.9522	3.4259	3.9703	4.5950	6.1304	8.1372	9.3576	14.129	18.488	35.527
17	1.1843	1.4002	1.6528	1.9479	2.2920	2.6928	3.1588	3.7000	4.3276	5.0545	6.8660	9.2765	10.761	16.672	22.186	44.409
18	1.1961	1.4282	1.7024	2.0258	2.4066	2.8543	3.3799	3.9960	4.7171	5.5599	7.6900	10.575	12.375	19.673	26.623	55.511
19	1.2081	1.4568	1.7535	2.1068	2.5270	3.0256	3.6165	4.3157	5.1417	6.1159	8.6128	12.056	14.232	23.214	31.948	69.389
20	1.2202	1.4859	1.8061	2.1911	2.6533	3.2071	3.8697	4.6610	5.6044	6.7275	9.6463	13.743	16.367	27.393	38.338	86.736
21	1.2324	1.5157	1.8603	2.2788	2.7860	3.3996	4.1406	5.0338	6.1088	7.4002	10.804	15.668	18.822	32.324	46.005	108.42
22	1.2447	1.5460	1.9161	2.3699	2.9253	3.6035	4.4304	5.4365	6.6586	8.1403	12.100	17.861	21.645	38.142	52.206	135.53
23	1.2572	1.5769	1.9736	2.4647	3.0715	3.8197	4.7405	5.8715	7.2579	8.9543	13.552	20.362	24.891	45.008	66.247	169.41
24	1.2697	1.6084	2.0328	2.5633	3.2251	4.0489	5.0724	6.3412	7.9111	9.8497	15.179	23.212	28.625	53.109	79.497	211.76
25	1.2824	1.6406	2.0938	2.6658	3.3864	4.2919	5.4274	6.8485	8.6231	10.835	17.000	26.462	32.919	62.669	95.396	264.70
30	1.3478	1.8114	2.4273	3.2434	4.3219	5.7435	7.6123	10.063	13.268	17.449	29.960	50.950	66.212	143.37	237.38	807.79
35	1.4166	1.9999	2.8139	3.9461	5.5160	7.6861	10.677	14.785	20.414	28.102	52.800	98.100	133.18	328.00	590.67	2465.2
40	1.4889	2.2080	3.2620	4.8010	7.0400	10.286	14.974	21.725	31.409	45.259	93.051	188.88	267.86	750.38	1469.8	7523.2
45	1.5648	2.4379	3.7816	5.8412	8.9850	13.765	21.002	31.920	48.327	72.890	163.99	363.68	538.77	1716.7	3657.3	22958
50	1.6446	2.6916	4.3839	7.1067	11.467	18.420	29.457	46.902	74.358	117.39	289.00	700.23	1083.7	3927.4	9100.4	70064

TABLE A.2 PRESENT VALUE OF A SINGLE FUTURE PAYMENT OF $1 $= \dfrac{1}{(1+k)^n}$

n/k	1%	2%	3%	4%	5%	6%	7%	8%	9%	10%	12%	14%	15%	18%	20%	25%
1	0.9901	0.9804	0.9709	0.9615	0.9524	0.9434	0.9346	0.9259	0.9174	0.9091	0.8929	0.8772	0.8696	0.8475	0.8333	0.8000
2	0.9803	0.9612	0.9426	0.9246	0.9070	0.8900	0.8734	0.8573	0.8417	0.8264	0.7972	0.7695	0.7561	0.7182	0.6944	0.6400
3	0.9706	0.9423	0.9151	0.8890	0.8638	0.8396	0.8163	0.7938	0.7722	0.7513	0.7118	0.6750	0.6575	0.6086	0.5787	0.5120
4	0.9610	0.9238	0.8885	0.8548	0.8227	0.7921	0.7629	0.7350	0.7084	0.6830	0.6355	0.5921	0.5718	0.5158	0.4823	0.4096
5	0.9515	0.9057	0.8626	0.8219	0.7835	0.7473	0.7130	0.6806	0.6499	0.6209	0.5674	0.5194	0.4972	0.4371	0.4019	0.3277
6	0.9420	0.8880	0.8375	0.7903	0.7462	0.7050	0.6663	0.6302	0.5963	0.5645	0.5066	0.4556	0.4323	0.3704	0.3349	0.2621
7	0.9327	0.8706	0.8131	0.7599	0.7107	0.6651	0.6227	0.5835	0.5470	0.5132	0.4523	0.3996	0.3759	0.3139	0.2791	0.2097
8	0.9235	0.8535	0.7894	0.7307	0.6768	0.6274	0.5820	0.5403	0.5019	0.4665	0.4039	0.3506	0.3269	0.2660	0.2326	0.1678
9	0.9143	0.8368	0.7664	0.7026	0.6446	0.5919	0.5439	0.5002	0.4604	0.4241	0.3606	0.3075	0.2843	0.2255	0.1938	0.1342
10	0.9053	0.8203	0.7441	0.6756	0.6139	0.5584	0.5083	0.4632	0.4224	0.3855	0.3220	0.2697	0.2472	0.1911	0.1615	0.1074
11	0.8963	0.8043	0.7224	0.6496	0.5847	0.5268	0.4751	0.4289	0.3875	0.3505	0.2875	0.2366	0.2149	0.1619	0.1346	0.0859
12	0.8874	0.7885	0.7014	0.6246	0.5568	0.4970	0.4440	0.3971	0.3555	0.3186	0.2567	0.2076	0.1869	0.1372	0.1122	0.0687
13	0.8787	0.7730	0.6810	0.6006	0.5303	0.4688	0.4150	0.3677	0.3262	0.2897	0.2292	0.1821	0.1625	0.1163	0.0935	0.0550
14	0.8700	0.7579	0.6611	0.5775	0.5051	0.4423	0.3878	0.3405	0.2992	0.2633	0.2046	0.1597	0.1413	0.0985	0.0779	0.0440
15	0.8613	0.7430	0.6419	0.5553	0.4810	0.4173	0.3624	0.3152	0.2745	0.2394	0.1827	0.1401	0.1229	0.0835	0.0649	0.0352
16	0.8528	0.7284	0.6232	0.5339	0.4581	0.3936	0.3387	0.2919	0.2519	0.2176	0.1631	0.1229	0.1069	0.0708	0.0541	0.0281
17	0.8444	0.7142	0.6050	0.5134	0.4363	0.3714	0.3166	0.2703	0.2311	0.1978	0.1456	0.1078	0.0929	0.0600	0.0451	0.0225
18	0.8360	0.7002	0.5874	0.4936	0.4155	0.3503	0.2959	0.2502	0.2120	0.1799	0.1300	0.0946	0.0808	0.0508	0.0376	0.0180
19	0.8277	0.6864	0.5703	0.4746	0.3957	0.3305	0.2765	0.2317	0.1945	0.1635	0.1161	0.0829	0.0703	0.0431	0.0313	0.0144
20	0.8195	0.6730	0.5537	0.4564	0.3769	0.3118	0.2584	0.2145	0.1784	0.1486	0.1037	0.0728	0.0611	0.0365	0.0261	0.0115
21	0.8114	0.6598	0.5375	0.4388	0.3589	0.2942	0.2415	0.1987	0.1637	0.1351	0.0926	0.0638	0.0531	0.0309	0.0217	0.0092
22	0.8034	0.6468	0.5219	0.4220	0.3418	0.2775	0.2257	0.1839	0.1502	0.1228	0.0826	0.0560	0.0462	0.0262	0.0181	0.0074
23	0.7954	0.6342	0.5067	0.4057	0.3256	0.2618	0.2109	0.1703	0.1378	0.1117	0.0738	0.0491	0.0402	0.0222	0.0151	0.0059
24	0.7876	0.6217	0.4919	0.3901	0.3101	0.2470	0.1971	0.1577	0.1264	0.1015	0.0659	0.0431	0.0349	0.0188	0.0126	0.0047
25	0.7798	0.6095	0.4776	0.3751	0.2953	0.2330	0.1842	0.1460	0.1160	0.0923	0.0588	0.0378	0.0304	0.0160	0.0105	0.0038
30	0.7419	0.5521	0.4120	0.3083	0.2314	0.1741	0.1314	0.0994	0.0754	0.0573	0.0334	0.0196	0.0151	0.0070	0.0042	0.0012
35	0.7059	0.5000	0.3554	0.2534	0.1813	0.1301	0.0937	0.0676	0.0490	0.0356	0.0189	0.0102	0.0075	0.0030	0.0017	0.0004
40	0.6717	0.4529	0.3066	0.2083	0.1420	0.0972	0.0668	0.0460	0.0318	0.0221	0.0107	0.0053	0.0037	0.0013	0.0007	0.0001
45	0.6391	0.4102	0.2644	0.1712	0.1113	0.0727	0.0476	0.0313	0.0207	0.0137	0.0061	0.0027	0.0019	0.0006	0.0003	0.0000
50	0.6080	0.3715	0.2281	0.1407	0.0872	0.0543	0.0339	0.0213	0.0134	0.0085	0.0035	0.0014	0.0009	0.0003	0.0001	0.0000

TABLE A.3 FUTURE VALUE OF AN ANNUITY OF $1 $= \dfrac{(1+k)^n - 1}{k}$

n/k	1%	2%	3%	4%	5%	6%	7%	8%	9%	10%	12%	14%	15%	18%	20%	25%
1	1.0000	1.0000	1.0000	1.0000	1.0000	1.0000	1.0000	1.0000	1.0000	1.0000	1.0000	1.0000	1.0000	1.0000	1.0000	1.0000
2	2.0100	2.0200	2.0300	2.0400	2.0500	2.0600	2.0700	2.0800	2.0900	2.1000	2.1200	2.1400	2.1500	2.1800	2.2000	2.2500
3	3.0301	3.0604	3.0909	3.1216	3.1525	3.1836	3.2149	3.2464	3.2781	3.3100	3.3744	3.4396	3.4725	3.5724	3.6400	3.8125
4	4.0604	4.1216	4.1836	4.2465	4.3101	4.3746	4.4399	4.5061	4.5731	4.6410	4.7793	4.9211	4.9934	5.2154	5.3680	5.7656
5	5.1010	5.2040	5.3091	5.4163	5.5256	5.6371	5.7507	5.8666	5.9847	6.1051	6.3528	6.6101	6.7424	7.1542	7.4416	8.2070
6	6.1520	6.3081	6.4684	6.6330	6.8019	6.9753	7.1533	7.3359	7.5233	7.7156	8.1152	8.5355	8.7537	9.4420	9.9299	11.259
7	7.2135	7.4343	7.6625	7.8983	8.1420	8.3938	8.6540	8.9228	9.2004	9.4872	10.089	10.730	11.067	12.142	12.916	15.073
8	8.2857	8.5830	8.8923	9.2142	9.5491	9.8975	10.260	10.637	11.028	11.436	12.300	13.233	13.727	15.327	16.499	19.842
9	9.3685	9.7546	10.159	10.583	11.027	11.491	11.978	12.488	13.021	13.579	14.776	16.085	16.786	19.086	20.799	25.802
10	10.462	10.950	11.464	12.006	12.578	13.181	13.816	14.487	15.193	15.937	17.549	19.337	20.304	23.521	25.959	33.253
11	11.567	12.169	12.808	13.486	14.207	14.972	15.784	16.645	17.560	18.531	20.655	23.045	24.349	28.755	32.150	42.566
12	12.683	13.412	14.192	15.026	15.917	16.870	17.888	18.977	20.141	21.384	24.133	27.271	29.002	34.931	39.581	54.208
13	13.809	14.680	15.618	16.627	17.713	18.882	20.141	21.495	22.953	24.523	28.029	32.089	34.352	42.219	48.497	68.760
14	14.947	15.974	17.086	18.292	19.599	21.015	22.550	24.215	26.019	27.975	32.393	37.581	40.505	50.818	59.196	86.949
15	16.097	17.293	18.599	20.024	21.579	23.276	25.129	27.152	29.361	31.772	37.280	43.842	47.850	60.965	72.035	109.68
16	17.258	18.639	20.157	21.825	23.657	25.673	27.888	30.324	33.003	35.950	42.753	50.980	55.717	72.939	87.442	138.10
17	18.430	20.012	21.762	23.698	25.840	28.213	30.840	33.750	36.974	40.545	48.884	59.118	65.075	87.068	105.93	173.63
18	19.615	21.412	23.414	25.645	28.132	30.906	33.999	37.450	41.301	45.599	55.750	68.394	75.836	103.74	128.11	218.04
19	20.811	22.841	25.117	27.671	30.539	33.760	37.379	41.446	46.018	51.159	63.440	78.969	88.212	123.41	154.73	273.55
20	22.019	24.397	26.870	29.778	33.066	36.786	40.995	45.762	51.160	52.275	72.052	91.025	102.44	146.62	186.68	342.94
21	23.239	25.783	28.676	31.969	35.719	39.993	44.865	50.423	56.765	64.002	81.699	104.76	118.81	174.02	225.02	429.68
22	24.472	27.299	30.537	34.248	38.505	43.392	49.006	55.457	62.873	71.403	92.503	120.43	137.63	206.34	271.03	538.10
23	25.716	28.845	32.453	36.618	41.430	46.996	53.436	60.893	69.532	79.543	104.60	138.29	159.27	244.48	326.23	673.62
24	26.973	30.422	34.426	39.083	44.502	50.816	58.177	66.765	76.790	88.497	118.15	158.65	184.16	288.49	392.48	843.03
25	28.243	32.030	36.459	41.646	47.727	54.865	63.249	73.106	84.701	98.347	133.33	181.87	212.79	342.60	471.98	1054.7
30	34.785	40.568	47.575	56.085	66.439	79.058	94.461	113.28	136.31	164.49	241.33	356.79	434.75	790.95	1181.8	3227.1
35	41.660	49.994	60.462	73.652	90.320	111.43	138.24	172.32	215.71	271.02	431.66	693.57	881.17	1816.7	2948.3	9856.8
40	48.886	60.402	75.401	95.026	120.80	154.76	199.64	259.06	337.88	442.59	767.09	1342.0	1779.1	4163.2	7343.8	30088
45	56.481	71.893	92.720	121.03	159.70	212.74	285.75	386.51	525.86	718.90	1358.2	2590.6	3585.1	9531.5	18281	91831
50	64.463	84.579	112.80	152.67	209.35	290.34	406.53	573.77	815.08	1163.9	2400.0	4994.5	7217.7	21813	45497	280255

Table A.4 Present Value of an Annuity of $1 $= \dfrac{1 - 1/(1+k)^n}{k}$

n/k	1%	2%	3%	4%	5%	6%	7%	8%	9%	10%	12%	14%	15%	18%	20%	25%
1	0.9901	0.9804	0.9709	0.9615	0.9524	0.9434	0.9346	0.9259	0.9174	0.9091	0.8929	0.8772	0.8696	0.8475	0.8333	0.8000
2	1.9704	1.9416	1.9135	1.8861	1.8594	1.8334	1.8080	1.7833	1.7591	1.7355	1.6901	1.6467	1.6257	1.5656	1.5278	1.4400
3	2.9410	2.8839	2.8286	2.7751	2.7232	2.6730	2.6243	2.5771	2.5313	2.4869	2.4018	2.3216	2.2832	2.1743	2.1065	1.9520
4	3.9020	3.8077	3.7171	3.6299	3.5460	3.4651	3.3872	3.3121	3.2397	3.1699	3.0373	2.9137	2.8550	2.6901	2.5887	2.3616
5	4.8534	4.7135	4.5797	4.4518	4.3295	4.2124	4.1002	3.9927	3.8897	3.7908	3.6048	3.4331	3.3522	3.1272	2.9906	2.6893
6	5.7955	5.6014	5.4172	5.2421	5.0757	4.9173	4.7665	4.6229	4.4859	4.3553	4.1114	3.8887	3.7845	3.4976	3.3255	2.9514
7	6.7282	6.4720	6.2303	6.0021	5.7864	5.5824	5.3893	5.2064	5.0330	4.8684	4.5638	4.2883	4.1604	3.8115	3.6046	3.1611
8	7.6517	7.3255	7.0197	6.7327	6.4632	6.2098	5.9713	5.7466	5.5348	5.3349	4.9676	4.6389	4.4873	4.0776	3.8372	3.3289
9	8.5660	8.1622	7.7861	7.4353	7.1078	6.8017	6.5152	6.2469	5.9952	5.7590	5.3282	4.9464	4.7716	4.3030	4.0310	3.4631
10	9.4713	8.9826	8.5302	8.1109	7.7217	7.3601	7.0236	6.7101	6.4177	6.1446	5.6502	5.2161	5.0188	4.4941	4.1925	3.5705
11	10.368	9.7868	9.2526	8.7605	8.3064	7.8869	7.4987	7.1390	6.8052	6.4951	5.9377	5.4527	5.2337	4.6560	4.3271	3.6564
12	11.255	10.575	9.9540	9.3851	8.8633	8.3838	7.9427	7.5361	7.1607	6.8137	6.1944	5.6603	5.4206	4.7932	4.4392	3.7251
13	12.134	11.348	10.635	9.9856	9.3936	8.8527	8.3577	7.9038	7.4869	7.1034	6.4235	5.8424	5.5831	4.9095	4.5327	3.7801
14	13.004	12.106	11.296	10.563	9.8986	9.2950	8.7455	8.2442	7.7862	7.3667	6.6282	6.0021	5.7245	5.0081	4.6106	3.8241
15	13.865	12.849	11.938	11.118	10.380	9.7122	9.1079	8.5595	8.0607	7.6061	6.8109	6.1422	5.8474	5.0916	4.6755	3.8593
16	14.718	13.578	12.561	11.652	10.106	10.106	9.4466	8.8514	8.3126	7.8237	6.9740	6.2651	5.9542	5.1624	4.7296	3.8874
17	15.562	14.292	13.166	12.166	11.274	10.477	9.7632	9.1216	8.5436	8.0216	7.1196	6.3729	6.0472	5.2223	4.7746	3.9099
18	16.398	14.992	13.754	12.659	11.690	10.828	10.059	9.3719	8.7556	8.2014	7.2497	6.4674	6.1280	5.2732	4.8122	3.9279
19	17.226	15.678	14.324	13.134	12.085	11.158	10.336	9.6036	8.9501	8.3649	7.3658	6.5504	6.1982	5.3162	4.8435	3.9424
20	18.046	16.351	14.877	13.590	12.462	11.470	10.594	9.8181	9.1285	8.5136	7.4694	6.6231	6.2593	5.3527	4.8696	3.9539
21	18.857	17.011	15.415	14.029	12.821	11.764	10.836	10.017	9.2922	8.6487	7.5620	6.6870	6.3125	5.3837	4.8913	3.9631
22	19.660	17.658	15.937	14.451	13.163	12.042	11.061	10.201	9.4424	8.7715	7.6446	6.7429	6.3587	5.4099	4.9094	3.9705
23	20.456	18.292	16.444	14.857	13.489	12.303	11.272	10.371	9.5802	8.8832	7.7184	6.7921	6.3988	5.4321	4.9245	3.9764
24	21.243	18.914	16.936	15.247	13.799	12.550	11.469	10.529	9.7066	8.9847	7.7843	6.8351	6.4338	5.4509	4.9371	3.9811
25	22.023	19.523	17.413	15.622	14.094	12.783	11.654	10.675	9.8226	9.0770	7.8431	6.8729	6.4641	5.4669	4.9476	3.9849
30	25.808	22.396	19.600	17.292	15.372	13.765	12.409	11.258	10.274	9.4269	8.0552	7.0027	6.5660	5.5168	4.9789	3.9950
35	29.409	24.999	21.487	18.665	16.374	14.498	12.948	11.655	10.567	9.6442	8.1755	7.0700	6.6166	5.5386	4.9915	3.9984
40	32.835	27.355	23.115	19.793	17.159	15.046	13.332	11.925	10.757	9.7791	8.2438	7.1050	6.6418	5.5482	4.9966	3.9995
45	36.095	29.490	24.519	20.720	17.774	15.456	13.606	12.108	10.881	9.8628	8.2825	7.1232	6.6543	5.5523	4.9986	3.9998
50	39.196	31.424	25.730	21.482	18.256	15.762	13.801	12.233	10.962	9.9148	8.3045	7.1327	6.6605	5.5541	4.9995	3.9999

TABLE A.5 CONTINUOUS COMPOUNDING FUTURE VALUE OF A SINGLE PAYMENT OF $1 = e^{k'n}$

n/k'	1%	2%	3%	4%	5%	6%	7%	8%	9%	10%	12%	14%	15%	18%	20%	25%
1	1.0101	1.0202	1.0305	1.0408	1.0513	1.0618	1.0725	1.0833	1.0942	1.1052	1.1275	1.1503	1.1618	1.1972	1.2214	1.2840
2	1.0202	1.0408	1.0618	1.0833	1.1052	1.1275	1.1503	1.1735	1.1972	1.2214	1.2712	1.3231	1.3499	1.4333	1.4918	1.6487
3	1.0305	1.0618	1.0942	1.1275	1.1618	1.1972	1.2337	1.2712	1.3100	1.3499	1.4333	1.5220	1.5683	1.7160	1.8221	2.1170
4	1.0408	1.0833	1.1275	1.1735	1.2214	1.2712	1.3231	1.3771	1.4333	1.4918	1.6161	1.7507	1.8221	2.0544	2.2255	2.7183
5	1.0513	1.1052	1.1618	1.2214	1.2840	1.3499	1.4191	1.4918	1.5683	1.6487	1.8221	2.0138	2.1170	2.4596	2.7183	3.4903
6	1.0618	1.1275	1.1972	1.2712	1.3499	1.4333	1.5220	1.6161	1.7160	1.8221	2.0544	2.3164	2.4596	2.9447	3.3201	4.4817
7	1.0725	1.1503	1.2337	1.3231	1.4191	1.5220	1.6323	1.7507	1.8775	2.0138	2.3164	2.6645	2.8577	3.5254	4.0552	5.7546
8	1.0833	1.1735	1.2712	1.3771	1.4918	1.6161	1.7507	1.8965	2.0544	2.2255	2.6117	3.0649	3.3201	4.2207	4.9530	7.3891
9	1.0942	1.1972	1.3100	1.4333	1.5683	1.7160	1.8776	2.0544	2.2479	2.4596	2.9447	3.5254	3.8574	5.0531	6.0496	9.4877
10	1.1052	1.2214	1.3499	1.4918	1.6487	1.8221	2.0138	2.2255	2.4596	2.7183	3.3201	4.0552	4.4817	6.0496	7.3891	12.182
11	1.1163	1.2461	1.3910	1.5527	1.7333	1.9348	2.1598	2.4109	2.6912	3.0042	3.7434	4.6646	5.2070	7.2427	9.0250	15.643
12	1.1275	1.2712	1.4333	1.6161	1.8221	2.0544	2.3164	2.6117	2.9447	3.3201	4.2207	5.3656	6.0496	8.6711	11.023	20.086
13	1.1388	1.2969	1.4770	1.6820	1.9155	2.1815	2.4843	2.8292	3.2220	3.6693	4.7588	6.1719	7.0287	10.381	13.464	25.790
14	1.1503	1.3231	1.5220	1.7507	2.0138	2.3164	2.6645	3.0649	3.5254	4.0552	5.3656	7.0993	8.1662	12.429	16.445	33.115
15	1.1618	1.3499	1.5683	1.8221	2.1170	2.4596	2.8577	3.3201	3.8574	4.4817	6.0496	8.1662	9.4877	14.880	20.086	45.251
16	1.1735	1.3771	1.6161	1.8965	2.2255	2.6117	3.0649	3.5966	4.2207	4.9530	6.8210	9.3933	11.023	17.814	24.533	54.598
17	1.1853	1.4049	1.6653	1.9739	2.3396	2.7732	3.2871	3.8962	4.6182	5.4739	7.6906	10.805	12.807	21.328	29.964	70.105
18	1.1972	1.4333	1.7160	2.0544	2.4596	2.9447	3.5254	4.2207	5.0531	6.0496	8.6711	12.429	14.880	25.534	36.598	90.017
19	1.2092	1.4623	1.7683	2.1383	2.5857	3.1268	3.7810	4.5722	5.5290	6.6859	9.7767	14.296	17.288	30.569	44.701	115.58
20	1.2214	1.4918	1.8221	2.2255	2.7183	3.3201	4.0552	4.9530	6.0496	7.3891	11.023	16.445	20.086	36.598	54.598	148.41
21	1.2337	1.5220	1.8776	2.3164	2.8577	3.5254	4.3492	5.3656	6.6194	8.1662	12.429	18.916	23.336	43.816	66.686	190.57
22	1.2461	1.5527	1.9348	2.4109	3.0042	3.7434	4.6646	5.8124	7.2427	9.0250	14.013	21.758	27.113	52.457	81.451	244.69
23	1.2586	1.5841	1.9937	2.5093	3.1582	3.9749	5.0028	6.2965	7.9248	9.9742	15.800	25.028	31.500	62.803	99.484	314.19
24	1.2712	1.6161	2.0544	2.6117	3.3201	4.2207	5.3656	6.8210	8.6711	11.023	17.814	28.789	36.598	75.189	121.51	403.43
25	1.2840	1.6487	2.1170	2.7183	3.4903	4.4817	5.7546	7.3891	9.4877	12.182	20.086	33.115	42.521	90.017	148.41	518.01
30	1.3499	1.8221	2.4596	3.3201	4.4817	6.0496	8.1662	11.023	14.880	20.086	36.598	66.686	90.017	221.4	403.4	1808.0
35	1.4191	2.0138	2.8577	4.0552	5.7546	8.1662	11.588	16.445	23.336	33.115	66.686	134.29	190.57	544.57	1096.6	6310.7
40	1.4918	2.2255	3.3201	4.9530	7.3891	11.023	16.445	24.533	36.598	54.598	121.51	270.43	403.43	1339.4	2981.0	22026
45	1.5683	2.4596	3.8574	6.0496	9.4877	14.880	23.336	36.598	57.397	90.017	221.41	544.57	854.06	3294.5	8103.1	76880
50	1.6487	2.7183	4.4817	7.3891	12.182	20.086	33.115	54.598	90.017	148.41	403.43	1096.6	1808.0	8103.1	22026	268337

Appendix B |

The Standard Normal Distribution

z	.00	.01	.02	.03	.04	.05	.06	.07	.08	.09
0.0	.0000	.0040	.0080	.0120	.0160	.0199	.0239	.0279	.0319	.0359
0.1	.0398	.0438	.0478	.0517	.0557	.0596	.0636	.0675	.0714	.0753
0.2	.0793	.0832	.0871	.0910	.0948	.0987	.1026	.1064	.1103	.1141
0.3	.1179	.1217	.1255	.1293	.1331	.1398	.1406	.1443	.1480	.1517
0.4	.1554	.1591	.1628	.1664	.1700	.1736	.1772	.1808	.1844	.1879
0.5	.1915	.1950	.1985	.2019	.2054	.2088	.2123	.2157	.2190	.2224
0.6	.2257	.2291	.2324	.2357	.2389	.2422	.2454	.2486	.2517	.2549
0.7	.2580	.2611	.2642	.2673	.2704	.2734	.2764	.2794	.2823	.2852
0.8	.2881	.2910	.2939	.2967	.2995	.3023	.3051	.3078	.3106	.3133
0.9	.3159	.3186	.3212	.3238	.3264	.3289	.3315	.3340	.3365	.3389
1.0	.3413	.3438	.3461	.3485	.3508	.3531	.3554	.3577	.3599	.3621
1.1	.3643	.3665	.3686	.3708	.3729	.3749	.3770	.3790	.3810	.3830
1.2	.3849	.3869	.3888	.3907	.3925	.3944	.3962	.3980	.3997	.4015
1.3	.4032	.4049	.4066	.4082	.4099	.4115	.4131	.4147	.4162	.4177
1.4	.4192	.4207	.4222	.4236	.4251	.4265	.4279	.4292	.4306	.4319
1.5	.4332	.4345	.4357	.4370	.4382	.4394	.4406	.4418	.4429	.4441
1.6	.4452	.4463	.4474	.4484	.4495	.4505	.4515	.4525	.4535	.4545
1.7	.4554	.4564	.4573	.4582	.4591	.4599	.4608	.4616	.4625	.4633
1.8	.4641	.4649	.4656	.4664	.4671	.4678	.4686	.4693	.4699	.4706
1.9	.4713	.4719	.4726	.4732	.4738	.4744	.4750	.4756	.4761	.4767
2.0	.4772	.4778	.4783	.4788	.4793	.4798	.4803	.4808	.4812	.4817
2.1	.4821	.4826	.4830	.4834	.4838	.4842	.4846	.4850	.4854	.4857
2.2	.4861	.4864	.4868	.4871	.4875	.4878	.4881	.4884	.4887	.4890
2.3	.4893	.4896	.4898	.4901	.4904	.4906	.4909	.4911	.4913	.4916
2.4	.4918	.4920	.4922	.4925	.4927	.4929	.4931	.4932	.4934	.4936
2.5	.4938	.4940	.4941	.4943	.4945	.4946	.4948	.4949	.4951	.4952
2.6	.4953	.4955	.4956	.4957	.4959	.4960	.4961	.4962	.4963	.4964
2.7	.4965	.4966	.4967	.4968	.4969	.4970	.4971	.4972	.4973	.4974
2.8	.4974	.4975	.4976	.4977	.4977	.4978	.4979	.4979	.4980	.4981
2.9	.4981	.4982	.4982	.4983	.4984	.4984	.4985	.4985	.4986	.4986
3.0	.4987	.4987	.4987	.4988	.4988	.4989	.4989	.4989	.4990	.4990